OXFORD TREASURY OF Sayings and Quotations

OXFORD TREASURY OF Sayings and Quotations

Fourth Edition

Edited by SUSAN RATCLIFFE

OXFORD
UNIVERSITY PRESS

OXFORD
UNIVERSITY PRESS

Great Clarendon Street, Oxford OX2 6DP

Oxford University Press is a department of the University of Oxford.
It furthers the University's objective of excellence in research, scholarship,
and education by publishing worldwide in

Oxford New York

Auckland Cape Town Dar es Salaam Hong Kong Karachi
Kuala Lumpur Madrid Melbourne Mexico City Nairobi
New Delhi Shanghai Taipei Toronto

With offices in

Argentina Austria Brazil Chile Czech Republic France Greece
Guatemala Hungary Italy Japan Poland Portugal Singapore
South Korea Switzerland Thailand Turkey Ukraine Vietnam

Oxford is a registered trade mark of Oxford University Press
in the UK and in certain other countries

Published in the United States
by Oxford University Press, Inc., New York

First published 1997
Second edition 2002
Third edition 2006
Fourth edition 2011
Previous editions published as *Oxford Dictionary of Phrase, Saying, and Quotation*

British Library Cataloguing in Publication Data

Data available

Library of Congress Cataloging in Publication Data

Data available

Typeset by Datagrafix, Inc.
Printed in Great Britain
on acid-free paper by
Clays Ltd., St Ives plc

ISBN 978-0-19-960912-3

10 9 8 7 6 5 4 3 2 1

Contents

Introduction to the Fourth Edition

The *Oxford Treasury of Sayings and Quotations* is a truly unique reference book which answers the question 'what has been said about this subject?' without restricting its coverage to any one area of the language. It is not a dictionary of quotations, or a dictionary of proverbs, or a dictionary of idioms and phrases, but a combination of all three, which explains the origins of sayings of all kinds and explores the links between them. Here, quotations, proverbs, phrases, and traditional or modern sayings on topics such as **Love**, **Anger**, or **Weather** are gathered together, whatever their 'official' form, to offer a selection of words which have been found over many years to express familiar truths in an apt, witty, or beautiful manner.

In fact, the distinction between a proverb, a phrase, and a quotation is often far from clear-cut. Many of the most familiar proverbs in English derive from the Bible, and can be found in dictionaries of quotations in a slightly unfamiliar form. Thus *The leopard does not change his spots*, proverbial in English since the 16th century, derives from the question 'Can the Ethiopian change his skin, or the leopard his spots?' in the book of Jeremiah, while the advice *Never let the sun go down on your anger* is a summary of St Paul's letter to the Ephesians: 'Be ye angry and sin not: let not the sun go down upon your wrath.' The reference to the Ethiopian has also entered the language, in the phrase *change one's skin*. All these various sayings can be found here, with appropriate explanations and cross references.

A few proverbs have started life as quotations, such as *Variety is the spice of life* from the poet William Cowper, while many quotations develop (or contradict) proverbial ideas: Oscar Wilde's 'Nothing succeeds like excess' depends heavily on the proverb *Nothing succeeds like success* for its effect. Modern sayings—perhaps the proverbs of the future—often derive from advertisements or television programmes: a hundred years ago Doan's Backache Kidney Pills first suggested *Every picture tells a story*, while more recently *Star Trek* gave us *Resistance is futile.* In today's *global village* (a phrase which began life from a quotation) many proverbs have entered English from other cultures, some at a specific moment, such as when Ronald Reagan famously quoted the Russian maxim 'Trust, but verify', others because they express an idea not previously found in English, such as the Japanese saying *The nail that sticks up is certain to be hammered down.* Many of these colourful additions to our language have been included here.

Commonly used phrases often link in one way or another to a quotation: *fresh fields and pastures new* is a misquotation of a line from the poet John Milton, while *the plot thickens* is a line from an eighteenth-century play. Depression was characterized as *the black dog* by the lexicographer Samuel Johnson, while an event in the life of Julius Caesar gave us *cross the Rubicon.*

More than a thousand new items have been added to this fourth edition, and subjects such as **Colours** and **India**, **Neighbours** and **Wisdom** appear for the first time. New quotations range from the classical ('All wish to possess knowledge, but no one is willing to pay the price', from Juvenal on **Knowledge**) to the very modern ('I'm just trying to change the world one sequin at a time', said by Lady Gaga on **Style**). There are additional sayings from famous wordsmiths such as Mae West 'Too much of a good thing can be wonderful' and Albert Einstein 'I think that only daring speculation can lead us further and not accumulation of facts.' Elsewhere are remarks from those such as the American clergyman Ralph Sockman, remembered only for the single line 'The larger the island of knowledge, the longer the shoreline of wonder' or those more famous for other reasons: Cindy Crawford's realistic comment on **Appearance** 'Even I don't wake up looking like Cindy Crawford.' Sometimes pursuing a quotation to its roots reveals a widespread error: William J. Boetcker's 'You cannot strengthen the weak by weakening the strong' is commonly, but wrongly, attributed to Abraham Lincoln.

A new gloss on the well-known proverb on **Honesty** is provided by George Bernard Shaw: 'I am afraid we must make the world honest before we can honestly say to our children that honesty is the best policy.' More new proverbs have been added from traditional sources: a Chinese view on **Fame** *A tall tree attracts the wind* and a German view on **Achievement** *He who* *likes cherries soon learns to climb*, together with modern sayings such as *If you snooze, you lose* or *Iron sharpens iron*, the latter deriving ultimately from the Bible. Other additions from recent years include Barbie's line *Math class is tough* and the Adidas advertising slogan *Impossible is nothing*, frequently wrongly attributed to Muhammad Ali who appeared in the campaign.

As always, phrases too have come from many sources. More classical references such *as fiddle while Rome burns* and *Parthian shot* are explained, and more phrases of literary origin such as *Banquo's ghost*, *Big Brother*, and *Lady Bountiful* added. Others are more recent: *the goldilocks principle*, *Portillo moment*, *white van man*, and of course, the *big society*.

An African proverb to be found at **Cooperation** tells us that *A single bracelet does not jingle*, and many people have contributed to this book. In particular I should like to thank Elizabeth Knowles, editor of the first edition, Joanna Harris, Commissioning Editor for Quotations, Ralph Bates for library research, Jean Harker and Verity Mason for contributions to the Quotations reading programme, and Susanne Charlett for data capture.

Walt Disney said that 'There is more treasure in books than in all the pirates' loot on Treasure Island.' It sometimes seems as if a book such as this can indeed be summed up as pirates' loot—after all, the words are not the editor's, but those of many men and women, some famous and others unknown, from many times and lands. But that it is treasure I hope there can be no doubt, and I trust the reader will enjoy the golden words and pearls of wisdom to be found in it.

SUSAN RATCLIFFE

Oxford 2011

How to Use the Treasury

Finding a saying...

...on a subject

The treasury is arranged by subject, so phrases, sayings, proverbs, and quotations about **Courage** or **Love** are grouped together. Some subjects cover related topics such as **Apology and Excuses**, and others cover opposites such as **Winning and Losing**. A list of all the subjects can be found on page xiii.

...if you know the words

If you want to find out about a particular quotation or saying, you can find it by looking in the Keyword Index, where the most significant words from each entry are indexed with a reference to help you find it (see **Using the index** below).

About the order...

...of subjects

The subjects are arranged in alphabetical order from **Ability** to **Youth**. For joint subjects such as **Chance and Luck** the main entry is found at **Chance**, and a cross-reference will direct you there from **Luck**.

...of phrases, sayings, and proverbs

Sayings and proverbs appear first in each theme, and are arranged in alphabetical order, ignoring 'the' and 'a.' Each saying is followed by a note describing its meaning, where this is not transparent, and its origin. Phrases follow, again in alphabetical order with a short definition and description of origin. Note that sometimes there may be no sayings or phrases on a subject.

...of quotations

Quotations are given in date order, with the oldest quotations first. After the text of each quotation the author is given, followed by the source.

Looking elsewhere in the book...

...for related subjects

After each heading, cross references are given to any related subjects which may also be relevant: for example '**Argument** see also **Opinion**.'

...for related sayings and quotations

Cross references are also given to phrases, sayings, proverbs, and quotations which are linked to an entry. Such references are to the name of the subject (sometimes in shortened form), followed by the number of the item within the subject: **HASTE 5** means the fifth item in the subject **Haste and Delay**.

Using the index...

...keywords

The most significant words from each item appear in the Keyword Index. Each instance of a keyword, abbreviated to its initial letter, is given with a short section of the surrounding text to help identify it. In the index, both the headwords and the sections of text are in alphabetical order. To simplify searching, words are indexed in their standard British English form, regardless of spelling in the original.

...references

Index references are to the name of the subject (sometimes in shortened form), followed by the number of the item within the subject: **EARTH 7** means the seventh item in the subject **The Earth**.

List of Themes

Sayings and Quotations

Ability

proverbs and sayings ▸

1 **...But I know a man who can.**
advertising slogan for the Automobile Association

2 **Horses for courses.**
originally (in horse-racing) meaning that different horses are suited to different race-courses; now used more generally to mean that different people are suited to different roles; English proverb, late 19th century

3 **If you can talk, you can sing, and if you can walk, you can dance.**
African proverb (Shona)

4 **Inside the forest there are many birds.**
people are of many different kinds and abilities ('many birds' = 'birds of many kinds'); Chinese proverb

5 **In the country of the blind the one eyed man is king.**
someone of moderate ability will dominate those with none; English proverb, early 16th century

6 **A sow may whistle, though it has an ill mouth for it.**
someone not naturally suited to a task will perform it badly; English proverb, early 19th century

phrases ▸

7 **all-singing all-dancing**
with every possible attribute, able to perform any necessary function; a phrase applied particularly in the area of computer technology, but originally coming from descriptions of show business acts. The term may derive ultimately from a series of posters produced in 1929 to promote the new sound cinema such as that advertising the Hollywood musical *Broadway Melody*, which proclaimed the words *All talking All singing All dancing*

8 **jack of all trades**
a person who can do many different kinds of work; see EXCELLENCE 3

quotations ▸

9 ***Non omnia possumus omnes.***
We can't all do everything.
Virgil 70–19 BC: *Eclogues*

10 **Natural abilities are like natural plants, that need pruning by study.**
Francis Bacon 1561–1626: *Essays* (1625) 'Of Studies'

11 **If a man write a better book, preach a better sermon, or make a better mouse-trap than his neighbour, tho' he build his house in the woods, the world will make a beaten path to his door.**
Ralph Waldo Emerson 1803–82: attributed to Emerson in Sarah S. B. Yule *Borrowings* (1889); Mrs Yule states in *The Docket* February 1912 that she copied this in her handbook from a lecture delivered by Emerson; the quotation was the occasion of a long controversy owing to Elbert Hubbard's claim to its authorship

12 **BETTER DROWNED THAN DUFFERS IF NOT DUFFERS WONT DROWN.**
Arthur Ransome 1884–1967: *Swallows and Amazons* (1930)

13 **Intelligence is quickness to apprehend as distinct from ability, which is capacity to act wisely on the thing apprehended.**
Alfred North Whitehead 1861–1947: *Dialogues* (1954) 15 December 1939

14 **I could have had class. I could have been a contender.**
Budd Schulberg 1914–2009: *On the Waterfront* (1954 film); spoken by Marlon Brando

Absence
see also MEETING

proverbs and sayings ▸

1 **Absence makes the heart grow fonder.**
affection for a person is strengthened by missing them; English proverb, mid 19th century, 1st century BC in Latin

2 **Absence of evidence is not evidence of absence.**
traditional saying, recorded from the 19th century

3 **He who is absent is always in the wrong.**
someone who is not present cannot defend themselves from blame; English proverb, mid 15th century

4 A little absence does much good.
American proverb, mid 20th century

5 Out of sight, out of mind.
someone who is not present is easily forgotten; see ABSENCE 9; English proverb, mid 13th century

phrases ▶

6 gone with the wind
gone completely, disappeared without trace, from Ernest Dowson (see MEMORY 15); subsequently popularized by the title of Margaret Mitchell's novel (1936) on the American Civil War

7 Hamlet without the Prince
a performance or event taking place without the principal actor or central figure, from an account given in the *Morning Post*, September 1775, of a theatrical company in which the actor who was to play the hero ran off with the innkeeper's daughter; when the play was announced, the audience was told 'the part of Hamlet to be left out, for that night'

quotations ▶

8 The Lord watch between me and thee, when we are absent one from another.
Bible: Genesis

9 Today the man is here; tomorrow he is gone. And when he is 'out of sight', quickly also is he out of mind.
Thomas à Kempis 1380–1471: *De Imitatione Christi*; see ABSENCE 5

10 Absence diminishes commonplace passions and increases great ones, as the wind extinguishes candles and kindles fire.
Duc de la Rochefoucauld 1613–80: *Maximes* (1678)

11 *Partir c'est mourir un peu,*
C'est mourir à ce qu'on aime.
To go away is to die a little, it is to die to that which one loves.
Edmond Haraucourt 1856–1941: 'Rondel de l'Adieu' (1891)

12 The more he looked inside the more Piglet wasn't there.
A. A. Milne 1882–1956: *The House at Pooh Corner* (1928)

13 The heart may think it knows better: the senses know that absence blots people out. We have really no absent friends.
Elizabeth Bowen 1899–1973: *Death of the Heart* (1938)

14 When I came back to Dublin, I was courtmartialled in my absence and sentenced to death in my absence, so I said they could shoot me in my absence.
Brendan Behan 1923–64: *Hostage* (1958)

15 Omissions are not accidents.
Marianne Moore 1887–1972: *Complete Poems* (1967) epigraph

16 Most of what matters in your life takes place in your absence.
Salman Rushdie 1947– : *Midnight's Children* (1981)

17 I wasn't even in the index.
on the omission of their affair from John Major's autobiography
Edwina Currie 1946– : in *Times* 28 September 2002

Achievement

see also AMBITION, EFFORT, PROBLEMS, SUCCESS

proverbs and sayings ▶

1 Didn't she [*or* he *or* they] do well?
catchphrase used by Bruce Forsyth in 'The Generation Game' on BBC Television, 1971–7

2 The difficult is done at once, the impossible takes a little longer.
slogan of the US Armed Forces; recorded earlier as a quotation by Charles Alexandre de Calonne (1734–1802) in the form 'Madam, if a thing is possible, consider it done; the impossible?—that will be done'

3 The hand will not reach for what the heart does not long for.
desire is essential for achievement; Welsh proverb

4 He who likes cherries soon learns to climb.
achievement seen as the result of motivation; German proverb

5 In a calm sea every man is a pilot.
apparent achievement may not have been tested by circumstances; English proverb, early 19th century

6 Palmam qui meruit, ferat.
Latin, *Let him who has won it bear the palm*, adopted by Lord Nelson (1758–1805) as his motto, from John Jortin *Lusus Poetici* (3rd ed., 1748) 'Ad Ventos'

7 **Per ardua ad astra.**
Latin, *through struggle to the stars*, motto of the Mulvany family, quoted and translated by Rider Haggard in *The People of the Mist* (1894), and still in use as motto of the RAF, having been approved by King George V in 1913

8 **Seekers are finders.**
success is the result of effort; Persian proverb; see ACTION 12

9 **Seriously, though, he's doing a grand job!**
catchphrase used by David Frost in 'That Was The Week That Was', on BBC Television, 1962–3

10 **Whatever man has done, man may do.**
anything that has been achieved once can be achieved again; English proverb, mid 19th century; see INVENTIONS 14

11 **While the grass grows, the steed starves.**
by the time hopes or expectations can be satisfied, it may be too late; English proverb, mid 14th century

12 **You cannot have your cake and eat it.**
you cannot have things both ways; English proverb, mid 16th century

phrases ▸

13 **bite off more than one can chew**
take on a commitment one cannot fulfil

14 **low-hanging fruit**
something easily achieved or overcome; the expression dates from the late 20th century, and the image may be associated with the idea in *cherry-pick*: choose selectively (as the most beneficial or profitable items or opportunities) from what is available

quotations ▸

15 **The desire accomplished is sweet to the soul.**
Bible: Proverbs

16 **I have fought a good fight, I have finished my course, I have kept the faith.**
Bible: II Timothy

17 **None climbs so high as he who knows not whither he is going.**
Oliver Cromwell 1599–1658: attributed

18 **The General [Wolfe]...repeated nearly the whole of Gray's Elegy...adding, as he concluded, that he would prefer being the author of that poem to the glory of beating the French to-morrow.**
James Wolfe 1727–59: J. Playfair *Biographical Account of J. Robinson* (1815)

19 **The distance is nothing; it is only the first step that is difficult.**
commenting on the legend that St Denis, carrying his head in his hands, walked two leagues
Mme Du Deffand 1697–1780: letter to Jean Le Rond d'Alembert, 7 July 1763; see BEGINNING 5

20 **He has, indeed, done it very well; but it is a foolish thing well done.**
on Goldsmith's apology in the *London Chronicle* for physically assaulting Thomas Evans, who had published a letter mocking Goldsmith
Samuel Johnson 1709–84: James Boswell *Life of Johnson* (1791) 3 April 1773

21 **Now, gentlemen, let us do something today which the world may talk of hereafter.**
Admiral Collingwood 1748–1810: before the Battle of Trafalgar, 21 October 1805; G. L. Newnham Collingwood (ed.) *A Selection from the Correspondence of Lord Collingwood* (1828)

22 ***J'ai vécu.***
I survived.
when asked what he had done during the French Revolution
Emmanuel Joseph Sieyès 1748–1836: F. A. M. Mignet *Notice historique sur la vie et les travaux de M. le Comte de Sieyès* (1836)

23 **The reward of a thing well done, is to have done it.**
Ralph Waldo Emerson 1803–82: *Essays: Second Series* (1844) 'New England Reformers'

24 **That low man seeks a little thing to do,**
Sees it and does it:
This high man, with a great thing to pursue,
Dies ere he knows it.
That low man goes on adding one to one,
His hundred's soon hit:
This high man, aiming at a million,
Misses an unit.
Robert Browning 1812–89: 'A Grammarian's Funeral' (1855)

25 **He who does *something* at the head of one regiment, will eclipse him who does *nothing* at the head of a hundred.**
Abraham Lincoln 1809–65: letter to Major-General David Hunter, 31 December 1861

26 So little done, so much to do.
Cecil Rhodes 1853–1902: said on the day of his death; Lewis Michell *Life of Rhodes* (1910)

27 There are two tragedies in life. One is not to get your heart's desire. The other is to get it.
George Bernard Shaw 1856–1950: *Man and Superman* (1903)

28 Give us the tools and we will finish the job.
Winston Churchill 1874–1965: radio broadcast, 9 February 1941

29 That's one small step for man, one giant leap for mankind.
Neil Armstrong 1930– : in *New York Times* 21 July 1969; interference in the transmission obliterated 'a' between 'for' and 'man'

30 We can lift ourselves out of ignorance, we can find ourselves as creatures of excellence and intelligence and skill.
Richard Bach 1936– : *Jonathan Livingston Seagull* (1970)

31 At the end of your life you will never regret not having passed one more test, winning one more verdict or not closing one more deal. You will regret time not spent with a husband, a child, a friend or a parent.
Barbara Bush 1925– : in *Washington Post* 2 June 1990

Acting

see also CINEMA, THEATRE

proverbs and sayings ▸

1 Anyone for tennis?
a typical entrance or exit line given to a young man in a superficial drawing-room comedy

phrases ▸

2 the Jersey Lily
the actresss Lillie Langtry, (1853–1929); born in Jersey, she was noted for her beauty and became known as 'the Jersey Lily' from the title of a portrait of her painted by Millais

3 sock and buskin
comedy and tragedy: the *sock* was a light shoe worn by comic actors on the Greek and Roman stage, and the *buskin* a thick-soled laced boot worn by Athenian tragic actors; see THEATRE 9

quotations ▸

4 Suit the action to the word, the word to the action; with this special observance, that you o'erstep not the modesty of nature; for anything so overdone is from the purpose of playing, whose end, both at the first and now, was and is, to hold, as 'twere, the mirror up to nature.
William Shakespeare 1564–1616: *Hamlet* (1601)

5 To see him act, is like reading Shakespeare by flashes of lightning.
on Edmund Kean
Samuel Taylor Coleridge 1772–1834: *Table Talk* (1835) 27 April 1823

6 She ran the whole gamut of the emotions from A to B.
of Katharine Hepburn at a Broadway first night, 1933
Dorothy Parker 1893–1967: attributed

7 Don't put your daughter on the stage,
Mrs Worthington,
Don't put your daughter on the stage.
Noël Coward 1899–1973: 'Mrs Worthington' (1935 song)

8 Actors are cattle.
Alfred Hitchcock 1899–1980: in *Saturday Evening Post* 22 May 1943

9 Shakespeare is so tiring. You never get a chance to sit down unless you're a king.
George S. Kaufman 1889–1961 and **Howard Teichmann** 1916–87: *The Solid Gold Cadillac* (1953); spoken by Josephine Hull

10 The basic essential of a great actor is that he loves himself in acting.
Charlie Chaplin 1889–1977: *My Autobiography* (1964)

11 Just say the lines and don't trip over the furniture.
advice on acting
Noël Coward 1899–1973: D. Richards *The Wit of Noël Coward* (1968)

12 To grasp the full significance of life is the actor's duty, to interpret it is his problem, and to express it his dedication.
Marlon Brando 1924–2004: David Shipman *Marlon Brando* (1974)

13 Acting is a masochistic form of

exhibitionism. It is not quite the occupation of an adult.

Laurence Olivier 1907–89: in *Time* 3 July 1978

Action and Inaction

see also IDLENESS, WORDS AND DEEDS

proverbs and sayings ▸

1 **Action is worry's worst enemy.**
advocating the control of fruitless worry by taking a decision and acting upon it; American proverb, mid 20th century

2 **Action this day.**
annotation as used by Winston Churchill at the Admiralty in 1940

3 **Action without thought is like shooting without aim.**
American proverb, mid 20th century

4 **A barking dog never bites.**
noisy threats often do not presage real danger; English proverb, 16th century, 13th century in French

5 **Better to light one candle than to curse the darkness.**
motto of the American Christopher Society, founded 1945; see HUMAN RIGHTS 19

6 **If it ain't broke, don't fix it.**
warning against interference with something that is working satisfactorily, late 20th century saying

7 **If you want something done, ask a busy person.**
implying that a busy person is most likely to have learned how to manage their time efficiently, late 20th century saying

8 **It is as cheap sitting as standing.**
often used literally; English proverb, mid 17th century

9 **Just do it.**
advertising slogan for Nike sports shoes, 1988

10 **Lookers-on see most of the game.**
those who are not participating are able to take an overall view; English proverb, early 16th century

11 **The road to hell is paved with good intentions.**
English proverb, late 16th century; earlier forms omit the first three words; see FESTIVALS 69

12 **Seek and ye shall find.**
an active search for something wanted is likely to be rewarded; English proverb, mid 16th century; see ACHIEVEMENT 8, PRAYER 8

13 **The shrimp that falls asleep is swept away by the current.**
those who get distracted will fall behind; Spanish proverb; see OPPORTUNITY 7

14 **When in doubt, do nowt.**
advising against taking action when one is unsure of one's ground; English proverb, mid 19th century

phrases ▸

15 **have many (or other) irons in the fire**
have a range of options or courses of action available, or be involved in many activities or commitments at the same time

16 **the line of least resistance**
an option avoiding difficulty or unpleasantness; the easiest course of action

17 **no peace for the wicked**
no rest or tranquillity for the speaker; incessant activity, responsibility, or work; from the Bible (Isaiah), see GOOD 14

quotations ▸

18 **Nowher so bisy a man as he ther nas,**
And yet he semed bisier than he was.
Geoffrey Chaucer 1343–1400: *The Canterbury Tales* 'The General Prologue'

19 **Iron rusts from disuse; stagnant water loses its purity and in cold weather becomes frozen; even so does inaction sap the vigour of the mind.**
Leonardo da Vinci 1452–1519: Edward McCurdy (ed. and trans.) *Leonardo da Vinci's Notebooks* (1906)

20 **But men must know, that in this theatre of man's life it is reserved only for God and angels to be lookers on.**
Francis Bacon 1561–1626: *The Advancement of Learning* (1605)

21 **If it were done when 'tis done, then 'twere well**
It were done quickly.
William Shakespeare 1564–1616: *Macbeth* (1606)

22 **A first impulse was never a crime.**
Pierre Corneille 1606–84: *Horace* (1640)

23 **You have sat too long here for any**

good you have been doing. Depart, I say, and let us have done with you. In the name of God, go!

addressing the Rump Parliament, 20 April 1653; quoted by Leo Amery to Neville Chamberlain in the House of Commons, 7 May 1940. Chamberlain resigned three days later
Oliver Cromwell 1599–1658: oral tradition

24 We have left undone those things which we ought to have done; And we have done those things which we ought not to have done; And there is no health in us.

The Book of Common Prayer 1662: *Morning Prayer* General Confession

25 They also serve who only stand and wait.

John Milton 1608–74: 'When I consider how my light is spent' (1673)

26 He who desires but acts not, breeds pestilence.

William Blake 1757–1827: *The Marriage of Heaven and Hell* (1790–3) 'Proverbs of Hell'

27 Think nothing done while aught remains to do.

Samuel Rogers 1763–1855: 'Human Life' (1819)

28 It is vain to say that human beings ought to be satisfied with tranquillity: they must have action; and they will make it if they cannot find it.

Charlotte Brontë 1816–55: *Jane Eyre* (1847)

29 Action is consolatory. It is the enemy of thought and the friend of flattering illusions.

Joseph Conrad 1857–1924: *Nostromo* (1904)

30 Inactivity is death.

Benito Mussolini 1883–1945: *Fascism: Doctrine and Institutions* (1935) 'Fundamental Ideas'

31 Under conditions of tyranny it is far easier to act than to think.

Hannah Arendt 1906–75: W. H. Auden *A Certain World* (1970)

32 The world can only be grasped by action, not by contemplation... The hand is the cutting edge of the mind.

Jacob Bronowski 1908–74: *The Ascent of Man* (1973)

33 I grew up in the Thirties with our unemployed father. He did not riot, he got on his bike and looked for work.

Norman Tebbit 1931– : speech at Conservative Party Conference, 15 October 1981

34 In this very real world, good doesn't drive out evil. Evil doesn't drive out good. But the energetic displaces the passive.

Bill Bernbach 1911–82: *Bill Bernbach said* (1989)

35 Vision without action is merely a dream. Action without vision just passes the time. Vision with action can change the world.

Joel Arthur Barker: *The Power of Vision* (1991 video); see IDEALISM 1

36 Let's go to work.

Quentin Tarantino 1963– : *Reservoir Dogs* (1992 film); spoken by Lawrence Tierney

Administration

see also MANAGEMENT

proverbs and sayings ▸

1 A committee is a group of the unwilling, chosen from the unfit, to do the unnecessary.

20th century saying

phrases ▸

2 men in suits

bureaucrats, faceless administrators, regarded as representatives of an organization rather than creative individuals; probably related to *suit* = a man who wears a business suit at work, a business executive

3 red tape

excessive bureaucracy or adherence to rules and formalities, especially in public business; the expression refers to the reddish-pink tape which is commonly used for securing legal and official documents; see ADMINISTRATION 5

quotations ▸

4 For forms of government let fools contest;
Whate'er is best administered is best.

Alexander Pope 1688–1744: *An Essay on Man* Epistle 3 (1733)

5 Let Wilmington, with grave, contracted brow,

Red tape and wisdom at the council show.
Lord Hervey 1696–1743: 'To the Queen' (1736); see ADMINISTRATION 3

6 I have in general no very exalted opinion of the virtue of paper government.
Edmund Burke 1729–97: *On Conciliation with America* (1775)

7 If any man will draw up his case, and put his name at the foot of the first page, I will give him an immediate reply. Where he compels me to turn over the sheet, he must wait my leisure.
on appeals made by officers to the Navy Board
Lord Sandwich 1718–92: N. W. Wraxall *Memoirs* (1884) vol. 1

8 Whatever was required to be done, the Circumlocution Office was beforehand with all the public departments in the art of perceiving—HOW NOT TO DO IT.
Charles Dickens 1812–70: *Little Dorrit* (1857)

9 A place for everything and everything in its place.
Mrs Beeton 1836–65: *The Book of Household Management* (1861); often attributed to Samuel Smiles; see ORDER 3

10 Sack the lot!
on overmanning and overspending within government departments
John Arbuthnot Fisher 1841–1920: letter to *Times*, 2 September 1919

11 Where there is officialism every human relationship suffers.
E. M. Forster 1879–1970: *A Passage to India* (1924)

12 Official dignity tends to increase in inverse ratio to the importance of the country in which the office is held.
Aldous Huxley 1894–1963: *Beyond the Mexique Bay* (1934)

13 This island is made mainly of coal and surrounded by fish. Only an organizing genius could produce a shortage of coal and fish at the same time.
Aneurin Bevan 1897–1960: speech at Blackpool 24 May 1945

14 Committee—a group of men who individually can do nothing but as a group decide that nothing can be done.
Fred Allen 1894–1956: attributed

15 Time spent on any item of the agenda will be in inverse proportion to the sum involved.
C. Northcote Parkinson 1909–93: *Parkinson's Law* (1958)

16 Bureaucracy, the rule of no one, has become the modern form of despotism.
Mary McCarthy 1912–89: *On the Contrary* (1961) 'The *Vita Activa*'

17 In a hierarchy every employee tends to rise to his level of incompetence.
Laurence J. Peter 1919–90: *The Peter Principle* (1969); see MANAGEMENT 5

18 Guidelines for bureaucrats: (1) When in charge, ponder. (2) When in trouble, delegate. (3) When in doubt, mumble.
James H. Boren 1925– : in *New York Times* 8 November 1970

19 A memorandum is written not to inform the reader but to protect the writer.
Dean Acheson 1893–1971: in *Wall Street Journal* 8 September 1977

20 A desk is a dangerous place from which to watch the world.
John le Carré 1931– : *The Honourable Schoolboy* (1977)

21 Back in the East you can't do much without the right papers, but *with* the right papers you can do *anything*. They *believe* in papers. Papers are power.
Tom Stoppard 1937– : *Neutral Ground* (1983)

22 A camel is a horse designed by a committee.
Alec Issigonis 1906–88: attributed; in *Guardian* 14 January 1991 'Notes and Queries'

Adversity

see also MISFORTUNES, SUFFERING

proverbs and sayings ►

1 Adversity makes strange bedfellows.
shared difficulties may bring together very different people; see MISFORTUNES 21; English proverb, mid 19th century

2 After hardship comes relief.
African proverb (Swahili)

3 **A dose of adversity is often as needful as a dose of medicine.**
American proverb, mid 20th century

4 **If life hands you lemons, make lemonade.**
an adjuration to make the best of difficult circumstances; late 20th century saying

phrases ▸

5 **gall and wormwood**
a source of bitter mortification or vexation, originally with allusion to the Bible (Genesis) 'lest there should be among you a root that beareth gall and wormwood'; *gall* = bile, the secretion of the liver, *wormwood* = an aromatic plant with a bitter taste; taken together as the type of something causing bitterness and grief

6 **the iron entered into his soul**
he became deeply and permanently affected by captivity or ill treatment; from the Bible (Psalms), from Latin mistranslation of Hebrew for 'his person entered into the iron', i.e. fetters

7 **light at the end of the tunnel**
a long-awaited sign that a period of hardship or adversity is nearing an end; see OPTIMISM 39

8 **locust years**
years of poverty and hardship; coined by Winston Churchill in his *History of the Second World War* (1948) to describe Britain in the 1930s; from the Bible (Joel) 'I will restore to you the years that the locust hath eaten'

9 **school of hard knocks**
the experience of a life of hardship, considered as a means of instruction; originally US

10 **a thorn in one's side**
a constant annoyance or problem, a source of continual trouble or annoyance; from the Bible (Numbers) 'those which ye let remain of them shall be…thorns in your sides'

11 **under the harrow**
in distress; *harrow* = a heavy frame set with iron teeth or tines, drawn over ploughed land to break up clods and root up weeds; see SUFFERING 25

quotations ▸

12 **Fire is the test of gold; adversity, of strong men.**
Seneca ('the Younger') c.4 BC–AD 65: *Moral Essays*

13 **Sweet are the uses of adversity,**
Which like the toad, ugly and venomous,
Wears yet a precious jewel in his head.
William Shakespeare 1564–1616: *As You Like It* (1599)

14 **Prosperity doth best discover vice, but adversity doth best discover virtue.**
Francis Bacon 1561–1626: *Essays* (1625) 'Of Adversity'

15 **Adversity is sometimes hard upon a man; but for one man who can stand prosperity, there are a hundred that will stand adversity.**
Thomas Carlyle 1795–1881: *On Heroes, Hero-Worship, and the Heroic* (1841)

16 **Into each life some rain must fall,**
Some days must be dark and dreary.
Henry Wadsworth Longfellow 1807–82: 'The Rainy Day' (1842)

17 **When fortune empties her chamberpot on your head, smile—and say 'we are going to have a summer shower'.**
John A. Macdonald 1815–91: spoken 1875 when Leader of the Opposition

18 **But there, everything has its drawbacks, as the man said when his mother-in-law died, and they came down upon him for the funeral expenses.**
Jerome K. Jerome 1859–1927: *Three Men in a Boat* (1889)

19 **By trying we can easily learn to endure adversity. Another man's, I mean.**
Mark Twain 1835–1910: *Following the Equator* (1897)

20 **Life is not meant to be easy.**
Malcolm Fraser 1930– : 5th Alfred Deakin lecture, 20 July 1971; see LIFE 47

21 **A woman is like a teabag—only in hot water do you realise how strong she is.**
Nancy Reagan 1923– : in *Observer* 29 March 1981

Advertising

proverbs and sayings ▸

1 **Any publicity is good publicity.**
it is always preferable to have attention focused on a name than to be unnoticed; see FAME 28; English proverb, early 20th century

2 **Good wine needs no bush.**
there is no need to advertise or boast about something of good quality as people will always discover its merits; a bunch of ivy was formerly the sign of a vintner's shop; English proverb, early 15th century; see ADVERTISING 15

3 **It pays to advertise.**
American proverb, mid 20th century

4 **Let's run it up the flagpole and see if anyone salutes it.**
recorded as an established expression in the 1960s, suggesting the testing of a new idea or product

phrases ▸

5 **proclaim from the housetops**
announce publicly, announce loudly; from the Bible (Luke) 'that which ye have spoken in the ear in closets shall be proclaimed upon the housetops'

quotations ▸

6 **Promise, large promise, is the soul of an advertisement.**
Samuel Johnson 1709–84: in *The Idler* 20 January 1759

7 **It is far easier to write ten passably effective sonnets, good enough to take in the not too enquiring critic, than one effective advertisement that will take in a few thousand of the uncritical buying public.**
Aldous Huxley 1894–1963: *On the Margin* (1923) 'Advertisement'

8 **Advertising may be described as the science of arresting human intelligence long enough to get money from it.**
Stephen Leacock 1869–1944: *Garden of Folly* (1924) 'The Perfect Salesman'

9 **Half the money I spend on advertising is wasted, and the trouble is I don't know which half.**
Lord Leverhulme 1851–1925: David Ogilvy *Confessions of an Advertising Man* (1963)

10 **Advertising is the rattling of a stick inside a swill bucket.**
George Orwell 1903–50: *Keep the Aspidistra Flying* (1936)

11 **It is not necessary to advertise food to hungry people, fuel to cold people, or houses to the homeless.**
J. K. Galbraith 1908–2006: *American Capitalism* (1952)

12 **The hidden persuaders.**
Vance Packard 1914–97: title of a study of the advertising industry (1957)

13 **The consumer isn't a moron; she is your wife.**
David Ogilvy 1911–99: *Confessions of an Advertising Man* (1963)

14 **A good poster is a visual telegram.**
A. M. Cassandre 1901–68: attributed

15 **Good wine needs no bush,**
And perhaps products that people
really want need no hard-sell or
soft-sell TV push.
Why not?
Look at pot.
Ogden Nash 1902–71: 'Most Doctors Recommend or Yours For Fast, Fast, Fast Relief' (1972); see ADVERTISING 2

16 **Advertising is the greatest art form of the twentieth century.**
Marshall McLuhan 1911–80: in *Advertising Age* 3 September 1976

17 **Society drives people crazy with lust and calls it advertising.**
John Lahr 1941– : in *Guardian* 2 August 1989

18 **Word of mouth is the best medium of all.**
Bill Bernbach 1911–82: *Bill Bernbach said* (1989)

Advice

proverbs and sayings ▸

1 **Don't teach your grandmother to suck eggs.**
a caution against offering advice to the wise and experienced; English proverb, early 18th century

2 **A fool may give a wise man counsel.**
sometimes used as a warning against overconfidence in one's judgement; English proverb, mid 14th century

3 **Night brings counsel.**
sometimes used as a warning against taking a hasty action or decision; English proverb, late 16th century

4 **A nod's as good as a wink to a blind horse.**
the slightest hint is enough to convey one's meaning in a particular case; English proverb, late 18th century

5 **A word to the wise is enough.**
only a very brief warning is necessary to an intelligent person; English proverb, early 16th century; earlier in Latin '*verbum sat sapienti* [a word is sufficient to a wise man]': see ADVICE 9

phrases ►

6 **counsel of perfection**
advice designed to guide one towards moral perfection, often seen as ideal but impracticable; sometimes with reference to the Bible (Matthew), 'If thou wilt be perfect, go and sell all that thou hast, and give to the poor'

7 **Delphic oracle**
the oracle of Apollo at Delphi in classical antiquity, where a priestess, the Pythia, acted as a medium through whom advice or prophecy was sought from the gods. The characteristic riddling responses have given rise to the use of *Delphic* to mean deliberately obscure or ambiguous

8 **Miss Lonelyhearts**
a journalist who gives advice in a newspaper or magazine to people who are lonely or in difficulties; see ADVICE 20

9 **a word to the wise**
used to imply that further explanation of or comment on a statement or situation is unnecessary; from the proverb: see ADVICE 5

quotations ►

10 **A word spoken in due season, how good is it!**
Bible: Proverbs

11 **Books will speak plain when counsellors blanch.**
Francis Bacon 1561–1626: *Essays* (1625) 'Of Counsel'

12 **Advice is seldom welcome; and those who want it the most always like it the least.**
Lord Chesterfield 1694–1773: *Letters to his Son* (1774) 29 January 1748

13 **Fools need advice most, but wise men only are the better for it.**
Benjamin Franklin 1706–90: *Poor Richard's Almanac* (1758) January

14 **It was, perhaps, one of those cases in which advice is good or bad only as the event decides.**
Jane Austen 1775–1817: *Persuasion* (1818)

15 **Of all the horrid, hideous notes of woe,**
Sadder than owl-songs or the midnight blast,
Is that portentous phrase, 'I told you so.'
Lord Byron 1788–1824: *Don Juan* (1819–24)

16 **Get the advice of everybody whose advice is worth having—they are very few—and then do what you think best yourself.**
Charles Stewart Parnell 1846–91: Conor Cruise O'Brien *Parnell* (1957)

17 **I always pass on good advice. It is the only thing to do with it. It is never of any use to oneself.**
Oscar Wilde 1854–1900: *An Ideal Husband* (1895)

18 **To ask advice is in nine cases out of ten to tout for flattery.**
John Churton Collins 1848–1908: L. C. Collins *Life of John Churton Collins* (1912)

19 **Well, if you knows of a better 'ole, go to it.**
caption to a cartoon of Old Bill and a friend in a shellhole under fire
Bruce Bairnsfather 1888–1959: *Fragments from France* (1915)

20 **The Miss Lonelyhearts are the priests of twentieth-century America.**
Nathaniel West 1903–40: *Miss Lonelyhearts* (1933); see ADVICE 8

21 **After all, when you seek advice from someone it's certainly not because you want them to give it. You just want them to be there while you talk to yourself.**
Terry Pratchett 1948– : *Jingo* (1997)

Africa

proverbs and sayings ▸

1 Always something new out of Africa.
from Pliny: see AFRICA 7; English proverb, mid 16th century

phrases ▸

2 African Eve
the hypothesis (based on study of mitochondrial DNA) that modern humans have a common female ancestor who lived in Africa around 200,000 years ago

3 the Dark Continent
Africa, referring to the time before it was fully explored by Europeans, first recorded in H. M. Stanley *Through the Dark Continent* (1878)

4 the Gold Coast
a former name (until 1957) for Ghana, so called because it was an important source of gold

5 the Slave Coast
part of the west coast of Africa, between the Volta River and Mount Cameroon, an area from which slaves were exported in the 16th–19th centuries

6 the white man's grave
equatorial West Africa, traditionally considered as being particularly unhealthy for whites

quotations ▸

7 *Semper aliquid novi Africam adferre.*
Africa always brings [us] something new.
originally referring to hybridization of African animals
Pliny the Elder AD 23–79: *Historia Naturalis*; see AFRICA 1

8 We are...a nation of dancers, singers and poets.
of the Ibo people
Olaudah Equiano c.1745–c.97: *Narrative of the Life of Olaudah Equiano* (1789)

9 The wind of change is blowing through this continent.
Harold Macmillan 1894–1986: speech at Cape Town, 3 February 1960

10 In Africa a thing is true at first light and a lie by noon.
Ernest Hemingway 1899–1961: *True at First Light* (1999)

11 The shape of Africa resembles a revolver, and the Congo is the trigger.
Frantz Fanon 1925–61: attributed

12 I who have cursed
The drunken officer of British rule, how choose
Between this Africa and the English tongue I love?
Derek Walcott 1930– : 'A Far Cry From Africa' (1962)

13 I have dedicated my life to this struggle of the African people. I have fought against white domination, and I have fought against black domination. I have cherished the ideal of a democratic and free society in which all persons live together in harmony with equal opportunities. It is an ideal which I hope to live for, and to achieve. But my lord, if needs be, it is an ideal for which I am prepared to die.
Nelson Mandela 1918– : speech at his trial in Pretoria, 20 April 1964, which he quoted on his release in Cape Town, 11 February 1990

14 Let there be work, bread, water and salt for all.
Nelson Mandela 1918– : inaugural address as President of South Africa, 10 May 1994

15 The state of Africa is a scar on the conscience of the world.
Tony Blair 1953– : speech to Labour Party Conference, 2 October 2001

16 Africa is not poor, it is poorly managed.
Ellen Johnson-Sirleaf 1938– : *Why is Africa Poor?* BBC World Service 24 August 2009

Alcohol
see also DRUNKENNESS

proverbs and sayings ▸

1 Don't ask a man to drink and drive.
British road safety slogan, from 1964

2 Guinness is good for you.
reply universally given to researchers asking people why they drank Guinness; advertising slogan for Guinness, from 1929

3 Heineken refreshes the parts other beers cannot reach.
slogan for Heineken lager, from 1975 onwards

4 I'm only here for the beer.
slogan for Double Diamond beer, 1971 onwards

5 Let's get out of these wet clothes and into a dry Martini.
line coined in the 1920s by Robert Benchley's press agent and adopted by Mae West in *Every Day's a Holiday* (1937 film)

6 Vodka is an aunt of wine.
Russian proverb

phrases ▸

7 shaken, not stirred
popular summary of the directions for making the perfect martini given by James Bond, from Fleming; see ALCOHOL 27

quotations ▸

8 Wine is a mocker, strong drink is raging.
Bible: Proverbs

9 No verse can give pleasure for long, nor last, that is written by drinkers of water.
Horace 65–8 BC: *Epistles*

10 Use a little wine for thy stomach's sake.
Bible: I Timothy

11 Claret is the liquor for boys; port, for men; but he who aspires to be a hero (smiling) must drink brandy.
Samuel Johnson 1709–84: James Boswell *Life of Johnson* (1791) 7 April 1779

12 Freedom and Whisky gang thegither!
Robert Burns 1759–96: 'The Author's Earnest Cry and Prayer' (1786)

13 O for a beaker full of the warm South,
Full of the true, the blushful
Hippocrene,
With beaded bubbles winking at the
brim,
And purple-stainèd mouth.
John Keats 1795–1821: 'Ode to a Nightingale' (1820)

14 Man wants but little drink below,
But wants that little strong.
Oliver Wendell Holmes 1809–94: 'A Song of other Days' (1848); see LIFE 26

15 Your lips, on my own, when they
printed 'Farewell',
Had never been soiled by the
'beverage of hell';
But they come to me now with the
bacchanal sign,
And the lips that touch liquor must
never touch mine.
George W. Young 1846–1919: 'The Lips That Touch Liquor Must Never Touch Mine' (1870); also attributed, in a different form, to Harriet A. Glazebrook, 1874

16 Wine may well be considered the most healthful and most hygienic of beverages.
Louis Pasteur 1822–95: *Études sur le vin* (1873)

17 Wine is bottled poetry.
Robert Louis Stevenson 1850–94: *The Silverado Squatters* (1883)

18 Fifteen men on the dead man's chest
Yo-ho-ho, and a bottle of rum!
Drink and the devil had done for the
rest—
Yo-ho-ho, and a bottle of rum!
Robert Louis Stevenson 1850–94: *Treasure Island* (1883)

19 And malt does more than Milton can
To justify God's ways to man.
A. E. Housman 1859–1936: *A Shropshire Lad* (1896); see WRITING 19

20 I'm only a beer teetotaller, not a champagne teetotaller.
George Bernard Shaw 1856–1950: *Candida* (1898)

21 Gin was mother's milk to her.
George Bernard Shaw 1856–1950: *Pygmalion* (1916); see LIKES 7

22 Our country has deliberately undertaken a great social and economic experiment, noble in motive and far-reaching in purpose.
on the Eighteenth Amendment enacting Prohibition
Herbert Hoover 1874–1964: letter to Senator W. H. Borah, 23 February 1928

23 Prohibition makes you want to cry into your beer and denies you the beer to cry into.
Don Marquis 1878–1937: *Sun Dial Time* (1936)

24 It's a naïve domestic Burgundy without any breeding, but I think you'll be amused by its presumption.
James Thurber 1894–1961: cartoon caption in *New Yorker* 27 March 1937

25 Some weasel took the cork out of my lunch.
W. C. Fields 1880–1946: *You Can't Cheat an Honest Man* (1939 film)

26 A good general rule is to state that the bouquet is better than the taste, and vice versa.
on wine-tasting
Stephen Potter 1900–69: *One-Upmanship* (1952)

27 A medium Vodka dry Martini—with a slice of lemon peel. Shaken and not stirred.
Ian Fleming 1908–64: *Dr No* (1958); see ALCOHOL 7

28 One reason why I don't drink is because I wish to know when I am having a good time.
Nancy Astor 1879–1964: in *Christian Herald* June 1960

29 A man shouldn't fool with booze until he's fifty; then he's a damn fool if he doesn't.
William Faulkner 1897–1962: James M. Webb and A. Wigfall Green *William Faulkner of Oxford* (1965)

30 I have taken more out of alcohol than alcohol has taken out of me.
Winston Churchill 1874–1965: Quentin Reynolds *By Quentin Reynolds* (1964)

31 I'd hate to be a teetotaller. Imagine getting up in the morning and knowing that's as good as you're going to feel all day.
Dean Martin 1917–95: attributed; also attributed to Jimmy Durante

Ambition

see also ACHIEVEMENT, SUCCESS

proverbs and sayings ▸

1 Hasty climbers have sudden falls.
the over-ambitious often fail to take necessary precautions; English proverb, mid 15th century

2 The higher the monkey climbs the more he shows his tail.
the further an unsuitable person is advanced, the more their inadequacies are apparent; English proverb, late 14th century

3 It's ill waiting for dead men's shoes.
often used of a situation in which one is hoping for a position currently occupied by another; English proverb, mid 16th century; see POSSESSIONS 9

4 Many go out for wool and come home shorn.
many who seek to better themselves or make themselves rich, end by losing what they already have; English proverb, late 16th century

5 There is always room at the top.
as a response to being advised against joining the overcrowded legal profession, it is also attributed to the American politician and lawyer Daniel Webster (1782–1852); English proverb, early 20th century; see OPPORTUNITY 25

quotations ▸

6 [I] had rather be first in a village than second at Rome.
Julius Caesar 100–44 BC: Francis Bacon *The Advancement of Learning*; based on Plutarch *Parallel Lives*

7 *Aut Caesar, aut nihil.*
Caesar or nothing.
Cesare Borgia 1476–1507: motto inscribed on his sword; John Leslie Garner *Caesar Borgia* (1912)

8 Who shoots at the mid-day sun, though he be sure he shall never hit the mark; yet as sure he is he shall shoot higher than who aims but at a bush.
Philip Sidney 1554–86: *Arcadia* ('New Arcadia', 1590)

9 When that the poor have cried, Caesar hath wept;
Ambition should be made of sterner stuff.
William Shakespeare 1564–1616: *Julius Caesar* (1599)

10 WALTER RALEGH: Fain would I climb, yet fear I to fall.
ELIZABETH: If thy heart fails thee, climb not at all.
Elizabeth I 1533–1603: lines written on a window-pane; Thomas Fuller *Worthies of England* (1662)

11 Cromwell, I charge thee, fling away ambition:
By that sin fell the angels.
William Shakespeare 1564–1616: *Henry VIII* (1613)

12 Better to reign in hell, than serve in heaven.
John Milton 1608–74: *Paradise Lost* (1667)

13 No bird soars too high, if he soars with his own wings.
William Blake 1757–1827: *The Marriage of Heaven and Hell* (1790–3)

14 Well is it known that ambition can creep as well as soar.
Edmund Burke 1729–97: *Third Letter...on the Proposals for Peace with the Regicide Directory* (1797)

15 Remember that there is not one of you who does not carry in his cartridge-pouch the marshal's baton of the duke of Reggio; it is up to you to bring it forth.
Louis XVIII 1755–1824: speech to Saint-Cyr cadets, 9 August 1819

16 I had rather be right than be President.
Henry Clay 1777–1852: to Senator Preston of South Carolina, 1839; S. W. McCall *Life of Thomas Brackett Reed* (1914)

17 Ah, but a man's reach should exceed his grasp,
Or what's a heaven for?
Robert Browning 1812–89: 'Andrea del Sarto' (1855)

18 The path of social advancement is, and must be, strewn with broken friendships.
H. G. Wells 1866–1946: *Kipps* (1905)

19 At the age of six I wanted to be a cook. At seven I wanted to be Napoleon. And my ambition has been growing steadily ever since.
Salvador Dali 1904–89: *The Secret Life of Salvador Dali* (1948)

20 Do you sincerely want to be rich?
stock question to salesmen
Bernard Cornfeld 1927–95: Charles Raw et al. *Do You Sincerely Want to be Rich?* (1971)

21 Yo I'll tell you what I want, what I really really want
so tell me what you want, what you really really want.
The Spice Girls: 'Wannabe' (1996 song, with Matthew Rowbottom and Richard Stannard)

America

see also AMERICAN CITIES

proverbs and sayings ▸

1 America is a tune. It must be sung together.
American proverb, mid 20th century

2 Good Americans when they die go to Paris.
coinage attributed to Thomas Gold Appleton (1812–84); American proverb, mid 19th century

phrases ▸

3 the American dream
the ideal of a democratic and prosperous society which is the traditional aim of the American people; American social or material values in general; see IDEALISM 19

4 the Bird of Freedom
the emblematic bald eagle of the US

5 founding father
an American statesman at the time of the Revolution, especially a member of the Federal Constitutional Convention of 1787; see AMERICA 26

6 Land of the Free
the United States of America, from 'The Star-Spangled Banner': see AMERICA 13

7 Old Glory
the national flag of the United States; attributed to Captain William Driver (1803–86), who is reported to have said, 'I name thee Old Glory!', when saluting a new flag flown on his ship in 1831

8 the Stars and Bars
the flag of the Confederate States of America; it had three bars, and a circle of eleven stars for the eleven states of the Confederacy

9 the Stars and Stripes
the national flag of the United States; when first adopted in 1777 it contained 13 stripes and 13 stars, representing the 13 states of the Union; it now has 13 stripes and 50 stars

quotations ▸

10 We must consider that we shall be a city upon a hill, the eyes of all people are on us; so that if we shall deal falsely with our God in this work we have undertaken, and so cause Him

to withdraw His present help from us, we shall be made a story and a byword through the world.

John Winthrop 1588–1649: *Christian Charity, A Model Hereof* (sermon, 1630)

11 Then join hand in hand, brave Americans all,—
By uniting we stand, by dividing we fall.

John Dickinson 1732–1808: 'The Liberty Song' (1768); see COOPERATION 20

12 Where today are the Pequot? Where are the Narragansett, the Mohican, the Pokanoket, and many other once powerful tribes of our people? They have vanished before the avarice and oppression of the white man, as snow before the summer sun.

Tecumseh 1768–1813: Dee Brown *Bury My Heart at Wounded Knee* (1970)

13 'Tis the star-spangled banner; O long may it wave
O'er the land of the free, and the home of the brave!

Francis Scott Key 1779–1843: 'The Star-Spangled Banner' (1814); see AMERICA 6

14 But this momentous question [the Missouri Compromise], like a firebell in the night awakened and filled me with terror. I considered it the knell of the Union.

Thomas Jefferson 1743–1826: letter to John Holmes, 22 April 1820; see DANGER 16

15 I called the New World into existence, to redress the balance of the Old.

George Canning 1770–1827: speech on the affairs of Portugal, House of Commons, 12 December 1826

16 I was born an American; I will live an American; I shall die an American.

Daniel Webster 1782–1852: speech in the Senate on 'The Compromise Bill', 17 July 1850

17 Go West, young man, and grow up with the country.

Horace Greeley 1811–72: *Hints toward Reforms* (1850); see EXPLORATION 7

18 The United States themselves are essentially the greatest poem.

Walt Whitman 1819–92: *Leaves of Grass* (1855)

19 What law have I broken? Is it wrong for me to love my own? Is it wicked for me because my skin is red? Because I am Sioux; because I was born where my fathers lived; because I would die for my people and my country?

Sitting Bull 1831–90: to Major Brotherton, recorded July 1881; Gary C. Anderson *Sitting Bull* (1996)

20 Give me your tired, your poor,
Your huddled masses yearning to breathe free.

inscription on the Statue of Liberty, New York

Emma Lazarus 1849–87: 'The New Colossus' (1883)

21 I pledge allegiance to the flag of the United States of America and to the republic for which it stands, one nation under God, indivisible, with liberty and justice for all.

Francis Bellamy 1856–1931: *The Pledge of Allegiance to the Flag* (1892)

22 Isn't this a billion dollar country?

responding to a Democratic gibe about a 'million dollar Congress'

Charles Foster 1828–1904: at the 51st Congress, in *North American Review* March 1892; also attributed to Thomas B. Reed

23 America! America!
God shed His grace on thee
And crown thy good with brotherhood
From sea to shining sea!

Katherine Lee Bates 1859–1929: 'America the Beautiful' (1893)

24 I'm a Yankee Doodle Dandy,
A Yankee Doodle, do or die;
A real live nephew of my Uncle Sam's,
Born on the fourth of July.

George M. Cohan 1878–1942: 'Yankee Doodle Boy' (1904 song)

25 America is God's Crucible, the great Melting-Pot where all the races of Europe are melting and re-forming!

Israel Zangwill 1864–1926: *The Melting Pot* (1908)

26 I must utter my belief in the divine inspiration of the founding fathers.

Warren G. Harding 1865–1923: inaugural address, 4 March 1921; see AMERICA 5

27 The chief business of the American people is business.

Calvin Coolidge 1872–1933: speech in Washington, 17 January 1925

28 The American system of rugged individualism.
Herbert Hoover 1874–1964: speech in New York City, 22 October 1928

29 I pledge you, I pledge myself, to a new deal for the American people.
Franklin D. Roosevelt 1882–1945: speech to the Democratic Convention in Chicago, 2 July 1932, accepting the presidential nomination

30 In the United States there is more space where nobody is than where anybody is. That is what makes America what it is.
Gertrude Stein 1874–1946: *The Geographical History of America* (1936)

31 God bless America,
Land that I love,
Stand beside her and guide her
Thru the night with a light from above.
Irving Berlin 1888–1989: 'God Bless America' (1939 song)

32 This land is your land, this land is my land,
From California to the New York Island.
From the redwood forest to the Gulf Stream waters
This land was made for you and me.
Woody Guthrie 1912–67: 'This Land is Your Land' (1956 song)

33 I like to be in America!
O.K. by me in America!
Ev'rything free in America
For a small fee in America!
Stephen Sondheim 1930– : 'America' (1957 song)

34 America is a vast conspiracy to make you happy.
John Updike 1932–2009: *Problems* (1980) 'How to love America and Leave it at the Same Time'

35 America is not a lie, it is a disappointment. But it can be a disappointment only because it is also a hope.
Samuel Huntington 1927–2008: *American Politics: the Promise of Disharmony* (1981)

36 There is nothing wrong with America that cannot be fixed by what is right with America.
William Jefferson ('Bill') Clinton 1946– : inaugural address, 1993

37 There is not a black America and a white America and Latino America and Asian America; there's the United States of America.
Barack Obama 1961– : Democratic National Convention keynote address, 27 July 2004

American Cities and States

phrases ▸

1 **the Aloha State**
Hawaii; *aloha* = Hawaiian word used when greeting or parting from someone

2 **the Bay State**
Massachusetts; the original colony was sited around Massachusetts Bay

3 **the Bear State**
Arkansas

4 **the Big Apple**
New York City

5 **the Big Easy**
New Orleans

6 **the Buckeye State**
Ohio, where buckeye trees are abundant

7 **the Centennial State**
Colorado, admitted as a state in 1876, the centennial year of the United States

8 **City of the Angels**
Los Angeles, California

9 **City of Elms**
New Haven, Connecticut

10 **City of Magnificent Distances**
Washington, DC

11 **the Crescent City**
New Orleans: the city is built on a curve of the Mississippi

12 **the dark and bloody ground**
Kentucky, sometimes said to be the meaning of Kentucky as an Indian term; alternatively, said to derive from a warning given by a Cherokee chief in the late 18th century, that the land was already 'a bloody ground' from earlier hunting and fighting, and that it would be dark for prospective settlers

13 **the Diamond State**
Delaware, said to be so named because it was seen as small in size but of great importance

14 **the Empire City**
New York

15 **the Empire State**
New York State

16 **the Empire State of the South**
Georgia

17 **the Equality State**
Wyoming, the first state to give women the vote

18 **the Forest City**
Cleveland, Ohio

19 **the Garden State**
New Jersey

20 **the Golden State**
California

21 **the Gopher State**
Minnesota

22 **the Granite State**
New Hampshire

23 **the Great White Way**
Broadway in New York City, referring to the brilliant street illumination

24 **the Hawkeye State**
Iowa

25 **the Keystone State**
Pennsylvania, the seventh or central one of the original thirteen States

26 **Land of Enchantment**
an informal name for New Mexico

27 **the Lone Star State**
Texas

28 **the Magnolia State**
Mississippi; the state's emblem is the magnolia flower

29 **the Monumental City**
the city of Baltimore, Maryland, named after the Washington Monument

30 **Mother of Presidents**
informal name for the state of Virginia and (later) Ohio; Virginia was the birthplace of Washington, Jefferson, and Monroe, and Ohio the birthplace of Garfield and Taft

31 **the North Star State**
Minnesota; *North Star* the polestar

32 **the Nutmeg State**
Connecticut; the inhabitants of Connecticut reputedly passed off as the spice nutmeg-shaped pieces of wood; see DECEPTION 11

33 **the Old Dominion**
Virginia

34 **the Palmetto State**
South Carolina

35 **the Pelican State**
Louisiana

36 **the Prairie State**
Illinois

37 **the Prairie States**
Illinois, Wisconsin, Iowa, Minnesota, and other states to the south

38 **Quaker City**
Philadelphia, founded by the Quaker William Penn in 1681

39 **the Quaker State**
Pennsylvania

40 **Queen of the West**
Cincinnati, Ohio

41 **the Silver State**
Nevada, referring to its silver mines

42 **Soul City**
the Harlem area of New York city, referring to the prevalence of soul music

43 **the Sunflower State**
Kansas; the sunflower is the state flower

44 **the Tarheel State**
North Carolina, with allusion to tar as a principal product of that state

45 **the Treasure State**
Montana, noted for its gold, silver, copper, and coal mines

46 **the Turpentine State**
North Carolina, from the quantity of turpentine obtained from its pine forests

47 **the Volunteer State**
Tennessee, from which large numbers volunteered for the Mexican War of 1847

48 **the Windy City**
Chicago

49 **the Wolverine State**
Michigan, where wolverines are found

quotations ▸

50 **Times are not good here. The city is crumbling into ashes...But it is better to live here in sackcloth and ashes, than to own the whole state of Ohio.**
of New Orleans
Lafcadio Hearn 1850–1904: letter to H. E. Krehbiel, 1880; Elizabeth Bisland *Life and Letters of Lafcadio Hearn* (1906)

51 A Boston man is the east wind made flesh.

Thomas Gold Appleton 1812–84: attributed

52 And this is good old Boston,
The home of the bean and the cod,
Where the Lowells talk to the Cabots
And the Cabots talk only to God.

John Collins Bossidy 1860–1928: verse spoken at Holy Cross College alumni dinner in Boston, Massachusetts, 1910

53 Hog Butcher for the World,
Tool Maker, Stacker of Wheat,
Player with Railroads and the Nation's
Freight Handler;
Stormy, husky, brawling,
City of the Big Shoulders.

Carl Sandburg 1878–1967: 'Chicago' (1916)

54 There is no there there.

on her hometown of Oakland, California, often misquoted as being said of Los Angeles

Gertrude Stein 1874–1946: *Everybody's Autobiography* (1937)

55 California is a fine place to live—if you happen to be an orange.

Fred Allen 1894–1956: *American Magazine* December 1945

56 New York, New York,—a helluva town,
The Bronx is up but the Battery's
down.

Betty Comden 1917–2006 and **Adolph Green** 1915–2002: 'New York, New York' (1945 song)

57 The state with the prettiest name,
the state that floats in brackish water,
held together by mangrove roots.

Elizabeth Bishop 1911–79: 'Florida' (1946)

58 Last week, I went to Philadelphia, but it was closed.

W. C. Fields 1880–1946: Richard J. Anobile *Godfrey Daniels* (1975)

59 A hundred times I have thought:
New York is a catastrophe, and fifty times: it is a beautiful catastrophe.

Le Corbusier 1887–1965: *When the Cathedrals were White* (1947) 'The Fairy Catastrophe'

60 A big hard-boiled city with no more personality than a paper cup.

of Los Angeles

Raymond Chandler 1888–1959: *The Little Sister* (1949)

61 Hollywood is a place where people from Iowa mistake each other for stars.

Fred Allen 1894–1956: Maurice Zolotow *No People like Show People* (1951)

62 I left my heart in San Francisco
High on a hill it calls to me.

Douglas Cross: 'I Left My Heart in San Francisco' (1954 song)

63 Washington is a city of southern efficiency and northern charm.

John F. Kennedy 1917–63: Arthur M. Schlesinger Jr. *A Thousand Days* (1965)

64 I had forgotten just how flat and empty it [middle America] is. Stand on two phone books almost anywhere in Iowa and you get a view.

Bill Bryson 1951– : *The Lost Continent* (1989)

Anger

proverbs and sayings ▸

1 Anger improves nothing but the arch of a cat's back.

American proverb, mid 20th century

2 He that will be angry for anything will be angry for nothing.

Scottish proverb

3 A little pot is soon hot.

a small person quickly becomes angry or passionate; English proverb, mid 16th century

4 When angry count a hundred.

advising against precipitate response (the number proposed varies, and sometimes the advice is '…recite the alphabet'); English proverb, late 16th century; see ANGER 14, ANGER 16

phrases ▸

5 look back in anger

reflect on the past with indignation and resentment; with allusion to John Osborne's play *Look Back in Anger*. see GENERATION GAP 2

6 make someone's blood boil

infuriate someone

7 red rag to a bull

an object, utterance, or act which is certain to provoke someone, from the traditional belief (recorded from the late 16th century) that this colour is particularly irritating to the animal

quotations ▸

8 A soft answer turneth away wrath.
Bible: Proverbs; see DIPLOMACY 1

9 Anger is a short madness.
Horace 65–8 BC: *Epistles*

10 Be ye angry and sin not: let the sun go down upon your wrath.
Bible: Ephesians; see FORGIVENESS 4

11 Anger makes dull men witty, but it keeps them poor.
Francis Bacon 1561–1626: 'Baconiana' (1859); often attributed to Queen Elizabeth I from a misreading of the text

12 Anger is never without an argument, but seldom with a good one.
Lord Halifax 1633–95: *Political, Moral, and Miscellaneous Thoughts and Reflections* (1750)

13 The tygers of wrath are wiser than the horses of instruction.
William Blake 1757–1827: *The Marriage of Heaven and Hell* (1790–3) 'Proverbs of Hell'

14 When angry, count ten before you speak; if very angry a hundred.
Thomas Jefferson 1743–1826: letter to Thomas Jefferson Smith, 21 February 1825; see ANGER 4, ANGER 16

15 We boil at different degrees.
Ralph Waldo Emerson 1803–82: *Society and Solitude* (1870)

16 When angry, count four; when very angry, swear.
Mark Twain 1835–1910: *Pudd'nhead Wilson* (1894); see ANGER 4, ANGER 14

17 It's my rule never to lose me temper till it would be dethrimental to keep it.
Sean O'Casey 1880–1964: *The Plough and the Stars* (1926)

18 Usually, when people are sad, they don't do anything. They just cry over their condition. But when they get angry, they bring about a change.
Malcolm X 1925–65: speech at rally in support of Fannie Lou Hamer, 20 December 1964

19 I'm mad as hell, and I'm not going to take this anymore!
Paddy Chayefsky 1923–81: *Network* (1976 film), spoken by Peter Finch as Howard Beale

Animals

see also BIRDS, CATS, DOGS

proverbs and sayings ▸

1 Care, and not fine stables, makes a good horse.
Danish proverb

2 Feed a dog for three days and he will remember your kindness for three years. Feed a cat for three years and she will forget your kindness in three days.
Japanese proverb

3 From beavers, bees should learn to
mend their ways.
A bee works; a beaver works and plays.
American proverb, mid 20th century

4 A howlin' coyote ain't stealin' no chickens.
American proverb, mid 20th century

5 If you want to live and thrive, let the spider run alive.
it was traditionally unlucky to harm a spider or a spider's web; English proverb, mid 19th century

6 No foot, no horse.
relating to horse care, and recorded in North America as 'no hoof, no horse'; English proverb, mid 18th century

7 One white foot, buy him; two white feet, try him; three white feet, look well about him; four white feet, go without him.
on horse-dealing, categorizing features in a horse which are believed to be unlucky; English proverb, recorded in various forms from the 15th century

8 Three things are not to be trusted; a cow's horn, a dog's tooth, and a horse's hoof.
one may be gored, bitten, or kicked without warning; English proverb, late 14th century

9 The wind of heaven is that which blows between a horse's ears.
saying, said to be an Arab proverb

phrases ▸

10 the king of beasts
the lion

11 the lion's provider
the jackal

12 the little gentleman in black velvet
the mole, in a Jacobite toast, from the belief that the death of William III was caused by his horse's stumbling over a molehill

13 the ship of the desert
the camel

quotations ►

14 There went in two and two unto Noah into the Ark, the male and the female.
Bible: Genesis

15 A righteous man regardeth the life of his beast: but the tender mercies of the wicked are cruel.
Bible: Proverbs; see SYMPATHY 11

16 All breathing, existing, living, sentient creatures should not be slain, nor treated with violence, nor abused, nor tormented, nor driven away.
This is the pure, unchangeable, eternal law.
Jaina Sutras 6th century BC: *Ācārānga Sutra*

17 Nature's great masterpiece, an elephant,
The only harmless great thing.
John Donne 1572–1631: 'The Progress of the Soul' (1601)

18 The serpent subtlest beast of all the field.
John Milton 1608–74: *Paradise Lost* (1667)

19 The question is not, Can they reason? nor, Can they talk? but, Can they suffer?
Jeremy Bentham 1748–1832: *Principles of Morals and Legislation* (1789)

20 Tyger Tyger, burning bright,
In the forests of the night;
What immortal hand or eye,
Could frame thy fearful symmetry?
William Blake 1757–1827: *Songs of Experience* (1794) 'The Tiger'

21 Animals, whom we have made our slaves, we do not like to consider our equal.
Charles Darwin 1809–82: Notebook B (1837–8)

22 All things bright and beautiful,
All creatures great and small,
All things wise and wonderful,
The Lord God made them all.
Cecil Frances Alexander 1818–95: 'All Things Bright and Beautiful' (1848)

23 I think I could turn and live with animals, they are so placid and self-contained,
I stand and look at them long and long.
They do not sweat and whine about their condition,
They do not lie awake in the dark and weep for their sins.
Walt Whitman 1819–92: 'Song of Myself' (written 1855)

24 Animals are such agreeable friends—they ask no questions, they pass no criticism.
George Eliot 1819–80: *Scenes of Clerical Life* (1858)

25 All animals, except man, know that the principal business of life is to enjoy it—and they do enjoy it as much as man and other circumstances will allow.
Samuel Butler 1835–1902: *The Way of All Flesh* (1903)

26 God in His wisdom made the fly
And then forgot to tell us why.
Ogden Nash 1902–71: 'The Fly' (1942)

27 A four-legged friend, a four-legged friend,
He'll never let you down.
sung by Roy Rogers about his horse Trigger
J. Brooks: 'A Four Legged Friend' (1952 song)

28 Where in this wide world can man find nobility without pride,
Friendship without envy, or beauty without vanity?
Ronald Duncan 1914–82: 'In Praise of the Horse' (1962)

29 I am fond of pigs. Dogs look up to us. Cats look down on us. Pigs treat us as equals.
Winston Churchill 1874–1965: attributed; M. Gilbert *Never Despair* (1988)

30 I hate a word like 'pets': it sounds so much
Like something with no living of its own.
Elizabeth Jennings 1926–2001: 'My Animals' (1966)

31 I gave my beauty and my youth to men. I am going to give my wisdom and experience to animals.
Brigitte Bardot 1934– : attributed, June 1987

Apology and Excuses

proverbs and sayings ▸

1 **Apology is only egoism wrong side out.**
American proverb, mid 20th century

2 **A bad excuse is better than none.**
it is better to attempt to give some kind of explanation, even a weak one; English proverb, mid 16th century

3 **A bad workman blames his tools.**
often used as a comment on someone's excuses for their lack of success; English proverb, early 17th century, late 13th century in French; see APOLOGY 7

4 **Don't make excuses, make good.**
American proverb, early 20th century

5 **He who excuses, accuses himself.**
often used to mean that attempts to excuse oneself show a guilty conscience; English proverb, early 17th century

6 **It is easy to find a stick to beat a dog.**
it is easy to find reasons to criticize someone who is vulnerable; English proverb, mid 16th century; see ARGUMENT 18

7 **One who cannot dance blames the uneven floor.**
Indian proverb; see APOLOGY 3

8 **When you are in a hole, stop digging.**
complicated explanations and attempts to exculpate oneself often make a bad situation worse; late 20th century saying, often associated with the British Labour politician Denis Healey; see CIRCUMSTANCE 12

phrases ▸

9 **eat crow**
in North American usage, be humiliated by having to admit one's defeats or mistakes; *crow* taken as a type of poor and unpalatable food; see APOLOGY 22

10 **eat humble pie**
make a humble apology and accept humiliation. *Humble pie* is from a pun based on *umbles* 'offal', considered as inferior food

11 **mea culpa**
an acknowledgement of one's guilt or responsibility for an error; Latin, literally '(through) my own fault': from the prayer of confession in the Latin liturgy of the Church

12 **a sop to Cerberus**
something offered in propitiation; *Cerberus* = the three-headed watchdog of classical mythology which guarded the entrance of Hades; in the *Aeneid*, Aeneas was able to pass him safely by drugging him with a specially prepared cake

quotations ▸

13 **Never make a defence or apology before you be accused.**
Charles I 1600–49: letter to Lord Wentworth, 3 September 1636

14 **A man should never be ashamed to own he has been in the wrong, which is but saying, in other words, that he is wiser to-day than he was yesterday.**
Alexander Pope 1688–1744: *Miscellanies* (1727) vol. 2 'Thoughts on Various Subjects'

15 **Never complain and never explain.**
Benjamin Disraeli 1804–81: J. Morley *Life of William Ewart Gladstone* (1903); see APOLOGY 18

16 **Beware of too much explaining, lest we end by too much excusing.**
Lord Acton 1834–1902: attributed by Acton to the Duc de Broglie, lecture delivered Cambridge, June 1895

17 **I have invented an invaluable permanent invalid called Bunbury, in order that I may be able to go down into the country whenever I choose.**
Oscar Wilde 1854–1900: *The Importance of Being Earnest* (1899)

18 **Never explain—your friends do not need it and your enemies will not believe you anyway.**
Elbert Hubbard 1859–1915: *The Motto Book* (1907); see APOLOGY 15

19 **It is a good rule in life never to apologize. The right sort of people do not want apologies, and the wrong sort take a mean advantage of them.**
P. G. Wodehouse 1881–1975: *The Man Upstairs* (1914)

20 **Very sorry can't come. Lie follows by post.**
telegraphed message to the Prince of Wales, on being summoned to dine at the eleventh hour
Lord Charles Beresford 1846–1919: Ralph Nevill *The World of Fashion 1837–1922* (1923)

21 **Several excuses are always less convincing than one.**
Aldous Huxley 1894–1963: *Point Counter Point* (1928)

22 **If you have to eat crow, eat it while it's hot.**
Alben W. Barkley 1877–1956: attributed; see APOLOGY 9

23 **I have expressed a degree of regret that can be equated with an apology.**
on permitting British sailors to sell their stories of their capture by Iran to the press
Des Browne 1952– : speech in the House of Commons, 16 April 2007

Appearance
see also BODY

proverbs and sayings ▶

1 **Appearances are deceptive.**
the outward form of something may not be a true guide to its real nature; English proverb, mid 17th century

2 **A blind man's wife needs no paint.**
there is no point in making efforts that cannot be appreciated; English proverb, mid 17th century

3 **A carpenter is known by his chips.**
the nature of a person's occupation or interest is demonstrated by the traces left behind; English proverb, mid 16th century

4 **The cowl does not make the monk.**
warning against judging nature and moral character by appearance; English proverb, late 14th century

5 **Distance lends enchantment to the view.**
English proverb, late 18th century, from Campbell: see COUNTRY 12

6 **A good horse cannot be of a bad colour.**
colour is not an indicator of a horse's quality; English proverb, early 17th century

7 **Keep that schoolgirl complexion.**
advertising slogan for Palmolive soap, from 1917

8 **Matching lips and fingertips.**
advertising slogan for Revlon cosmetics, 1940

9 **Never choose your women or linen by candlelight.**
warning against being deceived by apparent attractions seen in a poor light; English proverb, late 16th century

10 **What you see is what you get.**
a late 20th century computing expression, from which the acronym *wysiwyg* derives. The expression is used generally to mean that the function and value of something can be deduced from its outward appearance; there are no hidden drawbacks or advantages

11 **You can't tell a book by its cover.**
outward appearance is not a guide to a person's real nature; English proverb, early 20th century

phrases ▶

12 **the acceptable face of —**
the tolerable manifestation or aspect of (something usually considered suspect or immoral); see CAPITALISM 28

13 **the cut of someone's jib**
the appearance or look of someone. Originally a nautical expression suggested by the prominence and characteristic form of the jib (a triangular sail set forward of the foremast) as the identifying characteristic of a ship

quotations ▶

14 **A merry heart maketh a cheerful countenance.**
Bible: Proverbs

15 **Fine words and an insinuating appearance are seldom associated with true virtue.**
Confucius 551–479 BC: *Analects*

16 **There's no art**
To find the mind's construction in the face;
William Shakespeare 1564–1616: *Macbeth* (1606)

17 **Had Cleopatra's nose been shorter, the whole face of the world would have changed.**
Blaise Pascal 1623–62: *Pensées* (1670)

18 **An unforgiving eye, and a damned disinheriting countenance!**
Richard Brinsley Sheridan 1751–1816: *The School for Scandal* (1777)

19 **Like the silver plate on a coffin.**
describing Robert Peel's smile
John Philpot Curran 1750–1817: quoted by Daniel O'Connell, House of Commons, 26 February 1835

20 **The Lord prefers common-looking people. That is why he makes so**

many of them.
Abraham Lincoln 1809–65: attributed; James Morgan *Our Presidents* (1928)

21 It's as large as life, and twice as natural!
Lewis Carroll 1832–98: *Through the Looking-Glass* (1872)

22 She may very well pass for forty-three
In the dusk with a light behind her!
W. S. Gilbert 1836–1911: *Trial by Jury* (1875)

23 It is only shallow people who do not judge by appearances.
Oscar Wilde 1854–1900: *The Picture of Dorian Gray* (1891)

24 Most women are not so young as they are painted.
Max Beerbohm 1872–1956: *The Yellow Book* (1894)

25 A man's face is his autobiography.
A woman's face is her work of fiction.
Oscar Wilde 1854–1900: in 1898, H. Montgomery Hyde *Oscar Wilde* (1976)

26 Men seldom make passes
At girls who wear glasses.
Dorothy Parker 1893–1967: 'News Item' (1937)

27 Sure, deck your lower limbs in pants;
Yours are the limbs, my sweeting.
You look divine as you advance—
Have you seen yourself retreating?
Ogden Nash 1902–71: 'What's the Use?' (1940)

28 At 50, everyone has the face he deserves.
George Orwell 1903–50: last words in his notebook, 17 April 1949

29 My face looks like a wedding cake left out in the rain.
W. H. Auden 1907–73: Humphrey Carpenter *W. H. Auden* (1981)

30 You can never be too rich or too thin.
Duchess of Windsor 1896–1986: attributed

31 I think your whole life shows in your face and you should be proud of that.
Lauren Bacall 1924– : in *Daily Telegraph* 2 March 1988

32 It costs a lot of money to look this cheap.
Dolly Parton 1946– : attributed, perhaps apocryphal

33 Even I don't wake up looking like Cindy Crawford.
Cindy Crawford 1966– : attributed, in *The Age* [Melbourne] 17 August 1994

Architecture

proverbs and sayings ▸

1 In settling an island, the first building erected by a Spaniard will be a church; by a Frenchman, a fort; by a Dutchman, a warehouse; and by an Englishman, an alehouse.
English proverb, late 18th century

2 It is easier to build two chimneys than to maintain one.
the cost of using and maintaining a building may be much greater than the cost of building it; English proverb, mid 16th century

3 No good building without a good foundation.
English proverb, late 15th century

4 Si monumentum requiris, circumspice.
Latin, *If you seek a monument, gaze around*, inscription in St Paul's Cathedral, London, attributed to the son of Sir Christopher Wren, its architect

phrases ▸

5 the Seven Wonders of the World
the seven most spectacular man-made structures of the ancient world: traditionally they comprised the pyramids of Egypt, the Hanging Gardens of Babylon, the Mausoleum of Halicarnassus, the temple of Artemis at Ephesus in Asia Minor, the Colossus of Rhodes, the huge ivory and gold statue of Zeus at Olympia in the Peloponnese, and the Pharos of Alexandria (or in some lists, the walls of Babylon); see EXCELLENCE 6

quotations ▸

6 Now these should be so carried out that account is taken of strength, utility, grace.
of building works
Vitruvius fl. 1st century BC: *On Architecture*; see ARCHITECTURE 7

7 Well building hath three conditions. Commodity, firmness, and delight.
Henry Wotton 1568–1639: *Elements of Architecture* (1624); see ARCHITECTURE 6

8 Houses are built to live in and not to look on; therefore let use be preferred before uniformity, except where both

may be had.
Francis Bacon 1561–1626: *Essays* (1625) 'Of Building'

9 Light (God's eldest daughter) is a principal beauty in a building.
Thomas Fuller 1608–61: *The Holy State and the Profane State* (1642)

10 Architecture in general is frozen music.
Friedrich von Schelling 1775–1854: *Philosophie der Kunst* (1809)

11 Form follows function.
Louis Henri Sullivan 1856–1924: *The Tall Office Building Artistically Considered* (1896); see BEAUTY 38

12 A house is a machine for living in.
Le Corbusier 1887–1965: *Vers une architecture* (1923)

13 Architecture, of all the arts, is the one which acts the most slowly, but the most surely, on the soul.
Ernest Dimnet: *What We Live By* (1932)

14 We shape our buildings, and afterwards our buildings shape us.
Winston Churchill 1874–1965: in the House of Commons, 28 October 1943

15 A bicycle shed is a building; Lincoln Cathedral is a piece of architecture. Nearly everything that encloses space on a scale sufficient for a human being to move in is a building; the term architecture applies only to buildings designed with a view to aesthetic appeal.
Nikolaus Pevsner 1902–83: *An Outline of European Architecture* (1943)

16 Less is more.
Ludwig Mies van der Rohe 1886–1969: P. Johnson *Mies van der Rohe* (1947); see EXCESS 8

17 The physician can bury his mistakes, but the architect can only advise his client to plant vines—so they should go as far as possible from home to build their first buildings.
Frank Lloyd Wright 1867–1959: in *New York Times* 4 October 1953; see MEDICINE 16

18 Architecture is the art of how to waste space.
Philip Johnson 1906–2005: in *New York Times* 27 December 1964

19 The materials of city planning are sky, space, trees, steel and cement in that order and in that hierarchy.
Le Corbusier 1887–1965: in *Times* 1965

20 God is in the details.
Ludwig Mies van der Rohe 1886–1969: attributed, in *New York Times* 19 August 1969; see ORDER 2

21 A monstrous carbuncle on the face of a much-loved and elegant friend.
on the proposed extension to the National Gallery, London
Prince Charles 1948– : speech to the Royal Institute of British Architects, 30 May 1984

Argument

see also OPINION

proverbs and sayings ▸

1 Birds in their little nests agree.
used as a direction that young children should not argue among themselves; a nursery proverb from Isaac Watts *Divine Songs* (1715)

2 It takes two to make a quarrel.
some responsibility for a disagreement rests with each party to it; English proverb, early 18th century; see ARGUMENT 17

3 The more arguments you win, the less friends you will have.
American proverb, mid 20th century

4 While two dogs are fighting for a bone, a third runs away with it.
while the attention of the disputants is on their quarrel, both may lose possession of what they are fighting over to a third party; English proverb, late 14th century; see ARGUMENT 6

phrases ▸

5 apple of discord
a subject of dissension, from the golden apple inscribed 'for the fairest' contended for by Hera, Athene, and Aphrodite; the result of Paris's awarding the apple to Aphrodite was that Hera through jealousy brought about the Trojan War

6 bone of contention
a subject or issue over which there is continuing disagreement; from a bone thrown between two dogs as the type of something which causes a quarrel; see ARGUMENT 4

7 man of straw
originally, a dummy or image made of straw; from this, a person compared to a straw image, a sham; a sham argument set up to be defeated

8 Punch and Judy
quarrelsome and argumentative; *Punch and Judy* a traditional English puppet show in which Punch is shown nagging, beating, and finally killing a succession of characters, including his wife Judy; see PARLIAMENT 30, PLEASURE 5

quotations ▸

9 It is better to dwell in a corner of the housetop, than with a brawling woman in a wide house.
Bible: Proverbs

10 Our disputants put me in mind of the skuttle fish, that when he is unable to extricate himself, blackens all the water about him, till he becomes invisible.
Joseph Addison 1672–1719: in *The Spectator* 5 September 1712

11 There is no arguing with Johnson; for when his pistol misses fire, he knocks you down with the butt end of it.
Oliver Goldsmith 1728–74: James Boswell *Life of Johnson* (1791) 26 October 1769

12 I hate a fellow whom pride, or cowardice, or laziness drives into a corner, and who does nothing when he is there but sit and *growl*; let him come out as I do, and *bark*.
Samuel Johnson 1709–84: James Boswell *Life of Johnson* 10 October 1782

13 Who can refute a sneer?
William Paley 1743–1805: *Principles of Moral and Political Philosophy* (1785)

14 Persuasion is the resource of the feeble; and the feeble can seldom persuade.
Edward Gibbon 1737–94: *The Decline and Fall of the Roman Empire* (1776–88)

15 There is no good in arguing with the inevitable. The only argument available with an east wind is to put on your overcoat.
James Russell Lowell 1819–91: *Democracy and other Addresses* (1887)

16 Fear not those who argue but those who dodge.
Marie von Ebner-Eschenbach 1830–1916: *Aphorisms* (1905)

17 It takes in reality only one to make a quarrel. It is useless for the sheep to pass resolutions in favour of vegetarianism, while the wolf remains of a different opinion.
William Ralph Inge 1860–1954: *Outspoken Essays: First Series* (1919) 'Patriotism'; see ARGUMENT 2

18 Any stigma, as the old saying is, will serve to beat a dogma.
Philip Guedalla 1889–1944: *Masters and Men* (1923); see APOLOGY 6

19 The argument of the broken window pane is the most valuable argument in modern politics.
Emmeline Pankhurst 1858–1928: George Dangerfield *The Strange Death of Liberal England* (1936)

20 Making noise is an effective means of opposition.
Joseph Goebbels 1897–1945: Ernest K. Bramsted *Goebbels and National Socialist Propaganda 1925–45* (1965)

21 The Catholic and the Communist are alike in assuming that an opponent cannot be both honest and intelligent.
George Orwell 1903–50: in *Polemic* January 1946

22 For your own good is a persuasive argument that will eventually make a man agree to his own destruction.
Janet Frame 1924–2004: *Faces in the Water* (1961)

23 Get your tanks off my lawn, Hughie.
to the trade union leader Hugh Scanlon, at Chequers in June 1969
Harold Wilson 1916–95: Peter Jenkins *The Battle of Downing Street* (1970)

The Armed Forces

see also WARFARE, WARS, WORLD WAR I, WORLD WAR II

proverbs and sayings ▸

1 A bloody war and a sickly season.
naval toast in the time of Nelson, when an increased death rate meant more rapid promotion

2 Daddy, what did you do in the Great War?
daughter to father in First World War recruiting poster

3 **The first duty of a soldier is obedience.**
English proverb, mid 19th century

4 **If it moves, salute it; if it doesn't move, pick it up; and if you can't pick it up, paint it.**
1940s saying

5 **Old soldiers never die.**
English proverb, early 20th century; see ARMED FORCES 39

6 **One of our aircraft is missing.**
title of film (1941), an alteration of the customary formula used by BBC news in the Second World War, 'One of our aircraft failed to return'

7 **Providence is always on the side of the big battalions.**
English proverb, early 19th century; see GOD 23, STRENGTH 21, WARFARE 24

8 **A soldier of the Great War known unto God.**
adopted by the War Graves Commission as the standard epitaph for the unidentified dead of World War One

9 **Touching the sky with glory.**
motto of the Indian Air Force, taken from the Bhagavadgita

10 **A willing foe and sea room.**
naval toast in the time of Nelson

11 **Your King and Country need you.**
1914 recruiting advertisement, showing Lord Kitchener with pointing finger

phrases ▶

12 **the awkward squad**
a squad composed of recruits and soldiers who need further training; shortly before his death Robert Burns (1759–96) said, 'don't let the awkward squad fire over my grave'

13 **take the king's (or queen's) shilling**
enlist in the army. The reference is to the *shilling* formerly given to a recruit on enlistment

14 **the thin red line**
the British army; William Howard Russell said of the Russians charging the British at Balaclava, 'They dashed on towards that thin red line tipped with steel'; Russell's original dispatch to *The Times*, 14 November 1854, reads 'That thin red streak topped with a line of steel'; see LAW 16

15 **the wooden walls**
ships or shipping as a defensive force; the Athenian statesman Themistocles interpreted the Delphic oracle's reference to 'safety promised in a wooden wall' as referring to the Greek ships with which the decisive victory over the Persian fleet at Salamis was achieved; see SEA 13

quotations ▶

16 **Then a soldier,**
Full of strange oaths, and bearded like the pard,
Jealous in honour, sudden and quick in quarrel,
Seeking the bubble reputation
Even in the cannon's mouth.
William Shakespeare 1564–1616: *As You Like It* (1599)

17 **I would rather have a plain russet-coated captain that knows what he fights for, and loves what he knows, than that which you call 'a gentleman' and is nothing else.**
Oliver Cromwell 1599–1658: letter to Sir William Spring, September 1643

18 **It is upon the navy under the good Providence of God that the safety, honour, and welfare of this realm do chiefly depend.**
Charles II 1630–85: 'Articles of War' preamble; Sir Geoffrey Callender *The Naval Side of British History* (1952); probably a modern paraphrase

19 **Rascals, would you live for ever?**
to hesitant Guards at Kolin, 18 June 1757
Frederick the Great 1712–86: attributed

20 **Heart of oak are our ships,**
Heart of oak are our men:
We always are ready;
Steady, boys, steady;
We'll fight and we'll conquer again and again.
David Garrick 1717–79: 'Heart of Oak' (1759 song); see CHARACTER 24

21 **Discipline is the soul of an army. It makes small numbers formidable; procures success to the weak and esteem to all.**
George Washington 1732–99: letter to the captains of the Virginia Regiments, July 1759

22 **Every man thinks meanly of himself for not having been a soldier, or not**

having been at sea.

Samuel Johnson 1709–84: James Boswell *Life of Samuel Johnson* (1791) 10 April 1778

23 The courage of a soldier is found to be the cheapest and most common quality of human nature.

Edward Gibbon 1737–94: *The Decline and Fall of the Roman Empire* (1776–1788)

24 Who is the happy Warrior? Who is he
Whom every man in arms should wish to be?

William Wordsworth 1770–1850: 'Character of the Happy Warrior' (1807); see ARMED FORCES 37

25 As Lord Chesterfield said of the generals of his day, 'I only hope that when the enemy reads the list of their names, he trembles as I do.'

usually quoted as 'I don't know what effect these men will have upon the enemy, but, by God, they frighten me'

Duke of Wellington 1769–1852: letter, 29 August 1810

26 *La Garde meurt, mais ne se rend pas.*
The Guards die but do not surrender.

when called upon to surrender at Waterloo, 1815

Pierre, Baron de Cambronne 1770–1842: attributed to Cambronne, but later denied by him; H. Houssaye *La Garde meurt et ne se rend pas* (1907)

27 An army marches on its stomach.

Napoleon I 1769–1821: attributed, but probably condensed from a long passage in E. A. de Las Cases *Mémorial de Ste-Hélène* (1823) vol. 4, 14 November 1816; also attributed to Frederick the Great

28 Ours [our army] is composed of the scum of the earth—the mere scum of the earth.

Duke of Wellington 1769–1852: Philip Henry Stanhope *Notes of Conversations with the Duke of Wellington* (1888) 4 November 1831

29 *C'est magnifique, mais ce n'est pas la guerre.*
It is magnificent, but it is not war.

on the charge of the Light Brigade at Balaclava, 25 October 1854

Pierre Bosquet 1810–61: Cecil Woodham-Smith *The Reason Why* (1953)

30 Theirs not to make reply,
Theirs not to reason why,
Theirs but to do and die:
Into the valley of Death
Rode the six hundred.

Alfred, Lord Tennyson 1809–92: 'The Charge of the Light Brigade' (1854)

31 There is only one way for a young man to get on in the army. He must try and get killed in every way he possibly can!

Garnet Wolseley 1833–1913: in *Strand Magazine* May 1892; see SATISFACTION 10

32 The 'eathen in 'is blindness must end where 'e began.
But the backbone of the Army is the non-commissioned man!

Rudyard Kipling 1865–1936: 'The 'Eathen' (1896); see RELIGION 21

33 You can always tell an old soldier by the inside of his holsters and cartridge boxes. The young ones carry pistols and cartridges; the old ones, grub.

George Bernard Shaw 1856–1950: *Arms and the Man* (1898)

34 We're foot—slog—slog—slog—sloggin' over Africa!—
Foot—foot—foot—foot—sloggin' over Africa—
(Boots—boots—boots—boots—movin' up and down again!)
There's no discharge in the war!

Rudyard Kipling 1865–1936: 'Boots' (1903); the final line is from the Bible (Ecclesiastes)

35 They shall grow not old, as we that are left grow old.
Age shall not weary them, nor the years condemn.
At the going down of the sun and in the morning
We will remember them.

particularly associated with Remembrance Day services

Laurence Binyon 1869–1943: 'For the Fallen' (1914)

36 When you go home, tell them of us and say,
'For your tomorrows these gave their today.'

particularly associated with the dead of the Burma campaign of the Second World War, in the form 'For your tomorrow we gave our today'

John Maxwell Edmonds 1875–1958: *Inscriptions Suggested for War Memorials* (1919)

37 I saw him stab
And stab again
A well-killed Boche.

This is the happy warrior,
This is he...

Herbert Read 1893–1968: 'The Happy Warrior' (1919); see ARMED FORCES 24

38 Nor law, nor duty bade me fight,
Nor public men, nor cheering crowds,
A lonely impulse of delight
Drove to this tumult in the clouds.

W. B. Yeats 1865–1939: 'An Irish Airman Foresees his Death' (1919)

39 Old soldiers never die,
They simply fade away.

J. Foley 1906–70: 'Old Soldiers Never Die' (1920 song); possibly a 'folk-song' from the First World War; see ARMED FORCES 5

40 I divide my officers into four classes as follows: the clever, the industrious, the lazy, and the stupid. Each officer always possesses two of these qualities. Those who are clever and industrious I appoint to the General Staff. Use can under certain circumstances be made of those who are stupid and lazy. The man who is clever and lazy qualifies for the highest leadership posts. He has the requisite and the mental clarity for difficult decisions. But whoever is stupid and industrious must be got rid of, for he is too dangerous.

Kurt von Hammerstein-Equord 1878–1943: attributed, 1933; possibly apocryphal

41 Wars may be fought with weapons, but they are won by men.

George S. Patton 1885–1945: in *Cavalry Journal* September 1933

42 There is no difference between the Johnnies and the Mehmets to us where they lie side by side in this country of ours. You, the mothers, who sent their sons from faraway countries, wipe away your tears. Your sons are now lying in our bosom and are in peace. After having lost their lives on this land, they have become our sons as well.

Kemal Atatürk 1881–1938: address to a group of visiting Australians at Anzac Cove, Gallipoli, 1934; subsequently inscribed on the memorial there, and on the Atatürk memorials in Canberra and Wellington

43 You'll get no promotion this side of the ocean,
So cheer up, my lads, Bless 'em all!
Bless 'em all! Bless 'em all! The long and the short and the tall.

Jimmy Hughes and **Frank Lake**: 'Bless 'Em All' (1940 song)

44 An army without culture is a dull-witted army, and a dull-witted army cannot defeat the enemy.

Mao Zedong 1893–1976: *The United Front in Cultural Work* 30 October 1944

45 Naval tradition? Monstrous. Nothing but rum, sodomy, prayers, and the lash.

often quoted as, 'rum, sodomy, and the lash', as in Peter Gretton *Former Naval Person* (1968)

Winston Churchill 1874–1965: Harold Nicolson diary, 17 August 1950

46 To save your world you asked this man to die:
Would this man, could he see you now, ask why?

W. H. Auden 1907–73: 'Epitaph for the Unknown Soldier' (1955)

47 In bombers named for girls, we burned
The cities we had learned about in school—
Till our lives wore out.

Randall Jarrell 1914–65: 'Losses' (1963)

48 The sergeant is the army.

Dwight D. Eisenhower 1890–1969: attributed; see ARMED FORCES 32

49 How do you ask a man to be the last man to die in Vietnam? How do you ask a man to be the last man to die for a mistake?

John Kerry 1943– : speech to Senate Committee, 23 April 1971

50 When I was in the military, they gave me a medal for killing two men and a discharge for loving one.

Leonard Matlovich 1943–88: attributed

51 I expect you to rock their world. Wipe them out if that is what they choose. But if you are ferocious in battle remember to be magnanimous in victory.

Tim Collins 1960– : speech to the men under his command on arrival in Iraq, 20 March 2003

The Arts

see also ACTING, ARTS AND SCIENCES, MUSIC, PAINTING, PHOTOGRAPHY, SCULPTURE, WRITING

proverbs and sayings ▸

1 All arts are brothers; each is a light to the other.

American proverb, mid 19th century

2 Art is long and life is short.

originally from Hippocrates (see MEDICINE 8), comparing the difficulties encountered in learning the art of medicine or healing with the shortness of human life ('Art' is now commonly understood in the proverb in a less specific sense); English proverb, late 14th century; see also EDUCATION 17

3 Art is power.

American proverb, mid 19th century; see KNOWLEDGE 3

phrases ▸

4 ars gratia artis

art for art's sake; Latin, taken as the motto of Metro-Goldwyn-Mayer film studios, and apparently intended to say 'Art is beholden to the artists'; see ARTS 9

5 art for art's sake

used to convey the idea that the chief or only aim of a work of art is the self-expression of the individual artist who creates it, and associated with the Aesthetic movement of the 1880s; see ARTS 9, WRITERS 1

quotations ▸

6 Painting is silent poetry, poetry is eloquent painting.

Simonides *c.*556–468 BC: Plutarch *Moralia*

7 The poet ranks far below the painter in the representation of visible things, and far below the musician in that of invisible things.

Leonardo da Vinci 1452–1519: Irma A. Richter (ed.) *Selections from the Notebooks of Leonardo da Vinci* (1952)

8 In art the best is good enough.

Johann Wolfgang von Goethe 1749–1832: *Italienische Reise* (1816–17) 3 March 1787

9 Art for art's sake, with no purpose, for any purpose perverts art. But art achieves a purpose which is not its own.

Benjamin Constant 1767–1834: diary, 11 February 1804; see ARTS 4, ARTS 5, ARTS 14

10 What is art, monsieur, but nature concentrated?

Honoré de Balzac 1799–1850: *Lost Illusions* (1837–43)

11 God help the Minister that meddles with art!

Lord Melbourne 1779–1848: Lord David Cecil *Lord M* (1954)

12 The artist must be in his work as God is in creation, invisible and all-powerful; one must sense him everywhere but never see him.

Gustave Flaubert 1821–80: letter to Mademoiselle Leroyer de Chantepie, 18 March 1857

13 Art is a jealous mistress.

Ralph Waldo Emerson 1803–82: *The Conduct of Life* (1860)

14 Art for art's sake is an empty phrase. Art for the sake of the true, art for the sake of the good and the beautiful, that is the faith I am searching for.

George Sand 1804–76: letter to Alexandre Saint-Jean, 1872; see ARTS 9

15 All that I desire to point out is the general principle that Life imitates Art far more than Art imitates Life.

Oscar Wilde 1854–1900: *Intentions* (1891)

16 Art never expresses anything but itself.

Oscar Wilde 1854–1900: *Intentions* (1891) 'The Decay of Lying'

17 The Devil whoops, as he whooped of
old: 'It's clever, but is it Art?'

Rudyard Kipling 1865–1936: 'The Conundrum of the Workshops' (1892)

18 We work in the dark—we do what we can—we give what we have. Our doubt is our passion and our passion is our task. The rest is the madness of art.

Henry James 1843–1916: 'The Middle Years' (short story, 1893)

19 I always said God was against art and I still believe it.

Edward Elgar 1857–1934: letter to A. J. Jaeger, 9 October 1900

20 The history of art is the history of revivals.

Samuel Butler 1835–1902: *Notebooks* (1912)

21 In art one is either a plagiarist or a revolutionary.

usually quoted as 'Art is either plagiarism or revolution'

Paul Gauguin 1848–1903: attributed; James Huneker *The Pathos of Distance* (1913)

22 The true artist will let his wife starve, his children go barefoot, his mother drudge for his living at seventy, sooner than work at anything but his art.

George Bernard Shaw 1856–1950: *Man and Superman* (1903)

23 Art is vice. You don't marry it legitimately, you rape it.

Edgar Degas 1834–1917: Paul Lafond *Degas* (1918)

24 Another unsettling element in modern art is that common symptom of immaturity, the dread of doing what has been done before.

Edith Wharton 1862–1937: *The Writing of Fiction* (1925)

25 The artist is not a special kind of man, but every man is a special kind of artist.

Ananda Coomaraswamy 1877–1947: *Transformation of Nature in Art* (1934)

26 The proletarian state must bring up thousands of excellent 'mechanics of culture', 'engineers of the soul'.

Maxim Gorky 1868–1936: speech at the Writers' Congress 1934; see ARTS 31

27 Without tradition, art is a flock of sheep without a shepherd. Without innovation, it is a corpse.

Winston Churchill 1874–1965: speech at the Royal Academy, 30 April 1938

28 I suppose art is the only thing that can go on mattering once it has stopped hurting.

Elizabeth Bowen 1899–1973: *Heat of the Day* (1949)

29 Art is born of humiliation.

W. H. Auden 1907–73: Stephen Spender *World Within World* (1951)

30 An artist cannot speak about his art any more than a plant can discuss horticulture.

Jean Cocteau 1889–1963: in *Newsweek* 16 May 1955

31 In free society art is not a weapon... Artists are not engineers of the soul.

John F. Kennedy 1917–63: speech at Amherst College, Mass., 26 October 1963; see ARTS 26

32 We all know that Art is not truth. Art is a lie that makes us realize truth.

Pablo Picasso 1881–1973: Dore Ashton *Picasso on Art* (1972)

33 An artist is someone who produces things that people don't need to have but that he — for *some reason* — thinks it would be a good idea to give them.

Andy Warhol 1927–87: *Philosophy of Andy Warhol (From A to B and Back Again)* (1975)

34 Filling a space in a beautiful way. That's what art means to me.

Georgia O'Keefe 1887–1986: in *Art News* December 1977

35 Art has to move you and design does not, unless it's a good design for a bus.

David Hockney 1937– : in *Guardian* 26 October 1988

Arts and Sciences

phrases ▸

1 the nine Muses

in classical mythology the nine goddesses, daughters of Zeus and Mnemosyne, who preside over the arts and sciences

2 the two cultures

the arts and the sciences, from C. P. Snow *The Two Cultures and the Scientific Revolution* (1959)

quotations ▸

3 Histories make men wise; poets, witty; the mathematics, subtile; natural philosophy, deep; moral, grave; logic and rhetoric, able to contend.

Francis Bacon 1561–1626: *Essays* (1625) 'Of Studies'

4 In science, read, by preference, the newest works; in literature, the oldest.

Edward Bulwer-Lytton 1803–73: *Caxtoniana* (1863) 'Hints on Mental Culture'

5 Don't talk to me of your Archimedes' lever. He was an absent-minded person with a mathematical imagination. Mathematics commands all my respect, but I have no use for engines.

Give me the right word and the right accent and I will move the world.
Joseph Conrad 1857–1924: *A Personal Record* (1919); see TECHNOLOGY 6

6 Even if I could be Shakespeare, I think I should still choose to be Faraday.
Aldous Huxley 1894–1963: in 1925, attributed; Walter M. Elsasser *Memoirs of a Physicist in the Atomic Age* (1978)

7 Art is meant to disturb, science reassures.
Georges Braque 1882–1963: *Le Jour et la nuit: Cahiers 1917–52*

8 Science must begin with myths, and with the criticism of myths.
Karl Popper 1902–94: 'The Philosophy of Science'; C. A. Mace (ed.) *British Philosophy in the Mid-Century* (1957)

9 Once or twice I have been provoked and have asked the company how many of them could describe the Second Law of Thermodynamics. The response was cold: it was also negative. Yet I was asking something which is about the scientific equivalent of: *Have you read a work of Shakespeare's?*
C. P. Snow 1905–80: *The Two Cultures* (1959); see PHYSICAL 4

10 When I find myself in the company of scientists, I feel like a shabby curate who has strayed by mistake into a drawing room full of dukes.
W. H. Auden 1907–73: *The Dyer's Hand* (1963) 'The Poet and the City'

11 If a scientist were to cut his ear off, no one would take it as evidence of a heightened sensibility.
Peter Medawar 1915–87: 'J. B. S.' (1968)

12 Shakespeare would have grasped wave functions, Donne would have understood complementarity and relative time. They would have been excited. What richness! They would have plundered this new science for their imagery.
Ian McEwan 1948– : *The Child in Time* (1987)

13 Scientists are explorers, philosophers are tourists.
Richard Feynman 1918–88: Christopher Sykes (ed.) *No Ordinary Genius* (1994)

14 If Watson and Crick had not discovered the nature of DNA, one can be virtually certain that other scientists would eventually have determined it. With art—whether painting, music or literature — it is quite different. If Shakespeare had not written *Hamlet*, no other playwright would have done so.
Lewis Wolpert 1929– : *The Unnatural Nature of Science* (1993)

Australia

see also TOWNS

proverbs and sayings ▸

1 Advance Australia.
catchphrase used as a patriotic slogan or motto, mid 19th century onwards; see AUSTRALIA 17

2 Australians wouldn't give a XXXX for anything else.
advertising slogan for Castlemaine lager, 1986 onwards

3 Those who lose dreaming are lost.
modern saying, said to be an Aboriginal proverb

phrases ▸

4 Apple Island
Tasmania, popularly identified as an apple-growing region

5 beyond the black stump
in the remote outback; *black stump* an imaginary marker at the limits of settled and, by implication, civilized country

6 Cabbage Garden
the state of Victoria

7 First Fleet
the eleven British ships under the command of Arthur Phillip, first governor of New South Wales, which arrived in Australia in January 1788

8 the Lucky Country
Australia; see AUSTRALIA 23

9 the Never Never Land
the unpopulated northern part of the Northern Territory and Queensland; the desert country of the interior of Australia

10 stolen generation
the Aboriginal people forcibly removed from their families as children between the 1900s and the 1960s, to be brought up by white foster families or in institutions; see AUSTRALIA 26

11 Top End
(the northern part of) the Northern Territory of Australia

quotations ▶

12 From what I have said of the natives of New Holland, they may appear to some to be the most wretched people upon earth; but in reality they are far happier than we Europeans; being wholly unacquainted not only with the superfluous but the necessary conveniences so much sought after in Europe, they are happy in not knowing the use of them.
James Cook 1728–79: diary, August 1770

13 The loss of America what can repay?
New colonies seek for at Botany Bay.
John Freeth 1731–1808: 'Botany Bay' (1786)

14 True patriots we; for be it understood,
We left our country for our country's good.
prologue, written for, but not recited at, the opening of the Playhouse, Sydney, New South Wales, 16 January 1796, when the actors were principally convicts
Henry Carter d. 1806: A. W. Jose and H. J. Carter (eds.) *The Australian Encyclopaedia* (1927); previously attributed to George Barrington (b. 1755)

15 Who knows but that England may revive in New South Wales when it has sunk in Europe.
Joseph Banks 1743–1820: letter to Governor Hunter, 30 March 1797

16 Earth is here so kind, that just tickle her with a hoe and she laughs with a harvest.
Douglas Jerrold 1803–57: *The Wit and Opinions of Douglas Jerrold* (1859)

17 In joyful strains then let us sing
Advance Australia fair.
the national anthem of Australia, which officially replaced 'God Save the Queen' in 1984; see AUSTRALIA 1
P. D. McCormick 1834–1916: 'Advance Australia Fair' (1878 song)

18 The crimson thread of kinship runs through us all.
on Australian federation
Henry Parkes 1815–95: speech at banquet in Melbourne 6 February 1890; *The Federal Government of Australasia* (1890)

19 A nation for a continent and a continent for a nation.
on Australian federation
Edmund Barton 1849–1920: quoted in Robert Garran *The Coming Commonwealth* (1897)

20 Once a jolly swagman camped by a billabong,
Under the shade of a coolibah tree;
And he sang as he watched and waited till his 'Billy' boiled:
'You'll come a-waltzing, Matilda, with me.'
'Banjo' Paterson 1864–1941: 'Waltzing Matilda' (1903 song)

21 What Great Britain calls the Far East is to us the near north.
Robert Gordon Menzies 1894–1978: in *Sydney Morning Herald* 27 April 1939

22 Above our writers—and other artists—looms the intimidating mass of Anglo-Saxon culture. Such a situation almost inevitably produces the characteristic Australian Cultural Cringe.
Arthur Angell Phillips 1900–85: *Meanjin* (1950) 'The Cultural Cringe'

23 Australia is a lucky country run mainly by second-rate people who share its luck.
Donald Richmond Horne 1921– : *The Lucky Country: Australia in the Sixties* (1964); see AUSTRALIA 8

24 In all directions stretched the great Australian Emptiness, in which the mind is the least of possessions.
Patrick White 1912–90: *The Vital Decade* (1968) 'The Prodigal Son'

25 When New Zealanders emigrate to Australia, it raises the average IQ of both countries.
Robert Muldoon 1921–92: attributed

26 I was so angry because they were denying they had done anything wrong, denying that a whole generation was stolen.
of official response to concerns about the 'stolen generation'
Cathy Freeman 1973– : interview in *Daily Telegraph* 16 July 2000; see AUSTRALIA 10

Beauty

see also BODY

proverbs and sayings ▸

1 **Beauty draws with a single hair.**
asserting the powerful attraction of a woman's beauty (often shown as outdoing great physical strength); see WOMEN 24; English proverb, late 16th century

2 **Beauty is a good letter of introduction.**
American proverb, mid 20th century; see BEAUTY 10

3 **Beauty is in the eye of the beholder.**
beauty is not judged objectively, but according to the beholder's estimation; English proverb, mid 18th century

4 **Beauty is only skin deep.**
physical beauty is no guarantee of a good character or temperament; English proverb, early 17th century; see BEAUTY 35

5 **Beauty is power.**
advertising slogan for Helena Rubinstein's Valaze Skin Food, 1904

6 **Mirror, mirror on the wall, Who is the fairest of them all?**
in the early 19th-century translation of the Grimm Brothers' *Fairytales*, the customary invocation of Snow White's wicked stepmother, which in due time received the reply that Snow White rather than herself was now the most beautiful

7 **Monday's child is fair of face.**
traditional rhyme, mid 19th century; see also GIFTS 2, SORROW 2, TRAVEL 8, WORK 7

8 **Please your eye and plague your heart.**
contrasting the pleasure given by the appearance of a beautiful person with the heartache they may cause; English proverb, early 17th century

phrases ▸

9 **Beauty and the Beast**
characters in a fairy story by the French writer for children Madame de Beaumont (1711–80), translated into English in 1757. In the story Beauty, the youngest daughter of a merchant, goes to live in the Beast's palace and agrees to marry him; she discovers that he is a prince who has been put under a spell, which is destroyed by her love for him, and her ability to see his true worth beneath the hideous exterior; see BEAUTY 34

quotations ▸

10 A beautiful face is a mute recommendation.
Publilius Syrus: *Sententiae*; see BEAUTY 2

11 Consider the lilies of the field, how they grow; they toil not, neither do they spin:
And yet I say unto you, That even Solomon in all his glory was not arrayed like one of these.
Bible: St Matthew

12 And she was fayr as is the rose in May.
Geoffrey Chaucer 1343–1400: *The Legend of Good Women* 'Cleopatra'

13 Was this the face that launched a thousand ships,
And burnt the topless towers of Ilium?
Sweet Helen, make me immortal with a kiss!
Christopher Marlowe 1564–93: *Doctor Faustus* (1604)

14 Love built on beauty, soon as beauty, dies.
John Donne 1572–1631: *Elegies* 'The Anagram' (1595)

15 O! she doth teach the torches to burn bright.
It seems she hangs upon the cheek of night
Like a rich jewel in an Ethiop's ear;
Beauty too rich for use, for earth too dear.
William Shakespeare 1564–1616: *Romeo and Juliet* (1595)

16 There is no excellent beauty that hath not some strangeness in the proportion.
Francis Bacon 1561–1626: *Essays* (1625) 'Of Beauty'

17 Beauty is the lover's gift.
William Congreve 1670–1729: *The Way of the World* (1700)

18 The flowers anew, returning seasons bring;
But beauty faded has no second spring.
Ambrose Philips 1675–1749: *The First Pastoral* (1708)

19 Beauty is no quality in things themselves. It exists merely in the mind which contemplates them.
David Hume 1711–76: *Essays, Moral, Political, and Literary* (ed. T. H. Green and T. H. Grose, 1875) 'Of the Standard of Taste' (1757)

20 She walks in beauty, like the night
Of cloudless climes and starry skies.
Lord Byron 1788–1824: 'She Walks in Beauty' (1815)

21 A thing of beauty is a joy for ever.
John Keats 1795–1821: *Endymion* (1818); see MEN 15

22 'Beauty is truth, truth beauty,'—that is all
Ye know on earth, and all ye need to know.
John Keats 1795–1821: 'Ode on a Grecian Urn' (1820); see TRUTH 26

23 Beauty is only a promise of happiness.
Stendhal 1783–1842: *L'Amour* (1822)

24 There is nothing ugly; *I never saw an ugly thing in my life*: for let the form of an object be what it may,—light, shade, and perspective will always make it beautiful.
John Constable 1776–1837: C. R. Leslie *Memoirs of the Life of John Constable* (1843)

25 There are as many kinds of beauty as there are habitual ways of seeking happiness.
Charles Baudelaire 1821–67: *The Salon of 1846* (1846) 'What is Romanticism?'

26 Remember that the most beautiful things in the world are the most useless; peacocks and lilies for instance.
John Ruskin 1819–1900: *Stones of Venice* vol. 1 (1851)

27 If you get simple beauty and naught else,
You get about the best thing God invents.
Robert Browning 1812–89: 'Fra Lippo Lippi' (1855)

28 Beauty will save the world.
Fedor Dostoevsky 1821–81: *The Idiot* (1868)

29 The awful thing is that beauty is mysterious as well as terrible. God and devil are fighting there, and the battlefield is the heart of man.
Fedor Dostoevsky 1821–81: *The Brothers Karamazov* (1879–80)

30 It is amazing how complete is the delusion that beauty is goodness.
Leo Tolstoy 1828–1910: 'The Kreutzer Sonata' (1889)

31 When a woman isn't beautiful, people always say, 'You have lovely eyes, you have lovely hair.'
Anton Chekhov 1860–1904: *Uncle Vanya* (1897)

32 Beauty is all very well at first sight; but who ever looks at it when it has been in the house three days?
George Bernard Shaw 1856–1950: *Man and Superman* (1903)

33 A pretty girl is like a melody
That haunts you night and day.
Irving Berlin 1888–1989: 'A Pretty Girl is like a Melody' (1919 song)

34 Oh no, it wasn't the aeroplanes. It was Beauty killed the Beast.
James Creelman 1901–41 and **Ruth Rose**: *King Kong* (1933 film) final words; see BEAUTY 9

35 I'm tired of all this nonsense about beauty being only skin-deep. That's deep enough. What do you want—an adorable pancreas?
Jean Kerr 1923–2003: *The Snake has all the Lines* (1958); see BEAUTY 4

36 There are no ugly women, only lazy ones.
Helena Rubinstein 1882–1965: *My Life for Beauty* (1966)

37 At some point in life the world's beauty becomes enough. You don't need to photograph, paint or even remember it. It is enough.
Toni Morrison 1931– : *Tar Baby* (1981)

38 'Form follows profit' is the aesthetic principle of our times.
Richard Rogers 1933– : in *Times* 13 February 1991; see ARCHITECTURE 11

39 Being thought of as a beautiful woman has spared me nothing in life. No heartache, no trouble. Beauty is essentially meaningless.
Halle Berry 1968– : in *Observer* 8 August 2004

Beginning

see also CHANGE, ENDING

proverbs and sayings ▸

1 Are you sitting comfortably? Then we'll begin.
Julia Lang (1921–), introduction to stories on *Listen with Mother*, BBC Radio programme for small children, 1950–82

2 **First impressions are the most lasting.**
English proverb, early 18th century

3 **A good beginning makes a good ending.**
getting things right at the outset is likely to ensure success; English proverb, early 14th century

4 **It is easier to raise the Devil than to lay him.**
sometimes used to mean that it is easier to start a process than to stop it; English proverb, mid 17th century

5 **It is the first step that is difficult.**
English proverb, late 16th century; see ACHIEVEMENT 19

6 **It was a dark and stormy night.**
now a cliché as an opening line intended to convey a threatening and doom-laden atmosphere; first used by the novelist Edward Bulwer-Lytton (1803–73) in his novel *Paul Clifford* (1830)

7 **I've started so I'll finish.**
said by Magnus Magnusson when a contestant's time runs out while a question is being put, on *Mastermind*, BBC television (1972–97)

8 **The longest journey begins with a single step.**
often used to emphasize how important a single decision may be; late 20th century saying, ultimately derived from Lao Tzu: see BEGINNING 20

9 **The sooner begun, the sooner done.**
used as a warning against putting off a necessary but unwanted task; English proverb, late 16th century

10 **There is always a first time.**
English proverb, late 16th century

11 **Well begun is half done.**
emphasizing the importance of a successful beginning to the completion of a project; English proverb, early 15th century

phrases ▶

12 **back to square one**
back to the starting-point, with no progress made (*square one* may be a reference to a board-game such as Snakes and Ladders, or derive from the notional division of a football pitch into eight numbered sections for the purpose of early radio commentaries)

13 **back to the drawing board**
used to indicate that an idea, scheme, or proposal has been unsuccessful and that a new one must be devised; *drawing board* = a large flat board on which paper may be spread for artists or designers to work on; see INVENTIONS 22

14 **D-Day**
the day on which an important operation is to begin or a change to take effect; from the day (6 June 1944) in the Second World War on which Allied forces invaded northern France by means of beach landings in Normandy; see WORLD WAR II 20

15 **First Cause**
in philosophy, a supposed ultimate cause of all events, which does not itself have a cause, identified with God; see GOD 15

16 **fons et origo**
the source and origin; Latin, earliest in *fons et origo mali* (*mali* = of evil)

17 **primum mobile**
an originator of an action or event, an initiator, an initial source of activity; medieval Latin, literally 'first moving thing', in the medieval version of the Ptolemaic system, an outermost sphere supposed to revolve round the earth in twenty-four hours, carrying with it the inner spheres

18 **vita nuova**
a fresh start or new direction in life, especially after some powerful emotional experience; Italian = new life, a work by Dante describing his love for Beatrice

quotations ▶

19 **In the beginning God created the heaven and the earth. And the earth was without form, and void; and darkness was upon the face of the deep.**
Bible: Genesis

20 **A tower of nine storeys begins with a heap of earth.**
The journey of a thousand *li* starts from where one stands.
Lao Tzu c.604–c.531 BC: *Tao-te Ching*; see BEGINNING 8

21 **Ere time and place were, time and place were not;**
Where primitive nothing something straight begot;

Then all proceeded from the great united what.
John Wilmot, Lord Rochester 1647–80: 'Upon Nothing' (1680)

22 **'Where shall I begin, please your Majesty?' he asked. 'Begin at the beginning,' the King said, gravely, 'and go on till you come to the end: then stop.'**
Lewis Carroll 1832–98: *Alice's Adventures in Wonderland* (1865)

23 **In my beginning is my end.**
T. S. Eliot 1888–1965: *Four Quartets* 'East Coker' (1940); see ENDING 6

24 **All this will not be finished in the first 100 days. Nor will it be finished in the first 1,000 days, nor in the life of this Administration, nor even perhaps in our lifetime on this planet. But let us begin.**
John F. Kennedy 1917–63: inaugural address, 20 January 1961

Behaviour
see also MANNERS, WORDS AND DEEDS

proverbs and sayings ▸

1 **Be what you would seem to be.**
English proverb, late 14th century; earlier in classical sources

2 **By a sweet tongue and kindness, you can drag an elephant by a hair.**
Middle Eastern proverb; commonly found in this form in Arabic, the equivalent proverb in Persian has 'drag a snake'

3 **Cleanliness is next to godliness.**
next here means 'immediately following', as in serial order, and is now often used humorously to mean, 'the second most desirable quality possible'; English proverb, late 18th century; see DRESS 7

4 **Evil communications corrupt good manners.**
proper conduct is harmfully influenced by false information or knowledge; the saying is also used to assert the deleterious effect of bad example; English proverb, early 15th century, from the Bible: see MANNERS 8

5 **Handsome is as handsome does.**
handsome here originally referred to chivalrous or genteel behaviour, although it is often popularly taken to refer to good looks; English proverb, late 16th century; see BEHAVIOUR 7

6 **He is a good dog who goes to church.**
good character is shown by moral custom and practice; English proverb, early 19th century

7 **Pretty is as pretty does.**
American proverb, mid 19th century, equivalent of BEHAVIOUR 5

8 **When in Rome, do as the Romans do.**
English proverb, late 15th century, from St Ambrose; see BEHAVIOUR 18

phrases ▸

9 **add insult to injury**
act in a way that makes a bad or displeasing situation worse, from Edward Moore's *The Foundling* (1748), 'This is adding insult to injuries'

10 **beyond the pale**
outside the bounds of acceptable behaviour; *pale* = former term for an area within determined bounds, or subject to a particular jurisdiction, as in *the Pale*, used to designate the English Pale in medieval Ireland, the territory of Calais in northern France when under English jurisdiction, and those areas of Tsarist Russia to which Jewish residence was restricted (known more fully as the Pale of Settlement)

11 **conduct unbecoming**
unsuitable or inappropriate behaviour, from *Articles of War* (1872) 'Any officer who shall behave in a scandalous manner, unbecoming the character of an officer and a gentleman shall…be CASHIERED'; the Naval Discipline Act, 10 August 1860 uses the words 'conduct unbecoming the character of an Officer'

12 **dirty work at the crossroads**
dishonourable, illicit, or underhand behaviour. The term may reflect a view of *crossroads* as a sinister place, where suicides were traditionally buried

13 **prunes and prisms**
(marked by) prim, mincing affectation of speech; offered by Mrs General in Dickens's *Little Dorrit* (1857) as a phrase giving 'a pretty form to the lips'

14 **the Queensberry Rules**
standard rules of polite or acceptable behaviour; a code of rules drawn up in 1867 under the supervision of Sir John Sholto Douglas (1844–1900), eighth Marquis of *Queensberry*, to govern the sport of boxing in Great Britain; the standard rules of modern boxing

15 **sweetness and light**
extreme (and uncharacteristic) mildness and reason in manner and behaviour, from Swift (1704): see VIRTUE 25

16 **to the manner born**
naturally fitted for some position or employment, from Shakespeare *Hamlet*: see CUSTOM 11

quotations ►

17 *O tempora, O mores!*
Oh, the times! Oh, the manners!
Cicero 106–43 BC: *In Catilinam*

18 When I go to Rome, I fast on Saturday, but here [Milan] I do not. Do you also follow the custom of whatever church you attend, if you do not want to give or receive scandal.
St Ambrose c.339–397: 'Letter 54 to Januarius' (AD c.400); see BEHAVIOUR 8

19 Careless she is with artful care,
Affecting to seem unaffected.
William Congreve 1670–1729: 'Amoret'

20 Take the tone of the company that you are in.
Lord Chesterfield 1694–1773: *Letters to his Son* (1774) 16 October 1747

21 They teach the morals of a whore, and the manners of a dancing master.
of the *Letters* of Lord Chesterfield
Samuel Johnson 1709–84: James Boswell *Life of Samuel Johnson* (1791) 1754

22 Always ding, dinging Dame Grundy into my ears—what will Mrs Grundy zay? What will Mrs Grundy think?
Thomas Morton 1764–1838: *Speed the Plough* (1798); see MORALITY 7

23 May I ask whether these pleasing attentions proceed from the impulse of the moment, or are the result of previous study?
Jane Austen 1775–1817: *Pride and Prejudice* (1813)

24 There was a little girl
Who had a little curl
Right in the middle of her forehead,
When she was good
She was very, very good,
But when she was bad she was horrid.
composed for, and sung to, his second daughter while a babe in arms, 1850
Henry Wadsworth Longfellow 1807–82: B. R. Tucker-Macchetta *The Home Life of Henry W. Longfellow* (1882)

25 He only does it to annoy,
Because he knows it teases.
Lewis Carroll 1832–98: *Alice's Adventures in Wonderland* (1865)

26 Go directly—see what she's doing, and tell her she mustn't.
Punch: 1872

27 Conduct is three-fourths of our life and its largest concern.
Matthew Arnold 1822–88: *Literature and Dogma* (1873)

28 Be a good animal, true to your instincts.
D. H. Lawrence 1885–1930: *The White Peacock* (1911)

29 Vulgarity has its uses. Vulgarity often cuts ice which refinement scrapes at vainly.
Max Beerbohm 1872–1956: letter, 21 May 1921

30 Being tactful in audacity is knowing how far one can go too far.
Jean Cocteau 1889–1963: *Le Rappel à l'ordre* (1926)

31 Private faces in public places
Are wiser and nicer
Than public faces in private places.
W. H. Auden 1907–73: *Orators* (1932)

32 I get too hungry for dinner at eight.
I like the theatre, but never come late.
I never bother with people I hate.
That's why the lady is a tramp.
Lorenz Hart 1895–1943: 'The Lady is a Tramp' (1937 song)

33 Perfect behaviour is born of complete indifference.
Cesare Pavese 1908–50: diary, 21 February 1940

34 The basis of all good human behaviour is kindness.
Eleanor Roosevelt 1884–1962: *Book of Common Sense Etiquette* (1962)

35 **When people are on their best behaviour they aren't always at their best.**

Alan Bennett 1934– : *Dinner at Noon* (BBC television, 1988)

Belief

see also CERTAINTY, FAITH

proverbs and sayings ▸

1 **Believe nothing of what you hear, and only half of what you see.**

English proverb, mid 19th century; a related Middle English saying warns that you should not believe everything that is said or that you hear

2 **A believer is a songless bird in a cage.**

American proverb, late 19th century; see BELIEF 24

3 **Believing has a core of unbelieving.**

American proverb, mid 19th century

4 **Pigs may fly, but they are very unlikely birds.**

English proverb, mid 19th century; see BELIEF 8

5 **Seeing is believing.**

acceptance of the existence of something depends on actual demonstration; English proverb, early 17th century

6 **Tell that to the marines.**

a scornful expression of disbelief, from the saying *that will do for the marines but the sailors won't believe it* (the marines were originally soldiers enlisted and trained to serve on board ship). The expression is recorded from the early 19th century, although a late 19th-century hoax attributing the origin to a remark made by Charles II to Samuel Pepys has been widely reprinted; see BELIEF 21

phrases ▸

7 **a doubting Thomas**

a person who refuses to believe something without incontrovertible proof; a sceptic, from the story of the apostle *Thomas*, who said that he would not believe that Christ had risen again until he had seen and touched his wounds; from the Bible (John)

8 **pigs might fly**

an expression of ironical disbelief, from the proverb: see BELIEF 4

9 **swallow a camel**

make no difficulty about something incredible or unreasonable, from the Bible (Matthew) 'Ye blind guides, which strain at a gnat, and swallow a camel'

10 **take something with a pinch (or grain) of salt**

regard something as exaggerated; believe only part of something (from the modern Latin phrase *cum grano salis* 'with a grain of salt', recorded from the mid 17th century)

quotations ▸

11 **It is convenient that there be gods, and, as it is convenient, let us believe that there are.**

Ovid 43 BC–C. AD 17: *Ars Amatoria*

12 **Lord, I believe; help thou mine unbelief.**

Bible: St Mark

13 **Except ye see signs and wonders, ye will not believe.**

Bible: St John

14 ***Certum est quia impossibile est.***
It is certain because it is impossible.

often quoted as '*Credo quia impossibile* [I believe because it is impossible]'

Tertullian C. AD 160–*c.*225: *De Carne Christi*

15 **Nothing is so firmly believed as that which we least know.**

Montaigne 1533–92: *Essays* (1580)

16 **For what a man would like to be true, that he more readily believes.**

Francis Bacon 1561–1626: *Novum Organum* (1620)

17 **By night an atheist half believes a God.**

Edward Young 1683–1765: *Night Thoughts* (1742–5) 'Night 5'

18 **Truth, Sir, is a cow, that will yield such people [sceptics] no more milk, and so they are gone to milk the bull.**

Samuel Johnson 1709–84: James Boswell *Life of Samuel Johnson* (1791) 21 July 1763

19 **Confidence is a plant of slow growth in an aged bosom: youth is the season of credulity.**

William Pitt, Earl of Chatham 1708–78: speech, House of Commons, 14 January 1766

20 **Credulity is the man's weakness, but the child's strength.**

Charles Lamb 1775–1834: *Essays of Elia* (1823) 'Witches, and Other Night-Fears'

21 Tell that to the marines—the sailors won't believe it.

Sir Walter Scott 1771–1832: *Redgauntlet* (1824); see BELIEF 6

22 *We can believe what we choose.* We are answerable for what we choose to believe.

John Henry Newman 1801–90: letter to Mrs William Froude, 27 June 1848

23 Why, sometimes I've believed as many as six impossible things before breakfast.

Lewis Carroll 1832–98: *Through the Looking-Glass* (1872)

24 A believer is a songless bird in a cage, a freethinker is an eagle parting the clouds with tireless wings.

Robert G. Ingersoll 1833–99: *An Arraignment of the Church, and a Plea for Individuality* (1877); see BELIEF 2

25 It is wrong, always, everywhere and for any one, to believe anything upon insufficient evidence.

William Clifford 1845–79: 'The Ethics of Belief', lecture, 1879

26 What is wanted is not the will to believe, but the wish to find out, which is its exact opposite.

Bertrand Russell 1872–1970: *Free Thought and Official Propaganda* (1922)

27 I do not pretend to know where many ignorant men are sure — that is all that agnosticism means.

Clarence Darrow 1857–1938: speech at the trial of John Thomas Scopes, 15 July 1925

28 Of course not, but I am told it works even if you don't believe in it.

when asked whether he really believed a horseshoe hanging over his door would bring him luck, 1930

Niels Bohr 1885–1962: A. Pais *Inward Bound* (1986)

29 When men stop believing in God they don't believe in nothing; they believe in anything.

G. K. Chesterton 1874–1936: widely attributed, although not traced in his works

30 Man is a credulous animal, and must believe *something*; in the absence of good grounds for belief, he will be satisfied with bad ones.

Bertrand Russell 1872–1970: *Unpopular Essays* (1950) 'Outline of Intellectual Rubbish'

31 I do not believe...I know.

Carl Gustav Jung 1875–1961: L. van der Post *Jung and the Story of our Time* (1976)

32 I confused things with their names: that is belief.

Jean-Paul Sartre 1905–80: *Les Mots* (1964)

The Bible

phrases ▸

1 the Authorized Version

the King James Bible of 1611; this translation became widely popular following its publication, and although in fact never officially 'authorized' it remained for centuries the Bible of every English-speaking country; see BIBLE 3

2 the Breeches Bible

the Geneva bible of 1560, so named because the word *breeches* is used in Genesis 3:7 for the garments made by Adam and Eve, rendered *aprons* in the King James bible

3 the King James Bible

the 1611 English translation of the Bible, ordered to be made by James I, and produced by about fifty scholars; see BIBLE 1

4 Sin On Bible

an edition of 1716, the first English-language Bible to be printed in Ireland, so named because John 5:14 reads 'sin on more' instead of 'sin no more'

5 the Treacle Bible

a translation which has 'treacle' where other translations have 'balm', as in Jeremiah 8:22 'Is there no treacle in Gilead?'

6 the Wicked Bible

an edition of 1631, in which the seventh commandment was misprinted 'Thou shalt commit adultery'

quotations ▸

7 Holy writ is the scripture of peoples, for it is made, that all peoples should know it.

St Jerome C.AD 342–420: attributed

8 The devil can cite Scripture for his purpose.

William Shakespeare 1564–1616: *The Merchant of Venice* (1596–8); see QUOTATIONS 1

9 The pencil of the Holy Ghost hath laboured more in describing the afflictions of Job than the felicities of Solomon.

Francis Bacon 1561–1626: *Essays* (1625) 'Of Adversity'

10 *Scrutamini scripturas* [Let us look at the scriptures]. These two words have undone the world.

John Selden 1584–1654: *Table Talk* (1689) 'Bible Scripture'

11 We present you with this Book, the most valuable thing that this world affords. Here is wisdom; this is the royal Law; these are the lively Oracles of God.

Coronation Service 1689: The Presenting of the Holy Bible

12 The English Bible, a book which, if everything else in our language should perish, would alone suffice to show the whole extent of its beauty and power.

Lord Macaulay 1800–59: 'John Dryden' (1828)

13 There's a great text in Galatians,
Once you trip on it, entails
Twenty-nine distinct damnations,
One sure, if another fails.

Robert Browning 1812–89: 'Soliloquy of the Spanish Cloister' (1842)

14 We have used the Bible as if it was a constable's handbook—an opium-dose for keeping beasts of burden patient while they are being overloaded.

Charles Kingsley 1819–75: *Letters to the Chartists*

15 LORD ILLINGWORTH: The Book of Life begins with a man and a woman in a garden.
MRS ALLONBY: It ends with Revelations.

Oscar Wilde 1854–1900: *A Woman of No Importance* (1893)

16 An apology for the Devil: It must be remembered that we have only heard one side of the case. God has written all the books.

Samuel Butler 1835–1902: *Notebooks* (1912)

17 It ain't necessarily so,
De t'ings dat yo' li'ble
To read in de Bible
It ain't necessarily so.

Du Bose Heyward 1885–1940 and **Ira Gershwin** 1896–1989: 'It ain't necessarily so' (1935)

18 I know of no book which has been a source of brutality and sadistic conduct, both public and private, that can compare with the Bible.

Reginald Paget 1908–90: in *Observer* 28 June 1964

19 There's a Bible on that shelf there. But I keep it next to Voltaire—poison and antidote.

Bertrand Russell 1872–1970: in *Kenneth Harris Talking To* (1971) 'Bertrand Russell'

20 Anyone who thinks that politics and religion don't mix is not reading the same Bible I am.

Desmond Tutu 1931– : attributed; David Rogers *Politics, Prayer and Parliament* (2000)

Biography

phrases ▸

1 lues Boswelliana

a biographer's tendency to magnify his or her subject, regarded as a disease, from Latin *lues* (= plague) and the name of James *Boswell* (1740–95) as the friend and biographer of Samuel Johnson

2 who's who

a list or directory of facts about notable people; the annual biographical dictionary *Who's Who* was first issued in 1849 but took its present form in 1897. The entries are compiled with the assistance of the subjects themselves, and contain some agreeable eccentricities particularly in the section labelled 'Recreations'

quotations ▸

3 Many brave men lived before Agamemnon's time; but they are all, unmourned and unknown, covered by the long night, because they lack their sacred poet.

Horace 65–8 BC: *Odes*; see REPUTATION 1

4 Nobody can write the life of a man, but those who have eat and drunk and lived in social intercourse with him.

Samuel Johnson 1709–84: James Boswell *Life of Samuel Johnson* (1791) 31 March 1772

5 Lives of great men all remind us
We can make our lives sublime,
And, departing, leave behind us
Footprints on the sands of time.
Henry Wadsworth Longfellow 1807–82: 'A Psalm of Life' (1838)

6 A well-written Life is almost as rare as a well-spent one.
Thomas Carlyle 1795–1881: *Critical and Miscellaneous Essays* (1838) 'Jean Paul Friedrich Richter'

7 There is properly no history; only biography.
Ralph Waldo Emerson 1803–82: *Essays* (1841) 'History'

8 Then there is my noble and biographical friend who has added a new terror to death.
on Lord Campbell's *Lives of the Lord Chancellors* being written without the consent of heirs or executors
Charles Wetherell 1770–1846: Lord St Leonards *Misrepresentations in Campbell's Lives of Lyndhurst and Brougham* (1869); also attributed to Lord Lyndhurst (1772–1863)

9 refusing an offer to write his memoirs:
I should be trading on the blood of my men.
Robert E. Lee 1807–70: attributed, perhaps apocryphal

10 Every great man nowadays has his disciples, and it is always Judas who writes the biography.
Oscar Wilde 1854–1900: *Intentions* (1891) 'The Critic as Artist'

11 It is not a Life at all. It is a Reticence, in three volumes.
on J. W. Cross's *Life of George Eliot*
W. E. Gladstone 1809–98: E. F. Benson *As We Were* (1930)

12 The Art of Biography
Is different from Geography.
Geography is about Maps,
But Biography is about Chaps.
Edmund Clerihew Bentley 1875–1956: *Biography for Beginners* (1905)

13 And kept his heart a secret to the end
From all the picklocks of biographers.
of Robert E. Lee
Stephen Vincent Benét 1898–1943: *John Brown's Body* (1928)

14 Discretion is not the better part of biography.
Lytton Strachey 1880–1932: Michael Holroyd *Lytton Strachey* vol. 1 (1967)

15 Reformers are always finally neglected, while the memoirs of the frivolous will always eagerly be read.
Chips Channon 1897–1958: diary, 7 July 1936

16 To write one's memoirs is to speak ill of everybody except oneself.
Henri Philippe Pétain 1856–1951: in *Observer* 26 May 1946

17 If you really want to hear about it, the first thing you'll probably want to know is where I was born, and what my lousy childhood was like, and how my parents were occupied and all before they had me, and all that David Copperfield kind of crap, but I don't feel like going into it.
J. D. Salinger 1919–2010: *Catcher in the Rye* (1951)

18 An autobiography is an obituary in serial form with the last instalment missing.
Quentin Crisp 1908–99: *The Naked Civil Servant* (1968)

19 Biography is the mesh through which real life escapes.
Tom Stoppard 1937– : *The Invention of Love* (1997)

Birds

see also ANIMALS

proverbs and sayings ▸

1 The cuckoo comes in April,
He sings his song in May;
In the middle of June
He changes his tune,
And then he flies away.
traditional rhyme

2 A mockingbird has no voice of his own.
the mockingbird is noted for its mimicry of the calls and songs of other birds; American proverb, mid 19th century

3 One for sorrow; two for mirth; three for a wedding, four for a birth.
a traditional rhyme found in a variety of forms, referring to the number of magpies seen on a particular occasion; English proverb, mid 19th century

4 The robin and the wren are God's cock and hen; the martin and the swallow are God's mate and marrow.
there was a traditional belief that the robin and the wren were sacred birds, and that to harm them in any way would be unlucky (*marrow* = 'companion'); English proverb, late 18th century

5 The white heron is a bird of a single flight.
the white heron is very rare; Maori proverb; see ORIGINALITY 4

phrases ▸

6 the bird of Jove
the eagle

7 the bird of Juno
the peacock

8 Mother Carey's chicken
the storm petrel

quotations ▸

9 The silver swan, who, living had no note,
When death approached unlocked her silent throat.
Orlando Gibbons 1583–1625: 'The Silver Swan' (1612 song)

10 I wish the bald eagle had not been chosen as the representative of our country; he is a bird of bad moral character.
Benjamin Franklin 1706–90: letter to Mrs Bache, 26 January 1784

11 A robin red breast in a cage
Puts all Heaven in a rage.
William Blake 1757–1827: 'Auguries of Innocence' (1803)

12 O Cuckoo! Shall I call thee bird,
Or but a wandering voice?
William Wordsworth 1770–1850: 'To the Cuckoo' (1807)

13 Hail to thee, blithe Spirit!
Bird thou never wert,
That from Heaven, or near it,
Pourest thy full heart
In profuse strains of unpremeditated art.
Percy Bysshe Shelley 1792–1822: 'To a Skylark' (1819)

14 Alone and warming his five wits,
The white owl in the belfry sits.
Alfred, Lord Tennyson 1809–92: 'Song—The Owl' (1830)

15 That's the wise thrush; he sings each song twice over,
Lest you should think he never could recapture
The first fine careless rapture!
Robert Browning 1812–89: 'Home-Thoughts, from Abroad' (1845)

16 I once had a sparrow alight upon my shoulder for a moment while I was hoeing in a village garden, and I felt that I was more distinguished by that circumstance than I should have been by any epaulette I could have worn.
Henry David Thoreau 1817–62: *Walden* (1854) 'Winter Animals'

17 I caught this morning morning's minion, kingdom of daylight's dauphin, dapple-dawn-drawn Falcon.
Gerard Manley Hopkins 1844–89: 'The Windhover' (written 1877)

18 It was the Rainbow gave thee birth,
And left thee all her lovely hues.
W. H. Davies 1871–1940: 'Kingfisher' (1910)

19 Oh, a wondrous bird is the pelican!
His beak will hold more than his belican.
He can take in his beak
Enough food for a week.
But I'm damned if I see how the helican.
Dixon Lanier Merritt 1879–1972: adapted from the original in *Nashville Banner* 22 April 1913

20 It took the whole of Creation
To produce my foot, my each feather:
Now I hold Creation in my foot.
Ted Hughes 1930–98: 'Hawk Roosting' (1960)

21 Blackbirds are the cellos of the deep farms.
Anne Stevenson 1933– : 'Green Mountain, Black Mountain' (1982)

22 I live in a city. I know sparrows from starlings. After that everything's a duck as far as I'm concerned.
Terry Pratchett 1948– : *Monstrous Regiment* (2003)

Birth

see PREGNANCY AND BIRTH

The Body

see also APPEARANCE, SENSES

proverbs and sayings ▸

1 Cold hands, warm heart.
the outward sign may contradict the inward reality; English proverb, early 20th century

2 Does my bum look big in this?
catchphrase used by Arabella Weir in *The Fast Show* on BBC Television 1994–97

3 The eyes are the window of the soul.
it is in the eyes that a person's true nature can be discerned; English proverb, mid 16th century

phrases ▸

4 a boneless wonder
a contortionist; see POLITICIANS 26

5 crowning glory
a woman's hair; the most beautiful feature or possession, the greatest achievement; see BODY 10

6 Cupid's bow
a particular shape of (the upper edge of) the upper lip, referring to the double-curved bow traditionally carried by Cupid

7 lump of clay
the human body regarded as purely material, without a soul; linked to the biblical use of *clay* = a material of which the human body was formed, as in Genesis: 'I also am formed out of the clay'

8 unruly member
the tongue, after the Bible (James) 'the tongue is a little member...the tongue can no man tame; it is an unruly evil'

quotations ▸

9 I will give thanks unto thee, for I am fearfully and wonderfully made.
Bible: Psalm 139

10 Doth not even nature itself teach you, that if a man have long hair, it is a shame unto him?
But if a woman have long hair, it is a glory to her.
Bible: I Corinthians; see BODY 5

11 Our bodies are our gardens, to which our wills are gardeners.
William Shakespeare 1564–1616: *Othello* (1602–4)

12 Every tooth in a man's head is more valuable than a diamond.
Cervantes 1547–1616: *Don Quixote* (1605)

13 Why has not man a microscopic eye?
For this plain reason, man is not a fly.
Alexander Pope 1688–1744: *An Essay on Man* Epistle 1 (1733)

14 Every man is the builder of a temple, called his body.
Henry David Thoreau 1817–62: *Walden* (1854) 'Higher Laws'

15 I sing the body electric.
Walt Whitman 1819–92: title of poem (1855)

16 Our body is a machine for living. It is organized for that, it is its nature. Let life go on in it unhindered and let it defend itself, it will do more than if you paralyse it by encumbering it with remedies.
Leo Tolstoy 1828–1910: *War and Peace* (1865–9)

17 A large nose is in fact the sign of an affable man, good, courteous, witty, liberal, courageous, such as I am.
Edmond Rostand 1868–1918: *Cyrano de Bergerac* (1897)

18 An impersonal and scientific knowledge of the structure of our bodies is the surest safeguard against prurient curiosity and lascivious gloating.
Marie Stopes 1880–1958: *Married Love* (1918)

19 Anatomy is destiny.
Sigmund Freud 1856–1939: *Collected Writings* (1924)

20 There is more felicity on the far side of baldness than young men can possibly imagine.
Logan Pearsall Smith 1865–1946: *Afterthoughts* (1931)

21 Only God, my dear,
Could love you for yourself alone
And not your yellow hair.
W. B. Yeats 1865–1939: 'Anne Gregory' (1932)

22 Imprisoned in every fat man a thin one is wildly signalling to be let out.
Cyril Connolly 1903–74: *The Unquiet Grave* (1944)

23 The human body is the best picture of the human soul.
Ludwig Wittgenstein 1889–1951: *Philosophical Investigations* (1953)

24 I came in here in all good faith to help my country. I don't mind giving a reasonable amount [of blood], but a pint...why that's very nearly an armful.

Ray Galton 1930– and **Alan Simpson** 1929– : *The Blood Donor* (1961 BBC television programme) words spoken by Tony Hancock

25 A woman watches her body uneasily, as though it were an unreliable ally in the battle for love.

Leonard Cohen 1934– : *The Favourite Game* (1963)

26 My brain? It's my second favourite organ.

Woody Allen 1935– : *Sleeper* (1973 film, with Marshall Brickman)

27 Fat is a feminist issue.

Susie Orbach 1946– : title of book (1978)

28 The leg, a source of much delight, which carries weight and governs
height.

Ian Dury 1942–2000: 'The Body Song' (1981)

29 The body says what words cannot. Nothing is more revealing than movement.

Martha Graham 1894–1991: interview, *New York Times* 31 March 1985

30 My disability is that I cannot use my legs. My handicap is your negative perception of that disability, and thus of me.

Rick Hansen 1957– : *Rick Hansen: Man in Motion* (1987, with Jim Taylor)

31 Modern bodybuilding is ritual, religion, sport, art, and science, awash in Western chemistry and mathematics. Defying nature, it surpasses it.

Camille Paglia 1947– : *Sex, Art, and American Culture* (1992)

32 Nothing tastes as good as skinny feels.

Kate Moss 1974– : when asked for her motto, in *Women's Wear Daily* 13 November 2009

Books

see also FICTION, LIBRARIES, READING, WRITING

proverbs and sayings ▸

1 Beware of the man of one book.

warning against the person who places too much confidence in a single authority; Latin proverb

2 A book is like a garden carried in the pocket.

Middle Eastern saying

3 A great book is a great evil.

a long book is likely to be verbose and badly written; English proverb, early 17th century: a contraction of Callimachus (305–240 BC) 'the great book is equal to a great evil'

4 It is a tie between men to have read the same book.

American proverb, mid 19th century

quotations ▸

5 Of making many books there is no end; and much study is a weariness of the flesh.

Bible: Ecclesiastes

6 There is no book so bad that some good cannot be got out of it.

Pliny the Elder AD 23–79: Pliny the Younger *Letters*

7 Some books are to be tasted, others to be swallowed, and some few to be chewed and digested; that is, some books are to be read only in parts; others to be read but not curiously; and some few to be read wholly, and with diligence and attention. Some books also may be read by deputy, and extracts made of them by others.

Francis Bacon 1561–1626: *Essays* (1625) 'Of Studies'

8 A good book is the precious lifeblood of a master spirit, embalmed and treasured up on purpose to a life beyond life.

John Milton 1608–74: *Areopagitica* (1644)

9 An empty book is like an infant's soul, in which anything may be written. It is capable of all things,

but containeth nothing.

Thomas Traherne 1637–74: *Centuries of Meditations*

10 I hate books; they only teach us to talk about things we know nothing about.

Jean-Jacques Rousseau 1712–78: *Émile* (1762)

11 Your *borrowers of books*—those mutilators of collections, spoilers of the symmetry of shelves, and creators of odd volumes.

Charles Lamb 1775–1834: *Essays of Elia* (1823) 'The Two Races of Men'

12 A good book is the best of friends, the same to-day and for ever.

Martin Tupper 1810–89: *Proverbial Philosophy* Series I (1838) 'Of Reading'

13 No furniture so charming as books.

Sydney Smith 1771–1845: Lady Holland *Memoir* (1855)

14 'What is the use of a book,' thought Alice, 'without pictures or conversations?'

Lewis Carroll 1832–98: *Alice's Adventures in Wonderland* (1865)

15 There is no such thing as a moral or an immoral book. Books are well written, or badly written.

Oscar Wilde 1854–1900: *The Picture of Dorian Gray* (1891)

16 '*Classic*.' A book which people praise and don't read.

Mark Twain 1835–1910: *Following the Equator* (1897)

17 A book must be the axe for the frozen sea within us.

Franz Kafka 1883–1924: letter, 27 January 1904

18 A bad book is as much of a labour to write as a good one; it comes as sincerely from the author's soul.

Aldous Huxley 1894–1963: *Point Counter Point* (1928)

19 A best-seller is the gilded tomb of a mediocre talent.

Logan Pearsall Smith 1865–1946: *Afterthoughts* (1931)

20 Books can not be killed by fire. People die, but books never die. No man and no force can abolish memory...In this war, we know, books are weapons. And it is a part of your dedication always to make them weapons for man's freedom.

Franklin D. Roosevelt 1882–1945: 'Message to the Booksellers of America' 6 May 1942

21 The principle of procrastinated rape is said to be the ruling one in all the great best-sellers.

V. S. Pritchett 1900–97: *The Living Novel* (1946) 'Clarissa'

22 I suggest that the only books that influence us are those for which we are ready, and which have gone a little farther down our particular path than we have yet got ourselves.

E. M. Forster 1879–1970: *Two Cheers for Democracy* (1951)

23 Some books are undeservedly forgotten; none are undeservedly remembered.

W. H. Auden 1907–73: *The Dyer's Hand* (1963) 'Reading'

24 There is more treasure in books than in all the pirates' loot on Treasure Island.

Walt Disney 1901–66: attributed, Laurence J. Peter *Quotations for Our Time* (1977)

25 The possession of a book becomes a substitute for reading it.

Anthony Burgess 1917–93: in *New York Times Book Review* 4 December 1966

26 The good of a book lies in its being read.

Umberto Eco 1932– : *The Name of the Rose* (1981)

27 A classic is a book that has never finished saying what it has to say.

Italo Calvino 1923–85: 'Why Read the Classics?' in *L'Espresso* 28 June 1981

28 Books say: she did this because. Life says: she did this. Books are where things are explained to you; life is where things aren't.

Julian Barnes 1946– : *Flaubert's Parrot* (1984)

29 I don't trust books. They're all fact, no heart.

Stephen Colbert 1964– : *The Colbert Report* 17 October 2005

Boredom

phrases ▶

1 been there, done that
used to express past experience of or familiarity with something, especially something now regarded as boring or unwelcome; see TRAVEL 1

2 harp on the same string
dwell tediously on the same subject; see BOREDOM 3

quotations ▶

3 Harp not on that string.
William Shakespeare 1564–1616: *Richard III* (1591); see BOREDOM 2

4 People by whom one must not be bored are almost always boring.
Duc de la Rochefoucauld 1613–80: *Maxims* (1678)

5 The secret of being a bore...is to tell everything.
Voltaire 1694–1778: *Discours en vers sur l'homme* (1737)

6 He is not only dull in himself, but the cause of dullness in others.
on a law lord
Samuel Foote 1720–77: James Boswell *Life of Samuel Johnson* (1791) 1783

7 Society is now one polished horde,
Formed of two mighty tribes, the *Bores* and *Bored*.
Lord Byron 1788–1824: *Don Juan* (1819–24)

8 A desire for desires—boredom.
Leo Tolstoy 1828–1910: *Anna Karenina* (1873–6)

9 Boredom is...a vital problem for the moralist, since half the sins of mankind are caused by the fear of it.
Bertrand Russell 1872–1970: *The Conquest of Happiness* (1930)

10 Someone has somewhere commented on the fact that millions long for immortality who don't know what to do with themselves on a rainy Sunday afternoon.
Susan Ertz 1894–1985: *Anger in the Sky* (1943)

11 Nothing happens, nobody comes, nobody goes, it's awful!
Samuel Beckett 1906–89: *Waiting for Godot* (1955)

12 Nothing, like something, happens anywhere.
Philip Larkin 1922–85: 'I Remember, I Remember' (1955)

13 Life, friends, is boring. We must not say so...
And moreover my mother told me as a boy
(repeatingly) 'Ever to confess you're bored
means you have no
Inner Resources.' I conclude now I have no
inner resources, because I am heavy bored.
John Berryman 1914–72: *77 Dream Songs* (1964) no. 14

14 What's wrong with being a boring kind of guy?
during the campaign for the Republican nomination
George Bush 1924– : in *Daily Telegraph* 28 April 1988

Borrowing
see DEBT AND BORROWING

Britain
see also ENGLAND, SCOTLAND, WALES

phrases ▶

1 Cool Britannia
Britain, perceived as a stylish and fashionable place, especially (in the late 1990s) as represented by the international success of and interest in contemporary British art, popular music, film, and fashion

2 from Land's End to John o'Groats
from one end of Britain to the other; *Land's End* a rocky promontory in SW Cornwall, which forms the westernmost point of England; *John o'Groats* a village at the extreme NE point of the Scottish mainland

3 the Mother of Parliaments
the British parliament, from Bright: see PARLIAMENT 22

4 **the red, white, and blue**
the Union flag of the United Kingdom, from the colours of the three crosses making up the Union flag, the red on white cross of St George (for England), the white on blue cross saltire of St Andrew (for Scotland), and the red on white cross saltire of St Patrick (for Ireland)

5 **twist the lion's tail**
provoke the resentment of the British; a *lion* as the symbol of the British Empire

quotations ▸

6 Rule, Britannia, rule the waves;
Britons never will be slaves.
James Thomson 1700–48: *Alfred: a Masque* (1740)

7 It must be owned, that the Graces do not seem to be natives of Great Britain; and I doubt, the best of us here have more of rough than polished diamond.
Lord Chesterfield 1694–1773: *Letters to his Son* (1774) 18 November 1748

8 Born and educated in this country,
I glory in the name of Briton.
George III 1738–1820: *The King's Speech on Opening the Session* 18 November 1760

9 He [the Briton] is a barbarian, and thinks that the customs of his tribe and island are the laws of nature.
George Bernard Shaw 1856–1950: *Caesar and Cleopatra* (1901)

10 Other nations use 'force'; we Britons alone use 'Might'.
Evelyn Waugh 1903–66: *Scoop* (1938)

11 The British nation is unique in this respect. They are the only people who like to be told how bad things are, who like to be told the worst.
Winston Churchill 1874–1965: speech in the House of Commons, 10 June 1941

12 Britain will be honoured by historians more for the way she disposed of an empire than for the way in which she acquired it.
Lord Harlech 1918–85: in *New York Times* 28 October 1962

13 Great Britain has lost an empire and has not yet found a role.
Dean Acheson 1893–1971: speech at the Military Academy, West Point, 5 December 1962

14 Fifty years on from now, Britain will still be the country of long shadows on county [cricket] grounds, warm beer, invincible green suburbs, dog lovers, and—as George Orwell said—old maids bicycling to Holy Communion through the morning mist.
John Major 1943– : speech to the Conservative Group for Europe, 22 April 1993; see ENGLAND 24

15 You cannot trust people who have such bad cuisine. It is the country with the worst food after Finland.
on the British
Jacques Chirac 1932– : in *Times* 5 July 2005

British Towns and Regions

proverbs and sayings ▸

1 **Essex stiles, Kentish miles, Norfolk wiles, many a man beguiles.**
traditional saying, early 17th century

2 **From Hell, Hull, and Halifax, good Lord deliver us.**
traditional saying, late 16th century

3 **Glasgow's miles better.**
slogan introduced by Provost Michael Kelly, 1980s

4 **Kirton was a borough town**
When Exon was a vuzzy down.
on the relative age of Crediton (*Kirton*) and Exeter (*Exon*); traditional saying

5 **Lincoln was, London is, and York shall be.**
referring to which is the greatest city; traditional saying, late 16th century

6 **London Bridge is broken down**
My fair lady.
traditional nursery rhyme, early 18th century

7 **May God in His mercy look down on Belfast.**
traditional refrain; see BRITISH TOWNS 42

8 **Northamptonshire for squires and spires.**
traditional saying, late 19th century

9 **Peebles for pleasure.**
the town of *Peebles* in the Scottish Borders has traditionally been a favoured holiday resort; traditional saying, late 19th century

10 **Some places of Kent have health and**

no wealth, some wealth and no health, some health and wealth.
referring to the north and east of the county, Romney Marsh, and the Weald respectively; traditional saying, late 16th century

11 **Sussex won't be druv.**
asserting that Sussex people have minds of their own, and cannot be forced against their will (*druv* is a dialect version of *drove*, meaning *driven*); English proverb, early 20th century

12 **Take away Aberdeen and twelve miles round, and where are you?**
reflecting local pride; Scottish saying

13 **There are more saints in Cornwall than in heaven.**
referring to the number of West Country saints known through their local cult; traditional saying

14 **What Manchester says today, the rest of England says tomorrow.**
English proverb, late 19th century, occurring in a variety of forms

15 **Yorkshire born and Yorkshire bred, strong in the arm and weak in the head.**
the names of other (chiefly northern) English counties and towns are also used instead of Yorkshire; English proverb, mid 19th century

***phrases* ▸**

16 **the Athens of the North**
Edinburgh, alluding to its academic and intellectual traditions, and to the predominantly neoclassical style of architecture in its city centre

17 **Auld Reekie**
Edinburgh, literally 'Old Smoky'

18 **the big Smoke**
London

19 **City of Bon-accord**
Aberdeen; *bon-accord* in Scottish usage (from French) means 'good will, fellowship'

20 **City of Dreaming Spires**
Oxford, deriving originally from Matthew Arnold's 'Thyrsis' (1866): 'And that sweet City with her dreaming Spires'; see UNIVERSITIES 21

21 **the garden of England**
Kent; the Vale of Evesham

22 **the Granite City**
the city of Aberdeen, Scotland

23 **the great wen**
London, as the type of a large and overcrowded city, from William Cobbett *Rural Rides* (1822) 'But what is to be the fate of the great wen of all?'

24 **the land of the broad acres**
Yorkshire, NE England

***quotations* ▸**

25 **London, thou art the flower of cities all!**
Anonymous: 'London' (poem of unknown authorship, previously attributed to William Dunbar, 1465–1530)

26 **That shire which we the Heart of England well may call.**
of Warwickshire
Michael Drayton 1563–1631: *Poly-Olbion* (1612–22)

27 **When a man is tired of London, he is tired of life; for there is in London all that life can afford.**
Samuel Johnson 1709–84: James Boswell *Life of Samuel Johnson* (1791) 20 September 1777

28 **Earth has not anything to show more fair:**
Dull would he be of soul who could pass by
A sight so touching in its majesty.
William Wordsworth 1770–1850: 'Composed upon Westminster Bridge' (1807)

29 ***Was für Plunder!***
What rubbish!
of London as seen from the Monument in June 1814; often misquoted as '*Was für plündern* [What a place to plunder]!'
Gebhard Lebrecht Blücher 1742–1819: Evelyn Princess Blücher *Memoirs of Prince Blücher* (1932)

30 **One has no great hopes from Birmingham. I always say there is something direful in the sound.**
Jane Austen 1775–1817: *Emma* (1816)

31 **Oh! who can ever be tired of Bath?**
Jane Austen 1775–1817: *Northanger Abbey* (1818)

32 **It is from the midst of this putrid sewer that the greatest river of human industry springs up and carries fertility to the whole world. From this foul drain pure gold flows forth.**
of Manchester
Alexis de Tocqueville 1805–59: *Voyage en Angleterre et en Irlande de 1835* 2 July 1835

33 **Kent, sir—everybody knows Kent—apples, cherries, hops, and women.**
Charles Dickens 1812–70: *Pickwick Papers* (1837)

34 Towery city and branchy between towers;
Cuckoo-echoing, bell-swarmèd, lark-charmèd, rook-racked, river-rounded.
Gerard Manley Hopkins 1844–89: 'Duns Scotus's Oxford' (written 1879)

35 When Adam and Eve were dispossessed
Of the garden hard by Heaven,
They planted another one down in the west,
'Twas Devon, glorious Devon!
Harold Edwin Boulton 1859–1935: 'Glorious Devon' (1902)

36 For Cambridge people rarely smile,
Being urban, squat, and packed with guile.
Rupert Brooke 1887–1915: 'The Old Vicarage, Grantchester' (1915)

37 I belong to Glasgow
Dear Old Glasgow town!
Will Fyffe 1885–1947: 'I Belong to Glasgow' (1920 song)

38 Bugger Bognor.
comment made either in 1929, when it was proposed that the town be renamed Bognor Regis following the king's convalescence there; or on his deathbed when someone said 'Cheer up, your Majesty, you will soon be at Bognor again.'
George V 1865–1936: Kenneth Rose *King George V* (1983)

39 Very flat, Norfolk.
Noël Coward 1899–1973: *Private Lives* (1930)

40 London Pride has been handed down to us.
London Pride is a flower that's free.
London Pride means our own dear town to us,
And our pride it for ever will be.
Noël Coward 1899–1973: 'London Pride' (1941 song)

41 Maybe it's because I'm a Londoner
That I love London so.
Hubert Gregg 1914–2004: 'Maybe It's Because I'm a Londoner' (1947 song)

42 O the bricks they will bleed and the rain it will weep
And the damp Lagan fog lull the city to sleep;
It's to hell with the future and live on the past:
May the Lord in His mercy be kind to Belfast.
Maurice James Craig 1919– : 'Ballad to a Traditional Refrain' (1974); see BRITISH TOWNS 7

Broadcasting

proverbs and sayings ▸

1 **Nation shall speak peace unto nation.**
motto of the BBC, adapted from the Bible (Isaiah) by Montague John Rendall (1862–1950); see PEACE 8

2 **So much chewing gum for the eyes.**
small boy's definition of certain television programmes, 1950s

3 **To inform, educate, and entertain.**
traditional expression of the mission of the BBC, associated with Lord Reith (1889–1971)

phrases ▸

4 **couch potato**
a person who takes little or no exercise and watches a lot of television, coined in the US from a pun on *boob tube* as a slang expression for television; someone given to continuous viewing was a *boob tuber*, and the cartoonist Robert Armstrong drew the most familiar tuber, a potato, reclining on a couch watching TV

5 **jump the shark**
(of a television series) reach a point when the inclusion of far-fetched events for the sake of novelty marks a decline. The origin is said to be an episode in the long-running US television series *Happy Days*, in which the central character (the Fonz) jumped over a shark when waterskiing

6 **soap opera**
a television or radio drama serial dealing typically with daily events in the lives of the same group of characters; so named because such serials were originally sponsored in the US by soap manufacturers in the 1930s

quotations ▸

7 He who prides himself on giving what he thinks the public wants is often creating a fictitious demand for lower standards which he will then satisfy.
Lord Reith 1889–1971: memo to Crawford Committee 1926; Andrew Boyle *Only the Wind Will Listen* (1972); see BROADCASTING 10

8 *Television*? The word is half Greek, half Latin. No good can come of it.
C. P. Scott 1846–1932: Asa Briggs *The BBC: the First Fifty Years* (1985)

9 I hate television. I hate it as much as peanuts. But I can't stop eating peanuts.
Orson Welles 1915–85: in *New York Herald Tribune* 12 October 1956

10 Those who say they give the public what it wants begin by underestimating public taste, and end by debauching it.
T. S. Eliot 1888–1965: in *Pilkington Report* (1962); anonymous observation later attributed to Eliot in Richard Hoggart *A Sort of Clowning* (1990); see BROADCASTING 7

11 It's just like having a licence to print your own money.
on the profitability of commercial television in Britain
Roy Thomson 1894–1976: R. Braddon *Roy Thomson* (1965)

12 Television brought the brutality of war into the comfort of the living room. Vietnam was lost in the living rooms of America—not the battlefields of Vietnam.
Marshall McLuhan 1911–80: in *Montreal Gazette* 16 May 1975

13 Let's face it, there are no plain women on television.
Anna Ford 1943– : in *Observer* 23 September 1979

14 Anyone afraid of what he thinks television does to the world is probably just afraid of the world.
Clive James 1939– : *Glued to the Box* (1981)

15 Television contracts the imagination and radio expands it.
Terry Wogan 1938– : attributed, 1984

16 Television...thrives on unreason, and unreason thrives on television...[It] strikes at the emotions rather than the intellect.
Robin Day 1923–2000: *Grand Inquisitor* (1989)

17 57 channels (and nothin' on).
Bruce Springsteen 1949– : title of song, 1992

18 Television has made dictatorship impossible, but democracy unbearable.
Shimon Peres 1923– : at a Davos meeting, in *Financial Times* 31 January 1995

Business

see also BUYING

proverbs and sayings ►

1 The bulls make money, the bears make money, but the hogs get slaughtered.
money can be made through buying or selling stock, but greed is fatal; modern saying

2 Business before pleasure.
often used to encourage a course of action; English proverb, mid 19th century

3 Business goes where it is invited and stays where it is well-treated.
American proverb, mid 20th century

4 Business is like a car: it will not run by itself except downhill.
American proverb, mid 20th century

5 Business is war.
modern saying, said to derive from a Japanese proverb

6 Business neglected is business lost.
North American proverb, mid 20th century

7 The customer is always right.
English proverb, early 20th century; see BUSINESS 37

8 Don't be evil.
informal corporate motto of the search engine Google

9 If you don't speculate, you can't accumulate.
outlay (and some degree of risk) is necessary if real gain is to be achieved; English proverb, mid 20th century

10 I liked it so much, I bought the company!
advertising slogan for Remington Shavers, coined by owner Victor Kiam (1926–2001)

11 Keep your own shop and your shop will keep you.
recommending attention to what is essential to one's livelihood; English proverb, early 17th century

12 **Never knowingly undersold.**
motto, from 1920, of the John Lewis partnership

13 **No cure, no pay.**
known principally from its use on Lloyd's of London's Standard Form of Salvage Agreement; English proverb, late 19th century

14 **No penny, no paternoster.**
if you want a thing you must pay for it (the reference is to priests insisting on being paid for performing services); English proverb, early 16th century

15 **Pay beforehand was never well served.**
payment in advance removes the incentive to finish the work; English proverb, late 16th century

16 **Pile it high, sell it cheap.**
slogan coined by Jack Cohen (1898–1979), founder of the Tesco supermarket chain

17 **Sell in May and go away (come back on St Leger's day).**
saying relating to the cycle of activity on the London Stock Exchange. May, shortly after the start of the financial year, was traditionally a busy time, but during the summer months trading was slack as Londoners (including stockbrokers) took their holiday breaks away from the capital. The full form of the saying refers to the classic *St Leger* horse race, taken as marking the end of the English summer social calendar

18 **There are tricks in every trade.**
the practice of every skill is likely to involve some trickery or dishonesty; English proverb, mid 17th century

19 **Trade follows the flag.**
commercial development is likely to follow military intervention; English proverb, late 19th century

phrases ▸

20 **bear market**
a market in which share prices are falling encouraging selling. In Stock Exchange usage, a *bear* is a person who sells shares hoping to buy them back again later at a lower price. The dealer in this kind of stock was known as the bearskin jobber, and it seems likely that the original phrase was 'sell the bearskin'; see OPTIMISM 8. The associated *bull* is of later date, and may perhaps have been suggested by the existence of *bear* in this sense: see BUSINESS 22

21 **blue-chip**
denoting companies or their shares considered to be a reliable investment, though less secure than gilt-edged stock; US, early 20th century, from the *blue chip* used in gambling games, which usually has a high value

22 **bull market**
a market in which share prices are rising, encouraging buying; see BUSINESS 20

23 **Chinese wall**
on the Stock Exchange, a prohibition against the passing of confidential information from one department of a financial institution to another, alluding to the Great Wall of China, as an insurmountable barrier to understanding

24 **the triple-witching hour**
in the US, informal name for the unpredictable final hour of trading on the US Stock Exchange before the simultaneous expiry of three different kinds of options; a development of *witching* hour: see DAY 4

25 **a white knight**
a welcome company bidding for a company facing an unwelcome takeover bid, likened to a traditional figure of chivalry rescuing someone from danger

quotations ▸

26 **A merchant shall hardly keep himself from doing wrong.**
Bible: Ecclesiasticus

27 **They [corporations] cannot commit treason, nor be outlawed, nor excommunicate, for they have no souls.**
Edward Coke 1552–1634: *The Reports of Sir Edward Coke* (1658) 'The case of Sutton's Hospital'; see BUSINESS 33

28 **A Company for carrying on an undertaking of Great Advantage, but no one to know what it is.**
Anonymous: Company Prospectus at the time of the South Sea Bubble (1711)

29 **There is nothing more requisite in business than dispatch.**
Joseph Addison 1672–1719: *The Drummer* (1716)

30 **It is the nature of all greatness not to be exact; and great trade will always be attended with considerable abuses.**
Edmund Burke 1729–97: *On American Taxation* (1775)

31 People of the same trade seldom meet together, even for merriment and diversion, but the conversation ends in a conspiracy against the public, or in some contrivance to raise prices.
Adam Smith 1723–90: *Wealth of Nations* (1776)

32 To found a great empire for the sole purpose of raising up a people of customers, may at first sight appear a project fit only for a nation of shopkeepers. It is, however, a project altogether unfit for a nation of shopkeepers; but extremely fit for a nation whose government is influenced by shopkeepers.
Adam Smith 1723–90: *Wealth of Nations* (1776); see ENGLAND 14

33 Corporations have neither bodies to be punished, nor souls to be condemned, they therefore do as they like.
often quoted as 'Did you ever expect a corporation to have a conscience, when it has no soul to be damned, and no body to be kicked?'
Lord Thurlow 1731–1806: John Poynder *Literary Extracts* (1844); see BUSINESS 27

34 Here's the rule for bargains: 'Do other men, for they would do you.' That's the true business precept.
Charles Dickens 1812–70: *Martin Chuzzlewit* (1844)

35 The public be damned! I'm working for my stockholders.
William H. Vanderbilt 1821–85: comment to a news reporter, 2 October 1882

36 The growth of a large business is merely a survival of the fittest.
John D. Rockefeller 1839–1937: W. J. Ghent *Our Benevolent Feudalism* (1902); see LIFE SCIENCES 9

37 The customer is never wrong.
César Ritz 1850–1918: R. Nevill and C. E. Jerningham *Piccadilly to Pall Mall* (1908); see BUSINESS 7

38 The best of all monopoly profits is a quiet life.
J. R. Hicks 1904–89: *Econometrica* (1935)

39 For a salesman, there is no rock bottom to the life...A salesman is got to dream, boy. It comes with the territory.
Arthur Miller 1915–2005: *Death of a Salesman* (1949)

40 How to succeed in business without really trying.
Shepherd Mead 1914–94: title of book (1952)

41 For years I thought what was good for our country was good for General Motors and vice versa.
Charles E. Wilson 1890–1961: testimony to the Senate Armed Services Committee on his proposed nomination for Secretary of Defence, 15 January 1953

42 You cannot be a success in any business without believing that it is the greatest business in the world...You have to put your heart in the business and the business in your heart.
Thomas Watson Snr. 1874–1956: Robert Sobel *IBM: Colossus in Transition* (1981)

43 If business always made the right decisions, business wouldn't be business.
J. Paul Getty 1892–1976: *How to be Rich* (1965)

44 The most striking thing about modern industry is that it requires so much and accomplishes so little. Modern industry seems to be inefficient to a degree that surpasses one's ordinary powers of imagination. Its inefficiency therefore remains unnoticed.
E. F. Schumacher 1911–77: *Small is Beautiful* (1973)

45 After a certain point money is meaningless. It ceases to be the goal. The game is what counts.
Aristotle Onassis 1906–75: attributed, perhaps apocryphal

46 In the factory we make cosmetics; in the store we sell hope.
Charles Revson 1906–75: A. Tobias *Fire and Ice* (1976)

47 Rule No 1: never lose money. Rule No 2: never forget rule No 1.
Warren Buffett 1930– : in *Forbes 400* 27 October 1986

48 Deals are my art form. Other people paint beautifully on canvas or write wonderful poetry. I like making deals, preferably big deals. That's how I get my kicks.
Donald Trump 1946– : Donald Trump and Tony Schwartz *The Art of the Deal* (1987)

49 Nothing is illegal if one hundred well-

placed business men decide to do it.
Andrew Young 1932– : Morris K. Udall *Too Funny to be President* (1988)

50 There is only one boss. The customer. And he can fire everybody in the company from the chairman on down, simply by spending his money somewhere else.
Sam Walton 1919–92: *Sam Walton: Made in America, My Story*, with J. Huey (1990)

51 We used to build civilizations. Now we build shopping malls.
Bill Bryson 1951– : *Neither Here Nor There* (1991)

52 Investment must be rational; if you can't understand it, don't do it.
usually quoted as 'Never invest in a business you cannot understand'
Warren Buffett 1930– : in *Forbes 400* 21 October 1991

53 Only the paranoid survive.
dictum on which he has long run his company, the Intel Corporation
Andrew Grove 1936– : in *New York Times* 18 December 1994

54 Drill, baby, drill.
on the oil industry
Michael Steele 1958– : speech, Republican National Convention, Saint Paul, Minnesota, 3 September 2008, subsequently associated with Sarah Palin

55 Making money from money should be replaced with making money from making.
James Dyson 1947– : in *Observer* 8 February 2009

Buying and Selling

see also BUSINESS

proverbs and sayings ▸

1 The buyer has need of a hundred eyes, the seller of but one.
stressing the responsibility of a purchaser to examine goods on offer; English proverb, mid 17th century

2 Let the buyer beware.
warning that it is up to the buyer to establish the nature and value of a purchase before completing the transaction; English proverb, early 16th century. The Latin tag *caveat emptor* is also found

3 You buy land, you buy stones; you buy meat, you buy bones.
every purchase has its drawbacks; English proverb, late 17th century

phrases ▸

4 lipstick effect
the tendency for sales of small indulgences, such as *lipstick*, to rise during a recession, as a substitute for major purchases

quotations ▸

5 It is naught, it is naught, saith the buyer: but when he is gone his way, then he boasteth.
Bible: Proverbs

6 I have heard of a man who had a mind to sell his house, and therefore carried a piece of brick in his pocket, which he showed as a pattern to encourage purchasers.
Jonathan Swift 1667–1745: *The Drapier's Letters* (1724)

7 I often wonder what the Vintners buy
One half so precious as the Goods
they sell.
Edward Fitzgerald 1809–83: *The Rubáiyát of Omar Khayyám* (1859)

8 Every one lives by selling something.
Robert Louis Stevenson 1850–94: *Across the Plains* (1892) 'Beggars'

9 Only a fool holds out for the top dollar.
selling stock before the Wall Street crash of 1929
Joseph P. Kennedy 1888–1969: Richard J. Whalen *The Founding Father: the story of Joseph P. Kennedy* (1964)

10 The consumer, so it is said, is the king...each is a voter who uses his money as votes to get the things done that he wants done.
Paul A. Samuelson 1915–2009: *Economics* (8th ed., 1970)

11 In a consumer society there are inevitably two kinds of slaves: the prisoners of addiction and the prisoners of envy.
Ivan Illich 1926–2002: *Tools for Conviviality* (1973)

12 Buying is much more American than thinking and I'm as American

as they come.
Andy Warhol 1927–87: *Philosophy of Andy Warhol (From A to B and Back Again)* (1975)

13 When buying and selling are controlled by legislation, the first things to be bought and sold are legislators.
P. J. O'Rourke 1947– : *Parliament of Whores* (1991)

14 I love the smell of commerce in the morning.
Kevin Smith 1970– : *Mallrats* (1995 film), spoken by Jason Lee as Brodie

Canada

proverbs and sayings ►

1 A mari usque ad mare.
Latin, *From sea unto sea*, motto of Canada, taken from the Bible (Psalm 72) 'He shall have dominion also from sea to sea, and from the river unto the ends of the earth'

2 The Mounties always get their man.
unofficial motto of the Royal Canadian Mounted Police

phrases ►

3 the land God gave to Cain
a name for Labrador, from Cartier (see CANADA 5), referring to Cain's banishment by God to a desolate land 'east of Eden'; see also MURDER 7, ORDER 8, TRAVEL 14

4 the Land of the Little Sticks
the subarctic tundra region of northern Canada, characterized by its stunted vegetation; Chinook *stik* = wood, tree, forest

quotations ►

5 I am rather inclined to believe that this is the land God gave to Cain.
on discovering the northern shore of the Gulf of St Lawrence in 1534; see CANADA 3
Jacques Cartier 1491–1557: *La Première Relation*

6 These two nations have been at war over a few acres of snow near Canada, and... they are spending on this fine struggle more than Canada itself is worth.
of the struggle between the French and the British for the control of colonial north Canada
Voltaire 1694–1778: *Candide* (1759)

7 Fair these broad meads, these hoary woods are grand;
But we are exiles from our fathers' land.
John Galt 1779–1839: 'Canadian Boat Song' (1829); translated from the Gaelic; attributed

8 I expected to find a contest between a government and a people: I found two nations warring in the bosom of a single state.
John George Lambton, Lord Durham 1792–1840: *Report of the Affairs of British North America* (1839)

9 The twentieth century belongs to Canada.
encapsulation of a view expressed in a speech to the Canadian Club of Ottawa, 18 January 1904, 'The nineteenth century was the century of the United States. I think we can claim that it is Canada that shall fill the twentieth century'
Wilfrid Laurier 1841–1919: popularly attributed in this form

10 *O Canada! Terre de nos aïeux,*
Ton front est ceint de fleurons glorieux!
Car ton bras sait porter l'épée,
Il sait porter la croix!
O Canada! Our home and native land!
True patriot love in all thy sons command.
With glowing hearts we see thee rise,
The True North strong and free!
Robert Stanley Weir 1856–1926: 'Oh Canada' (1908 song); French words written in 1880 by Adolphe-Basile Routhier (1839–1920)

11 Building that railroad would have made a Canadian out of the German Emperor.
on the construction of the Canadian Pacific Railway
William Cornelius Van Horne 1843–1915: in *Canadian Encyclopedia* (1988) vol. 1

12 If some countries have too much history, we have too much geography.
William Lyon Mackenzie King 1874–1950: speech on Canada as an international power, 18 June 1936

13 Americans are benevolently ignorant about Canada, while Canadians are malevolently well-informed about the United States.
John Bartlet Brebner 1895–1957: attributed

14 We French, we English, never lost our civil war,

endure it still, a bloodless civil bore;
no wounded lying about, no Whitman
wanted.
It's only by our lack of ghosts we're
haunted.

Earle Birney 1904–95: 'Can.Lit.' (1962)

15 *Mon pays ce n'est pas un pays, c'est l'hiver.*
My country is not a country, it is winter.

Gilles Vigneault 1928– : 'Mon Pays' (1964)

16 Canada could have enjoyed:
English government,
French culture,
and American know-how.
Instead it ended up with:
English know-how,
French government,
and American culture.

a similar (prose) summary has been attributed to Lester Pearson (1897–1972), 'Canada was supposed to get British government, French culture, and American know-how. Instead it got French government, American culture, and British know-how'

John Robert Colombo 1936– : 'O Canada' (1965)

17 *Vive Le Québec Libre.*
Long Live Free Quebec.

Charles de Gaulle 1890–1970: speech in Montreal, 24 July 1967

18 When the white man came we had the land and they had the bibles; now they have the land and we have the bibles.

Dan George 1899–1981: Gerald Walsh *Indians in Transition: An Inquiry Approach* (1971)

19 A Canadian is somebody who knows how to make love in a canoe.

Pierre Berton 1920–2004: in *The Canadian* 22 December 1973

20 I see Canada as a country torn between a very northern, rather extraordinary, mystical spirit which it fears and its desire to present itself to the world as a Scotch banker.

Robertson Davies 1913–95: *The Enthusiasms of Robertson Davies* (1990)

21 I don't have a moral plan. I'm a Canadian.

David Cronenberg 1943– : attributed

Capitalism and Communism

see also CLASS, POLITICAL PARTIES

proverbs and sayings ►

1 All power to the Soviets.

slogan of workers in Petrograd, 1917

2 Are you now or have you ever been a member of the Communist Party?

formal question put to those appearing before the Committee on UnAmerican Activities during the McCarthy campaign of 1950–4 against alleged Communists in the US government and other institutions; the allusive form *are you now or have you ever been?* derives from this

3 Better red than dead.

slogan of nuclear disarmament campaigners, late 1950s

4 We pretend to work, and they pretend to pay us.

Russian saying of the Soviet era

phrases ►

5 the bamboo curtain

a political and economic barrier between China and non-Communist countries, after *iron curtain*: see CAPITALISM 7

6 dictatorship of the proletariat

the Communist ideal of proletarian supremacy following the overthrow of capitalism and preceding the classless state

7 the iron curtain

a notional barrier to the passage of people and information between the Soviet bloc and the West; in this specific sense from Churchill (see CAPITALISM 21), but the figurative use of *iron curtain* (literally a fire-curtain in a theatre) is recorded earlier; see also CAPITALISM 5

8 reds under the bed

denoting an exaggerated fear of the presence and harmful influence of Communist sympathizers within a society or institution

quotations ►

9 The Riches and Goods of Christians are not common, as touching the right, title, and possession of the same, as certain Anabaptists do falsely boast.

The Book of Common Prayer 1662: *Articles of Religion* (1562)

10 In the first stone which he [the savage] flings at the wild animals he pursues, in the first stick that he seizes to strike down the fruit which hangs above his reach, we see the appropriation of one article for the purpose of aiding in the acquisition of another, and thus discover the origin of capital.

Robert Torrens 1780–1864: *An Essay on the Production of Wealth* (1821)

11 A spectre is haunting Europe—the spectre of Communism.

Karl Marx 1818–83 and **Friedrich Engels** 1820–95: *The Communist Manifesto* (1848)

12 What is a communist? One who hath yearnings
For equal division of unequal earnings.

Ebenezer Elliott 1781–1849: 'Epigram' (1850)

13 All I know is that I am not a Marxist.

Karl Marx 1818–83: attributed in a letter from Friedrich Engels to Conrad Schmidt, 5 August 1890

14 Imperialism is the monopoly stage of capitalism.

Lenin 1870–1924: *Imperialism as the Last Stage of Capitalism* (1916) 'Briefest possible definition of imperialism'

15 I have seen the future; and it works.

following a visit to the Soviet Union in 1919
Lincoln Steffens 1866–1936: *Letters* (1938)

16 Communism is Soviet power plus the electrification of the whole country.

Lenin 1870–1924: Report to 8th Congress, 1920

17 The State is an instrument in the hands of the ruling class, used to break the resistance of the adversaries of that class.

Joseph Stalin 1879–1953: *Foundations of Leninism* (1924)

18 Communism is like prohibition, it's a good idea but it won't work.

Will Rogers 1879–1935: in 1927; *Weekly Articles* (1981)

19 Capital as such is not evil, it is its wrong use that is evil. Capital in some form or other will always be needed.

Mahatma Gandhi 1869–1948: in *Harijan* 28 July 1940

20 The inherent vice of capitalism is the unequal sharing of blessings. The inherent virtue of socialism is the equal sharing of miseries.

Winston Churchill 1874–1965: speech, House of Commons, 22 October 1945

21 From Stettin in the Baltic to Trieste in the Adriatic an iron curtain has descended across the Continent.

the expression 'iron curtain' previously had been applied by others to the Soviet Union or her sphere of influence
Winston Churchill 1874–1965: speech at Westminster College, Fulton, Missouri, 5 March 1946; see CAPITALISM 7

22 Whether you like it or not, history is on our side. We will bury you.

Nikita Khrushchev 1894–1971: speech to Western diplomats in Moscow, 18 November 1956

23 Capitalism, it is said, is a system wherein man exploits man. And communism—is vice versa.

quoting 'a Polish intellectual'
Daniel Bell 1919– : *The End of Ideology* (1960)

24 Normally speaking, it may be said that the forces of a capitalist society, if left unchecked, tend to make the rich richer and the poor poorer and thus increase the gap between them.

Jawaharlal Nehru 1889–1964: 'Basic Approach' in Vincent Shean *Nehru…* (1960)

25 History suggests that capitalism is a necessary condition for political freedom. Clearly it is not a sufficient condition for it.

Milton Friedman 1912–2006: *Capitalism and Freedom* (1962)

26 Capitalism is using its money; we socialists throw it away.

Fidel Castro 1927– : in *Observer* 8 November 1964

27 In the service of the people we followed such a policy that socialism would not lose its human face.

Alexander Dubček 1921–92: in *Rudé Právo* 19 July 1968

28 The unpleasant and unacceptable face of capitalism.

on the Lonrho affair
Edward Heath 1916–2005: speech, House of Commons, 15 May 1973; see APPEARANCE 12

29 Socialist governments traditionally do make a financial mess. They always run out of other people's money.

often quoted as 'the problem with socialism is that eventually you run out of other people's money'

Margaret Thatcher 1925– : interview, *This Week* Thames TV, 5 February 1976

30 It would be simplistic to say that Divine Providence caused the fall of communism. It fell by itself as a consequence of its own mistakes and abuses. It fell by itself because of its own inherent weaknesses.

Pope John Paul II 1920–2005: Carl Bernstein and Marco Politi *His Holiness: John Paul II and the Hidden History of our Time* (1996)

31 Yes to the market economy, No to the market society.

Lionel Jospin 1937– : in *Independent* 16 September 1998

Cats
see also ANIMALS

proverbs and sayings ▶

1 A cat always lands on its feet.

a cat's natural agility typifies its ability to escape from trouble; traditional saying

2 A cat has nine lives.

traditional saying

3 Touch not the cat but a glove.

but = without, the cat here is a wild cat; Scottish proverb, early 19th century

phrases ▶

4 Cheshire cat

a cat depicted with a broad fixed grin, as popularized through Lewis Carroll's *Alice's Adventures in Wonderland* (1865). The origin is unknown, but it is said that *Cheshire* cheeses used to be marked with the face of a smiling cat; see GOD 33, WAYS 11

5 fight like Kilkenny cats

two cats from Kilkenny in Ireland which, according to legend, fought until only their tails remained

quotations ▶

6 When I play with my cat, who knows whether she isn't amusing herself with me more than I am with her?

Montaigne 1533–92: *Essays* (1580)

7 For I will consider my Cat Jeoffrey....
For he counteracts the powers of darkness by his electrical skin and glaring eyes.
For he counteracts the Devil, who is death, by brisking about the life.

Christopher Smart 1722–71: *Jubilate Agno* (1758–63)

8 He walked by himself, and all places were alike to him.

Rudyard Kipling 1865–1936: *Just So Stories* (1902) 'The Cat that Walked by Himself'

9 Cats, no less liquid than their shadows,
Offer no angles to the wind.
They slip, diminished, neat, through loopholes
Less than themselves.

A. S. J. Tessimond 1902–62: *Cats* (1934)

10 The Naming of Cats is a difficult matter,
It isn't just one of your holiday games;
You may think at first I'm as mad as a hatter
When I tell you, a cat must have THREE DIFFERENT NAMES.

T. S. Eliot 1888–1965: 'The Naming of Cats' (1939); see MADNESS 2

11 The trouble with a kitten is
THAT
Eventually it becomes a
CAT.

Ogden Nash 1902–71: 'The Kitten' (1940)

12 Cats seem to go on the principle that it never does any harm to ask for what you want.

Joseph Wood Krutch 1893–1970: *Twelve Seasons* (1949)

13 If a fish is the movement of water embodied, given shape, then cat is a diagram and pattern of subtle air.

Doris Lessing 1919– : *Particularly Cats* (1967)

14 Cats, I always think, only jump into your lap to check if you are cold enough, yet, to eat.

Anne Enright 1962– : *The Gathering* (2007)

Causes and Consequences

proverbs and sayings ▸

1 **After the feast comes the reckoning.**
a period of pleasure or indulgence has to be paid for; English proverb, early 17th century, but now chiefly in modern North American use

2 **As you bake so shall you brew.**
as you begin, so shall you proceed; English proverb, late 16th century

3 **As you brew, so shall you bake.**
your circumstances will be shaped by your own initial actions; English proverb, late 16th century

4 **As you make your bed, so you must lie upon it.**
as you begin, so shall you proceed; English proverb, late 16th century

5 **As you sow, so you reap.**
you will have to endure the consequences of your actions; English proverb, late 15th century; see CAUSES 11, CAUSES 18, CAUSES 20

6 **Good seed makes a good crop.**
something which has a sound basis will do well; English proverb, mid 16th century

7 **Great oaks from little acorns grow.**
great results may ensue from apparently small beginnings; English proverb, late 14th century

8 **He who plants thorns must not expect to gather roses.**
Arabic proverb; see PRACTICALITY 2

9 **If you want to see heaven, you have to die yourself.**
Indian proverb

10 **The mother of mischief is no bigger than a midge's wing.**
the origin of difficulties can be very small; English proverb, early 17th century

11 **They that sow the wind, shall reap the whirlwind.**
those who have initiated a dangerous course must suffer the consequences; English proverb, late 16th century; see CAUSES 5, CAUSES 18, CAUSES 20

12 **Who won't be ruled by the rudder must be ruled by the rock.**
a ship which is not being steered on its course will run on to a rock; English proverb, mid 17th century

phrases ▸

13 **the butterfly effect**
the effect of a very small change in the initial conditions of a system which makes a significant difference to the outcome, from Lorenz: see CHANCE 37

14 **a grain of mustard seed**
a small thing capable of vast development, from the great height attained by black mustard in Palestine, as in the Bible (Matthew) 'a mustard seed…indeed is the least of all seeds: but when it is grown, it is the greatest among herbs'

15 **hoist with one's own petard**
ruined by one's own devices against others; literally blown up by one's own bomb, after Shakespeare *Hamlet* 'For 'tis the sport to have the engineer Hoist with his own petar'; *petar* = a petard, a small bomb made of a metal or wooden box filled with powder, used to blow in a door or to make a hole in a wall

16 **poetic justice**
the ideal justice in distribution of rewards and punishments supposed to befit a poem or other work of imagination; well-deserved unforeseen retribution or reward; from Pope *The Dunciad* 'Poetic Justice, with her lifted scale'

quotations ▸

17 **He that diggeth a pit shall fall into it.**
Bible: Ecclesiastes

18 **They have sown the wind, and they shall reap the whirlwind.**
Bible: Hosea; see CAUSES 5, CAUSES 11, CAUSES 20

19 **Whenever anything which has several parts is such that the whole is something over and above its parts, and not just the sum of them all, like a heap, then it always has some cause.**
Aristotle 384–322 BC: *Metaphysica*; see QUANTITIES 12

20 **Whatsoever a man soweth, that shall he also reap.**
Bible: Galatians; see CAUSES 5, CAUSES 11, CAUSES 18

21 **One leak will sink a ship, and one sin will destroy a sinner.**
John Bunyan 1628–88: *The Pilgrim's Progress* (1684)

22 **Whoever wills the end, wills also (so far as reason decides his conduct)**

the means in his power which are indispensably necessary thereto.
Immanuel Kant 1724–1804: *Fundamental Principles of the Metaphysics of Ethics* (1785)

23 Sow an act, and you reap a habit. Sow a habit and you reap a character. Sow a character, and you reap a destiny.
Charles Reade 1814–84: attributed; in *Notes and Queries* 17 October 1903

24 The present contains nothing more than the past, and what is found in the effect was already in the cause.
Henri Bergson 1859–1941: *L'Évolution créatrice* (1907)

25 And that after this is accomplished,
and the brave new world begins
When all men are paid for existing and
no man must pay for his sins,
As surely as Water will wet us, as
surely as Fire will burn,
The Gods of the Copybook Headings
with terror and slaughter return!
Rudyard Kipling 1865–1936: 'The Gods of the Copybook Headings' (1919); see REPUTATION 14

26 You have a row of dominoes set up. You knock over the first one, and what will happen to the last one is that it will go over very quickly. So you have the beginning of a disintegration that would have the most profound influences.
Dwight D. Eisenhower 1890–1969: speech at press conference, 7 April 1954; see INTERNATIONAL 4

27 The structure of a play is always the story of how the birds came home to roost.
Arthur Miller 1915–2005: in *Harper's Magazine* August 1958

28 Every positive value has its price in negative terms...The genius of Einstein leads to Hiroshima.
Pablo Picasso 1881–1973: F. Gilot and C. Lake *Life With Picasso* (1964)

29 I fear we have only awakened a sleeping giant, and his reaction will be terrible.
of the attack on Pearl Harbor, 1941
Larry Forrester: *Tora! Tora! Tora!* (1970 film), spoken by Soh Yamamura as the Japanese admiral Isoruko Yamamoto (1884–1943), although there is no evidence that Yamamoto used these words

30 If you wish to make an apple pie from scratch, you must first invent the universe.
Carl Sagan 1934–96: *Cosmos* (1980)

Caution

see also DANGER

proverbs and sayings ▸

1 Better be safe than sorry.
urging the wisdom of taking precautions; English proverb, mid 19th century

2 A bird in the hand is worth two in the bush.
it is better to accept what one has than to try to get more and risk losing everything; English proverb, mid 15th century; see CERTAINTY 5

3 Call on God, but row away from the rocks.
make an effort to avoid a dangerous situation; Indian proverb

4 A cat in gloves catches no mice.
deliberate restraint and caution (or 'pussyfooting') often result in nothing being achieved; English proverb, late 16th century

5 Caution is the parent of safety.
American proverb, early 18th century

6 Delhi is far away.
warning that unexpected events may intervene; Indian proverb, deriving from the response of the 14th-century Sufi mystic Nizamuddin Aulia to a threat from the Sultan of Delhi: the Sultan died before arriving home. Compare GOVERNMENT 3, GOVERNMENT 4

7 Discretion is the better part of valour.
often used to explain caution, and sometimes with allusion to Shakespeare's *1 Henry IV* (1597), 'The better part of valour is discretion'; English proverb, late 16th century

8 Don't put all your eggs in one basket.
you should not chance everything on a single venture, but spread the risk; English proverb, mid 17th century; see CAUTION 33

9 Full cup, steady hand.
used especially to caution against spoiling a comfortable or otherwise enviable situation by careless action; English proverb, early 11th century

10 **He who fights and runs away, may live to fight another day.**
English proverb, mid 16th century

11 **He who has been scalded by hot milk, blows even on cold lassi before drinking it.**
lassi = an Indian drink, traditionally based on diluted buttermilk or yoghurt, and usually served chilled; Indian proverb; see CAUTION 20, EXPERIENCE 8

12 **He who sups with the Devil should have a long spoon.**
one should be cautious when dealing with dangerous persons; English proverb, late 14th century

13 **If you can't be good, be careful.**
often used as a humorous warning; English proverb, early 20th century. The same idea is found in 11th-century Latin, *si non caste tamen caute*

14 **Let's be careful out there.**
catchphrase from *Hill Street Blues* (police procedural television series, 1981–7), written by Steven Bochco and Michael Kozoll

15 **Let sleeping dogs lie.**
something which may be dangerous or difficult to handle is better left undisturbed; English proverb, late 14th century; see CAUTION 21, CAUTION 23

16 **Let well alone.**
often used as a warning against raising problems which will then be difficult to resolve; English proverb, late 16th century

17 **Look before you leap.**
used to advise caution before committing oneself to a course of action; English proverb, mid 14th century

18 **The more you stir it [a turd] the worse it stinks.**
disturbance of something naturally unpleasant will only make it more disagreeable; English proverb, mid 16th century

19 **Never trouble trouble till trouble troubles you.**
another version of the advice that one should let well alone; English proverb, late 19th century

20 **Once bitten by a snake, a man will be afraid of a piece of rope for three years.**
Chinese proverb; see CAUTION 11, EXPERIENCE 8, TRUST 39

21 **Poke a bush, a snake comes out.**
warning against unnecessary disturbance; Japanese proverb; see CAUTION 15

22 **Safe bind, safe find.**
something kept securely will be readily found again; English proverb, mid 16th century

23 **Saw wood and say nothing.**
warning against unnecessary disturbance; American proverb, late 19th century; see CAUTION 15

24 **Second thoughts are best.**
it is dangerous to act on one's first impulse without due thought; English proverb, late 16th century; see CAUTION 31

25 **A stitch in time saves nine.**
a small but timely intervention will ensure against the need for much more substantial repair later; English proverb, early 18th century

26 **Stop-look-and-listen.**
road safety slogan, current in the US from 1912

27 **Those who play at bowls must look out for rubbers.**
one must beware of difficulties associated with a particular activity; a *rubber* here is an alteration of *rub*, an obstacle or impediment to the course of a bowl; English proverb, mid 18th century

28 **Trust in Allah, but tie up your camel.**
Arab proverb; see PRACTICALITY 3

quotations ▸

29 **Beware of desperate steps. The darkest day**
(Live till tomorrow) will have passed away.
William Cowper 1731–1800: 'The Needless Alarm' (written 1790)

30 **Prudence is a rich, ugly, old maid courted by Incapacity.**
William Blake 1757–1827: *The Marriage of Heaven and Hell* (1790–3) 'Proverbs of Hell'

31 **Have no truck with first impulses for they are always generous ones.**
Casimir, Comte de Montrond 1768–1843: attributed; Comte J. d'Estourmel *Derniers Souvenirs* (1860), where the alternative attribution to Talleyrand is denied; see CAUTION 24

32 **Tar-baby ain't sayin' nuthin', en Brer Fox, he lay low.**
Joel Chandler Harris 1848–1908: *Uncle Remus and His Legends of the Old Plantation* (1881)

33 Put all your eggs in the one basket, and—WATCH THAT BASKET.
Mark Twain 1835–1910: *Pudd'nhead Wilson* (1894); see CAUTION 8

34 Them that asks no questions isn't told a lie.
Watch the wall, my darling, while the Gentlemen go by!
Rudyard Kipling 1865–1936: 'A Smuggler's Song' (1906)

35 Of all forms of caution, caution in love is perhaps the most fatal to true happiness.
Bertrand Russell 1872–1970: *The Conquest of Happiness* (1930)

36 Hesitation increases in relation to risk in equal proportion to age.
Ernest Hemingway 1899–1961: A. E. Hotchner *Papa Hemingway* (1966)

37 You can put up a sign on the door, 'beware of the dog,' without having a dog.
Hans Blix 1928– : in *Guardian* (online edition) 18 September 2003; see DOGS 1

Celebrations
see FESTIVALS AND CELEBRATIONS

Censorship

phrases ▸

1 blue-pencil
censor or make cuts in a manuscript; a blue 'lead' pencil was traditionally used for marking corrections and deletions

2 thought control
the attempt to restrict ideas and impose opinions through censorship and the control of curricula in schools

quotations ▸

3 If these writings of the Greeks agree with the book of God, they are useless and need not be preserved; if they disagree, they are pernicious and ought to be destroyed.
on burning the library of Alexandria, AD 641
Caliph Omar d. 644: Edward Gibbon *The Decline and Fall of the Roman Empire* (1776–88)

4 As good almost kill a man as kill a good book: who kills a man kills a reasonable creature, God's image; but he who destroys a good book, kills reason itself, kills the image of God, as it were in the eye.
John Milton 1608–74: *Areopagitica* (1644)

5 It is a bad cause which cannot bear the words of a dying man.
as drums and trumpets were ordered to sound at his execution to drown anything he might say
Henry Vane 1613–62: Charles Dickens *A Child's History of England* (1853)

6 I disapprove of what you say, but I will defend to the death your right to say it.
his attitude towards Helvétius following the burning of the latter's *De l'esprit* in 1759
Voltaire 1694–1778: attributed to Voltaire, the words are in fact S. G. Tallentyre's summary; *The Friends of Voltaire* (1907)

7 Wherever books will be burned, men also, in the end, are burned.
Heinrich Heine 1797–1856: *Almansor* (1823)

8 As to the evil which results from a censorship, it is impossible to measure it, because it is impossible to tell where it ends.
Jeremy Bentham 1748–1832: *Theory of Legislation* (1864) 'Principles of the Penal Code'

9 Those whom books will hurt will not be proof against events. Events, not books, should be forbid.
Herman Melville 1819–91: *The Piazza Tales* (1856)

10 You have not converted a man, because you have silenced him.
Lord Morley 1838–1923: *On Compromise* (1874)

11 The dirtiest book in all the world is the expurgated book.
Walt Whitman 1819–92: Horace Traubel *With Walt Whitman in Camden* vol. 1 (1906) 9 May 1888

12 Assassination is the extreme form of censorship.
George Bernard Shaw 1856–1950: *The Showing-Up of Blanco Posnet* (1911)

13 It is obvious that 'obscenity' is not a term capable of exact legal definition; in the practice of the Courts, it means 'anything that shocks the magistrate'.

Bertrand Russell 1872–1970: *Sceptical Essays* (1928) 'The Recrudescence of Puritanism'

14 Don't you see that the whole aim of Newspeak is to narrow the range of thought? In the end we shall make thoughtcrime literally impossible, because there will be no words in which to express it.

George Orwell 1903–50: *Nineteen Eighty-Four* (1949)

15 Those who want the Government to regulate matters of the mind and spirit are like men who are so afraid of being murdered that they commit suicide to avoid assassination.

Harry S. Truman 1884–1972: address at the National Archives, Washington, D.C., 15 December 1952

16 Is it a book you would even wish your wife or your servants to read?

of D. H. Lawrence's *Lady Chatterley's Lover*
Mervyn Griffith-Jones 1909–79: speech for the prosecution at the Central Criminal Court, Old Bailey, 20 October 1960

17 The state has no place in the nation's bedrooms.

Pierre Trudeau 1919–2000: interview, Ottawa, 22 December 1967

18 If decade after decade the truth cannot be told, each person's mind begins to roam irretrievably. One's fellow countrymen become harder to understand than Martians.

Alexander Solzhenitsyn 1918–2008: *Cancer Ward* (1968)

19 Vietnam was the first war ever fought without censorship. Without censorship, things can get terribly confused in the public mind.

William C. Westmoreland 1914–2005: attributed, 1982

20 What is freedom of expression? Without the freedom to offend, it ceases to exist.

Salman Rushdie 1947– : in *Weekend Guardian* 10 February 1990

Certainty and Doubt

see also BELIEF, FAITH, INDECISION

proverbs and sayings ▸

1 Does she...or doesn't she?

advertising slogan for Clairol hair colouring, 1950s

2 Don't be vague, ask for Haig.

advertising slogan for Haig whisky, 1936

3 In matters of principle, stand like a rock; in matters of taste, swim with the current.

late 19th century saying, from the mid 20th century associated with Thomas Jefferson, in the form 'In matters of style, swim with the current; in matters of principle, stand like a rock'

4 Nothing is certain but death and taxes.

summarizing what in life is inevitable and inescapable; English proverb, early 18th century; see PREGNANCY 11, TAXES 13

phrases ▸

5 a bird in the hand

something certain (as implicitly contrasted with the prospect of a greater but less certain advantage), from the proverb: see CAUTION 2

6 Lombard Street to a China orange

great wealth against one ordinary object, virtual certainty; *Lombard Street* a street in London, originally occupied by Lombard bankers and still containing many of the principal London banks; *China orange* taken as the type of something worthless

7 twist in the wind

be left in a state of suspense or uncertainty; see HASTE 20

quotations ▸

8 How long halt ye between two opinions?

Bible: I Kings

9 I lived uncertain, I die doubtful: O thou Being of beings, have mercy upon me!

Aristotle 384–322 BC: attributed last words, probably apocryphal; a Latin version was current in the early 17th century

10 O thou of little faith, wherefore didst thou doubt?

Bible: St Matthew

11 The only certainty is that nothing is certain.
Pliny the Elder AD 23–79: *Historia Naturalis*

12 Our doubts are traitors
And make us lose the good we oft
might win
By fearing to attempt.
William Shakespeare 1564–1616: *Measure for Measure* (1604)

13 If a man will begin with certainties, he shall end in doubts; but if he will be content to begin with doubts, he shall end in certainties.
Francis Bacon 1561–1626: *The Advancement of Learning* (1605)

14 I beseech you, in the bowels of Christ, think it possible you may be mistaken.
Oliver Cromwell 1599–1658: letter to the General Assembly of the Kirk of Scotland, 3 August 1650

15 Doubt is not a pleasant condition. But certainty is an absurd one.
Voltaire 1694–1778: letter to Frederick the Great, 28 November 1770

16 Negative Capability, that is when man is capable of being in uncertainties, mysteries, doubts, without any irritable reaching after fact and reason.
John Keats 1795–1821: letter to George and Thomas Keats, 21 December 1817

17 I wish I was as cocksure of anything as Tom Macaulay is of everything.
Lord Melbourne 1779–1848: Lord Cowper's preface to *Lord Melbourne's Papers* (1889)

18 There lives more faith in honest doubt,
Believe me, than in half the creeds.
Alfred, Lord Tennyson 1809–92: *In Memoriam A. H. H.* (1850)

19 Ah, what a dusty answer gets the soul
When hot for certainties in this our
life!
George Meredith 1828–1909: *Modern Love* (1862); see SATISFACTION 12

20 Ten thousand difficulties do not make one doubt.
John Henry Newman 1801–90: *Apologia pro Vita Sua* (1864)

21 What, never?
No, never!
What, *never*?
Hardly ever!
W. S. Gilbert 1836–1911: *HMS Pinafore* (1878)

22 I am too much of a sceptic to deny the possibility of anything.
T. H. Huxley 1825–95: letter to Herbert Spencer, 22 March 1886

23 Oh! let us never, never doubt
What nobody is sure about!
Hilaire Belloc 1870–1953: 'The Microbe' (1897)

24 Life is doubt,
And faith without doubt is nothing but
death.
Miguel de Unamuno 1864–1937: 'Salmo II' (1907)

25 I respect faith but doubt is what gets you an education.
Wilson Mizner 1876–1933: H. L. Mencken *A New Dictionary of Quotations* (1942)

26 My mind is not a bed to be made and re-made.
James Agate 1877–1947: *Ego 6* (1944) 9 June 1943

27 Human beings are perhaps never more frightening than when they are convinced beyond doubt that they are right.
Laurens van der Post 1906–96: *The Lost World of the Kalahari* (1958)

28 The trouble with the world is that the stupid are cocksure and the intelligent are full of doubt.
Bertrand Russell 1872–1970: attributed

Chance and Luck

proverbs and sayings ►

1 Accidents will happen (in the best-regulated families).
the most orderly arrangements cannot prevent accidents from occurring; English proverb, mid 18th century

2 Blind chance sweeps the world along.
American proverb, mid 20th century

3 The devil looks after his own.
often used to comment on the good fortune of someone undeserving; English proverb, early 18th century; see CHANCE 4

4 **The devil's children have the devil's luck.**
commenting on the good fortune of someone undeserving; English proverb, late 17th century; see CHANCE 3

5 **Diligence is the mother of good luck.**
success results more from application and practice than from good fortune; English proverb, late 16th century

6 **Fools for luck.**
a foolish person is traditionally fortunate; English proverb, mid 19th century

7 **A great fortune depends on luck; a small one on diligence.**
for outstanding success we need good luck as well as the capacity for hard work; Chinese proverb

8 **The harder I work, the luckier I get.**
modern saying

9 **It could be you.**
advertising slogan for the British national lottery, 1994

10 **It is better to be born lucky than rich.**
often with the implication that riches can be lost or spent, but that good luck gives one the capacity to improve one's fortunes; English proverb, mid 17th century

11 **Lightning never strikes the same place twice.**
often used as an encouragement that a particular misfortune will not be repeated; English proverb, mid 19th century

12 **Lucky at cards, unlucky in love.**
suggesting that good fortune in gambling is balanced by lack of success in love; English proverb, mid 19th century

13 **See a pin and pick it up, all the day you'll have good luck; see a pin and let it lie, bad luck you'll have all day.**
extolling the virtues of thrift in small matters; English proverb, mid 19th century

14 **There is luck in odd numbers.**
English proverb, late 16th century

15 **Third time lucky.**
reflecting the idea that three is a lucky number; often used to suggest making another effort after initial failure; English proverb, mid 19th century

16 **Throw a lucky man into the sea, and he will come up with a fish in his mouth.**
a fortunate person will have further luck; Arab proverb

17 **You have two chances, Buckley's and none.**
Australian proverb; see CHANCE 20

phrases ▸

18 **Aladdin's lamp**
a talisman enabling the holder to gratify any wish; in the *Arabian Nights*, an old lamp found by Aladdin in a cave, which when rubbed brought a genie to obey his will; see WEALTH 8

19 **a bow at a venture**
a chance attempt at something; from the Bible: see CHANCE 23

20 **Buckley's chance**
in Australia, a slim chance, no chance at all, sometimes said to be from the name of William *Buckley* (died 1856), who, despite dire predictions as to his chances of survival, lived with the Aboriginals for many years; see CHANCE 17

21 **in the lap of the gods**
subject to fate; see FATE 10

22 **wheel of Fortune**
the wheel which the deity Fortune is represented as turning as a symbol of random luck or change; see CIRCUMSTANCE 9

quotations ▸

23 **And a certain man drew a bow at a venture, and smote the king of Israel between the joints of the harness.**
Bible: I Kings; see CHANCE 19

24 **Cast thy bread upon the waters: for thou shalt find it after many days.**
Bible: Ecclesiastes; see FUTURE 9

25 **Is he lucky?**
first question on being requested to take anyone into his service, later associated with Napoleon
Cardinal Mazarin 1602–61: attributed; Elizabeth Charlotte, Duchess of Orleans *Secret Memoirs of the Court of Louis XIV, and of the Regency* (1824)

26 **Care and diligence bring luck.**
Thomas Fuller 1654–1734: *Gnomologia* (1732)

27 **The chapter of knowledge is a very short, but the chapter of accidents is a very long one.**
Lord Chesterfield 1694–1773: letter to Solomon Dayrolles, 16 February 1753; see MISFORTUNES 10

28 O! many a shaft, at random sent,
Finds mark the archer little meant!
And many a word, at random spoken,
May soothe or wound a heart that's
broken.

Sir Walter Scott 1771–1832: *The Lord of the Isles* (1813)

29 All you know about it [luck] for certain is that it's bound to change.

Bret Harte 1836–1902: *The Outcasts of Poker Flat* (1871)

30 Some folk want their luck buttered.

Thomas Hardy 1840–1928: *The Mayor of Casterbridge* (1886)

31 A throw of the dice will never eliminate chance.

Stéphane Mallarmé 1842–98: title of poem (1897)

32 If there were no coincidence, it would be the greatest coincidence of all.

G. K. Chesterton 1874–1936: 'The Human Will and the Decline of Empire' in *Illustrated London News* 4 August 1906

33 At any rate, I am convinced that *He* [God] does not play dice.

often quoted as 'God does not play dice'
Albert Einstein 1879–1955: letter to Max Born, 4 December 1926

34 If an army of monkeys were strumming on typewriters they *might* write all the books in the British Museum.

Arthur Eddington 1882–1944: *The Nature of the Physical World* (1928); see COMPUTERS 17

35 Miracles do happen, but one has to work very hard for them.

Chaim Weizmann 1874–1952: Isaiah Berlin *Personal Impressions* (1998)

36 Mr Bond, they have a saying in Chicago: 'Once is happenstance. Twice is coincidence. The third time it's enemy action.'

Ian Fleming 1908–64: *Goldfinger* (1959)

37 Predictability: Does the flap of a butterfly's wings in Brazil set off a tornado in Texas?

Edward N. Lorenz 1917–2008: title of paper given to the American Association for the Advancement of Science, Washington, 29 December 1979; see CAUSES 13

38 What we call luck is the inner man externalized. We make things happen to us.

Robertson Davies 1913–95: *What's Bred in the Bone* (1985)

39 Luck is preparation meeting opportunity.

Oprah Winfrey 1954– : interview, Academy of Achievement, 21 February 1991

Change

see also BEGINNING, ENDING, PROGRESS

proverbs and sayings ▸

1 And now for something completely different.

catchphrase popularized in *Monty Python's Flying Circus* (BBC TV programme, 1969–74)

2 A change is as good as a rest.

suggesting that a change of activity can be refreshing; English proverb, late 19th century

3 It is never too late to mend.

one can always try to improve; English proverb, late 16th century

4 The leopard does not change his spots.

a person cannot change their essential nature, from the Bible: see CHANGE 20, CHANGE 28, CHARACTER 4; English proverb, mid 16th century

5 Never say never.

used as a warning against over-confidence that circumstances cannot change; late 20th century saying; see TIME 4

6 New brooms sweep clean.

often used in the context of someone newly appointed to a post who is making changes in personnel and procedures; English proverb, mid 16th century

7 New lords, new laws.

new authorities are likely to change existing rules; English proverb, mid 16th century

8 No matter how long a log floats in the river, it will never become a crocodile.

essential characteristics will not change; African proverb; see CHARACTER 8

9 No more Mr Nice Guy.

said to assert that one will no longer be amiable or cooperative; mid 20th century saying

10 Nothing is for ever.

late 20th century saying

11 **Other times, other manners.**
used in resignation or consolation; English proverb, late 16th century

12 **Semper eadem.**
Latin, *ever the same*, motto of Elizabeth I (1533–1603)

13 **There are no birds in last year's nest.**
circumstances have changed, and former opportunities are no longer there; English proverb, early 17th century

14 **Three removals are as bad as a fire.**
moving house is so disruptive and unsettling, that the effects of doing it three times are as destructive as a house fire; English proverb, mid 18th century

15 **Times change and we with time.**
we adapt in response to changes in the world around us; English proverb, late 16th century

16 **Variety is the spice of life.**
English proverb, late 18th century, originally with allusion to Cowper: see CHANGE 35

17 **You can't put new wine in old bottles.**
often used in relation to the introduction of new ideas or practices; English proverb, early 20th century, from the Bible (Matthew) 'Neither do men put new wine into old bottles: else the bottles break, and the wine runneth out, and the bottles perish'; see CHANGE 25

phrases ▸

18 **be subdued to what one works in**
become reduced in capacity or ability to the standard of one's material; in allusion to Shakespeare *Sonnets*: see CIRCUMSTANCE 26

19 **change horses in midstream**
change one's ideas or plans in the middle of a project or process; also in proverbial form, 'Don't change horses in midstream'

20 **change one's skin**
undergo a change of character regarded as fundamentally impossible, probably originally with reference to the Bible (Jeremiah): see CHANGE 4, CHANGE 28

21 **fresh fields and pastures new**
new areas of activity, from a misquotation of Milton: see CHANGE 31

22 **the law of the Medes and Persians**
a rule which cannot be altered in any circumstances, from the Bible (Daniel) 'The thing is true, according to the law of the Medes and Persians, which altereth not'

23 **mover and shaker**
a person who influences events, a person who gets things done; see MUSICIANS 7

24 **move the goalposts**
unfairly alter the conditions or rules of a procedure during its course. The term has been current since the late 1980s, and provides a useful image for the idea of making an important (and usually unheralded) alteration to terms and conditions previously agreed

25 **new wine in old bottles**
something new or innovatory added to an existing or established system or organization; from the proverb: see CHANGE 17

26 **road to Damascus**
a sudden and complete personal conversion to a cause or principle which one has formerly rejected, in allusion to the conversion of St Paul on the road to Damascus, told in the Bible (Acts)

27 **sea change**
a profound or notable transformation, from Shakespeare's *Tempest*: see SEA 11

quotations ▸

28 **Can the Ethiopian change his skin, or the leopard his spots?**
Bible: Jeremiah; see CHANGE 4, CHANGE 20

29 **Everything flows and nothing stays… You can't step twice into the same river.**
Heraclitus c.540–c.480 BC: Plato *Cratylus*

30 **He that will not apply new remedies must expect new evils; for time is the greatest innovator.**
Francis Bacon 1561–1626: *Essays* (1625) 'Of Innovations'

31 **At last he rose, and twitched his**
mantle blue:
Tomorrow to fresh woods, and
pastures new.
John Milton 1608–74: 'Lycidas' (1638); see CHANGE 21

32 **When it is not necessary to change, it is necessary not to change.**
Lucius Cary, Lord Falkland 1610–43: 'A Speech concerning Episcopacy' delivered in 1641

33 **Change is not made without inconvenience, even from worse to better.**
Samuel Johnson 1709–84: *A Dictionary of the English Language* (1755)

34 If we do not find anything pleasant, at least we shall find something new.
Voltaire 1694–1778: *Candide* (1759)

35 Variety's the very spice of life,
That gives it all its flavour.
William Cowper 1731–1800: *The Task* (1785) bk. 2 'The Timepiece'; see CHANGE 16

36 There is a certain relief in change, even though it be from bad to worse... it is often a comfort to shift one's position and be bruised in a new place.
Washington Irving 1783–1859: *Tales of a Traveller* (1824)

37 There are three things which the public will always clamour for, sooner or later: namely, novelty, novelty, novelty.
Thomas Hood 1799–1845: *Announcement of Comic Annual for 1836*

38 A foolish consistency is the hobgoblin of little minds, adored by little statesmen and philosophers and divines. With consistency a great soul has simply nothing to do.
Ralph Waldo Emerson 1803–82: *Essays* (1841) 'Self-Reliance'

39 Forward, forward let us range,
Let the great world spin for ever down the ringing grooves of change.
Alfred, Lord Tennyson 1809–92: 'Locksley Hall' (1842)

40 Change and decay in all around I see;
O Thou, who changest not, abide with me.
Henry Francis Lyte 1793–1847: 'Abide with Me' (probably written in 1847)

41 *Plus ça change, plus c'est la même chose.*
The more things change, the more they are the same.
Alphonse Karr 1808–90: *Les Guêpes* January 1849

42 The old order changeth, yielding place to new,
And God fulfils himself in many ways,
Lest one good custom should corrupt the world.
Alfred, Lord Tennyson 1809–92: *Idylls of the King* 'The Passing of Arthur' (1869)

43 All conservatism is based upon the idea that if you leave things alone you leave them as they are. But you do not. If you leave a thing alone you leave it to a torrent of change.
G. K. Chesterton 1874–1936: *Orthodoxy* (1908)

44 Most of the change we think we see in life
Is due to truths being in and out of favour.
Robert Frost 1874–1963: 'The Black Cottage' (1914)

45 All changed, changed utterly:
A terrible beauty is born.
W. B. Yeats 1865–1939: 'Easter, 1916' (1921)

46 Consistency is contrary to nature, contrary to life. The only completely consistent people are the dead.
Aldous Huxley 1894–1963: *Do What You Will* (1929)

47 Toto, I've a feeling we're not in Kansas any more.
Noel Langley 1911–80: *The Wizard of Oz* (1939 film), spoken by Judy Garland as Dorothy

48 We must be the change we wish to see in the world.
Mahatma Gandhi 1869–1948: not traced in Gandhi's writings, but said to be a favourite saying; attributed (1989) in *Yale Book of Quotations*

49 God, give us the serenity to accept what cannot be changed;
Give us the courage to change what should be changed;
Give us the wisdom to distinguish one from the other.
Reinhold Niebuhr 1892–1971: prayer said to have been first published in 1951; Richard Wightman Fox *Reinhold Niebuhr* (1985)

50 If we want things to stay as they are, things will have to change.
Giuseppe di Lampedusa 1896–1957: *The Leopard* (1957)

51 He not busy being born
Is busy dying.
Bob Dylan 1941– : 'It's Alright Ma (I'm Only Bleeding)' (1965 song)

Chaos

see ORDER AND CHAOS

Character

see also HUMAN NATURE

proverbs and sayings ►

1 **An ape's an ape, a varlet's a varlet, though they be clad in silk or scarlet.**
inward nature cannot be overcome by outward show; English proverb, mid 16th century

2 **A bad penny always turns up.**
referring to the inevitable return of an unwanted or disreputable person; English proverb, mid 18th century

3 **Better a good cow than a cow of a good kind.**
good character is more important than distinguished lineage; English proverb, early 20th century

4 **By seeing one spot, you know the entire leopard.**
Japanese proverb; see CHANGE 4

5 **Character is what we are; reputation is what others think we are.**
American proverb, mid 20th century

6 **The child is the father of the man.**
asserting the unity of character from childhood to adult life; English proverb, early 19th century, from Wordsworth: see CHILDREN 14

7 **Eagles don't catch flies.**
great or important persons do not concern themselves with trifling matters; English proverb, mid 16th century

8 **Feeding a snake with milk will not change its poisonous nature.**
kindness will not alter a bad character; Indian proverb; see CHANGE 8

9 **Iron sharpens iron.**
friends of the same calibre can strengthen one another; modern saying, from the Bible (Proverbs) 'Iron sharpeneth iron; so a man sharpeneth the countenance of his friend'

10 **It takes all sorts to make a world.**
often used in recognition that a particular group may encompass a wide range of character and background; English proverb, early 17th century

11 **Like a fence, character cannot be strengthened by whitewash.**
American proverb, mid 20th century

12 **The man who is born in a stable is not a horse.**
sometimes attributed to the Duke of Wellington, who asserted that being born in Ireland did not make him Irish; English proverb, mid 19th century

13 **Once a —, always a —.**
a particular way of life produces traits that cannot be eradicated; English proverb, early 17th century, see CLERGY 4

14 **The same fire that hardens the egg melts the butter.**
different people will react in different ways to the same experiences; modern saying, see SIMILARITY 19

15 **Still waters run deep.**
now commonly used to assert that a placid exterior hides a passionate nature; English proverb, early 15th century

16 **A stream cannot rise above its source.**
used to suggest that a person's natural level is set by their ultimate origin; English proverb, mid 17th century

17 **The tree is known by its fruit.**
a person is judged by what they do and produce; English proverb, early 16th century

18 **There's many a good cock come out of a tattered bag.**
something good may emerge from unpromising surroundings (the reference is to cockfighting); English proverb, late 19th century

19 **What can you expect from a pig but a grunt.**
used rhetorically of coarse or boorish behaviour; English proverb, mid 18th century

20 **What's bred in the bone will come out in the flesh.**
inherent characteristics will in the end become apparent; English proverb, late 15th century

21 **When the going gets tough, the tough get going.**
pressure acts as a stimulus to the strong; English proverb, mid 20th century, often used by Joseph Kennedy (1888–1969) as an injunction to his children

phrases ►

22 **a curate's egg**
something of very mixed character, partly good and partly bad; from the *Punch* cartoon: see SATISFACTION 34

23 **feet of clay**
fundamental weakness in a person who has appeared to be of great merit; from the Bible (Daniel) 'This image's head was of fine gold... his feet part of iron and part of clay'

24 **heart of oak**
a person with a strong, courageous nature; literally, the solid central part of the tree; see ARMED FORCES 20

25 **Jekyll-and-Hyde**
someone with violent and unpredictable changes of mood and personality; from the central character of Robert Louis Stevenson's story *The Strange Case of Dr Jekyll and Mr Hyde* (1886). He discovers a drug which creates a separate personality (appearing in the character of Mr Hyde) into which Jekyll's evil impulses are channelled

26 **a man for all seasons**
a person who is ready for any situation or contingency, or adaptable to any circumstance; from Whittington on Thomas More: see CHARACTER 32

27 **neither fish, nor flesh, nor good red herring**
of indefinite character; from distinctions made by early religious dietary laws; see FOOD 10, LOGIC 7

28 **of shreds and patches**
made up of rags or scraps, patched together; from Shakespeare *Hamlet* 'A King of shreds and patches'; see SINGING 9

quotations ▸

29 A man's character is his fate.
Heraclitus c.540–c.480 BC: *On the Universe*

30 I am made all things to all men.
Bible: I Corinthians; see CONFORMITY 3

31 He was a verray, parfit gentil knyght.
Geoffrey Chaucer 1343–1400: *The Canterbury Tales* 'The General Prologue'

32 As time requireth, a man of marvellous mirth and pastimes, and sometime of as sad gravity, as who say: a man for all seasons.
of Sir Thomas More
Robert Whittington c.1480–1553?: *Vulgaria* (1521); see CHARACTER 26

33 Nature is often hidden, sometimes overcome, seldom extinguished.
Francis Bacon 1561–1626: *Essays* (1625) 'Of Nature in Men'

34 Youth, what man's age is like to be
doth show;
We may our ends by our beginnings
know.
John Denham 1615–69: 'Of Prudence' (1668)

35 There are people whose defects become them, and others who are ill served by their good qualities.
Duc de la Rochefoucauld 1613–80: *Maxims* (1678)

36 A propensity to hope and joy is real riches: one to fear and sorrow, real poverty.
David Hume 1711–76: 'The Sceptic' (1741–2)

37 It is not in the still calm of life, or the repose of a pacific station, that great characters are formed...Great necessities call out great virtues.
Abigail Adams 1744–1818: letter to John Quincy Adams, 19 January 1780

38 Talent develops in quiet places, character in the full current of human life.
Johann Wolfgang von Goethe 1749–1832: *Torquato Tasso* (1790)

39 Nothing gives one person so great advantage over another, as to remain always cool and unruffled under all circumstances.
Thomas Jefferson 1743–1826: letter to Francis Wayles Eppes, 21 May 1816

40 I am not at all the sort of person you and I took me for.
Jane Carlyle 1801–66: letter to Thomas Carlyle, 7 May 1822

41 Though I've belted you and flayed you,
By the livin' Gawd that made you,
You're a better man than I am, Gunga
Din!
Rudyard Kipling 1865–1936: 'Gunga Din' (1892)

42 A man of great common sense and good taste, meaning thereby a man without originality or moral courage.
George Bernard Shaw 1856–1950: *Notes to Caesar and Cleopatra* (1901) 'Julius Caesar'

43 The two kinds of people on earth I
mean
Are the people who lift, and the
people who lean.
Ella Wheeler Wilcox 1855–1919: 'Which Are You?' (1904)

44 McKinley has no more backbone than a chocolate éclair!

Theodore Roosevelt 1858–1919: H. T. Peck *Twenty Years of the Republic* (1906)

45 If you can trust yourself when all men doubt you,
But make allowance for their doubting too;
If you can wait and not be tired by waiting,
Or being lied about, don't deal in lies,
Or being hated, don't give way to hating,
And yet don't look too good, nor talk too wise.

Rudyard Kipling 1865–1936: 'If—' (1910)

46 Slice him where you like, a hellhound is always a hellhound.

P. G. Wodehouse 1881–1975: *The Code of the Woosters* (1938)

47 It is the nature, and the advantage, of strong people that they can bring out the crucial questions and form a clear opinion about them. The weak always have to decide between alternatives that are not their own.

Dietrich Bonhoeffer 1906–45: *Widerstand und Ergebung* (Resistance and Submission, 1951)

48 There exists a great chasm between those, on one side, who relate everything to a single central vision... and, on the other side, those who pursue many ends, often unrelated and even contradictory...The first kind of intellectual and artistic personality belongs to the hedgehogs, the second to the foxes.

Isaiah Berlin 1909–97: *The Hedgehog and the Fox* (1953); see KNOWLEDGE 14

49 A thick skin is a gift from God.

Konrad Adenauer 1876–1967: in *New York Times* 30 December 1959

50 We are what we pretend to be.

Kurt Vonnegut 1922–2007: *Mother Night* (1961)

51 We are all worms. But I do believe that I am a glow-worm.

Winston Churchill 1874–1965: Violet Bonham-Carter *Winston Churchill as I Knew Him* (1965)

52 Those who stand for nothing fall for anything.

Alex Hamilton 1936– : 'Born Old' (radio broadcast), in *Listener* 9 November 1978

53 You can tell a lot about a fellow's character by his way of eating jellybeans.

Ronald Reagan 1911–2004: in *New York Times* 15 January 1981

54 Do not underestimate the determination of a quiet man.

Iain Duncan Smith 1954– : speech to the Conservative Party Conference, 10 October 2002

Charity

see also GIFTS

proverbs and sayings ▸

1 Charity begins at home.

you should look first to needs in your immediate vicinity; English proverb, late 14th century

2 Charity is not a bone you throw to a dog but a bone you share with a dog.

the recipient of one's charity should not be treated as an inferior; American proverb, mid 20th century

3 Charity sees the need, not the cause.

true charity succours need regardless of whether the needy person is responsible for their own situation; German proverb

4 Give a man a fish, and you feed him for a day; show him how to catch fish, and you feed him for a lifetime.

mid 20th century saying, perhaps deriving from a Chinese proverb: see TEACHING 6

5 Keep your own fish-guts for your own sea-maws.

any surplus product should be offered first to those in need who are closest to you; Scottish proverb, early 18th century

6 The roots of charity are always green.

true generosity constantly renews itself; American proverb, mid 20th century

7 Service is the rent we pay for our room on earth.

modern saying, deriving from the admission ceremony of Toc H, a society, originally of ex-servicemen and women, founded by Tubby Clayton (1885–1972) after the First World War to promote Christian fellowship and social service

phrases ▸

8 **blood out of a stone**
pity from the hard-hearted or money from the impecunious or avaricious; see FUTILITY 5

9 **a good Samaritan**
a charitable or helpful person; from the Bible (Luke) 'A certain Samaritan...had compassion on him', in the parable of the man who fell among thieves, in which the succouring Samaritan had been preceded by a priest and a Levite, both of whom 'passed by on the other side'; see CHARITY 22, INDIFFERENCE 6

10 **ladies who lunch**
women who organize and take part in fashionable lunches to raise funds for charitable projects; from 'The Ladies who Lunch', 1970 song by Stephen Sondheim (1930–) 'A toast to that invincible bunch...Let's hear it for the ladies who lunch'

11 **Lady Bountiful**
a patronizingly generous woman, named from a character in Farquhar's *The Beaux' Stratagem* (1707)

12 **a ministering angel**
a kind-hearted person, especially a woman, who nurses or comforts others; originally from Shakespeare *Hamlet* 'A ministering angel shall my sister be, When thou liest howling'; later reinforced by Scott: see WOMEN 28

13 **a widow's mite**
a person's modest contribution to a cause or charity, representing the most the giver can manage; from the Bible (Mark) in the parable of the poor widow who contributed two *mites* (coins of low value) to the treasury, and of whom Jesus said that 'this poor widow hath cast more in, than all they which have cast into the treasury', because she 'of her want did cast in all that she had'

quotations ▸

14 When thou doest alms, let not thy left hand know what thy right hand doeth.
Bible: St Matthew

15 Friends, I have lost a day.
on reflecting that he had done nothing to help anybody all day
Titus AD 39–81: Suetonius *Lives of the Caesars* 'Titus'

16 Thy necessity is yet greater than mine.
on giving his water-bottle to a dying soldier on the battle-field of Zutphen, 1586; commonly quoted 'thy need is greater than mine'
Philip Sidney 1554–86: Fulke Greville *Life of Sir Philip Sidney* (1652)

17 'Tis not enough to help the feeble up,
But to support him after.
William Shakespeare 1564–1616: *Timon of Athens* (1607)

18 The living need charity more than the dead.
George Arnold 1834–65: 'The Jolly Old Pedagogue' (1866)

19 Without trampling down twelve others
You cannot help one poor man.
Bertolt Brecht 1898–1956: *The Good Woman of Setzuan* (1938)

20 I have always depended on the kindness of strangers.
Tennessee Williams 1911–83: *A Streetcar Named Desire* (1947)

21 We ourselves feel that what we are doing is just a drop in the ocean. But if that drop was not in the ocean, I think the ocean would be less because of that missing drop.
Mother Teresa 1910–97: *A Gift for God* (1975)

22 No one would remember the Good Samaritan if he'd only had good intentions. He had money as well.
Margaret Thatcher 1925– : television interview, 6 January 1980; see CHARITY 9

23 Feed the world
Let them know it's Christmas time again.
Bob Geldof 1954– and **Midge Ure** 1953– : 'Do They Know it's Christmas?' (1984 song)

24 Charity begins today. Today somebody is suffering, today somebody is in the street, today somebody is hungry. Our work is for today, yesterday has gone, tomorrow has not yet come. We have only today.
Mother Teresa 1910–97: in *Osservatore Romano* 8 April 1991; see PRESENT 4

25 My idea is to have nothing left. Absolutely nothing. Money is counterproductive—it prevents happiness to come.
on giving away his £3 million fortune to charity
Karl Rabeder: in *Daily Telegraph* 8 February 2010

Child Care

see also CHILDREN, FAMILY, PARENTS

proverbs and sayings ▸

1 It takes a (whole) village to raise a child.
many in the community have a role in a child's development; African proverb (Yoruba)

2 Spare the rod and spoil the child.
the result of not disciplining a child is to spoil it; English proverb, early 11th century; see CRIME 20

quotations ▸

3 Train up a child in the way he should go: and when he is old, he will not depart from it.
Bible: Proverbs

4 Diogenes struck the father when the son swore.
Robert Burton 1577–1640: *The Anatomy of Melancholy* (1621–51)

5 Who ran to help me when I fell,
And would some pretty story tell,
Or kiss the place to make it well?
My Mother.
Ann Taylor 1782–1866 and **Jane Taylor** 1783–1824: 'My Mother' (1804)

6 There never was a child so lovely but his mother was glad to get him asleep.
Ralph Waldo Emerson 1803–82: *Journal* 1836

7 You will find as the children grow up that as a rule children are a bitter disappointment—their greatest object being to do precisely what their parents do not wish and have anxiously tried to prevent.
Queen Victoria 1819–1901: letter to the Crown Princess of Prussia, 5 January 1876

8 If you must hold yourself up to your children as an object lesson (which is not at all necessary), hold yourself up as a warning and not as an example.
George Bernard Shaw 1856–1950: *Parents and Children* (1914)

9 If there is anything that we wish to change in the child, we should first examine it and see whether it is not something that could better be changed in ourselves.
Carl Gustav Jung 1875–1961: 'Vom Werden der Persönlichkeit' (1932)

10 Oh, what a tangled web do parents weave
When they think that their children are naïve.
Ogden Nash 1902–71: 'Baby, What Makes the Sky Blue' (1940); after Scott: see DECEPTION 19

11 There is no finer investment for any community than putting milk into babies.
Winston Churchill 1874–1965: radio broadcast, 21 March 1943

12 You know more than you think you do.
Benjamin Spock 1903–98: *Baby and Child Care* (1946) opening words

13 If you bungle raising your children I don't think whatever else you do well matters very much.
Jacqueline Kennedy Onassis 1929–94: Theodore C. Sorenson *Kennedy* (1965)

14 They fuck you up, your mum and dad.
They may not mean to, but they do.
They fill you with the faults they had
And add some extra, just for you.
Philip Larkin 1922–85: 'This Be The Verse' (1974)

15 I don't work that way...The very idea that all children want to be cuddled by a complete stranger, I find completely amazing.
on her work for Save the Children
Anne, Princess Royal 1950– : in *Daily Telegraph* 17 January 1998

16 Kids are the best, Apu. You can teach them to hate the things you hate. And they practically raise themselves, what with the internet and all.
Homer Simpson
Matt Groening 1954– : *The Simpsons* 'Eight Misbehavin'' (1999) written by Matt Selman

Children

see also CHILD CARE, FAMILY, PARENTS, SCHOOLS, YOUTH

proverbs and sayings ▸

1 Children should be seen and not heard.
originally applied specifically to (young) women; English proverb, early 15th century

2 Children: one is one, two is fun, three is a houseful.
American proverb, mid 20th century

phrases ▶

3 the young idea
the child's mind, from Thomson: see TEACHING 11

quotations ▶

4 Like as the arrows in the hand of the giant: even so are the young children. Happy is the man that hath his quiver full of them.
Bible: Psalm 127

5 Suffer the little children to come unto me, and forbid them not: for of such is the kingdom of God.
Bible: St Mark

6 A child is owed the greatest respect; if you ever have something disgraceful in mind, don't ignore your son's tender years.
Juvenal c. AD 60–c. 140: *Satires*

7 A child is not a vase to be filled, but a fire to be lit.
François Rabelais c. 1494–c. 1553: attributed; see MIND 8

8 It should be noted that children at play are not playing about; their games should be seen as their most serious-minded activity.
Montaigne 1533–92: *Essays* (1580)

9 At first the infant,
Mewling and puking in the nurse's arms.
And then the whining schoolboy, with his satchel,
And shining morning face, creeping like snail
Unwillingly to school.
William Shakespeare 1564–1616: *As You Like It* (1599)

10 Children sweeten labours, but they make misfortunes more bitter.
Francis Bacon 1561–1626: *Essays* (1625) 'Of Parents and Children'

11 Men are generally more careful of the breed of their horses and dogs than of their children.
William Penn 1644–1718: *Some Fruits of Solitude* (1693)

12 Behold the child, by Nature's kindly law
Pleased with a rattle, tickled with a straw.
Alexander Pope 1688–1744: *An Essay on Man* Epistle 2 (1733)

13 Alas, regardless of their doom,
The little victims play!
Thomas Gray 1716–71: *Ode on a Distant Prospect of Eton College* (1747)

14 The Child is father of the Man;
And I could wish my days to be
Bound each to each by natural piety.
William Wordsworth 1770–1850: 'My heart leaps up when I behold' (1807); see CHARACTER 6

15 Oh, for an hour of Herod!
at the first night of J. M. Barrie's *Peter Pan* in 1904; see FESTIVALS 30
Anthony Hope 1863–1933: Denis Mackail *The Story of JMB* (1941)

16 Childhood is the kingdom where nobody dies.
Nobody that matters, that is.
Edna St Vincent Millay 1892–1950: 'Childhood is the Kingdom where Nobody dies' (1934)

17 There is always one moment in childhood when the door opens and lets the future in.
Graham Greene 1904–91: *The Power and the Glory* (1940)

18 Our greatest natural resource is the minds of our children.
Walt Disney 1901–66: in 1959, on wall of American Adventure, Epcot Centre, Walt Disney World

19 Childhood is measured out by sounds and smells
And sights, before the dark of reason grows.
John Betjeman 1906–84: *Summoned by Bells* (1960)

20 Literature is mostly about having sex and not much about having children. Life is the other way round.
David Lodge 1935– : *The British Museum is Falling Down* (1965)

21 A child becomes an adult when he realizes that he has a right not only to be right but also to be wrong.
Thomas Szasz 1920– : *The Second Sin* (1973)

22 There is no such thing as other people's children.
Hillary Rodham Clinton 1947– : in *Newsweek* 15 January 1996

23 We don't need any more kids—we have plenty of people on this planet.
Cameron Diaz 1972– : in *Cosmopolitan* July 2009

Choice
see also INDECISION

proverbs and sayings ▸

1 Different strokes for different folks.
different ways of doing something are appropriate for different people (the saying is of US origin, and *strokes* here means, 'comforting gestures of approval'); late 20th century saying

2 A door must be either shut or open.
said of two mutually exclusive alternatives; English proverb, mid 18th century

3 He that has a choice has trouble.
choosing between two things or persons may cause difficulties; American proverb, mid 20th century

4 No man can serve two masters.
English proverb, early 14th century; see MONEY 27

5 Of two evils choose the less.
English proverb, late 14th century; see CHOICE 11, CHOICE 22

6 Small choice in rotten apples.
if all options are unpalatable there is little choice to be had; English proverb, late 16th century

7 They offered death so you would be happy with a fever.
a worse possibility makes something inherently unwelcome acceptable; Persian proverb

8 Whose finger do you want on the trigger?
headline in *Daily Mirror* 21 September 1951, alluding to the atom bomb, apropos the failure of both the Labour and Conservative parties to purge their leaders of proven failures

9 You pays your money and you takes your choice.
said when there is little or nothing to choose between two options; English proverb, mid 19th century

phrases ▸

10 Hobson's choice
the option of taking what is offered or nothing; no choice; from *Hobson* (1554–1631), a Cambridge carrier who gave his customers a choice between the next horse or none at all

11 the lesser of two evils
the less harmful of two evil things; the alternative that has fewer drawbacks; see CHOICE 5, CHOICE 22

12 Morton's fork
a situation in which there are two choices or alternatives whose consequences are equally unpleasant, from John *Morton* (1420–1500) Archbishop of Canterbury and minister of Henry VII; *Morton's fork* = the argument (used by Morton to extract loans) that the obviously rich must have money and the frugal must have savings

quotations ▸

13 For many are called, but few are chosen.
Bible: St Matthew

14 To be, or not to be: that is the question.
William Shakespeare 1564–1616: *Hamlet* (1601)

15 How happy could I be with either,
Were t'other dear charmer away!
John Gay 1685–1732: *The Beggar's Opera* (1728)

16 From this day you must be a stranger to one of your parents.—Your mother will never see you again if you do *not* marry Mr Collins, and I will never see you again if you *do*.
Jane Austen 1775–1817: *Pride and Prejudice* (1813)

17 What man wants is simply *independent* choice, whatever that independence may cost and wherever it may lead.
Fedor Dostoevsky 1821–81: *Notes from Underground* (1864)

18 White shall not neutralize the black, nor good
Compensate bad in man, absolve him so:
Life's business being just the terrible choice.
Robert Browning 1812–89: *The Ring and the Book* (1868–9)

19 Any customer can have a car painted any colour that he wants so long as it is black.
on the Model T Ford, 1909
Henry Ford 1863–1947: *My Life and Work* (with Samuel Crowther, 1922)

20 Two roads diverged in a wood, and I—
I took the one less travelled by,
And that has made all the difference.

Robert Frost 1874–1963: 'The Road Not Taken' (1916)

21 If it has to choose who is to be crucified, the crowd will always save Barabbas.

Jean Cocteau 1889–1963: *Le Rappel à l'ordre* (1926)

22 Between two evils, I always pick the one I never tried before.

Mae West 1892–1980: *Klondike Annie* (1936 film); see CHOICE 5, CHOICE 11

23 If one cannot catch the bird of paradise, better take a wet hen.

Nikita Khrushchev 1894–1971: in *Time* 6 January 1958

24 Chips with everything.

Arnold Wesker 1932– : title of play (1962)

25 Was there ever in anyone's life span a point free in time, devoid of memory, a night when choice was any more than the sum of all the choices gone before?

Joan Didion 1934– : *Run River* (1963)

26 I'll make him an offer he can't refuse.

Mario Puzo 1920–99: *The Godfather* (1969)

27 There is no real alternative.

popularly encapsulated in the acronym TINA
Margaret Thatcher 1925– : speech at Conservative Women's Conference, 21 May 1980

28 A compromise in the sense that being bitten in half by a shark is a compromise with being swallowed whole.

P. J. O'Rourke 1947– : *Parliament of Whores* (1991)

29 DUMBLEDORE: It is our choices, Harry, that show what we truly are, far more than our abilities.

J. K. Rowling 1965– : *Harry Potter and the Chamber of Secrets* (1998)

The Christian Church

see also CLERGY, GOD, RELIGION

proverbs and sayings ▸

1 The blood of the martyrs is the seed of the Church.

persecution causes the Church to grow; English proverb, mid 16th century: see CHRISTIAN CHURCH 14

2 Christ has no body now on earth but yours, no hands but yours, no feet but yours, yours are the eyes through which he looks compassion on this world, yours are the feet with which he is to go about doing good.

modern saying, often attributed to St Teresa of Ávila (1512–82), but not found in her writings

3 The Christians to the lions!

saying reported by the Roman theologian Tertullian (c.160–c.225): 'If the Tiber rises, if the Nile does not rise, if the heavens give no rain, if there is an earthquake, famine, or pestilence, straightway the cry is...' *Apologeticus* ch. 40; see DANGER 26, HASTE 16

4 The church is an anvil which has worn out many hammers.

the passive strength of Christianity will outlast aggression; English proverb, mid 19th century; see CHRISTIAN CHURCH 17

5 The nearer the church, the farther from God.

sometimes used to indicate a lack of true spirituality where it is most likely to be found; English proverb, early 14th century

6 Meat and mass never hindered man.

indicating human need for physical and spiritual sustenance; English proverb, early 17th century

phrases ▸

7 God's Acre

a churchyard; German *Gottesacker* = 'God's seed-field' in which the bodies of the dead are 'sown'; from the Bible (I Corinthians)

8 muscular Christianity

Christian life characterized by cheerful physical activity or robust good works; Christianity without asceticism; as described in the writings of Charles Kingsley; see CHRISTIAN CHURCH 25

9 the Old Hundredth

the traditional tune to which the hymn 'All people that on earth do dwell' is sung, and the hymn itself. The hymn (which appears first in the Geneva Psalter of 1561) is an early metrical version of Psalm 100

10 the second Adam

Jesus Christ; from the Bible (I Corinthians) 'The first man Adam was made a living soul; the last Adam was made a quickening spirit... The second man is the Lord from heaven'; see HUMAN NATURE 5

11 **the Sermon on the Mount**
the discourse in the Bible (Matthew) in which teachings of Jesus, including the Lord's Prayer and the Beatitudes, are presented. It is introduced by the words, 'he went up into a mountain ...and taught them, saying'; see SCIENCE AND RELIGION 14

quotations ▸

12 Thou art Peter, and upon this rock I will build my church; and the gates of hell shall not prevail against it.
Bible: St Matthew

13 I am the way, the truth, and the life: no man cometh unto the Father, but by me.
Bible: St John; see also CUSTOM 9

14 As often as we are mown down by you, the more we grow in numbers; the blood of Christians is the seed.
Tertullian C.AD 160–c.225: *Apologeticus*; see CHRISTIAN CHURCH 1

15 He cannot have God for his father who has not the church for his mother.
St Cyprian C.AD 200–258: *De Ecclesiae Catholicae Unitate*

16 *In hoc signo vinces.*
In this sign shalt thou conquer.
traditional form of Constantine's vision of the cross (AD 312)
Constantine the Great C.AD 288–337: reported in Greek 'By this, conquer'; Eusebius *Life of Constantine*

17 It is the peculiarity of the Church of God...to endure blows, not to give them; but yet you will be pleased to remember, that it is an anvil on which many a hammer has been broken.
reply to the King of Navarre after the massacre of the Huguenots at Vassey in March 1562
Theodore Beza 1519–1605: G. de Félice *Histoire des protestants de France* (1851); see CHRISTIAN CHURCH 4

18 The papacy is not other than the ghost of the deceased Roman Empire, sitting crowned upon the grave thereof.
Thomas Hobbes 1588–1679: *Leviathan* (1651)

19 As some to church repair,
Not for the doctrine, but the music there.
Alexander Pope 1688–1744: *An Essay on Criticism* (1711)

20 The Gospel of Christ knows of no religion but social; no holiness but social holiness.
John Wesley 1703–91: *Hymns and Sacred Poems* (1739) preface

21 The Christian religion not only was at first attended with miracles, but even at this day cannot be believed by any reasonable person without one.
David Hume 1711–76: *An Enquiry Concerning Human Understanding* (1748)

22 Christians have burnt each other, quite persuaded
That all the Apostles would have done as they did.
Lord Byron 1788–1824: *Don Juan* (1819–24)

23 He who begins by loving Christianity better than Truth will proceed by loving his own sect or church better than Christianity, and end by loving himself better than all.
Samuel Taylor Coleridge 1772–1834: *Aids to Reflection* (1825)

24 A church is God between four walls.
Victor Hugo 1802–85: *Ninety-Three* (1873)

25 His Christianity was muscular.
Benjamin Disraeli 1804–81: *Endymion* (1880); see CHRISTIAN CHURCH 8

26 Scratch the Christian and you find the pagan—spoiled.
Israel Zangwill 1864–1926: *Children of the Ghetto* (1892)

27 The Christian ideal has not been tried and found wanting. It has been found difficult; and left untried.
G. K. Chesterton 1874–1936: *What's Wrong with the World* (1910)

28 The Church should go forward along the path of progress and be no longer satisfied only to represent the Conservative Party at prayer.
Maude Royden 1876–1956: address at Queen's Hall, London, 16 July 1917

29 The chief contribution of Protestantism to human thought is its massive proof that God is a bore.
H. L. Mencken 1880–1956: *Minority Report* (1956)

30 I want to throw open the windows of the Church so that we can see out and the people can see in.
Pope John XXIII 1881–1963: attributed

31 You have no idea how much nastier I would be if I was not a Catholic. Without supernatural aid I would hardly be a human being.
Evelyn Waugh 1903–66: Noel Annan *Our Age* (1990)

32 We're more popular than Jesus now; I don't know which will go first—rock 'n' roll or Christianity.
of The Beatles
John Lennon 1940–80: interview in *Evening Standard* 4 March 1966

33 We are an Easter people and Alleluia is our song.
Pope John Paul II 1920–2005: speech in Harlem, New York, 2 October 1979

34 If you're going to do a thing, you should do it thoroughly. If you're going to be a Christian, you may as well be a Catholic.
Muriel Spark 1918–2006: in *Independent* 2 August 1989

Christmas

proverbs and sayings ►

1 Christmas comes but once a year, and when it comes it brings good cheer.
English proverb, late 16th century

2 Christmas is coming, and the goose is getting fat.
traditional rhyme, recorded from the 19th century (goose was traditional Christmas fare)

3 A green Yule makes a fat churchyard.
a mild winter is traditionally unhealthy (*Yule* = archaic term for Christmas); English proverb, mid 17th century; see WEATHER 38

4 Only — shopping days to Christmas.
the imminence of Christmas expressed in commercial terms

phrases ►

5 the twelve days of Christmas
the traditional period of Christmas festivities, from Christmas Day to the Feast of the Epiphany; see GIFTS 6

6 a white Christmas
Christmas with snow on the ground, from Irving Berlin: see CHRISTMAS 15

quotations ►

7 For unto us a child is born, unto us a son is given: and the government shall be upon his shoulder: and his name shall be called Wonderful, Counsellor, The mighty God, The everlasting Father, The Prince of Peace.
Bible: Isaiah

8 She brought forth her firstborn son, and wrapped him in swaddling clothes, and laid him in a manger; because there was no room for them in the inn.
Bible: St Luke

9 Welcome, all wonders in one sight!
Eternity shut in a span.
Richard Crashaw 1612–49: 'Hymn of the Nativity' (1652)

10 'Twas the night before Christmas, when all through the house
Not a creature was stirring, not even a mouse.
Clement C. Moore 1779–1863: 'A Visit from St Nicholas' (December 1823)

11 'Bah,' said Scrooge. 'Humbug!'
Charles Dickens 1812–70: *A Christmas Carol* (1843)

12 Christmas won't be Christmas without any presents.
Louisa May Alcott 1832–88: *Little Women* (1868–9)

13 It is Christmas Day in the Workhouse.
George R. Sims 1847–1922: 'In the Workhouse—Christmas Day' (1879)

14 Yes, Virginia, there is a Santa Claus.
replying to a letter from eight-year-old Virginia O'Hanlon
Francis Pharcellus Church 1839–1906: editorial in New York *Sun*, 21 September 1897

15 I'm dreaming of a white Christmas,
Just like the ones I used to know.
Irving Berlin 1888–1989: 'White Christmas' (1942 song); see CHRISTMAS 6

16 And girls in slacks remember Dad,
And oafish louts remember Mum,
And sleepless children's hearts are glad,
And Christmas-morning bells say 'Come!'
John Betjeman 1906–84: 'Christmas' (1954)

17 A lovely thing about Christmas is that it's compulsory, like a thunderstorm, and we all go through it together.
Garrison Keillor 1942– : *Leaving Home* (1987) 'Exiles'

18 Be nice to yu turkeys dis Christmas
Cos' turkeys just wanna hav fun.
Benjamin Zephaniah 1958– : 'Talking Turkeys!!' (1994)

19 Christmas is the Disneyfication of Christianity.
Don Cupitt 1934– : in *Independent* 19 December 1996

20 Christmas is one of the great European exports. You'll meet Santa Claus and his reindeer in Shanghai and Dar es Salaam; a long way from the North Pole.
Rowan Williams 1950– : in *Radio Times* 11 December 2010

The Cinema

see also ACTING, THEATRE

proverbs and sayings ▸

1 Come with me to the Casbah.
often attributed to Charles Boyer in the film *Algiers* (1938), but not found there

2 Have gun, will travel.
supposedly characteristic statement of a hired gunman in a western; popularized as the title of an American television series (1957–64)

3 Play it again, Sam.
popular misquotation of Humphrey Bogart in *Casablanca* (1942), subsequently used as the title of a play (1969) and film (1972) by Woody Allen

4 You dirty rat.
frequently attributed to James Cagney in a gangster part, but not found in this precise form in any of his films

quotations ▸

5 It is like writing history with lightning. And my only regret is that it is all so terribly true.
on seeing D. W. Griffith's film *The Birth of a Nation*
Woodrow Wilson 1856–1924: at the White House, 18 February 1915

6 The lunatics have taken charge of the asylum.
on the take-over of United Artists by Charles Chaplin, Mary Pickford, Douglas Fairbanks and D. W. Griffith
Richard Rowland 1881–1947: Terry Ramsaye *A Million and One Nights* (1926)

7 There is only one thing that can kill the movies, and that is education.
Will Rogers 1879–1935: *Autobiography of Will Rogers* (1949)

8 Bring on the empty horses!
said while directing the 1936 film *The Charge of the Light Brigade*
Michael Curtiz 1888–1962: David Niven *Bring on the Empty Horses* (1975)

9 If we'd had as many soldiers as that, we'd have won the war!
on seeing the number of Confederate troops in *Gone with the Wind* at the 1939 premiere
Margaret Mitchell 1900–49: W. G. Harris *Gable and Lombard* (1976)

10 If my books had been any worse, I should not have been invited to Hollywood, and if they had been any better, I should not have come.
Raymond Chandler 1888–1959: letter to Charles W. Morton, 12 December 1945

11 This is the biggest electric train a boy ever had!
of the RKO studios
Orson Welles 1915–85: Roy Fowler *Orson Welles* (1946)

12 JOE GILLIS: You used to be in pictures. You used to be big.
NORMA DESMOND: I am big. It's the pictures that got small.
Charles Brackett 1892–1969, **Billy Wilder** 1906–2002, and **D.M. Marshman Jr.**: *Sunset Boulevard* (1950 film)

13 If I made Cinderella, the audience would immediately be looking for a body in the coach.
Alfred Hitchcock 1899–1980: in *Newsweek* 11 June 1956

14 Why should people go out and pay to see bad movies when they can stay at home and see bad television for nothing?
Sam Goldwyn 1882–1974: in *Observer* 9 September 1956

15 Photography is truth. The cinema is

truth 24 times per second.
Jean-Luc Godard 1930– : *Le Petit Soldat* (1960 film)

16 All I need to make a comedy is a park, a policeman and a pretty girl.
Charlie Chaplin 1889–1977: *My Autobiography* (1964)

17 The words 'Kiss Kiss Bang Bang' which I saw on an Italian movie poster, are perhaps the briefest statement imaginable of the basic appeal of movies.
Pauline Kael 1919–2001: *Kiss Kiss Bang Bang* (1968)

18 Pictures are for entertainment, messages should be delivered by Western Union.
Sam Goldwyn 1882–1974: Arthur Marx *Goldwyn* (1976)

19 GEORGES FRANJU: Movies should have a beginning, a middle and an end.
JEAN-LUC GODARD: Certainly. But not necessarily in that order.
Jean-Luc Godard 1930– : in *Time* 14 September 1981; see FICTION 22, QUANTITIES 25

20 Nobody knows anything.
on the film industry
William Goldman 1931– : *Adventures in the Screen Trade* (1984)

21 There are no rules in filmmaking. Only sins. And the cardinal sin is dullness.
Frank Capra 1897–1991: in *People* 16 September 1991

Circumstance and Situation

proverbs and sayings ▸

1 Circumstances alter cases.
a general principle may be modified in the light of particular circumstances; English proverb, late 17th century

2 If you live in the river, you should make friends with the crocodile.
Indian proverb

3 May you live in interesting times.
used ironically, as eventful times are generally dangerous or unpleasant; modern saying, said to derive from a Chinese curse, but likely to be apocryphal; see CIRCUMSTANCE 36

4 No rose without a thorn.
even the pleasantest circumstances have their drawbacks; English proverb, mid 15th century; see PRACTICALITY 2, SATISFACTION 4

5 One day honey, one day onions.
Arab proverb

6 One man's loss is another man's gain.
often said by the gainer in self-congratulation; English proverb, early 16th century

7 There's a time and place for everything.
often used as a warning against doing or saying something at a particular time or in a particular situation; English proverb, early 16th century

8 There's no great loss without some gain.
said in consolation or resignation; English proverb, mid 17th century

9 The wheel has come full circle.
the situation has returned to what it was in the past, as if completing a cycle, with reference to Shakespeare's *King Lear* 'The wheel is come full circle'; see CHANCE 22

phrases ▸

10 catch-22
a dilemma or difficult circumstance from which there is no escape because of mutually conflicting or dependent conditions, from Joseph Heller's novel: see MADNESS 14

11 cuckoo in the nest
an unwelcome intruder in a place or situation

12 dig oneself into a hole
get oneself into an awkward or restrictive situation; see APOLOGY 8

13 elephant in the room
an unwelcome fact which is not directly referred to but of which everyone is aware; other variants include *moose on the table*

14 a fish out of water
a person in a completely unsuitable environment or situation

15 fit for purpose
well equipped or well suited for its designated role or purpose, deriving from the requirements of the *Sale of Goods Act* (1979); see CIRCUMSTANCE 37

16 in the wrong box
unsuitably or awkwardly placed; in a difficulty, at a disadvantage

17 **on the horns of a dilemma**
faced with a decision involving equally unfavourable alternatives; *dilemma* in Rhetoric, a form of argument involving an adversary in the choice of two alternatives (the 'horns'), either of which is or appears to be equally unfavourable

18 **the plot thickens**
the situation becomes more difficult and complex, from George Villiers *The Rehearsal* (1671): see THEATRE 10

19 **a square peg in a round hole**
a person in a situation unsuited to his or her capacities or disposition, a misfit; see CIRCUMSTANCE 29

20 **swings and roundabouts**
a state of affairs in which different actions result in no eventual gain or loss, from the saying: see WINNING 3

quotations ▸

21 Every honourable action has its proper time and season, or rather it is this propriety or observance which distinguishes an honourable action from its opposite.
Agesilaus 444–360 BC: Plutarch *Lives* 'Agesilaus'

22 These things never happened, but are always.
Sallustius fl. C.AD 363: *On the Gods and the World*

23 In it is what is in it.
Jalal ad-Din ar-Rumi 1207–73: title of a collection of discourses, in Persian *Fihi ma Fihi*

24 But for the grace of God there goes John Bradford.
on seeing a group of criminals being led to their execution; usually quoted as, 'There but for the grace of God go I'
John Bradford 1510–55: in *Dictionary of National Biography* (1917–)

25 The time is out of joint; O cursèd spite,
That ever I was born to set it right!
William Shakespeare 1564–1616: *Hamlet* (1601)

26 My nature is subdued
To what it works in, like the dyer's hand.
William Shakespeare 1564–1616: sonnet 111; see CHANGE 18

27 And, spite of Pride, in erring Reason's spite,
One truth is clear, 'Whatever IS, is RIGHT.'
Alexander Pope 1688–1744: *An Essay on Man* Epistle 1 (1733)

28 *No se puede mirar.*
One cannot look at this.
Goya 1746–1828: *The Disasters of War* (1863) title of etching

29 We shall generally find that the triangular person has got into the square hole, the oblong into the triangular, and a square person has squeezed himself into the round hole. The officer and the office, the doer and the thing done, seldom fit so exactly that we can say they were almost made for each other.
Sydney Smith 1771–1845: *Sketches of Moral Philosophy* (1849); see CIRCUMSTANCE 19

30 For of all sad words of tongue or pen,
The saddest are these: 'It might have been!'
John Greenleaf Whittier 1807–92: 'Maud Muller' (1854); see CIRCUMSTANCE 32

31 It was the best of times, it was the worst of times.
Charles Dickens 1812–70: *A Tale of Two Cities* (1859)

32 If, of all words of tongue and pen,
The saddest are, 'It might have been,'
More sad are these we daily see:
'It is, but hadn't ought to be!'
Bret Harte 1836–1902: 'Mrs Judge Jenkins' (1867); see CIRCUMSTANCE 30

33 Watch out w'en you'er gittin all you want. Fattenin' hogs ain't in luck.
Joel Chandler Harris 1848–1908: *Uncle Remus: His Songs and His Sayings* (1880)

34 Isn't it pretty to think so?
Ernest Hemingway 1899–1961: *The Sun Also Rises* (1926)

35 Anyone who isn't confused doesn't really understand the situation.
on the Vietnam War
Ed Murrow 1908–65: Walter Bryan *The Improbable Irish* (1969)

36 There is a Chinese curse which says 'May he live in interesting times.' Like it or not we live in interesting times. They are times of danger and

uncertainty; but they are also more open to the creative energy of men than any other time in history.

Robert Kennedy 1925–68: speech, Cape Town, 6 June 1966; see CIRCUMSTANCE 3

37 Our system is not fit for purpose.

on the Home Office Immigration and Nationality Directorate (IND)

John Reid 1947– : speaking to the Commons Home Affairs Committee, 23 May 2006; see CIRCUMSTANCE 15

Cities

see TOWNS AND CITIES

Civilization

see CULTURE AND CIVILIZATION

Class

see also CAPITALISM, RANK

proverbs and sayings ▸

1 It takes three generations to make a gentleman.

English proverb, early 19th century; the idea that it took three generations before the possession of wealth conferred the status of gentleman occurs from the late 16th century

2 When Adam delved and Eve span, who was then the gentleman?

traditional rhyme from Richard Rolle (see CLASS 9), taken in this form by John Ball as the text of his revolutionary sermon on the outbreak of the Peasants' Revolt, 1381

phrases ▸

3 airs and graces

an affectation of superiority

4 Essex man

derogatory term for a type of British Conservative voter in the late 1980s, associated particularly with the county of Essex, and characterized as a brash, amoral, self-made young businessman, of right-wing views and few or no cultural or intellectual interests, devoted to the acquisition of goods and material wealth; see WOMEN 12

5 the gentlemen and the players

distinguishing between the amateur (gentlemen) and professional (players) players of cricket, and hence other sports; figuratively, a player means a lower-class person

6 Islington person

a middle-class, socially aware person with left-wing views, characteristics supposedly typical of Islington residents, seen as a typical supporter of New Labour who, while rejecting the brash self-interest of Essex man, is nevertheless similarly insulated by material wealth from the harshest pressures of modern society

7 the many-headed monster

an archaic term for the people, the populace, after Horace *Epistles* 'The people are a many-headed beast'; see THEATRE 12

8 Sloane Ranger

a fashionable and conventional upper-class young woman, especially one living in London; a play on *Sloane* Square, London, and *Lone Ranger*, a fictitious cowboy hero; coined in 1975 in the magazine *Harpers & Queen*

quotations ▸

9 When Adam dalfe and Eve spane
Go spire if thou may spede,
Where was than the pride of man
That now merres his mede?

Richard Rolle de Hampole 1290–1349: G. G. Perry *Religious Pieces* (1914); see CLASS 2

10 I must have the gentleman to haul and draw with the mariner, and the mariner with the gentleman...I would know him, that would refuse to set his hand to a rope, but I know there is not any such here.

Francis Drake 1540–96: J. S. Corbett *Drake and the Tudor Navy* (1898)

11 That in the captain's but a choleric word,
Which in the soldier is flat blasphemy.

William Shakespeare 1564–1616: *Measure for Measure* (1604)

12 He told me...that mine was the middle state, or what might be called the upper station of low life, which he had found by long experience was the best state in the world, the most suited to human happiness.

Daniel Defoe 1660–1731: *Robinson Crusoe* (1719)

13 O let us love our occupations,
Bless the squire and his relations,
Live upon our daily rations,
And always know our proper stations.
Charles Dickens 1812–70: *The Chimes* (1844) 'The Second Quarter'

14 The proletarians have nothing to lose but their chains. They have a world to win. WORKING MEN OF ALL COUNTRIES, UNITE!
commonly rendered as 'Workers of the world, unite!'
Karl Marx 1818–83 and **Friedrich Engels** 1820–95: *The Communist Manifesto* (1848); see CLASS 23

15 The rich man in his castle,
The poor man at his gate,
God made them, high or lowly,
And ordered their estate.
Cecil Frances Alexander 1818–95: 'All Things Bright and Beautiful' (1848)

16 *Il faut épater le bourgeois.*
One must astonish the bourgeois.
Charles Baudelaire 1821–67: attributed; also attributed to Privat d'Anglemont (1820–59) in the form '*Je les ai épatés, les bourgeois* [I flabbergasted them, the bourgeois]'

17 All the world over, I will back the masses against the classes.
W. E. Gladstone 1809–98: speech in Liverpool, 28 June 1886

18 The bourgeois are other people.
Jules Renard 1864–1910: diary, 28 January 1890

19 The curse of the working class is the fewness of their wants, the poverty of their desires.
John Burns 1858–1943: *Brains Better Than Bets or Beer* (1902)

20 You may tempt the upper classes
With your villainous demi-tasses,
But; Heaven will protect a
working-girl!
Edgar Smith 1857–1938: 'Heaven Will Protect the Working-Girl' (1909 song)

21 The bourgeois prefers comfort to pleasure, convenience to liberty, and a pleasant temperature to the deathly inner consuming fire.
Hermann Hesse 1877–1962: *Der Steppenwolf* (1927)

22 Civilization has made the peasantry its pack animal. The bourgeoisie in the long run only changed the form of the pack.
Leon Trotsky 1879–1940: *History of the Russian Revolution* (1933)

23 We of the sinking middle class...may sink without further struggles into the working class where we belong, and probably when we get there it will not be so dreadful as we feared, for, after all, we have nothing to lose but our aitches.
George Orwell 1903–50: *The Road to Wigan Pier* (1937); see CLASS 14

24 Will the people in the cheaper seats clap your hands? All the rest of you, if you'll just rattle your jewellery.
John Lennon 1940–80: at the Royal Variety Performance, 4 November 1963

25 The worst fault of the working classes is telling their children they're not going to succeed, saying: 'There is life, but it's not for you.'
John Mortimer 1923–2009: in *Daily Mail* 31 May 1988

26 It's where you are going to, not where you have come from that matters.
David Cameron 1966– : in *Sunday Times* 22 May 2005

Clergy

see also CHRISTIAN CHURCH

proverbs and sayings ▸

1 Clergymen's sons always turn out badly.
the implication is that the weight of expectation on clergyman's children is often in itself damaging; English proverb, late 19th century

2 Like people, like priest.
English proverb, late 16th century; from the Bible (Hosea) 'And there shall be like people, like priest'

3 Nobody is born learned; bishops are made of men.
American proverb, mid 20th century

4 Once a priest, always a priest.
English proverb, mid 19th century; see CHARACTER 13

phrases ►

5 the Angelic Doctor
St Thomas Aquinas (1225–74), Italian philosopher, theologian, and Dominican friar

6 benefit of clergy
historically, exemption from ordinary courts of law because of membership of the clergy or (later) literacy or scholarship; exemption from the sentence for certain first offences because of literacy

quotations ►

7 A bishop then must be blameless, the husband of one wife, vigilant, sober, of good behaviour, given to hospitality, apt to teach;
Not given to wine, no striker, not greedy of filthy lucre; but patient, not a brawler, not covetous.
Bible: I Timothy; see MONEY 19

8 In old time we had treen chalices and golden priests, but now we have treen priests and golden chalices.
John Jewel 1522–71: *Certain Sermons Preached Before the Queen's Majesty* (1609)

9 A single life doth well with churchmen, for charity will hardly water the ground where it must first fill a pool.
Francis Bacon 1561–1626: *Essays* (1625) 'Of Marriage and the Single Life'

10 New *Presbyter* is but old *Priest* writ
large.
John Milton 1608–74: 'On the New Forcers of Conscience under the Long Parliament' (1646)

11 And of all plagues with which
mankind are curst,
Ecclesiastic tyranny's the worst.
Daniel Defoe 1660–1731: *The True-Born Englishman* (1701)

12 I look upon all the world as my parish.
John Wesley 1703–91: *Journal* 11 June 1739

13 In all ages of the world, priests have been enemies of liberty.
David Hume 1711–76: *Essays, Moral, Political, and Literary* (1875) 'Of the Parties of Great Britain' (1741–2)

14 I never saw, heard, nor read, that the clergy were beloved in any nation where Christianity was the religion of the country. Nothing can render them popular, but some degree of persecution.
Jonathan Swift 1667–1745: *Thoughts on Religion* (1765)

15 *Merit*, indeed!...We are come to a pretty pass if they talk of *merit* for a bishopric.
John Fane, Lord Westmorland 1759–1841: Lady Salisbury's diary, 9 December 1835

16 How can a bishop marry? How can he flirt? The most he can say is, 'I will see you in the vestry after service.'
Sydney Smith 1771–1845: Lady Holland *Memoir* (1855)

17 Pray remember, Mr Dean, no dogma, no Dean.
Benjamin Disraeli 1804–81: W. Monypenny and G. Buckle *Life of Benjamin Disraeli* vol. 4 (1916)

18 I wouldn't take the Pope too seriously. He's a Pole first, a pope second, and maybe a Christian third.
Muriel Spark 1918–2006: in *International Herald Tribune* 29 May 1989

19 Pastors need to start where people are and not where we think they should be.
Basil Hume 1923–99: in *Independent* 18 June 1999

Colours

proverbs and sayings ►

1 Blue and green should never be seen.
traditional warning against wearing the two colours together

2 Richard of York gave battle in vain.
traditional mnemonic for the colours of the rainbow (red, orange, yellow, green, blue, indigo, violet)

quotations ►

3 If I could find anything blacker than black, I'd use it.
J. M. W. Turner 1775–1851: remark, 1844

4 Colour has taken hold of me; no longer do I have to chase after it.
I know that it has hold of me for ever.
Paul Klee 1879–1940: on a visit to Tunis in 1914; Herbert Read *A Concise History of Modern Painting* (1968)

5 Green how I love you green.
Green wind.
Green boughs.
The ship on the sea
and the horse on the mountain.
Federico García Lorca 1899–1936: *Romance sonámbulo* (1924–7)

6 I cannot pretend to feel impartial about the colours. I rejoice with the brilliant ones, and am genuinely sorry for the poor browns.
Winston Churchill 1874–1965: *Thoughts and Adventures* (1932)

7 It's not that easy being green.
sung by the Kermit the frog
Joe Raposo 1937–89: 'Bein' Green', song from Jim Henson's *Sesame Street* (TV show, 1969–)

8 I wear the black for the poor and the
beaten down,
Living in the hopeless hungry side of
town.
Johnny Cash 1932–2003: 'Man in Black' (1971 song)

9 Pink is the navy blue of India.
Diana Vreeland 1903–89: in *Rolling Stone* 11 August 1977; compare FASHION 4

10 I think it pisses God off if you walk by the colour purple in a field somewhere and don't notice it.
Alice Walker 1944– : *The Colour Purple* (1982)

Communism

see CAPITALISM AND COMMUNISM

Computers and the Internet

proverbs and sayings ▶

1 Computer says No.
catchphrase used by Matt Lucas as 'Carol' in *Little Britain* (BBC TV series 2, 2004), written by Matt Lucas and David Walliams

2 Do not fold, spindle or mutilate.
instruction on punched cards (1950s, and in differing forms from the 1930s)

3 Garbage in, garbage out.
in computing, incorrect or faulty input will always cause poor output; mid 20th century saying; see COMPUTERS 13

4 If you can't do it in Fortran, do it in assembly language. If you can't do it in assembly language, it isn't worth doing.
saying on computer programming

5 I think there is a world market for maybe five computers.
commonly attributed to Thomas Watson Snr. (1874–1956), Chairman of IBM 1914–52, but not traced; stated by IBM to derive from a misunderstanding of an occasion on 28 April 1953 when Thomas Watson Jnr. informed a meeting of IBM stockholders that 'we expected to get orders for five machines, we came home with orders for 18'

6 It's not a bug, it's a feature.
bug = an error in a computer program or system; late 20th century saying

7 No manager ever got fired for buying IBM.
IBM advertising slogan

8 To err is human but to really foul things up requires a computer.
late 20th century saying; see MISTAKES 6

phrases ▶

9 bells and whistles
in computing, speciously attractive but superfluous facilities, with allusion to the various bells and whistles of old fairground organs

10 Moore's law
the principle that a new type of microprocessor chip is released every 12 to 24 months, with each new version having approximately twice as many logical elements as its predecessor, and that this trend is likely to continue, resulting in an exponential rise in computing power per chip over a period of time; an observation and prediction originally made in 1965 by Gordon Earle *Moore* (1929–)

11 Trojan horse
a program designed to breach the security of a computer system while ostensibly performing some innocuous function; from a hollow wooden statue of a horse in which the Greeks are said to have concealed themselves to enter Troy; see TRUST 16

quotations ►

12 The Analytical Engine weaves algebraic patterns just as the Jacquard loom weaves flowers and leaves.
of Babbage's mechanical computer
Ada Lovelace 1815–52: Luigi Menabrea *Sketch of the Analytical Engine invented by Charles Babbage* (1843), translated and annotated by Ada Lovelace, Note A

13 Now, Mr Babbage, there is only one thing that I want to know. If you put the question in wrong, will the answer come out right?
question put by a lady to Charles Babbage (1791–1871), inventor of the mechanical computer; see COMPUTERS 3
Anonymous: Harriet Martineau *Autobiography* (1877)

14 Computers are composed of nothing more than logic gates stretched out to the horizon in a vast numerical irrigation system.
Stan Augarten: *State of the Art: A Photographic History of the Integrated Circuit* (1983)

15 A modern computer hovers between the obsolescent and the nonexistent.
Sydney Brenner 1927– : attributed in *Science* 5 January 1990

16 On the Internet, nobody knows you're a dog.
Peter Steiner 1940– : cartoon caption in *New Yorker* 5 July 1993

17 We've all heard that a million monkeys banging on a million typewriters will eventually reproduce the entire works of Shakespeare. Now, thanks to the Internet, we know this is not true.
Robert Wilensky 1951– : in *Mail on Sunday* 16 February 1997; see CHANCE 34

18 You have zero privacy anyway. Get over it.
Scott McNealy 1954– : on the introduction of Jini networking technology; quoted in *Wired News* (online edition), 26 January 1999

19 The email of the species is deadlier than the mail.
Stephen Fry 1957– : in *Sunday Telegraph* 23 December 2001

20 Google is white bread for the mind.
Tara Brabazon 1969– : title of inaugural lecture at the University of Brighton, 16 January 2008, in *Times* 14 January 2008

21 I think computer viruses should count as life. Maybe it says something about human nature, that the only form of life we have created so far is purely destructive.
Stephen Hawking 1942– : 'Life in the Universe', undated lecture on www.hawking.org (September 2008)

22 YouTube if you want to.
of Gordon Brown's YouTube videos
Hazel Blears 1956– : in *Observer* 3 May 2009

23 The Internet's completely over... Anyway, all these computers and digital gadgets are no good. They just fill your head with numbers and that can't be good for you.
Prince 1960– : in *Daily Mirror* 5 July 2010

Conformity

proverbs and sayings ►

1 The nail that sticks up is certain to be hammered down.
Japanese proverb

2 Obey orders, if you break owners.
the saying is nautical, and means that orders should be followed even if it is clear that they are wrong; English proverb, late 18th century

phrases ►

3 be all things to all men
please everyone, typically by fitting in with their needs or expectations; originally probably in allusion to the Bible; see CHARACTER 30

4 marching to a different drum
conforming to different principles and practices from those around one; ultimately from Thoreau: see CONFORMITY 10

5 Stepford wife
someone who is regarded as robotically conformist or obedient; from *The Stepford Wives*, the title of a 1972 novel by the American writer Ira Levin (1929–2007), in which *Stepford* is the name of a fictional idyllic suburb where the men have replaced their wives with robots

quotations ►

6 While we were talking came by several poor creatures carried by, by constables, for being at a

conventicle...I would to God they would either conform, or be more wise, and not be catched!

Samuel Pepys 1633–1703: diary, 7 August 1664

7 'It's always best on these occasions to do what the mob do.' 'But suppose there are two mobs?' suggested Mr Snodgrass. 'Shout with the largest,' replied Mr Pickwick.

Charles Dickens 1812–70: *Pickwick Papers* (1837)

8 Whoso would be a man must be a nonconformist.

Ralph Waldo Emerson 1803–82: *Essays* (1841) 'Self-Reliance'

9 Teach him to think for himself? Oh, my God, teach him rather to think like other people!

on her son's education

Mary Shelley 1797–1851: Matthew Arnold *Essays in Criticism* Second Series (1888) 'Shelley'

10 If a man does not keep pace with his companions, perhaps it is because he hears a different drummer. Let him step to the music which he hears, however measured or far away.

Henry David Thoreau 1817–62: *Walden* (1854); see CONFORMITY 4

11 My duty is to obey orders.

Thomas Jonathan 'Stonewall' Jackson 1824–63: attributed

12 You cannot make a man by standing a sheep on its hind-legs. But by standing a flock of sheep in that position you can make a crowd of men.

Max Beerbohm 1872–1956: *Zuleika Dobson* (1911)

13 Imitation lies at the root of most human actions. A respectable person is one who conforms to custom. People are called good when they do as others do.

Anatole France 1844–1924: *Crainquebille* (1923)

14 A dead thing can go with the stream, but only a living thing can go against it.

G. K. Chesterton 1874–1936: *The Everlasting Man* (1925); see CONFORMITY 16

15 The Party line is that there is no Party line.

Milovan Djilas 1911– : comment on reforms of the Yugoslavian Communist Party, November 1952; Fitzroy Maclean *Disputed Barricade* (1957)

16 Never forget that only dead fish swim with the stream.

Malcolm Muggeridge 1903–90: quoting a supporter; in *Radio Times* 9 July 1964; see CONFORMITY 14

17 In America, through pressure of conformity, there is freedom of choice, but nothing to choose from.

Peter Ustinov 1921–2004: Dick Richards *The Wit of Peter Ustinov* (1969)

18 The Normal is the good smile in a child's eyes—all right. It is also the dead stare in a million adults. It both sustains and kills—like a God. It is the Ordinary made beautiful; it is also the Average made lethal.

Peter Shaffer 1926– : *Equus* (1983 ed.)

Conscience

see also FORGIVENESS, SIN

proverbs and sayings ▸

1 A clean conscience is a good pillow.

a clear conscience enables its possessor to sleep soundly; English proverb, early 18th century

2 Conscience gets a lot of credit that belongs to cold feet.

American proverb, mid 20th century

3 Do right and fear no man.

English proverb, mid 15th century

4 Evil doers are evil dreaders.

someone engaged in wrongdoing is likely to be nervous and suspicious of others; English proverb, mid 16th century

5 A guilty conscience needs no accuser.

awareness of one's own guilt has the same effect as an accusation; English proverb, late 14th century

6 Let your conscience be your guide.

American proverb, mid 20th century

7 A quiet conscience sleeps in thunder.

someone with an untroubled conscience will sleep undisturbed whatever the noise; English proverb, late 16th century

phrases ▸

8 agenbite of inwit

remorse, used as a conscious archaism derived from James Joyce's *Ulysses*; see CONSCIENCE 18

9 prick of conscience

compunction, remorse, guilt; used as the title of a devotional treatise by the English mystic Richard Rolle of Hampole (1290–1349)

quotations ▸

10 Then I, however, showed again, by action, not in word only, that I did not care a whit for death...but that I did care with all my might not to do anything unjust or unholy.

on being ordered by the Thirty Commissioners to take part in the liquidation of Leon of Salamis
Socrates 469–399 BC: Plato *Apology*

11 *O dignitosa coscienza e netta,*
Come t'è picciol fallo amaro morso!
O pure and noble conscience, how bitter a sting to thee is a little fault!

Dante 1265–1321: *Divina Commedia* 'Purgatorio'

12 Thus conscience doth make cowards of us all.

William Shakespeare 1564–1616: *Hamlet* (1601)

13 In many walks of life, a conscience is a more expensive encumbrance than a wife or a carriage.

Thomas De Quincey 1785–1859: *Confessions of an English Opium-Eater* (1822)

14 If I am obliged to bring religion into after-dinner toasts (which indeed does not seem quite the thing) I shall drink—to the Pope, if you please—still, to Conscience first, and to the Pope afterwards.

John Henry Newman 1801–90: *A Letter Addressed to the Duke of Norfolk...* (1875)

15 It is easier to cope with a bad conscience than to cope with a bad reputation.

Friedrich Nietzsche 1844–1900: *The Gay Science* (1882)

16 Conscience is thoroughly well-bred and soon leaves off talking to those who do not wish to hear it.

Samuel Butler 1835–1902: *Further Extracts from Notebooks* (1934)

17 Conscience: the inner voice which warns us that someone may be looking.

H. L. Mencken 1880–1956: *A Little Book in C major* (1916)

18 They wash and tub and scrub.
Agenbite of inwit. Conscience.

James Joyce 1882–1941: *Ulysses* (1922); see CONSCIENCE 8

19 Most people sell their souls, and live with a good conscience on the proceeds.

Logan Pearsall Smith 1865–1946: *Afterthoughts* (1931)

20 Sufficient conscience to bother him, but not sufficient to keep him straight.

of Ramsay MacDonald
David Lloyd George 1863–1945: A. J. Sylvester *Life with Lloyd George* (1975)

21 I cannot and will not cut my conscience to fit this year's fashions.

Lillian Hellman 1905–84: letter to John S. Wood, 19 May 1952

22 The one thing that doesn't abide by majority rule is a person's conscience.

Harper Lee 1926– : *To Kill a Mockingbird* (1962)

Consequences

see CAUSES AND CONSEQUENCES

Consolation

see SYMPATHY AND CONSOLATION

Constancy and Inconstancy

proverbs and sayings ▸

1 Love me little, love me long.

love of great intensity is unlikely to last; English proverb, early 16th century

2 Quickly come, quickly go.

English proverb, late 16th century

3 A rolling stone gathers no moss.

used to imply that someone who does not settle down will not prosper, or form lasting ties; English proverb, mid 14th century

phrases ▸

4 true as Troilus
completely devoted, alluding to Shakespeare *Troilus and Cressida* ' "As true as Troilus" shall crown up the verse'

quotations ▸

5 My true love hath my heart and I have his,
By just exchange one for the other giv'n.
Philip Sidney 1554–86: *Arcadia* (1581)

6 But I am constant as the northern star,
Of whose true-fixed and resting quality
There is no fellow in the firmament.
William Shakespeare 1564–1616: *Julius Caesar* (1599)

7 No, the heart that has truly loved never forgets,
But as truly loves on to the close,
As the sunflower turns on her god, when he sets,
The same look which she turned when he rose.
Thomas Moore 1779–1852: 'Believe me, if all those endearing young charms' (1807)

8 Bright star, would I were steadfast as thou art—.
John Keats 1795–1821: 'Bright star, would I were steadfast as thou art' (written 1819)

9 His honour rooted in dishonour stood,
And faith unfaithful kept him falsely true.
Alfred, Lord Tennyson 1809–92: *Idylls of the King* 'Lancelot and Elaine' (1859)

10 I have been faithful to thee, Cynara! in my fashion.
Ernest Dowson 1867–1900: 'Non Sum Qualis Eram' (1896); also known as 'Cynara'; see CONSTANCY 11; MEMORY 15

11 But I'm always true to you, darlin', in my fashion.
Yes I'm always true to you, darlin', in my way.
Cole Porter 1891–1964: 'Always True to You in my Fashion' (1949 song); see CONSTANCY 10

12 Your idea of fidelity is not having more than one man in bed at the same time.
Frederic Raphael 1931– : *Darling* (1965)

13 You're...turning into a kind of serial monogamist.
Richard Curtis 1956– : *Four Weddings and a Funeral* (1994 film)

14 Why fool around with hamburger when you have steak at home?
when asked if he had difficulty staying faithful to his wife Joanne Woodward
Paul Newman 1925–2008: attributed

Conversation

see also GOSSIP, SPEECH, SPEECHES

proverbs and sayings ▸

1 It's good to talk.
advertising slogan for British Telecom, from 1994

phrases ▸

2 feast of reason
intellectual discussion, from Pope 'The feast of reason and the flow of soul'; see CONVERSATION 3

3 flow of soul
genial conversation, as complementary to intellectual discussion, from Pope: see CONVERSATION 2

4 glittering generalities
platitudes, clichés, superficially convincing but empty phrases; see HUMAN RIGHTS 11

quotations ▸

5 All use metaphors in conversation, as well as proper and appropriate words.
Aristotle 384–322 BC: *The Art of Rhetoric*

6 Must I always be a mere listener?
Juvenal C.AD 60–C.140: *Satires*

7 I am not bound to please thee with my answer.
William Shakespeare 1564–1616: *The Merchant of Venice* (1596–8)

8 With thee conversing I forget all time.
John Milton 1608–74: *Paradise Lost* (1667)

9 JOHNSON: Well, we had a good talk.
BOSWELL: Yes, Sir; you tossed and gored several persons.
James Boswell 1740–95: *Life of Samuel Johnson* (1791) Summer 1768

10 Religion is by no means a proper subject of conversation in a mixed company.
Lord Chesterfield 1694–1773: *Letters…to his Godson and Successor* (1890) Letter 142

11 Questioning is not the mode of conversation among gentlemen. It is assuming a superiority.
Samuel Johnson 1709–84: James Boswell *Life of Samuel Johnson* (1791) 25 March 1776

12 He talked on for ever; and you wished him to talk on for ever.
of Coleridge
William Hazlitt 1778–1830: *Lectures on the English Poets* (1818)

13 Two may talk and one may hear, but three cannot take part in a conversation of the most sincere and searching sort.
Ralph Waldo Emerson 1803–82: *Essays* (1841) 'Friendship'

14 'The time has come,' the Walrus said,
'To talk of many things:
Of shoes—and ships—and sealing wax—
Of cabbages—and kings.
Lewis Carroll 1832–98: *Through the Looking-Glass* (1872)

15 It is the province of knowledge to speak and it is the privilege of wisdom to listen.
Oliver Wendell Holmes 1809–94: *The Poet at the Breakfast-Table* (1872)

16 He speaks to Me as if I was a public meeting.
of Gladstone
Queen Victoria 1819–1901: G. W. E. Russell *Collections and Recollections* (1898)

17 Although there exist many thousand subjects for elegant conversation, there are persons who cannot meet a cripple without talking about feet.
Ernest Bramah 1868–1942: *The Wallet of Kai Lung* (1900)

18 There is no such thing as conversation. It is an illusion. There are intersecting monologues, that is all.
Rebecca West 1892–1983: *There is No Conversation* (1935)

19 Someone to tell it to is one of the fundamental needs of human beings.
Miles Franklin 1879–1954: *Childhood at Brindabella* (1963)

20 Too much agreement kills a chat.
Eldridge Cleaver 1935–98: *Soul on Ice* (1968) 'Letters from Prison'

Cooking and Eating

see also FOOD, GREED

proverbs and sayings ▶

1 After dinner rest a while, after supper walk a mile.
the implication is that dinner is a heavy meal, while supper is a light one; English proverb, late 16th century

2 After meat, mustard.
traditional comment on some essential ingredient which is brought too late of be of use; English proverb, late 16th century

3 Breakfast like a king, lunch like a prince, and dine like a pauper.
recommending lighter meals as you move through the day; modern saying

4 Eat to live, not live to eat.
distinguishing between necessity and indulgence; English proverb, late 14th century

5 Fingers were made before forks.
commonly used as a polite excuse for eating with one's hands at table; English proverb, mid 18th century. The earlier variant 'God made hands before knives' is found in the mid 16th century

6 God sends meat, but the Devil sends cooks.
anything which is in itself good or useful may be spoiled or perverted by the use to which it is put; English proverb, mid 16th century

7 Go to work on an egg.
advertising slogan for the British Egg Marketing Board, from 1957; perhaps written by Fay Weldon or Mary Gowing

8 Hunger is the best sauce.
food which is needed will be received most readily; English proverb, early 16th century

9 The way one eats is the way one works.
Czech proverb

10 We must eat a peck of dirt before we die.
often used as a consolatory remark in literal contexts; English proverb, mid 18th century

11 You are what you eat.
English proverb, mid 20th century; see COOKING 21

phrases ▸

12 Barmecide feast
an illusory or imaginary feast, from the name of a prince in the *Arabian Nights*, who gave a beggar a feast consisting of ornate but empty dishes

13 dine with Duke Humphrey
in archaic usage, go without dinner, go hungry; possibly originally associated with a part of Old St Paul's, wrongly believed to be the site of the tomb of Duke Humphrey of Gloucester, where people walked instead of dining

quotations ▸

14 The guest will judge better of a feast than the cook.
Aristotle 384–322 BC: *Politics*

15 You won't be surprised that diseases are innumerable—count the cooks.
Seneca c.4 BC–AD 65: *Epistles*

16 Now good digestion wait on appetite,
And health on both!
William Shakespeare 1564–1616: *Macbeth* (1606)

17 Strange to see how a good dinner and feasting reconciles everybody.
Samuel Pepys 1633–1703: diary, 9 November 1665

18 We not only dig our graves with our teeth.
Daniel Defoe 1660–1731: *Conjugal Lewdness* (1727)

19 I look upon it, that he who does not mind his belly will hardly mind anything else.
Samuel Johnson 1709–84: James Boswell *Life of Samuel Johnson* (1791) 5 August 1763

20 Some hae meat and canna eat,
And some wad eat that want it:
But we hae meat and we can eat,
And sae the Lord be thankit.
Robert Burns 1759–96: 'The Kirkcudbright Grace' (1790), also known as 'The Selkirk Grace'

21 Tell me what you eat and I will tell you what you are.
Anthelme Brillat-Savarin 1755–1826: *Physiologie du Goût* (1825); see COOKING 11

22 Anyone who tells a lie has not a pure heart, and cannot make a good soup.
Ludwig van Beethoven 1770–1827: Ludwig Nohl *Beethoven Depicted by his Contemporaries* (1880)

23 Let onion atoms lurk within the bowl,
And, scarce-suspected, animate the whole.
Sydney Smith 1771–1845: Lady Holland *Memoir* (1855) 'Receipt for a Salad'

24 One can say everything best over a meal.
George Eliot 1819–80: *Adam Bede* (1859)

25 Kissing don't last: cookery do!
George Meredith 1828–1909: *The Ordeal of Richard Feverel* (1859)

26 He sows hurry and reaps indigestion.
Robert Louis Stevenson 1850–94: *Virginibus Puerisque* (1881) 'An Apology for Idlers'

27 The cook was a good cook, as cooks go; and as cooks go, she went.
Saki 1870–1916: *Reginald* (1904)

28 Time for a little something.
A. A. Milne 1882–1956: *Winnie-the-Pooh* (1926)

29 One cannot think well, love well, sleep well, if one has not dined well.
Virginia Woolf 1882–1941: *A Room of One's Own* (1929)

30 Be content to remember that those who can make omelettes properly can do nothing else.
Hilaire Belloc 1870–1953: *A Conversation with a Cat* (1931)

31 Good food is always a trouble and its preparation should be regarded as a labour of love.
Elizabeth David 1913–92: *French Country Cooking* (1951) introduction

32 Hot on Sunday,
Cold on Monday,
Hashed on Tuesday,
Minced on Wednesday,
Curried Thursday,
Broth on Friday,
Cottage pie Saturday.
Dorothy Hartley 1893–1985: *Food in England* (1954) 'Vicarage Mutton'

33 Gluttony is an emotional escape, a sign something is eating us.
Peter De Vries 1910–93: *Comfort Me With Apples* (1956)

34 Lunch? You gotta be kidding. Lunch is for wimps.
Stanley Weiser and **Oliver Stone** 1946– : *Wall Street* (1987 film)

35 I don't eat anything with a face.
Linda McCartney 1941–98: quoted in *BBC News* (online edition) 19 April 1998; obituary

36 If God had not intended for us to eat animals, how come He made them out of meat?
Sarah Palin 1964– : *Going Rogue* (2009)

Cooperation

proverbs and sayings ▸

1 A chain is no stronger than its weakest link.
often used when identifying a particular point of vulnerability; English proverb, mid 19th century; see STRENGTH 10

2 Dog does not eat dog.
people of the same profession should not attack each other; English proverb, mid 16th century

3 Each of us at a handle of the basket.
Maori proverb

4 Every little helps.
English proverb, early 17th century

5 Four eyes see more than two.
two people are more observant than one alone; English proverb, late 16th century

6 Hawks will not pick out hawks' eyes.
powerful people from the same group will not attack one another; English proverb, late 16th century

7 If you don't believe in cooperation, watch what happens to a wagon when one wheel comes off.
American proverb, mid 20th century

8 It takes two to make a bargain.
often used to imply that both parties must be prepared to give some ground; English proverb, late 16th century

9 It takes two to tango.
meaning that a cooperative venture requires a contribution from both participants; mid 20th century saying, from the 1952 song by Al Hoffman and Dick Manning

10 Little birds that can sing and won't sing must be made to sing.
those who refuse to obey or cooperate will be forced to do so; English proverb, late 17th century

11 Many hands make light work.
often used as an encouragement to join in with assistance; English proverb, mid 14th century

12 One good turn deserves another.
English proverb, early 15th century

13 One hand washes the other.
referring to cooperation between two closely linked persons or organizations; English proverb, late 16th century

14 Phone a friend.
advice to contestants uncertain of the correct answer, said by Chris Tarrant, host of the ITV quiz show *Who Wants to be a Millionaire* (1998–)

15 A single arrow is easily broken, but not ten in a bundle.
Japanese proverb

16 A single bracelet does not jingle.
to make an effect we need the help of others; African proverb

17 There is honour among thieves.
sometimes used ironically; English proverb, early 19th century

18 A trouble shared is a trouble halved.
discussing a problem will lessen its impact; English proverb, mid 20th century

19 Union is strength.
English proverb, mid 17th century; *unity* is a popular alternative for *union*, especially when used as a trade-union slogan

20 United we stand, divided we fall.
a watchword of the American Revolution, English proverb, late 18th century; see AMERICA 11

21 When spider webs unite, they can tie up a lion.
African proverb

22 With your food basket, and with my food basket, the guest will have enough.
Maori proverb

quotations ▸

23 The wolf also shall dwell with the lamb, and the leopard shall lie down with the kid; and the calf and the young lion and the fatling together.
Bible: Isaiah; see COOPERATION 34

24 If a house be divided against itself, that house cannot stand.
Bible: St Mark

25 Bear ye one another's burdens.
Bible: Galatians

26 If someone claps his hand a sound arises. Listen to the sound of the single hand!
Hakuin 1686–1769: attributed

27 When bad men combine, the good must associate; else they will fall, one by one, an unpitied sacrifice in a contemptible struggle.
Edmund Burke 1729–97: *Thoughts on the Cause of the Present Discontents* (1770)

28 We must indeed all hang together, or, most assuredly, we shall all hang separately.
Benjamin Franklin 1706–90: at the signing of the Declaration of Independence, 4 July 1776; possibly not original

29 Now who will stand on either hand,
And keep the bridge with me?
Lord Macaulay 1800–59: 'Horatius' (1842)

30 All for one, one for all.
motto of the Three Musketeers
Alexandre Dumas 1802–70: *Les Trois Mousquetaires* (1844); see FRIENDSHIP 8

31 Government and cooperation are in all things the laws of life; anarchy and competition the laws of death.
John Ruskin 1819–1900: *Unto this Last* (1862)

32 Why don't you do something to *help* me?
Stan Laurel 1890–1965: *Drivers' Licence Sketch* (1947 film); words spoken by Oliver Hardy

33 We must learn to live together as brothers or perish together as fools.
Martin Luther King 1929–68: speech at St Louis, 22 March 1964

34 The lion and the calf shall lie down together but the calf won't get much sleep.
Woody Allen 1935– : in *New Republic* 31 August 1974; see COOPERATION 23

Corruption

proverbs and sayings ▸

1 Every man has his price.
everyone is susceptible to the right bribe; English proverb, mid 18th century: see CORRUPTION 10

2 A golden key can open any door.
any access is guaranteed if enough money is offered; English proverb, late 16th century

3 It's not what you know, it's who you know.
stressing the importance of personal influence; late 20th century saying

4 The rotten apple injures its neighbour.
often used to mean that one corrupt person in an organization is likely to affect others; English proverb, mid 14th century

5 When money speaks, the truth keeps silent.
Russian proverb

phrases ▸

6 itching palm
avarice, originally with reference to Shakespeare; see CORRUPTION 9

quotations ▸

7 *...Omnia Romae*
Cum pretio.
Everything in Rome—at a price.
Juvenal C.AD 60–C.140: *Satires*

8 If gold ruste, what shall iren do?
Geoffrey Chaucer 1343–1400: *The Canterbury Tales* 'The General Prologue'

9 Let me tell you, Cassius, you yourself
Are much condemned to have an
itching palm.
William Shakespeare 1564–1616: *Julius Caesar* (1599); see CORRUPTION 6

10 **All those men have their price.**
of fellow parliamentarians
Robert Walpole 1676–1745: W. Coxe *Memoirs of Sir Robert Walpole* (1798); see CORRUPTION 1

11 **I am not worth purchasing, but such as I am, the King of Great Britain is not rich enough to do it.**
replying to an offer from Governor George Johnstone of £10,000, and any office in the Colonies in the King's gift, if he were able successfully to promote a Union between Britain and America
Joseph Reed 1741–85: W. B. Read *Life and Correspondence of Joseph Reed* (1847)

12 **But the jingling of the guinea helps the hurt that Honour feels.**
Alfred, Lord Tennyson 1809–92: 'Locksley Hall' (1842)

13 **There's an honest graft, and I'm an example of how it works. I might sum up the whole thing by sayin': 'I seen my opportunities and I took 'em.'**
George Washington Plunkitt 1842–1924: 'Honest Graft and Dishonest Graft' in William L. Riordon *Plunkitt of Tammany Hall* (1905)

14 **And that is called paying the Danegeld;**
But we've proved it again and again,
That if once you have paid him the Danegeld
You never get rid of the Dane.
Rudyard Kipling 1865–1936: 'What Danegeld means' (1911)

15 **Men are more often bribed by their loyalties and ambitions than money.**
Robert H. Jackson 1892–1954: dissenting opinion in *United States v. Wunderlich* 1951

16 **I stuffed their mouths with gold.**
on his handling of the consultants during the establishment of the National Health Service
Aneurin Bevan 1897–1960: Brian Abel-Smith *The Hospitals 1800–1948* (1964)

17 **Follow the money.**
William Goldman 1931– : *All the President's Men* (1976 film); spoken by Hal Holbrook as Deep Throat to Bob Woodward

18 **The flood of money that gushes into politics today is a pollution of democracy.**
Theodore H. White 1915–86: in *Time* 19 November 1984

Countries and Peoples

see also AFRICA, AMERICA, AUSTRALIA, CANADA, ENGLAND, FRANCE, INDIA, INTERNATIONAL, IRELAND, RUSSIA, SCOTLAND, TOWNS, WALES

proverbs and sayings ▸

1 **Every land has its own law.**
Scottish proverb, early 17th century, used to emphasize the individuality of a nation or group

phrases ▸

2 **the Celestial Empire**
Imperial China; translation of a Chinese honorific title

3 **the children of Israel**
the Jewish people; people whose descent is traditionally traced from the patriarch Jacob (also called *Israel*), each of whose twelve sons became the founder of a tribe

4 **the chosen people**
the Jewish people; the people specially favoured by God; compare the Bible (1 Peter) 'but ye are a chosen generation, a royal priesthood, an holy nation, a peculiar people'

5 **the Holy Land**
a region on the eastern shores of the Mediterranean, in what is now Israel and Palestine, with religious significance for Judaism, Christianity, and Islam; medieval Latin *terra sancta*, French *la terre sainte*, applied to the region with reference to its having been the scene of the Incarnation and also to the existing sacred sites there, especially the Holy Sepulchre at Jerusalem

6 **the Holy Roman Empire**
the empire set up in western Europe following the coronation of Charlemagne as emperor in the year 800. It was created by the medieval papacy in an attempt to unite Christendom under one rule. At times the territory of the empire was extensive and included Germany, Austria, Switzerland, and parts of Italy and the Netherlands; see COUNTRIES 14

7 **the Land of the Long White Cloud**
New Zealand

8 **land of the midnight sun**
any of the most northerly European countries, in which it never gets fully dark during the summer months

9 **land of the rising sun**
Japan; the Japanese name of the country is *Nippon*, literally 'rising sun'

10 **the Lost Tribes**
Asher, Dan, Gad, Issachar, Levi, Manasseh, Naphtali, Reuben, Simeon, and Zebulun, ten of the twelve divisions of ancient Israel, each traditionally descended from one of the sons of Jacob; the ten tribes of Israel taken away 720 BC by Sargon II to captivity in Assyria, from which they are believed never to have returned, while the tribes of Benjamin and Judah remained

11 **on which the sun never sets**
(of an empire, originally the Spanish and later the British) worldwide

12 **the sick man of Europe**
Turkey in the late 19th century, originally with reference to the view expressed by Nicholas I, Russian Emperor from 1825, 'Turkey is a dying man. We may endeavour to keep him alive, but we shall not succeed. He will, he must die'

quotations ►

13 The Netherlands have been for many years, as one may say, the very cockpit of Christendom.
James Howell 1594–1666: *Instructions for Foreign Travel* (1642); see EUROPE 1

14 This agglomeration which was called and which still calls itself the Holy Roman Empire was neither holy, nor Roman, nor an empire.
Voltaire 1694–1778: *Essai sur l'histoire générale et sur les moeurs et l'esprit des nations* (1756); see COUNTRIES 6

15 As your ambassador can see for himself we possess all things. I set no value on objects strange or ingenious, and have no use for your country's manufactures.
writing to George III after the first British trade mission had reached Beijing
Qianlong 1711–99: 'The First Edict' September 1793

16 She has made me in love with a cold climate, and frost and snow, with a northern moonlight.
on Mary Wollstonecraft's letters from Sweden and Norway
Robert Southey 1774–1843: letter to his brother Thomas, 28 April 1797

17 If one should ask you concerning the spirit of a true Japanese, point to the wild cherry blossom shining in the sun.
Motoori Norinaga 1730–1801: attributed

18 I look upon Switzerland as an inferior sort of Scotland.
Sydney Smith 1771–1845: letter to Lord Holland, 1815

19 The isles of Greece, the isles of Greece!
Where burning Sappho loved and sung.
Lord Byron 1788–1824: *Don Juan* (1819–24)

20 A quiet, pilfering, unprotected race.
John Clare 1793–1864: 'The Gipsy Camp' (1841)

21 You may have the universe, if I may have Italy.
Giuseppe Verdi 1813–1901: *Attila* (1846), libretto by Temistocle Solera (1815–78)

22 Except the blind forces of Nature, nothing moves in this world which is not Greek in its origin.
Henry Maine 1822–88: *Village Communities* (3rd ed., 1876)

23 I'm Charley's aunt from Brazil—where the nuts come from.
Brandon Thomas 1856–1914: *Charley's Aunt* (1892)

24 Poor Mexico, so far from God and so close to the United States.
Porfirio Diaz 1830–1915: attributed

25 The sailor lives, and stands beside us, paying
Out into time's wave
The stain of blood that writes an island story.
of New Zealand
Allen Curnow 1911–2001: 'Landfall in Unknown Seas' (1943)

26 Latins are tenderly enthusiastic. In Brazil they throw flowers at you. In Argentina they throw themselves.
Marlene Dietrich 1901–92: in *Newsweek* 24 August 1959

27 A country is a piece of land surrounded on all sides by boundaries, usually unnatural.
Joseph Heller 1923–99: *Catch-22* (1961)

28 To the Europeans, South America is a man with a moustache, a guitar and a gun.
Gabriel García Márquez 1928– : *No One Writes to the Colonel* (1961)

29 History is built around creation and achievement, and nothing was created in the West Indies.

V. S. Naipaul 1932– : *The Middle Passage* (1962); see COUNTRIES 32

30 The architecture of our future is not only unfinished; the scaffolding has hardly gone up.

George Lamming 1927– : 'The West Indian People' (1966)

31 Nothing and no one can destroy the Chinese people. They are relentless survivors. They are the oldest civilized people on earth. Their civilization passes through phases but its basic characteristics remain the same. They yield, they bend to the wind, but they do not break.

Pearl S. Buck 1892–1973: *China, Past and Present* (1972)

32 Nothing will always be created in the West Indies for quite long time, because what will come out of there is like nothing one has ever seen before.

in response to V. S. Naipaul's comment: see COUNTRIES 29

Derek Walcott 1930– : 'The Caribbean: Culture or Mimicry?' in *Journal of Interamerican Studies and World Affairs* February 1974

33 If you take Greece apart, in the end you will see remaining to you an olive tree, a vineyard and a ship. Which means: with just so much you can put her back together.

Odysseus Elytis 1911– : 'The Little Seafarer' (1988)

The Country and the Town

see also FARMING

proverbs and sayings ▸

1 An everyday story of country folk.

traditional summary of the BBC's long-running radio soap opera *The Archers* (1951–)

2 God made the country and man made the town.

contrasting rural and urban life; English proverb, mid 17th century, in this form from Cowper: see COUNTRY 11

3 You can take the boy out of the country but you can't take the country out of the boy.

even when a person moves away from the place they were brought up in, they retain its essential manners and customs; English proverb, mid 20th century

phrases ▸

4 concrete jungle

a city with a high density of large, unattractive, modern buildings and which is perceived as an unpleasant living environment, after Morris: see COUNTRY 21

5 a country mouse

a person from a rural area unfamiliar with urban life, from one of Aesop's fables in which the *country mouse* and the *town mouse* visit each other, and each in the end is convinced of the superiority of its own home; see COUNTRY 7

6 rus in urbe

an illusion of countryside created by a building or garden within a city; an urban building which has this effect; Latin, literally 'country in city', from Martial (AD *c.*40–*c.*104)

7 a town mouse

a person with an urban lifestyle unfamiliar with rural life; see COUNTRY 5

quotations ▸

8 The country places and the trees won't teach me anything, and the people in the city do.

Plato 429–347 BC: *Phaedrus*, spoken by Socrates

9 What is the city but the people?

William Shakespeare 1564–1616: *Coriolanus* (1608)

10 God the first garden made, and the first city Cain.

Abraham Cowley 1618–67: 'The Garden' (1668); see COUNTRY 11

11 God made the country, and man made the town.

William Cowper 1731–1800: *The Task* (1785) bk. 1 'The Sofa'; see COUNTRY 2, COUNTRY 10

12 'Tis distance lends enchantment to the view,
And robes the mountain in its azure hue.

Thomas Campbell 1777–1844: *Pleasures of Hope* (1799); see APPEARANCE 5

13 We do not look in great cities for our best morality.
   Jane Austen 1775–1817: *Mansfield Park* (1814)

14 I have no relish for the country; it is a kind of healthy grave.
   Sydney Smith 1771–1845: letter to Miss G. Harcourt, 1838

15 Cities give us collision.
   Ralph Waldo Emerson 1803–82: *The Conduct of Life* (1860) 'Culture'

16 Anybody can be good in the country.
   Oscar Wilde 1854–1900: *The Picture of Dorian Gray* (1891)

17 It is my belief, Watson, founded upon my experience, that the lowest and vilest alleys in London do not present a more dreadful record of sin than does the smiling and beautiful countryside.
   Arthur Conan Doyle 1859–1930: *The Adventures of Sherlock Holmes* (1892) 'The Copper Beeches'

18 Wiv a ladder and some glasses,
You could see to 'Ackney Marshes,
If it wasn't for the 'ouses in between.
   Edgar Bateman and **George Le Brunn**: 'If it wasn't for the 'Ouses in between' (1894 song)

19 Oh, give me land, lots of land under
   starry skies above,
Don't fence me in.
Let me ride through the wide open
   country that I love,
Don't fence me in.
   Cole Porter 1891–1964: 'Don't Fence Me In' (1944 song)

20 Commuters give the city its tidal restlessness; natives give it solidity and continuity; but the settlers give it passion.
   E. B. White 1899–1985: *Here is New York* (1949)

21 The city is not a concrete jungle, it is a human zoo.
   Desmond Morris 1928– : *The Human Zoo* (1969); see COUNTRY 4

22 A city is a place where there is no need to wait for next week to get the answer to a question, to taste the food of any country, to find new voices to listen to and familiar ones to listen to again.
   Margaret Mead 1901–78: *World Enough* (1975)

23 Villages, unlike towns, have always been ruled by conformism, isolation, petty surveillance, boredom and repetitive malicious gossip about the same families. Which is a precise enough description of the global spectacle's present vulgarity.
   on the concept of the 'global village'
   Guy Debord 1931–94: *Comments on the Society of the Spectacle* (1988); see EARTH 6, TECHNOLOGY 17

Courage

see also FEAR

proverbs and sayings ▸

1 Attack is the best form of defence.
   English proverb, late 18th century; see COURAGE 2

2 The best defence is a good offence.
   late 20th-century American version of COURAGE 1

3 A bully is always a coward.
   English proverb, early 19th century

4 Courage is fear that has said its prayers.
   American proverb, mid 20th century

5 Don't cry before you're hurt.
   sometimes used as a warning against appealing for sympathy on the assumption of an unpleasant outcome; English proverb, mid 16th century

6 Faint heart never won fair lady.
   often used as an encouragement to action; English proverb, mid 16th century

7 Fortune favours the brave.
   a person who acts bravely is likely to be successful; English proverb, late 14th century, originally often with allusion to Terence *Phormio* 'Fortune assists the brave' and Virgil *Aeneid* 'Fortune assists the bold'

8 None but the brave deserve the fair.
   English proverb, late 17th century, from Dryden: see COURAGE 17

9 You never know what you can do till you try.
   often used as encouragement to the reluctant; English proverb, early 19th century

phrases ▸

10 Blitz spirit

stoicism and determination in a difficult or dangerous situation; from the *Blitz*, the German air raids on Britain in 1940–1, abbreviating German *blitzkrieg* = lightning war

11 grasp the nettle

tackle a difficulty or danger with courage or boldness; see COURAGE 18, DANGER 29

quotations ▸

12 Happiness depends on being free, and freedom depends on being courageous.

Thucydides c.455–c.400 BC: *History of the Peloponnesian War*

13 Cowards die many times before their deaths;
The valiant never taste of death but once.

William Shakespeare 1564–1616: *Julius Caesar* (1599); see FEAR 2

14 Boldness be my friend!
Arm me, audacity.

William Shakespeare 1564–1616: *Cymbeline* (1609–10)

15 He either fears his fate too much,
Or his deserts are small,
That puts it not unto the touch
To win or lose it all.

James Graham, Marquess of Montrose 1612–50: 'My Dear and Only Love' (written 1642)

16 For all men would be cowards if they durst.

John Wilmot, Lord Rochester 1647–80: 'A Satire against Mankind' (1679)

17 None but the brave deserves the fair.

John Dryden 1631–1700: *Alexander's Feast* (1697); see COURAGE 8

18 Tender-handed stroke a nettle,
And it stings you for your pains;
Grasp it like a man of mettle,
And it soft as silk remains.

Aaron Hill 1685–1750: 'Verses Written on a Window in Scotland'; see COURAGE 11, DANGER 29

19 Boldness, and again boldness, and always boldness!

Georges Jacques Danton 1759–94: speech to the Legislative Committee of General Defence, 2 September 1792

20 As to moral courage, I have very rarely met with two o'clock in the morning courage: I mean instantaneous courage.

Napoleon I 1769–1821: E. A. de Las Cases *Mémorial de Ste-Hélène* (1823) 4–5 December 1815

21 Was none who would be foremost
To lead such dire attack;
But those behind cried 'Forward!'
And those before cried 'Back!'

Lord Macaulay 1800–59: 'Horatius' (1842)

22 No coward soul is mine,
No trembler in the world's storm-troubled sphere:
I see Heaven's glories shine,
And faith shines equal, arming me from fear.

Emily Brontë 1818–48: 'No coward soul is mine' (1846)

23 In the fell clutch of circumstance,
I have not winced nor cried aloud:
Under the bludgeonings of chance
My head is bloody, but unbowed.

W. E. Henley 1849–1903: 'Invictus. In Memoriam R.T.H.B.' (1888)

24 Had we lived, I should have had a tale to tell of the hardihood, endurance, and courage of my companions which would have stirred the heart of every Englishman. These rough notes and our dead bodies must tell the tale.

Robert Falcon Scott 1868–1912: 'Message to the Public' in late editions of *Times* 11 February 1913

25 Courage is the thing. All goes if courage goes!

J. M. Barrie 1860–1937: Rectorial Address at St Andrews, 3 May 1922

26 Courage is the price that Life exacts for granting peace,
The soul that knows it not, knows no release
From little things.

Amelia Earhart 1898–1937: 'Courage' (1927)

27 Grace under pressure.

when asked what he meant by 'guts', in an interview with Dorothy Parker

Ernest Hemingway 1899–1961: in *New Yorker* 30 November 1929

28 Courage is rightly esteemed the first of human qualities because as has been said, it is the quality which guarantees all others.
Winston Churchill 1874–1965: *Great Contemporaries* (1932); see COURAGE 30

29 Life shrinks or expands in proportion to one's courage.
Anaïs Nin 1903–77: *The Diary of Anaïs Nin* vol. 3 (1971) June 1941

30 Courage is not simply *one* of the virtues but the form of every virtue at the testing point.
C. S. Lewis 1898–1963: *The Screwtape Letters* (1942); see COURAGE 28

31 What counts is not necessarily the size of the dog in the fight — it's the size of the fight in the dog.
Dwight D. Eisenhower 1890–1969: remark, Republican National Committee Breakfast, 31 January 1958

32 For every ten men who are willing to face the guns of an enemy there is only one willing to brave the disapproval of his fellow, the censure of his colleagues, the wrath of his society. Moral courage is a rarer commodity than bravery in battle or great intelligence.
Robert Kennedy 1925–68: speech in Cape Town, 6 June 1966

Courtship

see also LOVE

proverbs and sayings ▸

1 Can you make me a cambric shirt,
Parsley, sage, rosemary, and thyme,
Without any seam or needlework?
And you shall be a true lover of mine.
traditional song

2 Happy's the wooing that is not long a-doing.
English proverb, late 16th century, reflecting a traditional belief

quotations ▸

3 She is a woman, therefore may be wooed;
She is a woman, therefore may be won.
William Shakespeare 1564–1616: *Titus Andronicus* (1590)

4 Why so pale and wan, fond lover?
Prithee, why so pale?
Will, when looking well can't move her,
Looking ill prevail?
John Suckling 1609–42: *Aglaura* (1637)

5 Had we but world enough, and time,
This coyness, lady, were no crime.
Andrew Marvell 1621–78: 'To His Coy Mistress' (1681)

6 Courtship to marriage, as a very witty prologue to a very dull play.
William Congreve 1670–1729: *The Old Bachelor* (1693)

7 There are very few of us who have heart enough to be really in love without encouragement. In nine cases out of ten, a woman had better show *more* affection than she feels.
Jane Austen 1775–1817: *Pride and Prejudice* (1813)

8 If you want to win her hand,
Let the maiden understand
That she's not the only pebble on the beach.
Harry Braisted: 'You're Not the Only Pebble on the Beach' (1896 song)

9 Holding hands at midnight
'Neath a starry sky,
Nice work if you can get it,
And you can get it if you try.
Ira Gershwin 1896–1989: 'Nice Work If You Can Get It' (1937 song); see ENVY 5

10 A man chases a girl (until she catches him).
Irving Berlin 1888–1989: title of song (1949)

11 Everyone knows that dating in your thirties is not the happy-go-lucky free-for-all it was when you were twenty-two.
Helen Fielding 1958– : *Bridget Jones's Diary* (1996)

Creativity

proverbs and sayings ▸

1 If you don't make mistakes you don't make anything.
English proverb, late 19th century; see MISTAKES 21

phrases ▸

2 the tenth Muse
a spirit of inspiration; a muse of inspiration imagined as added to the nine of classical mythology; see ARTS AND SCIENCES 1

quotations ▸

3 Nothing can be created out of nothing.
Lucretius c.94–55 BC: *De Rerum Natura*

4 All things were made by him; and without him was not any thing made that was made.
Bible: St John

5 The whole, though it be long, stands almost complete and finished in my mind, so that I can survey it, like a fine picture or a beautiful statue, at a glance. Nor do I hear in my imagination the parts *successively*, but I hear them, as it were, all at once. What a delight this is I cannot tell!
on his method of composition
Wolfgang Amadeus Mozart 1756–91: letter, Edward Holmes *The Life of Mozart* (1845)

6 That which is creative must create itself.
John Keats 1795–1821: letter to Hessey, 8 October 1818

7 The urge for destruction is also a creative urge!
Michael Bakunin 1814–76: *Jahrbuch für Wissenschaft und Kunst* (1842) 'Die Reaktion in Deutschland' (under the pseudonym 'Jules Elysard')

8 Urge and urge and urge,
Always the procreant urge of the world.
Walt Whitman 1819–92: 'Song of Myself' (written 1855)

9 Birds build—but not I build; no, but strain,
Time's eunuch, and not breed one work that wakes.
Gerard Manley Hopkins 1844–89: 'Thou art indeed just, Lord' (written 1889)

10 Poems are made by fools like me,
But only God can make a tree.
Joyce Kilmer 1886–1918: 'Trees' (1914)

11 Like a piece of ice on a hot stove the poem must ride on its own melting. A poem may be worked over once it is in being, but may not be worried into being.
Robert Frost 1874–1963: *Collected Poems* (1939) 'The Figure a Poem Makes'

12 The more you reason, the less you create.
Raymond Chandler 1888–1959: letter, 28 October 1947

13 Think before you speak is criticism's motto; speak before you think creation's.
E. M. Forster 1879–1970: *Two Cheers for Democracy* (1951)

14 All men are creative but few are artists.
Paul Goodman 1911–72: *Growing up Absurd* (1961)

15 The worst crime is to leave a man's hands empty.
Men are born makers, with that primal simplicity
In every maker since Adam.
Derek Walcott 1930– : *Omeros* (1990)

Cricket

phrases ▸

1 barmy army
a self-designation of (a group of) the supporters of a particular team, particularly a group of young, vociferous followers of the England cricket team

2 break one's duck
in cricket, score one's first run, in allusion to the origin of duck for a score of 0, as resembling a duck's egg in shape

3 sticky wicket
a cricket pitch that has been drying after rain and is difficult to bat on; figuratively, a tricky or awkward situation

quotations ►

4 It's more than a game. It's an institution.

of cricket

Thomas Hughes 1822–96: *Tom Brown's Schooldays* (1857)

5 In Affectionate Remembrance
of
ENGLISH CRICKET,
Which Died at The Oval
on
29th August, 1882.
Deeply lamented by a large circle of sorrowing friends and acquaintances.
R. I. P.
N. B.—The body will be cremated and the ashes taken to Australia.

following England's defeat by the Australians

Anonymous: in *Sporting Times* 2 September 1882

6 There's a breathless hush in the Close to-night—
Ten to make and the match to win—
A bumping pitch and a blinding light,
An hour to play and the last man in.

Henry Newbolt 1862–1938: 'Vitaï Lampada' (1897); see SPORTS 13

7 Then ye returned to your trinkets; then ye contented your souls
With the flannelled fools at the wicket or the muddied oafs at the goals.

Rudyard Kipling 1865–1936: 'The Islanders' (1903)

8 What do they know of cricket who only cricket know?

C. L. R. James 1901–89: *Beyond a Boundary* (1963); see ENGLAND 16

9 Cricket—a game which the English, not being a spiritual people, have invented in order to give themselves some conception of eternity.

Lord Mancroft 1914–87: *Bees in Some Bonnets* (1979)

10 Cricket civilizes people and creates good gentlemen. I want everyone to play cricket in Zimbabwe; I want ours to be a nation of gentlemen.

Robert Mugabe 1924– : in *Sunday Times* 26 February 1984

Crime and Punishment

see also GUILT, JUSTICE, LAW, MURDER

proverbs and sayings ►

1 A conservative is a liberal who's been mugged.

American saying, 1980s; see CRIME 43

2 Crime doesn't pay.

American proverb, early 20th century; a slogan of the FBI and the cartoon detective Dick Tracy

3 Crime must be concealed by crime.

American proverb, mid 20th century

4 Hang a thief when he's young, and he'll no' steal when he's old.

Scottish proverbial saying, early 19th century

5 If there were no receivers, there would be no thieves.

English proverb, late 14th century

6 Ill gotten goods never thrive.

something which is acquired dishonestly is unlikely to be the basis of lasting prosperity; English proverb, early 16th century

7 Little thieves are hanged, but great ones escape.

sufficient power and influence can ensure that a wrongdoer is not punished; English proverb, mid 17th century

8 Opportunity makes a thief.

often used to imply that the carelessness of the person who is robbed has contributed to the crime; English proverb, early 13th century

9 Three strikes and you're out.

referring to legislation which provides that an offender's third felony is punishable by life imprisonment or other severe sentence; deriving from the terminology of baseball, in which a batter who has had three strikes, or three fair opportunities of hitting the ball, is out; late 20th century saying

10 When thieves fall out, honest men come by their own.

meaning that it is through thieves quarrelling over their stolen goods that they are likely to be caught, and the goods recovered; English proverb, mid 16th century

11 You'll die facing the monument.

warning of the end of a life of crime; in Glasgow, prisoners were hanged facing Nelson's Monument on Glasgow Green; Scottish proverb *phrases ▸*

12 **cruel and unusual punishment**
punishment which is seen to exceed the bounds of what is regarded as an appropriate penal remedy for a civilized society; from the Eighth Amendment (1791): see CRIME 27

13 **dead-end kid**
a young slum-dwelling tough, a juvenile delinquent; the *Dead End Kids* were the juvenile delinquents in the films *Dead End* (1937) and *Angels with Dirty Faces* (1938)

14 **double jeopardy**
the prosecution or punishment of a person twice for the same offence; from the Fifth Amendment (1791) 'Nor shall any person subject for the same offence to be twice put in jeopardy of life or limb'

15 **lash of scorpions**
an instrument of vengeance or repression; a whip of torture made of knotted cords or armed with metal spikes, especially in allusion to the Bible (1 Kings): see CRIME 21

16 **read the Riot Act**
reprimand or caution sternly; the *Riot Act*, passed in 1715 and repealed in 1967, made it a felony for an assembly of more than twelve people to refuse to disperse after the reading of a specified portion of it by lawful authority

17 **short sharp shock**
a form of corrective treatment for young offenders in which the deterrent value was seen in the harshness of the regime rather than the length of the sentence; advocated by the Home Secretary, William Whitelaw, to the Conservative Party Conference in 1979; see CRIME 33

18 **smite hip and thigh**
punish unsparingly, originally referring to the Bible (Judges) 'He smote them hip and thigh with a mighty plague'

quotations ▸

19 I the Lord thy God am a jealous God, visiting the iniquity of the fathers upon the children unto the third and fourth generation of them that hate me.
'the sins of the fathers' in the Book of Common Prayer (1662)
Bible: Exodus

20 He that spareth his rod hateth his son.
Bible: Proverbs; see CHILD CARE 2

21 My father hath chastised you with whips, but I will chastise you with scorpions.
Bible: I Kings; see CRIME 15

22 This is the first of punishments, that no guilty man is acquitted if judged by himself.
Juvenal C. AD 60–C. 140: *Satires*

23 Hanging is too good for him, said Mr Cruelty.
John Bunyan 1628–88: *The Pilgrim's Progress* (1678)

24 The crime and not the scaffold makes the shame.
Thomas Corneille 1625–1709: *Le Comte d'Essex* (1678)

25 Men are not hanged for stealing horses, but that horses may not be stolen.
Lord Halifax 1633–95: *Political, Moral, and Miscellaneous Thoughts and Reflections* (1750) 'Of Punishment'

26 All punishment is mischief: all punishment in itself is evil.
Jeremy Bentham 1748–1832: *Principles of Morals and Legislation* (1789)

27 Excessive bail shall not be required, nor excessive fines imposed, nor cruel and unusual punishment inflicted.
Constitution of the United States 1787– : *Eighth Amendment* (1791); see CRIME 12

28 Whenever the offence inspires less horror than the punishment, the rigour of penal law is obliged to give way to the common feelings of mankind.
Edward Gibbon 1737–94: attributed

29 Punishment is not for revenge, but to lessen crime and reform the criminal.
Elizabeth Fry 1780–1845: Rachel E. Cresswell and Katharine Fry *Memoir of the Life of Elizabeth Fry* (1848)

30 Better build schoolrooms for 'the boy,'
Than cells and gibbets for 'the man.'
Eliza Cook 1818–89: 'A Song for the Ragged Schools' (1853)

31 Thou shalt not steal; an empty feat,
When it's so lucrative to cheat.
Arthur Hugh Clough 1819–61: 'The Latest Decalogue' (1862)

32 If my life teaches the public that men are made mad by bad treatment, and

if the police are taught that they may not exasperate to madness men they persecute and ill treat, my life will not be entirely thrown away.

Ned Kelly 1855–80: interview in Beechworth Prison, in *The Age* 9 August 1880

33 Awaiting the sensation of a short,
sharp shock,
From a cheap and chippy chopper on
a big black block.

W. S. Gilbert 1836–1911: *The Mikado* (1885); see CRIME 17

34 My object all sublime
I shall achieve in time—
To let the punishment fit the crime—
The punishment fit the crime.

W. S. Gilbert 1836–1911: *The Mikado* (1885)

35 Singularity is almost invariably a clue. The more featureless and commonplace a crime is, the more difficult is it to bring it home.

Arthur Conan Doyle 1859–1930: *The Adventures of Sherlock Holmes* (1892) 'The Boscombe Valley Mystery'

36 Thieves respect property. They merely wish the property to become their property that they may more perfectly respect it.

G. K. Chesterton 1874–1936: *The Man who was Thursday* (1908)

37 The mood and temper of the public in regard to the treatment of crime and criminals is one of the most unfailing tests of the civilization of any country.

Winston Churchill 1874–1965: speech, House of Commons, 20 July 1910

38 Once in the racket you're always in it.

Al Capone 1899–1947: in *Philadelphia Public Ledger* 18 May 1929

39 Major Strasser has been shot. Round up the usual suspects.

Julius J. Epstein 1909–2001: *Casablanca* (1942 film), spoken by Claude Rains

40 Crime isn't a disease, it's a symptom. Cops are like a doctor that gives you aspirin for a brain tumour.

Raymond Chandler 1888–1959: *The Long Good-Bye* (1953)

41 The fear of burglars is not only the fear of being robbed, but also the fear of a sudden and unexpected clutch out of the darkness.

Elias Canetti 1905–94: *Crowds and Power* (1960)

42 I hate victims who respect their executioners.

Jean-Paul Sartre 1905–80: *Les Séquestrés d'Altona* (1960)

43 A liberal is a conservative who has been arrested.

Tom Wolfe 1931– : *The Bonfire of the Vanities* (1987); see CRIME 1

44 Society needs to condemn a little more and understand a little less.

John Major 1943– : interview with *Mail on Sunday* 21 February 1993

45 Labour is the party of law and order in Britain today. Tough on crime and tough on the causes of crime.

Tony Blair 1953– : speech at the Labour Party Conference, 30 September 1993

46 Prison is a most expensive way of making bad people worse.

Lord Ackner 1920–2005: speech, House of Lords, 23 October 1997

47 Cameron's empty idea seems to be 'let's hug a hoodie', whatever they have done.

Vernon Coaker 1953– : commenting on the text of a forthcoming speech by David Cameron, in *Observer* 9 July 2006: see CRIME 48

48 We—the people in suits—often see hoodies as aggressive, the uniform of a rebel army of gangsters. But hoodies are more defensive than offensive. They're a way to stay invisible in the street.

David Cameron 1966– : speech to Centre for Social Justice, 10 July 2006; see CRIME 47

Crises

proverbs and sayings ▸

1 Duck and cover.

US advice in the event of a missile attack, 1950; associated particularly with children's cartoon character 'Bert the Turtle'

2 Go in, stay in, tune in.

British government advice on preparing for emergencies, 2004

3 **Keep calm and carry on.**
poster designed by the Ministry of Information in 1939 but not used in World War II; re-discovered and popularized in the early 21st century

4 **Ohhh, I don't *believe* it!**
catchphrase used by Victor Meldrew in *One Foot in the Grave* (BBC television series, 1989–2000), written by David Renwick

5 **We won't make a drama out of a crisis.**
advertising slogan for Commercial Union insurance

6 **When disaster strikes and all hope is gone, get down on your knees and pray for Shackleton.**
modern saying, paraphrase of Apsley Cherry-Garrard by British geologist Raymond Priestley (1886–1974) in a lecture 'Twentieth Century Man against Antarctica' (1950); see EXPLORATION 13

phrases ▸

7 **cross the Rubicon**
take a decisive or irrevocable step; the *Rubicon* was a stream in North-East Italy which marked the ancient boundary with Cisalpine Gaul; by taking his army across it into Italy from his own province in 49 BC, Julius Caesar broke the law forbidding a general to lead an army out of his province, and so committed himself to war against the Senate and Pompey; see CRISES 14

8 **the Dunkirk spirit**
the refusal to surrender or despair in a time of crisis; from the evacuation of the British Expeditionary Force from Dunkirk in 1940; see CRISES 23, WORLD WAR II 11

9 **fiddle while Rome burns**
be concerned with relatively trivial matters while ignoring the serious or disastrous events going on around one; the original reference is to the behaviour of the emperor Nero, who according to Suetonius sang the whole of 'The Sack of Ilium' in his preferred stage costume to celebrate the beauty of the flames as Rome burned

10 **the final straw**
a slight addition to a burden or difficulty that makes it finally unbearable, from the proverb: see EXCESS 5

11 **moment of truth**
a crisis, a turning-point; a testing situation; Spanish *el momento de la verdad* = the time of the final sword-thrust in a bullfight

12 **the parting of the ways**
the moment at which a choice must be made; after the Bible (Ezekiel) 'The king of Babylon stood at the parting of the ways'

13 **the sky is falling**
a warning of imminent disaster, especially one which is regarded as unduly alarmist; from the nursery story in which Chicken Little and other animals repeatedly warn the king that the sky is falling down; see FEAR 5

quotations ▸

14 **The die is cast.**
at the crossing of the Rubicon (see CRISES 7); often quoted in Latin *'Iacta alea est'* but originally spoken in Greek
Julius Caesar 100–44 BC: Suetonius *Lives of the Caesars* 'Divus Julius'; Plutarch *Parallel Lives* 'Pompey'

15 **For it is your business, when the wall next door catches fire.**
Horace 65–8 BC: *Epistles*

16 **We have the wolf by the ears; and we can neither hold him, nor safely let him go. Justice is in one scale, and self-preservation in the other.**
on slavery
Thomas Jefferson 1743–1826: letter to John Holmes, 22 April 1820; see DANGER 18

17 **Swimming for his life, a man does not see much of the country through which the river winds.**
W. E. Gladstone 1809–98: diary, 31 December 1868

18 **If you can keep your head when all about you**
Are losing theirs and blaming it on you...
Rudyard Kipling 1865–1936: 'If—' (1910); see CRISES 22

19 **The British people have taken for themselves this motto—'Business carried on as usual during alterations on the map of Europe'.**
Winston Churchill 1874–1965: speech at Guildhall, 9 November 1914

20 **The crisis consists precisely in the fact that the old is dying and the new cannot be born; in this interregnum a great variety of morbid symptoms appear.**
Antonio Gramsci 1891–1937: in 1930, *Selections from the Prison Notebooks* (1971)

21 Comin' in on a wing and a pray'r.
the contemporary comment of a war pilot, speaking from a disabled plane to ground control
Harold Adamson 1906–80: title of song (1943); see NECESSITY 15

22 As someone pointed out recently, if you can keep your head when all about you are losing theirs, it's just possible you haven't grasped the situation.
Jean Kerr 1923–2003: *Please Don't Eat the Daisies* (1957); see CRISES 18

23 I myself have always deprecated... in crisis after crisis, appeals to the Dunkirk spirit as an answer to our problems.
Harold Wilson 1916–95: in the House of Commons, 26 July 1961; see CRISES 8

24 We're eyeball to eyeball, and I think the other fellow just blinked.
on the Cuban missile crisis
Dean Rusk 1909–94: comment, 24 October 1962; see DEFIANCE 6

25 In bygone days, commanders were taught that when in doubt, they should march their troops towards the sound of gunfire. I intend to march my troops towards the sound of gunfire.
Jo Grimond 1913–93: speech at Liberal Party Annual Assembly, 14 September 1963

26 There cannot be a crisis next week. My schedule is already full.
Henry Kissinger 1923– : in *New York Times Magazine* 1 June 1969

27 Does any one know where the love of
God goes
When the waves turn the minutes to
hours?
Gordon Lightfoot 1938– : 'The Wreck of the Edmund Fitzgerald' (1976 song)

28 Crisis? What Crisis?
headline summarizing James Callaghan's remark of 10 January 1979: 'I don't think other people in the world would share the view there is mounting chaos'
Anonymous: in *Sun* 11 January 1979

29 Don't panic.
Douglas Adams 1952–2001: *Hitch Hiker's Guide to the Galaxy* (1979)

30 You never want a serious crisis to go to waste.
often quoted as 'Never waste a good crisis'
Rahm Emanuel 1959– : to business leaders, 18 November 2008, in *Globe and Mail* (Canada) 20 November 2008

31 *Estamos bien en el refugio, los 33.*
We are OK in the refuge, the 33.
José Ojeda: note attached to drill bit searching for 33 miners trapped in the San José mine, Copiapó, Chile, 22 August 2010

Criticism

see also LIKES, TASTE

proverbs and sayings ▸

1 Criticism is something you can avoid by saying nothing, doing nothing, and being nothing.
abstaining from criticism will result in complete inaction; American proverb, mid 20th century

2 Don't judge a man till you've walked two moons in his moccasins.
warning against judging without understanding circumstances; modern saying, said to be of native American origin

phrases ▸

3 cast the first stone
be the first to make an accusation, especially when not oneself guiltless, with allusion to the Bible (John): see GUILT 8

4 the pot calling the kettle black
used to convey that the criticisms a person is aiming at someone else could equally well apply to themselves

quotations ▸

5 There is more business in interpreting interpretations than in interpreting things, and more books on books than on any other subject: all we do is gloss each other.
Montaigne 1533–92: *Essays* (1580)

6 One should look long and carefully at oneself before one considers judging others.
Molière 1622–73: *Le Misanthrope* (1666)

7 You *may* abuse a tragedy, though you cannot write one. You may scold a

carpenter who has made you a bad table, though you cannot make a table. It is not your trade to make tables.

on literary criticism

Samuel Johnson 1709–84: James Boswell *Life of Samuel Johnson* (1791) 25 June 1763

8 A man must serve his time to every trade
Save censure—critics all are ready made.

Lord Byron 1788–1824: *English Bards and Scotch Reviewers* (1809)

9 This will never do.

on Wordsworth's *The Excursion* (1814)

Francis, Lord Jeffrey 1773–1850: in *Edinburgh Review* November 1814

10 I never read a book before reviewing it; it prejudices a man so.

Sydney Smith 1771–1845: H. Pearson *The Smith of Smiths* (1934)

11 You know who the critics are? The men who have failed in literature and art.

Benjamin Disraeli 1804–81: *Lothair* (1870)

12 I am sitting in the smallest room of my house. I have your review before me. In a moment it will be behind me.

responding to a savage review by Rudolph Louis in *Münchener Neueste Nachrichten*, 7 February 1906

Max Reger 1873–1916: Nicolas Slonimsky *Lexicon of Musical Invective* (1953)

13 She was one of the people who say 'I don't know anything about music really, but I know what I like.'

Max Beerbohm 1872–1956: *Zuleika Dobson* (1911)

14 I have derived continued benefit from criticism at all periods of my life and I do not remember any time when I was ever short of it.

Winston Churchill 1874–1965: speech in House of Commons 27 November 1914

15 People ask you for criticism, but they only want praise.

W. Somerset Maugham 1874–1965: *Of Human Bondage* (1915)

16 Parodies and caricatures are the most penetrating of criticisms.

Aldous Huxley 1894–1963: *Point Counter Point* (1928)

17 Remember, a statue has never been set up in honour of a critic!

Jean Sibelius 1865–1957: Bengt de Törne *Sibelius: A Close-Up* (1937)

18 Whom the gods wish to destroy they first call promising.

Cyril Connolly 1903–74: *Enemies of Promise* (1938); see MADNESS 1

19 When the reviews are bad I tell my staff that they can join me as I cry all the way to the bank.

Liberace 1919–87: *Autobiography* (1973); an earlier version was reported in *Collier's* 17 September 1954

20 I have never found, in a long experience of politics, that criticism is ever inhibited by ignorance.

Harold Macmillan 1894–1986: in *Wall Street Journal* 13 August 1963

21 Interpretation is the revenge of the intellect upon art.

Susan Sontag 1933–2004: in *Evergreen Review* December 1964

22 A critic is a man who knows the way but can't drive the car.

Kenneth Tynan 1927–80: in *New York Times Magazine* 9 January 1966

23 *Il n'y a pas de hors-texte.*
There is nothing outside of the text.

Jacques Derrida 1930–2004: *Of Grammatology* (1967)

24 If you are not criticized, you may not be doing much.

Donald Rumsfeld 1932– : *Rumsfeld's Rules* (2001)

Cruelty

proverbs and sayings ▸

1 It takes 40 dumb animals to make a fur coat, but only one to wear it.

slogan of an anti-fur campaign poster, 1980s, sometimes attributed to David Bailey (1938–)

phrases ▸

2 out-Herod Herod

behave with extreme cruelty or tyranny; *Herod* = a blustering tyrant in miracle plays, representing Herod the ruler of Judaea at the time of Jesus' birth (see FESTIVALS 30); after Shakespeare *Hamlet* 'I would have such a fellow whipp'd for o'erdoing Termagant; it out-herods Herod'

3 reign of terror

a period of remorseless repression or bloodshed, in particular (*Reign of Terror*) the period of the Terror during the French Revolution between mid 1793 and July 1794 when the ruling Jacobin faction, dominated by Robespierre, ruthlessly executed anyone considered a threat to their regime

4 Roman holiday

an event occasioning enjoyment or profit derived from the suffering or discomfort of others, from Byron: see CRUELTY 9

quotations ▶

5 Boys throw stones at frogs for fun, but the frogs don't die for 'fun,' but in sober earnest.

Bion c.325–c.255 BC: Plutarch *Moralia*

6 Strike him so that he can feel that he is dying.

Caligula AD 12–41: Suetonius *Lives of the Caesars* 'Gaius Caligula'

7 I must be cruel only to be kind.

William Shakespeare 1564–1616: *Hamlet* (1601)

8 Man's inhumanity to man
Makes countless thousands mourn!

Robert Burns 1759–96: 'Man was made to Mourn' (1786)

9 *There* were his young barbarians all at play,
There was their Dacian mother—he, their sire,
Butchered to make a Roman holiday.

Lord Byron 1788–1824: *Childe Harold's Pilgrimage* (1812–18); see CRUELTY 4

10 Cruelty, like every other vice, requires no motive outside itself—it only requires opportunity.

George Eliot 1819–80: *Scenes of Clerical Life* (1858)

11 The infliction of cruelty with a good conscience is a delight to moralists. That is why they invented Hell.

Bertrand Russell 1872–1970: *Sceptical Essays* (1928) 'On the Value of Scepticism'

12 The healthy man does not torture others—generally it is the tortured who turn into torturers.

Carl Gustav Jung 1875–1961: in *Du* May 1941

13 The wish to hurt, the momentary intoxication with pain, is the loophole through which the pervert climbs into the minds of ordinary men.

Jacob Bronowski 1908–74: *The Face of Violence* (1954)

14 Our language lacks words to express this offence, the demolition of a man.

of a year spent in Auschwitz

Primo Levi 1919–87: *If This is a Man* (1958)

15 All cruel people describe themselves as paragons of frankness.

Tennessee Williams 1911–83: *The Milk Train Doesn't Stop Here any More* (1963)

Culture and Civilization

proverbs and sayings ▶

1 An ace caff with quite a nice museum attached.

advertising slogan for the Victoria and Albert Museum, February 1989

2 A man without culture is like a zebra without stripes.

African proverb (Masai)

phrases ▶

3 the age of reason

the late 17th and 18th centuries in western Europe, during which cultural life was characterized by faith in human reason; the enlightenment

4 the end of civilization as we know it

the complete collapse of ordered society; supposedly a cinematic cliché, and actually used in the film *Citizen Kane* (1941) 'a project which would mean the end of civilization as we know it'

5 the golden age

an idyllic past time of prosperity, happiness, and innocence; the period of a nation's greatest prosperity or literary and artistic merit

6 the noble savage

primitive man, conceived of in the manner of Rousseau as morally superior to civilized man; see also CULTURE 9

quotations ▸

7 Our love of what is beautiful does not lead to extravagance; our love of the things of the mind does not make us soft.

Pericles c.495–429 BC: funeral oration, Athens, 430 BC; Thucydides *History of the Peloponnesian War*

8 In the youth of a state arms do flourish; in the middle age of a state, learning; and then both of them together for a time; in the declining age of a state, mechanical arts and merchandise.

Francis Bacon 1561–1626: *Essays* (1625) 'Of Vicissitude of Things'

9 I am as free as nature first made man,
Ere the base laws of servitude began,
When wild in woods the noble savage ran.

John Dryden 1631–1700: *The Conquest of Granada* (1670); see CULTURE 6

10 I must study politics and war that my sons may have liberty to study mathematics and philosophy. My sons ought to study mathematics and philosophy, geography, natural history, naval architecture, navigation, commerce, and agriculture, in order to give their children a right to study painting, poetry, music, architecture, statuary, tapestry, and porcelain.

John Adams 1735–1826: letter to Abigail Adams, 12 May 1780

11 If a nation expects to be ignorant and free, in a state of civilization, it expects what never was and never will be.

Thomas Jefferson 1743–1826: letter to Colonel Charles Yancey, 6 January 1816

12 The three great elements of modern civilization, Gunpowder, Printing, and the Protestant Religion.

Thomas Carlyle 1795–1881: *Critical and Miscellaneous Essays* (1838) 'The State of German Literature'; see INVENTIONS 6

13 Civilization advances by extending the number of important operations which we can perform without thinking about them.

Alfred North Whitehead 1861–1947: *Introduction to Mathematics* (1911)

14 Mrs Ballinger is one of the ladies who pursue Culture in bands, as though it were dangerous to meet it alone.

Edith Wharton 1862–1937: *Xingu and Other Stories* (1916)

15 All civilization has from time to time become a thin crust over a volcano of revolution.

Havelock Ellis 1859–1939: *Little Essays of Love and Virtue* (1922)

16 Cultured people are merely the glittering scum which floats upon the deep river of production.

on hearing his son Randolph criticize the lack of culture of the Calgary oil magnates, probably 1929

Winston Churchill 1874–1965: Martin Gilbert *In Search of Churchill* (1994)

17 JOURNALIST: Mr Gandhi, what do you think of modern civilization?
GANDHI: That would be a good idea.

Mahatma Gandhi 1869–1948: on arriving in England in 1930; E. F. Schumacher *Good Work* (1979)

18 Whenever I hear the word culture...I release the safety-catch of my Browning!

often quoted: 'Whenever I hear the word culture, I reach for my pistol!'

Hanns Johst 1890–1978: *Schlageter* (1933); often attributed to Hermann Goering

19 Culture may even be described simply as that which makes life worth living.

T. S. Eliot 1888–1965: *Notes Towards a Definition of Culture* (1948)

20 In Italy for thirty years under the Borgias they had warfare, terror, murder, bloodshed —they produced Michelangelo, Leonardo da Vinci and the Renaissance. In Switzerland they had brotherly love, five hundred years of democracy and peace and what did that produce...? The cuckoo clock.

Orson Welles 1915–85: *The Third Man* (1949 film); words added by Welles to Graham Greene's script

21 If civilization had been left in female hands, we would still be living in grass huts.

Camille Paglia 1947– : *Sexual Personae* (1990)

22 A cultural Chernobyl.

of Euro Disney

Ariane Mnouchkine 1934– : in *Harper's Magazine* July 1992

23 A nation stays alive when its culture stays alive.
Anonymous: notice over the door of the Kabul museum after the expulsion of the Taliban from Afghanistan, 2002

Custom and Habit

proverbs and sayings ▸

1 Old habits die hard.
it is difficult to break long-established habits; English proverb, mid 18th century

2 What is new cannot be true.
used to imply that innovation is less soundly based than custom which has been proved by experience; English proverb, mid 17th century

3 You cannot shift an old tree without it dying.
often used to suggest the risk involved in moving an elderly person who has lived in the same place for many years; English proverb, early 16th century

4 You can't teach an old dog new tricks.
someone who is already set in their ways is not able to learn new ways of doing things; English proverb, mid 16th century

phrases ▸

5 pass on the torch
pass on a tradition, from Lucretius 'Some races increase, others are reduced, and in a short while the generations of living creatures are changed and like runners relay the torch of life'

quotations ▸

6 Without ritual, courtesy is tiresome, prudence is timid; without ritual, bravery is quarrelsome, frankness is hurtful.
Confucius 551–479 BC: *Analects*

7 If one were to order all mankind to choose the best set of rules in the world, each group would, after due consideration, choose its own customs; each group regards its own as being by far the best.
Herodotus c.485–c.425 BC: *Histories*

8 Neither by nature, then, nor contrary to nature do the virtues arise in us; nature gives us the capacity to receive them, and this capacity is brought to maturity by habit.
often quoted in the form 'We are what we repeatedly do'
Aristotle 384–322 BC: *Nicomachean Ethics*

9 The Lord says in the gospel; 'I am the Truth.' He does not say 'I am custom.' Therefore, when the truth is made manifest, custom must give way to truth.
Bishop Libosus of Vaga fl. AD 256: St Augustine of Hippo *On Baptism*; see CHRISTIAN CHURCH 13

10 *Consuetudo est altera natura.*
Habit is second nature.
Auctoritates Aristotelis: a compilation of medieval propositions

11 But to my mind,—though I am native here,
And to the manner born,—it is a custom
More honoured in the breach than the observance.
William Shakespeare 1564–1616: *Hamlet* (1601); see BEHAVIOUR 16

12 Custom, that unwritten law,
By which the people keep even kings in awe.
Charles D'Avenant 1656–1714: *Circe* (1677)

13 Custom reconciles us to everything.
Edmund Burke 1729–97: *On the Sublime and Beautiful* (1757)

14 Habit with him was all the test of truth,
'It must be right: I've done it from my youth.'
George Crabbe 1754–1832: *The Borough* (1810)

15 People wish to be settled: only as far as they are unsettled is there any hope for them.
Ralph Waldo Emerson 1803–82: *Essays* (1841) 'Circles'

16 The tradition of all the dead generations weighs like a nightmare on the brain of the living.
Karl Marx 1818–83: *The Eighteenth Brumaire of Louis Bonaparte* (1852)

17 The less of routine, the more of life.
Amos Bronson Alcott 1799–1888: *Table Talk* (1877)

18 Laws are sand, customs are rock. Laws can be evaded and punishment escaped, but an openly transgressed custom brings sure punishment.
Mark Twain 1835–1910: *The Gorky Incident* (1906)

19 Tradition means giving votes to the most obscure of all classes, our ancestors. It is the democracy of the dead.
G. K. Chesterton 1874–1936: *Orthodoxy* (1908)

20 Every public action, which is not customary, either is wrong, or, if it is right, is a dangerous precedent. It follows that nothing should ever be done for the first time.
Francis M. Cornford 1874–1943: *Microcosmographia Academica* (1908)

21 I confess myself to be a great admirer of tradition. The longer you can look back, the farther you can look forward.
Winston Churchill 1874–1965: speech, March 1944

22 The air is full of our cries. (*He listens*) But habit is a great deadener.
Samuel Beckett 1906–89: *Waiting for Godot* (1955)

23 *Good* habits: they are never good, because they are habits.
Jean-Paul Sartre 1905–80: attributed

Cynicism

see DISILLUSION AND CYNICISM

Dance

proverbs and sayings ▸

1 We're fools whether we dance or not, so we might as well dance.
modern saying, claimed to be a Japanese proverb

2 When you go to dance, take heed whom you take by the hand.
English proverb, early 17th century

3 You need more than dancing shoes to be a dancer.
American proverb, mid 20th century

phrases ▸

4 antic hay
an absurd dance, from Marlowe; see DANCE 6

5 trip the light fantastic
dance, originally with allusion to Milton: see DANCE 9

quotations ▸

6 My men, like satyrs grazing on the lawns,
Shall with their goat feet dance an antic hay.
Christopher Marlowe 1564–93: *Edward II* (1593); see DANCE 4

7 This wondrous miracle did Love devise,
For dancing is love's proper exercise.
John Davies 1569–1626: 'Orchestra, or a Poem of Dancing' (1596)

8 A dance is a measured pace, as a verse is a measured speech.
Francis Bacon 1561–1626: *The Advancement of Learning* (1605)

9 Come, and trip it as ye go
On the light fantastic toe.
John Milton 1608–74: 'L'Allegro' (1645); see DANCE 5

10 On with the dance! let joy be unconfined.
Lord Byron 1788–1824: *Childe Harold's Pilgrimage* (1812–18)

11 Will you, won't you, will you, won't you, will you join the dance?
Lewis Carroll 1832–98: *Alice's Adventures in Wonderland* (1865)

12 O body swayed to music, O brightening glance
How can we know the dancer from the dance?
W. B. Yeats 1865–1939: 'Among School Children' (1928)

13 Heaven—I'm in Heaven—And my heart beats so that I can hardly speak;
And I seem to find the happiness I seek
When we're out together dancing cheek-to-cheek.
Irving Berlin 1888–1989: 'Cheek-to-Cheek' (1935 song)

14 There may be trouble ahead,
But while there's moonlight and music
and love and romance,
Let's face the music and dance.

Irving Berlin 1888–1989: 'Let's Face the Music and Dance' (1936 song)

15 [Dancing is] a perpendicular expression of a horizontal desire.

George Bernard Shaw 1856–1950: in *New Statesman* 23 March 1962

16 The truest expression of a people is in its dances and its music. Bodies never lie.

Agnes de Mille 1908–93: in *New York Times Magazine* 11 May 1975

17 Dance is the hidden language of the soul.

Martha Graham 1894–1991: *Blood Memory* (1991)

18 Tango is a feeling that can be danced, and that feeling, of course, is passion.

Hernán Lombardi: Minister for Culture, Buenos Aires, in *Times* 1 October 2009

Danger

see also CAUTION, COURAGE

proverbs and sayings ▸

1 Adventures are to the adventurous.

the person who wants exciting things to happen must take the initiative; English proverb, mid 19th century

2 Heaven protects children, sailors, and drunken men.

often used (in a number of variant forms) to imply that someone unable to look after themselves has been undeservedly lucky; English proverb, mid 19th century

3 He who rides a tiger is afraid to dismount.

once a dangerous or troublesome venture is begun, the safest course is to carry it through to the end; see DANGER 17, DANGER 23; English proverb, late 19th century

4 If you play with fire you get burnt.

if you involve yourself with something potentially dangerous you are likely to be hurt; English proverb, late 19th century

5 It is the calm and silent water that drowns a man.

the greatest danger may be concealed beneath an innocent appearance; African proverb

6 Just when you thought it was safe to go back in the water.

advertising copy for the film *Jaws 2* (1978), featuring the return of the great white shark

7 Light the blue touch paper and retire immediately.

traditional instruction for lighting fireworks

8 More than one yew bow in Chester.

you may escape danger once, but not a second time (*Chester* representing the English, the traditional enemy); Welsh proverb

9 The post of honour is the post of danger.

English proverb, mid 16th century

10 When the lion shows its teeth, don't assume that it is smiling.

a warning sign should not be taken lightly; Arab proverb

11 Who dares wins.

motto of the British Special Air Service regiment, from 1942

12 Women and children first.

order given on a ship in difficulty, indicating that women and children should be allowed on to the lifeboats before men; in allusive (and often humorous) use, warning of a risky or unpleasant situation; from the mid 19th century

phrases ▸

13 bell the cat

take the danger of a shared enterprise upon oneself, from the fable in which mice proposed hanging a bell around a cat's neck so as to be warned of its approach

14 between Scylla and Charybdis

a situation involving two dangers in which an attempt to avoid one increases the risk from the other; in Greek mythology, *Scylla* was a female sea monster who devoured sailors when they tried to navigate the narrow channel between her cave and the whirlpool *Charybdis*

15 cry wolf

raise repeated false alarms, so that a genuine cry for help goes unheeded, from the fable of the shepherd boy who tricked people with false cries of 'Wolf!'; when he was actually attacked and killed, his genuine appeals for help were ignored

16 **firebell in the night**
a warning of danger; from Thomas Jefferson's expression of alarm at the implications of the Missouri Compromise (which established that slavery should be excluded from the northern states); see AMERICA 14

17 **have a tiger by the tail**
have embarked on a course of action which proves unexpectedly difficult but which cannot easily or safely be abandoned; see DANGER 3

18 **have a wolf by the ears**
be in a precarious situation; be in a predicament where any course of action presents problems; see CRISES 16

19 **a lion in the way**
a danger or obstacle, especially an imaginary one; from the Bible (Proverbs) 'The slothful man saith, There is a lion in the way'

20 **the lion's mouth**
a place or situation of great peril, with reference to the Bible (Psalms) 'Save me from the lion's mouth' and (2 Timothy) 'I was delivered out of the mouth of the lion'

21 **a pad in the straw**
a lurking or hidden danger; *pad* = a toad, regarded as a venomous creature

22 **pull the chestnuts out of the fire**
succeed in a hazardous undertaking on behalf of or through the agency of another, in allusion to the fable of a monkey using a cat's paw to get roasting chestnuts from a fire; see DUTY 6

23 **ride a tiger**
take on a responsibility or embark on a course of action which subsequently cannot easily or safely be abandoned, from the proverb: see DANGER 3

24 **a snake in the grass**
a secret enemy, a lurking danger; after Virgil *Eclogues* 'There's a snake hidden in the grass'

25 **a sword of Damocles**
an imminent danger; a constant threat, especially in the midst of prosperity; *Damocles* = a legendary courtier who extravagantly praised the happiness of Dionysius I, ruler of Syracuse, and whom Dionysius feasted while a sword hung by a hair above him

26 **throw someone to the lions**
to put in an unpleasant or dangerous situation, originally with reference to the practice in imperial Rome of throwing religious and political dissidents, especially Christians, to wild beasts as a method of execution; see CHRISTIAN CHURCH 3

27 **the valley of the shadow of death**
a place or period of intense gloom or peril, from the Bible (Psalms) 'Though I walk through the valley of the shadow of death, I will fear no evil'

quotations ►

28 I am escaped with the skin of my teeth.
Bible: Job

29 Out of this nettle, danger, we pluck this flower, safety.
William Shakespeare 1564–1616: *Henry IV, Part 1* (1597); see COURAGE 11

30 When there is no peril in the fight, there is no glory in the triumph.
Pierre Corneille 1606–84: *Le Cid* (1637)

31 Dangers by being despised grow great.
Edmund Burke 1729–97: speech on the Petition of the Unitarians, 11 May 1792

32 In skating over thin ice, our safety is in our speed.
Ralph Waldo Emerson 1803–82: *Essays* (1841) 'Prudence'

33 Nothing in life is so exhilarating as to be shot at without result.
Winston Churchill 1874–1965: *The Story of the Malakand Field Force* (1898)

34 We took risks, we knew we took them; things have come out against us, and therefore we have no cause for complaint.
Robert Falcon Scott 1868–1912: 'The Last Message' in *Scott's Last Expedition* (1913)

35 Considering how dangerous everything is, nothing is really very frightening!
Gertrude Stein 1874–1946: *Everybody's Autobiography* (1937)

36 Security is mostly a superstition. It does not exist in nature, nor do the children of men as a whole experience it. Avoiding danger is no safer in the long run than outright exposure. Life is either a daring adventure, or nothing.
Helen Keller 1880–1968: *The Open Door* (1957)

37 Security is when everything is settled, when nothing can happen to you; security is the denial of life.
Germaine Greer 1939– : *The Female Eunuch* (1970)

38 Risk comes from not knowing what you're doing.
Warren Buffett 1930– : in *Omaha World-Herald* 2 January 1994

Day and Night

proverbs and sayings ▸

1 Be the day weary or be the day long, at last it ringeth to evensong.
even the most difficult time will come to an end; English proverb, early 16th century

2 The morning daylight appears plainer when you put out your candle.
American proverb

phrases ▸

3 the watches of the night
the night-time; *watch* = originally each of the three or four periods of time, during which a watch or guard was kept, into which the night was divided by the Jews and Romans

4 the witching hour
midnight; the time when witches are proverbially active; after Shakespeare: see DAY 6; see also BUSINESS 24

quotations ▸

5 Night's candles are burnt out, and jocund day
Stands tiptoe on the misty mountain tops.
William Shakespeare 1564–1616: *Romeo and Juliet* (1595)

6 'Tis now the very witching time of night,
When churchyards yawn and hell itself breathes out
Contagion to this world.
William Shakespeare 1564–1616: *Hamlet* (1601); see DAY 4

7 Lighten our darkness, we beseech thee, O Lord; and by thy great mercy defend us from all perils and dangers of this night.
The Book of Common Prayer 1662: *Evening Prayer*

8 Now came still evening on, and twilight grey
Had in her sober livery all things clad.
John Milton 1608–74: *Paradise Lost* (1667)

9 The curfew tolls the knell of parting day,
The lowing herd wind slowly o'er the lea,
The ploughman homeward plods his weary way,
And leaves the world to darkness and to me.
Thomas Gray 1716–71: *Elegy Written in a Country Churchyard* (1751)

10 The Sun's rim dips; the stars rush out;
At one stride comes the dark.
Samuel Taylor Coleridge 1772–1834: 'The Rime of the Ancient Mariner' (1798)

11 The cares that infest the day
Shall fold their tents, like the Arabs,
And as silently steal away.
Henry Wadsworth Longfellow 1807–82: 'The Day is Done' (1844)

12 Awake! for Morning in the bowl of night
Has flung the stone that puts the stars to flight.
Edward Fitzgerald 1809–83: *The Rubáiyát of Omar Khayyám* (1859)

13 There midnight's all a glimmer, and noon a purple glow,
And evening full of the linnet's wings.
W. B. Yeats 1865–1939: 'The Lake Isle of Innisfree' (1892)

14 Let us go then, you and I,
When the evening is spread out against the sky
Like a patient etherized upon a table.
T. S. Eliot 1888–1965: 'The Love Song of J. Alfred Prufrock' (1917); see POETRY 32

15 I have a horror of sunsets, they're so romantic, so operatic.
Marcel Proust 1871–1922: *Cities of the Plain* (1922)

16 I have been one acquainted with the night.
Robert Frost 1874–1963: 'Acquainted with the Night' (1928)

17 Morning has broken
Like the first morning,
Blackbird has spoken
Like the first bird.
Eleanor Farjeon 1881–1965: 'A Morning Song (for the First Day of Spring)' (1957)

18 I cannot walk through the suburbs in the solitude of the night without

thinking that the night pleases us because it suppresses idle details, just as our memory does.

Jorge Luis Borges 1899–1986: *Labyrinths* (1962)

19 What are days for?
Days are where we live.

Philip Larkin 1922–85: 'Days' (1964)

20 It's been a hard day's night.

John Lennon 1940–80 and **Paul McCartney** 1942– : 'A Hard Day's Night' (1964 song)

Death

see also MOURNING, MURDER, SUICIDE

proverbs and sayings ▸

1 As a tree falls, so shall it lie.

one should not change from one's long established practices and customs because of approaching death; English proverb, mid 16th century, from the Bible (Ecclesiastes) 'in the place where the tree falleth, there let it lie.'

2 Blessed are the dead that the rain rains on.

English proverb, early 17th century

3 [Death is] nature's way of telling you to slow down.

American life insurance saying, in *Newsweek* 25 April 1960

4 Death is only an horizon, and an horizon is only the limit of our sight.

traditional saying, sometimes attributed to William Penn (1644–1718)

5 Death is the great leveller.

all people will be equal in death, whatever their material prosperity; English proverb, early 18th century

6 Death pays all debts.

the death of a person cancels out their obligations; English proverb, early 17th century: see DEATH 41

7 Et in Arcadia ego.

Latin tomb inscription 'And I too in Arcadia', of disputed meaning, often depicted in classical paintings, notably by Poussin in 1655

8 Hodie mihi, cras tibi.

traditional Latin inscription on gravestones 'It is my lot today, yours tomorrow'

9 One funeral makes many.

sometimes with the implication that attendance at a deathbed or funeral may have fatal consequences; English proverb, late 19th century

10 Stone-dead hath no fellow.

traditionally used by advocates of the death penalty, or to suggest that only when a dangerous person is dead can one be sure that they will cause no further trouble; English proverb, mid 17th century

11 There is a remedy for everything except death.

English proverb, mid 15th century

12 This ae nighte, this ae nighte,
—Every nighte and alle,
Fire and fleet and candle-lighte,
And Christe receive thy saule.

'Lyke-Wake Dirge', traditional ballad; *fleet* = corruption of *flet*: see HOME 12

13 You can only die once.

used to encourage someone in a dangerous or difficult enterprise; English proverb, mid 15th century

14 Young men may die, but old men must die.

death is inevitable for all, and can at best be postponed until old age; English proverb, mid 16th century

phrases ▸

15 beyond the veil

in the unknown state of being after death; originally with reference to Tyndale 'Christ hath brought us all in into the inner temple within the veil', taken as referring to the next world

16 go the way of all flesh

die; alteration of the Bible (I Kings) 'I go the way of all the earth' (Douay Bible 1609 'I enter into the way of all flesh')

17 Grim Reaper

a personification of death in the form of a cloaked skeleton wielding a large scythe; *reaper* in this sense is recorded from the mid 19th century; see LIFE SCIENCES 32

18 hic jacet

an epitaph; Latin, literally 'here lies', the traditional first two words of a Latin epitaph; see DEATH 42

19 join the great majority

die; Edward Young *The Revenge* (1721) 'Death joins us to the great majority'; see DEATH 32

20 **memento mori**
an object serving as a warning or reminder of death, such as a skull; Latin, literally 'remember (that you have) to die'

21 **the potter's field**
a burial place for paupers or strangers, in reference to the Bible (Matthew), of how the chief priests and elders made use of the thirty pieces of silver returned to them by Judas after the Crucifixion, 'And they took counsel, and bought with them the potter's field, to bury strangers in'; see TRUST 15

22 **Seven Last Words**
the last seven utterances of Christ on the Cross

23 **smite under the fifth rib**
stab to the heart, kill; originally with reference to the Bible (II Samuel) 'Abner…smote him under the fifth rib'

24 **turn one's face to the wall**
(of a dying person) turn away one's face in awareness of impending death

quotations ▸

25 I would rather be tied to the soil as another man's serf, even a poor man's, who hadn't much to live on himself, than be King of all these the dead and destroyed.
Homer: *The Odyssey*

26 For dust thou art, and unto dust shalt thou return.
Bible: Genesis; see DEATH 49

27 If any man thinks he slays, and if another thinks he is slain, neither knows the ways of truth. The Eternal in man cannot kill: the Eternal in man cannot die.
The Upanishads 800–200 BC: *Katha Upanishad*

28 To fear death, my friends, is only to think ourselves wise, without being wise: for it is to think that we know what we do not know.
Socrates 469–399 BC: Plato *Apology*

29 Death, therefore, the most awful of evils, is nothing to us, seeing that, when we are death is not come, and when death is come, we are not.
Epicurus 341–271 BC: Diogenes Laertius *Lives of Eminent Philosophers*

30 *Non omnis moriar.*
I shall not altogether die.
Horace 65–8 BC: *Odes*

31 O death, where is thy sting? O grave, where is thy victory?
Bible: I Corinthians; see WORLD WAR I 20

32 *Abiit ad plures.*
He's gone to join the majority [the dead].
Petronius d. AD 65: *Satyricon*; see DEATH 19

33 Anyone can stop a man's life, but no one his death; a thousand doors open on to it.
Seneca ('the Younger') c.4 BC–AD 65: *Phoenissae*; see DEATH 44

34 Finally he paid the debt of nature.
Robert Fabyan d. 1513: *The New Chronicles of England and France* (1516)

35 O Death, thou comest when I had thee least in mind.
Anonymous: *Everyman* (*c.*1509–19)

36 I am going to seek a great perhaps.
François Rabelais c.1494–c.1553: attributed last words, though none of his contemporaries authenticated the remark, which has become part of the 'Rabelaisian legend'; Jean Fleury *Rabelais et ses oeuvres* (1877)

37 I care not; a man can die but once; we owe God a death.
William Shakespeare 1564–1616: *Henry IV, Part 2* (1597); see DEATH 13

38 To die, to sleep;
To sleep: perchance to dream: ay, there's the rub;
For in that sleep of death what dreams may come
When we have shuffled off this mortal coil,
Must give us pause.
William Shakespeare 1564–1616: *Hamlet* (1601); see LIFE 15, PROBLEMS 18

39 Nothing in his life
Became him like the leaving it.
William Shakespeare 1564–1616: *Macbeth* (1606)

40 Death be not proud, though some have called thee
Mighty and dreadful, for thou art not so.
John Donne 1572–1631: *Holy Sonnets* (1609)

41 He that dies pays all debts.
William Shakespeare 1564–1616: *The Tempest* (1611); see DEATH 6

42 O eloquent, just, and mighty Death!… thou hast drawn together all the

farstretched greatness, all the pride, cruelty, and ambition of man, and covered it all over with these two narrow words, *Hic jacet.*

Walter Ralegh 1552–1618: *The History of the World* (1614); see DEATH 18

43 Only we die in earnest, that's no jest.

Walter Ralegh 1552–1618: 'On the Life of Man'

44 I know death hath ten thousand several doors
For men to take their exits.

John Webster c.1580–c.1625: *The Duchess of Malfi* (1623); see DEATH 33

45 Any man's death diminishes me, because I am involved in Mankind; And therefore never send to know for whom the bell tolls; it tolls for thee.

John Donne 1572–1631: *Devotions upon Emergent Occasions* (1624)

46 The long habit of living indisposeth us for dying.

Thomas Browne 1605–82: *Hydriotaphia* (Urn Burial, 1658)

47 We shall die alone.

Blaise Pascal 1623–62: *Pensées* (1670)

48 In the midst of life we are in death.

The Book of Common Prayer 1662: *The Burial of the Dead*; see DEBT 21

49 Forasmuch as it hath pleased Almighty God of his great mercy to take unto himself the soul of our dear brother here departed, we therefore commit his body to the ground; earth to earth, ashes to ashes, dust to dust; in sure and certain hope of the Resurrection to eternal life.

The Book of Common Prayer 1662: *The Burial of the Dead* Interment; see DEATH 26

50 I am about to take my last voyage, a great leap in the dark.

Thomas Hobbes 1588–1679: last words; John Watkins *Anecdotes of Men of Learning* (1808)

51 Death never takes the wise man by surprise; he is always ready to go.

Jean de la Fontaine 1621–95: *Fables* (1678–9) 'La Mort et le Mourant'

52 They that die by famine die by inches.

Matthew Henry 1662–1714: *An Exposition on the Old and New Testament* (1710)

53 Can storied urn or animated bust
Back to its mansion call the fleeting breath?

Thomas Gray 1716–71: *Elegy Written in a Country Churchyard* (1751)

54 It matters not how a man dies, but how he lives. The act of dying is not of importance, it lasts so short a time.

Samuel Johnson 1709–84: James Boswell *Life of Samuel Johnson* (1791) 26 October 1769

55 Depend upon it, Sir, when a man knows he is to be hanged in a fortnight, it concentrates his mind wonderfully.

on the execution of Dr Dodd

Samuel Johnson 1709–84: James Boswell *Life of Samuel Johnson* (1791) 19 September 1777

56 Now more than ever seems it rich to die,
To cease upon the midnight with no pain.

John Keats 1795–1821: 'Ode to a Nightingale' (1820)

57 This quiet Dust was Gentlemen and Ladies
And Lads and Girls—
Was laughter and ability and Sighing
And Frocks and Curls.

Emily Dickinson 1830–86: 'This quiet Dust was Gentlemen and Ladies' (1864)

58 Die, my dear Doctor, that's the last thing I shall do!

Lord Palmerston 1784–1865: last words, E. Latham *Famous Sayings and their Authors* (1904)

59 And all our calm is in that balm—
Not lost but gone before.

Caroline Norton 1808–77: 'Not Lost but Gone Before'

60 For though from out our bourne of time and place
The flood may bear me far,
I hope to see my pilot face to face
When I have crossed the bar.

Alfred, Lord Tennyson 1809–92: 'Crossing the Bar' (1889)

61 In the arts of life man invents nothing; but in the arts of death he outdoes Nature herself, and produces by chemistry and machinery all the slaughter of plague, pestilence and famine.

George Bernard Shaw 1856–1950: *Man and Superman* (1903)

62 Death is nothing at all; it does not count. I have only slipped away into the next room.
Henry Scott Holland 1847–1918: sermon preached on Whitsunday 1910

63 Why fear death? It is the most beautiful adventure in life.
Charles Frohman 1860–1915: before drowning in the *Lusitania*, 7 May 1915; see DEATH 66

64 Webster was much possessed by death
And saw the skull beneath the skin.
T. S. Eliot 1888–1965: 'Whispers of Immortality' (1919)

65 A man's dying is more the survivors' affair than his own.
Thomas Mann 1875–1955: *The Magic Mountain* (1924)

66 To die will be an awfully big adventure.
J. M. Barrie 1860–1937: *Peter Pan* (1928); see DEATH 63

67 If this is dying, then I don't think much of it.
Lytton Strachey 1880–1932: last words, Michael Holroyd *Lytton Strachey* vol. 2 (1968)

68 Nor dread nor hope attend
A dying animal;
A man awaits his end
Dreading and hoping all.
W. B. Yeats 1865–1939: 'Death' (1933)

69 Though lovers be lost love shall not;
And death shall have no dominion.
Dylan Thomas 1914–53: 'And death shall have no dominion' (1936)

70 He shouts play death more sweetly
this Death is a master from Deutschland.
Paul Celan 1920–70: 'Deathfugue' (written 1944)

71 One death is a tragedy, a million deaths a statistic.
Joseph Stalin 1879–1953: attributed

72 How long does a man spend dying?
Pablo Neruda 1904–73: 'And How Long?' (1958)

73 This parrot is no more! It has ceased to be! It's expired and gone to meet its maker! This is a late parrot! It's a stiff! Bereft of life it rests in peace — if you hadn't nailed it to the perch it would be pushing up the daisies! It's rung down the curtain and joined the choir invisible! THIS IS AN EX-PARROT!
Graham Chapman 1941–89, John Cleese 1939– , and others: *Monty Python's Flying Circus* (BBC TV programme, 1969)

74 So it goes.
Kurt Vonnegut 1922–2007: *Slaughterhouse Five* (1969)

75 Death is nothing if one can approach it as such. I was just a tiny night-light, suffocated in its own wax, and on the point of expiring.
E. M. Forster 1879–1970: Philip Gardner (ed.) *E. M. Forster: Commonplace Book* (1985)

76 It's not that I'm afraid to die. I just don't want to be there when it happens.
Woody Allen 1935– : *Death* (1975)

77 Even death is unreliable: instead of zero it may be some ghastly hallucination, such as the square root of minus one.
Samuel Beckett 1906–89: attributed

78 We die containing a richness of lovers and tribes, tastes we have swallowed, bodies we have plunged into and swum up as if rivers of wisdom, characters we have climbed into as if trees, fears we have hidden as if in caves.
Michael Ondaatje 1943– : *The English Patient* (1992)

79 There should be a booth on every corner where you can get a martini and a medal.
on euthanasia
Martin Amis 1949– : in *Sunday Times* 24 January 2010

Debt and Borrowing

see also THRIFT

proverbs and sayings ►

1 Access—your flexible friend.
advertising slogan for Access credit card, 1981 onwards

2 American Express?...That'll do nicely, sir.
advertising slogan for American Express credit card, 1970s

3 **Better to go to bed supperless than to rise in debt.**
English proverb, mid 17th century; see DEBT 17

4 **Have a horse of your own, and then you may borrow another's.**
evidence that you have resources of your own makes it more likely that you will be lent something; English proverb, mid 17th century

5 **He that goes a-borrowing, goes a sorrowing.**
involving oneself in debt is likely to lead to unhappiness; English proverb, late 15th century

6 **Lend your money and lose your friend.**
debt puts a strain on friendship; English proverb, late 15th century

7 **A man in debt is caught in a net.**
American proverb, mid 20th century

8 **A national debt, if it is not excessive, will be to us a national blessing.**
American proverb; often attributed to Alexander Hamilton (1757–1804)

9 **Neither a borrower, nor a lender be.**
advising caution in financial dealings with others; English proverb, early 17th century, from Shakespeare: see DEBT 16

10 **Out of debt, out of danger.**
someone in debt is vulnerable and at risk from others; English proverb, mid 17th century

11 **Short reckonings make long friends.**
the prompt settlement of any debt between friends ensures that their friendship will not be damaged; English proverb, mid 16th century

phrases ▸

12 **a pound of flesh**
a payment or penalty which is strictly due but which it is ruthless or inhuman to demand, with allusion to Shakespeare *The Merchant of Venice*, and Shylock's insistence that he had the right to take the pound of Antonio's flesh promised in the bargain between them

13 **rob Peter to pay Paul**
take away from one person to pay another; discharge one debt by incurring another; probably referring to the Apostles St *Peter* and St *Paul* as founders of the Church; see GOVERNMENT 36

quotations ▸

14 **Be not made a beggar by banqueting upon borrowing.**
Bible: Ecclesiasticus

15 **A small debt makes a man your debtor; a large one, an enemy.**
Seneca ('the Younger') c.4 BC–AD 65: *Epistulae ad Lucilium*

16 **Neither a borrower, nor a lender be;**
For loan oft loses both itself and friend,
And borrowing dulls the edge of husbandry.
William Shakespeare 1564–1616: *Hamlet* (1601); see DEBT 9

17 **Rather go to bed supperless than run in debt for a breakfast.**
Benjamin Franklin 1706–90: *Poor Richard's Almanac* (1739) May; see DEBT 3

18 **The human species, according to the best theory I can form of it, is composed of two distinct races, *the men who borrow*, and *the men who lend.***
Charles Lamb 1775–1834: *Essays of Elia* (1823) 'The Two Races of Men'

19 **Annual income twenty pounds, annual expenditure nineteen nineteen six, result happiness. Annual income twenty pounds, annual expenditure twenty pounds ought and six, result misery.**
Charles Dickens 1812–70: *David Copperfield* (1850)

20 **One must have some sort of occupation nowadays. If I hadn't my debts I shouldn't have anything to think about.**
Oscar Wilde 1854–1900: *A Woman of No Importance* (1893)

21 **In the midst of life we are in debt.**
Ethel Watts Mumford 1878–1940: *Altogether New Cynic's Calendar* (1907); see DEATH 48

22 **They hired the money, didn't they?**
on the subject of war debts incurred by England and others
Calvin Coolidge 1872–1933: John H. McKee *Coolidge: Wit and Wisdom* (1933)

23 **Sixteen tons, what do you get?**
Another day older and deeper in debt.
Say brother, don't you call me 'cause I can't go
I owe my soul to the company store.
Merle Travis 1917–83: 'Sixteen Tons' (1947 song)

24 **Should we really let our people starve so we can pay our debts?**
Julius Nyerere 1922–99: in *Guardian* 21 March 1985

25 You can't put your VISA bill on your American Express card.

P. J. O'Rourke 1947– : *The Bachelor Home Companion* (1987)

26 I don't borrow on credit cards because it is too expensive.

view of the chief executive of Barclays Bank
Matt Barrett 1944– : in *Independent* 17 October 2003

Deception

see also HONESTY, HYPOCRISY, LIES

proverbs and sayings ▸

1 Cheats never prosper.

English proverb, early 19th century

2 Fool me once, shame on you; fool me twice, shame on me.

if someone is deceived twice their own stupidity is to blame; late 20th century saying

phrases ▸

3 all done with mirrors

an apparent achievement with an element of trickery, alluding to explanations of the art of a conjuror

4 be caught with chaff

be easily deceived or trapped; *chaff* = the husks of corn separated from the grain by threshing; from the proverb: see EXPERIENCE 11

5 borrowed plumes

a pretentious display not of one's own making, with reference to the fable of the jay which decked itself in the peacock's feathers

6 hand a person a lemon

pass off a substandard article as good; swindle a person, do a person down; *lemon* = the type of a bad, unsatisfactory, or disappointing thing; see SATISFACTION 2

7 mare's nest

an illusory discovery, originally in the phrase *to have found* (or *spied*) *a mare's nest* (i.e. something that does not exist), used in the sense 'to have discovered something amazing'

8 a Potemkin village

a sham or unreal thing; any of a number of sham villages reputedly built on the orders of *Potemkin*, favourite of Empress Catherine II of Russia, for her tour of the Crimea in 1787

9 smell a rat

begin to suspect trickery or deception; see DECEPTION 18

10 a wolf in sheep's clothing

a person whose hostile or malicious intentions are concealed by a pretence of gentleness or friendliness, with reference to the Bible (Matthew): see HYPOCRISY 9

11 wooden nutmeg

in US usage, a false or fraudulent thing, from a piece of wood shaped to resemble a nutmeg and fraudulently sold; see AMERICAN CITIES 32

quotations ▸

12 Deceive boys with toys, but men with oaths.

Lysander d. 395 BC: Plutarch *Parallel Lives* 'Lysander'

13 And if, to be sure, sometimes you need to conceal a fact with words, do it in such a way that it does not become known, or, if it does become known, that you have a ready and quick defence.

Niccolò Machiavelli 1469–1527: 'Advice to Raffaello Girolami when he went as Ambassador to the Emperor' (October 1522)

14 A false report, if believed during three days, may be of great service to a government.

Catherine de' Medici 1518–89: Isaac D'Israeli *Curiosities of Literature* Second Series vol. 2 (1849)

15 Doubtless the pleasure is as great
Of being cheated, as to cheat.
As lookers-on feel most delight,
That least perceive a juggler's sleight.

Samuel Butler 1612–80: *Hudibras* pt. 2 (1664)

16 One is easily fooled by that which one loves.

Molière 1622–73: *Le Tartuffe* (1669)

17 An open foe may prove a curse,
But a pretended friend is worse.

John Gay 1685–1732: *Fables* (1727) 'The Shepherd's Dog and the Wolf'

18 Mr Speaker, I smell a rat; I see him forming in the air and darkening the sky; but I'll nip him in the bud.

Boyle Roche 1743–1807: attributed; see DECEPTION 9

19 O what a tangled web we weave,

When first we practise to deceive!
Sir Walter Scott 1771–1832: *Marmion* (1808); see CHILD CARE 10

20 A deception that elevates us is dearer than a host of low truths.
Alexander Pushkin 1799–1837: 'Hero' (1830)

21 You may fool all the people some of the time; you can even fool some of the people all the time; but you can't fool all of the people all the time.
Abraham Lincoln 1809–65: Alexander K. McClure *Lincoln's Yarns and Stories* (1904); also attributed to Phineas Barnum; see POLITICS 20

22 It was beautiful and simple as all truly great swindles are.
O. Henry 1862–1910: *Gentle Grafter* (1908)

23 In wartime...truth is so precious that she should always be attended by a bodyguard of lies.
Winston Churchill 1874–1965: *The Second World War* vol. 5 (1951)

24 Propaganda is a soft weapon: hold it in your hands too long, and it will move about like a snake, and strike the other way.
Jean Anouilh 1910–87: *The Lark* (adapted by Lillian Hellman, 1955)

25 It is now a very good day to get out anything we want to bury.
email sent in the aftermath of the terrorist action in America, 11 September 2001; often quoted as 'a good day to bury bad news'
Jo Moore: in *Daily Telegraph* 10 October 2001

Deeds
see WORDS AND DEEDS

Defiance
see also DETERMINATION

proverbs and sayings ►

1 Nemo me impune lacessit.
Latin, *No one provokes me with impunity*, motto of the Crown of Scotland and of all Scottish regiments

2 No surrender!
Protestant Northern Irish slogan originating with the defenders of Derry against the Catholic forces of James II in 1689

3 They haif said: Quhat say they? Lat thame say.
motto of the Earls Marischal of Scotland, inscribed at Marischal College, Aberdeen, 1593; a similarly defiant motto in Greek has been found engraved in remains from classical antiquity

4 You can take a horse to the water, but you can't make him drink.
even if you create the right circumstances, you cannot persuade someone to do something against their will; English proverb, late 12th century

phrases ►

5 die in the last ditch
die desperately defending something, die fighting to the last extremity; see DEFIANCE 13

6 eyeball to eyeball
confronting closely; with neither party yielding; see CRISES 24

7 kick against the pricks
rebel, be recalcitrant, especially to one's own hurt; with reference to the Bible (Acts) 'It is hard for thee to kick against the pricks'

8 nail one's colours to the mast
persist, refuse to give in; be undeterred in one's support for a party or plan of action; *colours* = the flag or ensign of a ship; see INDECISION 16

quotations ►

9 They are as venomous as the poison of a serpent: even like the deaf adder that stoppeth her ears;
Which refuseth to hear the voice of the charmer: charm he never so wisely.
Bible: Psalm 58; see SENSES 3

10 He will give him seven feet of English ground, or as much more as he may be taller than other men.
his offer to the invader Harald Hardrada, before the battle of Stamford Bridge
Harold II 1019–66: Snorri Sturluson *Heimskringla* (1260) 'King Harald's Saga'

11 I grow, I prosper;
Now, gods, stand up for bastards!
William Shakespeare 1564–1616: *King Lear* (1605–6)

12 ...What though the field be lost?
All is not lost; the unconquerable will,
And study of revenge, immortal hate,
And courage never to submit or yield:
And what is else not to be overcome?
John Milton 1608–74: *Paradise Lost* (1667)

13 'Do you not see your country is lost?' asked the Duke of Buckingham. 'There is one way never to see it lost' replied William, 'and that is to die in the last ditch.'

William III 1650–1702: Bishop Gilbert Burnet *History of My Own Time* (1838 ed.); see DEFIANCE 5

14 Should the whole frame of nature
round him break,
In ruin and confusion hurled,
He, unconcerned, would hear the
mighty crack,
And stand secure amidst a falling world.

Joseph Addison 1672–1719: translation of Horace *Odes*

15 I was ever a fighter, so—one fight more,
The best and the last!

Robert Browning 1812–89: 'Prospice' (1864)

16 *No pasarán.*
They shall not pass.

Dolores Ibarruri 1895–1989: radio broadcast, Madrid, 19 July 1936; see WORLD WAR I 1

17 Get up, stand up
Stand up for your rights
Get up, stand up
Never give up the fight.

Bob Marley 1945–81: 'Get up, Stand up' (1973 song)

18 She won't go quietly, that's the problem. I'll fight to the end.

Diana, Princess of Wales 1961–97: interview on *Panorama*, BBC1 TV, 20 November 1995

Delay

see HASTE AND DELAY

Democracy

see also ELECTIONS, POLITICS

proverbs and sayings ►

1 Democracy is better than tyranny.

an imperfect system is better than a bad one; American proverb

2 The voice of the people is the voice of God.

English version of the Latin *vox populi, vox dei*; English proverb, early 15th century: see DEMOCRACY 3

quotations ►

3 And those people should not be listened to who keep saying the voice of the people is the voice of God, since the riotousness of the crowd is always very close to madness.

Alcuin 735–804: letter 164; *Works* (1863); see DEMOCRACY 2

4 Let no one oppose this belief of mine with that well-worn proverb: 'He who builds on the people builds on mud.'

Niccolò Machiavelli 1469–1527: *The Prince* (written 1513)

5 Nor is the people's judgement always
true:
The most may err as grossly as the
few.

John Dryden 1631–1700: *Absalom and Achitophel* (1681)

6 I never could believe that Providence had sent a few men into the world, ready booted and spurred to ride, and millions ready saddled and bridled to be ridden.

Richard Rumbold 1622–85: on the scaffold; T. B. Macaulay *History of England* vol. 1 (1849)

7 One man shall have one vote.

John Cartwright 1740–1824: *The People's Barrier Against Undue Influence* (1780)

8 All, too, will bear in mind this sacred principle, that though the will of the majority is in all cases to prevail, that will to be rightful must be reasonable; that the minority possess their equal rights, which equal law must protect, and to violate would be oppression.

Thomas Jefferson 1743–1826: inaugural address, 4 March, 1801

9 Fourscore and seven years ago our fathers brought forth upon this continent a new nation, conceived in liberty, and dedicated to the proposition that all men are created equal...we here highly resolve that the dead shall not have died in vain, that this nation, under God, shall have a new birth of freedom; and that government of the people, by the

people, and for the people, shall not perish from the earth.

the Lincoln Memorial inscription reads 'by the people, for the people'

Abraham Lincoln 1809–65: address at the Dedication of the National Cemetery at Gettysburg, 19 November 1863, as reported the following day

10 The cure for the ills of Democracy is more Democracy.

Jane Addams 1860–1935: *Democracy and Social Ethics* (1902)

11 Democracy substitutes election by the incompetent many for appointment by the corrupt few.

George Bernard Shaw 1856–1950: *Man and Superman* (1903) 'Maxims: Democracy'

12 The world must be made safe for democracy.

Woodrow Wilson 1856–1924: speech to Congress, 2 April 1917

13 No, Democracy is *not* identical with majority rule. Democracy is a *State* which recognizes the subjection of the minority to the majority, that is, an organization for the systematic use of *force* by one class against the other, by one part of the population against another.

Lenin 1870–1924: *State and Revolution* (1919)

14 Man's capacity for justice makes democracy possible, but man's inclination to injustice makes democracy necessary.

Reinhold Niebuhr 1892–1971: *Children of Light and Children of Darkness* (1944)

15 No one pretends that democracy is perfect or all-wise. Indeed, it has been said that democracy is the worst form of Government except all those other forms that have been tried from time to time.

Winston Churchill 1874–1965: speech, House of Commons, 11 November 1947

16 After each war there is a little less democracy to save.

Brooks Atkinson 1894–1984: *Once Around the Sun* (1951)

17 So Two cheers for Democracy: one because it admits variety and two because it permits criticism. Two cheers are quite enough: there is no occasion to give three. Only Love the Beloved Republic deserves that.

E. M. Forster 1879–1970: *Two Cheers for Democracy* (1951)

18 Democracy means government by discussion, but it is only effective if you can stop people talking.

Clement Attlee 1883–1967: speech at Oxford, 14 June 1957

19 It's not the voting that's democracy, it's the counting.

Tom Stoppard 1937– : *Jumpers* (1972); see ELECTIONS 16

20 Democracy is the best revenge.

Benazir Bhutto 1953–2007: attributed, in *Washington Post* 11 June 1989, and quoted by her son Bilawal after her assassination

21 Every government is a parliament of whores. The trouble is, in a democracy the whores are us.

P. J. O'Rourke 1947– : *Parliament of Whores* (1991)

22 Democracy must be something more than two wolves and a sheep voting on what to have for dinner.

James Bovard 1956– : *Lost Rights* (1994)

Despair

see also HOPE, OPTIMISM, SORROW

phrases ▸

1 black dog

a metaphorical representation of melancholy or depression, used particularly by Samuel Johnson (see DESPAIR 6) and later by Winston Churchill when alluding to his own periodic bouts of depression

2 dark night of the soul

a period of anguish or despair; a period of spiritual aridity suffered by a mystic, 'Dark night of the soul' being a translation of the Spanish title of a work by St John of the Cross, known in English as *The Ascent of Mount Carmel* (1578–80); see DESPAIR 14

3 legion of the lost ones

people who are destitute or abandoned, regarded as beyond hope or help, after Kipling 'Gentleman-Rankers' (1892) 'To the legion of the lost ones, to the cohort of the damned, to my brethren in their sorrow overseas'

quotations ▸

4 My God, my God, look upon me; why hast thou forsaken me?

Bible: Psalm 22

5 Magnanimous Despair alone
Could show me so divine a thing,
Where feeble Hope could ne'er have flown
But vainly flapped its tinsel wing.

Andrew Marvell 1621–78: 'The Definition of Love' (1681)

6 The black dog I hope always to resist, and in time to drive, though I am deprived of almost all those that used to help me.

on his attacks of melancholia

Samuel Johnson 1709–84: letter to Mrs Thrale, 28 June 1783; see DESPAIR 1

7 Everywhere I see bliss, from which I alone am irrevocably excluded.

Mary Shelley 1797–1851: *Frankenstein* (1818)

8 I am in that temper that if I were under water I would scarcely kick to come to the top.

John Keats 1795–1821: letter to Benjamin Bailey, 25 May 1818

9 I give the fight up: let there be an end,
A privacy, an obscure nook for me.
I want to be forgotten even by God.

Robert Browning 1812–89: *Paracelsus* (1835)

10 Take thy beak from out my heart, and take thy form from off my door!
Quoth the Raven, 'Nevermore.'

Edgar Allan Poe 1809–49: 'The Raven' (1845)

11 There is no despair so absolute as that which comes with the first moments of our first great sorrow, when we have not yet known what it is to have suffered and be healed, to have despaired and have recovered hope.

George Eliot 1819–80: *Adam Bede* (1859)

12 In despair there are the most intense enjoyments, especially when one is very acutely conscious of the hopelessness of one's position.

Fedor Dostoevsky 1821–81: *Notes from Underground* (1864)

13 Not, I'll not, carrion comfort, Despair, not feast on thee;
Not untwist—slack they may be—these last strands of man
In me or, most weary, cry *I can no more*. I can;
Can something, hope, wish day come, not choose not to be.

Gerard Manley Hopkins 1844–89: 'Carrion Comfort' (written 1885)

14 In a real dark night of the soul it is always three o'clock in the morning.

F. Scott Fitzgerald 1896–1940: 'Handle with Care' in *Esquire* March 1936; see DESPAIR 2

15 Human life begins on the far side of despair.

Jean-Paul Sartre 1905–80: *Les Mouches* (1943)

16 Despair is the price one pays for setting oneself an impossible aim.

Graham Greene 1904–91: *Heart of the Matter* (1948)

17 Despair, in short, seeks its own environment as surely as water finds its own level.

Alfred Alvarez 1929– : *The Savage God* (1971)

Determination and Perseverance

see also DEFIANCE

proverbs and sayings ▸

1 Constant dropping wears away a stone.

primarily used to mean that persistence will achieve a difficult or unlikely objective; English proverb, mid 13th century; see DETERMINATION 30

2 A determined fellow can do more with a rusty monkey wrench than a lot of people can with a machine shop.

American proverb, mid 20th century

3 Fall seven times, stand up eight.

Japanese proverb; see DETERMINATION 6

4 He that will to Cupar maun to Cupar.

if someone is determined on an end they will not be dissuaded; *Cupar* is a town in Fife, Scotland; Scottish traditional saying, early 18th century

5 He who wills the end, wills the means.

someone sufficiently determined upon an outcome will also be ready to accept whatever is necessary to achieve it; English proverb, late 17th century

6 **If at first you don't succeed, try, try, try again.**
English proverb, mid 19th century; see DETERMINATION 48

7 **It is idle to swallow the cow and choke on the tail.**
when a serious matter has been accepted, there is no point in quibbling over a trifle, or that it is senseless to give up when a great task is almost completed; English proverb, mid 17th century

8 **It's dogged as does it.**
steady perseverance will bring success; English proverb, mid 19th century

9 **Little strokes fell great oaks.**
a person or thing of size and stature can be brought down by a series of small blows; English proverb, early 15th century

10 **Nil carborundum illegitimi.**
cod Latin for 'Don't let the bastards grind you down', in circulation during the Second World War, though possibly of earlier origin; often quoted as, '*nil carborundum*' or '*illegitimi non carborundum*'

11 **Put a stout heart to a stey brae.**
determination is needed to climb a steep ('stey') hillside; Scottish proverb, late 16th century

12 **Revenons à ces moutons.**
an exhortation to stop digressing and get back to the subject in hand; French, literally 'Let us return to these sheep', with allusion to the confused court scene in the Old French *Farce de Maistre Pierre Pathelin* (1470)

13 **The show must go on.**
American proverb, mid 19th century

14 **Slow and steady wins the race.**
from the story of the race between the hare and the tortoise, in Aesop's *Fables*, in which the winner was the slow but persistent tortoise and not the swift but easily distracted hare; mid 18th century saying; see DETERMINATION 22

15 **A stern chase is a long chase.**
a *stern chase* is a chase in which the pursuing ship follows directly in the wake of the pursued; English proverb, early 19th century

16 **The third time pays for all.**
success after initial failure makes up for earlier disappointment; English proverb, late 16th century

17 **We shall not be moved.**
title of labour and civil rights song (1931), adapted from an earlier gospel hymn

18 **We shall overcome.**
title of song, originating from before the American Civil War, adapted as a Baptist hymn ('I'll Overcome Some Day', 1901) by C. Albert Tindley; revived in 1946 as a protest song by black tobacco workers, and in 1963 during the black Civil Rights Campaign

19 **Where there's a will there's a way.**
anything can be done if one has sufficient determination; English proverb, mid 17th century

20 **A wilful man must have his way.**
a person set on their own ends will disregard advice in pursuing their chosen course; English proverb, early 19th century

phrases ▶

21 **gird up one's loins**
prepare oneself for mental and physical effort, summon one's courage and determination; of biblical origin, as in II Kings 'Then said he to Gehazi, Gird up thy loins, and take my staff in thine hand, and go thy way'

22 **hare and tortoise**
the defeat of ability by persistence, in allusion to Aesop's fable: see DETERMINATION 14

23 **make a spoon or spoil a horn**
make a determined effort to achieve something, whatever the cost. With reference to the practice of making spoons out of the horns of cattle or sheep

24 **put one's hand to the plough**
undertake a task; enter on a course of life or conduct, from the Bible (Luke): see DETERMINATION 26

quotations ▶

25 **Faint, yet pursuing.**
Bible: Judges

26 **No man, having put his hand to the plough, and looking back, is fit for the kingdom of God.**
Bible: St Luke; see DETERMINATION 24

27 ***Hoc volo, sic iubeo, sit pro ratione voluntas.***
I will have this done, so I order it done; let my will replace reasoned judgement.
Juvenal c. AD 60–c. 140: *Satires*

28 **Thought shall be the harder, heart the keener, courage the greater, as our might lessens.**
Anonymous: *The Battle of Maldon* (1000)

29 Here stand I. I can do no other. God help me. Amen.
Martin Luther 1483–1546: speech at the Diet of Worms, 18 April 1521; attributed

30 The drop of rain maketh a hole in the stone, not by violence, but by oft falling.
Hugh Latimer 1485–1555: *The Second Sermon preached before the King's Majesty*, 19 April 1549; see DETERMINATION 1

31 Perseverance, dear my lord,
Keeps honour bright.
William Shakespeare 1564–1616: *Troilus and Cressida* (1602)

32 Obstinacy in a bad cause, is but constancy in a good.
Thomas Browne 1605–82: *Religio Medici* (1643)

33 Who would true valour see,
Let him come hither;
One here will constant be,
Come wind, come weather.
John Bunyan 1628–88: *The Pilgrim's Progress* (1684)

34 I have not yet begun to fight.
as his ship was sinking, 23 September 1779, having been asked whether he had lowered his flag
John Paul Jones 1747–92: Mrs Reginald De Koven *Life and Letters of John Paul Jones* (1914)

35 I have only one eye,—I have a right to be blind sometimes...I really do not see the signal!
at the battle of Copenhagen, 1801
Horatio, Lord Nelson 1758–1805: Robert Southey *Life of Nelson* (1813); see IGNORANCE 14

36 I am in earnest—I will not equivocate—I will not excuse—I will not retreat a single inch—and I will be heard!
William Lloyd Garrison 1805–79: in *The Liberator* 1 January 1831

37 Let us, then, be up and doing,
With a heart for any fate;
Still achieving, still pursuing,
Learn to labour and to wait.
Henry Wadsworth Longfellow 1807–82: 'A Psalm of Life' (1838)

38 That which we are, we are;
One equal temper of heroic hearts,
Made weak by time and fate, but strong in will
To strive, to seek, to find, and not to yield.
Alfred, Lord Tennyson 1809–92: 'Ulysses' (1842)

39 I purpose to fight it out on this line, if it takes all summer.
Ulysses S. Grant 1822–85: dispatch to Washington, from head-quarters in the field, 11 May 1864

40 Children, if you are tired, keep going; if you are scared, keep going; if you are hungry, keep going; if you want to taste freedom, keep going.
Harriet Tubman c.1820–1913: during 1850s–60s; attributed, but apparently a modern paraphrase of her views

41 Patience and tenacity of purpose are worth more than twice their weight of cleverness.
T. H. Huxley 1825–95: 'On Medical Education' (address at University College, 1870)

42 The best way out is always through.
Robert Frost 1874–1963: 'A Servant to Servants' (1914)

43 Keep right on to the end of the road,
Keep right on to the end.
Harry Lauder 1870–1950: 'The End of the Road' (1924 song)

44 One man that has a mind and knows it can always beat ten men who haven't and don't.
George Bernard Shaw 1856–1950: *The Apple Cart* (1930)

45 Nothing in the world can take the place of persistence. Talent will not; nothing is more common than unsuccessful men with talent. Genius will not; unrewarded genius is almost a proverb. Education will not; the world is full of educated derelicts. Persistence and determination are omnipotent. The slogan 'press on' has solved and always will solve the problems of the human race.
Calvin Coolidge 1872–1933: attributed in the programme of a memorial service for Coolidge in 1933

46 Pick yourself up,
Dust yourself off,
Start all over again.
Dorothy Fields 1905–74: 'Pick Yourself Up' (1936 song)

47 Never give in. Never give in, *never, never, never, never*—in nothing, great or small, large or petty—never give in, except to convictions of honour and good sense. Never yield to force: never yield to the apparently overwhelming might of the enemy.

Winston Churchill 1874–1965: speech to boys at Harrow School, 29 October 1941

48 If at first you don't succeed, try, try again. Then quit. No use being a damn fool about it.

W. C. Fields 1880–1946: attributed; see DETERMINATION 6

49 On, on, on.

last words after collapsing on Mont Ventoux in the Tour de France; commonly quoted as, 'Put me back on my bike'

Tom Simpson 1937–67: William Fotheringham *Put Me Back on My Bike* (2002)

50 We shall not be diverted from our course. To those waiting with bated breath for that favourite media catchphrase, the U-turn, I have only this to say. 'You turn if you want to; the lady's not for turning.'

final line from alteration of the title of Christopher Fry's 1949 play *The Lady's Not For Burning*

Margaret Thatcher 1925– : speech at Conservative Party Conference in Brighton, 10 October 1980

51 Got to kick at the darkness 'til it bleeds daylight.

Bruce Cockburn 1945– : 'Lovers in a Dangerous Time' (1984 song)

52 The comeback kid!

Bill Clinton 1946– : description of himself after coming second in the New Hampshire primary, 1992

53 I can only go one way. I've not got a reverse gear.

Tony Blair 1953– : speech, Labour Party Conference, Bournemouth, 30 September 2003

54 What's the difference between a hockey mom and a pitbull? Lipstick.

Sarah Palin 1964– : speech to Republican Party convention, 3 September 2008

55 While we breathe, we hope, and where we are met with cynicism, and doubt, and those who tell us that we can't, we will respond with that timeless creed that sums up the spirit of a people: yes we can.

Barack Obama 1961– : speech on winning the Presidency, Chicago, 4 November 2008

Difference

see SIMILARITY AND DIFFERENCE

Diplomacy

see also INTERNATIONAL

proverbs and sayings ►

1 A soft answer turneth away wrath.

refraining from defending oneself against verbal attack may defuse a situation; English proverb, late 14th century, from the Bible: see ANGER 8

2 We have no friends but the mountains.

inhospitable terrain is more reliable than an ally as a source of safety; Kurdish proverb

phrases ►

3 coalition of the willing

a group of nations agreeing to act together, especially with military involvement; particularly associated with those countries giving active support to American intervention in Iraq in 2003

4 honest broker

an impartial mediator in international, industrial, or other disputes, from Bismarck: see DIPLOMACY 10

quotations ►

5 An ambassador is an honest man sent to lie abroad for the good of his country.

Henry Wotton 1568–1639: written in the album of Christopher Fleckmore in 1604; Izaak Walton *Reliquiae Wottonianae* (1651)

6 We are prepared to go to the gates of Hell—but no further.

attempting to reach an agreement with Napoleon, 1800–1

Pope Pius VII 1742–1823: J. M. Robinson *Cardinal Consalvi* (1987)

7 The Congress makes no progress; it dances.

on the Congress of Vienna

Charles-Joseph, Prince de Ligne 1735–1814: Auguste de la Garde-Chambonas *Souvenirs du Congrès de Vienne* (1820)

8 The compact which exists between the North and the South is 'a covenant with death and an agreement with hell.'

William Lloyd Garrison 1805–79: resolution adopted by the Massachusetts Anti-Slavery Society, 27 January 1843; in allusion to the Bible (Isaiah) 'We have made a covenant with death, and with hell are we at agreement'

9 An ambassador is not simply an agent; he is also a spectacle.

Walter Bagehot 1826–77: *The English Constitution* (1867) 'The House of Lords'

10 I do not regard the procuring of peace as a matter in which we should play the role of arbiter between different opinions...more that of an honest broker who really wants to press the business forward.

Otto von Bismarck 1815–98: speech to the Reichstag, 19 February 1878; see DIPLOMACY 4

11 There is a homely old adage which runs: 'Speak softly and carry a big stick; you will go far.' If the American nation will speak softly, and yet build and keep at a pitch of the highest training a thoroughly efficient navy, the Monroe Doctrine will go far.

Theodore Roosevelt 1858–1919: speech in Chicago, 3 April 1903; see INTERNATIONAL 7, WOMAN'S ROLE 30

12 You can no more make an agreement with those leaders of Colombia than you can nail currant jelly to the wall. And the failure to nail currant jelly to the wall is not due to the nail. It's due to the currant jelly.

at the time of the Panama revolution, 1903

Theodore Roosevelt 1858–1919: attributed; see FUTILITY 12

13 An appeaser is one who feeds a crocodile hoping it will eat him last.

Winston Churchill 1874–1965: in the House of Commons, January 1940

14 Negotiating with de Valera...is like trying to pick up mercury with a fork.

to which de Valera replied, 'Why doesn't he use a spoon?'

David Lloyd George 1863–1945: M. J. MacManus *Eamon de Valera* (1944)

15 To jaw-jaw is always better than to war-war.

Winston Churchill 1874–1965: speech at White House, 26 June 1954

16 Let us never negotiate out of fear. But let us never fear to negotiate.

John F. Kennedy 1917–63: inaugural address, 20 January 1961

17 One of the things I learnt when I was negotiating was that until I changed myself I could not change others.

Nelson Mandela 1918– : in *Sunday Times* 16 April 2000

Discontent

see SATISFACTION AND DISCONTENT

Discoveries

see INVENTIONS AND DISCOVERIES

Disillusion and Cynicism

proverbs and sayings ►

1 Blessed is he who expects nothing, for he shall never be disappointed.

English proverb, early 18th century; see DISILLUSION 12

phrases ►

2 Dead Sea fruit

any outwardly desirable object which on attainment turns out to be worthless; any hollow disappointing thing; from a legendary fruit, of attractive appearance, which dissolved into smoke and ashes when held; see DISILLUSION 3, DISILLUSION 5; POWER 42

3 dust and ashes

used to convey a feeling of great disappointment or disillusion about something; originally with allusion to the legend of the Dead Sea fruit; see DISILLUSION 2

4 take the gilt off the gingerbread

strip something of its attractions; gingerbread was traditionally made in decorative forms which were then gilded

5 turn to ashes in a person's mouth

turn out to be utterly disappointing or worthless; probably originally with allusion to the legend of Dead Sea fruit: see DISILLUSION 2

6 vanitas vanitatum
vanity of vanities, futility (frequently as an exclamation of disillusionment or pessimism); late Latin, from the Vulgate translation of the Bible; see FUTILITY 19, SATISFACTION 29

quotations ▸

7 To get practice in being refused.
on being asked why he was begging for alms from a statue
Diogenes 404–323 BC: Diogenes Laertius *Lives of the Philosophers*

8 Kill them all; God will recognize his own.
when asked how the true Catholics could be distinguished from the heretics at the massacre of Béziers, 1209
Arnald-Amaury, abbot of Citeaux d. 1225: Jonathan Sumption *The Albigensian Crusade* (1978)

9 Paris is well worth a mass.
Henri of Navarre, a Huguenot, on becoming King of France
Henri IV 1553–1610: attributed to Henri IV; alternatively to his minister Sully, in conversation with Henri

10 What makes all doctrines plain and clear?
About two hundred pounds a year.
And that which was proved true before,
Prove false again? Two hundred more.
Samuel Butler 1612–80: *Hudibras* pt. 3 (1680)

11 Everything has been said, and we are more than seven thousand years of human thought too late.
Jean de la Bruyère 1645–96: *Les Caractères ou les moeurs de ce siècle* (1688)

12 'Blessed is the man who expects nothing, for he shall never be disappointed' was the ninth beatitude.
Alexander Pope 1688–1744: letter to Fortescue, 23 September 1725; see DISILLUSION 1

13 Never glad confident morning again!
Robert Browning 1812–89: 'The Lost Leader' (1845)

14 Take the life-lie away from the average man and straight away you take away his happiness.
Henrik Ibsen 1828–1906: *The Wild Duck* (1884)

15 A man who knows the price of everything and the value of nothing.
definition of a cynic
Oscar Wilde 1854–1900: *Lady Windermere's Fan* (1892)

16 And nothing to look backward to with pride,
And nothing to look forward to with hope.
Robert Frost 1874–1963: 'The Death of the Hired Man' (1914)

17 Nothing matters very much and very few things matter at all.
Arthur James Balfour 1848–1930: Clodagh Anson *Book: discreet memoirs* (1931)

18 Cynicism is an unpleasant way of saying the truth.
Lillian Hellman 1905–84: *The Little Foxes* (1939)

19 Like all dreamers, I mistook disenchantment for truth.
Jean-Paul Sartre 1905–80: *Les Mots* (1964) 'Écrire'

20 Man hands on misery to man.
It deepens like a coastal shelf.
Get out as early as you can,
And don't have any kids yourself.
Philip Larkin 1922–85: 'This Be The Verse' (1974)

21 A cynic is what an idealist calls a realist.
Jonathan Lynn 1943– and **Antony Jay** 1930– : *Yes Minister* (BBC television, 1982), Sir Humphrey Appleby to Jim Hacker

22 Cynicism is our shared common language, the Esperanto that actually caught on.
Nick Hornby 1957– : *How to be Good* (2001)

Dislikes

see LIKES AND DISLIKES

Dogs

see also ANIMALS

proverbs and sayings ▸

1 Cave canem.
Latin, *beware of the dog*; deriving originally from Petronius (d. AD 65); see CAUTION 37

2 A dog is for life, not just for Christmas.
slogan of the National Canine Defence League (now Dogs Trust), from 1978

3 There is no good flock without a good shepherd, and no good shepherd without a good dog.
motto of the International Sheep Dog Society, said to derive from a Scottish proverb

quotations ▸

4 There will be little dogs, with golden hair, shining like precious stones.
Martin Luther 1483–1546: sermon on the resurrection, Easter Sunday, 1544

5 I am his Highness' dog at Kew;
Pray, tell me sir, whose dog are you?
Alexander Pope 1688–1744: 'Epigram Engraved on the Collar of a Dog which I gave to his Royal Highness' (1738)

6 Near this spot are deposited the remains of one who possessed beauty without vanity, strength without insolence, courage without ferocity, and all the virtues of Man, without his vices.
Lord Byron 1788–1824: 'Inscription on the Monument of a Newfoundland Dog' (1808)

7 The more one gets to know of men, the more one values dogs.
also attributed to Mme Roland in the form 'The more I see of men, the more I like dogs'
A. Toussenel 1803–85: *L'Esprit des bêtes* (1847)

8 In the whole history of the world there is but one thing that money cannot buy, to wit: the wag of a dog's tail.
sometimes quoted as 'Money will buy you a pretty good dog, but it won't buy the wag of his tail'
Josh Billings 1818–85: attributed

9 The dog is a gentleman; I hope to go to his heaven, not man's.
Mark Twain 1835–1910: letter to W. D. Howells, 2 April 1899

10 The great pleasure of a dog is that you may make a fool of yourself with him and not only will he not scold you, but he will make a fool of himself too.
Samuel Butler 1835–1902: *Notebooks* (1912)

11 Brothers and Sisters, I bid you beware
Of giving your heart to a dog to tear.
Rudyard Kipling 1865–1936: 'The Power of the Dog' (1909)

12 Any man who hates dogs and babies can't be all bad.
of W. C. Fields, and often attributed to him
Leo Rosten 1908–97: speech at Masquers' Club dinner, 16 February 1939

13 To his dog, every man is Napoleon: hence the constant popularity of dogs.
Aldous Huxley 1894–1963: attributed; Evan Esar *The Treasury of Humorous Quotations* (1951)

14 A door is what a dog is perpetually on the wrong side of.
Ogden Nash 1902–71: 'A Dog's Best Friend is his Illiteracy' (1953)

15 Happiness is a warm puppy.
Charles Monroe Schulz 1922– : title of book (1962); see HAPPINESS 32

16 Outside of a dog, a book is a man's best friend. Inside of a dog, it's too dark to read.
Groucho Marx 1890–1977: Groucho Marx and Stefan Kanfer *The Essential Groucho* (2000)

Doubt

see CERTAINTY AND DOUBT

Drawing

see PAINTING AND DRAWING

Dreams

see also SLEEP

proverbs and sayings ▸

1 Dream of a funeral and you hear of a marriage.
English proverb, mid 17th century

2 Dreams go by contraries.
English proverb, early 15th century

3 Dreams retain the infirmities of our character.
American proverb, late 19th century

4 Morning dreams come true.
English proverb, mid 16th century, recording a traditional superstition

phrases ▸

5 the gate of horn
in Greek legend, the gates through which true dreams pass

6 **the ivory gate**
in Greek legend, the gate through which false dreams pass; see DREAMS 8

quotations ▸

7 **O God! I could be bounded in a nut-shell, and count myself a king of infinite space, were it not that I have bad dreams.**
William Shakespeare 1564–1616: *Hamlet* (1601)

8 **That children dream not in the first half year, that men dream not in some countries, are to me sick men's dreams, dreams out of the ivory gate, and visions before midnight.**
Thomas Browne 1605–82: 'On Dreams'; see DREAMS 6

9 **The dream of reason produces monsters.**
Goya 1746–1828: *Los Caprichos* (1799)

10 **Was it a vision, or a waking dream?**
Fled is that music:—do I wake or sleep?
John Keats 1795–1821: 'Ode to a Nightingale' (1820)

11 **The quick Dreams,**
The passion-wingèd Ministers of thought.
Percy Bysshe Shelley 1792–1822: *Adonais* (1821)

12 **I have spread my dreams under your feet;**
Tread softly because you tread on my dreams.
W. B. Yeats 1865–1939: 'He Wishes for the Cloths of Heaven' (1899)

13 **The interpretation of dreams is the royal road to a knowledge of the unconscious activities of the mind.**
often quoted as, 'Dreams are the royal road to the unconscious'
Sigmund Freud 1856–1939: *The Interpretation of Dreams* (2nd ed., 1909)

14 **How many of our daydreams would darken into nightmares if there seemed any danger of their coming true!**
Logan Pearsall Smith 1865–1946: *Afterthoughts* (1931)

15 **All the things one has forgotten scream for help in dreams.**
Elias Canetti 1905–94: *Die Provinz der Menschen* (1973)

16 **Dreams come true; without that possibility nature would not incite us to have them.**
John Updike 1932–2009: *Self-Consciousness: Memoirs* (1989)

Dress

see also FASHION

proverbs and sayings ▸

1 **Clothes make the man.**
what one wears is taken by others as an essential signal of status; English proverb, early 15th century; see DRESS 15

2 **Fine feathers make fine birds.**
beautiful clothes confer beauty or style on the wearer; English proverb, late 16th century

3 **If you want to get ahead, get a hat.**
advertising slogan for the British Hat Council, 1965

4 **Ne'er cast a clout till May be out.**
warning against leaving off old or warm clothes until the end of the month of May (the saying is sometimes mistakenly understood to refer to may blossom); English proverb, early 18th century

5 **Nine tailors make a man.**
literally, a gentleman must select his attire from a number of sources (later also associated with bell-ringing, with the *nine tailors* or *tellers* indicating the nine knells traditionally rung for the death of a man); English proverb, early 17th century

quotations ▸

6 **Costly thy habit as thy purse can buy,**
But not expressed in fancy; rich, not gaudy;
For the apparel oft proclaims the man.
William Shakespeare 1564–1616: *Hamlet* (1601)

7 **Let it be observed, that slovenliness is no part of religion; that neither this, nor any text of Scripture, condemns neatness of apparel. Certainly this is a duty, not a sin. 'Cleanliness is, indeed, next to godliness.'**
John Wesley 1703–91: *Sermons on Several Occasions* (1788); see BEHAVIOUR 3

8 Beware of all enterprises that require new clothes.
Henry David Thoreau 1817–62: *Walden* (1854) 'Economy'

9 The sense of being well-dressed gives a feeling of inward tranquillity which religion is powerless to bestow.
Miss C. F. Forbes 1817–1911: R. W. Emerson *Letters and Social Aims* (1876)

10 You should never have your best trousers on when you go out to fight for freedom and truth.
Henrik Ibsen 1828–1906: *An Enemy of the People* (1882)

11 When you're all dressed up and have no place to go.
George Whiting: title of song (1912)

12 Where's the man could ease a heart like a satin gown?
Dorothy Parker 1893–1967: 'The Satin Dress' (1937)

13 When I was young, I found out that the big toe always ends up making a hole in a sock. So I stopped wearing socks.
Albert Einstein 1879–1955: to Philippe Halsman; A. P. French *Einstein: A Centenary Volume* (1979)

14 on being asked what she wore in bed:
Chanel No. 5.
Marilyn Monroe 1926–62: Pete Martin *Marilyn Monroe* (1956)

15 Clothes don't make the man...but they go a long way toward making a businessman.
Thomas Watson Snr. 1874–1956: Robert Sobel *IBM: Colossus in Transition* (1981); see DRESS 1

16 Look for the woman in the dress. If there is no woman, there is no dress.
Coco Chanel 1883–1971: in *New York Times* 23 August 1964

17 I have often said that I wish I had invented blue jeans: the most spectacular, the most practical, the most relaxed and nonchalant.
Yves Saint Laurent 1936–2008: in *Ritz* no. 85 (1984)

18 Haute Couture should be fun, foolish and almost unwearable.
Christian Lacroix 1951– : attributed, 1987

19 It is totally impossible to be well dressed in cheap shoes.
Hardy Amies 1909–2003: *The Englishman's Suit* (1994)

20 The clothes in themselves do not make a statement. The woman makes the statement and the dress helps.
Jean Muir 1928–95: in *Vogue* August 1995

21 Dress cute wherever you go. Life is too short to blend in.
Paris Hilton 1981– : *Confessions of an Heiress* (2004)

Drink

see FOOD AND DRINK

Drugs

proverbs and sayings ▶

1 Just say no.
motto of the Nancy Reagan Drug Abuse Fund, founded 1985

phrases ▶

2 chase the dragon
take heroin by heating it on a piece of folded tin foil and inhaling the fumes. The term is said to be translated from Chinese, and to arise from the fact that the fumes and the molten heroin powder move up and down the piece of tin foil with an undulating movement resembling the tail of the dragon in Chinese myths

3 cold turkey
the abrupt and complete cessation of taking a drug to which one is addicted; the phrase derives from one of the symptoms, the development of 'goose-flesh' on the skin from a sudden chill, caused by this

quotations ▶

4 Almighty God hath not bestowed on mankind a remedy of so universal an extent and so efficacious in curing divers maladies as opiates.
Thomas Sydenham 1624–89: *Observationes Medicae* (1676); MS version given in 1991 ed.

5 Thou hast the keys of Paradise, oh just, subtle, and mighty opium!
Thomas De Quincey 1785–1859: *Confessions of an English Opium Eater* (1822)

6 Cocaine habit-forming? Of course not. I ought to know. I've been using it for years.
Tallulah Bankhead 1903–68: *Tallulah* (1952)

7 In this country, don't forget, a habit is no damn private hell. There's no solitary confinement outside of jail. A habit is hell for those you love.
Billie Holiday 1915–59: *Lady Sings the Blues* (1956, with William F. Duffy)

8 Junk is the ideal product...the ultimate merchandise. No sales talk necessary. The client will crawl through a sewer and beg to buy.
William S. Burroughs 1914–97: *The Naked Lunch* (1959)

9 Every form of addiction is bad, no matter whether the narcotic be alcohol or morphine or idealism.
Carl Gustav Jung 1875–1961: *Erinnerungen, Träume, Gedanken* (1962)

10 I'll die young, but it's like kissing God.
on his drug addiction
Lenny Bruce 1925–66: attributed

11 I experimented with marijuana a time or two. And I didn't like it, and I didn't inhale.
Bill Clinton 1946– : in *Washington Post* 30 March 1992

12 Sure thing, man. I used to be a laboratory myself once.
on being asked to autograph a fan's school chemistry book
Keith Richards 1943– : in *Independent on Sunday* 7 August 1994

13 Go. Get busy living, or get busy dying.
advice to his son, a drug addict
Pierce Brosnan 1953– : in *Sunday Times* 13 November 2005

Drunkenness

see also ALCOHOL

proverbs and sayings ►

1 He that drinks beer, thinks beer.
warning against the effects of intoxication; English proverb, early 19th century

2 There is truth in wine.
a person who is drunk is more likely to speak the truth; English proverb, mid 16th century, the saying is found earlier in Latin as *in vino veritas*

3 When the wine is in, the wit is out.
when one is drunk one is likely to be indiscreet or to speak or act foolishly; English proverb, late 14th century

quotations ►

4 Drink, sir, is a great provoker of three things...nose-painting, sleep, and urine. Lechery, sir, it provokes, and unprovokes; it provokes the desire, but it takes away the performance.
William Shakespeare 1564–1616: *Macbeth* (1606)

5 A man who exposes himself when he is intoxicated, has not the art of getting drunk.
Samuel Johnson 1709–84: James Boswell *Life of Samuel Johnson* (1791) 24 April 1779

6 Not drunk is he, who from the floor
Can rise alone and still drink more;
But drunk is he, who prostrate lies,
Without the power to drink or rise.
Thomas Love Peacock 1785–1866: *The Misfortunes of Elphin* (1829)

7 It would be better that England should be free than that England should be compulsorily sober.
William Connor Magee 1821–91: speech on the Intoxicating Liquor Bill, House of Lords, 2 May 1872

8 Licker talks mighty loud w'en it git loose fum de jug.
Joel Chandler Harris 1848–1908: *Uncle Remus: His Songs and His Sayings* (1880)

9 First the man takes a drink,
Then the drink takes a drink,
Then the drink takes the man!
Edward Rowland Sill 1841–87: 'An Adage from the Orient' (1883), frequently quoted as a Japanese proverb

10 But I'm not so think as you drunk I am.
J. C. Squire 1884–1958: 'Ballade of Soporific Absorption' (1931)

11 Till a lady passing by was heard to say:
'You can tell a man who "boozes" by the company he chooses'
And the pig got up and slowly walked away.
of a pig and a drunk lying side by side in the gutter
Benjamin Hapgood Burt 1880–1950: 'The Pig Got Up and Slowly Walked Away' (1933 song)

12 Love makes the world go round? Not at all. Whisky makes it go round twice as fast.
Compton Mackenzie 1883–1972: *Whisky Galore* (1947); see LOVE 8

13 A man you don't like who drinks as much as you do.
definition of an alcoholic
Dylan Thomas 1914–53: Constantine Fitzgibbon *Life of Dylan Thomas* (1965)

14 One more drink and I'd have been under the host.
Dorothy Parker 1893–1967: Howard Teichmann *George S. Kaufman* (1972)

15 You're not drunk if you can lie on the floor without holding on.
Dean Martin 1917–95: Paul Dickson *Official Rules* (1978)

Duty and Responsibility

proverbs and sayings ▸

1 Don't care was made to care.
traditional rebuke to someone who asserts their lack of concern; first words of a children's rhyme ('Don't care was *made* to care, don't care was hung'); English saying, mid 20th century

2 Everybody's business is nobody's business.
when something is of some interest to everyone, no single person takes full responsibility for it; English proverb, early 17th century

3 Every herring must hang by its own gill.
everyone is accountable for their own actions; English proverb, early 17th century

4 Take what you want, and pay for it, says God.
traditional saying

5 Those who eat salty fish will have to accept being thirsty.
everyone is responsible for the consequences of their own actions; Chinese proverb

phrases ▸

6 cat's paw
a person who is used by another, typically to carry out an unpleasant or dangerous task; originally with allusion to the fable of a monkey which asked a cat to extract its roasted chestnuts from the fire; see DANGER 22

7 Nuremberg defence
a defence in which a person claims that they have no personal responsibility because they were following orders from a lawful superior; from the defence made by Nazis put on trial for war crimes at *Nuremberg* at the end of the Second World War

8 pass the buck
shift the responsibility for something to another person; *buck* = an article placed as a reminder before a player whose turn it is to deal at poker; see DUTY 25

9 wash one's hands of
renounce responsibility for; refuse to have any further dealings with; originally with allusion to the Bible; see GUILT 7, INDIFFERENCE 15

quotations ▸

10 And do thy duty, even if it be humble, rather than another's, even if it be great. To die in one's duty is life: to live in another's is death.
Bhagavadgita 250 BC–AD 250: ch. 3

11 Had I but served God as diligently as I have served the King, he would not have given me over in my grey hairs.
Thomas Wolsey 1475–1530: George Cavendish *Negotiations of Thomas Wolsey* (1641)

12 I could not love thee, Dear, so much,
Loved I not honour more.
Richard Lovelace 1618–58: 'To Lucasta, Going to the Wars' (1649)

13 England expects that every man will do his duty.
Horatio, Lord Nelson 1758–1805: at the battle of Trafalgar, 21 October 1805; Robert Southey *Life of Nelson* (1813)

14 Stern daughter of the voice of God!
O Duty!
William Wordsworth 1770–1850: 'Ode to Duty' (1807)

15 The brave man inattentive to his duty, is worth little more to his country,

than the coward who deserts her in the hour of danger.
to troops who had abandoned their lines during the battle of New Orleans, 8 January 1815
Andrew Jackson 1767–1845: attributed

16 The path of duty was the way to glory.
Alfred, Lord Tennyson 1809–92: 'Ode on the Death of the Duke of Wellington' (1852)

17 Do the work that's nearest,
Though it's dull at whiles,
Helping, when we meet them,
Lame dogs over stiles.
Charles Kingsley 1819–75: 'The Invitation. To Tom Hughes' (1856)

18 On an occasion of this kind it becomes more than a moral duty to speak one's mind. It becomes a pleasure.
Oscar Wilde 1854–1900: *The Importance of Being Earnest* (1895)

19 Take up the White Man's burden—
Send forth the best ye breed—
Go, bind your sons to exile
To serve your captives' need.
Rudyard Kipling 1865–1936: 'The White Man's Burden' (1899); see RACE 5

20 When a stupid man is doing something he is ashamed of, he always declares that it is his duty.
George Bernard Shaw 1856–1950: *Caesar and Cleopatra* (1901)

21 If we believe a thing to be bad, and if we have a right to prevent it, it is our duty to try to prevent it and to damn the consequences.
Lord Milner 1854–1925: speech in Glasgow, 26 November 1909

22 A sense of duty is useful in work, but offensive in personal relations. People wish to be liked, not to be endured with patient resignation.
Bertrand Russell 1872–1970: *The Conquest of Happiness* (1930)

23 Power without responsibility: the prerogative of the harlot throughout the ages.
summing up Lord Beaverbrook's political standpoint as a newspaper editor; Stanley Baldwin, Kipling's cousin, subsequently obtained permission to use the phrase in a speech in London on 18 March 1931
Rudyard Kipling 1865–1936: in *Kipling Journal* December 1971

24 I know this—a man got to do what he got to do.
John Steinbeck 1902–68: *Grapes of Wrath* (1939)

25 The buck stops here.
Harry S. Truman 1884–1972: unattributed motto on Truman's desk; see DUTY 8

26 Duty is what no-one else will do at the moment.
Penelope Fitzgerald 1916–2000: *Offshore* (1979)

The Earth

see also NATURE, POLLUTION, UNIVERSE

proverbs and sayings ▸

1 Touch the earth lightly.
modern saying, said to derive from an Australian Aboriginal proverb

2 We do not inherit the earth from our parents, we borrow it from our children.
modern saying, said to be of native American origin

phrases ▸

3 flood and field
sea and land, after Shakespeare *Othello* 'Of moving accidents by flood and field'

4 Gaia hypothesis
the theory, put forward by the English scientist James Lovelock (1919–) in 1969, that living matter on the earth collectively defines and regulates the material conditions necessary for the continuance of life; *Gaia* = in Greek mythology, the Earth personified as a goddess, daughter of Chaos; see EARTH 19

5 the glimpses of the moon
the earth by night; sublunary scenes; after Shakespeare *Hamlet* 'That thou, dead corse again in complete steel, Revisit'st thus the glimpses of the moon'

6 global village
the world considered as a single community linked by telecommunications, from McLuhan: see TECHNOLOGY 17; see also COUNTRY 23

7 under the sun
on earth; in existence (used in expressions emphasizing the large number of something); see FAMILIARITY 11, PROGRESS 5

quotations ▸

8 The earth is the Lord's, and all that therein is: the compass of the world, and they that dwell therein.
Bible: Psalm 24

9 Need for a knowledge of geography is greater than the need of gardens for water after the stars have failed to fulfil their promise of rain.
Yāqūt d. 1229: attributed

10 Above the smoke and stir of this dim spot,
Which men call earth.
John Milton 1608–74: *Comus* (1637)

11 Topography displays no favourites;
North's as near as West.
More delicate than the historians' are
the map-makers' colours.
Elizabeth Bishop 1911–79: 'The Map' (1946)

12 In every outthrust headland, in every curving beach, in every grain of sand there is a story of the earth.
Rachel Carson 1907–64: in *Holiday* July 1958

13 Now there is one outstandingly important fact regarding Spaceship Earth, and that is that no instruction book came with it.
R. Buckminster Fuller 1895–1983: *Operating Manual for Spaceship Earth* (1969)

14 God owns heaven
but He craves the earth.
Anne Sexton 1928–74: 'The Earth' (1975)

15 The earth is what we all have in common.
Wendell Berry 1934– : *The Unsettling of America* (1977)

16 How inappropriate to call this planet Earth when it is clearly Ocean.
Arthur C. Clarke 1917–2008: in *Nature* 1990; attributed

17 To me, it underscores our responsibility to deal more kindly with one another, and to preserve and cherish the pale blue dot, the only home we've ever known.
of Earth as photographed by Voyager 1
Carl Sagan 1934–96: *Pale Blue Dot* (1995)

18 Our planet is a lonely speck in the great enveloping cosmic dark. In our obscurity, in all this vastness, there is no hint that help will come from elsewhere to save us from ourselves.
Carl Sagan 1934–96: *Pale Blue Dot* (1995)

19 Gaia is a tough bitch. People think the earth is going to die and they have to save it, that's ridiculous...There's no doubt that Gaia can compensate for our output of greenhouse gases, but the environment that's left will not be happy for any people.
Lynn Margulis 1938– : in *New York Times Biographical Service* January 1996; see EARTH 4

20 Sand is overrated—it's just tiny little rocks.
Charlie Kaufman 1958– : *Eternal Sunshine of the Spotless Mind* (2004 film), spoken by Jim Carrey as Joel

Eating
see COOKING AND EATING

Economics
see also BUSINESS, DEBT, MONEY, THRIFT

proverbs and sayings ▸

1 Buy in the cheapest market and sell in the dearest.
sometimes with an implication of sharp practice; English proverb, late 16th century

2 The only free cheese is in a mousetrap.
Russian proverb; see also PREPARATION 12

3 There's no such thing as a free lunch.
colloquial axiom in American economics from the 1960s, much associated with Milton Friedman; first found in printed form in Robert Heinlein *The Moon is a Harsh Mistress* (1966); see UNIVERSE 16

phrases ▸

4 the dismal science
economics, from Thomas Carlyle *The Nigger Question* (1849), in a play on *gay science*: see POETRY 1

5 green shoots of recovery
signs of growth or renewal, especially of economic recovery; popular form of phrasing used by Norman Lamont: see ECONOMICS 25

6 selling off the family silver
parting with a valuable resource for immediate advantage; the reference is to Harold Macmillan's comparison of privatization to the sale of family assets by impoverished landowners: see ECONOMICS 22

7 tiger economy
a dynamic economy of one of the smaller East Asian countries, especially that of Singapore, Taiwan, or South Korea, from the early 1980s; see also IRELAND 2

quotations ▸

8 Demand for commodities is not demand for labour.
John Stuart Mill 1806–73: *Principles of Political Economy* (1848)

9 Finance is, as it were, the stomach of the country, from which all the other organs take their tone.
W. E. Gladstone 1809–98: article on finance, 1858; H. C. G. Matthew *Gladstone 1809–1874* (1986)

10 There can be no economy where there is no efficiency.
Benjamin Disraeli 1804–81: address to his constituents, 1 October 1868

11 Lenin was right. There is no subtler, no surer means of overturning the existing basis of society than to debauch the currency.
John Maynard Keynes 1883–1946: *The Economic Consequences of the Peace* (1919)

12 We have always known that heedless self-interest was bad morals; we know now that it is bad economics.
Franklin D. Roosevelt 1882–1945: second inaugural address, 20 January 1937

13 Economic progress, in capitalist society, means turmoil.
J. A. Schumpeter 1883–1950: *Capitalism, Socialism and Democracy* (1942)

14 What a country calls its vital economic interests are not the things which enable its citizens to live, but the things which enable it to make war.
Simone Weil 1909–43: W. H. Auden *A Certain World* (1971)

15 It's a recession when your neighbour loses his job; it's a depression when you lose yours.
Harry S. Truman 1884–1972: in *Observer* 13 April 1958

16 In a community where public services have failed to keep abreast of private consumption things are very different. Here, in an atmosphere of private opulence and public squalor, the private goods have full sway.
J. K. Galbraith 1908–2006: *The Affluent Society* (1958)

17 Expenditure rises to meet income.
C. Northcote Parkinson 1909–93: *The Law and the Profits* (1960)

18 Wall Street indexes predicted nine out of the last five recessions.
Paul A. Samuelson 1915–2009: in *Newsweek* 19 September 1966

19 Gross national product...measures everything, in short, except that which makes life worthwhile.
Robert Kennedy 1925–68: in *New York Times* 10 February 1968

20 Small is beautiful. A study of economics as if people mattered.
E. F. Schumacher 1911–77: title of book (1973); see QUANTITIES 8

21 Inflation is the one form of taxation that can be imposed without legislation.
Milton Friedman 1912–2006: in *Observer* 22 September 1974

22 First of all the Georgian silver goes, and then all that nice furniture that used to be in the saloon. Then the Canalettos go.
on privatization; see ECONOMICS 6
Harold Macmillan 1894–1986: speech to the Tory Reform Group, 8 November 1985

23 Government's view of the economy could be summed up in a few short phrases: If it moves, tax it. If it keeps moving, regulate it. And if it stops moving, subsidize it.
Ronald Reagan 1911–2004: National White House Conference on Small Business, 15 August 1986

24 If the policy isn't hurting, it isn't working.
on controlling inflation
John Major 1943– : speech in Northampton, 27 October 1989

25 The green shoots of economic spring are appearing once again.
Norman Lamont 1942– : speech at Conservative Party Conference, 9 October 1991; see ECONOMICS 5

26 All the current talk of no return to 'boom and bust' is somewhat premature to say the least.
Nigel Lawson 1932– : lecture, London School of Economics, 20 June 1994; see ECONOMICS 27, ECONOMICS 28

27 One of the guidelines which I have laid down throughout my chancellorship is no return to boom and bust.
Kenneth Clarke 1940– : speech, House of Commons, 30 October 1996; see ECONOMICS 26, ECONOMICS 28

28 No return to Tory boom and bust.
Gordon Brown 1951– : speech, Labour Party conference, 28 September 1998; see ECONOMICS 26, ECONOMICS 27

29 To those critics who are so pessimistic about our economy I say, don't be economic girlie men!
Arnold Schwarzenegger 1947– : speech to Republican National Convention, New York, 31 August 2004

30 The age of irresponsibility is giving way to the age of austerity.
David Cameron 1966– : speech, Conservative Party conference, 26 April 2009

Education

see also SCHOOLS, TEACHING, UNIVERSITIES

proverbs and sayings ▸

1 As the twig is bent, so is the tree inclined.
early influences have a permanent effect; English proverb, early 18th century

2 Education doesn't come by bumping your head against the school house.
American proverb, mid 20th century

3 Give me a child for the first seven years, and you may do what you like with him afterwards.
traditionally regarded as a Jesuit maxim; recorded in *Lean's Collectanea* vol. 3 (1903)

4 The ink of a scholar is holier than the blood of a martyr.
modern saying, said to derive from an Arab proverb, but of uncertain origin

5 It is never too late to learn.
English proverb, late 17th century

6 Never too old to learn.
English proverb, late 16th century

7 There is no royal road to learning.
English proverb, early 19th century, deriving from Euclid; see MATHS 9

8 When the pupil is ready, the master arrives.
Indian proverb, deriving from Sanskrit

phrases ▸

9 the groves of Academe
the academic community, from the Roman poet Horace (65–8 BC) *Epistles* 'And seek for truth in the groves of Academe'

quotations ▸

10 Get learning with a great sum of money, and get much gold by her.
Bible: Ecclesiasticus

11 In education there should be no class distinction.
Confucius 551–479 BC: *Analects*

12 We learn an art or craft by doing the things that we shall have to do when we have learnt it.
often quoted as 'What we have to learn to do, we learn by doing'
Aristotle 384–322 BC: *Nicomachean Ethics*

13 Whereas then a rattle is a suitable occupation for infant children, education serves as a rattle for young people when older.
Aristotle 384–322 BC: *Politics*

14 Say not, When I have leisure I will study; perchance thou wilt never have leisure.
Hillel 'The Elder' c.60 BC–c.AD 9: in *Talmud* Mishnah 'Pirqei Avot'

15 Study as if you were to live for ever; live as if you were to die tomorrow.
St Edmund of Abingdon c.1175–1240: John Crozier *St Edmund of Abingdon* (1982)

16 And gladly wolde he lerne and gladly teche.
Geoffrey Chaucer 1343–1400: *The Canterbury Tales* 'The General Prologue'

17 That lyf so short, the craft so long to lerne.

Geoffrey Chaucer 1343–1400: *The Parliament of Fowls*; see ARTS 2, MEDICINE 8

18 Studies serve for delight, for ornament, and for ability.

Francis Bacon 1561–1626: *Essays* (1625) 'Of Studies'

19 Go to the pine if you want to learn about the pine.

Matsuo Basho 1644–94: Nobuyuki Yuasa (ed.) *Basho. The Narrow Road to the Deep North* (1966) introduction

20 Wear your learning, like your watch in a private pocket: and do not merely pull it out and strike it, merely to show that you have one.

Lord Chesterfield 1694–1773: *Letters to his Son* (1774) 22 February 1748

21 Gie me ae spark o' Nature's fire,
That's a' the learning I desire.

Robert Burns 1759–96: 'Epistle to J. L[aprai]k' (1786)

22 Example is the school of mankind, and they will learn at no other.

Edmund Burke 1729–97: *Two Letters on the Proposals for Peace with the Regicide Directory* (9th ed., 1796)

23 What does education often do? It makes a straight-cut ditch of a free, meandering brook.

Henry David Thoreau 1817–62: *Journal* November 1850

24 Education makes a people easy to lead, but difficult to drive; easy to govern, but impossible to enslave.

Lord Brougham 1778–1868: attributed

25 Education is an admirable thing, but it is well to remember from time to time that nothing that is worth knowing can be taught.

Oscar Wilde 1854–1900: *Intentions* (1891)

26 The aim of education is the knowledge not of facts but of values.

William Ralph Inge 1860–1954: 'The Training of the Reason' in A. C. Benson (ed.) *Cambridge Essays on Education* (1917)

27 The best thing for being sad...is to learn something.

T. H. White 1906–64: *The Sword in the Stone* (1938)

28 The empires of the future are the empires of the mind.

Winston Churchill 1874–1965: speech at Harvard, 6 September 1943

29 The task of the modern educator is not to cut down jungles but to irrigate deserts.

C. S. Lewis 1898–1963: *The Abolition of Man* (1943)

30 If you educate a man you educate one person, but if you educate a woman you educate a family.

Ruby Manikan: in *Observer* 30 March 1947

31 Education is the ability to listen to almost anything without losing your temper or your self-confidence.

Robert Frost 1874–1963: in *Reader's Digest* April 1960

32 Education is what survives when what has been learned has been forgotten.

B. F. Skinner 1904–90: in *New Scientist* 21 May 1964

33 Education is the most powerful weapon which you can use to change the world.

Nelson Mandela 1918– : speech, Madison Park High School, Boston, 23 June 1990; reported in various forms including '...weapon which you can use in order to prepare our youth for their role as leaders of tomorrow' on CBS News 23 June 1990 and '...weapon we will need' in *New York Times* 24 June 1990

34 Education costs money, but then so does ignorance.

Claus Moser 1922– : speech to the British Association for the Advancement of Science, Swansea, 20 August 1990

35 Ask me my three main priorities for Government, and I tell you: education, education and education.

Tony Blair 1953– : speech at the Labour Party Conference, 1 October 1996; see POLITICS 14

Effort

see also ACHIEVEMENT

proverbs and sayings ▸

1 And all because the lady loves Milk Tray.

advertising slogan for Cadbury's Milk Tray chocolates, 1968 onwards, showing the obstacles overcome to deliver the chocolates

2 **The best fish swim near the bottom.**
patience and persistence are necessary for the best results; English proverb, mid 16th century

3 **Easy come, easy go.**
something which is acquired without effort will be lost without regret; English proverb, mid 17th century

4 **He that would eat the fruit must climb the tree.**
someone who wishes to attain success must first make the necessary effort; English proverb, early 18th century

5 **I didn't get where I am today without—.**
managerial catchphrase in BBC television series *The Fall and Rise of Reginald Perrin* (1976–80), written by David Nobbs

6 **If a thing's worth doing, it's worth doing well.**
if something is worth any effort at all, it should be taken seriously; English proverb, mid 18th century; see WOMEN 37

7 **If the sky falls we shall catch larks.**
used dismissively to indicate that something will be attainable only in the most unlikely circumstances; English proverb, mid 15th century

8 **Much cry and little wool.**
referring to a disturbance without tangible result; in early usage, the image was that of shearing a pig, which cried loudly but produced no wool; English proverb, late 15th century

9 **No pain, no gain.**
nothing worth having can be achieved without effort; English proverb, late 16th century

10 **One cannot become a good sailor sailing in a tranquil sea.**
a person must be disciplined and educated to become a useful citizen; Chinese proverb

11 **We're number two. We try harder.**
advertising slogan for Avis car rentals

phrases ▶

12 **burn the candle at both ends**
draw on one's resources from two directions; especially, overtax one's strength by going to bed late and getting up early; see TRANSIENCE 15

13 **improve the shining hour**
make good use of time; make the most of one's time; after Isaac Watts (1674–1748): see WORK 26

14 **a labour of Hercules**
a task requiring great strength or effort; *Hercules* a hero of superhuman strength and courage who performed twelve immense tasks or 'labours' imposed on him

15 **leave no stone unturned**
try every possible expedient; the expression is used by Pliny in his Letters. The term was said by the sophist Zenobius to derive from a story of hidden Persian treasure

16 **smell of the lamp**
show signs of laborious study and effort; the reference is to an oil-lamp, and according to Plutarch the criticism was once made of the work of Demosthenes, 'His impromptus smell of the lamp', meaning that his speeches were written rather than spoken orations

quotations ▶

17 ***Parturient montes, nascetur ridiculus mus.***
Mountains will go into labour, and a silly little mouse will be born.
Horace 65–8 BC: *Ars Poetica*

18 **Also say to them, that they suffer him this day to win his spurs.**
speaking of the Black Prince at the battle of Crécy, 1346, and commonly quoted as 'Let the boy win his spurs'; see SUCCESS 21
Edward III 1312–77: *The Chronicle of Froissart* (translated by John Bourchier 1523–5)

19 **Things won are done; joy's soul lies in the doing.**
William Shakespeare 1564–1616: *Troilus and Cressida* (1602)

20 **I had done all that I could; and no man is well pleased to have his all neglected, be it ever so little.**
Samuel Johnson 1709–84: letter to Lord Chesterfield, 7 February 1755

21 **But the fruit that can fall without shaking,**
Indeed is too mellow for me.
Lady Mary Wortley Montagu 1689–1762: 'Answered, for Lord William Hamilton' (1758)

22 **Oh, how I am tired of the struggle!**
Johann Wolfgang von Goethe 1749–1832: *Wandrers Nachtlied* (1821)

23 **Say not the struggle naught availeth,**
The labour and the wounds are vain,
The enemy faints not, nor faileth,

And as things have been, things remain.
Arthur Hugh Clough 1819–61: 'Say not the struggle naught availeth' (1855)

24 Now, *here*, you see, it takes all the running *you* can do, to keep in the same place. If you want to get somewhere else, you must run at least twice as fast as that!
Lewis Carroll 1832–98: *Through the Looking-Glass* (1872); said by the Red Queen: see LIFE SCIENCES 7

25 Superhuman effort isn't worth a damn unless it achieves results.
Ernest Shackleton 1874–1922: to his navigator Frank Worsley, 1916; F. P. Worsley *Endurance* (1931)

26 The world is divided into people who do things and people who get the credit. Try, if you can, to belong to the first class. There's far less competition.
Dwight Morrow 1873–1931: letter to his son; Harold Nicolson *Dwight Morrow* (1935)

27 The world is an oyster, but you don't crack it open on a mattress.
Arthur Miller 1915–2005: *Death of a Salesman* (1949)

Elections

see also DEMOCRACY

proverbs and sayings ►

1 As Maine goes, so goes the nation.
American political saying, 1840; see ELECTIONS 10

2 A straw vote only shows which way the hot air blows.
American proverb, early 20th century

3 Vote early and vote often.
American election slogan, already current when quoted by William Porcher Miles in the House of Representatives, 31 March 1858

phrases ►

4 Portillo moment
the unexpected electoral defeat of a major political figure; from Conservative Cabinet Minister Michael *Portillo*'s loss of Enfield Southgate in the 1997 general election

quotations ►

5 Anyone who campaigns for public office becomes disqualified for holding any office at all.
Thomas More 1478–1535: *Utopia* (1516)

6 The English people believes itself to be free; it is gravely mistaken; it is free only during the election of Members of Parliament; as soon as the Members are elected, the people is enslaved; it is nothing.
Jean-Jacques Rousseau 1712–78: *Du Contrat social* (1762)

7 To give victory to the right, not bloody bullets, but peaceful ballots only, are necessary.
usually quoted as 'The ballot is stronger than the bullet'
Abraham Lincoln 1809–65: speech, 18 May 1858

8 An election is coming. Universal peace is declared, and the foxes have a sincere interest in prolonging the lives of the poultry.
George Eliot 1819–80: *Felix Holt* (1866)

9 As for our majority...one is enough.
now often associated with Churchill
Benjamin Disraeli 1804–81: *Endymion* (1880)

10 As Maine goes, so goes Vermont.
after predicting correctly that Franklin D. Roosevelt would carry all but two states in the election of 1936
James A. Farley 1888–1976: statement to the press, 4 November 1936; see ELECTIONS 1

11 Hell, I never vote *for* anybody. I always vote *against*.
W. C. Fields 1880–1946: Robert Lewis Taylor *W. C. Fields* (1950)

12 If there had been any formidable body of cannibals in the country he would have promised to provide them with free missionaries fattened at the taxpayer's expense.
of Harry Truman's success in the 1948 presidential campaign
H. L. Mencken 1880–1956: in *Baltimore Sun* 7 November 1948

13 Don't buy a single vote more than necessary. I'll be damned if I'm going to pay for a landslide.
telegraphed message from his father, read at a Gridiron dinner in Washington, 15 March 1958, and almost certainly JFK's invention
John F. Kennedy 1917–63: J. F. Cutler *Honey Fitz* (1962)

14 Vote for the man who promises least; he'll be the least disappointing.
Bernard Baruch 1870–1965: Meyer Berger *New York* (1960)

15 The people have spoke—the bastards.
after being defeated in the California Senate primary *c.*1962; usually quoted as 'The people have spoken—the bastards'
Dick Tuck 1924– : in *Time* 13 August 1973

16 You won the elections, but I won the count.
replying to an accusation of ballot-rigging
Anastasio Somoza 1925–80: in *Guardian* 17 June 1977; see DEMOCRACY 19

17 You campaign in poetry. You govern in prose.
Mario Cuomo 1932– : in *New Republic*, Washington, DC, 8 April 1985

18 If voting changed anything, they'd abolish it.
Ken Livingstone 1945– : title of book, 1987

19 I earned capital in the campaign, political capital, and I intend to spend it.
on his re-election as President
George W. Bush 1946– : in *New York Times* 5 November 2004 (online edition)

Emotions

proverbs and sayings ▸

1 Out of the fullness of the heart the mouth speaks.
overwhelming feeling will express itself in speech; English proverb, late 14th century, originally with allusion to the Bible (Matthew), 'Out of the abundance of the heart the mouth speaketh'

2 Sing before breakfast, cry before night.
warning against overconfidence in early happiness presaging a reversal of good fortune; English proverb, early 17th century

phrases ▸

3 hard as the nether millstone
callous and unyielding, without sympathy or pity; *nether millstone* = the lower of the two millstones by which corn is ground; with allusion to Job in the Geneva Bible (1560) 'His heart is as strong as a stone, and as hard as the nether millstone'

4 in cold blood
without feeling or mercy, ruthlessly. According to medieval physiology, blood was naturally hot, so this phrase refers to an unnatural state in which someone can do a (hot-blooded) deed of passion or violence without the normal heating of the blood; see VIOLENCE 8

5 the pathetic fallacy
the attribution of human emotion or responses to inanimate things or animals, especially in art and literature; from John Ruskin *Modern Painters* (1856) 'All violent feelings…produce…a falseness in…impressions of external things, which I would generally characterize as the "Pathetic fallacy"'

6 wear one's heart on one's sleeve
allow one's feelings to be obvious, from Shakespeare: see EMOTIONS 9

7 wring the withers
stir the emotions or sensibilities, after Shakespeare *Hamlet* 'let the galled jade wince, our withers are unwrung'

quotations ▸

8 Even as rain breaks not through a well-thatched house, passions break not through a well-guarded mind.
Pali Tripitaka 2nd century BC: *Dhammapada*

9 But I will wear my heart upon my sleeve
For daws to peck at: I am not what I am.
William Shakespeare 1564–1616: *Othello* (1602–4); see EMOTIONS 6

10 A man whose blood
Is very snow-broth; one who never feels
The wanton stings and motions of the sense.
William Shakespeare 1564–1616: *Measure for Measure* (1604)

11 Our passions are most like to floods and streams;
The shallow murmur, but the deep are dumb.
Walter Ralegh 1552–1618: 'Sir Walter Ralegh to the Queen' (1655)

12 The heart has its reasons which reason knows nothing of.
Blaise Pascal 1623–62: *Pensées* (1670)

13 Calm of mind, all passion spent.
John Milton 1608–74: *Samson Agonistes* (1671)

14 The ruling passion, be it what it will,
The ruling passion conquers reason still.
Alexander Pope 1688–1744: *Epistles to Several Persons* 'To Lord Bathurst' (1733)

15 We shall never learn to feel and respect our real calling and destiny, unless we have taught ourselves to consider every thing as moonshine, compared with the education of the heart.
Sir Walter Scott 1771–1832: to J. G. Lockhart, August 1825

16 Nothing great was ever achieved without enthusiasm.
Ralph Waldo Emerson 1803–82: *Essays* (1841) 'Circles'

17 As you pass from the tender years of youth into harsh and embittered manhood, make sure you take with you on your journey all the human emotions! Don't leave them on the road, for you will not pick them up afterwards!
Nikolai Gogol 1809–52: *Dead Souls* (1842)

18 The heart of another is a dark forest.
Ivan Turgenev 1818–83: *A Month in the Country* (1850)

19 on being told there was no English word equivalent to *sensibilité*
Yes we have. Humbug.
Lord Palmerston 1784–1865: attributed

20 We do not expect people to be deeply moved by what is not unusual. That element of tragedy which lies in the very fact of frequency, has not yet wrought itself into the coarse emotion of mankind.
George Eliot 1819–80: *Middlemarch* (1871–2)

21 There is a road from the eye to the heart that does not go through the intellect.
G. K. Chesterton 1874–1936: *The Defendant* (1901)

22 Time cools, time clarifies; no mood can be maintained quite unaltered through the course of hours.
Thomas Mann 1875–1955: *The Magic Mountain* (1924), tr. H. T. Lowe-Porter

23 The desires of the heart are as crooked as corkscrews.
W. H. Auden 1907–73: 'Death's Echo' (1937)

24 Now that my ladder's gone
I must lie down where all ladders start
In the foul rag and bone shop of the heart.
W. B. Yeats 1865–1939: 'The Circus Animals' Desertion' (1939)

25 It is only with the heart that one can see rightly; what is essential is invisible to the eye.
Antoine de Saint-Exupéry 1900–44: *Le Petit Prince* (1943)

26 Oh heavens, how I long for a little ordinary human enthusiasm. Just enthusiasm—that's all. I want to hear a warm, thrilling voice cry out Hallelujah! Hallelujah! I'm alive!
John Osborne 1929–94: *Look Back in Anger* (1956)

27 A man who has not passed through the inferno of his passions has never overcome them.
Carl Gustav Jung 1875–1961: *Erinnerungen, Träume, Gedanken* (1962)

28 Sentimentality is the emotional promiscuity of those who have no sentiment.
Norman Mailer 1923–2007: *Cannibals and Christians* (1966)

29 The heart is an organ of fire.
Michael Ondaatje 1943– : *The English Patient* (1992)

30 The human heart likes a little disorder in its geometry.
Louis de Bernières 1954– : *Captain Corelli's Mandolin* (1994)

Employment
see also WORK

proverbs and sayings ▸

1 The labourer is worthy of his hire.
someone should be properly recompensed for effort; English proverb, late 14th century, deriving from the Bible (Luke)

2 Like master, like man.
English proverb, mid 16th century; *man* here means 'servant'

phrases ▸

3 the butcher, the baker, the candlestick-maker

people of all trades, from the nursery rhyme 'Rub-a-dub-dub, Three men in a tub'

4 man Friday

a male personal assistant or servant, from *Friday*, a character in Defoe's novel *Robinson Crusoe* (1719), whom Crusoe often refers to as 'my man Friday'. From the 1940s the term *girl Friday* has been used for a female assistant, especially a junior office worker

5 the oldest profession

traditional euphemism for prostitution; see also POLITICS 29

6 winter of discontent

a period of difficulty, especially political or industrial unrest; particularly applied to the winter of 1978–79 in Britain, when widespread strikes forced the government out of power; after Shakespeare *Richard III* 'Now is the winter of our discontent'; see EMPLOYMENT 26

quotations ▸

7 For promotion cometh neither from the east, nor from the west: nor yet from the south.

Bible: Psalm 75

8 He who does not teach his son a craft, teaches him brigandage.

The Talmud: *Babylonian Talmud* Qiddushin

9 I hold every man a debtor to his profession.

Francis Bacon 1561–1626: *The Elements of the Common Law* (1596)

10 Thou art not for the fashion of these times,
Where none will sweat but for promotion.

William Shakespeare 1564–1616: *As You Like It* (1599)

11 It is wonderful, when a calculation is made, how little the mind is actually employed in the discharge of any profession.

Samuel Johnson 1709–84: James Boswell *Life of Samuel Johnson* (1791) 6 April 1775

12 To do nothing and get something, formed a boy's ideal of a manly career.

Benjamin Disraeli 1804–81: *Sybil* (1845)

13 Which of us...is to do the hard and dirty work for the rest—and for what pay? Who is to do the pleasant and clean work, and for what pay?

John Ruskin 1819–1900: *Sesame and Lilies* (1865)

14 Naturally, the workers are perfectly free; the manufacturer does not force them to take his materials and his cards, but he says to them...'If you don't like to be frizzled in my frying pan, you can take a walk into the fire.'

Friedrich Engels 1820–95: *The Condition of the Working Class in England in 1844* (1892); see MISFORTUNES 13

15 The labour of women in the house, certainly, enables men to produce more wealth than they otherwise could; and in this way women are economic factors in society. But so are horses.

Charlotte Perkins Gilman 1860–1935: *Women and Economics* (1898)

16 When domestic servants are treated as human beings it is not worth while to keep them.

George Bernard Shaw 1856–1950: *Man and Superman* (1903)

17 Lord Finchley tried to mend the Electric Light
Himself. It struck him dead: And serve him right!
It is the business of the wealthy man
To give employment to the artisan.

Hilaire Belloc 1870–1953: 'Lord Finchley' (1911)

18 All professions are conspiracies against the laity.

George Bernard Shaw 1856–1950: *The Doctor's Dilemma* (1911)

19 Not a penny off the pay, not a second on the day.

often quoted with 'minute' substituted for 'second'

A. J. Cook 1885–1931: speech at York, 3 April 1926

20 Work is of two kinds: first, altering the position of matter at or near the earth's surface relatively to other such matter; second, telling other people to do so. The first kind is unpleasant and ill paid; the second is pleasant and highly paid.

Bertrand Russell 1872–1970: *In Praise of Idleness and Other Essays* (1986) title essay (1932)

21 Give a man a dole and you save his body and destroy his spirit. Give him a job and pay him an assured wage and you save both body and spirit.
Harry Lloyd Hopkins 1890–1946: in 1934

22 It is difficult to get a man to understand something when his salary depends on his not understanding it.
Upton Sinclair 1878–1968: *I, Candidate for Governor* (1935)

23 A professional is a man who can do his job when he doesn't feel like it. An amateur is a man who can't do his job when he does feel like it.
James Agate 1877–1947: diary, 19 July 1945

24 By working faithfully eight hours a day, you may eventually get to be a boss and work twelve hours a day.
Robert Frost 1874–1963: attributed

25 You don't get me I'm part of the union.
John Ford 1948– and **Richard Hudson** 1948– : 'Part of the Union' (1974 song)

26 I had known it was going to be a 'winter of discontent'.
James Callaghan 1912–2005: television interview, 8 February 1979; see EMPLOYMENT 6

27 Gizza job.
Alan Bleasdale 1946– : *The Boys from the Blackstuff* (BBC television, 1982) 'Yosser's Story'

28 McJob: A low-pay, low-prestige, low-dignity, low benefit, no-future job in the service sector.
Douglas Coupland 1961– : *Generation X* (1991)

Ending

see also BEGINNING, CHANGE

proverbs and sayings ▸

1 All good things must come to an end.
nothing lasts; although the addition of 'good' is a later development; English proverb, mid 15th century

2 All's well that ends well.
often used with the implication that difficulties have been successfully negotiated; English proverb, late 14th century

3 And they all lived happily ever after.
traditional ending for a fairy story

4 The end crowns the work.
the fulfilment of a process is its finest and most notable part; English proverb, early 16th century

5 Everything has an end.
no condition lasts for ever; English proverb, late 14th century

6 In my end is my beginning.
motto of Mary, Queen of Scots (1542–87); see BEGINNING 23

7 The opera isn't over till the fat lady sings.
using an informal description of the culmination of a traditional opera to indicate that a process is not yet complete; late 20th century saying

8 That's all folks!
closing line of Warner Brothers *Looney Tunes* cartoons, originally introduced in *Porky's Duck Hunt* (1937)

phrases ▸

9 crack of doom
in archaic usage, the thunder-peal supposed to proclaim the Day of Judgement; originally often as a quotation from Shakespeare's *Macbeth*

10 the four last things
the four things (death, judgement, heaven, and hell) studied in eschatology

11 the last of the Mohicans
the sole survivors of a particular race or kind; in Fenimore Cooper's novel of that name (1826), the American Indian Uncas, the last survivor of the Mohicans (= Mohegans), an Algonquian people formerly inhabiting Connecticut and Massachusetts

12 when the kissing has to stop
when the honeymoon period finishes; when one is forced to recognize harsh realities; from Browning: see KISSING 6

quotations ▸

13 Better is the end of a thing than the beginning thereof.
Bible: Ecclesiastes

14 The rest is silence.
William Shakespeare 1564–1616: *Hamlet* (1601)

15 Finish, good lady; the bright day is done,
And we are for the dark.
William Shakespeare 1564–1616: *Antony and Cleopatra* (1606–7)

16 What if this present were the world's last night?
John Donne 1572–1631: *Holy Sonnets* (after 1609)

17 This is the beginning of the end.
on the announcement of Napoleon's Pyrrhic victory at Borodino, 1812
Charles-Maurice de Talleyrand 1754–1838: attributed; Sainte-Beuve *M. de Talleyrand* (1870); see ENDING 20

18 All tragedies are finished by a death,
All comedies are ended by a marriage;
The future states of both are left to faith.
Lord Byron 1788–1824: *Don Juan* (1819–24)

19 This is the way the world ends
Not with a bang but a whimper.
T. S. Eliot 1888–1965: 'The Hollow Men' (1925)

20 Now this is not the end. It is not even the beginning of the end. But it is, perhaps, the end of the beginning.
on the Battle of Egypt
Winston Churchill 1874–1965: speech at the Mansion House, London, 10 November 1942; see ENDING 17

21 The party's over, it's time to call it a day.
Betty Comden 1917–2006 and **Adolph Green** 1915–2002: 'The Party's Over' (1956 song)

22 They think it's all over—it is now.
Kenneth Wolstenholme 1920–2002: television commentary in closing moments of the World Cup Final, 30 July 1966

23 Eternity's a terrible thought. I mean, where's it all going to end?
Tom Stoppard 1937– : *Rosencrantz and Guildenstern are Dead* (1967)

24 It ain't over till it's over.
Yogi Berra 1925– : comment on National League pennant race, 1973, quoted in many versions

Enemies

see also HATRED

proverbs and sayings ►

1 Dead men don't bite.
killing an enemy puts an end to danger; English proverb, mid 16th century; see PRACTICALITY 6

2 Do not call a wolf to help you against the dogs.
advising against allying with an enemy which will destroy you in your turn; Russian proverb

3 The enemy of my enemy is my friend.
shared enmity provides common ground; American proverb, mid 20th century, said to be 'an old Arab proverb'; compare FAMILY 10

4 There is no little enemy.
any enemy can be dangerous; English proverb, mid 17th century

quotations ►

5 If thine enemy be hungry, give him bread to eat; and if he be thirsty, give him water to drink.
For thou shalt heap coals of fire upon his head, and the Lord shall reward thee.
Bible: Proverbs; see FORGIVENESS 7

6 *Delenda est Carthago.*
Carthage must be destroyed.
warning included in every speech made by Cato, whatever the subject; see PEACE 5
Cato the Elder 234–149 BC: Pliny the Elder *Naturalis Historia*

7 He that is not with me is against me.
Bible: St Matthew

8 Love your enemies, do good to them which hate you.
Bible: St Luke; see FORGIVENESS 14

9 There is nothing in the whole world so painful as feeling that one is not liked. It always seems to me that people who hate me must be suffering from some strange form of lunacy.
Sei Shōnagon c.966–c.1013: *The Pillow Book*

10 Heat not a furnace for your foe so hot
That it do singe yourself.
William Shakespeare 1564–1616: *Henry VIII* (1613)

11 People wish their enemies dead—but I do not; I say give them the gout, give them the stone!

Lady Mary Wortley Montagu 1689–1762: letter from Horace Walpole to George Harcourt, 17 September 1778

12 He that wrestles with us strengthens our nerves, and sharpens our skill. Our antagonist is our helper.

Edmund Burke 1729–97: *Reflections on the Revolution in France* (1790)

13 Respect was mingled with surprise,
And the stern joy which warriors feel
In foemen worthy of their steel.

Sir Walter Scott 1771–1832: *The Lady of the Lake* (1810)

14 He makes no friend who never made a foe.

Alfred, Lord Tennyson 1809–92: *Idylls of the King* 'Lancelot and Elaine' (1859)

15 a Spanish general, asked on his deathbed if he forgave his enemies:

I have none. I had them all shot.

Ramón María Narváez 1800–68: Antony Beevor *The Battle For Spain* (2006)

16 A man cannot be too careful in the choice of his enemies.

Oscar Wilde 1854–1900: *The Picture of Dorian Gray* (1891)

17 You shall judge of a man by his foes as well as by his friends.

Joseph Conrad 1857–1924: *Lord Jim* (1900)

18 Scratch a lover, and find a foe.

Dorothy Parker 1893–1967: 'Ballade of a Great Weariness' (1937)

19 Not while I'm alive 'e ain't!

reply to the observation that Nye Bevan was sometimes his own worst enemy

Ernest Bevin 1881–1951: Roderick Barclay *Ernest Bevin and the Foreign Office* (1975)

20 I ain't got no quarrel with the Viet Cong.

refusing to be drafted to fight in Vietnam

Muhammad Ali 1942– : at a press conference in Miami, Florida, February 1966

21 Better to have him inside the tent pissing out, than outside pissing in.

of J. Edgar Hoover

Lyndon Baines Johnson 1908–73: David Halberstam *The Best and the Brightest* (1972)

22 Keep your friends close, but your enemies closer.

often wrongly attributed to Sun Tzu (fl. c.400–320 BC)

Mario Puzo 1920–99 and **Francis Ford Coppola** 1939– : *The Godfather: Part II* (1974 film), spoken by Al Pacino as Michael Corleone

England

see also BRITAIN, BRITISH TOWNS

proverbs and sayings ▸

1 England is the paradise of women, the hell of horses, and the purgatory of servants.

English proverb, late 16th century

2 An Englishman's word is his bond.

a promise given is regarded as having the force of a legal agreement; English proverb, early 16th century

phrases ▸

3 Anglo-Saxon attitudes

behaviour regarded as typically English. The phrase was coined by Lewis Carroll in *Through the Looking-Glass* (1872) as a description of the Messenger who approaches 'skipping and wriggling', and with his hands spread out fanlike from his sides: 'He's an Anglo-Saxon Messenger—and those are Anglo-Saxon attitudes.' (The image may reflect the depiction of figures in medieval manuscripts)

4 perfidious Albion

England; translation of French *la perfide Albion*, of late 18th century origin, with reference to England's alleged habitual treachery to other nations; *Albion* is probably of Celtic origin and related to Latin *albus* 'white', in allusion to the white cliffs of Dover; see ENGLAND 5

5 white cliffs of Dover

the chalk cliffs on the Kent coast near Dover, taken as a national and patriotic symbol; see ENGLAND 4

quotations ▸

6 *Non Angli sed Angeli.*

Not Angles but Angels.

summarizing Bede *Historia Ecclesiastica* 'They answered that they were called Angles. "It is well," he said, "for they have the faces of angels, and such should be the co-heirs of the angels of heaven"'

Gregory the Great AD 540–604: oral tradition

7 This royal throne of kings, this sceptred isle,
This earth of majesty, this seat of Mars,
This other Eden, demi-paradise,
This fortress built by Nature for herself
Against infection and the hand of war,
This happy breed of men, this little world,
This precious stone set in the silver sea...
This blessèd plot, this earth, this realm, this England.
William Shakespeare 1564–1616: *Richard II* (1595)

8 Let not England forget her precedence of teaching nations how to live.
John Milton 1608–74: *The Doctrine and Discipline of Divorce* (1643)

9 The English are busy; they don't have time to be polite.
Montesquieu 1689–1755: *Pensées et fragments inédits...* vol. 2 (1901)

10 The froth at top, dregs at bottom, but the middle excellent.
comparing the English to their own beer
Voltaire 1694–1778: attributed, in *Edinburgh Magazine* (1786)

11 In England there are sixty different religions, and only one sauce.
Francesco Caracciolo 1752–99: attributed

12 We must be free or die, who speak the tongue
That Shakespeare spake; the faith and morals hold
Which Milton held.
William Wordsworth 1770–1850: 'It is not to be thought of that the Flood' (1807)

13 I will not cease from mental fight,
Nor shall my sword sleep in my hand,
Till we have built Jerusalem,
In England's green and pleasant land.
William Blake 1757–1827: *Milton* (1804–10) 'And did those feet in ancient time'

14 England is a nation of shopkeepers.
the phrase 'nation of shopkeepers' had been used earlier by Samuel Adams and Adam Smith
Napoleon I 1769–1821: Barry E. O'Meara *Napoleon in Exile* (1822); see BUSINESS 32

15 For he might have been a Roosian,
A French, or Turk, or Proosian,
Or perhaps Ital-ian!
But in spite of all temptations
To belong to other nations,
He remains an Englishman!
W. S. Gilbert 1836–1911: *HMS Pinafore* (1878)

16 Winds of the World, give answer! They are whimpering to and fro—
And what should they know of England who only England know?
Rudyard Kipling 1865–1936: 'The English Flag' (1892); see CRICKET 8

17 Ask any man what nationality he would prefer to be, and ninety-nine out of a hundred will tell you that they would prefer to be Englishmen.
Cecil Rhodes 1853–1902: Gordon Le Sueur *Cecil Rhodes* (1913)

18 Englishmen never will be slaves: they are free to do whatever the Government and public opinion allow them to do.
George Bernard Shaw 1856–1950: *Man and Superman* (1903)

19 Mad dogs and Englishmen
Go out in the midday sun.
Noël Coward 1899–1973: 'Mad Dogs and Englishmen' (1931 song)

20 Down here it was still the England I had known in my childhood: the railway cuttings smothered in wild flowers...the red buses, the blue policemen—all sleeping the deep, deep sleep of England, from which I sometimes fear that we shall never wake till we are jerked out of it by the roar of bombs.
George Orwell 1903–50: *Homage to Catalonia* (1938)

21 There'll always be an England
While there's a country lane,
Wherever there's a cottage small
Beside a field of grain.
Ross Parker 1914–74 and **Hugh Charles** 1907–95: 'There'll always be an England' (1939 song)

22 I am American bred,
I have seen much to hate here—much to forgive,
But in a world where England is finished and dead,
I do not wish to live.
Alice Duer Miller 1874–1942: *The White Cliffs* (1940)

23 Think of what our Nation stands for,
Books from Boots' and country lanes,
Free speech, free passes, class
distinction,
Democracy and proper drains.

John Betjeman 1906–84: 'In Westminster Abbey' (1940)

24 Old maids biking to Holy Communion through the mists of the autumn mornings...these are not only fragments, but *characteristic* fragments, of the English scene.

George Orwell 1903–50: *The Lion and the Unicorn* (1941) 'England Your England'; see BRITAIN 14

25 An Englishman, even if he is alone, forms an orderly queue of one.

George Mikes 1912–87: *How to be an Alien* (1946)

26 England's not a bad country...It's just a mean, cold, ugly, divided, tired, clapped-out, post-imperial, post-industrial slag-heap covered in polystyrene hamburger cartons.

Margaret Drabble 1939– : *A Natural Curiosity* (1989)

The Environment

see POLLUTION AND THE ENVIRONMENT

Envy and Jealousy

proverbs and sayings ►

1 Better be envied than pitied.

even if one is unhappy it is preferable to be rich and powerful than poor and vulnerable; English proverb, mid 16th century

2 Envy feeds on the living; it ceases when they are dead.

American proverb, mid 20th century

3 The grass is always greener on the other side of the fence.

something just out of reach always appears more desirable than what one already has; English proverb, mid 20th century

phrases ►

4 the green-eyed monster

jealousy, from Shakespeare: see ENVY 9

5 nice work if you can get it

expressing envy of what is perceived to be another's more favourable situation; title of Gershwin song (1937); see COURTSHIP 9

quotations ►

6 Thou shalt not covet thy neighbour's house, thou shalt not covet thy neighbour's wife.

Bible: Exodus; see ENVY 12, LIFESTYLES 13

7 Love is strong as death; jealousy is cruel as the grave.

Bible: Song of Solomon

8 Though jealousy be produced by love, as ashes are by fire, yet jealousy extinguishes love as ashes smother the flame.

Marguerite d'Angoulême 1492–1549: *The Heptameron* (1558)

9 O! beware, my lord, of jealousy;
It is the green-eyed monster which
doth mock
The meat it feeds on.

William Shakespeare 1564–1616: *Othello* (1602–4); see ENVY 4

10 Fools out of favour grudge at knaves
in place.

Daniel Defoe 1660–1731: *The True-Born Englishman* (1701)

11 If something pleasant happens to you, don't forget to tell it to your friends, to make them feel bad.

Casimir, Comte de Montrond 1768–1843: attributed; Comte J. d'Estourmel *Derniers Souvenirs* (1860)

12 Thou shalt not covet; but tradition
Approves all forms of competition.

Arthur Hugh Clough 1819–61: 'The Latest Decalogue' (1862); see ENVY 6

13 Jealousy is no more than feeling alone against smiling enemies.

Elizabeth Bowen 1899–1973: *The House in Paris* (1935)

14 To jealousy, nothing is more frightful than laughter.

Françoise Sagan 1935–2004: *La Chamade* (1965)

15 Jealousy is all the fun you *think* they had.

Erica Jong 1942– : *How to Save Your Own Life* (1977)

16 Sometimes you look in a field and see a cow. You think it is a better cow than the one you see in your field. It never really works out that way.
Alex Ferguson 1941– : commenting on a possible transfer move by Wayne Rooney, 20 October 2010

Equality

see also HUMAN RIGHTS

proverbs and sayings ▸

1 A cat may look at a king.
even someone in a lowly position has a right to observe a person of power and influence; English proverb, mid 16th century

2 Diamond cuts diamond.
used of persons who are evenly matched in wit or cunning (only a diamond is hard enough to cut another diamond); English proverb, early 17th century

3 Jack is as good as his master.
Jack is used variously as a familiar name for a sailor, a member of the common people, a serving man, and one who does odd jobs; English proverb, early 18th century

quotations ▸

4 He maketh his sun to rise on the evil and on the good, and sendeth rain on the just and on the unjust.
Bible: St Matthew; see WEATHER 42

5 SHYLOCK: If you prick us, do we not bleed? if you tickle us, do we not laugh? if you poison us, do we not die? and if you wrong us, shall we not revenge?
William Shakespeare 1564–1616: *The Merchant of Venice* (1596–8)

6 Night makes no difference 'twixt the
Priest and Clerk;
Joan as my Lady is as good i' th' dark.
Robert Herrick 1591–1674: 'No Difference i' th' Dark' (1648)

7 Sir, there is no settling the point of precedency between a louse and a flea.
on the relative merits of two minor poets
Samuel Johnson 1709–84: James Boswell *Life of Samuel Johnson* (1791) 1783

8 A man's a man for a' that.
Robert Burns 1759–96: 'For a' that and a' that' (1790)

9 Equality may perhaps be a right, but no power on earth can ever turn it into a fact.
Honoré de Balzac 1799–1850: *La Duchesse de Langeais* (1834)

10 There is no method by which men can be both free and equal.
Walter Bagehot 1826–77: in *The Economist* 5 September 1863 'France or England'

11 Make all men equal today, and God has so created them that they shall all be unequal tomorrow.
Anthony Trollope 1815–82: *Autobiography* (1883)

12 When every one is somebodee,
Then no one's anybody.
W. S. Gilbert 1836–1911: *The Gondoliers* (1889)

13 Oh, East is East, and West is West, and
never the twain shall meet,
Till Earth and Sky stand presently at
God's great Judgement Seat;
But there is neither East nor West,
Border, nor Breed, nor Birth,
When two strong men stand face to
face, tho' they come from the ends
of earth!
Rudyard Kipling 1865–1936: 'The Ballad of East and West' (1892); see SIMILARITY 4

14 While there is a lower class, I am in it; while there is a criminal element, I am of it; while there is a soul in prison, I am not free.
Eugene Victor Debs 1855–1926: speech at his trial for sedition in Cleveland, Ohio, 14 September 1918

15 The constitution does not provide for first and second class citizens.
Wendell Willkie 1892–1944: *An American Programme* (1944)

16 All animals are equal but some animals are more equal than others.
George Orwell 1903–50: *Animal Farm* (1945)

17 I have a dream that one day on the red hills of Georgia the sons of former slaves and the sons of former slave owners will be able to sit down together at the table of brotherhood.
Martin Luther King 1929–68: speech at Civil Rights March in Washington, 28 August 1963

Europe

see also COUNTRIES, INTERNATIONAL

phrases ▸

1 the cockpit of Europe
Belgium; see COUNTRIES 13

2 the Common Market
a name for the European Economic Community or European Union, used especially in the 1960s and 1970s

3 the Garden of Europe
a traditional name for Italy

quotations ▸

4 The age of chivalry is gone.— That of sophisters, economists, and calculators, has succeeded; and the glory of Europe is extinguished for ever.
Edmund Burke 1729–97: *Reflections on the Revolution in France* (1790)

5 Roll up that map; it will not be wanted these ten years.
of a map of Europe, on hearing of Napoleon's victory at Austerlitz, December 1805
William Pitt 1759–1806: Earl Stanhope *Life of the Rt. Hon. William Pitt* vol. 4 (1862)

6 Better fifty years of Europe than a
cycle of Cathay.
Alfred, Lord Tennyson 1809–92: 'Locksley Hall' (1842)

7 Whoever speaks of Europe is wrong, [it is] a geographical concept.
Otto von Bismarck 1815–98: marginal note on a letter from the Russian Chancellor Gorchakov, November 1876

8 We are part of the community of Europe and we must do our duty as such.
Lord Salisbury 1830–1903: speech at Caernarvon, 10 April 1888

9 The European view of a poet is not of much importance unless the poet writes in Esperanto.
A. E. Housman 1859–1936: in *Cambridge Review* 1915

10 Purity of race does not exist. Europe is a continent of energetic mongrels.
H. A. L. Fisher 1856–1940: *A History of Europe* (1935)

11 This is something you ought to know: each time we have to choose between Europe and the open sea, we shall always choose the open sea.
Winston Churchill 1874–1965: to de Gaulle, 4 June 1944; Charles de Gaulle *War Memoirs:Unity 1942–1944* (1959)

12 Fog in Channel—Continent isolated.
Russell Brockbank 1913–79: newspaper placard in cartoon, *Round the Bend with Brockbank* (1948)

13 If you open that Pandora's Box, you never know what Trojan 'orses will jump out.
on the Council of Europe
Ernest Bevin 1881–1951: Roderick Barclay *Ernest Bevin and the Foreign Office* (1975); see PROBLEMS 13

14 Yes, it is Europe, from the Atlantic to the Urals, it is Europe, it is the whole of Europe, that will decide the fate of the world.
Charles de Gaulle 1890–1970: speech to the people of Strasbourg, 23 November 1959

15 Without Britain Europe would remain only a torso.
Ludwig Erhard 1897–1977: remark on West German television, 27 May 1962

16 It means the end of a thousand years of history.
on a European federation
Hugh Gaitskell 1906–63: speech at Labour Party Conference, 3 October 1962

17 In the eighteenth and nineteenth centuries you weren't considered cultured unless you made the European tour, and so it should be.
Edward Heath 1916– : in *Observer* 18 November 1990

18 The policy of European integration is in reality a question of war and peace in the 21st century.
Helmut Kohl 1930– : speech at Louvain University, 2 February 1996

19 In my lifetime all our problems have come from mainland Europe and all the solutions have come from the English-speaking nations of the world.
Margaret Thatcher 1925– : in *Times* 6 October 1999

20 **You're thinking of Europe as Germany and France. I don't. I think that's old Europe.**
to journalists who asked him about European hostility to a possible war, 22 January 2003
Donald Rumsfeld 1932– : in *Independent* 21 February 2003

Evil

see GOOD AND EVIL

Excellence

see also PERFECTION

proverbs and sayings ▸

1 **Corruptio optimi pessima.**
Latin saying, *Corruption of the best becomes the worst*; found in English from the early 17th century

2 **If something sounds too good to be true, it probably is.**
late 20th century saying

3 **Jack of all trades and master of none.**
a person who tries to master too many skills will learn none of them properly; English proverb, early 17th century; see ABILITY 8

phrases ▸

4 **an admirable Crichton**
a person who excels in all kinds of studies and pursuits, or who is noted for supreme competence; originally from James *Crichton* of Clunie (1560–85?), a Scottish prodigy of intellectual and knightly accomplishments; later in allusion to J. M. Barrie's play *The Admirable Crichton* (1902) of which the eponymous hero is a butler who takes charge when his master's family is shipwrecked on a desert island

5 **the blue ribbon**
the greatest distinction, the first place or prize; a ribbon of blue silk, especially that of the Order of the Garter, worn as a badge of honour; see also SPORTS 6

6 **eighth wonder of the world**
a particularly impressive object; something worthy to rank with the Seven Wonders of the ancient world; see ARCHITECTURE 5

7 **the jewel in the crown**
the most valuable or successful part of something; see INDIA 4

8 **ne plus ultra**
the furthest limit reached or attainable; the point of highest attainment, the acme or highest point of a quality; Latin = not further beyond, the supposed inscription on the Pillars of Hercules (Strait of Gibraltar) prohibiting passage by ships

9 **with flying colours**
with distinction. In former military parlance, *flying colours* meant having the regimental flag flying as a sign of success or victory; a conquered army usually had to *lower (or strike) its colours*

quotations ▸

10 **Between us and excellence, the gods have placed the sweat of our brows.**
Hesiod fl. 700 BC: *Works and Days*

11 **Nature made him, and then broke the mould.**
Ludovico Ariosto 1474–1533: *Orlando Furioso* (1532); see ORIGINALITY 3

12 **All things excellent are as difficult as they are rare.**
Baruch Spinoza 1632–77: *Ethics* (1677)

13 **The danger chiefly lies in acting well;**
No crime's so great as daring to excel.
Charles Churchill 1731–64: *An Epistle to William Hogarth* (1763)

14 **The best is the enemy of the good.**
Voltaire 1694–1778: *Contes* (1772) 'La Begueule'; derived from an Italian proverb

15 **The best is the best, though a hundred judges have declared it so.**
Arthur Quiller-Couch 1863–1944: *Oxford Book of English Verse* (1900) preface

16 **The dullard's envy of brilliant men is always assuaged by the suspicion that they will come to a bad end.**
Max Beerbohm 1872–1956: *Zuleika Dobson* (1911)

17 **The best lack all conviction, while the worst**
Are full of passionate intensity.
W. B. Yeats 1865–1939: 'The Second Coming' (1921)

18 **There's only one real sin, and that is to persuade oneself that the second-best is anything but the second-best.**
Doris Lessing 1919– : *Golden Notebook* (1962)

Excess and Moderation

proverbs and sayings ▸

1 **Do not add legs to the snake after you have finished drawing it.**
advising against making superfluous and undesirable additions; Chinese proverb

2 **Enough is as good as a feast.**
used as a warning against overindulgence, or overdoing something; English proverb, late 14th century

3 **Enough is enough.**
originally used as an expression of content or satisfaction, but now more usually employed as a reprimand, warning someone against persisting in an inappropriate or excessive course of action; English proverb, mid 16th century

4 **The half is better than the whole.**
advising economy or restraint; English proverb, mid 16th century, from Hesiod *Works and Days* 'The half is greater than the whole'

5 **It is the last straw that breaks the camel's back.**
the addition of one quite minor problem may prove crushing to someone who is already overburdened; English proverb, mid 17th century; see CRISES 10

6 **Keep no more cats than will catch mice.**
recommending efficiency and the ethic of steady work to justify one's place; English proverb, late 17th century

7 **The last drop makes the cup run over.**
in which the addition of something in itself quite minor causes an excess; English proverb, mid 17th century

8 **Less is more.**
something simple often has more effect; English proverb, mid 19th century; see ARCHITECTURE 16

9 **Moderation in all things.**
English proverb, mid 19th century, from Hesiod *Works and Days* 'Observe due measure; moderation is best in all things'; see EXCESS 11

10 **The pitcher will go to the well once too often.**
one should not repeat a risky action too often, or push one's luck too far; English proverb, mid 14th century

11 **There is measure in all things.**
English proverb, late 14th century; see EXCESS 9

12 **You can have too much of a good thing.**
excess even of something which is good in itself can be damaging; English proverb, late 15th century; see EXCESS 39

phrases ▸

13 **break a butterfly on a wheel**
use unnecessary force in destroying something fragile; *break on the wheel* = fracture the bones of or dislocate on a wheel as a form of punishment or torture; from Pope: see FUTILITY 24

14 **corn in Egypt**
a plentiful supply; from the Bible (Genesis) 'Behold, I have heard that there is corn in Egypt: get you down thither and buy for us from thence'

15 **embarras de richesse(s)**
a superfluity of something, more than one needs or wants; French = embarrassment of riches, from *L'embarras des richesses* (1726), title of comedy by Abbé d'Allainval

16 **gild the lily**
embellish excessively, add ornament where none is needed; from alteration of Shakespeare: see EXCESS 27

17 **the golden mean**
the avoidance of extremes, moderation; from the Roman poet Horace (65–8 BC) *Odes* 'Someone who loves the golden mean'

18 **the goldilocks principle**
something regarded as falling in the centre of a range of possible values or conditions, rather than leaning to one extreme or the other; from *Goldilocks*, the heroine of the children's story 'The Three Bears', in which she eats and sleeps in their house without leave, and chooses the possessions of the smallest bear as being neither too large nor too small for her, but 'just right'

19 **the Matthew principle**
the principle that more will be given to those who already have; after the Bible (Matthew) 'Unto every one that hath shall be given, and he shall have abundance'

20 **pile Ossa upon Pelion**
add further problems to an existing difficulty; from Virgil 'three times they endeavoured to pile Ossa on Pelion, no less, and to roll leafy Olympus on top of Ossa', referring to the Greek legend of how the giants used the Thessalian mountains of Ossa and Pelion in an attempt to scale the heavens and overthrow the gods

quotations ►

21 Nothing in excess.
Anonymous: inscribed on the temple of Apollo at Delphi, and variously ascribed to the Seven Wise Men

22 May temperance befriend me,
the gods' most lovely gift.
Euripides c.485–c.406 BC: *Medea*

23 The animal needing something knows how much it needs, the man does not.
Democritus c.460–c.370 BC: fragment 198

24 You will go most safely by the middle way.
Ovid 43 BC–c.AD 17: *Metamorphoses*

25 Because thou art lukewarm, and neither cold nor hot, I will spew thee out of my mouth.
Bible: Revelation

26 To many, total abstinence is easier than perfect moderation.
St Augustine of Hippo AD 354–430: *On the Good of Marriage* (AD 401)

27 To gild refinèd gold, to paint the lily...
Is wasteful and ridiculous excess.
William Shakespeare 1564–1616: *King John* (1591–8); see EXCESS 16

28 Use, do not abuse...Neither abstinence nor excess ever renders man happy.
Voltaire 1694–1778: *Sept Discours en Vers sur l'Homme* (1738)

29 By God, Mr Chairman, at this moment I stand astonished at my own moderation!
Lord Clive 1725–74: reply during Parliamentary cross-examination, 1773; G. R. Gleig *The Life of Robert, First Lord Clive* (1848)

30 I know many have been taught to think that moderation, in a case like this, is a sort of treason.
Edmund Burke 1729–97: *Letter to the Sheriffs of Bristol* (1777)

31 The road of excess leads to the palace of wisdom.
William Blake 1757–1827: *The Marriage of Heaven and Hell* (1790–3) 'Proverbs of Hell'

32 Above all, gentlemen, not the slightest zeal.
Charles-Maurice de Talleyrand 1754–1838: P. Chasles *Voyages d'un critique à travers la vie et les livres* (1868)

33 Our life is frittered away by detail... Simplify, simplify.
Henry David Thoreau 1817–62: *Walden* (1854)

34 Moderation is a fatal thing, Lady Hunstanton. Nothing succeeds like excess.
Oscar Wilde 1854–1900: *A Woman of No Importance* (1893); see SUCCESS 6

35 Fanaticism consists in redoubling your effort when you have forgotten your aim.
George Santayana 1863–1952: *The Life of Reason* (1905)

36 Up to a point, Lord Copper.
meaning no
Evelyn Waugh 1903–66: *Scoop* (1938)

37 Perhaps too much of everything is as bad as too little.
Edna Ferber 1887–1968: *Giant* (1952)

38 We know what happens to people who stay in the middle of the road. They get run down.
Aneurin Bevan 1897–1960: in *Observer* 6 December 1953; see EXCESS 42

39 Too much of a good thing can be wonderful.
Mae West 1892–1980: *Goodness Had Nothing to Do With It* (1959); see EXCESS 12

40 I would remind you that extremism in the defence of liberty is no vice! And let me remind you also that moderation in the pursuit of justice is no virtue!
Barry Goldwater 1909–98: accepting the presidential nomination, 16 July 1964

41 You were only supposed to blow the bloody doors off!
Troy Kennedy-Martin 1932–2009: *The Italian Job* (1969 film); spoken by Michael Caine as Charlie Croker

42 There's nothing in the middle of the road but yellow stripes and dead armadillos.
Jim Hightower 1943– : attributed, 1984; see EXCESS 38

Excuses
see APOLOGY AND EXCUSES

Experience
see also MATURITY

proverbs and sayings ▸

1 Appetite comes with eating.
desire or facility increases as an activity proceeds; English proverb, mid 17th century

2 A burnt child dreads the fire.
the memory of past hurt may act as a safeguard in the future; English proverb, mid 13th century

3 Experience is a comb which fate gives a man when his hair is all gone.
American proverb, mid 20th century; see WARS 29

4 Experience is the best teacher.
sometimes used with the implication that learning by experience may be painful; English proverb, mid 16th century; see EXPERIENCE 17

5 Experience is the father of wisdom.
real understanding of something comes only from direct experience of it; English proverb, mid 16th century

6 Experience keeps a dear school.
lessons learned from experience can be painful; English proverb, mid 18th century

7 Live and learn.
often as a resigned or rueful comment on a disagreeable experience; English proverb, early 17th century

8 Once bitten, twice shy.
someone who has suffered an injury will in the future be very cautious of the cause; English proverb, mid 19th century; see CAUTION 20

9 They that live longest, see most.
often used to comment on the experience of old age; English proverb, early 17th century

10 Walking ten thousand miles is better than reading ten thousand books.
theoretical knowledge must be consolidated by practical experience; Chinese proverb, compare KNOWLEDGE 8

11 You cannot catch old birds with chaff.
the wise and experienced are not easily fooled; English proverb, late 15th century: see DECEPTION 4

12 You cannot put an old head on young shoulders.
you cannot expect someone who is young and inexperienced to show the wisdom and maturity of an older person; English proverb, late 16th century; see SCHOOLS 12

13 You should make a point of trying every experience once, excepting incest and folk-dancing.
20th century saying, repeated by Arnold Bax in *Farewell My Youth* (1943), quoting 'a sympathetic Scot'

phrases ▸

14 babes in the wood
inexperienced people in a situation calling for experience, with reference to an old ballad *The Children in the Wood*, in which a wicked uncle who wishes to steal the children's inheritance causes them to be abandoned in a forest where they die

15 walk before one can run
understand elementary points before proceeding to anything more difficult, from the proverb: see PATIENCE 20

quotations ▸

16 *Experto credite.*
Trust one who has gone through it.
Virgil 70–19 BC: *Aeneid*

17 *Experientia docuit.*
Experience has taught.
commonly quoted as '*Experientia docet* [experience teaches]'
Tacitus C.AD 56–after 117: *The Histories*; see EXPERIENCE 4, EXPERIENCE 26

18 No man's knowledge here can go beyond his experience.
John Locke 1632–1704: *An Essay concerning Human Understanding* (1690)

19 Courts and camps are the only places to learn the world in.
Lord Chesterfield 1694–1773: *Letters to his Son* (1774) 2 October 1747

20 The courtiers who surround him have forgotten nothing and learnt nothing.

of Louis XVIII, at the time of the Declaration of Verona, September 1795

Charles François du Périer Dumouriez 1739–1823: *Examen impartial d'un Écrit intitulé Déclaration de Louis XVIII* (1795); quoted by Napoleon in his Declaration to the French on his return from Elba; a similar saying is attributed to Talleyrand

21 He went like one that hath been
stunned,
And is of sense forlorn:
A sadder and a wiser man,
He rose the morrow morn.

Samuel Taylor Coleridge 1772–1834: 'The Rime of the Ancient Mariner' (1798)

22 The light which experience gives is a lantern on the stern, which shines only on the waves behind us!

Samuel Taylor Coleridge 1772–1834: *Table Talk* (1835) 18 December 1831

23 Experience is the best of schoolmasters, only the school fees are heavy.

Thomas Carlyle 1795–1881: *Miscellaneous Essays* (1838) 'Goethe's Helena'

24 The years teach much which the days never know.

Ralph Waldo Emerson 1803–82: *Essays. Second Series* (1844) 'Experience'

25 Grace is given of God, but knowledge
is bought in the market.

Arthur Hugh Clough 1819–61: *The Bothie of Tober-na-Vuolich* (1848)

26 Experientia does it—as papa used to say.

said by Mrs Micawber

Charles Dickens 1812–70: *David Copperfield* (1850); see EXPERIENCE 17

27 in his case against Ruskin, replying to the question, 'For two days' labour, you ask two hundred guineas?':

No, I ask it for the knowledge of a lifetime.

James McNeill Whistler 1834–1903: D. C. Seitz *Whistler Stories* (1913)

28 Experience is the name every one gives to their mistakes.

Oscar Wilde 1854–1900: *Lady Windermere's Fan* (1892)

29 All experience is an arch to build upon.

Henry Brooks Adams 1838–1918: *The Education of Henry Adams* (1907)

30 Experience is not what happens to a man; it is what a man does with what happens to him.

Aldous Huxley 1894–1963: *Texts and Pretexts* (1932)

31 I've been things and seen places.

Mae West 1892–1980: *I'm No Angel* (1933 film)

32 It's a funny old world—a man's lucky if he gets out of it alive.

Walter de Leon and **Paul M. Jones**: *You're Telling Me* (1934 film); spoken by W. C. Fields

33 Experience isn't interesting till it begins to repeat itself—in fact, till it does that, it hardly *is* experience.

Elizabeth Bowen 1899–1973: *Death of the Heart* (1938)

34 We had the experience but missed the meaning.

T. S. Eliot 1888–1965: *Four Quartets* 'The Dry Salvages' (1941)

35 I've looked at life from both sides
now,
From win and lose and still somehow
It's life's illusions I recall;
I really don't know life at all.

Joni Mitchell 1945– : 'Both Sides Now' (1967 song)

36 Education is when you read the fine print; experience is what you get when you don't.

Pete Seeger 1919– : L. Botts *Loose Talk* (1980)

37 It's not the years, honey, it's the mileage.

George Lucas 1944– : *Raiders of the Lost Ark* (1981 film, with Philip Kaufman), spoken by Harrison Ford as Indiana Jones

38 Damaged people are dangerous. They know they can survive.

Josephine Hart: *Damage* (1991)

Exploration
see also TRAVEL

proverbs and sayings ►

1 Here be dragons.
alluding to a traditional indication of early map-makers that a region was unexplored and potentially dangerous

phrases ►

2 to boldly go
explore freely, unhindered by fear of the unknown; from the brief given to the *Enterprise* in the television series *Star Trek*, written by Gene Roddenberry (from 1966), 'These are the voyages of the starship Enterprise. Its five-year mission…to boldly go where no man has gone before'

quotations ►

3 Now the boundary of Britain is revealed, and everything unknown is held to be glorious.
reporting the speech of a British leader, Calgacus
Tacitus C.AD 56–after 117: *Agricola*

4 There is no land unhabitable nor sea innavigable.
Robert Thorne d. 1527: Richard Hakluyt *The Principal Navigations, Voyages, and Discoveries of the English Nation* (1589)

5 They are ill discoverers that think there is no land, when they can see nothing but sea.
Francis Bacon 1561–1626: *The Advancement of Learning* (1605)

6 So geographers, in Afric-maps,
With savage-pictures fill their gaps;
And o'er unhabitable downs
Place elephants for want of towns.
Jonathan Swift 1667–1745: 'On Poetry' (1733)

7 Go West, young man, go West!
John L. B. Soule 1815–91: in *Terre Haute* [Indiana] *Express* (1851); see AMERICA 17

8 It is not down in any map; true places never are.
Herman Melville 1819–91: *Moby Dick* (1851)

9 We have an unknown distance yet to run, an unknown river to explore. What falls there are, we know not; what rocks beset the channel, we know not; what walls rise over the river, we know not.
John Wesley Powell 1834–1902: *Exploration of the Colorado River of the West and Its Tributaries* (1875)

10 Why do people so love to wander? I think the civilized parts of the world will suffice for me in the future.
Mary Cassatt 1844–1926: letter to Louisine Havemeyer, 11 February 1911

11 In fourteen hundred ninety-two,
Columbus sailed the ocean blue.
Winifred Sackville Stoner 1902–83: 'The History of The U.S.' (1919); versions of this line are on record from earlier in the 20th century

12 Polar exploration is at once the cleanest and most isolated way of having a bad time which has been devised.
Apsley Cherry-Garrard 1882–1959: *The Worst Journey in the World* (1922)

13 For a joint scientific and geographical piece of organization, give me Scott; for a Winter Journey, Wilson; for a dash to the pole and nothing else, Amundsen: and if I am in the devil of a hole and want to get out of it, give me Shackleton every time.
Apsley Cherry-Garrard 1882–1959: *The Worst Journey in the World* (1922); see CRISES 6

14 One doesn't discover new lands without consenting to lose sight of the shore for a very long time.
André Gide 1869–1951: *The Counterfeiters* (1925) tr. Dorothy Bussy

15 We shall not cease from exploration
And the end of all our exploring
Will be to arrive where we started
And know the place for the first time.
T. S. Eliot 1888–1965: *Four Quartets* 'Little Gidding' (1942)

16 Simply by sailing in a new direction
You could enlarge the world.
Allen Curnow 1911–2001: 'Landfall in Unknown Seas' (1943)

Extravagance
see THRIFT AND EXTRAVAGANCE

Fact

see HYPOTHESIS AND FACT

Failure

see SUCCESS AND FAILURE

Faith

see also BELIEF

proverbs and sayings ▶

1 Faith will move mountains.
with the help of faith something naturally impossible can be achieved; English proverb, late 19th century, in allusion to the Bible: see FAITH 3

phrases ▶

2 born-again
relating to or denoting a person who has converted to a personal faith in Christ, alluding to the Bible (John) 'Except a man be born again, he cannot see the kingdom of God'; figuratively, newly converted to and very enthusiastic about an idea or cause

quotations ▶

3 If ye have faith as a grain of mustard seed, ye shall say unto this mountain, Remove hence to yonder place; and it shall remove.
Bible: St Matthew; see FAITH 1

4 Faith without works is dead.
Bible: James

5 The confidence and faith of the heart alone make both God and an idol.
Martin Luther 1483–1546: *Large Catechism* (1529) 'The First Commandment'

6 Be of good comfort Master Ridley, and play the man. We shall this day light such a candle by God's grace in England, as (I trust) shall never be put out.
prior to being burned for heresy, 16 October 1555
Hugh Latimer 1485–1555: John Foxe *Actes and Monuments* (1570 ed.)

7 A man with God is always in the majority.
John Knox 1505–72: inscription on the Reformation Monument, Geneva

8 The way to see by faith is to shut the eye of reason.
Benjamin Franklin 1706–90: *Poor Richard's Almanac* (1758) July

9 It is necessary to the happiness of man that he be mentally faithful to himself. Infidelity does not consist in believing, or in disbelieving, it consists in professing to believe what one does not believe.
Thomas Paine 1737–1809: *The Age of Reason* pt. 1 (1794)

10 The faith that stands on authority is not faith.
Ralph Waldo Emerson 1803–82: *Essays* (1841) 'The Over-Soul'

11 The Sea of Faith
Was once, too, at the full, and round earth's shore
Lay like the folds of a bright girdle furled.
But now I only hear
Its melancholy, long, withdrawing roar.
Matthew Arnold 1822–88: 'Dover Beach' (1867)

12 You can do very little with faith, but you can do nothing without it.
Samuel Butler 1835–1902: *Notebooks* (1912)

13 The great act of faith is when a man decides he is not God.
Oliver Wendell Holmes Jr. 1841–1935: letter to William James, 24 March 1907

14 And I said to the man who stood at the gate of the year: 'Give me a light that I may tread safely into the unknown.'
And he replied:
'Go out into the darkness and put your hand into the Hand of God. That shall be to you better than light and safer than a known way.'
quoted by King George VI in his Christmas broadcast, 25 December 1939
Minnie Louise Haskins 1875–1957: *Desert* (1908) 'God Knows'

15 Booth died blind and still by faith he trod,
Eyes still dazzled by the ways of God.
Vachel Lindsay 1879–1931: 'General William Booth Enters into Heaven' (1913)

16 A miracle, my friend, is an event which creates faith. That is the purpose and nature of miracles...Frauds deceive. An event which creates faith does not deceive: therefore it is not a fraud, but a miracle.

George Bernard Shaw 1856–1950: *Saint Joan* (1924)

17 A faith is something you die for; a doctrine is something you kill for: there is all the difference in the world.

Tony Benn 1925– : in *Observer* 16 April 1989

Fame

see also REPUTATION

proverbs and sayings ▸

1 More people know Tom Fool than Tom Fool knows.

English proverb, mid 17th century; *Tom Fool* was a name given to the part of the fool in a play or morris dance

2 A tall tree attracts the wind.

fame may make you the subject of hostile attention; Chinese proverb

3 Who he?

an editorial interjection after the name of a (supposedly) little-known person, associated particularly with Harold Ross (1892–1951), editor of the *New Yorker*, repopularized in Britain by the satirical magazine *Private Eye*

phrases ▸

4 backing into the limelight

apparently shrinking from attention while actually seeking it; *limelight* = an intense white light obtained by heating lime, formerly used in theatres; figuratively, the focus of public attention. The phrase is particularly associated with T. E. Lawrence (1888–1935), and has been ascribed by oral tradition to Lord Berners. However, see FAME 24

5 famous for fifteen minutes

enjoying a brief period of fame before fading back into obscurity; coined by the American artist Andy Warhol: see FAME 29

6 a legend in their own lifetime

a very famous or notorious person; someone whose fame is comparable to that of a hero of legend or about whom similar stories are told; see FAME 31

7 nine days' wonder

a person who or thing which is briefly famous

8 a tall poppy

a privileged or distinguished person; perhaps originally in allusion to the legendary Roman king Tarquin striking the heads off poppies in his garden to demonstrate how to treat the leaders of a conquered city

quotations ▸

9 Let us now praise famous men, and our fathers that begat us.

Bible: Ecclesiasticus

10 Cattle die, kinsmen die,
the self must also die;
but glory never dies,
for the man who is able to achieve it.

Anonymous: *Hávamál* ('Sayings of the High One'), 10th century

11 So long as men can breathe, or eyes can see,
So long lives this, and this gives life to thee.

William Shakespeare 1564–1616: sonnet 18

12 Fame is like a river, that beareth up things light and swollen, and drowns things weighty and solid.

Francis Bacon 1561–1626: *Essays* (1625) 'Of Praise'

13 Fame is the spur that the clear spirit doth raise
(That last infirmity of noble mind)
To scorn delights, and live laborious days;

John Milton 1608–74: 'Lycidas' (1638)

14 To be nameless in worthy deeds
exceeds an infamous history.

Thomas Browne 1605–82: *Hydriotaphia* (Urn Burial, 1658)

15 Seven wealthy towns contend for HOMER dead
Through which the living HOMER begged his bread.

Anonymous: epilogue to *Aesop at Tunbridge; or, a Few Selected Fables in Verse* By No Person of Quality (1698)

16 Full many a flower is born to blush unseen,
And waste its sweetness on the desert air.

Thomas Gray 1716–71: *Elegy Written in a Country Churchyard* (1751)

17 Every man has a lurking wish to appear considerable in his native place.
Samuel Johnson 1709–84: letter to Joshua Reynolds, 17 July 1771; see FAMILIARITY 13

18 I awoke one morning and found myself famous.
on the instantaneous success of *Childe Harold*
Lord Byron 1788–1824: Thomas Moore *Letters and Journals of Lord Byron* (1830)

19 The deed is all, the glory nothing.
Johann Wolfgang von Goethe 1749–1832: *Faust* pt. 2 (1832) 'Hochgebirg'

20 Popularity? It is glory's small change.
Victor Hugo 1802–85: *Ruy Blas* (1838)

21 Fame is a fickle food
Upon a shifting plate.
Emily Dickinson 1830–86: 'Fame is a fickle food'

22 Martyrdom...the only way in which a man can become famous without ability.
George Bernard Shaw 1856–1950: *The Devil's Disciple* (1901)

23 I don't care what you say about me, as long as you say *something* about me, and as long as you spell my name right.
said to a newspaperman in 1912
George M. Cohan 1878–1942: John McCabe *George M. Cohan* (1973)

24 You always hide just in the middle of the limelight.
to T. E. Lawrence, who had complained of Press attention
George Bernard Shaw 1856–1950: Charles Kessler *The Diaries of a Cosmopolitan 1918–1937* (1971) 14 November 1929; see FAME 4

25 Now who is responsible for this work of development on which so much depends? To whom must the praise be given? To the boys in the back rooms. They do not sit in the limelight. But they are the men who do the work.
Lord Beaverbrook 1879–1964: in *Listener* 27 March 1941; see SCIENCE 3

26 The celebrity is a person who is known for his well-knownness.
Daniel J. Boorstin 1914– : *The Image* (1961)

27 I'm world famous, Dr Parks said, all over Canada.
Mordecai Richler 1931–2001: *The Incomparable Atuk* (1963)

28 There's no such thing as bad publicity except your own obituary.
Brendan Behan 1923–64: Dominic Behan *My Brother Brendan* (1965); see ADVERTISING 1

29 In the future everybody will be world famous for fifteen minutes.
Andy Warhol 1927–87: *Andy Warhol* (1968); see FAME 5

30 Celebrity is a mask that eats into the face.
John Updike 1932–2009: *Self-Consciousness: Memoirs* (1989)

31 She's not a legend. She's a beginner.
on Nicole Kidman
Lauren Bacall 1924– : in *Independent* 9 September 2004; see FAME 6

32 After a while you learn that privacy is something you can sell, but you can't buy it back.
Bob Dylan 1941– : *Chronicles Volume One* (2004)

Familiarity

proverbs and sayings ►

1 Better the devil you know than the devil you don't know.
understanding of the nature of a danger may give one an advantage, and is preferable to something which is completely unknown, and which may well be worse; English proverb, mid 19th century

2 Better wed over the mixen than over the moor.
it is better to marry a neighbour than a stranger (a *mixen* is a midden); English proverb, early 17th century

3 Blue are the hills that are far away.
a distant view lends enchantment; English proverb, 19th century

4 Come live with me and you'll know me.
the implication is that only by living with a person will you learn their real nature; English proverb, early 20th century

5 Familiarity breeds contempt.
we value least the things which are most familiar; English proverb, late 14th century; see FAMILIARITY 20

6 If you lie down with dogs, you will get up with fleas.
asserting that human failings, such as dishonesty and foolishness, are contagious; English proverb, late 16th century (earlier in Latin)

7 Local ginger is not hot.
modern saying, said to derive from a Chinese proverb; see FAMILIARITY 10

8 A man is known by the company he keeps.
originally used as a moral maxim or exhortation in the context of preparation for marriage; English proverb, mid 16th century

9 No man is a hero to his valet.
English proverb, mid 18th century; see HEROES 6

10 A prophet is not without honour save in his own country.
English proverb, late 15th century, from the Bible: see FAMILIARITY 7, FAMILIARITY 13

11 There is nothing new under the sun.
English proverb, late 16th century, from the Bible; see EARTH 7, PROGRESS 5

12 You should know a man seven years before you stir his fire.
used as a caution against over-familiarity on slight acquaintance; English proverb, early 19th century

quotations ▸

13 A prophet is not without honour, save in his own country, and in his own house.
Bible: St Matthew; see FAMILIARITY 10, FAME 17

14 There is nothing that God hath established in a constant course of nature, and which therefore is done every day, but would seem a Miracle, and exercise our admiration, if it were done but once.
John Donne 1572–1631: *LXXX Sermons* (1640) Easter Day, 25 March 1627

15 Old friends are best. King James used to call for his old shoes; they were easiest for his feet.
John Selden 1584–1654: *Table Talk* (1689) 'Friends'

16 We can scarcely hate any one that we know.
William Hazlitt 1778–1830: *Table Talk* (1822) 'On Criticism'

17 Think you, if Laura had been
Petrarch's wife,
He would have written sonnets all his
life?
Lord Byron 1788–1824: *Don Juan* (1819–24)

18 A maggot must be born i' the rotten cheese to like it.
George Eliot 1819–80: *Adam Bede* (1859)

19 There are no conditions of life to which a man cannot get accustomed, especially if he sees them accepted by everyone about him.
Leo Tolstoy 1828–1910: *Anna Karenina* (1875–7)

20 Familiarity breeds contempt—and children.
Mark Twain 1835–1910: *Notebooks* (1935); see FAMILIARITY 5

21 Only the unknown frightens men. But once a man has faced the unknown, that terror becomes known.
Antoine de Saint-Exupéry 1900–44: *Wind, Sand and Stars* (1939)

22 I've grown accustomed to the trace
Of something in the air;
Accustomed to her face.
Alan Jay Lerner 1918–86: 'I've Grown Accustomed to her Face' (1956 song)

23 The mind loves the unknown. It loves images whose meaning is unknown, since the meaning of the mind itself is unknown.
René Magritte 1898–1967: Suzy Gablik *Magritte* (1970)

The Family

see also CHILD CARE, CHILDREN, PARENTS

proverbs and sayings ▸

1 The apple never falls far from the tree.
family characteristics will assert themselves; English proverb, mid 19th century

2 Blood is thicker than water.
in the end family ties will always count; English proverb, early 19th century

3 Blood will tell.
family characteristics or heredity will in the end be dominant; English proverb, mid 19th century

4 The child of a frog is a frog.
Japanese proverb

5 Children are certain cares, but uncertain comforts.
emphasizing the continuing responsibility and anxiety of parenthood; English proverb, mid 17th century

6 Dragons beget dragons, phoenixes beget phoenixes, and burglars' children learn how to break into houses.
Chinese proverb; see FAMILY 8

7 I belong by blood relationship; therefore I am.
on the importance of family ties in a sense of identity; African proverb

8 Like father, like son.
often used to call attention to similarities in behaviour; English proverb, mid 14th century

9 Like mother, like daughter.
English proverb, early 14th century; the ultimate allusion is to the Bible (Ezekiel), 'As is the mother, so is her daughter'

10 My brother and I against my cousin and my cousin and I against the stranger.
Arab proverb; compare ENEMIES 3

11 The shoemaker's son always goes barefoot.
the family of a skilled or knowledgeable person are often the last to benefit from their expertise; English proverb, mid 16th century

phrases ▸

12 black sheep
a member of a family or group who is regarded as a disgrace to it

13 a chip off the old block
a child resembling a parent or ancestor, especially in character; *chip* = something forming a portion of, or derived from, a larger or more important thing, of which it retains the characteristic qualities; see SPEECHES 11

quotations ▸

14 Thy wife shall be as the fruitful vine: upon the walls of thine house.
Thy children like the olive-branches: round about thy table.
Bible: Psalm 128

15 A little more than kin, and less than kind.
William Shakespeare 1564–1616: *Hamlet* (1601)

16 He that hath wife and children hath given hostages to fortune; for they are impediments to great enterprises, either of virtue or mischief.
Francis Bacon 1561–1626: *Essays* (1625) 'Of Marriage and the Single Life'

17 We begin our public affections in our families. No cold relation is a zealous citizen.
Edmund Burke 1729–97: *Reflections on the Revolution in France* (1790)

18 If a man's character is to be abused, say what you will, there's nobody like a relation to do the business.
William Makepeace Thackeray 1811–63: *Vanity Fair* (1847–8)

19 All happy families resemble one another, but each unhappy family is unhappy in its own way.
Leo Tolstoy 1828–1910: *Anna Karenina* (1875–7)

20 Family!...the home of all social evil, a charitable institution for comfortable women, an anchorage for house-fathers, and a hell for children.
August Strindberg 1849–1912: *The Son of a Servant* (1886)

21 The awe and dread with which the untutored savage contemplates his mother-in-law are amongst the most familiar facts of anthropology.
James George Frazer 1854–1941: *The Golden Bough* (2nd ed., 1900)

22 I am the family face;
Flesh perishes, I live on.
Thomas Hardy 1840–1928: 'Heredity' (1917)

23 When our relatives are at home, we have to think of all their good points or it would be impossible to endure them. But when they are away, we console ourselves for their absence by dwelling on their vices.
George Bernard Shaw 1856–1950: *Heartbreak House* (1919)

24 One would be in less danger
From the wiles of the stranger
If one's own kin and kith
Were more fun to be with.
Ogden Nash 1902–71: 'Family Court' (1931)

25 The family—that dear octopus from whose tentacles we never quite escape.
Dodie Smith 1896–1990: *Dear Octopus* (1938)

26 It is no use telling me that there are bad aunts and good aunts. At the core, they are all alike. Sooner or later, out pops the cloven hoof.
P. G. Wodehouse 1881–1975: *The Code of the Woosters* (1938); see GOOD 9

27 Far from being the basis of the good society, the family, with its narrow privacy and tawdry secrets, is the source of all our discontents.
Edmund Leach 1910–89: BBC Reith Lectures, 1967

28 Every family has a secret, and the secret is that it's not like other families.
Alan Bennett 1934– : *Dinner at Noon* (BBC television, 1988)

29 Having one child makes you a parent; having two you are a referee.
David Frost 1939– : in *Independent* 16 September 1989

30 [It is] time to turn our attention to pressing challenges like...how to make American families more like the Waltons and a little bit less like the Simpsons.
George Bush 1924– : speech, Neenah, Wisconsin, 27 July 1992

31 As I leave the second most important job I could ever hold, I cherish even more the first—as a husband and father.
Gordon Brown 1951– : statement on resigning as Prime Minister, 11 May 2010

32 Like getting a telegram from the mortuary.
on becoming a grandfather
Martin Amis 1949– : speaking at Hay on Wye Literary Festival, 6 June 2010

Farming

proverbs and sayings ▸

1 Candlemas day, put beans in the clay; put candles and candlesticks away.
recording the tradition that the feast of Candlemas, on 2 February, was the time for planting beans; English proverb, late 17th century

2 One for the mouse, one for the crow, one to rot, one to grow.
traditionally used when sowing seed, and enumerating the ways in which some of the crop will be lost leaving a proportion to germinate; English proverb, mid 19th century

3 On Saint Thomas the Divine kill all turkeys, geese and swine.
21 December, the traditional feast-day in the Western Church of St Thomas the Apostle, taken as marking the season at which domestic animals not kept through the winter were to be slaughtered; English proverb, mid 18th century

4 Three acres and a cow.
regarded as the requirement for self-sufficiency; late 19th century political slogan

phrases ▸

5 first fruits
the first agricultural produce of a season, especially when given as an offering to God; originally alluding to the Bible (Numbers), 'the first fruits of them which they shall offer unto the Lord'

quotations ▸

6 A farm is like a man—however great the income, if there is extravagance but little is left.
Cato the Elder 234–149 BC: *On Agriculture*

7 O farmers excessively fortunate if only they recognized their blessings!
Virgil 70–19 BC: *Georgics*

8 Cultivators of the earth are the most valuable citizens. They are the most vigorous, the most independent, the most virtuous, and they are tied to their country and wedded to its liberty and interests by the most lasting bands.
Thomas Jefferson 1743–1826: letter to John Jay, 23 August 1785

9 Agriculture is the foundation of manufactures; since the productions of nature are the materials of art.
Edward Gibbon 1737–94: *The Decline and Fall of the Roman Empire* (1776–88)

10 The class of citizens who provide at once their own food and their own raiment, may be viewed as the most truly independent and happy.
James Madison 1751–1836: 'Republican Distribution of Citizens' in *National Gazette* 5 March 1792

11 We plough the fields, and scatter
The good seed on the land,
But it is fed and watered
By God's almighty hand.

Jane Montgomery Campbell 1817–78: 'We plough the fields, and scatter' (1861 hymn)

12 Our salvation can only come through the farmer. Neither the lawyers, nor the doctors, nor the rich landlords are going to secure it.

Mahatma Gandhi 1869–1948: speech, Benares, 4 February 1916

13 The Farmer will never be happy again;
He carries his heart in his boots;
For either the rain is destroying his grain
Or the drought is destroying his roots.

A. P. Herbert 1890–1971: 'The Farmer' (1922)

14 Farming looks mighty easy when your plough is a pencil, and you're a thousand miles from the corn field.

Dwight D. Eisenhower 1890–1969: speech, Peoria, 25 September 1956

Fashion

see also DRESS

phrases ▸

1 all the world and his wife

everyone with pretensions to fashion, from Swift *Polite Conversation* (1738) 'Pray, Madam, who were the Company?...Why, there was all the world, and his wife'

2 be out of the ark

be very old-fashioned; the *ark* (in the Bible) the ship built by Noah to save his family and two of every kind of animal from the Flood

3 flavour of the month

the current fashion; a person who or thing which is especially popular at a given time; a marketing phrase used in US ice-cream parlours in the 1940s, when a particular flavour of ice-cream would be singled out for the month for special promotion

4 the new black

something which is suddenly extremely popular or fashionable, from its use to describe a colour in such vogue with clothing designers as to rival the traditional role of black as a staple or background colour for garments; compare COLOURS 9

5 radical chic

the fashionable affectation of radical left-wing views or an associated style of dress or life, coined by Tom Wolfe: see FASHION 14

quotations ▸

6 The women come to see the show, they come to make a show themselves.

Ovid 43 BC–C. AD 17: *Ars Amatoria*

7 It is charming to totter into vogue.

Horace Walpole 1717–97: letter to George Selwyn, 2 December 1765

8 A little of what you call frippery is very necessary towards looking like the rest of the world.

Abigail Adams 1744–1818: letter to John Adams, 1 May 1780

9 Every generation laughs at the old fashions, but follows religiously the new.

Henry David Thoreau 1817–62: *Walden* (1854)

10 A fashion...is usually a form of ugliness so intolerable that we have to alter it every six months.

Oscar Wilde 1854–1900: in *Woman's World* November 1887

11 Fashion is something barbarous, for it produces innovation without reason and imitation without benefit.

George Santayana 1863–1952: *The Life of Reason* (1905)

12 You cannot be both fashionable and first-rate.

Logan Pearsall Smith 1865–1946: *Afterthoughts* (1931) 'In the World'

13 Fashion is made to become unfashionable.

Coco Chanel 1883–1971: in *Life* 19 August 1957

14 Radical Chic...is only radical in Style; in its heart it is part of Society and its tradition—Politics, like Rock, Pop, and Camp, has its uses.

Tom Wolfe 1931– : in *New York* 8 June 1970; see FASHION 5

15 I don't design clothes, I design dreams.

Ralph Lauren 1939– : in *New York Times* 19 April 1986

16 Fashion is more usually a gentle progression of revisited ideas.
Bruce Oldfield 1950– : in *Independent* 9 September 1989

17 I never cared for fashion much. Amusing little seams and witty little pleats. It was the girls I liked.
David Bailey 1938– : in *Independent* 5 November 1990

18 You dress elegant and sophisticated women, I dress sluts.
Gianni Versace 1946–97: to Giorgio Armani, attributed; in *Independent* 15 September 2000

Fate

proverbs and sayings ▸

1 Hanging and wiving go by destiny.
an expression of fatalism about the course of one's life; English proverb, mid 16th century

2 If you're born to be hanged then you'll never be drowned.
used to qualify apparent good luck which may have an unhappy outcome; English proverb, late 16th century

3 Man proposes, God disposes.
often now said in consolation or resignation when plans have been disrupted; English proverb, mid 15th century

4 The mills of God grind slowly, yet they grind exceeding small.
English proverb, mid 17th century; the current form is from Longfellow: see GOD 21

5 We're here
Because
We're here
Because
We're here
Because we're here.
soldiers' song of the First World War, sung to the tune of 'Auld Lang Syne'

6 What goes up must come down.
commonly associated with wartime bombing and anti-aircraft shrapnel, and often used with the implication that an exhilarating rise must be followed by a fall; early 20th century saying

7 What must be, must be.
used to acknowledge the force of circumstances; English proverb, late 14th century

phrases ▸

8 appointment in Samarra
an unavoidable meeting with death or fate, from a story by Somerset Maugham in the play *Sheppey* (1933), in which a man sees Death in Baghdad and flees to distant Samarra to escape, not realizing that Death had always intended to meet him that night in Samarra; see FATE 22

9 have a person's name and number on it
(of a bullet) be destined to kill a particular person; see FATE 17

10 in the lap of the gods
beyond human control, from Homer *The Iliad* 'It lies in the lap of the gods'; see CHANCE 21

11 the three sisters
the three goddesses of destiny, the Fates

quotations ▸

12 Canst thou bind the sweet influences of Pleiades, or loose the bands of Orion?
Bible: Job

13 Each man is the smith of his own fortune.
Appius Claudius Caecus fl. 312–279 BC: Sallust *Ad Caesarem Senem de Re Publica Oratio*; see SELF 2

14 *Dis aliter visum.*
The gods thought otherwise.
Virgil 70–19 BC: *Aeneid*

15 There's a divinity that shapes our ends,
Rough-hew them how we will.
William Shakespeare 1564–1616: *Hamlet* (1601)

16 We are merely the stars' tennis-balls, struck and bandied
Which way please them.
John Webster c.1580–c.1625: *The Duchess of Malfi* (1623)

17 Every bullet has its billet.
William III 1650–1702: John Wesley's diary, 6 June 1765; see FATE 9

18 I shall seize fate by the throat; it shall certainly never wholly overcome me.
Ludwig van Beethoven 1770–1827: letter to Franz Wegeler, 16 November 1801

19 Must it be? It must be.
Ludwig van Beethoven 1770–1827: String Quartet in F Major, Opus 135 (1827), epigraph

20 What we call fate does not come into us from the outside, but emerges from us.
Rainer Maria Rilke 1875–1926: *Letters to a Young Poet* (1929) 12 August 1904, tr. S. Mitchell

21 There once was a man who said, 'Damn!
It is borne in upon me I am
An engine that moves
In predestinate grooves,
I'm not even a bus, I'm a tram.'
Maurice Evan Hare 1886–1967: 'Limerick' (1905)

22 I [Death] was astonished to see him in Baghdad, for I had an appointment with him tonight in Samarra.
W. Somerset Maugham 1874–1965: *Sheppey* (1933); see FATE 8

23 Fate is not an eagle, it creeps like a rat.
Elizabeth Bowen 1899–1973: *The House in Paris* (1935)

24 I go the way that Providence dictates with the assurance of a sleepwalker.
Adolf Hitler 1889–1945: speech in Munich, 15 March 1936

25 We may become the makers of our fate when we have ceased to pose as its prophets.
Karl Popper 1902–94: *The Open Society and its Enemies* (1945)

Fear

proverbs and sayings ▸

1 Be afraid. Be very afraid.
advertising copy for the film *The Fly* (1986)

2 Cowards may die many times before their death.
English proverb, late 16th century; see COURAGE 13

3 Fear makes the wolf bigger than he is.
fear exaggerates what we are afraid of; German proverb

4 In space no one can hear you scream.
advertising copy for the film *Alien* (1979)

phrases ▸

5 Chicken Little
an alarmist, a person who panics at the first sign of a problem; from the name of a character in a nursery story who repeatedly warns that the sky is falling down; see CRISES 13

6 freeze one's blood
fill one with a sudden feeling of great fear or horror. The idea of the blood congealing at such a moment goes back to the late medieval period; the actual phrase is used in *Hamlet*, when the Ghost tells his son that he 'could a tale unfold whose lightest word Would…freeze thy young blood.'; see STYLE 14

7 make one's flesh creep
frighten, horrify, or disgust, especially with dread of the supernatural; indicating that there is a physical sensation of something crawling over the skin, and causing goose-pimples; see FEAR 15

quotations ▸

8 Thou shalt not be afraid for any terror by night: nor for the arrow that flieth by day;
For the pestilence that walketh in darkness: nor for the sickness that destroyeth in the noon-day.
Bible: Psalm 91

9 The thing I fear most is fear.
Montaigne 1533–92: *Essays* (1580); see FEAR 21

10 Letting 'I dare not' wait upon
'I would,'
Like the poor cat i' the adage?
William Shakespeare 1564–1616: *Macbeth* (1606)

11 Present fears
Are less than horrible imaginings.
William Shakespeare 1564–1616: *Macbeth* (1606)

12 Every drop of ink in my pen ran cold.
Horace Walpole 1717–97: letter to George Montagu, 30 July 1752

13 No passion so effectually robs the mind of all its powers of acting and reasoning as fear.
Edmund Burke 1729–97: *On the Sublime and Beautiful* (1757)

14 Wee, sleekit, cow'rin,' tim'rous
beastie,
O what a panic's in thy breastie!
Robert Burns 1759–96: 'To a Mouse' (1786)

15 I wants to make your flesh creep.
The Fat Boy
Charles Dickens 1812–70: *Pickwick Papers* (1837); see FEAR 7

16 Better be killed than frightened to death.
R. S. Surtees 1805–64: *Mr Facey Romford's Hounds* (1865)

17 It is my belief that six out of every dozen people who go out hunting are disagreeably conscious of a nervous system, and two out of six are in what is brutally called 'a blue funk'.
Edith Œ Somerville 1858–1949 and **Martin Ross** 1862–1915: *Some Experiences of an Irish R.M.* (1899)

18 The horror! The horror!
Joseph Conrad 1857–1924: *Heart of Darkness* (1902)

19 I will show you fear in a handful of
dust.
T. S. Eliot 1888–1965: *The Waste Land* (1922)

20 To fear love is to fear life, and those who fear life are already three parts dead.
Bertrand Russell 1872–1970: *Marriage and Morals* (1929)

21 The only thing we have to fear is fear itself.
Franklin D. Roosevelt 1882–1945: inaugural address, 4 March 1933; see FEAR 9

22 Nothing in life is to be feared, it is only to be understood.
Marie Curie 1867–1934: attributed

23 We must travel in the direction of our fear.
John Berryman 1914–72: 'A Point of Age' (1942)

24 Cowardice, as distinguished from panic, is almost always simply a lack of ability to suspend the functioning of the imagination.
Ernest Hemingway 1899–1961: *Men at War* (1942)

25 There is no terror in a bang, only in the anticipation of it.
Alfred Hitchcock 1899–1980: attributed

26 Terror...often arises from a pervasive sense of disestablishment; that things are in the unmaking.
Stephen King 1947– : *Danse Macabre* (1981)

27 It is not power that corrupts, but fear. Fear of losing power corrupts those who wield it and fear of the scourge of power corrupts those who are subject to it.
Aung San Suu Kyi 1945– : *Freedom from Fear* (1991); see POWER 33, POWER 38

Festivals and Celebrations

see also CHRISTMAS

proverbs and sayings ▸

1 Barnaby bright, Barnaby bright, the longest day and the shortest night.
in the Old Style calendar St Barnabas' Day, 11 June, was reckoned the longest day of the year; English proverb, mid 17th century

2 The better the day, the better the deed.
frequently used to justify working on a Sunday or Holy Day; English proverb, early 17th century

3 If Saint Paul's day be fair and clear, it will betide a happy year.
the feast of the conversion of St Paul is 25 January; English proverb, late 16th century

4 Natale con i tuoi, Pasqua con chi vuoi.
Italian proverb, meaning 'Christmas with the family, Easter with whomever you want'

5 A penny for the guy.
traditional saying, used by children displaying a guy to ask for money toward celebrations of Guy Fawkes Night; *guy* = an effigy representing Guy Fawkes: see FESTIVALS 26

phrases ▸

6 All Saints' Day
1 November, on which there is a general commemoration of the blessed dead, sometimes known as All Hallows Day; see FESTIVALS 58

7 All Souls' Day
2 November, on which the Roman Catholic Church makes supplications on behalf of the dead

8 April Fool's Day
the first of April; the custom of playing tricks on this day has been observed in many countries for hundreds of years, but its origin is unknown

9 Ash Wednesday
the first day of Lent, from the custom of marking the foreheads of penitents with ashes on that day

10 **Bastille Day**
14 July, celebrated as a national holiday in France; the date of the storming of the Bastille in 1789

11 **Bonfire Night**
5 November, Guy Fawkes Night; see FESTIVALS 26

12 **Burns Night**
25 January; the annual celebration in honour of the Scottish poet Robert *Burns* (1759–96), held worldwide on his birthday

13 **Canada Day**
1 July, observed as a public holiday in Canada, marking the day in 1867 when four of the former colonial provinces were united under one government as the Dominion of Canada

14 **counting of the omer**
in the Jewish religion, the formal enumeration of the 49 days from the offering at Passover to Pentecost; *omer* = a sheaf of corn presented as an offering on the second day of Passover

15 **Day of Atonement**
Yom Kippur; see FESTIVALS 62

16 **Ember days**
a group of three days in each season, observed as days of fasting and prayer in some Christian Churches, and now associated almost entirely with the ordination of ministers; *Ember* = perhaps alteration of Old English *ymbryne* = period, revolution of time; at first, there were apparently only three groups, perhaps taken over from pagan religious observances connected with seed-time, harvest, and autumn vintage

17 **Empire Day**
May 24, the birthday of Queen Victoria, formerly observed as a (school) holiday in the British Empire and instituted to commemorate assistance given to Britain by the colonies during the Boer War (1899-1902); now Commonwealth Day, and observed on the second Monday in March

18 **Father's Day**
a day, usually the third Sunday in June, established for a special tribute to fathers

19 **festival of lights**
Hanukkah (Hebrew 'consecration'), an eight-day Jewish festival with lights beginning in December, commemorating the rededication of the Temple in 165 BC after its desecration by the Syrians; Diwali, (from Hindustani 'row of lights') a Hindu festival with lights, held over three nights in the period October to November to celebrate the new season at the end of the monsoon, and particularly associated with Lakshmi, the goddess of prosperity

20 **first-foot**
the first person to cross a threshold in the New Year, in accordance with a Scottish custom

21 **Forefathers' Day**
in US usage, 21 December, the anniversary of the landing of the first settlers at Plymouth, Massachusetts

22 **Fourth of July**
4 July, a national holiday in the United States, the anniversary of the adoption of the Declaration of Independence in 1776; see FESTIVALS 23, FESTIVALS 29

23 **the Glorious Fourth**
the Fourth of July; see FESTIVALS 22

24 **the glorious Twelfth**
12 August, on which the grouse-shooting season opens

25 **Good Friday**
the Friday before Easter Day, observed as the anniversary of Jesus' Crucifixion

26 **Guy Fawkes Night**
5 November, Bonfire Night; *Guy Fawkes*, conspirator in the Gunpowder Plot to blow up James I and his Parliament on 5 November 1605, who was arrested in the cellars of the Houses of Parliament the day before the scheduled attack and betrayed his colleagues under torture; he was subsequently executed, and the plot is commemorated by bonfires and fireworks, with the burning of an effigy of Guy Fawkes, annually on 5 November; see FESTIVALS 5, FESTIVALS 11, TRUST 2

27 **harvest home**
the festival (now rarely held) celebrating bringing in the harvest

28 **Holy Week**
the week before Easter Sunday, after Italian *la settimana santa*, French *la semaine sainte*

29 **Independence Day**
the Fourth of July; see FESTIVALS 22

30 **Innocents' Day**
28 December, commemorating the massacre of the *innocents*, the young children killed by Herod the Great after the birth of Jesus; see CHILDREN 15, CRUELTY 2

31 **kill the fatted calf**
celebrate, especially at a prodigal's return; from the Bible (Luke): see HOSPITALITY 6, FORGIVENESS 8

32 **Labour Day**
1 May in many places; the first Monday of September in North America; a day celebrated in honour of workers, often as a public holiday

33 **Lady Day**
25 March, the feast of the Annunciation to the Virgin Mary

34 **Lammas Day**
1 August; *Lammas* from Old English 'loaf mass', later interpreted as from *lamb*; formerly observed as an English harvest festival at which loaves made from the first ripe corn were consecrated

35 **Low Sunday**
the Sunday after Easter, perhaps so named in contrast to the high days of Holy Week and Easter

36 **many happy returns of the day**
a greeting to a person on his or her birthday

37 **Mardi Gras**
Shrove Tuesday in some Catholic countries; French, = fat Tuesday, in reference to celebrations before the beginning of Lent; see FESTIVALS 55

38 **mark with a white stone**
regard as specially fortunate or happy, with allusion to the ancient practice of using a white stone as a memorial of a happy event

39 **Maundy Thursday**
the Thursday before Good Friday; *Maundy* comes ultimately from Latin *mandatum* commandment, mandate in *mandatum novum* a new commandment (with reference to the Bible (John) 'A new commandment give I unto you'), the opening of the first antiphon sung at the Maundy ceremony of washing the feet of a number of poor people, performed by royal or other eminent people or by ecclesiastics, on the Thursday before Easter, and commonly followed by the distribution of clothing, food, or money

40 **May Day**
1 May; a day of traditional springtime celebrations, probably associated with pre-Christian fertility rites; May Day was designated an international labour day by the International Socialist congress of 1889

41 **Memorial Day**
in the United States, 30 May, or the last Monday in May; a day on which those who died on active service are remembered

42 **Midsummer Day**
24 June, traditionally taken as marking the summer solstice

43 **Mothering Sunday**
the fourth Sunday in Lent; *mothering* = the custom of visiting, communicating with, or giving presents to one's mother (formerly, one's parents) on this day; see FESTIVALS 44

44 **Mothers' Day**
in North America, the second Sunday in May; in Britain, Mothering Sunday; a day on which mothers are particularly honoured; see FESTIVALS 43

45 **New Year's Day**
1 January; the first day of the year; see FESTIVALS 69

46 **Oak-Apple Day**
29 May, the anniversary of Charles II's restoration in 1660, when oak-apples or oak-leaves were worn in memory of his hiding in an oak after the battle of Worcester, 1651

47 **Palm Sunday**
the Sunday before Easter, on which Jesus's entry into Jerusalem is commemorated by processions in which branches of palms are carried

48 **Pancake Day**
Shrove Tuesday, on which pancakes are traditionally eaten; see FESTIVALS 55

49 **Poppy Day**
Remembrance Day, from the artificial red poppies made for wearing on Remembrance Day and sold in aid of needy ex-servicemen and ex-servicewomen (see WORLD WAR I 3); see FESTIVALS 51

50 **red letter day**
a pleasantly memorable, fortunate, or happy day; a saint's day or church festival traditionally indicated in the calendar by red letters

51 **Remembrance Day**
the Sunday nearest to 11 November, anniversary of the signing of the armistice that ended the First World War on 11 November 1918, when those killed in the wars of 1914–18 and 1939–45 are commemorated; see FESTIVALS 49

52 **Rogation Sunday**
the Sunday before Ascension Day; *rogation(s)* = solemn prayers consisting of the litany of the saints chanted on the three days before Ascension Day

53 **Rosh Hashana**
the Jewish New Year, celebrated on the first (and sometimes second) day of the month Tishri (September–October); Hebrew, = beginning (literally 'head') of the year

54 **St Valentine's day**
14 February, traditionally associated with the choosing of sweethearts and the mating of birds

55 **Shrove Tuesday**
the Tuesday before Ash Wednesday; *shrove* = past tense of *shrive* = hear the confession of, assign penance to, and absolve; the day preceding the start of Lent, when it was formerly customary to be shriven and to take part in festivities; see FESTIVALS 37, FESTIVALS 48; see also FOOD 11

56 **Stir-up Sunday**
the Sunday before the Sunday on which Advent begins, so called from the opening words of the collect for the day: 'Stir up, we beseech thee, O Lord, the hearts of thy faithful people'

57 **Trafalgar Day**
21 October, the anniversary of the battle of Trafalgar, 1805

58 **trick or treat**
a children's custom of calling at houses at Hallowe'en (31 October, the eve of All Saints' Day) with the threat of pranks if they are not given a small gift; Hallowe'en is of pre-Christian origin, being associated with Samhain, the Celtic festival marking the end of the year and the beginning of winter, when ghosts and spirits were thought to be abroad; it was adopted as a Christian festival but gradually became a secular rather than a Christian observance, involving the dressing up and wearing of masks, and was particularly strong in Scotland; these secular customs were popularized in the US in the late 19th century and later developed into the custom of children playing *trick or treat*; see FESTIVALS 6

59 **Trinity Sunday**
the next Sunday after Whit Sunday, celebrated in honour of the Holy Trinity

60 **Twelfth Night**
the evening of 5 January, the eve of the Epiphany, formerly the last day of the Christmas festivities

61 **Whit Sunday**
the seventh Sunday after Easter, literally 'white Sunday', probably from the white robes of the newly baptized at Pentecost; commemorating the descent of the Holy Spirit on the disciples

62 **Yom Kippur**
the most solemn religious fast of the Jewish Year, the last of the ten days of penitence that begin with Rosh Hashana, the Jewish New Year; Hebrew; see FESTIVALS 15

quotations ►

63 *Natalis grate numeras?*
Do you count your birthdays thankfully?
Horace 65–8 BC: *Epistles*

64 Our birthdays are feathers in the broad wing of time.
Jean Paul Richter 1763–1825: *Titan* (1803)

65 Tomorrow 'ill be the happiest time of all the glad New-year;
Of all the glad New-year, mother, the maddest merriest day;
For I'm to be Queen o' the May, mother, I'm to be Queen o' the May.
Alfred, Lord Tennyson 1809–92: 'The May Queen' (1832)

66 Gay are the Martian Calends:
December's Nones are gay:
But the proud Ides, when the squadron rides,
Shall be Rome's whitest day!
Lord Macaulay 1800–59: *Lays of Ancient Rome* (1842) 'The Battle of the Lake Regillus'

67 Ring out the old, ring in the new,
Ring, happy bells, across the snow:
The year is going, let him go;
Ring out the false, ring in the true.
Alfred, Lord Tennyson 1809–92: *In Memoriam A. H. H.* (1850)

68 Seasons pursuing each other the indescribable
crowd is gathered, it is the fourth of Seventh-
month, (what salutes of cannon and small-arms!)
Walt Whitman 1819–92: 'Song of Myself' (written 1855); see FESTIVALS 22

69 Now is the accepted time to make your regular annual good resolutions. Next week you can begin paving hell with them as usual.
Mark Twain 1835–1910: in *Territorial Enterprise* [Virginia City] 1 January 1863; see ACTION 11

70 The holiest of all holidays are those
Kept by ourselves in silence and apart;
The secret anniversaries of the heart.
Henry Wadsworth Longfellow 1807–82: 'Holidays' (1877)

71 *April 1*. This is the day upon which we are reminded of what we are on the other three hundred and sixty-four.
Mark Twain 1835–1910: *Pudd'nhead Wilson* (1894); see FESTIVALS 8

72 Hogmanay, like all festivals, being but a bank from which we can only draw what we put in.
J. M. Barrie 1860–1937: *Sentimental Tommy* (1896)

73 Time has no divisions to mark its passage, there is never a thunderstorm or blare of trumpets to announce the beginning of a new month or year. Even when a new century begins it is only we mortals who ring bells and fire off pistols.
Thomas Mann 1875–1955: *The Magic Mountain* (1924)

74 EEYORE: But after all, what *are* birthdays? Here today and gone tomorrow.
A. A. Milne 1882–1956: *The House at Pooh Corner* (1928)

75 One of the sadder things, I think,
Is how our birthdays slowly sink:
Presents and parties disappear,
The cards grow fewer year by year.
Philip Larkin 1922–85: 'Dear Charles, My Muse, alive or dead' (1982)

Fiction and Story-telling

see also WRITERS, WRITING

proverbs and sayings ▸

1 Fact is stranger than fiction.
English proverb, mid 19th century; see TRUTH 6, TRUTH 27

2 A long time ago in a galaxy far, far away...
advertising copy for the film *Star Wars* (1977)

phrases ▸

3 a Canterbury tale
a long tedious story; one of those told on the pilgrimage to the shrine of St Thomas at *Canterbury* in Chaucer's *Canterbury Tales*

4 a cock and bull story
a rambling inconsequential tale, an incredible story; probably originally with reference to a particular fable

5 shaggy-dog story
a long, rambling story or joke, typically one that is amusing only because it is absurdly inconsequential or pointless. The expression comes from an anecdote of this type, about a shaggy-haired dog (1945)

6 a tale of a tub
in archaic usage, an apocryphal or incredible tale; used as the title for a comedy by Jonson (1633) and a satire by Swift (1704), but of earlier origin

7 a whole Megillah
a long, tedious, or complicated story; *Megillah* = each of five books of the Hebrew Scriptures (the Song of Solomon, Ruth, Lamentations, Ecclesiastes, and Esther) appointed to be read on certain Jewish notable days

quotations ▸

8 Storys to rede ar delitabill,
Suppos that thai be nocht bot fabill.
John Barbour 1320–95: *The Bruce* (1375)

9 With a tale forsooth he [the poet] cometh unto you, with a tale which holdeth children from play, and old men from the chimney corner.
Philip Sidney 1554–86: *The Defence of Poetry* (1595)

10 If this were played upon a stage now, I could condemn it as an improbable fiction.
William Shakespeare 1564–1616: *Twelfth Night* (1601)

11 'Oh! it is only a novel!...only Cecilia, or Camilla, or Belinda:' or, in short, only some work in which the most thorough knowledge of human nature, the happiest delineation of its varieties, the liveliest effusions of wit and humour are conveyed to the world in the best chosen language.
Jane Austen 1775–1817: *Northanger Abbey* (1818)

12 I hate things all *fiction*...there should always be some foundation of fact for the most airy fabric and pure invention is but the talent of a liar.
Lord Byron 1788–1824: letter to John Murray, 2 April 1817

13 A novel is a mirror which passes over a highway. Sometimes it reflects to your eyes the blue of the skies, at others the churned-up mud of the road.
Stendhal 1783–1842: *Le Rouge et le noir* (1830)

14 NOTICE: Persons attempting to find a motive in this narrative will be prosecuted; persons attempting to find a moral in it will be banished; persons attempting to find a plot in it will be shot. BY ORDER OF THE AUTHOR.
Mark Twain 1835–1910: *The Adventures of Huckleberry Finn* (1884)

15 Merely corroborative detail, intended to give artistic verisimilitude to an otherwise bald and unconvincing narrative.
W. S. Gilbert 1836–1911: *The Mikado* (1885)

16 The good ended happily, and the bad unhappily. That is what fiction means.
Oscar Wilde 1854–1900: *The Importance of Being Earnest* (1895)

17 Literature is a luxury; fiction is a necessity.
G. K. Chesterton 1874–1936: *The Defendant* (1901) 'A Defence of Penny Dreadfuls'

18 The Story is just the spoiled child of art.
Henry James 1843–1916: *The Ambassadors* (1909 ed.) preface

19 Yes—oh dear yes—the novel tells a story.
E. M. Forster 1879–1970: *Aspects of the Novel* (1927)

20 When in doubt have a man come through the door with a gun in his hand.
Raymond Chandler 1888–1959: attributed

21 Men must have legends, else they will die of strangeness.
Les Murray 1938– : 'The Noonday Axeman' (1965)

22 A beginning, a muddle, and an end.
on the 'classic formula' for a novel
Philip Larkin 1922–85: in *New Fiction* January 1978; see CINEMA 19, QUANTITIES 25

23 We tell ourselves stories in order to live.
Joan Didion 1934– : *The White Album* (1979)

24 'Thou shalt not' might reach the head, but it takes 'Once upon a time' to reach the heart.
Philip Pullman 1946– : in *Independent* 18 July 1996

Fitness

see HEALTH AND FITNESS

Flattery

see PRAISE AND FLATTERY

Flowers

proverbs and sayings ▸

1 Say it with flowers.
slogan for the Society of American Florists, from 1917

quotations ▸

2 That wel by reson men it calle may
The 'dayesye,' or elles the 'ye of day,'
The emperice and flour of floures alle.
Geoffrey Chaucer 1343–1400: *The Legend of Good Women* 'The Prologue'

3 I know a bank whereon the wild thyme blows,
Where oxlips and the nodding violet grows
Quite over-canopied with luscious woodbine,
With sweet musk-roses, and with eglantine.
William Shakespeare 1564–1616: *A Midsummer Night's Dream* (1595–6)

4 Daffodils,
That come before the swallow dares, and take
The winds of March with beauty.
William Shakespeare 1564–1616: *The Winter's Tale* (1610–11)

5 I wandered lonely as a cloud
That floats on high o'er vales and hills,
When all at once I saw a crowd,
A host, of golden daffodils;

Beside the lake, beneath the trees,
Fluttering and dancing in the breeze.
William Wordsworth 1770–1850: 'I wandered lonely as a cloud' (1815 ed.)

6 Here are sweet peas, on tiptoe for a flight.
John Keats 1795–1821: 'I stood tip-toe upon a little hill' (1817)

7 Flowers...are a proud assertion that a ray of beauty outvalues all the utilities of the world.
Ralph Waldo Emerson 1803–82: *Essays* (Second Series, 1844)

8 Summer set lip to earth's bosom bare,
And left the flushed print in a poppy there.
Francis Thompson 1859–1907: 'The Poppy' (1913)

9 Oh, no man knows
Through what wild centuries
Roves back the rose.
Walter de la Mare 1873–1956: 'All That's Past' (1912)

10 Unkempt about those hedges blows
An English unofficial rose.
Rupert Brooke 1887–1915: 'The Old Vicarage, Grantchester' (1915)

11 The rose of all the world is not for me.
I want for my part
Only the little white rose of Scotland
That smells sharp and sweet—and breaks the heart.
Hugh MacDiarmid 1892–1978: 'The Little White Rose' (1934)

12 Hey, buds below, up is where to grow,
Up with which below can't compare with.
Hurry! It's lovely up here! *Hurry*!
Alan Jay Lerner 1918–86: 'It's Lovely Up Here' (1965)

13 People from a planet without flowers would think we must be mad with joy the whole time to have such things about us.
Iris Murdoch 1919–99: *A Fairly Honourable Defeat* (1970)

14 Flowers are essentially tarts; prostitutes for the bees.
Bruce Robinson 1946– : *Withnail and I* (1987 film); spoken by Richard Griffiths as Monty

Food and Drink

see also ALCOHOL, COOKING

proverbs and sayings ►

1 An apple-pie without some cheese is like a kiss without a squeeze.
traditional saying, early 20th century

2 Don't eat oysters unless there is an R in the month.
from the tradition that oysters were likely to be unsafe to eat in the warmer months between May and August

3 God never sends mouths but He sends meat.
used in resignation or consolation; English proverb, late 14th century

4 A hungry man is an angry man.
someone deprived of a basic necessity will not be easily placated; English proverb, mid 17th century

5 If you are cold, tea will warm you; if you are too heated, it will cool you; if you are depressed, it will cheer you; if you are excited, it will calm you.
modern saying, attributed to W. E. Gladstone (1809–98) since the mid 20th century

6 It's ill speaking between a full man and a fasting.
someone in need is never on good terms with someone who has all they want; English proverb, mid 17th century

7 No dinner without bread.
Russian proverb

8 Oxo gives a meal man-appeal.
advertising slogan for Oxo beef extract, *c.*1960

phrases ►

9 bread and water
a frugal diet that is eaten in poverty, chosen in abstinence, or given as a punishment

10 fish, flesh, and fowl
meat of all kinds, comprising fish, animals excluding birds, and poultry, originally relating to distinctions made by religious dietary laws; see CHARACTER 27

11 Lenten fare
food without meat; food appropriate to *Lent*, the period from Ash Wednesday to Holy Saturday, of which the 40 weekdays are devoted to fasting and penitence in commemoration of Jesus's fasting in the wilderness; see FESTIVALS 55

12 staff of life
bread, or a similar staple food of an area or people; from the Biblical phrase *break the staff of bread* diminish or cut off the supply of food (Leviticus)

quotations ▸

13 Methinks sometimes I have no more wit than a Christian or an ordinary man has; but I am a great eater of beef, and I believe that does harm to my wit.
William Shakespeare 1564–1616: *Twelfth Night* (1601)

14 Doubtless God could have made a better berry, but doubtless God never did.
on the strawberry
William Butler 1535–1618: Izaak Walton *The Compleat Angler* (3rd ed., 1661)

15 Coffee, (which makes the politician wise,
And see thro' all things with his half-shut eyes).
Alexander Pope 1688–1744: *The Rape of the Lock* (1714)

16 A cucumber should be well sliced, and dressed with pepper and vinegar, and then thrown out, as good for nothing.
Samuel Johnson 1709–84: James Boswell *Journal of a Tour to the Hebrides* (1785) 5 October 1773

17 Fair fa' your honest, sonsie face,
Great chieftain o' the puddin'-race!
Robert Burns 1759–96: 'To a Haggis' (1787)

18 An egg boiled very soft is not unwholesome.
Jane Austen 1775–1817: *Emma* (1816)

19 Many's the long night I've dreamed of cheese—toasted, mostly.
Robert Louis Stevenson 1850–94: *Treasure Island* (1883)

20 Cauliflower is nothing but cabbage with a college education.
Mark Twain 1835–1910: *Pudd'nhead Wilson* (1894)

21 Look here, Steward, if this is coffee, I want tea; but if this is tea, then I wish for coffee.
Punch: 1902

22 There is no love sincerer than the love of food.
George Bernard Shaw 1856–1950: *Man and Superman* (1903)

23 Tea, although an Oriental,
Is a gentleman at least;
Cocoa is a cad and coward,
Cocoa is a vulgar beast.
G. K. Chesterton 1874–1936: 'Song of Right and Wrong' (1914)

24 MOTHER: It's broccoli, dear.
CHILD: I say it's spinach, and I say the hell with it.
E. B. White 1899–1985: *New Yorker* 8 December 1928 (cartoon caption)

25 The ethical value of uncooked food is incomparable. Economically this food has possibilities which no cooked food can have.
Mahatma Gandhi 1869–1948: in *Young India* 13 June 1929

26 The ordinary human being would sooner starve than live on brown bread and raw carrots. And the peculiar evil is this, that the less money you have, the less inclined you feel to spend it on wholesome food... When you are underfed, harassed, bored and miserable, you don't *want* to eat dull wholesome food. You want something a little bit 'tasty.'
George Orwell 1903–50: *The Road to Wigan Pier* (1937)

27 Shake and shake
The catsup bottle.
None will come,
And then a lot'll.
Richard Armour 1906–89: 'Going to Extremes' (1949)

28 Milk's leap toward immortality.
of cheese
Clifton Fadiman 1904–99: *Any Number Can Play* (1957)

29 Take away that pudding—it has no theme.
Winston Churchill 1874–1965: Lord Home *The Way the Wind Blows* (1976)

30 In Europe, spices were the jewels and furs and brocades of the kitchen and the still-room.
Elizabeth David 1913–92: *Spices, Salt and Aromatics in the English Kitchen* (1970)

31 I'm President of the United States, and I'm not going to eat any more broccoli!
George Bush 1924– : in *New York Times* 23 March 1990

32 A hen's egg is, quite simply, a work of art, a masterpiece of design and construction with, it has to be said, brilliant packaging.
Delia Smith: *How To Cook* (1998)

Fools

see also INTELLIGENCE

proverbs and sayings ▸

1 Ask a silly question and you get a silly answer.
often used to indicate that the answer is so obvious that the question should not have been asked; English proverb, early 14th century

2 Empty vessels make the most sound.
foolish and empty-headed people make the most noise; English proverb, mid 15th century

3 A fool and his money are soon parted.
English proverb, late 16th century

4 Fools build houses and wise men live in them.
a shrewd person chooses to save themselves trouble, and benefit from the effort expended by another; English proverb, late 17th century

5 Fortune favours fools.
a foolish person is traditionally fortunate; English proverb, mid 16th century

phrases ▸

6 suffer fools (gladly)
tolerate incompetence or foolishness (usually in negative contexts), from the Bible: see FOOLS 13

7 wear motley
play the fool; *motley* = the multicoloured costume of a jester; see FOOLS 14

8 a wise man of Gotham
a fool; *Gotham* = a village proverbial for the folly of its inhabitants

9 with egg on one's face
appearing foolish or ridiculous

quotations ▸

10 Answer not a fool according to his folly, lest thou also be like unto him.
Answer a fool according to his folly, lest he be wise in his own conceit.
Bible: Proverbs

11 As the crackling of thorns under a pot, so is the laughter of a fool.
Bible: Ecclesiastes

12 *Misce stultitiam consiliis brevem:*
Dulce est desipere in loco.
Mix a little foolishness with your prudence: it's good to be silly at the right moment.
Horace 65–8 BC: *Odes*

13 For ye suffer fools gladly, seeing ye yourselves are wise.
Bible: II Corinthians; see FOOLS 6

14 A worthy fool! Motley's the only wear.
William Shakespeare 1564–1616: *As You Like It* (1599); see FOOLS 7

15 The world is full of fools, and he who would not see it should live alone and smash his mirror.
Anonymous: adaptation from an original form attributed to Claude Le Petit (1640–65); *Discours satiriques* (1686)

16 A knowledgeable fool is a greater fool than an ignorant fool.
Molière 1622–73: *Les Femmes savantes* (1672)

17 The rest to some faint meaning make pretence,
But Shadwell never deviates into sense.
John Dryden 1631–1700: *MacFlecknoe* (1682)

18 For fools rush in where angels fear to tread.
Alexander Pope 1688–1744: *An Essay on Criticism* (1711)

19 Be wise with speed;
A fool at forty is a fool indeed.
Edward Young 1683–1765: *The Love of Fame* (1725–8)

20 'Tis hard if all is false that I advance
A fool must now and then be right, by chance.
William Cowper 1731–1800: 'Conversation' (1782)

21 A fool sees not the same tree that a wise man sees.
William Blake 1757–1827: *The Marriage of Heaven and Hell* (1790–3) 'Proverbs of Hell'

22 With stupidity the gods themselves struggle in vain.
Friedrich von Schiller 1759–1805: *Die Jungfrau von Orleans* (1801)

23 The ae half of the warld thinks the tither daft.
Sir Walter Scott 1771–1832: *Redgauntlet* (1824)

24 The ultimate result of shielding men from the effects of folly, is to fill the world with fools.
Herbert Spencer 1820–1903: *Essays* (1891) vol. 3 'State Tamperings with Money and Banks'

25 There's a sucker born every minute.
Phineas T. Barnum 1810–91: attributed

26 Better to keep your mouth shut and appear stupid than to open it and remove all doubt.
Mark Twain 1835–1910: James Munson (ed.) *The Sayings of Mark Twain* (1992); attributed, perhaps apocryphal

27 Never give a sucker an even break.
W. C. Fields 1880–1946: title of a W. C. Fields film (1941); the catchphrase (Fields's own) is said to have originated in the musical comedy *Poppy* (1923)

28 So dumb he can't fart and chew gum at the same time.
of Gerald Ford
Lyndon Baines Johnson 1908–73: Richard Reeves *A Ford, not a Lincoln* (1975)

29 As we journey through life, discarding baggage along the way, we should keep an iron grip, to the very end, on the capacity for silliness. It preserves the soul from desiccation.
Humphrey Lyttelton 1922–2008: *It Just Occurred to Me* (2006)

Football

see also SPORTS

phrases ▸

1 the beautiful game
football; associated with Pelé: see FOOTBALL 10

2 golden goal
the first goal scored during extra time which ends the match and gives victory to the scoring side

3 the hand of frog
French footballer Thierry Henry's handball which knocked Ireland out of the 2010 World Cup, 18 November 2009; see FOOTBALL 11

quotations ▸

4 Football, wherein is nothing but beastly fury, and extreme violence, whereof proceedeth hurt, and consequently rancour and malice do remain with them that be wounded.
Thomas Elyot 1499–1546: *Book of the Governor* (1531)

5 Then ye returned to your trinkets; then ye contented your souls
With the flannelled fools at the wicket or the muddied oafs at the goals.
Rudyard Kipling 1865–1936: 'The Islanders' (1903)

6 To say that these men paid their shillings to watch twenty-two hirelings kick a ball is merely to say that a violin is wood and catgut, that *Hamlet* is so much paper and ink. For a shilling the Bruddersford United AFC offered you Conflict and Art.
J. B. Priestley 1894–1984: *Good Companions* (1929)

7 Oh, he's football crazy, he's football mad
And the football it has robbed him o' the wee bit sense he had.
And it would take a dozen skivvies, his clothes to wash and scrub,
Since our Jock became a member of that terrible football club.
Jimmie McGregor 1932– : 'Football Crazy' (1960 song)

8 The great fallacy is that the game is first and last about winning. It is nothing of the kind. The game is about glory, it is about doing things in style and with a flourish, about going out and beating the lot, not waiting for them to die of boredom.
Danny Blanchflower 1926–93: attributed, 1972

9 Some people think football is a matter of life and death...I can assure them it is much more serious than that.
Bill Shankly 1913–81: in *Guardian* 24 December 1973

10 My life and the beautiful game.
Pelé 1940– : title of autobiography (1977); see FOOTBALL 1

11 The goal was scored a little bit by the hand of God, another bit by head of Maradona.
on his controversial goal against England in the 1986 World Cup
Diego Maradona 1960– : in *Guardian* 1 July 1986; see FOOTBALL 3

12 The natural state of the football fan is bitter disappointment, no matter what the score.
Nick Hornby 1957– : *Fever Pitch* (1992)

13 Football is a simple game; 22 men chase a ball for 90 minutes and at the end, the Germans win.
Gary Lineker 1960– : attributed

Foresight
see also FUTURE

proverbs and sayings ▸

1 The afternoon knows what the morning never suspected.
Swedish proverb

2 An inch ahead is darkness.
we have no knowledge of the future; Japanese proverb

3 It is easy to be wise after the event.
the difficult thing is to make a correct judgement without the benefit of hindsight; English proverb, early 17th century

4 It's too late to shut the stable-door after the horse has bolted.
preventive measures taken after things have gone wrong are of little effect; English proverb, mid 14th century; see MISTAKES 11

5 Nothing is certain but the unforeseen.
warning against an overconfident belief in a future occurrence; English proverb, late 19th century

6 Prevention is better than cure.
English proverb, early 17th century

7 To know the road ahead, ask those coming back.
Chinese proverb

phrases ▸

8 cross a person's palm with silver
give a person a coin as payment for fortune-telling; originally, make the sign of the cross with a coin in the fortune-teller's palm

9 famous last words
said as an ironic comment on or reply to an overconfident assertion that may well be proved wrong by events

10 a pricking in one's thumbs
a premonition, a foreboding, with allusion to Shakespeare *Macbeth*: see GOOD 26

quotations ▸

11 For which of you, intending to build a tower, sitteth not down first, and counteth the cost, whether he have sufficient to finish it?
Bible: St Luke

12 The best way to suppose what may come, is to remember what is past.
Lord Halifax 1633–95: *Political, Moral, and Miscellaneous Thoughts and Reflections* (1750) 'Miscellaneous: Experience'

13 Prognostics do not always prove prophecies,—at least the wisest prophets make sure of the event first.
Horace Walpole 1717–97: letter to Thomas Walpole, 19 February 1785

14 The best laid schemes o' mice an' men
Gang aft a-gley.
Robert Burns 1759–96: 'To a Mouse' (1786); see LIFE 14

15 You can never plan the future by the past.
Edmund Burke 1729–97: *Letter to a Member of the National Assembly* (1791)

16 She felt that those who prepared for all the emergencies of life beforehand may equip themselves at the expense of joy.
E. M. Forster 1879–1970: *Howards End* (1910)

17 The man who has fed the chicken every day throughout its life at last wrings its neck instead, showing that a more refined view as to the uniformity of nature would have been useful to the chicken.
Bertrand Russell 1872–1970: *The Problems of Philosophy* (1912)

18 **God damn you all: I told you so.**
suggestion for his own epitaph, in conversation with Sir Ernest Barker, 1939
H. G. Wells 1866–1946: Ernest Barker *Age and Youth* (1953)

19 **Some of the jam we thought was for tomorrow, we've already eaten.**
Tony Benn 1925– : attributed, 1969; see PRESENT 12

20 **The best way to predict the future is to invent it.**
Alan Kay 1940– : in 1971, at the Palo Alto Research Center

21 **Science fiction writers foresee the inevitable, and although problems and catastrophes may be inevitable, solutions are not.**
Isaac Asimov 1920–92: in *Natural History* April 1975

22 **Forecasts usually tell us more of the forecaster than of the forecast.**
Warren Buffett 1930– : in *Fortune* 5 May 1977

23 **It was déjà vu all over again.**
Yogi Berra 1925– : attributed

Forgiveness and Repentance

proverbs and sayings ▸

1 **Charity covers a multitude of sins.**
charity as a virtue outweighs many faults; English proverb, early 17th century; see FORGIVENESS 13

2 **A fault confessed is half redressed.**
by confessing what you have done wrong you have begun to make amends; English proverb, mid 16th century

3 **Good to forgive, best to forget.**
it is even better to forget that you have been injured than to forgive the injury; North American proverb, mid 20th century; see FORGIVENESS 24, FORGIVENESS 28, FORGIVENESS 29

4 **Never let the sun go down on your anger.**
recommending a swift reconciliation after a quarrel; from the Bible: English proverb, mid 17th century; see ANGER 10

5 **Offenders never pardon.**
the experience of having wronged someone often fosters a continuing resentment of the victim; English proverb, mid 17th century

6 **To know all is to forgive all.**
English proverb, mid 20th century; see INSIGHT 11

phrases ▸

7 **heap coals of fire on a person's head**
cause remorse by returning good for evil; with allusion to the Bible (Proverbs): see ENEMIES 5

8 **a prodigal son**
a spendthrift who subsequently regrets such behaviour; a returned and repentant wanderer; from the parable in the Bible (Luke) telling the story of the wastrel younger son who repented and was received back and forgiven by his father, who killed the fatted calf to celebrate his return; see FESTIVALS 31, HOSPITALITY 6

9 **turn the other cheek**
refuse to retaliate, permit or invite another blow or attack; alluding to the Bible (Matthew): see VIOLENCE 4

10 **wipe the slate clean**
forgive or forget past faults or offences, make a fresh start. Shopkeepers and landlords used formerly to keep a record of what was owing to them by writing on a tablet or slate; a *clean slate* was one on which no debts were recorded

quotations ▸

11 **Though your sins be as scarlet, they shall be as white as snow.**
Bible: Isaiah

12 **Lord, how oft shall my brother sin against me, and I forgive him? till seven times?**
Jesus saith unto him I say not unto thee, Until seven times: but Until seventy times seven.
Bible: St Matthew

13 **Charity shall cover the multitude of sins.**
Bible: I Peter; see FORGIVENESS 1

14 **We read that we ought to forgive our enemies; but we do not read that we ought to forgive our friends.**
speaking of what Bacon refers to as 'perfidious friends'
Cosimo de' Medici 1389–1464: Francis Bacon *Apophthegms* (1625); see ENEMIES 8

15 And forgive us our trespasses, As we forgive them that trespass against us.
The Book of Common Prayer 1662: *Morning Prayer* The Lord's Prayer

16 Repentance is but want of power to sin.
John Dryden 1631–1700: *Palamon and Arcite* (1700)

17 To err is human; to forgive, divine.
Alexander Pope 1688–1744: *An Essay on Criticism* (1711); see COMPUTERS 8, MISTAKES 6

18 This is no time for making new enemies.
on being asked to renounce the Devil on his deathbed
Voltaire 1694–1778: attributed

19 It is easier to forgive an enemy than to forgive a friend.
William Blake 1757–1827: *Jerusalem* (1815)

20 But with the morning cool repentance came.
Sir Walter Scott 1771–1832: *Rob Roy* (1817)

21 And blessings on the falling out
That all the more endears,
When we fall out with those we love
And kiss again with tears!
Alfred, Lord Tennyson 1809–92: *The Princess* (1847), song (added 1850)

22 God will pardon me, it is His trade.
on his deathbed
Heinrich Heine 1797–1856: Alfred Meissner *Heinrich Heine. Erinnerungen* (1856); see POWER 26

23 After such knowledge, what forgiveness?
T. S. Eliot 1888–1965: 'Gerontion' (1920)

24 I never forgive but I always forget.
Arthur James Balfour 1848–1930: R. Blake *Conservative Party* (1970); see FORGIVENESS 3, FORGIVENESS 28, FORGIVENESS 29

25 Every one says forgiveness is a lovely idea, until they have something to forgive.
C. S. Lewis 1898–1963: *Mere Christianity* (1952)

26 When a deep injury is done to us, we never recover until we forgive.
Alan Paton 1903–88: *Too Late the Phalarope* (1953)

27 I ain't sayin' you treated me unkind
You could have done better but I don't mind
You just kinda wasted my precious time
But don't think twice, it's all right.
Bob Dylan 1941– : 'Don't Think Twice, It's All Right' (1963 song)

28 Forgive but never forget.
John F. Kennedy 1917–63: Theodore Sorensen *Kennedy* (1965); see FORGIVENESS 3, FORGIVENESS 24, FORGIVENESS 29

29 The stupid neither forgive nor forget; the naïve forgive and forget; the wise forgive but do not forget.
Thomas Szasz 1920– : *The Second Sin* (1973); see FORGIVENESS 3, FORGIVENESS 24, FORGIVENESS 28

30 True reconciliation does not consist in merely forgetting the past.
Nelson Mandela 1918– : speech, 7 January 1996

France

see also COUNTRIES, INTERNATIONAL, TOWNS

proverbs and sayings ►

1 One Englishman can beat three Frenchmen.
a boastful statement now used of other nationalities and in different proportions; English proverb, late 16th century

phrases ►

2 la Belle France
the country of France, especially viewed in a nostalgic or patriotic manner

3 the Corsican ogre
Napoleon I (1769–1821), Emperor of France, in reference to his Corsican birthplace; see FRANCE 5

4 the Entente Cordiale
the understanding between Britain and France reached in 1904, forming the basis of Anglo-French cooperation in the First World War; see FRANCE 22

5 the little Corporal
Napoleon I (1769–1821), referring to his rank in the French Revolutionary army, and his diminutive height; see FRANCE 3

6 the Maid of Orleans
Joan of Arc (1412–31); translation of French *la Pucelle*; *Orleans* in reference to her relieving of the besieged city in 1429

7 a sunny place for shady people
the Riviera; the phrase is commonly associated with W. Somerset Maugham *Strictly Personal* (1941), but occurs from the early years of the 20th century

quotations ▸

8 France, mother of arts, of warfare, and of laws.
Joachim Du Bellay 1522–60: *Les Regrets* (1558)

9 That sweet enemy, France.
Philip Sidney 1554–86: *Astrophil and Stella* (1591)

10 Tilling and grazing are the two breasts by which France is fed.
Maximilien de Béthune, Duc de Sully 1559–1641: *Mémoires* (1638)

11 They order, said I, this matter better in France.
Laurence Sterne 1713–68: *A Sentimental Journey* (1768)

12 What is not clear is not French.
Antoine de Rivarol 1753–1801: *Discours sur l'Universalité de la Langue Française* (1784)

13 France has more need of me than I have need of France.
Napoleon I 1769–1821: speech, Paris, 31 December 1813

14 Yet, who can help loving the land that has taught us
Six hundred and eighty-five ways to dress eggs?
Thomas Moore 1779–1852: *The Fudge Family in Paris* (1818)

15 France was long a despotism tempered by epigrams.
Thomas Carlyle 1795–1881: *History of the French Revolution* (1837)

16 France, famed in all great arts, in none supreme.
Matthew Arnold 1822–88: 'To a Republican Friend—Continued' (1849)

17 The French soul is stronger than the French mind, and Voltaire shatters against Joan of Arc.
Victor Hugo 1802–85: *Tas de pierres* (1942)

18 If the French noblesse had been capable of playing cricket with their peasants, their chateaux would never have been burnt.
G. M. Trevelyan 1876–1962: *English Social History* (1942)

19 Everything ends this way in France. Weddings, christenings, duels, burials, swindlings, affairs of state—everything is a pretext for a good dinner.
Jean Anouilh 1910–87: *Cécile* (1951)

20 How can you govern a country which has 246 varieties of cheese?
Charles de Gaulle 1890–1970: Ernest Mignon *Les Mots du Général* (1962)

21 France is the only place where you can make love in the afternoon without people hammering on your door.
Barbara Cartland 1901–2000: in *Guardian* 24 December 1984

22 *Vive la différence, mais vive l'entente cordiale.*
Long live the difference, but long live the Entente Cordiale.
Elizabeth II 1926– : speech, Paris, 5 April 2004; see FRANCE 4

Friendship

see also RELATIONSHIPS

proverbs and sayings ▸

1 Be kind to your friends: if it weren't for them, you would be a total stranger.
American proverb, mid 20th century

2 A friend in need is a friend indeed.
a *friend in need* is one who helps when one is in need or difficulty; English proverb, mid 11th century

3 Life without a friend, is death without a witness.
friendship gives meaning to life; Spanish proverb

4 Love me, love my dog.
English proverb, early 16th century

5 Save us from our friends.
the earnest help of friends can sometimes be unintentionally damaging; English proverb, late 15th century; see FRIENDSHIP 19

6 Two is company, but three is none.
often used with the alternative ending 'three's a crowd'; English proverb, early 18th century

phrases ▸

7 fidus Achates
a faithful friend and follower; Latin, 'faithful Achates'; *Achates* was a companion of Aeneas, whose loyalty to his friend was so exemplary as to become proverbial

8 three musketeers
three close associates, three inseparable friends; translation of French *Les Trois Mousquetaires* by Alexandre Dumas père; see COOPERATION 30

quotations ▸

9 Intreat me not to leave thee, or to return from following after thee: for whither thou goest, I will go; and where thou lodgest, I will lodge: thy people shall be my people, and thy God my God.
Bible: Ruth

10 There is a friend that sticketh closer than a brother.
Bible: Proverbs

11 One soul inhabiting two bodies.
reply when asked 'What is a friend?'
Aristotle 384–322 BC: Diogenes Laertius *Lives of Philosophers*

12 To like and dislike the same things, that is indeed true friendship.
Sallust 86–35 BC: *Catiline*

13 I count myself in nothing else so happy
As in a soul remembering my good friends.
William Shakespeare 1564–1616: *Richard II* (1595)

14 It redoubleth joys, and cutteth griefs in halves.
Francis Bacon 1561–1626: *Essays* (1625) 'Of Friendship'

15 If a man does not make new acquaintance as he advances through life, he will soon find himself left alone. A man, Sir, should keep his friendship in constant repair.
Samuel Johnson 1709–84: James Boswell *Life of Samuel Johnson* (1791) 1755

16 We must take our friends as they are.
James Boswell 1740–95: diary, 25 February 1791

17 The bird a nest, the spider a web, man friendship.
William Blake 1757–1827: *The Marriage of Heaven and Hell* (1790–3) 'Proverbs of Hell'

18 Should auld acquaintance be forgot
And never brought to mind?
Robert Burns 1759–96: 'Auld Lang Syne' (1796)

19 Give me the avowed, erect and manly foe;
Firm I can meet, perhaps return the blow;
But of all plagues, good Heaven, thy wrath can send,
Save me, oh, save me, from the candid friend.
George Canning 1770–1827: 'New Morality' (1821); see FRIENDSHIP 5

20 The only reward of virtue is virtue; the only way to have a friend is to be one.
Ralph Waldo Emerson 1803–82: *Essays* (1841) 'Friendship'

21 Oh, the comfort—the inexpressible comfort of feeling *safe* with a person—having neither to weigh thoughts, nor measure words, but pouring them all right out, just as they are, chaff and grain together; certain that a faithful hand will take and sift them, keep what is worth keeping, and then with the breath of kindness blow the rest away.
Dinah Mulock Craik 1826–87: *A Life for a Life* (1859)

22 [Grant] stood by me when I was crazy, and I stood by him when he was drunk; and now we stand by each other always.
William Sherman 1820–91: in 1864; Geoffrey C. Ward *The Civil War* (1991)

23 Friends are the sunshine of life.
John Hay 1838–1905: in 1871; William Roscoe Thayer *Life and Letters of John Hay* (1915)

24 Friendships begin with liking or gratitude—roots that can be pulled up.
George Eliot 1819–80: *Daniel Deronda* (1876)

25 The holy passion of friendship is of so sweet and steady and loyal and enduring a nature that it will last through a whole lifetime, if not asked to lend money.
Mark Twain 1835–1910: *Pudd'nhead Wilson* (1894)

26 Friendship is like money, easier made than kept.
Samuel Butler 1835–1902: *Notebooks* (1912)

27 To find a friend one must close one eye. To keep him—two.
Norman Douglas 1868–1952: *South Wind* (1917)

28 I have lost friends, some by death... others through sheer inability to cross the street.
Virginia Woolf 1882–1941: *The Waves* (1931)

29 Think where man's glory most begins and ends
And say my glory was I had such friends.
W. B. Yeats 1865–1939: 'The Municipal Gallery Re-visited' (1939)

30 HUMPHREY BOGART: Louis, I think this is the beginning of a beautiful friendship.
Julius J. Epstein 1909–2001: *Casablanca* (1942 film)

31 Friends...are God's apology for relations.
Hugh Kingsmill 1889–1949: Michael Holroyd *The Best of Hugh Kingsmill* (1970)

32 Champagne for my real friends, real pain for my sham friends.
Francis Bacon 1909–92: in the 1950s; Michael Peppiatt *Francis Bacon* (1996); forms of the toast have existed since the 1830s

33 Oh I get by with a little help from my friends,
Mm, I get high with a little help from my friends.
John Lennon 1940–80 and **Paul McCartney** 1942– : 'With a Little Help From My Friends' (1967 song)

34 I do not believe that friends are necessarily the people you like best, they are merely the people who got there first.
Peter Ustinov 1921–2004: *Dear Me* (1977)

35 My father always used to say that when you die, if you've got five real friends, you've had a great life.
Lee Iacocca 1924– : *Iacocca: An Autobiography* (1984)

Futility

proverbs and sayings ▸

1 Dogs bark, but the caravan goes on.
trivial criticism will not deflect the progress of something important; English proverb, late 19th century

2 In vain the net is spread in the sight of the bird.
a person who has seen the process by which someone intends to harm them is unlikely to be in danger; English proverb, late 14th century

3 Sue a beggar and catch a louse.
it is pointless to try to obtain restitution from someone without resources; English proverb, mid 17th century

4 You cannot get a quart into a pint pot.
used of any situation in which the prospective contents are too large for the container; English proverb, late 19th century

5 You cannot get blood from a stone.
often used, as a resigned admission, to mean that it is hopeless to try to extort money or sympathy from those who have none; English proverb, mid 17th century; see CHARITY 8

6 You cannot make bricks without straw.
nothing can be made or achieved if one does not have the correct materials; English proverb, mid 17th century, from the Bible (Exodus): see PROBLEMS 11

7 You can put lipstick on a pig, but it will still be a pig.
superficial improvements will not alter the fundamental structure; modern saying

8 You can't make a silk purse out of a sow's ear.
inherent nature cannot be overcome by nurture; English proverb, early 16th century

phrases ▸

9 at the end of the rainbow
something much sought after but impossible to attain; alluding to the story of a crock of gold supposedly to be found by anyone reaching the end of a rainbow

10 cast pearls before swine
offer a good or valuable thing to a person incapable of appreciating it, with allusion to the Bible (Matthew): see VALUE 24

11 caviar to the general
a good thing unappreciated by the ignorant, from Shakespeare *Hamlet*: see TASTE 3

12 nail jelly to the wall
the type of an impossible task; see DIPLOMACY 12

13 paint the Forth Bridge
used to indicate that a task is never-ending; the Forth railway bridge is so long that once its painters had reached one end, they would have to begin again at the other

14 plough the sand
labour uselessly; a proverbial type of fruitless activity; see REVOLUTION 18

15 rearrange the deckchairs on the Titanic
to make trivial improvements in a major crisis; see FUTILITY 34

16 tilt at windmills
attack an imaginary enemy or wrong, from a story in Cervantes *Don Quixote* (1605–15) in which Don Quixote attacked a group of windmills believing them to be giants

17 a voice in the wilderness
an unheeded advocate of reform, with allusion to the Bible (Matthew) 'The voice of one crying in the wilderness'; see also PREPARATION 18

18 a wild-goose chase
a foolish, fruitless, or hopeless quest, a pursuit of something unattainable; from a horse-race in which the second or any succeeding horse had to follow accurately the course of the leader, like a flight of wild geese; later, an erratic course taken by one person (or thing) and followed (or that may be followed) by another

quotations ▸

19 Vanity of vanities, saith the Preacher, vanity of vanities; all is vanity.
Bible: Ecclesiastes; see DISILLUSION 6

20 You will never make a crab walk straight.
Aristophanes c.450–c.385 BC: *Peace*

21 How weary, stale, flat, and unprofitable
Seem to me all the uses of this world.
William Shakespeare 1564–1616: *Hamlet* (1601)

22 To enlarge or illustrate this power and effect of love is to set a candle in the sun.
Robert Burton 1577–1640: *The Anatomy of Melancholy* (1621–51)

23 To endeavour to work upon the vulgar with fine sense, is like attempting to hew blocks with a razor.
Alexander Pope 1688–1744: *Miscellanies* (1727) 'Thoughts on Various Subjects'

24 Who breaks a butterfly upon a wheel?
Alexander Pope 1688–1744: 'An Epistle to Dr Arbuthnot' (1735); see EXCESS 13

25 'My name is Ozymandias, king of kings:
Look on my works, ye Mighty, and despair!'
Nothing beside remains. Round the decay
Of that colossal wreck, boundless and bare
The lone and level sands stretch far away.
Percy Bysshe Shelley 1792–1822: 'Ozymandias' (1819)

26 Useless! Useless!
John Wilkes Booth 1838–65: last words; Philip van Doren Stern *The Man Who Killed Lincoln* (1939)

27 Pathos, piety, courage—they exist, but are identical, and so is filth. Everything exists, nothing has value.
E. M. Forster 1879–1970: *A Passage to India* (1924)

28 We are the hollow men
We are the stuffed men
Leaning together
Headpiece filled with straw. Alas!
T. S. Eliot 1888–1965: 'The Hollow Men' (1925)

29 God made everything out of nothing.
But the nothingness shows through.
Paul Valéry 1871–1945: *Mauvaises pensées et autres* (1942)

30 Nothing to be done.
Samuel Beckett 1906–89: *Waiting for Godot* (1955)

31 Nothingness haunts being.
Jean-Paul Sartre 1905–80: *Being and Nothingness* (1956)

32 There aren't any good, brave causes left. If the big bang does come, and we all get killed off, it won't be in aid of the old-fashioned, grand design. It'll just be for the Brave New-nothing-very-much-thank-you.
John Osborne 1929–94: *Look Back in Anger* (1956)

33 **He's a real nowhere man**
Sitting in his nowhere land
Making all his nowhere plans for nobody.
John Lennon 1940–80 and **Paul McCartney** 1942– : 'Nowhere Man' (1966 song)

34 **I'm not going to rearrange the furniture on the deck of the Titanic.**
having lost five of the last six primaries as President Ford's campaign manager
Rogers Morton 1914–79: *Washington Post* 16 May 1976; see FUTILITY 15

The Future
see also FORESIGHT

proverbs and sayings ▸

1 **Coming events cast their shadow before.**
some initial effects indicating the nature of an event may be felt before it takes place; English proverb, early 19th century

2 **The future's bright, the future's Orange.**
advertising slogan for Orange telecom company, mid 1990s

3 **He that follows freits, freits will follow him.**
someone who looks for portents of the future will find himself dogged by them (*freits* are omens); Scottish proverb, early 18th century

4 **There is no future like the present.**
American proverb, mid 20th century

5 **Today you; tomorrow me.**
often used in the context of the inevitability of death to each person; English proverb, mid 13th century

6 **Tomorrow is another day.**
English proverb, early 16th century; see HOPE 21

7 **Tomorrow is often the busiest day of the year.**
commenting on the tendency to put off necessary work; Spanish proverb

8 **Tomorrow never comes.**
used in the context of something which is constantly predicted to be imminent, but which never occurs; English proverb, early 16th century

phrases ▸

9 **cast one's bread upon the waters**
give generously in the expectation of future repayment for one's present kindness, from the Bible (Ecclesiastes): see CHANCE 24

10 **pie in the sky**
something that is pleasant to contemplate but is very unlikely to be realized, from the song by Joe Hill: see FUTURE 21

11 **the shape of things to come**
the way in which future events will develop; the form the future will take; from the title of a book by H. G. Wells, 1933

12 **a straw in the wind**
a small but significant indicator of the future course of events; proverbial: see MEANING 2

13 **the writing on the wall**
evidence or a sign of approaching disaster; an ominously significant event or situation; with allusion to the biblical story in Daniel of the writing that appeared on the palace wall at a feast given by Belshazzar, last king of Babylon, foretelling that he would be killed and the city sacked; see also SUCCESS 19

quotations ▸

14 **Boast not thyself of to morrow; for thou knowest not what a day may bring forth.**
Bible: Proverbs

15 **Lord! we know what we are, but know not what we may be.**
William Shakespeare 1564–1616: *Hamlet* (1601)

16 **For present joys are more to flesh and blood**
Than a dull prospect of a distant good.
John Dryden 1631–1700: *The Hind and the Panther* (1687)

17 **'We are always doing,' says he, 'something for Posterity, but I would fain see Posterity do something for us.'**
Joseph Addison 1672–1719: in *The Spectator* 20 August 1714

18 **If there must be trouble, let it be in my day, that my child may have peace.**
Thomas Paine 1737–1809: *The Crisis* (December 1776)

19 **People will not look forward to posterity, who never look backward to their ancestors.**
Edmund Burke 1729–97: *Reflections on the Revolution in France* (1790)

20 You cannot fight against the future. Time is on our side.
W. E. Gladstone 1809–98: speech on the Reform Bill, House of Commons, 27 April 1866

21 You will eat, bye and bye,
In that glorious land above the sky;
Work and pray, live on hay,
You'll get pie in the sky when you die.
Joe Hill 1879–1915: 'Preacher and the Slave' (1911 song); see FUTURE 10

22 Make me a beautiful word for doing things tomorrow; for that surely is a great and blessed invention.
George Bernard Shaw 1856–1950: *Back to Methuselah* (1921)

23 *In the long run* we are all dead.
John Maynard Keynes 1883–1946: *A Tract on Monetary Reform* (1923)

24 I never think of the future. It comes soon enough.
Albert Einstein 1879–1955: in an interview given on the *Belgenland*, December 1930

25 We have trained them [men] to think of the Future as a promised land which favoured heroes attain—not as something which everyone reaches at the rate of sixty minutes an hour, whatever he does, whoever he is.
C. S. Lewis 1898–1963: *The Screwtape Letters* (1942)

26 If you want a picture of the future, imagine a boot stamping on a human face—for ever.
George Orwell 1903–50: *Nineteen Eighty-Four* (1949)

27 Predictions can be very difficult—especially about the future.
Niels Bohr 1885–1962: H. Rosovsky *The University: An Owners Manual* (1991)

28 The future ain't what it used to be.
Yogi Berra 1925– : attributed

29 And now, we can see a new world coming into view. A world in which there is the very real prospect of a new world order.
George Bush 1924– : speech, in *New York Times* 7 March 1991; see INTERNATIONAL 8

30 The future belongs to crowds.
Don DeLillo 1936– : *Mao II* (1992)

31 The visions we offer our children shape the future. It *matters* what those visions are. Often they become self-fulfilling prophecies. Dreams are maps.
Carl Sagan 1934–96: *Pale Blue Dot* (1995)

Games
see SPORTS AND GAMES

Gardens
see also FLOWERS, TREES

proverbs and sayings ▶

1 All the flowers of tomorrow are in the seeds of today.
Indian proverb; see TREES 4

2 The answer lies in the soil.
traditional gardening advice

3 Dig for victory.
Second World War slogan, encouraging production of food in gardens and allotments

4 If you would be happy for a week take a wife; if you would be happy for a month kill a pig; but if you would be happy all your life plant a garden.
the saying exists in a variety of forms, but marriage is nearly always given as one of the ephemeral forms of happiness; English proverb, mid 17th century

5 It is not enough for a gardener to love flowers; he must also hate weeds.
American proverb, mid 20th century

6 One year's seeding makes seven years weeding.
the allusion is to the danger of allowing weeds to grow and seed themselves; English proverb, late 19th century

7 Parsley seed goes nine times to the Devil.
it is often slow to germinate; there was a superstition that parsley, which belonged to the Devil, had to be sown nine times before it would come up; English proverb, mid 17th century

8 Select a proper site for your garden and half your work is done.
Chinese proverb

9 Sow dry and set wet.
seeds should be sown in dry ground and then given water; English proverb, mid 17th century

10 Walnuts and pears you plant for your heirs.
both trees are traditionally slow growing, so that the benefit will be felt by future generations; English proverb, mid 17th century

quotations ▸

11 And the Lord God planted a garden eastward in Eden.
Bible: Genesis

12 Nothing is more pleasant to the eye than green grass kept finely shorn.
Francis Bacon 1561–1626: *Essays* (1625) 'Of Gardens'

13 Annihilating all that's made
To a green thought in a green shade.
Andrew Marvell 1621–78: 'The Garden' (1681)

14 All gardening is landscape-painting.
Alexander Pope 1688–1744: Joseph Spence *Anecdotes* (1966)

15 But though an old man, I am but a young gardener.
Thomas Jefferson 1743–1826: letter to Charles Willson Peale, 20 August 1811

16 What a man needs in gardening is a cast iron back, with a hinge in it.
Charles Dudley Warner 1829–1900: *My Summer in a Garden* (1870)

17 What is a weed? A plant whose virtues have not been discovered.
Ralph Waldo Emerson 1803–82: *Fortune of the Republic* (1878)

18 The Glory of the Garden lies in more
than meets the eye.
Rudyard Kipling 1865–1936: 'The Glory of the Garden' (1911)

19 The kiss of the sun for pardon,
The song of the birds for mirth,
One is nearer God's Heart in a garden
Than anywhere else on earth.
Dorothy Frances Gurney 1858–1932: 'God's Garden' (1913)

20 Perennials are the ones that grow like weeds, biennials are the ones that die this year instead of next and hardy annuals are the ones that never come up at all.
Katharine Whitehorn 1928– : *Observations* (1970)

21 I just come and talk to the plants, really—very important to talk to them, they respond I find.
Prince Charles 1948– : television interview, 21 September 1986

The Generation Gap

see also OLD AGE, YOUTH

proverbs and sayings ▸

1 Young folks think old folks to be fools, but old folks know young folks to be fools.
asserting the value of the experience of life which comes with age over youth and inexperience; English proverb, late 16th century

phrases ▸

2 an angry young man
a young man who feels and expresses anger at the conventional values of the society around him; originally, a member of a group of socially conscious writers in the 1950s, including particularly the playwright John Osborne; the phrase, the title of a book (1951) by Leslie Paul, was used of Osborne in the publicity material for his play *Look Back in Anger* (1956), in which the characteristic views were articulated by the anti-hero Jimmy Porter; see ANGER 5, WRITERS 2

3 baby boomer
a person born during the temporary marked increase in the birth rate following the Second World War

4 Generation X
the generation born after that of the baby boomers (roughly from the early 1960s to mid 1970s), typically perceived to be disaffected and directionless; popularized by Douglas Coupland's book *Generation X: tales for an accelerated culture* (1991)

quotations ▸

5 Tiresome, complaining, a praiser of past times, when he was a boy, a castigator and censor of the young generation.
Horace 65–8 BC: *Ars Poetica*

6 Age is deformed, youth unkind,
We scorn their bodies, they our mind.
Thomas Bastard 1566–1618: *Chrestoleros* (1598)

7 Crabbed age and youth cannot live together:
Youth is full of pleasance, age is full of care.
William Shakespeare 1564–1616: *The Passionate Pilgrim* (1599)

8 O Man! that from thy fair and shining youth
Age might but take the things Youth needed not!
William Wordsworth 1770–1850: 'The Small Celandine' (1807)

9 The old believe everything: the middle-aged suspect everything: the young know everything.
Oscar Wilde 1854–1900: 'Phrases and Philosophies for the Use of the Young' (written 1894)

10 Youth, which is forgiven everything, forgives itself nothing: age, which forgives itself everything, is forgiven nothing.
George Bernard Shaw 1856–1950: *Man and Superman* (1903)

11 When I was a boy of 14, my father was so ignorant I could hardly stand to have the old man around. But when I got to be 21, I was astonished at how much the old man had learned in seven years.
Mark Twain 1835–1910: attributed in *Reader's Digest* September 1939, but not traced in his works

12 The young man who has not wept is a savage, and the old man who will not laugh is a fool.
George Santayana 1863–1952: *Dialogues in Limbo* (1925)

13 Every generation revolts against its fathers and makes friends with its grandfathers.
Lewis Mumford 1895–90: *The Brown Decades* (1931)

14 Grown-ups never understand anything for themselves, and it is tiresome for children to be always and forever explaining things to them.
Antoine de Saint-Exupéry 1900–44: *Le Petit Prince* (1943)

15 It is the one war in which everyone changes sides.
Cyril Connolly 1903–74: Tom Driberg speech in House of Commons, 30 October 1959

16 Come mothers and fathers,
Throughout the land
And don't criticize
What you can't understand.
Your sons and your daughters
Are beyond your command
Your old road is
Rapidly agin'
Please get out of the new one
If you can't lend your hand
For the times they are a-changin'!
Bob Dylan 1941– : 'The Times They Are A-Changing' (1964 song)

Genius

proverbs and sayings ▸

1 Genius is an infinite capacity for taking pains.
English proverb, late 19th century

2 Genius without education is like silver in the mine.
American proverb, mid 18th century

quotations ▸

3 Great wits are sure to madness near allied,
And thin partitions do their bounds divide.
John Dryden 1631–1700: *Absalom and Achitophel* (1681)

4 When a true genius appears in the world, you may know him by this sign, that the dunces are all in confederacy against him.
Jonathan Swift 1667–1745: *Thoughts on Various Subjects* (1711)

5 The true genius is a mind of large general powers, accidentally determined to some particular direction.
Samuel Johnson 1709–84: *Lives of the English Poets* (1779–81) 'Cowley'

6 Rules and models destroy genius and art.
William Hazlitt 1778–1830: *Sketches and Essays* (1839) 'On Taste'

7 I know of no genius but the genius of hard work.
J. M. W. Turner 1775–1851: John Ruskin *Notes by Mr Ruskin on His Collection of Drawings by the late J. M. W. Turner* (1878)

8 Since when was genius found respectable?
Elizabeth Barrett Browning 1806–61: *Aurora Leigh* (1857)

9 Genius does what it must, and Talent does what it can.
Owen Meredith 1831–91: 'Last Words of a Sensitive Second-Rate Poet' (1868)

10 I have nothing to declare except my genius.
Oscar Wilde 1854–1900: at the New York Custom House; Frank Harris *Oscar Wilde* (1918)

11 Genius is one per cent inspiration, ninety-nine per cent perspiration.
Thomas Alva Edison 1847–1931: said 1903, in *Harper's Monthly Magazine* September 1932

12 Little minds are interested in the extraordinary; great minds in the commonplace.
Elbert Hubbard 1859–1915: *Thousand and One Epigrams* (1911)

13 A man of genius makes no mistakes. His errors are volitional and are the portals of discovery.
James Joyce 1882–1941: *Ulysses* (1922)

14 This is the most extraordinary collection of talent, of human knowledge, that has ever been gathered together at the White House, with the possible exception of when Thomas Jefferson dined alone.
John F. Kennedy 1917–63: at a White House dinner honouring Nobel Prize winners in 1962; Arthur Schlesinger *A Thousand Days* (1965)

15 Geniuses are the luckiest of mortals because what they must do is the same as what they most want to do.
W. H. Auden 1907–73: Dag Hammarskjöld *Markings* (1964)

16 It's not fun being a genius. It's torture.
John Lennon 1940–80: interview for *Rolling Stone* magazine in December 1970, broadcast for the first time in the UK on 3 December 2005

17 Airing one's dirty linen never makes for a masterpiece.
François Truffaut 1932–84: *Bed and Board* (1972)

18 Genius is always allowed some leeway, once the hammer has been pried from its hands and the blood has been cleaned up.
Terry Pratchett 1948– : *Thief of Time* (2001)

Gifts

see also CHARITY

proverbs and sayings ▸

1 A bird never flew on one wing.
frequently used to justify a further gift, especially another drink; early 18th century proverb, mainly Scottish and Irish

2 Friday's child is loving and giving.
English proverb, mid 19th century; see also BEAUTY 7, SORROW 2, TRAVEL 8, WORK 7

3 Give a thing, and take a thing, to wear the devil's gold ring.
a schoolchildren's rhyme, chanted when a person gives something and then asks for it back; English proverb, late 16th century

4 He gives twice who gives quickly.
associating readiness to give with generosity; English proverb, mid 16th century

5 It is better to give than to receive.
English proverb, late 14th century; see GIFTS 12

6 On the first day of Christmas my true love sent to me
A partridge in a pear tree.
'The Twelve Days of Christmas', traditional song listing gifts sent on each day of the Christmas season; see CHRISTMAS 5

phrases ▸

7 Greek gift
a gift given with intent to harm, in allusion to Virgil: see TRUST 1, TRUST 19

8 manna from heaven
an unexpected or gratuitous benefit; *manna* in the Bible (Exodus), the substance miraculously supplied each day as food to the Israelites in the wilderness; see SATISFACTION 22

quotations ▸

9 A gift though small is welcome.
Homer 8th century BC: *Odyssey*

10 Enemies' gifts are no gifts and do no good.
Sophocles c.496–406 BC: *Ajax*

11 Give, and it shall be given unto you; good measure, pressed down, and shaken together, and running over.
Bible: St Luke

12 It is more blessed to give than to receive.
Bible: Acts of the Apostles; see GIFTS 5

13 God loveth a cheerful giver.
Bible: II Corinthians

14 Teach us, good Lord, to serve Thee as Thou deservest:
To give and not to count the cost.
St Ignatius Loyola: 'Prayer for Generosity' (1548)

15 I am not in the giving vein to-day.
William Shakespeare 1564–1616: *Richard III* (1591)

16 Presents, I often say, endear Absents.
Charles Lamb 1775–1834: *Essays of Elia* (1823) 'A Dissertation upon Roast Pig'

17 Behold, I do not give lectures or a little charity,
When I give I give myself.
Walt Whitman 1819–92: 'Song of Myself' (written 1855)

18 They gave it me,—for an un-birthday present.
Lewis Carroll 1832–98: *Through the Looking-Glass* (1872)

19 One must be poor to know the luxury of giving.
George Eliot 1819–80: *Middlemarch* (1871–2)

20 Generosity is giving more than you can, and pride is taking less than you need.
Kahlil Gibran 1883–1931: *Sand and Foam* (1926)

21 Why is it no one ever sent me yet
One perfect limousine, do you suppose?
Ah no, it's always just my luck to get
One perfect rose.
Dorothy Parker 1893–1967: 'One Perfect Rose' (1937)

22 I know it's not much, but it's the best I can do,
My gift is my song and this one's for you.
Elton John 1947– and **Bernie Taupin** 1950– : 'Your Song' (1970 song)

God

see also BELIEF, BIBLE, CHRISTIAN CHURCH, RELIGION

proverbs and sayings ►

1 All things are possible with God.
English proverb, late 17th century; see GOD 10

2 God helps them that help themselves.
often used in urging someone to action; English proverb, mid 16th century

3 The nature of God is a circle of which the centre is everywhere and the circumference is nowhere.
medieval saying, said to have been traced to a lost treatise of Empedocles; quoted in the *Roman de la Rose*, and by St Bonaventura (1221–74) in *Itinerarius Mentis in Deum*

4 There's probably no God. Now stop worrying and enjoy your life.
advertisement on London buses (2008), supported by English evolutionary biologist Richard Dawkins (1941–)

phrases ►

5 the Ancient of Days
God; a scriptural title in the Bible (Daniel) 'the Ancient of Days did sit, whose garments were white as snow'

6 the Lord of Sabaoth
the Lord of Hosts, God; Hebrew *Sabaoth* = the heavenly hosts

7 Pascal's wager
the argument that it is in one's own best interest to behave as if God exists, since the possibility of eternal punishment in hell outweighs any advantage in believing otherwise; see GOD 22

quotations ►

8 The Lord is my shepherd: therefore can I lack nothing.
He shall feed me in a green pasture: and lead me forth beside the waters of comfort.
Bible: Psalm 23

9 God is always doing geometry.
Plato 429–347 BC: Plutarch *Moralia*

10 With men this is impossible; but with God all things are possible.
Bible: St Matthew; see GOD 1

11 He that loveth not knoweth not God; for God is love.
Bible: I John

12 A living man is the glory of God.
St Irenaeus C.AD 130–*c.*200: *Against the Heresies*

13 Praise belongs to God, the Lord of all Being,
the All-merciful, the All-compassionate,
the Master of the Day of Doom.
The Koran: sura 1

14 Prayer carries us half way to God, fasting brings us to the door of his palace, and alms procure us admission.
Umar ibn Abd al-Aziz *c.*682–720: George Sale *The Koran* (1734) 'Preliminary Discourse'

15 Therefore it is necessary to arrive at a prime mover, put in motion by no other; and this everyone understands to be God.
St Thomas Aquinas 1225–74: *Summa Theologicae* (1265); see BEGINNING 15

16 Many roads lead to God. I have chosen that of music and dance.
Jalal ad-Din ar-Rumi 1207–73: attributed

17 Whatever your heart clings to and confides in, that is really your God.
Martin Luther 1483–1546: *Large Catechism* (1529) 'The First Commandment'

18 'Twas only fear first in the world made gods.
Ben Jonson 1573–1637: *Sejanus* (1603)

19 Batter my heart, three-personed God; for, you
As yet but knock, breathe, shine, and seek to mend.
John Donne 1572–1631: *Holy Sonnets* (after 1609)

20 I had rather believe all the fables in the legend, and the Talmud, and the Alcoran, than that this universal frame is without a mind.
Francis Bacon 1561–1626: *Essays* (1625) 'Of Atheism'

21 Though the mills of God grind slowly, yet they grind exceeding small;
Though with patience He stands waiting, with exactness grinds He all.
Friedrich von Logau 1604–55: *Sinnegedichte* (1654) translated by Longfellow; Von Logau's first line is itself a translation of an anonymous verse in Sextus Empiricus *Adversus Mathematicos*; see FATE 4

22 'God is or he is not.' But to which side shall we incline?...Let us weigh the gain and the loss in wagering that God is. Let us estimate the two chances. If you gain, you gain all; if you lose, you lose nothing. Wager then without hesitation that he is.
Blaise Pascal 1623–62: *Pensées* (1670); see GOD 7

23 As you know, God is usually on the side of the big squadrons against the small.
Comte de Bussy-Rabutin 1618–93: letter to the Comte de Limoges, 18 October 1677; see ARMED FORCES 7, WARFARE 24

24 If the triangles were to make a God they would give him three sides.
Montesquieu 1689–1755: *Lettres Persanes* (1721)

25 If God did not exist, it would be necessary to invent him.
Voltaire 1694–1778: *Épîtres* no. 96 'A l'Auteur du livre des trois imposteurs'

26 God moves in a mysterious way
His wonders to perform.
William Cowper 1731–1800: 'Light Shining out of Darkness' (1779 hymn)

27 Suppose I had found a *watch* upon the ground, and it should be enquired how the watch happened to be in that place...the inference, we think, is inevitable; that the watch must have had a maker, that there must have existed, at some time and at some place or other, an artificer or artificers, who formed it for the purpose which we find it actually to answer; who comprehended its construction, and designed its use.
William Paley 1743–1805: *Natural Theology* (1802); see LIFE SCIENCES 29

28 Mine eyes have seen the glory of the coming of the Lord:
He is trampling out the vintage where the grapes of wrath are stored;

He hath loosed the fateful lightning of
his terrible swift sword:
His truth is marching on.

Julia Ward Howe 1819–1910: 'Battle Hymn of the Republic' (1862)

29 I will call no being good, who is not what I mean when I apply that epithet to my fellow-creatures; and if such a being can sentence me to hell for not so calling him, to hell I will go.

John Stuart Mill 1806–73: *Examination of Sir William Hamilton's Philosophy* (1865)

30 An honest God is the noblest work of man.

Robert G. Ingersoll 1833–99: *The Gods* (1876); see HONESTY 12

31 God is dead: but considering the state the species Man is in, there will perhaps be caves, for ages yet, in which his shadow will be shown.

Friedrich Nietzsche 1844–1900: *Die fröhliche Wissenschaft* (1882)

32 God is subtle but he is not malicious.

Albert Einstein 1879–1955: remark made at Princeton University, May 1921; R. W. Clark *Einstein* (1973)

33 Operationally, God is beginning to resemble not a ruler but the last fading smile of a cosmic Cheshire cat.

Julian Huxley 1887–1975: *Religion without Revelation* (1957 ed.); see CATS 4

34 God has been replaced, as he has all over the West, with respectability and air-conditioning.

Imamu Amiri Baraka 1934– : *Midstream* (1963)

35 God seems to have left the receiver off the hook, and time is running out.

Arthur Koestler 1905–83: *The Ghost in the Machine* (1967)

36 The Buddha, the Godhead, resides quite as comfortably in the circuits of a digital computer or the gears of a cycle transmission as he does at the top of a mountain or in the petals of a flower.

Robert M. Pirsig 1928– : *Zen and the Art of Motorcycle Maintenance* (1974)

37 Any God I ever felt in church I brought in with me. And I think all the other folks did too. They come to church to *share* God not find God.

Alice Walker 1944– : *The Colour Purple* (1982)

38 I am not clear that God manoeuvres physical things...After all, a conjuring trick with bones only proves that it is as clever as a conjuring trick with bones.

of the Resurrection

David Jenkins 1925– : 'Poles Apart' (BBC radio, 4 October 1984)

Good and Evil

see also SIN, VIRTUE

proverbs and sayings ▸

1 The greater the sinner, the greater the saint.

a sinner who has reformed is likely to be more virtuous that someone who is morally neutral; English proverb, late 18th century

2 He that touches pitch shall be defiled.

a person who chooses to put themselves in contact with wrongdoing will be marked by it; English proverb, early 14th century; see GOOD 15

3 Honi soit qui mal y pense.

French, *Evil be to him who evil thinks*, the motto of the Order of the Garter, originated by Edward III, probably on 23 April of 1348 or 1349

4 Ill weeds grow apace.

used to comment on the apparent success enjoyed by an ill-doer; English proverb, late 15th century

5 The sun loses nothing by shining into a puddle.

something which is naturally clear and radiant cannot be tainted or diminished by association; English proverb, early 14th century, of classical origin

6 Two blacks don't make a white.

one injury or instance of wrongdoing does not justify another; English proverb, early 18th century

7 Two wrongs don't make a right.

a first injury does not justify a second in retaliation; English proverb, late 18th century; see GOOD 45

8 Where God builds a church, the Devil will build a chapel.

the establishment of something which is in itself good may also create the opening for something evil; English proverb, mid 16th century; see GOOD 24

phrases ▶

9 cloven hoof

the mark of an inherently evil nature; a divided hoof, as that of a goat, ascribed to a satyr, the god Pan, or to the Devil; see FAMILY 26

10 Lord of the Flies

Satan, the Devil; the meaning of the Hebrew word which is the origin of *Beelzebub*, in the Bible (II Kings) the god of the Philistine city Ekron, and in the Gospels, the prince of the devils, often identified with the Devil

11 the Prince of this world

Satan, the Devil; from the Bible (John) 'the prince of this world is judged'

12 separate the sheep from the goats

sort the good persons or things from the bad or inferior, from the Bible (Matthew) 'He shall separate the one from another, as a shepherd divideth his sheep from his goats. And he shall set the sheep on his right hand, but the goats on his left'

13 three wise monkeys

a conventional sculptured group of three monkeys; used allusively to refer to a person who chooses to ignore or keep silent about wrongdoing. One monkey is depicted with its paws over its mouth (taken as connoting 'speak no evil'), one with its paws over its eyes ('see no evil'), and one with its paws over its ears ('hear no evil'); see VIRTUE 5

quotations ▶

14 There is no peace, saith the Lord, unto the wicked.

Bible: Isaiah; see ACTION 17

15 He that toucheth pitch shall be defiled therewith.

Bible: Ecclesiasticus; see GOOD 2

16 It is never right to do wrong or to requite wrong with wrong, or when we suffer evil to defend ourselves by doing evil in return.

Socrates 469–399 BC: Plato *Crito*

17 Every art and every investigation, and likewise every practical pursuit or undertaking, seems to aim at some good: hence it has been well said that the Good is That at which all things aim.

Aristotle 384–322 BC: *Nicomachean Ethics*

18 How can Satan cast out Satan?

Bible: St Mark; see also WARFARE 38

19 For the good that I would I do not: but the evil which I would not, that I do.

Bible: Romans

20 Unto the pure all things are pure.

Bible: Titus; see GOOD 39

21 With love for mankind and hatred of sins.

often quoted as 'Love the sinner but hate the sin'

St Augustine of Hippo AD 354–430: letter 211; J.-P. Migne (ed.) *Patrologiae Latinae* (1845)

22 Good and evil shall not be held equal. Turn away evil with that which is better; and behold the man between whom and thyself there was enmity, shall become, as it were, thy warmest friend.

The Koran: sura 41

23 If all evil were prevented, much good would be absent from the universe. A lion would cease to live, if there were no slaying of animals; and there would be no patience of martyrs if there were no tyrannical persecution.

St Thomas Aquinas 1225–74: *Summa Theologicae* (1265)

24 For, where God built a church, there the devil would also build a chapel... In such sort is the devil always God's ape.

Martin Luther 1483–1546: *Colloquia Mensalia* (1566); see GOOD 8

25 There is nothing either good or bad, but thinking makes it so.

William Shakespeare 1564–1616: *Hamlet* (1601)

26 By the pricking of my thumbs,
Something wicked this way comes.

William Shakespeare 1564–1616: *Macbeth* (1606); see FORESIGHT 10

27 Farewell remorse! All good to me is lost;
Evil, be thou my good.

John Milton 1608–74: *Paradise Lost* (1667)

28 But if he does really think that there is no distinction between virtue and vice, why, Sir, when he leaves our houses, let us count our spoons.
Samuel Johnson 1709–84: James Boswell *Life of Samuel Johnson* (1791) 14 July 1763

29 Don't let us make imaginary evils, when you know we have so many real ones to encounter.
Oliver Goldsmith 1728–74: *The Good-Natured Man* (1768)

30 It is necessary only for the good man to do nothing for evil to triumph.
Edmund Burke 1729–97: attributed (in a number of forms) to Burke, but not found in his writings

31 One impulse from a vernal wood
May teach you more of man,
Of moral evil and of good,
Than all the sages can.
William Wordsworth 1770–1850: 'The Tables Turned' (1798)

32 He who would do good to another, must do it in minute particulars
General good is the plea of the scoundrel, hypocrite and flatterer.
William Blake 1757–1827: *Jerusalem* (1815)

33 There are a thousand hacking at the branches of evil to one who is striking at the root.
Henry David Thoreau 1817–62: *Walden* (1854) 'Economy'

34 It is better to fight for the good, than to rail at the ill.
Alfred, Lord Tennyson 1809–92: *Maud* (1855)

35 Imagine that you are creating a fabric of human destiny with the object of making men happy in the end, giving them peace and rest at last, but that it was essential and inevitable to torture to death only one tiny creature...and to found that edifice on its unavenged tears, would you consent to be the architect on those conditions?
Fedor Dostoevsky 1821–81: *The Brothers Karamazov* (1879–80)

36 A belief in a supernatural source of evil is not necessary; men alone are quite capable of every wickedness.
Joseph Conrad 1857–1924: *Under Western Eyes* (1911)

37 In my humble opinion, non-cooperation with evil is as much a duty as is cooperation with good.
Mahatma Gandhi 1869–1948: speech in Ahmadabad, 23 March 1922

38 What we call evil is simply ignorance bumping its head in the dark.
Henry Ford 1863–1947: in *Observer* 16 March 1930

39 To the Puritan all things are impure, as somebody says.
D. H. Lawrence 1885–1930: *Etruscan Places* (1932) 'Cerveteri'; see GOOD 20

40 Evil is unspectacular and always human,
And shares our bed and eats at our own table.
W. H. Auden 1907–73: 'Herman Melville' (1940)

41 I and the public know
What all schoolchildren learn,
Those to whom evil is done
Do evil in return.
W. H. Auden 1907–73: 'September 1, 1939' (1940)

42 As soon as men decide that all means are permitted to fight an evil, then their good becomes indistinguishable from the evil that they set out to destroy.
Christopher Dawson 1889–1970: *The Judgement of the Nations* (1942)

43 The face of 'evil' is always the face of total need.
William S. Burroughs 1914–97: *The Naked Lunch* (1959)

44 It was as though in those last minutes he [Eichmann] was summing up the lessons that this long course in human wickedness had taught us—the lesson of the fearsome, word-and-thought-defying *banality of evil*.
Hannah Arendt 1906–75: *Eichmann in Jerusalem* (1963)

45 Two wrongs don't make a right, but they make a good excuse.
Thomas Szasz 1920– : *The Second Sin* (1973); see GOOD 7

46 The sad truth of the matter is that most evil is done by people who never made up their minds to be or do either good or evil.
Hannah Arendt 1906–75: *The Life of the Mind* (1978)

47 The line dividing good and evil cuts through the heart of every human being. And who is willing to destroy a piece of his own heart?
Alexander Solzhenitsyn 1918–2008: *The Gulag Archipelago* (1973–5)

48 Mostly, we are good when it makes sense. A good society is one that makes sense of being good.
Ian McEwan 1948– : *Enduring Love* (1998)

Gossip

see also REPUTATION, SECRECY

proverbs and sayings ▸

1 Careless talk costs lives.
Second World War security slogan

2 A dog that will fetch a bone will carry a bone.
someone given to gossip carries talk both ways; English proverb, early 19th century

3 Give a dog a bad name and hang him.
once a person's reputation has been blackened his plight is hopeless; English proverb, early 18th century

4 Gossip is the lifeblood of society.
American proverb, mid 20th century

5 Gossip is vice enjoyed vicariously.
American proverb, early 20th century

6 The greater the truth, the greater the libel.
English proverb, late 18th century

7 Loose lips sink ships.
American Second World War security slogan

8 A tale never loses in the telling.
implying that a story is often exaggerated when it is repeated; English proverb, mid 16th century

9 Those who live in glass houses shouldn't throw stones.
it is unwise to criticize or slander another if you are vulnerable to retaliation; English proverb, mid 17th century

10 What the soldier said isn't evidence.
hearsay evidence alone cannot be relied on; English proverb, mid 19th century, originally from Dickens *Pickwick Papers* (1837) 'You must not tell us what the soldier, or any other man, said...it's not evidence'

phrases ▸

11 bush telegraph
a rapid informal spreading of information or a rumour; the network through which this takes place; see GOSSIP 13

12 Chinese whispers
a game in which a message is distorted by being passed around in a whisper; Russian scandal; see GOSSIP 14

13 hear on the grapevine
acquire information by rumour or unofficial communication; originally from an American Civil War usage, when news was said to be passed 'by grapevine telegraph'; see GOSSIP 11

14 Russian scandal
Chinese whispers; see GOSSIP 12

quotations ▸

15 Many have fallen by the edge of the sword: but not so many as have fallen by the tongue.
Bible: Ecclesiasticus

16 *Che ti fa ciò che quivi pispiglia? Vien dietro a me, e lascia dir le genti.*
What is it to thee what they whisper there? Come after me and let the people talk.
Dante Alighieri 1265–1321: *Divina Commedia* 'Purgatorio'

17 Enter Rumour, painted full of tongues.
William Shakespeare 1564–1616: *Henry IV, Part 2* (1597); stage direction

18 How these curiosities would be quite forgot, did not such idle fellows as I am put them down.
John Aubrey 1626–97: *Brief Lives* 'Venetia Digby'

19 Love and scandal are the best sweeteners of tea.
Henry Fielding 1707–54: *Love in Several Masques* (1728)

20 It is a matter of great interest what sovereigns are doing; but as to what Grand Duchesses are doing—Who cares?
Napoleon I 1769–1821: letter, 17 December 1811

21 Every man is surrounded by a neighbourhood of voluntary spies.
Jane Austen 1775–1817: *Northanger Abbey* (1818)

22 **Everyone in a crowd has the power to throw dirt: nine out of ten have the inclination.**
William Hazlitt 1778–1830: 'On Reading New Books' (1827)

23 **There is only one thing in the world worse than being talked about, and that is not being talked about.**
Oscar Wilde 1854–1900: *The Picture of Dorian Gray* (1891)

24 **It takes your enemy and your friend, working together, to hurt you to the heart: the one to slander you and the other to get the news to you.**
Mark Twain 1835–1910: *Following the Equator* (1897)

25 **Like all gossip—it's merely one of those half-alive things that try to crowd out real life.**
E. M. Forster 1879–1970: *A Passage to India* (1924)

26 **No one gossips about other people's secret virtues.**
Bertrand Russell 1872–1970: *On Education Especially in Early Childhood* (1926)

27 **Blood sport is brought to its ultimate refinement in the gossip columns.**
Bernard Ingham 1932– : speech, 5 February 1986

Government

see also INTERNATIONAL, PARLIAMENT, POLITICS, PRESIDENCY, SOCIETY

proverbs and sayings ▸

1 **The cat, the rat, and Lovell the dog, rule all England under the hog.**
contemporary rhyme referring to William *Catesby*, Richard *Ratcliffe*, and Francis *Lovell*, favourites of Richard III (1452–85), whose personal emblem was a white *boar*

2 **Divide and rule.**
government control is more easily exercised if possible opponents are separated into factions; English proverb, early 17th century

3 **God is high above, and the tsar is far away.**
the source of central power is out of the reach of local interests; Russian proverb; see GOVERNMENT 4, compare CAUTION 6

4 **The mountains are high, and the emperor is far away.**
the source of central power is out of the reach of local interests; Chinese proverb; see GOVERNMENT 3, compare CAUTION 6

phrases ▸

5 **appeal to Caesar**
appeal to the highest possible authority; particularly with allusion to the Bible (Acts), in which Paul the Apostle exercised his right as a Roman citizen to have his case heard in Rome, with the words 'I appeal unto Caesar'

6 **bread and circuses**
the public provision of subsistence and entertainment, especially to assuage the populace; from Juvenal: see GOVERNMENT 12

7 **checks and balances**
counterbalancing influences by which an organization or system is regulated, typically those ensuring that power in political institutions is not concentrated in the hands of particular individuals or groups

8 **the corridors of power**
the senior levels of government or administration, where covert influence is regarded as being exerted and significant decisions are made; from the title of C. P. Snow's novel *The Corridors of Power* (1964)

9 **the ship of state**
the state and its affairs, especially when regarded as being subject to adverse or changing circumstances; a *ship* as the type of something subject to adverse or changing weather

quotations ▸

10 **A ruler who governs his state by virtue is like the north polar star, which remains in its place while all the other stars revolve around it.**
Confucius 551–479 BC: *Analects*

11 **Let them hate, so long as they fear.**
Accius 170–c.86 BC: from *Atreus*; Seneca *Dialogues*

12 ***...Duas tantum res anxius optat, Panem et circenses.***
Only two things does he [the modern citizen] anxiously wish for—bread and circuses.
Juvenal c.AD 60–c.140: *Satires*; see GOVERNMENT 6

13 Because it is difficult to join them together, it is much safer for a prince to be feared than loved, if he is to fail in one of the two.
Niccolò Machiavelli 1469–1527: *The Prince* (written 1513)

14 Though God hath raised me high, yet this I count the glory of my crown: that I have reigned with your loves.
Elizabeth I 1533–1603: The Golden Speech, 1601

15 I will govern according to the common weal, but not according to the common will.
James I 1566–1625: in December, 1621; J. R. Green *History of the English People* vol. 3 (1879)

16 *L'État c'est moi.*
I am the State.
Louis XIV 1638–1715: before the Parlement de Paris, 13 April 1655; probably apocryphal

17 It is a 'beautiful maxim' that it is necessary to save five *sous* on unessential things, and to pour out millions when it is a question of your glory.
Jean-Baptiste Colbert 1619–83: letter to Louis XIV, 1666

18 Governments need both shepherds and butchers.
Voltaire 1694–1778: 'The Piccini Notebooks' (1735–50)

19 I would not give half a guinea to live under one form of government rather than another. It is of no moment to the happiness of an individual.
Samuel Johnson 1709–84: James Boswell *Life of Samuel Johnson* (1791) 31 March 1772

20 A government of laws, and not of men.
John Adams 1735–1826: *Boston Gazette* (1774) 'Novanglus' papers; later incorporated in the Massachusetts Constitution (1780)

21 The happiness of society is the end of government.
John Adams 1735–1826: *Thoughts on Government* (1776)

22 I am well aware of the toil and blood and treasure that it will cost us to maintain this declaration, and support and defend these states.
John Adams 1735–1826: letter to Abigail Adams, 3 July 1776

23 Government, even in its best state, is but a necessary evil...Government, like dress, is the badge of lost innocence; the palaces of kings are built upon the ruins of the bowers of paradise.
Thomas Paine 1737–1809: *Common Sense* (1776)

24 My people and I have come to an agreement which satisfies us both. They are to say what they please, and I am to do what I please.
his interpretation of benevolent despotism
Frederick the Great 1712–86: attributed

25 If men were angels, no government would be necessary.
James Madison 1751–1836: *The Federalist* (1788) no. 51

26 When, in countries that are called civilized, we see age going to the workhouse and youth to the gallows, something must be wrong in the system of government.
Thomas Paine 1737–1809: *The Rights of Man* pt. 2 (1792)

27 Away with the cant of 'Measures not men'!—the idle supposition that it is the harness and not the horses that draw the chariot along. If the comparison must be made, if the distinction must be taken, men are everything, measures comparatively nothing.
George Canning 1770–1827: speech on the Army estimates, 8 December 1802; the phrase 'measures not men' may be found as early as 1742 (in a letter from Chesterfield to Dr Chevenix, 6 March)

28 To govern is to choose.
Duc de Lévis 1764–1830: *Maximes et Réflexions* (1812 ed.)

29 The best government is that which governs least.
John L. O'Sullivan 1813–95: *United States Magazine and Democratic Review* (1837)

30 No Government can be long secure without a formidable Opposition.
Benjamin Disraeli 1804–81: *Coningsby* (1844)

31 The Crown is, according to the saying, the 'fountain of honour'; but the Treasury is the spring of business.
Walter Bagehot 1826–77: *The English Constitution* (1867) 'The Cabinet'; see ROYALTY 25

32 My faith in the people governing is, on the whole, infinitesimal; my faith in The People governed is, on the whole, illimitable.
Charles Dickens 1812–70: speech at Birmingham and Midland Institute, 27 September 1869

33 The State is not 'abolished', *it withers away.*
Friedrich Engels 1820–95: *Anti-Dühring* (1878)

34 The poor have sometimes objected to being governed badly; the rich have always objected to being governed at all.
G. K. Chesterton 1874–1936: *The Man who was Thursday* (1908)

35 While the State exists, there can be no freedom. When there is freedom there will be no State.
Lenin 1870–1924: *State and Revolution* (1919)

36 A government which robs Peter to pay Paul can always depend on the support of Paul.
George Bernard Shaw 1856–1950: *Everybody's Political What's What?* (1944); see DEBT 13

37 BIG BROTHER IS WATCHING YOU.
George Orwell 1903–50: *Nineteen Eighty-Four* (1949); see POWER 14

38 If the Government is big enough to give you everything you want, it is big enough to take away everything you have.
Gerald Ford 1909–2006: John F. Parker *If Elected* (1960)

39 The Civil Service is profoundly deferential — 'Yes, Minister! No, Minister! If you wish it, Minister!'
Richard Crossman 1907–74: diary, 22 October 1964

40 A billion here and a billion there, and pretty soon you're talking real money.
on federal spending
Everett Dirksen 1896–1969: attributed, perhaps apocryphal

41 Many journalists have fallen for the conspiracy theory of government. I do assure you that they would produce more accurate work if they adhered to the cock-up theory.
Bernard Ingham 1932– : in *Observer* 17 March 1985

42 I think it will be a clash between the political will and the administrative won't.
Jonathan Lynn 1943– and **Antony Jay** 1930– : *Yes Prime Minister* (1987) vol. 2

43 We give the impression of being in office but not in power.
Norman Lamont 1942– : speech, House of Commons, 9 June 1993

44 Dear chief secretary, I'm afraid to tell you there's no money left.
Liam Byrne 1970– : letter left for his successor as Chief Secretary to the Treasury, David Laws, as quoted by Laws, 17 May 2010

Gratitude and Ingratitude

proverbs and sayings ▸

1 The Devil was sick, the Devil a saint would be; the Devil was well, the devil a saint was he.
promises made in adversity may not be kept in prosperity; English proverb, early 17th century

2 Don't overload gratitude, if you do, she'll kick.
American proverb, mid 18th century

3 Never look a gift horse in the mouth.
warning against questioning the quality or use of a lucky chance or gift; referring to the fact that it is by a horse's teeth that its age is judged; English proverb, early 16th century

4 You never miss the water till the well runs dry.
applied to situations in which it is only when a source of support or sustenance has been withdrawn that its importance is understood; English proverb, early 17th century

phrases ▸

5 bite the hand that feeds one
injure a benefactor, act ungratefully; see GRATITUDE 16

quotations ▸

6 A joyful and pleasant thing it is to be thankful.
Bible: Psalm 147

7 No duty is more urgent than that of returning thanks.
St Ambrose c.339–397: attributed

8 Blow, blow, thou winter wind,
Thou art not so unkind
As man's ingratitude.
William Shakespeare 1564–1616: *As You Like It* (1599)

9 They say late thanks are ever best.
Francis Bacon 1561–1626: letter to Robert, Lord Cecil, July 1603

10 How sharper than a serpent's tooth it is
To have a thankless child!
William Shakespeare 1564–1616: *King Lear* (1605–6)

11 In most of mankind gratitude is merely a secret hope for greater favours.
Duc de la Rochefoucauld 1613–80: *Maximes* (1678)

12 When I'm not thanked at all, I'm thanked enough,
I've done my duty, and I've done no more.
Henry Fielding 1707–54: *Tom Thumb the Great* (1731)

13 There are minds so impatient of inferiority, that their gratitude is a species of revenge, and they return benefits, not because recompense is a pleasure, but because obligation is a pain.
Samuel Johnson 1709–84: in *The Rambler* 15 January 1751

14 When our perils are past shall our gratitude sleep?
George Canning 1770–1827: 'The Pilot that Weathered the Storm'

15 There's plenty of boys that will come hankering and grovelling around you when you've got an apple, and beg the core off of you; but when they've got one, and you beg for the core and remind them how you give them a core one time, they say thank you 'most to death, but there ain't-a-going to be no core.
Mark Twain 1835–1910: *Tom Sawyer Abroad* (1894)

16 That's the way with these directors, they're always biting the hand that lays the golden egg.
Sam Goldwyn 1882–1974: Alva Johnston *The Great Goldwyn* (1937); see GRATITUDE 5, GREED 6

17 Never in the field of human conflict was so much owed by so many to so few.
on the skill and courage of British airmen
Winston Churchill 1874–1965: speech, House of Commons, 20 August 1940

18 [Gratitude] is a sickness suffered by dogs.
Joseph Stalin 1879–1953: Nikolai Tolstoy *Stalin's Secret War* (1981)

19 What have the Romans ever done for us?
Graham Chapman 1941–89, **John Cleese** 1939– , and **others**: *Monty Python's Life of Brian* (1979 film)

Greatness

proverbs and sayings ▸

1 Behind every great man there is a great woman.
American proverb, mid 20th century

2 Great men have great faults.
English proverb, early 17th century

3 Great men's sons seldom do well.
English proverb, mid 16th century

quotations ▸

4 The beauty of Israel is slain upon thy high places: how are the mighty fallen!
Bible: II Samuel

5 But be not afraid of greatness: some men are born great, some achieve greatness, and some have greatness thrust upon them.
William Shakespeare 1564–1616: *Twelfth Night* (1601)

6 The glory of great men should always be measured against the means they used to acquire it.
Duc de la Rochefoucauld 1613–80: *Maxims* (1678)

7 What millions died—that Caesar might be great!
Thomas Campbell 1777–1844: *Pleasures of Hope* (1799)

8 Fleas know not whether they are upon the body of a giant or upon one of ordinary size.
Walter Savage Landor 1775–1864: *Imaginary Conversations* (1824)

9 If any man seeks for greatness, let him forget greatness, and ask for truth, and he will find both.
Horace Mann 1796–1859: diary, 29 October 1838

10 Is it so bad, then, to be misunderstood? Pythagoras was misunderstood, and Socrates, and Jesus, and Luther, and Copernicus, and Galileo, and Newton, and every pure and wise spirit that ever took flesh. To be great is to be misunderstood.
Ralph Waldo Emerson 1803–82: *Essays* (1841) 'Self-Reliance'

11 The first test of a truly great man is his humility.
John Ruskin 1819–1900: *Modern Painters* (1856)

12 In me there dwells
No greatness, save it be some far-off touch
Of greatness to know well I am not great.
Alfred, Lord Tennyson 1809–92: *Idylls of the King* 'Lancelot and Elaine' (1859)

13 In historical events great men—so-called—are but labels serving to give a name to the event, and like labels they have the least possible connection with the event itself.
Leo Tolstoy 1828–1910: *War and Peace* (1868–9)

14 A man is seldom ashamed of feeling that he cannot love a woman so well when he sees a certain greatness in her: nature having intended greatness for men.
George Eliot 1819–80: *Middlemarch* (1871–2)

15 If I am a great man, then all great men are frauds.
Andrew Bonar Law 1858–1923: Lord Beaverbrook *Politicians and the War* (1932)

16 A man does not attain the status of Galileo merely because he is persecuted; he must also be right.
Stephen Jay Gould 1941–2002: *Ever since Darwin* (1977)

17 I'm looking for a dare-to-be-great situation.
Cameron Crowe 1957– : *Say Anything* (1989 film), spoken by John Cusack as Lloyd Dobler

Greed

see also MONEY

proverbs and sayings ▸

1 The more you get the more you want.
English proverb, mid 14th century

2 Much would have more.
the ownership of substantial possessions creates in the owner the desire for still more; English proverb, mid 14th century

3 Pigs get fat, but hogs get slaughtered.
used as a warning against greed; modern saying

4 The sea refuses no river.
the sea's capacity is so great that anyone who chooses may find a place there; English proverb, early 17th century

5 Where the carcase is, there shall the eagles be gathered together.
English proverb, mid 16th century, from the Bible (Matthew) 'Wheresoever the carcase is, there will the eagles be gathered together'; *eagles* here as the type of carrion bird

phrases ▸

6 kill the goose that lays the golden eggs
sacrifice long-term advantage to short-term gain; referring to a traditional story, in which the owner of the goose killed it in the hope of possessing himself of a store of golden eggs instead of being contented with a daily ration; see GRATITUDE 16

quotations ▸

7 Greedy for the property of others, extravagant with his own.
Sallust 86–35 BC: *Catiline*

8 *Quid non mortalia pectora cogis,*
Auri sacra fames!
To what do you not drive human hearts, cursed craving for gold!
Virgil 70–19 BC: *Aeneid*

9 Bell, book, and candle shall not drive me back,

When gold and silver becks me to
come on.
William Shakespeare 1564–1616: *King John* (1591–8); see SUPERNATURAL 2

10 What a rare punishment
Is avarice to itself!
Ben Jonson 1573–1637: *Volpone* (1606)

11 Please, sir, I want some more.
Charles Dickens 1812–70: *Oliver Twist* (1838)

12 Wealth is like sea-water; the more we drink, the thirstier we become, and the same is true of fame.
Arthur Schopenhauer 1788–1860: *Parerga and Paralipomena* (1851)

13 I'll be sick tonight.
in reply to his mother's warning 'You'll be sick tomorrow', when stuffing himself with cakes at tea
Jack Llewelyn-Davies 1894–1959: Andrew Birkin *J. M. Barrie and the Lost Boys* (1979); Barrie used the line in *Little Mary* (1903)

14 If all the rich people in the world divided up their money among themselves there wouldn't be enough to go round.
Christina Stead 1902–83: *House of All Nations* (1938)

15 There is enough in the world for everyone's need, but not enough for everyone's greed.
Frank Buchman 1878–1961: *Remaking the World* (1947)

16 But the music that excels is the sound
of oil wells
As they slurp, slurp, slurp into the
barrels...
I want an old-fashioned house
With an old-fashioned fence
And an old-fashioned millionaire.
Marve Fisher: 'An Old-Fashioned Girl' (1954 song)

17 Greed is all right...Greed is healthy. You can be greedy and still feel good about yourself.
Ivan F. Boesky 1937– : commencement address, Berkeley, California, 18 May 1986

18 Be fearful when others are greedy, be greedy when others are fearful.
Warren Buffett 1930– : L. A. Cunningham *Essays of Warren Buffett* (1998) letter to shareholders 1986

19 Greed—for lack of a better word—is good. Greed is right. Greed works.
Stanley Weiser and **Oliver Stone** 1946– : *Wall Street* (1987 film)

Guilt and Innocence

proverbs and sayings ▸

1 Confess and be hanged.
guilt must be confessed and the due punishment accepted for true repentance; English proverb, late 16th century

2 The guilty flee when no man pursueth.
saying, from the Bible (Proverbs) 'The wicked flee when no man pursueth; but the righteous are bold as a lion'

3 We are all guilty.
supposedly typical of the liberal view that all members of society bear responsibility for its wrongs; used particularly as a catchphrase by the psychiatrist 'Dr Heinz Kiosk' in the satirical column of 'Peter Simple' (pseudonym of Michael Wharton)

4 We name the guilty men.
supposedly now a cliché of investigative journalism; *Guilty Men* (1940) was the title of a tract by Michael Foot, Frank Owen, and Peter Howard, published under the pseudonym of 'Cato', which attacked the supporters of Munich and the appeasement policy of Neville Chamberlain

phrases ▸

5 Banquo's ghost
someone from the past whose presence reminds a person of their past misdeeds; *Banquo* a character in Shakespeare's *Macbeth* who is murdered on Macbeth's orders, and whose ghost subsequently appears at Macbeth's banqueting table, invisible to all except Macbeth himself

quotations ▸

6 Everyone's quick to blame the alien.
Aeschylus c.525–456 BC: *The Suppliant Maidens*

7 When Pilate saw that he could prevail nothing...he took water, and washed his hands before the multitude, saying, I am innocent of the blood of this just person: see ye to it.
Bible: St Matthew; see DUTY 9

8 He that is without sin among you, let him first cast a stone at her.
Bible: St John; see CRITICISM 3

9 Suspicion always haunts the guilty mind;
The thief doth fear each bush an officer.
William Shakespeare 1564–1616: *Henry VI, Part 3* (1592)

10 Here's the smell of the blood still: all the perfumes of Arabia will not sweeten this little hand.
William Shakespeare 1564–1616: *Macbeth* (1606)

11 He that first cries out stop thief, is often he that has stolen the treasure.
William Congreve 1670–1729: *Love for Love* (1695)

12 It is better that ten guilty persons escape than one innocent suffer.
William Blackstone 1723–80: *Commentaries on the Laws of England* (1765)

13 What hangs people...is the unfortunate circumstance of guilt.
Robert Louis Stevenson 1850–94: *The Wrong Box* (with Lloyd Osbourne, 1889)

14 The innocent and the beautiful
Have no enemy but time.
W. B. Yeats 1865–1939: 'In Memory of Eva Gore Booth and Con Markiewicz' (1933)

15 It is not only our fate but our business to lose innocence, and once we have lost that, it is futile to attempt a picnic in Eden.
Elizabeth Bowen 1899–1973: 'Out of a Book' in *Orion III* (1946)

16 Innocence always calls mutely for protection, when we would be so much wiser to guard ourselves against it: innocence is like a dumb leper who has lost his bell, wandering the world meaning no harm.
Graham Greene 1904–91: *The Quiet American* (1955)

17 True guilt is guilt at the obligation one owes to oneself to be oneself. False guilt is guilt felt at not being what other people feel one ought to be or assume that one is.
R. D. Laing 1927–89: *Self and Others* (1961)

18 All things truly wicked start from an innocence.
Ernest Hemingway 1899–1961: *A Moveable Feast* (1964) ch. 20

19 To be absolutely honest, what I feel really bad about is that I don't feel worse. That's the ineffectual liberal's problem in a nutshell.
Michael Frayn 1933– : in *Observer* 8 August 1965

20 I brought myself down. I gave them a sword. And they stuck it in.
Richard Nixon 1913–94: television interview, 19 May 1977

21 Good women always think it is their fault when someone else is being offensive. Bad women never take the blame for anything.
Anita Brookner 1928– : *Hotel du Lac* (1984)

22 Which office do I go to to get my reputation back?
Raymond Donovan 1930– : leaving court on being acquitted of fraud charges, New York, 25 May 1987

23 There was a period of remorse and apology for banks—that period needs to be over.
Bob Diamond 1951– : to the Treasury Select Committee, 11 January 2011, in *Independent* 12 January 2011

Habit

see CUSTOM AND HABIT

Happiness

proverbs and sayings ▸

1 Blessings brighten as they take their flight.
it is only when something is lost that one realizes its value; English proverb, mid 18th century

2 Call no man happy till he dies.
traditionally attributed to the Athenian statesman and poet Solon (*c.*640–after 556 BC) in the form 'Call no man happy before he dies, he is at best but fortunate'; English proverb, mid 16th century

3 Happiness is the only thing we can give without having.
modern saying

4 Happiness is what you make of it.
American proverb, mid 19th century

5 If I keep a green bough in my heart the singing bird will come.
we have some role in creating our own happiness; Chinese proverb

6 It is a poor heart that never rejoices.
often used to explain a celebratory action, and implying that circumstances are not in general unrelievedly bad; English proverb, mid 19th century

phrases ▸

7 the gaiety of nations
general gaiety or amusement; from Samuel Johnson on the death of David Garrick (1779), 'that stroke of death, which has eclipsed the gaiety of nations'

quotations ▸

8 Happiness resides not in possessions and not in gold, the feeling of happiness dwells in the soul.
Democritus c.460–c.370 BC: attributed

9 The person who is searching for his own happiness should pull out the dart that he has stuck in himself, the arrow-head of grieving, of desiring, of despair.
Pali Tripitaka 2nd century BC: *Sutta-Nipāta* [Woven Cadences]

10 *Nil admirari prope res est una, Numici,*
Solaque quae possit facere et servare beatum.
To marvel at nothing is just about the one and only thing, Numicius, that can make a man happy and keep him that way.
Horace 65–8 BC: *Epistles*; see HAPPINESS 16

11 Happiness lies in conquering one's enemies, in driving them in front of oneself, in taking their property, in savouring their despair, in outraging their wives and daughters.
Genghis Khan 1162–1227: Witold Rodzinski *The Walled Kingdom: A History of China* (1979)

12 But headlong joy is ever on the wing.
John Milton 1608–74: 'The Passion' (1645)

13 One is never as unhappy as one thinks, nor as happy as one hopes.
Duc de la Rochefoucauld 1613–80: *Sentences et Maximes de Morale* (1664)

14 For all the happiness mankind can gain
Is not in pleasure, but in rest from pain.
John Dryden 1631–1700: *The Indian Emperor* (1665)

15 Mirth is like a flash of lightning that breaks through a gloom of clouds, and glitters for a moment: cheerfulness keeps up a kind of daylight in the mind, and fills it with a steady and perpetual serenity.
Joseph Addison 1672–1719: in *The Spectator* 17 May 1712

16 Not to admire, is all the art I know,
To make men happy, and to keep them so.
Alexander Pope 1688–1744: *Imitations of Horace* (1738); see HAPPINESS 10

17 That all who are happy, are equally happy, is not true. A peasant and a philosopher may be equally *satisfied*, but not equally *happy*. Happiness consists in the multiplicity of agreeable consciousness.
Samuel Johnson 1709–84: James Boswell *Life of Samuel Johnson* (1791) February 1766

18 *Freude, schöner Götterfunken,*
Tochter aus Elysium.
Joy, beautiful radiance of the gods,
daughter of Elysium.
Friedrich von Schiller 1759–1805: 'An die Freude' (1785)

19 Happiness is not an ideal of reason but of imagination.
Immanuel Kant 1724–1804: *Fundamental Principles of the Metaphysics of Ethics* (1785)

20 A large income is the best recipe for happiness I ever heard of. It certainly may secure all the myrtle and turkey part of it.
Jane Austen 1775–1817: *Mansfield Park* (1814)

21 To be stupid, and selfish, and to have good health are the three requirements for happiness, though if stupidity is lacking, the others are useless.
Gustave Flaubert 1821–80: letter to Louise Colet, 13 August 1846

22 Happiness is no laughing matter.
Richard Whately 1787–1863: *Apophthegms* (1854)

23 It is not how much we have, but how much we enjoy, that makes happiness.
C. H. Spurgeon 1834–92: in *The Sword and the Trowel* (1867)

24 Ask yourself whether you are happy, and you cease to be so.
John Stuart Mill 1806–73: *Autobiography* (1873)

25 But a lifetime of happiness! No man alive could bear it: it would be hell on earth.
George Bernard Shaw 1856–1950: *Man and Superman* (1903)

26 Happiness is a mystery like religion, and should never be rationalized.
G. K. Chesterton 1874–1936: *Heretics* (1905)

27 There's only one way of being comfortable, and that is to stop running round after happiness. If you make up your mind not to be happy there's no reason why you shouldn't have a fairly good time.
often quoted as 'If only we'd stop trying to be happy we could have a pretty good time'
Edith Wharton 1862–1937: *The Hermit and the Wild Woman and Other Stories* (1908) 'The Last Asset'

28 To be without some of the things you want is an indispensable part of happiness.
Bertrand Russell 1872–1970: *The Conquest of Happiness* (1930)

29 There may be Peace without Joy, and Joy without Peace, but the two combined make Happiness.
John Buchan 1875–1940: *Memory-Hold-the-Door* (1940)

30 Happiness makes up in height for what it lacks in length.
Robert Frost 1874–1963: title of poem (1942)

31 Point me out the happy man and I will point you out either egotism, selfishness, evil—or else an absolute ignorance.
Graham Greene 1904–91: *The Heart of the Matter* (1948)

32 Happiness is a warm gun.
John Lennon 1940–80: title of song (1968); see DOGS 15

33 Happiness is an imaginary condition, formerly often attributed by the living to the dead, now usually attributed by adults to children, and by children to adults.
Thomas Szasz 1920– : *The Second Sin* (1973)

34 Happiness writes white.
Philip Larkin 1922–85: attributed

Haste and Delay

proverbs and sayings ▸

1 Always in a hurry, always behind.
North American proverb, mid 20th century

2 Delays are dangerous.
used as a warning against procrastination; English proverb, late 16th century

3 Haste is from the Devil.
often used to mean that undue haste results in work being done badly or carelessly; English proverb, mid 17th century

4 Haste makes waste.
hurried work is likely to be wasteful; English proverb, late 14th century

5 Make haste slowly.
advising a course of careful preparation; English proverb, late 16th century; see HASTE 11

6 More haste, less speed.
speed here meant originally success rather than swiftness, and the meaning is that hurried work is likely to be less successful; English proverb, mid 14th century

7 Never put off till tomorrow what you can do today.
English proverb, late 14th century

8 Procrastination is the thief of time.
someone who continually puts things off ultimately achieves little; English proverb, mid 18th century, from Edward Young *Night Thoughts* (1742–5)

phrases ▸

9 at the eleventh hour
at the latest possible moment; with reference to the story in the Bible (Matthew) of the labourers who were hired 'about the eleventh hour' to work in the vineyard, and who were given the same payment as those who had worked all day

quotations ▸

10 Why tarry the wheels of his chariots?
Bible: Judges

11 *Festina lente.*
Make haste slowly.
Augustus 63 BC–AD 14: Suetonius *Lives of the Caesars* 'Divus Augustus'; see HASTE 5

12 I'll put a girdle round about the earth
In forty minutes.
William Shakespeare 1564–1616: *A Midsummer Night's Dream* (1595–6)

13 I knew a wise man that had it for a by-word, when he saw men hasten to a conclusion. 'Stay a little, that we may make an end the sooner.'
Francis Bacon 1561–1626: *Essays* (1625) 'Of Dispatch'

14 Though I am always in haste, I am never in a hurry.
John Wesley 1703–91: letter to Miss March, 10 December 1777

15 No admittance till the week after next!
Lewis Carroll 1832–98: *Through the Looking-Glass* (1872)

16 Never be a pioneer. It's the Early Christian that gets the fattest lion.
Saki 1870–1916: *Reginald* (1904) 'Reginald's Choir Treat'; see CHRISTIAN CHURCH 3

17 There is more to life than increasing its speed.
Mahatma Gandhi 1869–1948: attributed

18 ESTRAGON: Charming spot. Inspiring prospects. Let's go.
VLADIMIR: We can't.
ESTRAGON: Why not?
VLADIMIR: We're waiting for Godot.
Samuel Beckett 1906–89: *Waiting for Godot* (1955)

19 If anyone believes that our smiles involve abandonment of the teaching of Marx, Engels and Lenin he deceives himself. Those who wait for that must wait until a shrimp learns to whistle.
Nikita Khrushchev 1894–1971: speech in Moscow, 17 September 1955

20 I think we ought to let him hang there.
Let him twist slowly, slowly in the wind.
of Patrick Gray, regarding his nomination as director of the FBI, in a telephone conversation with John Dean
John Ehrlichman 1925–99: in *Washington Post* 27 July 1973; see CERTAINTY 7

Hatred

see also ENEMIES

proverbs and sayings ▸

1 Better a dinner of herbs than a stalled ox where hate is.
simple food accompanied by goodwill and affection is preferable to luxury in an atmosphere of ill-will; English proverb, mid 16th century: see HATRED 3

2 Curses, like chickens, come home to roost.
ill will directed at another is likely to rebound on the originator; English proverb, late 14th century

quotations ▸

3 Better is a dinner of herbs where love is, than a stalled ox and hatred therewith.
Bible: Proverbs; see HATRED 1

4 For hate is not conquered by hate: hate is conquered by love. This is a law eternal.
Pali Tripitaka 2nd century BC: *Dhammapada*

5 Now hatred is by far the longest pleasure;
Men love in haste, but they detest at leisure.
Lord Byron 1788–1824: *Don Juan* (1819–24)

6 Gr-r-r—there go, my heart's abhorrence!
Water your damned flower-pots, do!
If hate killed men, Brother Lawrence,
God's blood, would not mine kill you!
Robert Browning 1812–89: 'Soliloquy of the Spanish Cloister' (1842)

7 Hatred is a feeling which leads to the extinction of values.
José Ortega y Gasset 1883–1955: *Meditations on Quixote* (1914)

8 I tell you there is such a thing as creative hate!
Willa Cather 1873–1947: *The Song of the Lark* (1915)

9 If you hate a person, you hate something in him that is part of yourself. What isn't part of ourselves doesn't disturb us.
Hermann Hesse 1877–1962: *Demian* (1919)

10 Any kiddie in school can love like a fool,
But hating, my boy, is an art.
Ogden Nash 1902–71: 'Plea for Less Malice Toward None' (1933)

11 I never hated a man enough to give him diamonds back.
Zsa Zsa Gabor 1919– : in *Observer* 25 August 1957

12 Always remember, others may hate you. Those who hate you don't win unless you hate them. And then you destroy yourself.
Richard Nixon 1913–94: address to members of his staff after his resignation, 9 August 1974

13 No one is born hating another person because of the colour of his skin, or his background, or his religion. People must learn to hate, and if they can learn to hate, they can be taught to love, for love comes more naturally to the human heart than its opposite.
Nelson Mandela 1918– : *Long Walk to Freedom* (1994)

Health and Fitness

proverbs and sayings ▸

1 An apple a day keeps the doctor away.
eating an apple each day keeps one healthy; English proverb, mid 19th century; compare HEALTH 5

2 Don't die of ignorance.
Aids publicity campaign, 1987

3 Drinka Pinta Milka Day.
advertising slogan for National Dairy Council, 1958; coined by Bertrand Whitehead

4 Early to bed and early to rise, makes a man healthy, wealthy, and wise.
linking a healthy and sober lifestyle with material success; English proverb; late 15th century, see SLEEP 20

5 Eat leeks in March and ramsons in May, and all the year after physicians may play.
ramsons = wild garlic; Welsh proverb; compare HEALTH 1

6 Even your closest friends won't tell you.
advertising slogan for Listerine mouthwash, US, 1923

7 Every good quality is contained in ginger.
Indian proverb

8 He who has health has hope; and he who has hope has everything.
Arab proverb

9 I believe that every human being has a finite number of heartbeats available to him, and I don't intend to waste any of mine running around doing exercises.
attributed to the American astronaut Neil Armstrong (1930–) in *Life* 4 July 1969; but denied by Armstrong in *First on the Moon* (1970, with Michael Collins and Edwin E. Aldrin)

10 I was a seven-stone weakling.
advertising slogan for Charles Atlas body-building, originally in US

11 More die of food than famine.
American proverb, mid 20th century

12 Slip, slop, slap.
sun protection slogan, meaning *slip* on a T-shirt, *slop* on some suncream, *slap* on a hat; Australian health education programme, 1980s

13 There is nothing so good for the inside of a man as the outside of a horse.
recommending the healthful effects of horse-riding; English proverb, early 20th century

14 Those who do not find time for exercise will have to find time for illness.
traditional saying

15 Your food is your medicine.
Indian proverb

quotations ▸

16 Life's not just being alive, but being well.
Martial C.AD 40–C.104: *Epigrammata*

17 *Orandum est ut sit mens sana in corpore sano.*
You should pray to have a sound mind in a sound body.
Juvenal C.AD 60–C.140: *Satires*

18 Look to your health; and if you have it, praise God, and value it next to a good conscience; for health is the second blessing that we mortals are capable of; a blessing that money cannot buy.
Izaak Walton 1593–1683: *The Compleat Angler* (1653)

19 The wise, for cure, on exercise depend;
God never made his work for man to mend.
John Dryden 1631–1700: Epistle 'To my honoured kinsman John Driden' (1700)

20 The sovereign invigorator of the body is exercise, and of all the exercises, walking is best.
Thomas Jefferson 1743–1826: letter to Thomas Mann Randolph Jr., 27 August 1786

21 The first wealth is health.
Ralph Waldo Emerson 1803–82: *The Conduct of Life* (1860)

22 A bear, however hard he tries,
Grows tubby without exercise.
A. A. Milne 1882–1956: 'Teddy Bear' (1924)

23 Exercise is bunk. If you are healthy, you don't need it: if you are sick you shouldn't take it.
Henry Ford 1863–1947: attributed

24 Avoid running at all times.
Leroy ('Satchel') Paige 1906–82: *How To Stay Young* (1953)

25 I sometimes think that running has given me a glimpse of the greatest freedom a man can ever know, because it results in the simultaneous liberation of both body and mind.
Roger Bannister 1929– : *First Four Minutes* (1955)

26 Exercise is the yuppie version of bulimia.
Barbara Ehrenreich 1941– : *The Worst Years of Our Lives* (1991) 'Food Worship'

27 The first law of dietetics seems to be: if it tastes good, it's bad for you.
Isaac Asimov 1920–92: attributed

28 The only exercise I take is walking behind the coffins of friends who took exercise.
Peter O'Toole 1932– : in *Mail on Sunday* 27 December 1998

Heaven and Hell

proverbs and sayings ►

1 Hell is wherever heaven is not.
English proverb, late 16th century

phrases ►

2 Abraham's bosom
heaven, the place of rest for the souls of the blessed; *Abraham* the Hebrew patriarch from whom all Jews trace their descent; from the Bible (Luke) 'And it came to pass, that the beggar died, and was carried by the angels into Abraham's bosom'

3 fire and brimstone
torment in hell; deriving from biblical allusion, as in Revelation 'These both were cast alive into a lake of fire burning with brimstone'

4 the happy hunting-grounds
among Native Americans, a fabled country full of game to which warriors go after death

5 Land of Beulah
heaven; from John Bunyan's *Pilgrim's Progress*, where the Land of Beulah is a pleasant and fertile country beyond the Valley of the Shadow of Death, and within sight of the Heavenly City

6 New Jerusalem
the abode of the blessed in heaven; from the Bible (Revelation) 'And I, John, saw the holy city, new Jerusalem, coming down from God out of heaven'

quotations ►

7 But the children of the kingdom shall be cast out into outer darkness: there shall be weeping and gnashing of teeth.
Bible: St Matthew

8 And I saw a new heaven and a new earth: for the first heaven and the first earth were passed away; and there was no more sea.
Bible: Revelation

9 *Per me si va nella città dolente,*
Per me si va nell' eterno dolore,
Per me si va tra la perduta gente...
Lasciate ogni speranza voi ch'entrate!
Through me is the way to the sorrowful city. Through me is the way to eternal suffering. Through me is the

way to join the lost people...Abandon all hope, you who enter!
inscription at the entrance to Hell; the final sentence now often quoted as 'Abandon hope, all ye who enter here'
Dante Alighieri 1265–1321: *Divina Commedia* 'Inferno'

10 Why, this is hell, nor am I out of it:
Thinkst thou that I who saw the face of God,
And tasted the eternal joys of heaven,
Am not tormented with ten thousand hells
In being deprived of everlasting bliss!
Christopher Marlowe 1564–93: *Doctor Faustus* (1604)

11 He ascended into heaven, And sitteth on the right hand of God the Father Almighty; From thence he shall come to judge the quick and the dead.
quick = an archaic term for the living
The Book of Common Prayer 1662: *Morning Prayer* The Apostles' Creed; see TRANSPORT 17

12 Me miserable! which way shall I fly
Infinite wrath, and infinite despair?
Which way I fly is hell; myself am hell.
John Milton 1608–74: *Paradise Lost* (1667)

13 My idea of heaven is, eating *pâté de foie gras* to the sound of trumpets.
the view of Smith's friend Henry Luttrell
Sydney Smith 1771–1845: H. Pearson *The Smith of Smiths* (1934)

14 I will spend my heaven doing good on earth.
St Teresa 1873–97: T. N. Taylor (ed.) *Soeur Thérèse of Lisieux* (1912)

15 Heaven for climate, and hell for society.
Mark Twain 1835–1910: *Speeches* (1910)

16 The true paradises are the paradises that we have lost.
Marcel Proust 1871–1922: *Time Regained* (1926)

17 Hell, madam, is to love no more.
Georges Bernanos 1888–1948: *Journal d'un curé de campagne* (1936)

18 Whose love is given over-well
Shall look on Helen's face in hell
Whilst they whose love is thin and wise
Shall see John Knox in Paradise.
Dorothy Parker 1893–1967: 'Partial Comfort' (1937)

19 Hell is other people.
Jean-Paul Sartre 1905–80: *Huis Clos* (1944)

20 What is hell?
Hell is oneself,
Hell is alone, the other figures in it
Merely projections.
T. S. Eliot 1888–1965: *The Cocktail Party* (1950)

21 We are not bound for ever to the circles of the world, and beyond them is more than memory.
J. R. R. Tolkien 1892–1973: *The Lord of the Rings* pt. 3 *The Return of the King* (1955)

22 We may be surprised at the people we find in heaven. God has a soft spot for sinners. His standards are quite low.
Desmond Tutu 1931– : in *Sunday Times* 15 April 2001

Heroes

proverbs and sayings ▸

1 Better to have lived one day as a tiger than a thousand years as a sheep.
modern saying; see HEROES 8

2 For every Pharaoh there is a Moses.
a liberator will arise against every oppressor; Middle Eastern proverb

phrases ▸

3 the Age of Chivalry
the time when men behave with courage, honour, and courtesy; the period during which the knightly social and ethical system prevailed

4 great white hope
a person expected to bring much success to a team or organization; originally (in 1911) referring to a white boxer thought capable of beating Jack Johnson, the first black world heavyweight champion

5 knight in shining armour
a chivalrous rescuer or helper, especially of a woman

quotations ▸

6 No man is a hero to his valet.
Mme Cornuel 1605–94: *Lettres de Mlle Aïssé à Madame C* (1787) Letter 13 'De Paris, 1728'; see HEROES 10; FAMILIARITY 9

7 See, the conquering hero comes!
Sound the trumpets, beat the drums!
Thomas Morell 1703–84: *Judas Maccabeus* (1747)

8 In this world I would rather live two days like a tiger, than two hundred years like a sheep.
Tipu Sultan 1750–99: Alexander Beatson *A View of the Origin and Conduct of the War with Tippoo Sultaun* (1800); see HEROES 1

9 So faithful in love, and so dauntless in war,
There never was knight like the young Lochinvar.
Sir Walter Scott 1771–1832: *Marmion* (1808) 'Lochinvar'

10 In short, he was a perfect cavaliero,
And to his very valet seemed a hero.
Lord Byron 1788–1824: *Beppo* (1818); see HEROES 6

11 Every hero becomes a bore at last.
Ralph Waldo Emerson 1803–82: *Representative Men* (1850)

12 Hero-worship is strongest where there is least regard for human freedom.
Herbert Spencer 1820–1903: *Social Statics* (1850)

13 Men reject their prophets and slay them, but they love their martyrs and honour those whom they have slain.
Fedor Dostoevsky 1821–81: *The Brothers Karamazov* (1879–80)

14 A hero is the one who does what he can. The others don't.
Romain Rolland 1866–1944: *Jean-Christophe* (1904–12) 'L'Adolescent'

15 Heroing is one of the shortest-lived professions there is.
Will Rogers 1879–1935: newspaper article, 15 February 1925

16 ANDREA: Unhappy the land that has no heroes!...
GALILEO: No. Unhappy the land that needs heroes.
Bertolt Brecht 1898–1956: *The Life of Galileo* (1939)

17 Show me a hero and I will write you a tragedy.
F. Scott Fitzgerald 1896–1940: Edmund Wilson (ed.) *The Crack-Up* (1945) 'Note-Books E'

18 Faster than a speeding bullet!...Look! Up in the sky! It's a bird! It's a plane! It's Superman!
Anonymous: *Superman* (US radio show, 1940 onwards)

19 If the myth gets bigger than the man, print the myth.
Dorothy Johnson 1905–84: *Indian Country* (1953) 'The Man Who Shot Liberty Valance'; see also JOURNALISM 23

20 It was involuntary. They sank my boat.
on being asked how he became a war hero
John F. Kennedy 1917–63: Arthur M. Schlesinger Jr. *A Thousand Days* (1965)

21 In such a regime, I say, you died a good death if your life had inspired someone to come forward and shoot your murderer in the chest—without asking to be paid.
Chinua Achebe 1930– : *A Man of the People* (1966)

22 Ultimately a hero is a man who would argue with the Gods, and so awakens devils to contest his vision.
Norman Mailer 1923–2007: *The Presidential Papers* (1976)

23 We can be heroes
Just for one day.
David Bowie 1947– : 'Heroes' (1977 song)

History

proverbs and sayings ▶

1 Happy is the country which has no history.
memorable events are likely to be unhappy and disruptive; English proverb, early 19th century: see HISTORY 13

2 History is a fable agreed upon.
American proverb, mid 20th century

3 History is written by the victors.
modern saying

4 History repeats itself.
English proverb, mid 19th century; see HISTORY 17, HISTORY 22

5 Until the lions produce their own historian, the story of the hunt will glorify the hunter.
African proverb

phrases ▸

6 the Father of History

Herodotus (5th century BC), Greek historian; the first historian to collect materials systematically, test their accuracy to a certain extent, and arrange them in a well-constructed and vivid narrative

7 Whig historian

a historian who interprets history as the continuing and inevitable victory of progress over reaction; first recorded in George Bernard Shaw's preface to *St Joan* (1924)

quotations ▸

8 I have written my work, not as an essay which is to win the applause of the moment, but as a possession for all time.

Thucydides c.455–c.400 BC: *History of the Peloponnesian War*

9 To be ignorant of what occurred before you were born is to remain forever a child.

Cicero 106–43 BC: *De Oratore*

10 History is philosophy from examples.

Dionysius of Halicarnassus fl. 30–7 BC: *Ars Rhetorica*

11 If history records good things of good men, the thoughtful hearer is encouraged to imitate what is good.

The Venerable Bede AD 673–735: *Ecclesiastical History of the English People*

12 Whosoever, in writing a modern history, shall follow truth too near the heels, it may happily strike out his teeth.

Walter Ralegh 1552–1618: *The History of the World* (1614)

13 Happy the people whose annals are blank in history-books!

Montesquieu 1689–1755: attributed to Montesquieu by Thomas Carlyle *History of Frederick the Great*; see HISTORY 1

14 History...is, indeed, little more than the register of the crimes, follies, and misfortunes of mankind.

Edward Gibbon 1737–94: *The Decline and Fall of the Roman Empire* (1776–88)

15 What experience and history teach is this—that nations and governments have never learned anything from history, or acted upon any lessons they might have drawn from it.

G. W. F. Hegel 1770–1831: *Lectures on the Philosophy of World History: Introduction* (1830); see HISTORY 17

16 History is the essence of innumerable biographies.

Thomas Carlyle 1795–1881: *Critical and Miscellaneous Essays* (1838) 'On History'

17 Hegel says somewhere that all great events and personalities in world history reappear in one fashion or another. He forgot to add: the first time as tragedy, the second as farce.

Karl Marx 1818–83: *The Eighteenth Brumaire of Louis Bonaparte* (1852); see HISTORY 4, HISTORY 15

18 History is a gallery of pictures in which there are few originals and many copies.

Alexis de Tocqueville 1805–59: *L'Ancien régime* (1856)

19 Great nations write their autobiographies in three manuscripts;—the book of their deeds, the book of their words, and the book of their art.

John Ruskin 1819–1900: *St Mark's Rest* (1884)

20 History is past politics, and politics is present history.

E. A. Freeman 1823–92: *Methods of Historical Study* (1886)

21 It has been said that though God cannot alter the past, historians can; it is perhaps because they can be useful to Him in this respect that He tolerates their existence.

Samuel Butler 1835–1902: *Erewhon Revisited* (1901); see PAST 19

22 History repeats itself; historians repeat one another.

Rupert Brooke 1887–1915: letter to Geoffrey Keynes, 4 June 1906; see HISTORY 4

23 History is more or less bunk.

Henry Ford 1863–1947: interview with Charles N. Wheeler in *Chicago Tribune* 25 May 1916

24 Human history becomes more and more a race between education and catastrophe.

H. G. Wells 1866–1946: *The Outline of History* (1920)

25 History is not what you thought. *It is what you can remember.*
W. C. Sellar 1898–1951 and **R. J. Yeatman** 1898–1968: *1066 and All That* (1930)

26 For my part, I consider that it will be found much better by all Parties to leave the past to history, especially as I propose to write that history myself.
Winston Churchill 1874–1965: speech in the House of Commons, 23 January 1948

27 History is the sum total of the things that could have been avoided.
Konrad Adenauer 1876–1967: attributed

28 History gets thicker as it approaches recent times.
A. J. P. Taylor 1906–90: *English History 1914–45* (1965) bibliography

29 What we may be witnessing is not just the end of the Cold War but the end of history as such: that is, the end point of man's ideological evolution and the universalism of Western liberal democracy.
Francis Fukuyama 1952– : in *Independent* 20 September 1989

The Home
see also HOUSEWORK

proverbs and sayings ►

1 Chuck out the chintz.
advertising slogan for IKEA, 1990s

2 The dog is a lion in his own house.
Persian proverb

3 East, west, home's best.
English proverb, mid 19th century

4 An Englishman's home is his castle.
a person has the right to refuse entry to his home; reflecting a legal principle, as formulated by the English jurist Edward Coke (1552–1634) 'For a man's house is his castle, *et domus sua cuique est tutissimum refugium* [and each man's home is his safest refuge]'; English proverb, late 16th century

5 Every cock will crow upon his own dunghill.
everyone is confident and at ease on their home ground; English proverb, mid 13th century

6 Falling leaves have to return to their roots.
everything must ultimately return to its origins; Chinese proverb

7 Home is home though it's never so homely.
no place can compare with one's own home; English proverb, mid 16th century

8 Home is where the heart is.
one's true home is wherever the person one loves most is; English proverb, late 19th century

9 Home is where the mortgage is.
American proverb, mid 20th century

10 Lang may yer lum reek!
long may your chimney smoke, often used as a toast; Scottish proverb

11 There's no place like home.
English proverb, late 16th century; the saying is found earlier in Greek, in the work of the Greek poet Hesiod (700 BC); see HOME 17

phrases ►

12 fire and flet
fire and houseroom; *flet* = a dwelling, a house; see DEATH 12

13 lares and penates
the home; Latin *lares* = the protective gods of the household worshipped in ancient Rome; *penates* = the protective gods of the household, especially the storeroom

14 motherhood and apple pie
in North American usage, a cherished ideal of homeliness, representing the type of values regarded as deserving unquestioning support

quotations ►

15 The foxes have holes, and the birds of the air have nests; but the Son of man hath not where to lay his head.
Bible: St Matthew

16 The accent of one's birthplace lingers in the mind and in the heart as it does in one's speech.
Duc de la Rochefoucauld 1613–80: *Maximes* (1678)

17 Mid pleasures and palaces though we
may roam,

Be it ever so humble, there's no place like home.

J. H. Payne 1791–1852: *Clari, or, The Maid of Milan* (1823 opera) 'Home, Sweet Home'; see HOME 11

18 A comfortable house is a great source of happiness. It ranks immediately after health and a good conscience.

Sydney Smith 1771–1845: letter to Lord Murray, 29 September 1843

19 What's the good of a home if you are never in it?

George Grossmith 1847–1912 and **Weedon Grossmith** 1854–1919: *The Diary of a Nobody* (1894)

20 Any old place I can hang my hat is home sweet home to me.

William Jerome 1865–1932: title of song (1901)

21 Home is the girl's prison and the woman's workhouse.

George Bernard Shaw 1856–1950: *Man and Superman* (1903) 'Maxims: Women in the Home'

22 Home is the place where, when you have to go there,
They have to take you in.

Robert Frost 1874–1963: 'The Death of the Hired Man' (1914)

23 One never reaches home, but wherever friendly paths intersect the whole world looks like home for a time.

Hermann Hesse 1877–1962: *Demian* (1919)

24 The best
Thing we can do is to make wherever we're lost in
Look as much like home as we can.

Christopher Fry 1907– : *The Lady's not for Burning* (1949)

25 It takes a heap o' livin' in a house t' make it home.

Edgar A. Guest 1881–1959: 'Home'

26 Home is where you come to when you have nothing better to do.

Margaret Thatcher 1925– : in *Vanity Fair* May 1991

Honesty

see also DECEPTION, LIES, TRUTH

proverbs and sayings ►

1 Children and fools tell the truth.

implying that they lack the cunning to see possible danger; tradition sometimes adds drunkards; English proverb, mid 16th century

2 Confession is good for the soul.

confession is essential to repentance and forgiveness; English proverb, mid 17th century

3 Honesty is more praised than practised.

it is easier to advise another person to be honest than to be honest oneself; American proverb, mid 20th century

4 Honesty is the best policy.

as well as being right, to be honest may also achieve a more successful outcome; English proverb, early 17th century; see HONESTY 14, HONESTY 18

5 It's a sin to steal a pin.

even if what is stolen is of little value, the action is still wrong; English proverb, late 19th century

6 Nothing is stolen without hands.

if money or goods are missing, someone has stolen them; English proverb, early 17th century

quotations ►

7 Do not be too straight or too soft; straight trees are cut down, but crooked trees remain standing.

Kautilya (Chanakya) fl. *c.*300 BC: *Garuda Purana*

8 Honesty is praised and left to shiver.

Juvenal *c.*AD 60–*c.*140: *Satires*

9 Here lies he who neither feared nor flattered any flesh.

of John Knox

James Douglas, Earl of Morton 1516–81: said as he was buried, 26 November 1572; George R. Preedy *The Life of John Knox* (1940)

10 Speak what we feel, not what we ought to say.

William Shakespeare 1564–1616: *King Lear* (1605–6)

11 And those who paint 'em truest praise 'em most.

Joseph Addison 1672–1719: *The Campaign* (1705)

12 An honest man's the noblest work of God.
Alexander Pope 1688–1744: *An Essay on Man* Epistle 4 (1734); see GOD 30

13 'But the Emperor has nothing on at all!' cried a little child.
Hans Christian Andersen 1805–75: *Danish Fairy Legends and Tales* (1846) 'The Emperor's New Clothes'

14 Honesty is the best policy; but he who is governed by that maxim is not an honest man.
Richard Whately 1787–1863: *Apophthegms* (1854); see HONESTY 4

15 The louder he talked of his honour, the faster we counted our spoons.
Ralph Waldo Emerson 1803–82: *The Conduct of Life* (1860)

16 A little sincerity is a dangerous thing, and a great deal of it is absolutely fatal.
Oscar Wilde 1854–1900: *Intentions* (1891)

17 It is dangerous to be sincere unless you are also stupid.
George Bernard Shaw 1856–1950: *Man and Superman* (1903) 'The Revolutionist's Handbook'

18 I am afraid we must make the world honest before we can honestly say to our children that honesty is the best policy.
George Bernard Shaw 1856–1950: 'Rungs of the Ladder' BBC radio broadcast 11 July 1932; see HONESTY 4

19 honesty is a good
thing but
it is not profitable to
its possessor
unless it is
kept under control.
Don Marquis 1878–1937: *archys life of mehitabel* (1933)

20 Integrity has no need of rules.
Albert Camus 1913–60: *The Myth of Sisyphus* (1942)

21 This is hard to answer, so I'll tell the truth.
David Ben-Gurion 1886–1973: at the Zionist Actions Committee session, London, 14 August 1945

22 Always be sincere, even if you don't mean it.
Harry S. Truman 1884–1972: attributed

Hope

see also DESPAIR, OPTIMISM

proverbs and sayings ▸

1 A drowning man will clutch at a straw.
when hope is slipping away one grasps at the slightest chance; English proverb, mid 16th century

2 He that lives in hope dances to an ill tune.
hoping for something better may constrain one's freedom of action; English proverb, late 16th century

3 Hope deferred makes the heart sick.
implying that it is worse to have had one's hopes raised and then dashed, than to have been resigned to not having something; English proverb, late 14th century, from the Bible: see HOPE 10

4 Hope is a good breakfast but a bad supper.
while it is pleasant to begin something in a hopeful mood, the hopes need to have been fulfilled by the time it ends; English proverb, mid 17th century

5 Hope springs eternal.
English proverb, mid 18th century, from Pope: see HOPE 12

6 If it were not for hope, the heart would break.
referring to the role of hope in warding off complete despair; English proverb, mid 13th century

7 In the kingdom of hope, there is no winter.
Russian proverb

8 It is better to travel hopefully than to arrive.
often with the implication that something long sought may be disappointing when achieved; English proverb, late 19th century, from Stevenson: see TRAVEL 36

9 While there's life there's hope.
often used as encouragement not to despair in an unpromising situation; English proverb, mid 16th century

quotations ▸

10 Hope deferred maketh the heart sick: but when the desire cometh, it is a tree of life.
Bible: Proverbs; see HOPE 3

11 *Nil desperandum.*
Never despair.
Horace 65–8 BC: *Odes*

12 Hope springs eternal in the human breast:
Man never Is, but always To be blest.
Alexander Pope 1688–1744: *An Essay on Man* Epistle 1 (1733); see HOPE 5

13 He that lives upon hope will die fasting.
Benjamin Franklin 1706–90: *Poor Richard's Almanac* (1758)

14 What is hope? nothing but the paint on the face of Existence; the least touch of truth rubs it off, and then we see what a hollow-cheeked harlot we have got hold of.
Lord Byron 1788–1824: letter to Thomas Moore, 28 October 1815

15 O, Wind,
If Winter comes, can Spring be far behind?
Percy Bysshe Shelley 1792–1822: 'Ode to the West Wind' (1819)

16 Work without hope draws nectar in a sieve,
And hope without an object cannot live.
Samuel Taylor Coleridge 1772–1834: 'Work without Hope' (1828)

17 If hopes were dupes, fears may be liars.
Arthur Hugh Clough 1819–61: 'Say not the struggle naught availeth' (1855)

18 He who has never hoped can never despair.
George Bernard Shaw 1856–1950: *Caesar and Cleopatra* (1901)

19 Plenty of hope—for God—an abundance of hope—only not for us.
Franz Kafka 1883–1924: to Max Brod, 28 February 1920; Heinz Politzer *Franz Kafka: Parable and Paradox* (1962)

20 Hope is like a road in the country; there was never a road, but when many people walk on it, the road comes into existence.
Lu Xun 1881–1936: *The Wisdom of China* (1944) 'The Epigrams of Lusin'

21 After all, tomorrow is another day.
Margaret Mitchell 1900–49: *Gone with the Wind* (1936); see FUTURE 6

22 Walk on, walk on, with hope in your heart,
And you'll never walk alone.
Oscar Hammerstein II 1895–1960: 'You'll Never Walk Alone' (1945 song)

23 Hope, like faith, is nothing if it is not courageous; it is nothing if it is not ridiculous.
Thornton Wilder 1897–1975: *The Eighth Day* (1967)

24 Hope is definitely not the same thing as optimism. It is not the conviction that something will turn out well, but the certainty that something makes sense, regardless of how it turns out.
Václav Havel 1936– : *Disturbing the Peace* (1986)

25 The hope of a skinny kid with a funny name who believes that America has a place for him, too...The audacity of hope!
Barack Obama 1961– : Democratic National Convention keynote address, 27 July 2004

Hospitality

proverbs and sayings ▸

1 The company makes the feast.
the success of a social occasion depends on those present rather than on the food and drink provided; English proverb, mid 17th century

2 The first day a guest, the second day a guest, the third day a calamity.
Indian proverb; see HOSPITALITY 3

3 Fish and guests stink after three days.
one should not outstay one's welcome; English proverb, late 16th century; see HOSPITALITY 2

4 It is merry in hall when beards wag all.
when conversation is in full flow; English proverb, early 14th century

5 Treat your guest as a guest for two days; on the third day give him a hoe.
African proverb

quotations ▸

6 Bring hither the fatted calf, and kill it.
Bible: St Luke; see FESTIVALS 31, FORGIVENESS 8

7 Be not forgetful to entertain strangers: for thereby some have entertained angels unawares.
Bible: Hebrews

8 Unbidden guests
Are often welcomest when they are gone.
William Shakespeare 1564–1616: *Henry VI, Part 1* (1592)

9 For I, who hold sage Homer's rule the best,
Welcome the coming, speed the going guest.
Alexander Pope 1688–1744: *Imitations of Horace* (1734); 'speed the parting guest' in Pope's translation of *The Odyssey* (1725–6)

10 The sooner every party breaks up the better.
Jane Austen 1775–1817: *Emma* (1816)

11 It was a delightful visit;- perfect, in being much too short.
Jane Austen 1775–1817: *Emma* (1816)

12 Come in the evening, or come in the morning,
Come when you're looked for, or come without warning.
Thomas Davis 1814–45: 'The Welcome' (1846)

13 If one plays good music, people don't listen and if one plays bad music people don't talk.
Oscar Wilde 1854–1900: *The Importance of Being Earnest* (1895)

14 At a dinner party one should eat wisely but not too well, and talk well but not too wisely.
W. Somerset Maugham 1874–1965: *Writer's Notebook* (1949); written in 1896

15 Some people can stay longer in an hour than others can in a week.
William Dean Howells 1837–1920: attributed

16 Candy
Is dandy
But liquor
Is quicker.
Ogden Nash 1902–71: 'Reflections on Ice-breaking' (1931)

17 The tumult and the shouting dies,
The captains and the kings depart,
And we are left with large supplies
Of cold blancmange and rhubarb tart.
Ronald Knox 1888–1957: 'After the Party' (1959); see PRIDE 13

18 The best number for a dinner party is two—myself and a dam' good head waiter.
Nubar Gulbenkian 1896–1972: in *Daily Telegraph* 14 January 1965

19 At every party there are two kinds of people—those who want to go home and those who don't. The trouble is, they are usually married to each other.
Ann Landers 1918–2002: in *International Herald Tribune* 19 June 1991

Housework

see also HOME

proverbs and sayings ▸

1 He that will thrive must first ask his wife.
the husband's material welfare depends on the way in which his wife manages the household; English proverb, late 15th century

2 It beats as it sweeps as it cleans.
advertising slogan for Hoover vacuum cleaners, 1919

3 Persil washes whiter—and it shows.
advertising slogan for Persil washing powder, 1970s

4 They that wash on Monday
Have all the week to dry;
They that wash on Tuesday
Are not so much awry;
They that wash on Wednesday
Are not so much to blame;
They that wash on Thursday
Wash for very shame;
They that wash on Friday
Wash in sorry need;
And they that wash on Saturday,
Are lazy folk indeed.
traditional rhyme

5 A woman's work is never done.
reflecting the traditional responsibilities of the housewife; English proverb, late 16th century

phrases ▸

6 lay up in lavender
preserve carefully for future use; the flowers and stalks of *lavender* were customarily placed among linen or other clothes as a preservative against moths during storage

quotations ▸

7 There is scarcely any less bother in the running of a family than in that of an entire state. And domestic business is no less importunate for being less important.
Montaigne 1533–92: *Essays* (1580)

8 God walks among the pots and pans.
St Teresa of Ávila 1512–82: *Book of the Foundations* (1610)

9 Cleanliness, punctuality, order, and method, are essentials in the character of a housekeeper.
Isabella Beeton 1836–65: *Book of Cookery and Household Management* (1861)

10 Hatred of domestic work is a natural and admirable result of civilization.
Rebecca West 1892–1983: in *The Freewoman* 6 June 1912

11 At the worst, a house unkempt cannot be so distressing as a life unlived.
Rose Macaulay 1881–1958: *Problems of a Woman's Life* (1926)

12 Few tasks are more like the torture of Sisyphus than housework, with its endless repetition...The housewife wears herself out marking time: she makes nothing, simply perpetuates the present.
Simone de Beauvoir 1908–86: *The Second Sex* (1949)

13 Cleaning your house while your kids are still growing is like shovelling the walk before it stops snowing.
Phyllis Diller 1917– : *Phyllis Diller's Housekeeping Hints* (1966)

14 There was no need to do any housework at all. After the first four years the dirt doesn't get any worse.
Quentin Crisp 1908–99: *The Naked Civil Servant* (1968)

15 Conran's Law of Housework—it expands to fill the time available plus half an hour.
Shirley Conran 1932– : *Superwoman 2* (1977)

16 'I hate discussions of feminism that end up with who does the dishes,' she said. So do I. But at the end, there are always the damned dishes.
Marilyn French 1929–2009: *The Women's Room* (1977)

Human Nature

see also BEHAVIOUR, CHARACTER

proverbs and sayings ▸

1 The best of men are but men at best.
even someone of great moral worth is still human and fallible; English proverb, late 17th century

2 Man is a wolf to man.
English proverb, mid 16th century, from Plautus: see HUMAN NATURE 7

3 There's nowt so queer as folk.
English proverb, early 20th century

4 Young saint, old devil.
unnaturally good and moral behaviour at an early age is likely to change in later life; English proverb, early 15th century

phrases ▸

5 the old Adam
unregenerate human nature; fallen man as contrasted with the *second Adam*, Jesus Christ; see HUMAN NATURE 11; CHRISTIAN CHURCH 10

quotations ▸

6 By nature men are alike. Through practice they have become far apart.
Confucius 551–479 BC: *Analects*

7 A man is a wolf rather than a man to another man, when he hasn't yet found out what he's like.
Plautus c.250–184 BC: *Asinaria*; see HUMAN NATURE 2

8 It is part of human nature to hate the man you have hurt.
Tacitus c.AD 56–after 117: *Agricola*

9 One touch of nature makes the whole world kin.
William Shakespeare 1564–1616: *Troilus and Cressida* (1602)

10 God and the doctor we alike adore
But only when in danger, not before;
The danger o'er, both are alike requited,
God is forgotten, and the Doctor slighted.
John Owen 1563–1622: *Epigrams*

11 O merciful God, grant that the old Adam in this Child may be so buried,

that the new man may be raised up in him.
The Book of Common Prayer 1662: *Public Baptism of Infants*; see HUMAN NATURE 5

12 How selfish soever man may be supposed, there are evidently some principles in his nature, which interest him in the fortune of others, and render their happiness necessary to him, though he derives nothing from it except the pleasure of seeing it.
Adam Smith 1723–90: *The Theory of Moral Sentiments* (1759)

13 On ev'ry hand it will allow'd be,
He's just—nae better than he
shou'd be.
Robert Burns 1759–96: 'A Dedication to G[avin] H[amilton]' (1786)

14 Subdue your appetites my dears, and you've conquered human natur.
Charles Dickens 1812–70: *Nicholas Nickleby* (1839)

15 But good God, people don't do such things!
Henrik Ibsen 1828–1906: *Hedda Gabler* (1890)

16 Adam was but human—this explains it all. He did not want the apple for the apple's sake; he wanted it only because it was forbidden.
Mark Twain 1835–1910: *Pudd'nhead Wilson* (1894)

17 The natural man has only two primal passions, to get and beget.
William Osler 1849–1919: *Science and Immortality* (1904)

18 The terrorist and the policeman both come from the same basket.
Joseph Conrad 1857–1924: *The Secret Agent* (1907)

19 That is ever the way. 'Tis all jealousy to the bride and good wishes to the corpse.
J. M. Barrie 1860–1937: *Quality Street* (1913)

20 I still believe that people are really good at heart.
Anne Frank 1929–45: diary, 15 July 1944

21 Most human beings have an almost infinite capacity for taking things for granted.
Aldous Huxley 1894–1963: *Themes and Variations* (1950) 'Variations on a Philosopher'

22 Human nature is not black and white but black and grey.
Graham Greene 1904–91: 'The Lost Childhood' (1951)

23 There's a man all over for you, blaming on his boots the faults of his feet.
Samuel Beckett 1906–89: *Waiting for Godot* (1955)

The Human Race

proverbs and sayings ▸

1 God sleeps in the stone, dreams in the plant, stirs in the animal, and awakens in man.
traditional saying, frequently said to be of Indian origin; the wording varies in different languages

2 Man is the measure of all things.
everything could be understood in terms of humankind; English proverb, mid 16th century; see HUMAN RACE 9

3 What is the most important thing in life? It is people, people, people.
Maori proverb

phrases ▸

4 a man and a brother
a fellow human being; from the anti-slavery motto *Am I not a man and a brother?*: see RACE 1

5 the man on the Clapham omnibus
the average man; attributed, in the *Law Reports* of 1903, to the English judge Lord Bowen (1853–94)

6 the naked ape
present-day humans regarded as a species, from the title of a book (1967) by Desmond Morris

7 ship of fools
the world, humankind; after *The shyp of folys of the worlde* (1509) translation of German work *Das Narrenschiff* (1494), literally a ship whose passengers represent various types of vice, folly, or human failings

quotations ▸

8 And God said, Let us make man in our image, after our likeness: and let them have dominion over the fish of the sea, and over the fowl of the air, and over the cattle, and over all the earth

and over every creeping thing that creepeth upon the earth.
Bible: Genesis

9 Man is the measure of all things.
Protagoras b. *c.*485 BC: Plato *Theaetetus*; see HUMAN RACE 2

10 There are many wonderful things, and nothing is more wonderful than man.
Sophocles *c.*496–406 BC: *Antigone*

11 I am a man, I count nothing human foreign to me.
Terence *c.* 190–159 BC: *Heauton Timorumenos*

12 O mankind, We have created you male and female, and appointed you races and tribes, that you may know one another.
The Koran: sura 49

13 The children of Adam are limbs to each other, having been created of one essence.
Sadi *c.* 1213–*c.*91: *The Rose Garden*

14 *Considerate la vostra semenza:*
Fatti non foste a viver come bruti,
Ma per seguir virtute e conoscenza.
Consider your origins: you were not made to live as brutes, but to follow virtue and knowledge.
Dante Alighieri 1265–1321: *Divina Commedia* 'Inferno'

15 What a piece of work is a man!
How noble in reason! how infinite in faculty! in form, in moving, how express and admirable! in action how like an angel! in apprehension how like a god! the beauty of the world! the paragon of animals! And yet, to me, what is this quintessence of dust?
William Shakespeare 1564–1616: *Hamlet* (1601)

16 How beauteous mankind is! O brave new world,
That has such people in't.
William Shakespeare 1564–1616: *The Tempest* (1611); see PROGRESS 1

17 Man is only a reed, the weakest thing in nature; but he is a thinking reed.
Blaise Pascal 1623–62: *Pensées* (1670)

18 What is man in nature? A nothing in respect of that which is infinite, an all in respect of nothing, a middle betwixt nothing and all.
Blaise Pascal 1623–62: *Pensées* (1670)

19 Principally I hate and detest that animal called man; although I heartily love John, Peter, Thomas, and so forth.
Jonathan Swift 1667–1745: letter to Pope, 29 September 1725

20 Know then thyself, presume not God to scan;
The proper study of mankind is man.
Alexander Pope 1688–1744: *An Essay on Man* Epistle 2 (1733)

21 Man is a tool-making animal.
Benjamin Franklin 1706–90: James Boswell *Life of Samuel Johnson* (1791) 7 April 1778

22 Out of the crooked timber of humanity no straight thing can ever be made.
Immanuel Kant 1724–1804: *Idee zu einer allgemeinen Geschichte in weltbürgerlicher Absicht* (1784)

23 Drinking when we are not thirsty and making love all year round, madam; that is all there is to distinguish us from other animals.
Pierre-Augustin Caron de Beaumarchais 1732–99: *Le Mariage de Figaro* (1785)

24 Man is the only animal that laughs and weeps; for he is the only animal that is struck with the difference between what things are and what they ought to be.
William Hazlitt 1778–1830: *Lectures on the English Comic Writers* (1819)

25 Is man an ape or an angel? Now I am on the side of the angels.
Benjamin Disraeli 1804–81: speech at Oxford, 25 November 1864; see LIFE SCIENCES 15

26 I teach you the superman. Man is something to be surpassed.
Friedrich Nietzsche 1844–1900: *Also Sprach Zarathustra* (1883)

27 Man is the Only Animal that Blushes. Or needs to.
Mark Twain 1835–1910: *Following the Equator* (1897)

28 Man, biologically considered, and whatever else he may be into the bargain, is simply the most formidable of all the beasts of prey, and, indeed, the only one that preys systematically on its own species.
William James 1842–1910: in *Atlantic Monthly* December 1904

29 What is man, when you come to think upon him, but a minutely set, ingenious machine for turning, with infinite artfulness, the red wine of Shiraz into urine?

Isak Dinesen 1885–1962: *Seven Gothic Tales* (1934) 'The Dreamers'

30 Human kind
Cannot bear very much reality.

T. S. Eliot 1888–1965: *Four Quartets* 'Burnt Norton' (1936)

31 To say, for example, that a man is made up of certain chemical elements is a satisfactory description only for those who intend to use him as a fertilizer.

H. J. Muller 1890–1967: *Science and Criticism* (1943)

32 We're all of us guinea pigs in the laboratory of God. Humanity is just a work in progress.

Tennessee Williams 1911–83: *Camino Real* (1953)

33 We are born of risen apes, not fallen angels, and the apes were armed killers beside.

Robert Ardrey 1908–80: *African Genesis* (1961)

34 In the final analysis, our most basic common link is that we all inhabit this small planet. We all breathe the same air. We all cherish our children's future. And we are all mortal.

John F. Kennedy 1917–63: address at American University, Washington, DC, 10 June 1963

Human Rights

see also EQUALITY, JUSTICE

proverbs and sayings ▸

1 Liberté! Égalité! Fraternité!

French, *Freedom! Equality! Brotherhood!*: motto of the French Revolution, 1789, but of earlier origin

phrases ▸

2 bread and roses

slogan summarizing the right to food for both mind and body; associated with a strike by textile workers in Lawrence, Massachussetts in 1912; see HUMAN RIGHTS 13, LIFESTYLES 7

3 the four freedoms

four essential human freedoms as proclaimed in a speech to Congress by Franklin D. Roosevelt in 1941; see HUMAN RIGHTS 15

4 rights of man

rights held to be justifiably belonging to any person; human rights; associated with the Declaration of the Rights of Man and of the Citizen, adopted by the French National Assembly in 1789 and used as a preface to the French Constitution of 1791

quotations ▸

5 No free man shall be taken or imprisoned or dispossessed, or outlawed or exiled, or in any way destroyed, nor will we go upon him, nor will we send against him except by the lawful judgement of his peers or by the law of the land.

Magna Carta 1215: clause 39

6 Magna Charta is such a fellow, that he will have no sovereign.

on the Lords' Amendment to the Petition of Right, 17 May 1628

Edward Coke 1552–1634: J. Rushworth *Historical Collections* (1659)

7 We hold these truths to be self-evident, that all men are created equal, that they are endowed by their Creator with certain unalienable rights, that among these are life, liberty and the pursuit of happiness.

American Declaration of Independence: 4 July 1776; from a draft by Thomas Jefferson (1743–1826)

8 Whatever each man can separately do, without trespassing upon others, he has a right to do for himself; and he has a right to a fair portion of all which society, with all its combinations of skill and force, can do in his favour.

Edmund Burke 1729–97: *Reflections on the Revolution in France* (1790)

9 Any law which violates the inalienable rights of man is essentially unjust and tyrannical; it is not a law at all.

Maximilien Robespierre 1758–94: *Déclaration des droits de l'homme* 24 April 1793

10 Natural rights is simple nonsense: natural and imprescriptible rights,

rhetorical nonsense—nonsense upon stilts.

Jeremy Bentham 1748–1832: *Anarchical Fallacies* (1843)

11 Its constitution the glittering and sounding generalities of natural right which make up the Declaration of Independence.

Rufus Choate 1799–1859: letter to the Maine Whig State Central Committee, 9 August 1856; see CONVERSATION 4

12 No man can put a chain about the ankle of his fellow man without at last finding the other end fastened about his own neck.

Frederick Douglass 1818–95: speech at Civil Rights Mass Meeting, Washington, DC, 22 October 1883

13 Hearts starve as well as bodies: Give us Bread, but give us Roses.

James Oppenheim 1882–1932: 'Bread and Roses' (1911); see HUMAN RIGHTS 2

14 The most stringent protection of free speech would not protect a man falsely shouting fire in a theatre and causing a panic.

sometimes quoted as, 'shouting fire in a crowded theatre'

Oliver Wendell Holmes Jr. 1841–1935: in *Schenck v. United States* (1919)

15 We look forward to a world founded upon four essential human freedoms. The first is freedom of speech and expression—everywhere in the world. The second is freedom of every person to worship God in his own way—everywhere in the world. The third is freedom from want...everywhere in the world. The fourth is freedom from fear...anywhere in the world.

Franklin D. Roosevelt 1882–1945: message to Congress, 6 January 1941; see HUMAN RIGHTS 3

16 All human beings are born free and equal in dignity and rights.

Anonymous: *Universal Declaration of Human Rights* (1948) article 1

17 A right is not effectual by itself, but only in relation to the obligation to which it corresponds...An obligation which goes unrecognized by anybody loses none of the full force of its existence. A right which goes unrecognized by anybody is not worth very much.

Simone Weil 1909–43: *L'Enracinement* (1949)

18 The rights of man come not from the generosity of the state, but from the hand of God.

John F. Kennedy 1917–63: inaugural address, 20 January 1961

19 Better to light a candle than curse the darkness.

Peter Benenson 1921–2005: the founder of Amnesty International, at a Human Rights Day ceremony, 10 December 1961; see ACTION 5

20 We have talked long enough in this country about equal rights. We have talked for a hundred years or more. It is time now to write the next chapter, and to write it in the books of law.

Lyndon Baines Johnson 1908–73: speech to Congress, 27 November 1963

21 We could live in a world which is airy-fairy, libertarian, where everybody does precisely what they like and we believe the best of everybody and then they destroy us.

David Blunkett 1947– : interview on London Weekend Television, 11 November 2001; see IDEALISM 2

Humility

see PRIDE AND HUMILITY

Humour

see also WIT

phrases ▶

1 collapse of Stout Party

standard dénouement in Victorian humour; *stout party* = a fat person; the phrase is supposed to come from *Punch*, as the characteristic finishing line of a joke, but no actual example has been traced

2 Homeric laughter

irrepressible laughter, proverbially like that of Homer's gods in the *Iliad* as they watched lame Hephaestus hobbling

3 a merry Andrew

a comic entertainer; a buffoon, a clown. The suggestion of the antiquary Thomas Hearne (1678–1735) that the original 'merry Andrew' was the traveller and physician Dr Andrew Boorde (1490?–1549) is thought improbable

quotations ►

4 A merry heart doeth good like a medicine.

Bible: Proverbs; see MEDICINE 4

5 Delight hath a joy in it either permanent or present. Laughter hath only a scornful tickling.

Philip Sidney 1554–86: *The Defence of Poetry* (1595)

6 I love such mirth as does not make friends ashamed to look upon one another next morning.

Izaak Walton 1593–1683: *The Compleat Angler* (1653)

7 We must laugh before we are happy, for fear of dying without having laughed at all.

Jean de la Bruyère 1645–96: *Les Caractères ou les moeurs de ce siècle* (1688)

8 Life is a jest; and all things show it.
I thought so once; but now I know it.

John Gay 1685–1732: 'My Own Epitaph' (1720)

9 I make myself laugh at everything, for fear of having to weep at it.

Pierre-Augustin Caron de Beaumarchais 1732–99: *Le Barbier de Séville* (1775)

10 Of all days, the one most surely wasted is the one on which one has not laughed.

Nicolas-Sébastien Chamfort 1741–94: *Maximes et Pensées* (1796)

11 We are not amused.

Queen Victoria 1819–1901: attributed; Caroline Holland *Notebooks of a Spinster Lady* (1919) 2 January 1900

12 Against the assault of laughter nothing can stand.

Mark Twain 1835–1910: *The Mysterious Stranger* (1916)

13 Everything is funny as long as it is happening to Somebody Else.

Will Rogers 1879–1935: *The Illiterate Digest* (1924)

14 Fun is fun but no girl wants to laugh all of the time.

Anita Loos 1893–1981: *Gentlemen Prefer Blondes* (1925)

15 What do you mean, funny? Funny-peculiar or funny ha-ha?

Ian Hay 1876–1952: *The Housemaster* (1938)

16 Whatever is funny is subversive, every joke is ultimately a custard pie...A dirty joke is a sort of mental rebellion.

George Orwell 1903–50: in *Horizon* September 1941 'The Art of Donald McGill'

17 The funniest thing about comedy is that you never know why people laugh. I know *what* makes them laugh but trying to get your hands on the *why* of it is like trying to pick an eel out of a tub of water.

W. C. Fields 1880–1946: R. J. Anobile *A Flask of Fields* (1972)

18 Good taste and humour...are a contradiction in terms, like a chaste whore.

Malcolm Muggeridge 1903–90: in *Time* 14 September 1953

19 Laughter would be bereaved if snobbery died.

Peter Ustinov 1921–2004: in *Observer* 13 March 1955

20 Freud's theory was that when a joke opens a window and all those bats and bogeymen fly out, you get a marvellous feeling of relief and elation. The trouble with Freud is that he never had to play the old Glasgow Empire on a Saturday night after Rangers and Celtic had both lost.

Ken Dodd 1927– : in *Guardian* 30 April 1991; quoted in many, usually much contracted, forms since the mid-1960s

21 The marvellous thing about a joke with a double meaning is that it can only mean one thing.

Ronnie Barker 1929–2005: *Sauce* (1977)

22 Comedy is tragedy plus time.

Carol Burnett 1936– : frequent saying, quoting her mother; *One More Time* (1987)

23 Comedy is tragedy that happens to *other* people.

Angela Carter 1940–92: *Wise Children* (1991)

Hunting, Shooting, and Fishing

proverbs and sayings ▸

1 The bleating of the lamb excites the tiger.
Indian proverb; quoted by Kipling in the form 'The bleating of the kid…'

2 The gods do not subtract from a man's allotted span the time spent fishing.
modern saying, sometimes claimed to have originated in an Assyrian tablet

phrases ▸

3 big five
a name given by hunters to the five largest and most dangerous of the African mammals: rhinoceros, elephant, buffalo, lion, and leopard.

4 the one that got away
traditional angler's description of a large fish that just eluded capture; from the comment 'you should have seen the one that got away'

quotations ▸

5 As no man is born an artist, so no man is born an angler.
Izaak Walton 1593–1683: *The Compleat Angler* (1653)

6 Most of their discourse was about hunting, in a dialect I understand very little.
Samuel Pepys 1633–1703: diary, 22 November 1663

7 The dusky night rides down the sky,
And ushers in the morn;
The hounds all join in glorious cry,
The huntsman winds his horn:
And a-hunting we will go.
Henry Fielding 1707–54: *Don Quixote in England* (1733)

8 The sport of kings;
Image of war, without its guilt.
William Somerville 1675–1742: *The Chase* (1735); see HUNTING 12, SPORTS 9

9 Fly fishing may be a very pleasant amusement; but angling or float fishing I can only compare to a stick and a string, with a worm at one end and a fool at the other.
Samuel Johnson 1709–84: attributed; Hawker *Instructions to Young Sportsmen* (1859); also attributed to Jonathan Swift, in *The Indicator* 27 October 1819

10 It is very strange, and very melancholy, that the paucity of human pleasures should persuade us ever to call hunting one of them.
Samuel Johnson 1709–84: Hester Lynch Piozzi *Anecdotes of…Johnson* (1786)

11 D'ye ken John Peel with his coat so grey?
D'ye ken John Peel at the break of the day?
D'ye ken John Peel when he's far far away
With his hounds and his horn in the morning?
John Woodcock Graves 1795–1886: 'John Peel' (1820)

12 'Unting is all that's worth living for—all time is lost wot is not spent in 'unting—it is like the hair we breathe—if we have it not we die—it's the sport of kings, the image of war without its guilt, and only five-and-twenty per cent of its danger.
R. S. Surtees 1805–64: *Handley Cross* (1843); see HUNTING 8

13 The English country gentleman galloping after a fox—the unspeakable in full pursuit of the uneatable.
Oscar Wilde 1854–1900: *A Woman of No Importance* (1893)

14 When a man wants to murder a tiger he calls it sport; when a tiger wants to murder him, he calls it ferocity.
George Bernard Shaw 1856–1950: *Man and Superman* (1903)

15 The fascination of shooting as a sport depends almost wholly on whether you are at the right or wrong end of the gun.
P. G. Wodehouse 1881–1975: *Mr Mulliner Speaking* (1929)

16 A sportsman is a man who, every now and then, simply has to get out and kill something. Not that he's cruel. He wouldn't hurt a fly. It's not big enough.
Stephen Leacock 1869–1944: *My Remarkable Uncle* (1942)

17 It has always been my private conviction that any man who pits his intelligence against a fish and loses has it coming.
John Steinbeck 1902–68: in *Punch* 25 August 1954

18 All men are equal before fish.
Herbert Hoover 1874–1964: *Addresses Upon The American Road* (1955)

19 Fishing is unquestionably a form of madness but, happily, for the once-bitten there is no cure.
Lord Home 1903–95: *The Way the Wind Blows* (1976)

20 If fishing is a religion, fly fishing is high church.
Tom Brokaw 1940– : in *International Herald Tribune* 10 September 1991

Hypocrisy

see also DECEPTION

proverbs and sayings ▸

1 Do as I say, not as I do.
often used to imply hypocrisy; English proverb, mid 16th century

phrases ▸

2 curry favour with
ingratiate oneself with someone through obsequious behaviour; from an alteration of Middle English *curry favel*, from the name (*Favel* or *Fauvel*) of a chestnut horse in a 14th-century French romance who became a symbol of cunning and duplicity; hence 'to rub down Favel' meant to use the cunning which he personified

3 holier than thou
characterized by an attitude of self-conscious virtue and piety, from the Bible (Isaiah) 'Stand by thyself, come not near to me; for I am holier than thou'

4 holy Willie
a pious hypocrite, from Robert Burns's poem 'Holy Willie's Prayer' (1785)

5 shed crocodile tears
put on a display of insincere grief; from the belief that crocodiles wept while devouring or luring their prey

6 a whited sepulchre
a hypocrite, an ostensibly virtuous or pleasant person who is inwardly corrupt; from the Bible (Matthew): see HYPOCRISY 10

quotations ▸

7 Woe unto them that call evil good, and good evil.
Bible: Isaiah

8 My tongue swore, but my mind's unsworn.
on his breaking of an oath
Euripides *c.*485–*c.*406 BC: *Hippolytus*

9 Beware of false prophets, which come to you in sheep's clothing, but inwardly they are ravening wolves.
Bible: St Matthew; see DECEPTION 10

10 Ye are like unto whited sepulchres, which indeed appear beautiful outward, but are within full of dead men's bones, and of all uncleanness.
Bible: St Matthew; see HYPOCRISY 6

11 I want that glib and oily art
To speak and purpose not.
William Shakespeare 1564–1616: *King Lear* (1605–6)

12 For neither man nor angel can discern
Hypocrisy, the only evil that walks
Invisible, except to God alone.
John Milton 1608–74: *Paradise Lost* (1667)

13 Hypocrisy is a tribute which vice pays to virtue.
Duc de la Rochefoucauld 1613–80: *Maximes* (1678)

14 Keep up appearances; there lies the test;
The world will give thee credit for the rest.
Outward be fair, however foul within;
Sin if thou wilt, but then in secret sin.
Charles Churchill 1731–64: *Night* (1761)

15 I sit on a man's back, choking him and making him carry me, and yet assure myself and others that I am very sorry for him and wish to ease his lot by all possible means—except by getting off his back.
Leo Tolstoy 1828–1910: *What Then Must We Do?* (1886)

16 Hypocrisy is the most difficult and nerve-racking vice that any man

can pursue; it needs an unceasing vigilance and a rare detachment of spirit. It cannot, like adultery or gluttony, be practised at spare moments; it is a whole-time job.
W. Somerset Maugham 1874–1965: *Cakes and Ale* (1930)

17 All Reformers, however strict their social conscience, live in houses just as big as they can pay for.
Logan Pearsall Smith 1865–1946: *Afterthoughts* (1931) 'Other People'

18 What makes it so plausible to assume that hypocrisy is the vice of vices is that integrity can indeed exist under the cover of all other vices except this one. Only crime and the criminal, it is true, confront us with the perplexity of radical evil; but only the hypocrite is really rotten to the core.
Hannah Arendt 1906–75: *On Revolution* (1963)

Hypothesis and Fact

see also SCIENCE

proverbs and sayings ▸

1 The exception proves the rule.
originally this meant that the recognition of something as an exception proved the existence of a rule, but it is now more often used or understood as justifying divergence from a rule; see HYPOTHESIS 6; English proverb, mid 17th century

2 Facts are stubborn things.
used to indicate a core of reality that cannot be adjusted to people's wishes; English proverb, early 18th century

3 Nullius in verba.
Latin, *In the word of none*, motto of the Royal Society, emphasizing reliance on experiment rather than authority; adapted from Horace *Epistles*; see LIBERTY 6

4 One story is good till another is told.
doubt may be cast on an apparently convincing account by a second told from a different angle; English proverb, late 16th century

5 The proof of the pudding is in the eating.
the truth of an assertion will be demonstrated by how things actually turn out; *proof* here means 'test'; English proverb, early 14th century

6 There is an exception to every rule.
English proverb, late 16th century; see HYPOTHESIS 1

phrases ▸

7 chapter and verse
exact reference or authority; the precise reference for a passage of Scripture

8 dot the i's and cross the t's
particularize minutely, complete in every detail

quotations ▸

9 *Hypotheses non fingo.*
I do not feign hypotheses.
Isaac Newton 1642–1727: *Principia Mathematica* (1713 ed.)

10 It may be so, there is no arguing against facts and experiments.
when told of an experiment which appeared to destroy his theory
Isaac Newton 1642–1727: reported by John Conduit, 1726; D. Brewster *Memoirs of Sir Isaac Newton* (1855)

11 It is the nature of an hypothesis, when once a man has conceived it, that it assimilates every thing to itself, as proper nourishment; and, from the first moment of your begetting it, it generally grows the stronger by every thing you see, hear, read, or understand.
Laurence Sterne 1713–68: *Tristram Shandy* (1759–67)

12 Nothing is too wonderful to be true, if it be consistent with the laws of nature, and in such things as these, experiment is the best test of such consistency.
Michael Faraday 1791–1867: diary, 19 March 1849

13 Now, what I want is, Facts...Facts alone are wanted in life.
Charles Dickens 1812–70: *Hard Times* (1854)

14 False views, if supported by some evidence, do little harm, for everyone takes a salutary pleasure in proving their falseness.
Charles Darwin 1809–82: *The Descent of Man* (1871)

15 It is a capital mistake to theorize before you have all the evidence. It biases the judgement.
Arthur Conan Doyle 1859–1930: *A Study in Scarlet* (1888)

16 The great tragedy of Science—the slaying of a beautiful hypothesis by an ugly fact.

T. H. Huxley 1825–95: *Collected Essays* (1893–4) 'Biogenesis and Abiogenesis'

17 Roundabout the accredited and orderly facts of every science there ever floats a sort of dust cloud of exceptional observations, of occurrences minute and irregular and seldom met with, which it always proves more easy to ignore than to attend to.

William James 1842–1910: *The Will to Believe* (1897)

18 Get your facts first, and then you can distort 'em as much as you please.

Mark Twain 1835–1910: Rudyard Kipling *From Sea to Sea* (1899)

19 The best scale for an experiment is 12 inches to a foot.

John Arbuthnot Fisher 1841–1920: *Memories* (1919)

20 Facts do not cease to exist because they are ignored.

Aldous Huxley 1894–1963: *Proper Studies* (1927)

21 When the facts change, I change my mind.

John Maynard Keynes 1883–1946: in the 1930s, attributed; Alfred L. Malabre *Lost Prophets* (1994)

22 I don't think that makes any difference. A door-opener for the Communist party is worse than a member of the Communist party. When someone walks like a duck, swims like a duck, and quacks like a duck, he's a duck.

James B. Carey 1911–73: in *New York Times* 3 September 1948

23 The grand aim of all science [is] to cover the greatest number of empirical facts by logical deduction from the smallest possible number of hypotheses or axioms.

Albert Einstein 1879–1955: Lincoln Barnett *The Universe and Dr Einstein* (1950 ed.)

24 Aristotle maintained that women have fewer teeth than men; although he was twice married, it never occurred to him to verify this statement by examining his wives' mouths.

Bertrand Russell 1872–1970: *The Impact of Science on Society* (1952)

25 I think that only daring speculation can lead us further and not accumulation of facts.

Albert Einstein 1879–1955: letter to Michele Besso, 8 October 1952

26 It is a good morning exercise for a research scientist to discard a pet hypothesis every day before breakfast. It keeps him young.

Konrad Lorenz 1903–89: *Das Sogenannte Böse* (1963; translated by Marjorie Latzke as *On Aggression*, 1966)

27 An experiment is a device to make Nature speak intelligibly. After that one has only to listen.

George Wald 1904–97: in *Science* vol. 162 (1968)

28 If an elderly but distinguished scientist says that something is possible he is almost certainly right, but if he says that it is impossible he is very probably wrong.

Arthur C. Clarke 1917–2008: in *New Yorker* 9 August 1969; see HYPOTHESIS 30

29 All models are wrong but some are useful.

George Box 1919– : 'Robustness in the strategy of scientific model building' in R. L. Launer and G. N. Wilkinson (eds.) *Robustness in Statistics* (1979)

30 When, however, the lay public rallies around an idea that is denounced by distinguished but elderly scientists and supports that idea with great fervour and emotion—the distinguished but elderly scientists are then, after all, probably right.

corollary to Arthur C. Clarke's law; see HYPOTHESIS 28

Isaac Asimov 1920–92: Arthur C. Clarke 'Asimov's Corollary' in K. Frazier (ed.) *Paranormal Borderlands of Science* (1981)

31 Extraordinary claims require extraordinary evidence.

Carl Sagan 1934–96: *Billions and Billions: Thoughts on Life and Death at the Brink of the Millennium* (1997)

32 We have not found any smoking guns.
of weapons inspections in Iraq
Hans Blix 1928– : in *Newsweek* 20 January 2003; see SECRECY 23

33 What can be asserted without evidence can also be dismissed without evidence.
Christopher Hitchens 1949– : in *Slate Magazine* 20 October 2003

Idealism
see also HOPE

proverbs and sayings ▸

1 Vision without action is a daydream. Action without vision is a nightmare.
recommending a balance between idealism and reality; modern saying, said to derive from a Japanese proverb; see ACTION 35

phrases ▸

2 airy-fairy
impractical and foolishly idealistic. The phrase, originally used to mean 'delicate or light as a fairy', derives from Tennyson's 'airy, fairy Lilian' *(Lilian*, 1830); see HUMAN RIGHTS 21

3 flower power
the ideas of the flower people, hippies who wore flowers as symbols of peace and love; especially the promotion of these as a means of changing the world

4 starry-eyed
idealistic, uplifted, romantic

5 the vision thing
a political view encompassing the longer term, from the comment by George Bush: see IDEALISM 18

quotations ▸

6 Where there is no vision, the people perish.
Bible: Proverbs

7 Love and a cottage! Eh, Fanny! Ah, give me indifference and a coach and six!
George Colman, the Elder 1732–94 and **David Garrick** 1717–79: *The Clandestine Marriage* (1766); see LOVE 45, MARRIAGE 15

8 Hitch your wagon to a star.
Ralph Waldo Emerson 1803–82: *Society and Solitude* (1870)

9 We are all in the gutter, but some of us are looking at the stars.
Oscar Wilde 1854–1900: *Lady Windermere's Fan* (1892)

10 I am an idealist. I don't know where I'm going but I'm on the way.
Carl Sandburg 1878–1967: *Incidentals* (1907)

11 A cause may be inconvenient, but it's magnificent. It's like champagne or high heels, and one must be prepared to suffer for it.
Arnold Bennett 1867–1931: *The Title* (1918)

12 When they come downstairs from their Ivory Towers, Idealists are very apt to walk straight into the gutter.
Logan Pearsall Smith 1865–1946: *Afterthoughts* (1931) 'Other People'; see REALITY 6

13 The first thing a man will do for his ideals is lie.
J. A. Schumpeter 1883–1950: *History of Economic Analysis* (1954)

14 I submit to you that if a man hasn't discovered something he will die for, he isn't fit to live.
Martin Luther King 1929–68: speech in Detroit, 23 June 1963

15 To dream the impossible dream,
To reach the unreachable star!
Joe Darion 1917–2001: 'The Quest' (1965 song)

16 Each time a man stands up for an ideal, or acts to improve the lot of others, or strikes out against injustice, he sends forth a tiny ripple of hope, and crossing each other from a million different centres of energy and daring those ripples build a current which can sweep down the mightiest walls of oppression and resistance.
Robert Kennedy 1925–68: speech, Cape Town, 6 June 1966

17 I'm not a dreamer...but I believe in miracles. I have to.
planning a fund-raising run across Canada; he completed two thirds of his 'Marathon of Hope'
Terry Fox 1958–81: letter to the Canadian Cancer Society, 15 October 1979

18 Oh, the vision thing.
responding to the suggestion that he turn his attention from short-term campaign objectives and look to the longer term
George Bush 1924– : in *Time* 26 January 1987; see IDEALISM 5

19 We Americans used to say that the American Dream is worth dying for. The new European Dream is worth living for.
Jeremy Rifkin 1945– : *The European Dream: How Europe's vision of the Future is Quietly Eclipsing the American Dream* (2004); see AMERICA 3

Ideas

see also HYPOTHESIS, MIND, PROBLEMS, THINKING

proverbs and sayings ▸

1 I have a cunning plan.
Baldrick's habitual overoptimistic promise, first used in *Blackadder II* (1987 television series, written by Richard Curtis and Ben Elton)

2 There is one thing stronger than all the armies in the world; and that is an idea whose time has come.
mid 20th century saying; see IDEAS 8

phrases ▸

3 invita Minerva
lacking inspiration; Latin = *Minerva* (the goddess of wisdom) unwilling

4 King Charles's head
an obsession, an *idée fixe*; with reference to 'Mr Dick', in Dickens's *David Copperfield* (1850), who could not write or speak on any subject without King Charles's head intruding

quotations ▸

5 New opinions are always suspected, and usually opposed, without any other reason but because they are not already common.
John Locke 1632–1704: *An Essay concerning Human Understanding* (1690)

6 General notions are generally wrong.
Lady Mary Wortley Montagu 1689–1762: letter to Edward Wortley Montagu, 28 March 1710

7 He who receives an idea from me, receives instruction himself without lessening mine; as he who lights his taper at mine, receives light without darkening me.
Thomas Jefferson 1743–1826: letter to Isaac McPherson, 13 August 1813

8 A stand can be made against invasion by an army; no stand can be made against invasion by an idea.
Victor Hugo 1802–85: *Histoire d'un Crime* (written 1851–2, published 1877); see IDEAS 2

9 Every now and then a man's mind is stretched by a new idea or sensation, and never shrinks back to its former dimensions.
Oliver Wendell Holmes 1809–94: *Autocrat of the Breakfast-Table* (1858)

10 I share no one's ideas. I have my own.
Ivan Turgenev 1818–83: *Fathers and Sons* (1862)

11 You see things; and you say 'Why?' But I dream things that never were; and I say 'Why not?'
George Bernard Shaw 1856–1950: *Back to Methuselah* (1921)

12 Marvellous, what ideas the young people have these days. But I don't believe a word of it.
of the uncertainty principle
Albert Einstein 1879–1955: in 1927; see PHYSICAL 9

13 Nothing is more dangerous than an idea, when you have only one idea.
Alain 1868–1951: *Propos sur la religion* (1938)

14 *Ideas won't keep.* Something must be done about them.
Alfred North Whitehead 1861–1947: *Dialogues* (1954) 28 April 1938

15 No grand idea was ever born in a conference, but a lot of foolish ideas have died there.
F. Scott Fitzgerald 1896–1940: Edmund Wilson (ed.) *The Crack-Up* (1945) 'Note-Books E'

16 Madmen in authority, who hear voices in the air, are distilling their frenzy from some academic scribbler of a few years back.
John Maynard Keynes 1883–1946: *General Theory* (1947 ed.)

17 It is better to entertain an idea than to take it home to live with you for the rest of your life.
Randall Jarrell 1914–65: *Pictures from an Institution* (1954)

18 No ideas but in things.
William Carlos Williams 1883–1963: *Autobiography* (1967)

19 Hang on a minute lads, I've got a great idea.
Troy Kennedy-Martin 1932–2009: *The Italian Job* (1969 film); final words, spoken by Michael Caine as Charlie Croker

20 The English approach to ideas is not to kill them, but to let them die of neglect.
Jeremy Paxman 1950– : *The English: a portrait of a people* (1998)

Idleness

see also ACTION, WORDS AND DEEDS

proverbs and sayings ▸

1 As good be an addled egg as an idle bird.
an idle person will produce nothing; English proverb, late 16th century

2 Better to wear out than to rust out.
it is better to remain active than to succumb to idleness; in this form frequently attributed to Richard Cumberland, Bishop of Peterborough (1631–1718); English proverb, mid 16th century

3 The devil finds work for idle hands to do.
someone who has no work to do will get into mischief; English proverb, early 18th century

4 An idle brain is the devil's workshop.
those who do not apply themselves to their work are most likely to get into trouble; English proverb, early 17th century

5 Idle people have the least leisure.
lazy people are the least able to manage their time efficiently; English proverb, late 17th century

6 Idleness is never enjoyable unless there is plenty to do.
American proverb, mid 20th century: see IDLENESS 20

7 Idleness is the root of all evil.
English proverb, early 15th century; the idea has been attributed to the French theologian, monastic reformer, and abbot St Bernard of Clairvaux (1090–1153); see MONEY 28

8 If you won't work you shan't eat.
essential sustenance is seen as a reward for industry; English proverb, mid 16th century, from the Bible: see WORK 22

9 Who is more busy than he who hath least to do?
English proverb, early 17th century

phrases ▸

10 the bread of idleness
food or sustenance for which one has not worked, after the Bible (Proverbs) 'She…eateth not the bread of idleness'

11 lotus-eater
a person who spends their time indulging in pleasure and luxury rather than dealing with practical concerns. The *lotus-eaters* in Greek mythology were a people who lived on the fruit of the lotus, said to cause a dreamy forgetfulness and an unwillingness to depart; see IDLENESS 17

quotations ▸

12 Go to the ant thou sluggard; consider her ways, and be wise.
Bible: Proverbs

13 He that would thrive
Must rise at five;
He that hath thriven
May lie till seven.
John Clarke d. 1658: 'Diligentia' (1639)

14 Idleness is only the refuge of weak minds.
Lord Chesterfield 1694–1773: *Letters to his Son* (1774) 20 July 1749

15 If you are idle, be not solitary; if you are solitary, be not idle.
Samuel Johnson 1709–84: letter to Boswell, 27 October 1779

16 A man who has nothing to do with his own time has no conscience in his intrusion on that of others.
Jane Austen 1775–1817: *Sense and Sensibility* (1811)

17 Surely, surely, slumber is more sweet
than toil, the shore

Than labour in the deep mid-ocean, wind and wave and oar;
Oh rest ye, brother mariners, we will not wander more.
Alfred, Lord Tennyson 1809–92: 'The Lotos-Eaters' (1832); see IDLENESS 11

18 How dull it is to pause, to make an end,
To rust unburnished, not to shine in use!
As though to breathe were life.
Alfred, Lord Tennyson 1809–92: 'Ulysses' (1842)

19 Never do to-day what you can put off till to-morrow.
Punch: in 1849

20 It is impossible to enjoy idling thoroughly unless one has plenty of work to do.
Jerome K. Jerome 1859–1927: *Idle Thoughts of an Idle Fellow* (1886); see IDLENESS 6

21 Oh! how I hate to get up in the morning,
Oh! how I'd love to remain in bed.
Irving Berlin 1888–1989: *Oh! How I Hate to Get Up in the Morning* (1918 song)

22 The time you enjoy wasting is not wasted time.
commenting on a remark by Bertrand Russell; frequently attributed to Russell
Laurence J. Peter 1919–90: *Quotations for Our Time* (1977)

23 I was raised to feel that doing nothing was a sin. I had to learn to do nothing.
Jenny Joseph 1932– : in *Observer* 19 April 1998

Ignorance

proverbs and sayings ▸

1 The husband is always the last to know.
relating to marital infidelity; English proverb, early 17th century

2 Ignorance is a voluntary misfortune.
one has chosen not to remedy the condition; American proverb, mid 20th century

3 Ignorance is bliss.
English proverb, mid 18th century, from Gray: see IGNORANCE 19

4 It is dark at the foot of the lighthouse.
we often miss what is closest to us; Japanese proverb

5 The less you know, the better you sleep.
Russian saying of the Soviet era

6 Man is the enemy of that of which he is ignorant.
fear is a common response to the unknown; Arab proverb

7 Nothing so bold as a blind mare.
those who know least about a situation are least likely to be deterred by it; English proverb, early 17th century

8 A slice off a cut loaf isn't missed.
if something has already been diminished or damaged, further damage may go unnoticed; English proverb, late 16th century (first recorded in Shakespeare's *Titus Andronicus*, 1592)

9 What the eye doesn't see, the heart doesn't grieve over.
now sometimes used with the implication that information is being withheld to prevent difficulties; English proverb, mid 16th century

10 What you don't know can't hurt you.
English proverb, late 16th century

11 When the blind lead the blind, both shall fall into the ditch.
when a person is guided by someone equally inexperienced, both are likely to come to grief; English proverb, late 9th century, from the Bible: see LEADERSHIP 11

phrases ▸

12 all Greek to me
completely unintelligible; *Greek* for unintelligible language or gibberish is recorded from the late 16th century; see IGNORANCE 17

13 invincible ignorance
in theological terms, ignorance which the person concerned does not have the means to overcome; translation of scholastic Latin *ignorantia invincibilis*, in the *Summa Theologiae* of Thomas Aquinas

14 turn a Nelson eye to
turn a blind eye to, overlook, pretend ignorance of. Horatio *Nelson* (1758–1805), British admiral, was killed in the battle of Trafalgar, having suffered the loss of an eye and an arm in earlier conflicts: see DETERMINATION 35

quotations ▶

15 I see no other single hindrance such as this hindrance of ignorance, obstructed by which mankind for a long long time runs on and circles on.
Pali Tripitaka 2nd century BC: *Itivuttaka* [Thus Was Said]

16 If one does not know to which port one is sailing, no wind is favourable.
Seneca ('the Younger') c.4 BC–AD 65: *Epistulae Morales*

17 But those that understood him smiled at one another and shook their heads; but, for mine own part, it was Greek to me.
William Shakespeare 1564–1616: *Julius Caesar* (1599); see IGNORANCE 12

18 Lo! the poor Indian, whose untutored mind
Sees God in clouds, or hears him in the wind.
Alexander Pope 1688–1744: *An Essay on Man* Epistle 1 (1733)

19 Where ignorance is bliss,
'Tis folly to be wise.
Thomas Gray 1716–71: *Ode on a Distant Prospect of Eton College* (1747); see IGNORANCE 3

20 Ignorance, madam, pure ignorance.
on being asked why he had defined *pastern* as the 'knee' of a horse
Samuel Johnson 1709–84: James Boswell *Life of Samuel Johnson* (1791) 1755

21 Ignorance is preferable to error; and he is less remote from the truth who believes nothing, than he who believes what is wrong.
Thomas Jefferson 1743–1826: *Notes on the State of Virginia* (1781–5)

22 For most men, an ignorant enjoyment is better than an informed one; it is better to conceive the sky as a blue dome than a dark cavity; and the cloud as a golden throne than a sleety mist.
John Ruskin 1819–1900: *Modern Painters* (1856)

23 Ignorance more frequently begets confidence than does knowledge: it is those who know little, and not those who know much, who so positively assert that this or that problem will never be solved by science.
Charles Darwin 1809–82: *The Descent of Man* (1871)

24 Ignorance is not innocence but sin.
Robert Browning 1812–89: *The Inn Album* (1875)

25 *Only* ignorance! How can you talk about only *ignorance*! Don't you know that it is the worst thing in the world next to wickedness.
Anna Sewell 1820–78: *Black Beauty* (1877)

26 Ignorance is like a delicate exotic fruit; touch it and the bloom is gone.
Oscar Wilde 1854–1900: *The Importance of Being Earnest* (1895)

27 I know nothing—nobody tells me anything.
John Galsworthy 1867–1933: *Man of Property* (1906)

28 You know everybody is ignorant, only on different subjects.
Will Rogers 1879–1935: in *New York Times* 31 August 1924

29 Happy the hare at morning, for she cannot read
The Hunter's waking thoughts.
W. H. Auden 1907–73: *Dog beneath the Skin* (with Christopher Isherwood, 1935)

30 Ignorance is an evil weed, which dictators may cultivate among their dupes, but which no democracy can afford among its citizens.
William Henry Beveridge 1879–1963: *Full Employment in a Free Society* (1944)

31 As any fule kno.
Geoffrey Willans 1911–58 and **Ronald Searle** 1920– : *Down with Skool!* (1953)

32 Nothing in all the world is more dangerous than sincere ignorance and conscientious stupidity.
Martin Luther King 1929–68: *Strength to Love* (1963)

33 A bishop wrote gravely to the *Times* inviting all nations to destroy 'the formula' of the atomic bomb. There is no simple remedy for ignorance so abysmal.
Peter Medawar 1915–87: *The Hope of Progress* (1972)

34 It was absolutely marvellous working for Pauli. You could ask him anything. There was no worry that he would think a particular question was stupid, since he thought *all* questions were stupid.
Victor Weisskopf 1908–2002: in *American Journal of Physics* 1977

35 Learn to say, 'I don't know.' If used when appropriate, it will be often.
Donald Rumsfeld 1932– : 'Rumsfeld's Rules' (2001)

Imagination

phrases ▸

1 build castles in the air
form unsubstantial or visionary projects

2 a castle in Spain
a visionary project, a daydream unlikely to be realized; the expression is recorded from late Middle English, and it is possible that *Spain*, as the nearest Moorish country to Christendom, was taken as the type of a region in which the prospective castle-builder had no standing

3 the vision splendid
the dream of some glorious imagined time; from Wordsworth 'And by the vision splendid is on his way attended'

quotations ▸

4 For the imagination of man's heart is evil from his youth.
Bible: Genesis

5 The lunatic, the lover, and the poet,
Are of imagination all compact.
William Shakespeare 1564–1616: *A Midsummer Night's Dream* (1595–6)

6 Though our brother is on the rack, as long as we ourselves are at our ease, our senses will never inform us of what he suffers...It is by imagination that we can form any conception of what are his sensations.
Adam Smith 1723–90: *Theory of Moral Sentiments* (2nd ed., 1762)

7 Were it not for imagination, Sir, a man would be as happy in the arms of a chambermaid as of a Duchess.
Samuel Johnson 1709–84: James Boswell *Life of Samuel Johnson* (1791) 9 May 1778

8 Whither is fled the visionary gleam?
Where is it now, the glory and the dream?
William Wordsworth 1770–1850: 'Ode. Intimations of Immortality' (1807)

9 The same that oft-times hath
Charmed magic casements, opening on the foam
Of perilous seas, in faery lands forlorn.
John Keats 1795–1821: 'Ode to a Nightingale' (1820)

10 His imagination resembled the wings of an ostrich. It enabled him to run, though not to soar.
Lord Macaulay 1800–59: T. F. Ellis (ed.) *Miscellaneous Writings of Lord Macaulay* (1860) 'John Dryden' (1828)

11 I dreamed that I dwelt in marble halls
With vassals and serfs at my side.
Alfred Bunn c.1796–1860: *The Bohemian Girl* (1843) 'The Gipsy Girl's Dream'; see LIKES 11

12 Where there is no imagination there is no horror.
Arthur Conan Doyle 1859–1930: *A Study in Scarlet* (1888)

13 Must then a Christ perish in torment in every age to save those that have no imagination?
George Bernard Shaw 1856–1950: *Saint Joan* (1924)

14 Imagination is more important than knowledge.
Albert Einstein 1879–1955: in *Saturday Evening Post* 26 October 1929

15 The imagination is man's power over nature.
Wallace Stevens 1879–1955: 'Adagia' (1959)

16 When the imagination sleeps, words are emptied of their meaning.
Albert Camus 1913–60: *Resistance, Rebellion and Death* (1961)

17 Imagination is the highest kite that can fly.
Lauren Bacall 1924– : *Lauren Bacall by Myself* (1979)

18 Fantasy is like an exercise bicycle for the mind.
Terry Pratchett 1948– : Leonard S. Marcus *The Wand in the Word* (2006)

Inaction

see ACTION AND INACTION

Inconstancy

see CONSTANCY AND INCONSTANCY

Indecision

see also CERTAINTY

proverbs and sayings ▸

1 **Between two stools one falls to the ground.**
inability to choose between, or accommodate oneself to, alternative viewpoints or courses of action may end in disaster; English proverb, late 14th century

2 **The cat would eat fish, but would not wet her feet.**
commenting on a situation in which desire for something is checked by unwillingness to risk discomfort in acquiring it; English proverb, early 13th century

3 **Councils of war never fight.**
people discussing matters in a group never reach the decision to fight, which an individual would make; English proverb, mid 19th century

4 **First thoughts are best.**
advice to trust an instinctive reaction, often used as a warning against indecision; English proverb, early 20th century

5 **He who hesitates is lost.**
often used to urge decisive action on someone; English proverb, early 18th century, early usages refer specifically to women, as in Addison *Cato* (1713) 'The woman that deliberates is lost'

6 **If you run after two hares you will catch neither.**
one must decide on one's goal; English proverb, early 16th century

phrases ▸

7 **Buridan's ass**
a paradox whereby a hungry and thirsty donkey, placed between a bundle of hay and a pail of water, would die of hunger and thirst because there was no reason for him to choose one resource over the other. It is said to have been constructed by the French philosopher Jean Buridan (c.1295–c.1358)

8 **fudge and mudge**
evade comment or avoid making a decision on an issue by waffling; apply facile solutions to decisions while trying to appear resolved; coined as a political catchphrase by the Labour politician David Owen in an attack on the leadership of James Callaghan, 'We are fed up with fudging and mudging, with mush and slush. We need courage, conviction, and hard work'

quotations ▸

9 **Now, the melancholy god protect thee, and the tailor make thy doublet of changeable taffeta, for thy mind is a very opal.**
William Shakespeare 1564–1616: *Twelfth Night* (1601)

10 **Then indecision brings its own delays,
And days are lost lamenting o'er lost days.**
Johann Wolfgang von Goethe 1749–1832: *Faust* pt. 1 (1808) as translated by John Anster (1835)

11 **I must have a prodigious quantity of mind; it takes me as much as a week, sometimes, to make it up.**
Mark Twain 1835–1910: *The Innocents Abroad* (1869)

12 **There is no more miserable human being than one in whom nothing is habitual but indecision.**
William James 1842–1910: *The Principles of Psychology* (1890)

13 **The tragedy of a man who could not make up his mind.**
Laurence Olivier 1907–89: introduction to his 1948 screen adaptation of *Hamlet*

14 **I'll give you a definite maybe.**
Sam Goldwyn 1882–1974: attributed

15 **A wrong decision isn't forever; it can always be reversed. The losses from a delayed decision *are* forever; they can never be retrieved.**
J. K. Galbraith 1908–2006: *A Life in our Times* (1981)

16 **The archbishop is usually to be found nailing his colours to the fence.**
of Archbishop Runcie
Frank Field 1942– : attributed in *Crockfords 1987/88* (1987); Geoffrey Madan records in his *Notebooks* a similar comment was made about A. J. Balfour, 1904; see DEFIANCE 8

India

proverbs and sayings ▶

1 **A lass and a lakh a day.**
said to be an after-dinner toast of the East India Company; a *lakh* was 100,000 rupees; see INDIA 2

phrases ▶

2 **John Company**
East India Company: a trading company (informally, John Company) formed in 1600 to develop commerce in the newly colonized areas of SE Asia and India. In the 18th century it took administrative control of Bengal and other areas of India, and held it until the British Crown took over in 1858 in the wake of the Indian Mutiny; see INDIA 1

quotations ▶

3 **If there is a paradise on earth, it is this, it is this, it is this.**
Amir Khusrau 1253–1325: inscribed on the wall of the Diwan-i-Khas [the hall of special audience] in the Red Fort at Delhi

4 **The brightest jewel that now remained in his Majesty's crown.**
on India; see EXCELLENCE 7
Charles James Fox 1749–1806: speech in the House of Commons, 1782; William Cobbett *The Parliamentary History of England* (1814)

5 **Nothing has been left undone, either by man or Nature, to make India the most extraordinary country that the sun visits on his rounds.**
Mark Twain 1835–1910: *Following the Equator* (1897)

6 **Nothing in India is identifiable, the mere asking of a question causes it to disappear or to merge in something else.**
E. M. Forster 1879–1970: *A Passage to India* (1924)

7 **At the stroke of the midnight hour, while the world sleeps, India will awake to life and freedom.**
Jawaharlal Nehru 1889–1964: speech to the Indian Constituent Assembly, 14 August 1947

8 **India will go on.**
R. K. Narayan 1906–2001: remark to V. S. Naipaul in 1961, V. S. Naipaul *India: A Wounded Civilization* (1977)

9 **India...is not a place that one can pick up and put down again as if nothing had happened. In a way it's not so much a country as an experience, and whether it turns out to be a good or a bad one depends, I suppose, on oneself.**
Ruth Prawer Jhabvala 1927– : *Travellers* (1973)

10 **No one can make India kneel.**
after the bombings in Mumbai
Manmohan Singh 1932– : in *Hindu* 12 July 2006

Indifference

proverbs and sayings ▶

1 **Am I bovvered?**
catchphrase of teenager Lauren, in *The Catherine Tate Show* (BBC TV, 2004–6)

phrases ▶

2 **compassion fatigue**
indifference to charitable appeals on behalf of those who are suffering, experienced as a result of the frequency or number of such appeals

3 **leather or prunella**
something to which one is completely indifferent; a misinterpretation of lines from Alexander Pope's *Essay on Man* (1734): 'Worth makes the Man, and want of it the Fellow;/The rest, is all but Leather or Prunella.' In Pope's poem, a distinction is being drawn between the trade of a cobbler (*leather*) and the profession of a clergyman (*prunella* as the material from which a clerical gown is made). The phrase was however taken to denote something of no value

4 **pass by on the other side**
to be indifferent to someone who is suffering; from the story of the good Samaritan in the Bible (Luke); see CHARITY 9, INDIFFERENCE 6

quotations ▶

5 **They have mouths, and speak not: eyes have they, and see not.**
They have ears, and hear not: noses have they, and smell not.
They have hands, and handle not: feet have they, and walk not: neither speak they through their throat.
Bible: Psalm 115

6 He passed by on the other side.
Bible: St Luke; see CHARITY 9, INDIFFERENCE 4

7 All colours will agree in the dark.
Francis Bacon 1561–1626: *Essays* (1625) 'Of Unity in Religion'

8 And this the burthen of his song,
For ever used to be,
I care for nobody, not I,
If no one cares for me.
Isaac Bickerstaffe 1733–c.1808: *Love in a Village* (1762) 'The Miller of Dee'

9 Vacant heart and hand, and eye,—
Easy live and quiet die.
Sir Walter Scott 1771–1832: *The Bride of Lammermoor* (1819)

10 If Jesus Christ were to come to-day, people would not even crucify him. They would ask him to dinner, and hear what he had to say, and make fun of it.
Thomas Carlyle 1795–1881: D. A. Wilson *Carlyle at his Zenith* (1927)

11 The worst sin towards our fellow creatures is not to hate them, but to be indifferent to them: that's the essence of inhumanity.
George Bernard Shaw 1856–1950: *The Devil's Disciple* (1901)

12 Science may have found a cure for most evils; but it has found no remedy for the worst of them all—the apathy of human beings.
Helen Keller 1880–1968: *My Religion* (1927)

13 I wish I could care what you do or where you go but I can't...My dear, I don't give a damn.
'Frankly, my dear, I don't give a damn!' in the 1939 screen version by Sidney Howard
Margaret Mitchell 1900–49: *Gone with the Wind* (1936)

14 Cast a cold eye
On life, on death.
Horseman pass by!
W. B. Yeats 1865–1939: 'Under Ben Bulben' (1939)

15 Catholics and Communists have committed great crimes, but at least they have not stood aside, like an established society, and been indifferent. I would rather have blood on my hands than water like Pilate.
Graham Greene 1904–91: *The Comedians* (1966); see DUTY 9

16 In Germany they came first for the Communists, and I didn't speak up because I wasn't a Communist; and then they came for the trade unionists, and I didn't speak up because I wasn't a trade unionist; and then they came for the Jews, and I didn't speak up because I wasn't a Jew; and then...they came for me... and by that time there was no-one left to speak up.
Martin Niemöller 1892–1984: quoted in many versions since the Second World War; this version, in *'Quote Unquote' Newsletter* April 2001, was approved by Niemöller as the original in 1971

17 I come from a people who gave the ten commandments to the world. Time has come to strengthen them by three additional ones, which we ought to adopt and commit ourselves to: thou shalt not be a perpetrator; thou shalt not be a victim; and thou shalt never, but never, be a bystander.
Yehuda Bauer 1926– : speech to the German Bundestag, 1998, quoted in his own speech to the Stockholm International Forum on the Holocaust, 26 July 2000; see LIFESTYLES 13

Ingratitude

see GRATITUDE AND INGRATITUDE

Innocence

see GUILT AND INNOCENCE

Insight

see also SELF-KNOWLEDGE

proverbs and sayings ▸

1 I pointed out to you the stars and all you saw was the tip of my finger.
African proverb

phrases ▸

2 the penny drops
understanding dawns; referring to the mechanism of a penny-in-the-slot machine

3 **scales fall from a person's eyes**
a person receives sudden enlightenment or revelation; from the Bible (Acts) 'And immediately there fell from his eyes as it had been scales: and he received sight forthwith'

4 **third eye**
in Hinduism and Buddhism, the 'eye of insight' in the forehead of an image of a deity, especially the god Shiva

quotations ▶

5 For the Lord seeth not as man seeth: for man looketh on the outward appearance, but the Lord looketh on the heart.
Bible: I Samuel

6 He—in whose nature, is the ugly disposition
Sees not the peacock,—only his ugly foot.
Sadi c.1213–c.91: *The Bustan* (1257); see SELF-KNOWLEDGE 2

7 Each of us touches one place
and understands the whole in that way.
The palm and the fingers feeling in the dark are
how the senses explore the reality of the elephant.
If each of us held a candle there,
and if we went in together,
we could see it.
on the inferences drawn by men touching different parts of an elephant in the dark
Jalal ad-Din ar-Rumi 1207–73: *Mathnawi*; see KNOWLEDGE 22

8 Everything I have written seems like straw by comparison with what I have seen and what has been revealed to me.
following a mystical experience, after which he did no more teaching or writing
St Thomas Aquinas 1225–74: on 6 December 1273

9 I have striven not to laugh at human actions, not to weep at them, nor to hate them, but to understand them.
Baruch Spinoza 1632–77: *Tractatus Politicus* (1677)

10 If the doors of perception were cleansed everything would appear to man as it is, infinite.
William Blake 1757–1827: *The Marriage of Heaven and Hell* (1790–3)

11 *Tout comprendre rend très indulgent.*
To be totally understanding makes one very indulgent.
Mme de Staël 1766–1817: *Corinne* (1807); see FORGIVENESS 6

12 Every man takes the limits of his own field of vision for the limits of the world.
Arthur Schopenhauer 1788–1860: *Studies in Pessimism* (1851) 'Psychological Observations'

13 The veil of eternity was lifted. The one great truth which underlies all human experience, and is the key to all the mysteries that philosophy has sought in vain to solve, flashed upon me in a sudden revelation...staggering to my desk, I wrote...'*A strong smell of turpentine prevails throughout.*'
of his experiences under the influence of ether
Oliver Wendell Holmes 1809–94: *Mechanism in Thought and Morals* (1871)

14 If we had a keen vision and feeling of all ordinary human life, it would be like hearing the grass grow and the squirrel's heart beat, and we should die of that roar which lies on the other side of silence.
George Eliot 1819–80: *Middlemarch* (1871–2)

15 One sees great things from the valley; only small things from the peak.
G. K. Chesterton 1874–1936: *The Innocence of Father Brown* (1911)

16 [See] things not as they are, but as they might be.
Felix Adler 1851–1933: Kai Bird and Martin J. Sherwin *American Prometheus* (2006)

17 The crown of life is neither happiness nor annihilation; it is understanding.
Winifred Holtby 1898–1935: Vera Brittain *Testament of Friendship: the Story of Winifred Holtby* (1940)

18 The thing that is important is the thing that is not seen.
Antoine de Saint-Exupéry 1900–44: *The Little Prince* (1943), spoken by the Little Prince

19 Come to the edge.
We might fall.
Come to the edge.
It's too high!

COME TO THE EDGE!
And they came
and he pushed
and they flew...

Christopher Logue 1926– : 'Come to the edge' (1969)

20 To understand just one life, you have to swallow the world.

Salman Rushdie 1947– : *Midnight's Children* (1981)

21 The world is like a Mask dancing. If you want to see it well you do not stand in one place.

Chinua Achebe 1930– : *Arrow of God* (1988)

22 If we find the answer to that [why it is that we and the universe exist], it would be the ultimate triumph of human reason—for then we would know the mind of God.

Stephen Hawking 1942– : *A Brief History of Time* (1988)

23 Know what I mean, Harry?

Frank Bruno 1961– : supposed to have been said in interview with sports commentator Harry Carpenter, possibly apocryphal

Insults

proverbs and sayings ▸

1 Don't add insult to injury.

recommending not to treat someone one has hurt with contempt as well; American proverb, mid 18th century

phrases ▸

2 bite one's thumb at

insult by making the gesture of biting one's thumb; in Shakespeare's *Romeo and Juliet* (1595), in a scene between two quarrelling servants, one when challenged says to the other, 'I do not bite my thumb at you, sir; but I bite my thumb, sir'

3 Parthian shot

a final remark, typically a cutting one, made by someone at the moment of departure; so named because of the trick used by *Parthians* of shooting arrows backwards while in real or pretended flight. From *c.*250 BC to *c.*230 AD the Parthians ruled an empire stretching from the Euphrates to the Indus

quotations ▸

4 The devil damn thee black, thou
cream-faced loon!
Where gott'st thou that goose look?

William Shakespeare 1564–1616: *Macbeth* (1606)

5 How easy it is to call rogue and villain, and that wittily! But how hard to make a man appear a fool, a blockhead, or a knave, without using any of those opprobrious terms! To spare the grossness of the names, and to do the thing yet more severely, is to draw a full face, and to make the nose and cheeks stand out, and yet not to employ any depth of shadowing.

John Dryden 1631–1700: *Of Satire* (1693)

6 An injury is much sooner forgotten than an insult.

Lord Chesterfield 1694–1773: *Letters to his Son* (1774) 9 October 1746

7 The words she spoke of Mrs Harris, lambs could not forgive...nor worms forget.

Charles Dickens 1812–70: *Martin Chuzzlewit* (1844)

8 Silence is the most perfect expression of scorn.

George Bernard Shaw 1856–1950: *Back to Methuselah* (1921)

9 JUDGE: You are extremely offensive, young man.
SMITH: As a matter of fact, we both are, and the only difference between us is that I am trying to be, and you can't help it.

F. E. Smith 1872–1930: 2nd Earl of Birkenhead *Earl of Birkenhead* (1933)

10 Okie use' ta mean you was from Oklahoma. Now it means you're a dirty son-of-a-bitch. Okie means you're scum. Don't mean nothing itself, it's the way they say it.

John Steinbeck 1902–68: *The Grapes of Wrath* (1939)

11 BESSIE BRADDOCK: Winston, you're drunk.
CHURCHILL: Bessie, you're ugly. But tomorrow I shall be sober.

Winston Churchill 1874–1965: J. L. Lane (ed.) *Sayings of Churchill* (1992)

12 Like being savaged by a dead sheep.
on being criticized by Geoffrey Howe
Denis Healey 1917– : speech in the House of Commons, 14 June 1978

13 I am proud to be ginger and rodents do valuable work cleaning up mess others leave behind. Red squirrel deserves to survive, unlike Labour.
after Labour deputy leader Harriet Harman called him a 'ginger rodent'
Danny Alexander 1972– : tweet, 30 October 2010

Intelligence and Intellectuals

proverbs and sayings ▸

1 Elementary, my dear Watson.
remark attributed to Sherlock Holmes, but not found in this form in any book by Arthur Conan Doyle; first found in P.G. Wodehouse *Psmith Journalist* (1915)

2 To question and ask is a moment's shame, but to question and not ask is a lifetime's shame.
Japanese proverb

phrases ▸

3 the chattering classes
the articulate professional people given to free expression of (especially liberal) opinions on society and culture

4 know a hawk from a handsaw
have ordinary discernment; now chiefly in allusion to Shakespeare *Hamlet*: see MADNESS 5

5 little grey cells
intelligence; the expression used by Agatha Christie's detective Hercule Poirot; see INTELLIGENCE 14

6 too clever by half
far more clever than is satisfactory or desirable; see INTELLIGENCE 21

7 trahison des clercs
a betrayal of intellectual, artistic, or moral standards by writers, academics, or artists; French, 'treason of the scholars', title of a book by Julien Benda (1927)

quotations ▸

8 Mere cleverness is not wisdom.
Euripides c.485–c.406 BC: *Bacchae*

9 Whoever in discussion adduces authority uses not intellect but rather memory.
Leonardo da Vinci 1452–1519: Edward McCurdy (ed.) *Leonardo da Vinci's Notebooks* (1906)

10 The height of cleverness is to be able to conceal it.
Duc de la Rochefoucauld 1613–80: *Maximes* (1678)

11 You beat your pate, and fancy wit will come:
Knock as you please, there's nobody at home.
Alexander Pope 1688–1744: 'Epigram: You beat your pate' (1732)

12 Sir, I have found you an argument; but I am not obliged to find you an understanding.
Samuel Johnson 1709–84: James Boswell *Life of Samuel Johnson* (1791) June 1784

13 A man is not necessarily intelligent because he has plenty of ideas, any more than he is a good general because he has plenty of soldiers.
Nicolas-Sébastien Chamfort 1741–94: *Maximes et Pensées* (1796)

14 He [Hercule Poirot] tapped his forehead. 'These little grey cells. It is "up to them".'
Agatha Christie 1890–1976: *The Mysterious Affair at Styles* (1920); see INTELLIGENCE 5

15 No one in this world, so far as I know—and I have searched the records for years, and employed agents to help me—has ever lost money by underestimating the intelligence of the great masses of the plain people.
H. L. Mencken 1880–1956: in *Chicago Tribune* 19 September 1926

16 What is a highbrow? He is a man who has found something more interesting than women.
Edgar Wallace 1875–1932: in *New York Times* 24 January 1932

17 As a human being, one has been endowed with just enough

intelligence to be able to see clearly how utterly inadequate that intelligence is when confronted with what exists.

Albert Einstein 1879–1955: letter to Queen Elisabeth of Belgium, 19 September 1932

18 The test of a first-rate intelligence is the ability to hold two opposed ideas in the mind at the same time, and still retain the ability to function.

F. Scott Fitzgerald 1896–1940: 'The Crack-Up' in *Esquire* February 1936

19 To the man-in-the-street, who, I'm sorry to say,
Is a keen observer of life,
The word 'Intellectual' suggests straight away
A man who's untrue to his wife.

W. H. Auden 1907–73: *New Year Letter* (1941)

20 An intellectual is someone whose mind watches itself.

Albert Camus 1913–60: *Carnets, 1935–42* (1962)

21 Too clever by half.

of Iain Macleod; the term had been applied by an earlier Lord Salisbury (1830–1903) to Disraeli's amendment on Disestablishment, 30 March 1868; See INTELLIGENCE 6

Lord Salisbury 1893–1972: speech, House of Lords, 7 March 1961

22 It takes little talent to see clearly what lies under one's nose, a good deal of it to know in which direction to point that organ.

W. H. Auden 1907–73: *Dyer's Hand* (1963) 'Writing'

23 Rule no. 11: Be nice to nerds. Chances are you'll end up working for one.

often wrongly attributed to the American computer entrepreneur Bill Gates

Charles J. Sykes 1954– : 'Rules Kids Won't Learn in School' published in newspapers from c.1998 and in *50 Rules Kids Won't Learn in School* (2007)

International Relations

see also COUNTRIES, DIPLOMACY, GOVERNMENT, POLITICS

phrases ▸

1 the Auld Alliance

the political relationship of France and Scotland between the 14th and the 16th centuries; *auld* is a Scottish form of old

2 the balance of power

a state of international equilibrium with no nation predominant; originally *the balance of power in Europe*, as in *London Gazette* 1701 'Your glorious design of re-establishing a just balance of power in Europe', and associated with the political aspirations of Robert Walpole (1676–1745)

3 the cold war

the hostility between the Soviet bloc countries and the Western powers which began after the Second World War with the Soviet takeover of the countries of eastern Europe, and which was formally ended in November 1990; from a speech to the South Carolina Legislature 16 April 1947, 'Let us not be deceived—we are today in the midst of a cold war' by Bernard Baruch (1870–1965); the expression *cold war* was suggested to him by H. B. Swope, former editor of the *New York World*

4 domino theory

the theory that a political event in one country will cause similar events in neighbouring countries, like a falling domino causing an entire row of upended dominoes to fall; see CAUSES 26

5 ethical foreign policy

the conduct of foreign policy according to ethical as well as national considerations; after the British general election of 1997, the aspiration was particularly associated with the incumbency of Robin Cook as Foreign Secretary, but its precise application in individual cases has been controversial

6 hands across the sea

promoting closer international links, recorded from the late 19th century; see INTERNATIONAL 20, INTERNATIONAL 26

7 **the Monroe doctrine**
a principle of US policy, that any intervention by external powers in the politics of the Americas is a potentially hostile act against the US, originated by President James Monroe in his annual message to Congress, 2 December 1823; see DIPLOMACY 11

8 **a New World Order**
a vision of a world ordered differently from the way it is at present; in particular, an optimistic view of the world order or balance of power following the end of the Cold War; see FUTURE 29

9 **the special relationship**
the relationship between Britain and the US, regarded as particularly close in terms of common origin and language; associated with Winston Churchill, as in the House of Commons 7 November 1945, 'We should not abandon our special relationship with the United States and Canada'

10 **the Third World**
the developing countries of Asia, Africa, and Latin America; the phrase was first applied in the 1950s by French commentators who used *tiers monde* to distinguish the developing countries from the capitalist and Communist blocs; see JOURNALISM 24

11 **watchful waiting**
American policy towards Mexico during Mexico's revolutionary period, 1913–20; from Woodrow Wilson's State of the Union address, 2 December 1913, 'Our policy of watchful waiting'

quotations ▸

12 Excessive dealings with tyrants are not good for the security of free states.
Demosthenes c.384–c.322 BC: *Second Philippic*

13 *Il n'y a plus de Pyrénées.*
The Pyrenees are no more.
on the accession of his grandson to the throne of Spain, 1700
Louis XIV 1638–1715: attributed to Louis by Voltaire in *Siècle de Louis XIV* (1753); but to the Spanish Ambassador to France in the *Mercure Galant* (Paris) November 1700

14 Peace, commerce, and honest friendship with all nations—entangling alliances with none.
Thomas Jefferson 1743–1826: inaugural address, 4th of March 1801

15 If you wish to avoid foreign collision, you had better abandon the ocean.
Henry Clay 1777–1852: speech in the House of Representatives, 22 January 1812

16 In matters of commerce the fault of the Dutch
Is offering too little and asking too much.
The French are with equal advantage content,
So we clap on Dutch bottoms just twenty per cent.
George Canning 1770–1827: dispatch, in cipher, to the English ambassador at the Hague, 31 January 1826

17 The Continent will [not] suffer England to be the workshop of the world.
Benjamin Disraeli 1804–81: speech, House of Commons, 15 March 1838

18 Italy is a geographical expression.
discussing the Italian question with Palmerston in 1847
Prince Metternich 1773–1859: *Mémoires, Documents, etc. de Metternich publiés par son fils* (1883)

19 We have no eternal allies, and we have no perpetual enemies. Our interests are eternal and perpetual, and those interests it is our duty to follow.
Lord Palmerston 1784–1865: speech, House of Commons, 1 March 1848

20 Hands across the sea,
Feet on English ground,
The old blood is bold blood, the wide world round.
Byron Webber b. 1838: 'Hands across the Sea' (1860), in Burton Stevenson *The Home Book of Quotations* (1967 ed.); see INTERNATIONAL 6, INTERNATIONAL 26

21 Lord Palmerston, with characteristic levity had once said that only three men in Europe had ever understood [the Schleswig-Holstein question], and of these the Prince Consort was dead, a Danish statesman (unnamed) was in an asylum, and he himself had forgotten it.
Lord Palmerston 1784–1865: R. W. Seton-Watson *Britain in Europe 1789–1914* (1937)

22 Nations touch at their summits.
Walter Bagehot 1826–77: *The English Constitution* (1867)

23 This policy cannot succeed through speeches, and shooting-matches, and songs; it can only be carried out through blood and iron.

Otto von Bismarck 1815–98: speech in the Prussian House of Deputies, 28 January 1886; see WARFARE 7

24 In a word, we desire to throw no one into the shade [in East Asia], but we also demand our own place in the sun.

Bernhard von Bülow 1849–1929: speech, Reichstag, 6 December 1897; see SUCCESS 18

25 Just for a word 'neutrality'—a word which in wartime has so often been disregarded—just for a scrap of paper, Great Britain is going to make war on a kindred nation who desires nothing better than to be friends with her.

Theobald von Bethmann Hollweg 1856–1921: summary of a report by Sir E. Goschen to Sir Edward Grey; *The Diary of Edward Goschen 1900–1914* (1980) discusses the contentious origins of this statement; see TRUST 13

26 I have never used in peace or in war any such expression as 'hands across the sea,' and I emphatically disapprove of what it signifies save in so far as it means cordial friendship between us and every other nation that acts in accordance with the standards that we deem just and right.

Theodore Roosevelt 1858–1919: in *Metropolitan* October 1915; see INTERNATIONAL 6, INTERNATIONAL 20

27 Since the day of the air, the old frontiers are gone. When you think of the defence of England you no longer think of the chalk cliffs of Dover; you think of the Rhine. That is where our frontier lies.

Stanley Baldwin 1867–1947: speech, House of Commons, 30 July 1934

28 If Hitler invaded hell I would make at least a favourable reference to the devil in the House of Commons.

Winston Churchill 1874–1965: *The Second World War* (1950) vol. 3

29 If you carry this resolution you will send Britain's Foreign Secretary naked into the conference chamber.

on a motion proposing unilateral nuclear disarmament by the UK

Aneurin Bevan 1897–1960: speech at Labour Party Conference in Brighton, 3 October 1957

30 We face neither East nor West: we face forward.

Kwame Nkrumah 1900–72: conference speech, Accra, 7 April 1960

31 The great nations have always acted like gangsters, and the small nations like prostitutes.

Stanley Kubrick 1928–99: in *Guardian* 5 June 1963

32 *Ich bin ein Berliner.*
I am a Berliner.

expressing US commitment to the support and defence of West Berlin

John F. Kennedy 1917–63: speech in West Berlin, 26 June 1963

33 We hope that the world will not narrow into a neighbourhood before it has broadened into a brotherhood.

Lyndon Baines Johnson 1908–73: speech at the lighting of the Nation's Christmas Tree, 22 December 1963

34 Living next to you is in some ways like sleeping with an elephant. No matter how friendly and even-tempered the beast, one is affected by every twitch and grunt.

on relations between Canada and the US

Pierre Trudeau 1919–2000: speech at National Press Club, Washington D. C., 25 March 1969

35 They're Germans. Don't mention the war.

John Cleese 1939– and **Connie Booth** 1944– : *Fawlty Towers* 'The Germans' (BBC TV programme, 1975)

36 If Kuwait grew carrots we wouldn't give a damn.

Lawrence Korb 1939– : in *International Herald Tribune* 21 August 1990

37 More than ever before in human history, we share a common destiny. We can master it only if we face it together. And that, my friends, is why we have the United Nations.

Kofi Annan 1938– : in *Sunday Times* 2 January 2000

38 This is not a battle betweeen the United States and terrorism, but between the free and democratic world and terrorism. We therefore here in Britain stand shoulder to shoulder with our American friends in

this hour of tragedy and we, like them, will not rest until this evil is driven from our world.

Tony Blair 1953– : in Downing Street, London, 11 September 2001

39 States like these...constitute an axis of evil, arming to threaten the peace of this world.

of Iraq, Iran, and North Korea

George W. Bush 1946– : State of the Union address, in *Newsweek* 11 February 2002

40 Blair, keep your England and let me keep my Zimbabwe.

Robert Mugabe 1924– : at the Earth Summit in Johannesburg, 2 September 2002

41 We will extend a hand if you are willing to unclench your fist.

Barack Obama 1961– : inaugural address, 20 January 2009

The Internet

see COMPUTERS AND THE INTERNET

Inventions and Discoveries

see also SCIENCE, TECHNOLOGY

proverbs and sayings ▶

1 Turkey, heresy, hops, and beer came into England all in one year.

perhaps referring to 1521. The *turkey*, found domesticated in Mexico in 1518, was soon afterwards introduced into Europe; in 1521, the Pope conferred on Henry VIII the title Defender of the Faith, in recognition of his opposition to the Lutheran *heresy*; the *hop*-plant is believed to have been introduced into the south of England from Flanders between 1520 and 1524; and *beer* as the name of hopped malt liquor became common only in the 16th century; English proverb, late 16th century

phrases ▶

2 the best thing since sliced bread

a particularly notable invention or discovery

3 reinvent the wheel

be forced by necessity to construct a basic requirement again from the beginning; the *wheel* as an essential requirement of modern civilization

quotations ▶

4 God hath made man upright; but they have sought out many inventions.

Bible: Ecclesiastes

5 *Eureka!*
I've got it!

Archimedes c.287–212 BC: Vitruvius Pollio *De Architectura*

6 It is well to observe the force and virtue and consequence of discoveries, and these are to be seen nowhere more conspicuously than in those three which were unknown to the ancients, and of which the origins, though recent, are obscure and inglorious; namely, printing, gunpowder, and the mariner's needle [the compass]. For these three have changed the whole face and state of things throughout the world.

Francis Bacon 1561–1626: *Novum Organum* (1620); see CULTURE 12

7 SALVIATI: Now you see how easy it is to understand.
SAGREDO: So are all truths, once they are discovered.

often quoted as 'All truths are easy to understand, once they are discovered; the point is, to discover them'

Galileo Galilei 1564–1642: *Dialogue Concerning the two Chief World Systems* (1632) 'The Second Day' translated by Stillman Drake

8 I don't know what I may seem to the world, but as to myself, I seem to have been only like a boy playing on the sea-shore and diverting myself in now and then finding a smoother pebble or a prettier shell than ordinary, whilst the great ocean of truth lay all undiscovered before me.

Isaac Newton 1642–1727: Joseph Spence *Anecdotes* (ed. J. Osborn, 1966)

9 What is the use of a new-born child?

when asked what was the use of a new invention

Benjamin Franklin 1706–90: J. Parton *Life and Times of Benjamin Franklin* (1864)

10 Then felt I like some watcher of the
skies
When a new planet swims into his
ken;
Or like stout Cortez when with eagle
eyes

He stared at the Pacific—and all his men
Looked at each other with a wild surmise—
Silent, upon a peak in Darien.

John Keats 1795–1821: 'On First Looking into Chapman's Homer' (1817)

11 The discovery of a new dish does more for human happiness than the discovery of a star.

Anthelme Brillat-Savarin 1755–1826: *Physiologie du Goût* (1826)

12 Why sir, there is every possibility that you will soon be able to tax it!

to Gladstone, when asked about the usefulness of electricity

Michael Faraday 1791–1867: W. E. H. Lecky *Democracy and Liberty* (1899 ed.)

13 My reflection, when I first made myself master of the central idea of the 'Origin,' was, How extremely stupid not to have thought of that!

T. H. Huxley 1825–95: 'On the Reception of the "Origin of Species"' in F. Darwin *Life and Letters of Charles Darwin* vol. 2 (1888)

14 What one man can invent another can discover.

Arthur Conan Doyle 1859–1930: *The Return of Sherlock Holmes* (1905) 'The Dancing Men'; see ACHIEVEMENT 10

15 Name the greatest of all the inventors. Accident.

Mark Twain 1835–1910: *Notebook* (1935)

16 When man wanted to make a machine that would walk he created the wheel, which does not resemble a leg.

Guillaume Apollinaire 1880–1918: *Les Mamelles de Tirésias* (1918)

17 Yes, wonderful things.

when asked what he could see on first looking into the tomb of Tutankhamun, 26 November 1922; his notebook records the words as 'Yes, it is wonderful'

Howard Carter 1874–1939: H. V. F. Winstone *Howard Carter and the discovery of the tomb of Tutankhamun* (1993)

18 Whatever Nature has in store for mankind, unpleasant as it may be, men must accept, for ignorance is never better than knowledge.

Enrico Fermi 1901–54: Laura Fermi *Atoms in the Family* (1955)

19 Discovery consists of seeing what everybody has seen and thinking what nobody has thought.

Albert von Szent-Györgyi 1893–1986: Irving Good (ed.) *The Scientist Speculates* (1962)

20 praise without end the go-ahead zeal
of whoever it was invented the wheel;
but never a word for the poor soul's sake
that thought ahead, and invented the brake.

Howard Nemerov 1920–91: 'To the Congress of the United States, Entering Its Third Century' 26 February 1989

21 After the idea, there is plenty of time to learn the technology.

James Dyson 1947– : *Against the Odds* (1997)

22 When the inventor of the drawing board messed things up, what did he go back to?

Bob Monkhouse 1928–2003: attributed; in *Guardian* 29 December 2003 (online edition); see BEGINNING 13

Ireland

proverbs and sayings ▸

1 England's difficulty is Ireland's opportunity.

associated with the aspirations of Irish nationalism; English proverb, mid 19th century

phrases ▸

2 Celtic tiger

the Irish economy, during a period of rapid growth in the 1990s and early 2000s; see ECONOMICS 7

3 Celtic twilight

the romantic fairy tale atmosphere of Irish folklore; literature conveying this; from the title of an anthology collected by W. B. Yeats, 1893

4 the Emerald Isle

Ireland; from William Drennan *Erin* (1795) 'Nor one feeling of vengeance presume to defile The cause, or the men, of the Emerald Isle'

5 the Flight of the Earls

the flight into exile from Ireland of the two Catholic leaders, Hugh O'Neill, Earl of Tyrone, and Rory O'Donnell, Earl of Tyrconnell, 1607

6 Land of Saints and Scholars

Ireland; *saint* meaning 'monk' or 'anchorite', alluding to the traditional view of medieval Ireland as a monastic and scholarly land

7 the Wild Geese

the Irish Jacobites who fled from Ireland to the Continent after the defeat of James II at the Battle of the Boyne (1690), many of whom later took service with the French forces; recorded in a poem by M. J. Barry in *Spirit of the Nation* (1845) 'The wild geese—the wild geese,—'Tis long since they flew, O'er the billowy ocean's bright bosom of blue'

quotations ▸

8 Icham of Irlaunde
Ant of the holy londe of irlonde
Gode sir pray ich ye
for of saynte charite,
come ant daunce wyt me,
in irlaunde.

Anonymous: fourteenth century

9 I met wid Napper Tandy, and he took me by the hand,
And he said, 'How's poor ould Ireland, and how does she stand?'
She's the most disthressful country that iver yet was seen,
For they're hangin' men an' women for the wearin' o' the Green.

Anonymous: 'The Wearin' o' the Green' (1795 ballad)

10 The moment the very name of Ireland is mentioned, the English seem to bid adieu to common feeling, common prudence, and common sense, and to act with the barbarity of tyrants, and the fatuity of idiots.

Sydney Smith 1771–1845: *Letters of Peter Plymley* (1807)

11 The harp that once through Tara's halls
The soul of music shed,
Now hangs as mute on Tara's walls
As if that soul were fled.

Thomas Moore 1779–1852: 'The harp that once through Tara's halls'(1807)

12 Thus you have a starving population, an absentee aristocracy, and an alien Church, and in addition the weakest executive in the world. That is the Irish Question.

Benjamin Disraeli 1804–81: speech in the House of Commons, 16 February 1844

13 I decided some time ago that if the G.O.M. [Gladstone] went for Home Rule, the Orange card would be the one to play. Please God it may turn out the ace of trumps and not the two.

Lord Randolph Churchill 1849–94: letter to Lord Justice FitzGibbon, 16 February 1886; see WAYS 28

14 Ulster will fight; Ulster will be right.

Lord Randolph Churchill 1849–94: public letter, 7 May 1886

15 For the great Gaels of Ireland
Are the men that God made mad,
For all their wars are merry,
And all their songs are sad.

G. K. Chesterton 1874–1936: *The Ballad of the White Horse* (1911)

16 Ireland is the old sow that eats her farrow.

James Joyce 1882–1941: *A Portrait of the Artist as a Young Man* (1916)

17 In Ireland the inevitable never happens and the unexpected constantly occurs.

John Pentland Mahaffy 1839–1919: W. B. Stanford and R. B. McDowell *Mahaffy* (1971)

18 Out of Ireland have we come.
Great hatred, little room,
Maimed us at the start.

W. B. Yeats 1865–1939: 'Remorse for Intemperate Speech' (1933)

19 Spenser's Ireland
has not altered;—
a place as kind as it is green,
the greenest place I've never seen.

Marianne Moore 1887–1972: 'Spenser's Ireland' (1941)

20 Clay is the word and clay is the flesh
Where the potato-gatherers like mechanized scarecrows move
Along the side-fall of the hill—
Maguire and his men.

Patrick Kavanagh 1904–67: 'The Great Hunger' (1947)

21 The famous
Northern reticence, the tight gag of place
And times: yes, yes. Of the 'wee six' I sing.

Seamus Heaney 1939– : 'Whatever You Say Say Nothing' (1975)

22 I'm Irish. We think sideways.
Spike Milligan 1918–2002: in *Independent on Sunday* 20 June 1999

Jazz
see also MUSIC

phrases ▸

1 beat generation
a movement of young people in the 1950s and early 1960s who rejected conventional society, valuing free self-expression and favouring modern jazz; the phrase was supposedly coined by Jack Kerouac (1922–69) in the course of a conversation

quotations ▸

2 Jazz will endure, just as long as people hear it through their feet instead of their brains.
John Philip Sousa 1854–1932: Nat Shapiro (ed.) *An Encyclopedia of Quotations about Music* (1978)

3 It don't mean a thing
If it ain't got that swing.
Irving Mills 1894–1985: 'It Don't Mean a Thing' (1932 song; music by Duke Ellington)

4 Jazz music is to be played sweet, soft, plenty rhythm.
Jelly Roll Morton 1885–1941: *Mister Jelly Roll* (1950)

5 What a terrible revenge by the culture of the Negroes on that of the whites!
Ignacy Jan Paderewski 1860–1941: Nat Shapiro (ed.) *An Encyclopedia of Quotations about Music* (1978)

6 Playing 'Bop' is like scrabble with all the vowels missing.
Duke Ellington 1899–1974: in *Look* 10 August 1954

7 A jazz musician is a juggler who uses harmonies instead of oranges.
Benny Green 1927– : *The Reluctant Art* (1962)

8 Jazz is the only music in which the same note can be played night after night but differently each time.
Ornette Coleman 1930– : W. H. Mellers *Music in a New Found Land* (1964)

9 If you still have to ask...shame on you.
when asked what jazz is; sometimes quoted as, 'Man, if you gotta ask you'll never know'
Louis Armstrong 1901–71: Max Jones et al. *Salute to Satchmo* (1970)

10 [Charlie] Parker was a modern jazz player just as Picasso was a modern painter and Pound a modern poet. I hadn't realized that jazz had gone from Lascaux to Jackson Pollock in fifty years.
Philip Larkin 1922–85: *Required Writing* (1983)

Jealousy
see ENVY AND JEALOUSY

Journalism
see also NEWS

proverbs and sayings ▸

1 All the news that's fit to print.
motto of the *New York Times*, from 1896; coined by Adolph S. Ochs (1858–1935)

2 Top people take *The Times*.
advertising slogan for *The Times* newspaper, from January 1959

3 Watch this space!
further developments are expected and more information will be given later; *space* = an area of a newspaper available for a specific purpose, especially for advertising

phrases ▸

4 the fourth estate
the press; a group regarded as having power in the land equivalent to that of one of the three Estates of the Realm, the Crown, the House of Lords, and the House of Commons; from Lord Macaulay in 1843, 'The gallery in which the reporters sit has become a fourth estate of the realm'

5 Grub Street
used in reference to a world or class of impoverished journalists and writers, from the name of a street (later Milton Street) in Moorgate, London, inhabited by such authors in the 17th century

6 Page Three

a British trademark term for a feature which formerly appeared daily on page three of the *Sun* newspaper and included a picture of a topless young woman; see JOURNALISM 28, WOMEN 15

7 the silly season

the months of August and September, when newspapers make up for the lack of serious news with articles on trivial topics; the time when Parliament and the law courts are in recess; recorded in 1861, when the *Saturday Review* of 13 July spoke of 'the Silly Season of 1861 setting in a month or two before its time'

quotations ▸

8 Our liberty depends on freedom of the press, and that cannot be limited without being lost.

Thomas Jefferson 1743–1826: letter to James Currie, 28 January 1786

9 Nothing can now be believed which is seen in a newspaper. Truth itself becomes suspicious by being put into that polluted vehicle.

Thomas Jefferson 1743–1826: letter to John Norvell, 14 June 1807, in *The Portable Thomas Jefferson* (1977)

10 *The Times* has made many ministries.

Walter Bagehot 1826–77: *The English Constitution* (1867) 'The Cabinet'

11 There are laws to protect the freedom of the press's speech, but none that are worth anything to protect the people from the press.

Mark Twain 1835–1910: 'License of the Press' (1873)

12 You furnish the pictures and I'll furnish the war.

message to the artist Frederic Remington in Havana, Cuba, during the Spanish-American War of 1898

William Randolph Hearst 1863–1951: attributed

13 By office boys for office boys.

of the *Daily Mail*

Lord Salisbury 1830–1903: H. Hamilton Fyfe *Northcliffe, an Intimate Biography* (1930)

14 The men with the muck-rakes are often indispensable to the well-being of society; but only if they know when to stop raking the muck.

Theodore Roosevelt 1858–1919: speech in Washington, 14 April 1906

15 A cynical, mercenary, demagogic, corrupt press will produce in time a people as base as itself.

Joseph Pulitzer 1847–1911: inscribed on the gateway to the Columbia School of Journalism in New York

16 The power of the press is very great, but not so great as the power of suppress.

Lord Northcliffe 1865–1922: office message, *Daily Mail* 1918; Reginald Rose and Geoffrey Harmsworth *Northcliffe* (1959)

17 Comment is free, but facts are sacred.

C. P. Scott 1846–1932: in *Manchester Guardian* 5 May 1921; see JOURNALISM 25

18 You cannot hope
to bribe or twist,
thank God! the
British journalist.

But, seeing what
the man will do
unbribed, there's
no occasion to.

Humbert Wolfe 1886–1940: 'Over the Fire' (1930)

19 Journalism—an ability to meet the challenge of filling the space.

Rebecca West 1892–1983: in *New York Herald Tribune* 22 April 1956

20 Anyone here been raped and speaks English?

shouted by a British TV reporter in a crowd of Belgian civilians waiting to be airlifted out of the Belgian Congo, 1960

Anonymous: Edward Behr *Anyone Here been Raped and Speaks English?* (1981)

21 A good newspaper, I suppose, is a nation talking to itself.

Arthur Miller 1915–2005: in *Observer* 26 November 1961

22 Freedom of the press in Britain means freedom to print such of the proprietor's prejudices as the advertisers don't object to.

Hannen Swaffer 1879–1962: Tom Driberg *Swaff* (1974)

23 When the legend becomes fact, print the legend.

Willis Goldbeck and **James Warner Bellah**: *The Man who Shot Liberty Valance* (1962 film); see also HEROES 19

24 The Third World never sold a newspaper.
Rupert Murdoch 1931– : in *Observer* 1 January 1978; see INTERNATIONAL 10

25 Comment is free but facts are on expenses.
Tom Stoppard 1937– : *Night and Day* (1978); see JOURNALISM 17

26 Rock journalism is people who can't write interviewing people who can't talk for people who can't read.
Frank Zappa 1940–93: Linda Botts *Loose Talk* (1980)

27 Go to where the silence is and say something.
accepting an award from Columbia University for her coverage of the 1991 massacre in East Timor by Indonesian troops
Amy Goodman 1957– : in *Columbia Journalism Review* March/April 1994

28 I don't know. The editor did it when I was away.
when asked why he had allowed Page 3 to develop
Rupert Murdoch 1931– : in *Guardian* 25 February 1994; see JOURNALISM 6

29 When seagulls follow a trawler, it is because they think sardines will be thrown into the sea.
to the media at the end of a press conference, 31 March 1995
Eric Cantona 1966– : in *Times* 1 April 1995

Justice

see also LAW

proverbs and sayings ▸

1 All's fair in love and war.
in certain conditions rules do not apply, and any measures are acceptable; English proverb, early 17th century

2 Be just before you're generous.
often used in the context of advising that one should settle any obligations before indulging in generosity; English proverb, mid 18th century

3 A fair exchange is no robbery.
sometimes used of an action regarded as cancelling out an obligation which has been incurred; English proverb, mid 16th century

4 Fair play's a jewel.
applauding the value of honest dealing; English proverb, early 19th century

5 A fox should not be on the jury at a goose's trial.
a member of a jury should be unbiased; English proverb, early 18th century

6 Give and take is fair play.
English proverb, late 18th century

7 Give the Devil his due.
one should acknowledge the strengths and capabilities of even the most unpleasant person; English proverb, late 16th century

8 One law for the rich and another for the poor.
English proverb, mid 19th century

9 There are two sides to every question.
a problem can be seen from more than one angle; English proverb, early 19th century

10 Turn about is fair play.
recommending equality of opportunity; English proverb, mid 18th century

11 We all love justice—at our neighbour's expense.
American proverb, mid 20th century

12 We must guard even our enemies against injustice.
Graham Greene's version of Thomas Paine's *Dissertation on the First Principles of Government*, modern saying; see LIBERTY 16

13 What goes around comes around.
often used as a comment on someone becoming subject to what they have visited on others; late 20th century, of US origin

14 What's sauce for the goose is sauce for the gander.
originally meaning that what is suitable for a woman is also suitable for a man, but now sometimes used in wider contexts; English proverb, late 17th century

phrases ▸

15 a fair field and no favour
equal conditions in a contest, not unduly favouring or hindering either side

16 Jedburgh justice
summary justice; such as that meted out to Border reivers at *Jedburgh* in southern Scotland in the 16th century

17 Jedem das Seine

German = 'To each his own'; inscription on the gate of Buchenwald concentration camp, 1937; often quoted as 'Everyone gets what he deserves'

18 a Roland for an Oliver

an appropriate retaliation for a verbal or physical attack, a quid pro quo; *Roland* was the legendary nephew of Charlemagne, celebrated with his comrade *Oliver* in the medieval romance *Chanson de Roland*

quotations ▸

19 Life for life,
Eye for eye, tooth for tooth.

Bible: Exodus; see REVENGE 3, REVENGE 9

20 What I say is that 'just' or 'right' means nothing but what is in the interest of the stronger party.

Plato 429–347 BC: *The Republic*, spoken by Thrasymachus

21 Judge not, that ye be not judged.

Bible: St Matthew; see PREJUDICE 1

22 *Nulla iniuria est, quae in volentem fiat.*

No injustice is done to someone who wants that thing done.

usually quoted as '*Volenti non fit iniuria*'
Ulpian d. 228: *Corpus Iuris Civilis* Digests

23 Justice is the constant and perpetual wish to render to every one his due.

Justinian AD 483–565: *Institutes*

24 To no man will we sell, or deny, or delay, right or justice.

Magna Carta 1215: clause 40; see JUSTICE 34

25 If the parties will at my hands call for justice, then, all were it my father stood on the one side, and the Devil on the other, his cause being good, the Devil should have right.

Thomas More 1478–1535: William Roper *Life of Sir Thomas More*

26 *Fiat justitia et pereat mundus.*

Let justice be done, though the world perish.

Ferdinand I 1503–64: motto; Johannes Manlius *Locorum Communium Collectanea* (1563)

27 The quality of mercy is not strained,
It droppeth as the gentle rain from
heaven
Upon the place beneath.

William Shakespeare 1564–1616: *The Merchant of Venice* (1596–8)

28 You manifestly wrong even the poorest ploughman, if you demand not his free consent.

Charles I 1600–49: The King's Reasons for declining the jurisdiction of the High Court of Justice, 21 January 1649

29 I'm armed with more than complete steel—The justice of my quarrel.

Anonymous: *Lust's Dominion* (1657); attributed to Marlowe, though of doubtful authorship

30 It is justice, not charity, that is wanting in the world.

Mary Wollstonecraft 1759–97: *A Vindication of the Rights of Woman* (1792)

31 Consider what you think justice requires, and decide accordingly. But never give your reasons; for your judgement will probably be right, but your reasons will certainly be wrong.

advice to a newly appointed colonial governor ignorant in the law
William Murray, Lord Mansfield 1705–93: Lord Campbell *The Lives of the Chief Justices of England* (1849)

32 Publicity is the very soul of justice. It is the keenest spur to exertion, and the surest of all guards against improbity.

Jeremy Bentham 1748–1832: *Publicity in the Courts of Justice* (1843)

33 Justice is truth in action.

Benjamin Disraeli 1804–81: speech, House of Commons, 11 February 1851

34 Justice delayed is justice denied.

W. E. Gladstone 1809–98: speech on the state of Ireland, House of Commons, 16 March 1868; see JUSTICE 24

35 When I hear of an 'equity' in a case like this, I am reminded of a blind man in a dark room—looking for a black hat—which isn't there.

Lord Bowen 1835–94: John Alderson Foote *Pie-Powder* (1911)

36 *J'accuse.*

I accuse.

on the Dreyfus affair
Émile Zola 1840–1902: title of an open letter to the President of the French Republic in *L'Aurore* 13 January 1898

37 A man who is good enough to shed his blood for the country is good enough to be given a square deal afterwards. More than that no man is entitled to, and less than that no man shall have.

Theodore Roosevelt 1858–1919: speech at the Lincoln Monument, Springfield, Illinois, 4 June 1903

38 In England, justice is open to all—like the Ritz Hotel.

James Mathew 1830–1908: R. E. Megarry *Miscellany-at-Law* (1955)

39 Injustice is relatively easy to bear; what stings is justice.

H. L. Mencken 1880–1956: *Prejudices, Third Series* (1922)

40 A long line of cases shows that it is not merely of some importance, but is of fundamental importance that justice should not only be done, but should manifestly and undoubtedly be seen to be done.

Gordon Hewart 1870–1943: Rex v Sussex Justices, 9 November 1923

41 Injustice anywhere is a threat to justice everywhere.

Martin Luther King 1929–68: letter from Birmingham Jail, Alabama, 16 April 1963

42 We shall overcome because the arc of a moral universe is long, but it bends toward justice.

Martin Luther King 1929–68: sermon at the National Cathedral, Washington, 31 March 1968; see JUSTICE 45

43 Once in a lifetime
The longed-for tidal wave
Of justice can rise up
And hope and history rhyme.

Seamus Heaney 1939– : *The Cure at Troy* (version of Sophocles' *Philoctetes*, 1990)

44 If it falls to me to start a fight to cut out the cancer of bent and twisted journalism in our country with the simple sword of truth and the trusty shield of British fair play, so be it.

Jonathan Aitken 1942– : statement, London, 10 April 1995

45 The arc of history is long but it bends towards justice.

Barack Obama 1961– : speech, George Mason University, 2 February 2007; see JUSTICE 42

Kissing

proverbs and sayings ▸

1 Kissing goes by favour.

a kiss is often given as a reward for something done; English proverb, early 17th century

2 When the gorse is out of bloom, kissing's out of fashion.

the idea behind the saying is that gorse is always in flower somewhere: see LOVE 15; English proverb, mid 19th century

quotations ▸

3 *Da mi basia mille, deinde centum,*
Dein mille altera, dein secunda centum,
Deinde usque altera mille, deinde centum.

Give me a thousand kisses, then a hundred, then another thousand, then a second hundred, then yet another thousand, then a hundred.

Catullus c.84–c.54 BC: *Carmina*

4 I kissed thee ere I killed thee, no way but this,
Killing myself to die upon a kiss.

William Shakespeare 1564–1616: *Othello* (1602–4)

5 O Love, O fire! once he drew
With one long kiss my whole soul through
My lips, as sunlight drinketh dew.

Alfred, Lord Tennyson 1809–92: 'Fatima' (1832)

6 What of soul was left, I wonder, when the kissing had to stop?

Robert Browning 1812–89: 'A Toccata of Galuppi's' (1855); see ENDING 12

7 I wonder who's kissing her now.

Frank Adams and **Will M. Hough**: title of song (1909)

8 You must remember this, a kiss is still a kiss,
A sigh is just a sigh;
The fundamental things apply,
As time goes by.

Herman Hupfeld 1894–1951: 'As Time Goes By' (1931 song)

9 A fine romance with no kisses.
A fine romance, my friend, this is.

Dorothy Fields 1905–74: 'A Fine Romance' (1936 song)

10 **Where do the noses go? I always wondered where the noses would go.**
Ernest Hemingway 1899–1961: *For Whom the Bell Tolls* (1940)

11 **A kiss can be a comma, a question mark or an exclamation point. That's basic spelling that every woman ought to know.**
Mistinguett 1875–1956: in *Theatre Arts* December 1955

12 **I wasn't kissing her, I was just whispering in her mouth.**
on being discovered by his wife with a chorus girl
Chico Marx 1891–1961: Groucho Marx and Richard J. Anobile *Marx Brothers Scrapbook* (1973)

13 **Oh, innocent victims of Cupid,**
Remember this terse little verse;
To let a fool kiss you is stupid,
To let a kiss fool you is worse.
E. Y. Harburg 1898–1981: 'Inscriptions on a Lipstick' (1965)

14 **A kiss is a lovely trick designed by nature to stop speech when words become superfluous.**
Ingrid Bergman 1915–82: attributed

Knowledge

see also WISDOM

proverbs and sayings ▶

1 **The cobbler to his last and the gunner to his linstock.**
a fanciful extension of 'Let the cobbler stick to his last' (see KNOWLEDGE 5). The gunner's *linstock* was a long pole used to hold a match for firing a cannon; English proverb, mid 18th century

2 **Knowledge and timber shouldn't be much used until they are seasoned.**
American proverb, mid 19th century

3 **Knowledge is power.**
English proverb, late 16th century; see KNOWLEDGE 26, ARTS 3

4 **Learning is better than house and land.**
reflecting on the difference between knowledge and material, and therefore ephemeral, possessions; English proverb, late 18th century

5 **Let the cobbler stick to his last.**
people should only concern themselves with things they know something about (the cobbler's *last* is a shoemaker's model for shaping or repairing a shoe or boot); English proverb, mid 16th century; see also KNOWLEDGE 1

6 **A little knowledge is a dangerous thing.**
English proverb, early 18th century; alteration of Pope: see KNOWLEDGE 29, KNOWLEDGE 40

7 **The sea of learning has no end.**
Chinese proverb

8 **Walking ten thousand miles; reading ten thousand books.**
theoretical knowledge and practical experience are of equal value; Chinese proverb, compare EXPERIENCE 10

9 **When house and land are gone and spent, then learning is most excellent.**
contrasting the value of learning with the ephemeral nature of material possessions; English proverb, mid 18th century

phrases ▶

10 **have the right sow by the ear**
have the correct understanding of a situation; see PRACTICALITY 5

11 **milk for babes**
something easy and pleasant to learn; especially in allusion to the Bible (I Corinthians) 'I…speak unto you…even as unto babes in Christ. I have fed you with milk, and not with meat'

12 **'satiable curiosity**
a thirst for knowledge that cannot be satisfied, as exemplified by the Elephant's Child in Kipling's *Just So Stories*, who was 'full of 'satiable curtiosity': see also KNOWLEDGE 43

13 **the tree of knowledge**
knowledge in general, comprising all its branches; the tree in the Garden of Eden bearing the apple eaten by Eve

quotations ▶

14 **The fox knows many things—the hedgehog one *big* one.**
Archilochus 7th century BC: E. Diehl (ed.) *Anthologia Lyrica Graeca* (3rd ed., 1949–52); see CHARACTER 48

15 **He who knows does not speak.**
He who speaks does not know.
Lao Tzu c.604–c.531 BC: *Tao-te Ching*

16 He that increaseth knowledge increaseth sorrow.
Bible: Ecclesiastes

17 I know nothing except the fact of my ignorance.
Socrates 469–399 BC: Diogenes Laertius *Lives of the Philosophers*

18 All men by nature desire knowledge.
Aristotle 384–322 BC: *Metaphysics*

19 Paul, thou art beside thyself; much learning doth make thee mad.
Bible: Acts of the Apostles

20 For now we see through a glass, darkly; but then face to face: now I know in part; but then shall I know even as also I am known.
Bible: I Corinthians

21 All wish to possess knowledge, but no one is willing to pay the price.
Juvenal C. AD 60–C. 140: *Satires* no. 7

22 Each had but known one part, and no man all;
Hence into deadly error each did fall.
No way to know the All man's heart can find:
Can knowledge e'er accompany the blind?
on blind men's conclusions on touching different parts of an elephant
Sana'i d. c.1131: 'The Blind Men and the Elephant'; see INSIGHT 7

23 Everyman, I will go with thee, and be thy guide,
In thy most need to go by thy side.
spoken by 'Knowledge'
Anonymous: *Everyman* (1509–19)

24 Knowledge without conscience is but the ruin of the soul.
François Rabelais c.1494–c.1553: *Gargantua and Pantagruel* (1532–64)

25 *Que sais-je?*
What do I know?
on the position of the sceptic
Montaigne 1533–92: *Essais* (1580)

26 Knowledge itself is power.
Francis Bacon 1561–1626: *Meditationes Sacrae* (1597) 'Of Heresies'; see KNOWLEDGE 3

27 What song the Syrens sang, or what name Achilles assumed when he hid himself among women, though puzzling questions, are not beyond all conjecture.
Thomas Browne 1605–82: *Hydriotaphia* (Urn Burial, 1658)

28 We have first raised a dust and then complain we cannot see.
George Berkeley 1685–1753: *A Treatise Concerning the Principles of Human Knowledge* (1710)

29 A little learning is a dangerous thing;
Drink deep, or taste not the Pierian spring.
Alexander Pope 1688–1744: *An Essay on Criticism* (1711); see KNOWLEDGE 6, POETRY 3

30 Action is the proper fruit of knowledge.
Thomas Fuller 1654–1734: *Gnomologia* (1732)

31 Knowledge may give weight, but accomplishments give lustre, and many more people see than weigh.
Lord Chesterfield 1694–1773: *Maxims* (1774)

32 Knowledge is of two kinds. We know a subject ourselves, or we know where we can find information upon it.
Samuel Johnson 1709–84: James Boswell *Life of Samuel Johnson* (1791) 18 April 1775

33 Dare to know! Have the courage to use your own reason! This is the motto of the Enlightenment.
Immanuel Kant 1724–1804: *What is Enlightenment?* (1784)

34 Only through beauty's gate, can you penetrate the land of knowledge.
Friedrich von Schiller 1759–1805: 'Die Künstler' (1789)

35 Knowledge advances by steps, and not by leaps.
Lord Macaulay 1800–59: T. F. Ellis (ed.) *Miscellaneous Writings of Lord Macaulay* (1860) 'History' (1828)

36 Knowledge comes, but wisdom lingers.
Alfred, Lord Tennyson 1809–92: 'Locksley Hall' (1842)

37 You will find it a very good practice always to verify your references, sir!
Martin Joseph Routh 1755–1854: John William Burgon *Lives of Twelve Good Men* (1888 ed.)

38 It is better to know nothing than to know what ain't so.
Josh Billings 1818–85: *Proverb* (1874)

39 No lesson seems to be so deeply inculcated by the experience of life as that you never should trust experts. If you believe the doctors, nothing is wholesome: if you believe the theologians, nothing is innocent: if you believe the soldiers, nothing is safe. They all require to have their strong wine diluted by a very large admixture of insipid common sense.
Lord Salisbury 1830–1903: letter to Lord Lytton, 15 June 1877

40 If a little knowledge is dangerous, where is the man who has so much as to be out of danger?
T. H. Huxley 1825–95: *Collected Essays* vol. 3 (1895) 'On Elementary Instruction in Physiology' (written 1877); see KNOWLEDGE 6

41 Now that I do know it, I shall do my best to forget it.
Arthur Conan Doyle 1859–1930: *A Study in Scarlet* (1887)

42 The motto of all the mongoose family is, 'Run and find out.'
Rudyard Kipling 1865–1936: *The Jungle Book* (1894)

43 I keep six honest serving-men
(They taught me all I knew);
Their names are What and Why and
When
And How and Where and Who.
Rudyard Kipling 1865–1936: *Just So Stories* (1902) 'The Elephant's Child'; see KNOWLEDGE 12

44 There is no such thing on earth as an uninteresting subject; the only thing that can exist is an uninterested person.
G. K. Chesterton 1874–1936: *Heretics* (1905)

45 The clever men at Oxford
Know all that there is to be knowed.
But they none of them know one half
as much
As intelligent Mr Toad!
Kenneth Grahame 1859–1932: *Wind in the Willows* (1908)

46 For lust of knowing what should not
be known,
We take the Golden Road to
Samarkand.
James Elroy Flecker 1884–1915: *The Golden Journey to Samarkand* (1913)

47 Owl hasn't exactly got Brain, but he Knows Things.
A. A. Milne 1882–1956: *Winnie-the-Pooh* (1926)

48 We have learned the answers, all the
answers:
It is the question that we do not
know.
Archibald MacLeish 1892–1982: *The Hamlet of A. McLeish* (1928)

49 Pedantry is the dotage of knowledge.
Holbrook Jackson 1874–1948: *Anatomy of Bibliomania* (1930)

50 Where is the wisdom we have lost in
knowledge?
Where is the knowledge we have lost
in information?
T. S. Eliot 1888–1965: *The Rock* (1934)

51 Our knowledge has made us cynical,
our cleverness hard and unkind.
Charlie Chaplin 1889–1977: *The Great Dictator* (1940 film)

52 We must know,
We will know.
David Hilbert 1862–1943: epitaph on his tombstone

53 Everybody gets so much information all day long that they lose their common sense.
Gertrude Stein 1874–1946: *Reflection on the Atomic Bomb* (1946)

54 An expert is one who knows more and more about less and less.
Nicholas Murray Butler 1862–1947: commencement address at Columbia University; attributed

55 The larger the island of knowledge, the longer the shoreline of wonder.
Ralph W. Sockman 1889–1970: attributed since the 1940s

56 An expert is someone who knows some of the worst mistakes that can be made in his subject and who manages to avoid them.
Werner Heisenberg 1901–76: *Der Teil und das Ganze* (1969)

57 Not many people know that.
Michael Caine 1933– : title of book (1984)

58 That was a little bit more information than I needed to know.
Quentin Tarantino 1963– : *Pulp Fiction* (1994 film); spoken by Uma Thurman

Language
see also MEANING, SPEECH, SWEARING, WORDS

proverbs and sayings ▸

1 The quick brown fox jumps over the lazy dog.
traditional sentence used by keyboarders to ensure that all letters of the alphabet are functioning

phrases ▸

2 weasel words
words or statements that are intentionally ambiguous or misleading; the expression was popularized by Theodore Roosevelt: see LANGUAGE 18

3 winged words
highly significant or apposite words; travelling as directly as arrows to the mark; from Homer *The Iliad*

quotations ▸

4 A word fitly spoken is like apples of gold in pictures of silver.
Bible: Proverbs

5 The chief merit of language is clearness, and we know that nothing detracts so much from this as do unfamiliar terms.
Galen AD 129–199: *On the Natural Faculties*

6 Grammer, the ground of al.
William Langland c.1330–c.1400: *The Vision of Piers Plowman*

7 Syllables govern the world.
John Selden 1584–1654: *Table Talk* (1689)

8 Good heavens! For more than forty years I have been speaking prose without knowing it.
Molière 1622–73: *Le Bourgeois Gentilhomme* (1671)

9 The true use of speech is not so much to express our wants as to conceal them.
Oliver Goldsmith 1728–74: in *The Bee* 20 October 1759 'On the Use of Language'

10 Language is the dress of thought.
Samuel Johnson 1709–84: *Lives of the English Poets* (1779–81)

11 In language, the ignorant have prescribed laws to the learned.
Richard Duppa 1770–1831: *Maxims* (1830)

12 He who understands baboon would do more towards metaphysics than Locke.
Charles Darwin 1809–82: Notebook M (16 August 1838)

13 Language is fossil poetry.
Ralph Waldo Emerson 1803–82: *Essays. Second Series* (1844) 'The Poet'

14 It is hard for a woman to define her feelings in language which is chiefly made by men to express theirs.
Thomas Hardy 1840–1928: *Far from the Madding Crowd* (1874)

15 I will not go down to posterity talking bad grammar.
while correcting proofs of his last Parliamentary speech, 31 March 1881
Benjamin Disraeli 1804–81: Robert Blake *Disraeli* (1966)

16 The mystery of language was revealed to me. I knew then that 'w-a-t-e-r' meant the wonderful cool something that was flowing over my hand. That living word awakened my soul, gave it light, joy, set it free!
Helen Keller 1880–1968: *The Story of My Life* (1902)

17 A definition is the enclosing a wilderness of idea within a wall of words.
Samuel Butler 1835–1902: *Notebooks* (1912)

18 One of our defects as a nation is a tendency to use what have been called 'weasel words.' When a weasel sucks eggs the meat is sucked out of the egg. If you use a 'weasel word' after another, there is nothing left of the other.
Theodore Roosevelt 1858–1919: speech in St Louis, 31 May 1916; see LANGUAGE 2

19 The limits of my language mean the limits of my world.
Ludwig Wittgenstein 1889–1951: *Tractatus Logico-Philosophicus* (1922)

20 One picture is worth ten thousand words.
Frederick R. Barnard: in *Printers' Ink* 10 March 1927; see WORDS AND DEEDS 5

21 The subjunctive mood is in its death throes, and the best thing to do is to put it out of its misery as soon as possible.
W. Somerset Maugham 1874–1965: *A Writer's Notebook* (1949) written in 1941

22 At the very best, a mind enclosed in language is in prison.
Simone Weil 1909–43: 'Human Personality' (1943)

23 Would you convey my compliments to the purist who reads your proofs and tell him or her that I write in a sort of broken-down patois which is something like the way a Swiss waiter talks, and that when I split an infinitive, God damn it, I split it so it will stay split.
Raymond Chandler 1888–1959: letter to Edward Weeks, 18 January 1947

24 This is the sort of English up with which I will not put.
Winston Churchill 1874–1965: Ernest Gowers *Plain Words* (1948)

25 Colourless green ideas sleep furiously.
illustrating that grammatical structure is independent of meaning
Noam Chomsky 1928– : *Syntactic Structures* (1957)

26 Slang is a language that rolls up its sleeves, spits on its hands and goes to work.
Carl Sandburg 1878–1967: in *New York Times* 13 February 1959

27 Different persons growing up in the same language are like different bushes trimmed and trained to take the shape of identical elephants. The anatomical details of twigs and branches will fulfill the elephantine form differently from bush to bush, but the overall outward results are alike.
W. V. O. Quine 1908–2000: *Word and Object* (1960)

28 Save the gerund and screw the whale.
Tom Stoppard 1937– : *The Real Thing* (1988 rev. ed.); see POLLUTION 2

29 I believe that political correctness can be a form of linguistic fascism, and it sends shivers down the spine of my generation who went to war against fascism.
P. D. James 1920– : in *Paris Review* 1995; see PREJUDICE 6

30 I went to give a talk at my old school and the girls were all doing 'likes' and 'innits?' and 'it aint's', which drives me insane.
Emma Thompson 1959– : in *Radio Times* 2 October 2010

Languages
see also TRANSLATION

proverbs and sayings ▸

1 A nation without a language is a nation without a heart.
Welsh proverb; see LANGUAGES 13

phrases ▸

2 the gift of tongues
the power of speaking in unknown languages, regarded as one of the gifts of the Holy Spirit; from the account in the Bible (Acts) of the coming of the Holy Spirit to the disciples at Pentecost, after which those to whom the disciples preached 'heard them speak with tongues, and magnify God'

3 the Tower of Babel
a tower built in an attempt to reach heaven, which God frustrated by confusing the languages of its builders so that they could not understand one another; from the biblical story (Genesis), which was probably inspired by the Babylonian ziggurat, and may be an attempt to explain the existence of different languages; see LANGUAGES 9

quotations ▸

4 And Frenssh she spak ful faire and fetisly,
After the scole of Stratford atte Bowe,

For Frenssh of Parys was to hire
unknowe.
Geoffrey Chaucer 1343–1400: *The Canterbury Tales* 'The General Prologue'

5 To God I speak Spanish, to women Italian, to men French, and to my horse—German.
Charles V 1500–58: attributed; Lord Chesterfield *Letters to his Son* (1774)

6 It is a thing plainly repugnant to the Word of God, and the custom of the Primitive Church, to have publick Prayer in the Church, or to minister the Sacraments in a tongue not understanded of the people.
The Book of Common Prayer 1662: *Articles of Religion* (1562)

7 Thou hadst small Latin, and less
Greek.
Ben Jonson 1573–1637: 'To the Memory of My Beloved, the Author, Mr William Shakespeare' (1623)

8 Poets that lasting marble seek
Must carve in Latin or in Greek.
Edmund Waller 1606–87: 'Of English Verse' (1645)

9 I am not like a lady at the court of Versailles, who said: 'What a dreadful pity that the bother at the tower of Babel should have got language all mixed up; but for that, everyone would always have spoken French.'
Voltaire 1694–1778: letter to Catherine the Great, 26 May 1767; see LANGUAGES 3

10 I am always sorry when any language is lost, because languages are the pedigree of nations.
Samuel Johnson 1709–84: James Boswell *Journal of a Tour to the Hebrides* (1785) 18 September 1773

11 My English text is chaste, and all licentious passages are left in the obscurity of a learned language.
parodied as 'decent obscurity' in the *Anti-Jacobin*, 1797–8
Edward Gibbon 1737–94: *Memoirs of My Life* (1796)

12 He who does not know foreign languages knows nothing of his own.
Johann Wolfgang von Goethe 1749–1832: *Maximen und Reflexionen* (1821)

13 A people without a language of its own is only half a nation.
Thomas Davis 1814–45: 'The National Language'; see LANGUAGES 1

14 The great breeding people had gone out and multiplied; colonies in every clime attest our success; French is the *patois* of Europe; English is the language of the world.
Walter Bagehot 1826–77: in *National Review* January 1856 'Edward Gibbon'

15 I like to be beholden to the great metropolitan English speech, the sea which receives tributaries from every region under heaven.
Ralph Waldo Emerson 1803–82: *Society and Solitude* (1870) 'Books'

16 A language is a dialect with an army and a navy.
Max Weinreich 1894–1969: in *Yivo Bleter* January–February 1945

17 England and America are two countries divided by a common language.
George Bernard Shaw 1856–1950: attributed in this and other forms, but not found in Shaw's published writings

18 There even are places where English
completely disappears.
In America, they haven't used it for
years!
Why can't the English teach their
children how to speak?
Alan Jay Lerner 1918–86: 'Why Can't the English?' (1956 song)

19 Waiting for the German verb is surely the ultimate thrill.
Flann O'Brien 1911–66: *The Hair of the Dogma* (1977)

20 The English language is nobody's special property. It is the property of the imagination: it is the property of the language itself.
Derek Walcott 1930– : Edward Hirsch 'The Art of Poetry' (1986) in R. Hanmer (ed.) *Critical Perspectives on Derek Walcott* (1993)

21 We are walking lexicons. In a single sentence of idle chatter we preserve Latin, Anglo-Saxon, Norse; we carry a museum inside our heads, each day we commemorate peoples of whom we have never heard.
Penelope Lively 1933– : *Moon Tiger* (1987)

The Law

see also CRIME, JUSTICE

proverbs and sayings ▸

1 **The devil makes his Christmas pies of lawyers' tongues and clerks' fingers.**
the lawyers' tongues and clerks' fingers stand for the words and actions of the legal profession as welcomed by the Devil; English proverb, late 16th century

2 **Gray's Inn for walks,**
Lincoln's Inn for a wall,
The Inner Temple for a garden,
And the Middle Temple for a hall.
on the four Inns of Court; traditional rhyme, mid 17th century

3 **Hard cases make bad law.**
difficult cases cause the clarity of the law to be obscured by exceptions and strained interpretations; the saying may now also be used to imply that a law framed in response to a particularly distressing case may not be well-thought-out or well-based; English proverb, mid 19th century

4 **Home is home, as the Devil said when he found himself in the Court of Session.**
the *Court of Session* is the supreme civil tribunal of Scotland, established in 1532; Scottish proverbial saying, mid 19th century

5 **Ignorance of the law is no excuse for breaking it.**
English proverb, early 15th century; see LAW 23

6 **Laws are like sausages. It's better not to see them being made.**
modern saying, often attributed to Bismarck, but not traced and probably apocryphal

7 **A man who is his own lawyer has a fool for his client.**
English proverb, early 19th century

8 **The more laws, the more thieves and bandits.**
a rigid and over-detailed code of law is likely to foster rather than prevent lawbreaking; English proverb, late 16th century; see LAW 18, LAW 21

9 **No one should be judge in his own cause.**
it is impossible to be impartial where your own interest is involved; English proverb, mid 15th century

10 **Possession is nine points of the law.**
although it does not reflect any specific legal ruling, in early use the satisfaction of ten (sometimes twelve) points was commonly asserted to attest to full entitlement or ownership; possession, represented by nine (or eleven) points is therefore the closest substitute for this; English proverb, early 17th century

11 **Rules are made to be broken.**
English proverb, mid 20th century; see LAW 28

12 **Where the law is uncertain, there is no law.**
legal saying, late 18th century; earliest found in Latin 'Ubi jus incertum, ibi jus nullum'

phrases ▸

13 **good cop, bad cop**
used to refer to a police interrogation technique in which one officer feigns a sympathetic or protective attitude while another adopts an aggressive approach

14 **habeas corpus**
a writ requiring a person under arrest to be brought before a judge or into court, especially to secure the person's release unless lawful grounds are shown for their detention; Latin, literally 'thou shalt have the body (in court)'; see LAW 29

15 **myrmidon of the law**
a police officer, a minor administrative officer of the law; *Myrmidon* = a member of a warlike people of ancient Thessaly, whom, according to a Homeric story, Achilles led to the siege of Troy

16 **the thin blue line**
the police as a defensive barrier of the law; alteration of *thin red line*: see ARMED FORCES 14

17 **twelve good men and true**
a jury; traditionally composed of twelve men

quotations ▸

18 **The more laws and orders are made prominent,**
The more thieves and bandits there will be.
Lao Tzu c.604–c.531 BC: *Tao-te Ching*; see LAW 8, LAW 21

19 **Written laws are like spider's webs; they will catch, it is true, the weak and poor, but would be torn in pieces by the rich and powerful.**
Anacharsis 6th century BC: Plutarch *Parallel Lives* 'Solon'

20 *Salus populi suprema est lex.*
The good of the people is the chief law.
Cicero 106–43 BC: *De Legibus*

21 The more corrupt the state, the more numerous the laws.
Tacitus c. AD 56–after 117: *Annals*; see LAW 8, LAW 18

22 How long soever it hath continued, if it be against reason, it is of no force in law.
Edward Coke 1552–1634: *The First Part of the Institutes of the Laws of England* (1628)

23 Ignorance of the law excuses no man; not that all men know the law, but because 'tis an excuse every man will plead, and no man can tell how to confute him.
John Selden 1584–1654: *Table Talk* (1689) 'Law'; see LAW 5

24 Law is a bottomless pit.
John Arbuthnot 1667–1735: *The History of John Bull* (1712)

25 The hungry judges soon the sentence sign,
And wretches hang that jury-men may dine.
Alexander Pope 1688–1744: *The Rape of the Lock* (1714)

26 Laws, like houses, lean on one another.
Edmund Burke 1729–97: *A Tract on the Popery Laws* (planned 1765)

27 Bad laws are the worst sort of tyranny.
Edmund Burke 1729–97: *Speech at Bristol, previous to the Late Election* (1780)

28 Laws were made to be broken.
Christopher North 1785–1854: in *Blackwood's Magazine* (May 1830); see LAW 11

29 The have-his-carcase, next to the perpetual motion, is vun of the blessedest things as wos ever made.
Charles Dickens 1812–70: *Pickwick Papers* (1837); see LAW 14

30 'If the law supposes that,' said Mr Bumble...'the law is a ass—a idiot.'
Charles Dickens 1812–70: *Oliver Twist* (1838)

31 English law does not permit good persons, as such, to strangle bad persons, as such.
T. H. Huxley 1825–95: letter in *Pall Mall Gazette*, 31 October 1866

32 I know no method to secure the repeal of bad or obnoxious laws so effective as their stringent execution.
Ulysses S. Grant 1822–85: inaugural address, 4 March 1869

33 When constabulary duty's to be done,
A policeman's lot is not a happy one.
W. S. Gilbert 1836–1911: *The Pirates of Penzance* (1879)

34 The Law is the true embodiment
Of everything that's excellent.
It has no kind of fault or flaw,
And I, my Lords, embody the Law.
the Lord Chancellor
W. S. Gilbert 1836–1911: *Iolanthe* (1882)

35 I don't know as I want a lawyer to tell me what I cannot do. I hire him to tell me how to do what I want to do.
J. P. Morgan 1837–1913: Ida M. Tarbell *The Life of Elbert H. Gary* (1925)

36 Regulations—they're written for the obedience of fools and the guidance of wise men.
Harry Day: to Douglas Bader, 1931; Paul Brickhill *Reach for the Sky* (1954)

37 No poet ever interpreted nature as freely as a lawyer interprets the truth.
Jean Giraudoux 1882–1944: *La Guerre de Troie n'aura pas lieu* (1935)

38 A verbal contract isn't worth the paper it is written on.
Sam Goldwyn 1882–1974: Alva Johnston *The Great Goldwyn* (1937)

39 Everything not forbidden is compulsory.
T. H. White 1906–64: *The Sword in the Stone* (1938)

40 We are not final because we are infallible, but we are infallible only because we are final.
of the Supreme Court
Robert H. Jackson 1892–1954: *Brown v. Allen* (1953)

41 Every society gets the kind of criminal it deserves. What is equally true is that every community gets the kind of law enforcement it insists on.
Robert Kennedy 1925–68: *The Pursuit of Justice* (1964)

42 A lawyer with his briefcase can steal more than a hundred men with guns.
Mario Puzo 1920–99: *The Godfather* (1969)

43 The big print giveth, and the fine print taketh away.

Fulton J. Sheen 1895–1979: attributed

44 Asking the ignorant to use the incomprehensible to decide the unknowable.

on the jury system

Hiller B. Zobel 1932– : 'The Jury on Trial' in *American Heritage* July–August 1995

45 Not only did we play the race card, we played it from the bottom of the deck.

on the defence's conduct of the O. J. Simpson trial

Robert Shapiro 1942– : interview, 3 October 1995, in *Times* 5 October 1995; see WAYS 28

Leadership

proverbs and sayings ▸

1 As one fern frond dies, another is born to take its place.

Maori proverb, applied particularly to chiefs

2 The fish always stinks from the head downwards.

as the freshness of a dead fish can be judged from the condition of its head, any corruption in a country or organization will be manifested first in its leaders; English proverb, late 16th century

3 A good leader is also a good follower.

American proverb, mid 20th century

4 He that cannot obey cannot command.

the experience of being under orders teaches one how they should be given; English proverb, late 15th century

5 If you are not the lead dog, the view never changes.

Canadian saying

6 One mountain cannot accommodate two tigers.

there cannot be two leaders; Chinese proverb

7 Take me to your leader.

catchphrase from science-fiction stories

phrases ▸

8 the Nelson touch

a masterly or sympathetic approach to a problem by the person in charge, supposedly characteristic of Nelson's style of leadership: see LEADERSHIP 14

quotations ▸

9 A leader is best when people barely know he exists...He acts without unnecessary speech, and when the work is done the people say 'We did it ourselves'.

Lao Tzu c.604–c.531 BC: *Tao-te Ching*

10 If you desire what is good, the people will be good. The character of a ruler is like wind and that of the people is like grass. In whatever direction the wind blows the grass always bends.

Confucius 551–479 BC: *Analects*

11 They be blind leaders of the blind. And if the blind lead the blind, both shall fall into the ditch.

Bible: St Matthew; see IGNORANCE 11

12 Since, then, a prince is necessitated to play the animal well, he chooses among the beasts the fox and the lion, because the lion does not protect himself from traps; the fox does not protect himself from wolves. The prince must be a fox, therefore, to recognize the traps and a lion to frighten the wolves.

Niccolò Machiavelli 1469–1527: *The Prince* (written 1513)

13 The first method for estimating the intelligence of a ruler is to look at the men he has around him.

Niccolò Machiavelli 1469–1527: *The Prince* (written 1513)

14 I believe my arrival was most welcome, not only to the Commander of the Fleet but almost to every individual in it; and when I came to explain to them the *'Nelson touch'*, it was like an electric shock. Some shed tears, all approved—'It was new—it was singular—it was simple!'

Horatio, Lord Nelson 1758–1805: letter to Lady Hamilton, 1 October 1805; see LEADERSHIP 8

15 I used to say of him [Napoleon] that his presence on the field made the difference of forty thousand men.

Duke of Wellington 1769–1852: Philip Henry Stanhope *Notes of Conversations with the Duke of Wellington* (1888) 2 November 1831

16 By the structure of the world we often want, at the sudden occurrence

of a grave tempest, to change the helmsman—to replace the pilot of the calm by the pilot of the storm.

Walter Bagehot 1826–77: *The English Constitution* (1867) 'The Cabinet'

17 The art of leadership...consists in consolidating the attention of the people against a single adversary and taking care that nothing will split up that attention.

Adolf Hitler 1889–1945: *Mein Kampf* (1925)

18 So long as men worship the Caesars and Napoleons, Caesars and Napoleons will duly arise and make them miserable.

Aldous Huxley 1894–1963: *Ends and Means* (1937)

19 The final test of a leader is that he leaves behind him in other men the conviction and the will to carry on.

Walter Lippmann 1889–1974: in *New York Herald Tribune* 14 April 1945

20 The loyalties which centre upon number one are enormous. If he trips he must be sustained. If he makes mistakes they must be covered. If he sleeps he must not be wantonly disturbed. If he is no good he must be pole-axed. But this last extreme process cannot be carried out every day; and certainly not in the days just after he has been chosen.

Winston Churchill 1874–1965: *The Second World War* vol. 2 (1949)

21 I know that the right kind of leader for the Labour Party is a desiccated calculating machine who must not in any way permit himself to be swayed by indignation.

generally taken as referring to Hugh Gaitskell, although Bevan specifically denied it

Aneurin Bevan 1897–1960: Michael Foot *Aneurin Bevan* (1973)

22 Ultimately a genuine leader is not a searcher for consensus, but a moulder of consensus.

Martin Luther King 1929–68: *Where Do We Go From Here?* (1967)

23 A leader who doesn't hesitate before he sends his nation into battle is not fit to be a leader.

Golda Meir 1898–1978: Israel and Mary Shenka *As Good as Golda* (1970)

24 I don't mind how much my Ministers talk, so long as they do what I say.

Margaret Thatcher 1925– : in *Observer* 27 January 1980

25 Leadership means making people feel good.

Jean Chrétien 1934– : in *Toronto Star* 7 June 1984

26 To grasp and hold a vision, that is the very essence of successful leadership—not only on the movie set where I learned it, but everywhere.

Ronald Reagan 1911–2004: in *The Wilson Quarterly* Winter 1994; attributed

27 The art of leadership is saying no, not yes. It is very easy to say yes.

Tony Blair 1953– : in *Mail on Sunday* 2 October 1994

28 Leadership is not about being nice. It's about being right and being strong.

Paul Keating 1944– : in *Time* 9 January 1995

29 You can't lead the people if you don't love the people, and you can't save the people if you won't serve the people.

Cornel West 1953– : interview, *The Tavis Smiley Show* National Public Radio 26 May 2004

Leisure

see also WORK

proverbs and sayings ▶

1 All work and no play makes Jack a dull boy.

warning against a lifestyle without any form of relaxation; English proverb, mid 17th century

2 The busiest men have the most leisure.

someone who is habitually busy is likely to make best use of their time; English proverb, late 19th century

3 Have a break, have a Kit-Kat.

advertising slogan for Rowntree's Kit-Kat, from 1955

quotations ▶

4 The wisdom of a learned man cometh by opportunity of leisure: and he that hath little business shall become wise.

Bible: Ecclesiasticus

5 The thing which is the most outstanding and chiefly to be desired by all healthy and good and well-off persons, is leisure with honour.
Cicero 106–43 BC: *Pro Sestio*

6 Take rest; a field that has rested gives a bountiful crop.
Ovid 43 BC–C. AD 17: *Ars Amatoria*

7 If all the year were playing holidays,
To sport would be as tedious as to work;
But when they seldom come, they wished for come.
William Shakespeare 1564–1616: *Henry IV, Part 1* (1597)

8 Repose is a good thing, but boredom is its brother.
Voltaire 1694–1778: attributed, 1921

9 Man is so made that he can only find relaxation from one kind of labour by taking up another.
Anatole France 1844–1924: *The Crime of Sylvestre Bonnard* (1881)

10 What is this life if, full of care,
We have no time to stand and stare.
W. H. Davies 1871–1940: 'Leisure' (1911)

11 A perpetual holiday is a good working definition of hell.
George Bernard Shaw 1856–1950: *Parents and Children* (1914)

12 There's sand in the porridge and sand in the bed,
And if this is pleasure we'd rather be dead.
Noël Coward 1899–1973: 'The English Lido' (1928)

13 To be able to fill leisure intelligently is the last product of civilization.
Bertrand Russell 1872–1970: *The Conquest of Happiness* (1930)

14 We are closer to the ants than to the butterflies. Very few people can endure much leisure.
Gerald Brenan 1894–1987: *Thoughts in a Dry Season* (1978)

15 To many people holidays are no voyage of discovery, but a ritual of reassurance.
Phillip Adams 1939– : in *Age* 10 September 1983

16 If I am doing nothing, I like to be doing nothing to some purpose. That is what leisure means.
Alan Bennett 1934– : *A Question of Attribution* (1989)

Letters

proverbs and sayings ▸

1 A love letter sometimes costs more than a three-cent stamp.
American proverb, mid 20th century

2 Someone, somewhere, wants a letter from you.
advertising slogan for the British Post Office in the 1960s

quotations ▸

3 Ye see how large a letter I have written unto you with mine own hand.
Bible: Galatians

4 There is nothing to write about, you say. Well then, write and let me know just this—that there is nothing to write about; or tell me in the good old style if you are well.
Pliny the Younger C. AD 61–C. 112: *Letters*

5 Sir, more than kisses, letters mingle souls.
John Donne 1572–1631: 'To Sir Henry Wotton' (1597–8)

6 I knew one that when he wrote a letter he would put that which was most material in the postscript, as if it had been a bymatter.
Francis Bacon 1561–1626: *Essays* (1625) 'Of Cunning'

7 All letters, methinks, should be free and easy as one's discourse, not studied as an oration, nor made up of hard words like a charm.
Dorothy Osborne 1627–95: letter to William Temple, September 1653

8 I have made this [letter] longer than usual, only because I have not had the time to make it shorter.
Blaise Pascal 1623–62: *Lettres Provinciales* (1657)

9 A woman seldom writes her mind but in her postscript.
Richard Steele 1672–1729: in *The Spectator* 31 May 1711

10 She'll vish there wos more, and that's the great art o' letter writin'.
Charles Dickens 1812–70: *Pickwick Papers* (1837–8)

11 Correspondences are like small-clothes before the invention of suspenders; it is impossible to keep them up.
Sydney Smith 1771–1845: letter to Catherine Crowe, 31 January 1841

12 It is wonderful how much news there is when people write every other day; if they wait for a month, there is nothing that seems worth telling.
O. Douglas 1877–1948: *Penny Plain* (1920)

13 Letters of thanks, letters from banks,
Letters of joy from girl and boy,
Receipted bills and invitations
To inspect new stock or to visit relations,
And applications for situations,
And timid lovers' declarations,
And gossip, gossip from all the nations.
W. H. Auden 1907–73: 'Night Mail' (1936)

14 It does me good to write a letter which is not a response to a demand, a gratuitous letter, so to speak, which has accumulated in me like the waters of a reservoir.
Henry Miller 1891–1980: *The Books in My Life* (1951)

Liberty

proverbs and sayings ▶

1 Lean liberty is better than fat slavery.
asserting that freedom matters more than any material comfort; English proverb, early 17th century

phrases ▶

2 the bird has flown
the prisoner or fugitive has escaped; see PARLIAMENT 15

3 Liberty Hall
a place where one may do as one likes; from Goldmith's *She Stoops to Conquer* (1773): 'This is Liberty-hall, gentlemen. You may do just as you please'

4 Underground Railroad
in the US, a secret network for helping slaves escape from the South to the North and Canada in the years before the American Civil War

quotations ▶

5 Let my people go.
Bible: Exodus

6 *Nullius addictus iurare in verba magistri,*
Quo me cumque rapit tempestas, deferor hospes.
Not bound to swear allegiance to any master, wherever the wind takes me I travel as a visitor.
Horace 65–8 BC: *Epistles*

7 One Cartwright brought a Slave from Russia, and would scourge him, for which he was questioned: and it was resolved, That England was too pure an Air for Slaves to breathe in.
Anonymous: 'In the 11th of Elizabeth' (1568–1569); John Rushworth *Historical Collections* (1680–1722)

8 Stone walls do not a prison make,
Nor iron bars a cage.
Richard Lovelace 1618–58: 'To Althea, From Prison' (1649)

9 None can love freedom heartily, but good men; the rest love not freedom, but licence.
John Milton 1608–74: *The Tenure of Kings and Magistrates* (1649)

10 Man was born free, and everywhere he is in chains.
Jean-Jacques Rousseau 1712–78: *Du Contrat social* (1762)

11 I know not what course others may take; but as for me, give me liberty, or give me death!
Patrick Henry 1736–99: speech in Virginia Convention, 23 March 1775

12 The tree of liberty must be refreshed from time to time with the blood of

patriots and tyrants. It is its natural manure.

Thomas Jefferson 1743–1826: letter to W. S. Smith, 13 November 1787

13 I believe there are more instances of the abridgement of the freedom of the people by gradual and silent encroachments of those in power than by violent and sudden usurpations.

James Madison 1751–1836: speech in Virginia Convention, 16 June 1788

14 The condition upon which God hath given liberty to man is eternal vigilance; which condition if he break, servitude is at once the consequence of his crime, and the punishment of his guilt.

John Philpot Curran 1750–1817: speech on the right of election of the Lord Mayor of Dublin, 10 July 1790

15 O liberty! O liberty! what crimes are committed in thy name!

Mme Roland 1754–93: A. de Lamartine *Histoire des Girondins* (1847)

16 He that would make his own liberty secure must guard even his enemy from oppression; for if he violates this duty he establishes a precedent that will reach to himself.

Thomas Paine 1737–1809: *Dissertation on First Principles of Government* (1795); see JUSTICE 12

17 If men are to wait for liberty till they become wise and good in slavery, they may indeed wait for ever.

Lord Macaulay 1800–59: *Essays Contributed to the Edinburgh Review* (1843) 'Milton'

18 The liberty of the individual must be thus far limited; he must not make himself a nuisance to other people.

John Stuart Mill 1806–73: *On Liberty* (1859)

19 The word 'freedom' means for me not a point of departure but a genuine point of arrival. The point of departure is defined by the word 'order'. Freedom cannot exist without the concept of order.

Prince Metternich 1773–1859: *Mein Politisches Testament* (1880)

20 In giving freedom to the slave, we assure freedom to the free—honourable alike in what we give and what we preserve. We shall nobly save, or meanly lose, the last, best hope of earth.

Abraham Lincoln 1809–65: annual message to Congress, 1 December 1862

21 I had reasoned this out in my mind. There were two things I had a right to, liberty and death. If I could not have one, I would have the other, for no man should take me alive.

Harriet Tubman c.1820–1913: Sarah H. Bradford *Harriet, the Moses of Her People* (1869)

22 Liberty means responsibility. That is why most men dread it.

George Bernard Shaw 1856–1950: *Man and Superman* (1903) 'Maxims: Liberty and Equality'

23 The cost of liberty is less than the price of repression.

W. E. B. Du Bois 1868–1963: *John Brown* (1909)

24 Tyranny is always better organized than freedom.

Charles Péguy 1873–1914: *Basic Verities* (1943) 'War and Peace'

25 Freedom is always and exclusively freedom for the one who thinks differently.

Rosa Luxemburg 1871–1919: *Die Russische Revolution* (1918)

26 Liberty is precious—so precious that it must be rationed.

Lenin 1870–1924: Sidney and Beatrice Webb *Soviet Communism* (1936)

27 It's often better to be in chains than to be free.

Franz Kafka 1883–1924: *The Trial* (1925)

28 Those who won our independence... believed liberty to be the secret of happiness and courage to be the secret of liberty.

Louis D. Brandeis 1856–1941: in *Whitney v California* (1927)

29 It is better to die on your feet than to live on your knees.

Dolores Ibarruri 1895–1989: speech in Paris, 3 September 1936; also attributed to Emiliano Zapata

30 I am condemned to be free.

Jean-Paul Sartre 1905–80: *L'Être et le néant* (1943)

31 If liberty means anything at all it means the right to tell people what they do not want to hear.
George Orwell 1903–50: 'The Freedom of the Press' (written 1944), in *Times Literary Supplement* 15 September 1972

32 The enemies of Freedom do not argue; they shout and they shoot.
William Ralph Inge 1860–1954: *End of an Age* (1948)

33 Freedom is the freedom to say that two plus two make four. If that is granted, all else follows.
George Orwell 1903–50: *Nineteen Eighty-Four* (1949)

34 The moment the slave resolves that he will no longer be a slave, his fetters fall. He frees himself and shows the way to others. Freedom and slavery are mental states.
Mahatma Gandhi 1869–1948: *Non-Violence in Peace and War* (1949)

35 Freedom is not something that one people can bestow on another as a gift. They claim it as their own and none can keep it from them.
Kwame Nkrumah 1900–72: speech in Accra, 10 July 1953

36 Liberty is always unfinished business.
American Civil Liberties Union: title of 36th Annual Report, 1 July 1955–30 June 1956

37 Liberty is liberty, not equality or fairness or justice or human happiness or a quiet conscience.
Isaiah Berlin 1909–97: *Two Concepts of Liberty* (1958)

38 Let every nation know, whether it wishes us well or ill, that we shall pay any price, bear any burden, meet any hardship, support any friend, oppose any foe to assure the survival and the success of liberty.
John F. Kennedy 1917–63: inaugural address, 20 January 1961

39 Freedom's just another word for
nothin' left to lose,
Nothin' ain't worth nothin,' but it's
free.
Kris Kristofferson 1936– : 'Me and Bobby McGee' (1969 song, with Fred Foster)

40 Let freedom reign. The sun shall never set on so glorious a human achievement.
Nelson Mandela 1918– : inaugural address as President of South Africa, 10 May 1994

41 Freedom is about the willingness of every single human being to cede to lawful authority a great deal of discretion about what you do, and how you do it.
Rudy Giuliani 1944– : attributed, in *Independent* 10 July 1999

42 Real freedom is freedom from fear, and unless you can live free from fear you cannot live a dignified human life.
Aung San Suu Kyi 1945– : undated interview with the BBC; transcript on BBC World Service website

Libraries

see also BOOKS, READING

proverbs and sayings ▸

1 A library is a repository of medicine for the mind.
American proverb, mid 20th century

quotations ▸

2 Medicine for the soul.
inscription on the library of Ramses II at Thebes (1292–1225 BC)
Anonymous: Diodorus Siculus *Bibliotheca Historica* (60–30 BC)

3 Let your bookcases and your shelves be your gardens and your pleasure-grounds. Pluck the fruit that grows therein, gather the roses, the spices and the myrrh.
Judah Ibn Tibbon 1120–90: Israel Abrahams *Jewish Life in the Middle Ages* (1932)

4 Come, and take choice of all my
library,
And so beguile thy sorrow.
William Shakespeare 1564–1616: *Titus Andronicus* (1590)

5 To make it fit and handsome with seats and shelves and desks and all that may be needful, to stir up other

men's benevolence to help to furnish it with books.

Thomas Bodley 1546–1613: letter to the Vice-Chancellor of the University of Oxford, 23 February 1597, proposing to restore the university library

6 No place affords a more striking conviction of the vanity of human hopes, than a public library.

Samuel Johnson 1709–84: in *The Rambler* 23 March 1751

7 With awe, around these silent walks
I tread;
These are the lasting mansions of the
dead.

George Crabbe 1754–1832: 'The Library' (1808)

8 What a sad want I am in of libraries, of books to gather facts from! Why is there not a Majesty's library in every county town? There is a Majesty's jail and gallows in every one.

Thomas Carlyle 1795–1881: diary, 18 May 1832

9 We call ourselves a rich nation, and we are filthy and foolish enough to thumb each other's books out of circulating libraries!

John Ruskin 1819–1900: *Sesame and Lilies* (1865)

10 A man should keep his little brain attic stocked with all the furniture that he is likely to use, and the rest he can put away in the lumber room of his library, where he can get it if he wants it.

Arthur Conan Doyle 1859–1930: *The Adventures of Sherlock Holmes* (1892)

11 I've been drunk for about a week now, and I thought it might sober me up to sit in a library.

F. Scott Fitzgerald 1896–1940: *The Great Gatsby* (1925)

12 Much have I travelled in the realms
of gold
For which I thank the Paddington and
Westminster
Public Libraries.

Peter Porter 1929– : 'The Sanitized Sonnets' 4 (1970); see READING 14

13 What is more important in a library than anything else—than everything else—is the fact that it exists.

Archibald MacLeish 1892–1982: 'The Premise of Meaning' in *American Scholar* 5 June 1972

14 I have always imagined Paradise as a kind of library.

Jorge Luis Borges 1899–1986: *Seven Nights* (1984) 'Blindness'

15 Libraries are reservoirs of strength, grace and wit, reminders of order, calm, continuity, lakes of mental energy, neither warm nor cold, light nor dark. The pleasure they give is steady, unorgiastic, reliable, deep and long-lasting.

Germaine Greer 1939– : *Daddy, We Hardly Knew You* (1989)

Lies

see also DECEPTION, TRUTH

proverbs and sayings ▸

1 An abomination unto the Lord, but a very present help in time of trouble.

definition of a lie, an amalgamation of lines from the Bible (Proverbs and Psalms), often attributed to the American politician Adlai Stevenson (1900–65)

2 Half the truth is often a whole lie.

something which is partially true can still convey a completely false impression; English proverb, mid 18th century

3 A liar ought to have a good memory.

implying that one lie is likely to lead to the need for another; English proverb, mid 16th century, 1st century AD in Latin

4 The liar's candle lasts till evening.

a lie will be exposed sooner or later; Turkish proverb

5 A lie can go around the world and back again while the truth is lacing up its boots.

American proverb, late 19th century; see LIES 17

6 One seldom meets a lonely lie.

implying that one lie is likely to lead to the need for another; American proverb, mid 20th century

7 To tell a falsehood is like the cut of a sabre, for though the wound may heal the scar will remain.

Persian proverb

phrases ►

8 economical with the truth

a person or statement that lies or deliberately withholds information; used euphemistically, and deriving from a statement given in evidence by Sir Robert Armstrong: see TRUTH 41

9 the liar paradox

the paradox involved in a speaker's statement that he or she is lying or is a (habitual) liar; said to have been created by the semi-legendary Cretan poet Epimenides, asserting that all Cretans are liars; by this definition, if he is a Cretan, then what he says cannot be true, and Cretans are honest

quotations ►

10 It is the penalty of a liar, that should he even tell the truth, he is not listened to.

The Talmud: *Babylonian Talmud* Sanhedrin

11 Man's mind is so formed that it is far more susceptible to falsehood than to truth.

Erasmus c.1469–1536: *In Praise of Folly* (1509)

12 The retort courteous...the quip modest...the reply churlish...the reproof valiant...the countercheck quarrelsome...the lie circumstantial... the lie direct.

of the degrees of a lie

William Shakespeare 1564–1616: *As You Like It* (1599)

13 A mixture of a lie doth ever add pleasure.

Francis Bacon 1561–1626: *Essays* (1625) 'Of Truth'

14 He replied that I must needs be mistaken, or that I *said the thing which was not.* (For they have no word in their language to express lying or falsehood.)

Jonathan Swift 1667–1745: *Gulliver's Travels* (1726)

15 Whoever would lie usefully should lie seldom.

Lord Hervey 1696–1743: *Memoirs of the Reign of George II* (ed. J. W. Croker, 1848)

16 as a child, when asked whether he had cut down a cherry tree:

I can't tell a lie, Pa; you know I can't tell a lie. I did cut it with my hatchet.

George Washington 1732–99: M. L. Weems *Life of George Washington* (10th ed., 1810); see LIES 18

17 If you want truth to go round the world you must hire an express train to pull it; but if you want a lie to go round the world, it will fly: it is as light as a feather, and a breath will carry it. It is well said in the old proverb, 'a lie will go round the world while truth is pulling its boots on.'

C. H. Spurgeon 1834–92: *Gems from Spurgeon* (1859); see LIES 5

18 I am different from Washington. I have a higher and grander stand of principle. Washington could not lie. I *can* lie but I won't.

Mark Twain 1835–1910: in *Chicago Tribune* 20 December 1871; see LIES 16

19 Great is the power of steady misrepresentation.

Charles Darwin 1809–82: *The Origin of Species* (6th ed., 1872)

20 The cruellest lies are often told in silence.

Robert Louis Stevenson 1850–94: *Virginibus Puerisque* (1881)

21 Matilda told such Dreadful Lies,
It made one Gasp and Stretch one's
Eyes.

Hilaire Belloc 1870–1953: *Cautionary Tales* (1907) 'Matilda'

22 A little inaccuracy sometimes saves tons of explanation.

Saki 1870–1916: *The Square Egg* (1924)

23 Without lies humanity would perish of despair and boredom.

Anatole France 1844–1924: *La Vie en fleur* (1922)

24 The broad mass of a nation...will more easily fall victim to a big lie than to a small one.

Adolf Hitler 1889–1945: *Mein Kampf* (1925)

25 Truth, like light, blinds. Falsehood, on the contrary, is a beautiful twilight, that enhances every object.

Albert Camus 1913–60: *The Fall* (1956)

26 In our country the lie has become not just a moral category but a pillar of the State.

Alexander Solzhenitsyn 1918–2008: 1974 interview, in *The Oak and the Calf* (1975)

Life

see also LIFE SCIENCES, LIFESTYLES

proverbs and sayings ▸

1 Be happy while y'er leevin,
For y'er a lang time deid.
Scottish motto for a house

2 Life is a sexually transmitted disease.
graffito found on the London Underground

3 Life is harder than crossing a field.
Russian proverb

4 Life isn't all beer and skittles.
life is not unalloyed pleasure or relaxation; English proverb, mid 19th century

5 Life is the best gift; the rest is extra.
African proverb (Swahili)

6 Life's a bitch, and then you die.
modern saying, late 20th century

7 A live dog is better than a dead lion.
often used in the context of a lesser person taking the place of a greater one who has died; English proverb, late 14th century, from the Bible: see VALUE 23

8 Man cannot live by bread alone.
one needs spiritual as well as physical sustenance; English proverb, late 19th century, after the Bible (Matthew) 'Man shall not live by bread alone, but by every word that proceedeth out of the mouth of God'

9 Tout passe, tout casse, tout lasse.
French = everything passes, everything perishes, everything palls

phrases ▸

10 all flesh
whatever has bodily life; from the Bible: see TRANSIENCE 7

11 all human life is there
every variety of human experience; used as an advertising slogan for the *News of the World* in the late 1950s: see LIFE 38

12 the elixir of life
a supposed drug or essence capable of prolonging life indefinitely; translation of medieval Latin *elixir vitae*

13 life's rich pageant
all the variety of human experience; the first recorded use is by Arthur Marshall (1910–89) in the monologue *The Games Mistress* (1937)

14 mouse and man
every living thing; alliterative association of the types of animal and human kind; probably popularized by Robert Burns: see FORESIGHT 14

15 this mortal coil
the turmoil of life, from Shakespeare *Hamlet*: see DEATH 38

quotations ▸

16 All that a man hath will he give for his life.
Bible: Job

17 Not to be born is, past all prizing, best.
Sophocles c.496–406 BC: *Oedipus Coloneus*; see LIFE 45

18 And life is given to none freehold, but it is leasehold for all.
Lucretius c.94–55 BC: *De Rerum Natura*

19 'Such,' he said, 'O King, seems to me the present life of men on earth, in comparison with that time which to us is uncertain, as if when on a winter's night you sit feasting with your ealdormen and thegns,—a single sparrow should fly swiftly into the hall, and coming in at one door, instantly fly out through another.'
The Venerable Bede AD 673–735: *Ecclesiastical History of the English People*

20 Life well spent is long.
Leonardo da Vinci 1452–1519: Edward McCurdy (ed.) *Leonardo da Vinci's Notebooks* (1906)

21 All the world's a stage,
And all the men and women merely players:
They have their exits and their entrances;
And one man in his time plays many parts,
His acts being seven ages.
William Shakespeare 1564–1616: *As You Like It* (1599)

22 Life's but a walking shadow, a poor player,
That struts and frets his hour upon the stage,
And then is heard no more; it is a tale
Told by an idiot, full of sound and fury,
Signifying nothing.
William Shakespeare 1564–1616: *Macbeth* (1606)

23 No arts; no letters; no society; and which is worst of all, continual fear and danger of violent death; and the life of man, solitary, poor, nasty, brutish, and short.

Thomas Hobbes 1588–1679: *Leviathan* (1651)

24 Life is an incurable disease.

Abraham Cowley 1618–67: 'To Dr Scarborough' (1656)

25 Man that is born of a woman hath but a short time to live, and is full of misery.

The Book of Common Prayer 1662: *The Burial of the Dead*

26 Man wants but little here below,
Nor wants that little long.

Oliver Goldsmith 1728–74: 'Edwin and Angelina, or the Hermit' (1766); see ALCOHOL 14

27 This world is a comedy to those that think, a tragedy to those that feel.

Horace Walpole 1717–97: letter to Anne, Countess of Upper Ossory, 16 August 1776

28 Life, like a dome of many-coloured glass,
Stains the white radiance of Eternity,
Until Death tramples it to fragments.

Percy Bysshe Shelley 1792–1822: *Adonais* (1821)

29 Life is real! Life is earnest!
And the grave is not its goal;
Dust thou art, to dust returnest,
Was not spoken of the soul.

Henry Wadsworth Longfellow 1807–82: 'A Psalm of Life' (1838); see DEATH 26

30 I slept, and dreamed that life was beauty;
I woke, and found that life was duty.

Ellen Sturgis Hooper 1816–41: 'Beauty and Duty' (1840)

31 Life must be understood backwards; but...it must be lived forwards.

Sören Kierkegaard 1813–55: *Journals and Papers* (1843)

32 Youth is a blunder; Manhood a struggle; Old Age a regret.

Benjamin Disraeli 1804–81: *Coningsby* (1844)

33 The mass of men lead lives of quiet desperation.

Henry David Thoreau 1817–62: *Walden* (1854)

34 Life would be tolerable but for its amusements.

George Cornewall Lewis 1806–63: in *Times* 18 September 1872

35 Life is mostly froth and bubble,
Two things stand like stone,
Kindness in another's trouble,
Courage in your own.

Adam Lindsay Gordon 1833–70: *Ye Wearie Wayfarer* (1866)

36 Life is the farce which everyone has to perform.

Arthur Rimbaud 1854–91: *A Season in Hell* (1873)

37 Real life is elsewhere.

Arthur Rimbaud 1854–91: *A Season in Hell* (1873)

38 Cats and monkeys—monkeys and cats—all human life is there!

Henry James 1843–1916: *The Madonna of the Future* (1879); see LIFE 11

39 The life of every man is a diary in which he means to write one story, and writes another; and his humblest hour is when he compares the volume as it is with what he vowed to make it.

J. M. Barrie 1860–1937: *The Little Minister* (1891)

40 Life is like playing a violin solo in public and learning the instrument as one goes on.

Samuel Butler 1835–1902: speech at the Somerville Club, 27 February 1895

41 Life is just one damned thing after another.

Elbert Hubbard 1859–1915: in *Philistine* December 1909; often attributed to Frank Ward O'Malley

42 The same stream of life that runs through my veins night and day runs through the world and dances in rhythmic measures.

It is the same life that shoots in joy through the dust of the earth into numberless blades of grass and breaks into tumultuous waves of leaves and flowers.

Rabindranath Tagore 1861–1941: *Gitanjali* (1912)

43 I have measured out my life with coffee spoons.
T. S. Eliot 1888–1965: 'The Love Song of J. Alfred Prufrock' (1917)

44 Life is not a series of gig lamps symmetrically arranged; life is a luminous halo, a semi-transparent envelope surrounding us from the beginning of consciousness to the end.
Virginia Woolf 1882–1941: *The Common Reader* (1925)

45 Never to have lived is best, ancient writers say;
Never to have drawn the breath of life, never to have looked into the eye of day;
The second best's a gay goodnight and quickly turn away.
W. B. Yeats 1865–1939: 'From *Oedipus at Colonus*' (1928); see LIFE 17

46 Life is a horizontal fall.
Jean Cocteau 1889–1963: *Opium* (1930)

47 Life is not meant to be easy, my child; but take courage: it can be delightful.
George Bernard Shaw 1856–1950: *Back to Methuselah* (rev. ed., 1930); see ADVERSITY 20

48 Life is just a bowl of cherries.
Lew Brown 1893–1958: title of song (1931)

49 All that matters is love and work.
Sigmund Freud 1856–1939: attributed

50 Life is either a daring adventure or nothing.
Helen Keller 1880–1968: *Let Us Have Faith* (1940)

51 To live at all is miracle enough.
Mervyn Peake 1911–68: *The Glassblower* (1950)

52 Life is like a sewer. What you get out of it depends on what you put into it.
Tom Lehrer 1928– : 'We Will All Go Together When We Go' (1953 song)

53 Oh, isn't life a terrible thing, thank God?
Dylan Thomas 1914–53: *Under Milk Wood* (1954)

54 As far as we can discern, the sole purpose of human existence is to kindle a light in the darkness of mere being.
Carl Gustav Jung 1875–1961: *Erinnerungen, Träume, Gedanken* (1962)

55 Life is first boredom, then fear.
Philip Larkin 1922–85: 'Dockery & Son' (1964)

56 The secret of life is to have a task, something you devote your entire life to, something you bring everything to, every minute of the day for your whole life. And the most important thing is—it must be something you cannot possibly do!
Henry Moore 1898–1986: attributed, in Donald Hall *Henry Moore* (1966) introduction

57 Life is a tragedy when seen in close-up, but a comedy in long-shot.
Charlie Chaplin 1889–1977: in *Guardian* 28 December 1977

58 The Answer to the Great Question Of… Life, the Universe and Everything…[is] Forty-two.
Douglas Adams 1952–2001: *The Hitch Hiker's Guide to the Galaxy* (1979)

59 Life is a rainbow which also includes black.
Yevgeny Yevtushenko 1933– : in *Guardian* 11 August 1987

60 My momma always said life was like a box of chocolates…you never know what you're gonna get.
Eric Roth: *Forrest Gump* (1994 film), based on the novel (1986) by Winston Groom; spoken by Tom Hanks

Life Sciences

see also LIFE, NATURE, SCIENCE, SCIENCE AND RELIGION

proverbs and sayings ▸

1 What's hit is history, what's missed is mystery.
on the importance of securing a dead specimen of a new species; late 19th-century saying

phrases ▸

2 animal, vegetable, and mineral
the three traditional divisions into which natural objects have been classified, first recorded in English in the early 18th century (earlier in Latin)

3 Darwin's bulldog
the English biologist Thomas Huxley (1825–95), referring to his tenacity in defending Charles Darwin's theory of evolution by natural selection; see LIFE SCIENCES 18

4 **hopeful monster**
in some theories of macroevolution, an organism displaying a radical mutation which nevertheless permits it to survive, produce offspring, and so potentially give rise to a new and distinct group of organisms

5 **the missing link**
a hypothetical intermediate type between humans and apes; a Victorian concept, arising from a simplistic picture of human evolution, representing either a common evolutionary ancestor for both humans and apes, or, in popular thought, some kind of ape-man through which humans had evolved from the other higher primates; it is now clear that human evolution has been much more complex

6 **natural selection**
the process whereby organisms better adapted to their environment tend to survive and produce more offspring; the theory of its action was first fully expounded by Charles Darwin and it is now believed to be the main process that brings about evolution; see LIFE SCIENCES 13, LIFE SCIENCES 16

7 **Red Queen hypothesis**
the hypothesis that organisms are constantly struggling to keep up with one another in an evolutionary race between predator and prey species, named from Lewis Carroll's Red Queen; see EFFORT 24, see also STRENGTH 1

8 **the selfish gene**
hypothesized as the unit of heredity whose preservation is the ultimate explanation of and rationale for human existence; from the title of a book (1976) by Richard Dawkins, which did much to popularize the theory of sociobiology

9 **survival of the fittest**
the process or result of natural selection, from Spencer: see LIFE SCIENCES 16; see also BUSINESS 36, LIFE SCIENCES 6

quotations ▶

10 **That which *is* grows, while that which *is not* becomes.**
Galen AD 129–199: *On the Natural Faculties*

11 **But what if one should tell such people in future that there are more animals living in the scum on the teeth in a man's mouth than there are men in a whole kingdom?**
on his observations of micro-organisms
Antoni van Leeuwenhoek 1632–1723: letter to Francis Aston, 17 September 1683

12 **Population, when unchecked, increases in a geometrical ratio. Subsistence only increases in an arithmetical ratio.**
Thomas Robert Malthus 1766–1834: *Essay on the Principle of Population* (1798)

13 **I have called this principle, by which each slight variation, if useful, is preserved, by the term of Natural Selection.**
Charles Darwin 1809–82: *On the Origin of Species* (1859); see LIFE SCIENCES 3, LIFE SCIENCES 6

14 **From so simple a beginning endless forms most beautiful and most wonderful have been, and are being, evolved.**
Charles Darwin 1809–82: *On the Origin of Species* (1859)

15 **Was it through his grandfather or his grandmother that he claimed his descent from a monkey?**
addressed to T. H. Huxley in the debate on Darwin's theory of evolution
Samuel Wilberforce 1805–73: at a meeting of British Association in Oxford, 30 June 1860; see HUMAN RACE 25, SCIENCE AND RELIGION 10

16 **This survival of the fittest which I have here sought to express in mechanical terms, is that which Mr Darwin has called 'natural selection, or the preservation of favoured races in the struggle for life.'**
Herbert Spencer 1820–1903: *Principles of Biology* (1865); see LIFE SCIENCES 6, LIFE SCIENCES 13

17 **It has, I believe, been often remarked that a hen is only an egg's way of making another egg.**
Samuel Butler 1835–1902: *Life and Habit* (1877)

18 **You know, I have to take care of him; in fact, I have always been Darwin's bulldog.**
T. H. Huxley 1825–95: to Osborn, winter 1879; Henry Fairfield Osborn *Impressions of Great Naturalists* (1924); see LIFE SCIENCES 3

19 **The microbe is nothing, the terrain is everything.**
Louis Pasteur 1822–95: to Professor Rénon, on his deathbed; Hans Seyle *The Stress of Life* (1956)

20 Men will not be content to manufacture life: they will want to improve on it.
J. D. Bernal 1901–71: *The World, the Flesh and the Devil* (1929)

21 Life exists in the universe only because the carbon atom possesses certain exceptional properties.
James Jeans 1877–1946: *The Mysterious Universe* (1930)

22 It has not escaped our notice that the specific pairing we have postulated immediately suggests a possible copying mechanism for the genetic material.
proposing the double helix as the structure of DNA, and hence the chemical mechanism of heredity
Francis Crick 1916–2004 and **James D. Watson** 1928– : in *Nature* 25 April 1953

23 We have discovered the secret of life!
on the discovery of the structure of DNA, 1953
Francis Crick 1916–2004: James D. Watson *The Double Helix* (1968)

24 It was Darwin's chief contribution, not only to Biology but to the whole of natural science, to have brought to light a process by which contingencies *a priori* improbable are given, in the process of time, an increasing probability, until it is their non-occurrence, rather than their occurrence, which becomes highly improbable.
sometimes quoted as 'Natural selection is a mechanism for generating an exceedingly high degree of improbability'
R. A. Fisher 1890–1962: 'Retrospect of the criticisms of the Theory of Natural Selection' in Julian Huxley *Evolution as a Process* (1954); see LIFE SCIENCES 30

25 Evolution advances, not by a priori design, but by the selection of what works best out of whatever choices offer. We are the products of editing, rather than of authorship.
George Wald 1904–97: in *Annals of the New York Academy of Sciences* vol. 69 1957

26 I'd lay down my life for two brothers or eight cousins.
J. B. S. Haldane 1892–1964: attributed; in *New Scientist* 8 August 1974

27 The biologist passes, the frog remains.
sometimes quoted as 'Theories pass. The frog remains'
Jean Rostand 1894–1977: *Inquiétudes d'un Biologiste* (1967)

28 Water is life's *mater* and *matrix*, mother and medium. There is no life without water.
Albert von Szent-Györgyi 1893–1986: in *Perspectives in Biology and Medicine* Winter 1971

29 [Natural selection] has no vision, no foresight, no sight at all. If it can be said to play the role of watchmaker in nature, it is the *blind* watchmaker.
Richard Dawkins 1941– : *The Blind Watchmaker* (1986); see GOD 27

30 The essence of life is statistical improbability on a colossal scale.
Richard Dawkins 1941– : *The Blind Watchmaker* (1986); see LIFE SCIENCES 24

31 Almost all aspects of life are engineered at the molecular level, and without understanding molecules we can only have a very sketchy understanding of life itself.
Francis Crick 1916–2004: *What Mad Pursuit* (1988)

32 Life is a copiously branching bush, continually pruned by the grim reaper of extinction, not a ladder of predictable progress.
Stephen Jay Gould 1941–2002: *Wonderful Life* (1989); see DEATH 17

33 Biology is the search for the chemistry that works.
R. J. P. Williams 1926– : lecture in Oxford, June 1996

34 For the past 15 years at ever faster rates we have been digitizing biology. By that I mean going from the analog world of biology through DNA sequencing into the digital world of the computer.
J. Craig Venter 1946– : Richard Dimbleby Lecture, BBC1, 4 December 2007

Lifestyles
see also LIFE

proverbs and sayings ▸

1 **Anyone can carry his burden, however heavy, until nightfall. Anyone can do his work, however hard, for one day. Anyone can live sweetly, patiently, lovingly, purely, till the sun goes down. And this is all that life really means.**
traditional saying, late 19th century, associated with the writer Robert Louis Stevenson (1850–94) from the early 20th century

2 **Before enlightenment, chop wood, carry water. After enlightenment, chop wood, carry water.**
Zen saying; see LIFESTYLES 22

3 **Do as you would be done by.**
English proverb, late 16th century; in Charles Kingsley's *The Water-Babies* (1863), Mrs *Doasyouwouldbedoneby* is the motherly and benevolent figure who is contrasted with her stern sister, Mrs *Bedonebyasyoudid*

4 **Do unto others as you would they should do unto you.**
English proverb; early 10th century, from the Bible (Matthew): see LIFESTYLES 18; see also LIKES 14

5 **Eat, drink and be merry, for tomorrow we die.**
a conflation of two biblical sayings, Ecclesiastes (see LIFESTYLES 15) and Isaiah, 'Let us eat and drink; for to morrow we shall die'; English proverb, late 19th century

6 **Fear less, hope more; Eat less, chew more; Whine less, breathe more; Talk less, say more; Love more, and all good things will be yours.**
Swedish saying

7 **If you have two coins, use one to buy bread, the other to buy hyacinths.**
both the mind and the body should be fed; Middle Eastern proverb (sometimes roses or lilies are suggested instead); see LIFESTYLES 32, HUMAN RIGHTS 2

8 **Make love not war.**
student slogan, 1960s

phrases ▸

9 **the eleventh commandment**
a rule of conduct regarded as coming next in importance to the Ten Commandments; often defined as 'Thou shalt not be found out'; see LIFESTYLES 13

10 **plain living and high thinking**
a frugal and philosophic lifestyle, from Wordsworth: see SATISFACTION 26

11 **rake's progress**
a progressive degeneration or decline, especially through self-indulgence; from the title of a series of engravings (1735) by William Hogarth, tracing the rake's life from indulged childhood to the gallows

12 **sow one's wild oats**
commit youthful follies or excesses before settling down; *wild oat* = a wild grass related to the cultivated oat which was traditionally a weed of cornfields

13 **the Ten Commandments**
the divine rules of conduct given by God to Moses on Mount Sinai, as recounted in the Bible (Exodus); the commandments are generally enumerated as: have no other gods; do not make or worship idols; do not take the name of the Lord in vain; keep the sabbath holy; honour one's father and mother; do not kill; do not commit adultery; do not steal; do not give false evidence; do not covet another's property or wife; see ENVY 6, MURDER 8, PARENTS 8; see also LIFESTYLES 9, INDIFFERENCE 17

quotations ▸

14 **Thou shalt love thy neighbour as thyself.**
Bible: Leviticus; see also St Matthew

15 **A man hath no better thing under the sun, than to eat, and to drink, and to be merry.**
Bible: Ecclesiastes; see LIFESTYLES 5

16 **We live, not as we wish to, but as we can.**
Menander 342–*c.*292 BC: *The Lady of Andros*

17 **1) Refraining from taking life. 2) Refraining from taking what is not given. 3) Refraining from incontinence. 4) Refraining from falsehood. 5) Refraining from strong drink, intoxicants, and liquor, which are occasions of carelessness.**
The Five Precepts
Pali Tripitaka 2nd century BC: *Vinaya, Mahāv.* [Book of Discipline]

18 Therefore all things whatsoever ye would that men should do to you, do ye even so to them: for this is the law and the prophets.
Bible: Matthew; see LIFESTYLES 4, SUCCESS 16

19 The art of living is more like wrestling than dancing, for it requires that we should stand ready and firm to meet onsets which are sudden and unexpected.
Marcus Aurelius AD 121–180: *Meditations*

20 Love and do what you will.
St Augustine of Hippo AD 354–430: *In Epistolam Joannis ad Parthos* (AD 413)

21 God desires
ease for you, and desires not hardship for you.
The Koran: sura 2

22 Miraculous powers and marvellous activity—
Drawing water and hewing wood!
P'ang Yun d. 808: attributed; Alan Watts *The Way of Zen* (1957); see LIFESTYLES 2

23 *Fay ce que vouldras.*
Do what you like.
François Rabelais c.1494–c.1553: *Gargantua* (1534); see LIFESTYLES 33

24 Living is my job and my art.
Montaigne 1533–92: *Essays* (1580)

25 Six hours in sleep, in law's grave study six,
Four spend in prayer, the rest on Nature fix.
Edward Coke 1552–1634: translation of a quotation from Justinian *The Pandects*

26 May you live all the days of your life.
Jonathan Swift 1667–1745: *Polite Conversation* (1738) 'The Colonel'

27 Just trust yourself and you'll learn the art of living.
often quoted as '...and you will know how to live'
Johann Wolfgang von Goethe 1749–1832: *Faust* pt. 1 (1808) 'Studierzimmer'

28 Take short views, hope for the best, and trust in God.
Sydney Smith 1771–1845: Lady Holland *Memoir* (1855)

29 Believe me! The secret of reaping the greatest fruitfulness and the greatest enjoyment from life is *to live dangerously*!
Friedrich Nietzsche 1844–1900: *Die fröhliche Wissenschaft* (1882)

30 *Bramo assai, poco spero, nulla chieggio.*
I essay much, I hope little, I ask nothing.
Edward Elgar 1857–1934: inscribed at the end of *Enigma Variations* (1899); from Torquato Tasso (1544–95)

31 Live all you can; it's a mistake not to. It doesn't so much matter what you do in particular, so long as you have your life. If you haven't had that, what *have* you had?
Henry James 1843–1916: *The Ambassadors* (1903)

32 If I had but two loaves of bread
I would sell one of them, and buy
White Hyacinths to feed my soul.
Elbert Hubbard 1859–1915: *White Hyacinths* (1907); see LIFESTYLES 7

33 Do what thou wilt shall be the whole of the Law.
Aleister Crowley 1875–1947: *Book of the Law* (1909); see LIFESTYLES 23

34 We had better live as we think, otherwise sooner or later we shall end up by thinking as we have lived.
Paul Bourget 1852–1935: *Le Démon de Midi* (1914)

35 Where is the Life we have lost in living?
T. S. Eliot 1888–1965: *The Rock* (1934)

36 Cigareetes and whuskey and wild, wild women
They'll drive you crazy; they'll drive you insane.
Tim Spencer 1908–74: 'Cigareetes, Whuskey And Wild, Wild Women' (1947 song); see LIFESTYLES 47

37 Dream as if you'll live forever. Live as if you'll die today.
James Dean 1931–55: in 1955, George Perry *James Dean* (2005)

38 Never play cards with a man called Doc. Never eat at a place called Mom's. Never sleep with a woman

whose troubles are worse than your own.

Nelson Algren 1909–81: in *Newsweek* 2 July 1956

39 Man is born to live, not to prepare for life.

Boris Pasternak 1890–1960: *Doctor Zhivago* (1958)

40 Turn on, tune in and drop out.

Timothy Leary 1920– : lecture, June 1966; *The Politics of Ecstasy* (1968)

41 I've lived a life that's full, I've travelled each and ev'ry highway
And more, much more than this. I did it my way.

Paul Anka 1941– : 'My Way' (1969 song)

42 Expect nothing. Live frugally
on surprise.

Alice Walker 1944– : 'Expect nothing' (1973)

43 Everybody's a mad scientist, and life is their lab. We're all trying to experiment to find a way to live, to solve problems, to fend off madness and chaos.

David Cronenberg 1943– : Chris Rodley (ed.) *Cronenberg on Cronenberg* (1992)

44 You only live once, and the way I live, once is enough.

Frank Sinatra 1915–98: attributed, in *Times* 16 May 1998

45 What we do in life echoes in eternity.

David Franzoni 1947– and **others**: *Gladiator* (2000 film), spoken by Russell Crowe as Maximus

46 Your time is limited, so don't waste it living someone else's life...Stay hungry. Stay foolish.

Steve Jobs 1955– : commencement address, Stanford University, 12 June 2005

47 What is the secret of my long life?
I really don't know—cigarettes, whisky and wild, wild women!

the oldest British survivor of the First World War

Henry Allingham 1896–2009: in *Daily Telegraph* 10 November 2005 (online edition); see LIFESTYLES 36

Likes and Dislikes

see also CRITICISM, TASTE

proverbs and sayings ▸

1 Every man to his taste.

often used to comment on someone else's choice: English proverb, late 16th century

2 One man's meat is another man's poison.

pointing out that what may be necessary to one person is injurious to another; English proverb, late 16th century

3 Tastes differ.

different people will like or approve of different things; English proverb, early 19th century

4 There is no accounting for tastes.

often used in recognition of a difference in choice between two people; English proverb, late 18th century

5 You can't please everyone.

English proverb, late 15th century

6 You're going to like this...not a lot...
but you'll like it!

catchphrase used by Paul Daniels in his conjuring act, especially on television from 1981 onwards

phrases ▸

7 mother's milk

in figurative usage, something providing sustenance or regarded by a person as entirely appropriate to them; see ALCOHOL 21

quotations ▸

8 To business that we love we rise betime,
And go to 't with delight.

William Shakespeare 1564–1616: *Antony and Cleopatra* (1606–7)

9 I do not love thee, Dr Fell.
The reason why I cannot tell;
But this I know, and know full well,
I do not love thee, Dr Fell.

written while an undergraduate at Christ Church, Oxford, of which Dr Fell was Dean

Thomas Brown 1663–1704: translation of an epigram by Martial AD c.40–c.104

10 People who like this sort of thing will find this the sort of thing they like.

judgement of a book

Abraham Lincoln 1809–65: G. W. E. Russell *Collections and Recollections* (1898)

11 For I've read in many a novel that,
unless they've souls that grovel,
Folks *prefer* in fact a hovel to your
dreary marble halls.
C. S. Calverley 1831–84: 'In the Gloaming' (1872); see IMAGINATION 11

12 I don't care anything about reasons, but I know what I like.
Henry James 1843–1916: *Portrait of a Lady* (1881)

13 Take care to get what you like or you will be forced to like what you get.
George Bernard Shaw 1856–1950: *Man and Superman* (1903) 'Maxims: Stray Sayings'

14 Do not do unto others as you would that they should do unto you. Their tastes may not be the same.
George Bernard Shaw 1856–1950: *Man and Superman* (1903) 'Maxims for Revolutionists: The Golden Rule'; see LIFESTYLES 4, SUCCESS 16

15 A little of what you fancy does you good.
Fred W. Leigh d. 1924 and **George Arthurs**: title of song (1915)

16 Tiggers don't like honey.
A. A. Milne 1882–1956: *House at Pooh Corner* (1928)

17 One-fifth of the people are against everything all the time.
Robert Kennedy 1925–68: speech, University of Pennsylvania, 6 May 1964

18 You don't have to like everything.
proposing a notice for the National Gallery
Alan Bennett 1934– : in *Independent* 24 May 1995

19 The hippies wanted peace and love. We wanted Ferraris, blondes and switchblades.
Alice Cooper 1948– : in *Independent* 5 May 2001

Logic and Reason

proverbs and sayings ►

1 A little nonsense now and then, is relished by the wisest men.
American proverb, mid 20th century

2 There is reason in the roasting of eggs.
however odd an action may seem, there is a reason for it; English proverb, mid 17th century

phrases ►

3 chop logic
engage in pedantically logical arguments; *chop* = exchange or bandy words, later wrongly understood as 'cut into small pieces, mince'

4 ex pede Herculem
inferring the whole of something from an insignificant part; Latin, *from the foot of Hercules*, alluding to the story that Pythagoras calculated Hercules's height from the size of Hercules's foot

5 lucus a non lucendo
a paradoxical or otherwise absurd derivation; something of which the qualities are the opposite of what its name suggests; Latin, literally 'a grove from its not shining', i.e. *lucus* (a grove) is derived from *lucere* (shine) because there is no light there

6 method in one's madness
sense or reason in what appears to be foolish or abnormal behaviour, from Shakespeare: see MADNESS 6

7 a red herring
a distraction introduced to a discussion or argument to divert attention from a more serious question or matter; from the practice of using the scent of a smoked herring to train hounds to follow a trail; see CHARACTER 27

quotations ►

8 A hidden connection is stronger than an obvious one.
Heraclitus c.540–c.480 BC: Hippolytus *Refutatio*

9 I have no other but a woman's reason: I think him so, because I think him so.
William Shakespeare 1564–1616: *The Two Gentlemen of Verona* (1592–3)

10 Reasons are not like garments, the worse for wearing.
Robert Devereux, Earl of Essex 1566–1601: letter to Lord Willoughby, 4 January 1599

11 What ever sceptic could inquire for;
For every why he had a wherefore.
Samuel Butler 1612–80: *Hudibras* pt. 1 (1663)

12 It is useless to attempt to reason a man out of what he was never reasoned into.
Jonathan Swift 1667–1745: attributed from the mid nineteenth century, but not traced in Swift's works, probably apocryphal

13 I'll not listen to reason...Reason always means what someone else has got to say.
Elizabeth Gaskell 1810–65: *Cranford* (1853)

14 In fact the *a priori* reasoning is so entirely satisfactory to me that if the facts won't fit in, why so much the worse for the facts is my feeling.
after reading *The Origin of Species*
Erasmus Darwin 1804–81: letter to Charles Darwin, 23 November 1859

15 'Contrariwise,' continued Tweedledee, 'if it was so, it might be; and if it were so, it would be: but as it isn't, it ain't. That's logic.'
Lewis Carroll 1832–98: *Through the Looking-Glass* (1872)

16 Logical consequences are the scarecrows of fools and the beacons of wise men.
T. H. Huxley 1825–95: *Science and Culture and Other Essays* (1881) 'On the Hypothesis that Animals are Automata'

17 [Logic] is neither a science nor an art, but a dodge.
Benjamin Jowett 1817–93: Lionel A. Tollemache *Benjamin Jowett* (1895)

18 'Is there any other point to which you would wish to draw my attention?'
'To the curious incident of the dog in the night-time.'
'The dog did nothing in the night-time.'
'That was the curious incident,' remarked Sherlock Holmes.
Arthur Conan Doyle 1859–1930: *The Memoirs of Sherlock Holmes* (1894)

19 After all, what was a paradox but a statement of the obvious so as to make it sound untrue?
Ronald Knox 1888–1957: *A Spiritual Aeneid* (1918)

20 Logic must take care of itself.
Ludwig Wittgenstein 1889–1951: *Tractatus Logico-Philosophicus* (1922)

21 If we would guide by the light of reason, we must let our minds be bold.
Louis D. Brandeis 1856–1941: *Jay Burns Baking Co. v. Bryan* (1924) (dissenting)

22 The best causes tend to attract to their support the worst arguments.
R. A. Fisher 1890–1962: *Statistical Methods and Scientific Inference* (1956)

23 You can't think rationally on an empty stomach, and a whole lot of people can't do it on a full stomach either.
Lord Reith 1889–1971: D. Parker *Radio: The Great Years* (1977)

24 Even logical positivists are capable of love.
A. J. Ayer 1910–89: Kenneth Tynan *Profiles* (1989)

Losing
see WINNING AND LOSING

Love
see also COURTSHIP, KISSING, MARRIAGE, RELATIONSHIPS, SEX

proverbs and sayings ▸

1 The course of true love never did run smooth.
English proverb, late 16th century, originally from Shakespeare: see LOVE 29

2 It is best to be off with the old love before you are on with the new.
English proverb, early 19th century

3 Jove but laughs at lover's perjury.
English proverb, mid 16th century; from the Roman poet Tibullus (50–19 BC) and ultimately from the Greek poet Hesiod (700 BC)

4 Love and a cough cannot be hid.
love can no more be concealed than a cough can be suppressed; English proverb, early 14th century

5 Love begets love.
English proverb, early 16th century

6 Love is blind.
Cupid, the god of love, was traditionally portrayed as blind, shooting his arrows at random, but the saying is generally used to mean that a person is often unable to see faults in the one they love; English proverb, late 14th century; see RELATIONSHIPS 3

7 Love laughs at locksmiths.
love is too strong a force to be denied by ordinary barriers; English proverb, early 19th century, from the title of a play (1808) by George Colman, the Younger (1762–1836)

8 **Love makes the world go round.**
English proverb, mid 19th century, from a traditional French song; see DRUNKENNESS 12; MONEY 51

9 **Love means never having to say you're sorry.**
advertising copy for the film *Love Story* (1970); from the novel (1970) by Erich Segal (1937–2010)

10 **Love will find a way.**
love is a force which cannot be stemmed or denied; English proverb, early 17th century

11 **One cannot love and be wise.**
English proverb, early 16th century; the statement 'to love and be wise is scarcely allowed to God' is found in Latin in the writings of the 1st-century Roman writer Publilius Syrus; see TAXES 9

12 **The quarrel of lovers is the renewal of love.**
love can be renewed through reconciliation; English proverb, early 16th century

13 **There are as good fish in the sea as ever came out of it.**
now often used as a consolation to rejected lovers in the form, 'there are plenty more fish in the sea'; English proverb, late 16th century

14 **'Tis better to have loved and lost, than never to have loved at all.**
English proverb, early 18th century; see LOVE 51

15 **When the furze is in bloom, my love's in tune.**
with the implication that some furze can always be found in bloom; English proverb, mid 18th century; see also KISSING 2

phrases ▸

16 **Cupid's dart**
the conquering power of love; *Cupid* the Roman god of love, son of Mercury and Venus, represented as a beautiful naked winged boy with a bow and arrows

17 **love's young dream**
the relationship of young lovers; the object of someone's love; a man regarded as a perfect lover; see LOVE 44

18 **moonlight and roses**
romance; title of song by Black and Moret, 1925

19 **star-crossed lovers**
ill-fated lovers, from Shakespeare *Romeo and Juliet* 'A pair of star-crossed lovers'

20 **tender passion**
romantic love; the term is first recorded in Sheridan's *Duenna* (1775)

quotations ▸

21 **Many waters cannot quench love, neither can the floods drown it.**
Bible: Song of Solomon

22 ***Omnia vincit Amor: et nos cedamus Amori.***
Love conquers all things: let us too give in to Love.
Virgil 70–19 BC: *Eclogues*

23 **And now abideth faith, hope, charity, these three; but the greatest of these is charity.**
Bible: I Corinthians

24 **There is no fear in love; but perfect love casteth out fear.**
Bible: I John

25 **Lord, make me an instrument of Your peace!**
Where there is hatred let me sow love.
St Francis of Assisi 1181–1226: 'Prayer of St Francis'; attributed

26 **The love that moves the sun and the other stars.**
Dante Alighieri 1265–1321: *Divina Commedia* 'Paradiso'

27 **I find no peace, and I am not at war,**
I fear and hope, and burn and I am ice.
Petrarch 1304–74: *Canzoniere* no. 134 (1352) tr. Mark Musa

28 **Where both deliberate, the love is slight;**
Who ever loved that loved not at first sight?
Christopher Marlowe 1564–93: *Hero and Leander* (1598)

29 **The course of true love never did run smooth.**
William Shakespeare 1564–1616: *A Midsummer Night's Dream* (1595–6); see LOVE 1

30 **Whoever loves, if he do not propose**
The right true end of love, he's one that goes
To sea for nothing but to make him sick.
John Donne 1572–1631: 'Love's Progress' (1600)

31 Then, must you speak
Of one that loved not wisely but too well.
William Shakespeare 1564–1616: *Othello* (1602–4)

32 Let me not to the marriage of true minds
Admit impediments. Love is not love
Which alters when it alteration finds.
William Shakespeare 1564–1616: sonnet 116

33 But true love is a durable fire,
In the mind ever burning,
Never sick, never old, never dead,
From itself never turning.
Walter Ralegh 1552–1618: 'Walsinghame'

34 No cord nor cable can so forcibly draw, or hold so fast, as love can do with a twined thread.
Robert Burton 1577–1640: *The Anatomy of Melancholy* (1621–51)

35 Love is the fart
Of every heart:
It pains a man when 'tis kept close,
And others doth offend, when 'tis let loose.
John Suckling 1609–42: 'Love's Offence' (1646)

36 It's no longer a burning within my veins:
it's Venus entire latched onto her prey.
Jean Racine 1639–99: *Phèdre* (1677)

37 There is no disguise which can hide love for long where it exists, or feign it where it does not.
Duc de la Rochefoucauld 1613–80: *Maximes* (1678) no. 70

38 Say what you will, 'tis better to be left than never to have been loved.
William Congreve 1670–1729: *The Way of the World* (1700); see LOVE 51

39 We cease loving ourselves if no one loves us.
Mme de Staël 1766–1817: *Sophie* (1786)

40 Love seeketh not itself to please,
Nor for itself hath any care;
But for another gives its ease,
And builds a Heaven in Hell's despair.
William Blake 1757–1827: 'The Clod and the Pebble' (1794)

41 Love seeketh only Self to please,
To bind another to its delight,
Joys in another's loss of ease,
And builds a Hell in Heaven's despite.
William Blake 1757–1827: 'The Clod and the Pebble' (1794)

42 O, my Luve's like a red, red rose
That's newly sprung in June.
Robert Burns 1759–96: 'A Red Red Rose' (1796); derived from various folk-songs

43 If I love you, what does that matter to you!
Johann Wolfgang von Goethe 1749–1832: *Wilhelm Meister's Apprenticeship* (1795-6)

44 No, there's nothing half so sweet in life
As love's young dream.
Thomas Moore 1779–1852: 'Love's Young Dream' (1807); see LOVE 17

45 Love in a hut, with water and a crust,
Is—Love, forgive us!—cinders, ashes, dust;
Love in a palace is perhaps at last
More grievous torment than a hermit's fast.
John Keats 1795–1821: 'Lamia' (1820); see IDEALISM 7

46 The magic of first love is our ignorance that it can ever end.
Benjamin Disraeli 1804–81: *Henrietta Temple* (1837)

47 In the spring a young man's fancy lightly turns to thoughts of love.
Alfred, Lord Tennyson 1809–92: 'Locksley Hall' (1842)

48 What love is, if thou wouldst be taught,
Thy heart must teach alone—
Two souls with but a single thought,
Two hearts that beat as one.
Friedrich Halm 1806–71: *Der Sohn der Wildnis* (1842)

49 If thou must love me, let it be for nought
Except for love's sake only.
Elizabeth Barrett Browning 1806–61: *Sonnets from the Portuguese* (1850) no. 14

50 How do I love thee? Let me count the ways.
I love thee to the depth and breadth and height
My soul can reach.
Elizabeth Barrett Browning 1806–61: *Sonnets from the Portuguese* (1850) no. 43

51 'Tis better to have loved and lost
Than never to have loved at all.
Alfred, Lord Tennyson 1809–92: *In Memoriam A. H. H.* (1850); see LOVE 14, LOVE 38

52 Love's like the measles—all the worse when it comes late in life.
Douglas Jerrold 1803–57: *The Wit and Opinions of Douglas Jerrold* (1859)

53 Much love much trial, but what an utter desert is life without love.
Charles Darwin 1809–82: letter to Joseph Hooker, 27 November 1863

54 The love that lasts longest is the love that is never returned.
W. Somerset Maugham 1874–1965: *A Writer's Notebook* (1949) written in 1894

55 I am the Love that dare not speak its name.
Lord Alfred Douglas 1870–1945: 'Two Loves' (1896)

56 Yet each man kills the thing he loves,
By each let this be heard,
Some do it with a bitter look,
Some with a flattering word.
The coward does it with a kiss,
The brave man with a sword!
Oscar Wilde 1854–1900: *The Ballad of Reading Gaol* (1898)

57 Love consists in this, that two solitudes protect and touch and greet each other.
Rainer Maria Rilke 1875–1926: *Letters to a Young Poet* (1929) 14 May 1904 (tr. Hugh MacLennan)

58 The fate of love is that it always seems too little or too much.
Amelia E. Barr 1831–1919: *The Belle of Bolling Green* (1904)

59 Love is so short, forgetting is so long.
Pablo Neruda 1904–73: 'Tonight I Can Write' (1924)

60 Even memory is not necessary for love. There is a land of the living and a land of the dead and the bridge is love, the only survival, the only meaning.
Thornton Wilder 1897–1975: *The Bridge of San Luis Rey* (1927), closing words

61 Experience shows us that love does not consist in gazing at each other but in looking together in the same direction.
Antoine de Saint-Exupéry 1900–44: *Wind, Sand and Stars* (1939)

62 The life that I have
Is all that I have
And the life that I have
Is yours.

The love that I have
Of the life that I have
Is yours and yours and yours.
given to the British secret agent Violette Szabo (1921–45), for use with the Special Operations Executive
Leo Marks 1920–2001: 'The Life that I Have' (written 1943)

63 You know very well that love is, above all, the gift of oneself!
Jean Anouilh 1910–87: *Ardèle* (1949)

64 Birds do it, bees do it,
Even educated fleas do it.
Let's do it, let's fall in love.
Cole Porter 1891–1964: 'Let's Do It' (1954 song; words added to the 1928 original)

65 Love. Of course, love. Flames for a year, ashes for thirty.
Guiseppe di Lampedusa 1896–1957: *The Leopard* (1957)

66 Selfhood begins with a walking away,
And love is proved in the letting go.
C. Day-Lewis 1904–72: 'Walking Away' (1962)

67 To fall in love is to create a religion that has a fallible god.
Jorge Luis Borges 1899–1986: *Other Inquisitions 1937–1952* (1964) 'The Meeting of a Dream'

68 What will survive of us is love.
Philip Larkin 1922–85: 'An Arundel Tomb' (1964)

69 All you need is love.
John Lennon 1940–80 and **Paul McCartney** 1942– : title of song (1967)

70 Love is never any better than the lover. Wicked people love wickedly, violent people love violently, weak people love weakly, stupid people love stupidly, but the love of a free man is never safe. There is no gift for the beloved.
Toni Morrison 1931– : *The Bluest Eye* (1970)

71 Love doesn't just sit there, like a stone, it has to be made, like bread; remade all the time, made new.
Ursula K. Le Guin 1929– : *The Lathe of Heaven* (1971)

72 If equal affection cannot be,
Let the more loving one be me.
W. H. Auden 1907–73: 'The More Loving One' (1976)

73 When you realize you want to spend the rest of your life with somebody, you want the rest of your life to start as soon as possible.
Nora Ephron 1941– : *When Harry Met Sally* (1989 film)

74 Love itself is what is left over when being in love has burned away.
Louis de Bernières 1954– : *Captain Corelli's Mandolin* (1994)

75 If grass can grow through cement, love can find you at every time in your life.
Cher 1946– : in *Times* 30 May 1998

76 Love is free; it is not practised as a way of achieving other ends.
Pope Benedict XVI 1927– : *Deus Caritas Est* (God is Love, 2005)

Luck
see CHANCE AND LUCK

Luxury
see WEALTH AND LUXURY

Madness
see also FOOLS, MIND

proverbs and sayings ▸

1 Whom the gods would destroy, they first make mad.
often used to comment on a foolish action seen as self-destructive in its effect; English proverb, early 17th century; see MADNESS 4, CRITICISM 18

phrases ▸

2 mad as a hatter
completely insane. Hat-makers sometimes suffered from mercury poisoning as a result of the use of mercurous nitrate in the manufacture of felt hats, and the idea was personified in one of the two eccentric hosts (the *Mad Hatter*) at the 'mad tea party' in Lewis Carroll's *Alice's Adventures in Wonderland* (1865); see MADNESS 3, see also CATS 10

3 mad as a March hare
completely insane; the allusion here is to the running and leaping of hares in the breeding season, and was reinforced by the character created by Lewis Carroll in *Alice's Adventures in Wonderland* (1865); see MADNESS 2

quotations ▸

4 Whenever God prepares evil for a man, He first damages his mind, with which he deliberates.
Anonymous: scholiastic annotation to Sophocles's *Antigone*; see MADNESS 1

5 I am but mad north-north-west; when the wind is southerly, I know a hawk from a handsaw.
William Shakespeare 1564–1616: *Hamlet* (1601); see INTELLIGENCE 4

6 Though this be madness, yet there is method in't.
William Shakespeare 1564–1616: *Hamlet* (1601); see LOGIC 6

7 There is a pleasure sure,
In being mad, which none but madmen know!
John Dryden 1631–1700: *The Spanish Friar* (1681)

8 They called me mad, and I called them mad, and damn them, they outvoted me.
Nathaniel Lee 1653–92: R. Porter *A Social History of Madness* (1987)

9 Mad, is he? Then I hope he will *bite* some of my other generals.
replying to the Duke of Newcastle, who had complained that General Wolfe was a madman
George II 1683–1760: Henry Beckles Willson *Life and Letters of James Wolfe* (1909)

10 Babylon in all its desolation is a sight not so awful as that of the human mind in ruins.
Scrope Davies 1783–1852: letter to Thomas Raikes, May 1835

11 Dear Sir,—I am in a madhouse and quite forget your name or who you are.
John Clare 1793–1864: letter, 1860

12 Every one is more or less mad on one point.
Rudyard Kipling 1865–1936: *Plain Tales from the Hills* (1888)

13 As an experience, madness is terrific... and in its lava I still find most of the things I write about.
Virginia Woolf 1882–1941: letter to Ethel Smyth, 22 June 1930

14 There was only one catch and that was Catch-22, which specified that a concern for one's own safety in the face of dangers that were real and immediate was the process of a rational mind...Orr would be crazy to fly more missions and sane if he didn't, but if he was sane he had to fly them. If he flew them he was crazy and didn't have to; but if he didn't want to he was sane and had to.
Joseph Heller 1923–99: *Catch-22* (1961); see CIRCUMSTANCE 10

15 Madness need not be all breakdown. It may also be break-through.
R. D. Laing 1927–89: *The Politics of Experience* (1967)

16 If you talk to God, you are praying; if God talks to you, you have schizophrenia. If the dead talk to you, you are a spiritualist; if God talks to you, you are a schizophrenic.
Thomas Szasz 1920– : *The Second Sin* (1973)

Management
see also ADMINISTRATION

proverbs and sayings ▸

1 The eye of a master does more work than both his hands.
employees work harder when the person who is in charge is present; English proverb, mid 18th century

2 We trained hard...but it seemed that every time we were beginning to form up into teams we would be reorganized. I was to learn later in life that we tend to meet any new situation by reorganizing; and a wonderful method it can be for creating the illusion of progress while producing confusion, inefficiency, and demoralization.
late 20th century saying, frequently (and wrongly) attributed to Roman satirist Petronius Arbiter (d. AD 65)

3 Why keep a dog and bark yourself?
often used to advise against carrying out work which can be done for you by somebody else; English proverb, late 16th century

4 You're fired!
catchphrase of the American businessman Donald Trump (1946–) on *The Apprentice* NBC TV 2004–, in the UK associated with the English businessman Alan Sugar (1947–)

phrases ▸

5 the Peter Principle
the principle that members of a hierarchy are promoted until they reach a level at which they are no longer competent; from title of book by US educationalist and author Laurence J. Peter: see ADMINISTRATION 17

6 pour encourager les autres
as an example to others, to encourage others; French, from Voltaire: see WAYS 32

quotations ▸

7 There is nothing in the world which does not have its decisive moment, and the masterpiece of good management is to recognize and grasp this moment.
Cardinal de Retz 1613–79: *Mémoires* (1717); see PHOTOGRAPHY 4

8 Every time I make an appointment, I create a hundred malcontents and one ingrate.
Louis XIV 1638–1715: Voltaire *Siècle de Louis XIV* (1768 ed.)

9 Some great men owe most of their greatness to the ability of detecting in those they destine for their tools the exact quality of strength that matters for their work.
Joseph Conrad 1857–1924: *Lord Jim* (1900)

10 I tell you, sir, the only safeguard of order and discipline in the modern world is a standardized worker with interchangeable parts. That would solve the entire problem of management.
Jean Giraudoux 1882–1944: *The Madwoman of Chaillot* (1945)

11 A good plan violently executed *Now* is better than a perfect plan next week.
George S. Patton 1885–1945: *War As I Knew It* (1947)

12 Perfection of planned layout is achieved only by institutions on the point of collapse.
C. Northcote Parkinson 1909–93: *Parkinson's Law* (1958)

13 Who's in charge of the clattering train?
habitual question about an organization
Lord Beaverbrook 1879–1964: A. Chisholm and M. Davie *Beaverbrook* (1992)

14 Surround yourself with the best people you can find, delegate authority, and don't interfere.
Ronald Reagan 1911–2004: in *Fortune* September 1986

15 If you want people motivated to do a good job, give them a good job to do.
Frederick Herzberg 1923–2000: in *Industry Week* 21 September 1987

16 When you're up to your ears in alligators, it is difficult to remember that the reason you're there is to drain the swamp.
Donald Rumsfeld 1932– : *Rumsfeld's Rules* (2001)

Manners

see also BEHAVIOUR

proverbs and sayings ▸

1 Civility costs nothing.
one should behave with at least minimal courtesy; English proverb, early 18th century

2 A civil question deserves a civil answer.
English proverb, mid 19th century

3 Everyone speaks well of the bridge which carries him over.
someone is naturally well-disposed towards a source of help, whether or not it has been beneficial to others; English proverb, late 17th century

4 Manners maketh man.
motto of William of Wykeham (1324–1404), bishop of Winchester and founder of Winchester College; English proverb, mid 14th century

5 Striking manners are bad manners.
American proverb, mid 20th century

6 There is nothing lost by civility.
English proverb, late 19th century

quotations ▸

7 Leave off first for manners' sake.
Bible: Ecclesiasticus

8 Evil communications corrupt good manners.
Bible: I Corinthians; see BEHAVIOUR 4

9 Immodest words admit of no defence,
For want of decency is want of sense.
Wentworth Dillon, Lord Roscommon 1633–85: *Essay on Translated Verse* (1684)

10 In my mind, there is nothing so illiberal and so ill-bred, as audible laughter.
Lord Chesterfield 1694–1773: *Letters to his Son* (1774) 9 March 1748

11 He is the very pineapple of politeness!
Richard Brinsley Sheridan 1751–1816: *The Rivals* (1775)

12 The art of pleasing consists in being pleased.
William Hazlitt 1778–1830: *The Round Table* (1817) 'On Manner'

13 Curtsey while you're thinking what to say. It saves time.
Lewis Carroll 1832–98: *Through the Looking-Glass* (1872)

14 Very notable was his distinction between coarseness and vulgarity (coarseness, revealing something; vulgarity, concealing something).
E. M. Forster 1879–1970: *The Longest Journey* (1907)

15 Of Courtesy, it is much less
Than Courage of Heart or Holiness,
Yet in my Walks it seems to me
That the Grace of God is in Courtesy.
Hilaire Belloc 1870–1953: 'Courtesy' (1910)

16 Good breeding consists in concealing how much we think of ourselves and how little we think of the other person.
Mark Twain 1835–1910: *Notebooks* (1935)

17 When suave politeness, tempering bigot zeal,
Corrected *I believe* to *One does feel.*
Ronald Knox 1888–1957: 'Absolute and Abitofhell' (1913)

18 It is wise to apply the oil of refined politeness to the mechanism of friendship.
Colette 1873–1954: *The Pure and the Impure* (1932)

19 It's not a slam at *you* when people are rude—it's a slam at the people they've met before.
F. Scott Fitzgerald 1896–1940: *The Last Tycoon* (1941)

20 THUMPER: If you can't say something nice...don't say nothing at all.
Larry Morey 1905–71: *Bambi* (1942 film); from the novel by Felix Salten (1869–1945)

21 Phone for the fish-knives, Norman
As Cook is a little unnerved;
You kiddies have crumpled the serviettes
And I must have things daintily served.
John Betjeman 1906–84: 'How to get on in Society' (1954)

22 To Americans, English manners are far more frightening than none at all.
Randall Jarrell 1914–65: *Pictures from an Institution* (1954)

23 Manners are especially the need of the plain. The pretty can get away with anything.
Evelyn Waugh 1903–66: in *Observer* 15 April 1962

24 The Japanese have perfected good manners and made them indistinguishable from rudeness.
Paul Theroux 1941– : *The Great Railway Bazaar* (1975)

Marriage

see also COURTSHIP, LOVE, SEX, SINGLE, WEDDINGS

proverbs and sayings ▸

1 Better be an old man's darling than a young man's slave.
English proverb, mid 16th century

2 Better one house spoiled than two.
said of two wicked or foolish people joined in marriage; English proverb, late 16th century

3 Change the name and not the letter, change for the worse and not the better.
it is unlucky for a woman to marry a man whose surname begins with the same letter as her own; English proverb, mid 19th century

4 A deaf husband and a blind wife are always a happy couple.
each will remain unaware of drawbacks in the other. The saying is sometimes reversed to a blind husband and a deaf wife; English proverb, late 16th century

5 The grey mare is the better horse.
the wife rules, or is more competent than, the husband; English proverb, mid 16th century

6 Marriage is a lottery.
referring either to one's choice of partner, or more generally to the element of chance involved in how a marriage will turn out; English proverb, mid 17th century

7 Marriages are made in heaven.
often used ironically; English proverb, mid 16th century

8 Marry in haste and repent at leisure.
the formula is also applied to rash steps taken in other circumstances; English proverb, mid 16th century; see MARRIAGE 26

9 Needles and pins, needles and pins, when a man marries, his trouble begins.
traditional saying (originally a nursery rhyme), perhaps reflecting on the pressures of domestic life; English proverb, mid 19th century

10 Never marry for money, but marry where money is.
distinguishing between monetary gain as a primary objective and a side benefit; English proverb, late 19th century

11 There goes more to marriage than four bare legs in a bed.
physical compatibility is not enough for a successful marriage; English proverb, mid 16th century

12 Wedlock is a padlock.
English proverb, late 17th century

13 You do not marry the person you love, you love the person you marry.
Indian proverb

14 A young man married is a young man marred.
often used as an argument against marrying too young; English proverb, late 16th century; see MARRIAGE 22

phrases ▸

15 love in a cottage
marriage with insufficient means; after Colman: see IDEALISM 7

16 May and January
a young woman and an old man as husband and wife, as in Chaucer's *Merchant's Tale* (1395)

17 the weaker vessel
a wife, a female partner; originally in allusion to the Bible (I Peter) 'Giving honour unto the wife, as unto the weaker vessel'

quotations ►

18 Man's best possession is a sympathetic wife.
Euripides c.485–c.406 BC: fragment no. 164; Augustus Nauck *Tragicorum Graecorum Fragmenta*

19 What therefore God hath joined together, let not man put asunder.
Bible: St Matthew

20 It is better to marry than to burn.
Bible: I Corinthians

21 I am your clay.
You are my clay.
In life we share a single quilt.
In death we will share one coffin.
Kuan Tao-sheng 1262–1319: 'Married Love'

22 A young man married is a man that's marred.
William Shakespeare 1564–1616: *All's Well that Ends Well* (1603–4); see MARRIAGE 14

23 Wives are young men's mistresses, companions for middle age, and old men's nurses.
Francis Bacon 1561–1626: *Essays* (1625) 'Of Marriage and the Single Life'

24 Then be not coy, but use your time;
And while ye may, go marry:
For having lost but once your prime,
You may for ever tarry.
Robert Herrick 1591–1674: 'To the Virgins, to Make Much of Time' (1648)

25 To have and to hold from this day forward, for better for worse, for richer for poorer, in sickness and in health, to love, cherish, and to obey, till death us do part.
The Book of Common Prayer 1662: *Solemnization of Matrimony* Betrothal

26 SHARPER: Thus grief still treads upon the heels of pleasure:
Married in haste, we may repent at leisure.
SETTER: Some by experience find those words mis-placed:
At leisure married, they repent in haste.
William Congreve 1670–1729: *The Old Bachelor* (1693); see MARRIAGE 8

27 Keep your eyes wide open before marriage, half shut afterwards.
Benjamin Franklin 1706–90: *Poor Richard's Almanack* (1738)

28 I...chose my wife, as she did her wedding gown, not for a fine glossy surface, but such qualities as would wear well.
Oliver Goldsmith 1728–74: *The Vicar of Wakefield* (1766)

29 The triumph of hope over experience.
of a man who remarried immediately after the death of a wife with whom he had been unhappy
Samuel Johnson 1709–84: James Boswell *Life of Samuel Johnson* (1791) 1770

30 My definition of marriage...it resembles a pair of shears, so joined that they cannot be separated; often moving in opposite directions, yet always punishing anyone who comes between them.
Sydney Smith 1771–1845: Lady Holland *Memoir* (1855)

31 Marriage is like life in this—that it is a field of battle, and not a bed of roses.
Robert Louis Stevenson 1850–94: *Virginibus Puerisque* (1881)

32 The chains of marriage are so heavy that it takes two to bear them, and sometimes three.
Alexandre Dumas 1824–95: Léon Treich *L'Esprit d'Alexandre Dumas*

33 In married life three is company and two none.
Oscar Wilde 1854–1900: *The Importance of Being Earnest* (1895)

34 Love the quest; marriage the conquest; divorce the inquest.
Helen Rowland 1875–1950: *Reflections of a Bachelor Girl* (1903)

35 Marriage is popular because it combines the maximum of temptation with the maximum of opportunity.
George Bernard Shaw 1856–1950: *Man and Superman* (1903) 'Maxims: Marriage'

36 Being a husband is a whole-time job. That is why so many husbands fail. They cannot give their entire attention to it.
Arnold Bennett 1867–1931: *The Title* (1918)

37 But let there be spaces in your togetherness,
And let the winds of the heavens dance between you.
Love one another, but make not a bond of love:
Let it rather be a moving sea between the shores of your souls.
Kahlil Gibran 1883–1931: *The Prophet* (1923) 'On Marriage'

38 Marriage isn't a word...it's a *sentence*!
King Vidor 1895–1982: *The Crowd* (1928 film)

39 The deep, deep peace of the double-bed after the hurly-burly of the chaise-longue.
on her recent marriage
Mrs Patrick Campbell 1865–1940: Alexander Woollcott *While Rome Burns* (1934)

40 If you cannot have your dear husband for a comfort and a delight, for a breadwinner and a crosspatch, for a sofa, chair or a hot-water bottle, one can use him as a Cross to be Borne.
Stevie Smith 1902–71: *Novel on Yellow Paper* (1936); see SUFFERING 5

41 Marriage is a bribe to make a housekeeper think she's a householder.
Thornton Wilder 1897–1975: *The Merchant of Yonkers* (1939)

42 The value of marriage is not that adults produce children but that children produce adults.
Peter De Vries 1910–93: *The Tunnel of Love* (1954)

43 Love and marriage, love and marriage, Go together like a horse and carriage.
Sammy Cahn 1913–93: *Love and Marriage* (1955 song)

44 One doesn't have to get anywhere in a marriage. It's not a public conveyance.
Iris Murdoch 1919–99: *A Severed Head* (1961)

45 The freedom to marry has long been recognized as one of the vital personal rights essential to the orderly pursuit of happiness by free men.
Earl Warren 1891–1974: judgement in *Loving v. Virginia* 1967

46 I think everybody really will concede that on this, of all days, I should begin my speech with the words 'My husband and I'.
Elizabeth II 1926– : speech at Guildhall, London, on her 25th wedding anniversary, 20 November 1972

47 A divorce is like an amputation; you survive, but there's less of you.
Margaret Atwood 1939– : in *Time*, 1973

48 Marriage is a wonderful invention; but, then again, so is a bicycle repair kit.
Billy Connolly 1942– : Duncan Campbell *Billy Connolly* (1976)

49 Chains do not hold a marriage together. It is threads, hundreds of tiny threads which sew people together through the years. That is what makes a marriage last—more than passion or even sex!
Simone Signoret 1921–85: in *Daily Mail* 4 July 1978

50 The heart of marriage is memories.
Bill Cosby 1937– : *Love and Marriage* (1989)

51 There were three of us in this marriage, so it was a bit crowded.
Diana, Princess of Wales 1961–97: interview on *Panorama*, BBC1 TV, 20 November 1995

Mathematics

see also QUANTITIES, STATISTICS

proverbs and sayings ▸

1 The good Christian should beware of mathematicians, and all those who make empty prophecies. The danger already exists that mathematicians have made a covenant with the Devil to darken the spirit and to confine man in the bonds of Hell.
mistranslation of St Augustine's *De Genesi ad Litteram*; the Latin word *mathematicus* means both 'mathematician' and 'astrologer': see SUPERNATURAL 10

2 Math class is tough.
spoken by Teen Talk Barbie, often misquoted as 'Math is hard'; the doll was released in July 1992, but following criticism by the American Association of University Women this saying was removed in October 1992

phrases ▸

3 Delian problem
the problem of finding geometrically the side of a cube having twice the volume of a given cube; from the Delian oracle's pronouncement that a plague in Athens would cease if the cubical altar to Apollo were doubled in size

4 Fermat's last theorem
the conjecture that if *n* is greater than 2 then there is no integer whose *n*th power can be expressed as the sum of two smaller *n*th powers. The French lawyer and mathematician Pierre de *Fermat* (1601–65) noted that he had 'a truly wonderful proof' of the conjecture, but never wrote it down. In 1995 a general proof was published by the Princeton-based British mathematician Andrew Wiles

5 the golden section
the division of a line so that the whole is to the greater part as that part is to the smaller part, a proportion which is considered to be particularly pleasing to the eye; although the proportion has been known since the 4th century BC, and occurs in Euclid, the name *golden section* (now the usual term) is not recorded before the 19th century

6 pons asinorum
the fifth proposition of the first book of Euclid; Latin, = bridge of asses; so called from the difficulty which beginners find in 'getting over' it

7 square the circle
construct a square equal in area to a given circle (a problem incapable of a purely geometrical solution); thus, do something that is considered to be impossible

quotations ▸

8 Let no one enter who does not know geometry [mathematics].
inscription on Plato's door, probably at the Academy at Athens
Anonymous: Elias Philosophus *In Aristotelis Categorias Commentaria*

9 There is no 'royal road' to geometry.
Euclid fl. 300 BC: addressed to Ptolemy I; Proclus *Commentary on the First Book of Euclid's Elementa*; see EDUCATION 7

10 If in other sciences we should arrive at certainty without doubt and truth without error, it behoves us to place the foundations of knowledge in mathematics.
Roger Bacon c.1220–c.92: *Opus Majus*

11 Philosophy is written in that great book which ever lies before our eyes—I mean the universe...This book is written in mathematical language and its characters are triangles, circles and other geometrical figures, without whose help...one wanders in vain through a dark labyrinth.
often quoted as 'The book of nature is written...'
Galileo 1564–1642: *The Assayer* (1623)

12 They are neither finite quantities, or quantities infinitely small, nor yet nothing. May we not call them the ghosts of departed quantities?
on Newton's infinitesimals
George Berkeley 1685–1753: *The Analyst* (1734)

13 What would life be without arithmetic, but a scene of horrors?
Sydney Smith 1771–1845: letter to Miss [Lucie Austen], 22 July 1835

14 I used to love mathematics for its own sake, and I still do, because it allows for no hypocrisy and no vagueness, my two *bêtes noires*.
Stendhal 1783–1842: *La Vie d'Henri Brulard* (1890)

15 'What's the good of *Mercator's* North
Poles and Equators,
Tropics, Zones and Meridian lines?'
So the Bellman would cry: and the
crew would reply,
'They are merely conventional signs!'
Lewis Carroll 1832–98: *The Hunting of the Snark* (1876)

16 God made the integers, all the rest is the work of man.
Leopold Kronecker 1823–91: *Jahrsberichte der Deutschen Mathematiker Vereinigung*

17 I never could make out what those damned dots meant.
on decimal points
Lord Randolph Churchill 1849–94: W. S. Churchill *Lord Randolph Churchill* (1906)

18 Mathematics, rightly viewed, possesses not only truth, but supreme beauty—a beauty cold and austere, like that of sculpture.
Bertrand Russell 1872–1970: *Philosophical Essays* (1910)

19 An equation for me has no meaning unless it expresses a thought of God.
Srinivasa Ramanujan 1887–1920: Robert Kanigel *The Man Who Knew Infinity* (1992)

20 Beauty is the first test: there is no permanent place in the world for ugly mathematics.
Godfrey Harold Hardy 1877–1947: *A Mathematician's Apology* (1940)

21 One must divide one's time between politics and equations. But our equations are much more important to me.
Albert Einstein 1879–1955: C. P. Snow 'Einstein' in M. Goldsmith et al. (eds.) *Einstein* (1980)

22 In mathematics you don't understand things. You just get used to them.
John von Neumann 1903–57: Gary Zukav *The Dancing Wu Li Masters* (1979)

23 It is more important to have beauty in one's equations than to have them fit experiment.
he went on to say 'The discrepancy may well be due to minor features…that will get cleared up with further developments'
Paul Dirac 1902–84: in *Scientific American* May 1963

24 No-one could study mathematics intensively for more than five hours a day and remain sane.
J. B. S. Haldane 1892–1964: in *Perspectives in Biology and Medicine* (1966) 'An Autobiography in Brief'

25 Points
Have no parts or joints
How then can they combine
To form a line?
J. A. Lindon: M. Gardner *Wheels, Life and Other Mathematical Amusements* (1983)

26 Someone told me that each equation I included in the book would halve the sales.
Stephen Hawking 1942– : *A Brief History of Time* (1988)

27 Prime numbers are what is left when you have taken all the patterns away. I think prime numbers are like life.
Mark Haddon 1962– : *The Curious Incident of the Dog in the Night-time* (2003)

28 There are 10 types of people in the country: those who understand binary and those who don't.
Jeremy Paxman 1950– : in *Sunday Telegraph* 28 December 2003

Maturity

see also EXPERIENCE

proverbs and sayings ▸

1 Never send a boy to do a man's job.
someone who is young and inexperienced should not be given too much responsibility; English proverb, mid 20th century

2 Soon ripe, soon rotten.
a warning against precocity, meaning that notably early achievement is unlikely to be long-lasting; English proverb, late 14th century (earlier in Latin)

quotations ▸

3 More childish valorous than manly wise.
Christopher Marlowe 1564–93: *Tamburlaine the Great* (1590)

4 And so, from hour to hour, we ripe and ripe,
And then from hour to hour, we rot and rot:
And thereby hangs a tale.
William Shakespeare 1564–1616: *As You Like It* (1599)

5 Is not old wine wholesomest, old pippins toothsomest, old wood burn brightest, old linen wash whitest? Old soldiers, sweethearts, are surest, and old lovers are soundest.
John Webster c.1580–c.1625: *Westward Hoe* (1607)

6 Men are but children of a larger growth;
Our appetites as apt to change as theirs,
And full as craving too, and full as vain.
John Dryden 1631–1700: *All for Love* (1678)

7 At twenty years of age, the will reigns; at thirty, the wit; and at forty, the judgement.
Benjamin Franklin 1706–90: *Poor Richard's Almanac* (1741)

8 The imagination of a boy is healthy, and the mature imagination of a man is healthy; but there is a space of life

between, in which the soul is in a ferment, the character undecided, the way of life uncertain, the ambition thick-sighted: thence proceeds mawkishness.

John Keats 1795–1821: *Endymion* (1818) preface

9 A man's maturity consists in having found again the seriousness one had as a child at play.

Friedrich Nietzsche 1844–1900: *Beyond Good and Evil* (1886)

10 If you can talk with crowds and keep your virtue,
Or walk with Kings—nor lose the common touch,
If neither foes nor loving friends can hurt you,
If all men count with you, but none too much;
If you can fill the unforgiving minute
With sixty seconds' worth of distance run,
Yours is the Earth and everything that's in it,
And—which is more—you'll be a Man, my son!

Rudyard Kipling 1865–1936: 'If—' (1910)

11 To be adult is to be alone.

Jean Rostand 1894–1977: *Pensées d'un biologiste* (1954)

12 Immature love says: 'I love you because I need you.' Mature love says: 'I need you because I love you.'

Erich Fromm 1900–80: *The Art of Loving* (1956)

13 How many roads must a man walk down
Before you can call him a man?...
The answer, my friend, is blowin' in the wind,
The answer is blowin' in the wind.

Bob Dylan 1941– : 'Blowin' in the Wind' (1962 song)

14 One of the most obvious facts about grown-ups, to a child, is that they have forgotten what it is like to be a child.

Randall Jarrell 1914–65: Christina Stead *The Man Who Loved Children* (1965)

15 It's sad to grow old—but nice to ripen.

Brigitte Bardot 1934– : Tony Crawley *Bébé: the Films of Brigitte Bardot* (1975)

16 I had always thought that once you grew up you could do anything you wanted—stay up all night or eat ice-cream straight out of the container.

Bill Bryson 1951– : *The Lost Continent* (1989)

17 When adults stop being infants, children can be children.

Rowan Williams 1950– : in *Mail on Sunday* 17 April 2005

Meaning

see also WORDS

proverbs and sayings ►

1 Every picture tells a story.

advertisement for Doan's Backache Kidney Pills (early 1900s)

2 Straws tell which way the wind blows.

English proverb, mid 17th century; see FUTURE 12

phrases ►

3 gammon and spinach

nonsense, humbug; with a pun on *gammon* bacon, ham. The words *gammon and spinach* are part of the refrain to the song 'A frog he would a-wooing go', and the term is used by Dickens in *David Copperfield* and *Bleak House*

quotations ►

4 I pray thee, understand a plain man in his plain meaning.

William Shakespeare 1564–1616: *The Merchant of Venice* (1596–8)

5 Where more is meant than meets the ear.

John Milton 1608–74: 'Il Penseroso' (1645)

6 Egad I think the interpreter is the hardest to be understood of the two!

Richard Brinsley Sheridan 1751–1816: *The Critic* (1779)

7 God and I both knew what it meant once; now God alone knows.

also attributed to Browning, apropos *Sordello*, in the form 'When it was written, God and Robert Browning knew what it meant; now only God knows'

Friedrich Klopstock 1724–1803: C. Lombroso *The Man of Genius* (1891)

8 'Then you should say what you mean,' the March Hare went on. 'I do,' Alice hastily replied; 'at least—at least I mean what I say—that's the same thing, you know.' 'Not the same thing a bit!' said the Hatter. 'Why, you might just as well say that "I see what I eat" is the same thing as "I eat what I see!"'

Lewis Carroll 1832–98: *Alice's Adventures in Wonderland* (1865)

9 You see it's like a portmanteau—there are two meanings packed up into one word.

Lewis Carroll 1832–98: *Through the Looking-Glass* (1872)

10 The meaning doesn't matter if it's only idle chatter of a transcendental kind.

W. S. Gilbert 1836–1911: *Patience* (1881)

11 No one means all he says, and yet very few say all they mean, for words are slippery and thought is viscous.

Henry Brooks Adams 1838–1918: *The Education of Henry Adams* (1907)

12 The little girl had the making of a poet in her who, being told to be sure of her meaning before she spoke, said, 'How can I know what I think till I see what I say?'

Graham Wallas 1858–1932: *The Art of Thought* (1926)

13 Any general statement is like a cheque drawn on a bank. Its value depends on what is there to meet it.

Ezra Pound 1885–1972: *The ABC of Reading* (1934)

14 We had the experience but missed the meaning.

T. S. Eliot 1888–1965: *Four Quartets* 'The Dry Salvages' (1941)

15 It all depends what you mean by...

C. E. M. Joad 1891–1953: answering questions on 'The Brains Trust' (formerly 'Any Questions'), BBC radio (1941–8)

16 It depends on what the meaning of 'is' is.

Bill Clinton 1946– : videotaped evidence to the grand jury; tapes broadcast 21 September 1998

Means

see WAYS AND MEANS

Medicine

see also SICKNESS

proverbs and sayings ▸

1 **The best doctors are Dr Diet, Dr Quiet, and Dr Merryman.**

outline to an appropriate regime for someone who is ill; English proverb, mid 16th century

2 **Dr Williams' pink pills for pale people.**

patent medicine advertisement, from 1890 on

3 **Keep taking the tablets.**

supposedly traditional advice from a doctor, especially when little change in the patient's condition is envisaged

4 **Laughter is the best medicine.**

late 20th century saying; the idea is an ancient one: see HUMOUR 4

5 **Similia similibus curantur.**

Latin, 'Like cures like'; motto of homeopathic medicine attributed to S. Hahnemann (1755–1843), although not found in this form in Hahnemann's writings

phrases ▸

6 **the Lady of the Lamp**

Florence Nightingale (1820–1910), English nurse and medical reformer; from her nightly rounds in the army hospital at Scutari in the Crimean War

quotations ▸

7 Honour a physician with the honour due unto him for the uses which ye may have of him: for the Lord hath created him.

Bible: Ecclesiasticus

8 Life is short, the art long.

Hippocrates c.460–357 BC: *Aphorisms*; see ARTS 2

9 Healing is a matter of time, but it is sometimes also a matter of opportunity.

Hippocrates c.460–357 BC: *Precepts*

10 I am dying with the help of too many physicians.

Alexander the Great 356–323 BC: attributed

11 Physician, heal thyself.
Bible: St Luke

12 Confront disease at its onset.
Persius AD 34–62: *Satires*

13 Diseases desperate grown,
By desperate appliances are relieved,
Or not at all.
William Shakespeare 1564–1616: *Hamlet* (1601); see NECESSITY 3

14 Throw physic to the dogs; I'll none of it.
William Shakespeare 1564–1616: *Macbeth* (1606)

15 By medicine life may be prolonged, yet death
Will seize the doctor too.
William Shakespeare 1564–1616: *Cymbeline* (1609–10)

16 Physicians of all men are most happy; what good success soever they have, the world proclaimeth, and what faults they commit, the earth covereth.
Francis Quarles 1592–1644: *Hieroglyphics of the Life of Man* (1638); see ARCHITECTURE 17

17 Cured yesterday of my disease,
I died last night of my physician.
Matthew Prior 1664–1721: 'The Remedy Worse than the Disease' (1727)

18 It may seem a strange principle to enunciate as the very first requirement in a Hospital that it should do the sick no harm.
Florence Nightingale 1820–1910: *Notes on Hospitals* (1863 ed.) preface

19 Ah, well, then, I suppose that I shall have to die beyond my means.
at the mention of a huge fee for a surgical operation
Oscar Wilde 1854–1900: R. H. Sherard *Life of Oscar Wilde* (1906)

20 If a lot of cures are suggested for a disease, it means that the disease is incurable.
Anton Chekhov 1860–1904: *The Cherry Orchard* (1904)

21 There is at bottom only one genuinely scientific treatment for all diseases, and that is to stimulate the phagocytes.
George Bernard Shaw 1856–1950: *The Doctor's Dilemma* (1911)

22 Every day, in every way, I am getting better and better.
to be said 15 to 20 times, morning and evening
Émile Coué 1857–1926: *De la suggestion et de ses applications* (1915)

23 One finger in the throat and one in the rectum makes a good diagnostician.
William Osler 1849–1919: *Aphorisms from his Bedside Teachings* (1961)

24 We shall have to learn to refrain from doing things merely because we know how to do them.
Theodore Fox 1899–1989: speech to Royal College of Physicians, 18 October 1965

25 'Healing...
is not a science,
but the intuitive art
of wooing nature.'
W. H. Auden 1907–73: 'The Art of Healing' (1967)

26 Formerly, when religion was strong and science weak, men mistook magic for medicine; now, when science is strong and religion weak, men mistake medicine for magic.
Thomas Szasz 1920– : *The Second Sin* (1973)

27 A cousin of mine who was a casualty surgeon in Manhattan tells me that he and his colleagues had a one-word nickname for bikers: Donors.
Stephen Fry 1957– : *Paperweight* (1992)

28 The irony is that the healthier Western society becomes, the more medicine it craves.
Roy Porter 1946–2002: *The Greatest Benefit to Mankind* (1998)

Meeting and Parting

proverbs and sayings ►

1 The best of friends must part.
no friendship is so close that separation is impossible; English proverb, early 17th century

2 Nice to see you—to see you, nice.
catchphrase used by Bruce Forsyth in 'The Generation Game' on BBC Television, 1973 onwards

3 Talk of the Devil, and he is bound to appear.

to speak of the Devil may be to invite his presence; often abbreviated to *talk of the Devil*, and used when a person just spoken of is seen; English proverb, mid 17th century

phrases ▸

4 nunc dimittis

permission to depart, dismissal; Latin = now you let (your servant) depart, a canticle forming part of the Christian liturgy at evensong and compline, comprising the song of Simeon in the Bible (Luke) (in the Vulgate beginning *Nunc dimittis, Domine*)

5 ships that pass in the night

people whose contact or acquaintance is necessarily fleeting or transitory; from Longfellow: see RELATIONSHIPS 15

quotations ▸

6 *Atque in perpetuum, frater, ave atque vale.*
And so, my brother, hail, and farewell evermore!

Catullus c.84–c.54 BC: *Carmina*

7 Fare well my dear child and pray for me, and I shall for you and all your friends that we may merrily meet in heaven.

Thomas More 1478–1535: last letter to his daughter Margaret Roper, 5 July 1535

8 Good-night, good-night! parting is such sweet sorrow.

William Shakespeare 1564–1616: *Romeo and Juliet* (1595)

9 Ill met by moonlight, proud Titania.

William Shakespeare 1564–1616: *A Midsummer Night's Dream* (1595–6)

10 When shall we three meet again
In thunder, lightning, or in rain?

William Shakespeare 1564–1616: *Macbeth* (1606)

11 Since there's no help, come let us kiss and part,
Nay, I have done: you get no more of me.

Michael Drayton 1563–1631: *Idea* (1619) sonnet 61

12 Gin a body meet a body
Comin thro' the rye,
Gin a body kiss a body
Need a body cry?

Robert Burns 1759–96: 'Comin thro' the rye' (1796)

13 Not many sounds in life, and I include all urban and all rural sounds, exceed in interest a knock at the door.

Charles Lamb 1775–1834: *Essays of Elia* (1823) 'Valentine's Day'

14 In every parting there is an image of death.

George Eliot 1819–80: *Scenes of Clerical Life* (1858)

15 Dr Livingstone, I presume?

Henry Morton Stanley 1841–1904: *How I found Livingstone* (1872)

16 Parting is all we know of heaven,
And all we need of hell.

Emily Dickinson 1830–86: 'My life closed twice before its close'

17 'Is there anybody there?' said the Traveller,
Knocking on the moonlit door.

Walter de la Mare 1873–1956: 'The Listeners' (1912)

18 And ever has it been that love knows not its own depth until the hour of separation.

Kahlil Gibran 1883–1931: *The Prophet* (1923) 'The Coming of the Ship'

19 We live our lives, for ever taking leave.

Rainer Maria Rilke 1875–1926: *Duineser Elegien* (1948)

20 Goodnight, children...everywhere.

Derek McCulloch 1897–1967: *Children's Hour* (BBC Radio programme; closing words normally spoken by 'Uncle Mac' in the 1930s and 1940s)

21 Why don't you come up sometime, and see me?

usually quoted as 'Why don't you come up and see me sometime?'

Mae West 1892–1980: *She Done Him Wrong* (1933 film)

22 We'll meet again, don't know where,
Don't know when,
But I know we'll meet again some sunny day.

Ross Parker 1914–74 and **Hugh Charles** 1907–95: 'We'll Meet Again' (1939 song)

23 HUMPHREY BOGART: Of all the gin joints in all the towns in all the world, she walks into mine.
Julius J. Epstein 1909–2001: *Casablanca* (1942 film)

24 Some enchanted evening,
You may see a stranger,
You may see a stranger,
Across a crowded room.
Oscar Hammerstein II 1895–1960: 'Some Enchanted Evening' (1949 song)

25 CORBETT: It's goodnight from me.
BARKER: And it's goodnight from him.
Ronnie Barker 1929–2005 and **Ronnie Corbett** 1930– : in *The Two Ronnies* (BBC television series, 1971–87)

26 I'll be back.
James Cameron 1954– : *The Terminator* (1984 film, with Gale Anne Hurd); spoken by Arnold Schwarzenegger

Memory

phrases ►

1 down memory lane
recalling a pleasant past; *Down Memory Lane* (1949) title of a compilation of Mack Sennett comedy shorts

2 Kim's game
a memory-testing game in which players try to remember as many as possible of a set of objects briefly shown to them; *Kim* (the eponymous hero of) a book by Rudyard Kipling (1865–1936), in which a similar game is played.

3 recherche du temps perdu
an evocation of one's early life; French, literally 'in search of the lost time', title of Proust's novel sequence of 1913–27 (in English translation of 1922–31, 'Remembrance of things past'): see MEMORY 7, MEMORY 16, PAST 18

quotations ►

4 Maybe one day it will be cheering to remember even these things.
Virgil 70–19 BC: *Aeneid*

5 The memories of long love gather like drifting snow, poignant as the mandarin ducks who float side by side in sleep.
Murasaki Shikibu c.978–c.1031: *The Tale of Genji*

6 Old men forget: yet all shall be forgot,
But he'll remember with advantages
What feats he did that day.
William Shakespeare 1564–1616: *Henry V* (1599)

7 When to the sessions of sweet silent thought
I summon up remembrance of things past.
William Shakespeare 1564–1616: sonnet 30; see MEMORY 3

8 The true art of memory is the art of attention.
Samuel Johnson 1709–84: *The Idler* no. 74 (15 September 1759)

9 We'll tak a cup o' kindness yet,
For auld lang syne.
Robert Burns 1759–96: 'Auld Lang Syne' (1796); see PAST 10

10 You may break, you may shatter the vase, if you will,
But the scent of the roses will hang round it still.
Thomas Moore 1779–1852: 'Farewell!—but whenever' (1807)

11 In looking on the happy autumn-fields,
And thinking of the days that are no more.
Alfred, Lord Tennyson 1809–92: *The Princess* (1847) song (added 1850)

12 And we forget because we must
And not because we will.
Matthew Arnold 1822–88: 'Absence' (1852)

13 Better by far you should forget and smile
Than that you should remember and be sad.
Christina Rossetti 1830–94: 'Remember' (1862)

14 I've a grand memory for forgetting, David.
Robert Louis Stevenson 1850–94: *Kidnapped* (1886)

15 I have forgot much, Cynara! gone with the wind,
Flung roses, roses, riotously, with the throng,
Dancing, to put thy pale, lost lilies out of mind.
Ernest Dowson 1867–1900: 'Non Sum Qualis Eram' (1896); also known as 'Cynara'; see ABSENCE 6, CONSTANCY 10

16 And suddenly the memory revealed itself. The taste was that of the little piece of madeleine which on Sunday mornings at Combray...my aunt Léonie used to give me, dipping it first in her own cup of tea or tisane.

Marcel Proust 1871–1922: *Swann's Way* (1913, vol. 1 of *Remembrance of Things Past*); see MEMORY 3

17 Midnight shakes the memory
As a madman shakes a dead geranium.

T. S. Eliot 1888–1965: 'Rhapsody on a Windy Night' (1917)

18 Someone said that God gave us memory so that we might have roses in December.

J. M. Barrie 1860–1937: Rectorial Address at St Andrew's, 3 May 1922

19 In plucking the fruit of memory one runs the risk of spoiling its bloom.

Joseph Conrad 1857–1924: *The Arrow of Gold* (1924 ed.)

20 A cigarette that bears a lipstick's
traces,
An airline ticket to romantic places;
And still my heart has wings
These foolish things
Remind me of you.

Holt Marvell: 'These Foolish Things Remind Me of You' (1935 song)

21 Our memories are card-indexes consulted, and then put back in disorder by authorities whom we do not control.

Cyril Connolly 1903–74: *The Unquiet Grave* (1944)

22 We met at nine.
We met at eight.
I was on time.
No, you were late.
Ah yes! I remember it well.

Alan Jay Lerner 1918–86: 'I Remember it Well' (1958 song)

23 Poor people's memory is less nourished than that of the rich; it has fewer landmarks in space because they seldom leave the place where they live, and fewer reference points in time.

Albert Camus 1913–60: *The First Man* (1994)

24 Everyone seems to remember with great clarity what they were doing on November 22nd, 1963, at the precise moment they heard President Kennedy was dead.

Frederick Forsyth 1938– : *The Odessa File* (1972)

25 Your memory is a monster; *you* forget—*it* doesn't. It simply files things away. It keeps things for you, or hides things from you—and summons them to your recall with a will of its own. You think you have a memory; but it has you!

John Irving 1942– : *A Prayer for Owen Meany* (1989)

Men

proverbs and sayings ▸

1 Boys will be boys.

English proverb, early 17th century, often used ironically

2 I married my husband for life, not for lunch.

20th century saying, origin unknown

3 The odds are good, but the goods are odd.

of a high male to female ratio, originally referring to Alaska; American saying, mid 20th century

4 The way to a man's heart is through his stomach.

English proverb, early 19th century

phrases ▸

5 dead white European male

regarded as the stereotypical figure on which literary, cultural, and philosophical studies have traditionally centred; the acronym DWEM derives from this

6 good ol' boy

in US usage, a (usually white) male from the Southern States of America, regarded as one of a group conforming to a social and cultural masculine stereotype

quotations ▸

7 Sigh no more, ladies, sigh no more,
Men were deceivers ever.

William Shakespeare 1564–1616: *Much Ado About Nothing* (1598–9)

8 Man is to be held only by the *slightest* chains, with the idea that he can break them at pleasure, he submits to them in sport.
Maria Edgeworth 1767–1849: *Letters for Literary Ladies* (1795)

9 Men have had every advantage of us in telling their own story. Education has been theirs in so much higher a degree; the pen has been in their hands.
Jane Austen 1775–1817: *Persuasion* (1818)

10 A man...is *so* in the way in the house!
Elizabeth Gaskell 1810–65: *Cranford* (1853)

11 The three most important things a man has are, briefly, his private parts, his money, and his religious opinions.
Samuel Butler 1835–1902: *Further Extracts from Notebooks* (1934)

12 Every man over forty is a scoundrel.
George Bernard Shaw 1856–1950: *Man and Superman* (1903) 'Maxims: Stray Sayings'

13 If you wish—
...I'll be irreproachably tender;
not a man, but—a cloud in trousers!
Vladimir Mayakovsky 1893–1930: 'The Cloud in Trousers' (1915)

14 Men build bridges and throw railroads across deserts, and yet they contend successfully that the job of sewing on a button is beyond them. Accordingly, they don't have to sew buttons.
Heywood Broun 1888–1939: *Seeing Things at Night* (1921)

15 Somehow a bachelor never quite gets over the idea that he is a thing of beauty and a boy forever.
Helen Rowland 1875–1950: *A Guide to Men* (1922); see BEAUTY 21

16 How beautiful maleness is, if it finds its right expression.
D. H. Lawrence 1885–1930: *Sea and Sardinia* (1923)

17 It's not the men in my life that counts—it's the life in my men.
Mae West 1892–1980: *I'm No Angel* (1933 film)

18 Why can't a woman be more like a man?
Men are so honest, so thoroughly square;
Eternally noble, historically fair.
Alan Jay Lerner 1918–86: 'A Hymn to Him' (1956 song)

19 Am I not a man? And is not a man stupid? I'm a man, so I married. Wife, children, house, everything, the full catastrophe.
Michael Cacoyannis 1922– : *Zorba the Greek* (1964 film), spoken by Anthony Quinn as Zorba

20 There is, of course, no reason for the existence of the male sex except that sometimes one needs help with moving the piano.
Rebecca West 1892–1983: in *Sunday Telegraph* 28 June 1970

21 Whatever they may be in public life, whatever their relations with men, in their relations with women, all men are rapists, and that's all they are. They rape us with their eyes, their laws, and their codes.
Marilyn French 1929–2009: *The Women's Room* (1977)

22 Years ago, manhood was an opportunity for achievement, and now it is a problem to be overcome.
Garrison Keillor 1942– : *The Book of Guys* (1994)

Men and Women

see also MEN, WOMAN'S ROLE, WOMEN

proverbs and sayings ▸

1 Every Jack has his Jill.
all lovers have found a mate; English proverb, early 17th century

2 A good Jack makes a good Jill.
used of the effect of a husband on his wife; English proverb, early 17th century

3 A man is as old as he feels, and a woman as old as she looks.
both parts of the proverb are sometimes used on their own; English proverb, late 19th century

quotations ▸

4 Just such disparity
As is 'twixt air and angels' purity,
'Twixt women's love, and men's will ever be.
John Donne 1572–1631: 'Air and Angels'

5 He for God only, she for God in him.
John Milton 1608–74: *Paradise Lost* (1667)

6 In every age and country, the wiser, or at least the stronger, of the two sexes, has usurped the powers of the state, and confined the other to the cares and pleasures of domestic life.
Edward Gibbon 1737–94: *The Decline and Fall of the Roman Empire* (1776–88)

7 Man's love is of man's life a thing
apart,
'Tis woman's whole existence.
Lord Byron 1788–1824: *Don Juan* (1819–24)

8 The man's desire is for the woman; but the woman's desire is rarely other than for the desire of the man.
Samuel Taylor Coleridge 1772–1834: *Table Talk* (1835) 23 July 1827

9 Man is the hunter; woman is his
game.
Alfred, Lord Tennyson 1809–92: *The Princess* (1847)

10 'Tis strange what a man may do, and a woman yet think him an angel.
William Makepeace Thackeray 1811–63: *The History of Henry Esmond* (1852)

11 Man dreams of fame while woman
wakes to love.
Alfred, Lord Tennyson 1809–92: *Idylls of the King* 'Merlin and Vivien' (1859)

12 I expect that Woman will be the last thing civilized by Man.
George Meredith 1828–1909: *The Ordeal of Richard Feverel* (1859)

13 Take my word for it, the silliest woman can manage a clever man; but it takes a very clever woman to manage a fool.
Rudyard Kipling 1865–1936: *Plain Tales from the Hills* (1888)

14 All women become like their mothers. That is their tragedy. No man does. That's his.
Oscar Wilde 1854–1900: *The Importance of Being Earnest* (1895)

15 Women deprived of the company of men pine, men deprived of the company of women become stupid.
Anton Chekhov 1860–1904: *Notebooks* (1921)

16 A woman can forgive a man for the harm he does her, but she can never forgive him for the sacrifices he makes on her account.
W. Somerset Maugham 1874–1965: *The Moon and Sixpence* (1919)

17 Women have served all these centuries as looking-glasses possessing the magic and delicious power of reflecting the figure of a man at twice its natural size.
Virginia Woolf 1882–1941: *A Room of One's Own* (1929)

18 Me Tarzan, you Jane.
summing up his role in *Tarzan, the Ape Man* (1932 film)
Johnny Weissmuller 1904–84: in *Photoplay Magazine* June 1932; the words occur neither in the film nor the original novel, by Edgar Rice Burroughs

19 It is not in giving life but in risking life that man is raised above the animal; that is why superiority has been accorded in humanity not to the sex that brings forth but to that which kills.
Simone de Beauvoir 1908–86: *The Second Sex* (1949)

20 There is more difference within the sexes than between them.
Ivy Compton-Burnett 1884–1969: *Mother and Son* (1955)

21 Every woman adores a Fascist,
The boot in the face, the brute
Brute heart of a brute like you.
Sylvia Plath 1932–63: 'Daddy' (1963)

22 Whatever women do they must do twice as well as men to be thought half as good.
Charlotte Whitton 1896–1975: in *Canada Month* June 1963

23 Stand by your man.
Tammy Wynette 1942–98 and **Billy Sherrill**: title of song (1968)

24 A woman needs a man like a fish needs a bicycle.
Irina Dunn: graffito written 1970; attributed by Gloria Steinem in *Time* 9 October 2000

25 Women have very little idea of how much men hate them.
Germaine Greer 1939– : *The Female Eunuch* (1971)

26 Sure he was great, but don't forget that Ginger Rogers did everything he did backwards...and in high heels!
caption to 'Frank and Ernest' cartoon, *c.*1982, showing a Fred Astaire film festival
Bob Thaves 1924–2006: Ginger Rogers *Ginger: My Story* (1991)

27 My mother said it was simple to keep a man, you must be a maid in the living room, a cook in the kitchen and a whore in the bedroom. I said I'd hire the other two and take care of the bedroom bit.
Jerry Hall: in *Observer* 6 October 1985

28 A man has every season, while a woman has only the right to spring.
Jane Fonda 1937– : in *Daily Mail* 13 September 1989

29 Men are from Mars, women are from Venus.
John Gray 1951– : title of book (1992)

30 In societies where men are truly confident of their own worth, women are not merely tolerated but valued.
Aung San Suu Kyi 1945– : videotape speech at NGO Forum on Women, China, early September 1995

31 Like a compass needle that points north, a man's accusing finger always finds a woman.
Khaled Hosseini 1965– : *A Thousand Splendid Suns* (2007)

Middle Age

proverbs and sayings ▸

1 A fool at forty is a fool indeed.
someone who has not learned wisdom by the age of forty will never learn it; in this form from Edward Young *Universal Passion* (1725) 'Be wise with speed; A fool at forty is a fool indeed'; English proverb, early 16th century

2 Life begins at forty.
English proverb, mid 20th century, from title of book (1932) by Walter B. Pitkin

quotations ▸

3 *Nel mezzo del cammin di nostra vita.*
Midway along the path of our life.
Dante Alighieri 1265–1321: *Divina Commedia* 'Inferno'

4 He who thinks to realize when he is older the hopes and desires of youth is always deceiving himself, for every decade of a man's life possesses its own kind of happiness, its own hopes and prospects.
Johann Wolfgang von Goethe 1749–1832: *Elective Affinities* (1809)

5 My days are in the yellow leaf;
The flowers and fruits of love are gone;
The worm, the canker, and the grief
Are mine alone!
Lord Byron 1788–1824: 'On This Day I Complete my Thirty-Sixth Year' (1824); see OLD AGE 16

6 I am past thirty, and three parts iced over.
Matthew Arnold 1822–88: letter to Arthur Hugh Clough, 12 February 1853

7 Few women, I fear, have had such reason as I have to think the long sad years of youth were worth living for the sake of middle age.
George Eliot 1819–80: letter, 1857

8 Thirty-five is a very attractive age. London society is full of women of the very highest birth who have, of their own free choice, remained thirty-five for years.
Oscar Wilde 1854–1900: *The Importance of Being Earnest* (1895)

9 At eighteen our convictions are hills from which we look; at forty-five they are caves in which we hide.
F. Scott Fitzgerald 1896–1940: 'Bernice Bobs her Hair' (1920)

10 The afternoon of human life must also have a significance of its own and cannot be merely a pitiful appendage to life's morning.
Carl Gustav Jung 1875–1961: *The Stages of Life* (1930)

11 One of the pleasures of middle age is to *find out* that one WAS right, and that one was much righter than one knew at say 17 or 23.
Ezra Pound 1885–1972: *ABC of Reading* (1934)

12 Years ago we discovered the exact point, the dead centre of middle age.

It occurs when you are too young to take up golf and too old to rush up to the net.
Franklin P. Adams 1881–1960: *Nods and Becks* (1944)

13 Middle age is when you've met so many people that every new person you meet reminds you of someone else.
Ogden Nash 1902–71: 'Let's Not Climb the Washington Monument Tonight' (1949)

14 At forty-five,
What next, what next?
At every corner,
I meet my Father,
my age, still alive.
Robert Lowell 1917–77: 'Middle Age' (1964)

15 After forty a woman has to choose between losing her figure or her face. My advice is to keep your face, and stay sitting down.
Barbara Cartland 1901–2000: Libby Purves 'Luncheon à la Cartland'; in *Times* 6 October 1993

16 By the time you hit 50, I reckon you've earned your wrinkles, so why not be proud of them?
Twiggy 1949– : in *Observer* 8 September 2002

The Mind

see also IDEAS, LOGIC, MADNESS, THINKING

proverbs and sayings ▸

1 An imaginary ailment is worse than a disease.
Yiddish proverb

2 Mind has no sex.
modern saying, from Mary Wollstonecraft: see MIND 14

3 A mind is a terrible thing to waste.
motto of the United Negro College Fund; see MIND 26

phrases ▸

4 the five wits
the five (bodily) senses of hearing, sight, smell, taste, and touch

5 the ghost in the machine
the mind viewed as distinct from the body; a term coined by the philosopher Gilbert Ryle in *The Concept of Mind* (1949), for a viewpoint which he regarded as completely misleading

6 nature and nurture
heredity and environment as influences on, or the determinants of, personality or behaviour; there has been a long debate on which, if either, is dominant; see MIND 27

quotations ▸

7 The mind of the perfect man is like a mirror. It does not lean forward or backward in its response to things. It responds to things but conceals nothing of its own.
Chuang Tzu c.369–286 BC: *Chuang Tzu*

8 The mind does not require filling like a bottle, but rather, like wood, it only requires kindling to create in it an impulse to think independently and an ardent desire for the truth.
Plutarch c.AD 46–c.120: *Moralia*; see CHILDREN 7

9 My mind to me a kingdom is.
Such perfect joy therein I find.
Edward Dyer d. 1607: 'In praise of a contented mind' (1588); attributed

10 It is not enough to have a good mind; the main thing is to use it well.
René Descartes 1596–1650: *Le Discours de la méthode* (1637) pt. 1

11 The mind is its own place, and in itself
Can make a heaven of hell, a hell of heaven.
John Milton 1608–74: *Paradise Lost* (1667)

12 Everyone complains of his memory, and no one complains of his judgement.
Duc de la Rochefoucauld 1613–80: *Maxims* (1678)

13 The mind is but a barren soil; a soil which is soon exhausted, and will produce no crop, or only one, unless it be continually fertilized and enriched with foreign matter.
Joshua Reynolds 1723–92: *Discourses on Art* 10 December 1774

14 To give a sex to mind was not very consistent with the principles of a man [Rousseau] who argued so warmly,

and so well, for the immortality of the soul.

Mary Wollstonecraft 1759–97: *A Vindication of the Rights of Woman* (1792); see MIND 2

15 The only means of strengthening one's intellect is to make up one's mind about nothing—to let the mind be a thoroughfare for all thoughts. Not a select party.

John Keats 1795–1821: letter to George and Georgiana Keats, 24 September 1819

16 What is Matter?—Never mind.
What is Mind?—No matter.

Punch: 1855

17 On earth there is nothing great but man; in man there is nothing great but mind.

William Hamilton 1788–1856: *Lectures on Metaphysics and Logic* (1859); attributed in a Latin form to Favorinus in Pico di Mirandola (1463–94) *Disputationes Adversus Astrologiam Divinatricem*

18 With me the horrid doubt always arises whether the convictions of man's mind which has been developed from the mind of the lower animals, are of any value or at all trustworthy.

Charles Darwin 1809–82: Francis Darwin (ed.) *The Life and Letters of Charles Darwin* (1887)

19 The mind of man is capable of anything.

Guy de Maupassant 1850–93: 'The Tress of Hair' (1884)

20 O the mind, mind has mountains; cliffs of fall
Frightful, sheer, no-man-fathomed. Hold them cheap
May who ne'er hung there.

Gerard Manley Hopkins 1844–89: 'No worst, there is none' (written 1885)

21 Minds are like parachutes. They only function when they are open.

James Dewar 1842–1923: attributed

22 If my mental processes are determined wholly by the motions of atoms in my brain, I have no reason for supposing that my beliefs are true. They may be sound chemically, but that does not make them sound logically. And hence I have no reason for supposing my brain to be composed of atoms.

J. B. S. Haldane 1892–1964: *Possible Worlds* (1927)

23 Noble deeds and hot baths are the best cures for depression.

Dodie Smith 1896–1990: *I Capture the Castle* (1949)

24 Purple haze is in my brain
Lately things don't seem the same.

Jimi Hendrix 1942–70: 'Purple Haze' (1967 song)

25 That's the classical mind at work, runs fine inside but looks dingy on the surface.

Robert M. Pirsig 1928– : *Zen and the Art of Motorcycle Maintenance* (1974)

26 What a waste it is to lose one's mind, or not to have a mind. How true that is.

Dan Quayle 1947– : speech to the United Negro College Fund, in *Times* 26 May 1989; see MIND 3

27 Every human brain is born not as a blank tablet (a *tabula rasa*) waiting to be filled in by experience but as 'an exposed negative waiting to be slipped into developer fluid.'

on the nature v. nurture debate; see MIND 6

Edward O. Wilson 1929– : attributed

Misfortunes

see also ADVERSITY

proverbs and sayings ▸

1 Bad things come in threes.

the belief that an accident or misfortune is likely to be accompanied by two more is traditional, although in this form it is only recorded from the late 20th century

2 The bread never falls but on its buttered side.

if something goes wrong, the outcome is likely to be as bad as possible; English proverb, mid 19th century

3 Help you to salt, help you to sorrow.

in which salt is regarded as a sign of bad luck (especially if spilt at table); English proverb, mid 17th century

4 I cried because I had no shoes, until I met a man who had no feet.

modern saying, deriving from a Persian original; see MISFORTUNES 20

5 **If anything can go wrong, it will.**
modern saying reflecting a supposed law of nature, said to have been coined in 1949 by George Nichols. Nichols is said to have developed the maxim from a remark made by a colleague, Captain E. Murphy, and the rule is otherwise known as Murphy's Law. See MISFORTUNES 12

6 **It is no use crying over spilt milk.**
it is pointless to repine when it is too late to prevent the misfortune; English proverb, mid 17th century

7 **It never rains but it pours.**
if one thing has gone wrong, worse will follow; English proverb, early 18th century

8 **Misfortunes never come singly.**
English proverb, early 14th century

9 **Never attribute to malice that which is adequately explained by stupidity.**
modern saying, often known as Hanlon's razor

phrases ►

10 **a chapter of accidents**
a series of misfortunes; see CHANCE 27

11 **damnosa hereditas**
an inheritance or tradition bringing more burden than profit; Latin = inheritance that causes loss, from *The Institutes* of the Roman jurist Gaius (AD 110–180)

12 **Murphy's law**
any of various aphoristic expressions of the apparent perverseness and unreasonableness of things; see MISFORTUNES 5

13 **out of the frying-pan into the fire**
from one unfortunate situation into an even worse one; see EMPLOYMENT 14

14 **perfect storm**
an especially bad situation caused by a combination of unfavourable circumstances; originally a particularly violent storm arising from a rare combination of adverse meteorological factors, especially a storm of this type which occurred off the north-eastern coast of the United States in October 1991

15 **a poisoned chalice**
an assignment, award, or honour which is likely to prove a disadvantage or source of problems to the recipient; originally from Shakespeare's *Macbeth* (1606): 'This even-handed justice Commends th'ingredience of our poison'd chalice To our own lips'

16 **shirt of Nessus**
a destructive or expurgatory force or influence; from the classical story of the centaur Nessus slain by Hercules, whose blood later poisoned Hercules after he was given a garment smeared with it to wear

17 **skeleton at the feast**
something that spoils one's pleasure; an intrusive worry or cause of grief; originally in allusion to an ancient Egyptian custom recorded in Herodotus's *Histories*, which tells of a wooden corpse in a coffin being carried round at parties, and shown to guests with the words, 'Look on this, for this will be your lot when you are dead'

18 **sow dragon's teeth**
take action that (perhaps unintentionally) brings about trouble; from the teeth of the dragon killed by Cadmus in Greek legend, which when sown in the ground sprouted up as armed men

quotations ►

19 **Man is born unto trouble, as the sparks fly upward.**
Bible: Job

20 **I never complained at the vicissitudes of fortune, nor murmured at the ordinances of Heaven, excepting once, when my feet were bare, and I had not the means of procuring myself shoes. I entered the great mosque at Cufah with a heavy heart when I beheld a man who had no feet. I offered up praise and thanksgiving to God for his bounty, and bore with patience the want of shoes.**
Sadi c.1213–c.91: *The Rose Garden* (1258); see MISFORTUNES 4

21 **Misery acquaints a man with strange bedfellows.**
William Shakespeare 1564–1616: *The Tempest* (1611); see ADVERSITY 1

22 **All the misfortunes of men derive from one single thing, which is their inability to be at ease in a room.**
Blaise Pascal 1623–62: *Pensées* (1670)

23 **In the misfortune of our best friends, we always find something which is not displeasing to us.**
Duc de la Rochefoucauld 1613–80: *Réflexions ou Maximes Morales* (1665)

24 If Gladstone fell into the Thames, that would be misfortune; and if anybody pulled him out, that, I suppose, would be a calamity.

Benjamin Disraeli 1804–81: Leon Harris *The Fine Art of Political Wit* (1965)

25 I had never had a piece of toast
Particularly long and wide,
But fell upon the sanded floor,
And always on the buttered side.

James Payn 1830–98: in *Chambers's Journal* 2 February 1884; see MISFORTUNES 2

26 I left the room with silent dignity, but caught my foot in the mat.

George Grossmith 1847–1912 and **Weedon Grossmith** 1854–1919: *The Diary of a Nobody* (1894)

27 And always keep a-hold of Nurse
For fear of finding something worse.

Hilaire Belloc 1870–1953: *Cautionary Tales* (1907) 'Jim'

28 One likes people much better when they're battered down by a prodigious siege of misfortune than when they triumph.

Virginia Woolf 1882–1941: diary, 13 August 1921

29 People will take balls,
Balls will be lost always, little boy,
And no one buys a ball back.

John Berryman 1914–72: 'The Ball Poem' (1948)

30 In the words of one of my more sympathetic correspondents, it has turned out to be an 'annus horribilis'.

Elizabeth II 1926– : speech at Guildhall, London, 24 November 1992; see TIME 10

Mistakes

proverbs and sayings ►

1 Even monkeys sometimes fall off a tree.

even the most adept can be careless and make errors; Japanese proverb

2 Homer sometimes nods.

even the greatest expert may make a mistake (*nods* here means 'becomes drowsy', implying a momentary lack of attention); English proverb, late 14th century; see MISTAKES 13

3 A miss is as good as a mile.

if you miss the target, it hardly matters by how much; the syntax has been distorted by abridgement: the original form was 'an inch in a miss is as good as an ell' (an *ell* being a former measure of length equal to about 1.1 metres); English proverb, early 17th century

4 Shome mishtake, shurely?

catchphrase in *Private Eye* magazine, from the 1980s

5 There's many a slip 'twixt cup and lip.

much can go wrong between the initiation of a process and its completion, often used as a warning; English proverb, mid 16th century

6 To err is human (to forgive divine).

English proverb, late 16th century (in its quoted form, from Pope, see FORGIVENESS 17); see also COMPUTERS 8, MISTAKES 30

7 Wink at sma' fauts, ye hae great anes yoursel.

avoid criticizing the mistakes of others, your own may be greater; Scottish proverb; see SELF-KNOWLEDGE 5

phrases ►

8 a beam in one's eye

a fault great compared to another's; from the Bible (Matthew): see SELF-KNOWLEDGE 5; see also MISTAKES 10

9 an error in the first concoction

a fault in the initial stage; the first of three stages of digestion formerly recognized

10 a mote in a person's eye

a fault observed in another person by a person who ignores a greater fault of his or her own; *mote* = an irritating particle in the eye; from the Bible (Matthew): see SELF-KNOWLEDGE 5; see also MISTAKES 8

11 shut the stable door when the horse has bolted

take preventive measures too late; from the proverb: see FORESIGHT 4

quotations ►

12 I would rather be wrong, by God, with Plato...than be correct with those men.

on Pythagoreans

Cicero 106–43 BC: *Tusculanae Disputationes*

13 I'm aggrieved when sometimes even excellent Homer nods.

Horace 65–8 BC: *Ars Poetica*; see MISTAKES 2, POETS 18

14 Leave no rubs nor botches in the work.
William Shakespeare 1564–1616: *Macbeth* (1606)

15 Errors, like straws, upon the surface flow;
He who would search for pearls must dive below.
John Dryden 1631–1700: *All for Love* (1678)

16 Crooked things may be as stiff and unflexible as straight: and men may be as positive in error as in truth.
John Locke 1632–1704: *An Essay concerning Human Understanding* (1690)

17 Truth lies within a little and certain compass, but error is immense.
Henry St John, Lord Bolingbroke 1678–1751: *Reflections upon Exile* (1716)

18 It is worse than a crime, it is a blunder.
on hearing of the execution of the Duc d'Enghien, 1804
Antoine Boulay de la Meurthe 1761–1840: C.-A. Sainte-Beuve *Nouveaux Lundis* (1870)

19 As she frequently remarked when she made any such mistake, it would be all the same a hundred years hence.
Charles Dickens 1812–70: *Nicholas Nickleby* (1839)

20 'Forward, the Light Brigade!'
Was there a man dismayed?
Not though the soldier knew
Some one had blundered.
Alfred, Lord Tennyson 1809–92: 'The Charge of the Light Brigade' (1854)

21 The man who makes no mistakes does not usually make anything.
Edward John Phelps 1822–1900: speech at the Mansion House, London, 24 January 1889; see CREATIVITY 1

22 To lose one parent, Mr Worthing, may be regarded as a misfortune; to lose both looks like carelessness.
Oscar Wilde 1854–1900: *The Importance of Being Earnest* (1895)

23 The report of my death was an exaggeration.
usually quoted as 'Reports of my death have been greatly exaggerated'
Mark Twain 1835–1910: in *New York Journal* 2 June 1897

24 It is better to be vaguely right than exactly wrong.
Carveth Read 1848–1931: *Logic, Deductive and Inductive* (1898)

25 Well, if I called the wrong number, why did you answer the phone?
James Thurber 1894–1961: cartoon caption in *New Yorker* 5 June 1937

26 One Galileo in two thousand years is enough.
on being asked to proscribe the works of Teilhard de Chardin
Pope Pius XII 1876–1958: attributed; Stafford Beer *Platform for Change* (1975)

27 The weak have one weapon: the errors of those who think they are strong.
Georges Bidault 1899–1983: in *Observer* 15 July 1962

28 Mistakes are a fact of life
It is the response to error that counts.
Nikki Giovanni 1943– : 'Of Liberation' (1970)

29 When people thought the Earth was flat, they were wrong. When people thought the Earth was spherical, they were wrong. But if *you* think that thinking the Earth is spherical is *just as wrong* as thinking the Earth is flat, then your view is wronger than both of them put together.
Isaac Asimov 1920–92: *The Relativity of Wrong* (1989)

30 To err is human, but it feels divine.
Dolly Parton 1946– : in *Observer* 7 August 2005; also attributed to Mae West (1892–1980); see MISTAKES 6

31 If I misspoke that was just a misstatement.
after wrongly claiming during her presidential campaign that she had been under sniper fire in Bosnia
Hillary Rodham Clinton 1947– : meeting with editorial board of the *Philadelphia Daily News*, 24 March 2008

Moderation

see EXCESS AND MODERATION

Money

see also GREED, POVERTY, THRIFT, WEALTH

proverbs and sayings ▸

1 **Bad money drives out good.**
money of lower intrinsic value tends to circulate more freely than money of higher intrinsic and equal nominal value, through what is recognized as money of higher value being hoarded, known as Gresham's law; English proverb, early 20th century; see MONEY 21

2 **The best things in life are free.**
English proverb, early 20th century; see POSSESSIONS 27

3 **Get the money honestly if you can.**
American proverb, early 19th century; see MONEY 26

4 **He that cannot pay, let him pray.**
if you have no material resources, prayer is your only resort; English proverb, early 17th century

5 **Money can't buy happiness.**
English proverb, mid 19th century

6 **Money has no smell.**
English proverb, early 20th century in this form, but originally deriving from a comment made by the Emperor Vespasian (AD 9–79); see TAXES 5

7 **Money isn't everything.**
often said in consolation or resignation; English proverb, early 20th century

8 **Money is power.**
English proverb, mid 18th century

9 **Money is the root of all evil.**
English proverb, mid 15th century, of biblical origin; see MONEY 28, MONEY 29

10 **Money, like manure, does no good till it is spread.**
English proverb, early 19th century; see MONEY 30

11 **Money makes the mare to go.**
referring to money as a source of power; English proverb, late 15th century

12 **Money talks.**
money has influence; English proverb, mid 17th century; see MONEY 50

13 **Shrouds have no pockets.**
worldly wealth cannot be kept and used after death; English proverb, mid 19th century

14 **Time is money.**
often used to mean that time spent fruitlessly on something represents a real loss of money which could have been earned in that time; English proverb, late 16th century; see TIME 36

15 **Where there's muck there's brass.**
dirty or unpleasant activities are also lucrative (*brass* here means 'money'); English proverb, late 17th century; see MONEY 30

16 **You cannot serve God and Mammon.**
now generally used of wealth regarded as an evil influence; English proverb, mid 16th century; see MONEY 27

phrases ▸

17 **the almighty dollar**
the power of money; originally with allusion to the American writer Washington Irving (1783–1859): 'The almighty dollar, that great object of universal veneration throughout our land'

18 **feather one's own nest**
make money, usually illicitly and at someone else's expense. With reference to the habit of some birds of using feathers (their own or another bird's) to line the interior of their nests

19 **filthy lucre**
money, especially when regarded as sordid or distasteful or gained in a dishonourable way; of biblical origin: see CLERGY 7

20 **the gnomes of Zurich**
Swiss financiers or bankers, regarded as having sinister influence; the phrase was popularized by the British Labour statesman Harold Wilson (1916–95)

21 **Gresham's Law**
the tendency for debased money to circulate more freely than money of higher intrinsic and equal nominal value; after Thomas *Gresham* (d. 1579), English financier and founder of the Royal Exchange; see MONEY 1

22 **the Old Lady of Threadneedle Street**
the Bank of England; *Threadneedle Street* in the City of London containing the premises of the Bank of England; the name is derived from *three-needle*, possibly from a tavern with the arms of the City of London Guild of Needlemakers

23 **a penny more and up goes the donkey**
inviting contributions to complete a sum of money; from the cry of a travelling showman

quotations ▸

24 Wine maketh merry: but money answereth all things.
Bible: Ecclesiastes

25 There's nothing in the world so demoralizing as money.
Sophocles c.496–406 BC: *Antigone*

26 If possible honestly, if not, somehow, make money.
Horace 65–8 BC: *Epistles*; see MONEY 3, WEALTH 23

27 No man can serve two masters...Ye cannot serve God and mammon.
Bible: St Matthew; see CHOICE 4, MONEY 16, WEALTH 13

28 The love of money is the root of all evil.
Bible: I Timothy; see IDLENESS 7, MONEY 9, MONEY 29, MONEY 45

29 Ah! The lack of money is all evil's root!
Sudraka fl. 2nd century BC–AD 5th century: *The Little Clay Cart*, tr. A. Ryder; see MONEY 9, MONEY 28

30 Money is like muck, not good except it be spread.
Francis Bacon 1561–1626: *Essays* (1625) 'Of Seditions and Troubles'; see MONEY 10, MONEY 15

31 Money speaks sense in a language all nations understand.
Aphra Behn 1640–89: *The Rover* pt. 2 (1681)

32 Money is the sinews of love, as of war.
George Farquhar 1678–1707: *Love and a Bottle* (1698); see WARFARE 18

33 Take care of the pence, and the pounds will take care of themselves.
William Lowndes 1652–1724: Lord Chesterfield *Letters to his Son* (1774) 5 February 1750; see THRIFT 9

34 Money...is none of the wheels of trade: it is the oil which renders the motion of the wheels more smooth and easy.
David Hume 1711–76: *Essays: Moral and Political* (1741–2) 'Of Money'

35 I want the whole of Europe to have one currency; it will make trading much easier.
Napoleon I 1769–1821: letter to his brother Louis, 6 May 1807

36 Banking establishments are more dangerous than standing armies.
Thomas Jefferson 1743–1826: letter to John Taylor, 28 May 1816

37 Put not your trust in money, but put your money in trust.
Oliver Wendell Holmes 1809–94: *The Autocrat of the Breakfast Table* (1858)

38 Money is like a sixth sense without which you cannot make a complete use of the other five.
W. Somerset Maugham 1874–1965: *Of Human Bondage* (1915)

39 I'm tired of Love: I'm still more tired
of Rhyme.
But Money gives me pleasure all the
time.
Hilaire Belloc 1870–1953: 'Fatigued' (1923)

40 When a feller says, 'It hain't the money, but th' principle o' th' thing,' it's the money.
Frank McKinney ('Kin') Hubbard 1868–1930: *Hoss Sense and Nonsense* (1926)

41 What is robbing a bank compared with founding a bank?
Bertolt Brecht 1898–1956: *Die Dreigroschenoper* (1928)

42 'My boy,' he says, 'always try to rub up against money, for if you rub up against money long enough, some of it may rub off on you.'
Damon Runyon 1884–1946: in *Cosmopolitan* August 1929, 'A Very Honourable Guy'

43 Money without brains is always dangerous.
Napoleon Hill 1883–1970: *Think and Grow Rich* (1934)

44 Money is always there but the pockets change.
Gertrude Stein 1874–1946: *Wars I Have Seen* (1945)

45 Until and unless you discover that money is the root of all good, you ask for your own destruction. When money ceases to become the means by which men deal with one another, then men become the tools of men. Blood, whips and guns—or dollars.
Ayn Rand 1905–82: *Atlas Shrugged* (1957); see MONEY 28

46 A bank is a place that will lend you money if you can prove that you don't need it.
Bob Hope 1903–2003: Alan Harrington *Life in the Crystal Palace* (1959)

47 Money, it turned out, was exactly like sex, you thought of nothing else if you didn't have it and thought of other things if you did.
James Baldwin 1924–87: in *Esquire* May 1961 'Black Boy looks at the White Boy'

48 A bank is a place where they lend you an umbrella in fair weather and ask for it back when it begins to rain.
Robert Frost 1874–1963: in *Muscatine Journal* 22 August 1961

49 For I don't care too much for money,
For money can't buy me love.
John Lennon 1940–80 and **Paul McCartney** 1942– : 'Can't Buy Me Love' (1964 song)

50 Money doesn't talk, it swears.
Bob Dylan 1941– : 'It's Alright, Ma (I'm Only Bleeding)' (1965 song); see MONEY 12

51 Money makes the world go around.
Fred Ebb 1932–2004: 'Money Money' (1965 song), from the musical *Cabaret*; see LOVE 8

52 From now the pound abroad is worth 14 per cent or so less in terms of other currencies. It does not mean, of course, that the pound here in Britain, in your pocket or purse or in your bank, has been devalued.
Harold Wilson 1916–95: ministerial broadcast, 19 November 1967

53 Those who have some means think that the most important thing in the world is love. The poor know that it is money.
Gerald Brenan 1894–1987: *Thoughts in a Dry Season* (1978)

54 Pennies don't fall from heaven. They have to be earned on earth.
Margaret Thatcher 1925– : in *Observer* 18 November 1979; see OPTIMISM 32

Morality

proverbs and sayings ▶

1 Never do evil that good may come of it.
the prospect of a good outcome cannot justify wrongdoing; English proverb, late 16th century

quotations ▶

2 Waste no more time arguing what a good man should be. Be one.
Marcus Aurelius AD 121–180: *Meditations*

3 *Cum finis est licitus, etiam media sunt licita.*
The end justifies the means.
Hermann Busenbaum 1600–68: *Medulla Theologiae Moralis* (1650); literally 'When the end is allowed, the means also are allowed'; see MORALITY 19, WAYS 3

4 That action is best, which procures the greatest happiness for the greatest numbers.
Francis Hutcheson 1694–1746: *An Inquiry into the Original of our Ideas of Beauty and Virtue* (1725); see SOCIETY 11

5 State a moral case to a ploughman and a professor. The former will decide it as well, and often better than the latter, because he has not been led astray by artificial rules.
Thomas Jefferson 1743–1826: letter to Peter Carr, 10 August 1787

6 We know no spectacle so ridiculous as the British public in one of its periodical fits of morality.
Lord Macaulay 1800–59: *Essays Contributed to the Edinburgh Review* (1843) 'Moore's *Life of Lord Byron*'

7 And many are afraid of God—
And more of Mrs Grundy.
Frederick Locker-Lampson 1821–95: 'The Jester's Plea' (1868); see BEHAVIOUR 22

8 The highest possible stage in moral culture is when we recognize that we ought to control our thoughts.
Charles Darwin 1809–82: *The Descent of Man* (1871)

9 Morality is the herd-instinct in the individual.
Friedrich Nietzsche 1844–1900: *Die fröhliche Wissenschaft* (1882)

10 If your morals make you dreary, depend upon it they are wrong.
Robert Louis Stevenson 1850–94: 'A Christmas Sermon' (1888)

11 Morality is a private and costly luxury.
Henry Brooks Adams 1838–1918: *The Education of Henry Adams* (1907)

12 The nation's morals are like its teeth: the more decayed they are the more it hurts to touch them.
George Bernard Shaw 1856–1950: *The Shewing-up of Blanco Posnet* (1911)

13 Moral indignation is jealousy with a halo.
H. G. Wells 1866–1946: *The Wife of Sir Isaac Harman* (1914)

14 You can't learn too soon that the most useful thing about a principle is that it can always be sacrificed to expediency.
W. Somerset Maugham 1874–1965: *The Circle* (1921)

15 Food comes first, then morals.
Bertolt Brecht 1898–1956: *The Threepenny Opera* (1928)

16 I know only that what is moral is what you feel good after and what is immoral is what you feel bad after.
Ernest Hemingway 1899–1961: *Death in the Afternoon* (1932)

17 In olden days a glimpse of stocking
Was looked on as something
shocking
Now, heaven knows,
Anything goes.
Cole Porter 1891–1964: 'Anything Goes' (1934 song)

18 The last temptation is the greatest
treason:
To do the right deed for the wrong
reason.
T. S. Eliot 1888–1965: *Murder in the Cathedral* (1935)

19 The end cannot justify the means, for the simple and obvious reason that the means employed determine the nature of the ends produced.
Aldous Huxley 1894–1963: *Ends and Means* (1937); see MORALITY 3

20 It is always easier to fight for one's principles than to live up to them.
Alfred Adler 1870–1937: Phyllis Bottome *Alfred Adler* (1939)

21 Morality's *not* practical. Morality's a gesture. A complicated gesture learned from books.
Robert Bolt 1924–95: *A Man for All Seasons* (1960)

22 Cowardice asks the question, 'Is it safe?' Expediency asks the question, 'Is it politic?' Vanity asks the question, 'Is it popular?' But Conscience asks the question, 'Is it right?'
Martin Luther King 1929–68: in 1967; in *Autobiography of Martin Luther King Jr.* (1999)

23 Even a purely moral act that has no hope of any immediate and visible political effect can gradually and indirectly, over time, gain in political significance.
Václav Havel 1936– : letter to Alexander Dubček, August 1969

24 Values are tapes we play on the Walkman of the mind: any tune we choose so long as it does not disturb others.
Jonathan Sacks 1948– : *The Persistence of Faith* (1991)

25 There is no good or evil, there is only power, and those too weak to seek it.
J. K. Rowling 1965– : *Harry Potter and the Philosopher's Stone* (1997)

Mountains

proverbs and sayings ▸

1 Two men may meet, but never two mountains.
American proverb

quotations ▸

2 Today I climbed the highest mountain in this region, which is not improperly called Ventosus (Windy). The only motive for my ascent was the wish to see what so great a height had to offer.
of Mont Ventoux in Provence, France
Petrarch 1304–74: letter to Dionisio da Borgo San Sepolcro 1336 (tr. Mark Musa)

3 Mountains are the beginning and the end of all natural scenery.
John Ruskin 1819–1900: *Modern Painters* (1856)

4 It is a fine thing to be out on the hills alone. A man can hardly be a beast or a fool alone on a great mountain.
Francis Kilvert 1840–79: diary, 29 May 1871

5 Do nothing in haste, look well to each step, and from the beginning think what may be the end.
Edward Whymper 1840–1911: *Scrambles Amongst the Alps* (1871)

6 Climb the mountains and get their good tidings.
John Muir 1838–1914: in *Atlantic Monthly* April 1898

7 Because it's there.
on being asked why he wanted to climb Mount Everest
George Leigh Mallory 1886–1924: in *New York Times* 18 March 1923

8 Well, we knocked the bastard off!
on conquering Mount Everest, 1953
Edmund Hillary 1919–2008: *Nothing Venture, Nothing Win* (1975)

9 My mountain did not seem to me a lifeless thing of rock and ice, but warm and friendly and living. She was a mother hen, and the other mountains were chicks under her wings.
on Everest
Tenzing Norgay 1914–86: *Man of Everest* (1975)

10 The Alps, the Rockies and all other mountains are related to the earth, the Himalayas to the heavens.
J. K. Galbraith 1908–2006: *A Life in our Times* (1981)

Mourning
see also SORROW

proverbs and sayings ▸

1 A bellowing cow soon forgets her calf.
the person who laments most loudly is the one who is soonest comforted; English proverb, late 19th century

2 Grief is the price we pay for love.
late 20th century saying; see MOURNING 24, MOURNING 27

3 He that conceals his grief, finds no remedy for it.
trying to hide distress means that you do not recover from it; proverb, said to be of Turkish origin

4 Let the dead bury the dead.
often used to mean that the past should be left undisturbed; English proverb, early 19th century, from the Bible (Matthew) 'Let the dead bury their dead'

5 No flowers by request.
an intimation that no flowers are desired at a funeral; see STYLE 18

6 You can shed tears that she is gone or you can smile because she has lived.
preface to the Order of Service at the funeral of Queen Elizabeth the Queen Mother, 2002

phrases ▸

7 sackcloth and ashes
a sign of penitence or mourning; used with biblical allusion to the wearing of sackcloth and having ashes sprinkled on the head, as in Matthew, 'if the mighty works, which were done in you, had been done in Tyre and Sidon, they would have repented long ago in sackcloth and ashes'

8 wear the green willow
grieve for the loss of a loved one, be in mourning; a branch or the leaves of the *willow* as a symbol of grief for unrequited love or the loss of a loved one

quotations ▸

9 Blessed are they that mourn: for they shall be comforted.
Bible: St Matthew

10 Grief fills the room up of my absent child,
Lies in his bed, walks up and down with me.
William Shakespeare 1564–1616: *King John* (1591–8)

11 All my pretty ones?
Did you say all? O hell-kite! All?
What! all my pretty chickens and their dam,
At one fell swoop?
William Shakespeare 1564–1616: *Macbeth* (1606); see THOROUGHNESS 6

12 He first deceased; she for a little tried
To live without him: liked it not, and died.
Henry Wotton 1568–1639: 'Upon the Death of Sir Albertus Moreton's Wife' (1651)

13 How often are we to die before we go quite off this stage? In every friend we lose a part of ourselves, and the best part.

Alexander Pope 1688–1744: letter to Jonathan Swift, 5 December 1732

14 I have had playmates, I have had companions,
In my days of childhood, in my joyful school-days,—
All, all are gone, the old familiar faces.

Charles Lamb 1775–1834: 'The Old Familiar Faces'

15 They told me, Heraclitus, they told me you were dead,
They brought me bitter news to hear and bitter tears to shed.
I wept as I remembered how often you and I
Had tired the sun with talking and sent him down the sky.

William Cory 1823–92: 'Heraclitus' (1858); translation of Callimachus 'Epigram'

16 The bitterest tears shed over graves are for words left unsaid and deeds left undone.

Harriet Beecher Stowe 1811–96: *Little Foxes* (1871)

17 Dead! and...never called me mother.

Mrs Henry Wood 1814–87: *East Lynne* (dramatized by T. A. Palmer, 1874, the words do not occur in the novel of 1861)

18 Time does not bring relief; you all have lied
Who told me time would ease me of my pain!
I miss him in the weeping of the rain;
I want him at the shrinking of the tide.

Edna St Vincent Millay 1892–1950: 'Time does not bring relief' (1917)

19 Do not stand at my grave and weep:
I am not there. I do not sleep.
I am a thousand winds that blow.
I am the diamond glints on snow...
Do not stand at my grave and cry;
I am not there, I did not die.

quoted in letter left by British soldier Stephen Cummins when killed by the IRA, March 1989
Mary E. Frye 1905–2004: originally circulated privately from 1932 on

20 He was my North, my South, my East and West,
My working week and my Sunday rest,
My noon, my midnight, my talk, my song;
I thought that love would last for ever: I was wrong.

W. H. Auden 1907–73: 'Funeral Blues' (1936)

21 Bereavement is a universal and integral part of our experience of love. It follows marriage as normally as marriage follows courtship or as autumn follows summer.

C. S. Lewis 1898–1963: *A Grief Observed* (1961)

22 All I have I would have given gladly not to be standing here today.

following the assassination of J. F. Kennedy
Lyndon Baines Johnson 1908–73: first speech to Congress as President, 27 November 1963

23 Widow. The word consumes itself.

Sylvia Plath 1932–63: 'Widow' (1971)

24 The pain of grief is just as much a part of life as the joy of love; it is, perhaps, the price we pay for love, the cost of commitment .

usually quoted as 'Grief is the price we pay for love'; see MOURNING 2, MOURNING 27
Colin Murray Parkes 1928– : *Bereavement: Studies of Grief in Adult Life* (1972)

25 I can't think of a more wonderful thanksgiving for the life I have had than that everyone should be jolly at my funeral.

Lord Mountbatten 1900–79: Richard Hough *Mountbatten* (1980)

26 The number of casualties will be more than any of us can bear.

following the destruction of the World Trade Center in New York, 11 September 2001
Rudy Giuliani 1944– : in *Times* 12 September 2001

27 Nothing that can be said can begin to take away the anguish and pain of these moments. Grief is the price we pay for love.

Elizabeth II 1926– : message to prayer service for the families of British victims of the terrorist attacks in New York, 21 September 2001; see MOURNING 2, MOURNING 24

Murder

see also DEATH

proverbs and sayings ▸

1 Blood will have blood.
killing will provoke further killing; English proverb, mid 15th century: in this form from Shakespeare *Macbeth* 'It will have blood, they say blood will have blood'

2 Guns don't kill people; people kill people.
National Rifle Association slogan; see MURDER 21

3 Killing no murder.
English proverb, mid 17th century; see MURDER 13

4 Lizzie Borden took an axe
And gave her mother forty whacks;
When she saw what she had done
She gave her father forty-one!
popular rhyme in circulation after the acquittal of Lizzie Borden, in June 1893, from the charge of murdering her father and stepmother at Fall River, Massachusetts on 4 August 1892

5 Murder will out.
the crime of murder can never be successfully concealed; English proverb, early 14th century; see MURDER 11

phrases ▸

6 licensed to kill
supposedly indicating that an agent is authorized by the Security Service to kill when engaged in counter-espionage; associated particularly with Ian Fleming's thriller-hero James Bond

7 mark of Cain
the stigma of a murderer, a sign of infamy; the sign placed on Cain after the murder of Abel, originally as a sign of divine protection in exile; see also CANADA 3, ORDER 8, TRAVEL 14

quotations ▸

8 Thou shalt not kill.
Bible: Exodus; see LIFESTYLES 13, MURDER 17

9 Whoso slays a soul not to retaliate for a soul slain, nor for corruption done in the land, shall be as if he had slain mankind altogether.
The Koran: sura 5

10 Will no one rid me of this turbulent priest?
of Thomas Becket, Archbishop of Canterbury, murdered in Canterbury Cathedral, December 1170
Henry II 1133–89: oral tradition

11 Mordre wol out; that se we day by day.
Geoffrey Chaucer 1343–1400: *The Canterbury Tales* 'The Nun's Priest's Tale'; see MURDER 5

12 Murder most foul, as in the best it is;
But this most foul, strange, and unnatural.
William Shakespeare 1564–1616: *Hamlet* (1601)

13 Killing no murder briefly discourst in three questions.
an apology for tyrannicide
Edward Sexby d. 1658: title of pamphlet (1657); see MURDER 3

14 Assassination is the quickest way.
Molière 1622–73: *Le Sicilien* (1668)

15 Murder considered as one of the fine arts.
Thomas De Quincey 1785–1859: in *Blackwood's Magazine* February 1827; essay title

16 In that case, if we are to abolish the death penalty, let the murderers take the first step.
Alphonse Karr 1808–90: in *Les Guêpes* January 1849

17 Thou shalt not kill; but need'st not strive
Officiously to keep alive.
Arthur Hugh Clough 1819–61: 'The Latest Decalogue' (1862); see MURDER 8

18 Kill a man, and you are an assassin. Kill millions of men, and you are a conqueror. Kill everyone, and you are a god.
Jean Rostand 1894–1977: *Pensées d'un biologiste* (1939)

19 Roast beef and Yorkshire, or roast pork and apple sauce, followed up by suet pudding and driven home, as it were, by a cup of mahogany-brown tea, have put you in just the right mood. Your pipe is drawing sweetly, the sofa cushions are soft underneath

you, the fire is well alight, the air is warm and stagnant. In these blissful circumstances, what is it that you want to read about?

Naturally, about a murder.

George Orwell 1903–50: *Decline of the English Murder and other essays* (1965) title essay, written 1946

20 Television has brought back murder into the home—where it belongs.

Alfred Hitchcock 1899–1980: in *Observer* 19 December 1965

21 The National Rifle Association says guns don't kill people, people do. But I think the gun helps. Just standing there, going 'Bang!'—that's not going to kill too many people.

Eddie Izzard 1962– : *Dress to Kill* (stageshow, San Francisco, 1998); see MURDER 2

22 I love you...That is what they were all saying down their phones, from the hijacked planes and the burning towers. There is only love, and then oblivion. Love was all they had to set against the hatred of their murderers.

of the last messages received from those trapped by terrorist attacks, 11 September 2001

Ian McEwan 1948– : in *Guardian* 15 September 2001

Music

see also JAZZ, MUSICIANS, SINGING

proverbs and sayings ▸

1 Every good boy deserves favour.

traditional mnemonic for the notes (E, G, B, D, F) on the lines of the treble clef stave

2 It takes seven years to make a piper.

Scottish proverb

3 Music helps not the toothache.

English proverb, mid 17th century

4 Writing about music is like dancing about architecture.

modern saying, attributed to Elvis Costello, David Bowie, Frank Zappa, and many others, but of unknown origin; also found in the form 'Talking about music...'

phrases ▸

5 music of the spheres

the harmonious sound supposed to be produced by the motion of the celestial globes imagined by the older astronomers as revolving round the earth and respectively carrying with them the moon, sun, planets, and fixed stars; see UNIVERSE 3

6 Tin Pan Alley

the world of composers and publishers of popular music; from the name given to a district in New York (28th Street, between 5th Avenue and Broadway) where many songwriters, arrangers, and music publishers were formerly based

7 the tune the old cow died of

a tedious badly played piece of music

quotations ▸

8 If music be the food of love, play on;
Give me excess of it, that, surfeiting,
The appetite may sicken, and so die.

William Shakespeare 1564–1616: *Twelfth Night* (1601)

9 Music has charms to soothe a savage breast.

William Congreve 1670–1729: *The Mourning Bride* (1697)

10 Music is the pleasure the human mind experiences from counting without being aware that it is counting.

Gottfried Wilhelm Leibniz 1646–1716: attributed

11 Too beautiful for our ears, and much too many notes, dear Mozart.

of *The Abduction from the Seraglio* (1782)

Joseph II 1741–90: F. X. Niemetschek *Life of Mozart* (1798)

12 Melody is the essence of music. I compare a good melodist to a fine racer, and counterpoints to hack post-horses.

Wolfgang Amadeus Mozart 1756–91: remark to Michael Kelly, 1786; Michael Kelly *Reminiscences* (1826)

13 But I struck one chord of music,
Like the sound of a great Amen.

Adelaide Ann Procter 1825–64: 'A Lost Chord' (1858)

14 Hell is full of musical amateurs: music is the brandy of the damned.

George Bernard Shaw 1856–1950: *Man and Superman* (1903)

15 There is music in the air.
Edward Elgar 1857–1934: R. J. Buckley *Sir Edward Elgar* (1905)

16 The symphony must be like the world. It must embrace everything.
Gustav Mahler 1860–1911: remark to Sibelius, Helsinki, 1907

17 It is only that which cannot be expressed otherwise that is worth expressing in music.
Frederick Delius 1862–1934: in *Sackbut* September 1920 'At the Crossroads'

18 Art is not national. It is international. Music is not written in red, white and blue; it is written with the heart's blood of the composer.
Nellie Melba 1861–1931: *Melodies and Memories* (1925)

19 Extraordinary how potent cheap music is.
Noël Coward 1899–1973: *Private Lives* (1930)

20 Music begins to atrophy when it departs too far from the dance...poetry begins to atrophy when it gets too far from music.
Ezra Pound 1885–1972: *The ABC of Reading* (1934)

21 Down the road someone is practising scales,
The notes like little fishes vanish with a wink of tails.
Louis MacNeice 1907–63: 'Sunday Morning' (1935)

22 The whole problem can be stated quite simply by asking, 'Is there a meaning to music?' My answer to that would be, 'Yes.' And 'Can you state in so many words what the meaning is?' My answer to that would be, 'No.'
Aaron Copland 1900–90: *What to Listen for in Music* (1939)

23 If I don't practise for one day, I know it; if I don't practise for two days, the critics know it; if I don't practise for three days, the audience knows it.
Ignacy Jan Paderewski 1860–1941: attributed; Nat Shapiro *An Encyclopedia of Quotations about Music* (1978)

24 Good music is that which penetrates the ear with facility and quits the memory with difficulty.
Thomas Beecham 1879–1961: speech, 1950; in *New York Times* 9 March 1961

25 The notes I handle no better than many pianists. But the pauses between the notes—ah, that is where the art resides!
Artur Schnabel 1882–1951: in *Chicago Daily News* 11 June 1958

26 Music is your own experience, your thoughts, your wisdom. If you don't live it, it won't come out of your horn.
Charlie Parker 1920–55: Nat Shapiro and Nat Hentoff *Hear Me Talkin' to Ya* (1955)

27 I don't know whether I like it, but it's what I meant.
on his 4th symphony
Ralph Vaughan Williams 1872–1958: Christopher Headington *Bodley Head History of Western Music* (1974)

28 The hills are alive with the sound of music,
With songs they have sung for a thousand years.
Oscar Hammerstein II 1895–1960: 'The Sound of Music' (1959 song)

29 This machine kills fascists.
Woody Guthrie 1912–67: slogan on his guitar

30 ANDRÉ PREVIN: You're playing all the wrong notes.
ERIC MORECAMBE: I'm playing all the *right* notes. But not *necessarily* in the right order.
on the Grieg Piano Concerto
Eddie Braben 1930– : *The Morecambe and Wise Show* (BBC TV, 25 December 1971)

31 Music...can name the unnameable, and communicate the unknowable.
Leonard Bernstein 1918–90: *The Unanswered Question* (1976)

32 You just pick a chord, go twang, and you've got music.
Sid Vicious 1957–79: attributed

33 Music is spiritual. The music business is not.
Van Morrison: in *Times* 6 July 1990

34 Why waste money on psychotherapy when you can listen to the B Minor Mass?
Michael Torke 1961– : in *Observer* 23 September 1990

35 Improvisation is too good to leave to chance.
Paul Simon 1942– : in *Observer* 30 December 1990

Musicians

see also JAZZ, MUSIC

phrases ▸

1 The Fab Four
George Harrison, John Lennon, Paul McCartney, and Ringo Starr; the four members of the pop and rock group the Beatles

2 the waltz king
Johann Strauss (1825–99), who composed many famous waltzes, such as *The Blue Danube* (1867)

quotations ▸

3 Tallis is dead and Music dies.
William Byrd 1543–1623: 'Ye Sacred Muses'

4 Difficult do you call it, Sir? I wish it were impossible.
on the performance of a celebrated violinist
Samuel Johnson 1709–84: William Seward *Supplement to the Anecdotes of Distinguished Persons* (1797)

5 Hats off, gentlemen—a genius!
on Chopin
Robert Schumann 1810–56: 'An Opus 2' (1831); H. Pleasants (ed.) *Schumann on Music* (1965)

6 This symphony is the Apotheosis of Dance herself.
on Beethoven's Seventh Symphony
Richard Wagner 1813–83: *The Art-Work of the Future* (1849)

7 We are the music makers,
We are the dreamers of dreams...
We are the movers and shakers
Of the world for ever, it seems.
Arthur O'Shaughnessy 1844–81: 'Ode' (1874); see CHANGE 23

8 Please do not shoot the pianist. He is doing his best.
printed notice in a dancing saloon
Anonymous: Oscar Wilde *Impressions of America* 'Leadville' (1882–3)

9 I have been told that Wagner's music is better than it sounds.
Bill Nye 1850–96: Mark Twain *Autobiography* (1924)

10 It will be generally admitted that Beethoven's Fifth Symphony is the most sublime noise that has ever penetrated into the ear of man.
E. M. Forster 1879–1970: *Howards End* (1910)

11 Wagner: a beautiful sunset which one mistook for a dawn.
Claude Debussy 1862–1918: *Monsieur Croche, antidilettante* (1921)

12 Ravel refuses the Legion of Honour, but all his music accepts it.
Erik Satie 1866–1925: Jean Cocteau *Le Discours d'Oxford* (1956)

13 Bach almost persuades me to be a Christian.
Roger Fry 1866–1934: Virginia Woolf *Roger Fry* (1940)

14 Children are given Mozart because of the small *quantity* of the notes; grown-ups avoid Mozart because of the great *quality* of the notes.
Artur Schnabel 1882–1951: *My Life and Music* (1961)

15 There are two golden rules for an orchestra: start together and finish together. The public doesn't give a damn what goes on in between.
Thomas Beecham 1879–1961: Harold Atkins and Archie Newman *Beecham Stories* (1978)

16 Whether the angels play only Bach in praising God I am not quite sure; I am sure, however, that en famille they play Mozart.
Karl Barth 1886–1968: in *New York Times* 11 December 1968

17 A musician, if he's a messenger, is like a child who hasn't been handled too many times by man, hasn't had too many fingerprints across his brain.
Jimi Hendrix 1942–70: in *Life Magazine* (1969)

18 Most people get into bands for three very simple rock and roll reasons: to get laid, to get fame, and to get rich.
Bob Geldof 1954– : in *Melody Maker* 27 August 1977

19 If anyone has conducted a Beethoven performance, and then doesn't have to go to an osteopath, then there's something wrong.
Simon Rattle 1955– : in *Guardian* 31 May 1990

20 Beethoven tells you what it's like to be Beethoven and Mozart tells you what it's like to be human. Bach tells you what it's like be the universe.
Douglas Adams 1952–2001: attributed, in *Independent* 17 May 2001

Names

proverbs and sayings ▸

1 By Tre, Pol, and Pen, you shall know the Cornish men.
traditional saying, referring to the frequency of these elements in Cornish names; English proverb, mid 16th century

2 If the cap fits, wear it.
used with reference to the assumed suitability of a name or description to a person's behaviour; English proverb, mid 18th century

3 If the shoe fits, wear it.
one has to accept it when a particular comment is shown to apply to oneself; found mainly in the US; English proverb, late 18th century

4 It is not what you call me. It is what I answer to.
African proverb

5 Only the camel knows the hundredth name of God.
saying from Arab folklore; see NAMES 6

phrases ▸

6 ninety-nine names of God
in Islam, the names for Allah (in the main taken or derived from the Koran); see NAMES 5

7 a rose by any other name
an allusive reference to Shakespeare, referring to the arbitrary nature of names: see NAMES 9

quotations ▸

8 God hath also highly exalted him, and given him a name which is above every name:
That at the name of Jesus every knee should bow.
Bible: Philippians

9 What's in a name? that which we call
a rose
By any other name would smell as
sweet.
William Shakespeare 1564–1616: *Romeo and Juliet* (1595); see NAMES 7

10 JAQUES: I do not like her name.
ORLANDO: There was no thought of pleasing you when she was christened.
William Shakespeare 1564–1616: *As You Like It* (1599)

11 If you should have a boy do not christen him John...'Tis a bad name and goes against a man. If my name had been Edmund I should have been more fortunate.
John Keats 1795–1821: letter to his sister-in-law, 13 January 1820

12 A nickname is the heaviest stone that the devil can throw at a man.
William Hazlitt 1778–1830: *Sketches and Essays* (1839) 'Nicknames'

13 With a name like yours, you might be any shape, almost.
Lewis Carroll 1832–98: *Through the Looking-Glass* (1872)

14 I have fallen in love with American
names,
The sharp, gaunt names that never
get fat,
The snakeskin-titles of mining-claims,
The plumed war-bonnet of Medicine
Hat,
Tucson and Deadwood and Lost Mule
Flat.
Stephen Vincent Benét 1898–1943: 'American Names' (1927)

15 Dear 338171 (May I call you 338?).
Noël Coward 1899–1973: letter to T. E. Lawrence, 25 August 1930

16 A self-made man may prefer a self-made name.
on Samuel Goldfish changing his name to Samuel Goldwyn
Learned Hand 1872–1961: Bosley Crowther *Lion's Share* (1957)

17 The name of a man is a numbing blow from which he never recovers.
Marshall McLuhan 1911–80: *Understanding Media* (1964)

18 Proper names are poetry in the raw. Like all poetry they are untranslatable.
W. H. Auden 1907–73: *A Certain World* (1970)

19 Every Tom, Dick and Harry is called Arthur.

to Arthur Hornblow, who was planning to name his son Arthur

Sam Goldwyn 1882–1974: Michael Freedland *The Goldwyn Touch* (1986)

20 No, I'm breaking it in for a friend.

when asked if Groucho were his real name

Groucho Marx 1890–1977: attributed

21 Colin is the sort of name you give your goldfish for a joke.

Colin Firth 1960– : in *Observer* 1 September 2002

22 We've put an accent over the first 'a' to make it a bit more exotic, and two 'i's at the end just to make it look a bit different.

on her daughter's name, Princess Tiáamii

Katie Price (Jordan) 1978– : in *Observer* 29 July 2007

Nature

see also EARTH, LIFE SCIENCES

proverbs and sayings ▸

1 Nature abhors a vacuum.

English proverb, mid 16th century; see NATURE 20

2 You can drive out nature with a pitchfork but she keeps on coming back.

English proverb, mid 16th century, from the Roman poet Horace (65–8 BC) *Epistles* 'You may drive out nature with a pitchfork, but she will always return'

phrases ▸

3 balance of nature

a state of equilibrium produced by the interaction of living organisms, ecological balance

4 Nature red in tooth and claw

a ruthless personification of the creative and regulative physical power conceived of as operating in the material world; from Tennyson: see NATURE 13

quotations ▸

5 Nature does nothing without purpose or uselessly.

Aristotle 384–322 BC: *Politics*

6 It is far from easy to judge whether she has proved a kind parent to man or a harsh step-mother.

on nature

Pliny the Elder AD 23–79: *Historia Naturalis*

7 The whole moon and the entire sky are reflected in dewdrops on the grass, or even in one drop of water.

often quoted as '…reflected in one dewdrop on the grass'

Dogen Kigen 1200–53: John M. Koller *Asian Philosophies* (2007)

8 In her inventions nothing is lacking, and nothing is superfluous.

Leonardo da Vinci 1452–1519: Edward McCurdy (ed.) *Leonardo da Vinci's Notebooks* (1906)

9 And this our life, exempt from public haunt,
Finds tongues in trees, books in the running brooks,
Sermons in stones, and good in everything.

William Shakespeare 1564–1616: *As You Like It* (1599)

10 The subtlety of nature is greater many times over than the subtlety of the senses and understanding.

Francis Bacon 1561–1626: *Novum Organum* (1620) tr. J. Spedding

11 All things are artificial, for nature is the art of God.

Thomas Browne 1605–82: *Religio Medici* (1643)

12 There is a pleasure in the pathless woods,
There is a rapture on the lonely shore,
There is society, where none intrudes,
By the deep sea, and music in its roar:
I love not man the less, but nature more.

Lord Byron 1788–1824: *Childe Harold's Pilgrimage* (1812–18)

13 Who trusted God was love indeed
And love Creation's final law—
Though Nature, red in tooth and claw
With ravine, shrieked against his creed.

Alfred, Lord Tennyson 1809–92: *In Memoriam A. H. H.* (1850); see NATURE 4

14 I believe a leaf of grass is no less than
the journey-work of the stars,
And the pismire is equally perfect,
and a grain of sand, and the egg of
the wren,
And the tree toad is a chef-d'oeuvre for
the highest,
And the running blackberry would
adorn the parlours of heaven.
Walt Whitman 1819–92: 'Song of Myself' (written 1855)

15 What a book a devil's chaplain might write on the clumsy, wasteful, blundering, low, and horridly cruel works of nature!
Charles Darwin 1809–82: letter to J. D. Hooker, 13 July 1856

16 Nature is not a temple, but a workshop, and man's the workman in it.
Ivan Turgenev 1818–83: *Fathers and Sons* (1862)

17 In nature there are neither rewards nor punishments—there are consequences.
Robert G. Ingersoll 1833–99: *Some Reasons Why* (1881)

18 For nature, heartless, witless nature,
Will neither care nor know
What stranger's feet may find the
meadow
And trespass there and go.
A. E. Housman 1859–1936: *Last Poems* (1922) no. 40

19 Nature, Mr Allnutt, is what we are put into this world to rise above.
James Agee 1909–55: *The African Queen* (1951 film); not in the novel by C. S. Forester

20 BRICK: Well, they say nature hates a vacuum, Big Daddy.
BIG DADDY: That's what they say, but sometimes I think that a vacuum is a hell of a lot better than some of the stuff that nature replaces it with.
Tennessee Williams 1911–83: *Cat on a Hot Tin Roof* (1955); see NATURE 1

21 People thought they could explain and conquer nature—yet the outcome is that they destroyed it and disinherited themselves from it.
Václav Havel 1936– : Lewis Wolpert *The Unnatural Nature of Science* (1993)

Necessity

proverbs and sayings ▸

1 **Any port in a storm.**
when one is in trouble or difficulty, support or shelter from any source is welcome; English proverb, mid 18th century

2 **Beggars can't be choosers.**
someone who is destitute is in no position to criticize what may be offered; English proverb, mid 16th century

3 **Desperate diseases must have desperate remedies.**
in a difficult or dangerous situation it may be necessary to take extreme and risky measures; English proverb, mid 16th century; see MEDICINE 13, REVOLUTION 8

4 **Even a worm will turn.**
even a meek person will resist or retaliate if pushed too far; English proverb, mid 16th century

5 **Hunger drives the wolf out of the wood.**
even the fiercest animal will be driven from shelter by acute need; English proverb, late 15th century

6 **If the mountain will not come to Mahomet, Mahomet must go to the mountain.**
used in the context of an apparently insoluble situation. The saying refers to a story of Muhammad recounted by Bacon in his *Essays*, in which the Prophet called a hill to him, and when it did not move, made this remark; English proverb, early 17th century

7 **Make a virtue of necessity.**
one should do with a good grace what is unavoidable; English proverb, late 14th century; see NECESSITY 17

8 **Necessity is the mother of invention.**
need is often a spur to the creative process; English proverb, mid 16th century

9 **Necessity knows no law.**
someone in extreme need will disregard rules or prohibitions; English proverb, late 14th century; see NECESSITY 20

10 **Necessity sharpens industry.**
American proverb, mid 20th century; see NECESSITY 8

11 Needs must when the devil drives.
used in recognition of overwhelming force of circumstance; English proverb, mid 15th century

12 When all fruit fails, welcome haws.
often used of someone taking of necessity an older or otherwise unsuitable lover (*haws*, the red fruit of the hawthorn, are contrasted with fruits generally eaten as food); English proverb, early 18th century

13 Who says A must say B.
only recorded in English from North American sources, and meaning that if a first step is taken, the second will inevitably follow; English proverb, mid 19th century

phrases ▸

14 the breath of life
a necessity for continuing existence; from the Bible (Genesis) 'all in whose nostrils was the breath of life'

15 a wing and a prayer
reliance on hope or the slightest chance in a desperate situation; from a song (1943) by H. Adamson, recounting an emergency landing by an aircraft: see CRISES 21

quotations ▸

16 Nothing have I found stronger than Necessity.
Euripides c.485–c.406 BC: *Alcestis*

17 All places that the eye of heaven visits
Are to a wise man ports and happy havens.
Teach thy necessity to reason thus;
There is no virtue like necessity.
William Shakespeare 1564–1616: *Richard II* (1595); see NECESSITY 7

18 Must! Is *must* a word to be addressed to princes? Little man, little man! thy father, if he had been alive, durst not have used that word.
to Robert Cecil, on his saying she must go to bed
Elizabeth I 1533–1603: J. R. Green *A Short History of the English People* (1874)

19 Cruel necessity.
on the execution of Charles I, 1649
Oliver Cromwell 1599–1658: Joseph Spence *Anecdotes* (1820)

20 Necessity hath no law. Feigned necessities, imaginary necessities... are the greatest cozenage that men can put upon the Providence of God, and make pretences to break known rules by.
Oliver Cromwell 1599–1658: speech to Parliament, 12 September 1654; see NECESSITY 9

21 Necessity never made a good bargain.
Benjamin Franklin 1706–90: *Poor Richard's Almanac* (1735)

22 The superfluous, a very necessary thing.
Voltaire 1694–1778: *Le Mondain* (1736)

23 Necessity is the plea for every infringement of human freedom: it is the argument of tyrants; it is the creed of slaves.
William Pitt 1759–1806: speech, House of Commons, 18 November 1783

24 What throws a monkey wrench in
A fella's good intention?
That nasty old invention—
Necessity!
E. Y. Harburg 1898–1981: 'Necessity' (1947)

25 Necessity has the face of a dog.
Gabriel García Márquez 1928– : *In Evil Hour* (1968)

Neighbours

proverbs and sayings ▸

1 Good fences make good neighbours.
this reduces the possibility of disputes over adjoining land; English proverb, mid 17th century; see NEIGHBOURS 11

2 A hedge between keeps friendship green.
it is wise to have a clear boundary between neighbours; English proverb, early 18th century

3 Love your neighbour, but don't pull down your hedge.
do not let feelings of friendship lead you to act unwisely; English proverb, mid 17th century

4 A wall between both best preserves friendship.
it is wise to have a clear boundary between neighbours; Spanish proverb

5 What a neighbour gets is not lost.
one is likely to benefit from the gain of a neighbour or friend; English proverb, mid 16th century

phrases ▸

6 keep up with the Joneses

strive not to be outdone socially by one's neighbours, from a comic-strip title, 'Keeping up with the Joneses—by Pop' in the New York *Globe* 1913; see NEIGHBOURS 14

quotations ▸

7 For what do we live, but to make sport for our neighbours, and laugh at them in our turn?

Jane Austen 1775–1817: *Pride and Prejudice* (1813)

8 If you would be known, and not know, vegetate in a village; if you would know, and not be known, live in a city.

Charles Caleb Colton 1780–1832: *Lacon* (1820)

9 The way to get on in the world is to be neither more nor less wise, neither better nor worse than your neighbours.

William Hazlitt 1778–1830: *Sketches and Essays* (1839) 'On Knowledge of the World'

10 We make our friends, we make our enemies; but God makes our next-door neighbour.

G. K. Chesterton 1874–1936: *Heretics* (1905)

11 My apple trees will never get across
And eat the cones under his pines,
I tell him.
He only says, 'Good fences make good
neighbours.'

Robert Frost 1874–1963: 'Mending Wall' (1914); see NEIGHBOURS 1

12 Your next-door neighbour...is not a man; he is an environment. He is the barking of a dog; he is the noise of a pianola; he is a dispute about a party wall; he is drains that are worse than yours, or roses that are better than yours.

G. K. Chesterton 1874–1936: *The Uses of Diversity* (1920)

13 The good neighbour looks beyond the external accidents and discerns those inner qualities that make all men human and, therefore, brothers.

Martin Luther King 1929–68: *Strength to Love* (1963)

14 Never try to keep up with the Joneses. Drag them down to your level. It's cheaper that way.

Quentin Crisp 1908–99: in *Times* 22 November 1999; see NEIGHBOURS 6

News

see also JOURNALISM

proverbs and sayings ▸

1 Bad news travels fast.

bad news is more likely to be talked about; English proverb, late 16th century

2 No news is good news.

often used in consolation or resignation; English proverb, early 17th century

3 One who sees something good must tell of it.

African proverb

phrases ▸

4 dodgy dossier

informal name for a government briefing document on Iraqi weaponry which was later withdrawn; from a reference in the leading article in the *Observer* newspaper, 9 February 2003, to 'Downing Street's dodgy dossier of "intelligence" about Iraq'

5 shoot the messenger

treat the bearer of bad news as if they were to blame for it; often in the form, *don't shoot (or kill) the messenger!*; see NEWS 10

quotations ▸

6 Tell it not in Gath, publish it not in the streets of Askelon.

Bible: II Samuel

7 How beautiful upon the mountains are the feet of him that bringeth good tidings.

Bible: Isaiah

8 What news on the Rialto?

William Shakespeare 1564–1616: *The Merchant of Venice* (1596–8)

9 Ill news hath wings, and with the wind
doth go,
Comfort's a cripple and comes ever
slow.

Michael Drayton 1563–1631: *The Barons' Wars* (1603)

10 The nature of bad news infects the teller.
William Shakespeare 1564–1616: *Antony and Cleopatra* (1606–7); see NEWS 5

11 A master passion is the love of news.
George Crabbe 1754–1832: 'The Newspaper' (1785)

12 If a dog bites a man it is not news, but if a man bites a dog it is.
often attributed to the American journalist John B. Bogart (1848–1921)
Charles A. Dana 1819–97: attributed, in *Bookman* February 1917; earlier sources do not attribute to a specific individual

13 News is what a chap who doesn't care much about anything wants to read. And it's only news until he's read it. After that it's dead.
Evelyn Waugh 1903–66: *Scoop* (1938)

14 News is something which somebody wants suppressed—all the rest is advertising.
William Randolph Hearst 1863–1951: attributed; Ian Gilmour *The Body Politic* (1969)

15 Ever noticed that no matter what happens in one day, it exactly fits in the newspaper?
Jerry Seinfeld 1954– : in *Mail on Sunday* 11 February 2007

Night
see DAY AND NIGHT

Old Age
see also MIDDLE AGE

proverbs and sayings ▸

1 For the unlearned, old age is winter; for the learned, it is the season of harvest.
Jewish saying

2 The gods send nuts to those who have no teeth.
opportunities or pleasures often come too late to be enjoyed; English proverb, early 20th century

3 The older the ginger the more pungent its flavour.
older people have more knowledge and experience than the young; Chinese proverb

4 An old horse does not spoil the furrow.
Russian proverb; see OLD AGE 5

5 There's many a good tune played on an old fiddle.
someone's abilities do not depend on their being young; English proverb, early 20th century

6 There's no fool like an old fool.
often used to suggest that folly in an older person, who should be wiser, is particularly acute; English proverb, mid 16th century

7 When an elder dies, it is as if a whole library has burned down.
African proverb

8 When drinking water, remember the source.
advocating filial piety; Chinese proverb

phrases ▸

9 Darby and Joan
a devoted old married couple, living in placid domestic harmony, from a poem (1735) in the *Gentleman's Magazine*

10 Indian summer
a tranquil late period of life; a period of fine weather in late autumn: see WEATHER 25

11 threescore and ten
the age of seventy; in reference to the biblical span of a person's life: see OLD AGE 13

quotations ▸

12 Then shall ye bring down my grey hairs with sorrow to the grave.
Bible: Genesis

13 The days of our age are threescore years and ten; and though men be so strong that they come to fourscore years: yet is their strength then but labour and sorrow; so soon passeth it away, and we are gone.
Bible: Psalm 90; see OLD AGE 11

14 Last scene of all,
That ends this strange eventful history,
Is second childishness, and mere oblivion,
Sans teeth, sans eyes, sans taste, sans everything.
William Shakespeare 1564–1616: *As You Like It* (1599)

15 No spring, nor summer beauty hath such grace,
As I have seen in one autumnal face.
John Donne 1572–1631: 'The Autumnal' (1600)

16 I have lived long enough: my way of life
Is fall'n into the sear, the yellow leaf.
William Shakespeare 1564–1616: *Macbeth* (1606); see MIDDLE AGE 5

17 Age will not be defied.
Francis Bacon 1561–1626: *Essays* (1625) 'Of Regimen of Health'

18 Every man desires to live long; but no man would be old.
Jonathan Swift 1667–1745: *Thoughts on Various Subjects* (1727 ed.)

19 Those that desire to write or say anything to me have no time to lose; for time has shaken me by the hand and death is not far behind.
John Wesley 1703–91: letter to Ezekiel Cooper, 1 February 1791

20 Age does not make us childish, as men tell,
It merely finds us children still at heart.
Johann Wolfgang von Goethe 1749–1832: *Faust* pt. 1 (1808)

21 Grow old along with me!
The best is yet to be.
Robert Browning 1812–89: 'Rabbi Ben Ezra' (1864)

22 We turn not older with years, but newer every day.
Emily Dickinson 1830–86: letter, 1874

23 It is better to be seventy years young than forty years old!
Oliver Wendell Holmes 1809–94: reply to invitation from Julia Ward Howe to her seventieth birthday party, 27 May 1889

24 The tragedy of old age is not that one is old, but that one is young.
Oscar Wilde 1854–1900: *The Picture of Dorian Grey* (1891)

25 When you are old and grey and full of sleep,
And nodding by the fire, take down this book
And slowly read and dream of the soft look
Your eyes had once, and of their shadows deep.
W. B. Yeats 1865–1939: 'When You Are Old' (1893)

26 Oh, to be seventy again!
on seeing a pretty girl on his eightieth birthday
Georges Clemenceau 1841–1929: James Agate diary, 19 April 1938; also attributed to Oliver Wendell Holmes Jnr.

27 From the earliest times the old have rubbed it into the young that they are wiser than they, and before the young had discovered what nonsense this was they were old too, and it profited them to carry on the imposture.
W. Somerset Maugham 1874–1965: *Cakes and Ale* (1930)

28 Bodily decrepitude is wisdom.
W. B. Yeats 1865–1939: 'After Long Silence' (1933)

29 Old age is the most unexpected of all things that happen to a man.
Leon Trotsky 1879–1940: diary, 8 May 1935

30 You will recognize, my boy, the first sign of old age: it is when you go out into the streets of London and realize for the first time how young the policemen look.
Seymour Hicks 1871–1949: C. R. D. Pulling *They Were Singing* (1952)

31 Do not go gentle into that good night,
Old age should burn and rave at close of day;
Rage, rage against the dying of the light.
Dylan Thomas 1914–53: 'Do Not Go Gentle into that Good Night' (1952)

32 To me old age is always fifteen years older than I am.
Bernard Baruch 1870–1965: in *Newsweek* 29 August 1955

33 Considering the alternative, it's not too bad at all.
when asked what he felt about the advancing years on his seventy-second birthday
Maurice Chevalier 1888–1972: Michael Freedland *Maurice Chevalier* (1981)

34 Hope I die before I get old.
Pete Townshend 1945– : 'My Generation' (1965 song)

35 Will you still need me, will you still feed me,
When I'm sixty four?
John Lennon 1940–80 and **Paul McCartney** 1942– : 'When I'm Sixty Four' (1967 song)

36 The man who works and is not bored is never old.
Pablo Casals 1876–1973: J. Lloyd Webber (ed.) *Song of the Birds* (1985)

37 When I am an old woman I shall wear purple
With a red hat which doesn't go, and doesn't suit me.
Jenny Joseph 1932– : 'Warning' (1974)

38 While there's snow on the roof, it doesn't mean the fire has gone out in the furnace.
John G. Diefenbaker 1895–1979: approaching his 80th birthday, Ottawa, 17 September 1975

39 With full-span lives having become the norm, people may need to learn how to be aged as they once had to learn how to be adult.
Ronald Blythe 1922– : *The View in Winter* (1979)

40 It's a good thing to be old, because that means you haven't died yet, right?
Penelope Cruz 1974– : in *Sunday Times* 1 August 2010 'Quotes of the Week'

Opinion

proverbs and sayings ▸

1 He that complies against his will is of his own opinion still.
English proverb, late 17th century, from Samuel Butler: see OPINION 16

2 So many men, so many opinions.
the greater the number of people involved, the greater the number of different opinions there will be; English proverb, late 14th century, from Terence (c. 190–159 BC) *Phormio* 'There are as many opinions as there are people: each has his own correct way'

3 Those who never retract their opinions, love themselves more than they love truth.
American proverb, mid 20th century

4 Thought is free.
while speech and action can be limited, one's powers of imagination and speculation cannot be regulated; English proverb, late 14th century

5 Where there are two Jews, there are three opinions.
Jewish saying

6 The wish is father to the thought.
one's opinions are often influenced by one's wishes; English proverb, late 16th century, from Shakespeare *2 Henry IV* 'Thy wish was father, Harry, to that thought'

phrases ▸

7 appeal from Philip drunk to Philip sober
suggest that an opinion or decision represents a passing mood only; alluding to Philip of Macedon, father of Alexander the Great, who is said to have been the subject of such an appeal

8 hearts and minds
people as represented by their emotions and intellect; originally with biblical allusion: see PEACE 9; see also OPINION 11, SPEECHES 14

9 no comment
I do not intend to express an opinion; traditional expression of refusal to answer journalists' questions

10 vox populi
expressed general opinion; Latin = voice of the people; see DEMOCRACY 2

11 win hearts and minds
gain emotional or intellectual support; especially used in the context of the Vietnam War: see OPINION 8

quotations ▸

12 People who only see one side of things
Engage in quarrels and disputes.
Pali Tripitaka 2nd century BC: *The Udāna* [Solemn Utterances]

13 A plague of opinion! a man may wear it on both sides, like a leather jerkin.
William Shakespeare 1564–1616: *Troilus and Cressida* (1602)

14 Opinion in good men is but knowledge in the making.
John Milton 1608–74: *Areopagitica* (1644)

15 They that approve a private opinion, call it opinion; but they that mislike it, heresy: and yet heresy signifies no more than private opinion.
Thomas Hobbes 1588–1679: *Leviathan* (1651)

16 He that complies against his will,
Is of his own opinion still.
Samuel Butler 1612–80: *Hudibras* pt. 3 (1680); see OPINION 1

17 Some praise at morning what they blame at night;
But always think the last opinion right.
Alexander Pope 1688–1744: *An Essay on Criticism* (1711)

18 Have not the wisest of men in all ages, not excepting Solomon himself,—have they not had their Hobby-Horses...and so long as a man rides his Hobby-Horse peaceably and quietly along the King's highway, and neither compels you or me to get up behind him,—pray, Sir, what have either you or I to do with it?
Laurence Sterne 1713–68: *Tristram Shandy* (1759–67)

19 Every man has a right to utter what he thinks truth, and every other man has a right to knock him down for it. Martyrdom is the test.
Samuel Johnson 1709–84: James Boswell *Life of Samuel Johnson* (1791) 1780

20 A man can brave opinion, a woman must submit to it.
Mme de Staël 1766–1817: *Delphine* (1802)

21 If all mankind minus one were of one opinion, and only one person were of the contrary opinion, mankind would be no more justified in silencing that one person, than he, if he had the power, would be justified in silencing mankind.
John Stuart Mill 1806–73: *On Liberty* (1859)

22 People seem not to see that their opinion of the world is also a confession of character.
Ralph Waldo Emerson 1803–82: *The Conduct of Life* (1860) 'Worship'

23 There are nine and sixty ways of constructing tribal lays,
And—every—single—one—of—them—is—right!
Rudyard Kipling 1865–1936: 'In the Neolithic Age' (1893)

24 It were not best that we should all think alike; it is difference of opinion that makes horse-races.
Mark Twain 1835–1910: *Pudd'nhead Wilson* (1894)

25 There is no opinion, however absurd, which men will not readily embrace as soon as they can be brought to the conviction that it is generally adopted.
Arthur Schopenhauer 1788–1860: *The Art of Controversy* (1896)

26 Thank God, in these days of enlightenment and establishment, everyone has a right to his own opinions, and chiefly to the opinion that nobody else has a right to theirs.
Ronald Knox 1888–1957: *Reunion All Round* (1914)

27 An intellectual hatred is the worst,
So let her think opinions are accursed.
W. B. Yeats 1865–1939: 'A Prayer for My Daughter' (1920)

28 The opinions that are held with passion are always those for which no good ground exists; indeed the passion is the measure of the holder's lack of rational conviction.
Bertrand Russell 1872–1970: *Sceptical Essays* (1928)

29 Why should you mind being wrong if someone can show you that you are?
A. J. Ayer 1910–89: attributed

30 You might very well think that.
I couldn't possibly comment.
the Chief Whip's habitual response to questioning
Michael Dobbs 1948– : *House of Cards* (televised 1990)

31 I've never had a humble opinion. If you've got an opinion, why be humble about it?
Joan Baez 1941– : in *Observer* 29 February 2004

Opportunity

proverbs and sayings ►

1 All is fish that comes to the net.
everything can be used to advantage; English proverb, early 16th century

2 All is grist that comes to the mill.
all experience or knowledge is useful (*grist* is corn that is ground to make flour); English proverb, mid 17th century

3 **A bleating sheep loses a bite.**
opportunities may be lost through idle chatter; English proverb, late 16th century

4 **Every dog has his day.**
everyone, however insignificant, has a moment of strength and power; English proverb, mid 16th century

5 **He that will not when he may, when he will he shall have nay.**
if an opportunity is not taken when offered, it may well not occur again; English proverb, late 10th century

6 **If the camel once gets his nose in the tent, his body will soon follow.**
an apparently insignificant opening is likely to lead to more serious developments; Arabic proverb

7 **If you snooze, you lose.**
it is advisable to stay alert to opportunities; modern saying; see ACTION 13

8 **It is good fishing in troubled waters.**
a difficult situation offers opportunities to those prepared to exploit it; English proverb, late 16th century

9 **It's not what you know, but whom you know.**
American proverb, mid 20th century

10 **Make hay while the sun shines.**
one should take advantage of favourable circumstances which may not last; English proverb, mid 16th century

11 **The mill cannot grind with the water that is past.**
an opportunity that has been missed cannot then be used; English proverb, early 17th century

12 **No time like the present.**
often used to urge swift and immediate action; English proverb, mid 16th century

13 **Opportunities look for you when you are worth finding.**
North American proverb, mid 20th century; see also OPPORTUNITY 14

14 **Opportunity never knocks for persons not worth a rap.**
American proverb, mid 20th century; see also OPPORTUNITY 13

15 **Opportunity never knocks twice at any man's door.**
a chance once missed will not occur again; English proverb, mid 16th century

16 **A person who misses his chance, and the monkey who misses his branch, can't be saved.**
Indian proverb; see OPPORTUNITY 15

17 **A postern door makes a thief.**
referring to the opportunity offered by a back or side entrance; English proverb, mid 15th century

18 **Strike while the iron is hot.**
one should take advantage of opportunity; the allusion was originally to the work of a blacksmith; English proverb, late 14th century; see OPPORTUNITY 35

19 **Take the goods the gods provide.**
one should accept and be grateful for unearned benefits; English proverb, late 17th century

20 **Time and tide wait for no man.**
often used as an exhortation to act, in the knowledge that a favourable moment will not last for ever; English proverb, late 14th century

21 **When one door shuts, another opens.**
as one possible course of action is closed off, another opportunity offers; English proverb, late 16th century

22 **When the cat's away, the mice will play.**
many will take advantage of a situation in which rules are not enforced or authority is lacking; English proverb, early 17th century

23 **The world is one's oyster.**
opportunities are unlimited; an *oyster* as a delicacy and a source of pearls. Perhaps originally with allusion to Shakespeare's *Merry Wives of Windsor* (1597), 'the world's mine oyster, which I, with sword will open'; English proverb, early 17th century

phrases ▸

24 **in the last chance saloon**
having been allowed one final opportunity to improve or get things right, from the fanciful idea of a saloon bar with this name

25 **room at the top**
opportunity to join an élite or the top ranks of a profession; see AMBITION 5

26 **second bite at the cherry**
another attempt or opportunity to do something; a *cherry* as the type of something to be consumed in a single bite (in original proverbial use, to *take two bites at the cherry* indicated a person's behaving with affected nicety)

27 streets paved with gold
proverbial view of a city in which opportunities for advancement are easy; as in George Colman the Younger's *The Heir at Law* (1797) 'Oh, London is a fine town, A very famous city, Where all the streets are paved with gold'

28 take time by the forelock
not let a chance slip away; from the personification of Time as bald except for a forelock; see OPPORTUNITY 34

29 window of opportunity
a free or suitable interval or period of time for a particular event or action; deriving from *launch window*, a period outside which the planned launch of a spacecraft cannot take place if the journey is to be completed, owing to the changing positions of the planets; especially used in connection with the US–Soviet arms race

quotations ▸

30 Time is that wherein there is opportunity, and opportunity is that wherein there is no great time.
Hippocrates c.460–357 BC: *Precepts*

31 How oft the sight of means to do ill deeds
Makes ill deeds done!
William Shakespeare 1564–1616: *King John* (1591–8)

32 There is a tide in the affairs of men,
Which, taken at the flood, leads on to fortune.
William Shakespeare 1564–1616: *Julius Caesar* (1599)

33 If any man can shew any just cause, why they may not lawfully be joined together, let him now speak, or else hereafter for ever hold his peace.
The Book of Common Prayer 1662: *Solemnization of Matrimony*

34 But on occasion's forelock watchful wait.
John Milton 1608–74: *Paradise Regained* (1671); see OPPORTUNITY 28

35 We must beat the iron while it is hot, but we may polish it at leisure.
John Dryden 1631–1700: *Aeneis* (1697); see OPPORTUNITY 18

36 *La carrière ouverte aux talents.*
The career open to the talents.
Napoleon I 1769–1821: Barry E. O'Meara *Napoleon in Exile* (1822); see OPPORTUNITY 37

37 To the very last he [Napoleon]
had a kind of idea; that, namely,
of *La carrière ouverte aux talents*,
The tools to him that can handle them.
Thomas Carlyle 1795–1881: *Critical and Miscellaneous Essays* (1838) 'Sir Walter Scott'; see OPPORTUNITY 36

38 Never the time and the place
And the loved one all together!
Robert Browning 1812–89: 'Never the Time and the Place' (1883)

39 If only I could get down to Sidcup! I've been waiting for the weather to break. He's got my papers, this man I left them with, it's got it all down there, I could prove everything.
Harold Pinter 1930–2008: *The Caretaker* (1960)

40 She's got a ticket to ride, but she don't care.
John Lennon 1940–80 and **Paul MacCartney** 1942– : 'Ticket to Ride' (1965 song)

41 I opened the door for a lot of people, and they just ran through and left me holding the knob.
Bo Diddley 1928–2008: in 1971; M. Wrenn *Bitch, Bitch, Bitch* (1988)

42 My friends, as I have discovered myself, there are no disasters, only opportunities. And, indeed, opportunities for fresh disasters.
Boris Johnson 1964– : in *Daily Telegraph* 2 December 2004

Optimism and Pessimism

see also DESPAIR, HOPE

proverbs and sayings ▸

1 All's for the best in the best of all possible worlds.
English proverb, early 20th century, from Voltaire; see OPTIMISM 19

2 Another day, another dollar.
a world-weary comment on routine toil to earn a living, originally referring to the custom of paying sailors by the day, so that the longer the voyage, the greater the financial reward; American proverb, mid 20th century

3 **Chickens are counted in autumn.**
Russian proverb; compare OPTIMISM 6

4 **The darkest hour is just before dawn.**
suggesting that the experience of complete despair may mean that matters have reached the lowest point and may shortly improve; English proverb, mid 17th century

5 **Don't bargain for fish that are still in the water.**
Indian proverb; see OPTIMISM 8

6 **Don't count your chickens before they are hatched.**
one should not make, or act upon, an assumption (usually favourable) which may turn out to be ill-founded; English proverb, late 16th century; see OPTIMISM 17; compare OPTIMISM 3

7 **Don't halloo till you are out of the wood.**
you should not exult until danger and difficulty are past (*halloo* means shout in order to attract attention); English proverb, late 18th century

8 **Don't sell the skin till you have caught the bear.**
do not act upon an assumption of success which may turn out to be ill-founded; English proverb, late 16th century. Early versions have *lion* or *beast*; see also BUSINESS 20

9 **Every cloud has a silver lining.**
even the gloomiest circumstance has some hopeful element in it; English proverb, mid 19th century; see OPTIMISM 34

10 **God's in his heaven; all's right with the world.**
English proverb, from early 16th century in the form 'God is where he was'; now largely replaced by this quotation from Browning; see OPTIMISM 21

11 **If ifs and ands were pots and pans, there'd be no work for tinkers' hands.**
traditional response to an over-optimistic conditional expression, in which *ands* is the plural form of *and* = 'if'; English proverb, mid 19th century

12 **If wishes were horses, beggars would ride.**
what one wishes is often far from reality; English proverb, early 17th century

13 **It's an ill wind that blows nobody any good.**
good luck may arise from the source of another's misfortune; English proverb, mid 16th century

14 **The sharper the storm, the sooner it's over.**
the more intense something is, the shorter time it is likely to last; English proverb, late 19th century

15 **Turn your face to the sun, and the shadows fall behind you.**
recommending a positive attitude; modern saying, said to derive from a Maori proverb

16 **When things are at the worst they begin to mend.**
when a bad situation has reached its worst possible point, the next change must reflect at least a small improvement; English proverb, mid 18th century

phrases ▸

17 **count one's chickens**
be overoptimistic, assume too much; from the proverb: see OPTIMISM 6

quotations ▸

18 **Sin is behovely, but all shall be well and all shall be well and all manner of thing shall be well.**
behovely = expedient, necessary
Julian of Norwich 1343–after 1416: *Revelations of Divine Love*

19 **In this best of possible worlds...all is for the best.**
usually quoted as 'All is for the best in the best of all possible worlds'
Voltaire 1694–1778: *Candide* (1759); see OPTIMISM 1, OPTIMISM 30

20 **There's a gude time coming.**
Sir Walter Scott 1771–1832: *Rob Roy* (1817)

21 **The lark's on the wing;**
The snail's on the thorn:
God's in his heaven—
All's right with the world!
Robert Browning 1812–89: *Pippa Passes* (1841); see OPTIMISM 10

22 **I have known him come home to supper with a flood of tears, and a declaration that nothing was now left but a jail; and go to bed making a calculation of the expense of putting bow-windows to the house, 'in case anything turned up,' which was his favourite expression.**
of Mr Micawber
Charles Dickens 1812–70: *David Copperfield* (1850)

23 In front the sun climbs slow, how slowly,
But westward, look, the land is bright.
Arthur Hugh Clough 1819–61: 'Say not the struggle naught availeth' (1855)

24 Nothing to do but work,
Nothing to eat but food,
Nothing to wear but clothes
To keep one from going nude.
Benjamin Franklin King 1857–94: 'The Pessimist'

25 If way to the Better there be, it exacts a full look at the worst.
Thomas Hardy 1840–1928: 'De Profundis' (1902)

26 Are we downhearted?
No! Let 'em all come!
Charles Knight and **Kenneth Lyle**: 'Here we are! Here we are again!!' (1914 song)

27 'Twixt the optimist and pessimist
The difference is droll:
The optimist sees the doughnut
But the pessimist sees the hole.
McLandburgh Wilson b. 1892: *Optimist and Pessimist* (1915)

28 Cheer up! the worst is yet to come!
Philander Chase Johnson 1866–1939: in *Everybody's Magazine* May 1920

29 Our motto is still alive and to the point: Pessimism of the intellect, optimism of the will.
the motto of the periodical *L'Ordine Nuovo* was borrowed from the French writer Romain Rolland (1866–1944)
Antonio Gramsci 1891–1937: in *L'Ordine Nuovo* 4 March 1921

30 The optimist proclaims that we live in the best of all possible worlds; and the pessimist fears this is true.
James Branch Cabell 1879–1958: *The Silver Stallion* (1926); see OPTIMISM 19

31 Leave your worry on the doorstep,
Just direct your feet
To the sunny side of the street.
Dorothy Fields 1905–74: 'On the Sunny Side of the Street' (1930 song)

32 Every time it rains, it rains
Pennies from heaven.
Don't you know each cloud contains
Pennies from heaven?
Johnny Burke 1908–64: 'Pennies from Heaven' (1936 song); see MONEY 54, SURPRISE 6

33 You've got to ac-cent-tchu-ate the positive
Elim-my-nate the negative
Latch on to the affirmative
Don't mess with Mister In-between.
Johnny Mercer 1909–76: 'Ac-cent-tchu-ate the Positive' (1944 song)

34 There are bad times just around the corner,
There are dark clouds travelling through the sky
And it's no good whining
About a silver lining
For we know from experience that they won't roll by.
Noël Coward 1899–1973: 'There are Bad Times Just Around the Corner' (1953 song); see OPTIMISM 9

35 Everything's coming up roses.
Stephen Sondheim 1930– : title of song (1959)

36 In the depths of winter, I finally learned that within me there lay an invincible summer.
Albert Camus 1913–60: *Lyrical and Critical* (1967)

37 When you're depressed, there *are* no molehills.
Randall Jarrell 1914–65: William H. Pritchard *Randall Jarrell: A Literary Life* (1990); see VALUE 18

38 I feel that life is—is divided up into the horrible and the miserable.
Woody Allen 1935– : *Annie Hall* (1977 film, with Marshall Brickman)

39 If we see light at the end of the tunnel,
It's the light of the oncoming train.
Robert Lowell 1917–77: 'Since 1939' (1977); see ADVERSITY 7

40 I don't consider myself a pessimist. I think of a pessimist as someone who is waiting for it to rain. And I feel soaked to the skin.
Leonard Cohen 1934– : in *Observer* 2 May 1993

Order and Chaos

proverbs and sayings ▸

1 **Better a century of tyranny than one day of chaos.**
stability under an oppressive regime may be preferable to anarchy (the number of years may fluctuate); modern saying, deriving from an Arab proverb; see ORDER 12

2 **The Devil is in the details.**
the most difficult part of planning and achieving something is the detailed specification rather than the overall concept; English proverb, late 20th century; see ARCHITECTURE 20

3 **A place for everything, and everything in its place.**
English proverb, mid 17th century, often associated with the 19th-century writer on self-help Samuel Smiles; see ADMINISTRATION 9

phrases ▸

4 **alarms and excursions**
confused noise and bustle; *alarums and excursions* an old stage-direction occurring in Shakespeare *3 Henry VI* and *Richard III*

5 **all hell let loose**
a state of utter confusion and uproar, utter pandemonium; from Milton: see ORDER 14

6 **flutter the dovecots**
startle or perturb a sedate or conventionally-minded community; from Shakespeare's *Coriolanus* 'like an eagle in a dove-cote, I Fluttered your Volscians in Corioli'

7 **a pretty kettle of fish**
an awkward state of affairs, a mess; *kettle* = a long pan for cooking fish in liquid

8 **raise Cain**
make a disturbance, cause trouble; *Cain* the eldest son of Adam, who in the Bible (Genesis) is said to have murdered his younger brother Abel; see also CANADA 3, MURDER 7, TRAVEL 14

9 **shipshape and Bristol fashion**
with all in good order; *Bristol* a city and port in the west of England; originally a nautical expression

10 **Sturm und Drang**
(a period of) emotion, stress, or turbulence; German, literally 'storm and stress', title of a 1776 play by Friedrich Maximilian Klinger (1752–1831)

11 **to the (four) winds**
in all directions; so as to be abandoned or neglected, from Milton's *Paradise Lost*: 'And fear of death deliver to the winds'; *the four winds* blowing from each of the points of the compass, and often personified as such

quotations ▸

12 **Sixty days of an unjust ruler are much better than one night of lawlessness.**
Ibn Taymiyyah 1263–1328: *Book of Divinely Ordered Politics* (c.1311–15); see ORDER 1

13 **All things began in order, so shall they end, and so shall they begin again; according to the ordainer of order and mystical mathematics of the city of heaven.**
Thomas Browne 1605–82: *The Garden of Cyrus* (1658)

14 **But wherefore thou alone? Wherefore with thee**
Came not all hell broke loose?
said by Gabriel to Satan
John Milton 1608–74: *Paradise Lost* (1667); see ORDER 5

15 **With ruin upon ruin, rout on rout,**
Confusion worse confounded.
John Milton 1608–74: *Paradise Lost* (1667)

16 **Good order is the foundation of all good things.**
Edmund Burke 1729–97: *Reflections on the Revolution in France* (1790)

17 **Chaos often breeds life, when order breeds habit.**
Henry Brooks Adams 1838–1918: *The Education of Henry Adams* (1907)

18 **Things fall apart; the centre cannot hold;**
Mere anarchy is loosed upon the world,
The blood-dimmed tide is loosed, and everywhere
The ceremony of innocence is drowned.
W. B. Yeats 1865–1939: 'The Second Coming' (1921)

19 **I'm interested in anything about revolt, disorder, chaos, especially activity that appears to have no meaning. It seems to me to be the road toward freedom.**
Jim Morrison 1943–71: in *Time* 24 January 1968

20 I'm at my best in a messy, middle-of-the-road muddle.

Harold Wilson 1916–95: remark in Cabinet, 21 January 1975; Philip Ziegler *Wilson* (1993)

Originality

proverbs and sayings ▸

1 Do not follow where the path may lead. Go instead where there is no path and leave a trail.

late 20th century saying, often attributed to Ralph Waldo Emerson (1803–82), but not found in his works

phrases ▸

2 an Arabian bird

a unique specimen; a phoenix, in allusion to Shakespeare *Cymbeline* 'She is alone the Arabian bird, and I Have lost the wager'

3 break the mould

make impossible the repetition of a certain type of creation; put an end to a pattern of events or behaviour by setting markedly different standards; originally with reference to Ariosto: see EXCELLENCE 11

4 rara avis

a person or thing of a kind rarely encountered; a unique or exceptional person; Latin, from the Roman satirist Juvenal (c.60–c.140) *Rara avis in terris nigroque simillima cycno.* 'A rare bird on this earth, like nothing so much as a black swan'; see BIRDS 5

5 a white crow

a rare thing or event; recorded from the 16th century

quotations ▸

6 Nothing has yet been said that's not been said before.

Terence c.190–159 BC: *Eunuchus*

7 It could be said of me that in this book I have only made up a bunch of other men's flowers, providing of my own only the string that ties them together.

Montaigne 1533–92: *Essais* (1580)

8 They lard their lean books with the fat of others' works.

Robert Burton 1577–1640: *The Anatomy of Melancholy* (1621–51)

9 The original writer is not he who refrains from imitating others, but he who can be imitated by none.

François-René Chateaubriand 1768–1848: *Le Génie du Christianisme* (1802)

10 Never forget what I believe was observed to you by Coleridge, that every great and original writer, in proportion as he is great and original, must himself create the taste by which he is to be relished.

William Wordsworth 1770–1850: letter to Lady Beaumont, 21 May 1807

11 Make copies, young man, many copies. You can only become a good artist by copying the masters.

Jean Ingres 1780–1867: to Degas; A. Vollard *Souvenirs d'un marchand de tableaux* (1937)

12 Everything has been said before. But since nobody listens we have to keep going back and beginning all over again.

André Gide 1869–1951: *Le Traite du Narcisse* (1892)

13 Most people are other people. Their thoughts are someone else's opinions, their lives a mimicry, their passions a quotation.

Oscar Wilde 1854–1900: *De Profundis* (1905)

14 Immature poets imitate; mature poets steal.

T. S. Eliot 1888–1965: *The Sacred Wood* (1920) 'Philip Massinger'

15 If you steal from one author, it's plagiarism; if you steal from many, it's research.

Wilson Mizner 1876–1933: Alva Johnston *The Legendary Mizners* (1953)

16 No plagiarist can excuse the wrong by showing how much of his work he did not pirate.

Learned Hand 1872–1961: *Sheldon v. Metro-Goldwyn Pictures Corp.* 1936

17 Be daring, be different, be impractical, be anything that will assert integrity of purpose and imaginative vision against the play-it-safers, the creatures of the commonplace, the slaves of the ordinary.

Cecil Beaton 1904–80: in *Theatre Arts* May 1957

18 Let's have some new clichés.
Sam Goldwyn 1882–1974: attributed, perhaps apocryphal

Painting and Drawing

see also ARTS

proverbs and sayings ►

1 Every painter paints himself.
Italian proverb, said to be of Renaissance origin

2 A good painter can draw a devil as well as an angel.
English proverb, late 16th century

3 Not a day without a line.
traditional saying, attributed to the Greek artist Apelles (fl. 325 BC) by Pliny the Elder

phrases ►

4 Giotto's O
the perfect circle supposedly drawn freehand by the Italian painter Giotto (1267–1337)

5 warts and all
including features or qualities that are not appealing or attractive; from Cromwell: see PAINTING 7

quotations ►

6 Good painters imitate nature, bad ones spew it up.
Cervantes 1547–1616: *El Licenciado Vidriera* (1613)

7 Remark all these roughnesses, pimples, warts, and everything as you see me; otherwise I will never pay a farthing for it.
to the painter Lely; see PAINTING 5
Oliver Cromwell 1599–1658: Horace Walpole *Anecdotes of Painting in England* vol. 3 (1763)

8 An imitation in lines and colours on any surface of all that is to be found under the sun.
of painting
Nicolas Poussin 1594–1665: letter to M. de Chambray, 1665

9 A mere copier of nature can never produce anything great.
Joshua Reynolds 1723–92: *Discourses on Art* 14 December 1770

10 There is no easy way of becoming a good painter.
Joshua Reynolds 1723–92: John Constable, letter to John Dunthorne, 29 May 1802

11 The sound of water escaping from mill-dams, etc., willows, old rotten planks, slimy posts, and brickwork... those scenes made me a painter and I am grateful.
John Constable 1776–1837: letter to John Fisher, 23 October 1821

12 *Le dessin est la probité de l'art.*
Drawing is the true test of art.
J. A. D. Ingres 1780–1867: *Pensées d'Ingres* (1922)

13 I have seen, and heard, much of Cockney impudence before now; but never expected to hear a coxcomb ask two hundred guineas for flinging a pot of paint in the public's face.
on Whistler's *Nocturne in Black and Gold*
John Ruskin 1819–1900: *Fors Clavigera* (1871–84) letter 79, 18 June 1877

14 I own I like definite form in what my eyes are to rest upon; and if landscapes were sold, like the sheets of characters of my boyhood, one penny plain and twopence coloured, I should go the length of twopence every day of my life.
Robert Louis Stevenson 1850–94: *Travels with a Donkey* (1879); see STYLE 3

15 A good picture is equivalent to a good deed.
Vincent Van Gogh 1853–90: letter to Albert Aurier, in *Complete Letters* (1958)

16 You should not paint the chair, but only what someone has felt about it.
Edvard Munch 1863–1944: written 1891; R. Heller *Munch* (1984)

17 Treat nature in terms of the cylinder, the sphere, the cone, all in perspective.
Paul Cézanne 1839–1906: letter to Emile Bernard, 1904; Emile Bernard *Paul Cézanne* (1925)

18 Monet is only an eye, but what an eye!
Paul Cézanne 1839–1906: attributed

19 What I dream of is an art of balance, of purity and serenity devoid of troubling or depressing subject matter...a soothing, calming influence on the

mind, rather like a good armchair which provides relaxation from physical fatigue.
Henri Matisse 1869–1954: *Notes d'un peintre* (1908)

20 It's with my brush that I make love.
often quoted as 'I paint with my prick'
Pierre Auguste Renoir 1841–1919: A. André *Renoir* (1919)

21 An active line on a walk, moving freely without a goal. A walk for walk's sake.
Paul Klee 1879–1940: *Pedagogical Sketchbook* (1925)

22 Every time I paint a portrait I lose a friend.
John Singer Sargent 1856–1925: N. Bentley and E. Esar *Treasury of Humorous Quotations* (1951)

23 This is not a pipe.
René Magritte 1898–1967: *The Treachery of Images* (1928–9), a painting of a tobacco pipe

24 A picture equals a movement in space.
Emily Carr 1871–1945: *Hundreds and Thousands: The Journals of Emily Carr* (1966) August 1935

25 No, painting is not made to decorate apartments. It's an offensive and defensive weapon against the enemy.
Pablo Picasso 1881–1973: interview with Simone Téry, 24 March 1945, in Alfred H. Barr *Picasso* (1946)

26 I paint my own reality.
Frida Kahlo 1907–54: Hayden Herrera *Frida* (1983)

27 There was a reviewer a while back who wrote that my pictures didn't have any beginning or any end. He didn't mean it as a compliment, but it was. It was a fine compliment.
Jackson Pollock 1912–56: Francis V. O'Connor *Jackson Pollock* (1967)

28 Painting is saying 'Ta' to God.
Stanley Spencer 1891–1959: letter from Spencer's daughter Shirin to *Observer* 7 February 1988

29 If Botticelli were alive today he'd be working for *Vogue*.
Peter Ustinov 1921–2004: in *Observer* 21 October 1962

30 A product of the untalented, sold by the unprincipled to the utterly bewildered.
on abstract art
Al Capp 1907–79: in *National Observer* 1 July 1963

31 I rarely draw what I see—I draw what I feel in my body.
Barbara Hepworth 1903–75: Alan Bowness *Barbara Hepworth—Drawings from a Sculptor's Landscape* (1966)

32 Mostly painting is like putting a message in a bottle and flinging it into the sea.
Howard Hodgkin 1932– : in *Observer* 10 June 2001

The Paranormal

see also SUPERNATURAL

proverbs and sayings ▸

1 It's life, Jim, but not as we know it.
late 20th century saying associated with the television series *Star Trek* (1966–); the saying does not occur in the series but derives from the 1987 song 'Star Trekkin' ' sung by The Firm

2 The truth is out there.
catchphrase from *The X Files* (American television series, 1993–2002), created by Chris Carter (1957–), in which two special agents repeatedly investigate cases which appear to involve the paranormal; final proof of extra-terrestrial activity, however, is always lacking

3 We are not alone.
advertising copy for the film *Close Encounters of the Third Kind* (1977); see PARANORMAL 5

phrases ▸

4 Bermuda triangle
a place where people or objects vanish without explanation; from an area of the West Atlantic Ocean where a disproportionately large number of ships and aeroplanes are said to have been mysteriously lost

5 Close Encounter
term used for a supposed encounter with a UFO; divided into categories, from a *Close Encounter of the First Kind* (sighting but no physical evidence), through Second (physical evidence left) and Third (extra-terrestrials beings observed) to a *Close Encounter of the Fourth Kind*, which involves abduction by aliens; see PARANORMAL 8

6 Fermi paradox

a paradox suggested by a question asked by the Italian-born American physicist Enrico Fermi (see PARANORMAL 13): if extraterrestrial civilizations exist throughout the galaxy, then they would have developed the technology to contact others, and evidence of such contact should be apparent on earth. But no such evidence has been observed

7 near-death experience

an unusual experience taking place on the brink of death and recounted by a person on recovery; see PARANORMAL 16, PARANORMAL 19

8 Unidentified Flying Object

a mysterious object seen in the sky for which it is claimed no orthodox scientific explanation can be found; often abbreviated to UFO. It is often supposed that UFOs, if real, must be vehicles carrying extraterrestrials, although other theories are put forward; see PARANORMAL 5

quotations ►

9 When the consciousness-principle getteth outside [the body it sayeth to itself] 'Am I dead or am I not dead?' It cannot determine. It seeth its relatives and connections as it had been used to seeing them before. It even heareth the wailings.

The Tibetan Book of the Dead 8th century: bk. 1, pt. 1

10 GLENDOWER: I can call spirits from the vasty deep.
HOTSPUR: Why, so can I, or so can any man;
But will they come when you do call for them?

William Shakespeare 1564–1616: *Henry IV, Part 1* (1597)

11 No testimony is sufficient to establish a miracle, unless the testimony be of such a kind, that its falsehood would be more miraculous than the fact which it endeavours to establish.

David Hume 1711–76: 'Of Miracles' (1748)

12 From the astrologer came the astronomer, from the alchemist the chemist, from the mesmerist the experimental psychologist. The quack of yesterday is the professor of tomorrow.

Arthur Conan Doyle 1859–1930: *Tales of Terror and Mystery* (1922)

13 But where is everybody?

on the existence of extraterrestrials

Enrico Fermi 1901–54: attributed, 1950; see PARANORMAL 6

14 About astrology and palmistry: they are good because they make people vivid and full of possibilities. They are communism at its best. Everybody has a birthday and almost everybody has a palm.

Kurt Vonnegut 1922–2007: *Wampeters, Foma and Granfalloons* (1974)

15 The fancy that extraterrestrial life is by definition of a higher order than our own is one that soothes all children, and many writers.

Joan Didion 1934– : *The White Album* (1979)

16 This was reality and all else an illusion.

on his near-death experience; see PARANORMAL 7

Michael Bentine 1922–96: *The Door Marked Summer* (1981)

17 If there's something strange in your neighbourhood,
Who you gonna call? Ghostbusters.

Ray Parker Jr. 1954– : 'Ghostbusters' (1984 song)

18 Black magic operates most effectively in preconscious, marginal areas. Casual curses are the most effective.

William S. Burroughs 1914–97: *The Western Lands* (1987)

19 Did you know that I was dead? The first time that I tried to cross the river I was frustrated, but my second attempt succeeded. It was most extraordinary. My thoughts became persons.

on his near-death experience; see PARANORMAL 7

A. J. Ayer 1910–89: in *Sunday Telegraph* 28 August 1988

20 Sometimes I think the surest sign that intelligent life exists elsewhere in the universe is that none of it has tried to contact us.

Bill Watterson 1958– : *Calvin and Hobbes* (comic strip) 8 November 1989

21 Mr Geller may have psychic powers by means of which he can bend spoons; if so, he appears to be doing it the hard way.

James Randi 1928– : *The Supernatural A-Z: the truth and the lies* (1995)

22 I don't believe in astrology; I'm a Sagittarius and we're sceptical.
Arthur C. Clarke 1917–2008: attributed; Nigel Rees *Cassell Dictionary of Humorous Quotations* (1999)

Parents
see also CHILD CARE, FAMILY

proverbs and sayings ▸

1 A father is a banker provided by nature.
French proverb

2 He who takes the child by the hand takes the mother by the heart.
Danish proverb

3 It is a wise child that knows its own father.
a child's legal paternity might not reflect an actual blood link; English proverb, late 16th century; see PARENTS 10

4 My son is my son till he gets him a wife, but my daughter's my daughter all the days of her life.
while a man who establishes his own family relegates former blood ties to second place, a woman's filial role is not affected by her marriage; English proverb, late 17th century

5 Parents want their children to become dragons.
parents want their children to be successful; Chinese proverb

6 Praise the child, and you make love to the mother.
English proverb, early 19th century

7 To understand your parents' love, you must raise children yourself.
Chinese proverb

quotations ▸

8 Honour thy father and thy mother.
Bible: Exodus; see LIFESTYLES 13

9 A wise son maketh a glad father: but a foolish son is the heaviness of his mother.
Bible: Proverbs

10 It is a wise father that knows his own child.
William Shakespeare 1564–1616: *The Merchant of Venice* (1596–8); see PARENTS 3

11 The joys of parents are secret, and so are their griefs and fears.
Francis Bacon 1561–1626: *Essays* (1625) 'Of Parents and Children'

12 A slavish bondage to parents cramps every faculty of the mind.
Mary Wollstonecraft 1759–97: *A Vindication of the Rights of Woman* (1792)

13 The mother's yearning, that completest type of the life in another life which is the essence of real human love, feels the presence of the cherished child even in the debased, degraded man.
George Eliot 1819–80: *Adam Bede* (1859)

14 A mother's arms are made of tenderness, and children sleep soundly in them.
Victor Hugo 1802–85: *Les Misérables* (1862)

15 What *do* girls do who haven't any mothers to help them through their troubles?
Louisa May Alcott 1832–88: *Little Women* (1869)

16 For the hand that rocks the cradle
Is the hand that rules the world.
William Ross Wallace 1819–81: 'What rules the world' (1865); see WOMEN 3

17 If I were damned of body and soul,
I know whose prayers would make me whole,
Mother o' mine, O mother o' mine.
Rudyard Kipling 1865–1936: *The Light That Failed* (1891)

18 Children begin by loving their parents; after a time they judge them; rarely, if ever, do they forgive them.
Oscar Wilde 1854–1900: *A Woman of No Importance* (1893)

19 Few misfortunes can befall a boy which bring worse consequences than to have a really affectionate mother.
W. Somerset Maugham 1874–1965: *A Writer's Notebook* (1949); written in 1896

20 The natural term of the affection of the human animal for its offspring is six years.
George Bernard Shaw 1856–1950: *Heartbreak House* (1919)

21 Your children are not your children.
They are the sons and daughters of
Life's longing for itself.

They came through you but not from you
And though they are with you yet they belong not to you.
Kahlil Gibran 1883–1931: *The Prophet* (1923) 'On Children'

22 The fundamental defect of fathers, in our competitive society, is that they want their children to be a credit to them.
Bertrand Russell 1872–1970: *Sceptical Essays* (1928) 'Freedom versus Authority in Education'

23 Children aren't happy with nothing to ignore,
And that's what parents were created for.
Ogden Nash 1902–71: 'The Parent' (1933)

24 Parents learn a lot from their children about coping with life.
Muriel Spark 1918–2006: *The Comforters* (1957)

25 Nothing has a stronger influence on their children than the unlived lives of their parents.
Carl Gustav Jung 1875–1961: attributed; in *Boston Magazine* June 1978

26 If you have never been hated by your child you have never been a parent.
Bette Davis 1908–89: *The Lonely Life* (1962)

27 No matter how old a mother is she watches her middle-aged children for signs of improvement.
Florida Scott-Maxwell: *Measure of my Days* (1968)

28 Children always assume the sexual lives of their parents come to a grinding halt at their conception.
Alan Bennett 1934– : *Getting On* (1972)

29 It doesn't matter who my father was; it matters who I remember he was.
Anne Sexton 1928–74: diary, 1 January 1972

30 Sometimes when I look at all my children, I say to myself: 'Lillian, you should have stayed a virgin.'
Lillian Carter 1898–1983: attributed, in *Newsweek* 29 December 1980

31 Love crawls with the baby, walks with the toddler, runs with the child, then stands aside to let the youth walk into adulthood.
Jo Ann Merrell: 'Love: A Variation on a Theme' (c.1986)

32 There must be many fathers around the country who have experienced the cruellest, most crushing rejection of all: their children have ended up supporting the wrong team.
Nick Hornby 1957– : *Fever Pitch* (1992)

33 I have reached the age when a woman begins to perceive that she is growing into the person she least plans to resemble: her mother.
Anita Brookner 1928– : *Incidents in the Rue Laugier* (1995)

34 Parents are the bones on which children sharpen their teeth.
Peter Ustinov 1921–2004: attributed, in *Times* 30 March 2004

35 You can't understand it until you experience the simple joy of the first time your son points at a seagull and says 'duck.'
on fatherhood
Russell Crowe 1964– : in *Observer* 29 May 2005

Parliament

proverbs and sayings ▸

1 I spy strangers!
the conventional formula demanding the exclusion from the House of Commons of non-members to whose presence attention is thus drawn

2 Who goes home?
formal question asked by the doorkeeper when the House of Commons adjourns

phrases ▸

3 Administration of All the Talents
a coalition government, ironically regarded; the Ministry of Lord Grenville, 1806–7, a short-lived coalition ironically regarded as possessing all possible talents in its members

4 another place
the other House of Parliament (traditionally used in the Commons to refer to the Lords, and vice versa)

5 apply for the Chiltern Hundreds
resign from the House of Commons; *Chiltern Hundreds* a crown manor, the administration of which is a nominal office under the Crown and so requires an MP to vacate his or her seat

6 **the best club in London**
the House of Commons

7 **Father of the House of Commons**
the member with the longest continuous service

8 **the Five Members**
the members of the Long Parliament, Pym, Hampden, Haselrig, Holles, and Strode, whose arrest was unsuccessfully attempted by Charles I on 4 January 1642 in the House of Commons; see PARLIAMENT 15

9 **His or Her Majesty's Opposition**
the principal party opposed to the governing party in the British Parliament; John Cam Hobhouse, in *Recollections of a Long Life* (1865), said of a debate in 1826, 'When I invented the phrase "His Majesty's Opposition" [Canning] paid me a compliment on the fortunate hit'

10 **Leader of the House**
(in the House of Commons) an MP chosen from the party in office to plan the Government's legislative programme and arrange the business of the House; (in the House of Lords) the peer who acts as spokesman for the Government

11 **Mr Balfour's poodle**
the House of Lords; title of a book by Roy Jenkins (1954), in allusion to Lloyd George's comment: see PARLIAMENT 26

12 **the West Lothian question**
the constitutional anomaly that MPs for Scottish and Welsh constituencies are unable to vote on Scottish or Welsh matters that have been devolved to those assemblies, but are able to vote on equivalent matters concerning England, whilst MPs for English constituencies have no reciprocal influence on Scottish or Welsh policy. *West Lothian* is the name of a former parliamentary constituency in Central Scotland, whose MP, Tam Dalyell, persistently raised this question in Parliament in debates on Scottish and Welsh devolution during 1977–8

quotations ►

13 **A parliament can do any thing but make a man a woman, and a woman a man.**
Henry Herbert, Lord Pembroke 1534–1601: quoted in 4th Earl of Pembroke's speech, 11 April 1648, proving himself Chancellor of Oxford

14 **I have neither eye to see, nor tongue to speak here, but as the House is pleased to direct me.**
the Speaker, on being asked if he had seen any of the five MPs whom the King had ordered to be arrested
William Lenthall 1591–1662: to Charles I, 4 January 1642; John Rushworth *Historical Collections. The Third Part* (1692)

15 **I see all the birds are flown.**
after attempting to arrest the Five Members; see PARLIAMENT 8
Charles I 1600–49: in the House of Commons, 4 January 1642; see LIBERTY 2

16 **Take away that fool's bauble, the mace.**
often quoted as, 'Take away these baubles'
Oliver Cromwell 1599–1658: at the dismissal of the Rump Parliament, 20 April 1653

17 **Your representative owes you, not his industry only, but his judgement; and he betrays, instead of serving you, if he sacrifices it to your opinion.**
Edmund Burke 1729–97: speech, Bristol, 3 November 1774

18 **Though we cannot out-vote them we will out-argue them.**
on the practical value of speeches in the House of Commons
Samuel Johnson 1709–84: James Boswell *Life of Samuel Johnson* (1791) 3 April 1778

19 **The duty of an Opposition [is] very simple...to oppose everything, and propose nothing.**
Edward Stanley, 14th Earl of Derby 1799–1869: quoting 'Mr Tierney, a great Whig authority', in the House of Commons, 4 June 1841

20 **Your business is not to govern the country but it is, if you think fit, to call to account those who do govern it.**
W. E. Gladstone 1809–98: speech to the House of Commons, 29 January 1855

21 **Definition of an independent Member of Parliament, viz. one that could not be depended upon.**
Edward Stanley, 14th Earl of Derby 1799–1869: memorandum by Prince Albert, 1 February 1855, in *The Letters of Queen Victoria* vol. 3 (1907)

22 England is the mother of Parliaments.
John Bright 1811–89: speech at Birmingham, 18 January 1865; see BRITAIN 3

23 A cabinet is a combining committee—a *hyphen* which joins, a *buckle* which fastens, the legislative part of the state to the executive part of the state.
Walter Bagehot 1826–77: *The English Constitution* (1867) 'The Cabinet'

24 I am dead; dead, but in the Elysian fields.
to a peer, on his elevation to the House of Lords
Benjamin Disraeli 1804–81: W. Monypenny and G. Buckle *Life of Benjamin Disraeli* vol. 5 (1920)

25 When in that House MPs divide,
If they've a brain and cerebellum too,
They have to leave that brain outside,
And vote just as their leaders tell
'em to.
W. S. Gilbert 1836–1911: *Iolanthe* (1882)

26 The leal and trusty mastiff which is to watch over our interests, but which runs away at the first snarl of the trade unions...A mastiff? It is the right hon. Gentleman's poodle.
on the House of Lords and A. J. Balfour
David Lloyd George 1863–1945: speech, House of Commons, 26 June 1907; see PARLIAMENT 11

27 Think of it! A second Chamber selected by the Whips. A seraglio of eunuchs.
Michael Foot 1913–2010: speech, *Hansard* 3 February 1969

28 The only safe pleasure for a parliamentarian is a bag of boiled sweets.
Julian Critchley 1930–2000: in *Listener* 10 June 1982

29 Being an MP is a good job, the sort of job all working-class parents want for their children—clean, indoors and no heavy lifting.
Diane Abbott 1953– : in *Independent* 18 January 1994

30 I'm fed up with the Punch and Judy politics of Westminster.
David Cameron 1966– : speech on becoming leader of the Conservative party, 6 December 2005; see ARGUMENT 8

Parting

see MEETING AND PARTING

The Past

see also HISTORY, MEMORY, PRESENT

proverbs and sayings ►

1 Nostalgia isn't what it used to be.
graffito; taken as title of book by Simone Signoret, 1978

2 Old sins cast long shadows.
current usage is likely to refer to the wrong done by one generation affecting its descendants; English proverb, early 20th century

3 The past always looks better than it was; it's only pleasant because it isn't here.
American proverb, late 19th century

4 The past at least is secure.
American proverb, early 19th century

5 The past is always ahead of us.
the past is a reminder of what has been and what may be; Maori proverb

6 Things past cannot be recalled.
what has already happened cannot be changed; English proverb, late 15th century

7 What's done cannot be undone.
English proverb, mid 15th century

8 You have drunk from wells you did not dig, and been warmed by fires you did not build.
the present generation depends on those who have gone before; modern saying, said to be of native American origin

phrases ►

9 ancien régime
the old system or style of things; French = former regime, the system of government in France before the Revolution of 1789

10 auld lang syne
times long past; literally 'old long since'; especially as the title and refrain of a traditional song (see MEMORY 9)

11 a fly in amber
a curious relic of the past, preserved into the present; alluding to the fossilized bodies of insects often found trapped in amber

12 **the good old days**
the past; regarded as better than the present; see PAST 35, PRESENT 16

13 **halcyon days**
a period of time in the past that was idyllically happy and peaceful; from *halcyon* a mythical bird said by ancient writers to breed in a nest floating at sea at the winter solstice, charming the wind and waves into calm

14 **the naughty nineties**
the 1890s; regarded as a time of liberalism and permissiveness, especially in Britain and France

15 **once upon a time**
at some vague time in the past; usually as a conventional opening of a story

16 **the roaring twenties**
the 1920s; regarded as a period of postwar buoyancy following the end of the First World War

17 **the swinging sixties**
the 1960s; regarded as a period of release from accepted social and cultural conventions

18 **temps perdu**
the past, contemplated with nostalgia and a sense of irretrievability; French, literally 'time lost', originally with allusion to Proust: see MEMORY 3

quotations ▸

19 Even a god cannot change the past.
literally 'The one thing which even God cannot do is to make undone what has been done'
Agathon b. *c.*445 BC: Aristotle *Nicomachaean Ethics*; see HISTORY 21

20 *Mais où sont les neiges d'antan?*
But where are the snows of yesteryear?
François Villon b. *c.*1431: *Le Grand Testament* (1461) 'Ballade des dames du temps jadis'

21 O! call back yesterday, bid time return.
William Shakespeare 1564–1616: *Richard II* (1595)

22 Antiquities are history defaced, or some remnants of history which have casually escaped the shipwreck of time.
Francis Bacon 1561–1626: *The Advancement of Learning* (1605)

23 Old mortality, the ruins of forgotten times.
Thomas Browne 1605–82: *Hydriotaphia* (Urn Burial, 1658)

24 Think of it, soldiers; from the summit of these pyramids, forty centuries look down upon you.
Napoleon I 1769–1821: speech, 21 July 1798, before the Battle of the Pyramids

25 Think only of the past as its remembrance gives you pleasure.
Jane Austen 1775–1817: *Pride and Prejudice* (1813) ch. 58

26 Thy Naiad airs have brought me home,
To the glory that was Greece
And the grandeur that was Rome.
Edgar Allan Poe 1809–49: 'To Helen' (1831)

27 The splendour falls on castle walls
And snowy summits old in story.
Alfred, Lord Tennyson 1809–92: *The Princess* (1847), song (added 1850)

28 The moving finger writes; and, having writ,
Moves on: nor all thy piety nor wit
Shall lure it back to cancel half a line,
Nor all thy tears wash out a word of it.
Edward Fitzgerald 1809–83: *The Rubáiyát of Omar Khayyám* (1859)

29 I have gazed upon the face of Agamemnon.
on discovering a gold mask at Mycenae, 1876; traditional version of his telegram to the minister at Athens: 'This one is very like the picture which my imagination formed of Agamemnon long ago'
Heinrich Schliemann 1822–90: W. M. Calder and D. A. Traill *Myth, Scandal, and History* (1986)

30 What are those blue remembered hills,
What spires, what farms are those?

That is the land of lost content,
I see it shining plain,
The happy highways where I went
And cannot come again.
A. E. Housman 1859–1936: *A Shropshire Lad* (1896)

31 Those who cannot remember the past are condemned to repeat it.
George Santayana 1863–1952: *The Life of Reason* (1905)

32 Stands the Church clock at ten to three?
And is there honey still for tea?
Rupert Brooke 1887–1915: 'The Old Vicarage, Grantchester' (1915)

33 I tell you the past is a bucket of ashes.
Carl Sandburg 1878–1967: 'Prairie' (1918)

34 Things ain't what they used to be.
Ted Persons: title of song (1941)

35 In every age 'the good old days' were a myth. No one ever thought they were good at the time. For every age has consisted of crises that seemed intolerable to the people who lived through them.
Brooks Atkinson 1894–1984: *Once Around the Sun* (1951); see PAST 12

36 The past is never dead. It's not even past.
William Faulkner 1897–1962: *Requiem for a Nun* (1951)

37 The past is a foreign country: they do things differently there.
L. P. Hartley 1895–1972: *The Go-Between* (1953)

38 Yesterday, all my troubles seemed so far away,
Now it looks as though they're here to stay.
Oh I believe in yesterday.
John Lennon 1940–80 and **Paul McCartney** 1942– : 'Yesterday' (1965 song)

39 Every age has the Stonehenge it deserves—or desires.
Jacquetta Hawkes 1910–96: in *Antiquity* no. 41, 1967

40 Hindsight is always twenty-twenty.
Billy Wilder 1906–2002: J. R. Columbo *Wit and Wisdom of the Moviemakers* (1979)

Patience

see also DETERMINATION, HASTE

proverbs and sayings ►

1 All commend patience, but none can endure to suffer.
American proverb, mid 20th century

2 All things come to those who wait.
often used as an adjuration to patience; English proverb, early 16th century

3 Bear and forbear.
recommending patience and tolerance; English proverb, late 16th century

4 Don't put the cart before the horse.
don't reverse the proper order of things; English proverb, early 16th century

5 First things first.
English proverb, late 19th century

6 Hurry no man's cattle.
sometimes used as an injunction to be patient with someone; English proverb, early 19th century

7 If you sit by the river long enough, you will see the body of your enemy float by.
advocating patience in the face of wrongs; modern saying, said to derive from a Japanese proverb

8 I sit on the shore, and wait for the wind.
what is expected will arrive sooner or later; Russian proverb

9 It is a long lane that has no turning.
commonly used as an assertion that an unfavourable situation will eventually change for the better; English proverb, mid 19th century

10 The longest way round is the shortest way home.
not trying to take a short cut is often the most effective way; English proverb, mid 17th century

11 The man who removes a mountain begins by carrying away small stones.
a major enterprise begins with small but essential tasks; modern saying, claimed to be a Chinese proverb

12 Nothing should be done in haste but gripping a flea.
used as a warning against rash action; English proverb, mid 17th century

13 One step at a time.
recommending cautious progression along a desired route; English proverb, mid 19th century

14 Patience is a virtue.
often used as an exhortation; English proverb, late 14th century

15 Rome was not built in a day.
used to warn against trying to achieve too much at once; English proverb, mid 16th century

16 Slow but sure.
sure here means 'sure-footed, deliberate'; English proverb, late 17th century

17 Softly, softly, catchee monkey.
advocating caution or guile as the best way to achieve an end; English proverb, early 20th century

18 **There is luck in leisure.**
it is often advisable to wait before acting; English proverb, late 17th century

19 **A watched pot never boils.**
to pay too close an attention to the development of a desired event appears to inhibit the result; English proverb, mid 19th century

20 **We must learn to walk before we can run.**
a solid foundation is necessary for faster progress; English proverb, mid 14th century; see EXPERIENCE 15

21 **What can't be cured must be endured.**
there is no point in complaining about what is unavoidable; English proverb, late 16th century

22 **Where water flows, a channel is formed.**
success will come when conditions are ripe; Chinese proverb

phrases ▸

23 **the patience of Job**
unending patience; from the patriarch *Job*, whose patience and exemplary piety were tried by dire and undeserved misfortunes, and who, in spite of his bitter lamentations, remained finally confident in the goodness and justice of God (see PATIENCE 24); see also SYMPATHY 8

quotations ▸

24 **The Lord gave, and the Lord hath taken away; blessed be the name of the Lord.**
Bible: Job; see PATIENCE 23

25 **Let patience have her perfect work.**
Bible: James

26 **Patience is a bitter thing, but its fruit is sweet.**
Sadi c.1213–c.91: 'Rose Garden'

27 **Let nothing trouble you, nothing frighten you. All things are passing; God never changes. Patient endurance attains all things.**
St Teresa of Ávila 1512–82: 'St Teresa's Bookmark'; found in her breviary after her death

28 **Still have I borne it with a patient shrug,**
For sufferance is the badge of all our tribe.
William Shakespeare 1564–1616: *The Merchant of Venice* (1596–8), spoken by Shylock

29 **Beware the fury of a patient man.**
John Dryden 1631–1700: *Absalom and Achitophel* (1681)

30 **Our patience will achieve more than our force.**
Edmund Burke 1729–97: *Reflections on the Revolution in France* (1790)

31 **All human wisdom is contained in these two words, Wait and Hope.**
Alexandre Dumas 1802–70: *The Count of Monte Cristo* (1845)

32 **The strongest of all warriors are these two—time and patience.**
Leo Tolstoy 1828–1910: *War and Peace* (1865–9) bk. 10, ch. 16

33 **Patience, that blending of moral courage with physical timidity.**
Thomas Hardy 1840–1928: *Tess of the d'Urbervilles* (1891)

34 **We had better wait and see.**
referring to the rumour that the House of Lords was to be flooded with new Liberal peers to ensure the passage of the Finance Bill
Herbert Asquith 1852–1928: phrase used repeatedly in speeches in 1910; Roy Jenkins *Asquith* (1964)

35 **Perhaps there is only one cardinal sin: impatience. Because of impatience we were driven out of Paradise; because of impatience we cannot return.**
Franz Kafka 1883–1924: *Collected Aphorisms* no. 3

36 **I am extraordinarily patient, provided I get my own way in the end.**
Margaret Thatcher 1925– : in *Observer* 4 April 1989

Patriotism

proverbs and sayings ▸

1 **I'm backing Britain.**
slogan coined by workers at the Colt factory, Surbiton, Surrey in 1968, and subsequently used in a national campaign

2 **It's an ill bird that fouls its own nest.**
a condemnation of a person who brings his own family, home, or country into disrepute by his words or actions; English proverb, mid 13th century

3 Lousy but loyal.
London East End slogan at George V's Jubilee (1935)

phrases ▸

4 King and country
the objects of allegiance for a patriot whose head of State is a king; see PATRIOTISM 26

5 Queen and country
the objects of allegiance for a patriot whose head of State is a queen

quotations ▸

6 I am not Athenian or Greek but a citizen of the world.
Socrates 469–399 BC: Plutarch *Moralia*

7 *Dulce et decorum est pro patria mori.*
Lovely and honourable it is to die for one's country.
Horace 65–8 BC: *Odes*; see WARFARE 43

8 Not that I loved Caesar less, but that I loved Rome more.
Brutus' reason for killing Caesar
William Shakespeare 1564–1616: *Julius Caesar* (1599)

9 Never was patriot yet, but was a fool.
John Dryden 1631–1700: *Absalom and Achitophel* (1681)

10 What pity is it
That we can die but once to serve our country!
Joseph Addison 1672–1719: *Cato* (1713)

11 Be England what she will,
With all her faults, she is my country still.
Charles Churchill 1731–64: *The Farewell* (1764)

12 Patriotism is the last refuge of a scoundrel.
Samuel Johnson 1709–84: James Boswell *Life of Samuel Johnson* (1791) 7 April 1775

13 I only regret that I have but one life to lose for my country.
prior to his execution by the British for spying
Nathan Hale 1755–76: Henry Phelps Johnston *Nathan Hale, 1776* (1914)

14 These are the times that try men's souls. The summer soldier and the sunshine patriot will, in this crisis, shrink from the service of their country; but he that stands it *now*, deserves the love and thanks of men and women.
Thomas Paine 1737–1809: *The Crisis* (December 1776)

15 Breathes there the man, with soul so dead,
Who never to himself hath said,
This is my own, my native land!
Sir Walter Scott 1771–1832: *The Lay of the Last Minstrel* (1805)

16 Our country! In her intercourse with foreign nations, may she always be in the right; but our country, right or wrong.
Stephen Decatur 1779–1820: toast at Norfolk, Virginia, April 1816; A. S. Mackenzie *Life of Stephen Decatur* (1846); see PATRIOTISM 17

17 My toast would be, may our country be always successful, but whether successful or otherwise, always right.
John Quincy Adams 1767–1848: letter to John Adams, 1 August 1816; see PATRIOTISM 16

18 A steady patriot of the world alone,
The friend of every country but his own.
on the Jacobins, extreme political radicals
George Canning 1770–1827: 'New Morality' (1821)

19 We don't want to fight, yet by jingo! if we do,
We've got the ships, we've got the men, and got the money too.
the origin of the term *jingoism*
G. W. Hunt c.1829–1904: 'We Don't Want to Fight' (1878 song)

20 If I should die, think only this of me:
That there's some corner of a foreign field
That is for ever England.
Rupert Brooke 1887–1915: 'The Soldier' (1914)

21 Standing, as I do, in view of God and eternity, I realize that patriotism is not enough. I must have no hatred or bitterness towards anyone.
on the eve of her execution for helping Allied soldiers to escape from occupied Belgium
Edith Cavell 1865–1915: in *Times* 23 October 1915

22 I vow to thee, my country—all earthly things above—

Entire and whole and perfect, the service of my love.
Cecil Spring-Rice 1859–1918: 'I Vow to Thee, My Country' (1918)

23 You'll never have a quiet world till you knock the patriotism out of the human race.
George Bernard Shaw 1856–1950: *O'Flaherty V.C.* (1919)

24 You think you are dying for your country; you die for the industrialists.
Anatole France 1844–1924: in *L'Humanité* 18 July 1922

25 Patriotism is a lively sense of collective responsibility. Nationalism is a silly cock crowing on its own dunghill.
Richard Aldington 1892–1962: *The Colonel's Daughter* (1931)

26 That this House will in no circumstances fight for its King and Country.
D. M. Graham 1911–99: motion worded by Graham for a debate at the Oxford Union, of which he was Librarian, 9 February 1933 (passed by 275 votes to 153); see PATRIOTISM 4

27 on H. G. Wells's comment on 'an alien and uninspiring court':
I may be uninspiring, but I'll be damned if I'm an alien!
George V 1865–1936: Sarah Bradford *George VI* (1989); attributed, perhaps apocryphal

28 If I had to choose between betraying my country and betraying my friend, I hope I should have the guts to betray my country.
E. M. Forster 1879–1970: *Two Cheers for Democracy* (1951)

29 And so, my fellow Americans: ask not what your country can do for you—ask what you can do for your country.
John F. Kennedy 1917–63: inaugural address, 20 January 1961

30 I would die for my country but I could never let my country die for me.
Neil Kinnock 1942– : speech at Labour Party Conference, 30 September 1986

31 The cricket test—which side do they cheer for?...Are you still looking back to where you came from or where you are?
on the loyalties of Britain's immigrant population
Norman Tebbit 1931– : interview in *Los Angeles Times*; in *Daily Telegraph* 20 April 1990

32 I worry that patriotism run amok will trample the very values that the country seeks to defend.
Dan Rather 1931– : in *Independent* 18 May 2002

33 I fell in love with my country when I was a prisoner in someone else's.
John McCain 1936– : speech at Republican National Convention, Minneapolis-St Paul, 4 September 2008

Peace

see also WARFARE

proverbs and sayings ▸

1 After a storm comes a calm.
often used with the implication that a calm situation is only achieved after stress and turmoil; English proverb, late 14th century

2 Ban the bomb.
US anti-nuclear slogan, 1953 onwards, adopted by the Campaign for Nuclear Disarmament

3 Nothing can bring you peace but yourself.
American proverb, mid 19th century

4 Peace is the dream of the wise; war is the history of man.
saying, recorded from the 19th century

phrases ▸

5 a Carthaginian peace
a peace settlement which imposes very severe terms on the defeated side; referring to the ultimate destruction of Carthage by Rome in the Punic Wars; see ENEMIES 6

6 an olive branch
a branch of an olive tree as an emblem of peace; any token of peace or goodwill; alluding to the Bible (Genesis) 'And the dove came in to him in the evening; and lo, in her mouth was an olive leave pluckt off: so Noah knew that the waters were abated from off the earth'

7 peace with honour
a phrase recorded from the 17th century, used most famously by Disraeli: see PEACE 14

quotations ▸

8 They shall beat their swords into plowshares, and their spears into pruninghooks: nation shall not lift up

sword against nation, neither shall they learn war any more.

Bible: Isaiah; see BROADCASTING 1

9 The peace of God, which passeth all understanding, shall keep your hearts and minds through Christ Jesus.

Bible: Philippians; see OPINION 8

10 They make a wilderness and call it peace.

Tacitus C. AD 56–after 117: *Agricola*

11 ...Peace hath her victories
No less renowned than war.

John Milton 1608–74: 'To the Lord General Cromwell' (written 1652)

12 It's a maxim not to be despised, 'Though peace be made, yet it's interest that keeps peace.'

Oliver Cromwell 1599–1658: speech to Parliament, 4 September 1654

13 Give peace in our time, O Lord.

The Book of Common Prayer 1662: *Morning Prayer*; see PEACE 22

14 Lord Salisbury and myself have brought you back peace—but a peace I hope with honour.

Benjamin Disraeli 1804–81: speech on returning from the Congress of Berlin, 16 July 1878; see PEACE 7, PEACE 22

15 In the arts of peace Man is a bungler.

George Bernard Shaw 1856–1950: *Man and Superman* (1903)

16 War makes rattling good history; but Peace is poor reading.

Thomas Hardy 1840–1928: *The Dynasts* (1904)

17 It is easier to make war than to make peace.

Georges Clemenceau 1841–1929: speech at Verdun, 20 July 1919

18 Peace is indivisible.

Maxim Litvinov 1876–1951: note to the Allies, 25 February 1920

19 If we are to reach real peace in this world, and if we are to carry on a real war against war, we shall have to begin with the children.

Mahatma Gandhi 1869–1948: in *Young India* 19 November 1921

20 I have many times asked myself whether there can be more potent advocates of peace upon earth through the years to come than this massed multitude of silent witnesses to the desolation of war.

George V 1865–1936: message read at Terlincthun Cemetery, Boulogne, 13 May 1922

21 I am not only a pacifist but a militant pacifist. I am willing to fight for peace. Nothing will end war unless the people themselves refuse to go to war.

Albert Einstein 1879–1955: interview with G. S. Viereck, January 1931

22 This is the second time in our history that there has come back from Germany to Downing Street peace with honour. I believe it is peace for our time.

Neville Chamberlain 1869–1940: speech from 10 Downing Street, 30 September 1938; see PEACE 7, PEACE 14

23 Go placidly amid the noise and the haste, and remember what peace there may be in silence.

Max Ehrmann 1872–1945: 'Desiderata' (1948); often wrongly dated to 1692, the date of foundation of a church in Baltimore whose vicar circulated the poem in 1956

24 The work, my friend, is peace. More than an end of this war—an end to the beginnings of all wars.

Franklin D. Roosevelt 1882–1945: undelivered address for Jefferson Day, 13 April 1945 (the day after Roosevelt died)

25 The grim fact is that we prepare for war like precocious giants and for peace like retarded pygmies.

Lester Pearson 1897–1972: speech in Toronto, 14 March 1955

26 I think that people want peace so much that one of these days governments had better get out of the way and let them have it.

Dwight D. Eisenhower 1890–1969: broadcast discussion, 31 August 1959

27 You can't separate peace from freedom because no one can be at peace unless he has his freedom.

Malcolm X 1925–65: speech in New York, 7 January 1965

28 Give peace a chance.

John Lennon 1940–80 and **Paul McCartney** 1942– : title of song (1969)

29 Enough of blood and tears. Enough.
Yitzhak Rabin 1922–95: at the signing of the Israel-Palestine Declaration, Washington, 13 September 1993

30 A war can perhaps be won single-handedly. But peace—lasting peace—cannot be secured without the support of all.
Luiz Inácio Lula da Silva 1945– : speech, United Nations, 23 September 2003

Peoples

see COUNTRIES AND PEOPLES

Perfection

see also EXCELLENCE

proverbs and sayings ▸

1 Trifles make perfection, but perfection is no trifle.
American proverb, mid 20th century; from Michelangelo: see PERFECTION 4

phrases ▸

2 not the rose but near it
not ideal but approaching or near this; the earliest version in English is found in an early 19th century translation of the *Gulistan* [Rose Garden] by the Persian poet Sadi (c.1213–c.91)

quotations ▸

3 Nothing is an unmixed blessing.
Horace 65–8 BC: *Odes*

4 Trifles make perfection, and perfection is no trifle.
Michelangelo 1475–1564: attributed; Samuel Smiles *Self-Help* (1859); see PERFECTION 1

5 How many things by season seasoned are
To their right praise and true perfection!
William Shakespeare 1564–1616: *The Merchant of Venice* (1596–8)

6 Perfection is the child of Time.
Joseph Hall 1574–1656: *Works* (1625)

7 Whoever thinks a faultless piece to see,
Thinks what ne'er was, nor is, nor e'er shall be.
Alexander Pope 1688–1744: *An Essay on Criticism* (1711)

8 Pictures of perfection as you know make me sick and wicked.
Jane Austen 1775–1817: letter to Fanny Knight, 23 March 1817

9 To live is to change, and to be perfect is to have changed often.
John Henry Newman 1801–90: *An Essay on the Development of Christian Doctrine* (1845)

10 Faultily faultless, icily regular, splendidly null,
Dead perfection, no more.
Alfred, Lord Tennyson 1809–92: *Maud* (1855)

11 Faultless to a fault.
Robert Browning 1812–89: *The Ring and the Book* (1868–9)

12 The pursuit of perfection, then, is the pursuit of sweetness and light...He who works for sweetness and light united, works to make reason and the will of God prevail.
Matthew Arnold 1822–88: *Culture and Anarchy* (1869); see VIRTUE 25

13 Finality is death. Perfection is finality.
Nothing is perfect. There are lumps in it.
James Stephens 1882–1950: *The Crock of Gold* (1912)

14 The intellect of man is forced to choose
Perfection of the life, or of the work.
W. B. Yeats 1865–1939: 'The Choice' (1933)

15 Perfection is finally attained not when there is no longer anything to add but when there is no longer anything to take away, when a body has been stripped down to its nakedness.
Antoine de Saint-Exupéry 1900–44: *Wind, Sand and Stars* (1939)

16 Perfection is terrible, it cannot have children.
Sylvia Plath 1932–63: 'The Munich Mannequins' (1965)

17 Forget your perfect offering
There is a crack in everything
That's how the light gets in.
Leonard Cohen 1934– : 'Anthem' (1992 song)

Perseverance

see DETERMINATION AND PERSEVERANCE

Pessimism

see OPTIMISM AND PESSIMISM

Philosophy

see also LOGIC

proverbs and sayings ▸

1 How many angels can dance on the head of a pin?

regarded satirically as a characteristic speculation of scholastic philosophy, particularly as exemplified by 'Doctor Scholasticus' (Anselm of Laon, d. 1117) and as used in medieval comedies; see PHILOSOPHY 8

phrases ▸

2 Occam's razor

the principle that in explaining a thing no more assumptions should be made than are necessary; an ancient philosophical principle often attributed to the English scholastic philosopher William of *Occam* (*c.*1285–1349), but earlier in origin; see PHILOSOPHY 6

3 the Socratic method

engaging in dialogue with others in an attempt to reach understanding and ethical concepts by exposing and dispelling error, after the Athenian philosopher *Socrates* (469–399 BC); see PHILOSOPHY 15

quotations ▸

4 The unexamined life is not worth living.

Socrates 469–399 BC: Plato *Apology*

5 There is nothing so absurd but some philosopher has said it.

Cicero 106–43 BC: *De Divinatione*

6 No more things should be presumed to exist than are absolutely necessary.

William of Occam c.1285–1349: not found in this form in his writings, although he frequently used similar expressions, e.g. 'Plurality should not be assumed unnecessarily'; *Quodlibeta* (1324); see PHILOSOPHY 2

7 How charming is divine philosophy!
Not harsh and crabbèd, as dull fools suppose,
But musical as is Apollo's lute.

John Milton 1608–74: *Comus* (1637)

8 Some who are far from atheists, may make themselves merry with that conceit of thousands of spirits dancing at once upon a needle's point.

Ralph Cudworth 1617–88: *The True Intellectual System of the Universe* (1678); see PHILOSOPHY 1

9 The same principles which at first view lead to scepticism, pursued to a certain point bring men back to common sense.

George Berkeley 1685–1753: *Three Dialogues between Hylas and Philonous* (1734)

10 Superstition sets the whole world in flames; philosophy quenches them.

Voltaire 1694–1778: *Dictionnaire philosophique* (1764) 'Superstition'

11 I have tried too in my time to be a philosopher; but, I don't know how, cheerfulness was always breaking in.

Oliver Edwards 1711–91: James Boswell *Life of Samuel Johnson* (1791) 17 April 1778

12 When philosophy paints its grey on grey, then has a shape of life grown old. By philosophy's grey on grey it cannot be rejuvenated but only understood. The owl of Minerva spreads its wings only with the falling of the dusk.

G. W. F. Hegel 1770–1831: *Philosophy of Right* (1821)

13 The philosophers have only interpreted the world in various ways; the point is to change it.

Karl Marx 1818–83: *Theses on Feuerbach* (written 1845, published 1888)

14 Metaphysics is the finding of bad reasons for what we believe upon instinct; but to find these reasons is no less an instinct.

F. H. Bradley 1846–1924: *Appearance and Reality* (1893)

15 The Socratic manner is not a game at which two can play.

Max Beerbohm 1872–1956: *Zuleika Dobson* (1911); see PHILOSOPHY 3

16 He [Wittgenstein] thinks nothing empirical is Knowable—I asked him to

admit that there was not a rhinoceros in the room, but he wouldn't.

Bertrand Russell 1872–1970: letter to Lady Ottoline Morrell, November 1911

17 The point of philosophy is to start with something so simple as not to seem worth stating, and to end with something so paradoxical that no one will believe it.

Bertrand Russell 1872–1970: *The Philosophy of Logical Atomism* (1918)

18 The safest general characterization of the European philosophical tradition is that it consists of a series of footnotes to Plato.

Alfred North Whitehead 1861–1947: *Process and Reality* (1929)

19 To ask the hard question is simple.

W. H. Auden 1907–73: title of poem (1933)

20 What is your aim in philosophy?—To show the fly the way out of the fly-bottle.

Ludwig Wittgenstein 1889–1951: *Philosophische Untersuchungen* (1953)

Photography

proverbs and sayings ▸

1 The camera never lies.

20th century saying; see PHOTOGRAPHY 8

2 You press the button, we do the rest.

advertising slogan to launch Kodak camera 1888, coined by George Eastman (1854–1932)

phrases ▸

3 candid camera

the technique of photographing or filming people without their knowledge, chiefly in situations set up for the amusement of television viewers

4 decisive moment

the moment in which a photographer recognizes the precise significance and organization of the picture to be taken; used as the title of an exhibition and book by the French photographer Henri Cartier-Bresson in 1952, and deriving ultimately from de Retz: see MANAGEMENT 7

quotations ▸

5 I longed to arrest all beauty that came before me, and at length the longing has been satisfied.

Julia Margaret Cameron 1815–79: *Annals of My Glass House* (1874)

6 The photographer is like the cod which produces a million eggs in order that one may reach maturity.

George Bernard Shaw 1856–1950: introduction to the catalogue for Alvin Langdon Coburn's exhibition at the Royal Photographic Society, 1906; Bill Jay and Margaret Moore *Bernard Shaw and Photography* (1989)

7 If your pictures aren't good enough, you aren't close enough.

of photojournalism

Robert Capa 1913–54: Russell Miller *Magnum: Fifty years at the Front Line of History* (1997)

8 The camera's eye
Does not lie,
But it cannot show
The life within.

W. H. Auden 1907–73: 'Runner' (1962); see PHOTOGRAPHY 1

9 A photograph is a secret about a secret. The more it tells you the less you know.

Diane Arbus 1923–71: Patricia Bosworth *Diane Arbus: a Biography* (1985)

10 In photography you've got to be quick, quick, quick, like an animal and a prey.

Henri Cartier-Bresson 1908–2004: interview, 1979

11 My idea of a good picture is one that's in focus and of a famous person doing something unfamous. It's being in the right place at the wrong time.

Andy Warhol 1927–87: *Andy Warhol's Exposures* (1979)

12 There are always two people in every picture: the photographer and the viewer.

Ansel Adams 1902–84: attributed

13 It takes a lot of imagination to be a good photographer. You need less imagination to be a painter, because you can invent things. But in photography everything is so ordinary; it takes a lot of looking before you learn to see the ordinary.

David Bailey 1938– : interview in *The Face* December 1984

14 Most things in life are moments of pleasure and a lifetime of embarrassment; photography is a

moment of embarrassment and a lifetime of pleasure.

Tony Benn 1925– : in *Independent* 21 October 1989

15 **It's more important to click with people than to click the shutter.**

Alfred Eisenstaedt 1898–1995: in *Life* 24 August 1995

16 **Photography deals exquisitely with appearances, but nothing is what it appears to be.**

Duane Michals 1932– : attributed

Physical Sciences

see also SCIENCE

proverbs and sayings ▸

1 **Laws of Thermodynamics:**
1) You cannot win, you can only break even.
2) You can only break even at absolute zero.
3) You cannot reach absolute zero.

folklore amongst physicists; see PHYSICAL 4

phrases ▸

2 **cold fusion**

nuclear fusion occurring at or close to room temperature; claims for its discovery in 1989 are generally held to have been mistaken

3 **fourth dimension**

a postulated spatial dimension additional to those determining length, area, and volume; the phrase is recorded from the late 19th century, and is now also used in physics to denote time as analogous to linear dimensions

4 **laws of thermodynamics**

three laws describing the general direction of physical change in the universe; see PHYSICAL 1, PHYSICAL 11, PHYSICAL 16; see also ARTS AND SCIENCES 9

5 **Maxwell's demon**

a hypothetical being imagined as controlling a hole in a partition dividing a gas-filled container into two parts, and allowing only fast-moving molecules to pass in one direction, and slow-moving molecules in the other. This would result in one side of the container becoming warmer and the other colder, in violation of the second law of thermodynamics. The name derives from the Scottish physicist James Clerk *Maxwell* (1831–79); see PHYSICAL 16

6 **perpetual motion**

the motion of a hypothetical machine which, once activated, would run forever unless subject to an external force or to wear. Although impossible according to the first and second laws of thermodynamics, the development of such a mechanism has been attempted by many inventors; see PHYSICAL 4

7 **quark confinement**

the hypothesis that free quarks can never be seen in isolation; *quark* = any of a number of subatomic particles carrying a fractional electric charge, postulated as building blocks of the hadrons. The name (originally *quork*) was invented in the 1960s by Murray Gell-Mann; it was changed by association with the line 'Three quarks for Muster Mark' in James Joyce's *Finnegans Wake* (1939)

8 **Schrödinger's cat**

a paradox concerning a cat in a sealed box containing a lethal device triggered by radioactive decay; an outside observer cannot know whether the device has been set off and the cat killed. According to quantum mechanics the cat is in an indeterminate state, some combination of alive and dead, until the box is opened, at which point it will be found to be one or the other. The paradox was suggested in 1935 by the Austrian theoretical physicist Erwin Schrödinger (1887–1961), to illustrate the conceptual difficulties of quantum mechanics

9 **uncertainty principle**

the principle that the momentum and position of a particle cannot both be precisely determined at the same time; see IDEAS 12

quotations ▸

10 **There was a young lady named Bright,**
Whose speed was far faster than light;
She set out one day
In a relative way
And returned on the previous night.

Arthur Buller 1874–1944: 'Relativity' in *Punch* 19 December 1923

11 **If someone points out to you that your pet theory of the universe is in disagreement with Maxwell's equations—then so much the worse for Maxwell's equations. If it is found to be contradicted by observation—well, these experimentalists do bungle things sometimes. But if your theory is found to be against the second law**

of thermodynamics I can give you no hope; there is nothing for it but to collapse in deepest humiliation.

Arthur Eddington 1882–1944: *The Nature of the Physical World* (1928); see PHYSICAL 4

12 If we assume that the last breath of, say, Julius Caesar has by now become thoroughly scattered through the atmosphere, then the chances are that each of us inhales one molecule of it with every breath we take.

James Jeans 1877–1946: *An Introduction to the Kinetic Theory of Gases* (1940)

13 I remembered the line from the Hindu scripture, the *Bhagavad Gita*...'I am become death, the destroyer of worlds.'

on the explosion of the first atomic bomb near Alamogordo, New Mexico, 16 July 1945

J. Robert Oppenheimer 1904–67: Len Giovannitti and Fred Freed *The Decision to Drop the Bomb* (1965)

14 In some sort of crude sense which no vulgarity, no humour, no overstatement can quite extinguish, the physicists have known sin; and this is a knowledge which they cannot lose.

J. Robert Oppenheimer 1904–67: lecture at Massachusetts Institute of Technology, 25 November 1947

15 If I could remember the names of all these particles I'd be a botanist.

Enrico Fermi 1901–54: R. L. Weber *More Random Walks in Science* (1973)

16 Heat won't pass from a cooler to a hotter,
You can try it if you like but you'd far better notter.

Michael Flanders 1922–75 and **Donald Swann** 1923–94: 'The First and Second Law' (1956 song); see PHYSICAL 4, PHYSICAL 5

17 It would be a poor thing to be an atom in a world without physicists. And physicists are made of atoms. A physicist is an atom's way of knowing about atoms.

George Wald 1904–97: foreword to L. J. Henderson *The Fitness of the Environment* (1958)

18 The great edifice of modern physics goes up, and the majority of the cleverest people in the western world have about as much insight into it as their neolithic ancestors would have had.

C. P. Snow 1905–80: *The Two Cultures* (1959)

19 Anybody who is not shocked by this subject has failed to understand it.

of quantum mechanics

Niels Bohr 1885–1962: attributed; in *Nature* 23 August 1990

20 Neutrinos, they are very small
They have no charge and have no mass
And do not interact at all.

John Updike 1932–2009: 'Cosmic Gall' (1964)

21 There is no democracy in physics. We can't say that some second-rate guy has as much right to opinion as Fermi.

Luis Walter Alvarez 1911–88: D. S. Greenberg *The Politics of Pure Science* (1969)

Pleasure

proverbs and sayings ▸

1 A good time was had by all.

title of a collection of poems published in 1937 by Stevie Smith (1902–71), taken from the characteristic conclusion of accounts of social events in parish magazines

2 Stop me and buy one.

Wall's ice cream, from spring 1922

phrases ▸

3 cakes and ale

merrymaking, good things; from Shakespeare *Twelfth Night*: see VIRTUE 22

4 forbidden fruit

illicit pleasure; the fruit forbidden to Adam in the Bible (Genesis) 'But of the tree of the knowledge of good and evil, thou shalt not eat of it'

5 pleased as Punch

showing or feeling great pleasure; *Punch* the grotesque hook-nosed humpbacked principal character of *Punch and Judy*, a traditional puppet-show in which Punch is shown nagging, beating, and finally killing a succession of characters, including his wife Judy; see ARGUMENT 8

6 **the primrose path**
the pursuit of pleasure, especially with disastrous consequences; in allusion to Shakespeare *Hamlet*: see WORDS AND DEEDS 12

7 **a song in one's heart**
a feeling of joy or pleasure; originally with allusion to Lorenz Hart 'With a Song in my Heart', 1930 song

8 **teddy bears' picnic**
an occasion of innocent enjoyment; from a song (1932) by Jimmy Kennedy and J. W. Bratton

9 **wine, women, and song**
proverbially required by men for carefree entertainment and pleasure; see PLEASURE 12

quotations ▸

10 Everyone is dragged on by their favourite pleasure.
Virgil 70–19 BC: *Eclogues*

11 The less we indulge our pleasures the more we enjoy them.
Juvenal C. AD 60–C. 140: *Satires*

12 Who loves not woman, wine, and song
Remains a fool his whole life long.
Martin Luther 1483–1546: attributed; later inscribed in the Luther room in the Wartburg, but with no proof of authorship; see PLEASURE 9, PLEASURE 19

13 Pleasure is nothing else but the intermission of pain.
John Selden 1584–1654: *Table Talk* (1689) 'Pleasure'

14 I shouldn't be surprised if the greatest rule of all weren't to give pleasure.
Molière 1622–73: *La Critique de l'école des femmes* (1663)

15 Music and women I cannot but give way to, whatever my business is.
Samuel Pepys 1633–1703: diary, 9 March 1666

16 Great lords have their pleasures, but the people have fun.
Montesquieu 1689–1755: *Pensées et fragments inédits…* vol. 2 (1901)

17 A man enjoys the happiness he feels, a woman the happiness she gives.
Pierre Choderlos de Laclos 1741–1803: *Les Liaisons dangereuses* (1782)

18 One half of the world cannot understand the pleasures of the other.
Jane Austen 1775–1817: *Emma* (1816)

19 Let us have wine and women, mirth and laughter,
Sermons and soda-water the day after.
Lord Byron 1788–1824: *Don Juan* (1819–24); see PLEASURE 12

20 The greatest pleasure I know, is to do a good action by stealth, and to have it found out by accident.
Charles Lamb 1775–1834: 'Table Talk by the late Elia' in *The Athenaeum* 4 January 1834

21 The Puritan hated bear-baiting, not because it gave pain to the bear, but because it gave pleasure to the spectators.
Lord Macaulay 1800–59: *History of England* vol. 1 (1849)

22 The great pleasure in life is doing what people say you cannot do.
Walter Bagehot 1826–77: in *Prospective Review* 1853 'Shakespeare'

23 A fool bolts pleasure, then complains of moral indigestion.
Minna Antrim 1861–1950: *Naked Truth and Veiled Allusions* (1902)

24 Lying in bed would be an altogether perfect and supreme experience if only one had a coloured pencil long enough to draw on the ceiling.
G. K. Chesterton 1874–1936: *Tremendous Trifles* (1909) 'On Lying in Bed'

25 Speed, it seems to me, provides the one genuinely modern pleasure.
Aldous Huxley 1894–1963: *Music at Night, and Other Essays* (1931) 'Wanted, A New Pleasure'

26 People must not do things for fun. We are not here for fun. There is no reference to fun in any Act of Parliament.
A. P. Herbert 1890–1971: *Uncommon Law* (1935)

27 All the things I really like to do are either illegal, immoral, or fattening.
Alexander Woollcott 1887–1943: R. E. Drennan *Wit's End* (1973)

28 There's no pleasure on earth that's worth sacrificing for the sake of an extra five years in the geriatric ward of the Sunset Old People's Home, Weston-Super-Mare.
John Mortimer 1923–2009: *Rumpole's Last Case* (1987); a similar saying has been attributed to Kingsley Amis

29 There's no greater bliss in life than when the plumber eventually comes to unblock your drains. No writer can give that sort of pleasure.
Victoria Glendinning 1937– : in *Observer* 3 January 1993

Poetry
see also WRITING

phrases ▸

1 the gay science
the art of poetry; Provencal *gai saber*, see ECONOMICS 4

2 Mount Parnassus
poetry; after a mountain in central Greece, just north of Delphi. Held to be sacred by the ancient Greeks, it was associated with Apollo and the Muses

3 the Pierian spring
the source of poetic inspiration; from Pieria, a district in northern Thessaly, that in classical mythology was reputed home of the Muses and the location of a spring sacred to them; see KNOWLEDGE 29

4 stuffed owl
of poetry which treats trivial or inconsequential subjects in a grandiose manner; *the stuffed owl* title of 'an anthology of bad verse' (1930); ultimately from Wordsworth *Miscellaneous Sonnets* (1827) 'The presence even of a stuffed owl for her Can cheat the time'

quotations ▸

5 Skilled or unskilled, we all scribble poems.
Horace 65–8 BC: *Epistles*

6 Poetry is devil's wine.
St. Augustine of Hippo AD 354–430: *Contra Academicos*

7 'By God,' quod he, 'for pleynly, at a word,
Thy drasty rymyng is nat worth a toord!'
Geoffrey Chaucer 1343–1400: *The Canterbury Tales* 'Sir Thopas'

8 I am two fools, I know,
For loving, and for saying so
In whining poetry.
John Donne 1572–1631: 'The Triple Fool'

9 All poets are mad.
Robert Burton 1577–1640: *The Anatomy of Melancholy* (1621–51) 'Democritus to the Reader'

10 Rhyme being no necessary adjunct or true ornament of poem or good verse, in longer works especially, but the invention of a barbarous age, to set off wretched matter and lame metre.
John Milton 1608–74: *Paradise Lost* (1667) 'The Verse' (preface, added 1668)

11 All that is not prose is verse; and all that is not verse is prose.
Molière 1622–73: *Le Bourgeois Gentilhomme* (1671)

12 BOSWELL: Sir, what is poetry?
JOHNSON: Why Sir, it is much easier to say what it is not. We all *know* what light is; but it is not easy to *tell* what it is.
Samuel Johnson 1709–84: James Boswell *Life of Samuel Johnson* (1791) 12 April 1776

13 Some rhyme a neebor's name to lash;
Some rhyme (vain thought!) for needfu' cash;
Some rhyme to court the countra clash,
An' raise a din;
For me, an aim I never fash;
I rhyme for fun.
Robert Burns 1759–96: 'To J. S[mith]' (1786)

14 Poetry is the spontaneous overflow of powerful feelings: it takes its origin from emotion recollected in tranquillity.
William Wordsworth 1770–1850: *Lyrical Ballads* (2nd ed., 1802)

15 That willing suspension of disbelief for the moment, which constitutes poetic faith.
Samuel Taylor Coleridge 1772–1834: *Biographia Literaria* (1817)

16 If poetry comes not as naturally as the leaves to a tree it had better not come at all.
John Keats 1795–1821: letter to John Taylor, 27 February 1818

17 Poetry is the record of the best and happiest moments of the happiest and best minds.
Percy Bysshe Shelley 1792–1822: *A Defence of Poetry* (written 1821)

18 Poets are the unacknowledged legislators of the world.
Percy Bysshe Shelley 1792–1822: *A Defence of Poetry* (written 1821)

19 Prose = words in their best order;—poetry = the *best* words in the best order.
Samuel Taylor Coleridge 1772–1834: *Table Talk* (1835) 12 July 1827

20 Scorn not the Sonnet; Critic, you have frowned,
Mindless of its just honours; with this key
Shakespeare unlocked his heart.
William Wordsworth 1770–1850: 'Scorn not the Sonnet' (1827)

21 Prose is when all the lines except the last go on to the end. Poetry is when some of them fall short of it.
Jeremy Bentham 1748–1832: M. St. J. Packe *The Life of John Stuart Mill* (1954)

22 If I read a book [and] it makes my whole body so cold no fire can ever warm me, I know *that* is poetry. If I feel physically as if the top of my head were taken off, I know *that* is poetry.
Emily Dickinson 1830–86: letter to T. W. Higginson, 16 August 1870

23 I said 'a line will take us hours maybe,
Yet if it does not seem a moment's thought
Our stitching and unstitching has been naught.'
W. B. Yeats 1865–1939: 'Adam's Curse' (1904)

24 All a poet can do today is warn.
Wilfred Owen 1893–1918: preface (written 1918) in *Poems* (1963)

25 Poetry is not a turning loose of emotion, but an escape from emotion; it is not the expression of personality but an escape from personality.
T. S. Eliot 1888–1965: *The Sacred Wood* (1920) 'Tradition and Individual Talent'

26 A poem should not mean
But be.
Archibald MacLeish 1892–1982: 'Ars Poetica' (1926)

27 In our language rhyme is a barrel. A barrel of dynamite. The line is a fuse. The line smoulders to the end and explodes; and the town is blown sky-high in a stanza.
Vladimir Mayakovsky 1893–1930: 'Conversation with an Inspector of Taxes about Poetry' (1926)

28 A poem is never finished; it's always an accident that puts a stop to it—i.e. gives it to the public.
often quoted in W. H. Auden' s paraphrase, 'A poem is never finished, only abandoned'
Paul Valéry 1871–1945: *Littérature* (1930)

29 Experience has taught me, when I am shaving of a morning, to keep watch over my thoughts, because, if a line of poetry strays into my memory, my skin bristles so that the razor ceases to act...The seat of this sensation is the pit of the stomach.
A. E. Housman 1859–1936: lecture at Cambridge, 9 May 1933

30 A poet writes always of his personal life, in his finest work out of its tragedy.
W. B. Yeats 1865–1939: 'A General Introduction for My Work' (written 1937, but not published)

31 There's nothing in the world for which a poet will give up writing, not even when he is a Jew and the language of his poems is German.
Paul Celan 1920–70: letter to relatives, 2 August 1948

32 For twenty years I've stared my level best
To see if evening—any evening —would suggest
A patient etherized upon a table;
In vain. I simply wasn't able.
on contemporary poetry
C. S. Lewis 1898–1963: 'A Confession' (1964); see DAY 14

33 I'd as soon write free verse as play tennis with the net down.
Robert Frost 1874–1963: Edward Lathem *Interviews with Robert Frost* (1966)

34 Most people ignore most poetry
because
most poetry ignores most people.
Adrian Mitchell 1932–2008: *Poems* (1964)

35 It is barbarous to write a poem after Auschwitz.

Theodor Adorno 1903–69: I. Buruma *Wages of Guilt* (1994)

36 A poet's hope: to be,
like some valley cheese,
local, but prized elsewhere.

W. H. Auden 1907–73: 'Shorts II' (1976)

37 Look around—there's only one thing of danger to you here—poetry.

watching from his deathbed as a military raid searched his garden, September 1973

Pablo Neruda 1904–73: Adam Feinstein *Pablo Neruda: A Passion for Life* (2004)

38 I think poetry should be alive. You should be able to dance it.

Benjamin Zephaniah 1958– : in *Sunday Times* 23 August 1987

Poets

phrases ▸

1 the Father of English poetry

Geoffrey Chaucer (1342–1400), regarded as traditional starting-point for English literature and as the first great English poet

2 the fleshly school of poetry

a group of late 19th-century poets associated with Dante Gabriel Rossetti; the term was coined in the *Contemporary Review* of October 1871 by the Scottish writer Robert Buchanan

3 the Good Gray Poet

the American poet Walt Whitman (1819–92); the sobriquet was first applied to him in a book of this title (1866) by his friend, the journalist William O'Connor

4 the Lake Poets

the poets Samuel Taylor Coleridge, Robert Southey, and William Wordsworth; they lived in and were inspired by the Lake District

5 the Peasant Poet

John Clare (1793–1864); his popularity became part of a vogue for rural poetry and 'ploughman' poets

6 Poet Laureate

an eminent poet appointed as a member of the British royal household; the Poet Laureate was formerly expected to write poems for state occasions, but since Victorian times the post has carried no specific duties

7 the Theban eagle

the Greek lyric poet Pindar (518–438 BC); the name derives from three passages in poems by Pindar in which an eagle is mentioned without its connection to the context being clear; traditionally, the bird has been taken as an image of the poet

quotations ▸

8 The worshipful father and first founder and embellisher of ornate eloquence in our English, I mean Master Geoffrey Chaucer.

William Caxton 1421–91: Caxton's edition (1478) of Chaucer's translation of Boethius *De Consolacione Philosophie*

9 Dr Donne's verses are like the peace of God; they pass all understanding.

James I 1566–1625: remark recorded by Archdeacon Plume (1630–1704)

10 'Tis sufficient to say, according to the proverb, that here is God's plenty.

of Chaucer

John Dryden 1631–1700: *Fables Ancient and Modern* (1700)

11 Ev'n copious Dryden, wanted, or forgot,
The last and greatest art, the art to blot.

Alexander Pope 1688–1744: *Imitations of Horace* (1737)

12 The living throne, the sapphire-blaze,
Where angels tremble, while they gaze,
He saw; but blasted with excess of light,
Closed his eyes in endless night.

of Milton

Thomas Gray 1716–71: *The Progress of Poesy* (1757)

13 Milton, Madam, was a genius that could cut a Colossus from a rock; but could not carve heads upon cherry-stones.

to Hannah More, who had expressed a wonder that the poet who had written *Paradise Lost* should write such poor sonnets

Samuel Johnson 1709–84: James Boswell *Life of Samuel Johnson* (1791) 13 June 1784

14 The reason Milton wrote in fetters when he wrote of Angels and God, and at liberty when of Devils and Hell, is

because he was a true Poet, and of the Devil's party without knowing it.
William Blake 1757–1827: *The Marriage of Heaven and Hell* (1790–3)

15 Mad, bad, and dangerous to know.
of Byron, after their first meeting
Lady Caroline Lamb 1785–1828: diary, March 1812; Elizabeth Jenkins *Lady Caroline Lamb* (1932)

16 With Donne, whose muse on dromedary trots,
Wreathe iron pokers into true-love knots.
Samuel Taylor Coleridge 1772–1834: 'On Donne's Poetry' (1818)

17 A cloud-encircled meteor of the air,
A hooded eagle among blinking owls.
of Coleridge
Percy Bysshe Shelley 1792–1822: 'Letter to Maria Gisborne' (1820)

18 We learn from Horace, Homer sometimes sleeps;
We feel without him: Wordsworth sometimes wakes.
Lord Byron 1788–1824: *Don Juan* (1819–24); see MISTAKES 13

19 In poetry, no less than in life, he is 'a beautiful and ineffectual angel, beating in the void his luminous wings in vain.'
Matthew Arnold 1822–88: *Essays in Criticism* Second Series (1888) 'Shelley' (quoting from his own essay on Byron in the same work)

20 Chaos, illumined by flashes of lightning.
on Robert Browning's 'style'
Oscar Wilde 1854–1900: Ada Leverson *Letters to the Sphinx* (1930)

21 How unpleasant to meet Mr Eliot!
With his features of clerical cut,
And his brow so grim
And his mouth so prim
And his conversation, so nicely
Restricted to What Precisely
And If and Perhaps and But.
T. S. Eliot 1888–1965: 'Five-Finger Exercises' (1936)

22 You were silly like us; your gift survived it all:
The parish of rich women, physical decay,
Yourself. Mad Ireland hurt you into poetry.
W. H. Auden 1907–73: 'In Memory of W. B. Yeats' (1940)

23 *Hugo—hélas!*
Hugo—alas!
when asked who was the greatest 19th-century poet
André Gide 1869–1951: Claude Martin *La Maturité d'André Gide* (1977)

24 For years a secret shame destroyed my peace—
I'd not read Eliot, Auden or MacNeice.
But then I had a thought that brought me hope—
Neither had Chaucer, Shakespeare, Milton, Pope.
Justin Richardson: 'Take Heart, Illiterates' (1966)

25 Self-contempt, well-grounded.
on the foundation of T. S. Eliot's work
F. R. Leavis 1895–1978: in *Times Literary Supplement* 21 October 1988; see SELF-ESTEEM 15

26 No death outside my immediate family has left me more bereft. No death in my lifetime has hurt poets more.
Seamus Heaney 1939– : funeral oration for Ted Hughes, 3 November 1998

Political Parties

see also CAPITALISM, POLITICIANS, POLITICS

proverbs and sayings ▸

1 I am a Marxist—of the Groucho tendency.
slogan found at Nanterre in Paris, 1968

2 Labour isn't working.
on a poster showing a long queue outside an unemployment office; British Conservative Party slogan, 1978

3 Meet the challenge—make the change.
Labour Party slogan, 1989

4 Not to be a republican at twenty is proof of want of heart; to be one at thirty is proof of want of head.
often used in the form 'Not to be a socialist…'; saying attributed by Georges Clemenceau (1841–1929) to François Guizot (1787–1874)

phrases ▸

5 **Big Blue Machine**
in Canada, informal name for the Ontario Progressive Conservative party, especially during the premiership of William Davis (1971–85), or for the group of people responsible for the party's campaigns and political organization

6 **big tent**
the doctrine or belief that a political party (or coalition of parties) should permit and encourage a broad spectrum of views and opinions among its members rather than insist on strict adherence to party policy; a party run on these lines

7 **clear blue water**
as seen by some Conservatives, the gap between their political aims and aspirations and those of the Labour Party; from blend of *clear water*, the distance between two boats, and *blue water*, the open sea, with a play on *blue* as the traditional colour of Conservatism

8 **the Grand Old Party**
the American Republican Party, recorded from the late 19th century

9 **the magic circle**
an inner group of politicians viewed as choosing the leader of the Conservative Party before this became an electoral matter; coined by Iain Macleod in a critical article in the *Spectator* on the 'emergence' of Alec Douglas-Home in succession to Harold Macmillan in 1963

10 **Selsdon man**
an advocate or adherent of the policies outlined at a conference of Conservative Party leaders held at the Selsdon Park Hotel, January 1970, from the view of a political opponent; from the *Selsdon* Park Hotel, Croydon, Surrey, after *Piltdown man* a fraudulent fossil composed of a human cranium and an ape jaw that was presented in 1912 as a genuine hominid of great antiquity

11 **somewhere to the right of Genghis Khan**
holding right-wing views of the most extreme kind; *Genghis Khan* (1162–1227), the founder of the Mongol empire, as the type of a repressive and tyrannical ruler

12 **yellow-dog Democrat**
in the US, a diehard Democrat, who will vote for a Democratic candidate, regardless of their personal qualities; the term implies someone who would vote for even a *yellow dog* if it were on the party ticket

quotations ▸

13 Party-spirit, which at best is but the madness of many for the gain of a few.
Alexander Pope 1688–1744: letter to Edward Blount, 27 August 1714

14 I have always said, the first Whig was the Devil.
Samuel Johnson 1709–84: James Boswell *Life of Johnson* (1791) 28 April 1778; see POLITICAL PARTIES 18

15 PRINCE OF WALES: True blue and Mrs Crewe.
MRS CREWE: Buff and blue and all of you.
toast proposed by George IV when Prince of Wales to Mrs Crewe, in honour of her support for the Whigs and Charles James Fox in the Westminster election of 1784 (buff and blue were the Whig colours)
George IV 1762–1830: at a dinner at Carlton House, May 1784; Amanda Foreman *Georgiana Duchess of Devonshire* (1998); see TRUST 17

16 If I could not go to Heaven but with a party, I would not go there at all.
Thomas Jefferson 1743–1826: letter to Francis Hopkinson, 13 March 1789

17 Let me...warn you in the most solemn manner against the baneful effects of the spirit of party.
George Washington 1732–99: President's address retiring from public life, 17 September 1796

18 God will not always be a Tory.
Lord Byron 1788–1824: letter 2 February 1821; see POLITICAL PARTIES 14

19 I always voted at my party's call,
And I never thought of thinking for
myself at all.
W. S. Gilbert 1836–1911: *HMS Pinafore* (1878)

20 Damn your principles! Stick to your party.
Benjamin Disraeli 1804–81: attributed to Disraeli and believed to have been said to Edward Bulwer-Lytton; E. Latham *Famous Sayings and their Authors* (1904)

21 We are Republicans and don't propose to leave our party and identify ourselves with the party whose antecedents are rum, Romanism, and rebellion.
Samuel Dickinson Burchard 1812–91: speech at the Fifth Avenue Hotel, New York, 29 October 1884

22 We are all socialists now.
during the passage of the 1888 budget, noted for the reduction of the National Debt
William Harcourt 1827–1904: attributed; Hubert Bland 'The Outlook' in G. B. Shaw (ed.) *Fabian Essays in Socialism* (1889)

23 Then raise the scarlet standard high!
Within its shade we'll live or die.
Tho' cowards flinch and traitors sneer,
We'll keep the red flag flying here.
James M. Connell 1852–1929: 'The Red Flag' (1889 song)

24 When in office, the Liberals forget their principles and the Tories remember their friends.
Thomas Kettle 1880–1916: Nicholas Mansergh *The Irish Question* (ed. 3, 1975)

25 I never dared be radical when young
For fear it would make me
conservative when old.
Robert Frost 1874–1963: 'Precaution' (1936)

26 I am reminded of four definitions: A Radical is a man with both feet firmly planted—in the air. A Conservative is a man with two perfectly good legs who, however, has never learned to walk forward. A Reactionary is a somnambulist walking backwards. A Liberal is a man who uses his legs and his hands at the behest—at the command—of his head.
Franklin D. Roosevelt 1882–1945: radio address to *New York Herald Tribune* Forum, 26 October 1939

27 The language of priorities is the religion of Socialism.
Aneurin Bevan 1897–1960: speech at Labour Party Conference in Blackpool, 8 June 1949

28 If they [the Republicans] will stop telling lies about the Democrats, we will stop telling the truth about them.
Adlai Stevenson 1900–65: speech during 1952 Presidential campaign; J. B. Martin *Adlai Stevenson and Illinois* (1976)

29 The Labour Party owes more to Methodism than to Marxism.
Morgan Phillips 1902–63: James Callaghan *Time and Chance* (1987); coined by Denis Healey as speechwriter for Phillips at the Socialist International Conference, Copenhagen, 1953

30 Under democracy one party always devotes its energies to trying to prove that the other party is unfit to rule—and both commonly succeed and are right.
H. L. Mencken 1880–1956: *Minority Report* (1956)

31 I am a free man, an American, a United States Senator, and a Democrat, in that order.
Lyndon Baines Johnson 1908–73: in *Texas Quarterly* Winter 1958

32 Fascism is not in itself a new order of society. It is the future refusing to be born.
Aneurin Bevan 1897–1960: Leon Harris *The Fine Art of Political Wit* (1965)

33 There are some of us...who will fight and fight and fight again to save the Party we love.
Hugh Gaitskell 1906–63: speech at Labour Party Conference, 5 October 1960

34 As usual the Liberals offer a mixture of sound and original ideas. Unfortunately none of the sound ideas is original and none of the original ideas is sound.
Harold Macmillan 1894–1986: speech to London Conservatives, 7 March 1961

35 Loyalty is the Tory's secret weapon.
Lord Kilmuir 1900–67: Anthony Sampson *Anatomy of Britain* (1962)

36 This party is a moral crusade or it is nothing.
Harold Wilson 1916–95: speech at the Labour Party Conference, 1 October 1962

37 The modern conservative is... engaged...in one of man's oldest, best financed, most applauded, and, on the whole, least successful exercises in moral philosophy. That is the search for a superior moral justification for selfishness.
J. K. Galbraith 1908–2006: in *Harper's Magazine* March 1964

38 An independent is a guy who wants to take the politics out of politics.
Adlai Stevenson 1900–65: Bill Adler *The Stevenson Wit* (1966)

39 The liberals can understand everything but people who don't understand them.
Lenny Bruce 1925–66: John Cohen (ed.) *The Essential Lenny Bruce* (1967)

40 They are going about the country stirring up complacency.
commonly quoted as '…stirring up apathy'
William Whitelaw 1918–99: of the Labour Party in the October 1974 election campaign; in *Independent* 13 June 1999

41 This party is a bit like an old stage-coach. If you drive along at a rapid rate, everyone aboard is either so exhilarated or so seasick that you don't have a lot of difficulty.
of the Labour Party
Harold Wilson 1916–95: Anthony Sampson *The Changing Anatomy of Britain* (1982)

42 Socialism can only arrive by bicycle.
José Antonio Viera Gallo 1943– : Ivan Illich *Energy and Equity* (1974) epigraph

43 The longest suicide note in history.
on the Labour Party's election manifesto *New Hope for Britain* (1983)
Gerald Kaufman 1930– : Denis Healey *The Time of My Life* (1989)

44 I have only one firm belief about the American political system, and that is this: God is a Republican and Santa Claus is a Democrat.
P. J. O'Rourke 1947– : *Parliament of Whores* (1991)

45 International life is right-wing, like nature. The social contract is left-wing, like humanity.
Régis Debray 1940– : *Charles de Gaulle* (1994)

46 You know what some people call us: the nasty party.
Theresa May 1956– : speech to the Conservative Conference, 7 October 2002

Politicians

see also POLITICAL PARTIES, POLITICS, SPEECHES

proverbs and sayings ▸

1 Mummy, what's that man for?
remark by a small child to its mother; commonly cited as originally said of a late 19th/early 20th century politician; the earliest known instance is a cartoon in *Punch* in 1906 where it is applied to a man carrying a bag of golf clubs; see also POLITICIANS 14

2 A politician is an animal who can sit on a fence and yet keep both ears to the ground.
American proverb, mid 20th century

phrases ▸

3 the Grand Old Man
William Ewart Gladstone (1809–98); recorded from 1882, and popularly abbreviated as *GOM*; Gladstone won his last election in 1892 at the age of eighty-three

4 the Iron Lady
Margaret Thatcher (1925–); name given to Margaret Thatcher in 1976 by the Soviet newspaper *Red Star*, which accused her of trying to revive the cold war

5 the People's William
William Ewart Gladstone (1809–98), British Liberal statesman; coined by the newspaper proprietor Edward Levy-Lawson (1833–1916)

6 spend more time with one's family
now used (often ironically) in the context of a politician's ostensible reason for resigning office, paraphrasing Norman Fowler's resignation in 1990: see POLITICIANS 39

quotations ▸

7 You have all the characteristics of a popular politician: a horrible voice, bad breeding and a vulgar manner.
Aristophanes c.450–c.385 BC: *The Knights* (424 BC)

8 Politicians also have no leisure, because they are always aiming at something beyond political life itself, power and glory, or happiness.
Aristotle 384–322 BC: *Nicomachean Ethics*

9 This judgement I have of you that you will not be corrupted by any manner of gift and that you will be faithful to the state; and that without respect of my private will you will give me that counsel which you think best.
to William Cecil, appointing him her Secretary of State in 1558
Elizabeth I 1533–1603: Conyers Read *Mr Secretary Cecil and Queen Elizabeth* (1955)

10 He that goeth about to persuade a multitude, that they are not so well governed as they ought to be, shall

never want attentive and favourable hearers.

Richard Hooker 1554–1600: *Of the Laws of Ecclesiastical Polity* (1593)

11 Get thee glass eyes;
And, like a scurvy politician, seem
To see the things thou dost not.

William Shakespeare 1564–1616: *King Lear* (1605–6)

12 The greatest art of a politician is to render vice serviceable to the cause of virtue.

Henry St John, Lord Bolingbroke 1678–1751: comment (1728); Joseph Spence *Observations, Anecdotes, and Characters* (1820)

13 A minister who moves about in society is in a position to read the signs of the times even in a festive gathering, but one who remains shut up in his office learns nothing.

Duc de Choiseul 1719–85: Jack F. Bernard *Talleyrand* (1973)

14 What is that fat gentleman in such a passion about?

as a child, on hearing Charles James Fox speak in Parliament

Charles Shaw-Lefevre, Lord Eversley 1794–1888: G. W. E. Russell *Collections and Recollections* (1898); see also POLITICIANS 1

15 If a due participation of office is a matter of right, how are vacancies to be obtained? Those by death are few; by resignation none.

usually quoted as, 'Few die and none resign'

Thomas Jefferson 1743–1826: letter to E. Shipman and others, 12 July 1801

16 The seagreen Incorruptible.

of Robespierre

Thomas Carlyle 1795–1881: *History of the French Revolution* (1837)

17 What I want is men who will support me when I am in the wrong.

replying to a politician who said 'I will support you as long as you are in the right'

Lord Melbourne 1779–1848: Lord David Cecil *Lord M* (1954)

18 The greatest gift of any statesman rests not in knowing what concessions to make, but recognising when to make them.

Prince Metternich 1773–1859: *Concessionen und Nichtconcessionen* (1852)

19 With malice toward none; with charity for all; with firmness in the right, as God gives us to see the right, let us strive on to finish the work we are in.

Abraham Lincoln 1809–65: Second Inaugural Address, 4 March 1865

20 An honest politician is one who when he's bought stays bought.

Simon Cameron 1799–1889: attributed

21 He knows nothing; and he thinks he knows everything. That points clearly to a political career.

George Bernard Shaw 1856–1950: *Major Barbara* (1907)

22 'Do you pray for the senators, Dr Hale?' 'No, I look at the senators and I pray for the country.'

Edward Everett Hale 1822–1909: Van Wyck Brooks *New England Indian Summer* (1940)

23 He [Labouchere] did not object to the old man always having a card up his sleeve, but he did object to his insinuating that the Almighty had placed it there.

on Gladstone's 'frequent appeals to a higher power'

Henry Labouchere 1831–1912: Earl Curzon *Modern Parliamentary Eloquence* (1913); see SECRECY 18

24 We all know that Prime Ministers are wedded to the truth, but like other married couples they sometimes live apart.

Saki 1870–1916: *The Unbearable Bassington* (1912)

25 If you want to succeed in politics, you must keep your conscience well under control.

David Lloyd George 1863–1945: Lord Riddell, diary, 23 April 1919

26 I remember, when I was a child, being taken to the celebrated Barnum's circus, which contained an exhibition of freaks and monstrosities, but the exhibit on the programme which I most desired to see was the one described as 'The Boneless Wonder'. My parents judged that that spectacle would be too revolting and demoralizing for my youthful eyes, and I have waited 50 years to see

the boneless wonder sitting on the Treasury Bench.

of Ramsay MacDonald

Winston Churchill 1874–1965: speech in the House of Commons, 28 January 1931; see BODY 4

27 Forever poised between a cliché and an indiscretion.

on the life of a Foreign Secretary

Harold Macmillan 1894–1986: in *Newsweek* 30 April 1956

28 I am not going to spend any time whatsoever in attacking the Foreign Secretary...If we complain about the tune, there is no reason to attack the monkey when the organ grinder is present.

during a debate on the Suez crisis

Aneurin Bevan 1897–1960: speech, House of Commons, 16 May 1957; see POWER 17

29 A statesman is a politician who's been dead 10 or 15 years.

Harry S. Truman 1884–1972: in *New York World Telegram and Sun* 12 April 1958

30 Politicians are the same all over. They promise to build a bridge where there is no river.

Nikita Khrushchev 1894–1971: at a press conference in New York, October 1960

31 The ability to foretell what is going to happen tomorrow, next week, next month, and next year. And to have the ability afterwards to explain why it didn't happen.

describing the qualifications desirable in a prospective politician

Winston Churchill 1874–1965: B. Adler *Churchill Wit* (1965)

32 I think a Prime Minister has to be a butcher and know the joints. That is perhaps where I have not been quite competent, in knowing all the ways that you can cut up a carcass.

R. A. Butler 1902–82: in *Listener* 28 June 1966

33 In politics, if you want anything said, ask a man. If you want anything done, ask a woman.

Margaret Thatcher 1925– : in 1970; in *People* (New York) 15 September 1975

34 If you want a friend in Washington, get a dog.

Harry S. Truman 1884–1972: attributed; popularized by the Reagan administration, *c.* 1988

35 A statesman is a politician who places himself at the service of the nation. A politician is a statesman who places the nation at his service.

Georges Pompidou 1911–74: in *Observer* 30 December 1973

36 All political lives, unless they are cut off in midstream at a happy juncture, end in failure, because that is the nature of politics and of human affairs.

Enoch Powell 1912–98: *Joseph Chamberlain* (1977)

37 It is not necessary that every time he rises he should give his famous imitation of a semi-house-trained polecat.

of Norman Tebbit

Michael Foot 1913–2010: speech, House of Commons, 2 March 1978

38 In politics you must always keep running with the pack. The moment that you falter and they sense that you are injured, the rest will turn on you like wolves.

R. A. Butler 1902–82: Dennis Walters *Not Always with the Pack* (1989)

39 I have a young family and for the next few years I should like to devote more time to them.

Margaret Thatcher replied that she understood 'your wish to be able to spend more time with your family': see POLITICIANS 6

Norman Fowler 1938– : resignation letter to the Prime Minister, in *Guardian* 4 January 1990

40 There are no true friends in politics. We are all sharks circling, and waiting, for traces of blood to appear in the water.

Alan Clark 1928–99: diary 30 November 1990

41 Three groups spend other people's money: children, thieves, politicians. All three need parental supervision.

Dick Armey 1940– : *The Freedom Revolution* (1995)

Politics

see also DEMOCRACY, ELECTIONS, GOVERNMENT, INTERNATIONAL, PARLIAMENT, POLITICAL PARTIES, POLITICIANS, PRESIDENCY

proverbs and sayings ►

1 **In politics a man must learn to rise above principle.**
American proverb, mid 20th century

2 **It'll play in Peoria.**
catchphrase of the Nixon administration (early 1970s) meaning 'it will be acceptable to middle America', but originating in a standard music hall joke of the 1930s

3 **The personal is political.**
1970s feminist slogan, coined by Carol Hanisch (1945–)

4 **Politics makes strange bedfellows.**
political alliances in a common cause may bring together those of widely differing views; English proverb, mid 19th century

phrases ►

5 **midnight appointment**
in US politics, an appointment made during the last hours of an administration; originally with particular reference to those made by the 2nd President John Adams (1735–1826)

6 **October surprise**
in the US, an unexpected but popular political act or speech made just prior to a November election in an attempt to win votes; used especially with reference to an alleged conspiracy in which members of the 1980 Republican campaign team are said to have made an arms deal with Iran to delay the release of US hostages in Iran until after the election

7 **a smoke-filled room**
regarded as the characteristic venue of those in control of a party meeting to arrange a political decision; from Kirke Simpson news report, filed 12 June 1920, '[Warren] Harding of Ohio was chosen by a group of men in a smoke-filled room early today as Republican candidate for President'; usually attributed to Harry Daugherty, one of Harding's supporters, who appears merely to have concurred with this version of events, when pressed for comment by Simpson.

8 **the third way**
in politics, a middle way between conventional right- and left-wing ideologies or policies; an ideology founded on political centrism or neutrality. In the 1990s the *third way* became identified with the political programmes of centre-left parties in Western Europe and North America, characterized by both market-driven economic policy and a concern for social justice

9 **the two nations**
the rich and poor members of a society seen as effectively divided into separate nations by the presence or absence of wealth; from Disraeli: see WEALTH 26

quotations ►

10 **Man is by nature a political animal.**
Aristotle 384–322 BC: *Politics*

11 **Most schemes of political improvement are very laughable things.**
Samuel Johnson 1709–84: James Boswell *Life of Samuel Johnson* (1791) 26 October 1769

12 **Magnanimity in politics is not seldom the truest wisdom; and a great empire and little minds go ill together.**
Edmund Burke 1729–97: *On Conciliation with America* (1775)

13 **I agree with you that in politics the middle way is none at all.**
John Adams 1735–1826: letter to Horatio Gates, 23 March 1776

14 **What is the first part of politics? Education. The second? Education. And the third? Education.**
Jules Michelet 1798–1874: *Le Peuple* (1846); see EDUCATION 35

15 **Finality is not the language of politics.**
Benjamin Disraeli 1804–81: speech, House of Commons, 28 February 1859

16 **Politics is the art of the possible.**
Otto von Bismarck 1815–98: in conversation with Meyer von Waldeck, 11 August 1867; see POLITICS 27, SCIENCE 27

17 **In politics, there is no use looking beyond the next fortnight.**
Joseph Chamberlain 1836–1914: letter from A. J. Balfour to 3rd Marquess of Salisbury, 24 March 1886; see POLITICS 28

18 A statesman...must wait until he hears the steps of God sounding through events; then leap up and grasp the hem of his garment.

Otto von Bismarck 1815–98: A. J. P. Taylor *Bismarck* (1955)

19 Politics is war without bloodshed while war is politics with bloodshed.

Mao Zedong 1893–1976: lecture, 1938; *Selected Works* (1965)

20 The trouble with this country is that there are too many politicians who believe, with a conviction based on experience, that you can fool all of the people all of the time.

Franklin P. Adams 1881–1960: *Nods and Becks* (1944); see DECEPTION 21

21 Politics is the art of looking for trouble, finding it everywhere, diagnosing it wrongly and applying unsuitable remedies.

Ernest Benn 1875–1954: attributed, Powell Spring *What Is Truth* (1944); often later associated with the American film comedian Groucho Marx (1890–1977)

22 All reactionaries are paper tigers. In appearance, the reactionaries are terrifying, but in reality they are not so powerful. From a long-term point of view, it is not the reactionaries but the people who are really powerful.

Mao Zedong 1893–1976: interview with Anne Louise Strong, August 1946; *Selected Works* (1961)

23 We have a great objective—the light on the hill—which we aim to reach by working for the betterment of mankind not only here but anywhere we may give a helping hand.

Joseph Benedict 'Ben' Chifley 1885–1951: speech to the Annual Conference of the New South Wales branch of the Australian Labor Party, 12 June 1949

24 Political language...is designed to make lies sound truthful and murder respectable, and to give an appearance of solidity to pure wind.

George Orwell 1903–50: *Shooting an Elephant* (1950) 'Politics and the English Language'

25 Men enter local politics solely as a result of being unhappily married.

C. Northcote Parkinson 1909–93: *Parkinson's Law* (1958)

26 Politics are too serious a matter to be left to the politicians.

responding to Attlee's remark that 'De Gaulle is a very good soldier and a very bad politician'

Charles de Gaulle 1890–1970: Clement Attlee *A Prime Minister Remembers* (1961); see WARFARE 45

27 Politics is not the art of the possible. It consists in choosing between the disastrous and the unpalatable.

J. K. Galbraith 1908–2006: letter to President Kennedy, 2 March 1962; see POLITICS 16

28 A week is a long time in politics.

probably first said at the time of the 1964 sterling crisis

Harold Wilson 1916–95: Nigel Rees *Sayings of the Century* (1984); see POLITICS 17

29 Politics is supposed to be the second oldest profession. I have come to realize that it bears a very close resemblance to the first.

Ronald Reagan 1911–2004: at a conference in Los Angeles, 2 March 1977; see EMPLOYMENT 5

30 Never doubt that a small group of thoughtful committed citizens can change the world. In fact, it's the only thing that ever has.

Margaret Mead 1901–78: attributed; Mary Bowman-Kruhm *Margaret Mead: a biography* (2003)

31 The opposition of events.

on his biggest problem; popularly quoted as, 'Events, dear boy. Events'

Harold Macmillan 1894–1986: David Dilks *The Office of Prime Minister in Twentieth Century Britain* (1993)

32 Politics is a marathon, not a sprint.

Ken Livingstone 1945– : in *New Statesman* 10 October 1997

33 The Big Society is our big idea.

David Cameron 1966– : speech to voters, Swindon 18 April 2010; the Big Society formed part of the Conservative Party manifesto launched on 13 April 2010; see SOCIETY 3

Pollution and the Environment

see also EARTH, NATURE

proverbs and sayings ▸

1 Kills all known germs.
advertising slogan for Domestos bleach, 1959

2 Save the whale.
environmental slogan associated with the alarm over the rapidly declining whale population which led in 1985 to a moratorium on commercial whaling; see also LANGUAGE 28

3 Think globally, act locally.
modern saying, mid 20th century, associated with Friends of the Earth from 1985

4 When the last tree is cut, the last river poisoned, and the last fish dead, we will discover that we can't eat money.
Canadian saying, sometimes said to be of native American origin

quotations ▸

5 Woe to her that is filthy and polluted, to the oppressing city!
Bible: Zephaniah

6 Woe unto them that join house to house, that lay field to field, till there be no place.
Bible: Isaiah

7 This most excellent canopy, the air, look you, this brave o'erhanging firmament, this majestical roof fretted with golden fire, why, it appears no other thing to me but a foul and pestilent congregation of vapours.
William Shakespeare 1564–1616: *Hamlet* (1601)

8 O all ye Green Things upon the Earth, bless ye the Lord: praise him, and magnify him for ever.
The Book of Common Prayer 1662: Benedicite

9 The parks are the lungs of London.
William Pitt, Earl of Chatham 1708–78: speech by William Windham, House of Commons, 30 June 1808

10 And did the Countenance Divine
Shine forth upon our clouded hills?
And was Jerusalem builded here
Among these dark Satanic mills?
William Blake 1757–1827: *Milton* (1804–10) 'And did those feet in ancient time'

11 The river Rhine, it is well known,
Doth wash your city of Cologne;
But tell me, Nymphs, what power divine
Shall henceforth wash the river Rhine?
Samuel Taylor Coleridge 1772–1834: 'Cologne' (1834)

12 In wildness is the preservation of the world.
Henry David Thoreau 1817–62: *Walking* (1862)

13 What would the world be, once bereft
Of wet and wildness? Let them be left,
O let them be left, wildness and wet;
Long live the weeds and the wilderness yet.
Gerard Manley Hopkins 1844–89: 'Inversnaid' (written 1881)

14 Dirt is only matter out of place.
John Chipman Gray 1839–1915: *Restraints on the Alienation of Property* (2nd ed., 1895)

15 Man has been endowed with reason, with the power to create, so that he can add to what he's been given. But up to now he hasn't been a creator, only a destroyer. Forests keep disappearing, rivers dry up, wild life's become extinct, the climate's ruined and the land grows poorer and uglier every day.
Anton Chekhov 1860–1904: *Uncle Vanya* (1897)

16 The sanitary and mechanical age we are now entering makes up for the mercy it grants to our sense of smell by the ferocity with which it assails our sense of hearing. As usual, what we call 'progress' is the exchange of one nuisance for another nuisance.
Havelock Ellis 1859–1939: *Impressions and Comments* (1914)

17 I think that I shall never see
A billboard lovely as a tree.
Perhaps, unless the billboards fall,
I'll never see a tree at all.
Ogden Nash 1902–71: 'Song of the Open Road' (1933); see TREES 17

18 Clear the air! clean the sky! wash the wind!
T. S. Eliot 1888–1965: *Murder in the Cathedral* (1935)

19 Come, friendly bombs, and fall on Slough!
It isn't fit for humans now,
There isn't grass to graze a cow.
Swarm over, Death!
John Betjeman 1906–84: 'Slough' (1937)

20 Over increasingly large areas of the United States, spring now comes unheralded by the return of the birds, and the early mornings are strangely silent where once they were filled with the beauty of bird song.
Rachel Carson 1907–64: *The Silent Spring* (1962)

21 Make it a *green* peace.
Bill Darnell: at a meeting of the Don't Make a Wave Committee, which preceded the formation of Greenpeace, in Vancouver, 1970; Robert Hunter *The Greenpeace Chronicle* (1979)

22 We have met the enemy and he is us.
the cartoon-strip character, Pogo the opossum, looking at litter under a tree; used as an Earth Day poster in 1971
Walt Kelly 1913–73: *Pogo* cartoon, 1970; see WINNING 15

23 The sea is the universal sewer.
Jacques Cousteau 1910–97: testimony before the House Committee on Science and Astronautics, 28 January 1971

24 It is not what they built. It is what they knocked down.
It is not the houses. It is the spaces between the houses.
It is not the streets that exist. It is the streets that no longer exist.
James Fenton 1949– : *German Requiem* (1981)

25 If I were a Brazilian without land or money or the means to feed my children, I would be burning the rain forest too.
Sting 1951– : in *International Herald Tribune* 14 April 1989

26 In my view, climate change is the most severe problem we are facing today—more serious even than the threat of terrorism.
David King 1939– : in *Science* 9 January 2004

27 Climate change is the greatest market failure the world has ever seen.
Nicholas Stern 1946– : *The Stern Review* (2006) Executive Summary

Possessions

proverbs and sayings ▸

1 **Finders keepers (losers weepers).**
English proverb, early 19th century

2 **Findings keepings.**
English proverb, mid 19th century

3 **If you have nothing, you have nothing to lose.**
modern saying, claimed to be an Arabic proverb

4 **Keep a thing seven years and you'll always find a use for it.**
recommending caution and thrift; English proverb, early 17th century

5 **Light come, light go.**
something gained without effort can be lost without much regret; English proverb, late 14th century

6 **What you have, hold.**
with reference to an uncompromising position based on a refusal to make any concessions; English proverb, mid 15th century

7 **What you spend, you have.**
the only real possessions one has are those of which one can dispose; English proverb, early 14th century

8 **You cannot lose what you never had.**
used in consolation or resignation; English proverb, late 16th century

phrases ▸

9 dead men's shoes
a property or position coveted by a prospective successor but available only on a person's death; from the proverb: see AMBITION 3

10 ewe lamb
a person's most cherished possession; from the Bible: see POSSESSIONS 13

11 goods and chattels
all kinds of personal property; a *chattel* is a movable possession

quotations ▸

12 The sage does not accumulate for himself.
The more he uses for others, the more he has himself.
The more he gives to others, the more he possesses of his own.
Lao Tzu c.604–c.531 BC: *Tao-te Ching*

13 The poor man had nothing, save one little ewe lamb.
Bible: II Samuel; see POSSESSIONS 10

14 How many things I can do without!
on looking at a multitude of wares exposed for sale
Socrates 469–399 BC: Diogenes Laertius *Lives of the Philosophers*

15 For we brought nothing into this world, and it is certain we can carry nothing out.
Bible: I Timothy

16 He is a wise man who does not grieve for the things which he has not, but rejoices for those which he has.
Epictetus C.AD 50–120: *The Enchiridion*

17 All my possessions for a moment of time.
Elizabeth I 1533–1603: attributed last words, but almost certainly apocryphal

18 There are only two families in the world, as a grandmother of mine used to say: the haves and the have-nots.
Cervantes 1547–1616: *Don Quixote* (1605)

19 Well! some people talk of morality, and some of religion, but give me a little snug property.
Maria Edgeworth 1767–1849: *The Absentee* (1812)

20 Property has its duties as well as its rights.
Thomas Drummond 1797–1840: letter to the Earl of Donoughmore, 22 May 1838

21 Property is theft.
Pierre-Joseph Proudhon 1809–65: *Qu'est-ce que la propriété?* (1840)

22 Things are in the saddle,
And ride mankind.
Ralph Waldo Emerson 1803–82: 'Ode' Inscribed to W. H. Channing (1847)

23 My riches consist, not in the extent of my possessions, but in the fewness of my wants.
responding to a slighting reference to the fortune that he had amassed in manufacturing
Joseph Brotherton 1783–1857: Joseph Johnson *Clever Boys of Our Time* (1860)

24 Have nothing in your houses that you do not know to be useful, or believe to be beautiful.
William Morris 1834–96: *Hopes and Fears for Art* (1882) 'Making the Best of It'

25 Possessions are generally diminished by possession.
Friedrich Nietzsche 1844–1900: *The Gay Science* (1882)

26 Conspicuous consumption of valuable goods is a means of reputability to the gentleman of leisure.
Thorstein Veblen 1857–1929: *Theory of the Leisure Class* (1899)

27 The moon belongs to everyone,
The best things in life are free.
Buddy De Sylva 1895–1950 and **Lew Brown** 1893–1958: 'The Best Things in Life are Free' (1927 song); see MONEY 2

28 If men are to respect each other for what they are, they must cease to respect each other for what they own.
R. H. Tawney 1880–1962: *Equality* (1931)

29 People don't resent having nothing nearly as much as too little.
Ivy Compton-Burnett 1884–1969: *A Family and a Fortune* (1939)

30 Man must choose whether to be rich in things or in the freedom to use them.
Ivan Illich 1926–2002: *Deschooling Society* (1971)

31 People who get through life dependent on other people's possessions are always the first to lecture you on how little possessions count.
Ben Elton 1959– : *Stark* (1989)

Poverty

see also MONEY, WEALTH

proverbs and sayings ►

1 Both poverty and prosperity come from spending money—prosperity from spending it wisely.
American proverb, mid 20th century

2 Empty sacks will never stand upright.
those in an extremity of need cannot survive; English proverb, mid 17th century

3 Make poverty history.
slogan of a campaign launched in 2005 by a coalition of charities and other groups to pressure governments to take action to reduce poverty

4 A moneyless man goes fast through the market.
someone without resources is unable to pause to buy anything (or, in a modern variant, rushes to wherever what they lack may be found); English proverb, early 18th century

5 Poverty comes from God, but not dirt.
American proverb, mid 20th century

6 Poverty is no disgrace, but it's a great inconvenience.
English proverb, late 16th century

7 Poverty is not a crime.
English proverb, late 16th century

8 When poverty comes in at the door, love flies out of the window.
the strains of living in poverty often destroy a loving relationship; English proverb, mid 17th century

phrases ▸

9 on one's beam-ends
at the end of one's financial resources; *beam-ends* are the ends of a ship's beams, and a ship *on her beam-ends* is one on its side, almost capsizing

10 on the breadline
in the poorest conditions in which it is possible to live; the *breadline* in North American usage was a queue of people waiting to receive free food

11 poor as Job
very poor; in the Bible (Job), the formerly wealthy figure of Job, deprived of his possessions, becomes a type of abject poverty

12 the submerged tenth
the supposed fraction of the population permanently living in poverty; from William Booth (1829–1912) *In Darkest England* (1890) 'This Submerged Tenth—is it, then, beyond the reach of the nine-tenths in the midst of whom they live?'

quotations ▸

13 What mean ye that ye beat my people to pieces, and grind the faces of the poor?
Bible: Isaiah

14 The poor always ye have with you.
Bible: St John

15 The misfortunes of poverty carry with them nothing harder to bear than that it makes men ridiculous.
Juvenal C. AD 60–C. 140: *Satires*

16 I can get no remedy against this consumption of the purse: borrowing only lingers and lingers it out, but the disease is incurable.
William Shakespeare 1564–1616: *Henry IV, Part 2* (1597)

17 I want there to be no peasant in my kingdom so poor that he is unable to have a chicken in his pot every Sunday.
Henri IV (of France) 1553–1610: Hardouin de Péréfixe *Histoire de Henry le Grand* (1681); see PROGRESS 15

18 Come away; poverty's catching.
Aphra Behn 1640–89: *The Rover* pt. 2 (1681)

19 Give me not poverty lest I steal.
Daniel Defoe 1660–1731: in *Review* 15 September 1711; later incorporated into *Moll Flanders* (1721)

20 Laws grind the poor, and rich men
rule the law.
Oliver Goldsmith 1728–74: *The Traveller* (1764)

21 Resolve not to be poor: whatever you have, spend less. Poverty is a great enemy to human happiness; it certainly destroys liberty, and it makes some virtues impracticable, and others extremely difficult.
Samuel Johnson 1709–84: letter to Boswell, 7 December 1782

22 Oh! God! that bread should be so
dear,
And flesh and blood so cheap!
Thomas Hood 1799–1845: 'The Song of the Shirt' (1843)

23 Like dear St Francis of Assisi I am wedded to Poverty: but in my case the marriage is not a success.
Oscar Wilde 1854–1900: letter June 1899

24 The greatest of evils and the worst of crimes is poverty.
George Bernard Shaw 1856–1950: *Major Barbara* (1907)

25 There's nothing surer,
The rich get rich and the poor get
children.
Gus Kahn 1886–1941 and **Raymond B. Egan** 1890–1952: 'Ain't We Got Fun' (1921 song)

26 Brother can you spare a dime?
E. Y. Harburg 1898–1981: title of song (1932)

27 How can you frighten a man whose hunger is not only in his own cramped stomach but in the wretched bellies of his children? You can't scare him—he has known a fear beyond every other.
John Steinbeck 1902–68: *The Grapes of Wrath* (1939)

28 The poor have the sufferings to which
they are fairly accustomed.
W. H. Auden 1907–73: 'In Memory of W. B. Yeats' (1940)

29 A hungry man is not a free man.
Adlai Stevenson 1900–65: speech at Kasson, Minnesota, 6 September 1952

30 Anyone who has ever struggled with poverty knows how extremely expensive it is to be poor.
James Baldwin 1924–87: *Nobody Knows My Name* (1961) 'Fifth Avenue, Uptown: a letter from Harlem'

31 Born down in a dead man's town
The first kick I took was when I hit the ground.
Bruce Springsteen 1949– : 'Born in the USA' (1984 song)

32 When I give food to the poor they call me a saint. When I ask why the poor have no food they call me a communist.
Helder Camara 1909–99: attributed

33 Poverty is a lot like childbirth—you know it is going to hurt before it happens, but you'll never know how much until you experience it.
J. K. Rowling 1965– : in *Mail on Sunday* 16 June 2002

34 The biggest deception of the past thousand years is this: to confuse poverty with stupidity.
Orhan Pamuk 1952– : *Snow* (2004)

35 Overcoming poverty is not a gesture of charity. It is an act of justice.
Nelson Mandela 1918– : speech in Trafalgar Square, London, 3 February 2005

Power

proverbs and sayings ▸

1 Better be the head of a dog than the tail of a lion.
it is preferable to be at the head of a small organization than in a lowly position in a large one; English proverb, late 16th century

2 Big fish eat little fish.
the rich and powerful are likely to prey on those who are less strong, and often used with the implication that each predator is in turn victim to a stronger one; English proverb, early 13th century

3 He who pays the piper calls the tune.
the person financially responsible for something can control what is done; English proverb, late 19th century; see POWER 18

4 Kings have long arms.
a king's power reaches a long way; English proverb, mid 16th century

5 Might is right.
English proverb, early 14th century

6 A mouse may help a lion.
alluding to Aesop's fable of the lion and the rat, in which a rat saved a lion which had become trapped in a net by gnawing through the cords which bound it; English proverb, mid 16th century

7 No fist is big enough to hide the sky.
there are limits to the powers of even the most repressive regime; African saying

8 Power corrupts.
English proverb, late 19th century; see POWER 33

9 Set a beggar on horseback, and he'll ride to the Devil.
a person unused to power will make unwise use of it; English proverb, late 16th century

10 They that dance must pay the fiddler.
you must be prepared to make recompense for the provision of an essential service; English proverb, mid 17th century

11 We have ways of making you talk.
supposedly the characteristic threat of an inquisitor in a 1930s film, but not traced in this form; 'We have ways of making men talk' occurs in *Lives of a Bengal Lancer* (1935)

12 **When elephants fight, it is the grass that gets hurt.**
the weak are likely to suffer as a result of the conflicts of the strong and powerful; African proverb (Swahili)

13 **You have the watches, but we have the time.**
early twenty-first century saying, said to be an Afghan saying addressed to ISAF/NATO forces

phrases ▸

14 **Big Brother**
a person or organization exercising total control over people's lives; from the name of the head of state in George Orwell's *Nineteen Eighty-Four* (1949); see GOVERNMENT 37

15 **éminence grise**
a person who exercises power or influence in a certain sphere without holding an official position; the term was originally applied to Cardinal Richelieu's grey-cloaked private secretary, Père Joseph (1577–1638)

16 **on the hip**
at a disadvantage (sometimes with allusion to Shakespeare's *Merchant of Venice*, 'Now, infidel, I have you on the hip')

17 **organ-grinder**
a person who is more important or powerful than another (usually contrasted with *monkey*). The allusion is to an itinerant street musician who played a barrel organ which was turned by hand, and who often had a pet monkey; see POLITICIANS 28

18 **pay the piper (and call the tune)**
pay the cost of (and so have the right to control) an activity or undertaking; from the proverb: see POWER 3

19 **the powers that be**
the authorities concerned, the people exercising political or social control; from the Bible (Romans), 'For there is no power but of God: the powers that be are ordained of God'

20 **speak truth to power**
challenge those who have a responsibility to act with the realities of a situation; the phrase was used in 1955 as the title of a document issued by the American Friends Service Committee, which claimed to derive the phrase from a charge given to Eighteenth Century Friends

quotations ▸

21 On the highest throne in the world, we still sit only on our bottom.
Montaigne 1533–92: *Essays* (1580)

22 Man, proud man,
Drest in a little brief authority.
William Shakespeare 1564–1616: *Measure for Measure* (1604)

23 All rising to great place is by a winding stair.
Francis Bacon 1561–1626: *Essays* (1625) 'Of Great Place'

24 Nature has left this tincture in the blood,
That all men would be tyrants if they could.
Daniel Defoe 1660–1731: *The History of the Kentish Petition* (1712–13)

25 Those who have been once intoxicated with power, and have derived any kind of emolument from it, even though for but one year, can never willingly abandon it.
Edmund Burke 1729–97: *Letter to a Member of the National Assembly* (1791)

26 I shall be an autocrat: that's my trade.
And the good Lord will forgive me: that's his.
Catherine the Great 1729–96: attributed; see FORGIVENESS 22

27 The good old rule
Sufficeth them, the simple plan,
That they should take who have the power,
And they should keep who can.
William Wordsworth 1770–1850: 'Rob Roy's Grave' (1807)

28 The fundamental article of my political creed is that despotism, or unlimited sovereignty, or absolute power, is the same in a majority of a popular assembly, an aristocratic council, an oligarchical junto, and a single emperor.
John Adams 1735–1826: letter to Thomas Jefferson, 13 November 1815

29 The tyrant grinds down his slaves and they don't turn against him, they crush those beneath them.
Emily Brontë 1818–48: *Wuthering Heights* (1847)

30 Power concedes nothing without a demand. It never did, and it never will.
Frederick Douglass 1818–95: letter to Gerrit Smith, 30 March 1849

31 I claim not to have controlled events, but confess plainly that events have controlled me.
Abraham Lincoln 1809–65: letter to A. G. Hodges, 4 April 1864

32 'The question is,' said Humpty Dumpty, 'which is to be master—that's all.'
Lewis Carroll 1832–98: *Through the Looking-Glass* (1872)

33 Power tends to corrupt and absolute power corrupts absolutely.
Lord Acton 1834–1902: letter to Bishop Mandell Creighton, 3 April 1887; see FEAR 27, POWER 8, POWER 38

34 Whatever happens we have got
The Maxim Gun, and they have not.
Hilaire Belloc 1870–1953: *The Modern Traveller* (1898)

35 Every Communist must grasp the truth, 'Political power grows out of the barrel of a gun.'
Mao Zedong 1893–1976: speech, 6 November 1938

36 The hate of men will pass, and dictators die, and the power they took from the people will return to the people.
Charlie Chaplin 1889–1977: *The Great Dictator* (1940 film)

37 Who controls the past controls the future: who controls the present controls the past.
George Orwell 1903–50: *Nineteen Eighty-Four* (1949)

38 Power does not corrupt. Fear corrupts, perhaps fear of a loss of power.
John Steinbeck 1902–68: *The Short Reign of Pippin IV* (1957); see FEAR 27, POWER 33

39 What is needed is a realization that power without love is reckless and abusive, and love without power is sentimental and anaemic. Power at its best is love implementing the demands of justice, and justice at its best is power correcting everything that stands against love.
Martin Luther King 1929–68: *Where Do We Go From Here?* (1967)

40 You only have power over people as long as you don't take *everything* away from them. But when you've robbed a man of *everything* he's no longer in your power — he's free again.
Alexander Solzhenitsyn 1918–2008: *The First Circle* (1968)

41 Power is the great aphrodisiac.
Henry Kissinger 1923– : in *New York Times* 19 January 1971

42 Power? It's like a Dead Sea fruit. When you achieve it, there is nothing there.
Harold Macmillan 1894–1986: Anthony Sampson *The New Anatomy of Britain* (1971); see DISILLUSION 2

43 When you make your peace with authority, you become an authority.
Jim Morrison 1943–71: Andrew Doe and John Tobler *In Their Own Words: The Doors* (1988)

44 The struggle of man against power is the struggle of memory against forgetting.
Milan Kundera 1929– : *The Book of Laughter and Forgetting* (1979)

45 Every dictator uses religion as a prop to keep himself in power.
Benazir Bhutto 1953–2007: interview on *60 Minutes*, CBS-TV, 8 August 1986

Practicality

proverbs and sayings ►

1 Cut your coat according to your cloth.
actions taken should suit one's circumstances or resources; English proverb, mid 16th century

2 He who wants a rose must respect the thorn.
someone wanting a desirable object needs to be aware of the dangers it brings with it; Persian proverb; see CIRCUMSTANCE 4, SATISFACTION 4

3 Put your trust in God, and keep your powder dry.
often attributed to Oliver Cromwell (1599–1658); English proverb, mid 19th century; see CAUTION 28

4 You cannot make an omelette without breaking eggs.
often used in the context of a regrettable political necessity which is said to be justified because it will benefit the majority; English proverb, mid 19th century

quotations ▸

5 This man hath the right sow by the ear.

of Thomas Cranmer, June 1529

Henry VIII 1491–1547: *Acts and Monuments of John Foxe* ['Fox's Book of Martyrs'], 1570; see KNOWLEDGE 10

6 A dead woman bites not.

pressing for the execution of Mary Queen of Scots in 1587

Patrick, Lord Gray d. 1612: oral tradition; William Camden *Annals of the Reign of Queen Elizabeth* (1615); see ENEMIES 1

7 My lord, we make use of you, not for your bad legs, but for your good head.

to William Cecil, who suffered from gout

Elizabeth I 1533–1603: F. Chamberlin *Sayings of Queen Elizabeth* (1923)

8 Common sense is the best distributed commodity in the world, for every man is convinced that he is well supplied with it.

René Descartes 1596–1650: *Le Discours de la méthode* (1637)

9 And he gave it for his opinion, that whoever could make two ears of corn or two blades of grass to grow upon a spot of ground where only one grew before, would deserve better of mankind, and do more essential service to his country than the whole race of politicians put together.

Jonathan Swift 1667–1745: *Gulliver's Travels* (1726) 'A Voyage to Brobdingnag'

10 'Tis use alone that sanctifies expense,
And splendour borrows all her rays
from sense.

Alexander Pope 1688–1744: *Epistles to Several Persons* 'To Lord Burlington' (1731)

11 Common sense is not so common.

Voltaire 1694–1778: *Dictionnaire philosophique* (1765) 'Sens Commun'

12 Whenever our neighbour's house is on fire, it cannot be amiss for the engines to play a little on our own.

Edmund Burke 1729–97: *Reflections on the Revolution in France* (1790)

13 It's grand, and you canna expect to be baith grand and comfortable.

J. M. Barrie 1860–1937: *The Little Minister* (1891)

14 Praise the Lord and pass the ammunition.

moving along a line of sailors passing ammunition by hand to the deck

Howell Forgy 1908–83: at Pearl Harbor, 7 December 1941; later the title of a song by Frank Loesser, 1942

15 Common sense is nothing more than a deposit of prejudices laid down in the mind before you reach eighteen.

Albert Einstein 1879–1955: Lincoln Barnett *The Universe and Dr Einstein* (1950 ed.)

16 Life is too short to stuff a mushroom.

Shirley Conran 1932– : *Superwoman* (1975)

Praise and Flattery

proverbs and sayings ▸

1 Flattery is soft soap, and soft soap is ninety percent lye.

lye = a strongly alkaline solution, especially of potassium hydroxide, used for washing or cleansing; American proverb, mid 19th century

2 Flattery, like perfume, should be smelled, not swallowed.

American proverb, mid 19th century; see PRAISE 17

3 Give credit where credit is due.

English proverb, late 18th century

4 Imitation is the sincerest form of flattery.

English proverb, early 19th century, from Charles Caleb Colton (1780–1832) *Lacon* (1820)

5 Praise from Sir Hubert is praise indeed.

popular saying, from Thomas Morton: see PRAISE 14

phrases ▸

6 damn with faint praise

commend so feebly as to imply disapproval; from Pope: see PRAISE 12

7 turn geese into swans

exaggerate the merits of people; see SELF-ESTEEM 18

quotations ▸

8 But when I tell him he hates flatterers,
He says he does, being then most
flattered.

William Shakespeare 1564–1616: *Julius Caesar* (1599)

9 It has been well said that 'the arch-flatterer with whom all the petty flatterers have intelligence is a man's self.'
Francis Bacon 1561–1626: *Essays* (1625) 'Of Love'

10 Of whom to be dispraised were no small praise.
John Milton 1608–74: *Paradise Regained* (1671)

11 He who discommendeth others obliquely commendeth himself.
Thomas Browne 1605–82: *Christian Morals* (1716)

12 Damn with faint praise, assent with civil leer,
And without sneering, teach the rest to sneer.
Alexander Pope 1688–1744: 'An Epistle to Dr Arbuthnot' (1735); see PRAISE 6

13 Madam, before you flatter a man so grossly to his face, you should consider whether or not your flattery is worth his having.
Samuel Johnson 1709–84: Fanny Burney's diary, August 1778

14 Approbation from Sir Hubert Stanley is praise indeed.
Thomas Morton c.1764–1838: *A Cure for the Heartache* (1797); see PRAISE 5

15 And even the ranks of Tuscany
Could scarce forbear to cheer.
Lord Macaulay 1800–59: *Lays of Ancient Rome* (1842) 'Horatius'

16 The advantage of doing one's praising for oneself is that one can lay it on so thick and exactly in the right places.
Samuel Butler 1835–1902: *The Way of All Flesh* (1903)

17 I suppose flattery hurts no one, that is, if he doesn't inhale.
Adlai Stevenson 1900–65: television broadcast, 30 March 1952; see PRAISE 2

18 The flattery of posterity is not worth much more than contemporary flattery, which is worth nothing.
Jorge Luis Borges 1899–1986: *Dreamtigers* (1964)

Prayer

proverbs and sayings ▸

1 The family that prays together stays together.
motto devised by Al Scalpone for the Roman Catholic Family Rosary Crusade, 1947

2 Laborare est orare.
Latin, *To work is to pray*, a traditional motto of the Benedictine order, also found in the form '*Ora, lege, et labora* [Pray, read, and work]'

3 Om mani padme hum.
used as a mantra or auspicious formula in prayer and meditation in Tibetan Buddhism; Sanskrit, commonly translated as 'Praise to the jewel in the lotus, hail'

phrases ▸

4 the Lord's Prayer
the prayer taught by Christ to his disciples, beginning 'Our Father'; the term is a translation of Latin *oratio Dominica*, and is first recorded in the Book of Common Prayer of 1549

5 sacrifice of praise (and thanksgiving)
an offering of praise to God; with reference to the Bible (Leviticus) 'He shall offer with the sacrifice of thanksgiving unleavened cakes mingled with oil'

6 tell one's beads
say one's prayers; the *beads* of a rosary or paternoster, used for keeping count of the prayers said

quotations ▸

7 O gods, grant me this in return for my piety.
Catullus c.84–c.54 BC: *Carmina*

8 Ask, and it shall be given you; seek, and ye shall find; knock, and it shall be opened unto you.
Bible: St Matthew; see ACTION 12

9 A man's prayer is only answered if he takes his heart into his hand.
The Talmud: *Babylonian Talmud* Taanit

10 Christ beside me,
Christ before me,
Christ behind me,
Christ within me,
Christ beneath me,
Christ above me.
St Patrick fl. 5th cent.: 'St Patrick's Breastplate'

11 Perform the prayer
at the sinking of the sun to the
darkening of the night
and the recital of dawn.
The Koran: sura 17

12 God be in my head,
And in my understanding.
Anonymous: *Sarum Missal* (11th century)

13 Prayer in my opinion is nothing else than an intimate sharing between friends.
St Teresa of Ávila 1512–82: *Life of the Mother Teresa of Jesus* (1611)

14 My words fly up, my thoughts remain below:
Words without thoughts never to heaven go.
William Shakespeare 1564–1616: *Hamlet* (1601)

15 I throw myself down in my Chamber, and I call in, and invite God, and his Angels thither, and when they are there, I neglect God and his Angels, for the noise of a fly, for the rattling of a coach, for the whining of a door.
John Donne 1572–1631: *LXXX Sermons* (1640) 12 December 1626 'At the Funeral of Sir William Cokayne'

16 O Lord! thou knowest how busy I must be this day: if I forget thee, do not thou forget me.
prayer before the Battle of Edgehill, 1642
Jacob Astley 1579–1652: Sir Philip Warwick *Memoires* (1701)

17 At my devotion I love to use the civility of my knee, my hat, and hand.
Thomas Browne 1605–82: *Religio Medici* (1643)

18 Be still and cool in thy own mind and spirit from thy own thoughts, and then thou wilt feel the principle of God to turn thy mind to the Lord God.
George Fox 1624–91: diary 1658

19 No praying, it spoils business.
Thomas Otway 1652–85: *Venice Preserved* (1682)

20 O God, if there be a God, save my soul, if I have a soul!
prayer of a common soldier before the battle of Blenheim, 1704
Anonymous: in *Notes and Queries* 9 October 1937

21 One single grateful thought raised to heaven is the most perfect prayer.
G. E. Lessing 1729–81: *Minna von Barnhelm* (1767)

22 He prayeth well, who loveth well
Both man and bird and beast.
Samuel Taylor Coleridge 1772–1834: 'The Rime of the Ancient Mariner' (1798)

23 And lips say, 'God be pitiful,'
Who ne'er said, 'God be praised.'
Elizabeth Barrett Browning 1806–61: 'The Cry of the Human' (1844)

24 More things are wrought by prayer
Than this world dreams of.
Alfred, Lord Tennyson 1809–92: *Idylls of the King* 'The Passing of Arthur' (1869)

25 Whatever a man prays for, he prays for a miracle. Every prayer reduces itself to this: Great God, grant that twice two be not four.
Ivan Turgenev 1818–83: *Poems in Prose* (1881) 'Prayer'

26 To lift up the hands in prayer gives God glory, but a man with a dungfork in his hand, a woman with a slop-pail, give him glory too. He is so great that all things give him glory if you mean they should.
Gerard Manley Hopkins 1844–89: 'The Principle or Foundation' (1882)

27 You can't pray a lie.
Mark Twain 1835–1910: *Adventures of Huckleberry Finn* (1885)

28 Often when I pray I wonder if I am not posting letters to a non-existent address.
C. S. Lewis 1898–1963: letter to Arthur Greeves, 24 December 1930; W. Hooper (ed.) *They Stand Together* (1979)

29 The wish for prayer is a prayer in itself.
Georges Bernanos 1888–1948: *Journal d'un curé de campagne* (1936)

30 Prayer is translation. A man translates himself into a child asking for all there is in a language he has barely mastered.
Leonard Cohen 1934– : *Beautiful Losers* (1966)

Pregnancy and Birth

proverbs and sayings ▸

1 And the child that is born of the
Sabbath day,
Is bonny, and blithe, and good and
gay.

traditional rhyme, mid 19th century; see also BEAUTY 7, GIFTS 2, SORROW 2, TRAVEL 8, WORK 7

2 Jeannie Jeannie, full of hopes
Read a book by Marie Stopes
But to judge from her condition
She must have read the wrong
edition.

1920s skipping rhyme; Marie Stopes (1880–1958) was a Scottish birth-control campaigner

3 No moon, no man.

recording the traditional belief that a child born at the time of the new moon or just before its appearance will not live to grow up; English proverb, late 19th century

quotations ▸

4 In sorrow thou shalt bring forth children.

Bible: Genesis

5 The hour which gives us life begins to take it away.

Seneca ('the Younger') c.4 BC–AD 65: *Hercules Furens*

6 The queen of Scots is this day leichter of a fair son, and I am but a barren stock.

Elizabeth I 1533–1603: in 1566; Sir James Melville *Memoirs of His Own Life* (1827 ed.)

7 Our birth is but a sleep and a
forgetting...
Not in entire forgetfulness,
And not in utter nakedness,
But trailing clouds of glory do we
come.

William Wordsworth 1770–1850: 'Ode. Intimations of Immortality' (1807)

8 It is a pleasant thing to reflect upon, and furnishes a complete answer to those who contend for the general degeneration of the human species, that every baby born into the world is a finer one than the last.

Charles Dickens 1812–70: *Nicholas Nickleby* (1838–9)

9 What you say of the pride of giving life to an immortal soul is very fine, dear, but I own I can not enter into that; I think much more of our being like a cow or a dog at such moments; when our poor nature becomes so very animal and unecstatic.

Queen Victoria 1819–1901: letter to the Princess Royal, 15 June 1858

10 We want better reasons for having children than not knowing how to prevent them.

Dora Russell 1894–1986: *Hypatia* (1925)

11 Death and taxes and childbirth! There's never any convenient time for any of them.

Margaret Mitchell 1900–49: *Gone with the Wind* (1936); see CERTAINTY 4

12 I am not yet born; O fill me
With strength against those who
would freeze my
humanity, would dragoon me into a
lethal automaton,
would make me a cog in a machine,
a thing with
one face, a thing.

Louis MacNeice 1907–63: 'Prayer Before Birth' (1944)

13 Abortions will not let you forget.
You remember the children you got
that you did not get...

Gwendolyn Brooks 1917–2000: 'The Mother' (1945)

14 A baby is God's opinion that life should go on.

Carl Sandburg 1878–1967: *Remembrance Rock* (1948)

15 Love set you going like a fat gold
watch.
The midwife slapped your footsoles,
and your bald cry
Took its place among the elements.

Sylvia Plath 1932–63: 'Morning Song' (1965)

16 A fast word about oral contraception. I asked a girl to go to bed with me and she said 'no'.

Woody Allen 1935– : at a nightclub in Washington, April 1965

17 If men could get pregnant, abortion would be a sacrament.

Florynce Kennedy 1916–2000: in *Ms.* March 1973

18 No test tube can breed love and affection. No frozen packet of semen ever read a story to a sleepy child.
Shirley Williams 1930– : in *Daily Mirror* 2 March 1978

19 If men had to have babies, they would only ever have one each.
Diana, Princess of Wales 1961–97: in *Observer* 29 July 1984

20 Having a baby is like getting a tattoo on your face. You really need to be certain it's what you want before you commit.
Elizabeth Gilbert 1969– : quoting her sister; *Eat, Pray, Love* (2006)

Prejudice and Tolerance

see also RACE

proverbs and sayings ▸

1 Judge not, that ye be not judged.
used as a warning against overhasty criticism of someone; English proverb, late 15th century, from the Bible (Matthew): see JUSTICE 21

2 Live and let live.
often used in the context of coexistence between deeply divided groups; English proverb, early 17th century

3 No tree takes so deep a root as a prejudice.
emphasizing how difficult it is to eradicate prejudice; American proverb, mid 20th century

4 There's none so blind as those who will not see.
used in reference to someone who is unwilling to recognize unwelcome facts; English proverb, mid 16th century

5 There's none so deaf as those who will not hear.
used to refer to someone who chooses not to listen to unwelcome information; English proverb, mid 16th century

phrases ▸

6 political correctness
the avoidance of forms of expression or action that are perceived to exclude, marginalize, or insult groups of people who are socially disadvantaged or discriminated against; see LANGUAGE 29

quotations ▸

7 *Sine ira et studio.*
With neither anger nor partiality.
Tacitus C. AD 56–after 117: *Annals*

8 Hear the other side.
St Augustine of Hippo AD 354–430: *De Duabus Animabus contra Manicheos*

9 Sir Roger told them, with the air of a man who would not give his judgement rashly, that much might be said on both sides.
Joseph Addison 1672–1719: in *The Spectator* 20 July 1711

10 There is, however, a limit at which forbearance ceases to be a virtue.
Edmund Burke 1729–97: *Observations on a late Publication on the Present State of the Nation* (2nd ed., 1769)

11 Drive out prejudices through the door, and they will return through the window.
Frederick the Great 1712–86: letter to Voltaire, 19 March 1771

12 Prejudice is the child of ignorance.
William Hazlitt 1778–1830: 'On Prejudice' (1830)

13 Prejudices, it is well known, are most difficult to eradicate from the heart whose soil has never been loosened or fertilised by education.
Charlotte Brontë 1816–55: *Jane Eyre* (1847)

14 Who's 'im, Bill?
A stranger!
'Eave 'arf a brick at 'im.
Punch: 1854

15 The mind of the bigot [is like] the pupil of the eye; the more light you pour on it, the more it contracts.
Oliver Wendell Holmes 1809–94: *The Autocrat of the Breakfast-Table* (1858)

16 Tolerance is only another name for indifference.
W. Somerset Maugham 1874–1965: *A Writer's Notebook* (1949) written in 1896

17 I decline utterly to be impartial as between the fire brigade and the fire.
replying to complaints of his bias in editing the *British Gazette* during the General Strike
Winston Churchill 1874–1965: speech, House of Commons, 7 July 1926

18 Bigotry tries to keep truth safe in its hand
With a grip that kills it.
Rabindranath Tagore 1861–1941: *Fireflies* (1928)

19 Oh who is that young sinner with the handcuffs on his wrists?
And what has he been after that they groan and shake their fists?
And wherefore is he wearing such a conscience-stricken air?
Oh they're taking him to prison for the colour of his hair.
A. E. Housman 1859–1936: *Collected Poems* (1939) 'Additional Poems' no. 18

20 You might as well fall flat on your face as lean over too far backward.
James Thurber 1894–1961: 'The Bear Who Let It Alone' in *New Yorker* 29 April 1939

21 Four legs good, two legs bad.
George Orwell 1903–50: *Animal Farm* (1945)

22 We should therefore claim, in the name of tolerance, the right not to tolerate the intolerant.
Karl Popper 1902–94: *The Open Society and Its Enemies* (1945)

23 PLEASE ACCEPT MY RESIGNATION. I DON'T WANT TO BELONG TO ANY CLUB THAT WILL ACCEPT ME AS A MEMBER.
Groucho Marx 1890–1977: *Groucho and Me* (1959)

24 What is objectionable, what is dangerous about extremists is not that they are extreme but that they are intolerant.
Robert Kennedy 1925–68: *The Pursuit of Justice* (1964)

25 Of my two 'handicaps,' being female put many more obstacles in my path than being black.
Shirley Chisholm 1924–2005: *Unbought and Unbossed* (1970) introduction

26 Human diversity makes tolerance more than a virtue, it makes it a requirement for survival.
René Dubos 1901–82: *Celebrations of Life* (1981)

Preparation and Readiness

proverbs and sayings ►

1 Be prepared.
motto of the Scout and Guide organizations, deriving from the initials of Robert Baden-Powell (1857–1941), the founder

2 Dig the well before you are thirsty.
make necessary preparations before you are in need; Japanese proverb

3 Don't cross the bridge till you come to it.
warning that you should not concern yourself with possible difficulties unless and until they arise; English proverb, mid 19th century

4 The early bird catches the worm.
someone who is energetic and efficient is most likely to be successful; English proverb, mid 17th century; see PREPARATION 12

5 The early man never borrows from the late man.
someone who has made their preparations has no need to turn to someone less efficient; English proverb, mid 17th century

6 Forewarned is forearmed.
if one has been warned in advance about a problem one can make preparations for dealing with it; English proverb, early 16th century

7 For want of a nail the shoe was lost; for want of a shoe the horse was lost; and for want of a horse the man was lost.
often quoted allusively to imply that one apparently small circumstance can result in a large-scale disaster; English proverb, early 17th century, late 15th century in French

8 Here's one I made earlier.
catchphrase popularized by children's television programme *Blue Peter*, from 1963, as a culmination to directions for making a model out of empty yoghurt pots, coat-hangers, and similar domestic items

9 He who fails to plan, plans to fail.
modern saying; see PREPARATION 16

10 Hope for the best and prepare for the worst.
recommending a balance between optimism and realism; English proverb, mid 16th century

11 If you want peace, you must prepare for war.
a country in a state of military preparedness is unlikely to be attacked; English proverb, mid 16th century; see WARFARE 16

12 It's the second mouse that gets the cheese.
modern addition to PREPARATION 4, suggesting the dangers of being the first to make a venture, and the possible benefits of following directly behind a pioneer; see also ECONOMICS 2

13 Measure seven times, cut once.
care taken in preparation will prevent errors (originally referring to carpentry and needlework); Russian proverb

14 No one was ever lost on a straight road.
if you know where you are going you will not make mistakes; Indian proverb

15 No plan survives first contact with the enemy.
modern saying, from von Moltke: see PREPARATION 25

16 To fail to prepare is to prepare to fail.
modern saying; see PREPARATION 9

phrases ▸

17 armed at all points
prepared in every particular; recorded from late Middle English, but often referring directly to a First Folio variant reading of Shakespeare *Hamlet*

quotations ▸

18 The voice of him that crieth in the wilderness, Prepare ye the way of the Lord.
Bible: Isaiah; see FUTILITY 17

19 The man who has planned badly, if fortune is on his side, may have had a stroke of luck; but his plan was a bad one nonetheless.
Herodotus c.485–c.425 BC: *Histories*

20 Watch therefore: for ye know not what hour your Lord doth come.
Bible: St Matthew

21 No time like the present.
Mrs Manley 1663–1724: *The Lost Lover* (1696)

22 Barkis is willin'.
Charles Dickens 1812–70: *David Copperfield* (1850)

23 I think the necessity of being *ready* increases. Look to it.
Abraham Lincoln 1809–65: the whole of a letter to Governor Andrew Curtin of Pennsylvania, 8 April 1861

24 Get there first with the most men.
often quoted as 'Git thar fustest with the mostest', though there is no evidence that non-standard speech was characteristic of Forrest
Nathan B. Forrest 1821–77: attributed

25 No plan of operations reaches with any certainty beyond the first encounter with the enemy's main force.
Helmuth von Moltke 1800–91: *Kriegsgechichtiche Einzelschriften* (1880); see PREPARATION 15

26 If we had had more time for discussion we should probably have made a great many more mistakes.
Leon Trotsky 1879–1940: *My Life* (1930)

27 In preparing for battle I have always found that plans are useless, but planning is indispensable.
Dwight D. Eisenhower 1890–1969: Richard Nixon *Six Crises* (1962); attributed

28 First things first, second things never.
Shirley Conran 1932– : *Superwoman* (1975)

29 Go ahead, make my day.
Joseph C. Stinson 1947– : *Sudden Impact* (1983 film); spoken by Clint Eastwood

30 We are ready for any unforeseen event which may or may not happen.
George W. Bush 1946– : in *Guardian* 30 December 2000

The Present

see also PAST

proverbs and sayings ▸

1 Better an egg today than a hen tomorrow.
take advantage of what is available now, rather than waiting for possible advantages later; English proverb, mid 17th century

2 Enjoy the present moment and don't grieve for the future.
American proverb, mid 20th century

3 Jam tomorrow and jam yesterday, but never jam today.
English proverb, late 19th century, from Carroll: see PRESENT 12

4 Yesterday has gone, tomorrow is yet to be. Today is the miracle.
modern saying; see PRESENT 5, CHARITY 24

5 Yesterday is ashes; tomorrow is wood. Only today does the fire burn brightly.
emphasizing the importance of enjoying and valuing the present rather than dwelling in the past, which cannot be changed, or the future, which has not yet happened; Canadian saying, said to be of Inuit origin; see PRESENT 4

quotations ▸

6 *Carpe diem, quam minimum credula postero.*
Seize the day, put no trust in the future.
Horace 65–8 BC: *Odes*

7 Take therefore no thought for the morrow: for the morrow shall take thought for the things of itself. Sufficient unto the day is the evil thereof.
Bible: St Matthew; see WORRY 4

8 Can ye not discern the signs of the times?
Bible: St Matthew

9 Praise they that will times past, I joy to see
My self now live: this age best pleaseth me.
Robert Herrick 1591–1674: 'The Present Time Best Pleaseth' (1648)

10 Unborn TO-MORROW, and dead YESTERDAY,
Why fret about them if TO-DAY be sweet!
Edward Fitzgerald 1809–83: *The Rubáiyát of Omar Khayyám* (1859)

11 Forever—is composed of nows.
Emily Dickinson 1830–86: 'Forever—is composed of nows' (*c.* 1863)

12 The rule is, jam to-morrow and jam yesterday—but never jam today.
Lewis Carroll 1832–98: *Through the Looking-Glass* (1872); see FORESIGHT 19, PRESENT 3

13 To-morrow for the young the poets exploding like bombs,
The walks by the lake, the weeks of perfect communion;
To-morrow the bicycle races
Through the suburbs on summer evenings: but to-day the struggle.
W. H. Auden 1907–73: 'Spain 1937' (1937)

14 Exhaust the little moment. Soon it dies.
And be it gash or gold it will not come
Again in this identical disguise.
Gwendolyn Brooks 1917–2000: 'Exhaust the little moment' (1949)

15 Things are both more trivial than they ever were, and more important than they ever were, and the difference between the trivial and the important doesn't seem to matter. But the nowness of everything is absolutely wondrous.
on his heightened awareness of things, in the face of his imminent death
Dennis Potter 1935–94: interview with Melvyn Bragg on Channel 4, March 1994, in *Seeing the Blossom* (1994)

16 It's not perfect, but to me on balance Right Now is a lot better than the Good Old Days.
Maeve Binchy 1940– : in *Irish Times* 15 November 1997; see PAST 12

The Presidency

see also AMERICA, POLITICIANS

phrases ▸

1 bully pulpit
a public office or position of authority that provides its occupant with an outstanding opportunity to speak out on any issue; from Roosevelt's personal view of the presidency: see PRESIDENCY 6

2 just a heart-beat away from the Presidency
the vice-president's position; from Adlai Stevenson (1900–65), speech at Cleveland, Ohio, 23 October 1952, 'The Republican party did not have to…encourage the excesses of its Vice-Presidential nominee [Richard Nixon]—the young man who asks you to set him one heart-beat from the Presidency of the United States'

quotations ▶

3 My country has in its wisdom contrived for me the most insignificant office that ever the invention of man contrived or his imagination conceived.

of the vice-presidency

John Adams 1735–1826: letter to Abigail Adams, 19 December 1793

4 A citizen, first in war, first in peace, and first in the hearts of his countrymen.

Henry Lee 1756–1818: *Funeral Oration on the death of General Washington* (1800)

5 As President, I have no eyes but constitutional eyes; I cannot see you.

Abraham Lincoln 1809–65: reply to the South Carolina Commissioners; attributed

6 I have got such a bully pulpit!

Theodore Roosevelt 1858–1919: in *Outlook* (New York) 27 February 1909; see PRESIDENCY 1, PRESIDENCY 16

7 Log-cabin to White House.

William Roscoe Thayer 1859–1923: title of biography (1910) of James Garfield (1831–81)

8 To announce that there must be no criticism of the president, or that we are to stand by the president, right or wrong, is not only unpatriotic and servile, but is morally treasonable to the American public.

Theodore Roosevelt 1858–1919: in *Kansas City Star* 7 May 1918

9 When I was a boy I was told that anybody could become President. I'm beginning to believe it.

Clarence Darrow 1857–1938: Irving Stone *Clarence Darrow for the Defence* (1941)

10 No easy problems ever come to the President of the United States. If they are easy to solve, somebody else has solved them.

Dwight D. Eisenhower 1890–1969: in *Parade Magazine* 8 April 1962

11 The lines he loved to hear were: 'Don't let it be forgot, that once there was a spot, for one brief shining moment that was known as Camelot.'...There'll be great Presidents again...but there'll never be another Camelot again.

on the Kennedy White House, quoting Alan Jay Lerner

Jacqueline Kennedy Onassis 1929–94: in *Life* 6 December 1963

12 The vice-presidency isn't worth a pitcher of warm piss.

John Nance Garner 1868–1967: O. C. Fisher *Cactus Jack* (1978)

13 There can be no whitewash at the White House.

on Watergate

Richard Nixon 1913–94: television speech, 30 April 1973

14 When the President does it, that means that it is not illegal.

Richard Nixon 1913–94: David Frost *I Gave Them a Sword* (1978)

15 Ronald Reagan...is attempting a great breakthrough in political technology—he has been perfecting the Teflon-coated Presidency. He sees to it that nothing sticks to him.

Patricia Schroeder 1940– : speech in the US House of Representatives, 2 August 1983

16 If the President has a bully pulpit, then the First Lady has a white glove pulpit...more refined, restricted, ceremonial, but it's a pulpit all the same.

Nancy Reagan 1923– : in *New York Times* 10 March 1988; see PRESIDENCY 6

17 Poor George [Bush], he can't help it—he was born with a silver foot in his mouth.

Ann Richards 1933–2006: keynote speech at the Democratic convention, in *Independent* 20 July 1988; see WEALTH 10

18 Somewhere out in this audience may even be someone who will one day follow in my footsteps, and preside over the White House as the President's spouse. I wish him well!

Barbara Bush 1925– : remarks at Wellesley College Commencement, 1 June 1990

19 To those of you who received honours, awards and distinctions, I say well done. And to the C students, I say you, too, can be president of the United States.

George W. Bush 1946– : in *Sunday Times* 27 May 2001

20 Although we weren't able to shatter that highest, hardest glass ceiling

this time, thanks to you, it has about 18 million cracks in it.

Hillary Rodham Clinton 1947– : speech to her supporters, conceding the Democratic party presidential nomination to Barack Obama, 7 June 2008

Pride and Humility

see also SELF-ESTEEM

proverbs and sayings ►

1 He that will not stoop for a pin [penny] will never be worth a point [pound].

if pride prevents you from taking a small benefit, you will not make further gains; English proverb, early 17th century

2 Pride feels no pain.

implying that inordinate self-esteem will not allow the admission that one might be suffering; English proverb, early 17th century

3 Pride goes before a fall.

often with the implication that proud and haughty behaviour will contribute to its own downfall; English proverb, late 14th century; see PRIDE 5

phrases ►

4 as proud as Lucifer

very proud, arrogant; *Lucifer* = the rebel angel whose fall from heaven Jerome and other early Christian writers considered was alluded to in the Bible (Isaiah, where the word is an epithet of the king of Babylon), and equivalent to Satan, the Devil

quotations ►

5 Pride goeth before destruction, and an haughty spirit before a fall.

Bible: Proverbs; see PRIDE 3

6 Blessed are the meek: for they shall inherit the earth.

Bible: St Matthew; see PRIDE 14

7 All virtues and duties are dependent on humility.

Bahya ibn Paquda fl. 1080: *The Duties of the Heart*

8 He that is down needs fear no fall,
He that is low no pride.
He that is humble ever shall
Have God to be his guide.

John Bunyan 1628–88: *The Pilgrim's Progress* (1684) 'Shepherd Boy's Song'

9 Proud people breed sad sorrows for themselves.

Emily Brontë 1818–48: *Wuthering Heights* (1847)

10 We are so very 'umble.

Charles Dickens 1812–70: *David Copperfield* (1850)

11 Pride helps us; and pride is not a bad thing when it only urges us to hide our own hurts, not to hurt others.

George Eliot 1819–80: *Middlemarch* (1871–2)

12 I can trace my ancestry back to a protoplasmal primordial atomic globule. Consequently, my family pride is something in-conceivable. I can't help it. I was born sneering.

W. S. Gilbert 1836–1911: *The Mikado* (1885)

13 The tumult and the shouting dies—
The captains and the kings depart—
Still stands Thine ancient Sacrifice,
An humble and a contrite heart.
Lord God of Hosts, be with us yet,
Lest we forget—lest we forget!

Rudyard Kipling 1865–1936: 'Recessional' (1897); see HOSPITALITY 17

14 We have the highest authority for believing that the meek shall inherit the earth; though I have never found any particular corroboration of this aphorism in the records of Somerset House.

F. E. Smith 1872–1930: *Contemporary Personalities* (1924); see PRIDE 6

15 I have often wished I had time to cultivate modesty...But I am too busy thinking about myself.

Edith Sitwell 1887–1964: in *Observer* 30 April 1950

16 No one can make you feel inferior without your consent.

Eleanor Roosevelt 1884–1962: in *Catholic Digest* August 1960

17 In 1969 I published a small book on Humility. It was a pioneering work which has not, to my knowledge, been superseded.

Lord Longford 1905–2001: in *Tablet* 22 January 1994

Problems and Solutions

see also WAYS

proverbs and sayings ▸

1 **If you lead your mule to the top of the minaret, then you must lead him down again.**

if you get yourself into a difficult position, you will have to extricate yourself; Arab proverb

2 **Impossible is nothing.**

Adidas advertising slogan, 2003, often associated with the American boxer Muhammad Ali, who appeared in the campaign

3 **Jim'll fix it.**

catchphrase of a BBC television series (1975–94) starring Jimmy Savile in which participants had their wishes fulfilled

4 **Never bid the Devil good morrow until you meet him.**

a warning against trying to deal with problems or difficulties before they have actually occurred; English proverb, late 19th century, said to be an old Irish saying

5 **When all you have is a hammer, everything looks like a nail.**

often used to comment on the wholesale application of one solution or method to the solution of any problem; English proverb, late 20th century (chiefly North American), from Maslow: see PROBLEMS 33

6 **Why did the chicken cross the road?**

traditional puzzle question, to which the answer is, to get to the other side; mid 19th century

phrases ▸

7 **a chicken-and-egg problem**

an unresolved question as to which of two things caused the other; from the riddle, *Which came first, the chicken or the egg?*

8 **cleanse the Augean stables**

a task or problem requiring so much effort to complete or solve as to seem impossible; the vast stables belonging to King Augeas had never been cleaned, and this was achieved (as the sixth of his Labours) by Hercules, who cleaned them in a day by diverting the River Alpheus to flow through them; often used figuratively to refer to corruption or waste developed over a long period

9 **cut the Gordian knot**

solve a problem by force or by evading the conditions; in allusion to an intricate knot tied by Gordius, king of Gordium, Phrygia, and cut through by Alexander the Great in response to the prophecy that only the future ruler of Asia could loosen it

10 **Frankenstein's monster**

something which has developed beyond the management or control of its originator; *Frankenstein* the title of a novel (1818) by Mary Shelley whose eponymous main character constructed and gave life to a human monster

11 **make bricks without straw**

perform a task without provision of the necessary materials or means; from the Bible (Exodus), in allusion to Pharaoh's decree to the taskmasters set over the Israelites in Egypt 'Ye shall no more give the people straw to make brick, as heretofore: let them go and gather straw for themselves'; see FUTILITY 6

12 **Open Sesame**

a (marvellous or irresistible) means of securing access to what would usually be inaccessible; the magic words by which, in the tale of Ali Baba and the Forty Thieves in the *Arabian Nights*, the door of the robbers' cave was made to open

13 **Pandora's box**

a thing which once activated will give rise to many unmanageable problems; in Greek mythology, the gift of Jupiter to *Pandōra*, 'all-gifted', the first mortal woman, on whom, when made by Vulcan, all the gods and goddesses bestowed gifts; the box enclosed all human ills, which flew out when it was foolishly opened (or in a later version, it contained all the blessings of the gods, which with the exception of hope escaped and were lost when the box was opened); see EUROPE 13

14 **philosophers' stone**

a universal cure or solution; the supreme object of alchemy, a substance supposed to change any metal into gold or silver and (according to some) to cure all diseases and prolong life indefinitely

15 **the sixty-four thousand dollar question**

the crucial issue, a difficult question, a dilemma; the top prize in a broadcast quiz show

16 **sorcerer's apprentice**

a person who having instigated a process is unable to control it; translating French *l'apprenti sorcier*, a symphonic poem by Paul Dukas (1897) after *der Zauberlehrling*, a ballad by Goethe (1797)

17 tar baby

a difficult problem which is only aggravated by attempts to solve it; origin with allusion to the doll smeared with tar as a trap for Brer Rabbit, in J. C. Harris's *Uncle Remus*

18 there's the rub

there is the difficulty; a *rub* here is literally an impediment in bowls by which a bowl is hindered in or diverted from its proper course; from Shakespeare: see DEATH 38

quotations ▶

19 Probable impossibilities are to be preferred to improbable possibilities.

Aristotle 384–322 BC: *Poetics*

20 The remedy is worse than the disease.

Francis Bacon 1561–1626: *Essays* (1625) 'Of Seditions and Troubles'

21 The fool wonders, the wise man asks.

Benjamin Disraeli 1804–81: *Contarini Fleming* (1832)

22 One hears only those questions for which one is able to find answers.

Friedrich Nietzsche 1844–1900: *The Gay Science* (1882)

23 How often have I said to you that when you have eliminated the impossible, whatever remains, *however improbable*, must be the truth?

Arthur Conan Doyle 1859–1930: *The Sign of Four* (1890)

24 Difficulties are just things to overcome after all.

Ernest Shackleton 1874–1922: diary, 11 December 1908, *The Heart of the Antarctic* (1909)

25 The fascination of what's difficult
Has dried the sap out of my veins, and rent
Spontaneous joy and natural content
Out of my heart.

W. B. Yeats 1865–1939: 'The Fascination of What's Difficult' (1910)

26 Man needs difficulties; they are necessary for health.

Carl Gustav Jung 1875–1961: 'The Transcendent Function' (1916)

27 For most of my life I refused to work at any problem unless its solution seemed to be capable of being put to commercial use.

Thomas Alva Edison 1847–1931: interview, in *New York Sun* February 1917

28 There is always a well-known solution to every human problem—neat, plausible, and wrong.

Henry Louis Mencken 1880–1956: *Prejudices* 2nd series (1920)

29 Another nice mess you've gotten me into.

usually quoted as 'another fine mess'

Stan Laurel 1890–1965: *Another Fine Mess* (1930 film) and many other Laurel and Hardy films; spoken by Oliver Hardy

30 It isn't that they can't see the solution. It is that they can't see the problem.

G. K. Chesterton 1874–1936: *Scandal of Father Brown* (1935)

31 We haven't got the money, so we've got to think!

Ernest Rutherford 1871–1937: in *Bulletin of the Institute of Physics* (1962)

32 Let me have the best solution worked out. Don't argue the matter. The difficulties will argue for themselves.

on the Mulberry floating harbours

Winston Churchill 1874–1965: minute to Lord Mountbatten, 30 May 1942

33 It is tempting, if the only tool you have is a hammer, to treat everything as if it were a nail.

Abraham Maslow 1908–70: *The Psychology of Science* (1966); see PROBLEMS 5

34 What we're saying today is that you're either part of the solution or you're part of the problem.

Eldridge Cleaver 1935–98: speech in San Francisco, 1968; R. Scheer *Eldridge Cleaver, Post Prison Writings and Speeches* (1969)

35 Problems worthy
of attack
prove their worth
by hitting back.

Piet Hein 1905–96: 'Problems' (1969)

36 Houston, we've had a problem.

on Apollo 13 space mission, 14 April 1970

James Lovell 1928– : in *Times* 15 April 1970

37 If a problem is too difficult to solve, one cannot claim that it is solved by

pointing at all the efforts made to solve it.

Hannes Alfven 1908–95: quoted by Lord Flowers in 1976; A. Sampson *The Changing Anatomy of Britain* (1982)

38 What I cannot create, I do not understand. Know how to solve every problem that has been solved.

written on his blackboard at Caltech, as he left it for the last time in January 1988

Richard Feynman 1918–88: Christopher Sykes (ed.) *No Ordinary Genius* (1994)

Progress

see also CHANGE

phrases ▸

1 brave new world

utopia produced by technological and social advance; title of a satirical novel by Aldous Huxley (1932), after Shakespeare *Tempest*: see HUMAN RACE 16

2 future shock

a state of distress or disorientation due to rapid social or technological change; from Alvin Toffler in *Horizon* 1965, 'The dizzying disorientation brought on by the premature arrival of the future'; definition of *future shock*

3 Great Leap Forward

an unsuccessful attempt made under Mao Zedong in China 1958–60 to hasten the process of industrialization and improve agricultural production

4 quantum leap

a sudden, significant or very evident (usually large) increase or advance; from the term *quantum jump* in Physics, referring to an abrupt transition from one quantum state to another

quotations ▸

5 The thing that hath been, it is that which shall be; and that which is done is that which shall be done: and there is no new thing under the sun.

Bible: Ecclesiastes; see EARTH 7, FAMILIARITY 11

6 Forgetting those things which are behind, and reaching forth unto those things which are before,
I press toward the mark.

Bible: Philippians

7 We are like dwarfs on the shoulders of giants, so that we can see more than they, and things at a greater distance, not by virtue of any sharpness of sight on our part, or any physical distinction, but because we are carried high and raised up by their giant size.

Bernard of Chartres d. c.1130: John of Salisbury *The Metalogicon* (1159); see PROGRESS 8

8 If I have seen further it is by standing on the shoulders of giants.

Isaac Newton 1642–1727: letter to Robert Hooke, 5 February 1676; see PROGRESS 7

9 Not to go back, is somewhat to advance,
And men must walk at least before
they dance.

Alexander Pope 1688–1744: *Imitations of Horace*

10 Nothing in progression can rest on its original plan. We may as well think of rocking a grown man in the cradle of an infant.

Edmund Burke 1729–97: *Letter to the Sheriffs of Bristol* (1777)

11 The European talks of progress because by an ingenious application of some scientific acquirements he has established a society which has mistaken comfort for civilization.

Benjamin Disraeli 1804–81: *Tancred* (1847)

12 The reasonable man adapts himself to the world: the unreasonable one persists in trying to adapt the world to himself. Therefore all progress depends on the unreasonable man.

George Bernard Shaw 1856–1950: *Man and Superman* (1903)

13 One step forward two steps back.

Lenin 1870–1924: title of book (1904)

14 The new growth in the plant swelling against the sheath, which at the same time imprisons and protects it, must still be the truest type of progress.

Jane Addams 1860–1935: *Democracy and Social Ethics* (1907)

15 The slogan of progress is changing from the full dinner pail to the full garage.

sometimes paraphrased as, 'a car in every garage and a chicken in every pot'

Herbert Hoover 1874–1964: speech in New York, 22 October 1928; see POVERTY 17

16 Want is one only of five giants on the road of reconstruction...the others are Disease, Ignorance, Squalor and Idleness.

William Henry Beveridge 1879–1963: *Social Insurance and Allied Services* (1942)

17 There's only one corner of the universe you can be certain of improving, and that's your own self.

Aldous Huxley 1894–1963: *Time Must Have a Stop* (1944)

18 'Change' is scientific, 'progress' is ethical; change is indubitable, whereas progress is a matter of controversy.

Bertrand Russell: *Unpopular Essays* (1950) 'Philosophy and Politics'

19 Forward ever, backward never.

Kwame Nkrumah 1900–72: motto of his Convention People's Party, *Autobiography* (1959)

20 Is it progress if a cannibal uses knife and fork?

Stanislaw Lec 1909–66: *Unkempt Thoughts* (1962)

21 The march of social progress is like a long and straggling parade, with the seers and prophets at its head and a smug minority bringing up the rear.

Pierre Berton 1920– : *The Smug Minority* (1968)

22 Things can only get better.

Jamie Petrie and **Peter Cunnah**: title of song (1992), used as a slogan by the Labour party in the 1997 general election campaign

23 For 80 per cent of humanity the Middle Ages ended suddenly in the 1950s; or perhaps better still, they were *felt* to end in the 1960s.

Eric Hobsbawm 1917– : *Age of Extremes* (1994)

24 The Stone Age came to an end not for a lack of stones, and the Oil Age will end, but not for a lack of oil.

Sheikh Yamani 1930– : to OPEC, September 2000, in *Guardian* 8 September 2000

Publishing

see also BOOKS

phrases ►

1 printer's devil

an errand-boy or junior assistant in a printing office; *devil* = a person employed in a subordinate position to work under the direction of or for a particular person; see PUBLISHING 8

2 river of white

a white line or streak down a printed page where spaces between words on consecutive lines are close together

quotations ►

3 I, according to my copy, have done set it in imprint, to the intent that noble men may see and learn the noble acts of chivalry, the gentle and virtuous deeds that some knights used in those days.

William Caxton 1421–91: Thomas Malory *Le Morte D'Arthur* (1485) prologue

4 You shall see them on a beautiful quarto page where a neat rivulet of text shall meander through a meadow of margin.

Richard Brinsley Sheridan 1751–1816: *The School for Scandal* (1777)

5 Never literary attempt was more unfortunate than my Treatise of Human Nature. It fell *dead-born from the press.*

David Hume 1711–76: *My Own Life* (1777)

6 The poem will please if it is lively—if it is stupid it will fail—but I will have none of your damned cutting and slashing.

Lord Byron 1788–1824: letter to his publisher John Murray, 6 April 1819

7 Publish and be damned.

replying to Harriette Wilson's blackmail threat, 1825

Duke of Wellington 1769–1852: attributed

8 For you know, dear—I may, without vanity, hint—
Though an angel should write, still 'tis *devils* must print.

Thomas Moore 1779–1852: *The Fudges in England* (1835); see PUBLISHING 1

9 Now Barabbas was a publisher.
alteration in a Bible of the verse 'Now Barabbas was a robber'
Thomas Campbell 1777–1844: attributed, in Samuel Smiles *A Publisher and his Friends* (1891); also attributed, wrongly, to Byron

10 University printing presses exist, and are subsidised by the Government for the purpose of producing books which no one can read; and they are true to their high calling.
Francis M. Cornford 1874–1943: *Microcosmographia Academica* (1908)

11 Gutenberg made everybody a reader. Xerox makes everybody a publisher.
Marshall McLuhan 1911–80: in *Guardian Weekly* 12 June 1977

12 When you publish a book, it's the world's book. The world edits it.
Philip Roth 1933– : in *New York Times Book Review* 2 September 1979

Punctuality

proverbs and sayings ▸

1 Better late than never.
even if one has missed the first chance of doing something, it is better to attempt it than not to do it at all; English proverb, early 14th century

2 Cathedral time is five minutes later than standard time.
order of service leaflet, Christ Church Cathedral, Oxford, 1990s

3 First come, first served.
English proverb, late 14th century

4 Punctuality is the art of guessing correctly how late the other party is going to be.
American proverb, mid 20th century

5 Punctuality is the politeness of princes.
English proverb, mid 19th century; see PUNCTUALITY 10

6 Punctuality is the soul of business.
English proverb, mid 19th century

quotations ▸

7 You come most carefully upon your hour.
William Shakespeare 1564–1616: *Hamlet* (1601)

8 I was nearly kept waiting.
Louis XIV 1638–1715: attribution queried, among others, by E. Fournier in *L'Esprit dans l'Histoire* (1857)

9 Recollect that painting and punctuality mix like oil and vinegar, and that genius and regularity are utter enemies, and must be to the end of time.
Thomas Gainsborough 1727–88: letter to the Hon. Edward Stratford, 1 May 1772

10 Punctuality is the politeness of kings.
Louis XVIII 1755–1824: *Souvenirs de J. Lafitte* (1844); attributed; see PUNCTUALITY 5

11 The only way of catching a train I have ever discovered is to miss the train before.
G. K. Chesterton 1874–1936: *Tremendous Trifles* (1909)

12 An artist must organize his life. Here is the exact timetable of my daily activities. Get up: 7.18 am; be inspired: 10.23 to 11.47 am. I take lunch at 12.11 pm and leave the table at 12.14 pm.
Erik Satie 1866–1925: *Memoirs of an Amnesiac* (1914)

13 But think how early I go.
when criticized for continually arriving late for work in the City in 1919
Lord Castlerosse 1891–1943: Leonard Mosley *Castlerosse* (1956); remark also claimed by Howard Dietz at MGM

14 We've been waiting 700 years, you can have the seven minutes.
on arriving at Dublin Castle for the handover by British forces on 16 January 1922, and being told that he was seven minutes late
Michael Collins 1880–1922: Tim Pat Coogan *Michael Collins* (1990); attributed, perhaps apocryphal

15 I have noticed that the people who are late are often so much jollier than the people who have to wait for them.
E. V. Lucas 1868–1938: *365 Days and One More* (1926)

16 We must leave exactly on time...From now on everything must function to perfection.
to a station-master
Benito Mussolini 1883–1945: Giorgio Pini *Mussolini* (1939)

17 **My Aunt Minnie would always be punctual and never hold up production, but who would pay to see my Aunt Minnie?**
on Marilyn Monroe's unpunctuality
Billy Wilder 1906–2002: P. F. Boller and R. L. Davis *Hollywood Anecdotes* (1988)

18 **Punctuality is the virtue of the bored.**
Evelyn Waugh 1903–66: diary 26 March 1962

19 **I love deadlines. I love the whooshing noise they make as they go by.**
Douglas Adams 1952–2001: in *Guardian* 14 May 2001

Punishment

see CRIME AND PUNISHMENT

Quantities and Qualities

proverbs and sayings ►

1 **Drops that gather one by one finally become a sea.**
Persian proverb

2 **How long is a piece of string?**
traditional saying, used to indicate that something cannot be given a finite measurement

3 **Little fish are sweet.**
small gifts are always acceptable; English proverb, early 19th century

4 **Many a little makes a mickle.**
the proper form of QUANTITIES 5 (*mickle* in Scottish usage means 'a great quantity or amount'); English proverb, mid 13th century

5 **Many a mickle makes a muckle.**
an alteration of QUANTITIES 4 which is actually nonsensical, since *muckle* is a variant of *mickle* and both mean 'a large quantity or amount'; English proverb, late 18th century

6 **The more the merrier.**
English proverb, late 14th century

7 **The nearer the bone, the sweeter the meat.**
the juiciest meat lies next to the bone, or that the meat closest to the bone is particularly precious because it may represent one's last scrap of food; English proverb, late 14th century

8 **Never mind the quality, feel the width.**
used as the title of a television comedy series (1967–9) about a tailoring business in the East End of London, ultimately probably an inversion of a cloth trade saying

9 **One spoonful of tar spoils a barrel of honey.**
Russian proverb

10 **Small is beautiful.**
title of a book by E. F. Schumacher, 1973; see ECONOMICS 20

11 **There is safety in numbers.**
now with the implication that a number of people will be unscathed where an individual might be in danger; English proverb, late 17th century

12 **The whole is more than the sum of the parts.**
traditional saying, probably deriving from Aristotle; see CAUSES 19

phrases ►

13 **Benjamin's portion**
the largest share; the youngest son of the patriarch Jacob, who according to the Bible (Genesis) was given a larger share than his other brothers by his brother Joseph, 'He took and sent messes [portions of food] unto them before him: but Benjamin's mess was five times so much as any of theirs'

14 **David and Goliath**
a type of apparently unequal combat; in the Bible (I Samuel), Goliath, a Philistine giant and warrior, according to legend was killed by David armed only with a sling and 'five smooth stones'

15 **E pluribus unum.**
Latin, 'out of many, one', selected as the motto for the American national seal in 1776 by a committee consisting of Thomas Jefferson, John Adams, and Benjamin Franklin

16 **the eye of a needle**
a minute opening or space through which it is difficult to pass; chiefly in echoes of the Bible (Matthew): see WEALTH 19

17 **grow like Topsy**
seem to have grown of itself without anyone's intention or direction; from the name of the young slave girl in Harriet Beecher Stowe's *Uncle Tom's Cabin* (1852), who says of herself 'I s'pect I growed. Don't think nobody never made me'

18 **horn of plenty**
a cornucopia, an overflowing stock; an abundant source; translation of Latin *cornu copiae* a mythical horn able to provide whatever is desired

19 **the lion's share**
the largest share of something

20 **the number of the beast**
six hundred and sixty-six; after the Bible (Revelation) 'Let him that hath understanding count the number of the beast: for it is the number of a man: and his number is six hundred threescore and six' (the beast was traditionally identified with Antichrist)

21 **their name is legion**
they are innumerable; from the story in the Bible (Mark) of the reply of the 'man with an unclean spirit' who was to be healed by Jesus, 'My name is Legion, for we are many'

22 **tip of the iceberg**
a known or recognizable part of something (especially a difficulty) evidently much larger; the part of an iceberg visible above the water

23 **Uncle Tom Cobley and all**
a whole lot of people; the last of a long list of people in the song 'Widecombe Fair'

24 **a widow's cruse**
a seemingly slight resource which is in fact not readily exhausted; in allusion to the story in the Bible (I Kings) of the cruse of oil and handful of meal belonging to the widow to whom Elijah was sent for sustenance: by God's decree neither meal nor oil were exhausted

quotations ▸

25 A whole is that which has a beginning, a middle, and an end.
Aristotle 384–322 BC: *Poetics*; see CINEMA 19, FICTION 22

26 The works of Creation are described as being completed in six days, the same formula for a day being repeated six times. The reason for this is that six is the number of perfection.
St. Augustine of Hippo AD 354–430: *The City of God*

27 Nobody can remember more than seven of anything.
reason for omitting the eight beatitudes from his catechism
Cardinal Robert Bellarmine 1542–1621: John Bossy *Christianity in the West 1400–1700* (1985)

28 Thick as autumnal leaves that strew
the brooks
In Vallombrosa.
John Milton 1608–74: *Paradise Lost* (1667)

29 So, naturalists observe, a flea
Hath smaller fleas that on him prey;
And these have smaller fleas to bite 'em,
And so proceed *ad infinitum.*
Jonathan Swift 1667–1745: 'On Poetry' (1733)

30 Nothing is more contrary to the organization of the mind, of the memory, and of the imagination...It's just tormenting the people with trivia!!!
on the introduction of the metric system
Napoleon I 1769–1821: *Mémoires...écrits à Ste-Hélène* (1823–5)

31 Oh, the little more, and how much it is!
And the little less, and what worlds
away!
Robert Browning 1812–89: 'By the Fireside' (1855)

32 I think no virtue goes with size.
Ralph Waldo Emerson 1803–82: 'The Titmouse' (1867)

33 It is our national joy to mistake for the first-rate, the fecund rate.
Dorothy Parker 1893–1967: review of Sinclair Lewis *Dodsworth*; in *New Yorker* 16 March 1929

34 Less is a bore.
Robert Venturi 1925– : *Complexity and Contradiction in Architecture* (1966); see ARCHITECTURE 16, EXCESS 8

35 I'm only a four-dimensional creature. Haven't got a clue how to visualise infinity. Even Einstein hadn't. I know because I asked him.
Patrick Moore 1923– : in *Sunday Times* 15 April 2001

Quotations

proverbs and sayings ▸

1 The devil can quote Scripture for his own ends.
it is possible for someone engaged in wrongdoing to quote selectively from the Bible in apparent support of their position, and alluding to the temptation of Christ by the Devil in the Bible (Matthew); English proverb, late 16th century: see BIBLE 8

2 Proverbs are the coins of the people.
Russian proverb

3 There is no proverb without a grain of truth.
Russian proverb

4 To understand the people acquaint yourself with their proverbs.
Arab proverb

phrases ▸

5 cap verses
reply to one previously quoted with another, that begins with the final or initial letter of the first, or that rhymes or otherwise corresponds with it

quotations ▸

6 Confound those who have said our remarks before us.
Aelius Donatus AD 4th century: St Jerome *Commentary on Ecclesiastes*

7 Classical quotation is the *parole* of literary men all over the world.
Samuel Johnson 1709–84: James Boswell *Life of Samuel Johnson* (1791) 8 May 1781

8 A proverb is one man's wit and all men's wisdom.
Lord John Russell 1792–1878: R. J. Mackintosh *Sir James Mackintosh* (1835)

9 I hate quotation. Tell me what you know.
Ralph Waldo Emerson 1803–82: diary May 1849

10 He wrapped himself in quotations—as a beggar would enfold himself in the purple of emperors.
Rudyard Kipling 1865–1936: *Many Inventions* (1893)

11 OSCAR WILDE: How I wish I had said that.
WHISTLER: You will, Oscar, you will.
James McNeill Whistler 1834–1903: R. Ellman *Oscar Wilde* (1987)

12 When a thing has been said and well said, have no scruple: take it and copy it.
Anatole France 1844–1924: 'The Creed', in Jean Jacques Brousson and John Pollock *Anatole France Himself: A Boswellian Record* (1925)

13 It is a good thing for an uneducated man to read books of quotations.
Winston Churchill 1874–1965: *My Early Life* (1930)

14 I always have a quotation for everything—it saves original thinking.
Dorothy L. Sayers 1893–1957: *Have His Carcase* (1932)

15 Misquotations are made by the people, not the poets.
Hesketh Pearson 1887–1964: *Common Misquotations* (1934)

16 Misquotation is, in fact, the pride and privilege of the learned. A widely-read man never quotes accurately, for the rather obvious reason that he has read too widely.
Hesketh Pearson 1887–1964: *Common Misquotations* (1934)

17 Brush up your Shakespeare,
Start quoting him now.
Brush up your Shakespeare
And the women you will wow.
Cole Porter 1891–1964: 'Brush Up your Shakespeare' (1948 song)

18 People who like quotations love meaningless generalizations.
Graham Greene 1904–91: *Travels With My Aunt* (1969)

19 Windbags can be right. Aphorists can be wrong. It is a tough world.
James Fenton 1949– : in *Times* 21 February 1985

Race and Racism

see also EQUALITY, PREJUDICE

proverbs and sayings ▸

1 Am I not a man and a brother.
motto on the seal of the British and Foreign Anti-Slavery Society, 1787, depicting a kneeling slave in chains uttering these words (subsequently a popular Wedgwood cameo); see HUMAN RACE 4

2 Black is beautiful.
slogan of American civil rights campaigners, mid-1960s

3 Power to the people.
slogan of the Black Panther movement, from 1968 onwards

phrases ►

4 rainbow coalition
a political alliance of minority peoples and other disadvantaged groups; from Jesse Jackson: see RACE 28

5 the white man's burden
the supposed task of whites to civilize blacks; from Kipling, originally in specific allusion to the United States' role in the Philippines: see DUTY 19

quotations ►

6 You call me misbeliever, cut-throat dog,
And spit upon my Jewish gabardine,
And all for use of that which is mine own.
William Shakespeare 1564–1616: *The Merchant of Venice* (1596–8), spoken by Shylock

7 Remember, Christians, Negroes black as Cain
May be refined, and join th' angelic train.
Phillis Wheatley c.1753–84: 'On Being Brought from Africa to America' (1773)

8 When I recovered a little I found some black people about me...I asked them if we were not to be eaten by those white men with horrible looks, red faces, and loose hair.
Olaudah Equiano c.1745–c.97: *Narrative of the Life of Olaudah Equiano* (1789)

9 You have seen how a man was made a slave; you shall see how a slave was made a man.
Frederick Douglass 1818–95: *Narrative of the Life of Frederick Douglass* (1845)

10 The only good Indian is a dead Indian.
at Fort Cobb, January 1869
Philip Henry Sheridan 1831–88: attributed

11 Because a man has a black face and a different religion from our own, there is no reason why he should be treated as a brute.
Edward VII 1841–1910: letter to Lord Granville, 30 November 1875

12 The gentleman will please remember that when his half-civilized ancestors were hunting the wild boar in Silesia, mine were princes of the earth.
in reply to a taunt by a Senator of German descent
Judah Benjamin 1811–84: B. Perley Poore *Perley's Reminiscences* (1886)

13 The so-called white races are really pinko-grey.
E. M. Forster 1879–1970: *A Passage to India* (1924)

14 How odd
Of God
To choose
The Jews.
to which Cecil Browne replied: 'But not so odd/As those who choose/A Jewish God/But spurn the Jews.'
William Norman Ewer 1885–1976: *Week-End Book* (1924)

15 I, too, sing America.

I am the darker brother.
They send me to eat in the kitchen
When company comes.
Langston Hughes 1902–67: 'I, Too' (1925)

16 If my theory of relativity is proven correct, Germany will claim me as a German and France will declare that I am a citizen of the world. Should my theory prove untrue, France will say that I am a German and Germany will declare that I am a Jew.
Albert Einstein 1879–1955: address at the Sorbonne, Paris, possibly early December 1929; in *New York Times* 16 February 1930

17 After all, who remembers today the extermination of the Armenians?
Adolf Hitler 1889–1945: comment, 22 August 1939

18 I herewith commission you to carry out all preparations with regard to...a *total solution* of the Jewish question in those territories of Europe which are under German influence.
Hermann Goering 1893–1946: instructions to Heydrich, 31 July 1941; W. L. Shirer *The Rise and Fall of the Third Reich* (1962)

19 The white man was *created* a devil, to bring chaos upon this earth.
Malcolm X 1925–65: speech, 1953; Malcolm X with Alex Haley *The Autobiography of Malcolm X* (1965)

20 My son, your troubled eyes search mine,
Puzzled and hurt by colour line.
Your black skin as soft as velvet shine;
What can I tell you, son of mine?
Oodgeroo Noonuccal 1920–93: 'Son of Mine (To Denis)' (1960)

21 I want to be the white man's brother, not his brother-in-law.

Martin Luther King 1929–68: in *New York Journal-American* 10 September 1962

22 Segregation now, segregation tomorrow and segregation forever!

George Wallace 1919– : inaugural speech as Governor of Alabama, 14 January 1963

23 There are no 'white' or 'coloured' signs on the foxholes or graveyards of battle.

John F. Kennedy 1917–63: message to Congress on proposed Civil Rights Bill, 19 June 1963

24 Being a star has made it possible for me to get insulted in places where the average Negro could never *hope* to go and get insulted.

Sammy Davis Jnr. 1925–90: *Yes I Can* (1965)

25 It comes as a great shock around the age of 5, 6 or 7 to discover that the flag to which you have pledged allegiance, along with everybody else, has not pledged allegiance to you. It comes as a great shock to see Gary Cooper killing off the Indians and, although you are rooting for Gary Cooper, that the Indians are you.

speaking for the proposition that 'The American Dream is at the expense of the American Negro'; see AMERICA 3

James Baldwin 1924–87: Cambridge Union, England, 17 February 1965

26 Though it be a thrilling and marvellous thing to be merely young and gifted in such times, it is doubly so, doubly dynamic—to be young, gifted and *black*.

Lorraine Hansberry 1930–65: *To be young, gifted and black: Lorraine Hansberry in her own words* (1969) adapted by Robert Nemiroff

27 As I look ahead, I am filled with foreboding. Like the Roman, I seem to see 'the River Tiber foaming with much blood'.

on the probable consequences of immigration

Enoch Powell 1912–98: speech at the Annual Meeting of the West Midlands Area Conservative Political Centre, Birmingham, 20 April 1968; see WARFARE 19

28 When I look out at this convention, I see the face of America, red, yellow, brown, black, and white. We are all precious in God's sight—the real rainbow coalition.

Jesse Jackson 1941– : speech at Democratic National Convention, Atlanta, 19 July 1988; see RACE 4

29 Growing up, I came up with this name: I'm a Cablinasian.

explaining his rejection of 'African-American' as the term to describe his Caucasian, Afro-American, Native American, Thai, and Chinese ancestry

Tiger Woods 1975– : interview, 21 April 1997

30 I hate the way they portray us in the media. You see a black family, it says 'They're looting.' You see a white family, it says, 'They're looking for food.'

Kanye West 1977– : fundraising concert for Hurricane Katrina, NBC TV 2 September 2005

31 She sat down in order that we all might stand up—and the walls of segregation came down.

of the civil rights activist Rosa Parks

Jesse Jackson 1941– : in *BBC News* (online edition) 25 October 2005

32 I don't have to be a symbol to anybody, I don't have to be a first to anybody. I don't have to be an imitation of a white woman that Hollywood sort of hoped I'd become. I'm me, and I'm like nobody else.

Lena Horne 1917–2010: attributed, in *Guardian* 11 May 2010

Rank and Title

see also CLASS

proverbs and sayings ▶

1 Everybody loves a lord.

English proverb, mid 19th century

2 If two ride on a horse, one must ride behind.

of two people engaged on the same task, one must take a subordinate role; English proverb, late 16th century

3 Where Macgregor sits is the head of the table.

sometimes attributed to 'Rob Roy' MacGregor. Other names are used as well as Macgregor; English proverb, mid 19th century

4 You may know a gentleman by his horse, his hawk, and his greyhound.
traditional accoutrements of leisure for those of rank; Welsh proverb

quotations ►

5 Virtue is the one and only nobility.
Juvenal C. AD 60–C. 140: *Satires*

6 I made the carles lords, but who made the carlines ladies?
of the wives of Scots Lords of Session
James I 1566–1625: E. Grenville Murray *Embassies and Foreign Courts* (1855)

7 What can ennoble sots, or slaves, or cowards?
Alas! Not all the blood of all the Howards.
Alexander Pope 1688–1744: *An Essay on Man* Epistle 4 (1734)

8 'Tis from high life high characters are drawn;
A saint in crape is twice a saint in lawn.
Alexander Pope 1688–1744: 'To Lord Cobham' (1734)

9 I bow to no man for I am considered a prince among my own people. But I will gladly shake your hand.
Canadian Mohawk leader, on being presented to George III
Joseph Brant (Thayendanegea) 1742–1807: attributed

10 Nobility is a graceful ornament to the civil order. It is the Corinthian capital of polished society.
Edmund Burke 1729–97: *Reflections on the Revolution in France* (1790)

11 The rank is but the guinea's stamp,
The man's the gowd for a' that!
Robert Burns 1759–96: 'For a' that and a' that' (1790)

12 I am an ancestor.
taunted on his lack of ancestry when made Duke of Abrantes by Napoleon, 1807
Marshal Junot 1771–1813: attributed

13 Kind hearts are more than coronets,
And simple faith than Norman blood.
Alfred, Lord Tennyson 1809–92: 'Lady Clara Vere de Vere' (1842)

14 What I like about the Order of the Garter is that there is no damned merit about it.
Lord Melbourne 1779–1848: Lord David Cecil *The Young Melbourne* (1939)

15 The stately homes of England,
How beautiful they stand!
Amidst their tall ancestral trees,
O'er all the pleasant land.
Felicia Hemans 1793–1835: 'The Homes of England' (1849); see RANK 19

16 Titles distinguish the mediocre, embarrass the superior, and are disgraced by the inferior.
George Bernard Shaw 1856–1950: *Man and Superman* (1903)

17 A fully-equipped duke costs as much to keep up as two Dreadnoughts; and dukes are just as great a terror and they last longer.
David Lloyd George 1863–1945: speech at Newcastle, 9 October 1909

18 When I want a peerage, I shall buy it like an honest man.
Lord Northcliffe 1865–1922: Tom Driberg *Swaff* (1974)

19 The Stately Homes of England,
How beautiful they stand,
To prove the upper classes
Have still the upper hand.
Noël Coward 1899–1973: 'The Stately Homes of England' (1938 song); see RANK 15

20 A medal glitters, but it also casts a shadow.
a reference to the envy caused by the award of honours
Winston Churchill 1874–1965: in 1941; Kenneth Rose *King George V* (1983)

21 There is no stronger craving in the world than that of the rich for titles, except perhaps that of the titled for riches.
Hesketh Pearson 1887–1964: *The Pilgrim Daughters* (1961)

22 What harm have I ever done to the Labour Party?
declining the offer of a peerage
R. H. Tawney 1880–1962: in *Evening Standard* 18 January 1962

23 She needed no royal title to continue to generate her particular brand of magic.
of his sister, Diana, Princess of Wales
Lord Spencer 1964– : tribute at her funeral, 7 September 1997

24 Gongs and medals and ribbons really belong on a Christmas tree.
J. G. Ballard 1930–2009: in *Independent* 14 July 2004

Readiness

see PREPARATION AND READINESS

Reading

see also BOOKS

proverbs and sayings ▶

1 Have you read any good books lately?
catchphrase used by Richard Murdoch in radio comedy series *Much-Binding-in-the-Marsh*, written by Richard Murdoch and Kenneth Horne, started 2 January 1947

2 He that runs may read.
meaning very clear and readable; English proverb, late 16th century, originally with allusion to the Bible (Habakkuk), reinforced by John Keble's 'Septuagesima' (1827), 'There is a book, who runs may read'

3 The man who reads is the man who leads.
American proverb, mid 20th century

quotations ▶

4 When he was reading, he drew his eyes along over the leaves, and his heart searched into the sense, but his voice and tongue were silent.
of St Ambrose
St Augustine of Hippo AD 354–430: *Confessions* (AD 397–8)

5 POLONIUS: What do you read, my lord?
HAMLET: Words, words, words.
William Shakespeare 1564–1616: *Hamlet* (1601)

6 Choose an author as you choose a friend.
Wentworth Dillon, Lord Roscommon 1633–85: *Essay on Translated Verse* (1684)

7 He had read much, if one considers his long life; but his contemplation was much more than his reading. He was wont to say that if he had read as much as other men, he should have known no more than other men.
John Aubrey 1626–97: *Brief Lives* 'Thomas Hobbes'

8 Reading is to the mind what exercise is to the body.
Richard Steele 1672–1729: in *The Tatler* 18 March 1710

9 The bookful blockhead, ignorantly read,
With loads of learned lumber in his head.
Alexander Pope 1688–1744: *An Essay on Criticism* (1711)

10 Much reading is an oppression of the mind, and extinguishes the natural candle, which is the reason of so many senseless scholars in the world.
William Penn 1644–1718: *Fruits of a Father's Love* (1726)

11 A man ought to read just as inclination leads him; for what he reads as a task will do him little good.
Samuel Johnson 1709–84: James Boswell *Life of Samuel Johnson* (1791) 14 July 1763

12 Digressions, incontestably, are the sunshine;—they are the life, the soul of reading;—take them out of this book for instance,—you might as well take the book along with them.
Laurence Sterne 1713–68: *Tristram Shandy* (1759–67)

13 To her kind lessons I ascribe my early and invincible love of reading, which I would not exchange for the treasures of India.
Edward Gibbon 1737–94: *The Decline and Fall of the Roman Empire* (1776–88) 'Memoirs of my Life and Reading'

14 Much have I travelled in the realms of gold,
And many goodly states and kingdoms seen.
John Keats 1795–1821: 'On First Looking into Chapman's Homer' (1817); see LIBRARIES 12

15 Literature is my Utopia.
Helen Keller 1880–1968: *The Story of my Life* (1903)

16 People say that life is the thing, but I prefer reading.
Logan Pearsall Smith 1865–1946: *Afterthoughts* (1931) 'Myself'

17 What do we ever get nowadays from reading to equal the excitement and the revelation in those first fourteen years?

Graham Greene 1904–91: *The Lost Childhood and Other Essays* (1951) title essay

18 What really knocks me out is a book that, when you're all done reading it, you wish the author that wrote it was a terrific friend of yours and you could call him up on the phone whenever you felt like it.

J. D. Salinger 1919–2010: *Catcher in the Rye* (1951)

19 By instructing students how to learn, unlearn and relearn, a powerful new dimension can be added to education... Tomorrow's illiterate will not be the man who can't read; he will be the man who has not learned how to learn.

now usually quoted as 'The illiterate of the 21st century will not be those who cannot read and write, but those who cannot learn, unlearn, and relearn'

Alvin Toffler 1928– : *Future Shock* (1970)

20 Curiously enough, one cannot *read* a book: one can only reread it. A good reader, a major reader, an active and creative reader is a rereader.

Vladimir Nabokov 1899–1977: *Lectures on Literature* (1980) 'Good Readers and Good Writers'

21 The world may be full of fourth-rate writers but it's also full of fourth-rate readers.

Stan Barstow 1928– : in *Daily Mail* 15 August 1989

Reality

see also APPEARANCE, HYPOTHESIS

proverbs and sayings ▶

1 All that glitters is not gold.

an attractive appearance is not necessarily evidence of intrinsic value; English proverb, early 13th century

2 Where's the beef?

advertising slogan for Wendy's Hamburgers in campaign launched 9 January 1984, and subsequently taken up by Walter Mondale in a televised debate with Gary Hart from Atlanta, 11 March 1984: 'When I hear your new ideas I'm reminded of that ad, "Where's the beef?"'

3 You can put your boots in the oven but that doesn't make them biscuits.

modern American saying

phrases ▶

4 cloud cuckoo land

a state of unrealistic or absurdly over-optimistic fantasy; a translation of Greek *Nephelokokkugia*, the name of the city built by the birds in the Greek poet Aristophanes' comedy *Birds* (414 BC)

5 in the cold light of day

when one has had time to consider a situation objectively

6 ivory tower

a state of privileged seclusion or separation from the facts and practicalities of the real world, translating French *tour d'ivoire*, used by the writer Sainte-Beuve (1804–69); see IDEALISM 12

7 Never-Never land

an imaginary, illusory, or Utopian place, often with allusion to the ideal country in J. M. Barrie's *Peter Pan*

8 opium of the people

something regarded as inducing a false and unrealistic sense of contentment among people; from Marx: see RELIGION 23; see also SPORTS 31

9 the real McCoy

the real thing, the genuine article; it is suggested that this originated from the phrase *the real Mackay*, an advertising slogan used by G. Mackay and Co, whisky distillers in Edinburgh in 1870. The form *McCoy* appears to be of US origin

10 the real Simon Pure

the real or genuine person or thing; a character in Centlivre's *A Bold Stroke for a Wife* (1717), who is impersonated by another character during part of the play

quotations ▶

11 Every thing, saith Epictetus, hath two handles, the one to be held by, the other not.

Robert Burton 1577–1640: *The Anatomy of Melancholy* (1621–51)

12 I refute it *thus*.

kicking a large stone by way of refuting Bishop Berkeley's theory of the non-existence of matter

Samuel Johnson 1709–84: James Boswell *Life of Samuel Johnson* (1791) 6 August 1763

13 All theory, dear friend, is grey, but the golden tree of actual life springs ever green.
Johann Wolfgang von Goethe 1749–1832: *Faust* pt. 1 (1808) 'Studierzimmer'

14 What is rational is actual and what is actual is rational.
G. W. F. Hegel 1770–1831: *Grundlinien der Philosophie des Rechts* (1821)

15 All that we see or seem
Is but a dream within a dream.
Edgar Allan Poe 1809–49: 'A Dream within a Dream' (1849)

16 Do you think that the things people make fools of themselves about are any less real and true than the things they behave sensibly about? They are more true: they are the only things that are true.
George Bernard Shaw 1856–1950: *Candida* (1898)

17 Between the idea
And the reality
Between the motion
And the act
Falls the Shadow.
T. S. Eliot 1888–1965: 'The Hollow Men' (1925)

18 They said, 'You have a blue guitar,
You do not play things as they are.'

The man replied, 'Things as they are
Are changed upon the blue guitar.'
Wallace Stevens 1879–1955: 'The Man with the Blue Guitar' (1937)

19 BLANCHE: I don't want realism.
MITCH: Naw, I guess not.
BLANCHE: I'll tell you what I want. Magic!
Tennessee Williams: *A Streetcar Named Desire* (1947)

20 In Israel, in order to be a realist, you must believe in miracles.
David Ben-Gurion 1886–1973: on CBS TV, 5 October 1956

21 Reality goes bounding past the satirist like a cheetah laughing as it lopes ahead of the greyhound.
Claud Cockburn 1904–81: *Crossing the Line* (1958)

22 The camera makes everyone a tourist in other people's reality, and eventually in one's own.
Susan Sontag 1933–2004: in *New York Review of Books* 18 April 1974

23 I keep trying to understand reality, but it always defeats me. I reinvent the world so that I can handle it.
Terry Gilliam 1940– : in *Observer* 12 September 2004

Reason

see LOGIC AND REASON

Rebellion

see REVOLUTION AND REBELLION

Relationships

see also FRIENDSHIP, HATRED, LOVE

proverbs and sayings ▸

1 I am because we are; we are because I am.
whatever affects the individual affects the whole community and whatever affects the whole community affects the individual; African proverb

2 It is easy to kindle a fire on a familiar hearth.
a relationship which has once existed can be revived; Welsh proverb

3 L'amour est aveugle; l'amitié ferme les yeux.
Love is blind; friendship closes its eyes; French proverb; see LOVE 6

4 There is always one who kisses, and one who turns (offers) the cheek.
traditional saying, said to be French in origin

5 Treat a man as he is, and that is what he remains. Treat a man as he can be, and that is what he becomes.
modern saying, from Goethe: see RELATIONSHIPS 12

quotations ▸

6 Am I my brother's keeper?
Bible: Genesis

7 Difficult or easy, pleasant or bitter, you are the same you: I cannot live with you—or without you.
Martial c.AD 40–c.104: *Epigrammata*

8 He who has a thousand friends has
not a friend to spare,
And he who has one enemy will meet
him everywhere.
Ali ibn-Abi-Talib 602–661: *A Hundred Sayings*

9 It is easier to know man in general than to know one man in particular.
Duc de la Rochefoucauld 1613–80: *Maxims* (1678)

10 In necessary things, unity; in doubtful things, liberty; in all things, charity.
Richard Baxter 1615–91: motto

11 Friendship is a disinterested commerce between equals; love, an abject intercourse between tyrants and slaves.
Oliver Goldsmith 1728–74: *The Good-Natured Man* (1768)

12 When we take people, thou wouldst say, merely as they are, we make them worse; when we treat them as if they were what they should be, we improve them as far as they can be improved.
Johann Wolfgang von Goethe 1749–1832: *Wilhelm Meisters Lehrjare* (1795–6), tr. Carlyle; see RELATIONSHIPS 5

13 Love is like the wild rose-briar;
Friendship like the holly-tree:
The holly is dark when the rose-briar
blooms,
But which will bloom most
constantly?
Emily Brontë 1818–48: 'Love and Friendship' (1846)

14 By loving people without cause he discovered indubitable causes for loving them.
Leo Tolstoy 1828–1910: *War and Peace* (1865–9)

15 Ships that pass in the night, and speak
each other in passing;
Only a signal shown and a distant
voice in the darkness;
So on the ocean of life we pass and
speak one another,
Only a look and a voice; then darkness
again and a silence.
Henry Wadsworth Longfellow 1807–82: *Tales of a Wayside Inn* pt. 3 (1874); see MEETING 5

16 Love, friendship, respect do not unite people as much as common hatred for something.
Anton Chekhov 1860–1904: *Notebooks* (1921)

17 Personal relations are the important thing for ever and ever, and not this outer life of telegrams and anger.
E. M. Forster 1879–1970: *Howards End* (1910)

18 I may be wrong, but I have never found deserting friends conciliates enemies.
Margot Asquith 1864–1945: *Lay Sermons* (1927)

19 No human relation gives one possession in another—every two souls are absolutely different. In friendship or in love, the two side by side raise hands together to find what one cannot reach alone.
Kahlil Gibran 1883–1931: *Beloved Prophet: the love letters of Kahlil Gibran and Mary Haskell and her private journal* (1972)

20 The meeting of two personalities is like the contact of two chemical substances: if there is any reaction, both are transformed.
Carl Gustav Jung 1875–1961: *Modern Man in Search of a Soul* (1933)

21 The time to make up your mind about people is never.
Donald Ogden Stewart 1894–1980: *The Philadelphia Story* (1940 film), spoken by Katharine Hepburn as Tracy Lord

22 In human relations kindness and lies are worth a thousand truths.
Graham Greene 1904–91: *The Heart of the Matter* (1948)

23 It is easier to live through someone else than to become complete yourself.
Betty Friedan 1921–2006: *The Feminine Mystique* (1963)

24 And it seems to me you lived your life
Like a candle in the wind.
Never knowing who to cling to
When the rain set in.
Elton John 1947– and **Bernie Taupin** 1950– : 'Candle in the Wind' (song, 1973)

25 Never marry a man who hates his mother, because he'll end up hating you.
Jill Bennett 1931–90: in *Observer* 12 September 1982

26 The ones we choose to love become
our anchor
when the hawser of the blood-tie's
hacked, or frays.
Tony Harrison 1937– : *v* (1985)

27 Men love women, women love children; children love hamsters—it's quite hopeless.
Alice Thomas Ellis 1932–2005: attributed, 1987

28 Their relationship consisted
In discussing if it existed.
Thom Gunn 1929–2004: 'Jamesian' (1992)

29 We have to learn to be human alongside all sorts of others, the ones whose company we don't greatly like.
Rowan Williams 1950– : in *Independent* 1 March 2003

Religion

see also BIBLE, CHRISTIAN CHURCH, CLERGY, GOD, PRAYER, SCIENCE AND RELIGION

proverbs and sayings ►

1 Man's extremity is God's opportunity.
great distress or danger may prompt a person to turn to God for help; English proverb, early 17th century

2 When you pray, move your feet.
advocating works as well as faith; saying, said to be of Quaker origin

phrases ►

3 graven image
an idol; in allusion to the second commandment in the Bible (Exodus) 'Thou shalt not make unto thee any graven image'; see LIFESTYLES 13

4 people of the Book
the Jews and Christians as regarded by Muslims; those whose religion entails adherence to a book of divine revelation

quotations ►

5 Is that which is holy loved by the gods because it is holy, or is it holy because it is loved by the gods?
Plato 429–347 BC: *Euthyphro*

6 *Tantum religio potuit suadere malorum.*
So much wrong could religion induce.
Lucretius c.94–55 BC: *De Rerum Natura*

7 Render therefore unto Caesar the things which are Caesar's; and unto God the things that are God's.
Bible: St Matthew

8 No compulsion is there in religion.
The Koran: sura 2

9 I go into the Muslim mosque and the Jewish synagogue and the Christian church and I see one altar.
Jalal ad-Din ar-Rumi 1207–73: Coleman Barks and John Moyne (eds.) *The Essential Rumi* (1999)

10 I count religion but a childish toy,
And hold there is no sin but
ignorance.
Christopher Marlowe 1564–93: *The Jew of Malta* (1592)

11 One religion is as true as another.
Robert Burton 1577–1640: *The Anatomy of Melancholy* (1621–51)

12 They are for religion when in rags and contempt; but I am for him when he walks in his golden slippers, in the sunshine and with applause.
John Bunyan 1628–88: *The Pilgrim's Progress* (1678)

13 'People differ in their discourse and profession about these matters, but men of sense are really but of one religion.'...'Pray, my lord, what religion is that which men of sense agree in?' 'Madam,' says the earl immediately, 'men of sense never tell it.'
1st Earl of Shaftesbury 1621–83: Bishop Gilbert Burnet *History of My Own Time* vol. 1 (1724)

14 To be furious in religion, is to be irreligiously religious.
William Penn 1644–1718: *Some Fruits of Solitude* (1693)

15 We have just enough religion to make us hate, but not enough to make us love one another.
Jonathan Swift 1667–1745: *Thoughts on Various Subjects* (1711)

16 I went to America to convert the Indians; but oh, who shall convert me?
John Wesley 1703–91: diary 24 January 1738

17 Putting moral virtues at the highest, and religion at the lowest, religion must still be allowed to be a collateral security, at least, to virtue; and every prudent man will sooner trust to two securities than to one.
Lord Chesterfield 1694–1773: *Letters to his Son* (1774) 8 January 1750

18 Orthodoxy is my doxy; heterodoxy is another man's doxy.
William Warburton 1698–1779: to Lord Sandwich; Joseph Priestley *Memoirs* (1807)

19 My country is the world, and my religion is to do good.
Thomas Paine 1737–1809: *The Rights of Man* pt. 2 (1792)

20 Any system of religion that has any thing in it that shocks the mind of a child cannot be a true system.
Thomas Paine 1737–1809: *The Age of Reason* pt. 1 (1794)

21 In vain with lavish kindness
The gifts of God are strown;
The heathen in his blindness
Bows down to wood and stone.
Reginald Heber 1783–1826: 'From Greenland's icy mountains' (1821 hymn); see ARMED FORCES 32

22 As men's prayers are a disease of the will, so are their creeds a disease of the intellect.
Ralph Waldo Emerson 1803–82: *Essays* (1841) 'Self-Reliance'

23 Religion...is the opium of the people.
Karl Marx 1818–83: *A Contribution to the Critique of Hegel's Philosophy of Right* (1843–4); see REALITY 8

24 Things have come to a pretty pass when religion is allowed to invade the sphere of private life.
on hearing an evangelical sermon
Lord Melbourne 1779–1848: G. W. E. Russell *Collections and Recollections* (1898)

25 So long as man remains free he strives for nothing so incessantly and so painfully as to find someone to worship.
Fedor Dostoevsky 1821–81: *The Brothers Karamazov* (1879–80)

26 So many gods, so many creeds,
So many paths that wind and wind,
While just the art of being kind
Is all the sad world needs.
Ella Wheeler Wilcox 1855–1919: 'The World's Need'

27 To become a popular religion, it is only necessary for a superstition to enslave a philosophy.
William Ralph Inge 1860–1954: *Idea of Progress* (1920)

28 There's no reason to bring religion into it. I think we ought to have as great a regard for religion as we can, so as to keep it out of as many things as possible.
Sean O'Casey 1880–1964: *The Plough and the Stars* (1926)

29 Zen...does not confuse spirituality with thinking about God while one is peeling potatoes. Zen spirituality is just to peel the potatoes.
Alan Watts 1915–73: *The Way of Zen* (1957)

30 Religion to me has always been the wound, not the bandage.
Dennis Potter 1935–94: interview with Melvyn Bragg on Channel 4, March 1994, in *Seeing the Blossom* (1994)

31 It is time the West confronted its ignorance of Islam. Jews, Muslims and Christians are all children of Abraham.
Tony Blair 1953– : Labour Party conference, Brighton, 2 October 2001

Repentance
see FORGIVENESS AND REPENTANCE

Reputation
see also FAME

proverbs and sayings ▸

1 Brave men lived before Agamemnon.
to be remembered the exploits of a hero must be recorded; English proverb, early 19th century, from Horace: see BIOGRAPHY 3

2 Common fame is seldom to blame.
reputation is generally founded on fact rather than rumour; English proverb, mid 17th century

3 De mortuis nil nisi bonum.
Latin, literally 'Of the dead, speak kindly or not at all'; see REPUTATION 8

4 **The devil is not so black as he is painted.**
someone may not be as bad as their reputation; English proverb, mid 16th century

5 **A good reputation stands still; a bad one runs.**
American proverb, mid 20th century

6 **He that has an ill name is half hanged.**
someone with a bad reputation is already half way to being condemned on any charge brought against him; English proverb, late 14th century

7 **A man's best reputation for his future is his record of the past.**
American proverb, mid 20th century

8 **Never speak ill of the dead.**
English proverb, mid 16th century; see REPUTATION 3

9 **No smoke without fire.**
rumour is generally founded on fact; English proverb, late 14th century, earlier in French and Latin

10 **One man may steal a horse, while another may not look over a hedge.**
while one person is endlessly indulged, another is treated with suspicion on the slightest evidence; English proverb, mid 16th century

11 **Speak as you find.**
English proverb, late 16th century

12 **Throw dirt enough, and some will stick.**
persistent slander will in the end be believed; English proverb, mid 17th century

13 **When a tiger dies it leaves its skin. When a man dies he leaves his name.**
a person leaves behind more than a body; Japanese proverb

phrases ▸

14 **blot one's copybook**
tarnish one's good reputation; a *copybook* was a book in which copies were written or printed for pupils to imitate, and *copybook* is applied allusively to maxims of a conventional or commonplace character; see CAUSES 25

15 **a blot on one's escutcheon**
a mark on one's reputation; *escutcheon* = an heraldic shield or emblem bearing one's coat of arms

16 **Caesar's wife**
a person required to be above suspicion; Julius Caesar, according to oral tradition, had divorced his wife after unfounded allegations were made against her: see REPUTATION 20

17 **rest on one's laurels**
cease to strive for further glory; *laurels* = leaves of the bay-tree as an emblem of victory or distinction; see SUCCESS 20

quotations ▸

18 **A good name is rather to be chosen than great riches.**
Bible: Proverbs

19 **And some there be, which have no memorial…and are become as though they had never been born…**
But these were merciful men, whose righteousness hath not been forgotten…
Their bodies are buried in peace; but their name liveth for evermore.
Bible: Ecclesiasticus

20 **Caesar's wife must be above suspicion.**
Julius Caesar 100–44 BC: oral tradition, based on Plutarch *Parallel Lives* 'Julius Caesar'; see REPUTATION 16

21 **Woe unto you, when all men shall speak well of you!**
Bible: St Luke

22 ***Non è il mondan romore altro che un fiato***
di vento, ch'or vien quinci ed or qien quindi,
e muta nome perchè muta lato.
The reputation which the world bestows
is like the wind, that shifts now here now there,
its name changed with the quarter whence it blows.
Dante Alighieri 1265–1321: *Divina Commedia* 'Purgatorio'

23 **Who steals my purse steals trash; 'tis something, nothing;**
'Twas mine, 'tis his, and has been slave to thousands;
But he that filches from me my good name

Robs me of that which not enriches him,
And makes me poor indeed.
William Shakespeare 1564–1616: *Othello* (1602–4)

24 They come together like the Coroner's Inquest, to sit upon the murdered reputations of the week.
William Congreve 1670–1729: *The Way of the World* (1700)

25 At ev'ry word a reputation dies.
Alexander Pope 1688–1744: *The Rape of the Lock* (1714)

26 Associate yourself with men of good quality, if you esteem your own reputation; for it is better to be alone than in bad company.
George Washington 1732–99: 'Rules of Civility', written *c.*1745; Jared Sparks *The Writings of George Washington* (1833) vol. 2

27 We owe respect to the living; to the dead we owe only truth.
Voltaire 1694–1778: 'Première Lettre sur Oedipe' in *Oeuvres* (1785)

28 How many people live on the reputation of the reputation they might have made.
Oliver Wendell Holmes 1809–94: *The Autocrat of the Breakfast-Table* (1858)

29 What is merit? The opinion one man entertains of another.
Lord Palmerston 1784–1865: Thomas Carlyle *Shooting Niagara: and After?* (1867)

30 Always providing you have enough courage—or money—you can do without a reputation.
Margaret Mitchell 1900–49: *Gone with the Wind* (1936)

31 Honour is like a match, you can only use it once.
Marcel Pagnol 1895–1974: *Marius* (1946)

32 I'm the girl who lost her reputation and never missed it.
Mae West 1892–1980: P. F. Boller and R. L. Davis *Hollywood Anecdotes* (1988)

33 You can't shame or humiliate modern celebrities. What used to be called shame and humiliation is now called publicity.
P. J. O'Rourke 1947– : *Give War a Chance* (1992)

Revenge

proverbs and sayings ▸

1 Don't cut off your nose to spite your face.
warning against spiteful revenge which is likely to result in your own hurt or loss; English proverb, mid 16th century

2 Don't get mad, get even.
late 20th century saying; see REVENGE 24

3 An eye for an eye makes the whole world blind.
modern saying, often attributed to Mahatma Gandhi (1869–1948); see JUSTICE 19, REVENGE 9

4 He laughs best who laughs last.
the most successful person is the one who is finally triumphant; English proverb, early 17th century

5 He who laughs last, laughs longest.
early 20th century development of REVENGE 4

6 If you want revenge, dig two graves.
pursuit of revenge is likely to be destructive to the pursuer as well as to their object; saying, claimed to be of Chinese or Japanese origin

7 Revenge is a dish that can be eaten cold.
vengeance need not be exacted immediately; English proverb, late 19th century

8 Revenge is sweet.
English proverb, mid 16th century

phrases ▸

9 an eye for an eye
revenge, retaliation in kind; from the Bible (Exodus): see JUSTICE 19, REVENGE 3

10 squeeze until the pips squeak
exact the maximum payment from; originally with reference to Eric Geddes: see REVENGE 21

quotations ▸

11 Vengeance is mine; I will repay, saith the Lord.
Bible: Romans

12 Indeed, revenge is always the pleasure of a paltry, feeble, tiny mind.
Juvenal *c.*AD 60–*c.*140: *Satires*

13 Men should be either treated generously or destroyed, because they

take revenge for slight injuries—for heavy ones they cannot.
Niccolò Machiavelli 1469–1527: *The Prince* (written 1513)

14 Caesar's spirit, ranging for revenge,
With Ate by his side, come hot from hell,
Shall in these confines, with a monarch's voice
Cry, 'Havoc!' and let slip the dogs of war.
William Shakespeare 1564–1616: *Julius Caesar* (1599); see WARFARE 8

15 Revenge is a kind of wild justice, which the more man's nature runs to, the more ought law to weed it out.
Francis Bacon 1561–1626: *Essays* (1625) 'Of Revenge'

16 A man that studieth revenge keeps his own wounds green.
Francis Bacon 1561–1626: *Essays* (1625) 'Of Revenge'

17 Heaven has no rage, like love to hatred turned,
Nor Hell a fury, like a woman scorned.
William Congreve 1670–1729: *The Mourning Bride* (1697); see WOMEN 4

18 We hand folks over to God's mercy, and show none ourselves.
George Eliot 1819–80: *Adam Bede* (1859)

19 *Sic semper tyrannis!* The South is avenged.
having shot President Lincoln, 14 April 1865
John Wilkes Booth 1838–65: '*Sic semper tyrannis* [Thus always to tyrants]'—motto of the State of Virginia; in *New York Times* 15 April 1865 (the second part of the statement possibly apocryphal)

20 Beware of the man who does not return your blow: he neither forgives you nor allows you to forgive yourself.
George Bernard Shaw 1856–1950: *Man and Superman* (1903)

21 The Germans, if this Government is returned, are going to pay every penny; they are going to be squeezed as a lemon is squeezed—until the pips squeak.
Eric Geddes 1875–1937: speech at Cambridge, 10 December 1918; see REVENGE 10

22 If you start throwing hedgehogs under me, I shall throw a couple of porcupines under you.
Nikita Khrushchev 1894–1971: in *New York Times* 7 November 1963

23 Get your retaliation in first.
Carwyn James 1929–83: attributed, 1971

24 Don't get mad, get everything.
advice to wronged wives
Ivana Trump 1949– : spoken in *The First Wives Club* (1996 film); see REVENGE 2

25 And I will have my vengeance, in this life or the next.
David Franzoni 1947– and **others**: *Gladiator* (2000 film), spoken by Russell Crowe as Maximus

Revolution and Rebellion

proverbs and sayings ▸

1 Every revolution was first a thought in one man's mind.
American proverb, mid 19th century

2 Peace to the cottages! War on the palaces!
French revolutionary slogan, 1790s

3 Revolutions are not made by men in spectacles.
American proverb, late 19th century; see REVOLUTION 4

4 Revolutions are not made with rosewater.
revolutions involve violence and ruthless behaviour; English proverb, early 19th century

5 Whosoever draws his sword against the prince must throw the scabbard away.
anyone who tries to assassinate or depose a monarch must remain constantly on the defence; English proverb, early 17th century; see WARFARE 9, WARFARE 13

phrases ▸

6 Boston Tea Party
a violent demonstration in 1773 by American colonists prior to the War of American Independence. Colonists boarded vessels in Boston harbour and threw the cargoes of tea into the water in protest at the imposition of a tax on tea by the British Parliament, in which the colonists had no representation

7 velvet revolution

a non-violent political revolution, especially the relatively smooth change from Communism to a Western-style democracy in Czechoslovakia at the end of 1989

quotations ▶

8 A desperate disease requires a dangerous remedy.

Guy Fawkes 1570–1606: remark, 6 November 1605; see NECESSITY 3

9 The surest way to prevent seditions (if the times do bear it) is to take away the matter of them.

Francis Bacon 1561–1626: *Essays* (1625) 'Of Seditions and Troubles'

10 Rebellion to tyrants is obedience to God.

John Bradshaw 1602–59: suppositious epitaph; Henry S. Randall *Life of Thomas Jefferson* (1865)

11 When the people contend for their liberty, they seldom get anything by their victory but new masters.

Lord Halifax 1633–95: *Political, Moral, and Miscellaneous Thoughts and Reflections* (1750) 'Of Prerogative, Power and Liberty'

12 He wished...that all the great men in the world and all the nobility could be hanged, and strangled with the guts of priests.

quoting 'an ignorant, uneducated man'; often quoted as 'I should like...the last of the kings to be strangled with the guts of the last priest'

Jean Meslier 1664–1733: *Testament* (1864)

13 *Après nous le déluge.*
After us the deluge.

Madame de Pompadour 1721–64: Madame du Hausset *Mémoires* (1824)

14 A little rebellion now and then is a good thing.

Thomas Jefferson 1743–1826: letter to James Madison, 30 January 1787

15 There was reason to fear that the Revolution, like Saturn, might devour in turn each one of her children.

Pierre Vergniaud 1753–93: Alphonse de Lamartine *Histoire des Girondins* (1847)

16 Bliss was it in that dawn to be alive,
But to be young was very heaven!

William Wordsworth 1770–1850: 'The French Revolution, as it Appeared to Enthusiasts' (1809)

17 A share in two revolutions is living to some purpose.

Thomas Paine 1737–1809: Eric Foner *Tom Paine and Revolutionary America* (1976)

18 Those who have served the cause of the revolution have ploughed the sea.

Simón Bolívar 1783–1830: attributed; see FUTILITY 14

19 Revolutions are not made; they come. A revolution is as natural a growth as an oak. It comes out of the past. Its foundations are laid far back.

Wendell Phillips 1811–84: speech, 8 January 1852

20 The social order destroyed by a revolution is almost always better than that which immediately preceded it, and experience shows that the most dangerous moment for a bad government is generally that in which it sets about reform.

Alexis de Tocqueville 1805–59: *L'Ancien régime* (1856)

21 Better to abolish serfdom from above than to wait till it begins to abolish itself from below.

Tsar Alexander II 1818–81: speech in Moscow, 30 March 1856

22 I will die like a true-blue rebel. Don't waste any time in mourning—organize.

prior to his death by firing squad

Joe Hill 1879–1915: farewell telegram to Bill Haywood, 18 November 1915

23 The Germans turned upon Russia the most grisly of all weapons. They transported Lenin in a sealed truck, like a plague bacillus, from Switzerland into Russia.

Winston Churchill 1874–1965: *The World Crisis* (1929)

24 To make war upon rebellion is messy and slow, like eating soup with a knife.

T. E. Lawrence 1888–1935: *Oriental Assembly* (1939)

25 Not believing in force is the same thing as not believing in gravitation.
Leon Trotsky 1879–1940: G. Maximov *The Guillotine at Work* (1940)

26 Come and see the blood
in the streets!
Pablo Neruda 1904–73: 'I'm Explaining a Few Things' (1947)

27 What is a rebel? A man who says no.
Albert Camus 1913–60: *L'Homme révolté* (1951)

28 Would it not be easier
In that case for the government
To dissolve the people
And elect another?
on the 1953 uprising in East Germany
Bertolt Brecht 1898–1956: 'The Solution' (1953)

29 History will absolve me.
Fidel Castro 1927– : title of pamphlet (1953)

30 Those who make peaceful revolution impossible will make violent revolution inevitable.
John F. Kennedy 1917–63: speech at the White House, 13 March 1962

31 The Revolution is made by man, but man must forge his revolutionary spirit from day to day.
Ernesto ('Che') Guevara 1928–67: *Socialism and Man in Cuba* (1968)

32 Ev'rywhere I hear the sound of
marching, charging feet, boy,
'Cause summer's here and the time is
right for fighting in the street, boy.
Mick Jagger 1943– and **Keith Richards** 1943– : 'Street Fighting Man' (1968 song)

33 The most radical revolutionary will become a conservative on the day after the revolution.
Hannah Arendt 1906–75: in *New Yorker* 12 September 1970

34 We must try to find ways to starve the terrorist and the hijacker of the oxygen of publicity on which they depend.
Margaret Thatcher 1925– : speech, 15 July 1985

35 We will make no distinction between the terrorists who committed these acts and those who harbour them.
after the terrorist attacks of 11 September
George W. Bush 1946– : televised address, 11 September 2001

Rivers

proverbs and sayings ▸

1 All rivers run into the sea.
English proverb, early 16th century; originally with biblical allusion to the Bible (Ecclesiastes), 'All the rivers run into the sea; yet the sea is not full; unto the place from whence the rivers come, thither they return again'

2 Says Tweed to Till—
'What gars ye rin sae still?'
Says Till to Tweed—
'Though ye rin with speed
And I rin slaw,
For ae man that ye droon
I droon twa.'
traditional Scottish rhyme

phrases ▸

3 the Father of Waters
the Mississippi; see RIVERS 4

4 Old Man River
the Mississippi; see RIVERS 3, RIVERS 15

quotations ▸

5 Because of you your land never pleads for showers, nor does its parched grass pray to Jupiter the Rain-giver.
of the River Nile
Tibullus c.50–19 BC: *Elegies*

6 Sweet Thames, run softly, till I end my song.
Edmund Spenser 1552–99: *Prothalamion* (1596)

7 I love any discourse of rivers, and fish and fishing.
Izaak Walton 1593–1683: *The Compleat Angler* (1653)

8 Oh, Tiber! father Tiber
To whom the Romans pray,
A Roman's life, a Roman's arms,
Take thou in charge this day!
Lord Macaulay 1800–59: *Lays of Ancient Rome* (1842) 'Horatius'

9 I come from haunts of coot and hern,
I make a sudden sally
And sparkle out among the fern,
To bicker down a valley.
Alfred, Lord Tennyson 1809–92: 'The Brook' (1855)

10 Even the weariest river
Winds somewhere safe to sea.
Algernon Charles Swinburne 1837–1909: 'The Garden of Proserpine' (1866)

11 The great grey-green, greasy,
Limpopo River, all set about with fever trees.
Rudyard Kipling 1865–1936: *Just So Stories* (1902) 'The Elephant's Child'

12 For soft is the song my paddle sings.
Pauline Johnson 1861–1913: 'The Song My Paddle Sings'

13 Then I saw the Congo, creeping through the black,
Cutting through the forest with a golden track.
Vachel Lindsay 1879–1931: 'The Congo' (1914)

14 I've known rivers:
I've known rivers ancient as the world and older than the flow of human blood in human veins.
Langston Hughes 1902–67: 'The Negro Speaks of Rivers' (1921)

15 Ol' man river, dat ol' man river,
He must know sumpin,' but don't say nothin,'
He jus' keeps rollin,'
He jus' keeps rollin' along.
Oscar Hammerstein II 1895–1960: 'Ol' Man River' (1927 song); see RIVERS 4

16 I do not know much about gods; but I think that the river
Is a strong brown god—sullen, untamed and intractable.
T. S. Eliot 1888–1965: *Four Quartets* 'The Dry Salvages' (1941)

17 The Thames is liquid history.
to an American who had compared the Thames disparagingly with the Mississippi
John Burns 1858–1943: in *Daily Mail* 25 January 1943

18 I may be smelly, and I may be old,
Rough in my pebbles, reedy in my pools,
But where my fish float by I bless their swimming
And I like people to bathe in me, especially women.
Stevie Smith 1902–71: 'The River God' (1950)

Royalty

proverbs and sayings ▸

1 Camels, fleas and princes exist everywhere.
referring to the large numbers of offspring of some rulers; Persian proverb

2 The king can do no wrong.
something cannot be wrong if it is done by someone of sovereign power, who alone is not subject to the laws of the land; translation of the Latin legal maxim *rex non potest peccare*; English proverb, mid 17th century

3 A king's chaff is worth more than other men's corn.
even minor benefits available to those attending on a sovereign are more substantial than the best that can be offered by those of lesser status; English proverb, early 17th century

phrases ▸

4 the Black Prince
Edward, Prince of Wales (1330–76), eldest son of Edward III of England; the name Black Prince apparently derives from the black armour he wore when fighting

5 Bonnie Prince Charlie
Charles Edward Stuart, the Young Pretender; Scottish appellation for Charles Edward Stuart, who led the Jacobite uprising of 1745–6; see ROYALTY 18

6 born in the purple
born into an imperial or royal reigning family; *purple* the dye traditionally used for fabric worn by persons of imperial or royal rank; see ROYALTY 15

7 the Chrysanthemum Throne
the throne of Japan; the chrysanthemum is the crest of the imperial family

8 the divine right of kings
the doctrine that monarchs have authority from God alone, independently of their subjects' will; see ROYALTY 30

9 the King over the Water
an exiled sovereign as seen by those loyal to his cause; 18th-century Jacobite toast to James Francis Edward Stuart (1688–1766) and his son Charles Edward Stuart (1720–88), who from exile in France and Italy asserted their right to the British throne against the House of Hanover; see ROYALTY 12, ROYALTY 18, ROYALTY 32

10 **the Merry Monarch**
Charles II (1630–85); from Rochester: see ROYALTY 28

11 **the Nine Days' Queen**
Lady Jane Grey (1537–54); named as his successor by her cousin, the dying Edward VI, she was deposed after nine days on the throne, and was executed in the following year

12 **the Old Pretender**
James Stuart (1688–1766), the son of the exiled James II of England, and focus of Jacobite loyalties; from his assertion of his claim to the British throne against the house of Hanover; see ROYALTY 18, ROYALTY 32

13 **the Peacock Throne**
the former throne of the Kings of Delhi, later that of the Shahs of Iran; adorned with precious stones forming an expanded peacock's tail, the throne was taken to Persia by Nadir Shah (1688–1747), king of Persia, who in 1739 captured Delhi

14 **Stupor Mundi**
Frederick II (1194–1250), Holy Roman Emperor; Latin = wonder of the world

15 **wear the purple**
hold the office of a sovereign or emperor; *purple* the dye traditionally used for fabric worn by persons of imperial or royal rank; see ROYALTY 6

16 **the Widow at Windsor**
Queen Victoria (1819–1901); the Queen's husband, Prince Albert, predeceased her by forty years

17 **the Young Chevalier**
Charles Edward Stuart, the Young Pretender; his father, James Stuart, the Old Pretender, was known by the sobriquet of *The Chevalier (de St George)*; see ROYALTY 5, ROYALTY 18

18 **the Young Pretender**
Charles Edward Stuart (1720–88); son of James Stuart, the Old Pretender, who asserted the Stuart claim to the British throne against the house of Hanover: see ROYALTY 5, ROYALTY 12, ROYALTY 17, ROYALTY 32

quotations ▸

19 Whoso pulleth out this sword of this stone and anvil is rightwise King born of all England.
Thomas Malory d. 1471: *Le Morte D'Arthur* (1470)

20 The anger of the sovereign is death.
Duke of Norfolk 1473–1554: William Roper *Life of Sir Thomas More*

21 I know I have the body of a weak and feeble woman, but I have the heart and stomach of a king, and of a king of England too.
Elizabeth I 1533–1603: speech to the troops at Tilbury on the approach of the Armada, 1588

22 Not all the water in the rough rude sea
Can wash the balm from an anointed king.
William Shakespeare 1564–1616: *Richard II* (1595)

23 Uneasy lies the head that wears a crown.
William Shakespeare 1564–1616: *Henry IV, Part 2* (1597)

24 To be a king and wear a crown is a thing more glorious to them that see it than it is pleasant to them that bear it.
Elizabeth I 1533–1603: The Golden Speech, 1601

25 He is the fountain of honour.
Francis Bacon 1561–1626: *An Essay of a King* (1642); attribution doubtful; see GOVERNMENT 31

26 A subject and a sovereign are clean different things.
Charles I 1600–49: speech on the scaffold, 30 January 1649

27 But methought it lessened my esteem of a king, that he should not be able to command the rain.
Samuel Pepys 1633–1703: diary 19 July 1662

28 A merry monarch, scandalous and poor.
John Wilmot, Lord Rochester 1647–80: 'A Satire on King Charles II' (1697); see ROYALTY 10

29 Titles are shadows, crowns are empty things,
The good of subjects is the end of kings.
Daniel Defoe 1660–1731: *The True-Born Englishman* (1701)

30 The Right Divine of Kings to govern wrong.
Alexander Pope 1688–1744: *The Dunciad* (1742); see ROYALTY 8

31 God save our gracious king!
Long live our noble king!
God save the king!

Anonymous: 'God save the King', attributed to various authors of the mid eighteenth century, including Henry Carey 1687–1743

32 God bless the King, I mean the Faith's Defender;
God bless—no harm in blessing—the Pretender;
But who Pretender is, or who is King,
God bless us all—that's quite another thing.

John Byrom 1692–1763: 'To an Officer in the Army, Extempore, Intended to allay the Violence of Party-Spirit' (1773); see ROYALTY 9, ROYALTY 12, ROYALTY 18

33 The influence of the Crown has increased, is increasing, and ought to be diminished.

John Dunning 1731–83: resolution passed in the House of Commons, 6 April 1780

34 Monarchy is only the string that ties the robber's bundle.

Percy Bysshe Shelley 1792–1822: *A Philosophical View of Reform* (written 1819–20)

35 The king neither administers nor governs, he reigns.

Louis Adolphe Thiers 1797–1877: in *Le National*, 4 February 1830

36 I will be good.

on being shown a chart of the line of succession, 11 March 1830

Queen Victoria 1819–1901: Theodore Martin *The Prince Consort* (1875)

37 The Emperor is everything, Vienna is nothing.

Prince Metternich 1773–1859: letter to Count Bombelles, 5 June 1848

38 Above all things our royalty is to be reverenced, and if you begin to poke about it you cannot reverence it...Its mystery is its life. We must not let in daylight upon magic.

Walter Bagehot 1826–77: *The English Constitution* (1867)

39 The Sovereign has, under a constitutional monarchy such as ours, three rights—the right to be consulted, the right to encourage, the right to warn.

Walter Bagehot 1826–77: *The English Constitution* (1867)

40 Everyone likes flattery; and when you come to Royalty you should lay it on with a trowel.

Benjamin Disraeli 1804–81: to Matthew Arnold; G. W. E. Russell *Collections and Recollections* (1898)

41 At long last I am able to say a few words of my own...you must believe me when I tell you that I have found it impossible to carry the heavy burden of responsibility and to discharge my duties as King as I would wish to do without the help and support of the woman I love.

Edward VIII 1894–1972: radio broadcast following his abdication, 11 December 1936

42 The whole world is in revolt. Soon there will be only five Kings left—the King of England, the King of Spades, the King of Clubs, the King of Hearts and the King of Diamonds.

King Farouk 1920–65: addressed to the author at a conference in Cairo, 1948; Lord Boyd-Orr *As I Recall* (1966)

43 The family firm.

description of the British monarchy

George VI 1895–1952: attributed

44 To be Prince of Wales is not a position. It is a predicament.

Alan Bennett 1934– : *The Madness of King George* (1995 film)

45 I'd like to be a queen in people's hearts but I don't see myself being Queen of this country.

Diana, Princess of Wales 1961–97: interview on *Panorama*, BBC1 TV, 20 November 1995

46 She was the People's Princess, and that is how she will stay...in our hearts and in our memories forever.

Tony Blair 1953– : on hearing of the death of Diana, Princess of Wales, 31 August 1997

Russia

proverbs and sayings ▸

1 Scratch a Russian and you find a Tartar.

if a person is harmed their real national character will be revealed; English proverb, early 19th century

quotations ►

2 God of frostbite, God of famine,
beggars, cripples by the yard,
farms with no crops to examine—
that's him, that's your Russian God.

Prince Peter Vyazemsky 1792–1878: 'The Russian God' (1828)

3 A land that does not like doing things by halves.

Nikolai Gogol 1809–52: *Dead Souls* (1842), tr. D. Magarshak

4 Russia has two generals in whom she can confide—Generals Janvier [January] and Février [February].

Nicholas I 1796–1855: attributed; *Punch* 10 March 1855

5 Every country has its own constitution; ours is absolutism moderated by assassination.

Anonymous: Ernst Friedrich Herbert, Count Münster, quoting 'an intelligent Russian', in *Political Sketches of the State of Europe, 1814–1867* (1868)

6 The Lord God has given us vast forests, immense fields, wide horizons; surely we ought to be giants, living in such a country as this.

Anton Chekhov 1860–1904: *The Cherry Orchard* (1904)

7 I cannot forecast to you the action of Russia. It is a riddle wrapped in a mystery inside an enigma.

Winston Churchill 1874–1965: radio broadcast, 1 October 1939

8 [Russian Communism is] the illegitimate child of Karl Marx and Catherine the Great.

Clement Attlee 1883–1967: speech at Aarhus University, 11 April 1956

9 The Soviet Union has indeed been our greatest menace, not so much because of what it has done, but because of the excuses it has provided us for our failures.

J. William Fulbright 1905–95: in *Observer* 21 December 1958

10 The idea of restructuring [perestroika]...combines continuity and innovation, the historical experience of Bolshevism and the contemporaneity of socialism.

Mikhail Sergeevich Gorbachev 1931– : speech on the seventieth anniversary of the Russian Revolution, 2 November 1987

11 Today is the last day of an era past.

at a Berlin ceremony to end the Soviet military presence in Germany

Boris Yeltsin 1931–2007: in *Guardian* 1 September 1994

12 The tree was already rotten. I just gave it a good shake and the rotten apples fell.

of the Soviet Union

Pope John Paul II 1920–2005: Carl Bernstein and Marco Politi *His Holiness: John Paul II and the Hidden History of our Time* (1996)

13 Anyone who doesn't regret the passing of the Soviet Union has no heart. Anyone who wants it restored has no brains.

Vladimir Putin 1952– : in *New York Times* 20 February 2000; a similar remark was attributed to General Alexander Lebed in *St Petersburg Times* (Florida) 28 June 1996

Satisfaction and Discontent

proverbs and sayings ►

1 Acorns were good till bread was found.

until something better is found, what one has will be judged satisfactory; English proverb, late 16th century

2 The answer is a lemon.

a *lemon* as the type of something unsatisfactory, perhaps referring to the least valuable symbol in a fruit machine; English proverb, early 20th century; see DECEPTION 6

3 Better are small fish than an empty dish.

a little is preferable to nothing at all; English proverb, late 17th century

4 Do not grieve that rose trees have thorns, rather rejoice that thorny bushes bear roses.

advocating an emphasis on positive aspects; Arab proverb; see CIRCUMSTANCE 4, PRACTICALITY 2

5 Go further and fare worse.
it is often wise to take what is on offer; English proverb, mid 16th century

6 Half a loaf is better than no bread.
to have part of something is better than having nothing at all; English proverb, mid 16th century

7 Something is better than nothing.
even a possession of intrinsically little value is preferable to being empty-handed; English proverb, mid 16th century

8 What you've never had you never miss.
English proverb, early 20th century

phrases ▸

9 all gas and gaiters
a satisfactory state of affairs; originally recorded in Dickens *Nicholas Nickleby* (1839) 'all is gas and gaiters'

10 all Sir Garnet
highly satisfactory, all right; Sir *Garnet* Wolseley (1833–1913), leader of several successful military expeditions; see ARMED FORCES 31

11 a chip on one's shoulder
a deeply ingrained grievance, typically about a particular thing. The phrase (originally US) is recorded from the 19th century, and may originate in a practice described in the *Long Island Telegraph* (Hempstead, New York), 20 May 1830, 'When two churlish boys were *determined* to fight, a *chip* would be placed on the shoulder of one, and the other demanded to knock it off at his peril'

12 a dusty answer
an unsatisfactory answer, a disappointing response; from Meredith: see CERTAINTY 19

13 a fly in the ointment
a trifling circumstance that spoils the enjoyment or agreeableness of a thing; after the Bible (Ecclesiastes) 'Dead flies cause the ointment of the apothecary to send forth a stinking savour'

14 rebel without a cause
a person who is dissatisfied with society but does not have a specific aim to fight for, from the title of a US film, starring James Dean, released in 1955

15 sour grapes
an expression or attitude of deliberate disparagement of a desired but unattainable object; alluding to Aesop's fable of 'The Fox and the Grapes', in which a fox unable to reach the grapes contented himself with the reflection that they must be sour

quotations ▸

16 My soul, do not seek immortal life, but exhaust the realm of the possible.
Pindar 518–438 BC: *Pythian Odes*

17 It is called Nirvana because of the getting rid of craving.
Pali Tripitaka 2nd century BC: *Samyutta-nikāya* [Kindred Sayings]

18 So long as the great majority of men are not deprived of either property or honour, they are satisfied.
Niccolò Machiavelli 1469–1527: *The Prince* (written 1513)

19 Some have too much, yet still do crave;
I little have, and seek no more.
They are but poor, though much they have,
And I am rich with little store.
Edward Dyer d. 1607: 'In praise of a contented mind' (1588)

20 'Tis just like a summer birdcage in a garden; the birds that are without despair to get in, and the birds that are within despair, and are in a consumption, for fear they shall never get out.
John Webster c.1580–c.1625: *The White Devil* (1612)

21 About six or seven o'clock, I walk out into a common that lies hard by the house, where a great many young wenches keep sheep and cows and sit in the shade singing of ballads...I talk to them, and find they want nothing to make them the happiest people in the world, but the knowledge that they are so.
Dorothy Osborne 1627–95: letter to William Temple, 2 June 1653

22 We loathe our manna, and we long for quails.
John Dryden 1631–1700: *The Medal* (1682); see GIFTS 8

23 The stoical scheme of supplying our wants, by lopping off our desires, is like cutting off our feet when we want shoes.
Jonathan Swift 1667–1745: *Thoughts on Various Subjects* (1711)

24 You never know what is enough unless you know what is more than enough.
William Blake 1757–1827: *The Marriage of Heaven and Hell* (1790–3) 'Proverbs of Hell'

25 Contented wi' little and cantie wi' mair,
Whene'er I forgather wi' Sorrow and Care,
I gie them a skelp, as they're creeping alang,
Wi' a cog o' gude swats and an auld Scotish sang.
Robert Burns 1759–96: 'Contented wi' little' (1796)

26 Plain living and high thinking are no more:
The homely beauty of the good old cause
Is gone.
William Wordsworth 1770–1850: 'O friend! I know not which way I must look' (1807); see LIFESTYLES 10

27 That all was wrong because not all was right.
George Crabbe 1754–1832: 'The Convert' (1812)

28 In pale contented sort of discontent.
John Keats 1795–1821: 'Lamia' (1820)

29 Ah! *Vanitas Vanitatum!* Which of us is happy in this world? Which of us has his desire? or, having it, is satisfied?
William Makepeace Thackeray 1811–63: *Vanity Fair* (1847–8); see DISILLUSION 6, FUTILITY 19

30 Were there none who were discontented with what they have, the world would never reach anything better.
Florence Nightingale 1820–1910: *Cassandra: an Essay* (1860)

31 It is better to be a human being dissatisfied than a pig satisfied; better to be Socrates dissatisfied than a fool satisfied.
John Stuart Mill 1806–73: *Utilitarianism* (1863)

32 It is an uneasy lot at best, to be what we call highly taught and yet not to enjoy: to be present at this great spectacle of life and never to be liberated from a small hungry shivering self.
George Eliot 1819–80: *Middlemarch* (1871–2)

33 A book of verses underneath the bough,
A jug of wine, a loaf of bread—and Thou
Beside me singing in the wilderness—
Oh, wilderness were paradise enow!
Edward Fitzgerald 1809–83: *The Rubáiyát of Omar Khayyám* (1879 ed.)

34 I'm afraid you've got a bad egg, Mr Jones.
Oh no, my Lord, I assure you! Parts of it are excellent!
Punch: cartoon caption, 1895, showing a curate breakfasting with his bishop; see CHARACTER 22

35 As long as I have a want, I have a reason for living. Satisfaction is death.
George Bernard Shaw 1856–1950: *Overruled* (1916)

36 He spoke with a certain what-is-it in his voice, and I could see that, if not actually disgruntled, he was far from being gruntled.
P. G. Wodehouse 1881–1975: *The Code of the Woosters* (1938)

37 When you don't have any money, the problem is food. When you have money, it's sex. When you have both it's health.
J. P. Donleavy 1926– : *The Ginger Man* (1955)

38 If I can think of it, it isn't what I want.
Randall Jarrell 1914–65: 'A Sick Child' (1955)

39 Let us be frank about it: most of our people have never had it so good.
Harold Macmillan 1894–1986: speech at Bedford, 20 July 1957; 'You Never Had It So Good' was the Democratic Party slogan during the 1952 US election campaign

40 I've had this business that anything is better than nothing. There are times when nothing has to be better than anything.
Penelope Gilliatt 1933–93: *Sunday, Bloody Sunday* (1971)

Schools

see also CHILDREN, EDUCATION, TEACHING

proverbs and sayings ▸

1 No more Latin, no more French,
No more sitting on a hard board bench.
traditional children's rhyme for the end of school term

phrases ▸

2 the happiest days of your life
school days; from the title of a film (1950) based on a play by John Dighton

quotations ▸

3 Public schools are the nurseries of all vice and immorality.
Henry Fielding 1707–54: *Joseph Andrews* (1742)

4 There is now less flogging in our great schools than formerly, but then less is learned there; so that what the boys get at one end they lose at the other.
Samuel Johnson 1709–84: James Boswell *Life of Samuel Johnson* (1791) 1775

5 My object will be, if possible, to form Christian men, for Christian boys I can scarcely hope to make.
on appointment to the Headmastership of Rugby School
Thomas Arnold 1795–1842: letter to Revd John Tucker, 2 March 1828

6 EDUCATION.—At Mr Wackford Squeers's Academy, Dotheboys Hall, at the delightful village of Dotheboys, near Greta Bridge in Yorkshire, Youth are boarded, clothed, booked, furnished with pocket-money, provided with all necessaries, instructed in all languages living and dead, mathematics, orthography, geometry, astronomy, trigonometry, the use of the globes, algebra, single stick (if required), writing, arithmetic, fortification, and every other branch of classical literature. Terms, twenty guineas per annum. No extras, no vacations, and diet unparalleled.
Charles Dickens 1812–70: *Nicholas Nickleby* (1839)

7 'I don't care a straw for Greek particles, or the digamma, no more does his mother. What is he sent to school for?…If he'll only turn out a brave, helpful, truth-telling Englishman, and a gentleman, and a Christian, that's all I want,' thought the Squire.
Thomas Hughes 1822–96: *Tom Brown's Schooldays* (1857)

8 You send your child to the schoolmaster, but 'tis the schoolboys who educate him.
Ralph Waldo Emerson 1803–82: *Conduct of Life* (1860) 'Culture'

9 Forty years on, when afar and asunder
Parted are those who are singing
to-day.
E. E. Bowen 1836–1901: 'Forty Years On' (Harrow School Song, published 1886)

10 Headmasters have powers at their disposal with which Prime Ministers have never yet been invested.
Winston Churchill 1874–1965: *My Early Life* (1930)

11 The dread of beatings! Dread of being
late!
And, greatest dread of all, the dread
of games!
John Betjeman 1906–84: *Summoned by Bells* (1960)

12 I am putting old heads on your young shoulders…all my pupils are the crème de la crème.
Muriel Spark 1918–2006: *The Prime of Miss Jean Brodie* (1961); see EXPERIENCE 12

13 The day of the bog-standard comprehensive is over.
Alastair Campbell 1957– : press briefing, 12 February 2001

14 Life isn't like coursework, baby. It's one damn essay crisis after another.
Boris Johnson 1964– : in *Observer* 15 May 2005

Science

see also ARTS AND SCIENCES, HYPOTHESIS, INVENTIONS, LIFE SCIENCES, PHYSICAL, SCIENCE AND RELIGION, TECHNOLOGY

proverbs and sayings ▸

1 Much science, much sorrow.
suggesting that learning may increase one's awareness of difficult questions; English proverb, early 17th century

2 Science has no enemy but the ignorant.
English proverb, mid 16th century, from Latin *Scientia non habet inimicum nisi ignorantem*

phrases ►

3 backroom boys

people who provide vital scientific and technical support for those in the field who become public figures; the expression derives from Lord Beaverbrook: see FAME 25

quotations ►

4 Lucky is he who has been able to understand the causes of things.

of Lucretius

Virgil 70–19 BC: *Georgics*

5 If anyone wishes to observe the works of nature, he should put his trust not in books of anatomy but in his own eyes.

Galen AD 129–199: *On the Usefulness of the Parts of the Body*

6 Books must follow sciences, and not sciences books.

Francis Bacon 1561–1626: *Resuscitatio* (1657)

7 The changing of bodies into light, and light into bodies, is very conformable to the course of Nature, which seems delighted with transmutations.

Isaac Newton 1642–1727: *Opticks* (1730 ed.)

8 Nature, and Nature's laws lay hid in night.
God said, *Let Newton be!* and all was light.

Alexander Pope 1688–1744: 'Epitaph: Intended for Sir Isaac Newton' (1730); see SCIENCE 17

9 Where observation is concerned, chance favours only the prepared mind.

Louis Pasteur 1822–95: address given on the inauguration of the Faculty of Science, University of Lille, 7 December 1854

10 I almost think it is the ultimate destiny of science to exterminate the human race.

Thomas Love Peacock 1785–1866: *Gryll Grange* (1861)

11 Science knows no country, because knowledge belongs to humanity.

Louis Pasteur 1822–95: toast at banquet of the International Congress of Sericulture, Milan, 1876, in Maurice B. Strauss *Familiar Medical Quotations* (1968)

12 When you can measure what you are speaking about, and express it in numbers, you know something about it; but when you cannot measure it, when you cannot express it in numbers, your knowledge is of a meagre and unsatisfactory kind: it may be the beginning of knowledge, but you have scarcely, in your thoughts, advanced to the stage of *science*, whatever the matter may be.

often quoted as 'If you cannot measure it, then it is not science'

Lord Kelvin 1824–1907: *Popular Lectures and Addresses* vol. 1 (1889) 'Electrical Units of Measurement', delivered 3 May 1883

13 Science is nothing but trained and organized common sense, differing from the latter only as a veteran may differ from a raw recruit: and its methods differ from those of common sense only as far as the guardsman's cut and thrust differ from the manner in which a savage wields his club.

T. H. Huxley 1825–95: *Collected Essays* (1893–4) 'The Method of Zadig'

14 In science, we must be interested in things, not in persons.

Marie Curie 1867–1934: in 1904; Eve Curie *Madame Curie* (1937)

15 Science is built up of facts, as a house is built of stones; but an accumulation of facts is no more a science than a heap of stones is a house.

Henri Poincaré 1854–1912: *Science and Hypothesis* (1905)

16 In science the credit goes to the man who convinces the world, not to the man to whom the idea first occurs.

Francis Darwin 1848–1925: in *Eugenics Review* April 1914 'Francis Galton'

17 It did not last: the Devil howling 'Ho! Let Einstein be!' restored the status quo.

J. C. Squire 1884–1958: 'In continuation of Pope on Newton' (1926); see SCIENCE 8

18 I ask you to look both ways. For the road to a knowledge of the stars leads through the atom; and important knowledge of the atom has been reached through the stars.

Arthur Eddington 1882–1944: *Stars and Atoms* (1928)

19 It is much easier to make measurements than to know exactly what you are measuring.

J. W. N. Sullivan 1886–1937: comment, 1928; R. L. Weber *More Random Walks in Science* (1982)

20 Science is always wrong; it is the very artifice of men. Science can never solve one problem without raising ten more problems.

George Bernard Shaw 1856–1950: BBC broadcast to USA, 28 October 1930

21 It can scarcely be denied that the supreme goal of all theory is to make the irreducible basic elements as simple and as few as possible without having to surrender the adequate representation of a single datum of experience.

often quoted as 'Everything should be made as simple as possible, but not simpler'

Albert Einstein 1879–1955: 'On the Method of Theoretical Physics', lecture delivered at Oxford, 10 June 1933

22 All science is either physics or stamp collecting.

Ernest Rutherford 1871–1937: J. B. Birks *Rutherford at Manchester* (1962)

23 The aim of science is not to open the door to infinite wisdom, but to set a limit to infinite error.

Bertolt Brecht 1898–1956: *Life of Galileo* (1939)

24 The importance of a scientific work can be measured by the number of previous publications it makes it superfluous to read.

David Hilbert 1862–1943: attributed; Lewis Wolpert *The Unnatural Nature of Science* (1993)

25 A new scientific truth does not triumph by convincing its opponents and making them see the light, but rather because its opponents eventually die, and a new generation grows up that is familiar with it.

Max Planck 1858–1947: *A Scientific Autobiography* (1949)

26 The scientific method, as far as it is a method, is nothing more than doing one's damnedest with one's mind, no holds barred.

Percy Williams Bridgeman 1882–1961: *Reflections of a Physicist* (1955)

27 If politics is the art of the possible, research is surely the art of the soluble. Both are immensely practical-minded affairs.

Peter Medawar 1915–87: in *New Statesman* 19 June 1964; see POLITICS 16

28 The world looks so different after learning science. For example, trees are made of air, primarily. When they are burned, they go back to air, and in the flaming heat is released the flaming heat of the sun which was bound in to convert the air into tree.

Richard Phillips Feynman 1918–88: speech to the 15th annual meeting of the National Science Teachers Association, New York City, 1966

29 Basic research is what I am doing when I don't know what I am doing.

Wernher von Braun 1912–77: R. L. Weber *A Random Walk in Science* (1973)

30 Science is an integral part of culture. It's not this foreign thing, done by an arcane priesthood. It's one of the glories of human intellectual tradition.

Stephen Jay Gould 1941–2002: in *Independent* 24 January 1990

Science and Religion

phrases ▸

1 creation science

the reinterpretation of scientific knowledge in accord with belief in the literal truth of the Bible; especially regarding the origin of matter, life, and humankind described in Genesis

2 God of the gaps

God as an explanation for phenomena not yet explained by science; God thought of as acting only in those spheres not otherwise accounted for; see SCIENCE AND RELIGION 11

3 intelligent design

the theory that life, or the universe, cannot have arisen by chance and was designed and created by some intelligent entity

quotations ▸

4 What has Athens to do with Jerusalem?

Tertullian C.AD 160–C.225: *De Proescriptione Haereticorum*

5 Science is for the cultivation of religion, not for worldly enjoyment.
Sadi c.1213–c.91: *The Rose Garden* (1258)

6 In disputes about natural phenomena one must begin not with the authority of Scriptural passage but with sensory experience and necessary demonstrations. For the Holy Scripture and nature derive equally from the Godhead, the former as the dictation of the Holy Spirit and the latter as the most obedient executrix of God's orders.
Galileo 1564–1642: letter to Christina Lotharinga, Archduchess of Tuscany

7 An Aristotle was but the rubbish of an Adam, and Athens but the rudiments of Paradise.
Robert South 1634–1716: *Twelve Sermons...* (1692)

8 If ignorance of nature gave birth to the Gods, knowledge of nature is destined to destroy them.
Paul Henri, Baron d'Holbach 1723–89: *Système de la Nature* (1770)

9 The atoms of Democritus
And Newton's particles of light
Are sands upon the Red Sea shore
Where Israel's tents do shine so bright.
William Blake 1757–1827: *MS Note-Book*

10 I asserted—and I repeat—that a man has no reason to be ashamed of having an ape for his grandfather. If there were an ancestor whom I should feel shame in recalling it would rather be a *man*—a man of restless and versatile intellect—who, not content with an equivocal success in his own sphere of activity, plunges into scientific questions with which he has no real acquaintance, only to obscure them by an aimless rhetoric, and distract the attention of his hearers from the real point at issue by eloquent digressions and skilled appeals to religious prejudice.
replying to Bishop Samuel Wilberforce in the debate on Darwin's theory of evolution
T. H. Huxley 1825–95: at a meeting of the British Association in Oxford, 30 June 1860; see LIFE SCIENCES 15

11 There are reverent minds who ceaselessly scan the fields of Nature and the books of Science in search of gaps—gaps which they will fill up with God. As if God lived in gaps?
Henry Drummond 1851–97: *The Ascent of Man* (1894); see SCIENCE AND RELIGION 2

12 The theory, coarsely enough, and to my Father's great indignation, was defined by a hasty press as being this—that God hid the fossils in the rocks in order to tempt geologists into infidelity.
on Philip Gosse's fundamentalist interpretation of geology (in *Omphalos*, 1857), subsequently applied to evolution
Edmund Gosse 1849–1928: *Father and Son* (1907)

13 Science without religion is lame, religion without science is blind.
Albert Einstein 1879–1955: *Science, Philosophy and Religion: a Symposium* (1941)

14 We have grasped the mystery of the atom and rejected the Sermon on the Mount.
Omar Bradley 1893–1981: speech on Armistice Day, 1948; see CHRISTIAN CHURCH 11

15 There is no evil in the atom; only in men's souls.
Adlai Stevenson 1900–65: speech at Hartford, Connecticut, 18 September 1952

16 The means by which we live have outdistanced the ends for which we live. Our scientific power has outrun our spiritual power. We have guided missiles and misguided men.
Martin Luther King 1929–68: *Strength to Love* (1963)

17 The priest persuades humble people to endure their hard lot; the politician urges them to rebel against it; and the scientist thinks of a method that does away with the hard lot altogether.
Max Perutz 1914–2002: *Is Science Necessary* (1989)

18 How is it that hardly any major religion has looked at science and concluded, 'This is better than we thought! The Universe is much bigger than our prophets said, grander, more subtle, more elegant'?
Carl Sagan 1934–96: *Pale Blue Dot* (1995)

19 The net, or magisterium, of science covers the empirical realm: what

is the universe made of (fact) and why it works that way (theory). The magisterium of religion extends over questions of ultimate meaning and moral value.

Stephen Jay Gould 1941–2002: *Rocks of Ages* (1999)

Scotland

see also BRITISH TOWNS

phrases ▸

1 the curse of Scotland

the nine of diamonds in a pack of cards; perhaps from its resemblance to the armorial bearings, nine lozenges on a saltire, of Lord Stair, from his part in sanctioning the Massacre of Glencoe in 1692; see SCOTLAND 7

2 the land of cakes

Scotland; *cake* = a piece of thin oaten bread

3 Scottish by formation

phrase coined by Scottish novelist Muriel Spark as a criterion for entrants to the Macallan/*Scotland on Sunday* short story competition in 1991

quotations ▸

4 So long as there shall but one hundred of us remain alive, we will never subject ourselves to the dominion of the English. For it is not glory, it is not riches, neither is it honour, but it is freedom alone that we fight and contend for, which no honest man will lose but with his life.

to the Pope, asserting the independence of Scotland

Declaration of Arbroath: letter sent by the Scottish Parliament, 6 April 1320

5 It came with a lass, and it will pass with a lass.

of the crown of Scotland, which had come to the Stuarts through the female line, on learning of the birth of Mary Queen of Scots, December 1542

James V 1512–42: Robert Lindsay of Pitscottie (1500–65) *History of Scotland* (1728)

6 Stands Scotland where it did?

William Shakespeare 1564–1616: *Macbeth* (1606)

7 It's a great work of charity to be exact in rooting out that damnable sept, the worst in all the Highlands.

on hearing that Alasdair Maclan, chief of the Glencoe MacDonalds, had been too late in taking the required oath of loyalty to William III; see SCOTLAND 1

Lord Stair 1648–1707: letter to Thomas Livingston, 11 January 1692

8 Now there's ane end of ane old song.

as he signed the engrossed exemplification of the Act of Union, 1706; see SCOTLAND 21

James Ogilvy, Lord Seafield 1664–1730: *The Lockhart Papers* (1817)

9 The noblest prospect which a Scotchman ever sees, is the high road that leads him to England!

Samuel Johnson 1709–84: James Boswell *Life of Samuel Johnson* (1791) 6 July 1763

10 My heart's in the Highlands, my heart is not here;
My heart's in the Highlands a-chasing the deer.

Robert Burns 1759–96: 'My Heart's in the Highlands' (1790)

11 Scots, wha hae wi' Wallace bled,
Scots, wham Bruce has aften led,
Welcome to your gory bed,—
Or to victorie.

Robert Burns 1759–96: 'Robert Bruce's March to Bannockburn' (1799) (also known as 'Scots, Wha Hae')

12 O Caledonia! stern and wild,
Meet nurse for a poetic child!

Sir Walter Scott 1771–1832: *The Lay of the Last Minstrel* (1805)

13 From the lone shieling of the misty island
Mountains divide us, and the waste of seas—
Yet still the blood is strong, the heart is Highland,
And we in dreams behold the Hebrides!

John Galt 1779–1839: 'Canadian Boat Song' (1829); translated from the Gaelic; attributed

14 They have barred us by barbed wire fences from the bens and glens: the peasant has been ruthlessly swept aside to make room for the pheasant, and the mountain hare now brings

forth her young on the hearthstone of the Gael!
Tom Johnston 1881–1965: *Our Scots Noble Families* (1909)

15 There are few more impressive sights in the world than a Scotsman on the make.
J. M. Barrie 1860–1937: *What Every Woman Knows* (1918)

16 It is never difficult to distinguish between a Scotsman with a grievance and a ray of sunshine.
P. G. Wodehouse 1881–1975: *Blandings Castle and Elsewhere* (1935)

17 O flower of Scotland, when will we see
your like again,
that fought and died for your wee bit
hill and glen
and stood against him, proud
Edward's army,
and sent him homeward tae think
again.
Roy Williamson 1936–90: 'O Flower of Scotland' (1968)

18 Scotland, land of the omnipotent No.
Alan Bold 1943– : 'A Memory of Death' (1969)

19 Scotland small? Our multiform, our
infinite Scotland *small*?
Only as a patch of hillside may be a
cliché corner
To a fool who cries 'Nothing but
heather!'
Hugh MacDiarmid 1892–1978: *Direadh* 1 (1974)

20 I don't want a Stormont. I don't want a wee pretendy government in Edinburgh.
on the prospective Scottish Parliament; often quoted as 'a wee pretendy Parliament'
Billy Connolly 1942– : interview on *Breakfast with Frost* (BBC TV), 9 February 1997

21 The Scottish Parliament which adjourned on 25 March in the year 1707 is hereby reconvened.
Winifred Ewing 1929– : in the Scottish Parliament, 12 May 1999; see SCOTLAND 8

Sculpture

phrases ▸

1 Elgin Marbles
a collection of classical Greek marble sculptures and architectural fragments, chiefly from the frieze and pediment of the Parthenon in Athens; they were brought to England in 1802–12 by the diplomat and art connoisseur Thomas Bruce (1766–1841), the 7th Earl of Elgin

2 fig leaf
representation of the leaf of a fig tree, often used for concealing the genitals in paintings and sculpture; with particular reference to the story of Adam and Eve in the Bible (Genesis), when having eaten of the tree of the knowledge of good and evil and become ashamed of their nakedness, 'they sewed fig leaves together, and made themselves aprons'

quotations ▸

3 The marble not yet carved can hold
the form
Of every thought the greatest artist has.
Michelangelo 1475–1564: Sonnet 15

4 All his statues are so constrained by agony that they seem to wish to break themselves. They all seem ready to succumb to the pressure of despair that fills them.
of Michelangelo
Auguste Rodin 1840–1917: *On Art and Artists* (1911)

5 Carving is interrelated masses conveying an emotion: a perfect relationship between the mind and the colour, light and weight which is the stone, made by the hand which feels.
Barbara Hepworth 1903–75: Herbert Read (ed.) *Unit One* (1934)

6 The first hole made through a piece of stone is a revelation.
Henry Moore 1898–1986: in *Listener* 18 August 1937

7 Sculpture is an art of the open air...I would rather have a piece of my sculpture put in a landscape, almost any landscape, than in, or on, the most beautiful building I know.
Henry Moore 1898–1986: A. D. B. Sylvester *Sculpture and Drawings by Henry Moore* (1951)

8 **Why don't they stick to murder and leave art to us?**
on hearing that his statue of Lazarus in New College chapel, Oxford, kept Khrushchev awake at night
Jacob Epstein 1880–1959: attributed

9 **When smashing monuments, save the pedestals—they always come in handy.**
Stanislaw Lec 1909–66: *Unkempt Thoughts* (1962)

10 **It's amazing what you can do with an E in A-level art, twisted imagination and a chainsaw.**
after winning the 1995 Turner Prize
Damien Hirst 1965– : in *Observer* 3 December 1995

The Sea

proverbs and sayings ▸

1 **The good seaman is known in bad weather.**
American proverb, mid 18th century

2 **He that would go to sea for pleasure would go to hell for a pastime.**
with reference to the dangers involved in going to sea; English proverb, late 19th century

3 **If the Bermudas let you pass, you must beware of Hatteras.**
traditional saying on the dangers of sailing in the Atlantic

4 **One hand for oneself and one for the ship.**
literally, hold on with one hand, and work the ship with the other; English proverb, late 18th century

phrases ▸

5 **Davy Jones's locker**
the deep, especially as the grave of those who are drowned at sea; *Davy Jones* = the evil spirit of the sea

6 **the long forties**
the sea area between the NE coast of Scotland and the SW coast of Norway; from its depth of over 40 fathoms

7 **price of admiralty**
the cost of maintaining command of the seas, often with reference to Kipling's line, 'If blood be the price of admiralty Good God, we ha' paid in full' ('Song of the English', 1893)

8 **the roaring forties**
stormy ocean tracts between latitude 40 and 50 degrees south

9 **the seven seas**
the Arctic, Antarctic, North and South Pacific, North and South Atlantic, and Indian Oceans

quotations ▸

10 **They that go down to the sea in ships: and occupy their business in great waters;**
These men see the works of the Lord: and his wonders in the deep.
Bible: Psalm 107

11 **Full fathom five thy father lies;**
Of his bones are coral made:
Those are pearls that were his eyes:
Nothing of him that doth fade,
But doth suffer a sea-change
Into something rich and strange.
William Shakespeare 1564–1616: *The Tempest* (1611); see CHANGE 27

12 **Whosoever commands the sea commands the trade; whosoever commands the trade of the world commands the riches of the world, and consequently the world itself.**
Walter Ralegh 1552–1618: 'A Discourse of the Invention of Ships, Anchors, Compass, &c.'

13 **The dominion of the sea, as it is an ancient and undoubted right of the crown of England, so it is the best security of the land...The wooden walls are the best walls of this kingdom.**
Thomas Coventry 1578–1640: speech to the Judges, 17 June 1635; see ARMED FORCES 15

14 **What is a ship but a prison?**
Robert Burton 1577–1640: *The Anatomy of Melancholy* (1621–51)

15 **Water, water, everywhere,**
And all the boards did shrink;
Water, water, everywhere,
Nor any drop to drink.
Samuel Taylor Coleridge 1772–1834: 'The Rime of the Ancient Mariner' (1798)

16 **It [the Channel] is a mere ditch, and will be crossed as soon as someone has the courage to attempt it.**
Napoleon I 1769–1821: letter to Consul Cambacérès, 16 November 1803

17 A wet sheet and a flowing sea,
A wind that follows fast
And fills the white and rustling sail
And bends the gallant mast.
Allan Cunningham 1784–1842: 'A Wet Sheet and a Flowing Sea' (1825)

18 Rocked in the cradle of the deep.
Emma Hart Willard 1787–1870: title of song (1840), inspired by a prospect of the Bristol Channel

19 Break, break, break,
On thy cold grey stones, O Sea!
And I would that my tongue could utter
The thoughts that arise in me.
Alfred, Lord Tennyson 1809–92: 'Break, Break, Break' (1842)

20 Meditation and water are wedded for ever.
Herman Melville 1819–91: *Moby Dick* (1851)

21 I must go down to the seas again, to the lonely sea and the sky,
And all I ask is a tall ship and a star to steer her by.
John Masefield 1878–1967: 'Sea Fever'; 'I must down to the seas' in the original of 1902, possibly a misprint

22 The dragon-green, the luminous, the dark, the serpent-haunted sea.
James Elroy Flecker 1884–1915: 'The Gates of Damascus' (1913)

23 The snotgreen sea. The scrotumtightening sea.
James Joyce 1882–1941: *Ulysses* (1922)

24 The sea hates a coward!
Eugene O'Neill 1888–1953: *Mourning becomes Electra* (1931)

25 It is an interesting biological fact that all of us have in our veins the exact same percentage of salt in our blood that exists in the ocean, and therefore, we have salt in our blood, in our sweat, in our tears. We are tied to the ocean. And when we go back to the sea—whether it is to sail or to watch it—we are going back from whence we came.
John F. Kennedy 1917–63: speech, Newport, Rhode Island, 14 September 1962

26 The sea is as near as we come to another world.
Anne Stevenson 1933– : 'North Sea off Carnoustie' (1977)

The Seasons

see also WEATHER

proverbs and sayings ▸

1 A cherry year, a merry year; a plum year, a dumb year.
recording the tradition that a good crop of cherries is a promising sign for the year; English proverb, late 17th century

2 A cold April the barn will fill.
cold weather in April is likely to mean a good harvest later in the year; traditional saying

3 If you do not sow in the spring, you will not reap in the autumn.
Irish proverb

4 It is not spring until you can plant your foot upon twelve daisies.
mild spring weather is only assured when daisies are flowering thickly on the grass; English proverb, mid 19th century

5 May chickens come cheeping.
the weakness of chickens born in May is apparent from their continuous feeble cries. The proverb has also been linked to the idea that marriage in May is unlucky, and that children of such marriages are less likely to survive; English proverb, late 19th century; see WEDDINGS 3

6 One swallow does not make a summer.
a single sign such as the arrival of one migratory swallow does not mean that the summer's settled weather has fully arrived; English proverb, mid 16th century

7 On the first of March, the crows begin to search.
crows traditionally pair off on this day; English proverb, mid 19th century

8 September dries up wells or breaks down bridges.
traditional saying

9 A swarm in May is worth a load of hay; a swarm in June is worth a silver spoon; but a swarm in July is not worth a fly.
traditional beekeepers' saying, meaning that the later in the year it is, the less time there will be for bees to collect pollen from flowers in blossom; English proverb, mid 17th century

10 Winter never rots in the sky.
the arrival of winter is not delayed; English proverb, early 17th century

phrases ▸

11 a blackthorn winter
a period of cold weather in early spring, at the time when the blackthorn is in flower

12 fall of the leaf
autumn

13 February fill-dyke
the month of February; referring to the month's rain and snows; see WEATHER 4

quotations ▸

14 Sumer is icumen in,
Lhude sing cuccu!
Anonymous: 'Cuckoo Song' (1250), sung annually at Reading Abbey gateway and first recorded by John Fornset, a monk of Reading Abbey; see SEASONS 27

15 In a somer seson, whan softe was the sonne.
William Langland c.1330–c.1400: *The Vision of Piers Plowman*

16 Whan that Aprill with his shoures soote
The droghte of March hath perced to the roote.
Geoffrey Chaucer 1343–1400: *The Canterbury Tales* 'The General Prologue'

17 I sing of brooks, of blossoms, birds, and bowers:
Of April, May, of June, and July-flowers.
I sing of May-poles, Hock-carts, wassails, wakes,
Of bride-grooms, brides, and of their bridal-cakes.
Robert Herrick 1591–1674: 'The Argument of his Book' from *Hesperides* (1648)

18 Early autumn—
rice field, ocean,
one green.
Matsuo Basho 1644–94: translated by Lucien Stryk

19 The way to ensure summer in England is to have it framed and glazed in a comfortable room.
Horace Walpole 1717–97: letter to Revd William Cole, 28 May 1774

20 Snowy, Flowy, Blowy,
Showery, Flowery, Bowery,
Hoppy, Croppy, Droppy,
Breezy, Sneezy, Freezy.
George Ellis 1753–1815: 'The Twelve Months'

21 Season of mists and mellow fruitfulness,
Close bosom-friend of the maturing sun;
Conspiring with him how to load and bless
With fruit the vines that round the thatch-eaves run.
John Keats 1795–1821: 'To Autumn' (1820)

22 In...the fall, the whole country goes to glory.
of North America
Frances Trollope 1780–1863: *Domestic Manners of the Americans* (1832)

23 A tedious season they await
Who hear November at the gate.
Alexander Pushkin 1799–1837: *Eugene Onegin* (1833)

24 No warmth, no cheerfulness, no healthful ease,
No comfortable feel in any member—
No shade, no shine, no butterflies, no bees,
No fruits, no flowers, no leaves, no birds,—
November!
Thomas Hood 1799–1845: 'No!' (1844)

25 Oh, to be in England
Now that April's there.
Robert Browning 1812–89: 'Home-Thoughts, from Abroad' (1845)

26 In winter I get up at night
And dress by yellow candle-light.
In summer, quite the other way,—
I have to go to bed by day.
Robert Louis Stevenson 1850–94: 'Bed in Summer' (1885)

27 Winter is icummen in,
Lhude sing Goddamm.
Ezra Pound 1885–1972: 'Ancient Music' (1917); see SEASONS 14

28 April is the cruellest month, breeding
Lilacs out of the dead land, mixing
Memory and desire, stirring
Dull roots with spring rain.
T. S. Eliot 1888–1965: *The Waste Land* (1922)

29 Summer time an' the livin' is easy,
Fish are jumpin' an' the cotton is high.
Du Bose Heyward 1885–1940 and **Ira Gershwin** 1896–1983: 'Summertime' (1935 song)

30 It is about five o'clock in an evening that the first hour of spring strikes—autumn arrives in the early morning, but spring at the close of a winter day.
Elizabeth Bowen 1899–1973: *The Death of the Heart* (1938)

31 'What is autumn?' 'A second spring, where every leaf is a flower.'
Albert Camus 1913–60: 'Le Malentendu' (1944)

32 June is bustin' out all over.
Oscar Hammerstein II 1895–1960: title of song (1945)

33 August creates as she slumbers, replete and satisfied.
Joseph Wood Krutch 1893–1970: *Twelve Seasons* (1949)

34 What of October, that ambiguous month, the month of tension, the unendurable month?
Doris Lessing 1919– : *Martha Quest* (1952)

35 For man, autumn is a time of harvest, of gathering together. For nature, it is a time of sowing, of scattering abroad.
Edwin Way Teale 1899–1980: *Autumn Across America* (1956)

36 Work seethes in the hands of spring, That strapping dairymaid.
Boris Pasternak 1890–1960: *Doctor Zhivago* (1958) 'Zhivago's Poems: March'

Secrecy

proverbs and sayings ▸

1 The day has eyes, the night has ears.
there is always someone watching or listening; traditional saying

2 Dead men tell no tales.
often used to imply that a person's knowledge of a secret will die with them; English proverb, mid 17th century

3 Don't ask, don't tell.
summary of the Clinton administration's compromise policy on homosexuals serving in the armed forces, as described by Sam Nunn (1938–) in May 1993

4 Fields have eyes and woods have ears.
one may always be spied on by unseen watchers or listeners; English proverb, early 13th century

5 Listeners never hear any good of themselves.
English proverb, mid 17th century

6 Little pitchers have large ears.
children overhear what is not meant for them (a pitcher's *ears* are its handles); English proverb, mid 16th century

7 My lips are sealed.
used to convey that one will not discuss or reveal something; popular version of Stanley Baldwin's speech on the Abyssinian crisis, 10 December 1935, when he told the House of Commons, 'My lips are not yet unsealed. Were these troubles over I would make a case, and I guarantee that not a man would go into the lobby against us.'

8 Never tell tales out of school.
a warning against indiscretion; English proverb, mid 16th century

9 No names, no pack-drill.
if nobody is named as being responsible, nobody can be blamed or punished (*pack-drill* = a military punishment of walking up and down carrying full equipment); English proverb, early 20th century, the expression is now used generally to express an unwillingness to provide detailed information

10 One does not wash one's dirty linen in public.
discreditable matters should be dealt with privately; English proverb, early 19th century

11 Sch...you know who.
advertising slogan for Schweppes mineral drinks, 1960s

12 See all your best work go unnoticed.
advertisement for staff for MI5, 2005

13 Those who hide can find.
those who have concealed something know where it is to be found; English proverb, early 15th century

14 Three may keep a secret, if two of them are dead.
the only way to keep a secret is to tell no-one else; English proverb, mid 16th century

15 Walls have ears.
care should be taken for possible eavesdroppers; English proverb, late 16th century

16 Will the real — please stand up?
catchphrase from an American TV game show (1955–66) in which a panel was asked to identify the 'real' one of three candidates all claiming to be a particular person; after the guesses were made, the compère would request the 'real' candidate to stand up

17 You can't hide an awl in a sack.
some things are too conspicuous to hide; Russian proverb

phrases ▶

18 an ace up one's sleeve
something effective held in reserve, a hidden advantage; an *ace* as the card of highest value in a card-game; see POLITICIANS 23

19 Chinese wall
an insurmountable barrier to understanding (alluding to the Great Wall of China); on the Stock Exchange, a prohibition against the passing of confidential information from one department of a financial institution to another

20 hidden agenda
a secret or ulterior motive for something

21 quiet American
a person suspected of being an undercover agent or spy; with allusion to Graham Greene's *The Quiet American* (1955)

22 a skeleton in the cupboard
a secret source of discredit, pain, or shame; brought into literary use by Thackeray in 1845, 'there is a skeleton in every house'

23 a smoking pistol
a piece of incontrovertible incriminating evidence; on the assumption that a person found with a smoking pistol or gun must be the guilty party; particularly associated with Barber B. Conable's comment on a Watergate tape revealing President Nixon's wish to limit FBI involvement in the investigation: 'I guess we have found the smoking pistol, haven't we?'; see HYPOTHESIS 32

24 something nasty in the woodshed
a traumatic experience or a concealed unpleasantness in a person's background; from Stella Gibbons *Cold Comfort Farm* (1932), the repeated assertion 'I saw something nasty in the woodshed' being Aunt Ada Doom's method of ensuring her family's continued attendance on her

25 under the rose
in secret, sometimes found in Latin = *sub rosa*; there is reason to believe that the phrase originated in Germany

quotations ▶

26 And whatsoever I shall see or hear in the course of my profession, as well as outside my profession in my intercourse with men, if it be what should not be published abroad, I will never divulge holding such things to be holy secrets.
Hippocrates c.460–357 BC: *The Hippocratic Oath* (tr. W. H. S. Jones)

27 DUKE: And what's her history?
VIOLA: A blank, my lord. She never
told her love,
But let concealment, like a worm i'
the bud,
Feed on her damask cheek.
William Shakespeare 1564–1616: *Twelfth Night* (1601)

28 I would not open windows into men's souls.
Elizabeth I 1533–1603: oral tradition, the words very possibly originating in a letter drafted by Bacon; J. B. Black *Reign of Elizabeth 1558–1603* (1936)

29 For secrets are edged tools,
And must be kept from children and
from fools.
John Dryden 1631–1700: *Sir Martin Mar-All* (1667)

30 Nothing weighs so heavy as a secret; women find it difficult to carry one far. And I know a lot of men who are just like women about this.
Jean de la Fontaine 1621–95: *Fables* bk. 8 (1678–9) 'The Women and the Secret'

31 The necessity of procuring good intelligence is apparent and need not be further urged.
George Washington 1732–99: letter, 26 July 1777

32 Secrets with girls, like loaded guns
with boys,
Are never valued till they make a noise.
George Crabbe 1754–1832: *Tales of the Hall* (1819) 'The Maid's Story'

33 A secret may be sometimes best kept by keeping the secret of its being a secret.
Henry Taylor 1800–86: *The Statesman* (1836)

34 We never knows wot's hidden in each other's hearts; and if we had glass winders there, we'd need keep the shutters up, some on us, I do assure you!
Charles Dickens 1812–70: *Martin Chuzzlewit* (1844)

35 After the first silence the small man said to the other: 'Where does a wise man hide a pebble?' And the tall man answered in a low voice: 'On the beach.' The small man nodded, and after a short silence said: 'Where does a wise man hide a leaf?' And the other answered: 'In the forest.'
G. K. Chesterton 1874–1936: *The Innocence of Father Brown* (1911)

36 We dance round in a ring and suppose,
But the Secret sits in the middle and knows.
Robert Frost 1874–1963: 'The Secret Sits' (1942)

37 Secrecy lies at the very core of power.
Elias Canetti 1905–94: *Crowds and Power* (1960)

38 Once the toothpaste is out of the tube, it is awfully hard to get it back in.
on the Watergate affair
H. R. Haldeman 1929– : to John Dean, 8 April 1973

39 That's another of those irregular verbs, isn't it? I give confidential briefings; you leak; he has been charged under Section 2a of the Official Secrets Act.
Jonathan Lynn 1943– and **Antony Jay** 1930– : *Yes Prime Minister* (1987) vol. 2 'Man Overboard'

40 I am deeply troubled about asserting these rights, because it may be perceived by some that I have something to hide.
invoking his Fifth Amendment protection and declining to answer Congress's questions on the Enron collapse; see SELF-INTEREST 18
Kenneth L. Lay 1942–2006: in *Newsweek* 25 February 2002

The Self

proverbs and sayings ▸

1 Deny self for self's sake.
the result of self-denial is likely to be self-improvement; American proverb, mid 18th century

2 Every man is the architect of his own fortune.
each person is ultimately responsible for what happens to them; English proverb, mid 16th century; see FATE 13

quotations ▸

3 The commander of three armies may be taken away but the will of even a common man may not be taken away from him.
Confucius 551–479 BC: *Analects*

4 If a man should conquer in battle a thousand and a thousand more, and another man should conquer himself, his would be the greater victory, because the greatest of victories is the victory over oneself.
Pali Tripitaka 2nd century BC: *Dhammapada*

5 If I am not for myself who is for me; and being for my own self what am I? If not now when?
Hillel 'The Elder' c.60 BC–c.AD 9: *Pirqe Aboth*

6 But by the grace of God I am what I am.
Bible: I Corinthians; see SELF 15

7 To study the self is to forget the self. To forget the self is to be authenticated by the myriad things.
often quoted as '…to become one with the ten thousand things'
Dogen Kigen 1200–53: William R. LaFleur (ed.) *Dogen Studies* (1985)

8 Every man's ordure well to his own sense doth smell.
Montaigne 1533–92: *Essays* (1580, Florio's translation of 1603), quoting the Latin of Erasmus (1469–1536)

9 This above all: to thine own self be true,
And it must follow, as the night the day,
Thou canst not then be false to any man.
William Shakespeare 1564–1616: *Hamlet* (1601)

10 Who is it that can tell me who I am?
William Shakespeare 1564–1616: *King Lear* (1605–6)

11 But I do nothing upon my self, and yet I am mine own *Executioner*.
John Donne 1572–1631: *Devotions upon Emergent Occasions* (1624)

12 It is the nature of extreme self-lovers, as they will set a house on fire, and it were but to roast their eggs.
Francis Bacon 1561–1626: *Essays* (1625) 'Of Wisdom for a Man's Self'

13 The self is hateful.
Blaise Pascal 1623–62: *Pensées* (1670)

14 It is not contrary to reason to prefer the destruction of the whole world to the scratching of my finger.
David Hume 1711–76: *A Treatise upon Human Nature* (1739)

15 Though not all these, not what I ought to be, not what I might be, not what I wish or hope to be, and not what I once was, I think I can truly say with the apostle, 'By the grace of God I am what I am.'
John Newton 1725–1807: speaking shortly before his death; *Letters* (1869); see SELF 6

16 I am—yet what I am, none cares or knows;
My friends forsake me like a memory lost:
I am the self-consumer of my woes.
John Clare 1793–1864: 'I Am' (1848)

17 Do I contradict myself?
Very well then I contradict myself,
(I am large, I contain multitudes.)
Walt Whitman 1819–92: 'Song of Myself' (written 1855)

18 It matters not how strait the gate,
How charged with punishments the scroll,
I am the master of my fate:
I am the captain of my soul.
W. E. Henley 1849–1903: 'Invictus. In Memoriam R.T.H.B.' (1888)

19 Rose is a rose is a rose is a rose, is a rose.
Gertrude Stein 1874–1946: *Sacred Emily* (1913)

20 I am I plus my surroundings, and if I do not preserve the latter I do not preserve myself.
José Ortega y Gasset 1883–1955: *Meditaciones del Quijote* (1914)

21 Through the Thou a person becomes I.
Martin Buber 1878–1965: *Ich und Du* (1923)

22 Whatever people think I am or say I am, that's what I'm not.
Alan Sillitoe 1928–2010: *Saturday Night and Sunday Morning* (1958)

23 The image of myself which I try to create in my own mind in order that I may love myself is very different from the image which I try to create in the minds of others in order that they may love me.
W. H. Auden 1907–73: *Dyer's Hand* (1963) 'Hic et Ille'

24 When a man points a finger at someone else, he should remember that four of his fingers are pointing to himself.
Louis Nizer 1902–94: *My Life in Court* (1963)

25 A man sets himself the task of portraying the world...Shortly before his death he discovers that that patient labyrinth of lines traces the image of his face.
Jorge Luis Borges 1899–1986: *Dreamtigers* (1964)

26 I am not a number, I am a free man!
Patrick McGoohan 1928–2009: Number Six, in *The Prisoner* (TV series 1967–68)

27 My one regret in life is that I am not someone else.
Woody Allen 1935– : Eric Lax *Woody Allen and his Comedy* (1975)

28 Whatever you are is never enough; you must find a way to accept something however small from the other to make you whole.
Chinua Achebe 1930– : *Anthills of the Savannah* (1987)

29 Personal isn't the same as important.
Terry Pratchett 1948– : *Men at Arms* (1993)

30 'You' your joys and your sorrows, your memories and ambitions, your sense of personal identity and free will, are in fact no more than the behaviour of a vast assembly of nerve cells and their associated molecules.
Francis Crick 1916–2004: *The Astonishing Hypothesis: The Scientific Search for the Soul* (1994)

Self-Esteem and Self-Assertion

see also PRIDE

proverbs and sayings ▸

1 Because I'm worth it.
advertising slogan for L'Oreal beauty products, from mid 1980s

2 The bigger the hat the smaller the property
Australian saying

3 Clever hawks conceal their claws.
it is not necessary to boast of one's abilities; Japanese proverb

4 A frog in a well knows nothing of the ocean.
one should be aware of the limitations of one's own experience; Japanese proverb

5 Here's tae us; wha's like us?
Gey few, and they're a' deid.
Scottish toast, probably of 19th-century origin

6 The kumara does not speak of its own sweetness.
one should not praise oneself (*kumara* = a sweet potato); Maori proverb

7 Self-praise is no recommendation.
a person's own favourable account of themselves is of dubious worth; English proverb, early 19th century

phrases ▸

8 a fly on the wheel
a person who overestimates his or her own influence; see SELF-ESTEEM 14

9 hide one's light under a bushel
conceal one's merits; with allusion to the Bible (Matthew) 'Neither do men light a candle, and put it under a bushel, but on a candlestick; and it giveth light unto all that are in the house'

10 little tin god
a self-important person; *tin* implicitly contrasted with precious metals; an object of unjustified veneration

11 pooh-bah
a person having much influence or holding many offices at the same time, especially one perceived as pompously self-important; from the name of a character in W. S. Gilbert's *The Mikado* (1885)

quotations ▸

12 Seest thou a man wise in his own conceit? There is more hope of a fool than of him.
Bible: Proverbs

13 Lord I am not worthy that thou shouldest come under my roof.
Bible: St Matthew

14 It was prettily devised of Aesop, 'The fly sat upon the axletree of the chariot-wheel and said, what a dust do I raise.'
Francis Bacon 1561–1626: *Essays* (1625) 'Of Vain-Glory'; see SELF-ESTEEM 8

15 Oft-times nothing profits more
Than self esteem, grounded on just and right
Well managed.
John Milton 1608–74: *Paradise Lost* (1667); see POETS 25

16 He that falls in love with himself will have no rivals.
Benjamin Franklin 1706–90: *Poor Richard's Almanac* May 1739

17 Where he falls short, 'tis Nature's fault alone;
Where he succeeds, the merit's all his own.
of the actor, Thomas Sheridan
Charles Churchill 1731–64: *The Rosciad* (1761)

18 All his own geese are swans, as the swans of others are geese.
of Joshua Reynolds
Horace Walpole 1717–97: letter to Anne, Countess of Upper Ossory, 1 December 1786; see PRAISE 7

19 The axis of the earth sticks out visibly through the centre of each and every town or city.
Oliver Wendell Holmes 1809–94: *The Autocrat of the Breakfast-Table* (1858)

20 He was like a cock who thought the sun had risen to hear him crow.
George Eliot 1819–80: *Adam Bede* (1859)

21 on the suggestion that his attacks on John Bright were too harsh as Bright was a self-made man:
I know he is and he adores his maker.
Benjamin Disraeli 1804–81: Leon Harris *The Fine Art of Political Wit* (1965)

22 You must stir it and stump it,
And blow your own trumpet,
Or trust me, you haven't a chance.
W. S. Gilbert 1836–1911: *Ruddigore* (1887)

23 It is easy—terribly easy— to shake a man's faith in himself. To take advantage of that to break a man's spirit is devil's work.
George Bernard Shaw 1856–1950: *Candida* (1898)

24 If you have no confidence in self you are twice defeated in the race of life. With confidence you have won even before you have started.

Marcus Garvey 1887–1940: *Philosophy and Opinions of Marcus Garvey* (1923)

25 Anything you can do, I can do better, I can do anything better than you.

Irving Berlin 1888–1989: 'Anything You Can Do' (1946 song)

26 Early in life I had to choose between honest arrogance and hypocritical humility. I chose honest arrogance and have seen no occasion to change.

Frank Lloyd Wright 1867–1959: Herbert Jacobs *Frank Lloyd Wright* (1965)

27 I'm the greatest.

Muhammad Ali (Cassius Clay) 1942– : catchphrase used from 1962, in *Louisville Times* 16 November 1962

28 It's easy to be independent when you've got money. But to be independent when you haven't got a thing—that's the Lord's test.

Mahalia Jackson 1911–72: *Movin' On Up* (with Evan McLoud Wylie 1966)

29 That's it baby, when you got it, flaunt it.

Mel Brooks 1926– : *The Producers* (1968 film)

30 Pretentious? *Moi*?

John Cleese 1939– and **Connie Booth** 1944– : *Fawlty Towers* 'The Psychiatrist' (BBC TV programme, 1979)

31 Shyness is just egotism out of its depth.

Penelope Keith 1940– : in *Daily Mail* 27 June 1988

32 Our deepest fear is not that we are inadequate. Our deepest fear is that we are powerful beyond measure. It is our light, not our darkness, that most frightens us.

Marianne Williamson 1953– : *A Return to Love* (1992)

33 Our mistreatment was just not right, and I was tired of it.

of her refusal, on 1 December 1955, to surrender her seat on a segregated bus in Alabama to a white man

Rosa Parks 1913–2005: *Quiet Strength* (1994)

Self-Interest

see also SELF-SACRIFICE

proverbs and sayings ▶

1 Every man for himself and God for us all.

ultimately God is concerned for humankind while individuals are concerned only for themselves; English proverb, mid 16th century

2 Every man for himself, and the Devil take the hindmost.

each person must look out for their own interests, and that the weakest is likely to come to disaster; English proverb, early 16th century

3 Hear all, see all, say nowt, tak'all, keep all, gie nowt, and if tha ever does owt for nowt do it for thysen.

now associated with Yorkshire, and caricaturing supposedly traditional Yorkshire attributes, in the picture of someone who is shrewd, taciturn, grasping, and selfish; English proverb, early 15th century

4 If you want a thing done well, do it yourself.

no-one else has so much interest in your own welfare; English proverb, mid 17th century

5 If you would be well served, serve yourself.

no-one else has so much interest in your own welfare; English proverb, mid 17th century

6 Near is my kirtle, but nearer is my smock.

used as a justification for putting one's own interests first (a *kirtle* is a woman's skirt or gown, and a *smock* is an undergarment); English proverb, mid 15th century

7 Near is my shirt, but nearer is my skin.

a justification of self-interest; English proverb, late 16th century

8 A satisfied person does not know the hungry person.

African proverb

9 Self-preservation is the first law of nature.

the instinct for self-preservation is inbuilt and instinctive; English proverb, mid 17th century

phrases ▸

10 **bow down in the house of Rimmon**
pay lip-service to a principle; sacrifice one's principles for the sake of conformity; *Rimmon* a deity worshipped in ancient Damascus; after the Bible (2 Kings) 'I bow myself in the house of Rimmon'

11 **cultivate one's garden**
attend to one's own affairs; after Voltaire: see SELF-INTEREST 25

12 **dog in the manger**
a person who selfishly refuses to let others enjoy benefits for which he or she personally has no use; from Aesop's fable of a dog which jumped into a manger and would not let the ox or horse eat the hay

13 **an eye to the main chance**
consideration for one's own interests; the *main chance* literally, in the game of hazard, a number (5, 6, 7, or 8) called by a player before throwing the dice

14 **I'm all right, Jack**
expressing selfish complacency and unconcern for others; originally in nautical use

15 **law of the jungle**
a system in which brute force and self-interest are paramount; the supposed code of survival in jungle life

16 **like turkeys voting for Christmas**
used to suggest that a particular action or decision is hopelessly self-defeating; see SELF-INTEREST 31

17 **not in my back yard**
expressing an objection to the siting of something regarded as unpleasant in one's own locality, while by implication finding it acceptable elsewhere; originating in the United States in derogatory references to the anti-nuclear movement, and in Britain particularly associated with reports of the then Environment Secretary Nicholas Ridley's opposition in 1988 to housing developments near his home; the acronym NIMBY derives from this

18 **take the Fifth (Amendment)**
in America, decline to incriminate oneself; appeal to Article V of the ten original amendments (1791) to the Constitution of the United States, which states that 'no person...shall be compelled in any criminal case to be a witness against himself'; see SECRECY 40

19 **throw someone to the wolves**
sacrifice another person in order to avert danger or difficulties for oneself; probably in allusion to stories of wolves in a pack pursuing travellers in a horse-drawn sleigh

quotations ▸

20 Nothing is easier than self-deceit. For what each man wishes, that he also believes to be true.
Demosthenes c.384–c.322 BC: *Third Olynthiac*; see SELF-INTEREST 22

21 *Cui bono?*
To whose profit?
Cicero 106–43 BC: *Pro Roscio Amerino*; quoting L. Cassius Longinus Ravilla

22 Men are nearly always willing to believe what they wish.
Julius Caesar 100–44 BC: *De Bello Gallico*; see SELF-INTEREST 20

23 Thus God and nature linked the gen'ral frame,
And bade self-love and social be the same.
Alexander Pope 1688–1744: *An Essay on Man* Epistle 3 (1733)

24 And this is law, I will maintain,
Unto my dying day, Sir,
That whatsoever King shall reign,
I will be the Vicar of Bray, sir!
Anonymous: 'The Vicar of Bray' (1734 song)

25 *Il faut cultiver notre jardin.*
We must cultivate our garden.
Voltaire 1694–1778: *Candide* (1759); see SELF-INTEREST 11

26 It is not from the benevolence of the butcher, the brewer, or the baker, that we expect our dinner, but from their regard to their own interest. We address ourselves not to their humanity but their self love.
Adam Smith 1723–90: *Wealth of Nations* (1776)

27 All sensible people are selfish, and nature is tugging at every contract to make the terms of it fair.
Ralph Waldo Emerson 1803–82: *The Conduct of Life* (1860)

28 He would, wouldn't he?
on being told that Lord Astor claimed that her allegations, concerning himself and his house parties at Cliveden, were untrue
Mandy Rice-Davies 1944– : at the trial of Stephen Ward, 29 June 1963

29 Fourteen heart attacks and he had to die in my week. In MY week.
when ex-President Eisenhower's death prevented her photograph appearing on the cover of *Newsweek*
Janis Joplin 1943–70: in *New Musical Express* 12 April 1969

30 We are now in the Me Decade—seeing the upward roll of...the third great religious wave in American history... and this one has the mightiest, holiest roll of all, the beat that goes...*Me... Me...Me...Me.*
Tom Wolfe 1931– : *Mauve Gloves and Madmen* (1976)

31 It's the first time in recorded history that turkeys have been known to vote for an early Christmas.
on the collapse of the pact between Labour and the Liberals; see SELF-INTEREST 16
James Callaghan 1912–2005: in the House of Commons, 28 March 1979

Self-Knowledge

proverbs and sayings ▸

1 Know thyself.
English proverb, late fourteenth century, inscribed in Greek on the temple of Apollo at Delphi; Plato, in *Protagoras*, ascribes the saying to the Seven Wise Men of the 6th century BC

2 The peacock is always happy because it never looks at its ugly feet.
a person does not see their own faults; Persian proverb: see INSIGHT 6

quotations ▸

3 He who knows others is wise;
He who knows himself is enlightened.
He who conquers others has physical strength.
He who conquers himself is strong.
Lao Tzu c.604–c.531 BC: *Tao-te Ching*

4 I do not know whether I was then a man dreaming I was a butterfly, or whether I am now a butterfly dreaming I am a man.
Chuang Tzu c.369–286 BC: *Chuang Tzu*

5 Why beholdest thou the mote that is in thy brother's eye, but considerest not the beam that is in thine own eye?
Bible: St Matthew; see MISTAKES 8, MISTAKES 10

6 He knows the universe and does not know himself.
Jean de la Fontaine 1621–95: *Fables* (1678–9) 'Démocrite et les Abdéritains'

7 Satire is a sort of glass, wherein beholders do generally discover everybody's face but their own.
Jonathan Swift 1667–1745: *The Battle of the Books* (1704)

8 All our knowledge is, ourselves to know.
Alexander Pope 1688–1744: *An Essay on Man* Epistle 4 (1734)

9 O wad some Pow'r the giftie gie us
To see oursels as others see us!
Robert Burns 1759–96: 'To a Louse' (1786)

10 How little do we know that which we are!
How less what we may be!
Lord Byron 1788–1824: *Don Juan* (1819–24)

11 I do not know myself, and God forbid that I should.
Johann Wolfgang von Goethe 1749–1832: J. P. Eckermann *Gespräche mit Goethe* (1836–48) 10 April 1829

12 Resolve to be thyself: and know, that he
Who finds himself, loses his misery.
Matthew Arnold 1822–88: 'Self-Dependence' (1852)

13 No, when the fight begins within himself,
A man's worth something.
Robert Browning 1812–89: 'Bishop Blougram's Apology' (1855)

14 The tragedy of a man who has found himself out.
J. M. Barrie 1860–1937: *What Every Woman Knows* (performed 1908, published 1918)

15 Between the ages of twenty and forty we are engaged in the process of discovering who we are, which involves learning the difference between accidental limitations which it is our duty to outgrow and the necessary limitations of our nature beyond which we cannot trespass with impunity.
W. H. Auden 1907–73: *Dyer's Hand* (1963) 'Reading'

16 [Alfred Hitchcock] thought of himself as looking like Cary Grant. That's tough, to think of yourself one way and look another.

Tippi Hedren 1930– : interview in California, 1982; P. F. Boller and R. L. Davis *Hollywood Anecdotes* (1988)

Self-Sacrifice

see also SELF-INTEREST

phrases ▸

1 labour of love

a task undertaken for the love of a person or for the work itself; from the Bible (I Thessalonians) 'Your work of faith and labour of love'

2 the supreme sacrifice

the laying down of one's life for another or for one's country; see SELF-SACRIFICE 12

quotations ▸

3 Go, tell the Spartans, thou who passest by,
That here obedient to their laws we lie.

epitaph for the Spartans who died at Thermopylae

Simonides c.556–468 BC: attributed; Herodotus *Histories*

4 Greater love hath no man than this, that a man lay down his life for his friends.

Bible: St John; see TRUST 37

5 True martyrdom is not determined by the penalty suffered, but by the cause.

St. Augustine of Hippo AD 354–430: Epistle 89 in Alois Goldbacher *S. Aureli Augustini Hipponensis Episcopi Epistulae* (1895) vol. 2

6 I am no longer my own, but yours. Put me to what you will, rank me with whom you will; put me to doing, put me to suffering.

Methodist Service Book: The Covenant Prayer (based on the words of Richard Alleine in the First Covenant Service, 1782)

7 Deny yourself! You must deny yourself!
That is the song that never ends.

Johann Wolfgang von Goethe 1749–1832: *Faust* pt. 1 (1808) 'Studierzimmer'

8 It is a far, far better thing that I do, than I have ever done; it is a far, far better rest that I go to, than I have ever known.

Sydney Carton's thoughts on the steps of the guillotine, taking the place of Charles Darnay whom he has smuggled out of prison

Charles Dickens 1812–70: *A Tale of Two Cities* (1859)

9 Self-sacrifice enables us to sacrifice other people without blushing.

George Bernard Shaw 1856–1950: *Man and Superman* (1903) 'Maxims: Self-Sacrifice'

10 I am just going outside and may be some time.

walking to his death in a blizzard

Captain Lawrence Oates 1880–1912: Scott's diary entry, 16–17 March 1912

11 I gave my life for freedom — This I know:
For those who bade me fight had told me so.

William Norman Ewer 1885–1976: 'Five Souls' (1917)

12 The love that never falters, the love that pays the price,
The love that makes undaunted the final sacrifice.

Cecil Spring-Rice 1859–1918: 'I Vow to Thee, My Country' (1918); see SELF-SACRIFICE 2

13 A woman will always sacrifice herself if you give her the opportunity. It is her favourite form of self-indulgence.

W. Somerset Maugham 1874–1965: *The Circle* (1921)

14 I have nothing to offer but blood, toil, tears and sweat.

Winston Churchill 1874–1965: speech, House of Commons, 13 May 1940

15 To gain that which is worth having, it may be necessary to lose everything else.

Bernadette Devlin McAliskey 1947– : preface to *The Price of My Soul* (1969)

Selling

see BUYING AND SELLING

The Senses

see also BODY

proverbs and sayings ▸

1 The eyes believe themselves; the ears believe other people.

Greek proverb

2 When a pine needle falls in the forest, the eagle sees it, the deer hears it, and the bear smells it.

modern saying, said to be of native American origin

phrases ▸

3 deaf as an adder

completely deaf; after the Bible: see DEFIANCE 9

4 the five senses

the special bodily faculties of sight, hearing, smell, taste, and touch

quotations ▸

5 I have heard of thee by the hearing of the ear: but now mine eye seeth thee.

The Bible: Job

6 Eyes and ears are bad witnesses
to men if they have souls that
understand not their language.

often quoted as 'poor witnesses to people if they have uncultured souls'

Heraclitus *c.*540–*c.*480 BC: fragment 42

7 By convention there is colour, by convention sweetness, by convention bitterness, but in reality there are atoms and space.

Democritus *c.*460–*c.*370 BC: fragment 125

8 When in recollection he withdraws all his senses from the attractions of the pleasures of sense, even as a tortoise withdraws all its limbs, then his is a serene wisdom.

Bhagavadgita: ch. 2

9 When I consider how my light is spent,
E're half my days, in this dark world and wide,
And that one talent which is death to hide
Lodged with me useless.

on his blindness

John Milton 1608–74: 'When I consider how my light is spent' (1673)

10 Whatever withdraws us from the power of our senses; whatever makes the past, the distant, or the future predominate over the present, advances us in the dignity of thinking beings.

Samuel Johnson 1709–84: *A Journey to the Western Islands of Scotland* (1775)

11 O for a life of sensations rather than of thoughts!

John Keats 1795–1821: letter to Benjamin Bailey, 22 November 1817

12 Any nose
May ravage with impunity a rose.

Robert Browning 1812–89: *Sordello* (1840)

13 Friday I tasted life. It was a vast morsel. A Circus passed the house—still I feel the red in my mind though the drums are out. The Lawn is full of south and the odours tangle, and I hear to-day for the first time the river in the tree.

Emily Dickinson 1830–86: letter to Mrs J. G. Holland, May 1866

14 You see, but you do not observe.

Arthur Conan Doyle 1859–1930: *The Adventures of Sherlock Holmes* (1892)

15 Fortissimo at last!

on seeing Niagara Falls

Gustav Mahler 1860–1911: K. Blaukopf *Gustav Mahler* (1973)

16 Does it matter?—losing your sight?...
There's such splendid work for the blind;
And people will always be kind,
As you sit on the terrace remembering
And turning your face to the light.

Siegfried Sassoon 1886–1967: 'Does it Matter?' (1918)

17 I test my bath before I sit,
And I'm always moved to wonderment
That what chills the finger not a bit
Is so frigid upon the fundament.

Ogden Nash 1902–71: 'Samson Agonistes' (1942)

18 Each day I live in a glass room
Unless I break it with the thrusting
Of my senses and pass through
The splintered walls to the great landscape.

Mervyn Peake 1911–68: 'Each day I live in a glass room' (1967)

19 My left hand is my thinking hand. The right is only a motor hand.
Barbara Hepworth 1903–75: *A Pictorial Autobiography* (1970)

20 I can hear people smile.
David Blunkett 1947– : in *Independent* 14 July 2001

21 To be able to feel the lightest touch is really a gift.
regaining some movement after being paralysed in a riding accident seven years before
Christopher Reeve 1952–2004: in *Sunday Times* 15 September 2002

Sex

see also LOVE, MARRIAGE, SINGLE

proverbs and sayings ▸

1 Did the earth move for you?
supposedly said to one's partner after sexual intercourse, after Hemingway: see SEX 26

2 Dirty water will quench fire.
mainly used to mean that a man's sexual needs can be satisfied by any woman, however ugly or immoral; English proverb, mid 16th century

3 Post coitum omne animal triste.
Latin = After coition every animal is sad

phrases ▸

4 the beast with two backs
a man and woman having sexual intercourse; from Shakespeare *Othello*: see SEX 13

5 a gay Lothario
a libertine, a rake; from Nicholas Rowe (1674–1718) *The Fair Penitent* (1703) 'Is this that haughty, gallant, gay Lothario?'

6 nudge nudge (wink wink)
used to draw attention to a sexual innuendo in the previous statement; a catchphrase from *Monty Python's Flying Circus*: see SEX 31; WORDS 29

quotations ▸

7 Someone asked Sophocles, 'How is your sex-life now? Are you still able to have a woman?' He replied, 'Hush, man; most gladly indeed am I rid of it all, as though I had escaped from a mad and savage master.'
Sophocles c.496–406 BC: Plato *Republic*

8 I have never yet seen anyone whose desire to build up his moral power was as strong as sexual desire.
Confucius 551–479 BC: *Analects*

9 Give me chastity and continency—but not yet!
St Augustine of Hippo AD 354–430: *Confessions* (AD 397–8)

10 And after wyn on Venus moste I thynke,
For al so siker as cold engendreth hayl,
A likerous mouth moste han a likerous tayl.
Geoffrey Chaucer 1343–1400: *The Canterbury Tales* 'The Wife of Bath's Prologue'

11 Licence my roving hands, and let them go,
Behind, before, above, between, below.
O my America, my new found land,
My kingdom, safeliest when with one man manned.
John Donne 1572–1631: 'To His Mistress Going to Bed' (1595)

12 Is it not strange that desire should so many years outlive performance?
William Shakespeare 1564–1616: *Henry IV, Part 2* (1597)

13 Your daughter and the Moor are now making the beast with two backs.
William Shakespeare 1564–1616: *Othello* (1602–4); see SEX 4

14 This trivial and vulgar way of coition; it is the foolishest act a wise man commits in all his life, nor is there any thing that will more deject his cooled imagination, when he shall consider what an odd and unworthy piece of folly he hath committed.
Thomas Browne 1605–82: *Religio Medici* (1643)

15 The Duke returned from the wars today and did pleasure me in his top-boots.
Sarah, Duchess of Marlborough 1660–1744: oral tradition, attributed in various forms; see I. Butler *Rule of Three* (1967)

16 I'll come no more behind your scenes, David; for the silk stockings and white bosoms of your actresses excite my amorous propensities.
Samuel Johnson 1709–84: James Boswell *Life of Samuel Johnson* (1791) 1750

17 The pleasure is momentary, the position ridiculous, and the expense damnable.

Lord Chesterfield 1694–1773: attributed

18 Not tonight, Josephine.

Napoleon I 1769–1821: attributed, but probably apocryphal; R. H. Horne *The History of Napoleon* (1841) describes the circumstances in which the affront may have occurred

19 'Tisn't beauty, so to speak, nor good talk necessarily. It's just It. Some women'll stay in a man's memory if they once walked down a street.

Rudyard Kipling 1865–1936: *Traffics and Discoveries* (1904); see WOMEN 14

20 When I hear his steps outside my door I lie down on my bed, close my eyes, open my legs, and think of England.

Lady Hillingdon 1857–1940: diary 1912 (original untraced, perhaps apocryphal); J. Gathorne-Hardy *The Rise and Fall of the British Nanny* (1972)

21 i like my body when it is with your body. It is so quite new a thing. Muscles better and nerves more.

e. e. cummings 1894–1962: 'Sonnets–Actualities' no. 8 (1925)

22 You're neither unnatural, nor abominable, nor mad; you're as much a part of what people call nature as anyone else; only you're unexplained as yet—you've not got your niche in creation.

on lesbianism

Radclyffe Hall 1883–1943: *The Well of Loneliness* (1928)

23 Chastity—the most unnatural of all the sexual perversions.

Aldous Huxley 1894–1963: *Eyeless in Gaza* (1936)

24 Pornography is the attempt to insult sex, to do dirt on it.

D. H. Lawrence 1885–1930: *Phoenix* (1936) 'Pornography and Obscenity'

25 Give a man a free hand and he'll try to put it all over you.

Mae West 1892–1980: *Klondike Annie* (1936 film)

26 But did thee feel the earth move?

Ernest Hemingway 1899–1961: *For Whom the Bell Tolls* (1940); see SEX 1

27 It doesn't matter what you do in the bedroom as long as you don't do it in the street and frighten the horses.

Mrs Patrick Campbell 1865–1940: Daphne Fielding *The Duchess of Jermyn Street* (1964)

28 The only unnatural sex act is that which you cannot perform.

Alfred Kinsey 1894–1956: attributed; in *Time* 21 January 1966

29 I can't get no satisfaction
I can't get no girl reaction.

Mick Jagger 1943– and **Keith Richards** 1943– : '(I Can't Get No) Satisfaction' (1965 song)

30 The orgasm has replaced the Cross as the focus of longing and the image of fulfilment.

Malcolm Muggeridge 1903–90: *Tread Softly* (1966)

31 Your wife interested in...*photographs*? Eh? Know what I mean—*photographs*? He asked him knowingly...nudge nudge, snap snap, grin grin, wink wink, say no more.

Graham Chapman 1941–89, **John Cleese** 1939– , and **others**: *Monty Python's Flying Circus* (BBC TV programme, 1969); see SEX 6

32 Is sex dirty? Only if it's done right.

Woody Allen 1935– : *Everything You Always Wanted to Know about Sex* (1972 film)

33 Traditionally, sex has been a very private, secretive activity. Herein perhaps lies its powerful force for uniting people in a strong bond. As we make sex less secretive, we may rob it of its power to hold men and women together.

Thomas Szasz 1920– : *The Second Sin* (1973)

34 Sexual intercourse began
In nineteen sixty-three
(Which was rather late for me) —
Between the end of the *Chatterley* ban
And the Beatles' first LP.

Philip Larkin 1922–85: 'Annus Mirabilis' (1974)

35 Is that a gun in your pocket, or are you just glad to see me?

usually quoted as 'Is that a pistol in your pocket...'

Mae West 1892–1980: Joseph Weintraub *Peel Me a Grape* (1975)

36 On bisexuality: It immediately doubles your chances for a date on Saturday night.
Woody Allen 1935– : in *New York Times* 1 December 1975

37 Don't knock masturbation. It's sex with someone I love.
Woody Allen 1935– : *Annie Hall* (1977 film, with Marshall Brickman)

38 That [sex] was the most fun I ever had without laughing.
Woody Allen 1935– : *Annie Hall* (1977 film, with Marshall Brickman)

39 Love is two minutes fifty-two seconds of squishing noises.
Johnny Rotten 1957– : in *Daily Mirror*, 1983

40 I'll have what she's having.
woman to waiter, seeing Sally acting an orgasm
Nora Ephron 1941– : *When Harry Met Sally* (1989 film)

41 Women need a reason to have sex, men just need a place.
Lowell Ganz 1948– and **Babaloo Mandel** 1949– : *City Slickers* (1991 film), spoken by Billy Crystal as Mitch Robbins

Sickness

see also HEALTH, MEDICINE

proverbs and sayings ▸

1 Coughs and sneezes spread diseases. Trap the germs in your handkerchief.
Second World War health slogan (1942)

2 A creaking door hangs longest.
someone who is apparently in poor health may well outlive the ostensibly stronger; English proverb, late 17th century

3 Diseases come on horseback but go away on foot.
sickness may occur swiftly, but recovery is likely to be slow; English proverb, late 16th century

4 Feed a cold and starve a fever.
probably intended as two separate admonitions, but sometimes interpreted to mean that if you feed a cold you will have to starve a fever later; English proverb, mid 19th century

5 From the bitterness of disease, man learns the sweetness of health.
Catalan proverb

phrases ▸

6 the Black Death
the great epidemic of plague in Europe in the 14th century; the name 'black death' is modern, and was apparently introduced by Mrs Penrose (Mrs Markham) in 1823; earlier writers call it the (great) pestilence, the plague, or the great death

7 the falling sickness
an archaic term for epilepsy

8 the king's evil
scrofula, from the belief that a cure could be obtained by the sovereign's touching the sores

9 white death
tuberculosis, after *Black Death*; see SICKNESS 6

quotations ▸

10 When two pains occur together, but not in the same place, the more violent obscures the other.
Hippocrates c.460–357 BC: *Aphorisms*

11 Diseases of the soul are both more dangerous and more numerous than those of the body.
Cicero 106–43 BC: *Tusculanae Disputationes*

12 Here am I, dying of a hundred good symptoms.
Alexander Pope 1688–1744: to George, Lord Lyttelton, 15 May 1744; Joseph Spence *Anecdotes* (ed. J. Osborn, 1966)

13 To know ourselves diseased, is half our cure.
Edward Young 1683–1765: *Night Thoughts* (1742–5) 'Night 9'

14 How few of his friends' houses would a man choose to be at when he is sick.
Samuel Johnson 1709–84: James Boswell *Life of Samuel Johnson* (1791) 1783

15 All diseases run into one, old age.
Ralph Waldo Emerson 1803–82: Journals, 1840

16 It is a most extraordinary thing, but I never read a patent medicine advertisement without being impelled to the conclusion that I am suffering from the particular disease therein dealt with in its most virulent form.
Jerome K. Jerome 1859–1927: *Three Men in a Boat* (1889)

17 'Ye can call it influenza if ye like,' said Mrs Machin. 'There was no influenza

in my young days. We called a cold a cold.'
Arnold Bennett 1867–1931: *The Card* (1911)

18 The desire to take medicine is perhaps the greatest feature which distinguishes man from animals.
William Osler 1849–1919: H. Cushing *Life of Sir William Osler* (1925)

19 I enjoy convalescence. It is the part that makes illness worth while.
George Bernard Shaw 1856–1950: *Back to Methuselah* (1921)

20 Illness is the doctor to whom we pay most heed; to kindness, to knowledge, we make promise only; pain we obey.
Marcel Proust 1871–1922: *Cities of the Plain* (1922)

21 Human nature seldom walks up to the word 'cancer'.
Rudyard Kipling 1865–1936: *Debits and Credits* (1926)

22 My final word, before I'm done,
Is 'Cancer can be rather fun'.
Thanks to the nurses and Nye Bevan
The NHS is quite like heaven
Provided one confronts the tumour
With a sufficient sense of humour.
J. B. S. Haldane 1892–1964: 'Cancer's a Funny Thing' (1968)

23 Did God who gave us flowers and trees,
Also provide the allergies?
E. Y. Harburg 1898–1981: 'A Nose is a Nose is a Nose' (1965)

24 A man's illness is his private territory and, no matter how much he loves you and how close you are, you stay an outsider. You are healthy.
Lauren Bacall 1924– : *By Myself* (1978)

25 Societies need to have one illness which becomes identified with evil, and attaches blame to its 'victims'.
Susan Sontag 1933–2004: *AIDS and its Metaphors* (1989)

26 You matter because you are you, and you matter to the last moment of your life. We will do all that we can not only to help you die peacefully, but also to live until you die.
Cicely Saunders 1916–2005: quoted in Robert Twycross 'A Tribute to Dame Cicely Saunders', Memorial Service, 8 March 2006

27 An embuggerance.
announcing that he had been diagnosed with an early-onset form of Alzheimer's disease
Terry Pratchett 1948– : on the website www.paulkidby.com/news 11 December 2007

Silence

see also SPEECH

proverbs and sayings ▸

1 A shut mouth catches no flies.
a warning against the dangers of idle talk; English proverb, late 16th century

2 Silence is a still noise.
American proverb, late 19th century

3 Silence means consent.
English proverb, late 14th century; translation of a Latin tag, '*qui tacet consentire videtur* [he who is silent seems to consent]', said to have been spoken by Thomas More (1478–1535) when asked at his trial why he was silent on being asked to acknowledge the king's supremacy over the Church. The principle is not accepted in modern English law

4 Speech is silver, but silence is golden.
discretion can be more valuable than the most eloquent words; English proverb, mid 19th century; see SPEECH 5

5 A still tongue makes a wise head.
a person who is not given to idle talk, and who listens to others, is likely to be wise; English proverb, mid 16th century

quotations ▸

6 Silence is a woman's finest ornament.
Auctoritates Aristotelis: a compilation of medieval propositions

7 Silence is the virtue of fools.
Francis Bacon 1561–1626: *De Dignitate et Augmentis Scientiarum* (1623)

8 Be silent, unless your speech is better than silence.
Salvator Rosa 1615–73: inscription on self portrait in the National Gallery, London

9 No voice; but oh! the silence sank
Like music on my heart.
Samuel Taylor Coleridge 1772–1834: 'The Rime of the Ancient Mariner' (1798)

10 Thou still unravished bride of quietness,
Thou foster-child of silence and slow time.
John Keats 1795–1821: 'Ode on a Grecian Urn' (1820)

11 Under all speech that is good for anything there lies a silence that is better. Silence is deep as Eternity; speech is shallow as Time.
Thomas Carlyle 1795–1881: *Critical and Miscellaneous Essays* (1838) 'Sir Walter Scott'

12 Speech is often barren; but silence also does not necessarily brood over a full nest. Your still fowl, blinking at you without remark, may all the while be sitting on one addled egg; and when it takes to cackling will have nothing to announce but that addled delusion.
George Eliot 1819–80: *Felix Holt* (1866)

13 Elected Silence, sing to me
And beat upon my whorlèd ear.
Gerard Manley Hopkins 1844–89: 'The Habit of Perfection' (written 1866)

14 Blessed is the man who, having nothing to say, abstains from giving us wordy evidence of the fact.
George Eliot 1819–80: *The Impressions of Theoprastus Such* (1879)

15 People talking without speaking
People hearing without listening
People writing songs that voices never share
And no one dare disturb the sound of silence.
Paul Simon 1942– : 'Sound of Silence' (1964 song)

Similarity and Difference

proverbs and sayings ►

1 All cats are grey in the dark.
darkness obscures inessential differences; English proverb, mid 16th century

2 Birds of a feather flock together.
people of the same (usually, unscrupulous) character associated together; English proverb, mid 16th century; see SIMILARITY 14

3 Comparisons are odious.
often used to suggest that to compare two different things or persons is unhelpful or misleading; English proverb, mid 15th century; see SIMILARITY 18

4 East is east, and west is west.
an assertion of ineradicable racial and cultural differences; English proverb, late 19th century, from Kipling: see EQUALITY 13

5 Extremes meet.
opposite extremes have much in common; English proverb, mid 18th century

6 From the sweetest wine, the tartest vinegar.
the strongest hate comes from former love; English proverb, late 16th century

7 Like breeds like.
a particular kind of event may well be the genesis of a similar occurrence; English proverb, mid 16th century

8 Like will to like.
those of similar nature and inclination are drawn together; English proverb, late 14th century

9 One nail drives out another.
like will counter like; English proverb, mid 13th century

10 Two of a trade never agree.
close association with someone makes disagreement over policy and principles more likely; English proverb, early 17th century

11 Two swords do not fit in one scabbard.
Indian proverb; see SIMILARITY 10

12 When Greek meets Greek, then comes the tug of war.
when two people of a similar kind are opposed, there is a struggle for supremacy; English proverb, late 17th century; see SIMILARITY 21

13 When the axe came into the forest, the trees said 'The handle is one of us!'
relying for safety on a supposed link with a potential aggressor may offer a false hope; Russian proverb

phrases ►

14 birds of a feather
those of like character; from the proverb: see SIMILARITY 2

15 **of the same leaven**
of the same sort or character; *leaven* = an agency which exercises a transforming influence from within, of biblical origin as in Matthew, 'Take heed and beware of the leaven of the Pharisees'; see SIN 3

16 **Tweedledum and Tweedledee**
a pair of people or things that are virtually indistinguishable; originally names applied to the composers Bononcini (1670–1747) and Handel, in a 1725 satire by John Byrom (1692–1763); they were later used for two identical characters in Lewis Carroll's *Through the Looking Glass*

quotations ▸

17 The road up and the road down are one and the same.
Heraclitus c.540–c.480 BC: H. Diels and W. Kranz *Die Fragmente der Vorsokratiker* (7th ed., 1954) fragment 60

18 Comparisons are odorous.
William Shakespeare 1564–1616: *Much Ado About Nothing* (1598–9); see SIMILARITY 3

19 In one and the same fire, clay grows hard and wax melts.
Francis Bacon 1561–1626: *History of Life and Death* (1623); see CHARACTER 14

20 Feel by turns the bitter change
Of fierce extremes, extremes by change more fierce.
John Milton 1608–74: *Paradise Lost* (1667)

21 When Greeks joined Greeks, then was the tug of war!
Nathaniel Lee 1653–92: *The Rival Queens* (1677); see SIMILARITY 12

22 No caparisons, Miss, if you please!—Caparisons don't become a young woman.
Richard Brinsley Sheridan 1751–1816: *The Rivals* (1775)

23 Near all the birds
Will sing at dawn,—and yet we do not take
The chaffering swallow for the holy lark.
Elizabeth Barrett Browning 1806–61: *Aurora Leigh* (1857)

24 One of the most common defects of half-instructed minds is to think much of that in which they differ from others, and little of that in which they agree with others.
on the evils of sectarianism
Walter Bagehot 1826–77: in *Economist* 11 June 1870

25 If every one were cast in the same mould, there would be no such thing as beauty.
Charles Darwin 1809–82: *The Descent of Man* (1871)

26 Whatever you may be sure of, be sure at least of this, that you are dreadfully like other people.
James Russell Lowell 1819–91: *My Study Windows* (1871)

27 Out of intense complexities intense simplicities emerge.
Winston Churchill 1874–1965: *The World Crisis* (1923–9)

28 World is crazier and more of it than we think,
Incorrigibly plural. I peel and portion
A tangerine and spit the pips and feel
The drunkenness of things being various.
Louis MacNeice 1907–63: 'Snow' (1935)

29 If we cannot end now our differences, at least we can help make the world safe for diversity.
John F. Kennedy 1917–63: address at American University, Washington, DC, 10 June 1963

30 Without deviation from the norm, progress is not possible.
Frank Zappa 1940–93: attributed, in *New York* 20 June 1994

31 I agree with Nick.
Gordon Brown 1951– : in the first televised Party Leaders' debate, ITV, 15 April 2010

Sin
see also GOOD

proverbs and sayings ▸

1 Satan rebuking sin.
originally meaning that the worst possible stage has been reached; in later use, an ironic comment on the nature of the person delivering the rebuke; English proverb, early 17th century

2 What is got over the Devil's back is spent under his belly.
what is gained improperly will be spent on folly and debauchery; English proverb, late 16th century

phrases ►

3 the old leaven
traces of an unregenerate condition; *leaven* = an agency which exercises a transforming influence from within, as in the Bible (1 Corinthians) 'Purge out therefore the old leaven'; see SIMILARITY 15

4 original sin
the tendency to evil supposedly innate in all humans, held to be inherited from Adam in consequence of the Fall of Man

5 the seven deadly sins
those entailing damnation; traditionally pride, covetousness, lust, envy, gluttony, anger, and sloth

6 the sin against the Holy Ghost
the only sin regarded as putting its perpetrator beyond redemption; an ultimate and irredeemable wrong; in Christian theology, based on the interpretation of several Gospel passages: see SIN 8

quotations ►

7 Be sure your sin will find you out.
Bible: Numbers

8 The blasphemy against the Holy Ghost shall not be forgiven unto men.
Bible: St Matthew; see SIN 6

9 The wages of sin is death.
Bible: Romans

10 No one ever suddenly became depraved.
Juvenal C. AD 60–C. 140: *Satires*

11 We make ourselves a ladder out of our vices if we trample the vices themselves underfoot.
St Augustine of Hippo AD 354–430: Sermon no. 176 ('On the Ascension of the Lord')

12 I have sinned exceedingly in thought, word, and deed, through my fault, through my fault, through my most grievous fault.
The Missal: *The Ordinary of the Mass*

13 Commit
The oldest sins the newest kind of ways.
William Shakespeare 1564–1616: *Henry IV, Part 2* (1597)

14 Nothing emboldens sin so much as mercy.
William Shakespeare 1564–1616: *Timon of Athens* (1607)

15 I should renounce the devil and all his works, the pomps and vanity of this wicked world, and all the sinful lusts of the flesh.
The Book of Common Prayer 1662: *Catechism*; see TEMPTATION 6

16 We have erred, and strayed from thy ways like lost sheep. We have followed too much the devices and desires of our own hearts.
The Book of Common Prayer 1662: *Morning Prayer* General Confession

17 It is public scandal that constitutes offence, and to sin in secret is not to sin at all.
Molière 1622–73: *Le Tartuffe* (1669)

18 Vice came in always at the door of necessity, not at the door of inclination.
Daniel Defoe 1660–1731: *Moll Flanders* (1721)

19 I waive the quantum o' the sin;
The hazard of concealing;
But och! it hardens a' within,
And petrifies the feeling!
Robert Burns 1759–96: 'Epistle to a Young Friend' (1786)

20 That Calvinistic sense of innate depravity and original sin from whose visitations, in some shape or other, no deeply thinking mind is always and wholly free.
Herman Melville 1819–91: *Hawthorne and His Mosses* (1850)

21 She [the Catholic Church] holds that it were better for sun and moon to drop from heaven, for the earth to fail, and for all the many millions who are upon it to die of starvation in extremest agony, as far as temporal affliction goes, than that one soul, I will not say, should be lost, but should commit one single venial sin, should tell one wilful untruth...or steal one poor farthing without excuse.
John Henry Newman 1801–90: *Lectures on Anglican Difficulties* (1852)

22 For the sin ye do by two and two ye must pay for one by one!
Rudyard Kipling 1865–1936: 'Tomlinson' (1892)

23 The only difference between the saint and the sinner is that every saint has a past, and every sinner has a future.
Oscar Wilde 1854–1900: *A Woman of No Importance* (1893)

24 When I'm good, I'm very, very good, but when I'm bad, I'm better.
Mae West 1892–1980: *I'm No Angel* (1933 film)

25 when asked by Mrs Coolidge what a sermon had been about:
'Sins,' he said. 'Well, what did he say about sin?' 'He was against it.'
Calvin Coolidge 1872–1933: John H. McKee *Coolidge: Wit and Wisdom* (1933); perhaps apocryphal

26 All sins are attempts to fill voids.
Simone Weil 1909–43: *La Pesanteur et la grâce* (1948)

27 There are different kinds of wrong. The people sinned against are not always the best.
Ivy Compton-Burnett 1884–1969: *The Mighty and their Fall* (1961)

28 All sin tends to be addictive, and the terminal point of addiction is what is called damnation.
W. H. Auden 1907–73: *A Certain World* (1970) 'Hell'

29 Sins become more subtle as you grow older. You commit sins of despair rather than lust.
Piers Paul Read 1941– : in *Daily Telegraph* 3 October 1990

Singing

see also MUSIC

proverbs and sayings ▸

1 Why should the devil have all the best tunes?
commonly attributed to the English evangelist Rowland Hill (1744–1833); many hymns are sung to popular secular melodies, and this practice was especially favoured by the Methodists

quotations ▸

2 The exercise of singing is delightful to Nature, and good to preserve the health of man. It doth strengthen all parts of the breast, and doth open the pipes.
William Byrd 1543–1623: *Psalms, Sonnets and Songs* (1588)

3 I can suck melancholy out of a song as a weasel sucks eggs.
William Shakespeare 1564–1616: *As You Like It* (1599)

4 If a man were permitted to make all the ballads, he need not care who should make the laws of a nation.
Andrew Fletcher of Saltoun 1655–1716: 'An Account of a Conversation concerning a Right Regulation of Government for the Good of Mankind. In a Letter to the Marquis of Montrose' (1704)

5 Nothing is capable of being well set to music that is not nonsense.
Joseph Addison 1672–1719: in *The Spectator* 21 March 1711

6 An exotic and irrational entertainment, which has been always combated, and always has prevailed.
of Italian opera
Samuel Johnson 1709–84: *Lives of the English Poets* (1779–81) 'Hughes'

7 Sentimentally I am disposed to harmony. But organically I am incapable of a tune.
Charles Lamb 1775–1834: *Essays of Elia* (1823) 'A Chapter on Ears'

8 Every tone [of the songs of the slaves] was a testimony against slavery, and a prayer to God for deliverance from chains.
Frederick Douglass 1818–95: *Narrative of the Life of Frederick Douglass* (1845)

9 A wandering minstrel I—
A thing of shreds and patches,
Of ballads, songs and snatches,
And dreamy lullaby!
W. S. Gilbert 1836–1911: *The Mikado* (1885); see CHARACTER 28

10 You think that's noise—you ain't heard nuttin' yet!
first said in a café, competing with the din from a neighbouring building site, in 1906; subsequently an aside in the 1927 film *The Jazz Singer*
Al Jolson 1886–1950: Martin Abramson *The Real Story of Al Jolson* (1950); also the title of a Jolson song, 1919, in the form 'You Ain't Heard Nothing Yet'

11 Everyone suddenly burst out singing;
And I was filled with such delight
As prisoned birds must find in
freedom.

Siegfried Sassoon 1886–1967: 'Everyone Sang' (1919)

12 Tenors get women by the score.

James Joyce 1882–1941: *Ulysses* (1922)

13 Words make you think a thought. Music makes you feel a feeling. A song makes you feel a thought.

E. Y. Harburg 1898–1981: lecture given at the New York YMCA in 1970

14 In writing songs I've learned as much from Cézanne as I have from Woody Guthrie.

Bob Dylan 1941– : Clinton Heylin *Dylan: Behind the Shades* (1991)

The Single Life

see also MARRIAGE

proverbs and sayings ▶

1 Why buy a cow when milk is so cheap?

putting forward an argument for choosing the least troublesome alternative; frequently used as an argument against marriage; English proverb, mid 17th century

phrases ▶

2 old maid

a single woman regarded as too old for marriage; figuratively, a prim and fussy person; see SINGLE 11

quotations ▶

3 If I am to disclose to you what I should prefer if I follow the inclination of my nature, it is this: beggar-woman and single, far rather than queen and married!

Elizabeth I 1533–1603: attributed reply to an imperial envoy, 1563; J. E. Neale *Queen Elizabeth I* (1979)

4 I would be married, but I'd have no
wife,
I would be married to a single life.

Richard Crashaw 1612–49: 'On Marriage' (1646)

5 Marriage has many pains, but celibacy has no pleasures.

Samuel Johnson 1709–84: *Rasselas* (1759)

6 It is amusing that a virtue is made of the vice of chastity; and it's a pretty odd sort of chastity at that, which leads men straight into the sin of Onan, and girls to the waning of their colour.

Voltaire 1694–1778: letter to M. Mariott, 28 March 1766

7 It is a truth universally acknowledged, that a single man in possession of a good fortune, must be in want of a wife.

Jane Austen 1775–1817: *Pride and Prejudice* (1813)

8 Marriage may often be a stormy lake, but celibacy is almost always a muddy horsepond.

Thomas Love Peacock 1785–1866: *Melincourt* (1817)

9 Single women have a dreadful propensity for being poor—which is one very strong argument in favour of matrimony.

Jane Austen 1775–1817: letter to Fanny Knight, 13 March 1817

10 Bachelors know more about women than married men. If they didn't they'd be married too.

H. L. Mencken 1880–1956: *A Little Book in C Major* (1916)

11 Being an old maid is like death by drowning, a really delightful sensation after you cease to struggle.

Edna Ferber 1887–1968: R. E. Drennan *Wit's End* (1973); see SINGLE 2

12 Nobody dies from lack of sex. It's lack of love we die from.

Margaret Atwood 1939– : *The Handmaid's Tale* (1986)

Situation

see CIRCUMSTANCE AND SITUATION

The Skies

see also UNIVERSE

phrases ▸

1 the evening star

the planet Venus, seen shining in the western sky after sunset; see SKIES 15

2 the Great Bear

in astronomy, the constellation Ursa Major; named from the story in Greek mythology that the nymph Callisto was turned into a bear and placed as a constellation in the heavens by Zeus. The seven brightest stars form a familiar formation variously called the Plough, Big Dipper, or Charles's Wain, and include the Pointers; see SKIES 7

3 the merry dancers

in Scotland, the aurora borealis; see SKIES 5

4 the mother of the months

the moon

5 the northern lights

the aurora borealis; alluding to the streamers of light appearing in the sky; see SKIES 3

6 the queen of tides

the moon

7 the seven stars

a former name for the Pleiades and the Great Bear; there are six stars in the Pleiades visible to the naked eye: the eldest Pleiad, Merope, was 'the lost Pleiad'; see also SKIES 2

quotations ▸

8 And God made two great lights; the greater light to rule the day, and the lesser light to rule the night: he made the stars also.

Bible: Genesis

9 And ther he saugh, with ful avysement
The erratik sterres, herkenyng armonye
With sownes ful of hevenyssh melodie.

Geoffrey Chaucer 1343–1400: *Troilus and Criseyde*

10 The fool will turn the whole art of astronomy inside out! But, as the Holy Scripture reports, Joshua ordered the sun to stand still and not the earth.

on Copernicus' suggestion that the earth moved round the sun

Martin Luther 1483–1546: *Table Talk*, 4 June 1539

11 Queen and huntress, chaste and fair,
Now the sun is laid to sleep,
Seated in thy silver chair,
State in wonted manner keep:
Hesperus entreats thy light,
Goddess, excellently bright.

Ben Jonson 1573–1637: *Cynthia's Revels* (1600)

12 The moon's an arrant thief,
And her pale fire she snatches from the sun.

William Shakespeare 1564–1616: *Timon of Athens* (1607)

13 Busy old fool, unruly sun,
Why dost thou thus,
Through windows, and through curtains call on us?

John Donne 1572–1631: 'The Sun Rising'

14 But it does move.

after his recantation, that the earth moves around the sun, in 1632

Galileo Galilei 1564–1642: attributed; Baretti *Italian Library* (1757) possibly has the earliest appearance of the phrase

15 The evening star,
Love's harbinger.

John Milton 1608–74: *Paradise Lost* (1667); see SKIES 1

16 The hornèd Moon, with one bright star
Within the nether tip.

Samuel Taylor Coleridge 1772–1834: 'The Rime of the Ancient Mariner' (1798)

17 Twinkle, twinkle, little star,
How I wonder what you are!
Up above the world so high,
Like a diamond in the sky!

Ann Taylor 1782–1866 and **Jane Taylor** 1783–1824: 'The Star' (1806)

18 I am the daughter of Earth and Water,
And the nursling of the Sky;
I pass through the pores of the ocean and shores;
I change, but I cannot die.

Percy Bysshe Shelley 1792–1822: 'The Cloud' (1819)

19 It may be that the stars of heaven appear to us fair and pure simply because we are at such a distance from them, and know nothing of their private life.

Heinrich Heine 1797–1856: *The Romantic School* (1833)

20 I have loved the stars too truly to be
fearful of the night.
Sarah Williams 1837–68: 'The Old Astronomer to His Pupil'

21 Look at the stars! look, look up at the
skies!
O look at all the fire-folk sitting in the
air!
Gerard Manley Hopkins 1844–89: 'The Starlight Night' (written 1877)

22 The night has a thousand eyes,
And the day but one;
Yet the light of the bright world dies,
With the dying sun.
F. W. Bourdillon 1852–1921: 'Light' (1878)

23 Slowly, silently, now the moon
Walks the night in her silver shoon.
Walter de la Mare 1873–1956: 'Silver' (1913)

24 The heaventree of stars hung with
humid nightblue fruit.
James Joyce 1882–1941: *Ulysses* (1922)

25 We have seen
The moon in lonely alleys make
A grail of laughter of an empty ash can.
Hart Crane 1899–1932: 'Chaplinesque' (1926)

26 Had I been a man I might have explored the Poles, or climbed Mount Everest, but as it was, my spirit found outlet in the air.
Amy Johnson 1903–41: Margot Asquith (ed.) *Myself When Young* (1938)

27 Don't tell me that man doesn't belong out there. Man belongs wherever he wants to go—and he'll do plenty well when he gets there.
Wernher von Braun 1912–77: in *Time* 17 February 1958

28 Houston, Tranquillity Base here. The Eagle has landed.
Neil Armstrong 1930– : on landing on the moon, on 20 July 1969

29 Looking up at the stars, I know quite
well
That for all they care, I can go to hell.
W. H. Auden 1907–73: 'The More Loving One' (1976)

30 Space isn't remote at all. It's only an hour's drive away if your car could go straight upwards.
Fred Hoyle 1915–2001: in *Observer* 9 September 1979

Sleep

see also DREAMS

proverbs and sayings ▶

1 The morning knows more than the evening.
the mind is clearer after sleep; Russian proverb

2 One hour's sleep before midnight is worth two after.
English proverb, mid 17th century

3 Six hours sleep for a man, seven for a woman, and eight for a fool.
implying that the more sleep a person needs, the less vigorous and effective they are likely to be; English proverb, early 17th century

4 Some sleep five hours; nature requires seven, laziness nine, and wickedness eleven.
American proverb, mid 20th century

5 We never sleep.
motto of the American detective agency founded by Allan Pinkerton (1855)

phrases ▶

6 the land of Nod
sleep; a pun on the biblical place-name in the Bible (Genesis) of the land to which Cain was exiled after the killing of Abel, after Swift *Polite Conversation* (1731–8) 'I'm going to the Land of Nod'; see also CANADA 3

quotations ▶

7 The sleep of a labouring man is sweet.
Bible: Ecclesiastes

8 Care-charmer Sleep, son of the sable
Night,
Brother to Death, in silent darkness
born.
Samuel Daniel 1563–1619: *Delia* (1592) sonnet 54

9 Not to be a-bed after midnight is to be up betimes.
William Shakespeare 1564–1616: *Twelfth Night* (1601)

10 Golden slumbers kiss your eyes,
Smiles awake you when you rise.
Thomas Dekker 1570–1641: *Patient Grissil* (1603)

11 Methought I heard a voice cry, 'Sleep
no more!

Macbeth does murder sleep,' the innocent sleep,
Sleep that knits up the ravelled sleave of care.
William Shakespeare 1564–1616: *Macbeth* (1606)

12 What hath night to do with sleep?
John Milton 1608–74: *Comus* (1637)

13 And so to bed.
Samuel Pepys 1633–1703: diary 20 April 1660

14 Tired Nature's sweet restorer, balmy sleep!
Edward Young 1683–1765: *Night Thoughts* (1742–5)

15 Turn the key deftly in the oilèd wards,
And seal the hushèd casket of my soul.
John Keats 1795–1821: 'Sonnet to Sleep' (written 1819)

16 A ruffled mind makes a restless pillow.
Charlotte Brontë 1816–55: *The Professor* (1857)

17 Sleeping is no mean art: for its sake one must stay awake all day.
Friedrich Nietzsche 1844–1900: *Thus Spake Zarathustra* (1883)

18 Must we to bed indeed? Well then,
Let us arise and go like men,
And face with an undaunted tread
The long black passage up to bed.
Robert Louis Stevenson 1850–94: 'North-West Passage. Good-Night' (1885)

19 The cool kindliness of sheets, that soon
Smooth away trouble; and the rough male kiss
Of blankets.
Rupert Brooke 1887–1915: 'The Great Lover' (1914)

20 Early to rise and early to bed makes a male healthy and wealthy and dead.
James Thurber 1894–1961: 'The Shrike and the Chipmunks' in *New Yorker* 18 February 1939; see HEALTH 4

21 Sleep is when all the unsorted stuff comes flying out as from a dustbin upset in a high wind.
William Golding 1911–93: *Pincher Martin* (1956)

22 I love sleep because it is both pleasant and safe to use.
Fran Lebowitz 1946– : *Metropolitan Life* (1978)

Smoking

proverbs and sayings ▸

1 Coffee without tobacco is like a Jew without a rabbi.
Moroccan proverb

2 Happiness is a cigar called Hamlet.
advertising slogan for Hamlet cigars, UK

3 More doctors smoke Camels than any other cigarette.
advertisement for Camel cigarettes, 1940s–50s

4 Smoking can seriously damage your health.
government health warning now required by British law to be printed on cigarette packets; in form 'Smoking can damage your health' from early 1970s

5 You're never alone with a Strand.
advertising slogan for Strand cigarettes, 1960; the image of loneliness was so strongly conveyed by the solitary smoker that sales were in fact adversely affected

quotations ▸

6 I do hold it, and will affirm it (before any prince in Europe) to be the most sovereign and precious weed that ever the earth tendered to the use of man.
of tobacco
Ben Jonson 1573–1637: *Every Man in His Humour* (1598)

7 A custom loathsome to the eye, hateful to the nose, harmful to the brain, dangerous to the lungs, and in the black, stinking fume thereof, nearest resembling the horrible Stygian smoke of the pit that is bottomless.
James I 1566–1625: *A Counterblast to Tobacco* (1604)

8 He who lives without tobacco is not worthy to live.
Molière 1622–73: *Don Juan* (performed 1665)

9 This very night I am going to leave off tobacco! Surely there must be some other world in which this unconquerable purpose shall be realized.
Charles Lamb 1775–1834: letter to Thomas Manning, 26 December 1815

10 The roots of tobacco plants must go clear through to hell.
Thomas Alva Edison 1847–1931: in *American Heritage* 12 July 1885

11 A woman is only a woman, but a good cigar is a Smoke.
Rudyard Kipling 1865–1936: 'The Betrothed' (1890)

12 A cigarette is the perfect type of a perfect pleasure. It is exquisite, and it leaves one unsatisfied. What more can one want?
Oscar Wilde 1854–1900: *The Picture of Dorian Gray* (1891)

13 What this country needs is a really good 5-cent cigar.
Thomas R. Marshall 1854–1925: in *New York Tribune* 4 January 1920

14 I smoked my first cigarette and kissed my first woman on the same day. I have never had time for tobacco since.
Arturo Toscanini 1867–1957: in *Observer* 30 June 1946

15 It has been said that cigarettes are the only product that, if used according to the manufacturer's instructions, have a very high chance of killing you.
Michael Buerk 1946– : in *Sunday Times* 11 July 1999

Society

see also GOVERNMENT, HUMAN RACE

proverbs and sayings ▸

1 If every man would sweep his own doorstep the city would soon be clean.
if everyone fulfils their own responsibilities, what is necessary will be done; English proverb, early 17th century

2 One half of the world does not know how the other half lives.
often used to comment on a lack of communication between neighbouring groups; English proverb, early 17th century

phrases ▸

3 big society
a concept whereby a significant amount of responsibility for the running of a society is devolved to local communities and volunteers; see POLITICS 33

4 body politic
the state viewed as an aggregate of its individual members; organized society

5 pillar of society
a person regarded as a particularly responsible citizen, a mainstay of the social fabric; *pillar* in the sense of a person regarded as a mainstay or support for something is recorded from Middle English; *Pillars of Society* was the English title (1888) of a play by Ibsen

quotations ▸

6 No man is an Island, entire of it self; every man is a piece of the Continent, a part of the main; if a clod be washed away by the sea, Europe is the less, as well as if a promontory were.
John Donne 1572–1631: *Devotions upon Emergent Occasions* (1624)

7 The only way by which any one divests himself of his natural liberty and puts on the bonds of civil society is by agreeing with other men to join and unite into a community.
John Locke 1632–1704: *Second Treatise of Civil Government* (1690)

8 Society is indeed a contract...it becomes a partnership not only between those who are living, but between those who are living, those who are dead, and those who are to be born.
Edmund Burke 1729–97: *Reflections on the Revolution in France* (1790)

9 The general will rules in society as the private will governs each separate individual.
Maximilien Robespierre 1758–94: *Lettres à ses commettans* (2nd series) 5 January 1793

10 Only in the state does man have a rational existence...Man owes his entire existence to the state, and has his being within it alone. Whatever worth and spiritual reality he possesses are his solely by virtue of the state.
G. W. F. Hegel 1770–1831: *Lectures on the Philosophy of World History: Introduction* (1830)

11 The greatest happiness of the greatest number is the foundation of morals

and legislation.

Jeremy Bentham 1748–1832: *The Commonplace Book*; Bentham claimed that either Joseph Priestley (1733–1804) or Cesare Beccaria (1738–94) passed on the 'sacred truth'; see MORALITY 4

12 Wherever a man goes, men will pursue him and paw him with their dirty institutions, and, if they can, constrain him to belong to their desperate oddfellow society.

Henry David Thoreau 1817–62: *Walden* (1854) 'The Village'

13 When society requires to be rebuilt, there is no use in attempting to rebuild it on the old plan.

John Stuart Mill 1806–73: *Dissertations and Discussions* vol. 1 (1859) 'Essay on Coleridge'

14 From each according to his abilities, to each according to his needs.

Karl Marx 1818–83: *Critique of the Gotha Programme* (written 1875, but of earlier origin)

15 The Social Contract is nothing more or less than a vast conspiracy of human beings to lie to and humbug themselves and one another for the general Good. Lies are the mortar that bind the savage individual man into the social masonry.

H. G. Wells 1866–1946: *Love and Mr Lewisham* (1900)

16 There is no such thing as the State
And no one exists alone;
Hunger allows no choice
To the citizen or the police;
We must love one another or die.

W. H. Auden 1907–73: 'September 1, 1939' (1940)

17 Society is based on the assumption that everyone is alike and no one is alive.

Hugh Kingsmill 1889–1949: Michael Holroyd *Hugh Kingsmill* (1964)

18 Economics is all about how people make choices. Sociology is all about why they don't have any choices to make.

James Stemble Duesenberry 1918– : *Demographic and Economic Change in the Developed World* (1960)

19 If a free society cannot help the many who are poor, it cannot save the few who are rich.

John F. Kennedy 1917–63: inaugural address, 20 January 1961

20 In your time we have the opportunity to move not only toward the rich society and the powerful society, but upward to the Great Society.

Lyndon Baines Johnson 1908–73: speech at University of Michigan, 22 May 1964

21 The citizen's first duty is unrest.

Günter Grass 1927– : *The Citizen's First Duty* address delivered 1967; in *Speak Out!* (1968)

22 We started off trying to set up a small anarchist community, but people wouldn't obey the rules.

Alan Bennett 1934– : *Getting On* (1972)

23 There is no such thing as Society. There are individual men and women, and there are families.

Margaret Thatcher 1925– : in *Woman's Own* 31 October 1987

24 There is such a thing as society, it's just not the same as the state.

David Cameron 1966– : in *Birmingham Post* 15 September 2005, later repeated on becoming leader of the Conservative party, 6 December 2005

Solitude

proverbs and sayings ▸

1 Better alone than in bad company.

American proverb, late 17th century

2 He travels fastest who travels alone.

implying that single-minded pursuit of an objective is more easily achieved by someone without family commitments; English proverb, late 19th century; see SOLITUDE 13

3 The lone sheep is in danger of the wolf.

stressing the importance of mutual support; English proverb, late 16th century

phrases ▸

4 send to Coventry

refuse to speak to; ostracize; perhaps after circumstances recorded in Clarendon *The History of the Rebellion* (1703) 'At Bromicham, a town so generally wicked, that it had risen upon small parties of the King's, and killed, or taken them prisoners, and sent them to Coventry' (Coventry being then strongly held for Parliament)

quotations ▸

5 It is not good that the man should be alone; I will make him an help meet for him.
Bible: Genesis; see SOLITUDE 18

6 He who is unable to live in society, or who has no need because he is sufficient for himself, must be either a beast or a god.
Aristotle 384–322 BC: *Politics*

7 Never less idle than when wholly idle, nor less alone than when wholly alone.
Scipio Africanus 236–*c.*184 BC: Cicero *De Officiis*

8 In solitude
What happiness? who can enjoy alone,
Or all enjoying, what contentment find?
John Milton 1608–74: *Paradise Lost* (1667)

9 Conversation enriches the understanding, but solitude is the school of genius.
Edward Gibbon 1737–94: *The Decline and Fall of the Roman Empire* (1776–88)

10 I am monarch of all I survey,
My right there is none to dispute;
From the centre all round to the sea
I am lord of the foul and the brute.
William Cowper 1731–1800: 'Verses Supposed to be Written by Alexander Selkirk' (1782); Selkirk (1621–1721) was the prototype of 'Robinson Crusoe'

11 Anythin' for a quiet life, as the man said wen he took the sitivation at the lighthouse.
Charles Dickens 1812–70: *Pickwick Papers* (1837)

12 One may have a blazing hearth in one's soul, and yet no one ever comes to sit by it.
Vincent Van Gogh 1853–90: letter to Theo Van Gogh, July 1880

13 Down to Gehenna or up to the Throne,
He travels the fastest who travels alone.
Rudyard Kipling 1865–1936: 'The Winners' (*The Story of the Gadsbys*, 1890); see SOLITUDE 2

14 My heart is a lonely hunter that hunts on a lonely hill.
Fiona McLeod 1855–1905: 'The Lonely Hunter' (1896); reworked by Carson McCullers as 'The heart is a lonely hunter' for the title of a novel, 1940

15 Man goes into the noisy crowd to drown his own clamour of silence.
Rabindranath Tagore 1861–1941: 'Stray Birds' (1916)

16 I want to be alone.
Greta Garbo 1905–90: *Grand Hotel* (1932 film), the phrase already being associated with Garbo

17 You come into the world alone and you go out of the world alone yet it seems to me you are more alone while living than even going and coming.
Emily Carr 1871–1945: *Hundreds and Thousands: The Journals of Emily Carr* (1966) 16 July 1933

18 God created man and, finding him not sufficiently alone, gave him a companion to make him feel his solitude more keenly.
Paul Valéry 1871–1945: *Tel Quel 1* (1941); see SOLITUDE 5

19 Oh, no no no, it was too cold always
(Still the dead one lay moaning)
I was much too far out all my life
And not waving but drowning.
Stevie Smith 1902–71: 'Not Waving but Drowning' (1957)

20 We're all of us sentenced to solitary confinement inside our own skins, for life!
Tennessee Williams 1911–83: *Orpheus Descending* (1958)

21 How does it feel
To be on your own
With no direction home
Like a complete unknown
Like a rolling stone?
Bob Dylan 1941– : *Like a Rolling Stone* (1965 song)

22 All the lonely people, where do they all come from?
John Lennon 1940–80 and **Paul McCartney** 1942– : 'Eleanor Rigby' (1966 song)

23 Loneliness and the feeling of being unwanted is the most terrible poverty.
Mother Teresa 1910–97: in *Time* Magazine 29 December 1975

24 We're born alone, we live alone, we die alone. Only through our love and friendship can we create the illusion for the moment that we're not alone.
Orson Welles 1915–85: *Someone to Love* (1987 film) words added by Welles to Henry Jaglom's script

Solutions
see PROBLEMS AND SOLUTIONS

Sorrow
see also MOURNING, SUFFERING

proverbs and sayings ▸

1 Misery loves company.
English proverb, late 16th century, now predominantly current in the United States

2 Wednesday's child is full of woe.
traditional rhyme, mid 19th century; see BEAUTY 7, GIFTS 2, TRAVEL 8, WORK 7

3 You cannot prevent the birds of sorrow from flying overhead, but you can prevent them from building nests in your hair.
sorrow may be unavoidable, but one can respond to it in different ways; Chinese proverb

phrases ▸

4 de profundis
a cry of appeal from the depths (of sorrow); Latin = from the depths, the initial words of Psalm 130: see SUFFERING 7

5 Man of Sorrows
a name for Jesus Christ, deriving from a prophecy in the Bible (Isaiah), 'He is despised and rejected of men; a man of sorrows, and acquainted with grief'

quotations ▸

6 By the waters of Babylon we sat down and wept: when we remembered thee, O Sion.
Bible: Psalm 137

7 *Sunt lacrimae rerum et mentem mortalia tangunt.*
There are tears shed for things even here and mortality touches the heart.
Virgil 70–19 BC: *Aeneid*

8 Small sorrows speak; great ones are silent.
Seneca ('the Younger') c.4 BC–AD 65: *Hippolytus*

9 ...*Nessun maggior dolore,*
Che ricordarsi del tempo felice
Nella miseria.
There is no greater pain than to remember a happy time when one is in misery.
Dante Alighieri 1265–1321: *Divina Commedia* 'Inferno'

10 If you have tears, prepare to shed them now.
William Shakespeare 1564–1616: *Julius Caesar* (1599)

11 When sorrows come, they come not single spies,
But in battalions.
William Shakespeare 1564–1616: *Hamlet* (1601)

12 We think caged birds sing, when indeed they cry.
John Webster c.1580–c.1625: *The White Devil* (1612)

13 All my joys to this are folly,
Naught so sweet as Melancholy.
Robert Burton 1577–1640: *The Anatomy of Melancholy* (1621–51)

14 Nothing is here for tears.
John Milton 1608–74: *Samson Agonistes* (1671)

15 Grief is a species of idleness.
Samuel Johnson 1709–84: letter to Mrs Thrale, 17 March 1773

16 I tell you, hopeless grief is passionless.
Elizabeth Barrett Browning 1806–61: 'Grief' (1844)

17 Tears, idle tears, I know not what they mean,
Tears from the depth of some divine despair.
Alfred, Lord Tennyson 1809–92: *The Princess* (1847), song (added 1850)

18 Pure and complete sorrow is as impossible as pure and complete joy.
Leo Tolstoy 1828–1910: *War and Peace* (1865)

19 Áh! ás the heart grows older
It will come to such sights colder

By and by, nor spare a sigh
Though worlds of wanwood leafmeal
lie;
And yet you *will* weep and know why.
Gerard Manley Hopkins 1844–89: 'Spring and Fall: to a young child' (written 1880)

20 MEDVEDENKO: Why do you wear black all the time?
MASHA: I'm in mourning for my life, I'm unhappy.
Anton Chekhov 1860–1904: *The Seagull* (1896)

21 Laugh and the world laughs with you;
Weep, and you weep alone.
Ella Wheeler Wilcox 1855–1919: 'Solitude'; see SYMPATHY 3

22 Between grief and nothing I will take grief.
William Faulkner 1897–1962: *The Wild Palms* (1931)

23 Now laughing friends deride tears
I cannot hide,
So I smile and say 'When a lovely
flame dies,
Smoke gets in your eyes.'
Otto Harbach 1873–1963: 'Smoke Gets in your Eyes' (1933 song)

24 He felt the loyalty we all feel to unhappiness—the sense that that is where we really belong.
Graham Greene 1904–91: *The Heart of the Matter* (1948)

25 No one ever told me that grief felt so like fear.
C. S. Lewis 1898–1963: *A Grief Observed* (1961)

Speech

see also CONVERSATION

proverbs and sayings ▸

1 How now, brown cow?
a traditional elocution exercise

2 Length begets loathing.
in reference to verbosity; English proverb, mid 18th century

3 Who knows most, speaks least.
English proverb, mid 17th century

phrases ▸

4 have kissed the Blarney stone
be eloquent and persuasive; a stone, at *Blarney* castle near Cork in Ireland, said to give the gift of persuasive speech to anyone who kisses it; the verb *to blarney* 'talk flatteringly' derives from this

5 a silver tongue
a gift of eloquence or persuasiveness; see SILENCE 4

6 without hesitation, deviation, or repetition
instruction for contestants' monologues on the panel show *Just a Minute* (BBC Radio, 1967–); coined by producer Ian Messiter (1920–99)

quotations ▸

7 The words of his mouth were softer than butter, having war in his heart: his words were smoother than oil, and yet they be very swords.
Bible: Psalm 55

8 Then said they unto him, Say now Shibboleth: and he said Sibboleth: for he could not frame to pronounce it right. Then they took him, and slew him.
Bible: Judges

9 The reason why we have two ears and only one mouth is that we may listen the more and talk the less.
to a youth who was talking nonsense
Zeno 333–261 BC: Diogenes Laertius *Lives of the Philosophers*

10 The tongue can no man tame; it is an unruly evil.
Bible: James; see BODY 8

11 Somwhat he lipsed, for his
wantownesse,
To make his Englissh sweete upon his
tonge.
Geoffrey Chaucer 1343–1400: *The Canterbury Tales* 'The General Prologue'

12 It has been well said, that heart speaks to heart, whereas language only speaks to the ears.
St Francis de Sales 1567–1622: letter to the Archbishop of Bourges, 5 October 1604, which John Henry Newman paraphrased for his motto as '*cor ad cor loquitur* [heart speaks to heart]'

13 Her voice was ever soft,
Gentle and low, an excellent thing in
woman.

William Shakespeare 1564–1616: *King Lear* (1605–6)

14 I do not much dislike the matter, but
The manner of his speech.

William Shakespeare 1564–1616: *Antony and Cleopatra* (1606–7)

15 Continual eloquence is tedious.

Blaise Pascal 1623–62: *Pensées* (1670)

16 Faith, that's as well said, as if I had said it myself.

Jonathan Swift 1667–1745: *Polite Conversation* (1738)

17 when asked if he found his stammering very inconvenient:

No, Sir, because I have time to think before I speak, and don't ask impertinent questions.

Erasmus Darwin 1731–1802: 'Reminiscences of My Father's Everyday Life', an appendix by Francis Darwin to his edition of Charles Darwin *Autobiography* (1877)

18 When you have nothing to say, say nothing.

Charles Caleb Colton 1780–1832: *Lacon* (1820)

19 And, when you stick on conversation's
burrs,
Don't strew your pathway with those
dreadful *urs*.

Oliver Wendell Holmes 1809–94: 'A Rhymed Lesson' (1848)

20 Human speech is like a cracked kettle on which we tap crude rhythms for bears to dance to, while we long to make music that will melt the stars.

Gustave Flaubert 1821–80: *Madame Bovary* (1857)

21 Take care of the sense, and the sounds will take care of themselves.

Lewis Carroll 1832–98: *Alice's Adventures in Wonderland* (1865); see THRIFT 9

22 I don't want to talk grammar, I want to talk like a lady.

George Bernard Shaw 1856–1950: *Pygmalion* (1916)

23 What can be said at all can be said clearly; and whereof one cannot speak thereof one must be silent.

Ludwig Wittgenstein 1889–1951: *Tractatus Logico-Philosophicus* (1922)

24 Speech is civilization itself. The word, even the most contradictory word, preserves contact — it is silence which isolates.

Thomas Mann 1875–1955: *The Magic Mountain* (1924)

25 You like potato and I like po-tah-to,
You like tomato and I like to-mah-to;
Potato, po-tah-to, tomato,
to-mah-to—
Let's call the whole thing off!

Ira Gershwin 1896–1983: 'Let's Call the Whole Thing Off' (1937 song)

26 Speech impelled us
To purify the dialect of the tribe
And urge the mind to aftersight and
foresight.

T. S. Eliot 1888–1965: *Four Quartets* 'Little Gidding' (1942)

27 Nagging is the repetition of unpalatable truths.

Edith Summerskill 1901–80: speech to the Married Women's Association, House of Commons, 14 July 1960

28 Never express yourself more clearly than you think.

Niels Bohr 1885–1962: Abraham Pais *Einstein Lived Here* (1994)

29 Lots of planets have a north.

explaining his northern accent

Russell T. Davies 1963– : *Doctor Who* BBC1 TV, 26 March 2005; spoken by Christopher Ecclestone as Doctor Who

Speeches

proverbs and sayings ▶

1 Unaccustomed as I am...

clichéistic opening words by a public speaker

phrases ▶

2 the rubber chicken circuit

the circuit followed by professional speakers; referring to what is regarded as the customary menu for the lunch or dinner preceding the speech

3 the Rupert of Debate

Edward Stanley (1799–1869), later 14th Earl of Derby; a description by the British novelist and politician Edward Bulwer-Lytton (1803–73), likening his parliamentary style to the dashing cavalry charges of Prince Rupert

4 talking to Buncombe

ostentatious and irrelevant speechmaking; from Felix Walker, excusing a long, dull, irrelevant speech in the House of Representatives, 1820, 'I'm talking to Buncombe', *Buncombe* being his constituency; the word *bunkum* derives from this

quotations ▶

5 What worse change can any one bring against an orator than that his words and his sentiments do not tally?

Demosthenes c.384–c.322 BC: *On the Crown*

6 When asked what was first in oratory, [he] replied to his questioner, 'action,' what second, 'action,' and again third, 'action.'

Demosthenes c.384–c.322 BC: Cicero *Brutus*

7 Grasp the subject, the words will follow.

Cato the Elder 234–149 BC: Caius Julius Victor *Ars Rhetorica*

8 Give brief orders; speeches that are too long are likely to be forgotten.

Abu Bakr 573–634: advice to his army, R. W. Maqsood *Sayings of Abu Bakr* (1989)

9 Friends, Romans, countrymen, lend
me your ears.

William Shakespeare 1564–1616: *Julius Caesar* (1599)

10 But all was false and hollow; though
his tongue
Dropped manna, and could make the
worse appear
The better reason.

John Milton 1608–74: *Paradise Lost* (1667)

11 Not merely a chip of the old 'block,' but the old block itself.

on the younger Pitt's maiden speech, February 1781

Edmund Burke 1729–97: N. W. Wraxall *Historical Memoirs of My Own Time* (1904 ed.); see FAMILY 13

12 The Right Honourable gentleman is indebted to his memory for his jests, and to his imagination for his facts.

Richard Brinsley Sheridan 1751–1816: speech in reply to Mr Dundas; T. Moore *Life of Sheridan* (1825)

13 A sophistical rhetorician, inebriated with the exuberance of his own verbosity.

of Gladstone

Benjamin Disraeli 1804–81: in *Times* 29 July 1878

14 [My ability] to put into words what is in their hearts and minds but not in their mouths.

when asked by Douglas MacArthur in 1906 to what he attributed his popularity

Theodore Roosevelt 1858–1919: William Safire *New Political Dictionary* (1978); see OPINION 8

15 He [Lord Charles Beresford] is one of those orators of whom it was well said, 'Before they get up, they do not know what they are going to say; when they are speaking, they do not know what they are saying; and when they have sat down, they do not know what they have said.'

Winston Churchill 1874–1965: speech, House of Commons, 20 December 1912

16 M. Clemenceau...is one of the greatest living orators, but he knows that the finest eloquence is that which gets things done and the worst is that which delays them.

David Lloyd George 1863–1945: speech at Paris Peace Conference, 18 January 1919

17 If I am to speak for ten minutes, I need a week for preparation; if fifteen minutes, three days; if half an hour, two days; if an hour, I am ready now.

Woodrow Wilson 1856–1924: Josephus Daniels *The Wilson Era* (1946)

18 If you don't say anything, you won't be called on to repeat it.

Calvin Coolidge 1872–1933: attributed

19 He [Winston Churchill] mobilized the English language and sent it into battle to steady his fellow countrymen and hearten those Europeans upon whom the long dark night of tyranny had descended.

Ed Murrow 1908–65: broadcast, 30 November 1954

20 I do not object to people looking at their watches when I am speaking. But I strongly object when they start shaking them to make certain they are still going.
Lord Birkett 1883–1962: in *Observer* 30 October 1960

21 Do you remember that in classical times when Cicero had finished speaking, the people said, 'How well he spoke', but when Demosthenes had finished speaking, they said, 'Let us march.'
introducing John F. Kennedy in 1960
Adlai Stevenson 1900–65: Bert Cochran *Adlai Stevenson*

22 This is not a time for soundbites.
of the final stage of the Northern Irish negotiations
Tony Blair 1953– : speech, Belfast, 8 April 1998

Sports and Games

see also CRICKET, FOOTBALL, HUNTING, WINNING

proverbs and sayings ▸

1 Chess is a sea where a gnat may drink and an elephant may bathe.
the game may be played at many levels; modern saying, said to derive from an Indian proverb

2 Citius, altius, fortius.
Latin, *Swifter, higher, stronger*, motto of the modern Olympic Games

3 Ka mate! Ka mate! Ka ora! Ka ora!
Maori, *I die! I die! I live! I live!*; haka, originally composed by Te Rauparaha (d. 1849) in the 1820s; now particularly associated with the New Zealand All Blacks rugby union team

4 Let me win. But if I cannot win, let me be brave in the attempt.
motto of the Special Olympics

5 Nice guys finish last.
modern saying, after Leo Durocher: see SPORTS 23

phrases ▸

6 the blue ribbon of the turf
the Derby, from Disraeli *Lord George Bentinck* (1852); a horse bred and sold by Lord George subsequently won the Derby, and Lord George coined this phrase in explaining to Disraeli his bitter disappointment at not still owning the horse, with the words 'you do not know what the Derby is'; see EXCELLENCE 5

7 no joy in Mudville
referring to the emotions (especially disappointment) felt by fans or a team according to the outcome of a game (especially in baseball); from the fictional town in E. L. Thayer's poem 'Casey at the Bat' (1888), which features the defeat of its baseball team

8 rumble in the jungle
the boxing match between Muhammad Ali and George Foreman in Zaire in 1974

9 the sport of kings
horse-racing; the term was originally applied to war and later hunting; see HUNTING 8, SPORTS 17

quotations ▸

10 There is plenty of time to win this game, and to thrash the Spaniards too.
receiving news of the Armada while playing bowls on Plymouth Hoe
Francis Drake 1540–96: attributed, in *Dictionary of National Biography* (1917–)

11 Chaos umpire sits,
And by decision more embroils the fray.
John Milton 1608–74: *Paradise Lost* (1667)

12 I am sorry I have not learned to play at cards. It is very useful in life: it generates kindness and consolidates society.
Samuel Johnson 1709–84: James Boswell *Journal of a Tour to the Hebrides* (1785) 21 November 1773

13 And it's not for the sake of a ribboned coat,
Or the selfish hope of a season's fame,
But his Captain's hand on his shoulder smote—
'Play up! play up! and play the game!'
Henry Newbolt 1862–1938: 'Vitaï Lampada' (1897)

14 To play billiards well is a sign of an ill-spent youth.
Charles Roupell: attributed; D. Duncan *Life of Herbert Spencer* (1908)

15 Take me out to the ball game,
Take me out with the crowd.
Buy me some peanuts and cracker-jack—
I don't care if I never get back.
Jack Norworth 1879–1959: 'Take Me Out to the Ball Game' (1908 song)

16 Golf is a good walk spoiled.
Mark Twain 1835–1910: Alex Ayres *Greatly Exaggerated: the Wit and Wisdom of Mark Twain* (1988); attributed

17 A royal sport for the natural kings of earth.
on surfing
Jack London 1876–1916: *The Cruise of the Snark* (1911); see SPORTS 9

18 Golf is so popular simply because it is the best game in the world at which to be bad.
A. A. Milne 1882–1956: *Not That It Matters* (1919)

19 We was robbed!
after Jack Sharkey beat Max Schmeling (of whom Jacobs was manager) in the heavyweight title fight, 21 June 1932
Joe Jacobs 1896–1940: Peter Heller *In This Corner* (1975)

20 He shoots! He scores!
Foster William Hewitt 1902–85: catchphrase used at ice-hockey games; first said over the radio 4 April 1933 at the game between the Toronto Maple Leafs and the Boston Bruins

21 For when the One Great Scorer comes
to mark against your name,
He writes—not that you won or lost—
but how you played the Game.
Grantland Rice 1880–1954: 'Alumnus Football' (1941)

22 Love-thirty, love-forty, oh! weakness
of joy,
The speed of a swallow, the grace of
a boy,
With carefullest carelessness, gaily
you won,
I am weak from your loveliness, Joan
Hunter Dunn.
John Betjeman 1906–84: 'A Subaltern's Love-Song' (1945)

23 I called off his players' names as they came marching up the steps behind him...All nice guys. They'll finish last. Nice guys. Finish last.
casual remark at a practice ground in the presence of a number of journalists, July 1946
Leo Durocher 1906–91: *Nice Guys Finish Last* (1975); see SPORTS 5

24 Serious sport has nothing to do with fair play...It is war minus the shooting.
George Orwell 1903–50: *Shooting an Elephant* (1950) 'I Write as I Please'

25 While all artists are not chess players, all chess players are artists.
Marcel Duchamp 1887–1968: address to New York State Chess Association, 30 August 1952

26 Don't look back. Something may be gaining on you.
a baseball pitcher's advice
Satchel Paige 1906–82: in *Collier's* 13 June 1953

27 If you watch a game, it's fun. If you play it, it's recreation. If you work at it, it's golf.
Bob Hope 1903–2003: in *Reader's Digest* October 1958

28 What I know most surely about morality and the duty of man I owe to sport.
often quoted as, '...I owe to football'
Albert Camus 1913–60: Herbert R. Lottman *Albert Camus* (1979)

29 A ball player's got to be kept hungry to become a big leaguer. That's why no boy from a rich family ever made the big leagues.
Joe DiMaggio 1914–99: in *New York Times* 30 April 1961

30 Float like a butterfly, sting like a bee.
summary of his boxing strategy
Muhammad Ali 1942– : G. Sullivan *Cassius Clay Story* (1964); probably originated by Drew 'Bundini' Brown

31 In America, it is sport that is the opiate of the masses.
Russell Baker 1925– : in *New York Times* 3 October 1967; see REALITY 8

32 It's gonna be a thrilla, a chilla, and a
killa,
When I get the gorilla in Manila.
of his fight with Joe Frazier
Muhammad Ali 1942– : in 1975

33 Think! How the hell are you gonna think and hit at the same time?
Yogi Berra 1925– : *Nice Guys Finish Seventh* (1976)

34 Sports do not build character. They reveal it.
Haywood Hale Broun 1918– : attributed; James Michener *Sports in America* (1976)

35 You cannot be serious!
John McEnroe 1959– : said to tennis umpire at Wimbledon, early 1980s

36 If people don't want to come out to the ball park, nobody's going to stop 'em.

Yogi Berra 1925– : attributed

37 The thing about sport, any sport, is that swearing is very much part of it.

Jimmy Greaves 1940– : in *Observer* 1 January 1989

38 Baseball, it is said, is only a game. True. And the Grand Canyon is only a hole in Arizona. Not all holes, or games, are created equal.

George F. Will 1941– : *Men At Work: The Craft of Baseball* (1990)

39 Boxing's just show business with blood.

Frank Bruno 1961– : in *Guardian* 20 November 1991; also attributed to David Belasco in 1915

40 If you can keep playing tennis when somebody is shooting a gun down the street, that's concentration. I didn't grow up playing at the country club.

Serena Williams 1981– : in *Sunday Times* 2 June 2002

41 Eat, sleep and swim. That's all I can do.

attributing his record number of Olympic gold medals to his high-calorie diet

Michael Phelps 1985– : in *Observer* 17 August 2008

42 I just blew my mind. And I blew the world's mind.

on winning the 200m at the Beijing Olympics

Usain Bolt 1986– : in *Independent* 21 August 2008

43 I say to the Chinese and I say to the world—ping pong is coming home.

on the 2012 London Olympics

Boris Johnson 1964– : at the conclusion of the Beijing Olympics; in *Independent* 25 August 2008

44 I play tennis for a living, even though I hate tennis, hate it with a dark and secret passion, and always have.

Andre Agassi 1970– : *Open* (2010)

45 I can cry like Roger, it's a shame I can't play like him.

after losing to Roger Federer in the final of the Australian Open Tennis Championship

Andy Murray 1987– : at Melbourne Park, Australia, 31 January 2010

Statistics

see also MATHS, QUANTITIES

phrases ▸

1 the law of averages

the supposed principle that future events are likely to turn out so that they balance any past deviation from a presumed average. The term derives initially from Henry Thomas Buckle's *The History of Civilization in England* (1857): 'The great advance made by the statisticians consists in applying to these inquiries [into crime] the doctrine of averages, which no one thought of doing before the eighteenth century'. The first (sceptical) reference to 'Mr Buckle's "Law of Averages" ' is found in 1875

2 vital statistics

quantitative data concerning the population, such as the number of births, marriages, and deaths; informally, the measurements of a woman's bust, waist, and hips

quotations ▸

3 We are just statistics, born to consume resources.

Horace 65–8 BC: *Epistles*

4 A witty statesman said, you might prove anything by figures.

Thomas Carlyle 1795–1881: *Chartism* (1839)

5 Every moment dies a man,
Every moment one is born.

Alfred, Lord Tennyson 1809–92: 'The Vision of Sin' (1842); see STATISTICS 6

6 Every moment dies a man,
Every moment 1¹⁄₁₆ is born.

Charles Babbage 1791–1871: parody of Tennyson's 'Vision of Sin' in an unpublished letter to the poet; in *New Scientist* 4 December 1958; see STATISTICS 5

7 There are three kinds of lies: lies, damned lies and statistics.

Benjamin Disraeli 1804–81: attributed; Mark Twain *Autobiography* (1924); anonymous versions of this occur earlier, e.g. in *Economic Journal* June 1892

8 Long and painful experience has taught me one great principle in managing business for other people,

viz., if you want to inspire confidence, *give plenty of statistics.*

Lewis Carroll 1832–98: C. L. Dodgson *Three Years in a Curatorship by One Whom It Has Tried* (1886)

9 You cannot feed the hungry on statistics.

David Lloyd George 1863–1945: speech in the House of Commons, 1904

10 He uses statistics as a drunken man uses lampposts—for support rather than for illumination.

Andrew Lang 1844–1912: attributed

11 [The War Office kept three sets of figures:] one to mislead the public, another to mislead the Cabinet, and the third to mislead itself.

Herbert Asquith 1852–1928: Alistair Horne *Price of Glory* (1962)

12 If your experiment needs statistics, you ought to have done a better experiment.

Ernest Rutherford 1871–1937: Norman T. J. Bailey *The Mathematical Approach to Biology and Medicine* (1967)

13 Statistics are the triumph of the quantitative method, and the quantitative method is the victory of sterility and death.

Hilaire Belloc 1870–1953: *The Silence of the Sea* (1941)

14 From the fact that there are 400,000 species of beetles on this planet, but only 8,000 species of mammals, he [Haldane] concluded that the Creator, if He exists, has a special preference for beetles.

J. B. S. Haldane 1892–1964: report of lecture, 7 April 1951

15 One of the thieves was saved. (*Pause*) It's a reasonable percentage.

Samuel Beckett 1906–89: *Waiting for Godot* (1955)

16 Any observed statistical regularity will tend to collapse once pressure is placed upon it for control purposes.

known as Goodhart's Law, and often quoted as 'When a measure becomes a target it ceases to be a good measure'

Charles Goodhart 1936– : *Monetary Theory and Practice: the UK Experience* (1984)

Story-telling

see FICTION AND STORY-TELLING

Strength and Weakness

proverbs and sayings ▸

1 The caribou feeds the wolf, but it is the wolf that keeps the caribou strong.

stressing the interrelationship between predator and prey; Inuit proverb; see LIFE SCIENCES 7

2 Every tub must stand on its own bottom.

it is necessary to support oneself by one's own efforts; English proverb, mid 16th century

3 If you don't like the heat, get out of the kitchen.

if you choose to work in a particular sphere you must also deal with its pressures; English proverb, mid 20th century; see STRENGTH 28

4 It is the pace that kills.

used as a warning against working under extreme pressure; English proverb, mid 19th century

5 Only an elephant can bear an elephant's load.

heavy responsibilities require significant strength; Indian proverb (Marathi)

6 A reed before the wind lives on, while mighty oaks do fall.

something which bends to the force of the wind is less likely to be broken than something which tries to withstand it; English proverb, late 14th century

7 Resistance is futile.

catchphrase of the Borg, first occurring in *Star Trek: The Next Generation* 'The Best of Both Worlds' pt. 1, 18 June 1990, written by Michael Piller (1948–2005)

8 Strength through joy.

German Labour Front slogan from 1933, coined by Robert Ley (1890–1945)

9 The weakest go to the wall.

usually said to derive from the installation of seating (around the walls) in the churches of the late Middle Ages; English proverb, early 16th century

10 You are the weakest link...goodbye.
catchphrase used by Anne Robinson on the television game-show *The Weakest Link* (2000–); see COOPERATION 1

phrases ▸

11 Achilles heel
a person's only vulnerable spot, a weak point; from the legend of the only point at which Achilles could be wounded after he was dipped into the River Styx, his mother having held him so that his heel was protected from the river water by her grasp

12 broken reed
a person who fails to give support, a weak or ineffectual person; from the Bible (Isaiah) 'thou trustest in the staff of this broken reed, on Egypt'

13 built on sand
lacking a firm foundation; unstable; ephemeral; from the parable in the Bible (Matthew) of the two houses founded respectively on rock and on sand

14 steal someone's thunder
use another person's idea, and spoil the effect the originator hoped to achieve by acting on it first; originally *thunder* as a stage effect, after John Dennis: see THEATRE 11

15 a tiger in one's tank
energy, spirit, animation; from an Esso petrol advertising slogan: see TRANSPORT 3

16 a tower of strength
a source of strong and reliable support; perhaps originally alluding to the *Book of Common Prayer* 'O Lord…be unto them a tower of strength'

quotations ▸

17 A threefold cord is not quickly broken.
Bible: Ecclesiastes

18 All the world knows that the weak
overcomes the strong and the soft
overcomes the hard.
But none can practice it.
Lao Tzu c.604–c.531 BC: *Tao-te Ching*

19 Choose rather to be strong in soul than strong of body.
Pythagoras 580–500 BC: Stobaeus *Sententiae*

20 If God be for us, who can be against us?
Bible: Romans

21 The gods are on the side of the stronger.
Tacitus C. AD 56–after 117: *Histories*; see ARMED FORCES 7

22 The concessions of the weak are the concessions of fear.
Edmund Burke 1729–97: *On Conciliation with America* (1775)

23 The thing is, you see, that the strongest man in the world is the man who stands most alone.
Henrik Ibsen 1828–1906: *An Enemy of the People* (1882)

24 I am as strong as a bull moose and you can use me to the limit.
'Bull Moose' subsequently became the popular name of the Progressive Party
Theodore Roosevelt 1858–1919: letter to Mark Hanna, 27 June 1900

25 This is the law of the Yukon, that only
the Strong shall thrive;
That surely the Weak shall perish, and
only the Fit survive.
Robert W. Service 1874–1958: 'The Law of the Yukon' (1907)

26 You cannot strengthen the weak by weakening the strong.
William J. H. Boetcker 1873–1962: 'Lincoln on Private Property' (1916); often wrongly attributed to Abraham Lincoln: the leaflet included Lincoln's words on one side and Boetcker's own on the other; later reprints missed out Boetcker's name, and implied that the whole was Lincoln's

27 A weak man has doubts before a decision; a strong man has them afterwards.
Karl Kraus 1874–1936: *Half-truths and One-and-a-Half-Truths* (1976)

28 If you can't stand the heat, get out of the kitchen.
Harry Vaughan: in *Time* 28 April 1952; associated with Harry S. Truman, but attributed by him to Vaughan, his 'military jester'; see STRENGTH 3

29 The most potent weapon in the hands of the oppressor is the mind of the oppressed.
Steve Biko 1946–77: statement as witness, 3 May 1976

30 A house built on granite and strong foundations, not even the onslaught

of pouring rain, gushing torrents and strong winds will be able to pull down.
Haile Selassie 1892–1975: *My Life and Ethiopia's Progress 1892–1937* (1976)

31 Toughness doesn't have to come in a pinstripe suit.
Dianne Feinstein 1933– : in *Time* 4 June 1984

Style
see also LANGUAGE

proverbs and sayings ▸

1 The style is the man.
one's chosen style reflects one's essential characteristics; English proverb, early 20th century; see STYLE 13

phrases ▸

2 neat but not gaudy
characterized by an elegant simplicity; see STYLE 11

3 penny plain
plain and simple; with reference to prints of characters sold for toy theatres, costing one penny for black-and-white ones, and two pennies for coloured ones; see PAINTING 14

4 purple patch
an ornate or elaborate passage in a literary composition; from Horace: see STYLE 6

quotations ▸

5 I strive to be brief, and I become obscure.
Horace 65–8 BC: *Ars Poetica*

6 Works of serious purpose and grand promises often have a purple patch or two stitched on, to shine far and wide.
Horace 65–8 BC: *Ars Poetica*; see STYLE 4

7 I have revered always not crude verbosity, but holy simplicity.
St Jerome C.AD 342–420: letter 'Ad Pammachium'

8 More matter with less art.
William Shakespeare 1564–1616: *Hamlet* (1601)

9 He does it with a better grace, but I do it more natural.
William Shakespeare 1564–1616: *Twelfth Night* (1601)

10 When we see a natural style, we are quite surprised and delighted, for we expected to see an author and we find a man.
Blaise Pascal 1623–62: *Pensées* (1670)

11 Style is the dress of thought; a modest dress,
Neat, but not gaudy, will true critics please.
Samuel Wesley 1662–1735: 'An Epistle to a Friend concerning Poetry' (1700); see STYLE 2

12 True wit is Nature to advantage dressed,
What oft was thought, but ne'er so well expressed.
Alexander Pope 1688–1744: *An Essay on Criticism* (1711)

13 These things [subject matter] are external to the man; style is the man.
Comte de Buffon 1707–88: *Discours sur le style*; address given to the Académie Française, 25 August 1753; see STYLE 1

14 The moving accident is not my trade;
To freeze the blood I have no ready arts:
'Tis my delight, alone in summer shade,
To pipe a simple song for thinking hearts.
William Wordsworth 1770–1850: 'Hart-Leap Well' (1800); see FEAR 6

15 Style is life! It is the very life-blood of thought!
Gustave Flaubert 1821–80: letter to Louise Colet, 7 September 1853

16 People think that I can teach them style. What stuff it all is! Have something to say, and say it as clearly as you can. That is the only secret of style.
Matthew Arnold 1822–88: G. W. E. Russell *Collections and Recollections* (1898)

17 As to the Adjective: when in doubt, strike it out.
Mark Twain 1835–1910: *Pudd'nhead Wilson* (1894)

18 No flowers, by request.
summarizing the principle of conciseness for contributors to the *Dictionary of National Biography*
Alfred Ainger 1837–1904: speech to contributors, 8 July 1897; see MOURNING 5

19 In matters of grave importance, style, not sincerity is the vital thing.

Oscar Wilde 1854–1900: *The Importance of Being Earnest* (1899)

20 'Feather-footed through the plashy fen passes the questing vole'...'Yes,' said the Managing Editor. 'That must be good style.'

Evelyn Waugh 1903–66: *Scoop* (1938)

21 The Mandarin style...is beloved by literary pundits, by those who would make the written word as unlike as possible to the spoken one.

Cyril Connolly 1903–74: *Enemies of Promise* (1938)

22 I am well aware that an addiction to silk underwear does not necessarily imply that one's feet are dirty. Nonetheless, style, like sheer silk, too often hides eczema.

Albert Camus 1913–60: *The Fall* (1956)

23 It's not what I do, but the way I do it. It's not what I say, but the way I say it.

Mae West 1892–1980: G. Eells and S. Musgrove *Mae West* (1989)

24 I'm just trying to change the world one sequin at a time.

Lady Gaga 1986– : in *Evening Chronicle* [Newcastle] 19 January 2009

Success and Failure

see also WINNING

proverbs and sayings ▸

1 The bigger they are, the harder they fall.

English proverb, early 20th century, commonly attributed in its current form to the fighter Robert Fitzsimmons, prior to a fight 1900

2 From clogs to clogs is only three generations.

the *clog*, a shoe with a thick wooden sole, was worn by manual workers in the north of England. The implication is that the energy and ability required to raise a person's material status from poverty is often not continued to the third generation, and that the success is therefore not sustained; English proverb, late 19th century, said to be a Lancashire proverb

3 From shirtsleeves to shirtsleeves in three generations.

wealth gained in one generation will be lost by the third; English proverb, early 20th century. The saying is often attributed to the Scottish-born American industrialist and philanthropist Andrew Carnegie (1835–1919) but is not found in his writings

4 From the sublime to the ridiculous is only one step.

English proverb, late 19th century; see SUCCESS 31, SUCCESS 32

5 Let them laugh that win.

triumphant laughter should be withheld until success is assured; English proverb, mid 16th century

6 Nothing succeeds like success.

someone already regarded as successful is likely to attract more support; English proverb, mid 19th century

7 The only place where success comes before work is in a dictionary.

modern saying

8 The race is not to the swift, nor the battle to the strong.

the person with the most apparent advantages will not necessarily be successful; English proverb, mid 17th century; see SUCCESS 22

9 A rising tide lifts all boats.

usually taken to mean that a prosperous society benefits everybody; in America the expression was particularly associated with John Fitzgerald Kennedy (1917–63); English proverb, mid 20th century

10 Rooster today, feather duster tomorrow.

one who is currently successful may subsequently find that circumstances change dramatically; Australian saying

11 Success has many fathers, while failure is an orphan.

once something is seen to succeed many people will claim to have initiated it, while responsibility for failure is likely to be disclaimed; English proverb, mid 20th century: see SUCCESS 45

12 Up like a rocket, down like a stick.

sudden marked success is likely to be followed by equally sudden failure; English proverb, late 19th century; see SUCCESS 30

13 **When an elephant is in trouble, even a frog can kick him.**
the weak can attack the strong when they are in difficulty; Indian proverb

14 **You win a few, you lose a few.**
one has to accept failure as well as success, and used as an expression of consolation or resignation; English proverb, mid 20th century

phrases ▶

15 **the bitch goddess**
material or worldly success as an object of attainment; from William James: see SUCCESS 39

16 **the golden rule**
a basic principle which should always be followed to ensure success in general or in a particular activity. The term is sometimes specifically used of the injunction given by Jesus in the Bible: see LIFESTYLES 18, LIKES 14

17 **one's finest hour**
the time of one's greatest success; now particularly associated with Churchill: see WORLD WAR II 13

18 **place in the sun**
one's share of good fortune or prosperity; a favourable situation or position, prominence; associated with German nationalism (see INTERNATIONAL 24) but earlier recorded in the writings of Pascal (translation 1688)

19 **weighed in the balance and found wanting**
having failed to meet the test of a particular situation; in the Bible (Daniel), part of the judgement made on King Belshazzar by the *writing on the wall*: see FUTURE 13

20 **win one's laurels**
succeed publicly, achieve one's due reward of acknowledgement and praise; *laurels* the foliage of the bay-tree (real or imaginary) as an emblem of victory or of distinction; see REPUTATION 17, YOUTH 14

21 **win one's spurs**
attain distinction, achieve one's first honours; *spurs* as an emblem of knighthood, especially gained by an act of valour; see EFFORT 18

quotations ▶

22 **The race is not to the swift, nor the battle to the strong.**
Bible: Ecclesiastes; see SUCCESS 8

23 ***Veni, vidi, vici.***
I came, I saw, I conquered.
Julius Caesar 100–44 BC: inscription displayed in Caesar's Pontic triumph, according to Suetonius *Lives of the Caesars* 'Divus Julius'; or, according to Plutarch *Parallel Lives* 'Julius Caesar', written in a letter by Caesar, announcing the victory of Zela which concluded the Pontic campaign

24 **For what shall it profit a man, if he shall gain the whole world, and lose his own soul?**
Bible: St Mark; see WALES 10

25 **You do well to weep as a woman over what you could not defend as a man.**
reproach to her son Boabdil (Muhammad XI, the last Sultan of Granada), who had surrendered Granada to Ferdinand and Isabella
Ayesha fl. 1492: traditional attribution; Washington Irving *The Alhambra* (1832; rev. ed. 1851)

26 **Of all I had, only honour and life have been spared.**
usually quoted 'All is lost save honour'
Francis I of France 1494–1547: letter to his mother following his defeat at Pavia, 1525

27 **MACBETH: If we should fail,—**
LADY MACBETH: We fail!
But screw your courage to the sticking-place,
And we'll not fail.
William Shakespeare 1564–1616: *Macbeth* (1606)

28 **'Tis not in mortals to command success,**
But we'll do more, Sempronius; we'll deserve it.
Joseph Addison 1672–1719: *Cato* (1713)

29 **In most things success depends on knowing how long it takes to succeed.**
Montesquieu 1689–1755: *Pensées et fragments inédits…* vol. 1 (1901)

30 **As he rose like a rocket, he fell like the stick.**
on Edmund Burke losing the parliamentary debate on the French Revolution to Charles James Fox
Thomas Paine 1737–1809: *Letter to the Addressers on the late Proclamation* (1792); see SUCCESS 12

31 **The sublime and the ridiculous are often so nearly related, that it is difficult to class them separately. One**

step above the sublime, makes the ridiculous; and one step above the ridiculous, makes the sublime again.

Thomas Paine 1737–1809: *The Age of Reason* pt. 2 (1795); see SUCCESS 4, SUCCESS 32

32 There is only one step from the sublime to the ridiculous.

to De Pradt, Polish ambassador, after the retreat from Moscow in 1812

Napoléon I 1769–1821: D. G. De Pradt *Histoire de l'Ambassade dans le grand-duché de Varsovie en 1812* (1815); see SUCCESS 4, SUCCESS 31

33 It was roses, roses, all the way.

Robert Browning 1812–89: 'The Patriot' (1855)

34 I have climbed to the top of the greasy pole.

on becoming Prime Minister

Benjamin Disraeli 1804–81: W. Monypenny and G. Buckle *Life of Benjamin Disraeli* vol. 4 (1916)

35 Success is a science; if you have the conditions, you get the result.

Oscar Wilde 1854–1900: letter ?March–April 1883

36 All you need in this life is ignorance and confidence; then success is sure.

Mark Twain 1835–1910: letter to Mrs Foote, 2 December 1887

37 Our business in this world is not to succeed, but to continue to fail, in good spirits.

Robert Louis Stevenson 1850–94: *Ethical Studies* (1924) 'Lay Morals and Other Ethical Papers'

38 He has achieved success who has lived well, laughed often, and loved much; who has enjoyed the trust of pure women, the respect of intelligent men, and the love of little children;... whose life was an inspiration, whose memory a benediction.

Bessie Anderson Stanley fl. 1905: 'What Constitutes Success', in *Modern Women* December 1905, and often wrongly attributed to Ralph Waldo Emerson or Robert Louis Stevenson; in *Notes and Queries* July 1976

39 The moral flabbiness born of the exclusive worship of the bitch-goddess *success*.

William James 1842–1910: letter to H. G. Wells, 11 September 1906; see SUCCESS 15

40 The world continues to offer glittering prizes to those who have stout hearts and sharp swords.

F. E. Smith 1872–1930: Rectorial Address, Glasgow University, 7 November 1923

41 You [the Mensheviks] are pitiful isolated individuals; you are bankrupts; your role is played out. Go where you belong from now on—into the dustbin of history!

Leon Trotsky 1879–1940: *History of the Russian Revolution* (1933)

42 How to win friends and influence people.

Dale Carnegie 1888–1955: title of book (1936)

43 History to the defeated
May say Alas but cannot help or
pardon.

W. H. Auden 1907–73: 'Spain 1937' (1937)

44 Success is relative:
It is what we can make of the mess we
have made of things.

T. S. Eliot 1888–1965: *The Family Reunion* (1939)

45 Victory has a hundred fathers, but no-one wants to recognise defeat as his own.

Count Galeazzo Ciano 1903–44: diary, 9 September 1942; see SUCCESS 11

46 If *A* is a success in life, then *A* equals *x* plus *y* plus *z*. Work is *x*; *y* is play; and *z* is keeping your mouth shut.

Albert Einstein 1879–1955: in *Observer* 15 January 1950

47 I cannot give you the formula for success, but I can give you the formula for failure: Try to please everybody.

Herbert Bayard Swope 1882–1958: Ely Jacques Kahn *The World of Swope* (1965)

48 Failure is not an option.

supposed announcement to ground crew in Houston, 14 April 1970, as Apollo 13 approached the critical earth-to-moon decision loop; this version was used in the film *Apollo 13* (1995), though his actual words were 'This crew is coming home'

Gene Kranz 1933– : title of autobiography, 2000

49 Whenever a friend succeeds, a little something in me dies.

Gore Vidal 1925– : in *Sunday Times Magazine* 16 September 1973

50 Is it possible to succeed without any act of betrayal?

Jean Renoir 1894–1979: *My Life and My Films* (1974)

51 Ever tried. Ever failed. No matter. Try again. Fail again. Fail better.

Samuel Beckett 1906–89: *Worstward Ho* (1983)

52 Success is more dangerous than failure, the ripples break over a wider coastline.

Graham Greene 1904–91: in *The Independent* 4 April 1991

53 Anybody seen in a bus over the age of thirty has been a failure in life.

Loelia, Duchess of Westminster 1902–93: in *Times* 4 November 1993 (obituary); habitual remark

54 Success is not the key to happiness. Happiness is the key to success.

Herman Cain 1945– : in *Omaha World Herald* 13 October 1996

Suffering

see also MOURNING, SORROW, SYMPATHY

proverbs and sayings ▸

1 Beauty without cruelty.

slogan for Animal Rights

2 Crosses are ladders that lead to heaven.

the way to heaven is through suffering; *crosses* refers either to the crucifix, or more generally to troubles or misfortunes; English proverb, early 17th century

3 Ee, it was agony, Ivy.

catchphrase from *Ray's a Laugh* (BBC radio programme, 1949–61), written by Ted Ray

4 No cross, no crown.

cross is here used punningly, as in SUFFERING 2; English proverb, early 17th century; see SUFFERING 17

phrases ▸

5 have one's cross to bear

suffer the troubles that life brings. The allusion is to Jesus (or Simon of Cyrene) carrying the Cross to Calvary for the Crucifixion; see MARRIAGE 40, SUFFERING 13, WORLD WAR II 25

quotations ▸

6 They that sow in tears: shall reap in joy.

Bible: Psalm 126

7 Out of the deep have I called unto thee, O Lord: Lord, hear my voice.

Bible: Psalm 130; see SORROW 4

8 The fool learns by suffering.

Hesiod fl. *c.*700 BC: *Works and Days*

9 Justice inclines her scales so that wisdom comes at the price of suffering.

Aeschylus *c.*525–456 BC: *Agamemnon* l. 250

10 Pain of mind is worse than pain of body.

Publilius Syrus fl. *c.*100 BC: *Sententiae* no. 166

11 Nothing happens to anybody which he is not fitted by nature to bear.

Marcus Aurelius AD 121–80: *Meditations*

12 All those who suffer in the world do so because of their desire for their own happiness.

Shantideva 685–763: *Bodhicaryāvatāra* ch. 8, v. 129

13 If you bear the cross gladly, it will bear you.

Thomas à Kempis 1380–1471: *The Imitation of Christ*; see SUFFERING 5

14 He jests at scars, that never felt a wound.

William Shakespeare 1564–1616: *Romeo and Juliet* (1595)

15 The worst is not,
So long as we can say, 'This is the worst.'

William Shakespeare 1564–1616: *King Lear* (1605–6)

16 Our torments also may in length of time
Become our elements.

John Milton 1608–74: *Paradise Lost* (1667)

17 No pain, no palm; no thorns, no throne; no gall, no glory; no cross, no crown.

William Penn 1644–1718: *No Cross, No Crown* (1669 pamphlet); see SUFFERING 4

18 To each his suff'rings, all are men,
Condemned alike to groan;
The tender for another's pain,
Th' unfeeling for his own.

Thomas Gray 1716–71: *Ode on a Distant Prospect of Eton College* (1747)

19 Thank you, madam, the agony is abated.
aged four, having had hot coffee spilt over his legs
Lord Macaulay 1800–59: G. O. Trevelyan *Life and Letters of Lord Macaulay* (1876)

20 Misery such as mine has no pride.
I care not who knows that I am wretched.
Jane Austen 1775–1817: *Sense and Sensibility* (1811)

21 Sorrow and silence are strong, and patient endurance is godlike.
Henry Wadsworth Longfellow 1807–82: *Evangeline* (1847)

22 For frequent tears have run
The colours from my life.
Elizabeth Barrett Browning 1806–61: *Sonnets from the Portuguese* (1850)

23 Endurance is nobler than strength.
John Ruskin 1819–1900: *The Two Paths* (1859) lecture 4

24 After great pain, a formal feeling comes—
The Nerves sit ceremonious, like Tombs—
The stiff Heart questions was it He, that bore,
And Yesterday, or Centuries before?
Emily Dickinson 1830–86: 'After great pain, a formal feeling comes' (1862)

25 The toad beneath the harrow knows
Exactly where each tooth-point goes;
The butterfly upon the road
Preaches contentment to that toad.
Rudyard Kipling 1865–1936: 'Pagett, MP' (1886); see ADVERSITY 11

26 What does not kill me makes me stronger.
Friedrich Nietzsche 1844–1900: *Twilight of the Idols* (1889)

27 Nothing begins, and nothing ends,
That is not paid with moan;
For we are born in other's pain,
And perish in our own.
Francis Thompson 1859–1907: 'Daisy' (1913)

28 It is not true that suffering ennobles the character; happiness does that sometimes, but suffering, for the most part, makes men petty and vindictive.
W. Somerset Maugham 1874–1965: *The Moon and Sixpence* (1919)

29 Too long a sacrifice
Can make a stone of the heart.
O when may it suffice?
W. B. Yeats 1865–1939: 'Easter, 1916' (1921)

30 The point is that nobody likes having salt rubbed into their wounds, even if it is the salt of the earth.
Rebecca West 1892–1983: *The Salt of the Earth* (1935); see VIRTUE 11

31 About suffering they were never wrong,
The Old Masters: how well they understood
Its human position; how it takes place
While someone else is eating or opening a window or just walking dully along.
W. H. Auden 1907–73: 'Musée des Beaux Arts' (1940)

32 Willy Loman never made a lot of money. His name was never in the paper. He's not the finest character that ever lived. But he's a human being, and a terrible thing is happening to him. So attention must be paid.
Arthur Miller 1915–2005: *Death of a Salesman* (1949)

33 Suffering is only intolerable when nobody cares.
Cicely Saunders 1916–2005: 'The Management of Patients in the Terminal Stage' in *Cancer* 1960 vol. 6

34 How can you expect a man who's warm to understand one who's cold?
Alexander Solzhenitsyn 1918–2008: *One Day in the Life of Ivan Denisovich* (1962)

35 Children's talent to endure stems from their ignorance of alternatives.
Maya Angelou 1928– : *I Know Why The Caged Bird Sings* (1969)

36 Scars have the strange power to remind us that our past is real.
Cormac McCarthy 1933– : *All the Pretty Horses* (1993)

Suicide

phrases ▸

1 assisted suicide
the suicide of a patient suffering from an incurable disease, effected by the taking of lethal drugs provided by a doctor for this purpose

2 kamikaze pilot
in the Second World War, the pilot of a Japanese aircraft loaded with explosives and making a deliberate suicidal crash on an enemy target; *kamikaze* = Japanese, from *kami* 'divinity' + *kaze* 'wind', originally referring to the gale that, in Japanese tradition, destroyed the fleet of invading Mongols in 1281

quotations ▸

3 For who would bear the whips and scorns of time,
The oppressor's wrong, the proud man's contumely,
The pangs of disprized love, the law's delay...
When he himself might his quietus make
With a bare bodkin?
William Shakespeare 1564–1616: *Hamlet* (1601)

4 All this buttoning and unbuttoning.
Anonymous: 18th-century suicide note

5 The suicide wills life, and is only dissatisfied with the conditions under which it has presented itself to him.
Arthur Schopenhauer 1788–1860: *The World as Will and Idea* (1819)

6 The thought of suicide is a great source of comfort: with it a calm passage is to be made across many a bad night.
Friedrich Nietzsche 1844–1900: *Jenseits von Gut und Böse* (1886)

7 In this life there's nothing new in dying,
But nor, of course, is living any newer.
his final poem, written in his own blood the day before he hanged himself in his Leningrad hotel room
Sergei Yesenin 1895–1925: 'Goodbye, my Friend, Goodbye' (1925)

8 Guns aren't lawful;
Nooses give;
Gas smells awful;
You might as well live.
Dorothy Parker 1893–1967: 'Résumé' (1937)

9 A suicide kills two people, Maggie, that's what it's for!
Arthur Miller 1915–2005: *After the Fall* (1964)

10 It's better to burn out
Than to fade away.
Neil Young 1945– : 'My My, Hey Hey (Out of the Blue)' (1978 song, with Jeff Blackburn); quoted by Kurt Cobain in his suicide note, 8 April 1994

11 Without the possibility of suicide, I would have killed myself long ago.
E. M. Cioran 1911–95: in *Independent* 2 December 1989

The Supernatural

see also PARANORMAL

proverbs and sayings ▸

1 From ghoulies and ghosties and long-leggety beasties
And things that go bump in the night,
Good Lord, deliver us!
'The Cornish or West Country Litany'; see SUPERNATURAL 4

phrases ▸

2 bell, book, and candle
the formulaic requirements for laying a curse on someone; with allusion to the rite of excommunication, 'Do to the book, quench the candle, ring the bell'; see GREED 9

3 the good neighbours
fairies; witches

4 things that go bump in the night
supernatural manifestations as a source of night-time terror; from 'The Cornish or West Country Litany': see SUPERNATURAL 1

5 the wee folk
fairies

6 a witch of Endor
a medium; from the story in the Bible (I Samuel) of 'a woman that hath a familiar spirit at Endor', who with its help conjured up the spirit of the dead prophet Samuel for Saul; see SUPERNATURAL 18

quotations ▸

7 Then a spirit passed before my face;
the hair of my flesh stood up.
Bible: Job

8 May the gods avert this omen.
Cicero 106–43 BC: *Third Philippic*

9 For we wrestle not against flesh and blood, but against principalities, against powers, against the rulers of the darkness of this world, against spiritual wickedness in high places.
Bible: Ephesians

10 Hence, a devout Christian must avoid astrologers and all impious soothsayers, especially when they tell the truth, for fear of leading his soul into error by consorting with demons and entangling himself with the bonds of such association.
St Augustine of Hippo AD 354–430: *De Genesi ad Litteram*; see MATHS 1

11 There are more things in heaven and earth, Horatio,
Than are dreamt of in your philosophy.
William Shakespeare 1564–1616: *Hamlet* (1601); see UNIVERSE 10

12 Double, double toil and trouble;
Fire burn and cauldron bubble.
William Shakespeare 1564–1616: *Macbeth* (1606)

13 There is a superstition in avoiding superstition.
Francis Bacon 1561–1626: *Essays* (1625) 'Of Superstition'

14 All argument is against it; but all belief is for it.
of the existence of ghosts
Samuel Johnson 1709–84: James Boswell *Life of Samuel Johnson* (1791) 31 March 1778

15 Superstition is the poetry of life.
Johann Wolfgang von Goethe 1749–1832: *Maximen und Reflexionen* (1819) 'Literatur und Sprache'

16 Up the airy mountain,
Down the rushy glen,
We daren't go a-hunting,
For fear of little men.
William Allingham 1824–89: 'The Fairies' (1850)

17 There are fairies at the bottom of our garden!
Rose Fyleman 1877–1957: 'The Fairies' (1918)

18 Oh, the road to En-dor is the oldest road
And the craziest road of all!
Straight it runs to the Witch's abode
As it did in the days of Saul,
And nothing has changed of the sorrow in store
For such as go down on the road to En-dor!
Rudyard Kipling 1865–1936: 'En-dor' (1914–19); see SUPERNATURAL 6

19 Every time a child says 'I don't believe in fairies' there is a little fairy somewhere that falls down dead.
J. M. Barrie 1860–1937: *Peter Pan* (1928)

20 Do not meddle in the affairs of Wizards, for they are subtle and quick to anger.
J. R. R. Tolkien 1892–1973: *The Lord of the Rings* pt. 1 *The Fellowship of the Ring* (1954)

21 The twilight is the crack between the worlds. It is the door to the unknown.
Carlos Castaneda 1925–98: *Tales of Power* (1974)

22 In every generation there is a Chosen One. She alone will stand against the vampires, the demons, and the forces of darkness. She is the Slayer.
Joss Whedon 1964– : *Buffy the Vampire Slayer* (TV series, 1997–2003), episode 1, opening words

Surprise

proverbs and sayings ▸

1 The age of miracles is past.
often used ironically, or as a comment on failure; English proverb, late 16th century

2 Nobody expects the Spanish Inquisition.
from a *Monty Python* script: see SURPRISE 15

3 The unexpected always happens.
warning against an overconfident belief that something cannot occur; English proverb, late 19th century

4 Wonders will never cease.
often used ironically to comment on an unusual circumstance; English proverb, late 18th century

5 You could have knocked me down with a feather.
expressing great surprise; English proverb, mid 19th century saying

phrases ▸

6 pennies from heaven
unexpected benefits, especially financial ones; song-title, 1936: see OPTIMISM 32

7 a Scarborough warning
very short notice, no notice at all; proverbial; explained by Thomas Fuller as relating to the surprise capture of Scarborough Castle by Thomas Stafford in 1557, but the first recorded use predates this by eleven years

quotations ▸

8 If you do not expect it, you will not find out the unexpected.
Heraclitus c.540–c.480 BC: *On the Universe*

9 O wonderful, wonderful, and most wonderful wonderful! and yet again wonderful, and after that, out of all whooping!
William Shakespeare 1564–1616: *As You Like It* (1599)

10 Surprises are foolish things. The pleasure is not enhanced, and the inconvenience is often considerable.
Jane Austen 1775–1817: *Emma* (1816)

11 I'm Gormed—and I can't say no fairer than that!
Charles Dickens 1812–70: *David Copperfield* (1850)

12 'Curiouser and curiouser!' cried Alice.
Lewis Carroll 1832–98: *Alice's Adventures in Wonderland* (1865)

13 I turned to Aunt Agatha, whose demeanour was now rather like that of one who, picking daisies on the railway, has just caught the down express in the small of the back.
P. G. Wodehouse 1881–1975: *The Inimitable Jeeves* (1923)

14 It was quite the most incredible event that has ever happened to me in my life. It was almost as incredible as if you fired a 15-inch shell at a piece of tissue paper and it came back and hit you.
on the back-scattering effect of metal foil on alpha-particles
Ernest Rutherford 1871–1937: E. N. da C. Andrade *Rutherford and the Nature of the Atom* (1964)

15 Nobody expects the Spanish Inquisition! Our chief weapon is surprise—surprise and fear...fear and surprise...our two weapons are fear and surprise—and ruthless efficiency...
Graham Chapman 1941–89, **John Cleese** 1939– , and **others**: *Monty Python's Flying Circus* (BBC TV programme, 1970); see SURPRISE 2

Swearing

proverbs and sayings ▸

1 Excuse (or pardon) my French.
an informal apology for swearing

phrases ▸

2 four-letter word
any of several short words referring to sexual or excretory functions, regarded as coarse or offensive

3 not Pygmalion likely
not bloody likely; a humorous euphemism deriving from Shaw's *Pygmalion* (1916), which caused a public sensation at the time of the first London production; see TRANSPORT 15

quotations ▸

4 Swear not at all; neither by heaven; for it is God's throne:
Nor by the earth; for it is his footstool.
Bible: St Matthew

5 You taught me language; and my profit on't
Is, I know how to curse: the red plague rid you,
For learning me your language!
William Shakespeare 1564–1616: *The Tempest* (1611)

6 Though 'Bother it' I may
Occasionally say,
I never use a big, big D—
W. S. Gilbert 1836–1911: *HMS Pinafore* (1878)

7 If ever I utter an oath again may my soul be blasted to eternal damnation!
George Bernard Shaw 1856–1950: *Saint Joan* (1924)

8 Orchestras only need to be sworn at, and a German is consequently at an advantage with them, as English profanity, except in America, has not gone beyond the limited terminology of perdition.
George Bernard Shaw 1856–1950: Harold Schonberg *The Great Conductors* (1967)

9 The man who first abused his fellows with swear words instead of bashing their brains out with a club should be counted among those who laid the foundations of civilization.
John Cohen 1911– : in *Observer* 21 November 1965

10 Don't swear, boy. It shows a lack of vocabulary.
Alan Bennett 1934– : *Forty Years On* (1969)

11 Expletive deleted.
Anonymous: *Submission of Recorded Presidential Conversations to the Committee on the Judiciary of the House of Representatives by President Richard M. Nixon* 30 April 1974

12 All pro athletes are bilingual. They speak English and profanity.
Gordie Howe 1928– : in *Toronto Star* 27 May 1975

Sympathy and Consolation

proverbs and sayings ▶

1 God makes the back to the burden.
an assertion that nothing is truly insupportable used in resignation or consolation; English proverb, early 19th century

2 God tempers the wind to the shorn lamb.
God so arranges it that bad luck does not unduly plague the weak or unfortunate; English proverb, mid 17th century

3 Laugh and the world laughs with you, weep and you weep alone.
English proverb, late 19th century; see SORROW 21

4 Nothing so bad but it might have been worse.
used in resignation or consolation; English proverb, late 19th century

5 One kind word warms three winter months.
Japanese proverb

6 Pity is akin to love.
English proverb, early 17th century

7 The rock in the water does not know the pain of the rock in the sun.
awareness of your own suffering prevents you from understanding the pain of those in different circumstances; Hawaiian proverb

phrases ▶

8 a Job's comforter
a person who aggravates distress while seeking to give comfort; *Job* the biblical patriarch, who responded to the exhortations of his friends, 'miserable comforters are ye all'; see PATIENCE 23

9 milk of human kindness
compassion, sympathy; originally from Shakespeare's Lady Macbeth: see SYMPATHY 18

10 tea and sympathy
hospitality and consolation offered to a distressed person; the phrase was used as the title of a play in 1953

11 tender mercies
a biblical phrase usually used ironically to refer to attention or treatment not in the best interests of its recipients; see ANIMALS 15

quotations ▶

12 Heaven and Earth are not ruthful;
To them the Ten Thousand Things are
but as straw dogs.
Ten Thousand Things all life forms; *straw dogs* sacrificial tokens
Lao Tzu c.604–c.531 BC: *Tao-Te Ching*

13 If you want me to weep, you must first feel grief yourself.
Horace 65–8 BC: *Ars Poetica*

14 O divine Master, grant that I may not
so much seek
To be consoled as to console;
To be understood as to understand.
St Francis of Assisi 1181–1226: 'Prayer of St Francis'; attributed

15 For pitee renneth soone in gentil herte.
Geoffrey Chaucer 1343–1400: *The Canterbury Tales* 'The Knight's Tale'

16 Honest plain words best pierce the ears of grief.
William Shakespeare 1564–1616: *Love's Labour's Lost* (1595)

17 But yet the pity of it, Iago! O! Iago, the pity of it, Iago!
William Shakespeare 1564–1616: *Othello* (1602–4)

18 Yet I do fear thy nature;
It is too full o' the milk of human kindness
To catch the nearest way.
William Shakespeare 1564–1616: *Macbeth* (1606); see SYMPATHY 9

19 We are all strong enough to bear the misfortunes of others.
Duc de la Rochefoucauld 1613–80: *Maximes* (1678)

20 If a madman were to come into this room with a stick in his hand, no doubt we should pity the state of his mind; but our primary consideration would be to take care of ourselves. We should knock him down first, and pity him afterwards.
Samuel Johnson 1709–84: House of Commons, 3 April 1776

21 Our sympathy is cold to the relation of distant misery.
Edward Gibbon 1737–94: *The Decline and Fall of the Roman Empire* (1776–88)

22 Then cherish pity, lest you drive an angel from your door.
William Blake 1757–1827: 'Holy Thursday' (1789)

23 [Edmund Burke] is not affected by the reality of distress touching his heart, but by the showy resemblance of it striking his imagination. He pities the plumage, but forgets the dying bird.
on Burke's *Reflections on the Revolution in France*
Thomas Paine 1737–1809: *The Rights of Man* (1791)

24 Nobody can tell what I suffer! But it is always so. Those who do not complain are never pitied.
Jane Austen 1775–1817: *Pride and Prejudice* (1813)

25 They charge me with fanaticism. If to be feelingly alive to the sufferings of my fellow-creatures is to be a fanatic, I am one of the most incurable fanatics ever permitted to be at large.
William Wilberforce 1759–1833: in House of Commons, 19 June 1816

26 Any victim demands allegiance.
Graham Greene 1904–91: *The Heart of the Matter* (1948)

27 True kindness presupposes the faculty of imagining as one's own the sufferings and joys of others.
André Gide 1869–1951: *Pretexts* (1959)

28 The fact that I have no remedy for the sorrows of the world is no reason for my accepting yours. It simply supports the strong probability that yours is a fake.
H. L. Mencken 1880–1956: *Minority Report* (1956)

29 When times get rough,
And friends just can't be found
Like a bridge over troubled water
I will lay me down.
Paul Simon 1942– : 'Bridge over Troubled Water' (1970 song)

30 Sometimes, I guess there just aren't enough rocks.
Eric Roth 1945– : *Forrest Gump* (1994 film), spoken by Tom Hanks as Forrest Gump

31 If you want others to be happy, practise compassion. If you want to be happy, practise compassion.
Dalai Lama 1935– : attributed

Taste

phrases ▸

1 arbiter elegantiarum
an authority on matters of taste or etiquette; Latin: see TASTE 2

quotations ▸

2 *Elegantiae arbiter.*
The arbiter of taste.
of Petronius
Tacitus C.AD 56–after 117: *Annals*; see TASTE 1

3 The play, I remember, pleased not the million; 'twas caviar to the general.
William Shakespeare 1564–1616: *Hamlet* (1601); see FUTILITY 11

4 Our tastes greatly alter. The lad does not care for the child's rattle, and the old man does not care for the young man's whore.
Samuel Johnson 1709–84: James Boswell *Life of Samuel Johnson* (1791) Spring 1766

5 Could we teach taste or genius by rules, they would be no longer taste and genius.
Joshua Reynolds 1723–92: *Discourses on Art* 14 December 1770

6 A difference of taste in jokes is a great strain on the affections.
George Eliot 1819–80: *Daniel Deronda* (1876)

7 It's worse than wicked, my dear, it's vulgar.
Punch: Almanac (1876)

8 Taste is the feminine of genius.
Edward Fitzgerald 1809–83: letter to J. R. Lowell, October 1877

9 of the wallpaper in the room where he was dying:
One of us must go.
Oscar Wilde 1854–1900: attributed, probably apocryphal

10 Good taste is better than bad taste, but bad taste is better than no taste.
Arnold Bennett 1867–1931: in *Evening Standard* 21 August 1930

11 The kind of people who always go on about whether a thing is in good taste invariably have very bad taste.
Joe Orton 1933–67: in *Transatlantic Review* Spring 1967

Taxes

proverbs and sayings ▸

1 Can't pay, won't pay.
anti-Poll Tax slogan, 1990; see TAXES 3

phrases ▸

2 Peter's pence
an annual tax of one penny from every householder having land of a certain value, paid to the papal see at Rome from Anglo-Saxon times until discontinued in 1534 after Henry VIII's break with Rome; St *Peter* regarded by Roman Catholics as the first bishop of the Church at Rome

3 poll tax
a tax levied on every adult, without reference to their income or resources. Such taxes were levied in England in 1377, 1379, and 1380; the last of these is generally regarded as having contributed to the 1381 Peasants' Revolt. From the mid 1980s, the term was used informally for the community charge, a usage which reflected the tax's deep unpopularity; see TAXES 1

quotations ▸

4 It is the part of the good shepherd to shear his flock, not skin it.
to governors who recommended burdensome taxes
Tiberius 42 BC–AD 37: Suetonius *Lives of the Caesars* 'Tiberius'

5 Money has no smell.
quashing an objection to a tax on public lavatories
Vespasian AD 9–79: traditional summary; Suetonius *Lives of the Caesars* 'Vespasian'; see MONEY 6

6 The art of taxation consists in so plucking the goose as to obtain the largest possible amount of feathers with the smallest possible amount of hissing.
Jean-Baptiste Colbert 1619–83: attributed

7 *Excise*. A hateful tax levied upon commodities.
Samuel Johnson 1709–84: *A Dictionary of the English Language* (1755)

8 Taxation without representation is tyranny.
James Otis 1725–83: watchword (1761) of the American Revolution; in *Dictionary of American Biography*

9 To tax and to please, no more than to love and to be wise, is not given to men.
Edmund Burke 1729–97: *On American Taxation* (1775); see LOVE 11

10 There is no art which one government sooner learns of another than that of draining money from the pockets of the people.
Adam Smith 1723–90: *Wealth of Nations* (1776)

11 The art of government is to make two-thirds of a nation pay all it possibly

can pay for the benefit of the other third.
Voltaire 1694–1778: attributed; Walter Bagehot *The English Constitution* (1867)

12 All taxes must, at last, fall upon agriculture.
Edward Gibbon 1737–94: quoting Artaxerxes, in *The Decline and Fall of the Roman Empire* (1776–88)

13 In this world nothing can be said to be certain, except death and taxes.
Benjamin Franklin 1706–90: letter to Jean Baptiste Le Roy, 13 November 1789; see CERTAINTY 4

14 The Chancellor of the Exchequer is a man whose duties make him more or less of a taxing machine. He is intrusted with a certain amount of misery which it is his duty to distribute as fairly as he can.
Robert Lowe 1811–92: speech, House of Commons, 11 April 1870

15 Death is the most convenient time to tax rich people.
David Lloyd George 1863–1945: in *Lord Riddell's Intimate Diary of the Peace Conference and After, 1918–23* (1933)

16 Income Tax has made more Liars out of the American people than Golf.
Will Rogers 1879–1935: *The Illiterate Digest* (1924) 'Helping the Girls with their Income Taxes'

17 Only the little people pay taxes.
Leona Helmsley 1920–2007: addressed to her housekeeper in 1983, and reported at her trial for tax evasion; in *New York Times* 12 July 1989

18 Read my lips: no new taxes.
campaign pledge on taxation
George Bush 1924– : in *New York Times* 19 August 1988

Teaching

see also EDUCATION, SCHOOLS, UNIVERSITIES

proverbs and sayings ▶

1 He teaches ill who teaches all.
English proverb, early 17th century

2 He that teaches himself has a fool for his master.
English proverb, early 17th century

3 Nobody forgets a good teacher.
Teacher Training Agency slogan, late 20th century

4 Teachers open the door, but you must enter by yourself.
learning requires effort on the part of the student; Chinese proverb

5 Tell me and I'll forget. Show me and I'll remember. Involve me and I'll be changed forever.
Japanese proverb

6 Who teaches me for a day is my father for a lifetime.
Chinese proverb; see CHARITY 4

quotations ▶

7 A man who reviews the old so as to find out the new is qualified to teach others.
Confucius 551–479 BC: *Analects*

8 Even while they teach, men learn.
Seneca ('the Younger') c.4 BC–AD 65: *Epistulae Morales*

9 There is no such whetstone, to sharpen a good wit and encourage a will to learning, as is praise.
Roger Ascham 1515–68: *The Schoolmaster* (1570)

10 Men must be taught as if you taught them not,
And things unknown proposed as things forgot.
Alexander Pope 1688–1744: *An Essay on Criticism* (1711)

11 Delightful task! to rear the tender thought,
To teach the young idea how to shoot.
James Thomson 1700–48: *The Seasons* (1746) 'Spring'; see CHILDREN 3

12 It is no matter what you teach them [children] first, any more than what leg you shall put into your breeches first.
Samuel Johnson 1709–84: James Boswell *Life of Samuel Johnson* (1791) 26 July 1763

13 Few have been taught to any purpose who have not been their own teachers.
Joshua Reynolds 1723–92: *Discourses on Art* 11 December 1769

14 C-l-e-a-n, clean, verb active, to make bright, to scour. W-i-n, win, d-e-r, der, winder, a casement. When the boy knows this out of the book, he goes and does it.

Charles Dickens 1812–70: *Nicholas Nickleby* (1839)

15 Be a governess! Better be a slave at once!

Charlotte Brontë 1816–55: *Shirley* (1849)

16 He who can, does. He who cannot, teaches.

George Bernard Shaw 1856–1950: *Man and Superman* (1903)

17 A teacher affects eternity; he can never tell where his influence stops.

Henry Brooks Adams 1838–1918: *The Education of Henry Adams* (1907)

18 We teachers can only help the work going on, as servants wait upon a master.

Maria Montessori 1870–1952: *The Absorbent Mind* (1949)

19 That is the difference between good teachers and great teachers: good teachers make the best of a pupil's means: great teachers foresee a pupil's ends.

Maria Callas 1923–77: *Kenneth Harris Talking To* (1971) 'Maria Callas'

20 A teacher should have maximal authority and minimal power.

Thomas Szasz 1920– : *The Second Sin* (1973) 'Education'

Technology

see also INVENTIONS, SCIENCE

proverbs and sayings ▸

1 Let your fingers do the walking.

1960s advertisement for Bell system Telephone Directory Yellow Pages

2 Science finds, industry applies, man conforms.

subtitle of guidebook to 1933 Chicago World's Fair

3 Vorsprung durch Technik.

German = Progress through technology; advertising slogan for Audi motors, from 1986

phrases ▸

4 grey goo

a mass of self-replicating nanoscale machines proliferating uncontrollably and destroying or damaging the biosphere, postulated as a danger of the use of nanotechnology; coined by the American engineer Eric Drexler in *Engines of Creation* (1986)

5 the white heat of technology

the most advanced form of technology; from a misquotation of Harold Wilson: see TECHNOLOGY 18

quotations ▸

6 Give me but one firm spot on which to stand, and I will move the earth.

on the action of a lever

Archimedes c.287–212 BC: Pappus *Synagoge*; see ARTS AND SCIENCES 5

7 I sell here, Sir, what all the world desires to have—POWER.

of his engineering works

Matthew Boulton 1728–1809: James Boswell *Life of Samuel Johnson* (1791) 22 March 1776

8 Man is a tool-using animal...Without tools he is nothing, with tools he is all.

Thomas Carlyle 1795–1881: *Sartor Resartus* (1834)

9 It is questionable if all the mechanical inventions yet made have lightened the day's toil of any human being.

John Stuart Mill 1806–73: *Principles of Political Economy* (1848)

10 One machine can do the work of fifty ordinary men. No machine can do the work of one extraordinary man.

Elbert Hubbard 1859–1915: *Thousand and One Epigrams* (1911)

11 Machines are worshipped because they are beautiful, and valued because they confer power; they are hated because they are hideous, and loathed because they impose slavery.

Bertrand Russell 1872–1970: *Sceptical Essays* (1928) 'Machines and Emotions'

12 This is not the age of pamphleteers. It is the age of the engineers. The spark-gap is mightier than the pen.

Lancelot Hogben 1895–1975: *Science for the Citizen* (1938); see WAYS 17

13 One servant is worth a thousand gadgets.
Joseph Alois Schumpeter 1883–1950: J. K. Galbraith *A Life in our Times* (1981)

14 When you see something that is technically sweet, you go ahead and do it and you argue about what to do about it only after you have had your technical success. That is the way it was with the atomic bomb.
J. Robert Oppenheimer 1904–67: in *In the Matter of J. Robert Oppenheimer, USAEC Transcript of Hearing Before Personnel Security Board* (1954)

15 It has been said that an engineer is a man who can do for ten shillings what any fool can do for a pound.
Nevil Shute 1899–1960: *Slide Rule* (1954)

16 Technology…the knack of so arranging the world that we need not experience it.
Max Frisch 1911–91: *Homo Faber* (1957)

17 The new electronic interdependence recreates the world in the image of a global village.
Marshall McLuhan 1911–80: *The Gutenberg Galaxy* (1962); see COUNTRY 23, EARTH 6

18 The Britain that is going to be forged in the white heat of this revolution will be no place for restrictive practices or for outdated methods on either side of industry.
referring to the 'technological revolution'
Harold Wilson 1916–95: speech at the Labour Party Conference, 1 October 1963; see TECHNOLOGY 5

19 The medium is the message.
Marshall McLuhan 1911–80: *Understanding Media* (1964)

20 When this circuit learns your job, what are you going to do?
Marshall McLuhan 1911–80: *The Medium is the Massage* (1967)

21 Inanimate objects are classified scientifically into three major categories—those that don't work, those that break down, and those that get lost.
Russell Baker 1925– : in *New York Times* 18 June 1968

22 The first rule of intelligent tinkering is to save all the parts.
Paul Ralph Ehrlich 1932– : in *Saturday Review* 5 June 1971

23 Any sufficiently advanced technology is indistinguishable from magic.
Arthur C. Clarke 1917–2008: *The Lost Worlds of 2001* (1972)

24 For a successful technology, reality must take precedence over public relations, for nature cannot be fooled.
Richard Phillips Feynman 1918–88: Appendix to the *Rogers Commission Report on the Space Shuttle Challenger Accident* 6 June 1986

25 The thing with high-tech is that you always end up using scissors.
David Hockney 1937– : in *Observer* 10 July 1994

26 Technology happens. It's not good, it's not bad. Is steel good or bad?
Andrew Grove 1936– : in *Time* 29 December 1997

Temptation

proverbs and sayings ▸

1 Fish follow the bait.
English proverb, mid 17th century

2 The fish will soon be caught that nibbles at every bait.
English proverb, 16th century

3 Naughty but nice.
advertising slogan for cream-cakes in the first half of the 1980s; earlier, the title of a 1939 film. 'It's Naughty but It's Nice' was the title of a music hall song of 1870 by Arthur Lloyd (1839–1904)

4 Stolen fruit is sweet.
the knowledge that something is forbidden makes it more attractive; English proverb, early 17th century

5 Stolen waters are sweet.
something which has been obtained secretly or illicitly seems particularly attractive; English proverb, late 14th century

phrases ▸

6 the pomps and vanities of this wicked world

ostentatious display as a type of worldly temptation; after the answer in the *Catechism*: see SIN 15

7 the world, the flesh, and the devil

the temptations of earthly life; from *Book of Common Prayer*. see TEMPTATION 12

quotations ▸

8 Get thee behind me, Satan.

Bible: St Matthew

9 And lead us not into temptation, but deliver us from evil.

Bible: St Matthew

10 Watch and pray, that ye enter not into temptation: the spirit indeed is willing but the flesh is weak.

Bible: St Matthew

11 Is this her fault or mine?
The tempter or the tempted, who sins most?

William Shakespeare 1564–1616: *Measure for Measure* (1604)

12 From all the deceits of the world, the flesh, and the devil,
Good Lord, deliver us.

The Book of Common Prayer 1662: *The Litany*; see TEMPTATION 7

13 What's done we partly may compute,
But know not what's resisted.

Robert Burns 1759–96: 'Address to the Unco Guid' (1787); see VIRTUE 13

14 I can resist everything except temptation.

Oscar Wilde 1854–1900: *Lady Windermere's Fan* (1892)

15 There are several good protections against temptations, but the surest is cowardice.

Mark Twain 1835–1910: *Following the Equator* (1897)

16 The Lord above made liquor for temptation
To see if man could turn away from sin.
The Lord above made liquor for temptation—but
With a little bit of luck,
With a little bit of luck,
When temptation comes you'll give right in!

Alan Jay Lerner 1918–86: 'With a Little Bit of Luck' (1956 song)

17 This extraordinary pride in being exempt from temptation that you have not yet risen to the level of! Eunuchs boasting of their chastity!

C. S. Lewis 1898–1963: 'Unreal Estates' in Kingsley Amis and Robert Conquest (eds.) *Spectrum IV* (1965)

18 I've looked on a lot of women with lust. I've committed adultery in my heart many times. This is something that God recognizes I will do — and I have done it — and God forgives me for it.

Jimmy Carter 1924– : in *Playboy* November 1976

The Theatre

see also ACTING

phrases ▸

1 the ghost walks

money is available and salaries will be paid; has been explained by the story that an actor playing the ghost of Hamlet's father refused to 'walk again' until the cast's overdue salaries had been paid

2 a mess of plottage

a theatrical production with a poorly constructed plot; by analogy with *mess of pottage*: see VALUE 19

3 the Scottish play

Shakespeare's *Macbeth*; in theatrical tradition it is regarded as unlucky to speak of this play by its title

quotations ▸

4 Tragedy is thus a representation of an action that is worth serious attention, complete in itself and of some amplitude...by means of pity and fear bringing about the purgation of such emotions.

Aristotle 384–322 BC: *Poetics*

5 For what's a play without a woman in it?

Thomas Kyd 1558–94: *The Spanish Tragedy* (1592)

6 Can this cockpit hold
The vasty fields of France? or may we cram
Within this wooden O the very casques
That did affright the air at Agincourt?
William Shakespeare 1564–1616: *Henry V* (1599)

7 The play's the thing
Wherein I'll catch the conscience of the king.
William Shakespeare 1564–1616: *Hamlet* (1601)

8 Four trestles, four boards, two actors, a passion.
all he needed to create a play
Lope de Vega 1562–1635: attributed; James Fitzmaurice-Kelly *Lope de Vega and the Spanish Drama* (1902)

9 Then to the well-trod stage anon,
If Jonson's learnèd sock be on,
Or sweetest Shakespeare fancy's child,
Warble his native wood-notes wild.
John Milton 1608–74: 'L'Allegro' (1645); see ACTING 3

10 Ay, now the plot thickens very much upon us.
George Villiers, Duke of Buckingham 1628–87: *The Rehearsal* (1672); see CIRCUMSTANCE 18

11 Damn them! They will not let my play run, but they steal my thunder!
on hearing his new thunder effects used at a performance of *Macbeth*, following the withdrawal of one of his own plays after only a short run
John Dennis 1657–1734: William S. Walsh *A Handy-Book of Literary Curiosities* (1893); see STRENGTH 14

12 There still remains, to mortify a wit,
The many-headed monster of the pit.
Alexander Pope 1688–1744: *Imitations of Horace*; see CLASS 7

13 Whaur's yer Wullie Shakespeare noo?
shout by an enthusiastic member of the audience at the opening of John Home's *Douglas* in Edinburgh, 1756
Anonymous: traditional

14 The composition of a tragedy requires *testicles.*
on being asked why no woman had ever written 'a tolerable tragedy'
Voltaire 1694–1778: letter from Byron to John Murray, 2 April 1817

15 Things on stage should be as complicated and as simple as in life. People dine, just dine, while their happiness is made and their lives are smashed. If in Act 1 you have a pistol hanging on the wall, then it must fire in the last act.
Anton Chekhov 1860–1904: attributed; Donald Rayfield *Anton Chekhov* (1997)

16 *Étonne-moi.*
Astonish me.
Sergei Diaghilev 1872–1929: to Jean Cocteau; Wallace Fowlie (ed.) *Journals of Jean Cocteau* (1956)

17 There's no business like show business.
Irving Berlin 1888–1989: title of song (1946)

18 We never closed.
of the Windmill Theatre, London, during the Second World War
Vivian van Damm 1889–1960: *Tonight and Every Night* (1952)

19 It's a sound you can't get in the movies or television...the sound of a wonderful, deep silence that means you've hit them where they live.
Shelley Winters 1922–2006: in *Theatre Arts* June 1956

20 Don't clap too hard—it's a very old building.
John Osborne 1929–94: *The Entertainer* (1957)

21 Satire is what closes Saturday night.
George S. Kaufman 1889–1961: Scott Meredith *George S. Kaufman and his Friends* (1974)

22 The weasel under the cocktail cabinet.
on being asked what his plays were about
Harold Pinter 1930–2008: J. Russell Taylor *Anger and After* (1962)

23 I can do you blood and love without the rhetoric, and I can do you blood and rhetoric without the love, and I can do you all three concurrent or consecutive, but I can't do you love and rhetoric without the blood. Blood is compulsory—they're all blood, you see.
Tom Stoppard 1937– : *Rosencrantz and Guildenstern are Dead* (1967)

Thinking

see also IDEAS, MIND

proverbs and sayings ►

1 Great minds think alike.

English proverb, early 17th century, now often used ironically

2 Perish the thought!

saying used, often ironically, to show that one finds a suggestion or idea completely ridiculous; the phrase probably derives from 'perish that thought!' in Colley Cibber's *Richard III* (1700)

3 Think different.

advertising slogan, Apple Computers, 1997

4 Two heads are better than one.

it is advisable to discuss a problem with another person; English proverb, late 14th century

phrases ►

5 an agonizing reappraisal

a reassessment of a policy or position painfully forced on one by a radical change of circumstance, or by a realization of what the existing circumstances really are; from John Foster Dulles (1888–1959) in 1953, 'If...the European Defence Community should not be effective; if France and Germany remain apart... That would compel an agonizing reappraisal of basic United States policy'

6 lateral thinking

a way of thinking which seeks the solution to intractable problems through unorthodox methods, or elements which would normally be ignored by logical thinking; from Edward de Bono (1933–) *The Use of Lateral Thinking* (1967) 'Some people are aware of another sort of thinking which...leads to those simple ideas that are obvious only after they have been thought of...the term "lateral thinking" has been coined to describe this other sort of thinking; "vertical thinking" is used to denote the conventional logical process'

7 positive thinking

the practice or result of concentrating one's mind on the good and constructive aspects of a matter so as to eliminate destructive attitudes and emotions; *The Power of Positive Thinking* title of a book (1952) by Norman Vincent Peale (1898–1993)

quotations ►

8 Learning without thought is labour lost; thought without learning is perilous.

often quoted as 'To study and not think is a waste. To think and not study is dangerous'
Confucius 551–479 BC: *Analects*

9 His thinking does not produce smoke after the flame, but light after smoke.

Horace 65–8 BC: *Ars Poetica*

10 Whatsoever things are true, whatsoever things are honest, whatsoever things are just, whatsoever things are pure, whatsoever things are lovely, whatsoever things are of good report; if there be any virtue and if there be any praise, think on these things.

Bible: Philippians

11 To change your mind and to follow him who sets you right is to be nonetheless the free agent that you were before.

Marcus Aurelius AD 121–80: *Meditations*

12 The important thing is not to think much but to love much.

St Teresa of Ávila 1512–82: *The Interior Castle* (1588)

13 Yond' Cassius has a lean and hungry
look;
He thinks too much: such men are
dangerous.

William Shakespeare 1564–1616: *Julius Caesar* (1599)

14 *Je pense, donc je suis.*
I think, therefore I am.

usually quoted as, 'Cogito, ergo sum', from the 1641 Latin edition
René Descartes 1596–1650: *Le Discours de la méthode* (1637); see THINKING 30

15 Two things fill the mind with ever new and increasing wonder and awe, the more often and the more seriously reflection concentrates upon them: the starry heaven above me and the moral law within me.

Immanuel Kant 1724–1804: *Critique of Practical Reason* (1788)

16 Stung by the splendour of a sudden
thought.

Robert Browning 1812–89: 'A Death in the Desert' (1864)

17 How often misused words generate misleading thoughts.
Herbert Spencer 1820–1903: *Principles of Ethics* (1879)

18 It is quite a three-pipe problem, and I beg that you won't speak to me for fifty minutes.
Arthur Conan Doyle 1859–1930: *The Adventures of Sherlock Holmes* (1892)

19 Three minutes' thought would suffice to find this out; but thought is irksome and three minutes is a long time.
A. E. Housman 1859–1936: *D. Iunii Iuvenalis Saturae* (1905)

20 Sometimes I sits and thinks, and then again I just sits.
Punch: 1906

21 How can I tell what I think till I see what I say?
E. M. Forster 1879–1970: *Aspects of the Novel* (1927)

22 When you are a Bear of Very Little Brain, and you Think of Things, you find sometimes that a Thing which seemed very Thingish inside you is quite different when it gets out into the open and has other people looking at it.
A. A. Milne 1882–1956: *The House at Pooh Corner* (1928)

23 A man of action forced into a state of thought is unhappy until he can get out of it.
John Galsworthy 1867–1933: *Maid in Waiting* (1931)

24 Many people would sooner die than think. In fact they do.
Bertrand Russell 1872–1970: attributed, c.1940

25 *Doublethink* means the power of holding two contradictory beliefs in one's mind simultaneously, and accepting both of them.
George Orwell 1903–50: *Nineteen Eighty-Four* (1949)

26 He can't think without his hat.
Samuel Beckett 1906–89: *Waiting for Godot* (1955)

27 It is a far, far better thing to have a firm anchor in nonsense than to put out on the troubled seas of thought.
J. K. Galbraith 1908–2006: *The Affluent Society* (1958)

28 What was once thought can never be unthought.
Friedrich Dürrenmatt 1921–90: *The Physicists* (1962)

29 The real question is not whether machines think but whether men do.
B. F. Skinner 1904–90: *Contingencies of Reinforcement* (1969)

30 *I think, therefore I am* is the statement of an intellectual who underrates toothaches.
Milan Kundera 1929– : *Immortality* (1991); see THINKING 14

Thoroughness

see also DETERMINATION

proverbs and sayings ▸

1 Do not spoil the ship for a ha'porth of tar.
used generally to warn against risking loss or failure through unwillingness to allow relatively trivial expenditure; *ship* is a dialectal pronunciation of *sheep*, and the original literal sense was 'do not allow sheep to die for the lack of a trifling amount of tar', tar being used to protect sores and wounds on sheep from flies; English proverb, early 17th century

2 In for a penny, in for a pound.
if one is to be involved at all, it may as well be fully; English proverb, late 17th century

3 Nothing venture, nothing gain.
a later variant of *nothing venture, nothing have*; English proverb, early 17th century

4 Nothing venture, nothing have.
one must be prepared to take some risks to achieve a desired end; English proverb, late 14th century

5 One might as well be hanged for a sheep as a lamb.
if one is going to incur a severe penalty it may as well be for something substantial; English proverb, late 17th century

phrases ▸

6 at one fell swoop
at a single blow, in one go; *swoop* = the sudden pouncing of a bird of prey from a height on its quarry, especially with allusion to Shakespeare *Macbeth*: see MOURNING 11

7 **flesh and fell**
entirely; the whole substance of the body (*fell* = the skin)

8 **go the extra mile**
make an extra effort, do more than is strictly asked or required; in a revue song (1957) by Joyce Grenfell, 'Ready…To go the extra mile', but perhaps ultimately in allusion to the Bible (Matthew) 'And whosoever shall compel thee to go a mile, go with him twain'

9 **to destroy root and branch**
to destroy thoroughly, radically; perhaps originally with reference to the Bible (Malachi), 'The day that cometh shall burn them up…that it shall leave them neither root nor branch'

quotations ►

10 **Whatsoever thy hand findeth to do, do it with thy might.**
Bible: Ecclesiastes

11 **Wherever you go, go with all your heart.**
Confucius 551–479 BC: *Shu Jing*

12 **There must be a beginning of any great matter, but the continuing unto the end until it be thoroughly finished yields the true glory.**
Francis Drake 1540–96: dispatch to Sir Francis Walsingham, 17 May 1587

13 **The shortest way to do many things is to do only one thing at once.**
Samuel Smiles 1812–1904: *Self-Help* (1859)

14 **Climb ev'ry mountain, ford ev'ry stream**
Follow ev'ry rainbow, till you find your dream!
Oscar Hammerstein II 1895–1960: *Climb Ev'ry Mountain* (1959 song)

Thrift and Extravagance

see also DEBT, POVERTY, WEALTH

proverbs and sayings ►

1 **Bang goes sixpence.**
ironic commentary on regretted expenditure, deriving from a cartoon in *Punch* of 5 December 1868, featuring a miserly Scotsman. The caption read: 'a had na' been the-erre abune Twa Hoours when—Bang—went Saxpence!'

2 **Make do and mend.**
wartime slogan, 1940s

3 **Most people consider thrift a fine virtue in ancestors.**
American proverb, mid 20th century

4 **A penny saved is a penny earned.**
used as an exhortation to thrift; English proverb, mid 17th century

5 **Penny wise and pound foolish.**
too much concern with saving small sums may result in larger loss if necessary expenditure on maintenance and safety has been withheld; English proverb, early 17th century

6 **Spare at the spigot, and let out the bung-hole.**
referring to the practice of being overcareful on the one hand, and carelessly generous on the other. A *spigot* is a peg or pin used to regulate the flow of liquid through a tap on a cask, and a *bung-hole* is a hole through which a cask is filled or emptied, and which is closed by a bung; English proverb, mid 17th century

7 **Spare well and have to spend.**
the person who is thrifty and careful with their resources can use them lavishly when the occasion offers; English proverb, mid 16th century

8 **Stretch your arm no further than your sleeve will reach.**
you should not spend more than you can afford; English proverb, mid 16th century

9 **Take care of the pence and the pounds will take care of themselves.**
thrift and small savings will grow to substantial wealth; English proverb, mid 18th century; see MONEY 33, SPEECH 21

10 **Thrift is a great revenue.**
care with expenditure is one of the best ways of providing an income for oneself; English proverb, mid 17th century

11 **Wilful waste makes woeful want.**
deliberate misuse of resources is likely to lead to severe shortage; English proverb, early 18th century

phrases ►

12 **play ducks and drakes with**
trifle with; treat frivolously or wastefully; *ducks and drakes* a game of throwing flat stones so that they skim along the surface of water

quotations ▸

13 Plenty has made me poor.
Ovid 43 BC–C.AD 17: *Metamorphoses*

14 Thrift, thrift, Horatio! the funeral baked meats
Did coldly furnish forth the marriage tables.
William Shakespeare 1564–1616: *Hamlet* (1601)

15 If you would be wealthy, think of saving as well as of getting.
Benjamin Franklin 1706–90: *The Way to Wealth* (1758)

16 Economy is going without something you do want in case you should, some day, want something you probably won't want.
Anthony Hope 1863–1933: *The Dolly Dialogues* (1894)

17 From the foregoing survey of conspicuous leisure and consumption, it appears that the utility of both alike for the purposes of reputability lies in the element of waste that is common to both. In the one case it is a waste of time and effort, in the other it is a waste of goods.
Thorstein Veblen 1857–1929: *Theory of the Leisure Class* (1899)

18 All decent people live beyond their incomes nowadays, and those who aren't respectable live beyond other peoples'.
Saki 1870–1916: *Chronicles of Clovis* (1911)

19 We could have saved sixpence. We have saved fivepence. (*Pause*) But at what cost?
Samuel Beckett 1906–89: *All That Fall* (1957)

20 I only feel angry when I see waste. When I see people throwing away things that we could use.
Mother Teresa 1910–97: *A Gift for God* (1975) 'Riches'

21 Prudence is the other woman in Gordon's life.
of Gordon Brown, Chancellor of the Exchequer
Anonymous: an unidentified aide, in March 1998

Time

see also TRANSIENCE

proverbs and sayings ▸

1 Give us back our eleven days.
slogan protesting against the adoption of the Gregorian Calendar in 1752, which meant that 14 September followed immediately after 2 September; see TIME 15

2 An inch of gold cannot buy an inch of time.
time cannot be bought by money; Chinese proverb

3 Man fears Time, but Time fears the Pyramids.
Egyptian proverb

4 Never is a long time.
often used to indicate that circumstances may ultimately change; English proverb, late 14th century; see CHANGE 5

5 Spring forward, fall back.
a reminder that clocks are moved *forward* in *spring* and *back* in the *fall* (autumn)

6 There is a time for everything.
there is always a suitable time to do something; English proverb, late 14th century, from the Bible: see TIME 21

7 Time is a great healer.
initial pain is felt less keenly with the passage of time; English proverb, late 14th century; see TIME 46

8 Time will tell.
the true nature of something is likely to emerge over a period of time, and that conversely it is only after time has passed that something can be regarded as settled; English proverb, mid 16th century

9 Time works wonders.
often used to suggest that with the passage of time something initially unknown and unwelcome will become familiar and acceptable; English proverb, late 16th century

phrases ▸

10 annus mirabilis
a remarkable or auspicious year; modern Latin = wonderful year in *Annus Mirabilis: the year of wonders*, title of poem (1667) by Dryden; see MISFORTUNES 30

11 **at the Greek Calends**
never; *calends* = the first day of the month in the ancient Roman calendar; the Greek Calends will never come as the Greeks did not use calends in reckoning time

12 **for the duration**
until the end of something, especially a war; hence, informally, for a very long time; used first of the 1914–18 war from the term of enlistment 'for four years or the duration of the war'

13 **half an hour later in Newfoundland**
Canadian broadcasting announcement, the island being half an hour ahead of the Atlantic time zone

14 **a movable feast**
an event which takes place at no regular time; a religious feast day (especially Easter Day and the other Christian holy days whose dates are related to it) which does not occur on the same calendar date each year; see TOWNS 26

15 **Old Style**
the method of calculating dates using the Julian calendar; in England and Wales it was superseded by the use of the Gregorian calendar in 1752; see TIME 1

16 **once in a blue moon**
very rarely, practically never; *to say that the moon is blue* is recorded in the sixteenth century as a proverbial assertion of something that could not be true

17 **till kingdom come**
for an indefinitely long period; *kingdom come* = the next world, eternity; from *thy kingdom come* in the Lord's Prayer

18 **time immemorial**
legally, a time up to the beginning of the reign of Richard I in 1189; generally, a longer time than anyone can remember or trace

19 **time's arrow**
the direction of travel from past to future in time considered as a physical dimension; from Arthur Eddington (1882–1944) *The Nature of the Physical World* (1928) 'Let us draw an arrow arbitrarily. If as we follow the arrow we find more and more of the random element in the world, then the arrow is pointing towards the future; if the random element decreases the arrow points towards the past…I shall use the phrase "time's arrow" to express this one-way property of time which has no analogue in space.'

20 **world without end**
for ever, eternally; translation of Late Latin *in saecula saeculorum* = to the ages of ages, as used in *Morning Prayer* and other services, 'As it was in the beginning, is now, and ever shall be: world without end.'

quotations ▸

21 To every thing there is a season, and a time to every purpose under the heaven:
A time to be born, and a time to die…
A time to weep, and a time to laugh;
a time to mourn, and a time to dance.
Bible: Ecclesiastes; see TIME 6

22 Wait for the wisest of all counsellors, Time.
Pericles c.495–429 BC: Plutarch *Parallel Lives* 'Pericles'

23 *Sed fugit interea, fugit inreparabile tempus.*
But meanwhile it is flying, irretrievable time is flying.
usually quoted as '*tempus fugit* [time flies]'
Virgil 70–19 BC: *Georgics*; see TRANSIENCE 3

24 *Tempus edax rerum.*
Time the devourer of everything.
Ovid 43 BC–c.AD 17: *Metamorphoses*

25 Every instant of time is a pinprick of eternity.
Marcus Aurelius AD 121–80: *Meditations*

26 I am Time grown old to destroy the world,
Embarked on the course of world annihilation.
Bhagavadgita 250 BC–AD 250: ch. 11

27 Time is…Time was…Time is past.
Robert Greene 1560–92: *Friar Bacon and Friar Bungay* (1594)

28 I wasted time, and now doth time waste me.
William Shakespeare 1564–1616: *Richard II* (1595)

29 Time hath, my lord, a wallet at his back,
Wherein he puts alms for oblivion.
William Shakespeare 1564–1616: *Troilus and Cressida* (1602)

30 To-morrow, and to-morrow, and to-morrow,

Creeps in this petty pace from day to day,
To the last syllable of recorded time;
And all our yesterdays have lighted fools
The way to dusty death.

William Shakespeare 1564–1616: *Macbeth* (1606)

31 Even such is Time, which takes in trust
Our youth, our joys, and all we have,
And pays us but with age and dust.

Walter Ralegh 1552–1618: written the night before his death, and found in his Bible in the Gate-house at Westminster

32 There was never any thing by the wit of man so well devised, or so sure established, which in continuance of time hath not been corrupted.

The Book of Common Prayer 1662: *The Preface* Concerning the Service of the Church

33 But at my back I always hear
Time's wingèd chariot hurrying near:
And yonder all before us lie
Deserts of vast eternity.

Andrew Marvell 1621–78: 'To His Coy Mistress' (1681)

34 Time, like an ever-rolling stream,
Bears all its sons away.

Isaac Watts 1674–1748: 'O God, our help in ages past' (1719 hymn)

35 I recommend to you to take care of minutes: for hours will take care of themselves.

Lord Chesterfield 1694–1773: *Letters to his Son* (1774) 6 November 1747

36 Remember that time is money.

Benjamin Franklin 1706–90: *Advice to a Young Tradesman* (1748); see MONEY 14

37 Men talk of killing time, while time quietly kills them.

Dion Boucicault 1820–90: *London Assurance* (1841)

38 Lost, yesterday, somewhere between Sunrise and Sunset, two golden hours, each set with sixty diamond minutes. No reward is offered, for they are gone forever.

Horace Mann 1796–1859: 'Lost, Two Golden Hours' in *Common School Journal* November 1844

39 Time is a great teacher but unfortunately it kills all its pupils.

Hector Berlioz 1803–69: attributed; in *Almanach des lettres françaises et étrangères* (1924) 11 May

40 Time is
Too slow for those who wait,
Too swift for those who fear,
Too long for those who grieve,
Too short for those who rejoice;
But for those who love,
Time is eternity.

Henry Van Dyke 1852–1933: 'Time is too slow for those who wait' (1905), read at the funeral of Diana, Princess of Wales; the original form of the last line is 'Time is not'

41 Time, you old gypsy man,
Will you not stay,
Put up your caravan
Just for one day?

Ralph Hodgson 1871–1962: 'Time, You Old Gipsy Man' (1917)

42 Ah! the clock is always slow;
It is later than you think.

Robert W. Service 1874–1958: 'It Is Later Than You Think' (1921)

43 Half our life is spent trying to find something to do with the time we have rushed through life trying to save.

Will Rogers 1879–1935: letter in *New York Times* 29 April 1930

44 Time present and time past
Are both perhaps present in time future,
And time future contained in time past.

T. S. Eliot 1888–1965: *Four Quartets* 'Burnt Norton' (1936)

45 Three o'clock is always too late or too early for anything you want to do.

Jean-Paul Sartre 1905–80: *La Nausée* (1938)

46 Time has too much credit...It is not a great healer. It is an indifferent and perfunctory one. Sometimes it does not heal at all. And sometimes when it seems to, no healing has been necessary.

Ivy Compton-Burnett 1884–1969: *Darkness and Day* (1951); see TIME 7

47 VLADIMIR: That passed the time.
ESTRAGON: It would have passed in any case.

VLADIMIR: Yes, but not so rapidly.
Samuel Beckett 1906–89: *Waiting for Godot* (1955)

48 The distinction between past, present and future is only an illusion, however persistent.
Albert Einstein 1879–1955: letter to Michelangelo Besso, 21 March 1955

49 Time is an illusion. Lunchtime doubly so.
Douglas Adams 1952–2001: *The Hitch Hiker's Guide to the Galaxy* (1979)

Title

see RANK AND TITLE

Tolerance

see PREJUDICE AND TOLERANCE

The Town

see COUNTRY

Towns and Cities

see also AMERICAN CITIES, BRITISH TOWNS

proverbs and sayings ▸

1 All roads lead to Rome.
English proverb, late 14th century, earlier in Latin

2 Isfahan is half the world.
Isfahan was the capital of Persia from 1598 until 1722; Persian proverb

3 New York is big but this is Biggar.
slogan for the town of Biggar in Saskatchewan, from 1909

4 Next year in Jerusalem!
traditionally the concluding words of the Jewish Passover service, expressing the hope of the Diaspora that Jews dispersed throughout the world would once more be reunited

5 See Naples and die.
implying that after seeing Naples, one could have nothing left on earth to wish for; Goethe noted it as an Italian proverb in his diary in 1787

phrases ▸

6 the cities of the plain
Sodom and Gomorrah, on the plain of Jordan in ancient Palestine; from the Bible (Genesis), the ancient cities destroyed by fire from heaven, because of the wickedness of their inhabitants

7 the City of the Seven Hills
Rome

8 City of the Tribes
Galway; the term *tribes of Galway* was used for Irish families or communities having the same surname

9 City of the Violated Treaty
Limerick; referring to the Treaty of Limerick of 1691

10 City of the Violet Crown
Athens; translating an epithet used by Pindar (518–438 BC) and Aristophanes (450–385 BC)

11 the Eternal City
Rome; translating the Latin *urbs aeterna*, occurring in Ovid and Tibullus, and frequently found in the official documents of the Empire

12 the Forbidden City
Lhasa; the centre of Tibetan Buddhism, closed to foreign visitors until the 20th century. The name *Forbidden City* is also given to an area of Beijing (Peking) containing the former imperial palaces

13 the Holy City
Jerusalem

14 the Venice of the North
St Petersburg

quotations ▸

15 He could boast that he inherited it brick and left it marble.
referring to the city of Rome
Augustus 63 BC–AD 14: Suetonius *Lives of the Caesars* 'Divus Augustus'

16 The spider weaves the curtains in the palace of the Caesars;
The owl calls the watches in the towers of Afrasiab.
quoting an anonymous Persian poet at the ruins of the Old Sacred Palace in Constantinople, 1453
Sultan Mehmed II 1430–81: attributed; Steven Runciman *Fall of Constantinople* (1965)

17 Once did she hold the gorgeous East in fee,
And was the safeguard of the West.
William Wordsworth 1770–1850: 'On the Extinction of the Venetian Republic' (1807)

18 While stands the Coliseum, Rome shall stand;
When falls the Coliseum, Rome shall fall;
And when Rome falls—the World.
Lord Byron 1788–1824: *Childe Harold's Pilgrimage* (1812–18)

19 Let there be light! said Liberty,
And like sunrise from the sea,
Athens arose!
Percy Bysshe Shelley 1792–1822: *Hellas* (1822)

20 Moscow: those syllables can start
A tumult in the Russian heart.
Alexander Pushkin 1799–1837: *Eugene Onegin* (1833)

21 Match me such marvel, save in Eastern clime,—
A rose-red city—half as old as Time!
John William Burgon 1813–88: *Petra* (1845)

22 Petersburg, the most abstract and premeditated city on earth.
Fedor Dostoevsky 1821–81: *Notes from Underground* (1864)

23 God made the harbour, and that's all right, but Satan made Sydney.
Anonymous: unnamed Sydney citizen; Mark Twain *More Tramps Abroad* (1897)

24 The last time I saw Paris
Her heart was warm and gay,
I heard the laughter of her heart in ev'ry street café.
Oscar Hammerstein II 1895–1960: 'The Last Time I saw Paris' (1941 song)

25 STREETS FLOODED. PLEASE ADVISE.
telegraph message on arriving in Venice
Robert Benchley 1889–1945: R. E. Drennan (ed.) *Wits End* (1973)

26 Paris is a movable feast.
Ernest Hemingway 1899–1961: *A Movable Feast* (1964) epigraph; see TIME 14

27 Venice is like eating an entire box of chocolate liqueurs in one go.
Truman Capote 1924–84: in *Observer* 26 November 1961

28 Some say that no one ever leaves Montreal, for that city, like Canada itself, is designed to preserve the past, a past that happened somewhere else.
Leonard Cohen 1934– : *The Favourite Game* (1963)

29 By God what a site! By man what a mess!
of Sydney
Clough Williams-Ellis 1883–1978: *Architect Errant* (1971)

30 Toronto is a kind of New York operated by the Swiss.
Peter Ustinov 1921–2004: in *Globe & Mail* 1 August 1987; attributed

Transience

see also OPPORTUNITY, TIME

proverbs and sayings ▸

1 And this, too, shall pass away.
traditional saying said to be true for all times and situations; the story is told by Edward Fitzgerald in *Polonius* (1852) 'The Sultan asked for a signet motto, that should hold good for Adversity or Prosperity. Solomon gave him—"This also shall pass away" '

2 Sic transit gloria mundi.
Latin = Thus passes the glory of the world; said during the coronation of a new Pope, while flax is burned (used at the coronation of Alexander V in Pisa, 7 July 1409, but earlier in origin)

3 Time flies.
English proverb, late 14th century, from Virgil: see TIME 23

quotations ▸

4 Like that of leaves is a generation of men.
Homer: *The Iliad*

5 For a thousand years in thy sight are but as yesterday: seeing that is past as a watch in the night.
Bible: Psalm 90

6 *Eheu fugaces, Postume, Postume,*
Labuntur anni.
Ah me, Postumus, Postumus, the fleeting years are slipping by.
Horace 65–8 BC: *Odes*

7 All flesh is as grass, and all the glory of man as the flower of grass. The grass withereth, and the flower thereof falleth away.
Bible: I Peter; see LIFE 10

8 Gather ye rosebuds while ye may,
Old Time is still a-flying:

And this same flower that smiles
to-day,
To-morrow will be dying.

Robert Herrick 1591–1674: 'To the Virgins, to Make Much of Time' (1648)

9 *Pourvu que ça dure!*
Let's hope it lasts!

on her son Napoleon becoming Emperor, 1804

Laetitia Bonaparte 1750–1836: attributed, possibly apocryphal

10 Though nothing can bring back the
hour
Of splendour in the grass, of glory in
the flower;
We will grieve not, rather find
Strength in what remains behind.

William Wordsworth 1770–1850: 'Ode. Intimations of Immortality' (1807)

11 I never nursed a dear gazelle,
To glad me with its soft black eye,
But when it came to know me well,
And love me, it was sure to die!

Thomas Moore 1779–1852: *Lalla Rookh* (1817) 'The Fire-Worshippers'; see VALUE 34

12 He who binds to himself a joy
Doth the winged life destroy
But he who kisses the joy as it flies
Lives in Eternity's sunrise.

William Blake 1757–1827: *MS Note-Book*

13 They are not long, the days of wine
and roses.

Ernest Dowson 1867–1900: 'Vitae Summa Brevis' (1896)

14 Look thy last on all things lovely,
Every hour.

Walter de la Mare 1873–1956: 'Fare Well' (1918)

15 My candle burns at both ends;
It will not last the night;
But ah, my foes, and oh, my friends—
It gives a lovely light.

Edna St Vincent Millay 1892–1950: *A Few Figs From Thistles* (1920) 'First Fig'; see EFFORT 12

16 The butterfly counts not months but
moments,
And has time enough.

Rabindranath Tagore 1861–1941: *Fireflies* (1928)

17 The sunlight on the garden
Hardens and grows cold,
We cannot cage the minute
Within its net of gold.

Louis MacNeice 1907–63: 'Sunlight on the Garden' (1938)

18 Treaties, you see, are like girls and roses: they last while they last.

Charles de Gaulle 1890–1970: speech at Elysée Palace, 2 July 1963

19 And it seems to me you lived your life
Like a candle in the wind.

of Marilyn Monroe, later revised for Diana Princess of Wales

Elton John 1947– and **Bernie Taupin** 1950– : 'Candle in the Wind' (song, 1973)

Translation

proverbs and sayings ▸

1 Traduttore traditore.

Italian, meaning 'translators, traitors'

phrases ▸

2 Translator General

Philemon Holland (1552–1637); he translated the work of Livy, Pliny, Plutarch, Suetonius, and others; Thomas Fuller named him the 'translator general in his age' and said that 'these books alone of his turning into English will make a country gentleman a competent library'

quotations ▸

3 Such is our pride, our folly, or our
fate,
That few, but such as cannot write,
translate.

John Denham 1615–69: 'To Richard Fanshaw' (1648)

4 He is translation's thief that addeth
more,
As much as he that taketh from the
store
Of the first author.

Andrew Marvell 1621–78: 'To His Worthy Friend Dr Witty' (1651)

5 It is a pretty poem, Mr Pope, but you must not call it Homer.

when pressed by Pope to comment on 'My Homer', i.e. his translation of Homer's *Iliad*

Richard Bentley 1662–1742: John Hawkins (ed.) *The Works of Samuel Johnson* (1787)

6 The vanity of translation; it were as wise to cast a violet into a crucible that you might discover the formal principle of its colour and odour, as seek to transfuse from one language to another the creations of a poet. The plant must spring again from its seed, or it will bear no flower.
Percy Bysshe Shelley 1792–1822: *A Defence of Poetry* (written 1821)

7 Dear me, our postilion has been struck by lightning.
reported phrase from a Magyar-English Manual of Conversation
Septimus Despencer (Ralph Butler): *Little Missions* (1932)

8 The original is unfaithful to the translation.
on Henley's translation of Beckford's *Vathek*
Jorge Luis Borges 1899–1986: *Sobre el 'Vathek' de William Beckford*; in *Obras Completas* (1974)

Transport

proverbs and sayings ▶

1 Clunk, click, every trip.
road safety campaign promoting the use of seat-belts, 1971

2 Let the train take the strain.
British Rail slogan, 1970 onwards

3 Put a tiger in your tank.
advertising slogan for Esso petrol, 1964; see STRENGTH 15

phrases ▶

4 a magic carpet
a means of sudden and effortless travel; a mythical carpet able to transport a person on it to any desired place

5 seven-league boots
the ability to travel very fast on foot; boots enabling the wearer to go seven leagues at each stride, from the fairy story of Hop o' my Thumb

6 white van man
an aggressive male driver of a delivery or workman's van (typically white in colour); a driver of such a van regarded as a social type, usually characterized as an ordinary working man with forthright views

quotations ▶

7 The driving is like the driving of Jehu, the son of Nimshi; for he driveth furiously.
Bible: II Kings

8 There was a rocky valley between Buxton and Bakewell...You enterprised a railroad...you blasted its rocks away...And now, every fool in Buxton can be at Bakewell in half-an-hour, and every fool in Bakewell at Buxton.
John Ruskin 1819–1900: *Praeterita* vol. 3 (1889)

9 The horseless vehicle is the coming wonder.
Thomas Alva Edison 1847–1931: interview, in *New York World* 17 November 1895

10 There is *nothing*—absolutely nothing—half so much worth doing as simply messing about in boats.
Kenneth Grahame 1859–1932: *The Wind in the Willows* (1908)

11 The poetry of motion! The *real* way to travel! The *only* way to travel! Here today—in next week tomorrow! Villages skipped, towns and cities jumped—always somebody else's horizon! O bliss! O poop-poop! O my! O my!
on the car
Kenneth Grahame 1859–1932: *The Wind in the Willows* (1908)

12 What good is speed if the brain has oozed out on the way?
Karl Kraus 1874–1936: in *Die Fackel* September 1909 'The Discovery of the North Pole'

13 Railway termini. They are our gates to the glorious and the unknown. Through them we pass out into adventure and sunshine, to them, alas! we return.
E. M. Forster 1879–1970: *Howards End* (1910)

14 Sir, Saturday morning, although recurring at regular and well-foreseen intervals, always seems to take this railway by surprise.
W. S. Gilbert 1836–1911: letter to the station-master at Baker Street, on the Metropolitan line; John Julius Norwich *Christmas Crackers* (1980)

15 Walk! Not bloody likely. I am going in a taxi.

George Bernard Shaw 1856–1950: *Pygmalion* (1916); see SWEARING 3

16 Men travel faster now, but I do not know if they go to better things.

Willa Cather 1873–1947: *Death Comes for the Archbishop* (1927)

17 [There are] only two classes of pedestrians in these days of reckless motor traffic—the quick, and the dead.

Lord Dewar 1864–1930: George Robey *Looking Back on Life* (1933); see HEAVEN 11

18 Home James, and don't spare the horses.

Fred Hillebrand 1893– : title of song (1934)

19 This is the Night Mail crossing the Border,
Bringing the cheque and the postal order,
Letters for the rich, letters for the poor,
The shop at the corner, the girl next door.

W. H. Auden 1907–73: 'Night Mail' (1936)

20 Oh! I have slipped the surly bonds of earth
And danced the skies on laughter-silvered wings;...
And, while with silent lifting mind I've trod
The high, untrespassed sanctity of space,
Put out my hand and touched the face of God.

quoted by Ronald Reagan following the explosion of the space shuttle *Challenger*, January 1986

John Gillespie Magee 1922–41: 'High Flight' (1943)

21 Take it easy driving—the life you save may be mine.

James Dean 1931–55: 29 July 1955, Val Holley *James Dean* (1995)

22 The car has become an article of dress without which we feel uncertain, unclad and incomplete in the urban compound.

Marshall McLuhan 1911–80: *Understanding Media* (1964)

23 I myself see the car crash as a tremendous sexual event really: a liberation of human and machine libido (if there is such a thing).

J. G. Ballard 1930–2009: in *Penthouse* September 1970

24 Ever since childhood, when I lived within earshot of the Boston and Maine, I have seldom heard a train go by and not wished I was on it.

Paul Theroux 1941– : *The Great Railway Bazaar* (1975)

25 There are only two emotions in a plane: boredom and terror.

Orson Welles 1915–85: interview to celebrate his 70th birthday, in *Times* 6 May 1985

Travel

see also COUNTRIES, EXPLORATION

proverbs and sayings ▸

1 Been there, done that, got the T-shirt.

evoking a jaded tourist as the image of someone who is bored by too much sight-seeing; see BOREDOM 1

2 Every two miles the water changes, every twelve miles the speech.

commenting on the changes experienced by travellers (the number of miles varies); Indian proverb

3 Go abroad and you'll hear news of home.

information about one's immediate vicinity may have become more widely publicized; English proverb, late 17th century

4 If it's Tuesday, this must be Belgium.

late 20th century saying, from the title of a 1969 film written by David Shaw

5 If you want to go fast, go alone. if you want to go far, go together.

modern saying, said to be an African proverb

6 Is your journey *really* necessary?

1939 slogan, coined to discourage Civil Servants from going home for Christmas

7 Take only photos, leave only footprints.

encouraging responsible behaviour when travelling in wilderness areas; mid 20th century saying, first found as 'Take nothing but pictures; leave nothing but footprints', and often attributed to Chief Seattle (1786–1866) of the Suquamish and Duwamish in the form 'Take only memories, leave only footprints'

8 **Thursday's child has far to go.**
traditional rhyme, mid 19th century; see also BEAUTY 7, GIFTS 2, PREGNANCY 1, SORROW 2, WORK 7

9 **Travel broadens the mind.**
English proverb, early 20th century

10 **Travelling is learning.**
African proverb

11 **Travelling is one way of lengthening life, at least in appearance.**
American proverb, mid 20th century

12 **A wise man will climb Mount Fuji once, but only a fool will climb it twice.**
Japanese proverb

phrases ►

13 **Cook's tour**
a rapid tour of many places; named after the travel firm founded by the English businessman Thomas Cook (1808–92). In 1841 he organized the first publicly advertised excursion train in England; the success of this venture led him to organize further excursions both in Britain and abroad

14 **curse of Cain**
the fate of someone compelled to lead a wandering life; after the Bible (Genesis) 'a fugitive…shalt thou [Cain] be in the earth'; see also CANADA 3, MURDER 7, ORDER 8

15 **genius loci**
the presiding god or spirit of a particular place; originally with reference to Virgil *Aeneid* 'He prays to the spirit of the place and to Earth'; later with *genius* taken as referring to the body of associations connected with or inspirations derived from a place, rather than to a tutelary deity

16 **port out, starboard home**
according to folk etymology, for which there is no supporting evidence, the adjective *posh* was formed from the initials of these words, referring to the more comfortable accommodation, out of the heat of the sun, on ships between England and India (in fact, it seems most likely that the origin is the earlier slang *posh*, denoting a dandy)

17 **round Robin Hood's barn**
by a circuitous route; *Robin Hood* = a popular English outlaw traditionally famous from medieval times, *Robin Hood's barn* = an out-of-the-way place

18 **Sabbath day's journey**
an easy journey; the distance a Jew might travel on the Sabbath (approximately two-thirds of a mile); in the Bible (Acts) the distance from Mount Olivet to Jerusalem is described as being 'a Sabbath day's journey'

19 **traveller's tale**
a story about the unusual characteristics or customs of a foreign country, regarded as typically exaggerated or untrue

20 **wild blue yonder**
the far distance; a remote place; from R. Crawford *Army Air Corps* (song, 1939) 'Off we go into the wild blue yonder, Climbing high into the sun'

quotations ►

21 **And the Lord said unto Satan, Whence comest thou? Then Satan answered the Lord, and said, From going to and fro in the earth, and from walking up and down in it.**
Bible: Job

22 **A good traveller leaves no track or trace.**
often quoted as 'A good traveller has no fixed plans'
Lao Tzu c.604–c.531 BC: *Tao Te Ching*

23 **They change their clime, not their frame of mind, who rush across the sea.**
Horace 65–8 BC: *Epistles*

24 **I have not told even half of the things that I have seen.**
when asked if he wished to deny any of his stories of his travels
Marco Polo c.1254–c.1324: attributed, but probably apocryphal

25 **Ay, now am I in Arden; the more fool I. When I was at home I was in a better place; but travellers must be content.**
William Shakespeare 1564–1616: *As You Like It* (1599)

26 **Travel, in the younger sort, is a part of education; in the elder, a part of experience. He that travelleth into a country before he hath some entrance into the language, goeth to school, and not to travel.**
Francis Bacon 1561–1626: *Essays* (1625) 'Of Travel'

27 See one promontory (said Socrates of old), one mountain, one sea, one river, and see all.
Robert Burton 1577–1640: *The Anatomy of Melancholy* (1621–51)

28 I always love to begin a journey on Sundays, because I shall have the prayers of the church, to preserve all that travel by land, or by water.
Jonathan Swift 1667–1745: *Polite Conversation* (1738)

29 A wise traveller never despises his own country.
Carlo Goldoni 1707–93: *Pamela* (1749)

30 So it is in travelling; a man must carry knowledge with him, if he would bring home knowledge.
Samuel Johnson 1709–84: James Boswell *Life of Samuel Johnson* (1791) 17 April 1778

31 Worth seeing, yes; but not worth going to see.
on the Giant's Causeway
Samuel Johnson 1709–84: James Boswell *Life of Samuel Johnson* (1791) 12 October 1779

32 Travelling is the ruin of all happiness! There's no looking at a building here after seeing Italy.
Fanny Burney 1752–1840: *Cecilia* (1782)

33 I am become a name;
For always roaming with a hungry heart.
Alfred, Lord Tennyson 1809–92: 'Ulysses' (1842)

34 Some minds improve by travel, others, rather
Resemble copper wire, or brass,
Which gets the narrower by going farther!
Thomas Hood 1799–1845: 'Ode to Rae Wilson, Esq.'

35 It is not worthwhile to go around the world to count the cats in Zanzibar.
Henry David Thoreau 1817–62: *Walden* (1854) 'Conclusion'

36 To travel hopefully is a better thing than to arrive, and the true success is to labour.
Robert Louis Stevenson 1850–94: *Virginibus Puerisque* (1881); see HOPE 8

37 The whole object of travel is not to set foot on foreign land; it is at last to set foot on one's own country as a foreign land.
G. K. Chesterton 1874–1936: *Tremendous Trifles* (1909) 'The Riddle of the Ivy'

38 A man travels the world in search of what he needs and returns home to find it.
George Moore 1852–1933: *The Brook Kerith* (1916)

39 *Caminante, no hay camino.*
Se hace camino al andar.
Traveller, there is no path. Paths are made by walking.
Antonio Machado 1875–1939: 'Proverbs and Songs' (1917)

40 How 'ya gonna keep 'em down on the farm (after they've seen Paree)?
Sam M. Lewis 1885–1959 and **Joe Young** 1889–1939: title of song (1919)

41 The real voyage of discovery...consists not in seeking new landscapes but in having new eyes.
Marcel Proust 1871–1922: *The Captive* (1923)

42 In America there are two classes of travel—first class, and with children.
Robert Benchley 1889–1945: *Pluck and Luck* (1925)

43 A good traveller is one who does not know where he is going to, and a perfect traveller does not know where he came from.
Lin Yutang 1895–1976: *The Importance of Living* (1938)

44 I did not fully understand the dread term 'terminal illness' until I saw Heathrow for myself.
Dennis Potter 1935–94: in *Sunday Times* 4 June 1978

45 I wouldn't mind seeing China if I could come back the same day.
Philip Larkin 1922–85: interview with *Observer*, 1979, in *Required Writing* (1983)

46 The Devil himself had probably re-designed Hell in the light of information he had gained from observing airport layouts.
Anthony Price 1928– : *The Memory Trap* (1989)

47 To infinity and beyond.
Joel Cohen and **others**: *Toy Story* (1995 film); spoken by Buzz Lightyear

Treachery

see TRUST AND TREACHERY

Trees

proverbs and sayings ▸

1 The best time to plant a tree was twenty years ago. The second best is now.
even if you regret not having already planted a tree, it is still worth doing so; modern saying

2 Beware of an oak, it draws the stroke; avoid an ash, it counts the flash; creep under the thorn, it can save you from harm.
recording traditional beliefs on where to shelter from lightning during a thunderstorm; English proverb, late 19th century

3 Every elm has its man.
perhaps referring to the readiness of the tree to drop its branches on the unwary. Elm wood was also traditionally used for coffins; English proverb, early 20th century

4 A seed hidden in the heart of an apple is an orchard invisible.
Welsh proverb; see GARDENS 1

5 Trees planted by the ancestors provide shade for their descendants.
Chinese proverb; see TREES 7

phrases ▸

6 upas tree
in folklore, a Javanese tree alleged to poison its surroundings and said to be fatal to approach; an account of the tree given in the *London Magazine* of 1783 was said to be translated from one written in Dutch by Mr Foersch, a surgeon at Samarang in 1773, but was in fact invented by the writer and critic George Steevens (1736–1800)

quotations ▸

7 He plants the trees to serve another age.
Caecilius Statius d. after 166 BC: *Synephebi*; quoted in Cicero 'De Senectute'; see TREES 5

8 Generations pass while some trees stand, and old families last not three oaks.
Thomas Browne 1605–82: *Hydriotaphia* (Urn Burial, 1658)

9 He that plants trees loves others beside himself.
Thomas Fuller 1654–1734: *Gnomologia* (1732)

10 The poplars are felled, farewell to the shade
And the whispering sound of the cool colonnade.
William Cowper 1731–1800: 'The Poplar-Field' (written 1784)

11 The tree which moves some to tears of joy is in the eyes of others only a green thing that stands in the way.
William Blake 1757–1827: letter to Rev. Dr Trusler, 23 August 1799

12 O leave this barren spot to me!
Spare, woodman, spare the beechen tree.
Thomas Campbell 1777–1844: 'The Beech-Tree's Petition' (1800)

13 He who plants a tree
Plants a hope.
Lucy Larcom 1824–93: 'Plant a Tree'

14 And since to look at things in bloom
Fifty springs are little room,
About the woodlands I will go
To see the cherry hung with snow.
A. E. Housman 1859–1936: *A Shropshire Lad* (1896)

15 Of all the trees that grow so fair,
Old England to adorn,
Greater are none beneath the Sun,
Than Oak, and Ash, and Thorn.
Rudyard Kipling 1865–1936: *Puck of Pook's Hill* (1906) 'A Tree Song'

16 I like trees because they seem more resigned to the way they have to live than other things do.
Willa Cather 1873–1947: *O Pioneers!* (1913)

17 I think that I shall never see
A poem lovely as a tree.
Joyce Kilmer 1886–1918: 'Trees' (1914); see POLLUTION 17

18 O chestnut-tree, great-rooted blossomer,
Are you the leaf, the blossom or the bole?
W. B. Yeats 1865–1939: 'Among School Children' (1928)

19 **In every wood, in every spring, there is a different green.**
J. R. R. Tolkien 1892–1973: *The Fellowship of the Ring* (1954)

20 **A culture is no better than its woods.**
W. H. Auden 1907–73: 'Woods' (1958)

Trust and Treachery

proverbs and sayings ▶

1 **Fear the Greeks bearing gifts.**
English proverb, late 19th century; originally from Virgil: see TRUST 19; see also GIFTS 7, TRUST 16

2 **Please to remember the Fifth of November,**
Gunpowder Treason and Plot.
We know no reason why gunpowder treason
Should ever be forgot.
traditional rhyme on the Gunpowder Plot (1605); see FESTIVALS 26

3 **Promises, like pie-crust, are made to be broken.**
English proverb, late 17th century

4 **Test before you trust.**
Russian proverb; see TRUST 41

5 **Would you buy a used car from this man?**
campaign slogan directed against Richard Nixon, 1968

6 **You cannot run with the hare and hunt with the hounds.**
you must take one of two opposing sides; English proverb, mid 15th century; see TRUST 12

phrases ▶

7 **drop the pilot**
abandon a trustworthy adviser; from *dropping the pilot*, caption to Tenniel's cartoon, and title of poem, on Bismarck's dismissal as German Chancellor by the young Kaiser; in *Punch* 29 March 1890

8 **fifth column**
an organized body sympathizing with and working for the enemy within a country at war or otherwise under attack; translating Spanish *quinta columna*, an extra body of supporters claimed by General Mola as being within Madrid when he besieged the city with four columns of Nationalist forces in 1936

9 **Judas kiss**
an act of betrayal; *Judas* Iscariot, the disciple who betrayed Jesus, after the Bible (Matthew), 'And he that betrayed him gave them a sign, saying, Whomsoever I shall kiss, that same is he: hold him fast'

10 **night of the long knives**
a ruthless or decisive action held to resemble a treacherous massacre; after the massacre (according to legend) of the Britons by Hengist in 472, or of Ernst Roehm and his associates by Hitler on 29–30 June 1934

11 **Punic faith**
treachery; from Latin *Punica fide* 'with Carthaginian trustworthiness' (Sallust *Jugurtha*), reflecting the traditional hostility of Rome to Carthage

12 **run with the hare and hunt with the hounds**
try to remain on good terms with both sides in a quarrel; play a double role; see TRUST 6

13 **a scrap of paper**
a treaty or pledge which one does not intend to honour; said to have been used by the German Chancellor, Bethmann-Hollweg (1856–1921) in connection with German violation of Belgian neutrality in August 1914; see INTERNATIONAL 25

14 **sell down the river**
let down, betray; originally of selling a troublesome slave to the owner of a sugar cane plantation on the lower Mississippi, where conditions were harsher than in the northern slave states

15 **thirty pieces of silver**
a material gain for which a principle has been betrayed; from the price for which Judas betrayed Jesus to the Jewish authorities, as told in the Bible (Matthew): 'and they covenanted with him for thirty pieces of silver'; see DEATH 21

16 **Trojan horse**
a person or device deliberately set to bring about an enemy's downfall or to undermine from within; a hollow wooden statue of a horse in which the Greeks are said to have concealed themselves to enter Troy: see TRUST 19; see also COMPUTERS 11

17 **true blue**
faithful, staunch, and unwavering; perhaps with regard to the blue of the sky, or to some specially fast dye; from the mid 17th century applied specifically to the Scottish Presbyterian or Whig party, and later (in the current sense), to the Tory, or Conservative, Party; see POLITICAL PARTIES 15

quotations ►

18 O put not your trust in princes, nor in any child of man: for there is no help in them.

Bible: Psalm 146

19 *Equo ne credite, Teucri.*
Quidquid id est, timeo Danaos et dona ferentes.
Do not trust the horse, Trojans.
Whatever it is, I fear the Greeks even when they bring gifts.

Virgil 70–19 BC: *Aeneid*; see TRUST 1, TRUST 16, see also GIFTS 7

20 *Et tu, Brute?*
You too, Brutus?

said to his friend Brutus as he was assassinated by him

Julius Caesar 100–44 BC: traditional rendering of Suetonius *Lives of the Caesars* 'Divus Julius'

21 This night, before the cock crow, thou shalt deny me thrice.

Bible: St Matthew

22 *Quis custodiet ipsos custodes?*
Who is to guard the guards themselves?

Juvenal C. AD 60–C. 140: *Satires*

23 The smylere with the knyf under the cloke.

Geoffrey Chaucer 1343–1400: *The Canterbury Tales* 'The Knight's Tale'

24 I know what it is to be a subject, what to be a Sovereign, what to have good neighbours, and sometimes meet evil-willers.

the traditional version concludes: 'and in trust I have found treason'

Elizabeth I 1533–1603: speech to a Parliamentary deputation at Richmond, 12 November 1586; John Neale *Elizabeth I and her Parliaments 1584–1601* (1957), from a report 'which the Queen herself heavily amended in her own hand'

25 Treason doth never prosper, what's the reason?
For if it prosper, none dare call it treason.

John Harington 1561–1612: *Epigrams* (1618)

26 There is nothing makes a man suspect much, more than to know little.

Francis Bacon 1561–1626: *Essays* (1625) 'Of Suspicion'

27 A man who does not trust himself will never really trust anybody.

Cardinal de Retz 1613–79: *Mémoires* (1717)

28 It is better to suffer wrong than to do it, and happier to be sometimes cheated than not to trust.

Samuel Johnson 1709–84: in *Rambler* 18 December 1750

29 Caesar had his Brutus—Charles the First, his Cromwell—and George the Third—('Treason,' cried the Speaker)...*may profit by their example.* If *this* be treason, make the most of it.

Patrick Henry 1736–99: speech in the Virginia assembly, May 1765

30 to the Emperor of Russia, who had spoken bitterly of those who had betrayed the cause of Europe:

That, Sire, is a question of dates.

often quoted as, 'treason is a matter of dates'

Charles-Maurice de Talleyrand 1754–1838: Duff Cooper *Talleyrand* (1932)

31 Just for a handful of silver he left us,
Just for a riband to stick in his coat.

of Wordsworth's apparent betrayal of his radical principles by accepting the position of poet laureate

Robert Browning 1812–89: 'The Lost Leader' (1845)

32 And trust me not at all or all in all.

Alfred, Lord Tennyson 1809–92: *Idylls of the King* 'Merlin and Vivien' (1859)

33 To promise not to do a thing is the surest way in the world to make a body want to go and do that very thing.

Mark Twain 1835–1910: *The Adventures of Tom Sawyer* (1876)

34 A promise made is a debt unpaid, and the trail has its own stern code.

Robert W. Service 1874–1958: 'The Cremation of Sam McGee' (1907)

35 Anyone can rat, but it takes a certain amount of ingenuity to re-rat.

on rejoining the Conservatives twenty years after leaving them for the Liberals, 1924

Winston Churchill 1874–1965: Kay Halle *Irrepressible Churchill* (1966)

36 He trusted neither of them as far as he could spit, and he was a poor spitter, lacking both distance and control.

P. G. Wodehouse 1881–1975: *Money in the Bank* (1946)

37 **Greater love hath no man than this, that he lay down his friends for his life.**

on Harold Macmillan sacking seven of his Cabinet on 13 July 1962

Jeremy Thorpe 1929– : D. E. Butler and Anthony King *The General Election of 1964* (1965); see SELF-SACRIFICE 4

38 **To betray, you must first belong.**

Kim Philby 1912–88: in *Sunday Times* 17 December 1967

39 **Frankly speaking it is difficult to trust the Chinese. Once bitten by a snake you feel suspicious even when you see a piece of rope.**

Dalai Lama 1935– : attributed, 1981; see CAUTION 20

40 **He who wields the knife never wears the crown.**

Michael Heseltine 1933– : in *New Society* 14 February 1986

41 **We have listened to the wisdom in an old Russian maxim. And I'm sure you're familiar with it, Mr General Secretary. The maxim is...'trust, but verify.'**

Ronald Reagan 1911–2004: at the signing of the INF treaty on arms limitation, 8 December 1987, and used frequently thereafter; see TRUST 4

42 **It is rather like sending your opening batsmen to the crease only for them to find the moment that the first balls are bowled that their bats have been broken before the game by the team captain.**

Geoffrey Howe 1926– : resignation speech as Deputy Prime Minister, House of Commons 13 November 1990

Truth

see also HONESTY, LIES

proverbs and sayings ▸

1 **Believe it or not.**

title of syndicated newspaper feature (from 1918), written by Robert L. Ripley

2 **Many a true word is spoken in jest.**

an apparent joke may often include a shrewd comment, or that what is spoken of as unlikely or improbable may in the future turn out to be true; English proverb, late 14th century

3 **An old error is always more popular than a new truth.**

German proverb

4 **Se non è vero, è molto ben trovato.**

Italian = If it is not true, it is a happy invention; common saying from the 16th century; see TRUTH 12

5 **Tell the truth and shame the devil.**

by telling the truth one is taking the right course however embarrassing or difficult it may be; English proverb, mid 16th century; see TRUTH 8

6 **Truth is stranger than fiction.**

implying that no invention can be as remarkable as what may actually happen; English proverb, early 19th century, from Byron: see TRUTH 27; see also FICTION 1

7 **Truth lies at the bottom of a well.**

sometimes used to imply that the truth of a situation can be hard to find; English proverb, mid 16th century

8 **Truth makes the Devil blush.**

English proverb, mid 20th century; see TRUTH 5

9 **Truth will out.**

in the end what has really happened will become apparent; English proverb, mid 15th century

10 **What everybody says must be true.**

sometimes used ironically to assert that popular gossip is often inaccurate; English proverb, late 14th century

11 **When you shoot an arrow of truth, dip its point in honey.**

advocating tact; Arab proverb

phrases ▸

12 **ben trovato**

happily invented; appropriate though untrue; Italian, literally 'well found': see TRUTH 4

13 **the truth, the whole truth, and nothing but the truth**

the absolute truth, without concealment or addition; part of the formula of the oath taken by witnesses in court

quotations ▸

14 **Great is Truth, and mighty above all things.**

Bible: I Esdras

15 **But, my dearest Agathon, it is truth which you cannot contradict; you**

can without any difficulty contradict Socrates.
Socrates 469–399 BC: Plato *Symposium*

16 Plato is dear to me, but dearer still is truth.
Aristotle 384–322 BC: attributed

17 And ye shall know the truth, and the truth shall make you free.
Bible: St John; see TRUTH 36

18 Truth will come to light; murder cannot be hid long.
William Shakespeare 1564–1616: *The Merchant of Venice* (1596–8)

19 What is truth? said jesting Pilate; and would not stay for an answer.
Francis Bacon 1561–1626: *Essays* (1625) 'Of Truth'

20 Though all the winds of doctrine were let loose to play upon the earth, so Truth be in the field, we do injuriously by licensing and prohibiting to misdoubt her strength. Let her and Falsehood grapple; who ever knew Truth put to the worse, in a free and open encounter?
John Milton 1608–74: *Areopagitica* (1644)

21 True and False are attributes of speech, not of things. And where speech is not, there is neither Truth nor Falsehood.
Thomas Hobbes 1588–1679: *Leviathan* (1651)

22 It is one thing to show a man that he is in error, and another to put him in possession of truth.
John Locke 1632–1704: *An Essay concerning Human Understanding* (1690)

23 It is commonly said, and more particularly by Lord Shaftesbury, that ridicule is the best test of truth.
Lord Chesterfield 1694–1773: *Letters to his Son* (1774) 6 February 1752

24 In lapidary inscriptions a man is not upon oath.
Samuel Johnson 1709–84: James Boswell *Life of Samuel Johnson* (1791) 1775

25 A truth that's told with bad intent
Beats all the lies you can invent.
William Blake 1757–1827: 'Auguries of Innocence' (1803)

26 I am certain of nothing but the holiness of the heart's affections and the truth of imagination—what the imagination seizes as beauty must be truth—whether it existed before or not.
John Keats 1795–1821: letter to Benjamin Bailey, 22 November 1817; see BEAUTY 22

27 'Tis strange—but true; for truth is always strange;
Stranger than fiction.
Lord Byron 1788–1824: *Don Juan* (1819–24); see TRUTH 6

28 Rather than love, than money, than fame, give me truth.
Henry David Thoreau 1817–62: *Walden* (1854) 'Conclusion'

29 What I tell you three times is true.
Lewis Carroll 1832–98: *The Hunting of the Snark* (1876)

30 It is the customary fate of new truths to begin as heresies and to end as superstitions.
T. H. Huxley 1825–95: *Science and Culture and Other Essays* (1881) 'The Coming of Age of the Origin of Species'

31 The truth is rarely pure, and never simple.
Oscar Wilde 1854–1900: *The Importance of Being Earnest* (1895)

32 Truth is the most valuable thing we have. Let us economize it.
Mark Twain 1835–1910: *Following the Equator* (1897); see TRUTH 41

33 A platitude is simply a truth repeated until people get tired of hearing it.
Stanley Baldwin 1867–1947: speech, House of Commons, 29 May 1924

34 An exaggeration is a truth that has lost its temper.
Kahlil Gibran 1883–1931: *Sand and Foam* (1926)

35 The truth is often a terrible weapon of aggression. It is possible to lie, and even to murder, for the truth.
Alfred Adler 1870–1937: *The Problems of Neurosis* (1929)

36 The truth which makes men free is for the most part the truth which men prefer not to hear.
Herbert Agar 1897–1980: *A Time for Greatness* (1942); see TRUTH 17

37 There are no whole truths; all truths are half-truths. It is trying to treat them as whole truths that plays the devil.

Alfred North Whitehead 1861–1947: *Dialogues* (1954)

38 Believe those who are seeking the truth; doubt those who find it.

André Gide 1869–1951: *So Be It* (1960)

39 Truth exists; only lies are invented.

Georges Braque 1882–1963: *Le Jour et la nuit: Cahiers 1917–52*

40 One of the favourite maxims of my father was the distinction between the two sorts of truths, profound truths recognized by the fact that the opposite is also a profound truth, in contrast to trivialities where opposites are obviously absurd.

Niels Bohr 1885–1962: S. Rozental *Niels Bohr* (1967)

41 It contains a misleading impression, not a lie. It was being economical with the truth.

the phrase 'economy of truth' was earlier used by Edmund Burke (1729–97)

Robert Armstrong 1927– : referring to a letter during the 'Spycatcher' trial, Supreme Court, New South Wales, in *Daily Telegraph* 19 November 1986; see LIES 8, TRUTH 32

The Universe

see also EARTH, SKIES

phrases ▸

1 big bang

the explosion of dense matter which according to current cosmological theories marked the origin of the universe; see UNIVERSE 15

2 the four elements

earth, air, fire, and water; collectively regarded as constituents of the material world by ancient and medieval philosophers

3 Ptolemaic system

the theory that the earth is the stationary centre of the universe, with the planets moving in epicyclic orbits within surrounding concentric spheres; after Ptolemy (2nd century), Greek astronomer and geographer; see UNIVERSE 6, see also MUSIC 5

quotations ▸

4 Is it not worthy of tears that, when the number of worlds is infinite, we have not yet become lords of a single one?

when asked why he wept on hearing from Anaxarchus that there was an infinite number of worlds

Alexander the Great 356–323 BC: Plutarch *Moralia*

5 The universe and I exist together, and all things and I are one.

Chuang Tzu c.369–286 BC: *Chuang Tzu*

6 Had I been present at the Creation, I would have given some useful hints for the better ordering of the universe.

on studying the Ptolemaic system

Alfonso 'the Wise' of Castile 1221–84: attributed; see UNIVERSE 3

7 The eternal silence of these infinite spaces [the heavens] terrifies me.

Blaise Pascal 1623–62: *Pensées* (1670)

8 on hearing that Margaret Fuller 'accepted the universe':

'Gad! she'd better!'

Thomas Carlyle 1795–1881: William James *Varieties of Religious Experience* (1902)

9 The world is everything that is the case.

Ludwig Wittgenstein 1889–1951: *Tractatus Logico-Philosophicus* (1922)

10 Now, my own suspicion is that the universe is not only queerer than we suppose, but queerer than we *can* suppose...I suspect that there are more things in heaven and earth than are dreamed of, or can be dreamed of, in any philosophy.

J. B. S. Haldane 1892–1964: *Possible Worlds and Other Essays* (1927) 'Possible Worlds'; see SUPERNATURAL 11

11 From the intrinsic evidence of his creation, the Great Architect of the Universe now begins to appear as a pure mathematician.

James Jeans 1877–1946: *The Mysterious Universe* (1930)

12 This, now, is the judgement of our scientific age—the third reaction of man upon the universe! This universe is not hostile, nor yet is it friendly. It is simply indifferent.

John H. Holmes 1879–1964: *The Sensible Man's View of Religion* (1932)

13 The eternal mystery of the world is its comprehensibility...The fact that it is comprehensible is a miracle.
usually quoted as 'The most incomprehensible fact about the universe is that it is comprehensible'
Albert Einstein 1879–1955: in *Franklin Institute Journal* March 1936 'Physics and Reality'

14 It is this, or that - all the universe or nothing. Which shall it be, Passworthy? Which shall it be?
H. G. Wells 1866–1946: *Things to Come* (1936 film), spoken by Raymond Massey

15 One [idea] was that the Universe started its life a finite time ago in a single huge explosion....This big bang idea seemed to me to be unsatisfactory.
Fred Hoyle 1915–2001: *The Nature of the Universe* (1950); see UNIVERSE 1

16 It is often said that there is no such thing as a free lunch. It now appears possible, however, that the Universe is a free lunch.
Alan Guth 1947– : '10^{-35} Seconds After the Big Bang' in J. Audouze and J. Tran Thanh Van *The Birth of the Universe* (1982); see ECONOMICS 3

17 What is it that breathes fire into the equations and makes a universe for them to describe...Why does the universe go to all the bother of existing?
Stephen Hawking 1942– : *A Brief History of Time* (1988)

18 Space is almost infinite. As a matter of fact, we think it is infinite.
Dan Quayle 1947– : in *Daily Telegraph* 8 March 1989

19 The Universe is not obliged to conform to what we consider comfortable or plausible.
Carl Sagan 1934–96: *Pale Blue Dot* (1995)

Universities

see also EDUCATION, TEACHING

proverbs and sayings ▸

1 Lady Margaret Hall for ladies,
St Hugh's for girls,
St Hilda's for wenches,
Somerville for women.
Oxford saying, 1930s

phrases ▸

2 the Ivy League
a group of long-established eastern US universities of high academic and social prestige, including Harvard, Yale, Princeton, and Columbia

3 redbrick university
a British university founded in the late 19th or early 20th century, usually in a large industrial city, and especially as contrasted with Oxford and Cambridge; see UNIVERSITIES 19

4 town and gown
non-members and members of a university in a particular place; *gown* as worn by members of a university

quotations ▸

5 A Clerk there was of Oxenford also,
That unto logyk hadde longe ygo.
As leene was his hors as is a rake,
And he was nat right fat, I undertake,
But looked holwe, and therto sobrely.
Geoffrey Chaucer 1343–1400: *The Canterbury Tales* 'The General Prologue'

6 Universities incline wits to sophistry and affectation.
Francis Bacon 1561–1626: *Valerius Terminus of the Interpretation of Nature*

7 The discipline of colleges and universities is in general contrived, not for the benefit of the students, but for the interest, or more properly speaking, for the ease of the masters.
Adam Smith 1723–90: *Wealth of Nations* (1776)

8 To the University of Oxford I acknowledge no obligation; and she will as cheerfully renounce me for a son, as I am willing to disclaim her for a mother. I spent fourteen months at Magdalen College: they proved the fourteen months the most idle and unprofitable of my whole life.
Edward Gibbon 1737–94: *Memoirs of My Life* (1796)

9 The true University of these days is a collection of books.
Thomas Carlyle 1795–1881: *On Heroes, Hero-Worship, and the Heroic* (1841)

10 A classic lecture, rich in sentiment,
With scraps of thundrous epic lilted out
By violet-hooded Doctors, elegies

And quoted odes, and jewels five-words-long,
That on the stretched forefinger of all Time
Sparkle for ever.

Alfred, Lord Tennyson 1809–92: *The Princess* (1847)

11 A whaleship was my Yale College and my Harvard.

Herman Melville 1819–91: *Moby Dick* (1851)

12 Nor can I do better, in conclusion, than impress upon you the study of Greek literature, which not only elevates above the vulgar herd, but leads not infrequently to positions of considerable emolument.

Thomas Gaisford 1779–1855: Christmas Day Sermon in the Cathedral, Oxford; W. Tuckwell *Reminiscences of Oxford* (2nd ed., 1907)

13 Home of lost causes, and forsaken beliefs, and unpopular names, and impossible loyalties!

of Oxford

Matthew Arnold 1822–88: *Essays in Criticism* First Series (1865)

14 A University should be a place of light, of liberty, and of learning.

Benjamin Disraeli 1804–81: speech, House of Commons, 11 March 1873

15 Gentlemen: I have not had your advantages. What poor education I have received has been gained in the University of Life.

Horatio Bottomley 1860–1933: speech at the Oxford Union, 2 December 1920

16 The value of an education in a liberal arts college is not the learning of many facts but the training of the mind to think something that cannot be learned from textbooks.

Albert Einstein 1879–1955: in 1921; Philipp Frank *Einstein: His Life and Times* (1947)

17 Our American professors like their literature clear and cold and pure and very dead.

Sinclair Lewis 1885–1951: Nobel Prize Address, 12 December 1930

18 Princeton is a wonderful little spot. A quaint and ceremonious village of puny demigods on stilts.

Albert Einstein 1879–1955: letter to Queen Elisabeth of Belgium, 20 November 1933

19 I don't think one 'comes down' from Jimmy's university. According to him, it's not even red brick, but white tile.

John Osborne 1929–94: *Look Back in Anger* (1956); see UNIVERSITIES 3

20 The delusion that there are thousands of young people about who are capable of benefiting from university training, but have somehow failed to find their way there, is...a necessary component of the expansionist case... More will mean worse.

Kingsley Amis 1922–95: in *Encounter* July 1960

21 City of perspiring dreams.

of Cambridge

Frederic Raphael 1931– : *The Glittering Prizes* (1976); see BRITISH TOWNS 20

22 There is one thing that a professor can be absolutely certain of: almost every student entering the university believes, or says he believes, that truth is relative.

Allan Bloom 1930–92: *The Closing of the American Mind* (1987)

23 Why am I the first Kinnock in a thousand generations to be able to get to a university?

later plagiarized by the American politician Joe Biden

Neil Kinnock 1942– : speech in party political broadcast, 21 May 1987

Value

proverbs and sayings ▶

1 Everything has a price, but jade is priceless.

modern saying, said to derive from a Chinese proverb extolling the value of jade

2 Gold may be bought too dear.

wealth may be acquired at too great a price; English proverb, mid 16th century

3 If you pay peanuts, you get monkeys.

a poor rate of pay will attract only poorly qualified and incompetent staff (*peanuts* here means 'a small sum of money'); English proverb, mid 20th century

4 **It is a poor dog that's not worth whistling for.**
a dog is of no value if the owner will not even go to the trouble of whistling for it; English proverb, mid 16th century

5 **Little things please little minds.**
English proverb, late 16th century

6 **Nothing comes of nothing.**
English proverb, late 14th century

7 **Nothing for nothing.**
summarizing the attitude that nothing will be offered unless a return is assured; English proverb, early 18th century

8 **One man's trash is another man's treasure.**
modern saying

9 **What can a monkey know of the taste of ginger?**
ginger was a rare and expensive delicacy; Indian proverb

10 **What do you think of the show so far? Rubbish!**
catchphrase of Eric Morecambe (1926–84) on *The Morecambe and Wise Show* (BBC Television, 1968–78; Thames Television, 1978–83)

11 **Worth a guinea a box.**
advertising slogan for Beecham's pills, from 1859, from the chance remark of a lady purchaser

12 **The worth of a thing is what it will bring.**
the real value of something can only be measured by what another person is willing to pay for it; English proverb, mid 16th century

phrases ▸

13 **bang for one's buck**
an informal US expression meaning value for money; the phrase was notably used in 1954 by Charles E. Wilson: see WARFARE 2

14 **elephants' graveyard**
a repository for unwanted goods, from the belief (recorded from the early 20th century) that elephants in the wild seek out a particular spot in which to die, where their remains then lie

15 **the end of the rainbow**
the place where something precious is found at last; with allusion to the proverbial belief in the existence of a crock of gold (or something else of great value) at the end of a rainbow; see VALUE 20

16 **golden calf**
something, especially wealth, as an object of excessive or unworthy worship; from the story in the Bible (Exodus) of the idol made and worshipped by the Israelites in disobedience to Moses

17 **holy of holies**
a thing regarded as sacrosanct; the inner chamber of the sanctuary in the Jewish Temple, separated by a veil from the outer chamber

18 **make a mountain out of a molehill**
laying unnecessary stress on a small matter; see OPTIMISM 37

19 **mess of pottage**
a material or trivial comfort gained at the expense of something more important; the price, according to the Bible (Genesis), for which Esau sold his birthright to his brother Jacob; see THEATRE 2

20 **pot of gold**
an imaginary reward; a jackpot; an ideal; supposedly to be found at *the end of the rainbow*. see VALUE 15

21 **pride of place**
the most prominent or important position among a group of things; in falconry, the high position from which a falcon or similar bird swoops down on its prey; first recorded in Shakespeare's *Macbeth*

quotations ▸

22 **Thirty spokes share the wheel's hub;**
It is the centre hole that makes it useful.
Shape clay into a vessel;
It is the space within that makes it useful.
Cut doors and windows for a room;
It is the holes which make it useful.
Therefore profit comes from what is there;
Usefulness from what is not there.
Lao Tzu c.604–c.531 BC: *Tao-Te Ching*

23 **A living dog is better than a dead lion.**
Bible: Ecclesiastes; see LIFE 7

24 **Neither cast ye your pearls before swine.**
Bible: St Matthew; see FUTILITY 10

25 **O monstrous! but one half-pennyworth of bread to this intolerable deal of sack!**
William Shakespeare 1564–1616: *Henry IV, Part 1* (1597)

26 Of one whose hand,
Like the base Indian, threw a pearl away
Richer than all his tribe.
William Shakespeare 1564–1616: *Othello* (1602–4)

27 The harder the conflict, the more glorious the triumph. What we obtain too cheap, we esteem too lightly: it is dearness only that gives everything its value.
Thomas Paine 1737–1809: *The Crisis* (December 1776)

28 Then on the shore
Of the wide world I stand alone and think
Till love and fame to nothingness do sink.
John Keats 1795–1821: 'When I have fears that I may cease to be' (written 1818)

29 It is not that pearls fetch a high price *because* men have dived for them; but on the contrary, men dive for them because they fetch a high price.
Richard Whately 1787–1863: *Introductory Lectures on Political Economy* (1832)

30 An acre in Middlesex is better than a principality in Utopia.
Lord Macaulay 1800–59: *Essays Contributed to the Edinburgh Review* (1843) 'Lord Bacon'

31 Every man is wanted, and no man is wanted much.
Ralph Waldo Emerson 1803–82: *Essays. Second Series* (1844) 'Nominalist and Realist'

32 You can calculate the worth of a man by the number of his enemies, and the importance of a work of art by the harm that is spoken of it.
Gustave Flaubert 1821–80: letter to Louise Colet, 14 June 1853

33 Nothink for nothink 'ere, and precious little for sixpence.
Punch: in 1869

34 I never loved a dear Gazelle—
Nor anything that cost me much:
High prices profit those who sell,
But why should I *be fond of such?*
Lewis Carroll 1832–98: *Phantasmagoria* (1869) 'Theme with Variations'; see TRANSIENCE 11

35 It has long been an axiom of mine that the little things are infinitely the most important.
Arthur Conan Doyle 1859–1930: *Adventures of Sherlock Holmes* (1892)

36 Price is what you pay. Value is what you get.
Warren Buffett 1930– : letter to partners, 20 January 1966, in *Warren Buffett Speaks* (2007)

37 Nothing that costs only a dollar is worth having.
Elizabeth Arden 1876–1966: attributed; in *Fortune* October 1973

Violence

proverbs and sayings ▸

1 Burn, baby, burn.
black extremist slogan in use during the Los Angeles riots, August 1965

phrases ▸

2 blood and thunder
violence and bloodshed, especially in fiction

quotations ▸

3 Force, unaided by judgement, collapses through its own weight.
Horace 65–8 BC: *Odes*

4 Resist not evil: but whosoever shall smite thee on thy right cheek, turn to him the other also.
Bible: St Matthew; see FORGIVENESS 9, VIOLENCE 7

5 All they that take the sword shall perish with the sword.
Bible: St Matthew

6 Who overcomes
By force, hath overcome but half his foe.
John Milton 1608–74: *Paradise Lost* (1667)

7 Wisdom has taught us to be calm and meek,
To take one blow, and turn the other cheek;
It is not written what a man shall do
If the rude caitiff smite the other too!
Oliver Wendell Holmes 1809–94: 'Non-Resistance' (1861); see VIOLENCE 4

8 If you strike a child take care that you strike it in anger, even at the risk of maiming it for life. A blow in cold blood neither can nor should be forgiven.
George Bernard Shaw 1856–1950: *Man and Superman* (1903) 'Maxims: How to Beat Children'; see EMOTIONS 4

9 Victory attained by violence is tantamount to a defeat, for it is momentary.
Mahatma Gandhi 1869–1948: *Satyagraha Leaflet no. 13* (1919)

10 Non-violence is the first article of my faith. It is also the last article of my creed.
Mahatma Gandhi 1869–1948: speech at Shahi Bag, 18 March 1922, on a charge of sedition

11 A man may build himself a throne of bayonets, but he cannot sit on it.
quoted by Boris Yeltsin at the time of the failed military coup in Russia, August 1991
William Ralph Inge 1860–1954: *Philosophy of Plotinus* (1923)

12 Where force is necessary, there it must be applied boldly, decisively and completely. But one must know the limitations of force; one must know when to blend force with a manoeuvre, a blow with an agreement.
Leon Trotsky 1879–1940: *What Next?* (1932)

13 Pale Ebenezer thought it wrong to fight,
But Roaring Bill (who killed him) thought it right.
Hilaire Belloc 1870–1953: 'The Pacifist' (1938)

14 Violence is the last refuge of the incompetent.
Isaac Asimov 1920–92: *Foundation* (1951)

15 In violence, we forget who we are.
Mary McCarthy 1912–89: *On the Contrary* (1961) 'Characters in Fiction'

16 I don't think there is anything particularly wrong about hitting a woman—although I don't recommend doing it in the same way that you'd hit a man.
Sean Connery 1930– : in *Playboy* November 1965

17 A riot is at bottom the language of the unheard.
Martin Luther King 1929–68: *Where Do We Go From Here?* (1967)

18 I say violence is necessary. It is as American as cherry pie.
H. Rap Brown 1943– : speech at Washington, 27 July 1967

19 What has violence ever accomplished? What has it ever created? No martyr's cause has ever been stilled by an assassin's bullet.
Robert Kennedy 1925–68: speech to Cleveland City Club, 5 April 1968

20 Keep violence in the mind
Where it belongs.
Brian Aldiss 1925– : *Barefoot in the Head* (1969) 'Charteris'

21 The only thing that's been a worse flop than the organization of non-violence has been the organization of violence.
Joan Baez 1941– : *Daybreak* (1970)

22 The quietly pacifist peaceful
always die
to make room for men
who shout.
Alice Walker 1944– : 'The QPP' (1973)

23 The terrible thing about terrorism is that ultimately it destroys those who practise it. Slowly but surely, as they try to extinguish life in others, the light within them dies.
Terry Waite 1939– : in *Guardian* 20 February 1992

Virtue

see also GOOD, SIN

proverbs and sayings ▸

1 The good die young.
English proverb, late 17th century, often used ironically; see YOUTH 3

2 Good men are scarce.
English proverb, early 17th century

3 He lives long who lives well.
the reputation derived from living a good and moral life will mean that one's name will last; English proverb, mid 16th century

4 **No good deed goes unpunished.**
modern humorous saying, sometimes attributed to Oscar Wilde but not traced in his writings

5 **See no evil, hear no evil, speak no evil.**
conventionally represented by 'the three wise monkeys' covering their eyes, ears, and mouth respectively with their hands, and used particularly to imply a deliberate refusal to notice something that is wrong; English proverb, early 20th century; see GOOD 13

6 **Virtue is its own reward.**
the satisfaction of knowing that one has observed appropriate moral standards should be all that is sought; English proverb, early 16th century

phrases ▸

7 **the book of life**
the record of those achieving salvation; after the Bible (Revelation) 'I will not blot out his name out of the book of life'

8 **a cardinal virtue**
a particular strength or attribute; each of the chief moral attributes (originally of scholastic philosophy), justice, prudence, temperance, and fortitude, which with the three theological virtues of faith, hope, and charity, comprise the seven virtues; *cardinal* meaning 'a hinge'

9 **odour of sanctity**
a state of holiness or saintliness; translation of French *odeur de sainteté* a sweet or balsamic odour reputedly emitted by the bodies of saints at or after death

10 **pure as the driven snow**
completely pure; *driven* of snow that has been piled into drifts or made smooth by the wind; see VIRTUE 40

11 **salt of the earth**
of complete kindness, honesty, and reliability; after the Bible (Matthew) 'Ye are the salt of the earth'

12 **sans peur et sans reproche**
without fear and without blame, fearless and blameless; French; *Chevalier sans peur et sans reproche* 'Fearless, blameless knight' was the description in contemporary chronicles of Pierre Bayard (1476–1524)

13 **the unco guid**
those who are professedly strict in matters of morals and religion; originally alluding to Robert Burns 'Address to the Unco Guid, or the Rigidly Righteous': see TEMPTATION 13

14 **Victorian values**
values based on high standards of self-reliance and personal morality supposedly typical of the reign of Queen Victoria (1819–1901), but alternatively regarded as representing a restrictive moral earnestness; associated particularly with Margaret Thatcher as Conservative Prime Minister: see VIRTUE 44

15 **without any spot or wrinkle**
without any moral stain or blemish; originally in Tyndale's translation of the Bible (Ephesians)

quotations ▸

16 **To be able under all circumstances to practise five things constitutes perfect virtue; these five things are gravity, generosity of soul, sincerity, earnestness and kindness.**
Confucius 551–479 BC: *Analects*

17 **Strait is the gate, and narrow is the way, which leadeth unto life, and few there be that find it.**
Bible: St Matthew

18 ***Puro e disposto a salire alle stelle.***
Pure and ready to mount to the stars.
Dante Alighieri 1265–1321: *Divina Commedia* 'Purgatorio'

19 **Would that we had spent one whole day well in this world!**
Thomas à Kempis 1380–1471: *The Imitation of Christ*

20 **Our goodness derives not from our capacity to think but to love.**
St Teresa of Ávila 1512–82: *Book of the Foundations* (1610)

21 **How far that little candle throws his beams!**
So shines a good deed in a naughty world.
William Shakespeare 1564–1616: *The Merchant of Venice* (1596–8)

22 **Dost thou think, because thou art virtuous, there shall be no more cakes and ale?**
William Shakespeare 1564–1616: *Twelfth Night* (1601); see PLEASURE 3

23 **Virtue is like a rich stone, best plain set.**
Francis Bacon 1561–1626: *Essays* (1625) 'Of Beauty'

24 **I cannot praise a fugitive and cloistered virtue, unexercised and unbreathed,**

that never sallies out and sees her adversary, but slinks out of the race, where that immortal garland is to be run for, not without dust and heat.
John Milton 1608–74: *Areopagitica* (1644)

25 Instead of dirt and poison we have rather chosen to fill our hives with honey and wax; thus furnishing mankind with the two noblest of things, which are sweetness and light.
Jonathan Swift 1667–1745: *The Battle of the Books* (1704); see BEHAVIOUR 15

26 Virtue she finds too painful an endeavour,
Content to dwell in decencies for ever.
Alexander Pope 1688–1744: *Epistles to Several Persons* 'To a Lady' (1735)

27 Let humble Allen, with an awkward shame,
Do good by stealth, and blush to find it fame.
Alexander Pope 1688–1744: *Imitations of Horace* (1738)

28 Virtue knows to a farthing what it has lost by not having been vice.
Horace Walpole 1717–97: L. Kronenberger *The Extraordinary Mr Wilkes* (1974)

29 That best portion of a good man's life,
His little, nameless, unremembered, acts
Of kindness and of love.
William Wordsworth 1770–1850: 'Lines composed a few miles above Tintern Abbey' (1798)

30 My strength is as the strength of ten,
Because my heart is pure.
Alfred, Lord Tennyson 1809–92: 'Sir Galahad' (1842)

31 More people are flattered into virtue than bullied out of vice.
R. S. Surtees 1805–64: *The Analysis of the Hunting Field* (1846)

32 I expect to pass through this world but once; any good thing therefore that I can do, or any kindness that I can show to any fellow-creature, let me do it now; let me not defer or neglect it, for I shall not pass this way again.
Stephen Grellet 1773–1855: attributed; see John o' London *Treasure Trove* (1925) for some of the many other claimants to authorship

33 Be good, sweet maid, and let who will be clever.
Charles Kingsley 1819–75: 'A Farewell' (1858)

34 If some great Power would agree to make me always think what is true and do what is right, on condition of being turned into a sort of clock and wound up every morning before I got out of bed, I should instantly close with the offer.
T. H. Huxley 1825–95: 'On Descartes' *Discourse on Method*' (written 1870)

35 Few things are harder to put up with than the annoyance of a good example.
Mark Twain 1835–1910: *Pudd'nhead Wilson* (1894)

36 No people do so much harm as those who go about doing good.
Mandell Creighton 1843–1901: *The Life and Letters of Mandell Creighton* by his wife (1904)

37 She was poor but she was honest
Victim of a rich man's game.
First he loved her, then he left her,
And she lost her maiden name...
Anonymous: 'She was Poor but she was Honest'; sung by British soldiers in the First World War

38 'Goodness, what beautiful diamonds!'
'Goodness had nothing to do with it.'
Mae West 1892–1980: *Night After Night* (1932 film)

39 If all the good people were clever,
And all clever people were good,
The world would be nicer than ever
We thought that it possibly could.
But somehow, 'tis seldom or never
The two hit it off as they should;
The good are so harsh to the clever,
The clever so rude to the good!
Elizabeth Wordsworth 1840–1932: 'Good and Clever'

40 I'm as pure as the driven slush.
Tallulah Bankhead 1903–68: in *Saturday Evening Post* 12 April 1947; see VIRTUE 10

41 Terrible is the temptation to be good.
Bertolt Brecht 1898–1956: *The Caucasian Chalk Circle* (1948)

42 What after all
Is a halo? It's only one more thing to keep clean.
Christopher Fry 1907– : *The Lady's not for Burning* (1949)

43 In our era, the road to holiness necessarily passes through the world of action.

Dag Hammarskjold 1905–61: diary, 25 December 1955, *Markings* (1964)

44 I was asked whether I was trying to restore Victorian values. I said straight out I was. And I am.

Margaret Thatcher 1925– : speech to the British Jewish Community, 21 July 1983, referring to an interview with Brian Walden on 17 January 1983; see VIRTUE 14

Wales

phrases ▸

1 Land of my Fathers

Wales; from the opening words of the first verse of the Welsh national anthem by Evan James; see WALES 6, WALES 9

2 Little England beyond Wales

the English-speaking area of Pembrokeshire (Dyfed); a name first recorded in Camden's *Britannia* (1586)

quotations ▸

3 Who dare compare the English, the most degraded of all the races under heaven, with the Welsh?

Giraldus Cambrensis c.1146–c.1220: attributed

4 Though it appear a little out of fashion,
There is much care and valour in this
Welshman.

William Shakespeare 1564–1616: *Henry V* (1599)

5 The English have forgot that they ever conquered the Welsh, but some ages will elapse before the Welsh forget that the English have conquered them.

George Borrow 1803–81: *Wild Wales* (1854)

6 Wales, Wales, sweet are thy hills and
vales,
Thy speech, thy song,
To thee belong,
O may they live ever in Wales.

Evan James 1809–78: 'Land of My Fathers' (1856); see WALES 1

7 Among our ancient mountains,
And from our lovely vales,
Oh, let the prayer re-echo:
'God bless the Prince of Wales!'

George Linley 1798–1865: 'God Bless the Prince of Wales' (1862 song); translated from the Welsh original by J. C. Hughes (1837–87)

8 'I often think,' he continued, 'that we can trace almost all the disasters of English history to the influence of Wales!'

Evelyn Waugh 1903–66: *Decline and Fall* (1928)

9 The land of my fathers. My fathers can have it.

Dylan Thomas 1914–53: in *Adam* December 1953; see WALES 1

10 It profits a man nothing to give his soul for the whole world...But for Wales—!

Robert Bolt 1924–95: *A Man for All Seasons* (1960); see SUCCESS 24

11 Everyday when I wake up, I thank the Lord I'm Welsh.

Cerys Matthews 1969– : 'International Velvet' (1998 song)

12 What are they for? They are always so pleased with themselves.

of the Welsh; comment made on BBC2's *Room 101* programme

Anne Robinson 1944– : in *Daily Telegraph* 7 March 2001

13 In these stones horizons sing.

Gwyneth Lewis 1959– : English words inscribed outside the Welsh Millennium Centre in Cardiff, 2004

Warfare

see also ARMED FORCES, PEACE, WARS

proverbs and sayings ▸

1 A bayonet is a weapon with a worker at each end.

British pacifist slogan (1940)

2 A bigger bang for a buck.

Charles E. Wilson's defence policy, in *Newsweek* 22 March 1954; see VALUE 13

3 58% don't want Pershing.

anti-nuclear weapons slogan on T-shirt worn by British fashion designer Katharine Hamnett (1952–) when she attended a drinks party at 10 Downing Street in 1984

4 **War is God's way of teaching Americans geography.**
modern saying, widely attributed to Ambrose Bierce (1842–*c.*1914), but not found before the early 1990s

5 **War will cease when men refuse to fight.**
pacifist slogan, from 1936; often quoted as 'Wars will cease...'

6 **When war is declared, Truth is the first casualty.**
epigraph to Arthur Ponsonby's *Falsehood in Wartime* (1928), perhaps deriving from Johnson: see WARFARE 25; attributed also to Hiram Johnson, speaking in the US Senate, 1918, but not recorded in his speech

phrases ▸

7 **blood and iron**
military force as distinguished from diplomacy; translation of German *Blut und Eisen*: see INTERNATIONAL 23

8 **dogs of war**
the havoc accompanying war; from Shakespeare *Julius Caesar*: see REVENGE 14

9 **draw one's sword against**
take up arms against, attack; see REVOLUTION 5

10 **fog of war**
used to describe the complexity of military conflicts. *Fog of war* is often attributed to the Prussian military theorist Karl von Clausewitz (1780–1831), but is in fact a paraphrase of what he said: 'War is the realm of uncertainty; three quarters of the factors on which action in war is based are wrapped in a fog of greater or lesser uncertainty.'

11 **just war**
a war which is deemed to be morally or theologically justifiable; in the Middle Ages, St Thomas Aquinas laid down three conditions which a *just war* must meet: it had to be authorized by the sovereign, the cause must be just, and those engaging in it must have the intention of advancing good or avoiding evil; see WARFARE 38

12 **shock and awe**
term for a military strategy based on achieving rapid dominance over an adversary by the initial imposition of overwhelming force and firepower. The concept was formulated by the American strategic analysts Harlan K. Ullman and James P. Wade in a Pentagon briefing document of 1996, and came to wider prominence during the campaign in Iraq in 2003

13 **throw away the scabbard**
abandon all thought of making peace; from the proverb: see REVOLUTION 5

quotations ▸

14 **War is the father of all and the king of all.**
Heraclitus *c.*540–*c.*480 BC: *On the Universe*

15 **Know the enemy and know yourself; in a hundred battles you will never be defeated.**
Sun Tzu fl. *c.*400–320 BC: *The Art of War*

16 **We make war that we may live in peace.**
Aristotle 384–322 BC: *Nicomachean Ethics*; see PREPARATION 11

17 **Laws are silent in time of war.**
Cicero 106–43 BC: *Pro Milone*

18 **The sinews of war, unlimited money.**
Cicero 106–43 BC: *Fifth Philippic*; see MONEY 32

19 **I see wars, horrible wars, and the Tiber foaming with much blood.**
Virgil 70–19 BC: *Aeneid*; see RACE 27

20 **Wars begin when you will, but they do not end when you please.**
Niccolò Machiavelli 1469–1527: *History of Florence* (1521–4)

21 **Once more unto the breach, dear friends, once more;**
Or close the wall up with our English dead!
In peace there's nothing so becomes a man
As modest stillness and humility:
But when the blast of war blows in our ears,
Then imitate the action of the tiger;
Stiffen the sinews, summon up the blood,
Disguise fair nature with hard-favoured rage.
William Shakespeare 1564–1616: *Henry V* (1599)

22 **For what can war, but endless war still breed?**
John Milton 1608–74: 'On the Lord General Fairfax at the Siege of Colchester' (written 1648)

23 **Force, and fraud, are in war the two cardinal virtues.**
Thomas Hobbes 1588–1679: *Leviathan* (1651)

24 God is on the side not of the heavy battalions, but of the best shots.

Voltaire 1694–1778: 'The Piccini Notebooks' (1735–50); see ARMED FORCES 7, GOD 23

25 Among the calamities of war may be jointly numbered the diminution of the love of truth, by the falsehoods which interest dictates and credulity encourages.

Samuel Johnson 1709–84: in *The Idler* 11 November 1758; see WARFARE 6

26 There never was a good war, or a bad peace.

Benjamin Franklin 1706–90: letter to Josiah Quincy, 11 September 1783

27 In war, three-quarters turns on personal character and relations; the balance of manpower and materials counts only for the remaining quarter.

Napoléon I 1769–1821: 'Observations sur les affaires d'Espagne, Saint-Cloud, 27 août 1808'

28 Next to a battle lost, the greatest misery is a battle gained.

Duke of Wellington 1769–1852: in *Diary of Frances, Lady Shelley 1787–1817* (ed. R. Edgcumbe)

29 Everything is very simple in war, but the simplest thing is difficult. These difficulties accumulate and produce a friction which no man can imagine exactly who has not seen war.

Karl von Clausewitz 1780–1831: *On War* (1832–4)

30 War is nothing but a continuation of politics with the admixture of other means.

commonly rendered as 'War is the continuation of politics by other means'

Karl von Clausewitz 1780–1831: *On War* (1832–4)

31 He knew that the essence of war is violence, and that moderation in war is imbecility.

Lord Macaulay 1800–59: *Essays Contributed to the Edinburgh Review* (1843) 'John Hampden'

32 All the business of war, and indeed all the business of life, is to endeavour to find out what you don't know by what you do; that's what I called 'guessing what was at the other side of the hill.'

Duke of Wellington 1769–1852: in *The Croker Papers* (1885)

33 It is well that war is so terrible. We should grow too fond of it.

Robert E. Lee 1807–70: after the battle of Fredericksburg, December 1862; attributed

34 Always mystify, mislead, and surprise the enemy, if possible.

his strategic motto during the Civil War

Thomas Jonathan 'Stonewall' Jackson 1824–63: M. Miner and H. Rawson *American Heritage Dictionary of American Quotations* (1997)

35 War is an ugly thing, but not the ugliest of things: the decayed and degraded state of moral and patriotic feeling which thinks nothing *worth* a war, is worse.

John Stuart Mill 1806–73: *Dissertations and Discussions* vol. 3 (1867) 'The Contest in America'

36 There is many a boy here to-day who looks on war as all glory, but, boys, it is all hell.

William Sherman 1820–91: speech at Columbus, Ohio, 11 August 1880

37 of possible German involvement in the Balkans:
Not worth the healthy bones of a single Pomeranian grenadier.

Otto von Bismarck 1815–98: George O. Kent *Bismarck and his Times* (1978); see WORLD WAR II 24

38 I do wish people would not deceive themselves by talk of a just war. There is no such thing as a just war. What we are doing is casting out Satan by Satan.

Charles Hamilton Sorley 1895–1915: letter to his mother from Aldershot, March 1915; see GOOD 18, WARFARE 11

39 War is hell, and all that, but it has a good deal to recommend it. It wipes out all the small nuisances of peace-time.

Ian Hay 1876–1952: *The First Hundred Thousand* (1915)

40 War is a game that is played with a smile. If you can't smile grin. If you can't grin keep out of the way till you can.

Winston Churchill 1874–1965: letter to Clementine Churchill, 27 January 1916

41 Once lead this people into war and they will forget there ever was such a thing as tolerance.

Woodrow Wilson 1856–1924: John Dos Passos *Mr Wilson's War* (1917)

42 My subject is War, and the pity of War. The Poetry is in the pity.

Wilfred Owen 1893–1918: preface (written 1918) in *Poems* (1963)

43 If you could hear, at every jolt, the blood
Come gargling from the froth-corrupted lungs,
Obscene as cancer, bitter as the cud
Of vile, incurable sores on innocent tongues,—
My friend, you would not tell with such high zest
To children ardent for some desperate glory,
The old Lie: Dulce et decorum est
Pro patria mori.

Wilfred Owen 1893–1918: 'Dulce et Decorum Est'; see PATRIOTISM 7

44 Waste of Blood, and waste of Tears,
Waste of youth's most precious years,
Waste of ways the saints have trod,
Waste of Glory, waste of God,
War!

G. A. Studdert Kennedy 1883–1929: 'Waste' (1919)

45 War is too serious a matter to entrust to military men.

Georges Clemenceau 1841–1929: attributed to Clemenceau, e.g. in Hampden Jackson *Clemenceau and the Third Republic* (1946); but also to Briand and Talleyrand; see POLITICS 26

46 The bomber will always get through. The only defence is in offence, which means that you have to kill more women and children more quickly than the enemy if you want to save yourselves.

Stanley Baldwin 1867–1947: speech, House of Commons, 10 November 1932

47 Wars may be fought with weapons, but they are won by men.

George S. Patton 1885–1945: in *Cavalry Journal* September 1933

48 We can manage without butter but not, for example, without guns. If we are attacked we can only defend ourselves with guns not with butter.

Joseph Goebbels 1897–1945: speech in Berlin, 17 January 1936; see WARFARE 49

49 We have no butter...but I ask you—would you rather have butter or guns?...preparedness makes us powerful. Butter merely makes us fat.

Hermann Goering 1893–1946: speech at Hamburg, 1936; W. Frischauer *Goering* (1951); see WARFARE 48

50 Little girl...Sometime they'll give a war and nobody will come.

Carl Sandburg 1878–1967: *The People, Yes* (1936); 'Suppose They Gave a War and Nobody Came?' was the title of a 1970 film

51 War always finds a way.

Bertolt Brecht 1898–1956: *Mother Courage* (1939)

52 War will be won by Blood and Guts alone.

George Patton 1885–1945: address to fellow officers, Fort Benning, Georgia, 1940; see WORLD WAR II 7

53 Probably the battle of Waterloo *was* won on the playing-fields of Eton, but the opening battles of all subsequent wars have been lost there.

George Orwell 1903–50: *The Lion and the Unicorn* (1941) 'England Your England'; see WARS 15

54 What difference does it make to the dead, the orphans and the homeless, whether the mad destruction
is wrought under the name of totalitarianism or the holy name of liberty or democracy?

Mahatma Gandhi 1869–1948: *Non-Violence in Peace and War* (1942)

55 War's tragedy is that it uses man's best to do man's worst.

Harry Emerson Fosdick 1878–1969: *On Being Fit to Live With* (1946)

56 The quickest way of ending a war is to lose it.

George Orwell 1903–50: in *Polemic* May 1946

57 In war: resolution. In defeat: defiance. In victory: magnanimity. In peace: goodwill.

Winston Churchill 1874–1965: *The Second World War* vol. 1 (1948)

58 Every gun that is made, every warship launched, every rocket fired signifies, in the final sense, a theft from those who hunger and are not fed, those who are cold and are not clothed. This world in arms is not spending money alone. It is spending the sweat of its labourers, the genius of its scientists, the hopes of its children.

Dwight D. Eisenhower 1890–1969: speech in Washington, 16 April 1953

59 Mankind must put an end to war or war will put an end to mankind.

John F. Kennedy 1917–63: speech to United Nations General Assembly, 25 September 1961

60 Rule 1, on page 1 of the book of war, is: 'Do not march on Moscow'...[Rule 2] is: 'Do not go fighting with your land armies in China.'

Lord Montgomery 1887–1976: speech, House of Lords, 30 May 1962

61 The conventional army loses if it does not win. The guerrilla wins if he does not lose.

Henry Kissinger 1923– : in *Foreign Affairs* January 1969

62 I love the smell of napalm in the morning. It smells like victory.

John Milius and **Francis Ford Coppola** 1939– : *Apocalypse Now* (1979 film)

Wars

see also WORLD WAR I, WORLD WAR II

proverbs and sayings ▸

1 Hey, hey, LBJ, how many kids have you killed today?

anti-Vietnam marching slogan

2 Not in my name.

slogan of protesters against the war in Iraq, 2003

3 Remember the Alamo!

Texan battle-cry at the battle of San Jacinto, 1836, referring to the defence of a Franciscan mission in the Texan War of Independence, in which all the defenders were killed

phrases ▸

4 the late unpleasantness

the war that took place recently; originally the American Civil War

quotations ▸

5 Men said openly that Christ and His saints slept.

of twelfth-century England during the civil war between Stephen and Matilda

Anonymous: *Anglo-Saxon Chronicle* for 1137

6 I hae brocht ye to the ring, now see gif ye can dance.

William Wallace c.1270–1305: before the battle of Falkirk, 1298; attributed in varying forms, including '...hop if ye can'; James MacKay *William Wallace: Brave Heart* (1996)

7 The singeing of the King of Spain's Beard.

on the expedition to Cadiz, 1587

Francis Drake 1540–96: Francis Bacon *Considerations touching a War with Spain* (1629)

8 The dimensions of this mercy are above my thoughts. It is, for aught I know, a crowning mercy.

on the battle of Worcester, 1651

Oliver Cromwell 1599–1658: letter to William Lenthall, Speaker of the Parliament of England, 4 September 1651

9 They now *ring* the bells, but they will soon *wring* their hands.

on the declaration of war with Spain, 1739

Robert Walpole 1676–1745: W. Coxe *Memoirs of Sir Robert Walpole* (1798)

10 What a glorious morning is this.

on hearing gunfire at Lexington, 19 April 1775; traditionally quoted 'What a glorious morning for America'

Samuel Adams 1722–1803: J. K. Hosmer *Samuel Adams* (1886)

11 Men, you are all marksmen—don't one of you fire until you see the white of their eyes.

Israel Putnam 1718–90: at Bunker Hill, 1775; R. Frothingham *History of the Siege of Boston* (1873) ; also attributed to William Prescott, 1726–95

12 *Guerra a cuchillo.*

War to the knife.

at the siege of Saragossa, 4 August 1808, replying to the suggestion that he should surrender

José de Palafox 1780–1847: as reported; he actually said: '*Guerra y cuchillo* [War and the knife]'; José Gòmez de Arteche y Moro *Guerra de la Independencia* (1875)

13 **Up Guards and at them!**
Duke of Wellington 1769–1852: in *The Battle of Waterloo* by a Near Observer [J. Booth] (1815); later denied by Wellington

14 **Hard pounding this, gentlemen; let's see who will pound longest.**
Duke of Wellington 1769–1852: at the battle of Waterloo, 1815; Sir Walter Scott *Paul's Letters* (1816)

15 **The battle of Waterloo was won on the playing fields of Eton.**
Duke of Wellington 1769–1852: oral tradition, but not found in this form of words; C. F. R. Montalembert *De l'avenir politique de l'Angleterre* (1856); see WARFARE 53

16 **Half a league, half a league,**
Half a league onward,
All in the valley of Death
Rode the six hundred...

Cannon to right of them,
Cannon to left of them,
Cannon in front of them
Volleyed and thundered.
Alfred, Lord Tennyson 1809–92: 'The Charge of the Light Brigade' (1854)

17 ***J'y suis, j'y reste.***
Here I am, and here I stay.
Comte de Macmahon 1808–93: at the taking of the Malakoff fortress during the Crimean War, 8 September 1855; G. Hanotaux *Histoire de la France Contemporaine* (1903–8)

18 **There is Jackson with his Virginians, standing like a stone wall. Let us determine to die here, and we will conquer.**
referring to General T. J. ('Stonewall') Jackson
Barnard Elliott Bee 1823–61: at the battle of Bull Run, 21 July, 1861; B. Perley Poore *Perley's Reminiscences* (1886)

19 **All quiet along the Potomac to-night,**
No sound save the rush of the river,
While soft falls the dew on the face of the dead—
The picket's off duty forever.
Ethel Lynn Beers 1827–79: 'The Picket Guard' (1861); the first line is also attributed to George B. McClellan (1826–85)

20 **Give them the cold steel, boys!**
Lewis Addison Armistead 1817–63: attributed during the American Civil War, 1863

21 **Hold out. Relief is coming.**
usually quoted as 'Hold the fort! I am coming!'
William Tecumseh Sherman 1820–91: flag signal from Kennesaw Mountain to General John Murray Corse at Allatoona Pass, 5 October 1864

22 **We are not about to send American boys 9 or 10,000 miles away from home to do what Asian boys ought to be doing for themselves.**
Lyndon Baines Johnson 1908–73: speech at Akron University, 21 October 1964

23 **They've got to draw in their horns and stop their aggression, or we're going to bomb them back into the Stone Age.**
on the North Vietnamese
Curtis E. LeMay 1906–90: *Mission with LeMay* (1965)

24 **It became necessary to destroy the town to save it.**
statement by unidentified US Army Major, referring to Ben Tre in Vietnam
Anonymous: Associated Press Report, *New York Times* 8 February 1968

25 **The pity in this war is that only one side can lose.**
of the Iran-Iraq war 1980–8, often quoted as 'A pity they can't both lose'
Henry Kissinger 1923– : *c.* 1980, attributed; Steven Greffenius *The Logic of Conflict: making war and peace in the Middle East* (1993)

26 **Just rejoice at that news and congratulate our forces and the Marines...Rejoice!**
on the recapture of South Georgia; usually quoted as 'Rejoice, rejoice'
Margaret Thatcher 1925– : to newsmen outside Downing Street, 25 April 1982

27 **I counted them all out and I counted them all back.**
on the number of British aeroplanes (which he was not permitted to disclose) joining the raid on Port Stanley in the Falkland Islands
Brian Hanrahan 1949–2011: BBC broadcast report, 1 May 1982

28 **GOTCHA!**
Anonymous: headline on the sinking of the *General Belgrano*, in *Sun* 4 May 1982

29 **The Falklands thing was a fight between two bald men over a comb.**
Jorge Luis Borges 1899–1986: in *Time* 14 February 1983; see EXPERIENCE 3

30 **The mother of battles.**
popular interpretation of his description of the approaching Gulf War
Saddam Hussein 1937–2006: speech in Baghdad, 6 January 1991; *Times*, 7 January 1991, reported that Saddam had no intention of relinquishing Kuwait and was ready for the 'mother of all wars'

31 **It is time for us to win the first war of the 21st century.**
of the 'war on terrorism'
George W. Bush 1946– : at a White House press conference, 16 September 2001

32 **Stuff happens.**
on looting in Iraq
Donald Rumsfeld 1932– : press conference, 11 April 2003

Ways and Means

proverbs and sayings ▸

1 **Catching's before hanging.**
an essential step must be taken before the consequence can ensue; English proverb, early 19th century

2 **Eat the mangoes. Do not count the trees.**
concentrate on the task in hand; Indian proverb

3 **The end justifies the means.**
English proverb, late 16th century; see MORALITY 3

4 **Fight fire with fire.**
one should counter like with like; English proverb, mid 19th century

5 **Fire is a good servant but a bad master.**
acknowledging that fire is both essential for living and potentially destructive; English proverb, early 17th century

6 **First catch your hare.**
referring to the first essential step that must be taken before a process can begin; English proverb, early 19th century, often attributed to the English cook Hannah Glasse (fl. 1747), but her directions for making hare soup are, 'Take your hare when it is cased' (*cased* here meaning 'skinned')

7 **Give a man enough rope and he will hang himself.**
often used to mean that someone given enough licence or freedom will defeat themselves through their own mistakes; English proverb, mid 17th century

8 **The hammer shatters glass but forges steel.**
modern saying, said to be of Russian origin

9 **Honey catches more flies than vinegar.**
soft or ingratiating words achieve more than sharpness; English proverb, mid 17th century

10 **If you can't beat them, join them.**
often used in consolation or resignation; English proverb, mid 20th century

11 **If you don't know where you are going, any road will take you there.**
modern saying, originally with allusion to Alice's conversation with the Cheshire Cat in Lewis Carroll's *Alice in Wonderland* (1865); see CATS 4

12 **It hardly matters if it is a white cat or a black cat that catches the mice.**
Chinese proverb; see WAYS 36

13 **It is good to make a bridge of gold to a flying enemy.**
it is wiser to give passage to an enemy in flight, who may be desperate; English proverb, late 16th century

14 **An old poacher makes the best gamekeeper.**
someone who has formerly taken part in wrongdoing knows best how to counter it in others; English proverb, late 14th century

15 **One size does not fit all.**
an assertion of individual requirements; earlier versions are based on the metaphor of different size shoes for different feet; English proverb, early 17th century

16 **The paths are many, but the goal is the same.**
Indian proverb, deriving from Sanskrit

17 **The pen is mightier than the sword.**
written words may often have more lasting force than military strength; English proverb, late 16th century; see TECHNOLOGY 12, WRITING 6, WRITING 31

18 **Set a thief to catch a thief.**
used to imply that the person best placed to catch someone out in dishonest practices is one whose own nature tends that way; English proverb, mid 17th century

19 **There are more ways of killing a cat than choking it with cream.**
there are more ways of achieving an end than giving an opponent a glut of what they most want; English proverb, mid 19th century

20 **There are more ways of killing a dog than choking it with butter.**
there are more ways of achieving an end than giving an opponent a glut of what they most want; English proverb, mid 19th century

21 **There are more ways of killing a dog than hanging it.**
there are more ways than one of achieving an end; English proverb, late 17th century

22 **There is more than one way to skin a cat.**
English proverb, mid 19th century

23 **There is nothing like leather.**
referring to the toughness and durability of leather. The saying comes from one of Aesop's fables, in which a leatherworker contributed this opinion to a discussion on how to fortify a city; English proverb, late 17th century

24 **What matters is what works.**
late 20th century saying

phrases ►

25 **drive a coach and six through**
make useless by the disregard of law or custom; from Stephen Rice (1637–1715) 'I will drive a coach and six horses through the Act of Settlement'

26 **iron hand (*or* fist) in a velvet glove**
firmness or ruthlessness cloaked in outward gentleness; attributed to Napoleon from the mid 19th century

27 **Golden Fleece**
a goal that is highly desirable but difficult to achieve; the *fleece* of a *golden* ram, guarded by an unsleeping dragon, and sought and won by Jason with the help of Medea

28 **play the — card**
introduce a specified (advantageous) factor; from Lord Randolph Churchill: see IRELAND 13; see also LAW 45

quotations ►

29 **I will either find a way, or make one.**
on crossing the Alps
Hannibal 247–182 BC: traditional attribution; see WAYS 35

30 **It is in life as it is in ways, the shortest way is commonly the foulest, and surely the fairer way is not much about.**
Francis Bacon 1561–1626: *The Advancement of Learning* (1605)

31 **There are no small steps in great affairs.**
Cardinal de Retz 1613–79: *Mémoires* (1717) bk. 2

32 ***Dans ce pays-ci il est bon de tuer de temps en temps un amiral pour encourager les autres.***
In this country [England] it is thought well to kill an admiral from time to time to encourage the others.
referring to the execution of Admiral John Byng, 1757
Voltaire 1694–1778: *Candide* (1759); see MANAGEMENT 6

33 **A servant's too often a negligent elf;**
—If it's business of consequence,
DO IT YOURSELF!
R. H. Barham 1788–1845: 'The Ingoldsby Penance!—Moral' (1842)

34 **They sought it with thimbles, they sought it with care;**
They pursued it with forks and hope;
They threatened its life with a railway-share;
They charmed it with smiles and soap.
Lewis Carroll 1832–98: *The Hunting of the Snark* (1876)

35 **I shall find a way or make one.**
Robert Peary 1856–1920: attributed as his motto in W. H. Hobbs *Peary* (1936); see WAYS 29

36 **The colour of the cat doesn't matter as long as it catches the mice.**
Deng Xiaoping 1904–97: in *Financial Times* 18 December 1986; see WAYS 12

Weakness

see STRENGTH AND WEAKNESS

Wealth and Luxury

see also MONEY, THRIFT

proverbs and sayings ▸

1 **A diamond is forever.**
advertising slogan for De Beers Consolidated Mines, 1940s onwards

2 **If you really want to make a million... the quickest way is to start your own religion.**
previously attributed to L. Ron Hubbard 1911–86 in B. Corydon and L. Ron Hubbard Jr. *L. Ron Hubbard* (1987), but attribution subsequently rejected by L. Ron Hubbard Jr., who also dissociated himself from the book

3 **Money is like sea water. The more you drink, the thirstier you become.**
possession of wealth creates an addiction to money; modern saying

4 **Money makes a man.**
possession of wealth confers status; English proverb, early 16th century

5 **Money makes money.**
implying that those who are already wealthy are likely to become more so; English proverb, late 16th century

6 **The rich man has his ice in the summer and the poor man gets his in the winter.**
contrasting luxury with hardship through apparent equality; English proverb, early 20th century

phrases ▸

7 **the affluent society**
a society in which material wealth is widely distributed, a rich society; usually in allusion to the book *The Affluent Society* (1958) by the Canadian-born economist John Kenneth Galbraith

8 **Aladdin's cave**
a place of great riches; in the *Arabian Nights*, the cave in which Aladdin found an old lamp which, when rubbed, brought a genie to obey his will; see CHANCE 18

9 **as rich as Croesus**
a person of great wealth; *Croesus* (6th century BC), last king of Lydia c.560–546 BC, renowned for his great wealth

10 **born with a silver spoon in one's mouth**
born in affluence; see PRESIDENCY 17

11 **gilded cage**
a luxurious but restrictive environment

12 **golden goose**
a continuing source of wealth or profit that may be exhausted if it is misused; in a traditional fairytale, a *goose* which laid *golden* eggs; it was killed in an attempt to possess the source of this wealth, which as a result was lost

13 **the Mammon of unrighteousness**
wealth ill-used or ill-gained; *Mammon* (ultimately from Hebrew *māmōn* money, wealth), in early use, (the proper name of) the devil of covetousness, later with personification, wealth regarded as an idol or an evil influence; see MONEY 27

14 **the Midas touch**
the ability to turn one's actions to financial advantage; *Midas*, in classical legend a king of Phrygia whose touch was said to turn all things to gold

15 **milk and honey**
abundance, comfort, prosperity; with allusion to the biblical description of the promised land: see WEALTH 18

16 **poor little rich girl**
a wealthy girl or woman whose money brings her no happiness; title of a 1925 song by Noël Coward

17 **Tom Tiddler's ground**
a place where money or profit is readily made; a children's game in which one player tries to catch the others who run on to his or her territory crying 'We're on Tom Tiddler's ground, picking up gold and silver'

quotations ▸

18 **A land flowing with milk and honey.**
Bible: Exodus; see WEALTH 15

19 **It is easier for a camel to go through the eye of a needle, than for a rich man to enter into the kingdom of God.**
Bible: St Matthew; see QUANTITIES 16

20 **Riches are for spending.**
Francis Bacon 1561–1626: *Essays* (1625) 'Of Expense'

21 **Let none admire**
That riches grow in hell; that soil may best
Deserve the precious bane.
John Milton 1608–74: *Paradise Lost* (1667)

22 It was very prettily said, that we may learn the little value of fortune by the persons on whom heaven is pleased to bestow it.
Richard Steele 1672–1729: in *The Tatler* 27 July 1710

23 Get place and wealth, if possible, with grace;
If not, by any means get wealth and place.
Alexander Pope 1688–1744: *Imitations of Horace* (1738); see MONEY 26

24 The chief enjoyment of riches consists in the parade of riches.
Adam Smith 1723–90: *Wealth of Nations* (1776)

25 We are not here to sell a parcel of boilers and vats, but the potentiality of growing rich, beyond the dreams of avarice.
at the sale of Thrale's brewery
Samuel Johnson 1709–84: James Boswell *Life of Samuel Johnson* (1791) 6 April 1781

26 'Two nations; between whom there is no intercourse and no sympathy; who are as ignorant of each other's habits, thoughts, and feelings, as if they were dwellers in different zones, or inhabitants of different planets...' 'You speak of—' said Egremont, hesitatingly, 'THE RICH AND THE POOR.'
Benjamin Disraeli 1804–81: *Sybil* (1845); see POLITICS 9

27 The man who dies...rich dies disgraced.
Andrew Carnegie 1835–1919: in *North American Review* June 1889 'Wealth'

28 The only way not to think about money is to have a great deal of it.
Edith Wharton 1862–1937: *The House of Mirth* (1905)

29 In every well-governed state, wealth is a sacred thing; in democracies it is the only sacred thing.
Anatole France 1844–1924: *L'Île des pingouins* (1908)

30 To be clever enough to get all that money, one must be stupid enough to want it.
G. K. Chesterton 1874–1936: *Wisdom of Father Brown* (1914)

31 Her voice is full of money.
F. Scott Fitzgerald 1896–1940: *The Great Gatsby* (1925)

32 Let me tell you about the very rich. They are different from you and me.
F. Scott Fitzgerald 1896–1940: *All the Sad Young Men* (1926) 'Rich Boy'; to which Ernest Hemingway replied, 'Yes, they have more money', in *Esquire* August 1936 'The Snows of Kilimanjaro'

33 I am absolutely convinced that no wealth in the world can help humanity forward, even in the hands of the most devoted worker in this cause... Can anyone imagine Moses, Jesus, or Gandhi with the moneybags of Carnegie?
Albert Einstein 1879–1955: *Mein Weltbild* (1934)

34 A kiss on the hand may be quite continental,
But diamonds are a girl's best friend.
Leo Robin 1900–84: 'Diamonds are a Girl's Best Friend' (1949 song)

35 If you can actually count your money, then you are not really a rich man.
J. Paul Getty 1892–1976: in *Observer* 3 November 1957

36 The greater the wealth, the thicker will be the dirt.
J. K. Galbraith 1908–2006: *The Affluent Society* (1958)

37 I want to spend, and spend, and spend.
said to reporters on arriving to collect her husband's football pools winnings of £152,000
Vivian Nicholson 1936– : in *Daily Herald* 28 September 1961

38 The saddest thing I can imagine is to get used to luxury.
Charlie Chaplin 1889–1977: *My Autobiography* (1964)

39 I've been rich and I've been poor: rich is better.
Sophie Tucker 1884–1966: attributed

40 The minute you walked in the joint,
I could see you were a man of distinction,
A real big spender...
Hey! big spender, spend a little time with me.
Dorothy Fields 1905–74: 'Big Spender' (1966 song)

41 **Money, money, money
Must be funny
In the rich man's world.**

Benny Andersson 1946– and **Björn Ulvaeus** 1945– : 'Money, Money, Money' (1976 song)

42 **[New Labour] is intensely relaxed about people getting filthy rich.**

Peter Mandelson 1953– : speech to executives in Silicon Valley, California, October 1999; Andrew Rawnsley *Servants of the People* (2000)

43 **I am grateful for the blessings of wealth, but it hasn't changed who I am. My feet are still on the ground. I'm just wearing better shoes.**

Oprah Winfrey 1954– : in *Independent on Sunday* 18 July 2004

44 **A very rich person should leave his kids enough to do anything but not enough to do nothing.**

Warren Buffett 1930– : quoted in *Fortune Magazine* (online edition) 25 June 2006

Weather

proverbs and sayings ▸

1 **April showers bring forth May flowers.**

referring to the value of rain during April to early growth; English proverb, mid 16th century

2 **As the day lengthens, so the cold strengthens.**

recording the tradition that the coldest weather arrives when days begin to grow lighter; English proverb, early 17th century

3 **A dripping June sets all in tune.**

rain in June is beneficial to all crops and plants; English proverb, mid 18th century

4 **February fill dyke, be it black or be it white.**

February is a month likely to bring heavy rain (black) or snow (white); English proverb, mid 16th century; see SEASONS 13

5 **If Candlemas day be sunny and bright, winter will have another flight; if Candlemas day be cloudy with rain, winter is gone and won't come again.**

in the Church calendar 2 February is the date of the feast of the Purification of the Virgin Mary and the Presentation of Christ in the Temple. This is known as *Candlemas Day* because candles are blessed at services on that day; English proverb, late 17th century

6 **If in February there be no rain, 'tis neither good for hay nor grain.**

a drought in February will be damaging to crops later in the year; English proverb, early 18th century

7 **Long foretold, long last; short notice, soon past.**

if there is a long gap between the signs that the weather will change and the change itself, then the predicted weather will last a long time. If the intervening period is a short one, then the predicted weather will be of correspondingly short duration; English proverb, mid 19th century

8 **March borrowed from April three days, and they were ill.**

traditional saying, implying that bad weather in early April reflects the influence of March; English proverb, mid 17th century; see WEATHER 22

9 **March comes in like a lion, and goes out like a lamb.**

weather is traditionally stormy at the beginning of March, but calm at the end; English proverb, early 17th century

10 **North wind doth blow, we shall have snow.**

traditional weather rhyme, deriving from a nursery rhyme of the early 19th century

11 **A peck of March dust is worth a king's ransom.**

March is traditionally a wet month, and dust is rare (a *peck* was a dry measure of two gallons); English proverb, early 16th century

12 **Rain before seven, fine before eleven.**

English proverb, mid 19th century

13 **Rain, rain, go away,
Come again another day.**

traditional rhyme, mid 17th century

14 **Red sky at night, shepherd's delight; red sky in the morning, shepherd's warning.**

good and bad weather respectively is presaged by a red sky at sunset and dawn; English proverb, late 14th century

15 **Robin Hood could brave all weathers but a thaw wind.**

a *thaw wind* is a cold wind which accompanies the breaking up of frost; English proverb, mid 19th century

16 **Saint Swithin's day, if thou be fair, for forty days it will remain; Saint**

Swithin's day, if thou bring rain, for forty days it will remain.
St Swithin's day is 15 July, and the tradition may have its origin in the heavy rain said to have occurred when his relics were to be transferred to a shrine in Winchester cathedral; English proverb, early 17th century

17 **September blow soft till the fruit's in the loft.**
expressing the hope that fine weather often traditional in September will hold until a crop of apples or other fruit has been picked and stored; English proverb, late 16th century

18 **So many mists in March, so many frosts in May.**
mist or fog in March presages frost in May; English proverb, early 17th century

19 **There is no such thing as bad weather, only the wrong clothes.**
late 20th century saying

20 **When the oak is before the ash, then you will only get a splash; when the ash is before the oak, then you may expect a soak.**
a traditional way of predicting whether the summer will be wet or dry on the basis of whether the oak or the ash is first to come into leaf in the spring; English proverb, mid 19th century

21 **When the wind is in the east, 'tis neither good for man nor beast.**
referring to the traditional bitterness of the east wind; English proverb, early 17th century

phrases ▸

22 **borrowed days**
in Scottish tradition, the last three days of March (Old Style), said to have been borrowed from April and to be particularly stormy; see WEATHER 8

23 **the bow of promise**
a rainbow; after the Bible (Genesis) 'I do set my bow in the cloud, and it shall be for a token of a covenant between me and the earth'

24 **Groundhog Day**
in North American usage, a day (in most areas 2 February) which, if sunny, is believed to indicate wintry weather to come; from the story that, if there is enough sun for the *groundhog* (a woodchuck) to see its shadow, it retires underground for further hibernation

25 **Indian summer**
a period of calm dry warm weather in late autumn in the northern US or elsewhere; see OLD AGE 10

26 **London particular**
a dense fog affecting London; see WEATHER 37

27 **queen's weather**
fine weather; of the kind supposedly associated with public appearances by Queen Victoria

28 **St Luke's summer**
a period of fine weather occurring about the feast of St Luke (18 October)

29 **St Martin's summer**
a period of fine weather occurring about Martinmas (11 November)

quotations ▸

30 **There is no such thing as bad weather. All weather is good because it is God's.**
St Teresa of Ávila 1512–82: attributed; H. Ward and J. Wild (eds.) *The Lion Christian Quotation Collection* (1997)

31 **The uncertain glory of an April day.**
William Shakespeare 1564–1616: *The Two Gentlemen of Verona* (1592–3)

32 **So foul and fair a day I have not seen.**
William Shakespeare 1564–1616: *Macbeth* (1606)

33 **When two Englishmen meet, their first talk is of the weather.**
Samuel Johnson 1709–84: in *The Idler* 24 June 1758

34 **What dreadful hot weather we have! It keeps one in a continual state of inelegance.**
Jane Austen 1775–1817: letter, 18 September 1796

35 **The frost performs its secret ministry,**
Unhelped by any wind.
Samuel Taylor Coleridge 1772–1834: 'Frost at Midnight' (1798)

36 **O wild West Wind, thou breath of Autumn's being,**
Thou, from whose unseen presence the leaves dead
Are driven, like ghosts from an enchanter fleeing.
Percy Bysshe Shelley 1792–1822: 'Ode to the West Wind' (1819)

37 This is a London particular...A fog, miss.
Charles Dickens 1812–70: *Bleak House* (1853); see WEATHER 26

38 They say a green Yule makes a fat churchyard; but so does a white Yule too.
George Eliot 1819–80: *The Sad Fortunes of the Reverend Amos Barton* (1858); see CHRISTMAS 3

39 Welcome, wild North-easter!
Shame it is to see
Odes to every zephyr;
Ne'er a verse to thee.
Charles Kingsley 1819–75: 'Ode to the North-East Wind' (1858)

40 There is a sumptuous variety about the New England weather that compels the stranger's admiration—and regret. The weather is always doing something there; always attending strictly to business; always getting up new designs and trying them on the people to see how they will go.
Mark Twain 1835–1910: speech to New England Society, 22 December 1876

41 The weather is like the Government, always in the wrong.
Jerome K. Jerome 1859–1927: *Idle Thoughts of an Idle Fellow* (1889)

42 The rain, it raineth on the just
And also on the unjust fella:
But chiefly on the just, because
The unjust steals the just's umbrella.
Lord Bowen 1835–94: Walter Sichel *Sands of Time* (1923); see EQUALITY 4

43 The yellow fog that rubs its back upon the window-panes.
T. S. Eliot 1888–1965: 'The Love Song of J. Alfred Prufrock' (1917)

44 No one can tell me,
Nobody knows,
Where the wind comes from,
Where the wind goes.
A. A. Milne 1882–1956: 'Wind on the Hill' (1927)

45 Thank heavens, the sun has gone in, and I don't have to go out and enjoy it.
Logan Pearsall Smith 1865–1946: *Afterthoughts* (1931)

46 It ain't a fit night out for man or beast.
W. C. Fields 1880–1946: adopted by Fields but claimed by him not to be original; letter, 8 February 1944

47 A woman rang to say she heard there was a hurricane on the way. Well don't worry, there isn't.
weather forecast on the night before serious gales in southern England
Michael Fish 1944– : BBC TV, 15 October 1987

48 Rain is grace; rain is the sky condescending to the earth; without rain, there would be no life.
John Updike 1932–2009: *Self-Consciousness: Memoirs* (1989)

49 We are having particular problems on this occasion with the type of snow, which is very dry and powdery and is actually penetrating all the protection we had on some of our locomotives.
spokesman explaining disruption on British Rail
Terry Worrall: in *Evening Standard* 11 February 1991; see WEATHER 50

50 British Rail, which last week predicted that it was ready for the worst the weather could do, now blames the near-total dislocation of its services on 'the wrong sort of snow'.
Anonymous: leader in *Evening Standard* 12 February 1991; WEATHER 49

Weddings
see also MARRIAGE

proverbs and sayings ▸

1 Always a bridesmaid, never a bride.
recording the belief that to be a bridesmaid too often is unlucky for one's own chances of marriage; English proverb, late 19th century

2 Happy is the bride that the sun shines on.
English proverb, mid 17th century

3 Marry in May, rue for aye.
English proverb, late 17th century; see SEASONS 5

4 Now you will feel no rain, for each of you will be shelter for the other. Now you will feel no cold, for each of you will be warmth for the other.
from the saying known as the 'Apache Blessing'

5 One wedding brings another.
English proverb, mid 17th century

quotations ▶

6 As the bridegroom rejoiceth over the bride.
Bible: Isaiah

7 Look, how my ring encompasseth thy finger,
Even so thy breast encloseth my poor heart;
Wear both of them, for both of them are thine.
William Shakespeare 1564–1616: *Venus and Adonis* (1593)

8 With this Ring I thee wed, with my body I thee worship, and with all my worldly goods I thee endow.
The Book of Common Prayer 1662: *Solemnization of Matrimony* Wedding

9 The flowers in the bride's hand are sadly like the garland which decked the heifers of sacrifice in old times.
Thomas Hardy 1840–1928: *Jude the Obscure* (1896)

10 If it were not for the presents, an elopement would be preferable.
George Ade 1866–1944: *Forty Modern Fables* (1901)

11 Why am I always the bridesmaid,
Never the blushing bride?
Fred W. Leigh d. 1924: 'Why Am I Always the Bridesmaid?' (1917 song, with Charles Collins and Lily Morris)

12 A man looks pretty small at a wedding, George. All those good women standing shoulder to shoulder, making sure that the knot's tied in a mighty public way.
Thornton Wilder 1897–1975: *Our Town* (1938)

13 I'm getting married in the morning,
Ding dong! The bells are gonna chime.
Pull out the stopper;
Let's have a whopper;
But get me to the church on time!
Alan Jay Lerner 1918–86: 'Get Me to the Church on Time' (1956 song)

14 The trouble
with being best man is, you don't get a chance to prove it.
Les A. Murray 1938– : *The Boys Who Stole the Funeral* (1989)

15 It's pretty easy. Just say 'I do' whenever anyone asks you a question.
Richard Curtis 1956– : *Four Weddings and a Funeral* (1994 film)

Winning and Losing

see also SUCCESS

proverbs and sayings ▶

1 All your base are belong to us.
deriving from the poor English translation of the Japanese video game Zero Wing, released 1989; late 20th century saying

2 Heads I win, tails you lose.
I win in any event; *heads* and *tails* the obverse and reverse images on a coin; English proverb, late 17th century

3 What you lose on the swings you gain on the roundabouts.
one's losses and gains tend to cancel one another out; English proverb, early 20th century; see CIRCUMSTANCE 20, WINNING 21

4 A winner never quits, and a quitter never wins.
American proverb, early 20th century

5 You can't win them all.
used as an expression of consolation or resignation; English proverb, mid 20th century

phrases ▶

6 Pyrrhic victory
a victory gained at too great a cost, like that of Pyrrhus over the Romans at Asculum in 279 BC: see WINNING 8

quotations ▶

7 To win one hundred victories in one hundred battles is not the acme of skill. To subdue the enemy without fighting is the acme of skill.
Sun Tzu fl. c.400–320 BC: *The Art of War*

8 One more such victory and we are lost.
on defeating the Romans at Asculum, 279 BC
Pyrrhus 319–272 BC: Plutarch *Parallel Lives* 'Pyrrhus'; see WINNING 6

9 The only safe course for the defeated is to expect no safety.
Virgil 70–19 BC: *Aeneid*

10 The happy state of winning the palm without the dust of racing.
Horace 65–8 BC: *Epistles*

11 Know ye not that they which run in a race run all, but one receiveth the prize.
Bible: I Corinthians

12 *Vae victis.*
Down with the defeated!
cry (already proverbial) of the Gallic King, Brennus, on capturing Rome (390 BC)
Livy 59 BC–AD 17: *Ab Urbe Condita*

13 Eclipse first, the rest nowhere.
comment on a horse-race at Epsom, 3 May 1769; *Eclipse* was the most famous racehorse of the 18th century, one of the ancestors in the direct male line of all thoroughbred racehorses throughout the world
Dennis O'Kelly 1720–87: in *Annals of Sporting* (1822); *Dictionary of National Biography* gives the occasion as the Queen's Plate at Winchester, 1769

14 When in doubt, win the trick.
Edmond Hoyle 1672–1769: *Hoyle's Games Improved* (ed. Charles Jones, 1790) 'Twenty-four Short Rules for Learners' (though attributed to Hoyle, this may well have been an editorial addition by Jones, since it is not found in earlier editions)

15 We have met the enemy and they are ours.
Oliver Hazard Perry 1785–1819: reporting his victory over the British in the battle of Lake Erie, 10 September 1813; see POLLUTION 22

16 'The game,' said he, 'is never lost till won.'
George Crabbe 1754–1832: *Tales of the Hall* (1819) 'Gretna Green'

17 The politicians of New York...see nothing wrong in the rule, that to the victor belong the spoils of the enemy.
William Learned Marcy 1786–1857: speech to the Senate, 25 January 1832

18 EVERYBODY has won, and all must have prizes.
Lewis Carroll 1832–98: *Alice's Adventures in Wonderland* (1865)

19 We are not interested in the possibilities of defeat; they do not exist.
on the Boer War during 'Black Week', December 1899
Queen Victoria 1819–1901: Lady Gwendolen Cecil *Life of Robert, Marquis of Salisbury* (1931)

20 The important thing in life is not the victory but the contest; the essential thing is not to have won but to have fought well.
Baron Pierre de Coubertin 1863–1937: speech on the Olympic Games, London, 24 July 1908

21 What's lost upon the roundabouts we pulls up on the swings!
Patrick Reginald Chalmers 1872–1942: 'Roundabouts and Swings' (1912); see WINNING 3

22 Honey, I just forgot to duck.
to his wife, on losing the World Heavyweight title, 23 September 1926
Jack Dempsey 1895–1983: J. and B. P. Dempsey *Dempsey* (1977); after a failed attempt on his life in 1981, Ronald Reagan quipped to his wife 'Honey, I forgot to duck'

23 What is our aim?...Victory, victory at all costs, victory in spite of all terror; victory, however long and hard the road may be; for without victory, there is no survival.
Winston Churchill 1874–1965: speech, House of Commons, 13 May 1940

24 The war situation has developed not necessarily to Japan's advantage.
announcing Japan's surrender, in a broadcast to his people after atom bombs had destroyed Hiroshima and Nagasaki
Emperor Hirohito 1901–89: on 15 August 1945

25 Man is not made for defeat. A man can be destroyed but not defeated.
Ernest Hemingway 1899–1961: *The Old Man and the Sea* (1952)

26 Sure, winning isn't everything. It's the only thing.
Henry 'Red' Sanders: in *Sports Illustrated* 26 December 1955; often attributed to Vince Lombardi

27 Show me a good loser and I'll show you a loser.
Vince Lombardi 1913–70: attributed

28 Defeat doesn't finish a man—quit does. A man is not finished when he's defeated. He's finished when he quits.
Richard Nixon 1913–94: William Safire *Before the Fall* (1975)

29 The moment of victory is much too short to live for that and nothing else.
Martina Navratilova 1956– : in *Independent* 21 June 1989

30 Winning is everything. The only ones who remember you when you come second are your wife and your dog.
Damon Hill 1960– : in *Sunday Times* 18 December 1994

31 Sometimes it is better to lose and do the right thing than to win and do the wrong thing.
Tony Blair 1953– : on losing the vote on the Terrorism Bill, 9 November 2005

Wisdom

see also KNOWLEDGE

proverbs and sayings ▶

1 Fools ask questions that wise men cannot answer.
a foolish person may put a question to which there is no simple or easily given answer; English proverb, mid 17th century

2 Out of the mouths of babes—.
young children may sometimes speak with disconcerting wisdom; English proverb, late 19th century, with allusion to the Bible (Psalms), 'Out of the mouth of very babes and sucklings hast thou ordained strength, because of thine enemies'

quotations ▶

3 In our sleep, pain which cannot forget falls drop by drop upon the heart until, in our own despair, against our will, comes wisdom through the awful grace of God.
quoted by Robert Kennedy on the night of the assassination of Martin Luther King
Aeschylus c.525–456 BC: *Agamemnon*

4 The price of wisdom is above rubies.
Bible: Job

5 No man is wise at all times.
Pliny the Elder AD 23–79: *Natural History*

6 Authority without wisdom is like a heavy axe without an edge, fitter to bruise than polish.
Anne Bradstreet c.1612–72: *The Tenth Muse* (1650)

7 Wisdom is not the purchase of a day.
Thomas Paine 1737–1809: *The Crisis* (December 1776)

8 Knowledge is proud that he has learned so much;
Wisdom is humble that he knows no more.
William Cowper 1731–1800: *The Task* (1785)

9 Does the eagle know what is in the pit?
Or wilt thou go ask the mole:
Can wisdom be put in a silver rod?
Or love in a golden bowl?
William Blake 1757–1827: *The Book of Thel* (1789) plate i 'Thel's Motto'

10 One would need to be already wise, in order to love wisdom.
Friedrich von Schiller 1759–1805: *On the Aesthetic Education of Man* (1795) letter 8

11 The art of being wise is the art of knowing what to overlook.
William James 1842–1910: *The Principles of Psychology* (1890)

12 Courage was mine, and I had mystery,
Wisdom was mine, and I had mastery.
Wilfred Owen 1893–1918: 'Strange Meeting' (written 1918)

13 It may be a mistake to mix different wines but old and new wisdom mix admirably.
Bertolt Brecht 1898–1956: *The Caucasian Chalk Circle* (1944)

Wit and Wordplay

see also HUMOUR

proverbs and sayings ▶

1 Brevity is the soul of wit.
English proverb, early 17th century, from Shakespeare: see WIT 6

phrases ▶

2 Attic salt
refined, delicate, poignant wit; *Attic* of Attica, district of ancient Greece, or Athens, its chief city

3 esprit de l'escalier
a clever remark that occurs to one after the opportunity to make it is lost; French = staircase wit, from Denis Diderot (1713–84) *Paradoxe sur le Comédien* (written 1773–8) 'The witty riposte one thinks of only when one has left the drawing-room and is already on the way downstairs'

quotations ▸

4 Wit is educated insolence.
Aristotle 384–322 BC: *The Art of Rhetoric*

5 I am not only witty in myself, but the cause that wit is in other men.
William Shakespeare 1564–1616: *Henry IV, Part 2* (1597)

6 Brevity is the soul of wit.
William Shakespeare 1564–1616: *Hamlet* (1601); see WIT 1, WIT 18

7 A thing well said will be wit in all languages.
John Dryden 1631–1700: *An Essay of Dramatic Poesy* (1668)

8 Wit will shine
Through the harsh cadence of a rugged line.
John Dryden 1631–1700: 'To the Memory of Mr Oldham' (1684)

9 A man who could make so vile a pun would not scruple to pick a pocket.
John Dennis 1657–1734: editorial note in *The Gentleman's Magazine* (1781)

10 Apt Alliteration's artful aid.
Charles Churchill 1731–64: *The Prophecy of Famine* (1763)

11 If I reprehend any thing in this world, it is the use of my oracular tongue, and a nice derangement of epitaphs!
Richard Brinsley Sheridan 1751–1816: *The Rivals* (1775)

12 There's no possibility of being witty without a little ill-nature; the malice of a good thing is the barb that makes it stick.
Richard Brinsley Sheridan 1751–1816: *The School for Scandal* (1777)

13 His wit invites you by his looks to come,
But when you knock it never is at home.
William Cowper 1731–1800: 'Conversation' (1782)

14 What is an Epigram? a dwarfish whole,
Its body brevity, and wit its soul.
Samuel Taylor Coleridge 1772–1834: 'Epigram' (1809)

15 Wit is the salt of conversation, not the food.
William Hazlitt 1778–1830: *Lectures on the English Comic Writers* (1819)

16 [A pun] is a pistol let off at the ear; not a feather to tickle the intellect.
Charles Lamb 1775–1834: *Last Essays of Elia* (1833) 'Popular Fallacies'

17 Wit is the epitaph of an emotion.
Friedrich Nietzsche 1844–1900: *Menschliches, Allzumenschliches* (1867–80)

18 Impropriety is the soul of wit.
W. Somerset Maugham 1874–1965: *The Moon and Sixpence* (1919); see WIT 6

19 If, with the literate, I am
Impelled to try an epigram,
I never seek to take the credit;
We all assume that Oscar said it.
Dorothy Parker 1893–1967: 'A Pig's-Eye View of Literature' (1937)

20 Satire is a lesson, parody is a game.
Vladimir Nabokov 1899–1977: *Strong Opinions* (1974)

Woman's Role
see also MEN AND WOMEN

proverbs and sayings ▸

1 Burn your bra.
feminist slogan, 1970s

2 Silence is a woman's best garment.
often used as recommending a traditionally submissive and discreet role for women; English proverb, mid 16th century

3 Votes for women.
slogan of the women's suffrage movement, adopted when it proved impossible to use a banner with the longer slogan 'Will the Liberal Party Give Votes for Women?' made by Emmeline Pankhurst, Christabel Pankhurst, and Annie Kenney

4 A woman's place is in the home.
reflecting the traditional view of a woman's role; English proverb, mid 19th century

phrases ▸

5 the angel in the house
a woman who is completely devoted to her husband and family; from the title of a poem (1854–62) by Coventry Patmore; now often used ironically

quotations ▸

6 Men are the managers of the affairs of women.
The Koran: sura 4

7 The First Blast of the Trumpet Against the Monstrous Regiment of Women.
regiment = rule or government over a country, directed against the rule of Mary Tudor in England and Mary of Lorraine in Scotland (as regent for her daughter Mary Queen of Scots)
John Knox 1505–72: title of pamphlet (1558)

8 I am obnoxious to each carping tongue,
Who says my hand a needle better fits,
A poet's pen, all scorn, I should thus wrong.
Anne Bradstreet 1612–72: 'The Prologue' (1650)

9 If all men are born free, how is it that all women are born slaves?
Mary Astell 1668–1731: *Some Reflections upon Marriage* (1706 ed.)

10 A woman's preaching is like a dog's walking on his hinder legs. It is not done well; but you are surprised to find it done at all.
Samuel Johnson 1709–84: James Boswell *Life of Samuel Johnson* (1791) 31 July 1763

11 In the new code of laws which I suppose it will be necessary for you to make I desire you would remember the ladies, and be more generous and favourable to them than your ancestors. Do not put such unlimited power into the hands of the husbands. Remember all men would be tyrants if they could.
Abigail Adams 1744–1818: letter to John Adams, 31 March 1776

12 A man is in general better pleased when he has a good dinner upon his table, than when his wife talks Greek.
Samuel Johnson 1709–84: John Hawkins (ed.) *The Works of Samuel Johnson* (1787) 'Apophthegms, Sentiments, Opinions, etc.'

13 I do not wish them [women] to have power over men; but over themselves.
Mary Wollstonecraft 1759–97: *A Vindication of the Rights of Woman* (1792)

14 That little man...he says women can't have as much rights as men, cause Christ wasn't a woman. Where did your Christ come from? From God and a woman. Man had nothing to do with Him.
Sojourner Truth 1797–1883: speech at Women's Rights Convention, Akron, Ohio, 1851

15 I should like to know what is the proper function of women, if it is not to make reasons for husbands to stay at home, and still stronger reasons for bachelors to go out.
George Eliot 1819–80: *The Mill on the Floss* (1860)

16 I want to be something so much worthier than the doll in the doll's house.
Charles Dickens 1812–70: *Our Mutual Friend* (1865)

17 Men, their rights, and nothing more; women, their rights, and nothing less.
Susan Brownell Anthony 1820–1906: motto of the newspaper *The Revolution*, 8 January 1868

18 The Queen is most anxious to enlist every one who can speak or write to join in checking this mad, wicked folly of 'Woman's Rights', with all its attendant horrors, on which her poor feeble sex is bent, forgetting every sense of womanly feeling and propriety.
Queen Victoria 1819–1901: letter to Theodore Martin, 29 May 1870

19 We are here to claim our right as women, not only to be free, but to fight for freedom. That it is our right as well as our duty.
Christabel Pankhurst 1880–1958: in *Votes for Women* 31 March 1911

20 I myself have never been able to find out precisely what feminism is: I only know that people call me a feminist whenever I express sentiments that differentiate me from a doormat or a prostitute.
Rebecca West 1892–1983: in *The Clarion* 14 November 1913

21 De nigger woman is de mule uh de world.
Zora Neale Hurston c.1901–60: *Their Eyes Were Watching God* (1937); see WOMAN'S ROLE 23

22 **Back of every great work we can find the self-sacrificing devotion of a woman.**
Anonymous: plaque on Brooklyn Bridge, New York, 1951, referring to the contribution of Emily Roebling (1843–1903) to its construction

23 **Woman is the nigger of the world.**
Yoko Ono 1933– : remark made in a 1968 interview for *Nova* magazine and adopted by John Lennon as the title of a song (1972); see WOMAN'S ROLE 21

24 **But if God had wanted us to think just with our wombs, why did He give us a brain?**
Clare Booth Luce 1903–87: in *Life* 16 October 1970

25 **Women's Liberation is just a lot of foolishness. It's the men who are discriminated against. They can't bear children. And no-one's likely to do anything about that.**
Golda Meir 1898–1978: in *Newsweek* 23 October 1972

26 **We are becoming the men we wanted to marry.**
Gloria Steinem 1934– : in *Ms* July/August 1982

27 **Womanist is to feminist as purple to lavender.**
Alice Walker 1944– : *In Search of Our Mother's Gardens* (1983), epigraph

28 **The freedom women were supposed to have found in the Sixties largely boiled down to easy contraception and abortion: things to make life easier for men, in fact.**
Julie Burchill 1960– : *Damaged Goods* (1986)

29 **I could have stayed home and baked cookies and had teas. But what I decided was to fulfil my profession, which I entered before my husband was in public life.**
Hillary Rodham Clinton 1947– : comment on questions raised by rival Democratic contender Edmund G. Brown Jr.; in *Albany Times-Union* 17 March 1992

30 **Women have been trained to speak softly and carry lipstick. Those days are over.**
Bella Abzug 1920–98: attributed; in *Times* 2 April 1998; see DIPLOMACY 11

31 **I want to deal with women's issues because I just don't think they clean behind the fridge enough.**
view of a UKIP MEP
Godfrey Bloom 1949– : in *Guardian* 21 July 2004

Women

see also MEN AND WOMEN

proverbs and sayings ▸

1 **Far-fetched and dear-bought is good for ladies.**
expensive or exotic articles are suitable for women; English proverb, mid 14th century

2 **The female of the species is more deadly than the male.**
English proverb, early 20th century; from Kipling: see WOMEN 38

3 **The hand that rocks the cradle rules the world.**
referring to the strength of a woman's indirect influence on the male world; English proverb, mid 19th century; see PARENTS 16

4 **Hell hath no fury like a woman scorned.**
a woman whose love has turned to hate is the most savage of creatures; a *fury* here may be either one of the avenging deities of classical mythology, or more generally someone in a state of frenzied rage; English proverb, late 17th century, see REVENGE 17

5 **Long and lazy, little and loud; fat and fulsome, pretty and proud.**
categorizing supposed physical and temperamental characteristics in women; English proverb, late 16th century

6 **The prettiest girl in the world can only give what she has.**
French proverb

7 **A whistling woman and a crowing hen are neither fit for God nor men.**
both the woman and the hen are considered unnatural, and therefore unlucky; English proverb, early 18th century

8 **A woman, a dog, and a walnut tree, the more you beat them the better they be.**
the walnut tree was beaten firstly to bring down the fruit, and then to break down long shoots and encourage short fruit-bearing ones; English proverb, late 16th century

9 A woman and a ship ever want mending.
both women and ships require constant attention and expenditure; English proverb, late 16th century

10 Women hold up half the sky.
women should be considered equal in status to men; Chinese proverb

phrases ▸

11 daughter of Eve
a woman, especially one regarded as showing a typically feminine trait

12 Essex girl
a derogatory term applied to a type of young woman, supposedly to be found in and around Essex, and variously characterized as unintelligent, promiscuous, and materialistic; she is typically the butt of politically incorrect jokes; see also CLASS 4

13 the fair sex
the female sex, women collectively; see WOMEN 33

14 It girl
an actress or model, usually vivacious and outgoing, considered to have particular sex appeal. In later use, also a young woman who has achieved celebrity because of her socialite lifestyle; coined by the screenwriter Elinor Glyn (1864–1943) and personified by the actress Clara Bow (1905–65). The use of *it* meaning sex appeal is first recorded in Kipling: see SEX 19

15 page three girl
a model whose nude or semi-nude photograph appears as part of a regular series in a tabloid newspaper; after the standard page position in the *Sun*, a British newspaper: see JOURNALISM 6

quotations ▸

16 This is now bone of my bones, and flesh of my flesh: she shall be called Woman, because she was taken out of Man.
Bible: Genesis

17 Who can find a virtuous woman? for her price is far above rubies.
Bible: Proverbs

18 The greatest glory of a woman is to be least talked about by men.
Pericles c.495–429 BC: Thucydides *History of the Peloponnesian War*

19 Men say of us that we live a life free from danger at home while they fight wars. How wrong they are! I would rather stand three times in the battle line than bear one child.
Euripides c.485–c.406 BC: *Medea*

20 *Varium et mutabile semper*
Femina.
Fickle and changeable always is woman.
Virgil 70–19 BC: *Aeneid*

21 Whoever has a daughter and does not bury her alive, nor insult her nor favour his son over her, Allah will enter him into Paradise.
Ahmad ibn Hanbal 780–855: Musnad no. 1957

22 Frailty, thy name is woman!
William Shakespeare 1564–1616: *Hamlet* (1601)

23 The weaker sex, to piety more prone.
William Alexander, Earl of Stirling 1567–1640: 'Doomsday' 5th Hour (1637)

24 She knows her man, and when you rant and swear,
Can draw you to her *with a single hair*.
John Dryden 1631–1700: translation of Persius *Satires*; see BEAUTY 1

25 Woman's at best a contradiction still.
Alexander Pope 1688–1744: *Epistles to Several Persons* 'To a Lady' (1735)

26 Women, then, are only children of a larger growth.
Lord Chesterfield 1694–1773: *Letters to his Son* (1774) 5 September 1748

27 Auld nature swears, the lovely dears
Her noblest work she classes, O;
Her prentice han' she tried on man,
An' then she made the lasses, O.
Robert Burns 1759–96: 'Green Grow the Rashes' (1787)

28 O Woman! in our hours of ease,
Uncertain, coy, and hard to please,
And variable as the shade
By the light quivering aspen made;
When pain and anguish wring the brow,
A ministering angel thou!
Sir Walter Scott 1771–1832: *Marmion* (1808); see CHARITY 12

29 All the privilege I claim for my own sex...is that of loving longest, when existence or when hope is gone.
Jane Austen 1775–1817: *Persuasion* (1818)

30 In her first passion woman loves her lover,
In all the others all she loves is love.
Lord Byron 1788–1824: *Don Juan* (1819–24)

31 Eternal Woman draws us upward.
Johann Wolfgang von Goethe 1749–1832: *Faust* pt. 2 (1832) 'Hochgebirg'

32 The woman is so hard
Upon the woman.
Alfred, Lord Tennyson 1809–92: *The Princess* (1847)

33 Only the male intellect, clouded by sexual impulse, could call the undersized, narrow-shouldered, broad-hipped, and short-legged sex the fair sex.
Arthur Schopenhauer 1788–1860: 'On Women' (1851); see WOMEN 13

34 The happiest women, like the happiest nations, have no history.
George Eliot 1819–80: *The Mill on the Floss* (1860)

35 Woman was God's second blunder.
Friedrich Nietzsche 1844–1900: *Der Antichrist* (1888)

36 When you get to a man in the case,
They're like as a row of pins—
For the Colonel's Lady an' Judy O'Grady
Are sisters under their skins!
Rudyard Kipling 1865–1936: 'The Ladies' (1896)

37 The prime truth of woman, the universal mother...that if a thing is worth doing, it is worth doing badly.
G. K. Chesterton 1874–1936: *What's Wrong with the World* (1910) 'Folly and Female Education'; see EFFORT 6

38 The female of the species is more deadly than the male.
Rudyard Kipling 1865–1936: 'The Female of the Species' (1919); see WOMEN 2

39 Certain women should be struck regularly, like gongs.
Noël Coward 1899–1973: *Private Lives* (1930)

40 The great and almost only comfort about being a woman is that one can always pretend to be more stupid than one is and no one is surprised.
Freya Stark 1893–1993: *The Valleys of the Assassins* (1934)

41 Woman may born you, love you, an' mourn you,
But a woman is a sometime thing.
Du Bose Heyward 1885–1940 and **Ira Gershwin** 1896–1983: 'A Woman is a Sometime Thing' (1935 song)

42 The great question that has never been answered and which I have not yet been able to answer, despite my thirty years of research into the feminine soul, is 'What does a woman want?'
Sigmund Freud 1856–1939: to Marie Bonaparte; Ernest Jones *Sigmund Freud: Life and Work* (1955)

43 One is not born a woman: one becomes one.
Simone de Beauvoir 1908–86: *Le deuxième sexe* (1949)

44 There is nothin' like a dame.
Oscar Hammerstein II 1895–1960: title of song (1949)

45 Thank heaven for little girls!
For little girls get bigger every day.
Alan Jay Lerner 1918–86: 'Thank Heaven for Little Girls' (1958 song)

46 I got a twenty dollar piece says
There ain't nothin' I can't do.
I can make a dress out of a feed bag an' I can make a man out of you.
'Cause I'm a woman
W-O-M-A-N
I'll say it again.
Jerry Leiber 1933– : 'I'm a Woman' (1962 song)

47 From birth to 18 a girl needs good parents. From 18 to 35, she needs good looks. From 35 to 55, good personality. From 55 on, she needs good cash.
Sophie Tucker 1884–1966: Michael Freedland *Sophie* (1978)

48 She takes just like a woman, yes, she does
She makes love just like a woman, yes, she does
And she aches just like a woman
But she breaks like a little girl.
Bob Dylan 1941– : 'Just Like a Woman' (1966 song)

49 Sisterhood is powerful.
Robin Morgan 1941– : title of book (1970)

50 Show me a woman who doesn't feel guilty and I'll show you a man.
Erica Jong 1942– : *Fear of Flying* (1973)

51 Well-behaved women seldom make history.
Laurel Thatcher Ulrich 1938– : in 1976; *Well-Behaved Women Seldom Make History* (2007)

52 Being a woman is of special interest only to aspiring male transsexuals. To actual women, it is merely a good excuse not to play football.
Fran Lebowitz 1946– : *Metropolitan Life* (1978)

53 You can now see the Female Eunuch the world over...spreading herself wherever blue jeans and Coca-Cola may go. Wherever you see nail varnish, lipstick, brassieres, and high heels, the Eunuch has set up her camp.
Germaine Greer 1939– : *The Female Eunuch* (20th anniversary ed., 1991)

54 You can have it all, but you can't do it all.
Michelle Pfeiffer 1959– : attributed; in *Guardian* 4 January 1996

Wordplay
see WIT AND WORDPLAY

Words
see also LANGUAGE, MEANING, NAMES, WORDS AND DEEDS

proverbs and sayings ▸

1 All words are pegs to hang ideas on.
American proverb, late 19th century

2 Hard words break no bones.
the damage done by verbal attack is limited; English proverb, late 17th century

3 I before e, except after c.
traditional spelling rule, 19th century

4 If you take hyphens seriously you will surely go mad.
said to be from a style book in use with Oxford University Press, New York; perhaps apocryphal

5 Sticks and stones may break my bones, but words will never hurt me.
verbal attack does no real injury; English proverb, late 19th century

6 The swiftest horse cannot overtake the word once spoken.
Chinese proverb; see WORDS 8

7 That blessed word Mesopotamia.
supposed to have greatly consoled a pious but illiterate old woman; traditional, from the 1860s; see WORDS 14

quotations ▸

8 And once sent out a word takes wing beyond recall.
Horace 65–8 BC: *Epistles*; see WORDS 6

9 But words are words; I never yet did hear
That the bruised heart was piercèd through the ear.
William Shakespeare 1564–1616: *Othello* (1602–4)

10 Words are wise men's counters, they do but reckon by them: but they are the money of fools, that value them by the authority of an Aristotle, a Cicero, or a Thomas, or any other doctor whatsoever, if but a man.
Thomas Hobbes 1588–1679: *Leviathan* (1651)

11 Words easy to be understood do often hit the mark; when high and learned ones do only pierce the air.
John Bunyan 1628–88: *The Holy City* (1665)

12 Words are like leaves; and where they most abound,
Much fruit of sense beneath is rarely found.
Alexander Pope 1688–1744: *An Essay on Criticism* (1711)

13 I am not yet so lost in lexicography as to forget that words are the daughters of earth, and that things are the sons of heaven.
Samuel Johnson 1709–84: *A Dictionary of the English Language* (1755)

14 He could make men weep or tremble by his varied utterances of the word 'Mesopotamia.'
on the moving voice of the English Methodist preacher George Whitefield (1714–70)
David Garrick 1717–79: A. C. H. Seymour *The Life and Times of Selina, Countess of Huntingdon* (1840); see WORDS 7

15 It's exactly where a thought is lacking
That, just in time, a word shows up instead.
Goethe 1749–1832: *Faust* (1808)

16 With words we govern men.
Benjamin Disraeli 1804–81: *Contarini Fleming* (1832) pt. 1, ch. 21

17 'Do you spell it with a "V" or a "W"?' inquired the judge. 'That depends upon the taste and fancy of the speller, my Lord,' replied Sam [Weller].
Charles Dickens 1812–70: *Pickwick Papers* (1837)

18 'When *I* use a word,' Humpty Dumpty said in a rather scornful tone, 'it means just what I choose it to mean—neither more nor less.'
Lewis Carroll 1832–98: *Through the Looking-Glass* (1872)

19 Some word that teems with hidden meaning—like Basingstoke.
W. S. Gilbert 1836–1911: *Ruddigore* (1887)

20 I fear those big words, Stephen said, which make us so unhappy.
James Joyce 1882–1941: *Ulysses* (1922)

21 Words are, of course, the most powerful drug used by mankind.
Rudyard Kipling 1865–1936: speech, 14 February 1923

22 My spelling is Wobbly. It's good spelling but it Wobbles, and the letters get in the wrong places.
A. A. Milne 1882–1956: *Winnie-the-Pooh* (1926)

23 The man is not wholly evil: he has a Thesaurus in his cabin.
of Captain Hook
J. M. Barrie 1860–1937: *Peter Pan* (1928)

24 The Greeks had a word for it.
Zoë Akins 1886–1958: title of play (1930)

25 I gotta use words when I talk to you.
T. S. Eliot 1888–1965: *Sweeney Agonistes* (1932)

26 Words ought to be a little wild, for they are the assault of thoughts upon the unthinking.
John Maynard Keynes 1883–1946: in *New Statesman and Nation* 15 July 1933

27 Words strain,
Crack and sometimes break, under the burden,
Under the tension, slip, slide, perish,
Decay with imprecision, will not stay in place,
Will not stay still.
T. S. Eliot 1888–1965: *Four Quartets* 'Burnt Norton' (1936)

28 Man does not live by words alone, despite the fact that he sometimes has to eat them.
Adlai Stevenson 1900–65: *The Wit and Wisdom of Adlai Stevenson* (1965)

29 If *Miss* means respectably unmarried, and *Mrs* respectably married, then *Ms* means nudge, nudge, wink, wink.
Angela Carter 1940–92: 'The Language of Sisterhood' in Christopher Ricks (ed.) *The State of the Language* (1980); see SEX 6

30 Euphemisms are unpleasant truths wearing diplomatic cologne.
Quentin Crisp 1908–99: *Manners from Heaven* (1984)

31 'Refudiate,' 'misunderestimate,' 'weewee'd up.' English is a living language. Shakespeare liked to coin words, too.
following controversy over her use of the word 'refudiate'
Sarah Palin 1964– : tweet, 18 July 2010, in *Guardian* 20 July 2010

Words and Deeds

proverbs and sayings ▸

1 Actions speak louder than words.
real feeling is expressed not by what someone says but by what they do; English proverb, early 17th century

2 Brag is a good dog, but Holdfast is better.
perseverance is a better quality than ostentation; English proverb, early 18th century

3 Example is better than precept.
English proverb, early 15th century

4 Fine words butter no parsnips.
nothing is ever achieved by fine words alone (*butter* was the traditional garnish for parsnips); English proverb, mid 17th century

5 One picture is worth ten thousand words.
English proverb, early 20th century; see LANGUAGE 20

6 An ounce of practice is worth a pound of precept.
a small amount of practical assistance is worth more than a great deal of advice; English proverb, late 16th century

7 Practise what you preach.
you should follow the advice you give to others; English proverb, late 14th century

8 Talk is cheap.
it is easier to say than to do something; English proverb, mid 19th century

9 Threatened men live long.
threats are often not put into effect, and those who express resentment are actually much less dangerous than those who conceal animosity; English proverb, mid 16th century

quotations ▸

10 But be ye doers of the word, and not hearers only.
Bible: James

11 Woord is but wynd; leff woord and tak the dede.
John Lydgate c.1370–c.1451: *Secrets of Old Philosophers*

12 Do not, as some ungracious pastors do,
Show me the steep and thorny way to heaven,
Whiles, like a puffed and reckless libertine,
Himself the primrose path of dalliance treads,
And recks not his own rede.
William Shakespeare 1564–1616: *Hamlet* (1601); see PLEASURE 6

13 Oh that thou hadst like others been all words,
And no performance.
Philip Massinger 1583–1640: *The Parliament of Love* (1624)

14 Here lies a great and mighty king
Whose promise none relies on;
He never said a foolish thing,
Nor ever did a wise one.
on Charles II
John Wilmot, Lord Rochester 1647–80: 'The King's Epitaph' (alternatively 'Here lies our sovereign lord the King'); in C. E. Doble et al. *Thomas Hearne: Remarks and Collections* (1885–1921) 17 November 1706; see WORDS AND DEEDS 15

15 This is very true: for my words are my own, and my actions are my ministers'.
reply to Lord Rochester's epitaph
Charles II 1630–85: in *Thomas Hearne: Remarks and Collections* (1885–1921) 17 November 1706; see WORDS AND DEEDS 14

16 Because half a dozen grasshoppers under a fern make the field ring with their importunate chink, whilst thousands of great cattle, reposed beneath the shadow of the British oak, chew the cud and are silent, pray do not imagine that those who make the noise are the only inhabitants of the field.
Edmund Burke 1729–97: *Reflections on the Revolution in France* (1790)

17 The end of man is an action and not a thought, though it were the noblest.
Thomas Carlyle 1795–1881: *Sartor Resartus* (1834)

18 It is by acts and not by ideas that people live.
Anatole France 1844–1924: *La Vie littéraire* (1888)

19 Considering how foolishly people act and how pleasantly they prattle, perhaps it would be better for the world if they talked more and did less.
W. Somerset Maugham 1874–1965: *A Writer's Notebook* (1949) written in 1892

20 Words without actions are the assassins of idealism.
Herbert Hoover 1874–1964: attributed, in *Capital Times* (Madison, Wisconsin) 15 April 1930

21 Enough of talking—it is time now to do.
Tony Blair 1953– : on taking office as Prime Minister; Downing Street, 2 May 1997

Work

see also EMPLOYMENT, IDLENESS, LEISURE

proverbs and sayings ▸

1 Arbeit macht frei.
German, *Work liberates*, words inscribed on the gates of Dachau concentration camp, 1933, and subsequently on those of Auschwitz

2 Every man to his trade.
one should operate within one's own area of expertise; English proverb, late 16th century

3 **Fools and bairns should never see half-done work.**
the unwise and the inexperienced may judge the quality of a finished article from its rough unfinished state; English proverb, early 18th century

4 **One volunteer is worth two pressed men.**
a *pressed man* was someone forcibly enlisted by the press gang, a body of men which in the 18th and 19th centuries was employed to enlist men forcibly into service in the army or navy; English proverb, early 18th century

5 **Practice makes perfect.**
often used as an encouragement; English proverb, mid 16th century

6 **Root, hog, or die.**
advocating hard work and independence: *root* (of an animal) = turn up the ground with its snout in search of food; American proverb, early 19th century

7 **Saturday's child works hard for its living.**
traditional rhyme, mid 19th century; see also BEAUTY 7, GIFTS 2, PREGNANCY 1, SORROW 2, TRAVEL 8

8 **A short horse is soon curried.**
a slight task is soon completed (literally, that it does not take long to rub down a short horse with a curry-comb); English proverb, mid 14th century

9 **Too many cooks spoil the broth.**
the involvement of too many people is likely to mean that something is done badly; English proverb, late 16th century

10 **Two boys are half a boy, and three boys are no boy at all.**
the more boys there are present, the less work will be done; English proverb, mid 20th century

11 **Where bees are, there is honey.**
industrious work is necessary to create riches; English proverb, early 17th century

12 **Work expands so as to fill the time available.**
English proverb, mid 20th century, from Parkinson: see WORK 39

phrases ▸

13 **the bread of idleness**
food or sustenance for which one has not worked; after the Bible (Proverbs) 'She…eateth not the bread of idleness'

14 **burn the midnight oil**
study late into the night; see WORK 25

15 **by the sweat of one's brow**
by one's own hard work; from the Bible: see WORK 20

16 **daily bread**
a livelihood; after the Bible (Matthew) 'Give us this day our daily bread' (part of the Lord's Prayer)

17 **a glutton for punishment**
a person who is always eager to undertake hard or unpleasant tasks. *Glutton of* — was used figuratively from the early 18th century for someone who is inordinately fond of the thing specified, especially translating the Latin phrase *helluo librorum* 'a glutton of books'. The current usage may originate with early 19th-century sporting slang

18 **ply the labouring oar**
do much of the work; *labouring oar* = the hardest to pull, originally with allusion to Dryden *Aeneid* 'three Trojans tug at ev'ry lab'ring oar'

19 **sing for one's supper**
provide a service in order to earn a benefit; after the nursery rhyme *Little Tommy Tucker*

quotations ▸

20 **In the sweat of thy face shalt thou eat bread.**
Bible: Genesis; see WORK 15

21 **Come unto me, all ye that labour and are heavy laden, and I will give you rest…**
For my yoke is easy, and my burden is light.
Bible: St Matthew

22 **If any would not work, neither should he eat.**
Bible: II Thessalonians; see IDLENESS 8

23 **Set thy heart upon thy work but never upon its reward. Work not for a reward: but never cease to do thy work.**
Bhagavadgita: ch. 2, v. 47

24 **The labour we delight in physics pain.**
William Shakespeare 1564–1616: *Macbeth* (1606)

25 **We spend our midday sweat, our midnight oil;**
We tire the night in thought, the day in toil.
Francis Quarles 1592–1644: *Emblems* (1635); see WORK 14

26 How doth the little busy bee
Improve each shining hour,
And gather honey all the day
From every opening flower!
Isaac Watts 1674–1748: 'Against Idleness and Mischief' (1715); see EFFORT 13

27 If you have great talents, industry will improve them: if you have but moderate abilities, industry will supply their deficiency.
Joshua Reynolds 1723–92: *Discourses on Art* 11 December 1769

28 The world is too much with us; late and soon,
Getting and spending, we lay waste our powers.
William Wordsworth 1770–1850: 'The world is too much with us' (1807)

29 My life is one demd horrid grind!
Charles Dickens 1812–70: *Nicholas Nickleby* (1839)

30 Blessèd are the horny hands of toil!
James Russell Lowell 1819–91: 'A Glance Behind the Curtain' (1844)

31 For men must work, and women must weep,
And there's little to earn, and many to keep,
Though the harbour bar be moaning.
Charles Kingsley 1819–75: 'The Three Fishers' (1858)

32 Labour without joy is base. Labour without sorrow is base. Sorrow without labour is base. Joy without labour is base.
John Ruskin 1819–1900: *Time and Tide* (1867)

33 Generations have trod, have trod, have trod;
And all is seared with trade; bleared, smeared with toil.
Gerard Manley Hopkins 1844–89: 'God's Grandeur' (written 1877)

34 I like work: it fascinates me. I can sit and look at it for hours. I love to keep it by me: the idea of getting rid of it nearly breaks my heart.
Jerome K. Jerome 1859–1927: *Three Men in a Boat* (1889)

35 Work is love made visible.
Kahlil Gibran 1883–1931: *The Prophet* (1923)

36 Who built Thebes of the seven gates?
In the books you will find the names of kings.
Did the kings haul up the lumps of rock?
Bertolt Brecht 1898–1956: 'Questions From A Worker Who Reads' (1935)

37 God give me work till my life shall end
And life till my work is done.
Winifred Holtby 1898–1935: epitaph; Vera Brittain *Testament of Friendship: the Story of Winifred Holtby* (1940)

38 Why should I let the toad *work*
Squat on my life?
Philip Larkin 1922–85: 'Toads' (1955)

39 Work expands so as to fill the time available for its completion.
C. Northcote Parkinson 1909–93: *Parkinson's Law* (1958); see WORK 12

40 Without work, all life goes rotten, but when work is soulless, life stifles and dies.
Albert Camus 1913–60: attributed; E. F. Schumacher *Good Work* (1979)

41 It has been my experience that one cannot, in any shape or form, depend on human relations for lasting reward. It is only work that truly satisfies.
Bette Davis 1908–89: *The Lonely Life* (1962)

42 Work was like a stick. It had two ends. When you worked for the knowing you gave them quality; when you worked for a fool you simply gave him eye-wash.
Alexander Solzhenitsyn 1918–2008: *One Day in the Life of Ivan Denisovich* (1962)

43 Work is much more fun than fun.
Noël Coward 1899–1973: in *Observer* 21 June 1963

44 It's true hard work never killed anybody, but I figure why take the chance?
Ronald Reagan 1911–2004: interview, *Guardian* 31 March 1987

45 I have long been of the opinion that if work were such a splendid thing the rich would have kept more of it for themselves.
Bruce Grocott 1940– : in *Observer* 22 May 1988

46 I have nothing to say of my working life, only that a tie is a noose, and

inverted though it is, it will hang a man nonetheless if he's not careful.
Yann Martel 1963– : *Life of Pi* (2001)

World War I

see also ARMED FORCES, WARFARE

proverbs and sayings ▸

1 Ils ne passeront pas.
French, *They shall not pass*, slogan used by the French army at the defence of Verdun in 1916; variously attributed to Marshal Pétain and to General Robert Nivelle, and taken up by the Republicans in the Spanish Civil War in the form '*No pasarán!*'; see DEFIANCE 16

phrases ▸

2 the Angels of Mons
protective spirits supposedly seen over the First World War battlefield. The origin was in fact a short story, 'The Angel of Mons' (1915) by Arthur Machen (1843–1947), which circulated widely by word of mouth as a factual account

3 Flanders poppy
a red poppy used as an emblem of the soldiers of the Allies who fell in the First World War; chosen as a flower which grew on the battlefields: see WORLD WAR I 15

4 lions led by donkeys
associated with British soldiers during the First World War; attributed to Max Hoffman (1869–1927) in Alan Clark *The Donkeys* (1961); this attribution has not been traced elsewhere, and the phrase is of much earlier origin

5 the Old Contemptibles
the British army in France in 1914; referring to the German Emperor's alleged mention of a 'contemptible little army'

6 the war to end wars
the war of 1914–18, as a war intended to make further wars impossible; after the title of book by H. G. Wells in 1914, *The War That Will End War*

quotations ▸

7 If there is ever another war in Europe, it will come out of some damned silly thing in the Balkans.
Otto von Bismarck 1815–98: quoted in speech, House of Commons, 16 August 1945

8 The lamps are going out all over Europe; we shall not see them lit again in our lifetime.
on the eve of the First World War
Edward Grey 1862–1933: *25 Years* (1925)

9 Do your duty bravely. Fear God. Honour the King.
Lord Kitchener 1850–1916: message to soldiers of the British Expeditionary Force, August 1914

10 *Gott strafe England!*
God punish England!
Alfred Funke 1869–1941: *Schwert und Myrte* (1914)

11 Belgium put the kibosh on the Kaiser.
Alf Ellerton: title of song (1914)

12 Now, God be thanked Who has matched us with His hour.
Rupert Brooke 1887–1915: 'Peace' (1914)

13 Oh! we don't want to lose you but we think you ought to go
For your King and your Country both need you so.
Paul Alfred Rubens 1875–1917: 'Your King and Country Want You' (1914 song)

14 My centre is giving way, my right is retreating, situation excellent, I am attacking.
Ferdinand Foch 1851–1929: message sent during the first Battle of the Marne, September 1914; R. Recouly *Foch* (1919)

15 In Flanders fields the poppies blow
Between the crosses, row on row.
John McCrae 1872–1918: 'In Flanders Fields' (1915); see WORLD WAR I 3

16 What passing-bells for these who die as cattle?
Only the monstrous anger of the guns.
Only the stuttering rifles' rapid rattle
Can patter out their hasty orisons.
Wilfred Owen 1893–1918: 'Anthem for Doomed Youth' (written 1917)

17 *Lafayette, nous voilà!*
Lafayette, we are here.
Charles E. Stanton 1859–1933: at the tomb of Lafayette in Paris, 4 July 1917

18 Over there, over there,
Send the word, send the word over there
That the Yanks are coming, the Yanks are coming...

We'll be over, we're coming over
And we won't come back till it's over,
over there.

George M. Cohan 1878–1942: 'Over There' (1917 song); see WORLD WAR II 1

19 If I were fierce, and bald, and short of
breath,
I'd live with scarlet Majors at the Base,
And speed glum heroes up the line to
death.

Siegfried Sassoon 1886–1967: 'Base Details' (1918)

20 O Death, where is thy
sting-a-ling-a-ling,
O grave, thy victory?
The bells of Hell go ting-a-ling-a-ling
For you but not for me.

Anonymous: 'For You But Not For Me' (First World War song); see DEATH 31

21 My home policy: I wage war; my foreign policy: I wage war. All the time I wage war.

Georges Clemenceau 1841–1929: speech to French Chamber of Deputies, 8 March 1918

22 At eleven o'clock this morning came to an end the cruellest and most terrible war that has ever scourged mankind. I hope we may say that thus, this fateful morning, came to an end all wars.

David Lloyd George 1863–1945: speech, House of Commons, 11 November 1918

23 You are all a lost generation.

of the young who served in the First World War; phrase borrowed (in translation) from a French garage mechanic, whom Stein heard address it disparagingly to an incompetent apprentice

Gertrude Stein 1874–1946: Ernest Hemingway subsequently took it as his epigraph to *The Sun Also Rises* (1926)

24 All quiet on the western front.

Erich Maria Remarque 1898–1970: English title of *Im Westen nichts Neues* (1929 novel)

25 See that little stream—we could walk to it in two minutes. It took the British a month to walk it—a whole empire walking very slowly, dying in front and pushing forward behind. And another empire walked very slowly backward a few inches a day, leaving the dead like a million bloody rugs.

F. Scott Fitzgerald 1896–1940: *Tender is the Night* (1934)

26 Oh what a lovely war.

Joan Littlewood 1914–2002 and **Charles Chilton** 1914– : title of stage show (1963)

World War II

see also WARFARE

proverbs and sayings ▸

1 Overpaid, overfed, oversexed, and over here.

of American troops in Britain during the Second World War; associated with Tommy Trinder, but probably not his invention; see WORLD WAR I 18

phrases ▸

2 the Baedeker raids

a series of German reprisal air raids in 1942 on places in Britain of cultural and historical importance; after the series of guidebooks published by Karl *Baedeker* (1801–59), German publisher

3 the Battle of Britain

a series of air battles fought over Britain (August–October 1940), in which the RAF successfully resisted raids by the numerically superior German air force; from Winston Churchill, 18 June 1940, 'What General Weygand called the Battle of France is over. I expect that the Battle of Britain is about to begin'; the words 'The Battle of Britain is about to begin' appeared in the order of the day for pilots on 10 July

4 the Desert Fox

Erwin Rommel (1891–1944), German Field Marshal, from his early successes in the North African campaign, 1941–2

5 the desert rats

soldiers of the 7th British armoured division in the North African desert campaign of 1941–2; the badge of the division was a jerboa

6 the forgotten army

the British army in Burma after the fall of Rangoon in 1942 and the evacuation west, and the subsequent cutting by the Japanese of the supply link from India to Nationalist China; said to derive from Lord Louis Mountbatten's encouragement to his troops after taking over as supreme Allied commander in South-East Asia, 'You are not the Forgotten Army—no one's even heard of you'

7 Old Blood and Guts
George Patton (1885–1945); name given to General Patton by his men; see WARFARE 52

quotations ▸

8 How horrible, fantastic, incredible it is that we should be digging trenches and trying on gas-masks here because of a quarrel in a far away country between people of whom we know nothing.
on Germany's annexation of the Sudetenland
Neville Chamberlain 1869–1940: radio broadcast, 27 September 1938

9 We're gonna hang out the washing on the Siegfried Line.
Jimmy Kennedy and **Michael Carr**: title of song (1939)

10 We shall not flag or fail. We shall go on to the end. We shall fight in France, we shall fight on the seas and oceans, we shall fight with growing confidence and growing strength in the air, we shall defend our island, whatever the cost may be. We shall fight on the beaches, we shall fight on the landing grounds, we shall fight in the fields and in the streets, we shall fight in the hills; we shall never surrender.
Winston Churchill 1874–1965: speech, House of Commons, 4 June 1940

11 This little steamer, like all her brave and battered sisters, is immortal. She'll go sailing proudly down the years in the epic of Dunkirk. And our great-grand-children, when they learn how we began this war by snatching glory out of defeat, and then swept on to victory, may also learn how the little holiday steamers made an excursion to hell and came back glorious.
J. B. Priestley 1894–1984: radio broadcast, 5 June 1940; see CRISES 8

12 France has lost a battle. But France has not lost the war!
Charles de Gaulle 1890–1970: proclamation, 18 June 1940

13 Let us therefore brace ourselves to our duty, and so bear ourselves that, if the British Empire and its Commonwealth lasts for a thousand years, men will still say, 'This was their finest hour.'
Winston Churchill 1874–1965: speech, House of Commons, 18 June 1940; see SUCCESS 17

14 I'm glad we've been bombed. It makes me feel I can look the East End in the face.
Queen Elizabeth, the Queen Mother 1900–2002: to a London policeman, 13 September 1940

15 We have the men—the skill—the wealth—and above all, the will...We must be the great arsenal of democracy.
Franklin D. Roosevelt 1882–1945: 'Fireside Chat' radio broadcast, 29 December 1940

16 Yesterday, December 7, 1941—a date which will live in infamy—the United States of America was suddenly and deliberately attacked by naval and air forces of the Empire of Japan.
Franklin D. Roosevelt 1882–1945: address to Congress, 8 December 1941

17 Sighted sub, sank same.
on sinking a Japanese submarine in the Atlantic region (the first US naval success in the war)
Donald Mason 1913– : radio message, 28 January 1942

18 I came through and I shall return.
on reaching Australia, having broken through Japanese lines en route from Corregidor
Douglas MacArthur 1880–1964: statement in Adelaide, 20 March 1942

19 Don't let's be beastly to the Germans
When our Victory is ultimately won.
Noël Coward 1899–1973: 'Don't Let's Be Beastly to the Germans' (1943 song)

20 The first twenty-four hours of the invasion will be decisive...for the Allies, as well as Germany, it will be the longest day.
Erwin Rommel – : to his aide, 22 April 1944; Cornelius Ryan *The Longest Day: June 6, 1944* (1959); see BEGINNING 14

21 I think we might be going a bridge too far.
expressing reservations about the Arnhem 'Market Garden' operation
Frederick ('Boy') Browning 1896–1965: to Field Marshal Montgomery on 10 September 1944

22 The Third Fleet's sunken and damaged ships have been salvaged and are retiring at high speed toward the enemy.
on hearing claims that the Japanese had virtually annihilated the US fleet
W. F. ('Bull') Halsey 1882–1959: report, 14 October 1944

23 Nuts!

Anthony McAuliffe 1898–1975: replying to the German demand for surrender at Bastogne, Belgium, 22 December 1944

24 I would not regard the whole of the remaining cities of Germany as worth the bones of one British Grenadier.

supporting the continued strategic bombing of German cities

Arthur Harris 1892–1984: letter to Norman Bottomley, deputy Chief of Air Staff, 29 March 1945; Max Hastings *Bomber Command* (1979); see WARFARE 37

25 Of all the crosses I have had to bear during this war, the heaviest has been the Cross of Lorraine.

the Cross of Lorraine was the symbol of the Free French forces, led by General de Gaulle

Edward Spears 1886–1974: attributed in *Times* 1 June 2006, and often attributed to Winston Churchill who subsequently used it; Martin Gilbert *Churchill: A Life* (1991); see SUFFERING 5

26 Who do you think you are kidding,
Mister Hitler?
If you think we're on the run?
We are the boys who will stop your
little game
We are the boys who will make you
think again.

Jimmy Perry 1923– : 'Who do you think you are kidding, Mister Hitler' (theme song of *Dad's Army*, BBC television, 1968–77)

Worry

proverbs and sayings ▸

1 Care killed the cat.

the meaning of *care* has shifted somewhat from 'worry, grief' to 'care, caution'; English proverb, late 16th century; see WORRY 7

2 Do not meet troubles half-way.

warning against anxiety about something that has not yet happened; English proverb, late 19th century

3 It is not work that kills, but worry.

direct effort is less stressful than constant concern; English proverb, late 19th century

4 Sufficient unto the day is the evil thereof.

dealing with unpleasant matters should be left until it becomes necessary; English proverb, mid 18th century, from the Bible: see PRESENT 7

5 Worry is interest paid on trouble before it falls due.

American proverb, early 20th century

quotations ▸

6 O polished perturbation! golden
care!
That keep'st the ports of slumber open
wide
To many a watchful night!

William Shakespeare 1564–1616: *Henry IV, Part 2* (1597)

7 What though care killed a cat, thou hast mettle enough in thee to kill care.

William Shakespeare 1564–1616: *Much Ado About Nothing* (1598–9); see WORRY 1

8 In trouble to be troubled
Is to have your trouble doubled.

Daniel Defoe 1660–1731: *The Farther Adventures of Robinson Crusoe* (1719)

9 Nothing puzzles me more than time and space; and yet nothing troubles me less, as I never think about them.

Charles Lamb 1775–1834: letter to Thomas Manning, 2 January 1810

10 What's the use of worrying?
It never was worth while,
So, pack up your troubles in your old
kit-bag,
And smile, smile, smile.

George Asaf 1880–1951: 'Pack up your Troubles' (1915 song)

11 Neurosis is the way of avoiding non-being by avoiding being.

Paul Tillich 1886–1965: *The Courage To Be* (1952)

12 A neurosis is a secret you don't know you're keeping.

Kenneth Tynan 1927–80: Kathleen Tynan *Life of Kenneth Tynan* (1987)

Writers

see also POETS

phrases ▸

1 Aesthetic Movement

a literary and artistic movement which flourished in England in the 1880s; devoted to 'art for art's sake' and rejecting the notion that art should have a social or moral purpose, its chief exponents included Oscar Wilde, Max Beerbohm, and others associated with the journal the *Yellow Book*; see ARTS 5

2 angry young men

a group of socially conscious writers in the 1950s, including particularly the playwright John Osborne; see GENERATION GAP 2

3 Bloomsbury Group

a group of writers, artists, and philosophers living in or associated with Bloomsbury in the early 20th century; the group included Virginia Woolf, Lytton Strachey, Vanessa Bell, Duncan Grant, and Roger Fry

4 Kaleyard School

a group of late 19th-century fiction writers, including J. M. Barrie; they described local town life in Scotland in a romantic vein and with much use of the vernacular; *kaleyard* in Scots means literally 'kitchen garden'

5 the Swan of Avon

Shakespeare, after Ben Jonson's line 'Sweet Swan of Avon' (1623)

quotations ▸

6 Will you have all in all for prose and verse? Take the miracle of our age, Sir Philip Sidney.

Richard Carew 1555–1620: William Camden *Remains concerning Britain* (1614) 'The Excellency of the English Tongue'

7 He was not of an age, but for all time!

Ben Jonson 1573–1637: 'To the Memory of My Beloved, the Author, Mr William Shakespeare' (1623)

8 That great Cham of literature, Samuel Johnson.

Tobias Smollett 1721–71: letter to John Wilkes, 16 March 1759

9 Why, Sir, if you were to read Richardson for the story, your impatience would be so much fretted that you would hang yourself.

Samuel Johnson 1709–84: James Boswell *Life of Samuel Johnson* (1791) 6 April 1772

10 What should I do with your strong, manly, spirited sketches, full of variety and glow?—How could I possibly join them on to the little bit (two inches wide) of ivory on which I work with so fine a brush, as produces little effect after much labour?

Jane Austen 1775–1817: letter to J. Edward Austen, 16 December 1816

11 The Big Bow-Wow strain I can do myself like any now going; but the exquisite touch, which renders ordinary commonplace things and characters interesting, from the truth of the description and the sentiment, is denied to me.

of Jane Austen

Sir Walter Scott 1771–1832: diary 14 March 1826

12 Thou large-brained woman and
large-hearted man.

Elizabeth Barrett Browning 1806–61: 'To George Sand—A Desire' (1844)

13 A rake among scholars, and a scholar among rakes.

of Richard Steele

Lord Macaulay 1800–59: *Essays Contributed to the Edinburgh Review* (1850) 'The Life and Writings of Addison'

14 He describes London like a special correspondent for posterity.

Walter Bagehot 1826–77: *National Review* 7 October 1858 'Charles Dickens'

15 *Madame Bovary, c'est moi.*

Madame Bovary is myself.

Gustave Flaubert 1821–80: attributed

16 With the single exception of Homer, there is no eminent writer, not even Sir Walter Scott, whom I can despise so entirely as I despise Shakespeare when I measure my mind against his.

George Bernard Shaw 1856–1950: in *Saturday Review* 26 September 1896

17 Shaw has not an enemy in the world; and none of his friends like him.

Oscar Wilde 1854–1900: letter from Bernard Shaw to Archibald Henderson, 22 February 1911

18 It is leviathan retrieving pebbles. It is a magnificent but painful

hippopotamus resolved at any cost, even at the cost of its dignity, upon picking up a pea which has got into a corner of its den.

of Henry James
H. G. Wells 1866–1946: *Boon* (1915)

19 E. M. Forster never gets any further than warming the teapot. He's a rare fine hand at that. Feel this teapot. Is it not beautifully warm? Yes, but there ain't going to be no tea.

Katherine Mansfield 1888–1923: diary, May 1917

20 English literature's performing flea.

of P. G. Wodehouse
Sean O'Casey 1880–1964: P. G. Wodehouse *Performing Flea* (1953)

21 When I read something saying I've not done anything as good as *Catch-22* I'm tempted to reply, 'Who has?'

Joseph Heller 1923–99: in *Times* 9 June 1993

Writing

see also BOOKS, FICTION, ORIGINALITY, POETRY, STYLE, WORDS

proverbs and sayings ▸

1 The art of writing is the art of applying the seat of the pants to the seat of the chair.

American proverb, mid 20th century

2 For most of history, Anonymous was a woman.

modern saying, mid 20th century, often associated with the English writer Virginia Woolf (1882–1941)

3 He who would write and can't write can surely review.

American proverb, mid 19th century

4 Paper bleeds little.

real casualties may result from carrying out what appears to be a good plan; Spanish proverb

5 Paper is patient.

paper allows the writer to put down what they choose; German proverb

6 What is written with a pen cannot be cut out with an axe.

words are more powerful than violence; Russian proverb; see WAYS 17

7 Writing is a picture of the writer's heart.

Chinese proverb

phrases ▸

8 cacoethes scribendi

an irresistible desire to write; from Juvenal (see WRITING 12); Latin from Greek *kakoēthes* use as noun of adjective *kakoēthes* ill-disposed

9 disjecta membra

scattered fragments, especially of a written work; Latin, an alteration of *disjecti membra poetae*, as used by the poet Horace, 'in our case you would not recognize, as you would in the case of Ennius, the limbs, even though you had dismembered him, of a poet'

quotations ▸

10 It is a foolish thing to make a long prologue, and to be short in the story itself.

Bible: II Maccabees

11 You will have written exceptionally well if, by skilful arrangement of your words, you have made an ordinary one seem original.

Horace 65–8 BC: *Ars Poetica*

12 *Tenet insanabile multos*
Scribendi cacoethes et aegro in corde senescit.
Many suffer from the incurable disease of writing, and it becomes chronic in their sick minds.

Juvenal C. AD 60–C. 140: *Satires*; see WRITING 8

13 If writing did not exist, what terrible depressions we should suffer from.

Sei Shōnagon c.966–c.1013: *The Pillow Book of Sei Shōnagon*

14 Go, litel bok, go, litel myn tragedye.

Geoffrey Chaucer 1343–1400: *Troilus and Criseyde*

15 And, as imagination bodies forth
The forms of things unknown, the poet's pen
Turns them to shapes, and gives to airy nothing
A local habitation and a name.

William Shakespeare 1564–1616: *A Midsummer Night's Dream* (1595–6)

16 If all the earth were paper white
And all the sea were ink

'Twere not enough for me to write
As my poor heart doth think.

John Lyly 1554–1606: 'If all the earth were paper white'

17 The last thing one knows in constructing a work is what to put first.

Blaise Pascal 1623–62: *Pensées* (1670)

18 Of every four words I write, I strike out three.

Nicolas Boileau 1636–1711: *Satire (2). A M. Molière* (1665)

19 What in me is dark
Illumine, what is low raise and support;
That to the height of this great argument
I may assert eternal providence,
And justify the ways of God to men.

John Milton 1608–74: *Paradise Lost* (1667); see ALCOHOL 19

20 Learn to write well, or not to write at all.

John Sheffield, Duke of Buckingham and Normanby 1648–1721: 'An Essay upon Satire' (1689)

21 The chief glory of every people arises from its authors.

Samuel Johnson 1709–84: *A Dictionary of the English Language* (1755)

22 Writing, when properly managed (as you may be sure I think mine is) is but a different name for conversation.

Laurence Sterne 1713–68: *Tristram Shandy* (1759–67)

23 Any fool may write a most valuable book by chance, if he will only tell us what he heard and saw with veracity.

Thomas Gray 1716–71: letter to Horace Walpole, 25 February 1768

24 You write with ease, to show your breeding,
But easy writing's vile hard reading.

Richard Brinsley Sheridan 1751–1816: 'Clio's Protest' (written 1771, published 1819)

25 Read over your compositions, and where ever you meet with a passage which you think is particularly fine, strike it out.

Samuel Johnson 1709–84: quoting a college tutor; James Boswell *Life of Samuel Johnson* (1791) 30 April 1773

26 No man but a blockhead ever wrote, except for money.

Samuel Johnson 1709–84: James Boswell *Life of Samuel Johnson* (1791) 5 April 1776

27 Another damned, thick, square book! Always scribble, scribble, scribble! Eh! Mr Gibbon?

William Henry, Duke of Gloucester 1743–1805: Henry Best *Personal and Literary Memorials* (1829); also attributed to the Duke of Cumberland and King George III; D. M. Low *Edward Gibbon* (1937)

28 Let other pens dwell on guilt and misery. I quit such odious subjects as soon as I can.

Jane Austen 1775–1817: *Mansfield Park* (1814)

29 Until you understand a writer's ignorance, presume yourself ignorant of his understanding.

Samuel Taylor Coleridge 1772–1834: *Biographia Literaria* (1817)

30 When my sonnet was rejected, I exclaimed, 'Damn the age; I will write for Antiquity!'

Charles Lamb 1775–1834: letter to B. W. Proctor 22 January 1829

31 Beneath the rule of men entirely great
The pen is mightier than the sword.

Edward George Bulwer-Lytton 1803–73: *Richelieu* (1839); see WAYS 17

32 A losing trade, I assure you, sir: literature is a drug.

George Borrow 1803–81: *Lavengro* (1851)

33 How vain it is to sit down to write when you have not stood up to live.

Henry David Thoreau 1817–62: diary, 19 August 1851

34 Writers, like teeth, are divided into incisors and grinders.

Walter Bagehot 1826–77: *Estimates of some Englishmen and Scotchmen* (1858) 'The First Edinburgh Reviewers'

35 The business of the poet and novelist is to show the sorriness underlying the grandest things, and the grandeur underlying the sorriest things.

Thomas Hardy 1840–1928: notebook entry for 19 April 1885

36 Only connect!...Only connect the prose and the passion, and both will

be exalted, and human love will be seen at its height.
E. M. Forster 1879–1970: *Howards End* (1910)

37 My theory of writing I can sum up in one sentence. An author ought to write for the youth of his own generation, the critics of the next, and the schoolmasters of ever after.
F. Scott Fitzgerald 1896–1940: letter to the Booksellers' Convention, April 1920

38 This writing business. Pencils and what-not. Over-rated, if you ask me. Silly stuff. Nothing in it.
A. A. Milne 1882–1956: *Winnie-the-Pooh* (1926)

39 A woman must have money and a room of her own if she is to write fiction.
Virginia Woolf 1882–1941: *A Room of One's Own* (1929)

40 I am a camera with its shutter open, quite passive, recording, not thinking.
Christopher Isherwood 1904–86: *Goodbye to Berlin* (1939) 'Berlin Diary' Autumn 1930

41 Remarks are not literature.
Gertrude Stein 1874–1946: *Autobiography of Alice B. Toklas* (1933)

42 Literature is news that STAYS news.
Ezra Pound 1885–1972: *The ABC of Reading* (1934)

43 Manuscripts don't burn.
Mikhail Bulgakov 1891–1940: *The Master and Margarita* (1966–67)

44 A writer's ambition should be...to trade a hundred contemporary readers for ten readers in ten years' time and for one reader in a hundred years.
Arthur Koestler 1905–83: in *New York Times Book Review* 1 April 1951

45 Writing is not a profession but a vocation of unhappiness.
Georges Simenon 1903–89: interview in *Paris Review* Summer 1955

46 The writer's only responsibility is to his art. He will be completely ruthless if he is a good one....If a writer has to rob his mother, he will not hesitate; the *Ode on a Grecian Urn* is worth any number of old ladies.
William Faulkner 1897–1962: in *Paris Review* Spring 1956

47 The most essential gift for a good writer is a built-in, shock-proof shit detector. This is the writer's radar and all great writers have had it.
Ernest Hemingway 1899–1961: in *Paris Review* Spring 1958

48 A writer must refuse, therefore, to allow himself to be transformed into an institution.
Jean-Paul Sartre 1905–80: refusing the Nobel Prize at Stockholm, 22 October 1964

49 Good prose is like a window-pane.
George Orwell 1903–50: *Collected Essays* (1968) vol. 1 'Why I Write'

50 Writing saved me from the sin and *inconvenience* of violence.
Alice Walker 1944– : 'One Child of One's Own' in Janet Sternburg *The Writer on her Work* (1980)

51 Writers don't give prescriptions. They give headaches.
Chinua Achebe 1930– : *Anthills of the Savannah* (1987)

Youth

see also CHILDREN, GENERATION GAP

proverbs and sayings ▸

1 The old net is cast aside while the new net goes fishing.
the future belongs to the young; Maori proverb

2 Wanton kittens make sober cats.
someone who in youth is light-minded and lascivious may be soberly behaved in later life; English proverb, early 18th century

3 Whom the gods love die young.
the happiest fate is to die before health and strength are lost; English proverb, mid 16th century; see VIRTUE 1, YOUTH 7

4 Youth must be served.
some indulgence should be given to the wishes and enthusiasms of youth; English proverb, early 19th century

phrases ▸

5 salad days
the period when one is young and inexperienced, one's time of youth; from Shakespeare's *Antony and Cleopatra* (1606–7) 'My salad days, When I was green in judgment'

6 an ugly duckling

a young person who shows no promise at all of the beauty and success that will eventually come with maturity; in allusion to a tale by Hans Andersen of a cygnet in a brood of ducks

quotations ▸

7 Whom the gods love dies young.

Menander 342–*c.*292 BC: *Dis Exapaton*; see VIRTUE 1, YOUTH 3

8 In delay there lies no plenty;
Then come kiss me, sweet and twenty,
Youth's a stuff will not endure.

William Shakespeare 1564–1616: *Twelfth Night* (1601)

9 Young men are fitter to invent than to judge, fitter for execution than for counsel, and fitter for new projects than for settled business.

Francis Bacon 1561–1626: *Essays* (1625) 'Of Youth and Age'

10 The atrocious crime of being a young man…I shall neither attempt to palliate nor deny.

William Pitt, Earl of Chatham 1708–78: speech, House of Commons, 2 March 1741

11 In gallant trim the gilded vessel goes;
Youth on the prow, and Pleasure at the helm.

Thomas Gray 1716–71: 'The Bard' (1757)

12 Heaven lies about us in our infancy!
Shades of the prison-house begin to close
Upon the growing boy,

William Wordsworth 1770–1850: 'Ode. Intimations of Immortality' (1807)

13 Live as long as you may, the first twenty years are the longest half of your life.

Robert Southey 1774–1843: *The Doctor* (1812)

14 Oh, talk not to me of a name great in story;
The days of our youth are the days of our glory;
And the myrtle and ivy of sweet two-and-twenty
Are worth all your laurels, though ever so plenty.

Lord Byron 1788–1824: 'Stanzas Written on the Road between Florence and Pisa, November 1821'; see SUCCESS 20

15 The Youth of a Nation are the trustees of Posterity.

Benjamin Disraeli 1804–81: *Sybil* (1845)

16 Youth is the one thing worth having.

Oscar Wilde 1854–1900: *The Picture of Dorian Gray* (1891)

17 I'm not young enough to know everything.

J. M. Barrie 1860–1937: *The Admirable Crichton* (performed 1902, published 1914)

18 Youth would be an ideal state if it came a little later in life.

Herbert Henry Asquith 1852–1928: in *Observer* 15 April 1923

19 Youth is happy because it has the ability to see beauty.

Franz Kafka 1883–1924: Gustav Janouch *Conversations with Kafka* (1971)

20 It is better to waste one's youth than to do nothing with it at all.

Georges Courteline 1858–1929: *La Philosophie de Georges Courteline* (1948)

21 The force that through the green fuse drives the flower
Drives my green age.

Dylan Thomas 1914–53: 'The force that through the green fuse drives the flower' (1934)

22 It's that second time you hear your love song sung,
Makes you think perhaps, that
Love like youth is wasted on the young.

Sammy Cahn 1913–93: 'The Second Time Around' (1960 song)

23 Youth is something very new: twenty years ago no one mentioned it.

Coco Chanel 1883–1971: Marcel Haedrich *Coco Chanel, Her Life, Her Secrets* (1971)

24 Make me young, make me young, make me young!

Kurt Vonnegut 1922–2007: *Breakfast of Champions* (1973)

25 Remember that as a teenager you are at the last stage in your life when you will be happy to hear that the phone is for you.

Fran Lebowitz 1946– : *Social Studies* (1981)

Keyword Index

Adam A. was but human HUMAN NATURE 16
old A. HUMAN NATURE 5
old A. in this child HUMAN NATURE 11
rubbish of an A. SCIENCE AND RELIGION 7
second A. CHRISTIAN CHURCH 10
When A. and Eve BRITISH TOWNS 35
When A. dalfe CLASS 9
When A. delved CLASS 2
add no longer anything to a. PERFECTION 15
adder a. that stoppeth her ears DEFIANCE 9
deaf as an a. SENSES 3
addeth translation's thief that a. TRANSLATION 4
addiction a. is bad DRUGS 9
prisoners of a. BUYING 11
addictive sin tends to be a. SIN 28
addled a. egg IDLENESS 1
one a. egg SILENCE 12
address letters to a non-existent a. PRAYER 28
adjective As to the A. STYLE 17
adjourned Parliament which a. SCOTLAND 21
administered a. is best ADMINISTRATION 4
administers a. nor governs ROYALTY 35
administration A. of All the Talents PARLIAMENT 3
administrative a. won't GOVERNMENT 42
admirable a. Crichton EXCELLENCE 4
admiral kill an a. from time to time WAYS 32
admiralty price of a. SEA 7
admirari *Nil a.* HAPPINESS 10
admiration exercise our a. FAMILIARITY 14
admire Not to a. HAPPINESS 16
admittance a. till the week after HASTE 15
adopted conviction that it is generally a. OPINION 25
adult a. is alone MATURITY 11
child becomes an a. CHILDREN 21
occupation of an a. ACTING 13
adultery committed a. in my heart TEMPTATION 18
adults a. produce children MARRIAGE 42
a. to children HAPPINESS 33
When a. stop being infants MATURITY 17
advance A. Australia AUSTRALIA 1
A. Australia AUSTRALIA 17
somewhat to a. PROGRESS 9
advanced sufficiently a. technology TECHNOLOGY 23
advancement path of social a. AMBITION 18
advantage not necessarily to Japan's a. WINNING 24
so great a. over another CHARACTER 39
take a mean a. APOLOGY 19
undertaking of great A. BUSINESS 28
with equal a. INTERNATIONAL 16
adventure awfully big a. DEATH 66
Life is either a daring a. LIFE 50
most beautiful a. DEATH 63
adventures A. are for the adventurous DANGER 1
adversary against a single a. LEADERSHIP 17
adversity a. doth best discover ADVERSITY 14
A. makes strange bedfellows ADVERSITY 1
a., of strong men ADVERSITY 12
dose of a. ADVERSITY 3
hundred that will stand a. ADVERSITY 15
learn to endure a. ADVERSITY 19
uses of a. ADVERSITY 13
advertise a. food to hungry people ADVERTISING 11
pays to a. ADVERTISING 3
advertisement one effective a. ADVERTISING 7
patent medicine a. SICKNESS 16
soul of an a. ADVERTISING 6
advertisers a. don't object to JOURNALISM 22
advertising A. is the greatest ADVERTISING 16
A. is the rattling ADVERTISING 10
A. may be described ADVERTISING 8
all the rest is a. NEWS 14
calls it a. ADVERTISING 17
money I spend on a. ADVERTISING 9
advice a. is good or bad ADVICE 14
A. is seldom welcome ADVICE 12
a. is worth having ADVICE 16
Fools need a. most ADVICE 13
pass on good a. ADVICE 17
To ask a. is in nine cases ADVICE 18
when you seek a. ADVICE 21
advocates a. of peace PEACE 20
aeroplanes it wasn't the a. BEAUTY 34
aesthetic A. Movement WRITERS 1
affable sign of an a. man BODY 17
affairs a. of men OPPORTUNITY 32
no small steps in great a. WAYS 31
affectation sophistry and a. UNIVERSITIES 6
affection a. of the human PARENTS 20
If equal a. cannot be LOVE 72
affections holiness of the heart's a. TRUTH 26
afflictions a. of Job BIBLE 9
affluent a. society WEALTH 7
afraid a. of God MORALITY 7
a. of what he thinks television BROADCASTING 14
a. to die DEATH 76
Be a. FEAR 1
Africa A. always brings AFRICA 7
A. and the English tongue AFRICA 12
A. a thing is true at first light AFRICA 10
A. is a scar AFRICA 15
A. resembles a revolver AFRICA 11
something new out of A. AFRICA 1
African A. Eve AFRICA 2
after happily ever a. ENDING 3
afternoon a. knows what the morning FORESIGHT 1
a. of human life MIDDLE AGE 10
make love in the a. FRANCE 21
again déjà vu all over a. FORESIGHT 23
against a. everything LIKES 17
God was a. art ARTS 19
He was a. it SIN 25
I always vote *a.* ELECTIONS 11
who can be a. us STRENGTH 20
with me is a. me ENEMIES 7
Agamemnon face of A. PAST 29
lived before A. REPUTATION 1
age A. does not make us childish OLD AGE 20
a. going to the workhouse GOVERNMENT 26
A. is deformed GENERATION GAP 6
a. is the most unexpected OLD AGE 29
A. might but take GENERATION GAP 8
A. shall not weary them ARMED FORCES 35
a., which forgives itself GENERATION GAP 10
A. will not be defied OLD AGE 17
All diseases run into one, old a. SICKNESS 15
Crabbed a. GENERATION GAP 7
days of our a. OLD AGE 13
very attractive a. MIDDLE AGE 8
was not of an a. WRITERS 7
with a. and dust TIME 31
aged learn how to be a. OLD AGE 39
agenbite a. of inwit CONSCIENCE 8
A. of inwit CONSCIENCE 18
agenda hidden a. SECRECY 20
item of the a. ADMINISTRATION 15
ages seven a. LIFE 21
agnosticism all that a. means BELIEF 27
agonizing a. reappraisal THINKING 5

agony a. is abated SUFFERING 19
constrained by a. SCULPTURE 4
it was a., Ivy SUFFERING 3
agree a. in the dark INDIFFERENCE 7
a. with others SIMILARITY 24
a. with the book of God CENSORSHIP 3
I a. with Nick SIMILARITY 31
trade never a. SIMILARITY 10
agreement a. with hell DIPLOMACY 8
blow with an a. VIOLENCE 12
Too much a. kills CONVERSATION 20
agriculture A. is the foundation FARMING 9
at last, fall upon a. TAXES 12
ahead a., get a hat DRESS 3
past is always a. of us PAST 5
aid Apt Alliteration's artful a. WIT 10
ailment imaginary a. is worse MIND 1
aim all things a. GOOD 17
forgotten your a. EXCESS 35
impossible a. DESPAIR 16
shooting without a. ACTION 3
aiming a. at a million ACHIEVEMENT 24
air a. and angels' purity MEN AND WOMEN 4
art of the open a. SCULPTURE 7
castles in the a. IMAGINATION 1
Clear the a. POLLUTION 18
excellent canopy, the a. POLLUTION 7
feet planted in the a. POLITICAL PARTIES 26
hot a. blows ELECTIONS 2
music in the a. MUSIC 15
outlet in the a. SKIES 26
pattern of subtle a. CATS 13
too pure an A. LIBERTY 7
trees are made of a. SCIENCE 28
air-conditioning respectability and a. GOD 34
aircraft a. is missing ARMED FORCES 6
airport observing a. layouts TRAVEL 46
airs a. and graces CLASS 3
airy a.-fairy IDEALISM 2
world which is a.-fairy HUMAN RIGHTS 21
aitches lose but our a. CLASS 23
Aladdin A.'s cave WEALTH 8
A.'s lamp CHANCE 18
Alamo Remember the A. WARS 3
alarms a. and excursions ORDER 4
alas Hugo—a. POETS 23
May say A. SUCCESS 43
Albion perfidious A. ENGLAND 4
alcohol a. has taken out of me ALCOHOL 30
a. or morphine DRUGS 9
ale cakes and a. PLEASURE 3
no more cakes and a. VIRTUE 22
alehouse by an Englishman, an a. ARCHITECTURE 1
algebraic weaves a. patterns COMPUTERS 12
alien damned if I'm an a. PATRIOTISM 27
quick to blame the a. GUILT 6
alike all places were a. CATS 8
everyone is a. SOCIETY 17
Great minds think a. THINKING 1
men are a. HUMAN NATURE 6
alive gets out of it a. EXPERIENCE 32
half-a. things GOSSIP 25
Hallelujah! I'm a. EMOTIONS 26
in that dawn to be a. REVOLUTION 16
Life's not just being a. HEALTH 16
no one is a. SOCIETY 17
Not while I'm a. ENEMIES 19
Officiously to keep a. MURDER 17
poetry should be a. POETRY 38
all A. for one COOPERATION 30
a. in respect of nothing HUMAN RACE 18
A.-merciful GOD 13
a. must have prizes WINNING 18
A. my pretty ones MOURNING 11
a. shall be well OPTIMISM 18
a. that a man hath LIFE 16
a. things to all men CHARACTER 30
a. things to all men CONFORMITY 3
God for us a. SELF-INTEREST 1
his a. neglected EFFORT 20
know a. is to forgive FORGIVENESS 6
man for a. seasons CHARACTER 32
not at all or a. in all TRUST 32
teaches ill who teaches a. TEACHING 1
That's a. folks ENDING 8
Will you have a. in all WRITERS 6
You can have it a. WOMEN 54
allegiance a. to any master LIBERTY 6
Any victim demands a. SYMPATHY 26
not pledged a. to you RACE 25
alleluia A. is our song CHRISTIAN CHURCH 33
allergies Also provide the a. SICKNESS 23
alley Tin Pan A. MUSIC 6
alliance Auld A. INTERNATIONAL 1
alliances a. with none INTERNATIONAL 14
allies no eternal a. INTERNATIONAL 19
alligators up to your ears in a. MANAGEMENT 16
alliteration Apt A.'s artful aid WIT 10
almighty a. dollar MONEY 17
A. had placed it there POLITICIANS 23
alms a. for oblivion TIME 29
a. procure us admission GOD 14
aloha A. State AMERICAN CITIES 1
alone adult is a. MATURITY 11
a. against smiling enemies ENVY 13
a. and smash his mirror FOOLS 15
Better a. SOLITUDE 1
better to be a. REPUTATION 26
I want to be a. SOLITUDE 16
Let well a. CAUTION 16
man should be a. SOLITUDE 5
man who stands most a. STRENGTH 23
more a. while living SOLITUDE 17
never a. with a Strand SMOKING 5
not sufficiently a. SOLITUDE 18
We are not a. PARANORMAL 3
weep and you weep a. SYMPATHY 3
We're born a., we live alone SOLITUDE 24
We shall die a. DEATH 47
when wholly a. SOLITUDE 7
who travels a. SOLITUDE 2
you'll never walk a. HOPE 22
alter a. it every six months FASHION 10
alteration when it a. finds LOVE 32
alternative Considering the a. OLD AGE 33
no real a. CHOICE 27
alternatives a. that are not their own CHARACTER 47
ignorance of a. SUFFERING 35
always a. be an England ENGLAND 21
never happened, but are a. CIRCUMSTANCE 22
Once a —, a. a — CHARACTER 13
am I a. what I am SELF 6
I a.—yet what I am SELF 16
I think, therefore I a. THINKING 14
people think I a. or say I am SELF 22
amateur a. is a man who can't EMPLOYMENT 23
amateurs full of musical a. MUSIC 14

architect (*cont.*)
consent to be the a. GOOD 35
Great A. of the Universe UNIVERSE 11
architecture a. applies only ARCHITECTURE 15
A. in general ARCHITECTURE 10
A. is the art ARCHITECTURE 18
A., of all the arts ARCHITECTURE 13
a. of our future COUNTRIES 30
like dancing about a. MUSIC 4
ardua Per a. ad astra ACHIEVEMENT 7
are a. what we pretend to be CHARACTER 50
a. what we repeatedly do CUSTOM 8
know that which we a. SELF-KNOWLEDGE 10
take our friends as they a. FRIENDSHIP 16
tell you what you a. COOKING 21
things not as they a. INSIGHT 16
we know what we a. FUTURE 15
You a. what you eat COOKING 11
argue a. about what to do TECHNOLOGY 14
a. but those who dodge ARGUMENT 16
a. with the Gods HEROES 22
difficulties will a. PROBLEMS 32
arguing a. what a good man should MORALITY 2
a. with the inevitable ARGUMENT 15
argument All a. is against it SUPERNATURAL 14
a. of the broken window ARGUMENT 19
I have found you an a. INTELLIGENCE 12
without an a. ANGER 12
arguments more a. you win ARGUMENT 3
support the worst a. LOGIC 22
Aristotle A. maintained that women HYPOTHESIS 24
A. was but the rubbish SCIENCE AND RELIGION 7
arithmetic life be without a. MATHS 13
ark A., the male and female ANIMALS 14
be out of the a. FASHION 2
arm Stretch your a. no further THRIFT 8
strong in the a. BRITISH TOWNS 15
armadillos stripes and dead a. EXCESS 42
armchair like a good a. PAINTING 19
armed a. at all points PREPARATION 17
a. with more JUSTICE 29
Armenians extermination of the A. RACE 17
armful nearly an a. BODY 24
armies commander of three a. SELF 3
stronger than all the a. IDEAS 2
armour knight in shining a. HEROES 5
arms a. do flourish CULTURE 8
Kings have long a. POWER 4
army a. marches on its stomach ARMED FORCES 27
a. without culture is a dull-witted ARMED FORCES 44
backbone of the A. ARMED FORCES 32
barmy a. CRICKET 1
dialect with an a. LANGUAGES 16
Discipline is the soul of an a. ARMED FORCES 21
forgotten a. WORLD WAR II 6
invasion by an a. IDEAS 8
[our a.] is composed ARMED FORCES 28
sergeant is the a. ARMED FORCES 48
to get on in the a. ARMED FORCES 31
around What goes a. JUSTICE 13
arranging knack of so a. the world TECHNOLOGY 16
arrest a. all beauty PHOTOGRAPHY 5
arrested conservative who has been a. CRIME 43
arrival point of a. LIBERTY 19
arrive a. where we started EXPLORATION 15
better thing than to a. TRAVEL 36
hopefully than to a. HOPE 8
arrogance honest a. SELF-ESTEEM 26
arrow a. that flieth by day FEAR 8
single a. is easily broken COOPERATION 15
time's a. TIME 19
arrowhead a. of grieving HAPPINESS 9
arrows a. in the hand of the giant CHILDREN 4
ars a. gratia artis ARTS 4
arsenal a. of democracy WORLD WAR II 15
art a. for art's sake ARTS 5
A. for art's sake ARTS 9
A. for the sake of the true ARTS 14
A. has to move you ARTS 35
A. is a jealous ARTS 13
A. is born of humiliation ARTS 29
A. is long ARTS 2
A. is meant to disturb ARTS AND SCIENCES 7
a. is not a weapon ARTS 31
A. is not truth ARTS 32
A. is power ARTS 3
a. is the only thing ARTS 28
A. is vice ARTS 23
a. long MEDICINE 8
A. never expresses anything ARTS 16
a. of God NATURE 11
a. of the possible POLITICS 16
clever, but is it A. ARTS 17
Deals are my a. form BUSINESS 48
destroy genius and a. GENIUS 6
E in A-level a. SCULPTURE 10
element in modern a. ARTS 24
God was against a. ARTS 19
greatest a. form ADVERTISING 16
hating, my boy, is an a. HATRED 10
history of a. ARTS 20
importance of a work of a. VALUE 32
In a. the best ARTS 8
intellect upon a. CRITICISM 21
last and greatest a. POETS 11
leave a. to us SCULPTURE 8
Life imitates A. ARTS 15
madness of a. ARTS 18
meddles with a. ARTS 11
More matter with less a. STYLE 8
my job and my a. LIFESTYLES 24
Sleeping is no mean a. SLEEP 17
spoiled child of a. FICTION 18
true test of a. PAINTING 12
what a. means to me ARTS 34
work of a. FOOD 32
artful Apt Alliteration's a. aid WIT 10
Arthur Harry is called A. NAMES 19
artificial led astray by a. rules MORALITY 5
artisan employment to the a. EMPLOYMENT 17
artist a. is someone ARTS 33
a. must be in his work ARTS 12
a. must organize his life PUNCTUALITY 12
a. will let his wife ARTS 22
become a good a. by copying ORIGINALITY 11
born an a. HUNTING 5
special kind of a. ARTS 25
artists all chess players are a. SPORTS 25
few are a. CREATIVITY 14
arts All a. are brothers ARTS 1
famed in all great a. FRANCE 16
mother of a. FRANCE 8
one of the fine a. MURDER 15
ash A. Wednesday FESTIVALS 9
avoid an a. TREES 2
Oak, and A., and Thorn TREES 15
oak is before the a. WEATHER 20

avis rara a. ORIGINALITY 4
avoid manages to a. them KNOWLEDGE 56
avoided things that could have been a. HISTORY 27
avoiding by a. being WORRY 11
Avon swan of A. WRITERS 5
awake A.! for Morning DAY 12
awakened a. a sleeping giant CAUSES 29
away one that got a. HUNTING 4
awe increasing wonder and a. THINKING 15
shock and a. WARFARE 12
awful it's a. BOREDOM 11
awkward a. squad ARMED FORCES 12
awl can't hide an a. in a sack SECRECY 17
awoke a. one morning FAME 18
axe a. for the frozen sea BOOKS 17
cannot be cut out with an a. WRITING 6
heavy a. without an edge WISDOM 6
Lizzie Borden took an a. MURDER 4
When the a. came into the forest SIMILARITY 13
axioms hypotheses or a. HYPOTHESIS 23
axis a. of evil INTERNATIONAL 39
a. of the earth SELF-ESTEEM 19
babel bother at the tower of B. LANGUAGES 9
Tower of B. LANGUAGES 3
babes b. in the wood EXPERIENCE 14
milk for b. KNOWLEDGE 11
mouths of b. WISDOM 2
babies hates dogs and b. DOGS 12
If men had to have b. PREGNANCY 19
putting milk into b. CHILD CARE 11
baboon He who understands b. LANGUAGE 12
baby b. boomer GENERATION GAP 3
b. is God's opinion that life PREGNANCY 14
b. is like getting a tattoo PREGNANCY 20
Burn, b., burn VIOLENCE 1
Drill, b., drill BUSINESS 54
every b. born into the world PREGNANCY 8
Love crawls with the b. PARENTS 31
tar b. PROBLEMS 17
Babylon B. in all its desolation MADNESS 10
waters of B. SORROW 6
Bach angels play only B. MUSICIANS 16
B. almost persuades me MUSICIANS 13
B. tells you MUSICIANS 20
bachelor b. never quite gets over MEN 15
bachelors B. know more about women SINGLE 10
reasons for b. to go out WOMAN'S ROLE 15
back b. to the drawing board BEGINNING 13
boys in the b. rooms FAME 25
cast iron b., with a hinge GARDENS 16
come b. the same day TRAVEL 45
Don't look b. SPORTS 26
I'll be b. MEETING 26
in the small of the b. SURPRISE 13
I sit on a man's b. HYPOCRISY 15
makes the b. to the burden SYMPATHY 1
not in my b. yard SELF-INTEREST 17
Not to go b. PROGRESS 9
over the Devil's b. SIN 2
those before cried 'b.!' COURAGE 21
what did he go b. to INVENTIONS 22
backbone b. of the Army ARMED FORCES 32
no more b. than CHARACTER 44
backing I'm b. Britain PATRIOTISM 1
backroom b. boys SCIENCE 3
backs beast with two b. SEX 4
beast with two b. SEX 13
backward b. to their ancestors FUTURE 19
Forward ever, b. never PROGRESS 19
backwards b.... and in high heels MEN AND WOMEN 26
understood b. LIFE 31
bad b. book is as much of a labour BOOKS 18
b. colour APPEARANCE 6
b. ended unhappily FICTION 16
b. excuse is better APOLOGY 2
B. laws are the worst LAW 27
b. men combine COOPERATION 27
B. money MONEY 1
b. news infects NEWS 10
B. news travels fast NEWS 1
b. penny always turns up CHARACTER 2
b. taste is better than TASTE 10
B. things come in threes MISFORTUNES 1
b. times just around OPTIMISM 34
B. women never take GUILT 21
come to a b. end EXCELLENCE 16
dog a b. name GOSSIP 3
feel really b. about GUILT 19
from b. to worse CHANGE 36
good or b. GOOD 25
Hard cases make b. law LAW 3
in b. company SOLITUDE 1
it's b. for you HEALTH 27
mad, b. and dangerous POETS 15
made mad by b. treatment CRIME 32
make them feel b. ENVY 11
no book so b. that BOOKS 6
no such thing as b. weather WEATHER 19
no such thing as b. weather WEATHER 30
Nothing so b. SYMPATHY 4
pay to see b. movies CINEMA 14
strangle b. persons LAW 31
thing as b. publicity FAME 28
two legs b. PREJUDICE 21
what you feel b. after MORALITY 16
when I'm b., I'm better SIN 24
when she was b. BEHAVIOUR 24
badge b. of all our tribe PATIENCE 28
badly always turn out b. CLERGY 1
man who has planned b. PREPARATION 19
worth doing b. WOMEN 37
Baedeker B. raids WORLD WAR II 2
bag out of a tattered b. CHARACTER 18
Baghdad astonished to see him in B. FATE 22
bah 'B.,' said Scrooge CHRISTMAS 11
bairns Fools and b. should never see WORK 3
bait Fish follow the b. TEMPTATION 1
nibbles at every b. TEMPTATION 2
bake b. so shall you brew CAUSES 2
so shall you b. CAUSES 3
baked home and b. cookies WOMAN'S ROLE 29
baker butcher, the b. EMPLOYMENT 3
Bakewell B. in half-an-hour TRANSPORT 8
balance art of b. PAINTING 19
b. of nature NATURE 3
b. of power INTERNATIONAL 2
redress the b. AMERICA 15
weighed in the b. SUCCESS 19
balances checks and b. GOVERNMENT 7
bald between two b. men over a comb WARS 29
baldness far side of b. BODY 20
Balfour B.'s poodle PARLIAMENT 11
Balkans damned silly thing in the B. WORLD WAR I 7
ball b. player's got to be kept hungry SPORTS 29
out to the b. game SPORTS 15
out to the b. park SPORTS 36
ballads make all the b. SINGING 4
ballot b. is stronger ELECTIONS 7

beastie tim'rous b. FEAR 14
beastly b. to the Germans WORLD WAR II 19
beasts king of b. ANIMALS 10
beat b. generation JAZZ 1
can't b. them, join them WAYS 10
more you b. them WOMEN 8
beatings dread of b. SCHOOLS 11
Beatles B.'s first LP SEX 34
beats b. as it sweeps HOUSEWORK 2
beauteous How b. mankind is HUMAN RACE 16
beautiful All things bright and b. ANIMALS 22
always make it b. BEAUTY 24
b. catastrophe AMERICAN CITIES 59
b. face is a mute BEAUTY 10
b. game FOOTBALL 1
b. game FOOTBALL 10
b. things in the world BEAUTY 26
b. upon the mountains NEWS 7
beginning of a b. friendship FRIENDSHIP 30
believe to be b. POSSESSIONS 24
Black is b. RACE 2
endless forms most b. LIFE SCIENCES 14
in a b. way ARTS 34
innocent and the b. GUILT 14
love of what is b. CULTURE 7
Small is b. ECONOMICS 20
Small is b. QUANTITIES 10
Too b. for our ears MUSIC 11
When a woman isn't b. BEAUTY 31
beauty ability to see b. YOUTH 19
arrest all b. PHOTOGRAPHY 5
as many kinds of b. BEAUTY 25
b. and my youth ANIMALS 31
b. and naught else BEAUTY 27
B. and the Beast BEAUTY 9
b. being only skin-deep BEAUTY 35
B. draws with a single BEAUTY 1
b. faded BEAUTY 18
b. in a building ARCHITECTURE 9
b. in one's equations MATHS 23
B. is a good letter BEAUTY 2
b. is a joy BEAUTY 21
B. is all very well BEAUTY 32
B. is essentially meaningless BEAUTY 39
B. is in the eye BEAUTY 3
b. is mysterious BEAUTY 29
B. is no quality BEAUTY 19
B. is only skin deep BEAUTY 4
B. is power BEAUTY 5
B. is the first test MATHS 20
B. is the lover's gift BEAUTY 17
B. is truth BEAUTY 22
B. killed the Beast BEAUTY 34
B. too rich for use BEAUTY 15
B. will save the world BEAUTY 28
B. without cruelty SUFFERING 1
b. without vanity ANIMALS 28
b. without vanity DOGS 6
delusion that b. is goodness BEAUTY 30
life was b. LIFE 30
Love built on b. BEAUTY 14
no excellent b. BEAUTY 16
no such thing as b. SIMILARITY 25
Only through b.'s gate KNOWLEDGE 34
ray of b. outvalues FLOWERS 7
terrible b. is born CHANGE 45
thing of b. MEN 15
truth, but supreme b. MATHS 18
walks in b. BEAUTY 20
winds of March with b. FLOWERS 4
world's b. becomes enough BEAUTY 37
beaver b. works and plays ANIMALS 3
because B. it's there MOUNTAINS 7
B. We're here FATE 5
she did this b. BOOKS 28
becomes that is what he b. RELATIONSHIPS 5
that which *is not* b. LIFE SCIENCES 10
bed And so to b. SLEEP 13
As you make your b. CAUSES 4
b. at the same time CONSTANCY 12
Better to go to b. supperless DEBT 3
Early to b. HEALTH 4
early to b. SLEEP 20
go to b. by day SEASONS 26
legs in a b. MARRIAGE 11
Lying in b. PLEASURE 24
mind is not a b. CERTAINTY 26
Not to be a-b. SLEEP 9
passage up to b. SLEEP 18
reds under the b. CAPITALISM 8
remain in b. IDLENESS 21
bedfellows Politics makes strange b. POLITICS 4
strange b. ADVERSITY 1
strange b. MISFORTUNES 21
bedroom what you do in the b. SEX 27
bedrooms in the nation's b. CENSORSHIP 17
bee b. works ANIMALS 3
How doth the little busy b. WORK 26
sting like a b. SPORTS 30
beechen spare the b. tree TREES 12
beef eater of b. FOOD 13
Where's the b. REALITY 2
been B. there BOREDOM 1
B. there TRAVEL 1
have you ever b. CAPITALISM 2
I've b. things EXPERIENCE 31
beer b. and skittles LIFE 4
b. teetotaller ALCOHOL 20
denies you the b. ALCOHOL 23
drinks b., thinks beer DRUNKENNESS 1
here for the b. ALCOHOL 4
heresy, hops, and b. INVENTIONS 1
warm b. BRITAIN 14
beers b. cannot reach ALCOHOL 3
bees Where b. are, there is honey WORK 11
Beethoven B.'s Fifth Symphony MUSICIANS 10
B. tells you MUSICIANS 20
conducted a B. MUSICIANS 19
beetles preference for b. STATISTICS 14
before Christ b. me PRAYER 10
I b. e, except after c WORDS 3
not been said b. ORIGINALITY 6
those b. cried 'Back!' COURAGE 21
beforehand Pay b. BUSINESS 15
beget to get and b. HUMAN NATURE 17
begets Love b. love LOVE 5
beggar b.-woman and single SINGLE 3
b. would enfold himself QUOTATIONS 10
Be not made a b. DEBT 14
Set a b. on horseback POWER 9
Sue a b. FUTILITY 3
beggars B. can't be choosers NECESSITY 2
b. would ride OPTIMISM 12
begged living HOMER b. FAME 15
begin B. at the beginning BEGINNING 22
b. with certainties CERTAINTY 13
But let us b. BEGINNING 24
Then we'll b. BEGINNING 1

Wars b. when you will WARFARE 20
beginner not a legend. She's a b. FAME 31
beginning b. all over again ORIGINALITY 12
b., a middle QUANTITIES 25
b., a muddle FICTION 22
b. is my end BEGINNING 23
b. of any great matter THOROUGHNESS 12
b. of the end ENDING 17
b. of the end ENDING 20
b. or any end PAINTING 27
end is my b. ENDING 6
good b. BEGINNING 3
In the b. BEGINNING 19
Movies should have a b. CINEMA 19
thing than the b. ENDING 13
beginnings ends by our b. know CHARACTER 34
begins b. with a single step BEGINNING 8
begun b. to fight DETERMINATION 34
sooner b. BEGINNING 9
Well b. BEGINNING 11
behaviour basis of all good human b. BEHAVIOUR 34
on their best b. BEHAVIOUR 35
Perfect b. is born of complete BEHAVIOUR 33
behind always b. HASTE 1
B., before, above SEX 11
B. every great man GREATNESS 1
Get thee b. me, Satan TEMPTATION 8
it will be b. me CRITICISM 12
one must ride b. RANK 2
those b. cried 'Forward!' COURAGE 21
beholder eye of the b. BEAUTY 3
being by avoiding b. WORRY 11
darkness of mere b. LIFE 54
I will call no b. good GOD 29
Nothingness haunts b. FUTILITY 31
worried into b. CREATIVITY 11
Belfast be kind to B. BRITISH TOWNS 42
look down on B. BRITISH TOWNS 7
Belgium B. put the kibosh on WORLD WAR I 11
must be B. TRAVEL 4
belief all b. is for it SUPERNATURAL 14
grounds for b. BELIEF 30
that is b. BELIEF 32
beliefs my b. are true MIND 22
believe b. anything upon insufficient BELIEF 25
b. in miracles IDEALISM 17
B. it or not TRUTH 1
B. nothing of what you hear BELIEF 1
b. what one does not FAITH 9
b. what they wish SELF-INTEREST 22
b. what we choose BELIEF 22
Corrected *I b.* MANNERS 17
even if you don't b. BELIEF 28
I b. in yesterday PAST 38
I do not b. BELIEF 31
I don't b. a word of it IDEAS 12
I don't b. in fairies SUPERNATURAL 19
I don't *b.* it CRISES 4
not the will to b. BELIEF 26
they b. in anything BELIEF 29
ye will not b. BELIEF 13
believed b. as many as six BELIEF 23
b. during three days DECEPTION 14
Nothing can now be b. JOURNALISM 9
Nothing is so firmly b. BELIEF 15
believer b. is a songless bird BELIEF 2
believes he more readily b. BELIEF 16
believing B. has a core BELIEF 3
Not b. in force REVOLUTION 25
Seeing is b. BELIEF 5
bell B., book, and candle GREED 9
b., book, and candle SUPERNATURAL 2
b. the cat DANGER 13
Cuckoo-echoing, b.-swarmèd BRITISH TOWNS 34
for whom the b. tolls DEATH 45
belle La B. France FRANCE 2
bellowing b. cow soon forgets MOURNING 1
bells b. and whistles COMPUTERS 9
mortals who ring b. FESTIVALS 73
belly mind his b. COOKING 19
spent under his b. SIN 2
belong All your base are b. to us WINNING 1
b. by blood relationship FAMILY 7
B. TO ANY CLUB PREJUDICE 23
doesn't b. out there SKIES 27
I b. to Glasgow BRITISH TOWNS 37
where we really b. SORROW 24
you must first b. TRUST 38
ben b. trovato TRUTH 12
bend b. to the wind COUNTRIES 31
he can b. spoons PARANORMAL 21
benefit b. of clergy CLERGY 6
benevolence b. of the butcher SELF-INTEREST 26
stir up other men's b. LIBRARIES 5
Benjamin B.'s portion QUANTITIES 13
bent twig is b. EDUCATION 1
bereaved Laughter would be b. HUMOUR 19
bereavement B. is a universal MOURNING 21
Berliner *Ich bin ein B.* INTERNATIONAL 32
Bermuda B. triangle PARANORMAL 4
Bermudas If the B. let you pass SEA 3
berry made a better b. FOOD 14
beside Christ b. me PRAYER 10
thou art b. thyself KNOWLEDGE 19
best administered is b. ADMINISTRATION 4
All is for the b. OPTIMISM 19
All's for the b. OPTIMISM 1
aren't always at their b. BEHAVIOUR 35
b. and happiest moments POETRY 17
b. is good enough ARTS 8
b. is the best EXCELLENCE 15
b. is the enemy EXCELLENCE 14
b. is yet to be OLD AGE 21
b. lack all conviction EXCELLENCE 17
b. of all possible worlds OPTIMISM 30
b. of friends MEETING 1
b. of men HUMAN NATURE 1
b. of times CIRCUMSTANCE 31
b. people you can find MANAGEMENT 14
b. thing since sliced INVENTIONS 2
b. things in life MONEY 2
b. things in life POSSESSIONS 27
b. way out DETERMINATION 42
b. words POETRY 19
Corruption of the b. EXCELLENCE 1
Hope for the b. PREPARATION 10
man's b. to do man's worst WARFARE 55
past all prizing, b. LIFE 17
trouble with being b. man WEDDINGS 14
best-seller b. is the gilded tomb BOOKS 19
best-sellers all the great b. BOOKS 21
betray guts to b. my country PATRIOTISM 28
To b., you must first TRUST 38
betrayal any act of b. SUCCESS 50
better b. and better MEDICINE 22
B. is the end ENDING 13
b. man than I am CHARACTER 41
b. mouse-trap ABILITY 11

better (*cont.*)
b. part of biography BIOGRAPHY 14
b. than he shou'd be HUMAN NATURE 13
b. than it sounds MUSICIANS 9
b. the day FESTIVALS 2
b. to have loved LOVE 51
could have done b. FORGIVENESS 27
Fail b. SUCCESS 51
far, far b. thing SELF-SACRIFICE 8
for b. for worse MARRIAGE 25
from worse to b. CHANGE 33
Gad! she'd b. UNIVERSE 8
go to b. things TRANSPORT 16
neither b. nor worse NEIGHBOURS 9
never reach anything b. SATISFACTION 30
nothing b. to do HOME 26
past always looks b. PAST 3
rich is b. WEALTH 39
Things can only get b. PROGRESS 22
way to the B. OPTIMISM 25
between B. two stools INDECISION 1
Beulah Land of B. HEAVEN 5
beware b. of giving your heart DOGS 11
b. of the dog CAUTION 37
Let the buyer b. BUYING 2
bewildered utterly b. PAINTING 30
beyond b. the pale BEHAVIOUR 10
b. the veil DEATH 15
Bible English B., a book BIBLE 12
not reading the same B. BIBLE 20
To read in de B. BIBLE 17
used the B. BIBLE 14
bibles they had the b. CANADA 18
bicker b. down a valley RIVERS 9
bicycle arrive by b. POLITICAL PARTIES 42
Fantasy is like an exercise b. IMAGINATION 18
like a fish needs a b. MEN AND WOMEN 24
so is a b. repair kit MARRIAGE 48
bicycling b. to Holy Communion BRITAIN 14
bid b. the Devil good morrow PROBLEMS 4
biennials b. are the ones that die GARDENS 20
big b. bang UNIVERSE 1
B. Blue machine POLITICAL PARTIES 5
B. Brother POWER 14
B. BROTHER IS WATCHING YOU GOVERNMENT 37
b. enough to take away GOVERNMENT 38
B. fish eat little POWER 2
b. five HUNTING 3
B. Society POLITICS 33
b. society SOCIETY 3
b. tent POLITICAL PARTIES 6
Does my bum look b. in this BODY 2
Hey! b. spender WEALTH 40
I am b. CINEMA 12
I fear those b. words WORDS 20
side of the b. squadrons GOD 23
This b. bang idea UNIVERSE 15
victim to a b. lie LIES 24
Biggar but this is B. TOWNS 3
bigger b. they are SUCCESS 1
Fear makes the wolf b. FEAR 3
Universe is much b. SCIENCE AND RELIGION 18
biggest b. electric train CINEMA 11
bigot mind of the b. PREJUDICE 15
bigotry B. tries to keep truth PREJUDICE 18
bike he got on his b. ACTION 33
Put me back on my b. DETERMINATION 49
bikers nickname for b.: donors MEDICINE 27
biking b. to Holy Communion ENGLAND 24
bilingual All pro athletes are b. SWEARING 12
billabong camped by a b. AUSTRALIA 20
billboard b. lovely as a tree POLLUTION 17
billet Every bullet has its b. FATE 17
billiards To play b. well SPORTS 14
billion b. dollar country AMERICA 22
b. here and a billion there GOVERNMENT 40
binary those who understand b. MATHS 28
bind b. the sweet influences FATE 12
Safe b. CAUTION 22
binds b. to himself a joy TRANSIENCE 12
biographers picklocks of b. BIOGRAPHY 13
biographical noble and b. friend BIOGRAPHY 8
biographies innumerable b. HISTORY 16
biography better part of b. BIOGRAPHY 14
B. is about Chaps BIOGRAPHY 12
B. is the mesh through BIOGRAPHY 19
Judas who writes the b. BIOGRAPHY 10
no history; only b. BIOGRAPHY 7
biologist b. passes LIFE SCIENCES 27
biology B. is the search LIFE SCIENCES 33
digitizing b. LIFE SCIENCES 34
bird Arabian b. ORIGINALITY 2
beauty of b. song POLLUTION 20
b. a nest, the spider a web FRIENDSHIP 17
b. has flown LIBERTY 2
b. in a cage BELIEF 2
b. in the hand CAUTION 2
b. in the hand CERTAINTY 5
b. never flew GIFTS 1
B. of Freedom AMERICA 4
catch the b. of paradise CHOICE 23
early b. catches PREPARATION 4
idle b. IDLENESS 1
It's a b. HEROES 18
It's an ill b. PATRIOTISM 2
No b. soars too high AMBITION 13
sight of the b. FUTILITY 2
birdcage like a summer b. SATISFACTION 20
birds b. are flown PARLIAMENT 15
B. build CREATIVITY 9
b. came home CAUSES 27
B. do it LOVE 64
b. in last year's nest CHANGE 13
B. in their little nests ARGUMENT 1
B. of a feather SIMILARITY 2
b. of a feather SIMILARITY 14
b. of the air HOME 15
cannot prevent the b. of sorrow SORROW 3
catch old b. EXPERIENCE 11
feathers make fine b. DRESS 2
Little b. that can sing COOPERATION 10
there are many b. ABILITY 4
We think caged b. sing SORROW 12
Birmingham hopes from B. BRITISH TOWNS 30
birth b. is but a sleep PREGNANCY 7
four for a b. BIRDS 3
Rainbow gave thee b. BIRDS 18
birthdays after all, what *are* b. FESTIVALS 74
b. are feathers FESTIVALS 64
count your b. thankfully FESTIVALS 63
how our b. slowly sink FESTIVALS 75
birthplace accent of one's b. HOME 16
bisexuality b.: It immediately SEX 36
bishop b. then must be blameless CLERGY 7
How can a b. marry CLERGY 16
bishopric *merit* for a b. CLERGY 15
bishops b. are made of men CLERGY 3
bitch b. goddess SUCCESS 15

blood (*cont.*)
Come and see the b. REVOLUTION 26
flesh and b. so cheap POVERTY 22
flow of human b. RIVERS 14
freeze one's b. FEAR 6
hawser of the b.-tie RELATIONSHIPS 26
in cold b. EMOTIONS 4
innocent of the b. GUILT 7
make someone's b. boil ANGER 6
Old B. and Guts WORLD WAR II 7
salt in our b. SEA 25
show business with b. SPORTS 39
stain of b. that writes COUNTRIES 25
summon up the b. WARFARE 21
Tiber foaming with much b. WARFARE 19
trading on the b. BIOGRAPHY 9
won by B. and Guts alone WARFARE 52
bloodshed war without b. POLITICS 19
bloody b. but unbowed COURAGE 23
b. war and a sickly season ARMED FORCES 1
dark and b. ground AMERICAN CITIES 12
Not b. likely TRANSPORT 15
bloom furze is in b. LOVE 15
gorse is out of b. KISSING 2
spoiling its b. MEMORY 19
Bloomsbury B. Group WRITERS 3
blossom b. or the bole TREES 18
blossoms b., birds, and bowers SEASONS 17
blot art to b. POETS 11
b. one's copybook REPUTATION 14
b. on one's escutcheon REPUTATION 15
blow b. the bloody doors off EXCESS 41
b., thou winter wind GRATITUDE 8
b. your own trumpet SELF-ESTEEM 22
not return your b. REVENGE 20
numbing b. from which NAMES 17
September b. soft WEATHER 17
blowing b. in the wind MATURITY 13
blows b. even on cold lassi CAUTION 11
blue Big B. Machine POLITICAL PARTIES 5
B. and green should never COLOURS 1
B. are the hills FAMILIARITY 3
b. funk FEAR 17
b.-pencil CENSORSHIP 1
b. remembered hills PAST 30
b. ribbon EXCELLENCE 5
b. ribbon of the turf SPORTS 6
b. touch paper DANGER 7
b. water POLITICAL PARTIES 7
cherish the pale b. dot EARTH 17
once in a b. moon TIME 16
red, white, and b. BRITAIN 4
thin b. line LAW 16
true b. TRUST 17
True b. and Mrs Crewe POLITICAL PARTIES 15
wild b. yonder TRAVEL 20
You have a b. guitar REALITY 18
blue-chip b. BUSINESS 21
blunder God's second b. WOMEN 35
it is a b. MISTAKES 18
Youth is a b. LIFE 32
blundered Some one had b. MISTAKES 20
blush b. to find it fame VIRTUE 27
born to b. unseen FAME 16
Truth makes the Devil b. TRUTH 8
blushes Animal that B. HUMAN RACE 27
board back to the drawing b. BEGINNING 13
boards four b., two actors THEATRE 8
boast B. not thyself of to morrow FUTURE 14
boasteth then he b. BUYING 5
boat They sank my b. HEROES 20
boats lifts all b. SUCCESS 9
messing about in b. TRANSPORT 10
Boche well-killed B. ARMED FORCES 37
bodies b. into light SCIENCE 7
b. never lie DANCE 16
b. we have plunged into DEATH 78
inhabiting two b. FRIENDSHIP 11
Our b. are our gardens BODY 11
our dead b. COURAGE 24
structure of our b. BODY 18
bodkin With a bare b. SUICIDE 3
body b. electric BODY 15
b. is a machine BODY 16
b. of a weak and feeble ROYALTY 21
b. politic SOCIETY 4
b. says what words cannot BODY 29
b. to be kicked BUSINESS 33
getteth outside [the b.] PARANORMAL 9
Gin a body meet a b. MEETING 12
human b. is the best picture BODY 23
i like my b. SEX 21
looking for a b. in the coach CINEMA 13
mind in a sound b. HEALTH 17
no b. now on earth CHRISTIAN CHURCH 2
save his b. and destroy EMPLOYMENT 21
temple, called his b. BODY 14
with my b. I thee worship WEDDINGS 8
woman watches her b. uneasily BODY 25
bodybuilding Modern b. is ritual BODY 31
bodyguard b. of lies DECEPTION 23
bog b.-standard comprehensive SCHOOLS 13
Bognor Bugger B. BRITISH TOWNS 38
boil b. at different degrees ANGER 15
make someone's blood b. ANGER 6
boils watched pot never b. PATIENCE 19
bold b. as a blind mare IGNORANCE 7
let our minds be b. LOGIC 21
boldly to b. go EXPLORATION 2
boldness B., and again boldness COURAGE 19
B. be my friend COURAGE 14
bolted horse has b. MISTAKES 11
bomb Ban the b. PEACE 2
b. them back into the Stone Age WARS 23
formula of the atom b. IGNORANCE 33
bombed glad we've been b. WORLD WAR II 14
bomber b. will always get through WARFARE 46
bombers b. named for girls ARMED FORCES 47
bombs Come, friendly b. POLLUTION 19
bon-accord City of B. BRITISH TOWNS 19
bond make not a b. of love MARRIAGE 37
word is his b. ENGLAND 2
bondage b. to parents PARENTS 12
bonds surly b. of earth TRANSPORT 20
bone b. of contention ARGUMENT 6
b. of my bones WOMEN 16
bred in the b. CHARACTER 20
Charity is not a b. CHARITY 2
fetch a b. GOSSIP 2
fighting for a b. ARGUMENT 4
nearer the b. QUANTITIES 7
boneless b. wonder BODY 4
b. wonder POLITICIANS 26
bones b. of one British Grenadier WORLD WAR II 24
conjuring trick with b. GOD 38
Hard words break no b. WORDS 2
Not worth the healthy b. WARFARE 37
Parents are the b. PARENTS 34

borrowing banqueting upon b. DEBT 14
b. dulls the edge DEBT 16
b. only lingers POVERTY 16
He that goes a-b. DEBT 5
borrows early man never b. PREPARATION 5
bosoms white b. of your actresses SEX 16
boss get to be a b. EMPLOYMENT 24
only one b. BUSINESS 50
Boston B. man is the east wind AMERICAN CITIES 51
B. Tea Party REVOLUTION 6
this is good old B. AMERICAN CITIES 52
Boswelliana lues B. BIOGRAPHY 1
botanist I'd be a b. PHYSICAL 15
Botany Bay seek for at B. AUSTRALIA 13
botches no rubs nor b. MISTAKES 14
both pity they can't b. lose WARS 25
bother Though 'B. it' I may SWEARING 6
bothered Am I b. INDIFFERENCE 1
Botticelli If B. were alive PAINTING 29
bottle message in a b. PAINTING 32
shake the catsup b. FOOD 27
bottles wine in old b. CHANGE 17
wine in old b. CHANGE 25
bottom at the b. of our garden SUPERNATURAL 17
best fish swim near the b. EFFORT 2
stand on its own b. STRENGTH 2
still sit only on our b. POWER 21
bottomless Law is a b. pit LAW 24
bought b. and sold are legislators BUYING 13
Gold may be b. too dear VALUE 2
I b. the company BUSINESS 10
one who when he's b. POLITICIANS 20
bound We are not b. forever HEAVEN 21
boundaries b., usually unnatural COUNTRIES 27
bounded b. in a nut-shell DREAMS 7
bountiful Lady B. CHARITY 11
bouquet b. is better ALCOHOL 26
bourgeois astonish the b. CLASS 16
b. are other people CLASS 18
b. prefers comfort CLASS 21
bourne b. of time and place DEATH 60
Bovary *Madame B., c'est moi* WRITERS 15
bovvered Am I b. INDIFFERENCE 1
bow b. at a venture CHANCE 19
b. down in the house SELF-INTEREST 10
b. of promise WEATHER 23
b. to no man RANK 9
Cupid's b. BODY 6
drew a b. at a venture CHANCE 23
More than one yew b. DANGER 8
bowels b. of Christ CERTAINTY 14
bowl b. of cherries LIFE 48
lurk within the b. COOKING 23
bowls those who play at b. CAUTION 27
bows B. down to wood RELIGION 21
bow windows b. to the house OPTIMISM 22
bow-wow Big B. strain WRITERS 11
box in the wrong b. CIRCUMSTANCE 16
Pandora's b. PROBLEMS 13
Worth a guinea a b. VALUE 11
boxing B.'s just show business SPORTS 39
boy b. forever MEN 15
b. playing on the sea-shore INVENTIONS 8
country out of the b. COUNTRY 3
good ol' b. MEN 6
misfortunes can befall a b. PARENTS 19
Never send a b. MATURITY 1
schoolrooms for 'the b.' CRIME 30
When I was a b. GENERATION GAP 11
boys backroom b. SCIENCE 3
b. get at one end SCHOOLS 4
b. in the back rooms FAME 25
B. will be boys MEN 1
Christian b. I can scarcely SCHOOLS 5
for office b. JOURNALISM 13
not about to send American b. WARS 22
Two b. are half a boy WORK 10
bra Burn your b. WOMAN'S ROLE 1
bracelet single b. does not jingle COOPERATION 16
brae stout heart to a stey b. DETERMINATION 11
brag B. is a good dog WORDS AND DEEDS 2
brain atoms in my b. MIND 22
Bear of Very Little B. THINKING 22
b. attic stocked LIBRARIES 10
b. has oozed out TRANSPORT 12
fingerprints across his b. MUSICIANS 17
harmful to the b. SMOKING 7
haze that is my b. MIND 24
human b. is born MIND 27
idle b. IDLENESS 4
leave that b. outside PARLIAMENT 25
My b.? It's my second BODY 26
Owl hasn't exactly got B. KNOWLEDGE 47
why did He give us a b. WOMAN'S ROLE 24
brained Thou large-b. woman WRITERS 12
brains feet instead of their b. JAZZ 2
Money without b. is always MONEY 43
brake invented the b. INVENTIONS 20
branch destroy root and b. THOROUGHNESS 9
monkey who misses his b. OPPORTUNITY 16
olive b. PEACE 6
branchy b. between towers BRITISH TOWNS 34
brandy b. of the damned MUSIC 14
must drink b. ALCOHOL 11
brass muck there's b. MONEY 15
brave b. deserve the fair COURAGE 8
b. in the attempt SPORTS 4
b. man inattentive DUTY 15
b. man with a sword LOVE 56
B. men lived before REPUTATION 1
B. New-nothing-very-much FUTILITY 32
b. new world PROGRESS 1
Fortune favours the b. COURAGE 7
home of the b. AMERICA 13
Many b. men lived before BIOGRAPHY 3
None but the b. COURAGE 17
O b. new world HUMAN RACE 16
brawling with a b. woman ARGUMENT 9
bray Vicar of B. SELF-INTEREST 24
Brazil Charley's aunt from B. COUNTRIES 23
In B. they throw flowers COUNTRIES 26
Brazilian B. without land POLLUTION 25
breach honoured in the b. CUSTOM 11
Once more unto the b. WARFARE 21
bread better than no b. SATISFACTION 6
b. and circuses GOVERNMENT 6
b. and circuses GOVERNMENT 12
b. and roses HUMAN RIGHTS 2
b. and water FOOD 9
b. never falls MISFORTUNES 2
b. of idleness IDLENESS 10
b. of idleness WORK 13
b. should be so dear POVERTY 22
b. upon the waters CHANCE 24
b. upon the waters FUTURE 9
daily b. WORK 16
Give us B., but give us Roses HUMAN RIGHTS 13
Google is white b. COMPUTERS 20

HOMER begged his b. FAME 15
live by b. alone LIFE 8
made like b. LOVE 71
No dinner without b. FOOD 7
one half-pennyworth of b. VALUE 25
shalt thou eat b. WORK 20
since sliced b. INVENTIONS 2
till b. was found SATISFACTION 1
use one to buy b. LIFESTYLES 7
work, b., water and salt AFRICA 14
breadline on the b. POVERTY 10
break B., break, break SEA 19
b. one's duck CRICKET 2
b. them at pleasure MEN 8
b. the mould ORIGINALITY 3
Have a b. LEISURE 3
heart would b. HOPE 6
nature round him b. DEFIANCE 14
sucker an even b. FOOLS 27
those that b. down TECHNOLOGY 21
breakdown need not be all b. MADNESS 15
breakfast B. like a king COOKING 3
Hope is a good b. HOPE 4
sing before b. EMOTIONS 2
things before b. BELIEF 23
breaking b. it in NAMES 20
breaks b. a butterfly FUTILITY 24
b. like a little girl WOMEN 48
party b. up the better HOSPITALITY 10
break-through may also be b. MADNESS 15
breast all parts of the b. SINGING 2
soothe a savage b. MUSIC 9
breastie panic's in thy b. FEAR 14
breasts b. by which France is fed FRANCE 10
breath b. of life NECESSITY 14
call the fleeting b. DEATH 53
last b. of, say, Julius Caesar PHYSICAL 12
breathe all b. the same air HUMAN RACE 34
As though to b. were life IDLENESS 18
men can b. FAME 11
breathes B. there the man PATRIOTISM 15
breathless b. hush in the Close CRICKET 6
bred b. in the bone CHARACTER 20
breeches B. Bible BIBLE 2
put into your b. TEACHING 12
breed b. of their horses CHILDREN 11
endless war still b. WARFARE 22
this happy b. ENGLAND 7
breeding Burgundy without any b. ALCOHOL 24
Good b. consists MANNERS 16
breeds Familiarity b. contempt FAMILIARITY 5
Like b. like SIMILARITY 7
brevity B. is the soul of wit WIT 1
B. is the soul of wit WIT 6
Its body b. WIT 14
brew b., so shall you bake CAUSES 3
so shall you b. CAUSES 2
bribe b. or twist JOURNALISM 18
Marriage is a b. MARRIAGE 41
bribed b. by their loyalties CORRUPTION 15
brick carried a piece of b. BUYING 6
'Eave 'arf a b. at 'im PREJUDICE 14
inherited it b. TOWNS 15
not even red b. UNIVERSITIES 19
bricks b. without straw FUTILITY 6
make b. without straw PROBLEMS 11
bride b. of quietness SILENCE 10
b. that the sun shines on WEDDINGS 2
flowers in the b.'s hand WEDDINGS 9
jealousy to the b. HUMAN NATURE 19
never a b. WEDDINGS 1
Never the blushing b. WEDDINGS 11
rejoiceth over the b. WEDDINGS 6
bridegroom b. rejoiceth over WEDDINGS 6
brides bride-grooms, b. SEASONS 17
bridesmaid Always a b. WEDDINGS 1
always the b. WEDDINGS 11
bridge b. is love LOVE 60
b. of asses MATHS 6
b. of gold to a flying enemy WAYS 13
b. over troubled water SYMPATHY 29
b. that carries him MANNERS 3
b. too far WORLD WAR II 21
b. where there is no river POLITICIANS 30
Don't cross the b. PREPARATION 3
keep the b. with me COOPERATION 29
London B. is broken down BRITISH TOWNS 6
paint the Forth B. FUTILITY 13
bridges breaks down b. SEASONS 8
brief little b. authority POWER 22
strive to be b. STYLE 5
brigandage teaches him b. EMPLOYMENT 8
bright All things b. and beautiful ANIMALS 22
b. day is done ENDING 15
future's b. FUTURE 2
land is b. OPTIMISM 23
brighten Blessings b. HAPPINESS 1
brilliant envy of b. men EXCELLENCE 16
brimstone fire and b. HEAVEN 3
bring what it will b. VALUE 12
brisking b. about the life CATS 7
Bristol B. fashion ORDER 9
Britain Battle of B. WORLD WAR II 3
boundary of B. is revealed EXPLORATION 3
I'm backing B. PATRIOTISM 1
Without B. Europe would EUROPE 15
Britannia Cool B. BRITAIN 1
Rule, B. BRITAIN 6
British bones of one B. Grenadier WORLD WAR II 24
B. is unique BRITAIN 11
officer of B. rule AFRICA 12
ridiculous as the B. MORALITY 6
Briton glory in the name of B. BRITAIN 8
Britons B. alone use 'Might' BRITAIN 10
B. never will be slaves BRITAIN 6
broad land of the b. acres BRITISH TOWNS 24
broadens Travel b. the mind TRAVEL 9
broccoli eat any more b. FOOD 31
It's b., dear FOOD 24
broke b. the mould EXCELLENCE 11
If it ain't b. ACTION 6
broken bats have been b. TRUST 42
b. reed STRENGTH 12
Laws were made to be b. LAW 28
made to be b. TRUST 3
not quickly b. STRENGTH 17
Rules are made to be b. LAW 11
broker honest b. DIPLOMACY 4
honest b. DIPLOMACY 10
brook free, meandering b. EDUCATION 23
brooms New b. sweep clean CHANGE 6
broth Too many cooks spoil the b. WORK 9
brother Am I my b.'s keeper RELATIONSHIPS 6
Big B. POWER 14
BIG B. IS WATCHING YOU GOVERNMENT 37
b. and I against my cousin FAMILY 10
B. can you spare a dime POVERTY 26
b. sin against me FORGIVENESS 12

brother (*cont.*)
B. to Death SLEEP 8
closer than a b. FRIENDSHIP 10
man and a b. HUMAN RACE 4
man and a b. RACE 1
white man's b. RACE 21
brotherhood broadened into a b. INTERNATIONAL 33
crown thy good with b. AMERICA 23
table of b. EQUALITY 17
brother-in-law not his b. RACE 21
brothers All arts are b. ARTS 1
b. or eight cousins LIFE SCIENCES 26
live together as b. COOPERATION 33
brow sweat of one's b. WORK 15
brown How now, b. cow SPEECH 1
strong b. god RIVERS 16
browns sorry for the poor b. COLOURS 6
bruised b. in a new place CHANGE 36
brush b. that I make love PAINTING 20
B. up your Shakespeare QUOTATIONS 17
work with so fine a b. WRITERS 10
brutality b. and sadistic conduct BIBLE 18
brute Brute heart of a b. MEN AND WOMEN 21
treated as a b. RACE 11
brutes made to live as b. HUMAN RACE 14
brutish b. and short LIFE 23
Brutus You too, B. TRUST 20
bubble b. reputation ARMED FORCES 16
froth and b. LIFE 35
buck bang for one's b. VALUE 13
bigger bang for a b. WARFARE 2
b. stops here DUTY 25
pass the b. DUTY 8
bucket b. of ashes PAST 33
stick inside a swill b. ADVERTISING 10
buckeye B. State AMERICAN CITIES 6
buckle *b.* which fastens PARLIAMENT 23
Buckley B.'s chance CHANCE 20
two chances, B.'s and none CHANCE 17
bud nip him in the b. DECEPTION 18
Buddha B., the Godhead GOD 36
buds Hey, b. below FLOWERS 12
bug not a b., it's a feature COMPUTERS 6
bugger B. Bognor BRITISH TOWNS 38
build Birds b. CREATIVITY 9
b. shopping malls BUSINESS 51
easier to b. two chimneys ARCHITECTURE 2
Fools b. houses FOOLS 4
building beauty in a b. ARCHITECTURE 9
first b. erected by ARCHITECTURE 1
it's a very old b. THEATRE 20
No good b. without ARCHITECTURE 3
buildings applies only to b. ARCHITECTURE 15
our b. shape us ARCHITECTURE 14
builds b. on mud DEMOCRACY 4
built b. in a day PATIENCE 15
b. on sand STRENGTH 13
b. Thebes of the seven gates WORK 36
bulimia yuppie version of b. HEALTH 26
bull b. market BUSINESS 22
milk the b. BELIEF 18
red rag to a b. ANGER 7
bulldog Darwin's b. LIFE SCIENCES 3
Darwin's b. LIFE SCIENCES 18
bullet Every b. has its billet FATE 17
stronger than the b. ELECTIONS 7
bullied b. out of vice VIRTUE 31
bulls b. make money BUSINESS 1
bully b. is always a coward COURAGE 3
b. pulpit PRESIDENCY 1
such a b. pulpit PRESIDENCY 6
bum Does my b. look big in this BODY 2
bump go b. in the night SUPERNATURAL 1
go b. in the night SUPERNATURAL 4
bumping b. your head EDUCATION 2
Bunbury invalid called B. APOLOGY 17
Buncombe talking to B. SPEECHES 4
bundle not ten in a b. COOPERATION 15
bung-hole let out the b. THRIFT 6
bungle b. raising your children CHILD CARE 13
bungler Man is a b. PEACE 15
bunk Exercise is b. HEALTH 23
more or less b. HISTORY 23
burden Anyone can carry his b. LIFESTYLES 1
bear any b. LIBERTY 38
heavy b. of responsibility ROYALTY 41
makes the back to the b. SYMPATHY 1
my b. is light WORK 21
White Man's b. DUTY 19
white man's b. RACE 5
burdens Bear ye one another's b. COOPERATION 25
bureaucracy B., the rule of ADMINISTRATION 16
bureaucrats Guidelines for b. ADMINISTRATION 18
burglars fear of b. is not only CRIME 41
burgundy naïve domestic B. ALCOHOL 24
burials b., swindlings, affairs of state FRANCE 19
Buridan B.'s ass INDECISION 7
burn better to b. out SUICIDE 10
b. and I am ice LOVE 27
B., baby, burn VIOLENCE 1
b. the candle at both ends EFFORT 12
b. the midnight oil WORK 14
B. your bra WOMAN'S ROLE 1
Manuscripts don't b. WRITING 43
marry than to b. MARRIAGE 20
burned being in love has b. away LOVE 74
in the end, are b. CENSORSHIP 7
burning b. the rain forest POLLUTION 25
b. within my veins LOVE 36
Tyger, b. bright ANIMALS 20
burns B. Night FESTIVALS 12
candle b. at both ends TRANSIENCE 15
fiddle while Rome b. CRISES 9
burnt b. child dreads EXPERIENCE 2
Christians have b. each other CHRISTIAN CHURCH 22
never have been b. FRANCE 18
bury b. bad news DECEPTION 25
b. his mistakes ARCHITECTURE 17
b. the dead MOURNING 4
does not b. her alive WOMEN 21
We will b. you CAPITALISM 22
bus Anybody seen in a b. SUCCESS 53
good design for a b. ARTS 35
I'm not even a b. FATE 21
buses red b. ENGLAND 20
bush aims at a b. AMBITION 8
b. telegraph GOSSIP 11
copiousy branching b. LIFE SCIENCES 32
good wine needs no b. ADVERTISING 2
Poke a b., a snake comes out CAUTION 21
thief doth fear each b. GUILT 9
two in the b. CAUTION 2
wine need no b. ADVERTISING 15
bushel light under a b. SELF-ESTEEM 9
bushes b. trimmed and trained LANGUAGE 27
busiest b. men have the most LEISURE 2
Tomorrow is often the b. day FUTURE 7
business American people is b. AMERICA 27

reap a c. CAUSES 23
Sports do not build c. SPORTS 34
three-quarters turns on personal c. WARFARE 27
characters c. we have climbed into DEATH 78
charge c. of the clattering train MANAGEMENT 13
chariot Time's wingèd c. TIME 33
chariots wheels of his c. HASTE 10
charitable c. institution FAMILY 20
charity C. begins at home CHARITY 1
C. covers a multitude FORGIVENESS 1
c. for all POLITICIANS 19
C. is not a bone CHARITY 2
C. sees the need CHARITY 3
C. shall cover FORGIVENESS 13
c. will hardly water CLERGY 9
faith, hope, c. LOVE 23
in all things, c. RELATIONSHIPS 10
justice, not c., that is wanting JUSTICE 30
lectures or a little c. GIFTS 17
living need c. CHARITY 18
not a gesture of c. POVERTY 35
roots of c. CHARITY 6
Charles C. the First, his Cromwell TRUST 29
King C.'s head IDEAS 4
Charlie Bonnie Prince C. ROYALTY 5
charm c. he never so wisely DEFIANCE 9
hard words like a c. LETTERS 7
northern c. AMERICAN CITIES 63
charmed C. magic casements IMAGINATION 9
charmer t'other dear c. away CHOICE 15
charming c. is divine philosophy PHILOSOPHY 7
charms Music has c. MUSIC 9
Charybdis between Scylla and C. DANGER 14
chase c. the dragon DRUGS 2
stern c. DETERMINATION 15
wild-goose c. FUTILITY 18
chases man c. a girl COURTSHIP 10
chaste c. and fair SKIES 11
c. whore HUMOUR 18
chastised c. you with whips CRIME 21
chastity c. and continence SEX 9
C.—the most unnatural SEX 23
Eunuchs boasting of their c. TEMPTATION 17
vice of c. SINGLE 6
chat agreement kills a c. CONVERSATION 20
chateaux c. would never have been FRANCE 18
chattels goods and c. POSSESSIONS 11
chatter idle c. MEANING 10
chattering c. classes INTELLIGENCE 3
Chatterley end of the *C.* ban SEX 34
Chaucer Master Geoffrey C. POETS 8
cheap as c. sitting ACTION 8
dressed in c. shoes DRESS 19
flesh and blood so c. POVERTY 22
how potent c. music is MUSIC 19
sell it c. BUSINESS 16
Talk is c. WORDS AND DEEDS 8
to look this c. APPEARANCE 32
What we obtain too c. VALUE 27
when milk is so c. SINGLE 1
cheaper people in the c. seats CLASS 24
cheapest Buy in the c. ECONOMICS 1
c. and most common quality ARMED FORCES 23
cheat lucrative to c. CRIME 31
cheated c., as to cheat DECEPTION 15
happier to be sometimes c. TRUST 28
cheats C. never prosper DECEPTION 1
checks c. and balances GOVERNMENT 7
cheek dancing c.-to-cheek DANCE 13
one who turns the c. RELATIONSHIPS 4
smite thee on thy right c. VIOLENCE 4
turn the other c. FORGIVENESS 9
turn the other c. VIOLENCE 7
cheeping chickens come c. SEASONS 5
cheer comes it brings good c. CHRISTMAS 1
could scarce forbear to c. PRAISE 15
which side do they c. for PATRIOTISM 31
cheerful c. countenance APPEARANCE 14
c. giver GIFTS 13
cheerfulness c. keeps up HAPPINESS 15
c. was always breaking in PHILOSOPHY 11
cheers Two c. for Democracy DEMOCRACY 17
cheese apple-pie without some c. FOOD 1
born i' the rotten c. FAMILIARITY 18
c.—toasted mostly FOOD 19
like some valley c. POETRY 36
only free c. ECONOMICS 2
second mouse that gets the c. PREPARATION 12
varieties of c. FRANCE 20
chemical certain c. elements HUMAN RACE 31
two c. substances RELATIONSHIPS 20
chemistry c. and machinery DEATH 61
c. that works LIFE SCIENCES 33
cheque statement is like a c. MEANING 13
Chernobyl cultural C. CULTURE 22
cherries bowl of c. LIFE 48
c., hops, and women BRITISH TOWNS 33
likes c. soon learns to climb ACHIEVEMENT 4
cherry as American as c. pie VIOLENCE 18
c. hung with snow TREES 14
c. year SEASONS 1
second bite at the c. OPPORTUNITY 26
wild c. blossom shining COUNTRIES 17
cherry-stones carve heads upon c. POETS 13
Cheshire C. cat CATS 4
cosmic C. cat GOD 33
chess all c. players are artists SPORTS 25
C. is a sea SPORTS 1
chestnut c.-tree, great-rooted blossomer TREES 18
chestnuts c. out of the fire DANGER 22
chevalier Young C. ROYALTY 17
chew more than one can c. ACHIEVEMENT 13
chewing gum c. for the eyes BROADCASTING 2
chic Radical C. FASHION 14
radical c. FASHION 5
chicken c.-and-egg problem PROBLEMS 7
c. cross the road PROBLEMS 6
c. in his pot POVERTY 17
C. Little FEAR 5
man who has fed the c. FORESIGHT 17
Mother Carey's c. BIRDS 8
rubber c. circuit SPEECHES 2
chickens all my pretty c. MOURNING 11
C. are counted in autumn OPTIMISM 3
count one's c. OPTIMISM 17
Curses, like c. HATRED 2
Don't count your c. OPTIMISM 6
May c. come SEASONS 5
stealin' no c. ANIMALS 4
chieftain c. of the puddin'-race FOOD 17
child battle line than bear one c. WOMEN 19
change in the c. CHILD CARE 9
cherished c. PARENTS 13
c. becomes an adult CHILDREN 21
C. is father of the Man CHILDREN 14
c. is not a vase CHILDREN 7
c. is owed the greatest respect CHILDREN 6
c. is the father CHARACTER 6

child (*cont.*)
c. makes you a parent FAMILY 29
c. of a frog is a frog FAMILY 4
c.'s strength BELIEF 20
Give me a c. EDUCATION 3
have a thankless c. GRATITUDE 10
If you strike a c. VIOLENCE 8
knows his own c. PARENTS 10
like to be a c. MATURITY 14
Monday's c. BEAUTY 7
my absent c. MOURNING 10
never been hated by your c. PARENTS 26
never was a c. so lovely CHILD CARE 6
Praise the c. PARENTS 6
remain forever a c. HISTORY 9
Saturday's c. works hard WORK 7
seriousness one had as a c. MATURITY 9
shocks the mind of a c. RELIGION 20
spoiled c. of art FICTION 18
spoil the c. CHILD CARE 2
that my c. may have peace FUTURE 18
Thursday's c. has far to go TRAVEL 8
Train up a c. CHILD CARE 3
unto us a c. is born CHRISTMAS 7
use of a new-born c. INVENTIONS 9
village to raise a c. CHILD CARE 1
Wednesday's c. SORROW 2
wise c. that knows PARENTS 3
childbirth Death and taxes and c. PREGNANCY 11
Poverty is a lot like c. POVERTY 33
childhood C. is the kingdom CHILDREN 16
one moment in c. CHILDREN 17
what my lousy c. was like BIOGRAPHY 17
childish Age does not make us c. OLD AGE 20
c. valorous MATURITY 3
childishness second c. OLD AGE 14
children begin with the c. PEACE 19
borrow it from our c. EARTH 2
breeds contempt—and c. FAMILIARITY 20
bring forth c. PREGNANCY 4
bungle raising your c. CHILD CARE 13
C. always assume PARENTS 28
C. and fools HONESTY 1
c. are a bitter disappointment CHILD CARE 7
C. are certain cares FAMILY 5
c. are not your children PARENTS 21
C. aren't happy PARENTS 23
c. at play CHILDREN 8
c. can be children MATURITY 17
c. how to speak LANGUAGES 18
c. like the olive-branches FAMILY 14
c. love hamsters RELATIONSHIPS 27
c. of Abraham RELIGION 31
c. of a larger growth MATURITY 6
c. of a larger growth WOMEN 26
c. of Israel COUNTRIES 3
c. produce adults MARRIAGE 42
C. should be seen CHILDREN 1
C.'s talent to endure SUFFERING 35
c. still at heart OLD AGE 20
c. to adults HAPPINESS 33
c. to be a credit PARENTS 22
devil's c. CHANCE 4
dogs than of their c. CHILDREN 11
each one of her c. REVOLUTION 15
first class, and with c. TRAVEL 42
Goodnight, c. MEETING 20
Heaven protects c. DANGER 2
hell for c. FAMILY 20
holdeth c. from play FICTION 9
it cannot have c. PERFECTION 16
kept from c. SECRECY 29
not much about having c. CHILDREN 20
other people's c. CHILDREN 22
poor get c. POVERTY 25
reasons for having c. PREGNANCY 10
Suffer the little c. CHILDREN 5
their c. are naïve CHILD CARE 10
They can't bear c. WOMAN'S ROLE 25
wife and c. FAMILY 16
Women and c. first DANGER 12
wretched bellies of his c. POVERTY 27
you must raise c. yourself PARENTS 7
You remember the c. PREGNANCY 13
Chiltern Hundreds apply for the C. PARLIAMENT 5
chimney old men from the c. FICTION 9
chimneys easier to build two c. ARCHITECTURE 2
china land armies in C. WARFARE 60
wouldn't mind seeing C. TRAVEL 45
Chinese C. wall BUSINESS 23
C. wall SECRECY 19
C. whispers GOSSIP 12
no one can destroy the C. COUNTRIES 31
trust the C. TRUST 39
chintz Chuck out the c. HOME 1
chip c. off the old block FAMILY 13
c. of the old 'block' SPEECHES 11
c. on one's shoulder SATISFACTION 11
chips C. with everything CHOICE 24
known by his c. APPEARANCE 3
chivalry Age of C. HEROES 3
age of c. EUROPE 4
noble acts of c. PUBLISHING 3
chocolate entire box of c. liqueurs TOWNS 27
than a c. éclair CHARACTER 44
chocolates box of c. LIFE 60
choice c. in rotten apples CHOICE 6
c. of all my library LIBRARIES 4
freedom of c., but CONFORMITY 17
has a c. has trouble CHOICE 3
Hobson's c. CHOICE 10
independent c. CHOICE 17
terrible c. CHOICE 18
you takes your c. CHOICE 9
choices c. that show what we truly CHOICE 29
don't have any c. to make SOCIETY 18
sum of all the c. CHOICE 25
choke c. on the tail DETERMINATION 7
choking c. him and making him HYPOCRISY 15
choleric captain's but a c. word CLASS 11
choose *believe what we c.* BELIEF 22
c. not to be DESPAIR 13
c. to be Faraday ARTS AND SCIENCES 6
nothing to c. from CONFORMITY 17
ones we c. to love RELATIONSHIPS 26
To c. The Jews RACE 14
To govern is to c. GOVERNMENT 28
choosers Beggars can't be c. NECESSITY 2
choosing c. between the disastrous POLITICS 27
chop Before enlightenment, c. wood LIFESTYLES 2
c. logic LOGIC 3
chord I struck one c. MUSIC 13
You just pick a c. MUSIC 32
chosen c. people COUNTRIES 4
few are c. CHOICE 13
Christ cause C. wasn't a woman WOMAN'S ROLE 14
C. and His saints slept WARS 5
C. beside me PRAYER 10

cocoa C. is a cad FOOD 23
cod photographer is like the c. PHOTOGRAPHY 6
code trail has its own stern c. TRUST 34
coffee c., I want tea FOOD 21
C., which makes the politician FOOD 15
C. without tobacco SMOKING 1
coffin In death we will share one c. MARRIAGE 21
plate on a c. APPEARANCE 19
coffins walking behind the c. HEALTH 28
cogito C., ergo sum THINKING 14
coil shuffled off this mortal c. DEATH 38
this mortal c. LIFE 15
coincidence If there were no c. CHANCE 32
Twice is c. CHANCE 36
coins Proverbs are the c. of the people QUOTATIONS 2
coition After c. SEX 3
vulgar way of c. SEX 14
cold called a c. a cold SICKNESS 17
can be eaten c. REVENGE 7
Cast a c. eye INDIFFERENCE 14
c. April the barn will fill SEASONS 2
c. enough, yet, to eat CATS 14
c. fusion PHYSICAL 2
C. hands BODY 1
C. on Monday COOKING 32
c. relation FAMILY 17
c. turkey DRUGS 3
c. war INTERNATIONAL 3
Feed a c. SICKNESS 4
fuel to c. people ADVERTISING 11
Give them the c. steel WARS 20
in c. blood EMOTIONS 4
ink in my pen ran c. FEAR 12
in love with a c. climate COUNTRIES 16
in the c. light of day REALITY 5
makes my whole body so c. POETRY 22
one who's c. SUFFERING 34
so the c. strengthens WEATHER 2
you will feel no c. WEDDINGS 4
Colin C. is the sort of name NAMES 21
Coliseum While stands the C. TOWNS 18
collapse c. of Stout Party HUMOUR 1
on the point of c. MANAGEMENT 12
college cabbage with a c. education FOOD 20
colleges discipline of c. UNIVERSITIES 7
Collins marry Mr C. CHOICE 16
collision avoid foreign c. INTERNATIONAL 15
Cities give us c. COUNTRY 15
Cologne wash your city of C. POLLUTION 11
cologne truths wearing diplomatic c. WORDS 30
colonies New c. seek for AUSTRALIA 13
Colossus C. from a rock POETS 13
colour any c. that he wants CHOICE 19
bad c. APPEARANCE 6
By convention there is c. SENSES 7
c. has taken hold of me COLOURS 4
c. of his hair PREJUDICE 19
c. of the cat doesn't matter WAYS 36
Puzzled and hurt by c. line RACE 20
coloured no 'white' or 'c.' signs RACE 23
twopence c. PAINTING 14
colourless C. green ideas LANGUAGE 25
colours c. from my life SUFFERING 22
c. to the fence INDECISION 16
c. will agree INDIFFERENCE 7
feel impartial about the c. COLOURS 6
lines and c. PAINTING 8
nail one's c. DEFIANCE 8
with flying c. EXCELLENCE 9
Columbus C. sailed the ocean blue EXPLORATION 11
column Fifth c. TRUST 8
comb between two bald men over a c. WARS 29
Experience is a c. EXPERIENCE 3
combine When bad men c. COOPERATION 27
come C. again another day WEATHER 13
C. in the evening HOSPITALITY 12
c. into the world alone SOLITUDE 17
c. out as I do ARGUMENT 12
C. to the edge INSIGHT 19
c. to those who wait PATIENCE 2
c. up and see me MEETING 21
C. with me to the Casbah CINEMA 1
death is not c. DEATH 29
Easy c., easy go EFFORT 3
First c., first served PUNCTUALITY 3
Light c., light go POSSESSIONS 5
nobody will c. WARFARE 50
not where you have c. from CLASS 26
people don't want to c. SPORTS 36
Quickly c. CONSTANCY 2
shape of things to c. FUTURE 11
suppose what may c. FORESIGHT 12
will they c. when you do call PARANORMAL 10
comeback c. kid DETERMINATION 52
comedies c. are ended ENDING 18
comedy c. in long-shot LIFE 57
c. is a park CINEMA 16
C. is tragedy HUMOUR 23
c. to those that think LIFE 27
comes goes around c. around JUSTICE 13
nobody c. BOREDOM 11
Tomorrow never c. FUTURE 8
Where the wind c. from WEATHER 44
comfort Be of good c. FAITH 6
bourgeois prefers c. CLASS 21
c. of feeling *safe* FRIENDSHIP 21
mistaken c. for civilization PROGRESS 11
comfortable baith grand and c. PRACTICALITY 13
c. house is a great source HOME 18
comfortably Are you sitting c. BEGINNING 1
comforted they shall be c. MOURNING 9
comforter Job's c. SYMPATHY 8
comforts uncertain c. FAMILY 5
coming C. events FUTURE 1
C. thro' the rye MEETING 12
c. up roses OPTIMISM 35
gude time c. OPTIMISM 20
vehicle is the c. wonder TRANSPORT 9
Yanks are c. WORLD WAR I 18
comma kiss can be a c. KISSING 11
command cannot obey cannot c. LEADERSHIP 4
c. the rain ROYALTY 27
to c. success SUCCESS 28
commander c. of three armies SELF 3
commandment eleventh c. LIFESTYLES 9
commandments Ten C. LIFESTYLES 13
commendeth obliquely c. himself PRAISE 11
comment C. is free JOURNALISM 17
C. is free JOURNALISM 25
I couldn't possibly c. OPINION 30
no c. OPINION 9
commerce c., and honest friendship INTERNATIONAL 14
matters of c. INTERNATIONAL 16
smell of c. in the morning BUYING 14
commercial put to c. use PROBLEMS 27
committee c. is a group ADMINISTRATION 1
C.—a group of men ADMINISTRATION 14

Crediton C. was a borough town BRITISH TOWNS 4
credo C. quia impossibile BELIEF 14
credulity C. is the man's weakness BELIEF 20
season of c. BELIEF 19
credulous Man is a c. animal BELIEF 30
creed last article of my c. VIOLENCE 10
creeds c. a disease of the intellect RELIGION 22
half the c. CERTAINTY 18
so many c. RELIGION 26
creep c. as well as soar AMBITION 14
make one's flesh c. FEAR 7
make your flesh c. FEAR 15
creeping c. through the black RIVERS 13
crème c. de la crème SCHOOLS 12
crescent C. City AMERICAN CITIES 11
Crewe True blue and Mrs C. POLITICAL PARTIES 15
Crichton admirable C. EXCELLENCE 4
cricket capable of playing c. FRANCE 18
county [c.] grounds BRITAIN 14
C. civilizes people CRICKET 10
c. test—which side PATRIOTISM 31
What do they know of c. CRICKET 8
crime commonplace a c. CRIME 35
consequence of his c. LIBERTY 14
c. and not the scaffold CRIME 24
C. doesn't pay CRIME 2
C. must be concealed CRIME 3
c. of being a young man YOUTH 10
impulse was never a c. ACTION 22
No c.'s so great EXCELLENCE 13
Poverty is not a c. POVERTY 7
punishment fit the c. CRIME 34
Tough on c. CRIME 45
treatment of c. and criminals CRIME 37
worse than a c. MISTAKES 18
crimes c. are committed LIBERTY 15
register of c. HISTORY 14
worst of c. is poverty POVERTY 24
criminal c. element, I am of it EQUALITY 14
c. it deserves LAW 41
reform the c. CRIME 29
crimson c. thread of kinship AUSTRALIA 18
cringe Cultural C. AUSTRALIA 22
cripple cannot meet a c. CONVERSATION 17
crises c. that seemed intolerable PAST 35
crisis C.? What Crisis CRISES 28
drama out of a c. CRISES 5
Never waste a good c. CRISES 30
There cannot be a c. CRISES 26
critic c. is a man who knows CRITICISM 22
in honour of a c. CRITICISM 17
criticism continued benefit from c. CRITICISM 14
c. is ever inhibited by ignorance CRITICISM 20
C. is something you can avoid CRITICISM 1
c.'s motto CREATIVITY 13
no c. of the president PRESIDENCY 8
People ask you for c. CRITICISM 15
criticisms most penetrating of c. CRITICISM 16
criticize c. what you can't GENERATION GAP 16
criticized If you are not c. CRITICISM 24
critics c. are all ready made CRITICISM 8
c. know it MUSIC 23
c. of the next WRITING 37
You know who the c. are CRITICISM 11
crocodile c. tears HYPOCRISY 5
make friends with the c. CIRCUMSTANCE 2
never become a c. CHANGE 8
one who feeds a c. DIPLOMACY 13
Croesus as rich as C. WEALTH 9
crooked c. as corkscrews EMOTIONS 23
C. things may be as stiff MISTAKES 16
c. timber of humanity HUMAN RACE 22
crop makes a good c. CAUSES 6
cross bear the c. gladly SUFFERING 13
c. a person's palm FORESIGHT 8
c. the Rubicon CRISES 7
c. the t's HYPOTHESIS 8
C. to be borne MARRIAGE 40
Don't c. the bridge PREPARATION 3
have one's c. to bear SUFFERING 5
heaviest has been the c. of Lorraine WORLD WAR II 25
inability to c. the street FRIENDSHIP 28
No c., no crown SUFFERING 4
no c., no crown SUFFERING 17
replaced the C. SEX 30
crosses Between the c., row on row WORLD WAR I 15
C. are ladders SUFFERING 2
crossroads dirty work at the c. BEHAVIOUR 12
crow before the cock c. TRUST 21
cock will c. HOME 5
eat c. APOLOGY 9
If you have to eat c. APOLOGY 22
one for the c. FARMING 2
risen to hear him c. SELF-ESTEEM 20
white c. ORIGINALITY 5
crowd c. of men CONFORMITY 12
c. will always save Barabbas CHOICE 21
crowded Across a c. room MEETING 24
it was a bit c. MARRIAGE 51
crowds future belongs to c. FUTURE 30
crowing whistling woman and a c. hen WOMEN 7
crown City of the Violet C. TOWNS 10
c. of life is neither happiness INSIGHT 17
c. thy good AMERICA 23
glory of my c. GOVERNMENT 14
head that wears a c. ROYALTY 23
influence of the C. ROYALTY 33
jewel in the c. EXCELLENCE 7
never wears the c. TRUST 40
No cross, no c. SUFFERING 4
no cross, no c. SUFFERING 17
remained in his Majesty's c. INDIA 4
crowning c. glory BODY 5
c. mercy WARS 8
crowns end c. the work ENDING 4
crows c. begin to search SEASONS 7
crucible America is God's C. AMERICA 25
cast a violet into a c. TRANSLATION 6
crucify would not even c. him INDIFFERENCE 10
cruel All c. people describe themselves CRUELTY 15
c. and unusual punishment CRIME 12
c. and unusual punishment CRIME 27
c. as the grave ENVY 7
C. necessity NECESSITY 19
c. only to be kind CRUELTY 7
c. works of nature NATURE 15
cruellest c. month SEASONS 28
cruelty Beauty without c. SUFFERING 1
C., like every other vice CRUELTY 10
c. with a good conscience CRUELTY 11
crusade party is a moral c. POLITICAL PARTIES 36
cruse widow's c. QUANTITIES 24
crush c. those beneath them POWER 29
crust c. over a volcano CULTURE 15
cry beer to c. into ALCOHOL 23
c. all the way to the bank CRITICISM 19
c. before night EMOTIONS 2
c. before you're hurt COURAGE 5

dance (*cont.*)
chosen that of music and d. GOD 16
d. is a measured pace DANCE 8
D. is the hidden language DANCE 17
d. must pay the fiddler POWER 10
d. on the head of a pin PHILOSOPHY 1
dancer form the d. DANCE 12
d. wyt me, in irlaunde IRELAND 8
departs too far from d. MUSIC 20
face the music and d. DANCE 14
fools whether we d. or not DANCE 1
if you can walk, you can d. ABILITY 3
now see gif ye can d. WARS 6
On with the d. DANCE 10
When you go to d. DANCE 2
will you join the d. DANCE 11
dancer d. from the dance DANCE 12
shoes to be a d. DANCE 3
dancers merry d. SKIES 3
nation of d. AFRICA 8
dances d. and its music DANCE 16
d. in rhythmic measures LIFE 42
d. to an ill tune HOPE 2
no progress; it d. DIPLOMACY 7
dancing all-singing all d. ABILITY 7
d. cheek-to-cheek DANCE 13
d. is love's proper DANCE 7
like a Mask d. INSIGHT 21
like d. about architecture MUSIC 4
manners of a d. master BEHAVIOUR 21
more like wrestling than d. LIFESTYLES 19
more than d. shoes DANCE 3
dandy I'm a Yankee Doodle D. AMERICA 24
Danegeld paying the D. CORRUPTION 14
danger as to be out of d. KNOWLEDGE 40
Avoiding d. is no safer DANGER 36
d. chiefly lies EXCELLENCE 13
nettle of d. DANGER 29
One would be in less d. FAMILY 24
only one thing of d. POETRY 37
only when in d. HUMAN NATURE 10
out of d. DEBT 10
post of d. DANGER 9
dangerous Damaged people are d. EXPERIENCE 38
d. to know POETS 15
Delays are d. HASTE 2
establishments are more d. MONEY 36
how d. everything is DANGER 35
knowledge is a d. thing KNOWLEDGE 6
learning is a d. thing KNOWLEDGE 29
most d. moment REVOLUTION 20
Nothing is more d. IDEAS 13
Success is more d. SUCCESS 52
dangerously *live d.* LIFESTYLES 29
dangers D. by being despised DANGER 31
perils and d. DAY 7
Darby D. and Joan OLD AGE 9
dare d.-to-be-great situation GREATNESS 17
D. to know KNOWLEDGE 33
Letting 'I d. not' FEAR 10
none d. call it treason TRUST 25
dares Who d. wins DANGER 11
Darien upon a peak in D. INVENTIONS 10
daring Be d., be different ORIGINALITY 17
dark agree in the d. INDIFFERENCE 7
as good i' th' d. EQUALITY 6
blind man in a d. room JUSTICE 35
d. and bloody ground AMERICAN CITIES 12
d. and stormy night BEGINNING 6
d. at the foot of the lighthouse IGNORANCE 4
D. Continent AFRICA 3
d. night of the soul DESPAIR 2
feeling in the d. INSIGHT 7
grey in the d. SIMILARITY 1
leap in the d. DEATH 50
one stride comes the d. DAY 10
too d. to read DOGS 16
we are for the d. ENDING 15
darker I am the d. brother RACE 15
darkest d. hour OPTIMISM 4
darkly through a glass, d. KNOWLEDGE 20
darkness cast out into outer d. HEAVEN 7
clutch out of the d. CRIME 41
Got to kick at the d. DETERMINATION 51
inch ahead is d. FORESIGHT 2
Lighten our d. DAY 7
light in the d. LIFE 54
rulers of the d. SUPERNATURAL 9
than curse the d. HUMAN RIGHTS 19
than to curse the d. ACTION 5
darling old man's d. MARRIAGE 1
dart Cupid's d. LOVE 16
Darwin D.'s bulldog LIFE SCIENCES 3
D.'s bulldog LIFE SCIENCES 18
date d. on Saturday night SEX 36
d. which will live in infamy WORLD WAR II 16
dates treason is a matter of d. TRUST 30
dating d. in your thirties COURTSHIP 11
daughter d. of Eve WOMEN 11
d. of the voice of God DUTY 14
d. on the stage ACTING 7
d.'s my daughter PARENTS 4
Like mother, like d. FAMILY 9
Whoever has a d. WOMEN 21
daughters d. of Life's longing PARENTS 21
words are the d. of earth WORDS 13
dauntless d. in war HEROES 9
dauphin daylight's d. BIRDS 17
David D. and Goliath QUANTITIES 14
Davy D. Jones's locker SEA 5
dawn Bliss was it in that d. REVOLUTION 16
just before d. OPTIMISM 4
sing at d. SIMILARITY 23
day Action this d. ACTION 2
Another d. OPTIMISM 2
another d. older DEBT 23
arrow that flieth by d. FEAR 8
As the d. lengthens WEATHER 2
Be the d. weary DAY 1
better the d. FESTIVALS 2
bright d. is done ENDING 15
built in a d. PATIENCE 15
call it a d. ENDING 21
cares that infest the d. DAY 11
D-D. BEGINNING 14
d. has eyes SECRECY 1
d. most surely wasted HUMOUR 10
d. upon which we are reminded FESTIVALS 71
dog has his d. OPPORTUNITY 4
hard d.'s night DAY 20
however hard, for one d. LIFESTYLES 1
I have lost a d. CHARITY 15
in the cold light of d. REALITY 5
jocund d. stands tiptoe DAY 5
Just for one d. HEROES 23
knell of parting d. DAY 9
lived one d. as a tiger HEROES 1
longest d. WORLD WAR II 20

discovery (*cont.*)
d. of a new dish INVENTIONS 11
no voyage of d. LEISURE 15
real voyage of d. TRAVEL 41
discretion d. about what you do LIBERTY 41
D. is not the better part BIOGRAPHY 14
D. is the better part CAUTION 7
discriminated men who are d. WOMAN'S ROLE 25
discussing d. if it existed RELATIONSHIPS 28
discussion government by d. DEMOCRACY 18
more time for d. PREPARATION 26
discussions d. of feminism HOUSEWORK 16
disease Cured yesterday of my d. MEDICINE 17
desperate d. requires REVOLUTION 8
d. at its onset MEDICINE 12
d. is incurable MEDICINE 20
From the bitterness of d. SICKNESS 5
incurable d. LIFE 24
incurable d. of writing WRITING 12
sexually transmitted d. LIFE 2
worse then the d. PROBLEMS 20
diseased To know ourselves d. SICKNESS 13
diseases All d. run into one, old age SICKNESS 15
Desperate d. NECESSITY 3
d. are innumerable COOKING 15
D. come on horseback SICKNESS 3
D. desperate grown MEDICINE 13
D. of the soul SICKNESS 11
spread d. SICKNESS 1
disenchantment d. for truth DISILLUSION 19
disestablishment pervasive sense of d. FEAR 26
disgrace Poverty is no d. POVERTY 6
disgraced dies...rich dies d. WEALTH 27
disgraceful something d. in mind CHILDREN 6
disgruntled not actually d. SATISFACTION 36
disguise d. which can hide love LOVE 37
dish discovery of a new d. INVENTIONS 11
than an empty d. SATISFACTION 3
dishes who does the d. HOUSEWORK 16
disinheriting d. countenance APPEARANCE 18
disjecta d. membra WRITING 9
dislike like and d. the same FRIENDSHIP 12
dismal d. science ECONOMICS 4
dismount afraid to d. DANGER 3
Disney of Euro D. CULTURE 22
Disneyfication D. of Christianity CHRISTMAS 19
disorder d., chaos ORDER 19
little d. in its geometry EMOTIONS 30
dispatch business than d. BUSINESS 29
disposed d. of an empire BRITAIN 12
disposes God d. FATE 3
dispraised Of whom to be d. PRAISE 10
disqualified d. for holding any office ELECTIONS 5
dissatisfied human being d. SATISFACTION 31
dissolve d. the people REVOLUTION 28
distance at such a d. from them SKIES 19
d. is nothing ACHIEVEMENT 19
D. lends enchantment APPEARANCE 5
d. lends enchantment COUNTRY 12
distances City of Magnificent D. AMERICAN CITIES 10
distant prospect of a d. good FUTURE 16
relation of d. misery SYMPATHY 21
distinction no class d. EDUCATION 11
distinguished d. by that circumstance BIRDS 16
distort d. 'em as much as you please HYPOTHESIS 18
disturb Art is meant to d. ARTS AND SCIENCES 7
ourselves doesn't d. us HATRED 9
ditch [Channel] is a mere d. SEA 16
die in the last d. DEFIANCE 5
die in the last d. DEFIANCE 13
fall into the d. IGNORANCE 11
makes a straight-cut d. EDUCATION 23
diversity Human d. makes tolerance PREJUDICE 26
world safe for d. SIMILARITY 29
divide D. and rule GOVERNMENT 2
divided d. against itself COOPERATION 24
d. by a common language LANGUAGES 17
d. we fall COOPERATION 20
dividing d. we fall AMERICA 11
divine d. as you advance APPEARANCE 27
D. Providence caused the fall CAPITALISM 30
d. right of kings ROYALTY 8
human, but it feels d. MISTAKES 30
Right D. of Kings ROYALTY 30
to forgive, d. FORGIVENESS 17
divinity d. that shapes our ends FATE 15
divorce d. is like an amputation MARRIAGE 47
d. the inquest MARRIAGE 34
DNA nature of D. ARTS AND SCIENCES 14
do Anything you can d. SELF-ESTEEM 25
are what we repeatedly d. CUSTOM 8
D. as I say HYPOCRISY 1
d. as the Romans BEHAVIOUR 8
D. as you would be done by LIFESTYLES 3
D. IT YOURSELF WAYS 33
Do not d. unto others LIKES 14
d. nothing EMPLOYMENT 12
d. only one thing THOROUGHNESS 13
D. other men BUSINESS 34
d. something to *help* COOPERATION 32
D. unto others LIFESTYLES 4
d. what I please GOVERNMENT 24
d. what I want to do LAW 35
D. what thou wilt LIFESTYLES 33
D. what you like LIFESTYLES 23
d. what you will LIFESTYLES 20
d. ye even so to them LIFESTYLES 18
HOW NOT TO D. IT ADMINISTRATION 8
I can d. no other DETERMINATION 29
it is time now to d. WORDS AND DEEDS 21
Just d. it ACTION 9
Just say 'I d.' WEDDINGS 15
Let's d. it LOVE 64
man got to d. DUTY 24
man may d. ACHIEVEMENT 10
people who d. things EFFORT 26
so much to d. ACHIEVEMENT 26
they d. what I say LEADERSHIP 24
way I d. it STYLE 23
We can't all d. everything ABILITY 9
you can't d. it all WOMEN 54
Doc with a man called D. LIFESTYLES 38
doctor Angelic D. CLERGY 5
death Will seize the d. too MEDICINE 15
God and the d. HUMAN NATURE 10
keeps the d. away HEALTH 1
doctors d. are Dr Diet MEDICINE 1
More d. smoke Camels SMOKING 3
doctrine all the winds of d. TRUTH 20
d. is something you kill FAITH 17
Not for the d. CHRISTIAN CHURCH 19
doctrines d. plain and clear DISILLUSION 10
dodge argue but those who d. ARGUMENT 16
nor an art, but a d. LOGIC 17
dodgy d. dossier NEWS 4
doers be ye d. of the word WORDS AND DEEDS 10
Evil d. CONSCIENCE 4
does as handsome d. BEHAVIOUR 5

drinka D. Pinta Milka Day HEALTH 3
drinking D. when we are not HUMAN RACE 23
drinks d. as much as you DRUNKENNESS 13
d. beer, thinks beer DRUNKENNESS 1
dripping d. June sets all in tune WEATHER 3
drive can't d. the car CRITICISM 22
difficult to d. EDUCATION 24
drink and d. ALCOHOL 1
d. a coach and six WAYS 25
drives when the devil d. NECESSITY 11
driving like the d. of Jehu TRANSPORT 7
Take it easy d. TRANSPORT 21
drop because of that missing d. CHARITY 21
d. makes the cup run EXCESS 7
d. out LIFESTYLES 40
d. the pilot TRUST 7
Nor any d. to drink SEA 15
dropping Constant d. wears away DETERMINATION 1
drops D. that gather one by one QUANTITIES 1
penny d. INSIGHT 2
drought d. is destroying his roots FARMING 13
d. of March SEASONS 16
drove Sussex won't be d. BRITISH TOWNS 11
drown I d. twa RIVERS 2
drowned BETTER D. THAN DUFFERS ABILITY 12
you'll never be d. FATE 2
drowning d. man will clutch HOPE 1
like death by d. SINGLE 11
not waving but d. SOLITUDE 19
drowns calm and silent water that d. DANGER 5
drudge his mother d. ARTS 22
drug literature is a d. WRITING 32
most powerful d. used WORDS 21
drum marching to a different d. CONFORMITY 4
drummer hears a different d. CONFORMITY 10
drunk appeal from Philip d. OPINION 7
art of getting d. DRUNKENNESS 5
d. for about a week LIBRARIES 11
Not d. is he DRUNKENNESS 6
think as you d. I am DRUNKENNESS 10
when he was d. FRIENDSHIP 22
Winston, you're d. INSULTS 11
You're not d. DRUNKENNESS 15
drunken d. man uses lampposts STATISTICS 10
sailors and d. men DANGER 2
drunkenness d. of things being SIMILARITY 28
dry into a d. Martini ALCOHOL 5
Sow d. GARDENS 9
till the well runs d. GRATITUDE 4
Dryden D. wanted, or forgot POETS 11
duchess chambermaid as of a D. IMAGINATION 7
duchesses D. are doing GOSSIP 20
duck After that everything's a d. BIRDS 22
break one's d. CRICKET 2
D. and cover CRISES 1
forgot to d. WINNING 22
seagull and says 'd.' PARENTS 35
When someone walks like a d. HYPOTHESIS 22
duckling ugly d. YOUTH 6
ducks d. who float MEMORY 5
play d. and drakes with THRIFT 12
due Give the Devil his d. JUSTICE 7
render everyone his d. JUSTICE 23
duffers BETTER DROWNED THAN D. ABILITY 12
dukes drawing room full of d. ARTS AND SCIENCES 10
d. are just as great RANK 17
dulce *D. et decorum est* PATRIOTISM 7
dull d. in himself BOREDOM 6
makes d. men witty ANGER 11
makes Jack a d. boy LEISURE 1
dullard d.'s envy EXCELLENCE 16
dullness cardinal sin is d. CINEMA 21
d. in others BOREDOM 6
dumb deep are d. EMOTIONS 11
d. year SEASONS 1
So d. he can't fart FOOLS 28
takes 40 d. animals CRUELTY 1
dunces d. are all in confederacy GENIUS 4
dungfork d. in his hand PRAYER 26
dunghill crowing on its own d. PATRIOTISM 25
crow upon his own d. HOME 5
Dunkirk appeals to the D. spirit CRISES 23
D. spirit CRISES 8
dupes If hopes were d. HOPE 17
duration for the d. TIME 12
dure *Pourvu que ça d.* TRANSIENCE 9
dusk d. with a light behind APPEARANCE 22
dust d. and ashes DISILLUSION 3
d. thou art DEATH 26
D. thou art LIFE 29
d. to dust DEATH 49
D. yourself off DETERMINATION 46
handful of d. FEAR 19
peck of March d. WEATHER 11
raised a d. KNOWLEDGE 28
shoots in joy through the d. LIFE 42
This quiet D. DEATH 57
what a d. do I raise SELF-ESTEEM 14
winning the palm without the d. WINNING 10
with age and d. TIME 31
dustbin d. of history SUCCESS 41
d. upset SLEEP 21
duster feather d. tomorrow SUCCESS 10
dusty d. answer CERTAINTY 19
d. answer SATISFACTION 12
Dutch fault of the D. INTERNATIONAL 16
duties Property has its d. POSSESSIONS 20
duty actor's d., to interpret ACTING 12
citizen's first d. SOCIETY 21
declares that it is his d. DUTY 20
die in one's d. is life DUTY 10
Do your d. bravely WORLD WAR I 9
d. bade me fight ARMED FORCES 38
d. is to obey orders CONFORMITY 11
d. is useful in work DUTY 22
D. is what no-one else will do DUTY 26
d. of a soldier ARMED FORCES 3
d. to speak one's mind DUTY 18
every man will do his d. DUTY 13
inattentive to his d. DUTY 15
I've done my d. GRATITUDE 12
life was d. LIFE 30
No d. is more urgent than GRATITUDE 7
path of d. was the way DUTY 16
voice of God! O D. DUTY 14
We must do our d. EUROPE 8
dwarfs d. on the shoulders PROGRESS 7
dyer like the d.'s hand CIRCUMSTANCE 26
dying attend a d. animal DEATH 68
d. is more the survivors' DEATH 65
d. of a hundred SICKNESS 12
d. of the light OLD AGE 31
d. without having laughed HUMOUR 7
d. with the help of too many physicians MEDICINE 10
feel that he is d. CRUELTY 6
get busy d. DRUGS 13
How long does a man spend d. DEATH 72
If this is d. DEATH 67

err (*cont.*)
To e. is human COMPUTERS 8
To e. is human FORGIVENESS 17
To e. is human MISTAKES 6
erred We have e. and strayed SIN 16
error e. in the first MISTAKES 9
e. is immense MISTAKES 17
e. that counts MISTAKES 28
Hence into deadly e. KNOWLEDGE 22
Ignorance is preferable to e. IGNORANCE 21
leading his soul into e. SUPERNATURAL 10
limit to infinite e. SCIENCE 23
old e. is always more popular TRUTH 3
positive in e. MISTAKES 16
show a man that he is in e. TRUTH 22
errors E., like straws MISTAKES 15
e. of those MISTAKES 27
His e. are volitional GENIUS 13
escalier esprit de l'e. WIT 3
escape e. from emotion POETRY 25
Gluttony is an emotional e. COOKING 33
great ones e. CRIME 7
escaped e. with the skin DANGER 28
escutcheon blot on one's e. REPUTATION 15
Esperanto E. that actually caught on DISILLUSION 22
poet writes in E. EUROPE 9
esprit e. de l'escalier WIT 3
essay e. much LIFESTYLES 30
one damn e. crisis after SCHOOLS 14
essence created of one e. HUMAN RACE 13
essential e. is invisible EMOTIONS 25
Essex E. girl WOMEN 12
E. man CLASS 4
E. stiles BRITISH TOWNS 1
established so sure e. TIME 32
estate fourth e. JOURNALISM 4
ordered their e. CLASS 15
esteem self e., grounded SELF-ESTEEM 15
état *L'É. c'est moi* GOVERNMENT 16
eternal E. City TOWNS 11
E. in man cannot kill DEATH 27
E. Woman draws us upward WOMEN 31
Hope springs e. HOPE 5
Hope springs e. HOPE 12
eternity conception of e. CRICKET 9
deep as E. SILENCE 11
do in life echoes in e. LIFESTYLES 45
E.'s a terrible thought ENDING 23
E. shut in a span CHRISTMAS 9
pinprick of e. TIME 25
radiance of E. LIFE 28
teacher affects e. TEACHING 17
Time is e. TIME 40
etherized e. upon a table DAY 14
E. upon a table POETRY 32
ethical e. foreign policy INTERNATIONAL 5
e. value of uncooked food FOOD 25
Ethiop jewel in an E.'s ear BEAUTY 15
Eton on the playing-fields of E. WARFARE 53
on the playing fields of E. WARS 15
eunuch Female E. WOMEN 53
Time's e. CREATIVITY 9
eunuchs E. boasting of their chastity TEMPTATION 17
seraglio of e. PARLIAMENT 27
euphemisms E. are unpleasant truths WORDS 30
Eureka E.! I've got it INVENTIONS 5
Europe between E. and the open sea EUROPE 11
cockpit of E. EUROPE 1
community of E. EUROPE 8
E. is a continent EUROPE 10
E. that will decide EUROPE 14
E. to have one currency MONEY 35
E. would remain a torso EUROPE 15
fifty years of E. EUROPE 6
from mainland E. EUROPE 19
Garden of E. EUROPE 3
glory of E. EUROPE 4
going out all over E. WORLD WAR I 8
sick man of E. COUNTRIES 12
sunk in E. AUSTRALIA 15
that's old E. EUROPE 20
Whoever speaks of E. EUROPE 7
European E. Dream is worth living for IDEALISM 19
E. integration EUROPE 18
E. male MEN 5
E. view of a poet EUROPE 9
unless you made the E. tour EUROPE 17
eve Adam dalfe and E. spane CLASS 9
Adam delved and E. span CLASS 2
African E. AFRICA 2
daughter of E. WOMEN 11
even get e. REVENGE 2
You can only break e. PHYSICAL 1
evening Come in the e. HOSPITALITY 12
e. full of the linnet's DAY 13
e. is spread out DAY 14
e. star SKIES 1
e. star SKIES 15
five o'clock in an e. SEASONS 30
morning knows more than the e. SLEEP 1
Now came still e. DAY 8
To see if e. POETRY 32
evensong ringeth to e. DAY 1
event as the e. decides ADVICE 14
name to the e. GREATNESS 13
wise after the e. FORESIGHT 3
events e. cast their shadow FUTURE 1
E., dear boy POLITICS 31
e. have controlled me POWER 31
E., not books, should be forbid CENSORSHIP 9
ever E. the same CHANGE 12
Hardly e. CERTAINTY 21
Nothing is for e. CHANGE 10
Everest climbed Mount E. SKIES 26
everlasting e. bliss HEAVEN 10
evermore name liveth for e. REPUTATION 19
every E. day, in every way MEDICINE 22
E. man for himself SELF-INTEREST 1
E. man for himself SELF-INTEREST 2
everybody E. has won WINNING 18
e. is ignorant IGNORANCE 28
E.'s business DUTY 2
What e. says TRUTH 10
where is e. PARANORMAL 13
everyday e. story COUNTRY 1
Everyman E., I will go with thee KNOWLEDGE 23
everyone e. is alike SOCIETY 17
E. suddenly burst out SINGING 11
You can't please e. LIKES 5
everything Chips with e. CHOICE 24
don't have to like e. LIKES 18
E. has an end ENDING 5
E. has been said DISILLUSION 11
e. in its place ADMINISTRATION 9
E. is funny HUMOUR 13
e. passes LIFE 9
e. that is the case UNIVERSE 9
get e. REVENGE 24

feeble f., tiny mind REVENGE 12
help the f. up CHARITY 17
resource of the f. ARGUMENT 14
feed F. a cold SICKNESS 4
F. the world CHARITY 23
will you still f. me OLD AGE 35
you f. him for a day CHARITY 4
feeds hand that f. GRATITUDE 5
feel as good as you're going to f. ALCOHOL 31
draw what I f. PAINTING 31
f. a thought SINGING 13
f. that he is dying CRUELTY 6
making people f. good LEADERSHIP 25
One does f. MANNERS 17
Speak what we f. HONESTY 10
tragedy to those that f. LIFE 27
feeling f. that can be danced DANCE 18
formal f. comes SUFFERING 24
petrifies the f. SIN 19
feelings f. in language LANGUAGE 14
feels as old as he f. MEN AND WOMEN 3
fees school f. are heavy EXPERIENCE 23
feet belongs to cold f. CONSCIENCE 2
cat always lands on its f. CATS 1
cutting off our f. SATISFACTION 23
die on your f. LIBERTY 29
f. are still on the ground WEALTH 43
f. of clay CHARACTER 23
f. of him that bringeth NEWS 7
hear it through their f. JAZZ 2
man who had no f. MISFORTUNES 20
man with no f. MISFORTUNES 4
never looks at its ugly f. SELF-KNOWLEDGE 2
seven f. of English ground DEFIANCE 10
When you pray, move your f. RELIGION 2
without talking about f. CONVERSATION 17
felicities f. of Solomon BIBLE 9
felicity f. on the far side BODY 20
fell flesh and f. THOROUGHNESS 7
help me when I f. CHILD CARE 5
I do not love thee, Dr F. LIKES 9
fellow Stone-dead hath no f. DEATH 10
felt what someone has f. PAINTING 16
female being f. put many more obstacles PREJUDICE 25
F. Eunuch WOMEN 53
f. of the species WOMEN 2
f. of the species WOMEN 38
left in f. hands CULTURE 21
feminine f. of genius TASTE 8
feminism discussions of f. HOUSEWORK 16
feminist Fat is a f. issue BODY 27
people call me a f. WOMAN'S ROLE 20
Womanist is to f. WOMAN'S ROLE 27
fence animal who can sit on a f. POLITICIANS 2
colours to the f. INDECISION 16
Don't f. me in COUNTRY 19
other side of the f. ENVY 3
fences barbed wire f. SCOTLAND 14
f. make good neighbours NEIGHBOURS 1
Fermat F.'s last theorem MATHS 4
Fermi F. paradox PARANORMAL 6
right to opinion as F. PHYSICAL 21
fern As one f. frond dies LEADERSHIP 1
ferocious f. in battle ARMED FORCES 51
ferocity he calls it f. HUNTING 14
Ferraris F., blondes and switchblades LIKES 19
fertilizer use him as a f. HUMAN RACE 31
festina *F. lente* HASTE 11
festival f. of lights FESTIVALS 19
fetters his f. fall LIBERTY 34
Milton wrote in f. POETS 14
fever happy with a f. CHOICE 7
starve a f. SICKNESS 4
few f. are chosen CHOICE 13
Gey f. SELF-ESTEEM 5
so many to so f. GRATITUDE 17
you win a f. SUCCESS 14
fickle Fame is a f. food FAME 21
F. and changeable always WOMEN 20
fiction face is her work of f. APPEARANCE 25
f. is a necessity FICTION 17
I hate things all *f.* FICTION 12
improbable f. FICTION 10
Stranger than f. TRUTH 27
stranger than f. FICTION 1
stranger than f. TRUTH 6
That is what f. means FICTION 16
fiddle f. while Rome burns CRISES 9
played on an old f. OLD AGE 5
fiddler dance must pay the f. POWER 10
fidelity Your idea of f. CONSTANCY 12
fidus f. Achates FRIENDSHIP 7
field corner of a foreign f. PATRIOTISM 20
f. that has rested gives LEISURE 6
flood and f. EARTH 3
harder than crossing a f. LIFE 3
lay f. to field POLLUTION 6
look in a f. and see a cow ENVY 16
only inhabitants of the f. WORDS AND DEEDS 16
potter's f. DEATH 21
fields F. have eyes SECRECY 4
fresh f. CHANGE 21
plough the f. FARMING 11
fierce by change more f. SIMILARITY 20
fifteen famous for f. minutes FAME 5
famous for f. minutes FAME 29
F. men on the dead ALCOHOL 18
f. years older OLD AGE 32
fifth f. column TRUST 8
take the F. (Amendment) SELF-INTEREST 18
under the f. rib DEATH 23
fifty booze until he's f. ALCOHOL 29
f., everyone has the face APPEARANCE 28
fig f. leaf SCULPTURE 2
fight Councils of war never f. INDECISION 3
duty bade me f. ARMED FORCES 38
f. against the future FUTURE 20
f. and fight and fight POLITICAL PARTIES 33
f. begins within himself SELF-KNOWLEDGE 13
F. fire with fire WAYS 4
f. for freedom DRESS 10
f. for its King PATRIOTISM 26
f. for one's principles MORALITY 20
f. for peace PEACE 21
f. for the good GOOD 34
f. it out DETERMINATION 39
f. like Kilkenny cats CATS 5
f. on the beaches WORLD WAR II 10
fought a good f. ACHIEVEMENT 16
I give the f. up DESPAIR 9
I'll f. to the end DEFIANCE 18
Never give up the f. DEFIANCE 17
not yet begun to f. DETERMINATION 34
size of the f. in the dog COURAGE 31
those who bade me f. SELF-SACRIFICE 11
thought it wrong to f. VIOLENCE 13
to f. for freedom WOMAN'S ROLE 19

freedom (*cont.*)
f. and truth DRESS 10
F. and Whisky ALCOHOL 12
f. depends on COURAGE 12
f. for the one LIBERTY 25
f. from fear LIBERTY 42
F. is not something LIBERTY 35
F. is the freedom to say LIBERTY 33
F. of the press JOURNALISM 22
F.'s just another word LIBERTY 39
f. there will be no State GOVERNMENT 35
f. to offend CENSORSHIP 20
f. to the slave LIBERTY 20
f. to use them POSSESSIONS 30
greatest f. a man can ever know HEALTH 25
infringement of human f. NECESSITY 23
Let f. reign LIBERTY 40
my life for f. SELF-SACRIFICE 11
not f., but licence LIBERTY 9
regard for human f. HEROES 12
road towards f. ORDER 19
separate peace from f. PEACE 27
to fight for f. WOMAN'S ROLE 19
freedoms four f. HUMAN RIGHTS 3
freehold given to none f. LIFE 18
freethinker f. is an eagle BELIEF 24
freeze f. my humanity PREGNANCY 12
f. one's blood FEAR 6
to f. the blood STYLE 14
freits He that follows f. FUTURE 3
French always have spoken F. LANGUAGES 9
clear is not F. FRANCE 12
Excuse my F. SWEARING 1
F. are with equal advantage INTERNATIONAL 16
F. is the *patois* LANGUAGES 14
F. noblesse had been FRANCE 18
F. she spak ful faire LANGUAGES 4
F. soul is stronger FRANCE 17
men, F. LANGUAGES 5
no more F. SCHOOLS 1
We F., we English CANADA 14
Frenchmen beat three F. FRANCE 1
frequency very fact of f. EMOTIONS 20
fresh f. fields CHANGE 21
f. woods CHANGE 31
Freud trouble with F. HUMOUR 20
Freude *F., schöner Götterfunken* HAPPINESS 18
friction f. which no man can imagine WARFARE 29
Friday F.'s child is loving GIFTS 2
Good F. FESTIVALS 25
man F. EMPLOYMENT 4
fridge clean behind the f. WOMAN'S ROLE 31
friend as you choose a f. READING 6
betraying my f. PATRIOTISM 28
Boldness be my f. COURAGE 14
breaking it in for a f. NAMES 20
candid f. FRIENDSHIP 19
enemy and your f. GOSSIP 24
enemy is my f. ENEMIES 3
four-legged f. ANIMALS 27
f. in need FRIENDSHIP 2
f. in Washington, get a dog POLITICIANS 34
f. is to be one FRIENDSHIP 20
f. of every country PATRIOTISM 18
f. that sticketh closer FRIENDSHIP 10
girl's best f. WEALTH 34
He makes no f. ENEMIES 14
In every f. we lose MOURNING 13
lose a f. PAINTING 22
lose your f. DEBT 6
man's best f. DOGS 16
much-loved and elegant f. ARCHITECTURE 21
Phone a f. COOPERATION 14
pretended f. is worse DECEPTION 17
To find a f. FRIENDSHIP 27
Whenever a f. succeeds SUCCESS 49
friends Animals are such agreeable f. ANIMALS 24
as well as by his f. ENEMIES 17
Be kind to your f. FRIENDSHIP 1
book is the best of f. BOOKS 12
Champagne for my real f. FRIENDSHIP 32
closest f. won't tell you HEALTH 6
deserting f. conciliates RELATIONSHIPS 18
few of his f.' houses SICKNESS 14
forgive our f. FORGIVENESS 14
f. are the sunshine of life FRIENDSHIP 23
f. ashamed to look HUMOUR 6
f. do not need it APOLOGY 18
f. in politics POLITICIANS 40
f. must part MEETING 1
F., Romans, countrymen SPEECHES 9
has a thousand f. RELATIONSHIPS 8
help from my f. FRIENDSHIP 33
his life for his f. SELF-SACRIFICE 4
How to win f. SUCCESS 42
I had such f. FRIENDSHIP 29
I have lost f. FRIENDSHIP 28
intimate sharing between f. PRAYER 13
lay down his f. for his life TRUST 37
less f. you will have ARGUMENT 3
make f. with the crocodile CIRCUMSTANCE 2
misfortune of our best f. MISFORTUNES 23
no absent f. ABSENCE 13
no f. but the mountains DIPLOMACY 2
none of his f. like him WRITERS 17
Old f. are best FAMILIARITY 15
reckonings make long f. DEBT 11
remembering my good f. FRIENDSHIP 13
Save us from our f. FRIENDSHIP 5
take our f. as they are FRIENDSHIP 16
tell it to your f. ENVY 11
Tories remember their f. POLITICAL PARTIES 24
We make our f. NEIGHBOURS 10
friendship beginning of a beautiful f. FRIENDSHIP 30
best preserves f. NEIGHBOURS 4
F. a disinterested commerce RELATIONSHIPS 11
f. closes its eyes RELATIONSHIPS 3
f. in constant repair FRIENDSHIP 15
F. is like money FRIENDSHIP 26
F. like the holly-tree RELATIONSHIPS 13
hedge between keeps f. green NEIGHBOURS 2
mechanism of f. MANNERS 18
spider a web, man f. FRIENDSHIP 17
that is true f. FRIENDSHIP 12
friendships strewn with broken f. AMBITION 18
frighten by God, they f. me ARMED FORCES 25
frightened f. to death FEAR 16
frightening never more f. CERTAINTY 27
nothing is really very f. DANGER 35
frightens Only the unknown f. FAMILIARITY 21
frippery what you call f. FASHION 8
frivolous memoirs of the f. BIOGRAPHY 15
frog child of a f. is a frog FAMILY 4
even a f. can kick him SUCCESS 13
f. in a well knows nothing SELF-ESTEEM 4
f. remains LIFE SCIENCES 27
hand of f. FOOTBALL 3
frogs f. don't die for 'fun' CRUELTY 5

goo grey g. TECHNOLOGY 4
good Acorns were g. SATISFACTION 1
All g. things ENDING 1
Anybody can be g. COUNTRY 16
arguing what a g. man should MORALITY 2
as g. as you're going to feel ALCOHOL 31
Be g., sweet maid VIRTUE 33
best is g. enough ARTS 8
Better a g. cow CHARACTER 3
cooperation with g. GOOD 37
could have a pretty g. time HAPPINESS 27
distant g. FUTURE 16
do a g. action PLEASURE 20
Do g. by stealth VIRTUE 27
drives out g. MONEY 1
enemy of the g. EXCELLENCE 14
Evil, be thou my g. GOOD 27
fight for the g. GOOD 34
For your own g. ARGUMENT 22
G. and evil shall not be held GOOD 22
g. and gay PREGNANCY 1
g. as his master EQUALITY 3
g. aunts and bad aunts FAMILY 26
g. becomes indistinguishable GOOD 42
g. beginning BEGINNING 3
g. boy deserves favour MUSIC 1
g. cop, bad cop LAW 13
g. deed in a naughty world VIRTUE 21
g. die young VIRTUE 1
g. doesn't drive out evil ACTION 34
g. ended happily FICTION 16
g. evil HYPOCRISY 7
G. fences NEIGHBOURS 1
g. for our country BUSINESS 41
G. Friday FESTIVALS 25
G. Gray Poet POETS 3
G. is that at which GOOD 17
g. Jack MEN AND WOMEN 2
g. leader is also LEADERSHIP 3
g. man to do nothing GOOD 30
g. may come of it MORALITY 1
G. men are scarce VIRTUE 2
g. must associate COOPERATION 27
g. name is rather REPUTATION 18
g. neighbours SUPERNATURAL 3
g. of subjects ROYALTY 29
g. of the people LAW 20
g. ol' boy MEN 6
g. old days PAST 12
g. old days PAST 35
g. on earth HEAVEN 14
g. or bad GOOD 25
g. publicity ADVERTISING 1
g. that I would do not GOOD 19
g. time coming OPTIMISM 20
g. time was had PLEASURE 1
g. to talk CONVERSATION 1
g. to them which hate ENEMIES 8
g. when it makes sense GOOD 48
g. when they do as others CONFORMITY 13
g. would be absent GOOD 23
Greed is g. GREED 19
Guinness is g. for you ALCOHOL 2
Hanging is too g. for him CRIME 23
having a g. time ALCOHOL 28
He who would do g. GOOD 32
If all the g. people were clever VIRTUE 39
If you can't be g. CAUTION 13
I will be g. ROYALTY 36
I will call no being g. GOD 29
Listeners never hear any g. SECRECY 5
made up their minds to be g. GOOD 46
make g. APOLOGY 4
making people feel g. LEADERSHIP 25
never g., because they are habits CUSTOM 23
never had it so g. SATISFACTION 39
No g. deed goes unpunished VIRTUE 4
not enough to have a g. mind MIND 10
odds are g. MEN 3
One g. turn COOPERATION 12
only g. Indian RACE 10
our country's g. AUSTRALIA 14
people are really g. at heart HUMAN NATURE 20
pictures aren't g. enough PHOTOGRAPHY 7
records g. things of good men HISTORY 11
sake of the g. and the beautiful ARTS 14
sees something g. NEWS 3
Show me a g. loser WINNING 27
sounds too g. to be true EXCELLENCE 2
Terrible is the temptation to be g. VIRTUE 41
thing is in g. taste TASTE 11
those who go about doing g. VIRTUE 36
thought half as g. MEN AND WOMEN 22
Too much of a g. thing EXCESS 39
too much of a g. thing EXCESS 12
twelve g. men LAW 17
very g. day DECEPTION 25
what you feel g. after MORALITY 16
When I'm g., I'm very SIN 24
When she was g. BEHAVIOUR 24
goodness delusion that beauty is g. BEAUTY 30
g. derives not from VIRTUE 20
G. had nothing to do with it VIRTUE 38
goodnight And it's g. from him MEETING 25
gay g. LIFE 45
G., children MEETING 20
goods g. and chattels POSSESSIONS 11
g. the gods provide OPPORTUNITY 19
Ill gotten g. CRIME 6
Riches and g. CAPITALISM 9
goodwill In peace: g. WARFARE 57
google G. is white bread COMPUTERS 20
goose golden g. WEALTH 12
g. is getting fat CHRISTMAS 2
g. that lays GREED 6
gott'st thou that g. look INSULTS 4
sauce for the g. JUSTICE 14
wild-g. chase FUTILITY 18
gopher G. State AMERICAN CITIES 21
Gordian cut the G. knot PROBLEMS 9
gored g. several persons CONVERSATION 9
gorilla g. in Manila SPORTS 32
gormed I'm G. SURPRISE 11
gorse g. is out of bloom KISSING 2
gory Welcome to your g. bed SCOTLAND 11
gossip g. from all the nations LETTERS 13
G. is the lifeblood GOSSIP 4
G. is vice GOSSIP 5
in the g. columns GOSSIP 27
repetitive malicious g. COUNTRY 23
gossips g. about other people's secret GOSSIP 26
got man g. to do DUTY 24
when you've g. it SELF-ESTEEM 29
gotcha G. WARS 28
Gotham wise man of G. FOOLS 8
gout give them the g. ENEMIES 11
govern g. a country FRANCE 20
g. in prose ELECTIONS 17

greed enough for everyone's g. GREED 15
G. is good GREED 19
greedy be g. when others are fearful GREED 18
G. for the property GREED 7
Greek all G. to me IGNORANCE 12
at the G. Calends TIME 11
G. gift GIFTS 7
G. in its origin COUNTRIES 22
half G., half Latin BROADCASTING 8
it was all G. to me IGNORANCE 17
Latin or in G. LANGUAGES 8
less G. LANGUAGES 7
straw for G. particles SCHOOLS 7
study of G. literature UNIVERSITIES 12
When G. meets Greek SIMILARITY 12
when his wife talks G. WOMAN'S ROLE 12
Greeks G. bearing gifts TRUST 1
G. had a word for it WORDS 24
I fear the G. even TRUST 19
When G. joined Greeks SIMILARITY 21
green all ye G. Things POLLUTION 8
Blue and g. should never COLOURS 1
charity are always g. CHARITY 6
Colourless g. ideas LANGUAGE 25
Drives my g. age YOUTH 21
g. and pleasant land ENGLAND 13
g. bough in my heart HAPPINESS 5
Green how I love you g. COLOURS 5
g. shoots of recovery ECONOMICS 5
g. thing that stands in the way TREES 11
g. Yule makes a fat churchyard CHRISTMAS 3
keeps his own wounds g. REVENGE 16
kind as it is g. IRELAND 19
life springs ever g. REALITY 13
Make it a g. peace POLLUTION 21
not that easy being g. COLOURS 7
One g. SEASONS 18
there is a different g. TREES 19
To a g. thought GARDENS 13
wearin' o' the G. IRELAND 9
greener grass is always g. ENVY 3
green-eyed g. monster ENVY 4
g. monster ENVY 9
greenhouse g. gases EARTH 19
grenadier bones of a single Pomeranian g. WARFARE 37
Gresham G.'s Law MONEY 21
grew once you g. up MATURITY 16
grey All cats are g. SIMILARITY 1
black and g. HUMAN NATURE 22
bring down my g. hairs OLD AGE 12
Good G. Poet POETS 3
g. goo TECHNOLOGY 4
g.-green, greasy, Limpopo RIVERS 11
in my g. hairs DUTY 11
little g. cells INTELLIGENCE 5
little g. cells INTELLIGENCE 14
philosophy paints its g. PHILOSOPHY 12
When you are old and g. OLD AGE 25
greyhound his horse, his hawk, and his g. RANK 4
grief best pierce the ears of g. SYMPATHY 16
Between g. and nothing SORROW 22
feel g. yourself SYMPATHY 13
g. felt so like fear SORROW 25
G. fills the room MOURNING 10
G. is a species SORROW 15
G. is the price MOURNING 2
G. is the price we pay MOURNING 27
He that conceals his g. MOURNING 3
hopeless g. SORROW 16
pain of g. is just as much a part MOURNING 24
griefs cutteth g. in halves FRIENDSHIP 14
grievance Scotsman with a g. SCOTLAND 16
grieve heart doesn't g. over IGNORANCE 9
not g. for the things POSSESSIONS 16
grieving arrow-head of g. HAPPINESS 9
grim G. Reaper DEATH 17
grin If you can't smile g. WARFARE 40
grind bastards g. you down DETERMINATION 10
g. the faces of the poor POVERTY 13
mill cannot g. OPPORTUNITY 11
mills of God g. GOD 21
mills of God g. slowly FATE 4
one demd horrid g. WORK 29
grinder organ-g. POWER 17
grinders divided into incisors and g. WRITING 34
grise éminence g. POWER 15
grist g. that comes to the mill OPPORTUNITY 2
grooves g. of change CHANGE 39
In predestinate g. FATE 21
Groucho G. tendency POLITICAL PARTIES 1
ground Grammer, the g. of al LANGUAGE 6
seven feet of English g. DEFIANCE 10
Tom Tiddler's g. WEALTH 17
when I hit the g. POVERTY 31
groundhog G. Day WEATHER 24
grounds g. for belief BELIEF 30
groves g. of Academe EDUCATION 9
grow one to g. FARMING 2
They shall g. not old ARMED FORCES 35
weeds g. apace GOOD 4
growl sit and g. ARGUMENT 12
grown-ups G. never understand GENERATION GAP 14
g., to a child MATURITY 14
grows That which *is* g. LIFE SCIENCES 10
growth children of a larger g. WOMEN 26
new g. in the plant PROGRESS 14
grub G. Street JOURNALISM 5
the old ones, g. ARMED FORCES 33
Grundy more of Mrs G. MORALITY 7
What will Mrs G. think BEHAVIOUR 22
grunt from a pig but a g. CHARACTER 19
gruntled far from being g. SATISFACTION 36
guarantees g. all others COURAGE 28
guard g. even his enemy LIBERTY 16
g. even our enemies against injustice JUSTICE 12
Who is to g. the guards TRUST 22
guards G. die ARMED FORCES 26
Up G. and at them WARS 13
guardsman G.'s cut and thrust SCIENCE 13
guerre *n'est pas la g.* ARMED FORCES 29
guerrilla g. wins if he does not lose WARFARE 61
guessing g. correctly how late PUNCTUALITY 4
g. what was at the other side WARFARE 32
guest first day a g. HOSPITALITY 2
g. will judge better of a feast COOKING 14
speed the going g. HOSPITALITY 9
Treat your guest as a g. HOSPITALITY 5
guests Fish and g. stink HOSPITALITY 3
Unbidden g. HOSPITALITY 8
guid unco g. VIRTUE 13
guidance g. of wise men LAW 36
guide be thy g. KNOWLEDGE 23
conscience be your g. CONSCIENCE 6
g. by the light of reason LOGIC 21
guided We have g. missiles SCIENCE AND RELIGION 16
guile packed with g. BRITISH TOWNS 36
guilt circumstance of g. GUILT 13

hand (*cont.*)
made by the h. SCULPTURE 5
man a free h. SEX 25
One h. for oneself SEA 4
One h. washes COOPERATION 13
sound of the single h. COOPERATION 26
steady h. CAUTION 9
sweeten this little h. GUILT 10
takes the child by the h. PARENTS 2
thinking h. SENSES 19
thy h. findeth to do THOROUGHNESS 10
what thy right h. doeth CHARITY 14
whom you take by the h. DANCE 2
written with mine own h. LETTERS 3
handbook constable's h. BIBLE 14
handful h. of dust FEAR 19
handicap My h. is your negative BODY 30
handle h. is one of us SIMILARITY 13
h. of the basket COOPERATION 3
him that can h. them OPPORTUNITY 37
handles Every thing hath two h. REALITY 11
hands Cold h. BODY 1
h. across the sea INTERNATIONAL 6
H. across the sea INTERNATIONAL 20
h. across the sea INTERNATIONAL 26
Holding h. at midnight COURTSHIP 9
horny h. of toil WORK 30
leave a man's h. empty CREATIVITY 15
Licence my roving h. SEX 11
Many h. make light work COOPERATION 11
more work than both his h. MANAGEMENT 1
no h. but yours CHRISTIAN CHURCH 2
Nothing is stolen without h. HONESTY 6
raise h. together RELATIONSHIPS 19
spits on its h. LANGUAGE 26
washed his h. GUILT 7
wash one's h. DUTY 9
work for idle h. IDLENESS 3
handsaw hawk from a h. INTELLIGENCE 4
hawk from a h. MADNESS 5
handsome H. is BEHAVIOUR 5
hang enough rope and he will h. himself WAYS 7
H. a thief when he's young CRIME 4
H. on a minute lads IDEAS 19
let him h. there HASTE 20
We must h. together COOPERATION 28
wretches h. LAW 25
hanged born to be h. FATE 2
Confess and be h. GUILT 1
h. for a sheep THOROUGHNESS 5
h. for stealing horses CRIME 25
h. in a fortnight DEATH 55
ill name is half h. REPUTATION 6
Little thieves are h. CRIME 7
hanging Catching's before h. WAYS 1
H. and wiving FATE 1
H. is too good for him CRIME 23
killing a dog than h. it WAYS 21
hangs What h. people GUILT 13
happen Accidents will h. CHANCE 1
h. tomorrow, next week POLITICIANS 31
may or may not h. PREPARATION 30
We make things h. CHANCE 38
happened never h., but are always CIRCUMSTANCE 22
happens h. anywhere BOREDOM 12
Nothing h. BOREDOM 11
Stuff h. WARS 32
there when it h. DEATH 76
what h. to a man EXPERIENCE 30
happenstance Once is h. CHANCE 36
happier h. than we Europeans AUSTRALIA 12
happiest h. and best minds POETRY 17
h. days of your life SCHOOLS 2
h. people in the world SATISFACTION 21
h. women, like the happiest nations WOMEN 34
happily h. ever after ENDING 3
happiness best recipe for h. HAPPINESS 20
desire for their own h. SUFFERING 12
fatal to true h. CAUTION 35
great enemy to human h. POVERTY 21
greatest h. MORALITY 4
greatest h. SOCIETY 11
H. depends on being free COURAGE 12
h. he feels PLEASURE 17
H. is a cigar SMOKING 2
H. is an imaginary condition HAPPINESS 33
H. is a warm gun HAPPINESS 32
H. is a warm puppy DOGS 15
h. I seek DANCE 13
H. is no laughing matter HAPPINESS 22
H. is what you make of it HAPPINESS 4
H. lies in conquering HAPPINESS 11
H. makes up in height HAPPINESS 30
h. mankind can gain HAPPINESS 14
h. of an individual GOVERNMENT 19
h. of society GOVERNMENT 21
house is a great source of h. HOME 18
In solitude, What h. SOLITUDE 8
its own kind of h. MIDDLE AGE 4
liberty to be the secret of h. LIBERTY 28
lifetime of h. HAPPINESS 25
Money can't buy h. MONEY 5
more for human h. INVENTIONS 11
only a promise of h. BEAUTY 23
pursuit of h. HUMAN RIGHTS 7
render their h. necessary HUMAN NATURE 12
result h. DEBT 19
ruin of all h. TRAVEL 32
Success is not the key to h. SUCCESS 54
suited to human h. CLASS 12
take away his h. DISILLUSION 14
two combined make H. HAPPINESS 29
ways of seeking h. BEAUTY 25
happy Call no man h. HAPPINESS 2
conspiracy to make you h. AMERICA 34
h. all your life GARDENS 4
h. as one hopes HAPPINESS 13
h. breed of men ENGLAND 7
h. could I be with either CHOICE 15
h. families resemble FAMILY 19
h. hunting-grounds HEAVEN 4
H. is the man CHILDREN 4
H.'s the wooing COURTSHIP 2
H. the hare IGNORANCE 29
H. the people whose annals HISTORY 13
h. while y'er leevin LIFE 1
lot is not a h. one LAW 33
man would be as h. IMAGINATION 7
many h. returns FESTIVALS 36
must laugh before we are h. HUMOUR 7
peacock is always h. SELF-KNOWLEDGE 2
Point me out the h. man HAPPINESS 31
remember a h. time SORROW 9
stop trying to be h. HAPPINESS 27
This is the h. warrior ARMED FORCES 37
to be h., practise compassion SYMPATHY 31
To make men h. HAPPINESS 16
whether you are h. HAPPINESS 24

Who is the h. Warrior ARMED FORCES 24
Youth is h. because YOUTH 19
happy-go-lucky h. free-for-all COURTSHIP 11
harbour God made the h. TOWNS 23
those who h. them REVOLUTION 35
hard ask the h. question PHILOSOPHY 19
doing it the h. way PARANORMAL 21
h. as the nether millstone EMOTIONS 3
H. cases make bad law LAW 3
h. day's night DAY 20
H. pounding this WARS 14
H. words break no bones WORDS 2
Math is h. MATHS 2
Old habits die h. CUSTOM 1
so h. Upon the woman WOMEN 32
hard-boiled big h. city AMERICAN CITIES 60
hardens fire that h. the egg CHARACTER 14
it h. a' within SIN 19
harder h. they fall SUCCESS 1
hardship After h. comes relief ADVERSITY 2
hare cannot run with the h. TRUST 6
First catch your h. WAYS 6
Happy the h. IGNORANCE 29
h. and tortoise DETERMINATION 22
mad as a March h. MADNESS 3
run with the h. TRUST 12
hares run after two h. INDECISION 6
harlot prerogative of the h. DUTY 23
harm do the sick no h. MEDICINE 18
forgive a man for the h. MEN AND WOMEN 16
h. to my wit FOOD 13
No people do so much h. VIRTUE 36
What h. have I ever done RANK 22
harmless elephant, the only h. ANIMALS 17
harmonies h. instead of oranges JAZZ 7
harmony disposed to h. SINGING 7
herkenyng h. SKIES 9
harness joints of the h. CHANCE 23
harp H. not on that string BOREDOM 3
h. on the same string BOREDOM 2
h. that once IRELAND 11
harrow under the h. ADVERSITY 11
Harvard my Yale College and my H. UNIVERSITIES 11
harvest h. home FESTIVALS 27
laughs with a h. AUSTRALIA 16
learned, it is the season of h. OLD AGE 1
haste done in h. PATIENCE 12
Do nothing in h. MOUNTAINS 5
H. is from the Devil HASTE 3
H. makes waste HASTE 4
I am always in h. HASTE 14
love in h. HATRED 5
Make h. slowly HASTE 5
Marry in h. MARRIAGE 8
More h., less speed HASTE 6
repent in h. MARRIAGE 26
hasty H. climbers AMBITION 1
hat ahead, get a h. DRESS 3
bigger the h. the smaller SELF-ESTEEM 2
can't think without his h. THINKING 26
hang my h. HOME 20
h. which doesn't go OLD AGE 37
my knee, my h. PRAYER 17
hatched before they are h. OPTIMISM 6
hatchet I did it with my little h. LIES 16
hate creative h. HATRED 8
don't win unless you h. them HATRED 12
even though I h. tennis SPORTS 44
good to them which h. ENEMIES 8
h. and detest HUMAN RACE 19
h. any one that we know FAMILIARITY 16
h. is conquered by love HATRED 4
h. of men will pass POWER 36
h. something in him HATRED 9
h. the man you have hurt HUMAN NATURE 8
h. the sin GOOD 21
h. to get up IDLENESS 21
how much men h. them MEN AND WOMEN 25
If h. killed men HATRED 6
I h. quotation QUOTATIONS 9
I h. television BROADCASTING 9
I have seen much to h. ENGLAND 22
immortal h. DEFIANCE 12
learn to h. HATRED 13
Let them h. GOVERNMENT 11
not to h. them INDIFFERENCE 11
people who h. me ENEMIES 9
religion to make us h. RELIGION 15
stalled ox where h. is HATRED 1
teach them to h. the things CHILD CARE 16
hated I never h. a man enough HATRED 11
never been h. by your child PARENTS 26
hates h. dogs and babies DOGS 12
man who h. his mother RELATIONSHIPS 25
tell him he h. flatterers PRAISE 8
hating don't give way to h. CHARACTER 45
h., my boy, is an art HATRED 10
hatred common h. for something RELATIONSHIPS 16
h., little room IRELAND 18
intellectual h. OPINION 27
love to h. turned REVENGE 17
set against the h. MURDER 22
stalled ox and h. HATRED 3
hats H. off, gentlemen MUSICIANS 5
hatter mad as a h. MADNESS 2
Hatteras you must beware of H. SEA 3
haunts h. of coot RIVERS 9
have h.-his-carcase, next to the perpetual LAW 29
h. to take you in HOME 22
I'll h. what she's having SEX 40
not how much we h. HAPPINESS 23
What you h., hold POSSESSIONS 6
What you spend, you h. POSSESSIONS 7
You can h. it all WOMEN 54
have-nots haves and the h. POSSESSIONS 18
haves h. and the have-nots POSSESSIONS 18
having thing we can give without h. HAPPINESS 3
havoc Cry, 'H.' REVENGE 14
hawk h. from a handsaw INTELLIGENCE 4
h. from a handsaw MADNESS 5
his horse, his h., and his greyhound RANK 4
hawkeye H. State AMERICAN CITIES 24
hawks Clever h. conceal their claws SELF-ESTEEM 3
H. will not pick out COOPERATION 6
haws welcome h. NECESSITY 12
hay antic h. DANCE 4
antic h. DANCE 6
h. while the sun shines OPPORTUNITY 10
worth a load of h. SEASONS 9
haze Purple h. MIND 24
he H. would SELF-INTEREST 28
Who h. FAME 3
head at the command—of his h. POLITICAL PARTIES 26
Better be the h. of a dog POWER 1
bumping its h. GOOD 38
for you good h. PRACTICALITY 7
God be in my h. PRAYER 12
h. on young shoulders EXPERIENCE 12

hero (*cont.*)
See, the conquering h. HEROES 7
Show me a h. HEROES 17
valet seemed a h. HEROES 10
who aspires to be a h. ALCOHOL 11
Herod Oh, for an hour of H. CHILDREN 15
out-Herod H. CRUELTY 2
heroes land that needs h. HEROES 16
speed glum h. up the line WORLD WAR I 19
We can be h. HEROES 23
heroing H. is one of the shortest HEROES 15
heron white h. is a bird BIRDS 5
hero-worship H. is strongest HEROES 12
herring Every h. must hang by DUTY 3
good red h. CHARACTER 27
red h. LOGIC 7
hesitate leader who doesn't h. before LEADERSHIP 23
hesitates h. is lost INDECISION 5
hesitation H. increases in relation to risk CAUTION 36
Without h., deviation SPEECH 6
heterodoxy h. is another man's RELIGION 18
hic h. jacet DEATH 18
H. jacet DEATH 42
hidden h. agenda SECRECY 20
h. connection is stronger LOGIC 8
h. in each other's hearts SECRECY 34
h. persuaders ADVERTISING 12
Nature is often h. CHARACTER 33
hide always h. just in the middle FAME 24
disguise which can h. love LOVE 37
h. one's light SELF-ESTEEM 9
h. our own hurts PRIDE 11
something to h. SECRECY 40
Those who h. can find SECRECY 13
wise man h. a leaf SECRECY 35
high h. man, with a great thing ACHIEVEMENT 24
h. thinking LIFESTYLES 10
None climbs so h. ACHIEVEMENT 17
Pile it h. BUSINESS 16
highbrow What is a h. INTELLIGENCE 16
higher h. the monkey climbs AMBITION 2
Swifter, h., stronger SPORTS 2
highland heart is H. SCOTLAND 13
highlands My heart's in the H. SCOTLAND 10
worst in all the H. SCOTLAND 7
high-tech thing with h. TECHNOLOGY 25
highway each and every h. LIFESTYLES 41
passes over a h. FICTION 13
hijacker terrorist and h. REVOLUTION 34
hill at the other side of the h. WARFARE 32
city upon a h. AMERICA 10
light on the h. POLITICS 23
hills Blue are the h. FAMILIARITY 3
blue remembered h. PAST 30
City of the Seven H. TOWNS 7
convictions are h. MIDDLE AGE 9
h. are alive MUSIC 28
sweet are thy h. and vales WALES 6
Himalayas H. to the heavens MOUNTAINS 10
himself Every man for h. SELF-INTEREST 1
Every man for h. SELF-INTEREST 2
hind-legs sheep on its h. CONFORMITY 12
hindmost Devil take the h. SELF-INTEREST 2
hindrance h. of ignorance IGNORANCE 15
hindsight h. is always twenty-twenty PAST 40
hinge cast iron back, with a h. GARDENS 16
hip on the h. POWER 16
smite h. and thigh CRIME 18
hippies h. wanted peace and love LIKES 19
Hippocrene blushful H. ALCOHOL 13
hippopotamus magnificent but painful h. WRITERS 18
hire worthy of his h. EMPLOYMENT 1
hired h. the money DEBT 22
Hiroshima Einstein leads to H. CAUSES 28
hissing smallest possible amount of h. TAXES 6
historian lions produce their own h. HISTORY 5
Whig h. HISTORY 7
historians h. can HISTORY 21
h. repeat one another HISTORY 22
history all the disasters of English h. WALES 8
arc of h. is long JUSTICE 45
country which has no h. HISTORY 1
dustbin of h. SUCCESS 41
end of h. HISTORY 29
Father of H. HISTORY 6
happiest women have no h. WOMEN 34
h. defaced PAST 22
H. gets thicker HISTORY 28
H. is a fable HISTORY 2
H. is bunk HISTORY 23
H. is not what you thought HISTORY 25
h. is on our side CAPITALISM 22
H. is past politics HISTORY 20
H. is the essence HISTORY 16
H. is written by the victors HISTORY 3
h. of art ARTS 20
h. records good things HISTORY 11
H. repeats itself HISTORY 4
H. repeats itself HISTORY 22
H. to the defeated SUCCESS 43
H. will absolve me REVOLUTION 29
h. with lightning CINEMA 5
hope and h. rhyme JUSTICE 43
learned anything from h. HISTORY 15
Make poverty h. POVERTY 3
no h.; only biography BIOGRAPHY 7
Thames is liquid h. RIVERS 17
thousand years of h. EUROPE 16
too much h. CANADA 12
War makes good h. PEACE 16
What's hit is h. LIFE SCIENCES 1
women seldom make h. WOMEN 51
writing a modern h. HISTORY 12
history-books blank in h. HISTORY 13
hit h. them where they live THEATRE 19
think and h. at the same time SPORTS 33
What's h. is history LIFE SCIENCES 1
hitch h. your wagon IDEALISM 8
Hitler H. invaded hell INTERNATIONAL 28
you are kidding, Mister H. WORLD WAR II 26
hitting worth by h. back PROBLEMS 35
wrong about h. a woman VIOLENCE 16
hobby horses had their H. OPINION 18
hobgoblin h. of little minds CHANGE 38
Hobson H.'s choice CHOICE 10
hockey h. mom and a pitbull DETERMINATION 54
hodie H. mihi, cras tibi DEATH 8
hoe third day give him a h. HOSPITALITY 5
tickle her with a h. AUSTRALIA 16
hog England under the h. GOVERNMENT 1
Root, h., or die WORK 6
Hogmanay H., like all festivals FESTIVALS 72
hogs h. get slaughtered BUSINESS 1
h. get slaughtered GREED 3
hoist h. with one's own petard CAUSES 15
hold H. the fort WARS 21

hope (*cont.*)
faith, h., charity LOVE 23
forward to with h. DISILLUSION 16
great white h. HEROES 4
He that lives in h. HOPE 2
He who has health has h. HEALTH 8
h. and history rhyme JUSTICE 43
H. deferred HOPE 3
H. deferred HOPE 10
h. for greater favours GRATITUDE 11
h. for the best LIFESTYLES 28
H. for the best PREPARATION 10
h. in your heart HOPE 22
H. is a good breakfast HOPE 4
h. little LIFESTYLES 30
h. over experience MARRIAGE 29
H. springs eternal HOPE 5
H. springs eternal HOPE 12
h.—only not for us HOPE 19
I fear and h. LOVE 27
If it were not for h. HOPE 6
In the kingdom of h. HOPE 7
last, best h. of earth LIBERTY 20
life there's h. HOPE 9
lives upon h. HOPE 13
Plants a h. TREES 13
recovered h. DESPAIR 11
tiny ripple of h. IDEALISM 16
Wait and H. PATIENCE 31
we sell h. BUSINESS 46
What is h. HOPE 14
when h. is gone WOMEN 29
While we breathe, we h. DETERMINATION 55
Work without h. HOPE 16
hoped He who has never h. HOPE 18
hopeful h. monster LIFE SCIENCES 4
hopefully better to travel h. HOPE 8
To travel h. TRAVEL 36
hopeless h. grief SORROW 16
hopelessness h. of one's position DESPAIR 12
hopes happy as one h. HAPPINESS 13
h. and prospects MIDDLE AGE 4
h. from Birmingham BRITISH TOWNS 30
If h. were dupes HOPE 17
vanity of human h. LIBRARIES 6
hops cherries, h., and women BRITISH TOWNS 33
heresy, h., and beer INVENTIONS 1
horizon Death is only an h. DEATH 4
horizons In these stones h. sing WALES 13
wide h. RUSSIA 6
horizontal h. desire DANCE 15
h. fall LIFE 46
horn come out of your h. MUSIC 26
cow's h. ANIMALS 8
gate of h. DREAMS 5
h. of plenty QUANTITIES 18
hounds and his h. HUNTING 11
spoil a h. DETERMINATION 23
horned h. Moon SKIES 16
horns h. of a dilemma CIRCUMSTANCE 17
horny h. hands of toil WORK 30
horribilis annus h. MISFORTUNES 30
horrible h. and the miserable OPTIMISM 38
h. imaginings FEAR 11
horror h.! The horror FEAR 18
h. of sunsets DAY 15
there is no h. IMAGINATION 12
horrors scene of h. MATHS 13
horse blows between a h.'s ears ANIMALS 9
camel is a h. ADMINISTRATION 22
cart before the h. PATIENCE 4
for want of a h. PREPARATION 7
gift h. in the mouth GRATITUDE 3
good h. APPEARANCE 6
Have a h. of your own DEBT 4
his h., his hawk, and his greyhound RANK 4
h. has bolted FORESIGHT 4
h. has bolted MISTAKES 11
h.'s hoof ANIMALS 8
h. to the water DEFIANCE 4
If two ride on a h. RANK 2
makes a good h. ANIMALS 1
mare is the better h. MARRIAGE 5
may steal a h. REPUTATION 10
No foot, no h. ANIMALS 6
old h. does not spoil the furrow OLD AGE 4
outside of a h. HEALTH 13
short h. is soon curried WORK 8
stable is not a h. CHARACTER 12
swiftest h. cannot overtake WORDS 6
Trojan h. TRUST 16
horseback Diseases come on h. SICKNESS 3
Set a beggar on h. POWER 9
horseless h. vehicle is the coming TRANSPORT 9
horseman H. pass by INDIFFERENCE 14
horsepond always a muddy h. SINGLE 8
horse races opinion that makes h. OPINION 24
horses breed of their h. CHILDREN 11
Bring on the empty h. CINEMA 8
don't spare the h. TRANSPORT 18
frighten the h. SEX 27
hell of h. ENGLAND 1
H. for courses ABILITY 2
h. in midstream CHANGE 19
h. may not be stolen CRIME 25
h. of instruction ANGER 13
If wishes were h. OPTIMISM 12
hospital requirement in a H. MEDICINE 18
host under the h. DRUNKENNESS 14
hostages h. to fortune FAMILY 16
hostile universe is not h. UNIVERSE 12
hot eat it while it's h. APOLOGY 22
H. on Sunday COOKING 32
Local ginger is not h. FAMILIARITY 7
pot is soon h. ANGER 3
What dreadful h. weather WEATHER 34
while the iron is h. OPPORTUNITY 18
hotter cooler to a h. PHYSICAL 16
hounds h. all join in HUNTING 7
h. and his horn HUNTING 11
hunt with the h. TRUST 6
hunt with the h. TRUST 12
hour at the eleventh h. HASTE 9
darkest h. OPTIMISM 4
finest h. SUCCESS 17
half an h. later TIME 13
h. which gives us life PREGNANCY 5
Improve each shining h. WORK 26
improve the shining h. EFFORT 13
longer in an h. HOSPITALITY 15
matched us with His h. WORLD WAR I 12
most carefully upon your h. PUNCTUALITY 7
Oh, for an h. of Herod CHILDREN 15
One h.'s sleep before SLEEP 2
their finest h. WORLD WAR II 13
witching h. DAY 4
ye know not what h. PREPARATION 20
hours eight h. a day EMPLOYMENT 24

hurt (*cont.*)
it is going to h. POVERTY 33
wish to h. CRUELTY 13
hurting after it has stopped h. ARTS 28
h., it isn't working ECONOMICS 24
hurts hide our own h. PRIDE 11
husband deaf h. MARRIAGE 4
h. for a comfort MARRIAGE 40
h. for life MEN 2
h. is always the last IGNORANCE 1
h. is a whole-time job MARRIAGE 36
My h. and I MARRIAGE 46
husbands reasons for h. to stay WOMAN'S ROLE 15
hush breathless h. in the Close CRICKET 6
hut Love in a h. LOVE 45
huts living in grass h. CULTURE 21
hyacinths buy White H. LIFESTYLES 32
other to buy h. LIFESTYLES 7
Hyde Jekyll-and-H. character CHARACTER 25
hygienic most h. of beverages ALCOHOL 16
hyphen *h.* which joins PARLIAMENT 23
hyphens If you take h. seriously WORDS 4
hypocrisy H. is the most difficult HYPOCRISY 16
H., the only evil HYPOCRISY 12
it allows for no h. MATHS 14
hypocrite h. is really rotten HYPOCRISY 18
hypotheses I do not feign H. HYPOTHESIS 9
hypothesis beautiful h. HYPOTHESIS 16
discard a pet h. HYPOTHESIS 26
nature of a h. HYPOTHESIS 11
i My husband and I MARRIAGE 46
IBM fired for buying I. COMPUTERS 7
ice burn and I am i. LOVE 27
i. on a hot stove CREATIVITY 11
rich man has his i. in the summer WEALTH 6
skating over thin i. DANGER 32
Vulgarity often cuts i. BEHAVIOUR 29
iceberg tip of the i. QUANTITIES 22
ice-cream i. out of the container MATURITY 16
iced three parts i. over MIDDLE AGE 6
idea After the i., plenty of time INVENTIONS 21
entertain an i. IDEAS 17
forgiveness is a lovely i. FORGIVENESS 25
good i. CAPITALISM 18
i. And the reality REALITY 17
i. first occurs SCIENCE 16
i. was ever born IDEAS 15
i. whose time IDEAS 2
invasion by an i. IDEAS 8
I've got a great i. IDEAS 19
more dangerous than an i. IDEAS 13
public rallies round an i. HYPOTHESIS 30
teach the young i. TEACHING 11
That would be a good i. CULTURE 17
wilderness of i. LANGUAGE 17
young i. CHILDREN 3
ideal i. for which I am prepared AFRICA 13
i. of reason HAPPINESS 19
idealism assassins of i. WORDS AND DEEDS 20
morphine or i. DRUGS 9
idealist I am an i. IDEALISM 10
what an i. calls a realist DISILLUSION 21
idealists I. are very apt to walk IDEALISM 12
ideals will do for his i. is lie IDEALISM 13
ideas because he has plenty of i. INTELLIGENCE 13
by acts and not by i. WORDS AND DEEDS 18
English approach to i. IDEAS 20
hold two opposed i. in the mind INTELLIGENCE 18
I. won't keep IDEAS 14
No i. but in things IDEAS 18
pegs to hang i. on WORDS 1
share no one's i. IDEAS 10
what i. the young people have IDEAS 12
identifiable Nothing in India is i. INDIA 6
ides proud I. FESTIVALS 66
idiot told by an i. LIFE 22
idiots fatuity of i. IRELAND 10
idle i. bird IDLENESS 1
i. brain IDLENESS 4
i. hands to do IDLENESS 3
i. people IDLENESS 5
most i. and unprofitable UNIVERSITIES 8
solitary be not i. IDLENESS 15
Tears, i. tears SORROW 17
when wholly i. SOLITUDE 7
idleness bread of i. IDLENESS 10
bread of i. WORK 13
I. is never enjoyable IDLENESS 6
I. is only the refuge IDLENESS 14
I. is the root IDLENESS 7
species of i. SORROW 15
idling impossible to enjoy i. IDLENESS 20
idol both God and an i. FAITH 5
ifs i. and ands OPTIMISM 11
ignorance but then so does i. EDUCATION 34
child of i. PREJUDICE 12
criticism is ever inhibited by i. CRITICISM 20
Don't die of i. HEALTH 2
else an absolute i. HAPPINESS 31
evil is simply i. GOOD 38
fact of my i. KNOWLEDGE 17
hindrance of i. IGNORANCE 15
i. and confidence SUCCESS 36
I. is an evil weed IGNORANCE 30
I. is a voluntary IGNORANCE 2
I. is bliss IGNORANCE 3
i. is bliss IGNORANCE 19
I. is like a delicate IGNORANCE 26
i. is never better INVENTIONS 18
I. is not innocence IGNORANCE 24
I. is preferable to error IGNORANCE 21
i. of nature SCIENCE AND RELIGION 8
I. of the law LAW 5
I. of the law LAW 23
i. so abysmal IGNORANCE 33
invincible i. IGNORANCE 13
lift ourselves out of i. ACHIEVEMENT 30
no sin but i. RELIGION 10
only i. IGNORANCE 25
pure i. IGNORANCE 20
sincere i. IGNORANCE 32
understand a writer's i. WRITING 29
ignorant Americans are benevolently i. CANADA 13
asking the i. LAW 44
everybody is i. IGNORANCE 28
i. and free CULTURE 11
i. enjoyment IGNORANCE 22
i. have prescribed laws LANGUAGE 11
i. men are sure BELIEF 27
i. of what occurred before HISTORY 9
no enemy but the i. SCIENCE 2
that of which he is i. IGNORANCE 6
ignore i. most poetry POETRY 34
nothing to i. PARENTS 23
ignored because they are i. HYPOTHESIS 20
ill I. gotten goods CRIME 6
I. met by moonlight MEETING 9
i. name is half hanged REPUTATION 6

line (*cont.*)
Not a day without a l. PAINTING 3
there is no Party l. CONFORMITY 15
thin blue l. LAW 16
thin red l. ARMED FORCES 14
linen Airing one's dirty l. GENIUS 17
wash one's dirty l. SECRECY 10
women or l. APPEARANCE 9
lines Just say the l. ACTING 11
l. and colours PAINTING 8
l. except the last POETRY 21
linguistic l. fascism LANGUAGE 29
lining cloud has a silver l. OPTIMISM 9
link missing l. LIFE SCIENCES 5
than its weakest l. COOPERATION 1
You are the weakest l. STRENGTH 10
linstock gunner to his l. KNOWLEDGE 1
lion better than a dead l. LIFE 7
dog is a l. in his own house HOME 2
gets the fattest l. HASTE 16
l. and the calf COOPERATION 34
l. in the way DANGER 19
l. shows its teeth DANGER 10
l.'s mouth DANGER 20
l.'s provider ANIMALS 11
l.'s share QUANTITIES 19
l. to frighten the wolves LEADERSHIP 12
living dog better than a dead l. VALUE 23
March comes in like a l. WEATHER 9
mouse may help a l. POWER 6
they can tie up a l. COOPERATION 21
twist the l.'s tail BRITAIN 5
lions Christians to the l. CHRISTIAN CHURCH 3
l. led by donkeys WORLD WAR I 4
l. produce their own historian HISTORY 5
throw someone to the l. DANGER 26
lip 'twixt cup and l. MISTAKES 5
lips l. that touch liquor ALCOHOL 15
Loose l. sink ships GOSSIP 7
Matching l. and fingertips APPEARANCE 8
My l. are sealed SECRECY 7
Read my l. TAXES 18
soul through My l. KISSING 5
lipsed Somwhat he l. SPEECH 11
lipstick l. effect BUYING 4
l.'s traces MEMORY 20
put l. on a pig FUTILITY 7
speak softly and carry l. WOMAN'S ROLE 30
liquid Cats, no less l. CATS 9
Thames is l. history RIVERS 17
liquor lips that touch l. ALCOHOL 15
l. is quicker HOSPITALITY 16
L. talks DRUNKENNESS 8
made l. for temptation TEMPTATION 16
listen good music, people don't l. HOSPITALITY 13
l. the more SPEECH 9
l. to almost anything EDUCATION 31
Stop-look-and-l. CAUTION 26
wisdom to l. CONVERSATION 15
listened he is not l. to LIES 10
listener always be a mere l. CONVERSATION 6
listeners L. never hear any good SECRECY 5
listens since nobody l. ORIGINALITY 12
literary parole of l. men QUOTATIONS 7
literature failed in l. CRITICISM 11
great Cham of l. WRITERS 8
like their l. clear UNIVERSITIES 17
l. is a drug WRITING 32
L. is a luxury FICTION 17
L. is mostly about having sex CHILDREN 20
L. is my Utopia READING 15
L. is news WRITING 42
l.'s performing flea WRITERS 20
l., the oldest ARTS AND SCIENCES 4
Remarks are not l. WRITING 41
little as bad as too l. EXCESS 37
as much as too l. POSSESSIONS 29
eat l. fish POWER 2
Every l. helps COOPERATION 4
Go, l. bok WRITING 14
l. absence ABSENCE 4
l. and loud WOMEN 5
l. Corporal FRANCE 5
L. fish are sweet QUANTITIES 3
l. knowledge KNOWLEDGE 6
l. man! thy father NECESSITY 18
l. more QUANTITIES 31
l. of what you fancy LIKES 15
l. pot is soon hot ANGER 3
L. strokes DETERMINATION 9
l. things are the most important VALUE 35
L. things please little minds VALUE 5
l. we think of the other MANNERS 16
Love me l. CONSTANCY 1
Man wants but l. LIFE 26
Many a l. makes QUANTITIES 4
no l. enemy ENEMIES 4
Only the l. people pay taxes TAXES 17
So l. done ACHIEVEMENT 26
too l. or too much LOVE 58
wants that l. strong ALCOHOL 14
live as if you were to l. for ever EDUCATION 15
better l. as we think LIFESTYLES 34
born to l. LIFESTYLES 39
cannot l. with you RELATIONSHIPS 7
Come l. with me FAMILIARITY 4
Days are where we l. DAY 19
Eat to l. COOKING 4
enable its citizens to l. ECONOMICS 14
find a way to l. LIFESTYLES 43
he isn't fit to l. IDEALISM 14
If you don't l. it MUSIC 26
l. all the days of your life LIFESTYLES 26
L. all you can LIFESTYLES 31
L. and learn EXPERIENCE 7
L. and let live PREJUDICE 2
L. as if you'll die today LIFESTYLES 37
l. at all is miracle LIFE 51
l. dangerously LIFESTYLES 29
l. dog is better LIFE 7
L. frugally LIFESTYLES 42
l. longest, see most EXPERIENCE 9
l., not as we wish LIFESTYLES 16
l. on your knees LIBERTY 29
l. our lives MEETING 19
l. through someone else RELATIONSHIPS 23
L. till tomorrow CAUTION 29
l. to fight another day CAUTION 10
l. together as brothers COOPERATION 33
l. up to them MORALITY 20
l. without him MOURNING 12
man desires to l. long OLD AGE 18
short time to l. LIFE 25
tell ourselves stories in order to l. FICTION 23
Threatened men l. long WORDS AND DEEDS 9
To l. is to change PERFECTION 9
would you l. for ever ARMED FORCES 19
You might as well l. SUICIDE 8

l. in a cottage MARRIAGE 15
l. in a golden bowl WISDOM 9
L. in a hut LOVE 45
l. in haste HATRED 5
l. in the afternoon FRANCE 21
l. is, above all, the gift LOVE 63
L. is a durable fire LOVE 33
L. is as strong as death ENVY 7
L. is blind LOVE 6
L. is blind RELATIONSHIPS 3
L. is like the wild rose-briar RELATIONSHIPS 13
L. is not love LOVE 32
l. is of man's life MEN AND WOMEN 7
L. is so short LOVE 59
L. is the fart LOVE 35
l. is to fear life FEAR 20
L. is two minutes SEX 39
L. laughs at locksmiths LOVE 7
L. like youth is wasted on YOUTH 22
L. makes the world DRUNKENNESS 12
L. makes the world LOVE 8
L. means not ever having LOVE 9
L. me little CONSTANCY 1
L. more, and all good things LIFESTYLES 6
l. my dog FRIENDSHIP 4
l. no more HEAVEN 17
l. not man the less NATURE 12
l. of money MONEY 28
l. one another or die SOCIETY 16
L. seeketh not itself to please LOVE 40
L. set you going PREGNANCY 15
L.'s harbinger SKIES 15
L.'s like a red, red rose LOVE 42
L.'s like the measles LOVE 52
l.'s proper exercise DANCE 7
l.'s young dream LOVE 17
l.'s young dream LOVE 44
L. that dare not speak LOVE 55
l. that I have LOVE 62
L. that lasts longest LOVE 54
l. that moves the sun LOVE 26
L. the Beloved Republic DEMOCRACY 17
l. themselves OPINION 3
l. the person you marry MARRIAGE 13
L. the quest MARRIAGE 34
L. the sinner GOOD 21
L.-thirty, love-forty SPORTS 22
l. thy neighbour LIFESTYLES 14
L. will find a way LOVE 10
l. would last for ever MOURNING 20
L. your enemies ENEMIES 8
magic of first l. LOVE 46
Make l. not war LIFESTYLES 8
memories of long l. MEMORY 5
No test tube can breed l. PREGNANCY 18
off with the old l. LOVE 2
ones we choose to l. RELATIONSHIPS 26
Pity is akin to l. SYMPATHY 6
power without l. is reckless POWER 39
price we pay for l. MOURNING 2
Rather than l., than money TRUTH 28
right true end of l. LOVE 30
service of my l. PATRIOTISM 22
sex with someone I l. SEX 37
sincerer than the l. of food FOOD 22
sinews of l. MONEY 32
support of the woman I l. ROYALTY 41
survive of us is l. LOVE 68
taught to l. HATRED 13
There is only l. MURDER 22
thoughts of l. LOVE 47
to think but to l. VIRTUE 20
To understand your parents' l. PARENTS 7
true l. sent to me GIFTS 6
'Twixt women's l. MEN AND WOMEN 4
unlucky in l. CHANCE 12
violent people l. violently LOVE 70
waters cannot quench l. LOVE 21
where the l. of God goes CRISES 27
Whom the gods l. die young YOUTH 3
woman wakes to l. MEN AND WOMEN 11
Work is l. made visible WORK 35
yet jealousy extinguishes l. ENVY 8
loved feared than to be l. GOVERNMENT 13
heart that has truly l. CONSTANCY 7
holy l. by the gods RELIGION 5
l. and lost LOVE 14
l. and lost LOVE 51
l. Caesar less PATRIOTISM 8
l. not at first sight LOVE 28
l. not wisely LOVE 31
l. one all together OPPORTUNITY 38
never to have been l. LOVE 38
love letter l. sometimes costs LETTERS 1
loveliness weak from your l. SPORTS 22
Lovell L. the dog GOVERNMENT 1
lovely Hurry! It's l. up here FLOWERS 12
on all things l. TRANSIENCE 14
what a l. war WORLD WAR I 26
You have l. eyes BEAUTY 31
lover Beauty is the l.'s gift BEAUTY 17
l., and the poet IMAGINATION 5
l.'s perjury LOVE 3
never any better than the l. LOVE 70
Scratch a l. ENEMIES 18
true l. of mine COURTSHIP 1
woman loves her l. WOMEN 30
lovers old l. are soundest MATURITY 5
quarrel of l. LOVE 12
star-crossed l. LOVE 19
loves all she l. is love WOMEN 30
Everybody l. a lord RANK 1
fooled by that which one l. DECEPTION 16
kills the thing he l. LOVE 56
lady l. Milk Tray EFFORT 1
l. himself in acting ACTING 10
reigned with your l. GOVERNMENT 14
loveth He that l. not GOD 11
prayeth well, who l. well PRAYER 22
loving By l. people without cause RELATIONSHIPS 14
cease l. ourselves if no one LOVE 39
discharge for l. ARMED FORCES 50
l. and giving GIFTS 2
l. longest WOMEN 29
one for l. POETRY 8
low l.-hanging fruit ACHIEVEMENT 14
l. man seeks ACHIEVEMENT 24
L. Sunday FESTIVALS 35
upper station of l. life CLASS 12
Lowells L. talk to the Cabots AMERICAN CITIES 52
loyal Lousy but l. PATRIOTISM 3
loyalties bribed by their l. CORRUPTION 15
l. which centre LEADERSHIP 20
loyalty L. is the Tory's secret POLITICAL PARTIES 35
l. we all feel SORROW 24
lucendo lucus a non l. LOGIC 5
Lucifer as proud as L. PRIDE 4
luck All you know about it [l.] CHANCE 29

majesty M.'s library LIBRARIES 8
majority As for our m. ELECTIONS 9
doesn't abide by m. rule CONSCIENCE 22
God is always in the m. FAITH 7
gone to join the m. DEATH 32
join the great m. DEATH 19
minority to the m. DEMOCRACY 13
will of the m. DEMOCRACY 8
majors live with scarlet M. WORLD WAR I 19
make does not m. anything MISTAKES 21
Don't m. excuses APOLOGY 4
find a way, or m. one WAYS 29
find a way or m. one WAYS 35
If you don't m. mistakes CREATIVITY 1
M. do and mend THRIFT 2
m. it up INDECISION 11
m. my day PREPARATION 29
Scotsman on the m. SCOTLAND 15
We m. things happen CHANCE 38
what you m. of it HAPPINESS 4
maker adores his m. SELF-ESTEEM 21
watch must have had a m. GOD 27
makers Men are born m. CREATIVITY 15
making making money from m. BUSINESS 55
malcontents create a hundred m. MANAGEMENT 8
male European m. MEN 5
existence of the m. MEN 20
more deadly than the m. WOMEN 2
more deadly than the m. WOMEN 38
maleness How beautiful m. is MEN 16
malice m. of a good thing is the barb WIT 12
m. toward none POLITICIANS 19
Never attribute to m. MISFORTUNES 9
malicious he is not m. GOD 32
malt m. does more than Milton ALCOHOL 19
mammon God and M. MONEY 16
God and m. MONEY 27
M. of unrighteousness WEALTH 13
man always get their m. CANADA 2
angry young m. GENERATION GAP 2
animal called m. HUMAN RACE 19
awakens in m. HUMAN RACE 1
Clothes make the m. DRESS 1
degraded m. PARENTS 13
demolition of a m. CRUELTY 14
do a m.'s job MATURITY 1
dreaming I am a m. SELF-KNOWLEDGE 4
drink takes the m. DRUNKENNESS 9
father of the M. CHILDREN 14
for m. or beast WEATHER 46
Grand Old M. POLITICIANS 3
if a m. bites a dog NEWS 12
I know a m. who can ABILITY 1
know one m. in particular RELATIONSHIPS 9
last thing civilized by M. MEN AND WOMEN 12
Like master, like m. EMPLOYMENT 2
make a m. a woman PARLIAMENT 13
m. and a brother HUMAN RACE 4
m. and a brother RACE 1
M., biologically considered HUMAN RACE 28
M. cannot live by bread LIFE 8
M. dreams of fame MEN AND WOMEN 11
m. for all seasons CHARACTER 26
m. for all seasons CHARACTER 32
m. Friday EMPLOYMENT 4
m. from animals SICKNESS 18
M. hands on misery DISILLUSION 20
m. in our image HUMAN RACE 8
M. is a tool-making animal HUMAN RACE 21
M. is a wolf to man HUMAN NATURE 2
m.... is *so* in the way MEN 10
M. is something to be surpassed HUMAN RACE 26
M. is the hunter MEN AND WOMEN 9
M. is the measure HUMAN RACE 2
M. is the measure HUMAN RACE 9
M. is the only Animal HUMAN RACE 27
M. is to be held MEN 8
m. must be a nonconformist CONFORMITY 8
Manners maketh m. MANNERS 4
M. of Sorrows SORROW 5
M. proposes FATE 3
m.'s a man for a' that EQUALITY 8
m.'s desire MEN AND WOMEN 8
M.'s inhumanity to man CRUELTY 8
M. wants but little LIFE 26
Money makes a m. WEALTH 4
more wonderful than m. HUMAN RACE 10
mouse and m. LIFE 14
Nine tailor make a m. DRESS 5
noblest work of m. GOD 30
No m. is an Island SOCIETY 6
no m. is wanted much VALUE 31
No moon, no m. PREGNANCY 3
nothing great but m. MIND 17
nowhere m. FUTILITY 33
Old M. River RIVERS 4
piece of work is a m. HUMAN RACE 15
rights of m. HUMAN RIGHTS 4
slave was made a m. RACE 9
Stand by your m. MEN AND WOMEN 23
what a m. may do MEN AND WOMEN 10
what's that m. for POLITICIANS 1
wolf rather than a m. HUMAN NATURE 7
woman be more like a m. MEN 18
you can call him a m. MATURITY 13
you'll be a M. MATURITY 10
managed not poor, it is poorly m. AFRICA 16
manager No m. ever got fired COMPUTERS 7
managers m. of affairs of women WOMAN'S ROLE 6
man-appeal gives a meal m. FOOD 8
Manchester What M. says today BRITISH TOWNS 14
mandarin M. style STYLE 21
manger dog in the m. SELF-INTEREST 12
laid him in a m. CHRISTMAS 8
mangoes Eat the m. WAYS 2
mangrove held together by m. roots AMERICAN CITIES 57
manhood m. was an opportunity MEN 22
Manila gorilla in M. SPORTS 32
mankind How beauteous m. is HUMAN RACE 16
M. must put an end to war WARFARE 59
proper study of m. HUMAN RACE 20
silencing m. OPINION 21
slain m. altogether MURDER 9
manly m. wise MATURITY 3
manna loathe our m. SATISFACTION 22
m. from heaven GIFTS 8
manner m. of his speech SPEECH 14
to the m. born BEHAVIOUR 16
to the m. born CUSTOM 11
manners corrupt good m. BEHAVIOUR 4
corrupt good m. MANNERS 8
for m.' sake MANNERS 7
M. are especially MANNERS 23
m. are more frightening MANNERS 22
M. maketh man MANNERS 4
m. of a dancing master BEHAVIOUR 21
Oh, the m. BEHAVIOUR 17

meat (*cont.*)
God sends m. COOKING 6
He made them out of m. COOKING 36
He sends m. FOOD 3
M. and mass CHRISTIAN CHURCH 6
One man's m. LIKES 2
Some hae m. and canna COOKING 20
sweeter the m. QUANTITIES 7
you buy m. BUYING 3
mechanical all the m. inventions yet TECHNOLOGY 9
m. arts CULTURE 8
mechanics m. of culture ARTS 26
medal get a martini and a m. DEATH 79
m. for killing two men ARMED FORCES 50
m. glitters RANK 20
medals Gongs and m. and ribbons RANK 24
meddle Do not m. in the affairs SUPERNATURAL 20
Medes M. and Persians CHANGE 22
medicine desire to take m. SICKNESS 18
good like a m. HUMOUR 4
Laughter is the best m. MEDICINE 4
m. for magic MEDICINE 26
m. for the mind LIBRARIES 1
M. for the soul LIBRARIES 2
more m. it craves MEDICINE 28
patent m. advertisement SICKNESS 16
Your food is your m. HEALTH 15
mediocre distinguish the m. RANK 16
meditation M. and water are wedded SEA 20
medium m. is the message TECHNOLOGY 19
meek Blessed are the M. PRIDE 6
m. shall inherit PRIDE 14
meet Extremes m. SIMILARITY 5
m. in heaven MEETING 7
m. troubles half-way WORRY 2
never the twain shall m. EQUALITY 13
Two men may m. MOUNTAINS 1
We'll m. again MEETING 22
we three m. again MEETING 10
meeting as if I was a public m. CONVERSATION 16
meets When Greek m. Greek SIMILARITY 12
Megillah whole M. FICTION 7
Mehmets between the Johnnies and the M. ARMED FORCES 42
melancholy m. out of a song SINGING 3
so sweet as M. SORROW 13
mellow too m. for me EFFORT 21
melody ful of hevenyssh m. SKIES 9
girl is like a m. BEAUTY 33
M. is the essence MUSIC 12
melting-pot great M. AMERICA 25
melts m. the butter CHARACTER 14
member ACCEPT ME AS A M. PREJUDICE 23
unruly m. BODY 8
members Five M. PARLIAMENT 8
membra disjecta m. WRITING 9
même c'est la m. chose CHANGE 41
memento m. mori DEATH 20
memoirs m. of the frivolous BIOGRAPHY 15
write one's m. BIOGRAPHY 16
memorandum m. is written not to inform ADMINISTRATION 19
memorial M. Day FESTIVALS 41
memories heart of marriage is m. MARRIAGE 50
m. are card-indexes MEMORY 21
m. of long love MEMORY 5
Take only m. TRAVEL 7
memory down m. lane MEMORY 1
Everyone complains of his m. MIND 12
fruit of m. MEMORY 19
God gave us m. MEMORY 18
have a good m. LIES 3
intellect but rather m. INTELLIGENCE 9
m. against forgetting POWER 44
m. for forgetting MEMORY 14
m. for his jests SPEECHES 12
m. is a monster MEMORY 25
m. is the art of attention MEMORY 8
m. revealed itself MEMORY 16
Midnight shakes the m. MEMORY 17
more than m. HEAVEN 21
no force can abolish m. BOOKS 20
quits the m. MUSIC 24
men all m. would be tyrants WOMAN'S ROLE 11
all things to all m. CHARACTER 30
best of m. HUMAN NATURE 1
company of m. MEN AND WOMEN 15
For fear of little m. SUPERNATURAL 16
have power over m. WOMAN'S ROLE 13
how much m. hate them MEN AND WOMEN 25
If m. could get pregnant PREGNANCY 17
If m. had to have babies PREGNANCY 19
intended greatness for m. GREATNESS 14
Measures not m. GOVERNMENT 27
m. are alike HUMAN NATURE 6
M. are but children MATURITY 6
m. are rapists MEN 21
m. become the tools of men MONEY 45
M. have had every advantage MEN 9
m. in my life MEN 17
M. seldom make passes APPEARANCE 26
M. were deceivers MEN 7
m. we wanted to marry WOMAN'S ROLE 26
m. who are discriminated WOMAN'S ROLE 25
more I see of m. DOGS 7
schemes o' mice an' m. FORESIGHT 14
So many m. OPINION 2
they are won by m. ARMED FORCES 41
menace our greatest m. RUSSIA 9
mend Make do and m. THRIFT 2
never too late to m. CHANGE 3
they begin to m. OPTIMISM 16
mending woman and a ship ever want m. WOMEN 9
mens *m. sana in corpore sano* HEALTH 17
mental m. states LIBERTY 34
merchandise mechanical arts and m. CULTURE 8
ultimate m. DRUGS 8
merchant m. shall hardly keep BUSINESS 26
mercies tender m. SYMPATHY 11
tender m. of the wicked ANIMALS 15
mercury m. with a fork DIPLOMACY 14
mercy crowning m. WARS 8
Lord in His m. be kind BRITISH TOWNS 42
over to God's m. REVENGE 18
quality of m. JUSTICE 27
so much as m. SIN 14
merit *m.* for a bishopric CLERGY 15
m.'s all his own SELF-ESTEEM 17
no damned m. about it RANK 14
What is m. REPUTATION 29
merrier more the m. QUANTITIES 6
merrily m. meet in heaven MEETING 7
merry drink, and to be m. LIFESTYLES 15
eat, drink and be m. LIFESTYLES 5
m. Andrew HUMOUR 3
m. dancers SKIES 3
m. heart APPEARANCE 14
m. heart HUMOUR 4

mind (*cont.*)
edge of the m. ACTION 32
empires of the m. EDUCATION 28
feeble, tiny m. REVENGE 12
frame is without a m. GOD 20
give a sex to m. MIND 14
had thee least in m. DEATH 35
just blew my m. SPORTS 42
Keep violence in the m. VIOLENCE 20
lose one's m. MIND 26
love of things of the m. CULTURE 7
make up his m. INDECISION 13
make up your m. about people RELATIONSHIPS 21
Man's m. is so formed LIES 11
matters of the m. CENSORSHIP 15
medicine for the m. LIBRARIES 1
m. be a thoroughfare MIND 15
m. being wrong OPINION 29
m. does not require filling MIND 8
m. enclosed in language LANGUAGE 22
m. has mountains MIND 20
M. has no sex MIND 2
m. his belly COOKING 19
m. in ruins MADNESS 10
m. is actually employed EMPLOYMENT 11
m. is a terrible thing MIND 3
m. is a very opal INDECISION 9
m. is but a barren MIND 13
m. is its own place MIND 11
m. is like a mirror MIND 7
m. is not a bed CERTAINTY 26
m. is stretched by a new idea IDEAS 9
m. is the least AUSTRALIA 24
m. loves the unknown FAMILIARITY 23
m. of God INSIGHT 22
m. of large general powers GENIUS 5
m. of man is capable of anything MIND 19
m. of the lower animals MIND 18
m. of the oppressed STRENGTH 29
m.'s construction APPEARANCE 16
m. to me a kingdom is MIND 9
m. watches itself INTELLIGENCE 20
m. which contemplates BEAUTY 19
my m.'s unsworn HYPOCRISY 8
not enough to have a good m. MIND 10
nothing great but m. MIND 17
not their frame of m. TRAVEL 23
One man that has a m. DETERMINATION 44
out of m. ABSENCE 5
out of m. ABSENCE 9
Pain of m. SUFFERING 10
prodigious quantity of m. INDECISION 11
Reading is to the m. READING 8
robs the m. FEAR 13
sound m. in a sound body HEALTH 17
To change your m. THINKING 11
Travel broadens the m. TRAVEL 9
vigour of the m. ACTION 19
Walkman of the m. MORALITY 24
well-guarded m. EMOTIONS 8
What is M. MIND 16
writes her m. LETTERS 9
minds great empire and little m. POLITICS 12
greatest natural resource is the m. CHILDREN 18
Great m. think alike THINKING 1
hearts and m. OPINION 8
in their hearts and m. SPEECHES 14
Little things please little m. VALUE 5
made up their m. to be good GOOD 46
marriage of true m. LOVE 32
M. are like parachutes MIND 21
win hearts and m. OPINION 11
mineral vegetable, and m. LIFE SCIENCES 2
Minerva invita M. IDEAS 3
owl of M. PHILOSOPHY 12
mining titles of m.-claims NAMES 14
minister M. that meddles ARTS 11
m. who moves about POLITICIANS 13
Yes, M. GOVERNMENT 39
ministering m. angel CHARITY 12
m. angel thou WOMEN 28
ministers how much my M. talk LEADERSHIP 24
M. of thought DREAMS 11
my actions are my m.' WORDS AND DEEDS 15
ministries *Times* has made many m. JOURNALISM 10
minority m. possess their equal DEMOCRACY 8
smug m. PROGRESS 21
subjection of the m. DEMOCRACY 13
minstrel wandering m. I SINGING 9
minus square root of m. one DEATH 77
minute cannot cage the m. TRANSIENCE 17
fill the unforgiving m. MATURITY 10
m. particulars GOOD 32
sucker born every m. FOOLS 25
minutes can have the seven m. PUNCTUALITY 14
famous for fifteen m. FAME 5
famous for fifteen m. FAME 29
In forty m. HASTE 12
sixty m. an hour FUTURE 25
take care of the m. TIME 35
Three m.' thought THINKING 19
two m. fifty-two seconds SEX 39
when the waves turn the m. CRISES 27
mirabilis annus m. TIME 10
miracle establish a m. PARANORMAL 11
m. enough LIFE 51
m., my friend FAITH 16
m. of our age WRITERS 6
would seem a M. FAMILIARITY 14
miracles age of m. is past SURPRISE 1
attended with m. CHRISTIAN CHURCH 21
believe in m. IDEALISM 17
M. do happen CHANCE 35
you must believe in m. REALITY 20
mirror mind is like a m. MIND 7
M., mirror on the wall BEAUTY 6
m. up to nature ACTING 4
novel is a m. FICTION 13
smash his m. FOOLS 15
mirrors all done with m. DECEPTION 3
mirth I love such m. HUMOUR 6
M. is like a flash HAPPINESS 15
two for m. BIRDS 3
mischief mother of m. CAUSES 10
punishment is m. CRIME 26
miserable horrible and the m. OPTIMISM 38
Me m. HEAVEN 12
m. human being INDECISION 12
miseries equal sharing of m. CAPITALISM 20
misery certain amount of m. TAXES 14
dwell on guilt and m. WRITING 28
greatest m. is a battle gained WARFARE 28
loses his m. SELF-KNOWLEDGE 12
Man hands on m. DISILLUSION 20
M. acquaints a man MISFORTUNES 21
M. loves company SORROW 1
M. such as mine SUFFERING 20
relation of distant m. SYMPATHY 21

I want some m. GREED 11
Less is m. ARCHITECTURE 16
Less is m. EXCESS 8
little m. QUANTITIES 31
m. about less KNOWLEDGE 54
m. equal than others EQUALITY 16
m. he has himself POSSESSIONS 12
m. Piglet wasn't there ABSENCE 12
m. the merrier QUANTITIES 6
m. things in heaven UNIVERSE 10
M. will mean worse UNIVERSITIES 20
m. you get GREED 1
Much would have m. GREED 2
She'll vish there wos m. LETTERS 10
their rights, and nothing m. WOMAN'S ROLE 17
mores O m. BEHAVIOUR 17
mori memento m. DEATH 20
moriar *Non omnis m.* DEATH 30
morning appendage to life's m. MIDDLE AGE 10
glad confident m. DISILLUSION 13
glorious m. for America WARS 10
hate to get up in the m. IDLENESS 21
in the early m. SEASONS 30
M. dreams come true DREAMS 4
M. has broken DAY 17
M. in the bowl of night DAY 12
m. knows more than the evening SLEEP 1
m. never suspected FORESIGHT 1
m.'s minion BIRDS 17
moron consumer isn't a m. ADVERTISING 13
morphine m. or idealism DRUGS 9
morrow bid the Devil good m. PROBLEMS 4
mortal this m. coil LIFE 15
mortality m., the ruins PAST 23
mortar Lies are the m. SOCIETY 15
mortgage where the m. is HOME 9
Morton M.'s fork CHOICE 12
mortuary telegram from the m. FAMILY 32
mortuis De m. nil REPUTATION 3
Moscow Do not march on M. WARFARE 60
M.: those syllables TOWNS 20
Moses every Pharaoh there is a M. HEROES 2
moss gathers no m. CONSTANCY 3
mostest fustest with the m. PREPARATION 24
mote beholdest thou the m. SELF-KNOWLEDGE 5
m. in a person's eye MISTAKES 10
mother affectionate m. PARENTS 19
church for his m. CHRISTIAN CHURCH 15
father and thy m. PARENTS 8
gave her m. forty whacks MURDER 4
how old a m. is PARENTS 27
Like m., like daughter FAMILY 9
make love to the m. PARENTS 6
man who hates his m. RELATIONSHIPS 25
M. Carey's chicken BIRDS 8
m. of battles WARS 30
m. of good luck CHANCE 5
m. of invention NECESSITY 8
m. of mischief CAUSES 10
M. of Parliaments BRITAIN 3
m. of Parliaments PARLIAMENT 22
M. of Presidents AMERICAN CITIES 30
m. of the months SKIES 4
M. o' mine PARENTS 17
m.'s arms are made of tenderness PARENTS 14
m.'s milk LIKES 7
m.'s yearning PARENTS 13
m. was glad to get him asleep CHILD CARE 6
never called me m. MOURNING 17
resemble: her m. PARENTS 33
takes the m. by the heart PARENTS 2
writer has to rob his m. WRITING 46
motherhood m. and apple pie HOME 14
mothering M. Sunday FESTIVALS 43
mother-in-law contemplates his m. FAMILY 21
when his m. died ADVERSITY 18
mothers M.' Day FESTIVALS 44
m. to help them PARENTS 15
women become like their m. MEN AND WOMEN 14
motion perpetual m. PHYSICAL 6
poetry of m. TRANSPORT 11
motivated m. to do a good job MANAGEMENT 15
motive m. in this narrative FICTION 14
requires no m. CRUELTY 10
motley M.'s the only wear FOOLS 14
wear m. FOOLS 7
mould break the m. ORIGINALITY 3
broke the m. EXCELLENCE 11
cast in the same m. SIMILARITY 25
mount Sermon on the M. CHRISTIAN CHURCH 11
mountain alone on a great m. MOUNTAINS 4
climbed the highest m. MOUNTAINS 2
Climb ev'ry m. THOROUGHNESS 14
man who removes a m. PATIENCE 11
m. out of a molehill VALUE 18
m. will not come NECESSITY 6
One m. cannot accommodate LEADERSHIP 6
top of a m. GOD 36
Up the airy m. SUPERNATURAL 16
mountains beautiful upon the m. NEWS 7
but never two m. MOUNTAINS 1
Climb the m. and get MOUNTAINS 6
Faith will move m. FAITH 1
mind has m. MIND 20
m. are high GOVERNMENT 4
m. are related MOUNTAINS 10
m. are the beginning MOUNTAINS 3
M. will go into labour EFFORT 17
no friends but the m. DIPLOMACY 2
other m. were chicks MOUNTAINS 9
Mounties M. always get CANADA 2
mourir *Partir c'est m. un peu* ABSENCE 11
mourn Blessed are they that m. MOURNING 9
countless thousands m. CRUELTY 8
mourning in m. for my life SORROW 20
waste any time in m. REVOLUTION 22
mouse country m. COUNTRY 5
m. and man LIFE 14
m. may help a lion POWER 6
m. will be born EFFORT 17
not even a m. CHRISTMAS 10
One for the m. FARMING 2
second m. that gets the cheese PREPARATION 12
town m. COUNTRY 7
mousetrap free cheese is in a m. ECONOMICS 2
mouse-trap make a better m. ABILITY 11
moustache m., a guitar and a gun COUNTRIES 28
mouth ashes in a person's m. DISILLUSION 5
gift horse in the m. GRATITUDE 3
ill m. for it ABILITY 6
keeping your m. shut SUCCESS 46
keep your m. shut FOOLS 26
likerous m. SEX 10
lion's m. DANGER 20
m. speaks EMOTIONS 1
shut m. catches SILENCE 1
silver foot in his m. PRESIDENCY 17
silver spoon in one's m. WEALTH 10

mouth (*cont.*)
spew thee out of my m. EXCESS 25
teeth in a man's m. LIFE SCIENCES 11
two ears and only one m. SPEECH 9
whispering in her m. KISSING 12
Word of m. is the best ADVERTISING 18
mouths God never sends m. FOOD 3
m., and speak not INDIFFERENCE 5
m. of babes WISDOM 2
stuffed their m. CORRUPTION 16
moutons Revenons à ces m. DETERMINATION 12
movable m. feast TIME 14
move Art has to m. you ARTS 35
But it does m. SKIES 14
Did the earth m. SEX 1
Faith will m. mountains FAITH 1
feel the earth m. SEX 26
I will m. the earth TECHNOLOGY 6
m. the goalposts CHANGE 24
moved We shall not be m. DETERMINATION 17
movement picture equals a m. PAINTING 24
mover m. and shaker CHANGE 23
prime m. GOD 15
movers m. and shakers MUSICIANS 7
moves If it m., salute it ARMED FORCES 4
If it m., tax it ECONOMICS 23
movie on the m. set LEADERSHIP 26
movies basic appeal of the m. CINEMA 17
kill the m. CINEMA 7
pay to see bad m. CINEMA 14
moving m. accident is not STYLE 14
m. finger writes PAST 28
Mozart Children are given M. MUSICIANS 14
M. tells you MUSICIANS 20
they play only M. MUSICIANS 16
MP M. is a good job PARLIAMENT 29
Mrs *M.* respectably married WORDS 29
Ms *M.* means nudge, nudge, wink, wink WORDS 29
much how m. we think of ourselves MANNERS 16
m. owed by so many GRATITUDE 17
M. would have more GREED 2
Some have too m. SATISFACTION 19
so m. to do ACHIEVEMENT 26
too little or too m. LOVE 58
Too m. of a good thing EXCESS 39
too m. of a good thing EXCESS 12
too m. of everything is as bad EXCESS 37
muck Money is like m. MONEY 30
stop raking the m. JOURNALISM 14
Where there's m. MONEY 15
muckle makes a m. QUANTITIES 5
mud builds on m. DEMOCRACY 4
muddle middle-of-the-road m. ORDER 20
m., and an end FICTION 22
mudge fudge and m. INDECISION 8
Mudville no joy in M. SPORTS 7
mugged liberal who's been m. CRIME 1
mule m. to the top of the minaret PROBLEMS 1
multitude m. of sins FORGIVENESS 1
m. of sins FORGIVENESS 13
multitudes I contain m. SELF 17
mum oafish louts remember M. CHRISTMAS 16
your m. and dad CHILD CARE 14
mumble when in doubt, m. ADMINISTRATION 18
mundi Stupor M. ROYALTY 14
murder Killing no m. MURDER 3
Killing no m. MURDER 13
lie, and even to m. TRUTH 35
Macbeth does m. sleep SLEEP 11
M. considered MURDER 15
m. in to the home MURDER 20
M. most foul MURDER 12
m. sound respectable POLITICS 24
M. will out MURDER 5
M. wol out MURDER 11
Naturally, about a m. MURDER 19
stick to m. SCULPTURE 8
murdered afraid of being m. CENSORSHIP 15
m. reputations REPUTATION 24
murderer shoot your m. HEROES 21
murderers m. take the first step MURDER 16
murmur shallow m. EMOTIONS 11
Murphy M.'s law MISFORTUNES 12
muscles M. better SEX 21
muscular His Christianity was m. CHRISTIAN CHURCH 25
m. Christianity CHRISTIAN CHURCH 8
muse m. on dromedary trots POETS 16
tenth M. CREATIVITY 2
muses nine M. ARTS AND SCIENCES 1
museum m. inside our heads LANGUAGES 21
nice m. attached CULTURE 1
mushroom stuff a m. PRACTICALITY 16
music being well set to m. SINGING 5
chosen that of m. and dance GOD 16
doctrine, but the m. CHRISTIAN CHURCH 19
expressing in m. MUSIC 17
Fled is that m. DREAMS 10
frozen m. ARCHITECTURE 10
good m., people don't listen HOSPITALITY 13
his m. accepts it MUSICIANS 12
how potent cheap m. is MUSIC 19
Let's face the m. DANCE 14
Like m. on my heart SILENCE 9
meaning to m. MUSIC 22
M. and women PLEASURE 15
m. be the food of love MUSIC 8
M. dies MUSICIANS 3
M. helps not MUSIC 3
m. in the air MUSIC 15
M. is not written in MUSIC 18
M. is spiritual MUSIC 33
m. is that which penetrates MUSIC 24
M. is the pleasure the human mind MUSIC 10
m. of the spheres MUSIC 5
m. that excels GREED 16
sound of m. MUSIC 28
twang, and you've got m. MUSIC 32
We are the m. makers MUSICIANS 7
musical m. as is Apollo's lute PHILOSOPHY 7
musician far below the m. ARTS 7
m., if he's a messenger MUSICIANS 17
musketeers three m. FRIENDSHIP 8
musk-roses m., and with eglantine FLOWERS 3
Muslim go into the M. mosque RELIGION 9
must forget because we m. MEMORY 12
Genius does what it m. GENIUS 9
Is *m.* a word NECESSITY 18
It m. be FATE 19
We m. know KNOWLEDGE 52
What m. be, must be FATE 7
mustard After meat, m. COOKING 2
grain of m. CAUSES 14
grain of m. FAITH 3
mute m. recommendation BEAUTY 10
mutilate fold, spindle or m. COMPUTERS 2
myrmidon m. of the law LAW 15
myrtle m. and turkey HAPPINESS 20

nature (*cont.*)
Habit is second n. CUSTOM 10
he outdoes N. DEATH 61
Holy Scripture and n. SCIENCE AND RELIGION 6
ignorance of n. SCIENCE AND RELIGION 8
In n. there are neither NATURE 17
intuitive art of wooing n. MEDICINE 25
man's power over n. IMAGINATION 15
mirror up to n. ACTING 4
N. abhors a vacuum NATURE 1
n. and nurture MIND 6
n. cannot be fooled TECHNOLOGY 24
n. concentrated ARTS 10
N. does nothing NATURE 5
N. has in store INVENTIONS 18
n. having intended GREATNESS 14
n., heartless NATURE 18
N. is not a temple NATURE 16
N. is often hidden CHARACTER 33
n. is subdued CIRCUMSTANCE 26
n. is the art NATURE 11
n. is tugging at SELF-INTEREST 27
N. made him EXCELLENCE 11
N., Mr Allnutt NATURE 19
N., red in tooth NATURE 13
n. replaces it with NATURE 20
N.'s great masterpiece ANIMALS 17
N.'s laws lay hid SCIENCE 8
N. speak intelligibly HYPOTHESIS 27
N.'s sweet restorer SLEEP 14
n.'s way of telling you DEATH 3
n. with a pitchfork NATURE 2
observe the works of n. SCIENCE 5
one touch of n. HUMAN NATURE 9
painters imitate n. PAINTING 6
poet ever interpreted n. LAW 37
productions of n. FARMING 9
spark o' N.'s fire EDUCATION 21
subtlety of n. NATURE 10
uniformity of n. FORESIGHT 17
naught it is n. BUYING 5
naughty good deed in a n. world VIRTUE 21
N. but nice TEMPTATION 3
n. nineties PAST 14
naval N. tradition ARMED FORCES 45
navy It is upon the n. ARMED FORCES 18
Pink is the n. blue COLOURS 9
near N. is my kirtle SELF-INTEREST 6
N. is my shirt SELF-INTEREST 7
near-death n. experience PARANORMAL 7
nearer n. God's Heart GARDENS 19
n. the bone QUANTITIES 7
n. the church CHRISTIAN CHURCH 5
nearly n. kept waiting PUNCTUALITY 8
neat n. but not gaudy STYLE 2
necessarily It ain't n. so BIBLE 17
necessary Is your journey *really* n. TRAVEL 6
n. condition CAPITALISM 25
n. not to change CHANGE 32
superfluous, a n. thing NECESSITY 22
than are absolutely n. PHILOSOPHY 6
necessities n. call out great virtues CHARACTER 37
necessity Cruel n. NECESSITY 19
door of n. SIN 18
fiction is a n. FICTION 17
Make a virtue of n. NECESSITY 7
nasty old invention—N. NECESSITY 24
N. has the face NECESSITY 25
N. hath no law NECESSITY 20
N. is the mother NECESSITY 8
N. is the plea NECESSITY 23
N. knows no law NECESSITY 9
N. never made NECESSITY 21
N. sharpens industry NECESSITY 10
no virtue like n. NECESSITY 17
stronger than N. NECESSITY 16
Thy n. is yet greater CHARITY 16
neck fastened about his own n. HUMAN RIGHTS 12
wrings its n. FORESIGHT 17
need All you n. is love LOVE 69
because I n. you MATURITY 12
Charity sees the n. CHARITY 3
face of total n. GOOD 43
for everyone's n. GREED 15
France has more n. of me FRANCE 13
friend in n. FRIENDSHIP 2
In thy most n. KNOWLEDGE 23
people don't n. ARTS 33
thy n. is greater CHARITY 16
Will you still n. me OLD AGE 35
needle eye of a n. QUANTITIES 16
go through the eye of a n. WEALTH 19
my hand a n. better fits WOMAN'S ROLE 8
upon a n.'s point PHILOSOPHY 8
When a pine n. falls SENSES 2
needles N. and pins MARRIAGE 9
needs according to his n. SOCIETY 14
knows how much it n. EXCESS 23
N. must NECESSITY 11
negative exposed n. MIND 27
N. Capability CERTAINTY 16
your n. perception BODY 30
neglect die of n. IDEAS 20
neglected always finally n. BIOGRAPHY 15
Business n. BUSINESS 6
his all n. EFFORT 20
negotiate n. out of fear DIPLOMACY 16
negotiating learnt when I was n. DIPLOMACY 17
N. with de Valera DIPLOMACY 14
Negro average N. could never *hope* RACE 24
Negroes culture of the N. JAZZ 5
N. black as Cain RACE 7
neighbour covet thy n.'s house ENVY 6
God makes our next-door n. NEIGHBOURS 10
justice at our n.'s expense JUSTICE 11
love thy n. LIFESTYLES 14
Love your n., but don't NEIGHBOURS 3
n. gets is not lost NEIGHBOURS 5
n.'s house is on fire PRACTICALITY 12
neighbourhood narrow into a n. INTERNATIONAL 33
n. of voluntary spies GOSSIP 21
neighbours fences make good n. NEIGHBOURS 1
good n. SUPERNATURAL 3
sport for our n. NEIGHBOURS 7
Nelson N. eye IGNORANCE 14
N. touch LEADERSHIP 8
'N. touch' LEADERSHIP 14
nemo N. me impune DEFIANCE 1
nerds Be nice to n. INTELLIGENCE 23
nervous conscious of a n. system FEAR 17
Nessus shirt of N. MISFORTUNES 16
nest cuckoo in the n. CIRCUMSTANCE 11
feather one's own n. MONEY 18
fouls its own n. PATRIOTISM 2
last year's n. CHANGE 13
mare's n. DECEPTION 7
nests Birds in their little n. ARGUMENT 1
birds of the air have n. HOME 15

original great and o. writer ORIGINALITY 10
made an ordinary one seem o. WRITING 11
o. is unfaithful TRANSLATION 8
o. sin SIN 4
o. writer is not he ORIGINALITY 9
saves o. thinking QUOTATIONS 14
sound and o. ideas POLITICAL PARTIES 34
originality o. or moral courage CHARACTER 42
originals few o. HISTORY 18
origins Consider your o. HUMAN RACE 14
Orion loose the bands of O. FATE 12
Orleans Maid of O. FRANCE 6
ornament Nobility is a graceful o. RANK 10
o., and for ability EDUCATION 18
woman's finest o. SILENCE 6
orphan failure is an o. SUCCESS 11
orthodoxy O. is my doxy RELIGION 18
Oscar all assume that O. said it WIT 19
Ossa O. upon Pelion EXCESS 20
osteopath have to go to an o. MUSICIANS 19
ostrich wings of an o. IMAGINATION 10
other bourgeois are o. people CLASS 18
dreadfully like o. people SIMILARITY 26
happens to *o.* people HUMOUR 23
Most people are o. people ORIGINALITY 13
o. half lives SOCIETY 2
o. people's children CHILDREN 22
run out of o. people's money CAPITALISM 29
something however small from the o. SELF 28
turn the o. cheek FORGIVENESS 9
Were t'o. dear charmer away CHOICE 15
others as o. see us SELF-KNOWLEDGE 9
Do not do unto o. LIKES 14
Do unto o. LIFESTYLES 4
I could not change o. DIPLOMACY 17
otherwise gods thought o. FATE 14
ought hadn't o. to be CIRCUMSTANCE 32
not what I o. to be SELF 15
o. to have done ACTION 24
ounce o. of practice is worth a pound WORDS AND DEEDS 6
ours met the enemy and they are o. WINNING 15
ourselves better be changed in o. CHILD CARE 9
We did it o. LEADERSHIP 9
out garbage o. COMPUTERS 3
Mordre wol o. MURDER 11
Murder will o. MURDER 5
o. of alcohol ALCOHOL 30
O. of sight ABSENCE 5
O. of the deep SUFFERING 7
Truth will o. TRUTH 9
out-argue we will o. them PARLIAMENT 18
outgrow duty to o. SELF-KNOWLEDGE 15
out-Herod o. Herod CRUELTY 2
outside come into us from the o. FATE 20
I am just going o. SELF-SACRIFICE 10
o. of a horse HEALTH 13
outsider stay an o. SICKNESS 24
outvote we cannot o. them PARLIAMENT 18
outvoted they o. me MADNESS 8
outward o. appearance INSIGHT 5
oven put your boots in the o. REALITY 3
over It ain't o. ENDING 24
opera isn't o. ENDING 7
oversexed, and o. here WORLD WAR II 1
Over there, o. there WORLD WAR I 18
party's o. ENDING 21
put it all o. you SEX 25
They think it's all o. ENDING 22
overcome has never o. them EMOTIONS 27
just things to o. PROBLEMS 24
often hidden, sometimes o. CHARACTER 33
We shall o. DETERMINATION 18
overcomes Who o. By force VIOLENCE 6
overload Don't o. gratitude GRATITUDE 2
overlook knowing what to o. WISDOM 11
overpaid O., overfed WORLD WAR II 1
overrated Sand is o. EARTH 20
over-rated O., if you ask me WRITING 38
oversexed o., and over here WORLD WAR II 1
owe o. God a death DEATH 37
owed o. by so many GRATITUDE 17
owl o. in the belfry BIRDS 14
o. of Minerva PHILOSOPHY 12
stuffed o. POETRY 4
owls eagle among blinking o. POETS 17
own devil looks after his o. CHANCE 3
for what they o. POSSESSIONS 28
God will recognize his o. DISILLUSION 8
room of her o. WRITING 39
To be on your o. SOLITUDE 21
To each his o. JUSTICE 17
owners if you break o. CONFORMITY 2
ox stalled o. and hatred HATRED 3
than a stalled o. HATRED 1
Oxenford Clerk there was of O. UNIVERSITIES 5
Oxford To the University of O. UNIVERSITIES 8
oxygen o. of publicity REVOLUTION 34
oyster world is an o. EFFORT 27
world is one's o. OPPORTUNITY 23
oysters Don't eat o. FOOD 2
Ozymandias My name is O. FUTILITY 25
pace measured p. DANCE 8
p. that kills STRENGTH 4
Pacific stared at the P. INVENTIONS 10
pacifist militant p. PEACE 21
quietly p. peaceful VIOLENCE 22
pack keep running with the p. POLITICIANS 38
p. up your troubles WORRY 10
peasantry its p. animal CLASS 22
packaging brilliant p. FOOD 32
pack-drill No names, no p. SECRECY 9
pad p. in the straw DANGER 21
paddle song my p. sings RIVERS 12
padlock Wedlock is a p. MARRIAGE 12
pagan you find the p. CHRISTIAN CHURCH 26
page foot of the first p. ADMINISTRATION 7
P. Three JOURNALISM 6
p. three girl WOMEN 15
pageant life's rich p. LIFE 13
pain After great p. SUFFERING 24
born in other's p. SUFFERING 27
intermission of p. PLEASURE 13
intoxication with p. CRUELTY 13
No p., no gain EFFORT 9
p. of mind SUFFERING 10
p. to the bear PLEASURE 21
p. we obey SICKNESS 20
p. which cannot forget WISDOM 3
physics p. WORK 24
Pride feels no p. PRIDE 2
rest from p. HAPPINESS 14
tender for another's p. SUFFERING 18
painful p. as feeling ENEMIES 9
pains capacity for taking p. GENIUS 1
When two p. occur together SICKNESS 10
paint flinging a pot of p. PAINTING 13
p. 'em truest HONESTY 11

people (*cont.*)
Not many p. know that KNOWLEDGE 57
One-fifth of the p. LIKES 17
opium of the p. REALITY 8
other p.'s children CHILDREN 22
p. as base as itself JOURNALISM 15
p. don't do such things HUMAN NATURE 15
p. have spoke—the bastards ELECTIONS 15
p. ignore most poetry POETRY 34
p. of the Book RELIGION 4
p., people, people HUMAN RACE 3
P.'s Princess ROYALTY 46
P.'s William POLITICIANS 5
plenty of p. on this planet CHILDREN 23
Power to the p. RACE 3
protect the p. JOURNALISM 11
shall be my p. FRIENDSHIP 9
start where p. are CLERGY 19
voice of the p. DEMOCRACY 2
voice of the p. DEMOCRACY 3
voice of the p. OPINION 10
What is the city but the p. COUNTRY 9
peoples scripture of p. BIBLE 7
Peoria It'll play in P. POLITICS 2
percentage reasonable p. STATISTICS 15
perception doors of p. INSIGHT 10
perdu recherche du temps p. MEMORY 3
temps p. PAST 18
pereat *p. mundus* JUSTICE 26
perennials P. are the ones that grow GARDENS 20
perestroika restructuring [p.] RUSSIA 10
perfect her p. work PATIENCE 25
One p. rose GIFTS 21
p. storm MISFORTUNES 14
pismire is equally p. NATURE 14
Practice makes p. WORK 5
perfection counsel of p. ADVICE 6
Dead p. PERFECTION 10
number of p. QUANTITIES 26
P. is terrble PERFECTION 16
P. is the child PERFECTION 6
P. of the life PERFECTION 14
Pictures of p. PERFECTION 8
praise and true p. PERFECTION 5
Trifles make p. PERFECTION 1
Trifles make p. PERFECTION 4
perfidious p. Albion ENGLAND 4
perform p. without thinking CULTURE 13
which you cannot p. SEX 28
performance all words, And no p. WORDS AND DEEDS 13
outlive p. SEX 12
takes away the p. DRUNKENNESS 4
perfume Flattery, like p. PRAISE 2
perfumes p. of Arabia GUILT 10
perhaps seek a great p. DEATH 36
peril p. in the fight DANGER 30
perils defend us from all p. DAY 7
When our p. are past GRATITUDE 14
period p. of remorse and apology GUILT 23
perish people p. IDEALISM 6
P. the thought THINKING 2
p. together as fools COOPERATION 33
p. with the sword VIOLENCE 5
though the world p. JUSTICE 26
perjury lover's p. LOVE 3
perpendicular p. expression DANCE 15
perpetrator thou shalt not be a p. INDIFFERENCE 17
perpetual p. motion PHYSICAL 6
persecuted merely because he is p. GREATNESS 16
persecution no tyrannical p. GOOD 23
some degree of p. CLERGY 14
perseverance P., dear my lord DETERMINATION 31
Pershing 58% don't want P. WARFARE 3
Persians Medes and P. CHANGE 22
persistence P. and determination DETERMINATION 45
person p. you and I took me for CHARACTER 40
uninterested p. KNOWLEDGE 44
personal P. isn't the same SELF 29
p. is political POLITICS 3
P. relations RELATIONSHIPS 17
writes always of his p. life POETRY 30
personalities meeting of two p. RELATIONSHIPS 20
personality escape from p. POETRY 25
From 35 to 55, good p. WOMEN 47
no more p. than AMERICAN CITIES 60
persons My thoughts became p. PARANORMAL 19
things, not p. SCIENCE 14
perspiration ninety-nine per cent p. GENIUS 11
perspiring City of p. dreams UNIVERSITIES 21
persuaders hidden p. ADVERTISING 12
persuasion P. is the resource ARGUMENT 14
persuasive p. argument ARGUMENT 22
perturbation O polished p. WORRY 6
perversions all the sexual p. SEX 23
pervert p. climbs into the minds CRUELTY 13
pessimism P. of the intellect OPTIMISM 29
pessimist consider myself a p. OPTIMISM 40
p. fears this is true OPTIMISM 30
p. sees the hole OPTIMISM 27
pestilence breeds p. ACTION 26
petard hoist with one's own p. CAUSES 15
Peter P. Principle MANAGEMENT 5
P.'s pence TAXES 2
rob P. DEBT 13
robs P. to pay Paul GOVERNMENT 36
Thou art P. CHRISTIAN CHURCH 12
Petersburg P., the most abstract TOWNS 22
petrifies p. the feeling SIN 19
pets I hate a word like 'p.' ANIMALS 30
petty p. and vindictive SUFFERING 28
peur sans p. et sans reproche VIRTUE 12
phagocytes stimulate the p. MEDICINE 21
pharaoh every P. there is a Moses HEROES 2
pheasant make room for the p. SCOTLAND 14
Philadelphia I went to P. AMERICAN CITIES 58
Philip appeal from P. drunk OPINION 7
philosopher peasant and a p. HAPPINESS 17
p. has said it PHILOSOPHY 5
p.'s stone PROBLEMS 14
time to be a p. PHILOSOPHY 11
philosophers p. are tourists ARTS AND SCIENCES 13
philosophical European p. tradition PHILOSOPHY 18
philosophy charming is divine p. PHILOSOPHY 7
dreamt of in your p. SUPERNATURAL 11
enslave a p. RELIGION 27
History is p. HISTORY 10
p., deep; moral ARTS AND SCIENCES 3
p. quenches them PHILOSOPHY 10
phoenixes p. beget phoenixes FAMILY 6
phone answer the p. MISTAKES 25
call him up on the p. READING 18
hear that the p. is for you YOUTH 25
P. a friend COOPERATION 14
stand on two p. books AMERICAN CITIES 64
photograph p. is a secret PHOTOGRAPHY 9
photographer p. and the viewer PHOTOGRAPHY 12

p. is like the cod PHOTOGRAPHY 6
photography P. deals exquisitely with appearances PHOTOGRAPHY 16
P. is truth CINEMA 15
p. you've got to be quick PHOTOGRAPHY 10
photos Take only p. TRAVEL 7
physic Throw p. to the dogs MEDICINE 14
physician died last night of my p. MEDICINE 17
Honour a p. MEDICINE 7
p. can bury his mistakes ARCHITECTURE 17
P., heal thyself MEDICINE 11
physicians dying with the help of too many p. MEDICINE 10
p. may play HEALTH 5
P. of all men MEDICINE 16
physicists p. are made of atoms PHYSICAL 17
p. have known sin PHYSICAL 14
physics edifice of modern p. PHYSICAL 18
no democracy in p. PHYSICAL 21
p. or stamp collecting SCIENCE 22
p. pain WORK 24
pianist shoot the p. MUSICIANS 8
pianists no better than many p. MUSIC 25
piano help with moving the p. MEN 20
pick p. it up CHANCE 13
p. the one I never tried CHOICE 22
P. yourself up DETERMINATION 46
picklocks p. of biographers BIOGRAPHY 13
picnic p. in Eden GUILT 15
teddy bears' p. PLEASURE 8
picture good p. is equivalent to PAINTING 15
One p. is worth ten thousand words WORDS AND DEEDS 5
p. equals a movement PAINTING 24
p. is worth ten thousand LANGUAGE 20
p. tells a story MEANING 1
pictures gallery of p. HISTORY 18
P. are for entertainment CINEMA 18
p. aren't good enough PHOTOGRAPHY 7
p. didn't have any beginning PAINTING 27
P. of perfection PERFECTION 8
p. or conversations BOOKS 14
p. that got small CINEMA 12
You furnish the p. JOURNALISM 12
pie eat humble p. APOLOGY 10
p. in the sky FUTURE 10
p. in the sky FUTURE 21
pie-crust Promises, like p. TRUST 3
Pierian P. spring POETRY 3
pies devil makes his Christmas p. LAW 1
piety in return for my p. PRAYER 7
pig expect from a p. CHARACTER 19
kill a p. GARDENS 4
p. got up DRUNKENNESS 11
p. satisfied SATISFACTION 31
put lipstick on a p. FUTILITY 7
pigs P. get fat, but hogs get GREED 3
P. may fly BELIEF 4
p. might fly BELIEF 8
P. treat us as equals ANIMALS 29
Pilate said jesting P. TRUTH 19
pile P. it high BUSINESS 16
p. Ossa upon Pelion EXCESS 20
pilfering p., unprotected race COUNTRIES 20
pillar p. of society SOCIETY 5
p. of the State LIES 26
pillow clean conscience is a good p. CONSCIENCE 1
pills pink p. for pale people MEDICINE 2
pilot drop the p. TRUST 7
every man is a p. ACHIEVEMENT 5
I hope to see my p. DEATH 60
kamikaze p. SUICIDE 2
p. of the calm LEADERSHIP 16
pin He that will not stoop for a p. PRIDE 1
on the head of a p. PHILOSOPHY 1
See a p. CHANCE 13
steal a p. HONESTY 5
pinch with a p. of salt BELIEF 10
pine want to learn about the p. EDUCATION 19
pineapple p. of politeness MANNERS 11
pines eat the cones under his p. NEIGHBOURS 11
ping pong p. is coming home SPORTS 43
pink P. is the navy blue COLOURS 9
p. pills for pale people MEDICINE 2
pinko-grey really p. RACE 13
pinprick p. of eternity TIME 25
pinstripe come in a p. suit STRENGTH 31
pint p....why that's very nearly BODY 24
quart into a p. pot FUTILITY 4
pinta P. Milka Day HEALTH 3
pipe This is not a p. PAINTING 23
three-p. problem THINKING 18
piper pays the p. POWER 3
pay the p. POWER 18
takes seven years to make a p. MUSIC 2
pipes open the p. SINGING 2
pips until the p. squeak REVENGE 10
until the p. squeak REVENGE 21
pirates p.' loot on Treasure Island BOOKS 24
piss pitcher of warm p. PRESIDENCY 12
pissing p. out ENEMIES 21
pistol p. hanging on the wall THEATRE 15
p. in your pocket SEX 35
p. let off at the ear WIT 16
p. misses fire ARGUMENT 11
reach for my p. CULTURE 18
smoking p. SECRECY 23
pistols p. and cartridges ARMED FORCES 33
pit diggeth a p. CAUSES 17
Law is a bottomless p. LAW 24
many-headed monster of the p. THEATRE 12
pitbull hockey mom and a p. DETERMINATION 54
pitch p. shall be defiled GOOD 2
p. shall be defiled GOOD 15
pitcher p. of warm piss PRESIDENCY 12
p. will go to the well EXCESS 10
pitchers Little p. have large SECRECY 6
pitchfork nature with a p. NATURE 2
pitied complain are never p. SYMPATHY 24
envied than p. ENVY 1
pities p. the plumage SYMPATHY 23
pitiful God be p. PRAYER 23
pity by means of p. and fear THEATRE 4
p. him afterwards SYMPATHY 20
P. is akin to love SYMPATHY 6
p. of it, Iago SYMPATHY 17
p. renneth soone SYMPATHY 15
Poetry is in the p. WARFARE 42
Then cherish p. SYMPATHY 22
place another p. PARLIAMENT 4
get wealth and p. WEALTH 23
no p. like home HOME 11
no p. to go DRESS 11
p. for everything ADMINISTRATION 9
p. for everything ORDER 3
p. in the sun INTERNATIONAL 24
p. in the sun SUCCESS 18
pride of p. VALUE 21

place (*cont.*)
tight gag of p. IRELAND 21
time and p. BEGINNING 21
time and p. for everything CIRCUMSTANCE 7
time and the p. OPPORTUNITY 38
woman's p. is in the home WOMAN'S ROLE 4
places all p. were alike CATS 8
true p. never are EXPLORATION 8
placidly p. amid the noise PEACE 23
plagiarism either p. or revolution ARTS 21
one author, it's p. ORIGINALITY 15
plagiarist p. can excuse the wrong ORIGINALITY 16
plague like a p. bacillus REVOLUTION 23
p. of opinion OPINION 13
p. your heart BEAUTY 8
plain best p. set VIRTUE 23
Books will speak p. ADVICE 11
cities of the p. TOWNS 6
masses of the p. people INTELLIGENCE 15
need of the p. MANNERS 23
one penny p. PAINTING 14
penny p. STYLE 3
p. living LIFESTYLES 10
P. living SATISFACTION 26
p. meaning MEANING 4
p. women on television BROADCASTING 13
plan don't have a moral p. CANADA 21
fails to p., plans to fail PREPARATION 9
I have a cunning p. IDEAS 1
No p. of operations PREPARATION 25
No p. survives first contact PREPARATION 15
on the old p. SOCIETY 13
p. the future FORESIGHT 15
p. violently executed MANAGEMENT 11
rest on its original p. PROGRESS 10
plane emotions in a p. TRANSPORT 25
It's a p. HEROES 18
planet all inhabit this small p. HUMAN RACE 34
Our p. is a lonely speck EARTH 18
p. swims into his ken INVENTIONS 10
p. without flowers FLOWERS 13
planets Lots of p. have a north SPEECH 29
planned man who has p. badly PREPARATION 19
p. layout is achieved MANAGEMENT 12
planning p. is indispensable PREPARATION 27
plans making all his nowhere p. FUTILITY 33
p. are useless PREPARATION 27
traveller has no fixed p. TRAVEL 22
plant best time to p. a tree TREES 1
dreams in the p. HUMAN RACE 1
new growth in the p. PROGRESS 14
p. can discuss horticulture ARTS 30
p. whose virtues GARDENS 17
plants abilities are like natural p. ABILITY 10
P. a hope TREES 13
p. trees loves others TREES 9
talk to the p. GARDENS 21
plashy through the p. fen STYLE 20
platitude p. is simply a truth repeated TRUTH 33
Plato footnotes to P. PHILOSOPHY 18
P. is dear to me TRUTH 16
wrong, by God, with P. MISTAKES 12
plausible neat, p., and wrong PROBLEMS 28
play All work and no p. LEISURE 1
children at p. CHILDREN 8
holdeth children from p. FICTION 9
It'll p. in Peoria POLITICS 2
little victims p. CHILDREN 13
mice will p. OPPORTUNITY 22
p. ducks and drakes with THRIFT 12
p. is played out SATISFACTION 29
P. it again, Sam CINEMA 3
p.'s the thing THEATRE 7
p. the game SPORTS 13
p. the race card LAW 45
p. the — card WAYS 28
p. with fire DANGER 4
p. with my cat CATS 6
p. without a woman in it THEATRE 5
prologue to a very dull p. COURTSHIP 6
Scottish p. THEATRE 3
shame I can't p. like him SPORTS 45
structure of a p. CAUSES 27
y is p. SUCCESS 46
played how you p. the Game SPORTS 21
players gentlemen and the p. CLASS 5
playing on the p. fields of Eton WARS 15
plays beaver works and p. ANIMALS 3
pleasant find anything p. CHANGE 34
green and p. land ENGLAND 13
p. because it isn't here PAST 3
p. happens to you ENVY 11
p. thing it is GRATITUDE 6
please do what I p. GOVERNMENT 24
p. thee with my answer CONVERSATION 7
P. your eye BEAUTY 8
To tax and to p. TAXES 9
Try to p. everybody SUCCESS 47
Uncertain, coy, and hard to p. WOMEN 28
You can't p. everyone LIKES 5
pleased always so p. with themselves WALES 12
consists in being p. MANNERS 12
p. as Punch PLEASURE 5
pleasing art of p. MANNERS 12
pleasure Business before p. BUSINESS 2
doth ever add p. LIES 13
except the p. of seeing it HUMAN NATURE 12
if this is p. LEISURE 12
Is not in p. HAPPINESS 14
It becomes a p. DUTY 18
lifetime of p. PHOTOGRAPHY 14
no p. on earth that's worth PLEASURE 28
Peebles for p. BRITISH TOWNS 9
perfect p. SMOKING 12
P. at the helm YOUTH 11
p. for a parliamentarian PARLIAMENT 28
p. in life PLEASURE 22
p. in the pathless woods NATURE 12
p. is momentary SEX 17
p. is not enhanced SURPRISE 10
P. is nothing else PLEASURE 13
p. me in his top-boots SEX 15
p. sure, In being mad MADNESS 7
p. they give is steady LIBRARIES 15
p. to the spectators PLEASURE 21
prefers comfort to p. CLASS 21
remembrance gives you p. PAST 25
their favourite p. PLEASURE 10
to sea for p. SEA 2
weren't to give p. PLEASURE 14
pleasures celibacy has no p. SINGLE 5
less we indulge our p. PLEASURE 11
lords have their p. PLEASURE 16
paucity of human p. HUNTING 10
p. and palaces HOME 17
p. of sense SENSES 8
p. of the other PLEASURE 18
pleats witty little p. FASHION 17

politician (*cont.*)
p. who's been dead POLITICIANS 29
popular p. POLITICIANS 7
politicians left to the p. POLITICS 26
P. have no leisure POLITICIANS 8
whole race of p. PRACTICALITY 9
politics continuation of p. by other means WARFARE 30
first part of p. POLITICS 14
in p. the middle way POLITICS 13
no true friends in p. POLITICIANS 40
p. and equations MATHS 21
p. and religion don't mix BIBLE 20
P. is a marathon POLITICS 32
p. is present history HISTORY 20
P. makes strange bedfellows POLITICS 4
p. out of politics POLITICAL PARTIES 38
p. with bloodshed POLITICS 19
Punch and Judy p. PARLIAMENT 30
to succeed in p. POLITICIANS 25
poll p. tax TAXES 3
Pollock from Lascaux to Jackson P. JAZZ 10
polluted filthy and p. POLLUTION 5
pollution p. of democracy CORRUPTION 18
Pomeranian bones of a single P. grenadier WARFARE 37
pomps p. and vanities TEMPTATION 6
p. and vanity SIN 15
pons p. asinorum MATHS 6
poodle Balfour's p. PARLIAMENT 11
hon. Gentleman's p. PARLIAMENT 26
pooh p.-bah SELF-ESTEEM 11
poop-poop O p. TRANSPORT 11
poor another for the p. JUSTICE 8
cannot help one p. man CHARITY 19
grind the faces of the p. POVERTY 13
how expensive it is to be p. POVERTY 30
Laws grind the p. POVERTY 20
many who are p. SOCIETY 19
not p., it is poorly managed AFRICA 16
peasant in my kingdom so p. POVERTY 17
Plenty has made me p. THRIFT 13
p. always ye have POVERTY 14
p. as Job POVERTY 11
p. but she was honest VIRTUE 37
p. get children POVERTY 25
p. have sometimes objected to being GOVERNMENT 34
p. have the sufferings to which POVERTY 28
p. know that it is money MONEY 53
p. little rich girl WEALTH 16
p. man at his gate CLASS 15
p. man had nothing POSSESSIONS 13
P. people's memory is less nourished MEMORY 23
p. poorer CAPITALISM 24
propensity for being p. SINGLE 9
why the p. have no food POVERTY 32
your tired, your p. AMERICA 20
poorer for richer for p. MARRIAGE 25
pope Pole first, a p. second CLERGY 18
P. afterwards CONSCIENCE 14
poplars p. are felled TREES 10
poppies In Flanders fields the p. blow WORLD WAR I 15
poppy Flanders p. WORLD WAR I 3
flushed print in a p. FLOWERS 8
P. Day FESTIVALS 49
tall p. FAME 8
popular more p. than Jesus CHRISTIAN CHURCH 32
p. politician POLITICIANS 7
popularity P.? It is glory's small change FAME 20
population P., when unchecked LIFE SCIENCES 12
populi vox p. OPINION 10
porcupines couple of p. REVENGE 22
pornography P. is the attempt SEX 24
porridge sand in the p. LEISURE 12
port p., for the men ALCOHOL 11
p. in a storm NECESSITY 1
p. one is sailing IGNORANCE 16
p. out, starboard home TRAVEL 16
Portillo P. moment ELECTIONS 4
portion Benjamin's p. QUANTITIES 13
portmanteau like a p. MEANING 9
portrait paint a p. PAINTING 22
position p. of matter EMPLOYMENT 20
p. ridiculous SEX 17
positive ac-cent-tchu-ate the p. OPTIMISM 33
p. thinking THINKING 7
p. value has its price CAUSES 28
positivists logical p. capable of love LOGIC 24
possession diminished by p. POSSESSIONS 25
Man's best p. MARRIAGE 18
No human relation gives one p. RELATIONSHIPS 19
p. for all time HISTORY 8
P. is nine points LAW 10
p. of a book BOOKS 25
title and p. CAPITALISM 9
possessions Happiness resides not in p. HAPPINESS 8
least of p. AUSTRALIA 24
other people's p. POSSESSIONS 31
p. for a moment POSSESSIONS 17
possibilities improbable p. PROBLEMS 19
not interested in the p. WINNING 19
possibility p. of anything CERTAINTY 22
p. of suicide SUICIDE 11
possible all p. worlds OPTIMISM 1
all p. worlds OPTIMISM 19
All things are p. GOD 1
all things are p. GOD 10
art of the p. POLITICS 16
as simple as p., but not SCIENCE 21
p. you may be mistaken CERTAINTY 14
realm of the p. SATISFACTION 16
something is p. HYPOTHESIS 28
possumus p. omnes ABILITY 9
post Lie follows by p. APOLOGY 20
p. of honour DANGER 9
poster p. is a visual telegram ADVERTISING 14
posterity flattery of p. is not worth PRAISE 18
forward to p. FUTURE 19
go down to p. LANGUAGE 15
something for P. FUTURE 17
special correspondent for p. WRITERS 14
trustees of P. YOUTH 15
postern p. door makes a thief OPPORTUNITY 17
postilion p. has been struck by lightning TRANSLATION 7
postscript material in the p. LETTERS 6
mind but in her p. LETTERS 9
pot chicken in his p. POVERTY 17
Look at p. ADVERTISING 15
p. calling the kettle black CRITICISM 4
p. is soon hot ANGER 3
p. never boils PATIENCE 19
p. of gold VALUE 20
potato couch p. BROADCASTING 4
Where the p.-gatherers IRELAND 20
You like p. SPEECH 25

potatoes just to peel the p. RELIGION 29
Potemkin P. village DECEPTION 8
potent p. cheap music is MUSIC 19
Potomac All quiet along the P. to-night WARS 19
pots among the p. and pans HOUSEWORK 8
p. and pans OPTIMISM 11
pottage mess of p. VALUE 19
potter p.'s field DEATH 21
poultry lives of the p. ELECTIONS 8
pound any fool can do for a p. TECHNOLOGY 15
in for a p. THOROUGHNESS 2
p. foolish THRIFT 5
p. in your pocket MONEY 52
p. of flesh DEBT 12
pounding Hard p. this WARS 14
pounds p. will take care MONEY 33
p. will take care of themselves THRIFT 9
two hundred p. a year DISILLUSION 10
pours rains but it p. MISFORTUNES 7
poverty Both p. and prosperity POVERTY 1
confuse p. with stupidity POVERTY 34
fear and sorrow, real p. CHARACTER 36
Make p. history POVERTY 3
misfortunes of p. POVERTY 15
not p. lest I steal POVERTY 19
Overcoming p. is not a gesture POVERTY 35
P. comes from God POVERTY 5
p. comes in at the door POVERTY 8
P. is a lot like childbirth POVERTY 33
P. is no disgrace POVERTY 6
P. is not a crime POVERTY 7
p. of their desires CLASS 19
p.'s catching POVERTY 18
wedded to P. POVERTY 23
worst of crimes is p. POVERTY 24
powder keep your p. dry PRACTICALITY 3
power absolute p. corrupts POWER 33
absolute p., is the same POWER 28
Art is p. ARTS 3
balance of p. INTERNATIONAL 2
Beauty is p. BEAUTY 5
corridors of p. GOVERNMENT 8
flower p. IDEALISM 3
have p. over men WOMAN'S ROLE 13
intoxicated with p. POWER 25
Knowledge is p. KNOWLEDGE 3
Knowledge itself is p. KNOWLEDGE 26
lies at the very core of p. SECRECY 37
maximal authority and minimal p. TEACHING 20
Money is p. MONEY 8
not p. that corrupts, but fear FEAR 27
office, but not in p. GOVERNMENT 43
only have p. over people POWER 40
Papers are p. ADMINISTRATION 21
Political p. grows out of POWER 35
P. concedes nothing POWER 30
P. corrupts POWER 8
P. is the great aphrodisiac POWER 41
p. of the press JOURNALISM 16
P. to the people RACE 3
p. to the Soviets CAPITALISM 1
p. without love is reckless POWER 39
P. without responsibility DUTY 23
some P. the giftie gie SELF-KNOWLEDGE 9
speak truth to p. POWER 20
struggle of man against p. POWER 44
take who have the p. POWER 27
there is only p. MORALITY 25
world desires to have—P. TECHNOLOGY 7
powerful p. beyond measure SELF-ESTEEM 32
powers Headmasters have p. SCHOOLS 10
p. that be POWER 19
practical Morality's *not* p. MORALITY 21
practice If I don't p. MUSIC 23
ounce of p. is worth a pound WORDS AND DEEDS 6
p. in being refused DISILLUSION 7
P. makes perfect WORK 5
p. they have become HUMAN NATURE 6
practise P. what you preach WORDS AND DEEDS 7
practised more praised than p. HONESTY 3
prairie P. State AMERICAN CITIES 36
P. States AMERICAN CITIES 37
praise Damn with faint p. PRAISE 12
damn with faint p. PRAISE 6
is p. indeed PRAISE 14
learning, as is p. TEACHING 9
p. and don't read BOOKS 16
p. and true perfection PERFECTION 5
p. at morning OPINION 17
P. belongs to God GOD 13
p. 'em most HONESTY 11
p. famous men FAME 9
P. from Sir Hubert PRAISE 5
P. the child PARENTS 6
P. the Lord and pass PRACTICALITY 14
P. they that will PRESENT 9
sacrifice of p. PRAYER 5
they only want p. CRITICISM 15
were no small p. PRAISE 10
praised God be p. PRAYER 23
Honesty is p. HONESTY 8
more p. than practised HONESTY 3
praiser p. of past times GENERATION GAP 5
praising doing one's p. for oneself PRAISE 16
prattle how pleasantly they p. WORDS AND DEEDS 19
pray can't p. a lie PRAYER 27
let him p. MONEY 4
p. for Shackleton CRISES 6
p. for the country POLITICIANS 22
To work is to p. PRAYER 2
When you p., move your feet RELIGION 2
prayer Conservative Party at p. CHRISTIAN CHURCH 28
Every p. reduces itself PRAYER 25
four spend in p. LIFESTYLES 25
Lord's P. PRAYER 4
most perfect p. PRAYER 21
p. at sinking of the sun PRAYER 11
P. carries us half way to God GOD 14
p. is only answered PRAYER 9
P. is translation PRAYER 30
things are wrought by p. PRAYER 24
wing and a p. CRISES 21
wing and a p. NECESSITY 15
wish for p. PRAYER 29
prayers fear that has said its p. COURAGE 4
p. are a disease of the will RELIGION 22
p. of the church TRAVEL 28
p. would make me whole PARENTS 17
prayeth p. well, who loveth well PRAYER 22
praying No p., it spoils business PRAYER 19
prays family that p. together PRAYER 1
preach Practise what you p. WORDS AND DEEDS 7
preaching woman's p. is like WOMAN'S ROLE 10
precedency p. between a louse EQUALITY 7
precedent dangerous p. CUSTOM 20
precept Example is better than p. WORDS AND DEEDS 3
worth a pound of p. WORDS AND DEEDS 6

promotion (*cont.*)
sweat but for p. EMPLOYMENT 10
You'll get no p. ARMED FORCES 43
pronounce p. it right SPEECH 8
proof p. of the pudding HYPOTHESIS 5
Proosian Turk, or P. ENGLAND 15
propaganda P. is a soft weapon DECEPTION 24
proper know our p. stations CLASS 13
p. study of mankind HUMAN RACE 20
property either p. or honour SATISFACTION 18
give me a little snug p. POSSESSIONS 19
nobody's special p. LANGUAGES 20
P. has its duties POSSESSIONS 20
P. is theft POSSESSIONS 21
p. of others GREED 7
smaller the p. SELF-ESTEEM 2
Thieves respect p. CRIME 36
prophecies always prove p. FORESIGHT 13
prophet p. is not without honour FAMILIARITY 10
p. is not without honour FAMILIARITY 13
prophets men reject their p. HEROES 13
pose as its p. FATE 25
p. make sure of the event FORESIGHT 13
proportion strangeness in the p. BEAUTY 16
propose p. nothing PARLIAMENT 19
proposes Man p. FATE 3
prose Good p. is like a window-pane WRITING 49
govern in p. ELECTIONS 17
P. = words in their best POETRY 19
p. is verse POETRY 11
P. is when all the lines POETRY 21
p. without knowing it LANGUAGE 8
prospect noblest p. which SCOTLAND 9
prosper Cheats never p. DECEPTION 1
I grow, I p. DEFIANCE 11
Treason doth never p. TRUST 25
prosperity Both poverty and p. POVERTY 1
man who can stand p. ADVERSITY 15
P. doth best discover ADVERSITY 14
prostitute doormat or a p. WOMAN'S ROLE 20
prostitutes small nations like p. INTERNATIONAL 31
protect p. a working-girl CLASS 20
p. the people JOURNALISM 11
p. the writer ADMINISTRATION 19
two solitudes p. LOVE 57
protection calls mutely for p. GUILT 16
protections p. against temptations TEMPTATION 15
protects imprisons and p. PROGRESS 14
Protestant Printing, and the P. CULTURE 12
Protestantism P. to human thought CHRISTIAN CHURCH 29
proud as p. as Lucifer PRIDE 4
Death be not p. DEATH 40
P. people breed sad sorrows PRIDE 9
prove I could p. everything OPPORTUNITY 39
p. anything by figures STATISTICS 4
proverb no p. without a grain of truth QUOTATIONS 3
p. is one man's wit QUOTATIONS 8
proverbs acquaint yourself with their p. QUOTATIONS 4
P. are the coins of the people QUOTATIONS 2
proves exception p. the rule HYPOTHESIS 1
provide goods the gods p. OPPORTUNITY 19
providence go the way that P. dictates FATE 24
P. is always on the side ARMED FORCES 7
provider lion's p. ANIMALS 11
proving p. their falseness HYPOTHESIS 14
provokes p. me with impunity DEFIANCE 1
prow Youth on the p. YOUTH 11
prudence P. is a rich CAUTION 30
P. is the other woman THRIFT 21
prunella leather or p. INDIFFERENCE 3
prunes p. and prisms BEHAVIOUR 13
pruning need p. by study ABILITY 10
prurient p. curiosity BODY 18
psychotherapy waste money on p. MUSIC 34
Ptolemaic P. system UNIVERSE 3
public as if I was a p. meeting CONVERSATION 16
faces in p. places BEHAVIOUR 31
give the p. what it wants BROADCASTING 10
Government and p. opinion ENGLAND 18
I and the p. know GOOD 41
mislead the p. STATISTICS 11
p. be damned BUSINESS 35
p. rallies round an idea HYPOTHESIS 30
p. squalor ECONOMICS 16
temper of the p. CRIME 37
what he thinks the p. wants BROADCASTING 7
publications previous p. SCIENCE 24
publicity good p. ADVERTISING 1
now called p. REPUTATION 33
oxygen of p. REVOLUTION 34
P. is the very soul of justice JUSTICE 32
thing as bad p. FAME 28
public relations precedence over p. TECHNOLOGY 24
publish P. and be damned PUBLISHING 7
p. it not in the streets NEWS 6
publisher Barabbas was a p. PUBLISHING 9
makes everybody a p. PUBLISHING 11
pudding chieftain o' the p.-race FOOD 17
proof of the p. HYPOTHESIS 5
Take away that p. FOOD 29
puddle shining into a p. GOOD 5
pulpit bully p. PRESIDENCY 1
such a bully p. PRESIDENCY 6
white glove p. PRESIDENCY 16
pun make so vile a p. WIT 9
[p.] is a pistol let off at the ear WIT 16
punch pleased as P. PLEASURE 5
P. and Judy ARGUMENT 8
P. and Judy politics PARLIAMENT 30
punctuality Cleanliness, p., order HOUSEWORK 9
painting and p. PUNCTUALITY 9
P. is the art PUNCTUALITY 4
P. is the politeness PUNCTUALITY 5
P. is the politeness PUNCTUALITY 10
P. is the soul PUNCTUALITY 6
Punic P. faith TRUST 11
punishment cruel and unusual p. CRIME 27
glutton for p. WORK 17
less horror than the p. CRIME 28
p. fit the crime CRIME 34
p. is avarice GREED 10
p. is mischief CRIME 26
P. is not for revenge CRIME 29
pupil make the best of a p.'s means TEACHING 19
p. of the eye PREJUDICE 15
When the p. is ready EDUCATION 8
pupils all my p. are the crème SCHOOLS 12
kills all its p. TIME 39
puppy Happiness is a warm p. DOGS 15
purchasing I am not worth p. CORRUPTION 11
pure all things are p. GOOD 20
Because my heart is p. VIRTUE 30
has not a p. heart COOKING 22
P. and complete sorrow SORROW 18
P. and ready to mount VIRTUE 18
p. as the driven slush VIRTUE 40

race (*cont.*)
they which run in a r. WINNING 11
unprotected r. COUNTRIES 20
wins the r. DETERMINATION 14
races r. and tribes, that you may HUMAN RACE 12
so-called white r. RACE 13
two distinct r. DEBT 18
racket Once in the r. CRIME 38
radical most r. revolutionary REVOLUTION 33
R. Chic FASHION 14
r. chic FASHION 5
R. is a man POLITICAL PARTIES 26
r. when young POLITICAL PARTIES 25
radio r. expands it BROADCASTING 15
rag r. and bone shop EMOTIONS 24
red r. to a bull ANGER 7
rage Heaven in a r. BIRDS 11
r. against the dying OLD AGE 31
rags for religion when in r. RELIGION 12
raids Baedeker r. WORLD WAR II 2
rail r. at the ill GOOD 34
railroad Building that r. CANADA 11
enterprised a r. TRANSPORT 8
Underground R. LIBERTY 4
railway r. cuttings ENGLAND 20
R. termini TRANSPORT 13
take this r. by surprise TRANSPORT 14
rain command the r. ROYALTY 27
gentle r. from heaven JUSTICE 27
If in February there be no r. WEATHER 6
Into each life some r. must fall ADVERSITY 16
Jupiter the R.-giver RIVERS 5
left out in the r. APPEARANCE 29
R. before seven WEATHER 12
r. breaks not EMOTIONS 8
r. is destroying his grain FARMING 13
R. is grace WEATHER 48
r., it raineth on the just WEATHER 42
r. maketh a hole DETERMINATION 30
R., rain, go away WEATHER 13
r. rains on DEATH 2
sendeth r. on the just EQUALITY 4
waiting for it to r. OPTIMISM 40
you will feel no r. WEDDINGS 4
rainbow at the end of the r. FUTILITY 9
end of the r. VALUE 15
Life is a r. LIFE 59
r. coalition RACE 4
R. gave thee birth BIRDS 18
real r. coalition RACE 28
raineth r. drop SEASONS 27
rains It never r. MISFORTUNES 7
r. Pennies from heaven OPTIMISM 32
rainy r. Sunday afternoon BOREDOM 10
raise easier to r. the Devil BEGINNING 4
r. Cain ORDER 8
raising bungle r. your children CHILD CARE 13
rake r. among scholars WRITERS 13
r.'s progress LIFESTYLES 11
random word, at r. spoken CHANCE 28
ranger Sloane R. CLASS 8
rank r. is but the guinea's stamp RANK 11
ranks even the r. of Tuscany PRAISE 15
rap persons not worth a r. OPPORTUNITY 14
rape procrastinated r. BOOKS 21
you r. it ARTS 23
raped r. and speaks English JOURNALISM 20
rapidly Yes, but not so r. TIME 47
rapists all men are r. MEN 21
rapture careless r. BIRDS 15
rara r. avis ORIGINALITY 4
rare as difficult as they are r. EXCELLENCE 12
rascals R., would you live ARMED FORCES 19
rat Anyone can r. TRUST 35
creeps like a r. FATE 23
r., and Lovell GOVERNMENT 1
smell a r. DECEPTION 9
smell a r. DECEPTION 18
You dirty r. CINEMA 4
rational r. is actual REALITY 14
rationalized should never be r. HAPPINESS 26
rationally think r. on empty stomach LOGIC 23
rationed it must be r. LIBERTY 26
rats desert r. WORLD WAR II 5
rattle care for the child's r. TASTE 4
pleased with a r. CHILDREN 12
serves as a r. EDUCATION 13
rattling r. of a stick ADVERTISING 10
ravage r. with impunity SENSES 12
Ravel R. refuses the Legion MUSICIANS 12
ravelled r. sleave of care SLEEP 11
raven Quoth the R., 'Nevermore' DESPAIR 10
raw names are poetry in the r. NAMES 18
razor hew blocks with a r. FUTILITY 23
Occam's r. PHILOSOPHY 2
reach beers cannot r. ALCOHOL 3
r. should exceed his grasp AMBITION 17
reaction can't get no girl r. SEX 29
if there is any r. RELATIONSHIPS 20
reactionaries r. are paper tigers POLITICS 22
reactionary R. is a somnambulist POLITICAL PARTIES 26
read books which no one can r. PUBLISHING 10
cannot *r.* a book READING 20
He that runs may r. READING 2
I'd not r. Eliot, Auden POETS 24
if he had r. as much READING 7
I never r. a book CRITICISM 10
lies in its being r. BOOKS 26
news until he's r. it NEWS 13
people who can't r. JOURNALISM 26
praise and don't r. BOOKS 16
Pray, r., and work PRAYER 2
r. any good books lately READING 1
r. by deputy BOOKS 7
r., by preference ARTS AND SCIENCES 4
r. just as inclination READING 11
R. my lips TAXES 18
r. Richardson for the story WRITERS 9
r. the Riot Act CRIME 16
r. the same book BOOKS 4
r. too widely QUOTATIONS 16
servants to r. CENSORSHIP 16
she cannot r. IGNORANCE 29
superfluous to r. SCIENCE 24
what is it you want to r. MURDER 19
reader made everybody a r. PUBLISHING 11
one r. in a hundred years WRITING 44
readers full of fourth-rate r. READING 21
reading early and invincible love of r. READING 13
easy writing's vile hard r. WRITING 24
he was r. READING 4
I prefer r. READING 16
Much r. is an oppression READING 10
Peace is poor r. PEACE 16
R. is to the mind READING 8
r. ten thousand books EXPERIENCE 10
r. ten thousand books KNOWLEDGE 8

rich (*cont.*)
r. in things POSSESSIONS 30
r. is better WEALTH 39
r. man has his ice in the summer WEALTH 6
r. man in his castle CLASS 15
r. men rule the law POVERTY 20
r. people in the world GREED 14
r. richer CAPITALISM 24
r. to die DEATH 56
r. with little store SATISFACTION 19
r. would have kept more of it WORK 45
sincerely want to be r. AMBITION 20
to get r. MUSICIANS 18
very r.. They are different WEALTH 32
You can never be too r. APPEARANCE 30
Richard R. of York gave battle COLOURS 2
richer for r. for poorer MARRIAGE 25
R. than all his tribe VALUE 26
riches chief enjoyment of r. WEALTH 24
embarrassment of r. EXCESS 15
hope and joy is real r. CHARACTER 36
R. are for spending WEALTH 20
r. consist, not in the extent POSSESSIONS 23
r. grow in hell WEALTH 21
Titled for r. RANK 21
richesse embarras de r. EXCESS 15
ridden bridled to be r. DEMOCRACY 6
riddle r. wrapped in a mystery RUSSIA 7
ride r. a tiger DANGER 23
spurred to r. DEMOCRACY 6
ticket to r. OPPORTUNITY 40
rides He who r. a tiger DANGER 3
ridicule r. is the best test of truth TRUTH 23
ridiculous makes men r. POVERTY 15
nothing if it is not r. HOPE 23
position r. SEX 17
r. as the British MORALITY 6
step above the r. SUCCESS 31
sublime to the r. SUCCESS 32
to the r. SUCCESS 4
Ridley comfort, Master R. FAITH 6
right all r., Jack SELF-INTEREST 14
all's r. with the world OPTIMISM 10
always r. PATRIOTISM 17
country, r. or wrong PATRIOTISM 16
customer is always r. BUSINESS 7
divine r. of kings ROYALTY 8
Do r. CONSCIENCE 3
do what is r. VIRTUE 34
Equality may perhaps be a r. EQUALITY 9
firmness in the r. POLITICIANS 19
generalities of natural r. HUMAN RIGHTS 11
he must also be r. GREATNESS 16
I had rather be r. AMBITION 16
It must be r. CUSTOM 14
It's about being r. LEADERSHIP 28
it's all r. FORGIVENESS 27
just not r. SELF-ESTEEM 33
lose and do the r. thing WINNING 31
Might is r. POWER 5
never r. to do wrong GOOD 16
not all was r. SATISFACTION 27
one WAS r. MIDDLE AGE 11
one—of—them—is—is—r. OPINION 23
Only if it's done r. SEX 32
question, 'Is it r.' MORALITY 22
r., by chance FOOLS 20
R. Divine of Kings ROYALTY 30
'r.' means nothing JUSTICE 20
r. of Genghis Khan POLITICAL PARTIES 11
r. sort of people APOLOGY 19
r. there is none to SOLITUDE 10
r. to a fair portion HUMAN RIGHTS 8
r. to his own opinions OPINION 26
r. to utter OPINION 19
r. which goes unrecognized HUMAN RIGHTS 17
r. with the world OPTIMISM 21
scientists are probably r. HYPOTHESIS 30
that they are r. CERTAINTY 27
To do the r. deed MORALITY 18
Ulster will be r. IRELAND 14
vaguely r. than exactly wrong MISTAKES 24
Whatever IS, is R. CIRCUMSTANCE 27
what is r. with America AMERICA 36
what thy r. hand doeth CHARITY 14
wrongs don't make a r. GOOD 7
wrongs don't make a r. GOOD 45
your r. to say it CENSORSHIP 6
righteous r. man regardeth the life ANIMALS 15
rights asserting these r. SECRECY 40
dignity and r. HUMAN RIGHTS 16
inalienable r. of man HUMAN RIGHTS 9
Natural r. is nonsense HUMAN RIGHTS 10
possess their equal r. DEMOCRACY 8
r. of man HUMAN RIGHTS 4
their r., and nothing more WOMAN'S ROLE 17
vital personal r. essential to MARRIAGE 45
wicked folly of 'Woman's R.' WOMAN'S ROLE 18
right-wing r., like nature POLITICAL PARTIES 45
Rimmon house of R. SELF-INTEREST 10
ring devil's gold r. GIFTS 3
I hae brocht ye to the r. WARS 6
r. encompasseth thy finger WEDDINGS 7
R. out the old FESTIVALS 67
They now *r.* the bells WARS 9
With this R. I thee wed WEDDINGS 8
riot read the R. Act CRIME 16
r. is at bottom the language VIOLENCE 17
ripe r. and ripe MATURITY 4
Soon r. MATURITY 2
ripen but nice to r. MATURITY 15
ripple tiny r. of hope IDEALISM 16
rise early to r. HEALTH 4
maketh his sun to r. EQUALITY 4
power to drink or r. DRUNKENNESS 6
r. above its source CHARACTER 16
r. above principle POLITICS 1
r. at five IDLENESS 13
this world to r. above NATURE 19
rising All r. to great place POWER 23
land of the r. sun COUNTRIES 9
r. tide lifts all SUCCESS 9
risk Hesitation increases in relation to r. CAUTION 36
R. comes from not knowing what DANGER 38
risking in r. life MEN AND WOMEN 19
risks We took r. DANGER 34
ritual Modern bodybuilding is r. BODY 31
Without r., courtesy is tiresome CUSTOM 6
Ritz like the R. Hotel JUSTICE 38
rivals himself will have no r. SELF-ESTEEM 16
river bridge where there is no r. POLITICIANS 30
Even the weariest r. RIVERS 10
Fame is like a r. FAME 12
If you live in the r. CIRCUMSTANCE 2
last r. poisoned POLLUTION 4
log floats in the r. CHANGE 8
Old Man R. RIVERS 4
Ol' man r. RIVERS 15

Saturday (*cont.*)
Glasgow Empire on a S. HUMOUR 20
S. morning, although TRANSPORT 14
S.'s child works hard WORK 7
sauce Hunger is the best s. COOKING 8
only one s. ENGLAND 11
s. for the goose JUSTICE 14
sausages Laws are like s. LAW 6
savage mad and s. master SEX 7
noble s. CULTURE 6
noble s. ran CULTURE 9
s. wields his club SCIENCE 13
soothe a s. breast MUSIC 9
untutored s. FAMILY 21
savaged s. by a dead sheep INSULTS 12
save Beauty will s. the world BEAUTY 28
destroy the town to s. it WARS 24
less democracy to s. DEMOCRACY 16
s. five *sous* on unessential things GOVERNMENT 17
s. my soul PRAYER 20
s. the Party POLITICAL PARTIES 33
S. the whale POLLUTION 2
s. those that have IMAGINATION 13
S. us from our friends FRIENDSHIP 5
through life trying to s. TIME 43
To s. your world ARMED FORCES 46
saved could have s. sixpence THRIFT 19
penny s. is a penny earned THRIFT 4
saving s. as well as of getting THRIFT 15
saw I came, I s. SUCCESS 23
S. wood and say nothing CAUTION 23
say Do as I s. HYPOCRISY 1
Have something to s. STYLE 16
having nothing to s., abstains SILENCE 14
I don't care what you s. FAME 23
If you can't s. something nice MANNERS 20
If you don't s. anything SPEECHES 18
Lat thame s. DEFIANCE 3
nothing to s. SPEECH 18
s. everything best over a meal COOKING 24
S. it with flowers FLOWERS 1
s. nowt SELF-INTEREST 3
s. what they please GOVERNMENT 24
s. what you mean MEANING 8
see what I s. MEANING 12
someone else has got to s. LOGIC 13
till I see what I s. THINKING 21
way I s. it STYLE 23
wink wink, s. no more SEX 31
your right to s. it CENSORSHIP 6
saying know what they are s. SPEECHES 15
says What everybody s. TRUTH 10
Who s. A NECESSITY 13
scabbard not fit in one s. SIMILARITY 11
throw away the s. WARFARE 13
throw the s. away REVOLUTION 5
scaffold crime and not the s. CRIME 24
scaffolding s. has hardly gone up COUNTRIES 30
scalded s. by hot milk CAUTION 11
scale encloses space on a s. ARCHITECTURE 15
s. for an experiment HYPOTHESIS 19
scales s. fall INSIGHT 3
someone is practising s. MUSIC 21
scandal Love and s. GOSSIP 19
public s. that constitutes SIN 17
Russian s. GOSSIP 14
scar s. on the conscience AFRICA 15
s. will remain LIES 7
Scarborough S. warning SURPRISE 7
scarce Good men are s. VIRTUE 2
scarecrows mechanized s. IRELAND 20
s. of fools LOGIC 16
scarlet raise the s. standard POLITICAL PARTIES 23
silk or s. CHARACTER 1
sins be s. FORGIVENESS 11
scars He jests at s. SUFFERING 14
s. have strange power SUFFERING 36
scatter s. the good seed FARMING 11
scattering of s. abroad SEASONS 35
scene English s. ENGLAND 24
scenery end of all natural s. MOUNTAINS 3
scent s. of the roses MEMORY 10
sceptic s. could inquire LOGIC 11
too much of a s. CERTAINTY 22
sceptical we're s. PARANORMAL 22
scepticism lead to s. PHILOSOPHY 9
sceptred s. isle ENGLAND 7
schedule s. is already full CRISES 26
schemes best-laid s. FORESIGHT 14
s. of political improvement POLITICS 11
schizophrenic you are a s. MADNESS 16
Schleswig-Holstein S. question INTERNATIONAL 21
scholar ink of a s. EDUCATION 4
s. among rakes WRITERS 13
scholars Saints and S. IRELAND 6
school Example is the s. EDUCATION 22
head against the s. house EDUCATION 2
keeps a dear s. EXPERIENCE 6
s. of hard knocks ADVERSITY 9
s. of Stratford atte Bowe LANGUAGES 4
sent to s. for SCHOOLS 7
tales out of s. SECRECY 8
unwillingly to s. CHILDREN 9
schoolboy s., with his satchel CHILDREN 9
schoolboys s. who educate him SCHOOLS 8
schoolchildren what all s. learn GOOD 41
schoolgirl s. complexion APPEARANCE 7
schoolmaster send your child to the s. SCHOOLS 8
schoolmasters Experience is the best of s. EXPERIENCE 23
s. of ever after WRITING 37
schoolrooms s. for 'the boy' CRIME 30
schools Public s. are the nurseries SCHOOLS 3
Schrödinger S.'s cat PHYSICAL 8
science aim of all s. HYPOTHESIS 23
creation s. SCIENCE AND RELIGION 1
destiny of s. to exterminate SCIENCE 10
dismal s. ECONOMICS 4
gay s. POETRY 1
it is not s. SCIENCE 12
magisterium, of s. covers SCIENCE AND RELIGION 19
Much s., much sorrow SCIENCE 1
never be solved by s. IGNORANCE 23
orderly facts of every s. HYPOTHESIS 17
S. finds TECHNOLOGY 2
S. has no enemy SCIENCE 2
S. is for the cultivation SCIENCE AND RELIGION 5
s. is strong MEDICINE 26
S. knows no country SCIENCE 11
S. must begin with myths ARTS AND SCIENCES 8
s., read, by preference ARTS AND SCIENCES 4
s. reassures ARTS AND SCIENCES 7
S. without religion SCIENCE AND RELIGION 13
Success is a s. SUCCESS 35
tragedy of S. HYPOTHESIS 16
sciences Books must follow s. SCIENCE 6
scientific importance of a s. SCIENCE 24
new s. truth SCIENCE 25

sentimentality S. is the emotional promiscuity EMOTIONS 28
sentiments his words and his s. SPEECHES 5
separately We shall all hang s. COOPERATION 28
separation until the hour of s. MEETING 18
sept that damnable s. SCOTLAND 7
September S. blow soft WEATHER 17
S. dries up wells SEASONS 8
sepulchre whited s. HYPOCRISY 6
sepulchres whited s. HYPOCRISY 10
sequin change the world one s. STYLE 24
seraglio s. of eunuchs PARLIAMENT 27
serenity s. to accept CHANGE 49
serf another man's s. DEATH 25
serfdom abolish s. REVOLUTION 21
sergeant s. is the army ARMED FORCES 48
serial kind of s. monogamist CONSTANCY 13
obituary in s. form BIOGRAPHY 18
serious too s. a matter POLITICS 26
War is too s. a matter WARFARE 45
You cannot be s. SPORTS 35
seriously S., though ACHIEVEMENT 9
seriousness s. one had as a child MATURITY 9
sermon S. on the Mount CHRISTIAN CHURCH 11
S. on the Mount SCIENCE AND RELIGION 14
sermons S. and soda-water PLEASURE 19
S. in stones NATURE 9
serpent s.-haunted sea SEA 22
s. subtlest beast ANIMALS 18
sharper than a s. tooth GRATITUDE 10
servant good s. but a bad master WAYS 5
s. is worth a thousand gadgets TECHNOLOGY 13
servants s. are treated as human EMPLOYMENT 16
s. to read CENSORSHIP 16
serve No man can s. CHOICE 4
s. God and Mammon MONEY 16
s. in heaven AMBITION 12
s. our country PATRIOTISM 10
s. two masters MONEY 27
They also s. ACTION 25
served first come, first s. PUNCTUALITY 3
Had I but s. God DUTY 11
never well s. BUSINESS 15
would be well s. SELF-INTEREST 5
Youth must be s. YOUTH 4
service no-future job in the s. sector EMPLOYMENT 28
S. is the rent we pay CHARITY 7
serviettes crumpled the s. MANNERS 21
serving-men six honest s. KNOWLEDGE 43
servitude s. is at once LIBERTY 14
sesame Open S. PROBLEMS 12
sets sun never s. COUNTRIES 11
settled People who wish to be s. CUSTOM 15
settlers s. give it passion COUNTRY 20
seven City of the S. Hills TOWNS 7
for the first s. years EDUCATION 3
Keep a thing s. years POSSESSIONS 4
Measure s. times PREPARATION 13
Rain before s. WEATHER 12
s. ages LIFE 21
s. deadly sins SIN 5
S. Last Words DEATH 22
s.-league boots TRANSPORT 5
s. of anything QUANTITIES 27
s. seas SEA 9
s. stars SKIES 7
s.-stone weakling HEALTH 10
seventy times s. FORGIVENESS 12
s. wealthy towns FAME 15
S. Wonders of the World ARCHITECTURE 5
seventy Oh, to be s. again OLD AGE 26
s. times seven FORGIVENESS 12
s. year young OLD AGE 23
sewer Life is like a s. LIFE 52
midst of this putrid s. BRITISH TOWNS 32
sea is the universal s. POLLUTION 23
sewing s. on a button MEN 14
sex exactly like s. MONEY 47
fair s. WOMEN 13
give a s. to mind MIND 14
have money, it's s. SATISFACTION 37
Is s. dirty SEX 32
make s. less secretive SEX 33
Mind has no s. MIND 2
mostly about having s. CHILDREN 20
Nobody dies from lack of s. SINGLE 12
only unnatural s. act SEX 28
s. with someone I love SEX 37
to insult s. SEX 24
weaker s., to piety more prone WOMEN 23
sexes difference within the s. MEN AND WOMEN 20
stronger, of the two s. MEN AND WOMEN 6
sexual car crash as a s. event TRANSPORT 23
S. intercourse began SEX 34
s. lives of their parents PARENTS 28
strong as s. desire SEX 8
sexually s. transmitted disease LIFE 2
Shackleton pray for S. CRISES 6
shade farewell to the s. TREES 10
s. for their descendants TREES 5
thought in a green s. GARDENS 13
shades S. of the prison-house YOUTH 12
shadow also casts a s. RANK 20
but a walking s. LIFE 22
events cast their s. FUTURE 1
Falls the S. REALITY 17
s. of death DANGER 27
s. will be shown GOD 31
shadowing employ any depth of s. INSULTS 5
shadows less liquid than their s. CATS 9
s. fall behind you OPTIMISM 15
sins cast long s. PAST 2
shady sunny place for s. people FRANCE 7
shaft s. at random sent CHANCE 28
shaggy s.-dog story FICTION 5
shake s. and the rotten apples fell RUSSIA 12
s. The catsup bottle FOOD 27
shaken S. and not stirred ALCOHOL 27
s. me by the hand OLD AGE 19
s., not stirred ALCOHOL 7
shaker mover and s. CHANGE 23
shakers movers and s. MUSICIANS 7
Shakespeare Brush up your S. QUOTATIONS 17
entire works of S. COMPUTERS 17
I could be S. ARTS AND SCIENCES 6
like reading S. ACTING 5
read a work of S.'s ARTS AND SCIENCES 9
S. had not written *Hamlet* ARTS AND SCIENCES 14
S. liked to coin words WORDS 31
S. would have grasped ARTS AND SCIENCES 12
tongue that S. spake ENGLAND 12
Whaur's yer Wullie S. THEATRE 13
shaking fall without s. EFFORT 21
start s. them SPEECHES 20
shallow only s. people who do not judge APPEARANCE 23
s. murmur EMOTIONS 11

shalt Thou s. not kill MURDER 8
'Thou s. not' might reach FICTION 24
sham real pain for my s. friends FRIENDSHIP 32
shame ask is a moment's s. INTELLIGENCE 2
fool me twice, s. on me DECEPTION 2
secret s. destroyed my peace POETS 24
s. and humiliation REPUTATION 33
s. on you JAZZ 9
s. the devil TRUTH 5
shape our buildings s. us ARCHITECTURE 14
s. of things to come FUTURE 11
you might be any s. NAMES 13
share church to *s.* God GOD 37
lion's s. QUANTITIES 19
s. in two revolutions REVOLUTION 17
s. no one's ideas IDEAS 10
shared trouble s. COOPERATION 18
sharing intimate s. between friends PRAYER 13
unequal s. of blessings CAPITALISM 20
shark bitten in half by a s. CHOICE 28
jump the s. BROADCASTING 5
sharks We are all s. POLITICIANS 40
sharp short, s. shock CRIME 33
short s. shock CRIME 17
sharpen children s. their teeth PARENTS 34
sharpens Iron s. iron CHARACTER 9
sharper s. than a serpent's tooth GRATITUDE 10
s. the storm OPTIMISM 14
shaving s. of a morning POETRY 29
she Does s....or doesn't she CERTAINTY 1
shear good shepherd to s. his flock TAXES 4
shears resembles a pair of s. MARRIAGE 30
shed prepare to s. them now SORROW 10
sheep black s. FAMILY 12
bleating s. loses OPPORTUNITY 3
hanged for a s. THOROUGHNESS 5
hundred years like a s. HEROES 8
Let us return to these s. DETERMINATION 12
like lost s. SIN 16
lone s. is in danger SOLITUDE 3
savaged by a dead s. INSULTS 12
s. from the goats GOOD 12
s. on its hind-legs CONFORMITY 12
s.'s clothing HYPOCRISY 9
s. to pass resolutions ARGUMENT 17
thousand years as a s. HEROES 1
two wolves and a s. voting DEMOCRACY 22
wolf in s.'s clothing DECEPTION 10
sheet wet s. and a flowing sea SEA 17
sheets kindliness of s. SLEEP 19
shell fired a 15-inch s. SURPRISE 14
shelter s. for the other WEDDINGS 4
shelves your bookcases and your s. LIBRARIES 3
shepherd good s. to shear his flock TAXES 4
Lord is my s. GOD 8
no good s. without a good dog DOGS 3
s.'s delight WEATHER 14
shepherds s. and butchers GOVERNMENT 18
shibboleth Say now S. SPEECH 8
shieling s. of the misty island SCOTLAND 13
shift s. an old tree CUSTOM 3
shifting food Upon a s. plate FAME 21
shilling take the king's s. ARMED FORCES 13
shillings can do for ten s. TECHNOLOGY 15
shines hay while the sun s. OPPORTUNITY 10
shining improve the s. hour EFFORT 13
s. morning face CHILDREN 9
ship Do not spoil the s. THOROUGHNESS 1
one for the s. SEA 4
one leak will sink a s. CAUSES 21
s. but a prison SEA 14
s. of fools HUMAN RACE 7
s. of state GOVERNMENT 9
s. of the desert ANIMALS 13
vineyard and a s. COUNTRIES 33
woman and a s. ever want mending WOMEN 9
ships down to the sea in s. SEA 10
launched a thousand s. BEAUTY 13
Loose lips sink s. GOSSIP 7
s. that pass MEETING 5
S. that pass in the night RELATIONSHIPS 15
sunken and damaged s. WORLD WAR II 22
shipshape s. and Bristol fashion ORDER 9
shipwreck s. of time PAST 22
shire s. which we the Heart BRITISH TOWNS 26
shirt Near is my s. SELF-INTEREST 7
s. of Nessus MISFORTUNES 16
shirtsleeves From s. to SUCCESS 3
shit shock-proof s. detector WRITING 47
shiver praised and left to s. HONESTY 8
shivering hungry s. self SATISFACTION 32
shock future s. PROGRESS 2
s. and awe WARFARE 12
short, sharp s. CRIME 33
short sharp s. CRIME 17
shocked s. by this subject PHYSICAL 19
shocking looked on as something s. MORALITY 17
shocks s. the magistrate CENSORSHIP 13
s. the mind of a child RELIGION 20
shoe If the s. fits NAMES 3
shoemaker s.'s son always goes barefoot FAMILY 11
shoes call for his old s. FAMILIARITY 15
dead men's s. AMBITION 3
dead men's s. POSSESSIONS 9
dressed in cheap s. DRESS 19
I had no s. MISFORTUNES 4
just wearing better s. WEALTH 43
more than dancing s. DANCE 3
want of s. MISFORTUNES 20
shoot he shall s. higher AMBITION 8
s. me in my absence ABSENCE 14
s. the messenger NEWS 5
s. the pianist MUSICIANS 8
s. your murderer HEROES 21
shout and they s. LIBERTY 32
shooting s. a gun SPORTS 40
s. as a sport HUNTING 15
s. without aim ACTION 3
war minus the s. SPORTS 24
shoots green s. of economic spring ECONOMICS 25
green s. of recovery ECONOMICS 5
He s.! He scores SPORTS 20
shop Keep your own s. BUSINESS 11
shopkeepers nation of s. BUSINESS 32
nation of s. ENGLAND 14
shopping Now we build s. malls BUSINESS 51
s. days to Christmas CHRISTMAS 4
shore I sit on the s. PATIENCE 8
lose sight of the s. EXPLORATION 14
shoreline s. of wonder KNOWLEDGE 55
shorn come home s. AMBITION 4
grass kept finely s. GARDENS 12
to the s. lamb SYMPATHY 2
short brutish and s. LIFE 23
Life is s. MEDICINE 8
life is s. ARTS 2
Life is too s. to PRACTICALITY 16
lyf so s. EDUCATION 17

sixpence Bang goes s. THRIFT 1
could have saved s. THRIFT 19
precious little for s. VALUE 33
sixties swinging s. PAST 17
sixty-four s. thousand dollar question PROBLEMS 15
When I'm s. OLD AGE 35
size no virtue goes with s. QUANTITIES 32
one of an ordinary s. GREATNESS 8
One s. does not fit all WAYS 15
s. of the fight in the dog COURAGE 31
skeleton s. at the feast MISFORTUNES 17
s. in the cupboard SECRECY 22
skelp gie them a s. SATISFACTION 25
skies watcher of the s. INVENTIONS 10
skilled S. or unskilled POETRY 5
skin beauty being only s.-deep BEAUTY 35
Beauty is only s. deep BEAUTY 4
because my s. is red AMERICA 19
change his s. CHANGE 28
change one's s. CHANGE 20
Don't sell the s. OPTIMISM 8
electrical s. and glaring eyes CATS 7
my s. bristles POETRY 29
nearer is my s. SELF-INTEREST 7
shear his flock, not s. it TAXES 4
s. of my teeth DANGER 28
skull beneath the s. DEATH 64
thick s. is a gift CHARACTER 49
way to s. a cat WAYS 22
skinny tastes as good as s. feels BODY 32
skins inside our own s. SOLITUDE 20
sisters under their s. WOMEN 36
skittles beer and s. LIFE 4
skull s. beneath the skin DEATH 64
skuttle fish mind of the s. ARGUMENT 10
sky big enough to hide the s. POWER 7
clean the s. POLLUTION 18
never rots in the s. SEASONS 10
nursling of the S. SKIES 18
pie in the s. FUTURE 10
Red s. at night WEATHER 14
s. as a blue dome IGNORANCE 22
s. falls we shall catch EFFORT 7
s. is falling CRISES 13
s., space, trees, steel ARCHITECTURE 19
Touching the s. with glory ARMED FORCES 9
Women hold up half the s. WOMEN 10
slacks girls in s. CHRISTMAS 16
slag-heap post-industrial s. ENGLAND 26
slain s., nor treated with violence ANIMALS 16
slam not a s. at *you* MANNERS 19
slander one to s. GOSSIP 24
slang S. is a language LANGUAGE 26
slap Slip, slop, s. HEALTH 12
slashing damned cutting and s. PUBLISHING 6
slate wipe the s. clean FORGIVENESS 10
slave Better be a s. TEACHING 15
freedom to the s. LIBERTY 20
moment the s. resolves LIBERTY 34
S. Coast AFRICA 5
s. was made a man RACE 9
young man's s. MARRIAGE 1
slavery fat s. LIBERTY 1
testimony against s. SINGING 8
wise and good in s. LIBERTY 17
slaves Air for S. to breathe LIBERTY 7
all women are born s. WOMAN'S ROLE 9
creed of s. NECESSITY 23
made our s. ANIMALS 21
never will be s. BRITAIN 6
never will be s. ENGLAND 18
sons of former s. EQUALITY 17
two kinds of s. BUYING 11
slayer She is the S. SUPERNATURAL 22
slays If any man thinks he s. DEATH 27
Whoso s. a soul MURDER 9
sleekit s., cow'rin' FEAR 14
sleep calf won't get much s. COOPERATION 34
Care-charmer S. SLEEP 8
deep s. of England ENGLAND 20
full of s. OLD AGE 25
ideas s. furiously LANGUAGE 25
I love s. SLEEP 22
less you know, the better you s. IGNORANCE 5
Macbeth does murder s. SLEEP 11
night to do with s. SLEEP 12
One hour's s. before SLEEP 2
Six hours in s. LIFESTYLES 25
Six hours s. SLEEP 3
s.: perchance to dream DEATH 38
s. and a forgetting PREGNANCY 7
s. five hours SLEEP 4
S. no more SLEEP 11
s. of a labouring man SLEEP 7
s. with a woman LIFESTYLES 38
We never s. SLEEP 5
sleeping awakened a s. giant CAUSES 29
Let s. dogs lie CAUTION 15
S. is no mean art SLEEP 17
s. with an elephant INTERNATIONAL 34
sleeps s. in thunder CONSCIENCE 7
When the imagination s. IMAGINATION 16
sleepwalker assurance of a s. FATE 24
sleeve ace up one's s. SECRECY 18
card up his s. POLITICIANS 23
heart on one's s. EMOTIONS 6
heart upon my s. EMOTIONS 9
your s. will reach THRIFT 8
sleeves rolls up its s. LANGUAGE 26
slept Christ and His saints s. WARS 5
slice S. him where you like CHARACTER 46
s. off a cut loaf IGNORANCE 8
sliced since s. bread INVENTIONS 2
slip many a s. MISTAKES 5
S., slop, slap HEALTH 12
slippers walks in his golden s. RELIGION 12
Sloane S. Ranger CLASS 8
slog s.—slog—slog ARMED FORCES 34
slop Slip, s., slap HEALTH 12
slough fall on S. POLLUTION 19
slovenliness s. is no part of religion DRESS 7
slow S. and steady DETERMINATION 14
S. but sure PATIENCE 16
telling you to s. down DEATH 3
Too s. for those who wait TIME 40
slowly Make haste s. HASTE 5
mills of God grind s. FATE 4
mills of God grind s. GOD 21
s. in the wind HASTE 20
sluggard Go to the ant thou s. IDLENESS 12
slumber keep'st the ports of s. WORRY 6
s. is more sweet than toil IDLENESS 17
slumbers Golden s. SLEEP 10
slurp s., slurp, slurp GREED 16
slush pure as the driven s. VIRTUE 40
sluts I dress s. FASHION 18
small Better are s. fish SATISFACTION 3
gift though s. is welcome GIFTS 9

small (*cont.*)
looks pretty s. at a wedding WEDDINGS 12
Neutrinos, they are very s. PHYSICAL 20
one s. step ACHIEVEMENT 29
pictures that got s. CINEMA 12
Scotland s. SCOTLAND 19
S. is beautiful ECONOMICS 20
S. is beautiful QUANTITIES 10
small-clothes like s. LETTERS 11
smaller s. fleas to bite 'em QUANTITIES 29
smell I love the s. of napalm WARFARE 62
Money has no s. MONEY 6
Money has no s. TAXES 5
our sense of s. POLLUTION 16
s. a rat DECEPTION 9
s. of commerce in the morning BUYING 14
s. of the lamp EFFORT 16
to his own sense doth s. SELF 8
would s. as sweet NAMES 9
smelled s., not swallowed PRAISE 2
smells by sounds and s. CHILDREN 19
smelly I may be s. RIVERS 18
smile Cambridge people rarely s. BRITISH TOWNS 36
forget and s. MEMORY 13
game that is played with a s. WARFARE 40
hear people s. SENSES 20
last fading s. GOD 33
s. because she has lived MOURNING 6
smiler s. with the knyf TRUST 23
smiles charmed it with s. and soap WAYS 34
smiling against s. enemies ENVY 13
assume that it is s. DANGER 10
smite rude caitiff s. the other too VIOLENCE 7
s. hip and thigh CRIME 18
s. under the fifth rib DEATH 23
smith s. of his own fortune FATE 13
smock nearer is my s. SELF-INTEREST 6
smoke big S. BRITISH TOWNS 18
good cigar is a S. SMOKING 11
horrible Stygian s. SMOKING 7
light after s. THINKING 9
No s. without fire REPUTATION 9
s. and stir EARTH 10
s.-filled room POLITICS 7
S. gets in your eyes SORROW 23
smoked s. my first cigarette SMOKING 14
smoking not found any s. guns HYPOTHESIS 32
S. can seriously damage SMOKING 4
s. pistol SECRECY 23
smooth never did run s. LOVE 1
never did run s. LOVE 29
smoother his words were s. SPEECH 7
smug s. minority PROGRESS 21
snake add legs to the s. EXCESS 1
bitten by a s. TRUST 39
drag a s. by a hair BEHAVIOUR 2
Feeding a s. with milk CHARACTER 8
move about like a s. DECEPTION 24
Once bitten by a s. CAUTION 20
Poke a bush, a s. comes out CAUTION 21
s. in the grass DANGER 24
snakeskin s.-titles NAMES 14
sneer Who can refute a s. ARGUMENT 13
sneering born s. PRIDE 12
sneezes Coughs and s. SICKNESS 1
sneezy Breezy, S., Freezy SEASONS 20
snobbery bereaved if s. died HUMOUR 19
snooze If you s., you lose OPPORTUNITY 7
snotgreen s. sea SEA 23
snow cherry hung with s. TREES 14
few acres of s. CANADA 6
gather like drifting s. MEMORY 5
pure as the driven s. VIRTUE 10
s. before the summer sun AMERICA 12
s. on the roof OLD AGE 38
type of s. WEATHER 49
we shall have s. WEATHER 10
wrong sort of s. WEATHER 50
snow-broth blood Is very s. EMOTIONS 10
snows s. of yesteryear PAST 20
snowy S., Flowy, Blowy SEASONS 20
so S. it goes DEATH 74
soak you may expect a s. WEATHER 20
soaked I feel s. to the skin OPTIMISM 40
soap charmed it with smiles and s. WAYS 34
Flattery is soft s. PRAISE 1
s. opera BROADCASTING 6
soar creep as well as s. AMBITION 14
run, though not to s. IMAGINATION 10
soars No bird s. too high AMBITION 13
sober compulsorily s. DRUNKENNESS 7
s. me up to sit in a library LIBRARIES 11
tomorrow I shall be s. INSULTS 11
Wanton kittens make s. cats YOUTH 2
social no religion but s. CHRISTIAN CHURCH 20
self-love and s. SELF-INTEREST 23
s. and economic ALCOHOL 22
socialism religion of S. POLITICAL PARTIES 27
S. can only arrive POLITICAL PARTIES 42
s. would not lose CAPITALISM 27
socialist be a s. at twenty POLITICAL PARTIES 4
socialists s. throw it away CAPITALISM 26
We are all s. now POLITICAL PARTIES 22
society affluent s. WEALTH 7
Big S. POLITICS 33
big s. SOCIETY 3
bonds of civil s. SOCIETY 7
desperate oddfellow s. SOCIETY 12
good s. GOOD 48
Great S. SOCIETY 20
happiness of s. GOVERNMENT 21
hell for s. HEAVEN 15
lifeblood of s. GOSSIP 4
no such thing as S. SOCIETY 23
No to the market s. CAPITALISM 31
pillar of s. SOCIETY 5
S. is now BOREDOM 7
S. needs to condemn CRIME 44
s., with all its combinations HUMAN RIGHTS 8
There is such a thing as s. SOCIETY 24
unable to live in s. SOLITUDE 6
sociology S. is all about why SOCIETY 18
sock Jonson's learnèd s. THEATRE 9
making a hole in a s. DRESS 13
s. and buskin ACTING 3
Socratic S. manner PHILOSOPHY 15
S. method PHILOSOPHY 3
soda water Sermons and s. PLEASURE 19
sodomy s., prayers ARMED FORCES 45
soft does not make us s. CULTURE 7
s. answer ANGER 8
s. answer turneth away wrath DIPLOMACY 1
s. spot for sinners HEAVEN 22
whan s. was the sonne SEASONS 15
softer s. than butter SPEECH 7
softly S., softly PATIENCE 17
Sweet Thames, run s. RIVERS 6
Tread s. DREAMS 12

soil answer lies in the s. GARDENS 2
barren s. MIND 13
soldier courage of a s. is found ARMED FORCES 23
duty of a s. ARMED FORCES 3
having been a s. ARMED FORCES 22
s., Full of strange oaths ARMED FORCES 16
s. is flat blasphemy CLASS 11
s. of the Great War ARMED FORCES 8
summer s. PATRIOTISM 14
tell an old s. ARMED FORCES 33
What the s. said GOSSIP 10
soldiers as many s. as that CINEMA 9
Old s. never die ARMED FORCES 39
s. never die ARMED FORCES 5
solitary s. be not idle IDLENESS 15
s. confinement SOLITUDE 20
solitude feel his s. more keenly SOLITUDE 18
In s., What happiness SOLITUDE 8
solitudes two s. protect LOVE 57
Solomon felicities of S. BIBLE 9
S. in all his glory BEAUTY 11
soluble art of the s. SCIENCE 27
solution always a well-known s. PROBLEMS 28
can't see the s. PROBLEMS 30
part of the s. PROBLEMS 34
total s. RACE 18
solutions all the s. EUROPE 19
s. are not FORESIGHT 21
solve s. every problem PROBLEMS 38
some fool s. of the people DECEPTION 21
somebody When every one is s. EQUALITY 12
someone not s. else SELF 27
S. had blundered MISTAKES 20
S., somewhere LETTERS 2
S. to tell it to CONVERSATION 19
Somerset House records of S. PRIDE 14
something do s. to *help* COOPERATION 32
He who does s. ACHIEVEMENT 25
s. completely different CHANGE 1
s. for Posterity FUTURE 17
S. is better than SATISFACTION 7
S. may be gaining SPORTS 26
s. to forgive FORGIVENESS 25
Time for a little s. COOKING 28
sometime come up and see me s. MEETING 21
woman is a s. thing WOMEN 41
somewhere Someone, s. LETTERS 2
somnambulist s. walking backwards POLITICAL PARTIES 26
son hateth his s. CRIME 20
leichter of a fair s. PREGNANCY 6
Like father, like s. FAMILY 8
prodigal s. FORGIVENESS 8
s. always goes barefoot FAMILY 11
s. is my son PARENTS 4
song end of an old s. SCOTLAND 8
melancholy out of a s. SINGING 3
My gift is my s. GIFTS 22
s. in one's heart PLEASURE 7
s. makes you feel SINGING 13
s. my paddle sings RIVERS 12
s. that never ends SELF-SACRIFICE 7
s. the Syrens sang KNOWLEDGE 27
Thy speech, thy s., To thee belong WALES 6
till I end my s. RIVERS 6
wine, and s. PLEASURE 12
women, and s. PLEASURE 9
songless s. bird in a cage BELIEF 2
s. bird in a cage BELIEF 24
songs In writing s. I've learned SINGING 14
s. are sad IRELAND 15
sonnet Scorn not the s. POETRY 20
sonnets passably effective s. ADVERTISING 7
written s. all his life FAMILIARITY 17
sons Clergymen's s. CLERGY 1
Great men's s. seldom do well GREATNESS 3
My s. ought to study mathematics CULTURE 10
s. and daughters of Life PARENTS 21
s. and your daughters GENERATION GAP 16
soon S. ripe MATURITY 2
sooner end the s. HASTE 13
s. begun BEGINNING 9
s. every party HOSPITALITY 10
s. it's over OPTIMISM 14
sop s. to Cerberus APOLOGY 12
sophistry s. and affectation UNIVERSITIES 6
sorcerer s.'s apprentice PROBLEMS 16
sorriness s. underlying the grandest things WRITING 35
sorrow beguile thy s. LIBRARIES 4
cannot prevent the birds of s. SORROW 3
first great s. DESPAIR 11
forgather wi' S. SATISFACTION 25
help you to s. MISFORTUNES 3
increaseth s. KNOWLEDGE 16
In s. thou shalt bring PREGNANCY 4
Labour without s. is base WORK 32
Much science, much s. SCIENCE 1
One for s. BIRDS 3
s. and silence SUFFERING 21
s. in store SUPERNATURAL 18
s. to the grave OLD AGE 12
such sweet s. MEETING 8
sorrowing goes a s. DEBT 5
sorrows Man of S. SORROW 5
Proud people breed sad s. PRIDE 9
remedy for the s. SYMPATHY 28
Small s. speak SORROW 8
sorry having to say you're s. LOVE 9
safe than s. CAUTION 1
Very s. can't come APOLOGY 20
sort not at all the s. of person CHARACTER 40
sorts It takes all s. CHARACTER 10
soul best picture of the human s. BODY 23
blazing hearth in one's s. SOLITUDE 12
captain of my s. SELF 18
casket of my s. SLEEP 15
dark night of the s. DESPAIR 2
dark night of the s. DESPAIR 14
Diseases of the s. SICKNESS 11
engineers of the s. ARTS 26
engineers of the s. ARTS 31
flow of s. CONVERSATION 3
French s. is stronger FRANCE 17
give his s. for the whole world WALES 10
giving life to an immortal s. PREGNANCY 9
good for the s. HONESTY 2
happiness dwells in the s. HAPPINESS 8
hidden language of the s. DANCE 17
Hyacinths to feed my s. LIFESTYLES 32
if I have a s. PRAYER 20
I owe my s. DEBT 23
iron entered into his s. ADVERSITY 6
like an infant's s. BOOKS 9
lose his own s. SUCCESS 24
Medicine for the s. LIBRARIES 2
most surely, on the s. ARCHITECTURE 13
No coward s. is mine COURAGE 22

soul (*cont.*)
rather to be strong in s. STRENGTH 19
s. be blasted SWEARING 7
S. City AMERICAN CITIES 42
s. inhabiting two bodies FRIENDSHIP 11
s. through My lips KISSING 5
than that one s. SIN 21
when it has no s. BUSINESS 33
window of the s. BODY 3
with s. so dead PATRIOTISM 15
soulless when work is s. WORK 40
souls All S.' Day FESTIVALS 7
letters mingle s. LETTERS 5
only in men's s. SCIENCE AND RELIGION 15
sell their s. CONSCIENCE 19
s. with but a single LOVE 48
they have no s. BUSINESS 27
windows into men's s. SECRECY 28
sound full of s. and fury LIFE 22
make the most s. FOOLS 2
mind in a s. body HEALTH 17
s. and original ideas POLITICAL PARTIES 34
s. of a great Amen MUSIC 13
s. of music MUSIC 28
s. of silence SILENCE 15
soundbites not a time for s. SPEECHES 22
sounds better than it s. MUSICIANS 9
by s. and smells CHILDREN 19
s. will take care SPEECH 21
soup cannot make a good s. COOKING 22
sour s. grapes SATISFACTION 15
source remember the s. OLD AGE 8
rise above its s. CHARACTER 16
s. and origin BEGINNING 16
south full of the warm S. ALCOHOL 13
S. is avenged REVENGE 19
sovereign anger of the s. ROYALTY 20
he will have no s. HUMAN RIGHTS 6
subject and a s. ROYALTY 26
sovereigns what s. are doing GOSSIP 20
Soviet Communism is S. power CAPITALISM 16
Soviets power to the S. CAPITALISM 1
sow out of a s.'s ear FUTILITY 8
right s. by the ear PRACTICALITY 5
S. an act CAUSES 23
s. by the ear KNOWLEDGE 10
s. dragon's teeth MISFORTUNES 18
s. dry GARDENS 9
s. in tears SUFFERING 6
s. may whistle ABILITY 6
s., so you reap CAUSES 5
s. that eats her farrow IRELAND 16
s. the wind CAUSES 11
soweth Whatsoever a man s. CAUSES 20
sowing time of s. SEASONS 35
sown s. the wind CAUSES 18
space fewer landmarks in s. MEMORY 23
Filling a s. ARTS 34
filling the s. JOURNALISM 19
how to waste s. ARCHITECTURE 18
In s., no one can hear you FEAR 4
king of infinite s. DREAMS 7
more than time and s. WORRY 9
S. is almost infinite UNIVERSE 18
S. isn't remote at all SKIES 30
s. where nobody is AMERICA 30
Watch this s. JOURNALISM 3
spaces silence of these infinite s. UNIVERSE 7
s. between the houses POLLUTION 24
s. in your togetherness MARRIAGE 37
spaceship S. Earth EARTH 13
Spain castle in S. IMAGINATION 2
singeing of the King of S.'s Beard WARS 7
Spaniards thrash the S. SPORTS 10
Spanish To God I speak S. LANGUAGES 5
spare Brother can you s. a dime POVERTY 26
don't s. the horses TRANSPORT 18
S. at the spigot THRIFT 6
s. the beechen tree TREES 12
S. the rod CHILD CARE 2
S. well and have to spend THRIFT 7
spared s. me nothing in life BEAUTY 39
spareth s. his rod CRIME 20
spark s. o' Nature's fire EDUCATION 21
spark-gap s. is mightier than the pen TECHNOLOGY 12
sparks s. fly upward MISFORTUNES 19
sparrow s. alight upon my shoulder BIRDS 16
s. should fly swiftly LIFE 19
sparrows know s. from starlings BIRDS 22
Spartans Go tell the S. SELF-SACRIFICE 3
speak artist cannot s. about his art ARTS 30
children how to s. LANGUAGES 18
dare not s. its name LOVE 55
I didn't s. up INDIFFERENCE 16
knowledge to s. CONVERSATION 15
let him now s. OPPORTUNITY 33
Small sorrows s. SORROW 8
s. and purpose not HYPOCRISY 11
S. as you find REPUTATION 11
s. before you think CREATIVITY 13
s. for ten minutes SPEECHES 17
s. ill of everybody BIOGRAPHY 16
s. ill of the dead REPUTATION 8
s. no evil VIRTUE 5
S. Out SOCIETY 21
S. softly DIPLOMACY 11
s. softly and carry lipstick WOMAN'S ROLE 30
s. well of you REPUTATION 21
S. what we feel HONESTY 10
whereof one cannot s. SPEECH 23
speaking It's ill s. FOOD 6
speaks heart s. to heart SPEECH 12
He s. to me as if CONVERSATION 16
mouth s. EMOTIONS 1
s. does not know KNOWLEDGE 15
s. least SPEECH 3
s. well of the bridge MANNERS 3
special s. kind of artist ARTS 25
s. relationship INTERNATIONAL 9
species female of the s. WOMEN 2
preys on its own s. HUMAN RACE 28
spectacle he is also a s. DIPLOMACY 9
spectacles not made by men in s. REVOLUTION 3
spectre s. of Communism CAPITALISM 11
speculate If you don't s. BUSINESS 9
speculation only daring s. can lead us HYPOTHESIS 25
speech as it does in one's s. HOME 16
Be silent, unless your s. SILENCE 8
every twelve miles the s. TRAVEL 2
freedom of s. HUMAN RIGHTS 15
Human s. is like SPEECH 20
manner of his s. SPEECH 14
S. is civilization SPEECH 24
S. is often barren SILENCE 12
s. is shallow SILENCE 11
S. is silver SILENCE 4
true use of s. LANGUAGE 9

squeak until the pips s. REVENGE 10
squeeze like a kiss without a s. FOOD 1
s. until the pips squeak REVENGE 10
squeezed s. as a lemon REVENGE 21
squire Bless the s. CLASS 13
squires s. and spires BRITISH TOWNS 8
squirrel s.'s heart beat INSIGHT 14
squishing s. noises SEX 39
stable born in a s. CHARACTER 12
stable-door late to shut the s. FORESIGHT 4
stables Care, and not fine s. ANIMALS 1
cleanse the Augean s. PROBLEMS 8
staff s. of life FOOD 12
stage daughter on the s. ACTING 7
played upon a s. FICTION 10
to the well-trod s. anon THEATRE 9
world's a s. LIFE 21
stage-coach like an old s. POLITICAL PARTIES 41
stair by a winding s. POWER 23
stale s., flat, and unprofitable FUTILITY 21
stammering s. very inconvenient SPEECH 17
stamp more than a three-cent s. LETTERS 1
physics or s. collecting SCIENCE 22
stand firm spot on which to s. TECHNOLOGY 6
Get up, s. up DEFIANCE 17
Here s. I DETERMINATION 29
real — please s. up SECRECY 16
seven times, s. up eight DETERMINATION 3
s. and stare LEISURE 10
s. and wait ACTION 25
s. by each other always FRIENDSHIP 22
S. by your man MEN AND WOMEN 23
s. for nothing CHARACTER 52
s. in one place INSIGHT 21
s. on either hand COOPERATION 29
s. up for bastards DEFIANCE 11
United we s. COOPERATION 20
uniting we s. AMERICA 11
standard bog-s. comprehensive SCHOOLS 13
raise the scarlet s. POLITICAL PARTIES 23
standardized s. worker with interchangeable MANAGEMENT 10
standards fictitious demand for lower s. BROADCASTING 7
His s. are quite low HEAVEN 22
standing as cheap sitting as s. ACTION 8
not to be s. here MOURNING 22
stands good reputation s. still REPUTATION 5
man who s. most alone STRENGTH 23
S. Scotland where SCOTLAND 6
starts from where one s. BEGINNING 20
While s. the Coliseum TOWNS 18
stanza sky-high in a s. POETRY 27
star Being a s. has made RACE 24
constant as the northern s. CONSTANCY 6
discovery of a s. INVENTIONS 11
evening s. SKIES 1
Lone S. State AMERICAN CITIES 27
North S. State AMERICAN CITIES 31
s. to steer her by SEA 21
s., would I were steadfast CONSTANCY 8
twinkle, little s. SKIES 17
unreachable s. IDEALISM 15
wagon to a s. IDEALISM 8
with one bright s. SKIES 16
starboard port out, s. home TRAVEL 16
star-crossed s. lovers LOVE 19
stare stand and s. LEISURE 10
starlings know sparrows from s. BIRDS 22
starry-eyed s. IDEALISM 4
stars erratik s. SKIES 9
heaventree of s. SKIES 24
journey-work of the s. NATURE 14
knowledge of the s. SCIENCE 18
looking at the s. IDEALISM 9
Looking up at the s. SKIES 29
Look up at the s. SKIES 21
loved the s. too truly SKIES 20
melt the s. SPEECH 20
mistake each other for s. AMERICAN CITIES 61
pointed out to you the s. INSIGHT 1
ready to mount to the s. VIRTUE 18
seven s. SKIES 7
S. and Bars AMERICA 8
S. and Stripes AMERICA 9
s. of heaven appear to us SKIES 19
s.' tennis-balls FATE 16
s. to flight DAY 12
sun and the other s. LOVE 26
star-spangled s. banner AMERICA 13
start rest of your life to s. LOVE 73
S. all over again DETERMINATION 46
s. together MUSICIANS 15
s. where people are CLERGY 19
started arrive where we s. EXPLORATION 15
s. so I'll finish BEGINNING 7
starve let his wife s. ARTS 22
let our people s. DEBT 24
s. a fever SICKNESS 4
would sooner s. FOOD 26
starves steed s. ACHIEVEMENT 11
starving s. population IRELAND 12
state bosom of a single s. CANADA 8
from the generosity of the s. HUMAN RIGHTS 18
I am the S. GOVERNMENT 16
not the same as the s. SOCIETY 24
Only in the s. SOCIETY 10
ship of s. GOVERNMENT 9
s. has no place in CENSORSHIP 17
S. is an instrument CAPITALISM 17
S. is not 'abolished' GOVERNMENT 33
s. with the prettiest name AMERICAN CITIES 57
such thing as the S. SOCIETY 16
While the S. exists GOVERNMENT 35
stately S. Homes of England RANK 19
s. homes of England RANK 15
statement s. is like a cheque MEANING 13
woman makes the s. DRESS 20
statesman gift of any s. POLITICIANS 18
s. is a politician POLITICIANS 29
s. is a politician POLITICIANS 35
stations know our proper s. CLASS 13
statistic million deaths a s. DEATH 71
statistical s. improbability LIFE SCIENCES 30
statistics damned lies and s. STATISTICS 7
experiment needs s. STATISTICS 12
feed the hungry on s. STATISTICS 9
give plenty of s. STATISTICS 8
uses s. as STATISTICS 10
vital s. STATISTICS 2
We are just s. STATISTICS 3
statue s. has never been set up CRITICISM 17
statues s. are so constrained SCULPTURE 4
status quo restored the s. SCIENCE 17
stay Go in, s. in, tune in CRISES 2
Here I am, and here I s. WARS 17
S. a little HASTE 13
s. as they are CHANGE 50

stormy dark and s. night BEGINNING 6
story cock and bull s. FICTION 4
means to write one s. LIFE 39
novel tells a s. FICTION 19
One s. is good HYPOTHESIS 4
picture tells a s. MEANING 1
read Richardson for the s. WRITERS 9
shaggy-dog s. FICTION 5
short in the s. itself WRITING 10
s. and a byword AMERICA 10
S. is just the spoiled child FICTION 18
stout collapse of S. Party HUMOUR 1
stove ice on a hot s. CREATIVITY 11
strafe Gott s. England WORLD WAR I 10
straight makes a s.-cut ditch EDUCATION 23
never make a crab walk s. FUTILITY 20
no s. thing HUMAN RACE 22
s. trees are cut down HONESTY 7
sufficient to keep him s. CONSCIENCE 20
unflexible as s. MISTAKES 16
strain train take the s. TRANSPORT 2
Words s., Crack WORDS 27
strait S. is the gate VIRTUE 17
strand never alone with a S. SMOKING 5
strange something s. in your neighbourhood PARANORMAL 17
strangeness s. in the proportion BEAUTY 16
will die of s. FICTION 21
stranger cousin and I against the s. FAMILY 10
cuddled by a complete s. CHILD CARE 15
s. than fiction FICTION 1
s. than fiction TRUTH 6
S. than fiction TRUTH 27
s. to one of your parents CHOICE 16
Who's 'im, Bill? A s. PREJUDICE 14
wiles of a s. FAMILY 24
you would be a total s. FRIENDSHIP 1
strangers entertain s. HOSPITALITY 7
I spy s. PARLIAMENT 1
kindness of s. CHARITY 20
strangle s. bad persons LAW 31
strangled s. with the guts REVOLUTION 12
Stratford scole of S. atte Bowe LANGUAGES 4
straw bricks without s. FUTILITY 6
but as s. dogs SYMPATHY 12
clutch at a s. HOPE 1
final s. CRISES 10
Headpiece filled with s. FUTILITY 28
last s. EXCESS 5
make bricks without s. PROBLEMS 11
man of s. ARGUMENT 7
pad in the s. DANGER 21
seems like s. INSIGHT 8
s. in the wind FUTURE 12
s. vote ELECTIONS 2
tickled with a s. CHILDREN 12
strawberry on the s. FOOD 14
straws Errors, like s. MISTAKES 15
S. tell which way MEANING 2
stream dead thing can go with the s. CONFORMITY 14
s. cannot rise CHARACTER 16
swim with the s. CONFORMITY 16
Time, like an ever-rolling s. TIME 34
street don't do it in the s. SEX 27
fighting in the s. REVOLUTION 32
Grub S. JOURNALISM 5
sunny side of the s. OPTIMISM 31
streets blood in the s. REVOLUTION 26
S. FLOODED TOWNS 25
s. paved with gold OPPORTUNITY 27
s. that no longer exist POLLUTION 24
strength as the s. of ten VIRTUE 30
child's s. BELIEF 20
Endurance is nobler than s. SUFFERING 23
exact quality of s. MANAGEMENT 9
S. in what remains behind TRANSIENCE 10
S. through joy STRENGTH 8
s., utility, grace ARCHITECTURE 6
s. without innocence DOGS 6
tower of s. STRENGTH 16
Union is s. COOPERATION 19
strengthen s. the weak by weakening STRENGTH 26
strengthened s. by whitewash CHARACTER 11
strengthens s. our nerves ENEMIES 12
stretched mind is s. by a new idea IDEAS 9
stride s. comes the dark DAY 10
strike If you s. a child VIOLENCE 8
S. him so that he can feel CRUELTY 6
s. it out STYLE 17
s. it out WRITING 25
S. while the iron OPPORTUNITY 18
strikes Lightning never s. CHANCE 11
Three s. and you're out CRIME 9
striking S. manners are bad MANNERS 5
string harp on the same s. BOREDOM 2
long is a piece of s. QUANTITIES 2
Monarchy is only the s. ROYALTY 34
s. that ties them ORIGINALITY 7
stripes Stars and S. AMERICA 9
s. and dead armadillos EXCESS 42
zebra without s. CULTURE 2
strive s., to seek DETERMINATION 38
strokes Different s. CHOICE 1
Little s. DETERMINATION 9
strong battle to the s. SUCCESS 8
battle to the s. SUCCESS 22
only the S. shall thrive STRENGTH 25
rather to be s. in soul STRENGTH 19
s. as a bull moose STRENGTH 24
s. enough to bear SYMPATHY 19
s. in the arm BRITISH TOWNS 15
s. men stand face to face EQUALITY 13
think they are s. MISTAKES 27
wants that little s. ALCOHOL 14
weak overcomes the s. STRENGTH 18
wolf that keeps the caribou s. STRENGTH 1
stronger interest of the s. party JUSTICE 20
makes me s. SUFFERING 26
side of the s. STRENGTH 21
s. by every thing HYPOTHESIS 11
s. than Necessity NECESSITY 16
strongest s. man in the world STRENGTH 23
s. of all warriors are these PATIENCE 32
struck Diogenes s. the father CHILD CARE 4
s. regularly, like gongs WOMEN 39
struggle cease to s. SINGLE 11
gods themselves s. FOOLS 22
Manhood a s. LIFE 32
s. naught availeth EFFORT 23
s. of man against power POWER 44
tired of the s. EFFORT 22
today the s. PRESENT 13
stubborn Facts are s. HYPOTHESIS 2
students benefit of the s. UNIVERSITIES 7
studies S. serve for delight EDUCATION 18
study I must s. politics and war CULTURE 10
leisure, I will s. EDUCATION 14
result of previous s. BEHAVIOUR 23

tooth (*cont.*)
red in t. NATURE 13
sharper than a serpent's t. GRATITUDE 10
t. for tooth JUSTICE 19
toothache helps not the t. MUSIC 3
toothaches intellectual who underrates t. THINKING 30
toothpaste t. is out of the tube SECRECY 38
top room at the t. AMBITION 5
room at the t. OPPORTUNITY 25
T. End AUSTRALIA 11
T. people take *The Times* JOURNALISM 2
topography T. displays no favourites EARTH 11
Topsy grow like T. QUANTITIES 17
torch pass on the t. CUSTOM 5
torches t. to burn bright BEAUTY 15
Tories T. remember their friends POLITICAL PARTIES 24
torment more grievous t. LOVE 45
tormenting just t. the people QUANTITIES 30
torments Our t. also SUFFERING 16
tornado t. in Texas CHANCE 37
Toronto T. is a kind TOWNS 30
torrent t. of change CHANGE 43
torso remain a t. EUROPE 15
tortoise hare and t. DETERMINATION 22
torture t. to death GOOD 35
tortured t. who turn into CRUELTY 12
torturers turn into t. CRUELTY 12
Tory always be a T. POLITICAL PARTIES 18
T.'s secret weapon POLITICAL PARTIES 35
tossed t. and gored CONVERSATION 9
total History is the sum t. HISTORY 27
t. solution RACE 18
totalitarianism under the name of t. WARFARE 54
totter t. into vogue FASHION 7
touch feel the lightest t. SENSES 21
Midas t. WEALTH 14
Nelson t. LEADERSHIP 8
'Nelson t.' LEADERSHIP 14
puts it not unto the t. COURAGE 15
T. not the cat CATS 3
t. of greatness GREATNESS 12
t. of nature HUMAN NATURE 9
touches Each of us t. one place INSIGHT 7
He that t. pitch GOOD 2
toucheth He that t. pitch GOOD 15
tough T. on crime CRIME 45
When the going gets t. CHARACTER 21
toughness T. doesn't have to STRENGTH 31
tour Cook's t. TRAVEL 13
unless you made the European t. EUROPE 17
tourist t. in other people's reality REALITY 22
tourists philosophers are t. ARTS AND SCIENCES 13
tout T. passe LIFE 9
tower build a t. FORESIGHT 11
ivory t. REALITY 6
T. of Babel LANGUAGES 3
t. of nine storeys BEGINNING 20
t. of strength STRENGTH 16
towery T. city and branchy BRITISH TOWNS 34
town destroy the t. to save it WARS 24
every t. or city SELF-ESTEEM 19
Kirton was a borough t. BRITISH TOWNS 4
man made the t. COUNTRY 2
man made the t. COUNTRY 11
t. and gown UNIVERSITIES 4
t. mouse COUNTRY 7
towns seven wealthy t. FAME 15
toys boys with t. DECEPTION 12
track traveller leaves no t. or trace TRAVEL 22
trade all is seared with t. WORK 33
autocrat: that's my t. POWER 26
Every man to his t. WORK 2
it is His t. FORGIVENESS 22
People of the same t. BUSINESS 31
T. follows the flag BUSINESS 19
t. will always be attended BUSINESS 30
tricks in every t. BUSINESS 18
Two of a t. SIMILARITY 10
wheels of t. MONEY 34
whosoever commands the t. SEA 12
trades Jack of all t. ABILITY 8
Jack of all t. EXCELLENCE 3
trading make t. much easier MONEY 35
t. on the blood BIOGRAPHY 9
tradition t. Approves all forms ENVY 12
T. means giving votes CUSTOM 19
t. of all the dead CUSTOM 16
Without t., art is a flock ARTS 27
traditore Traduttore t. TRANSLATION 1
traduttore T. traditore TRANSLATION 1
Trafalgar T. Day FESTIVALS 57
tragedies t. are finished ENDING 18
two t. in life ACHIEVEMENT 27
tragedy abuse a t. CRITICISM 7
Comedy is t. HUMOUR 23
Comedy is t. plus time HUMOUR 22
element of t. EMOTIONS 20
finest work out of its t. POETRY 30
first time as t. HISTORY 17
One death is a t. DEATH 71
T. is thus a representation THEATRE 4
t. of a man INDECISION 13
t. of a man SELF-KNOWLEDGE 14
t. of old age OLD AGE 24
t. of Science HYPOTHESIS 16
t. requires *testicles* THEATRE 14
t. to those that feel LIFE 27
t. when seen in close-up LIFE 57
write you a t. HEROES 17
trahison t. des clercs INTELLIGENCE 7
trail no path and leave a t. ORIGINALITY 1
t. has its own stern code TRUST 34
train biggest electric t. CINEMA 11
charge of the clattering t. MANAGEMENT 13
light of the oncoming t. OPTIMISM 39
miss the t. before PUNCTUALITY 11
seldom heard a t. go by TRANSPORT 24
t. take the strain TRANSPORT 2
T. up a child CHILD CARE 3
trained We t. hard MANAGEMENT 2
traitors Our doubts are t. CERTAINTY 12
tram I'm a t. FATE 21
tramp lady is a t. BEHAVIOUR 32
trample t. the very values PATRIOTISM 32
trampling t. down twelve others CHARITY 19
tranquil sailing in a t. sea EFFORT 10
tranquillity emotion recollected in t. POETRY 14
feeling of inward t. DRESS 9
satisfied with t. ACTION 28
T. Base here SKIES 28
transcendental t. kind MEANING 10
transit Sic t. gloria TRANSIENCE 2
translate such as cannot write, t. TRANSLATION 3
translation Prayer is t. PRAYER 30
t.'s thief that addeth TRANSLATION 4
unfaithful to the t. TRANSLATION 8
translator T. General TRANSLATION 2

vegetable v., and mineral LIFE SCIENCES 2
veil beyond the v. DEATH 15
vein giving v. GIFTS 15
velvet gentleman in black v. ANIMALS 12
iron hand in a v. glove WAYS 26
v. revolution REVOLUTION 7
vengeance I will have my v. REVENGE 25
V. is mine REVENGE 11
veni *V., vidi, vici* SUCCESS 23
Venice V. is like eating an entire TOWNS 27
V. of the North TOWNS 14
Ventosus not improperly called V. MOUNTAINS 2
venture bow at a v. CHANCE 19
drew a bow at a v. CHANCE 23
Nothing v., nothing gain THOROUGHNESS 3
Nothing v., nothing have THOROUGHNESS 4
Venus V. entire LOVE 36
women are from V. MEN AND WOMEN 29
veracity heard and saw with v. WRITING 23
verb Waiting for the German v. LANGUAGES 19
verba Nullius in v. HYPOTHESIS 3
verbal v. contract LAW 38
verbosity exuberance of his own v. SPEECHES 13
not crude v. STYLE 7
verify trust, but v. TRUST 41
v. your references KNOWLEDGE 37
verisimilitude artistic v. FICTION 15
veritas *in vino v.* DRUNKENNESS 2
Vermont so goes V. ELECTIONS 10
vernal impulse from a v. wood GOOD 31
verse chapter and v. HYPOTHESIS 7
No v. can give pleasure ALCOHOL 9
v. is prose POETRY 11
write free v. POETRY 33
verses cap v. QUOTATIONS 5
version Authorized V. BIBLE 1
very Be v. afraid FEAR 1
vessel weaker v. MARRIAGE 17
vessels Empty v. FOOLS 2
vestry I will see you in the v. CLERGY 16
vicar V. of Bray SELF-INTEREST 24
vicariously vice enjoyed v. GOSSIP 5
vice Art is v. ARTS 23
between virtue and v. GOOD 28
bullied out of v. VIRTUE 31
Gossip is v. GOSSIP 5
lost by not having been v. VIRTUE 28
nerve-racking v. HYPOCRISY 16
nurseries of all v. SCHOOLS 3
render v. serviceable POLITICIANS 12
V. came in always SIN 18
v. of chastity SINGLE 6
v. pays to virtue HYPOCRISY 13
vice-presidency v. isn't worth a pitcher PRESIDENCY 12
vices dwelling on their v. FAMILY 23
ladder of our v. SIN 11
victim Any v. demands allegiance SYMPATHY 26
thou shalt not be a v. INDIFFERENCE 17
victims I hate v. CRIME 42
little v. play CHILDREN 13
victis *Vae v.* WINNING 12
victor to the v. belong the spoils WINNING 17
Victorian V. values VIRTUE 14
V. values VIRTUE 44
victories Peace hath her v. PEACE 11
victors History is written by the v. HISTORY 3
victory Dig for v. GARDENS 3
grave, where is thy v. DEATH 31
In v.: magnanimity WARFARE 57
It smells like v. WARFARE 62
magnanimous in v. ARMED FORCES 51
moment of v. is much too short WINNING 29
not the v. but the contest WINNING 20
One more such v. WINNING 8
Pyrrhic v. WINNING 6
v. at all costs WINNING 23
V. attained by violence VIOLENCE 9
V. has a hundred fathers SUCCESS 45
v. over oneself SELF 4
Vienna V. is nothing ROYALTY 37
Viet Cong no quarrel with the V. ENEMIES 20
Vietnam last man to die in V. ARMED FORCES 49
V. was lost BROADCASTING 12
V. was the first CENSORSHIP 19
view enchantment to the v. COUNTRY 12
v. never changes LEADERSHIP 5
you get a v. AMERICAN CITIES 64
viewer photographer and the v. PHOTOGRAPHY 12
vigilance man is eternal v. LIBERTY 14
village first in a v. AMBITION 6
global v. EARTH 6
image of a global v. TECHNOLOGY 17
Potemkin v. DECEPTION 8
vegetate in a v. NEIGHBOURS 8
v. to raise a child CHILD CARE 1
villages V., unlike towns, have always COUNTRY 23
villain rogue and v. INSULTS 5
vindictive petty and v. SUFFERING 28
vine shall be as the fruitful v. FAMILY 14
vinegar catches more flies than v. WAYS 9
tartest v. SIMILARITY 6
vines client to plant v. ARCHITECTURE 17
vineyard v. and a ship COUNTRIES 33
vino *in v. veritas* DRUNKENNESS 2
vintners wonder what the V. buy BUYING 7
violated City of the V. Treaty TOWNS 9
violence essence of war is v. WARFARE 31
fury and extreme v. FOOTBALL 4
inconvenience of v. WRITING 50
In v., we forget who VIOLENCE 15
I say v. is necessary VIOLENCE 18
Keep v. in the mind VIOLENCE 20
slain, nor treated with v. ANIMALS 16
Victory attained by v. VIOLENCE 9
What has v. ever accomplished VIOLENCE 19
violent more v. obscures the other SICKNESS 10
v. and sudden usurpations LIBERTY 13
v. revolution inevitable REVOLUTION 30
violet cast a v. into a crucible TRANSLATION 6
City of the V. Crown TOWNS 10
violin playing a v. LIFE 40
v. is wood and catgut FOOTBALL 6
virgin should have stayed a v. PARENTS 30
virtue best discover v. ADVERSITY 14
cardinal v. VIRTUE 8
cause of v. POLITICIANS 12
every v. at the testing point COURAGE 30
fine v. in ancestors THRIFT 3
follow v. and knowledge HUMAN RACE 14
fugitive and cloistered v. VIRTUE 24
governs his state by v. GOVERNMENT 10
Make a v. of necessity NECESSITY 7
no v. like necessity NECESSITY 17
Patience is a v. PATIENCE 14
reward of v. FRIENDSHIP 20
vice pays to v. HYPOCRISY 13
v. and vice GOOD 28

weapon (*cont.*)
most potent w. STRENGTH 29
terrible w. of aggression TRUTH 35
Tory's secret w. POLITICAL PARTIES 35
weak have one w. MISTAKES 27
w. against the enemy PAINTING 25
w. with a worker at each end WARFARE 1
weapons books are w. BOOKS 20
Wars may be fought with w. ARMED FORCES 41
Wars may be fought with w. WARFARE 47
wear Better to w. out IDLENESS 2
qualities as would w. well MARRIAGE 28
w. motley FOOLS 7
w. the green willow MOURNING 8
w. the purple ROYALTY 15
weariest Even the w. river RIVERS 10
weariness w. of the flesh BOOKS 5
wearing w. o' the Green IRELAND 9
weary Age shall not w. them ARMED FORCES 35
Be the day w. DAY 1
w., stale, flat FUTILITY 21
weasel w. took the cork ALCOHOL 25
w. under the cocktail cabinet THEATRE 22
w. words LANGUAGE 2
w. words LANGUAGE 18
weather first talk is of the w. WEATHER 33
known in bad w. SEA 1
no such thing as bad w. WEATHER 19
no such thing as bad w. WEATHER 30
queen's w. WEATHER 27
variety about the New England w. WEATHER 40
w. is like the government WEATHER 41
weave tangled web we w. DECEPTION 19
web O what a tangled w. DECEPTION 19
webs laws are like spider's w. LAW 19
wed w. over the mixen FAMILIARITY 2
wedded w. to the truth POLITICIANS 24
wedding One w. brings another WEDDINGS 5
three for a w. BIRDS 3
wedding cake face looks like a w. APPEARANCE 29
weddings W., christenings, duels FRANCE 19
wedlock W. is a padlock MARRIAGE 12
Wednesday Ash W. FESTIVALS 9
W.'s child SORROW 2
wee w. folk SUPERNATURAL 5
w. pretendy government SCOTLAND 20
W., sleekit FEAR 14
weed evil w. IGNORANCE 30
precious w. SMOKING 6
What is a w. GARDENS 17
weeding seven year's w. GARDENS 6
weeds he must also love w. GARDENS 5
w. and the wilderness POLLUTION 13
w. grow apace GOOD 4
week die in my w. SELF-INTEREST 29
Holy W. FESTIVALS 28
next w. to get the answer COUNTRY 22
others can in a w. HOSPITALITY 15
w. after next HASTE 15
w. for preparation SPEECHES 17
w. is a long time POLITICS 28
weep fear of having to w. HUMOUR 9
If you want me to w. SYMPATHY 13
stand at my grave and w. MOURNING 19
w. and know why SORROW 19
W., and you weep alone SORROW 21
w. and you weep alone SYMPATHY 3
w. as a woman SUCCESS 25
women must w. WORK 31
weepers losers w. POSSESSIONS 1
weeping w. and gnashing of teeth HEAVEN 7
weeps only animal that laughs and w. HUMAN RACE 24
weighed w. in the balance SUCCESS 19
welcome Advice is seldom w. ADVICE 12
W., all wonders CHRISTMAS 9
W. the coming HOSPITALITY 9
W. to your gory bed SCOTLAND 11
welcomest w. when they are gone HOSPITALITY 8
welfare w. of this realm ARMED FORCES 18
well alive, but being w. HEALTH 16
all shall be w. OPTIMISM 18
All's w. ENDING 2
Didn't she do w. ACHIEVEMENT 1
Dig the w. before PREPARATION 2
foolish thing w. done ACHIEVEMENT 20
frog in a w. knows nothing SELF-ESTEEM 4
Let w. alone CAUTION 16
lies at the bottom of a w. TRUTH 7
lies in acting w. EXCELLENCE 13
not wisely but too w. LOVE 31
pitcher will go to the w. EXCESS 10
something will turn out w. HOPE 24
speak w. of you REPUTATION 21
that's as w. said SPEECH 16
thing done w. SELF-INTEREST 4
till the w. runs dry GRATITUDE 4
W. begun BEGINNING 11
Will, when looking w. COURTSHIP 4
worth doing w. EFFORT 6
well-behaved W. women seldom make WOMEN 51
well-bred Conscience is w. CONSCIENCE 16
well dressed sense of being w. DRESS 9
w. in cheap shoes DRESS 19
wells drunk from w. you did not dig PAST 8
well-spent rare as a w. one BIOGRAPHY 6
well-treated stays where it is w. BUSINESS 3
well-written w. Life BIOGRAPHY 6
Welsh before the W. forget WALES 5
compare the English with the W. WALES 3
thank the Lord I'm W. WALES 11
Welshman much care and valour in this W. WALES 4
wen great w. BRITISH TOWNS 23
wept sat down and w. SORROW 6
young man who has not w. GENERATION GAP 12
west down in the w. BRITISH TOWNS 35
Go W., young man AMERICA 17
Go W., young man EXPLORATION 7
O wild W. Wind WEATHER 36
Queen of the W. AMERICAN CITIES 40
safeguard of the W. TOWNS 17
w. is west SIMILARITY 4
W. Lothian question PARLIAMENT 12
western All quiet on the w. front WORLD WAR I 24
delivered by W. Union CINEMA 18
West Indies nothing was created in the W. COUNTRIES 29
westward w., look OPTIMISM 23
wet set w. GARDENS 9
w. and wildness POLLUTION 13
w. her feet INDECISION 2
w. sheet and a flowing sea SEA 17
whacks gave her mother forty w. MURDER 4
whale Save the w. POLLUTION 2
screw the w. LANGUAGE 28
whaleship w. was my Yale College UNIVERSITIES 11
what great united w. BEGINNING 21
It's not w. you know CORRUPTION 3

wife (*cont.*)
I chose my w. MARRIAGE 28
I'd have no w. SINGLE 4
in want of a w. SINGLE 7
Petrarch's w. FAMILIARITY 17
she is your w. ADVERTISING 13
Stepford w. CONFORMITY 5
sympathetic w. MARRIAGE 18
take a w. GARDENS 4
untrue to his w. INTELLIGENCE 19
when his w. talks Greek WOMAN'S ROLE 12
w. and children FAMILY 16
w. or servants CENSORSHIP 16
w. shall be as the fruitful vine FAMILY 14
world and his w. FASHION 1
wild Caledonia! stern and w. SCOTLAND 12
sow one's w. oats LIFESTYLES 12
W. Geese IRELAND 7
w.-goose chase FUTILITY 18
wilderness crieth in the w. PREPARATION 18
make a w. PEACE 10
voice in the w. FUTILITY 17
weeds and the w. POLLUTION 13
w. of idea LANGUAGE 17
w. were paradise enow SATISFACTION 33
wildness In w. is the preservation POLLUTION 12
wiles Norfolk w. BRITISH TOWNS 1
wilful w. man must have his way DETERMINATION 20
W. waste makes woeful want THRIFT 11
will common w. GOVERNMENT 15
complies against his w. OPINION 1
complies against his w. OPINION 16
general w. rules SOCIETY 9
let my w. replace DETERMINATION 27
not because we w. MEMORY 12
political w. GOVERNMENT 42
Where there's a w. DETERMINATION 19
w. not when he may OPPORTUNITY 5
w. of even common man SELF 3
w. reigns MATURITY 7
w. to carry on LEADERSHIP 19
w. to Cupar DETERMINATION 4
W. you, won't you DANCE 11
You w., Oscar QUOTATIONS 11
William People's W. POLITICIANS 5
Willie holy W. HYPOCRISY 4
willing Barkis is w. PREPARATION 22
coalition of the w. DIPLOMACY 3
spirit indeed is w. TEMPTATION 10
willow wear the green w. MOURNING 8
willows w., old rotten planks PAINTING 11
wills w. the end DETERMINATION 5
wilt Do what thou w. LIFESTYLES 33
wimps Lunch is for w. COOKING 34
win arguments you w. ARGUMENT 3
end, the Germans w. FOOTBALL 13
Heads I w. WINNING 2
How to w. friends SUCCESS 42
if I cannot w. SPORTS 4
laugh that w. SUCCESS 5
When in doubt, w. the trick WINNING 14
w. and do the wrong thing WINNING 31
w. his spurs EFFORT 18
w. one hundred victories WINNING 7
w. one's laurels SUCCESS 20
w. one's spurs SUCCESS 21
w. or lose it all COURAGE 15
w. unless you hate them HATRED 12
You cannot w. PHYSICAL 1
You can't w. them all WINNING 5
You w. a few SUCCESS 14
wind all weathers but a thaw w. WEATHER 15
available with an east w. ARGUMENT 15
blowin' in the w. MATURITY 13
blow, thou winter w. GRATITUDE 8
candle in the w. RELATIONSHIPS 24
east w. made flesh AMERICAN CITIES 51
God tempers the w. SYMPATHY 2
gone with the w. ABSENCE 6
gone with the w. MEMORY 15
how the w. doth ramm SEASONS 27
It's an ill w. OPTIMISM 13
Like a candle in the w. TRANSIENCE 19
like the w., that shifts REPUTATION 22
North w. doth blow WEATHER 10
no w. is favourable IGNORANCE 16
O wild West W. WEATHER 36
reed before the w. STRENGTH 6
ruler is like w. LEADERSHIP 10
slowly in the w. HASTE 20
solidity to pure w. POLITICS 24
sown the w. CAUSES 18
sow the w. CAUSES 11
straw in the w. FUTURE 12
twist in the w. CERTAINTY 7
Unhelped by any w. WEATHER 35
upset in a high w. SLEEP 21
wait for the w. PATIENCE 8
When the w. is in the east WEATHER 21
Where the w. comes from WEATHER 44
wherever the w. takes me LIBERTY 6
which way the w. blows MEANING 2
w. extinguishes candles ABSENCE 10
w. of change AFRICA 9
w. of heaven ANIMALS 9
Woord is but w. WORDS AND DEEDS 11
windbags W. can be right QUOTATIONS 19
winding by a w. stair POWER 23
windmills tilt at w. FUTILITY 16
window argument of the broken w. ARGUMENT 19
der, w., a casement TEACHING 14
Good prose is like a w.-pane WRITING 49
love flies out of the w. POVERTY 8
return through the w. PREJUDICE 11
w. of opportunity OPPORTUNITY 29
w. of the soul BODY 3
window-panes its back upon the w. WEATHER 43
windows w. into men's souls SECRECY 28
w. of the Church CHRISTIAN CHURCH 30
winds to the four w. ORDER 11
w. of March FLOWERS 4
W. of the World ENGLAND 16
Windsor Widow at W. ROYALTY 16
windy W. City AMERICAN CITIES 48
wine days of w. and roses TRANSIENCE 13
jug of w. SATISFACTION 33
old w. wholesomest MATURITY 5
Poetry is devil's w. POETRY 6
sweetest w. SIMILARITY 6
truth in w. DRUNKENNESS 2
Vodka is an aunt of w. ALCOHOL 6
w., and song PLEASURE 12
w. and women PLEASURE 19
w. for thy stomach's sake ALCOHOL 10
w. in old bottles CHANGE 17
w. in old bottles CHANGE 25
W. is a mocker ALCOHOL 8
W. is bottled poetry ALCOHOL 17

worship find someone to w. RELIGION 25
w. God in his own way HUMAN RIGHTS 15
w. of the bitch-goddess SUCCESS 39
worst full look at the w. OPTIMISM 25
man's best to do man's w. WARFARE 55
prepare for the w. PREPARATION 10
things are at the w. OPTIMISM 16
told the w. BRITAIN 11
w. are full of passionate EXCELLENCE 17
w. form of Government DEMOCRACY 15
w. is not SUFFERING 15
w. is yet to come OPTIMISM 28
w. of times CIRCUMSTANCE 31
worth Because I'm w. it SELF-ESTEEM 1
calculate the w. of a man VALUE 32
If a thing's w. doing EFFORT 6
makes life w. living CULTURE 19
man's w. something SELF-KNOWLEDGE 13
nothing that is w. knowing EDUCATION 25
not w. going to see TRAVEL 31
Ode on a Grecian Urn is w. WRITING 46
that which is w. having SELF-SACRIFICE 15
thinks nothing w. a war WARFARE 35
w. doing badly WOMEN 37
w. of a thing is what VALUE 12
your flattery is w. PRAISE 13
Youth is the one thing w. YOUTH 16
Worthington on the stage, Mrs W. ACTING 7
worthwhile that which makes life w. ECONOMICS 19
worthy Lord I am not w. SELF-ESTEEM 13
nameless in w. deeds FAME 14
w. of his hire EMPLOYMENT 1
w. of their steel ENEMIES 13
would He w. SELF-INTEREST 28
w. not, that I do GOOD 19
wound never felt a w. SUFFERING 14
w., not the bandage RELIGION 30
wounds keeps his own w. green REVENGE 16
rubbed into their w. SUFFERING 30
wrath down upon your w. ANGER 10
grapes of w. GOD 28
soft answer turneth away w. DIPLOMACY 1
turneth away w. ANGER 8
tygers of w. ANGER 13
wren robin and the w. BIRDS 4
wrench with a rusty monkey w. DETERMINATION 2
wrestling more like w. than dancing LIFESTYLES 19
wretched knows that I am w. SUFFERING 20
w. people upon earth AUSTRALIA 12
wring they will soon *w.* their hands WARS 9
w. the withers EMOTIONS 7
wrinkle without any spot or w. VIRTUE 15
wrinkles earned your w. MIDDLE AGE 16
write I will w. for Antiquity WRITING 30
Learn to w. well WRITING 20
nothing to w. about LETTERS 4
people who can't w. JOURNALISM 26
such as cannot w. TRANSLATION 3
things I w. about MADNESS 13
would write and can't w. WRITING 3
w. all the books CHANCE 34
w. that history myself HISTORY 26
w. the life of a man BIOGRAPHY 4
w. the next chapter HUMAN RIGHTS 20
writer original w. is not ORIGINALITY 9
picture of the w.'s heart WRITING 7
understand a w.'s ignorance WRITING 29
w. has to rob his mother WRITING 46
writers full of fourth-rate w. READING 21
W. don't give prescriptions WRITING 51
W., like teeth, are divided WRITING 34
writes Happiness w. white HAPPINESS 34
moving finger w. PAST 28
writing easy w.'s vile hard reading WRITING 24
If w. did not exist WRITING 13
incurable disease of w. WRITING 12
In w. songs I've learned SINGING 14
This w. business WRITING 38
W. is a picture WRITING 7
w. on the wall FUTURE 13
written anything may be w. BOOKS 9
Books are well w. BOOKS 15
What is w. with a pen WRITING 6
w. in red, white and blue MUSIC 18
w. seems like straw INSIGHT 8
w. word as unlike STYLE 21
wrong All models are w. HYPOTHESIS 29
all was w. SATISFACTION 27
always in the w. ABSENCE 3
always in the w. WEATHER 41
but also to be w. CHILDREN 21
called the w. number MISTAKES 25
country, right or w. PATRIOTISM 16
customer is never w. BUSINESS 37
different kinds of w. SIN 27
for the w. reason MORALITY 18
he has been in the w. APOLOGY 14
he is very probably w. HYPOTHESIS 28
If anything can go w. MISFORTUNES 5
If you put the question in w. COMPUTERS 13
in the w. POLITICIANS 17
in the w. box CIRCUMSTANCE 16
I was w. MOURNING 20
I would rather be w. MISTAKES 12
keep himself from doing w. BUSINESS 26
king can do no w. ROYALTY 2
mind being w. OPINION 29
neat, plausible, and w. PROBLEMS 28
notions are generally w. IDEAS 6
on the w. side of DOGS 14
requite w. with wrong GOOD 16
Science is always w. SCIENCE 20
So much w. RELIGION 6
thought it w. to fight VIOLENCE 13
to govern w. ROYALTY 30
vaguely right than exactly w. MISTAKES 24
win and do the w. thing WINNING 31
w. decision isn't forever INDECISION 15
w. end of the gun HUNTING 15
w. sort of snow WEATHER 50
wronger w. than both of them MISTAKES 29
wrongs w. don't make a right GOOD 7
w. don't make a right GOOD 45
wrote ever w., except for money WRITING 26
xerox X. makes everybody PUBLISHING 11
XXXX Australians wouldn't give a X. AUSTRALIA 2
Yale whaleship was my Y. College UNIVERSITIES 11
Yankee Doodle I'm a Y. Dandy AMERICA 24
Yanks Y. are coming WORLD WAR I 18
yard not in my back y. SELF-INTEREST 17
year Christmas comes but once a y. CHRISTMAS 1
gate of the y. FAITH 14
New Y.'s Day FESTIVALS 45
Next y. in Jerusalem TOWNS 4
years After the first four y. HOUSEWORK 14
for the first seven y. EDUCATION 3
Forty y. on SCHOOLS 9

years (*cont.*)
know a man seven y. FAMILIARITY 12
locust y. ADVERSITY 8
not the y., honey, it's the mileage EXPERIENCE 37
takes seven y. to make a piper MUSIC 2
thousand y. as a sheep HEROES 1
thousand y. in the sight TRANSIENCE 5
thousand y. of history EUROPE 16
waiting 700 y. PUNCTUALITY 14
We turn not older with y. OLD AGE 22
y. are slipping by TRANSIENCE 6
y. teach much EXPERIENCE 24
yellow y.-dog Democrat POLITICAL PARTIES 12
y. leaf OLD AGE 16
yes easy to say y. LEADERSHIP 27
Y., Minister GOVERNMENT 39
yesterday call back y. PAST 21
dead Y. PRESENT 10
jam y. PRESENT 12
Y., all my troubles PAST 38
y. has gone CHARITY 24
Y. has gone PRESENT 4
Y. is ashes PRESENT 5
yesterdays all our y. TIME 30
yesteryear snows of y. PAST 20
yet but not y. SEX 9
yew More than one y. bow DANGER 8
yield find, and not to y. DETERMINATION 38
yoke my y. is easy WORK 21
Yom Kippur Y. FESTIVALS 62
yonder wild blue y. TRAVEL 20
York Y. shall be BRITISH TOWNS 5
Yorkshire Y. born BRITISH TOWNS 15
you cannot live with y. RELATIONSHIPS 7
For y. but not for me WORLD WAR I 20
It could be y. CHANCE 9
You matter because y. are you SICKNESS 26
'Y.' your joys SELF 30
young angry y. man GENERATION GAP 2
angry y. men WRITERS 2
but that one is y. OLD AGE 24
censor of the y. GENERATION GAP 5
crime of being a y. man YOUTH 10
good die y. VIRTUE 1
I'll die y. DRUGS 10
love's y. dream LOVE 17
love's y. dream LOVE 44
Make me y. YOUTH 24
not y. enough to know everything YOUTH 17
radical when y. POLITICAL PARTIES 25
seventy years y. OLD AGE 23
thief when he's y. CRIME 4
too y. to take up golf MIDDLE AGE 12
what ideas the y. people have IDEAS 12
Whom the gods love dies y. YOUTH 7
Whom the gods love die y. YOUTH 3
y. as they are painted APPEARANCE 24
Y. Chevalier ROYALTY 17
Y. folks think old folks GENERATION GAP 1
y., gifted and *black* RACE 26
y. had discovered OLD AGE 27
y. idea CHILDREN 3
y. know everything GENERATION GAP 9
y. man married MARRIAGE 14
y. man married MARRIAGE 22
y. man's slave MARRIAGE 1
Y. men are fitter to invent YOUTH 9
Y. men may die DEATH 14
Y. Pretender ROYALTY 18
Y. saint HUMAN NATURE 4
y. the policemen look OLD AGE 30
y. who has not wept GENERATION GAP 12
yours no hands but y. CHRISTIAN CHURCH 2
y. and yours LOVE 62
yourself do it y. SELF-INTEREST 4
DO IT Y. WAYS 33
love you for y. BODY 21
peace but y. PEACE 3
serve y. SELF-INTEREST 5
youth better to waste one's y. YOUTH 20
Crabbed age and y. GENERATION GAP 7
evil from his y. IMAGINATION 4
Love like y. is wasted on YOUTH 22
sad years of y. MIDDLE AGE 7
sign of an ill-spent y. SPORTS 14
tender years of y. EMOTIONS 17
Y. is something very new YOUTH 23
y. is the season BELIEF 19
Y. must be served YOUTH 4
Y. needed not GENERATION GAP 8
Y. of a Nation are the trustees YOUTH 15
y. of his own generation WRITING 37
Y. on the prow YOUTH 11
Y.'s a stuff will not endure YOUTH 8
y. to the gallows GOVERNMENT 26
y. unkind GENERATION GAP 6
Y., what man's age is like CHARACTER 34
Y., which is forgiven GENERATION GAP 10
YouTube Y. if you want to COMPUTERS 22
Yukon law of the Y. STRENGTH 25
yule green Y. makes a fat churchyard CHRISTMAS 3
so does a white Y. too WEATHER 38
yuppie y. version of bulimia HEALTH 26
Zanzibar count the cats in Z. TRAVEL 35
zeal not the slightest z. EXCESS 32
zealous z. citizen FAMILY 17
zebra z. without stripes CULTURE 2
zen Z. spirituality is just RELIGION 29
zephyr Odes to every z. WEATHER 39
zero You cannot reach absolute z. PHYSICAL 1
You have z. privacy anyway COMPUTERS 18
Zimbabwe keep my Z. INTERNATIONAL 40
zoo human z. COUNTRY 21
Zurich gnomes of Z. MONEY 20